Hammer Complete

**2**

# Hammer Complete

*The Films, the Personnel, the Company*

HOWARD MAXFORD

## Volume 2

*(The Encyclopedia M–Z; Appendix; Notes;
Bibliography; Index)*

McFarland & Company, Inc., Publishers

*Jefferson, North Carolina*

# Volume 2

Library of Congress Cataloguing-in-Publication Data

Names: Maxford, Howard, author.
Title: Hammer complete : the films, the personnel, the company / Howard Maxford.
Description: Jefferson, North Carolina : McFarland & Company, Inc., Publishers, 2023. |
Includes bibliographical references and index.
Identifiers: LCCN 2017046834 | ISBN 9781476670072 (paperback : acid free paper) ∞
Subjects: LCSH: Hammer Film Productions—Encyclopedias.
Classification: LCC PN1999.H3 M37 2023 | DDC 791.43/6164—dc23
LC record available at https://lccn.loc.gov/2017046834

British Library cataloguing data are available

***2 volume set—***
**ISBN (print) 978-1-4766-9344-6**

Front cover: Veronica Carlson and Christopher Lee in the 1968 film
*Dracula Has Risen from the Grave* (Warner Bros./Photofest)

Printed in the United States of America

*McFarland & Company, Inc., Publishers
Box 611, Jefferson, North Carolina 28640
www.mcfarlandpub.com*

# Table of Contents

## M

### Ma, James

Ma can be seen as Hsi Ta, one of the brothers in Hammer's *The Legend of the 7 Golden Vampires* (1974). He then went on to appear as a Thai boxer in *Shatter* (1974), which was shot back-to-back with the vampire film. **Hammer credits:** *The Legend of the 7 Golden Vampires* (1974, as Hsi Ta), *Shatter* (1974, as Thai boxer)

### Maasz, Ronnie

This busy British cameraman (1926–2007) worked as an operator on two films for Hammer in the sixties, both of which were helmed by cinematographer-turned-director Freddie Francis, for whom he'd previously worked as a focus puller (both films were photographed by John Wilcox). In films from 1941 as an assistant in Ealing's camera maintenance department, he made his debut with *Went the Day Well?* (1942), on which he worked as the loader/clapper boy. He soon after moved to Shepherd's Bush, where he worked for Gainsborough on such films as *Waterloo Road* (1944). His other credits, first as focus puller then as operator or second unit cameraman, include *School for Randle* (1949), *That Lady* (1955), *The Entertainer* (1960), *The Guns of Navarone* (1961), *The Heroes of Telemark* (1965), *One More Time* (1969), *The Italian Job* (1969) and *Living Free* (1972), plus many corporate films and commercials. He also photographed the Children's Film Foundation adventures *Haunters of the Deep* (1984) and *Terry on the Fence* (1985). **Hammer credits:** *Nightmare* (1964), *The Evil of Frankenstein* (1964)

### Maben, Alvis *see* Maben, Alvys

### Maben, Alvys (Alvis)

This British actress (1922–1963, real name Alvyn Dorothy Mitchell) played the role of Joan Merrill in the Hammer thriller *The Stranger Came Home* (1954). She also appeared in *Murder by Proxy* (1955), in which she was billed as Alvis Maben. Her other credits include *The Trip to Biarritz* (1963), plus episodes of *BBC Sunday-Night Theatre* (1950–1959, TV), *Sherlock Holmes* (1951, TV), *Captain Gallant of the Foreign Legion* (1955–1957, TV) and *The Adventures of Sherlock Holmes* (1954–1955, TV). **Hammer credits:** *The Stranger Came Home* (1954, as Joan Merrill), *Murder by Proxy* (1955, as Lita Huntley)

### MacCagno, Yvonne Josephine *see* Carreras, Yvonne Josephine

### MacCorkindale, Simon

This dashing British leading man (1952–2010) first came to note in the Agatha Christie thriller *Death on the Nile* (1978), though he had in fact made his debut several years earlier in *Juggernaut* (1974). His other credits include *The Riddle of the Sands* (1978), *Caboblanco* (1979), *The Sword and the Sorcerer* (1982) and *Jaws 3-D* (1983). Also busy on television, especially in America, his credits here include *Jesus of Nazareth* (1977, TV), *Quatermass* (1979, TV), *Manimal* (1983, TV), in which he played Professor Jonathan Chase, *Falcon Crest* (1982–1991, TV), in which he played Greg Reardon between 1985 and 1987, and *Casualty* (1986–, TV), in which he played Harry Harper between 2002 and 2008. He also appeared in *Visitor from the Grave*, an episode of *Hammer House of Horror* (1980, TV). Married twice, his first wife was the actress Fiona Fullerton (1956–), to whom he was married between 1976 and 1982. His second wife was the actress Susan George (1950–), whom he married in 1984, and with whom he formed the production company Amy International, through which they made such films as *Stealing Heaven* (1988), which he produced, *That Summer of White Roses* (1989), which he co-wrote and produced, and *Such a Long Journey* (1998), which he produced. George appeared in *Czech Mate* (1984, TVM [episode of *Hammer House of Mystery and Suspense*]). **Hammer credits:** *Visitor from the Grave* (1980, TV [episode of *Hammer House of Horror*], as Harry Wells)

### MacDonald, Adrian

MacDonald worked as the first assistant editor on Hammer's *Scars of Dracula* (1970). His other credits include *The Day of the Triffids* (1962), on which he was an assistant editor, and *The Castle of Fu Manchu* (1969), on which he was the dubbing editor. **Hammer credits:** *Scars of Dracula* (1970 [uncredited])

### MacDonald, Aimi

Specializing in scatterbrained types, this British (Scottish) comedy actress and dancer (1942–) was a familiar face on television in the sixties and seventies in episodes of such series and quiz shows as *The Saint* (1962–1969, TV), *At Last the 1948 Show* (1967, TV), in which she was constantly referred to as "The lovely Aimi MacDonald," *Whodunnit?* (1972–1978, TV), *Celebrity Squares* (1975–1997, TV) and *Give Us a Clue* (1978–1982, TV). Her film credits are few, among them *Secrets of a Windmill Girl* (1966), *Take a Girl Like You* (1969), *Vampira* (1974) and Hammer's *Man About the House* (1974), in which she played Hazel Lovett, the ditzy girlfriend of a married MP (and for which she was billed as Aimi McDonald). Her other small screen credits include episodes of *Get Real* (1998, TV), *Doctors* (2000–, TV), *Baddiel's Syndrome* (2001, TV) and *Bob Monkhouse … The Million Joke Man* (2015, TV). Also on stage. Her daughter is the actress and dancer Lisa Mulidore. **Hammer credits:** *Man About the House* (1974, as Hazel Lovett)

### MacDonald, Alan *see* McDonald, Alan

### MacDonald, Richard

Having qualified from the Royal College of Art, this noted British production designer (1919–1993) went on to become a lecturer at Leeds College of Art, where he became head of painting. In the fifties, he became an art director in advertising, and was spotted by the director Joseph Losey, who invited him to join the art department on his first British film, *The Sleeping Tiger* (1954). MacDonald retained close ties with Losey, and went on to become his designer on *The Gypsy and The Gentleman* (1958), which he followed with *The Criminal* (1960), *Eva* (1962), *The Servant* (1963), *King and Country* (1964), which earned him a BAFTA nomination, *Modesty Blaise* (1966), *Secret Ceremony* (1968), *Boom!* (1968), *The Assassination of Trotsky* (1972), *Galileo* (1975) and *The Romantic Englishwoman* (1975). He also worked as Losey's production assistant on Hammer's *The Damned* (1963), which was designed in-house by Bernard Robinson. MacDonald's other credits include *Far from the Madding Crowd* (1967), *Jesus Christ Superstar* (1973), *Day of the Locust* (1974), which earned him a second BAFTA nomination, *Marathon Man* (1976), *Something Wicked This Way Comes* (1983), *Supergirl* (1984), *The Addams Family* (1991), which earned him a third BAFTA nomination, and *The Firm* (1993). He was married to the costume designer Ruth Myers (1940–), who worked with him on several films. **Hammer credits:** *The Damned* (1963 [uncredited])

### MacGinnis, Niall

Best remembered for playing the sinister occultist Dr. Karswell in *Night of the Demon* (1957), this noted Irish character actor (1913–1977) began his film career in England in 1935 with *Turn of the Tide*. Over sixty films followed, among them *The Luck of the Irish* (1935), *49th Parallel* (1941), *Henry V* (1944), *The Nun's Story* (1959), *Jason and the Argonauts* (1963), in which he played Zeus, *Island of Terror* (1966) and *The Mackintosh Man* (1973). He also played the defense counsel in Hammer's controversial child abuse drama *Never Take Sweets from a Stranger* (1960), Friar Tuck in *Sword of Sherwood Forest* (1960) and Tiberion in *The Viking Queen* (1967). His occasional television credits include episodes of *The Veil* (1958, TV), *The Saint* (1962–1969, TV) and *Danger Man* (1964–1966, TV). Also much on stage. **Hammer credits:** *Never Take Sweets from a Stranger* (1960, as Defense Counsel), *Sword of Sherwood Forest* (1960, as Friar Tuck), *The Viking Queen* (1967, as Tiberion)

### MacGowran, Jack

Best remembered for his last film, *The Exorcist* (1973), in which he played the foul-mouthed movie director Burke Dennings, this noted Irish character actor (1918–1973, real name John Joseph MacGowran) also gave memorable performances in two Roman Polanski films: *Cul-de-Sac* (1966) and *The Fearless Vampire Killers* (1967), playing Professor Abronsius in the latter. Following stage experience at the Abbey Theater, prior to which he worked as an insurance assessor, he broke into films in 1949 with a minor role as a chief engineer in the "unofficial" Hammer second feature *Jack of Diamonds* (1949), which led to over thirty big screen appearances in the likes of *No Resting Place* (1951), *The Quiet Man* (1952), *The Titfield Thunderbolt* (1953), *Darby O'Gill and the Little People* (1958), *Tom Jones* (1963), *Doctor Zhivago* (1965), *Wonderwall* (1968) and *A Day at the Beach* (1970). He also appeared as a "frightened man" in the Hammer pirate yarn *Captain Clegg* (1962). On stage for much of his career in both Britain and America, he was particularly admired for his performances in the works of Samuel Beckett and Sean O'Casey. His daughter is the actress Tara MacGowran (1964–). **Hammer credits:** *Jack of Diamonds* (1949, as Stephens [uncredited]), *Captain Clegg* (1962, as Frightened man)

## MacGregor, Scott

In films from 1941 as an assistant to art director Edward Carrick, this British (Scottish) designer (1914–1973, full name Ronald Scott MacGregor) came to films following stage experience. His early credits include *Target for Tonight* (1941) and *Western Approaches* (1944), although he is perhaps best know for taking over as Hammer's designer-in-chief following the death of Bernard Robinson. As such, he worked on such key productions as *Taste the Blood of Dracula* (1970), *Vampire Circus* (1972) and *Frankenstein and the Monster from Hell* (1973), although his first association with the company can be traced back to the wartime comedy *Don't Panic Chaps* (1959). Like his predecessor, MacGregor was adept at recycling sets again and again. For example, the disused church first seen in *Taste the Blood of Dracula* was subsequently much redressed, appearing as Castle Karnstein in *The Vampire Lovers* (1970) among others. Meanwhile, Frankenstein's baronial hall from *The Horror of Frankenstein* (1970) appeared as Dracula's castle in *Scars of Dracula* (1970); that both these films appeared on the same double bill may have given the game away, however.

In addition to the gothic films, MacGregor also designed Hammer's space western *Moon Zero Two* (1969). Recalled the designer of his work on this particular project, "The exterior of the space station work area was based on the work of the architect Candela…. The interior of the reception area would on earth be made of concrete but I wanted to give it a much lighter effect and used some translucent fabric stretched over the strengthening struts, made of tubular aluminium. We selected Swedish furniture…. The floor was paper on stretched burlap Hessian. It was painted white then varnished. It was perfectly good for ten days' wear."[1]

MacGregor's many other credits (usually as assistant art director) include *Life in Her Hands* (1951), *The Day They Robbed the Bank of England* (1960), *The Day of the Triffids* (1962), *Cleopatra* (1963), *It's All Happening* (1963) and *The Vengeance of Fu Manchu* (1967). He also worked on episodes of such TV series as *Fabian of the Yard* (1954–1956, TV), *O.S.S.* (1957–1958, TV) and *White Hunter* (1958–1959, TV).

Remembered MacGregor's wife, art director Peggy Gick (1911–2006), whom he married in 1940, "I don't think Mac had any specific traits that you could recognize in his work. I don't think he had any favorite films, just favorite sets. There were happy sets and unhappy sets. Mark you, the film he was on was awful and the film he had just been on was always marvellous. He was delighted to work with Terry Fisher on *Frankenstein and the Monster from Hell*, because he had such respect for him."[2] Indeed, his work on this film was particularly inspired, as he revealed to publicist Jean Garioch during production: "For this *Frankenstein* all my backgrounds are sepia toned. This way the drapes, set dressings and props stand out. So much depends on lighting. On this film [cinematographer] Brian Probyn and I have worked closely from the outset."[3] **Additional notes:** MacGregor can be seen as a mourner in the opening credits of *That's Your Funeral* (1973). Several sources claim that MacGregor died in 1971, which doesn't fit with his Hammer timeline. **Hammer credits:** *Don't Panic Chaps* (1959, art director), *Moon Zero Two* (1969, art director), *Crescendo* (1970, art director), *Taste the Blood of Dracula* (1970, art director), *The Vampire Lovers* (1970, art director), *Scars of Dracula* (1970, art director), *The Horror of Frankenstein* (1970, art director), *On the Buses* (1971, production designer), *Blood from the Mummy's Tomb* (1971, designer), *Vampire Circus* (1972, art director), *Straight on Till Morning* (1972, art director), *Mutiny on the Buses* (1972, production designer), *Nearest and Dearest* (1973, art director), *That's Your Funeral* (1973, art director, also uncredited cameo appearance as mourner), *Frankenstein and the Monster from Hell* (1974, art director)

## MacIlwraith, Bill

This British writer (1928–2016) had his caustic 1966 play *The Anniversary* turned into a film by Hammer in 1968 with a screenplay by Jimmy Sangster. MacIlwraith's own screenplays include *Linda* (1960), *The Big Day* (1960) and *This Is My Street* (1963), while his television work includes episodes of *No Hiding Place* (1969–1967, TV), *The Human Jungle* (1963–1964, TV), *Beryl's Lot* (1973–1977, TV), *Two's Company* (1975–1979, TV), which he also created, *Cribb* (1980–1981, TV) and *Seconds Out* (1981–1982, TV), which he also created. **Hammer credits:** *The Anniversary* (1968)

## MacIntyre, Jeanne

This British actress (1922–) had a minor role in Hammer's *Sporting Love* (1936). Her other credits include *The Howard Case* (1936) and *Two Minutes* (1939), plus the early TV play *The Moon in the Yellow River* (1938, TV). **Hammer credits:** *Sporting Love* (1936, unnamed role [uncredited])

## MacKenzie, Mary

Busy in the fifties, this British supporting actress (1922–1966) appeared in such films as *Wanted for Murder* (1946), *The Master Plan* (1954), *Cloak Without Dagger* (1955), *Yield to the Night* (1956) and *The Man Who Liked Funerals* (1959). She also popped up in two Hammer second features, her performance in the first of which was described by *Variety* as being "good" in comparison to the "adequate" work of the other supporting players. Also on television, her credits here include episodes of *BBC Sunday-Night Theatre* (1950–1959, TV), *Douglas Fairbanks, Jr. Presents* (1953–1957, TV) and *Ghost Squad* (1961–1964, TV). Also on radio. **Hammer credits:** *Stolen Face* (1952, as Lily), *Lady in the Fog* (1952, as Marilyn Durant)

## MacKenzie, Ross

MacKenzie worked as the assistant director on three films for Hammer, following which he was promoted to the position of production manager for three more. His other credits as a first assistant include *Small Hotel* (1957), *The Yellow Teddybears* (1963) and *Murder Elite* (1985), plus episodes of *Dial 999* (1958–1959, TV) and *International Detective* (1959–1961, TV). He also worked as the location manager on *The Ipcress File* (1965). **Hammer credits:** *Sands of the Desert* (1960, assistant director), *Paranoiac* (1963, assistant director), *Maniac* (1963, assistant director), *Dracula—Prince of Darkness* (1966, production manager), *Rasputin—The Mad Monk* (1966, production manager), *Slave Girls* (1968, production manager)

## Mackie, Philip

Noted for his television plays and series, this celebrated British dramatist (1918–1985) came to television in 1954 following experience in government-funded documentaries. Among his greatest successes were *The Caesars* (1968, TV), on which he also worked as a producer, *The Organization* (1972, TV), *Conjugal Rights* (1973) and, most famously, *The Naked Civil Servant* (1975, TVM). His film credits are rarer, among them his big screen debut, the overly-talkative Hammer featurette *The Right Person* (1956), the story for which had already been presented by the BBC in 1954, marking his small screen debut (it was subsequently remade for Australian and German television in 1957, the latter as *Der Mann, den ich suche*, thus making it a lucrative property). He also penned a handful of Edgar Wallace programers, including *Clue of the New Pin* (1961), *Clue of the Silver Key* (1961), *The Man at the Carlton Tower* (1961) and *The Sinister Man* (1961), as well as *All the Way Up* (1970), the latter of which he also produced. His other TV credits include episodes of *Mr. Rose* (1967–1968, TV), which he also created and frequently produced, *Raffles* (1975–1977, TV), *The Cleopatras* (1983, TV) and *Jemima Shore Investigates* (1983, TV). His plays include *The Whole Truth* (1955), which was presented for television in 1955 and filmed in 1958, *Maigret and the Lady* (1965) and *The Chairman* (1976). His granddaughter is actress Pearl Mackie (1987–). **Hammer credits:** *The Right Person* (1956)

## MacKinnon, Allan

This British scenarist (1912–1955) adapted Lester Powell's 1948 radio serial *Return from Darkness* for Hammer, which was subsequently re-titled

*The Black Widow* (1950). He also penned the script for *The Saint's Return* (1953) and the swashbuckler *Men of Sherwood Forest* (1954). His other credits include *This Man Is News* (1938), *Unpublished Story* (1942), *Vote for Huggett* (1949), *She Shall Have Murder* (1950), *Time Is My Enemy* (1954) and *Second Fiddle* (1957), as well as such early TV plays as *They're Off* (1938, TV), *Pest Control* (1938, TV) and *King of the Congo* (1938, TV). **Hammer credits:** *The Black Widow* (1950), *The Saint's Return* (1953), *Men of Sherwood Forest* (1954)

## Macklen, Peter

Macklen (sometimes Maclin) can be seen in a supporting role in *And the Wall Came Tumbling Down* (1984, TVM [episode of *Hammer House of Mystery and Suspense*]). His other credits include episodes of *Rumpole of the Bailey* (1978–1992, TV), *Tales of the Unexpected* (1979–1988, TV), *Richard III* (1983, TVM) and *Casualty* (1986–, TV). **Hammer credits:** *And the Wall Came Tumbling Down* (1984, TVM [episode of *Hammer House of Mystery and Suspense*], as Military Policeman)

## MacLennan, Elizabeth

This British (Scottish) actress (1938–2015) can be seen as the distraught Mrs. Wilson during the séance sequence in Hammer's *Hands of the Ripper* (1971). Her other credits include *Joanna* (1968) and *The House in Nightmare Park* (1973), plus episodes of *Storyboard* (1961, TV), *Z Cars* (1962–1978, TV) and *Play for Today* (1970–1984, TV). Also on stage. She was married to the writer, director and producer John McGrath (1935–2002) from 1962. **Hammer credits:** *Hands of the Ripper* (1971, as Mrs. Wilson)

## MacManus, Freddie

MacManus worked the wardrobe assistant on Hammer's *The Satanic Rites of Dracula* (1974). **Hammer credits:** *The Satanic Rites of Dracula* (1974 [uncredited])

## MacMillan, Tonie

MacMillan can be seen as the cook, Mrs. Thimble, in the Hammer comedy *What the Butler Saw* (1950). Her other credits include *Operation Diamond* (1948), *The Cure for Love* (1950), *Josephine and Men* (1955) and *The Chalk Garden* (1964), plus episodes of *Robin Hood* (1953, TV) and *Emergency—Ward 10* (1957–1967, TV). **Hammer credits:** *What the Butler Saw* (1950, as Mrs. Thimble)

## MacNaughtan, Alan

This busy British (Scottish) actor (1920–2002, aka Alan MacNaughton) played Kleve, the father of the tragic Christina in Hammer's *Frankenstein Created Woman* (1967). He also had a key role in an episode of *Journey to the Unknown* (1968, TV). In films from 1956 with *Bond of Fear*, his other screen credits include *Victim* (1961), *Family Life* (1971) and *The Commissioner* (1997), while his TV work includes episodes of *A Very British Coup* (1988, TV) and *Kavanagh Q.C.* (1995–2001, TV). Also on stage. **Hammer credits:** *Frankenstein Created Woman* (1967, as Kleve), *Jane Brown's Body* (1968, TV [episode of *Journey to the Unknown*], as Dr. Ian Denholt)

## MacNaughton, Ian

This British (Scottish) actor (1925–2002, full name Edward Ian MacNaughton) played the role of "Haggis" in the Hammer shocker *X—The Unknown* (1956), in which he comes to a sticky end when "slimed" by the title monster down a crevasse. His other credits include *Laxdale Hall* (1953), *The Safecracker* (1958) and *Lawrence of Arabia* (1962), plus episodes of *Hancock's Half Hour* (1956–1960, TV), *The Avengers* (1961–1969, TV) and *Redcap* (1964–1965, TV). He went on to become a highly successful producer and director on television, producing and directing over forty episodes of *Monty Python's Flying Circus* (1969–1974, TV), which won him one shared BAFTA and three further nominations, as well as an Emmy nomination. He also directed the Pythons' first film, *And Now for Something Completely Different* (1971). His other work as a director includes episodes of *Z Cars* (1962–1978, TV), *Dr. Finlay's Casebook* (1962–1971, TV) and *Rising Damp* (1974–1978, TV), as well as the short *Le Petomane* (1979). **Hammer credits:** *X—The Unknown* (1956, as "Haggis")

## Macnee, Patrick

Known the world over for playing John Steed in the ever-popular television series *The Avengers* (1961–1969), this dapper British actor (1922–2015, full name Daniel Patrick Macnee) began his film career working as an extra on such films as *Pygmalion* (1938) and *The Life and Death of Colonel Blimp* (1943). He began appearing in small roles in 1948 with *The Fatal Night*, and went on to play a supporting role in Hammer's third and final Dick Barton adventure, *Dick Barton at Bay* (1950), in which he gets shot in the opening minutes (the film's credits bill him as Patrick McNee). Macnee's other film credits include *Scrooge* (1951), *Les Girls* (1957), *The Sea Wolves* (1980), *The Howling* (1981), *A View to a Kill* (1985), in which he played Sir Godfrey Tibbett, *Waxwork* (1988) and *The Avengers* (1998), while on television he revived the role of John Steed in *The New Avengers* (1976–1977, TV). Married three times, his first wife was the actress Barbara Douglas (1921–2012), to whom he was married between 1942 and 1956. His second wife was the actress Catherine Woodville (1938–2013, aka Katherine Woodville), to whom he was married between 1965 and 1969; she appeared in Hammer's *The Brigand of Kandahar* (1965). His son (with Douglas) is the producer Rupert Macnee (1947–). He wrote about his life in *Blind in One Ear* (1989). **Additional notes:** In the big screen version of *The Avengers*, the role of John Steed was played by Ralph Fiennes, while Macnee made a vocal cameo as Invisible Jones. **Hammer credits:** *Dick Barton at Bay* (1950, as David Phillips)

## MacOwan, Norman

This British (Scottish) actor (1877–1961) played the role of the soon-to-retire lighthouse skipper Rigby in the Hammer quickie *The Dark Light* (1951). On stage from 1900, his screen credits include *Whisky Galore!* (1949), which marked his belated debut, *Valley of Eagles* (1951), *Laxdale Hall* (1953), *Kidnapped* (1959), *The Battle of the Sexes* (1960) and *The City of the Dead* (1960). He can also be seen in Hammer's *X—The Unknown* (1956) as Old Tom. He also worked as a playwright, among them *Glorious Morning* (1938), which was filmed for television twice, in 1938 and 1960. He also penned the television play *The Infinite Shoeblack* (1939, TV), which was re-made in 1952. His own television appearances include episodes of *BBC Sunday-Night Theatre* (1950–1959, TV) and *ITV Television Playhouse* (1955–1967, TV). **Hammer credits:** *The Dark Light* (1951, as Rigby), *X—The Unknown* (1956, as Old Tom)

## MacPherson, Peter

Macpherson played one of the inmates in Hammer's *Frankenstein and the Monster from Hell* (1974). **Hammer credits:** *Frankenstein and the Monster from Hell* (1974, as Inmate [uncredited])

## Madden, Ciaran

This RADA-trained British actress (1942–) played the role of Lady Marian Fitzwalter in *Wolfshead: The Legend of Robin Hood* (1969 [released 1973]), which was not made, but was subsequently bought, by Hammer. Her other credits include *Gawain and the Green Knight* (1973), *The Beast Must Die* (1974) and *Swing Kids* (1993). Busiest on television, her many credits here include episodes of *W. Somerset Maugham* (1969–1970, TV), *Star Maidens* (1976, TV), *Oxbridge Blues* (1984, TV), *Drummonds* (1985–1987, TV), in which she played Mary Drummond, *Maigret* (1992–1993, TV), in which she played Madame Maigret, and *Ivanhoe* (1997, TV). **Hammer credits:** *Wolfshead: The Legend of Robin Hood* (1969 [released 1973], as Lady Marian Fitzwalter)

## Madden, Peter

In films from 1937 with *Command Performance*, following experience as a stand up comedian and a racing driver, this sour-looking Malaysian born character actor (1904–1976) can be seen as Bert Darwin in the Hammer thriller *Hell Is a City* (1960). In over forty films, his other credits include *Tom Brown's School Days* (1940), *Rhythm Serenade* (1943), *The Wicked Lady* (1945), *Dr. Terror's House of Horrors* (1965), *Doctor Zhivago* (1965), *The Private Life of Sherlock Holmes* (1970) and *One of Our Dinosaurs Is Missing* (1975). He also returned to Hammer to appear in three horror films and two sitcom spin-offs. His small screen work includes episodes of *ITV Television Playhouse* (1955–1967, TV), *Espionage* (1963–1964, TV) and *Sherlock Holmes* (1965–1968, TV), in which he played Inspector Lestrade. His wife was actress Mary Jordan (1913–1973), whom he married in 1940. **Hammer credits:** *Hell Is a City* (1960, as Bert Darwin), *The Kiss of the Vampire* (1963, as Bruno), *Frankenstein Created Woman* (1967, as Police Chief), *On the Buses* (1971, as Mr. Brooks), *Nearest and Dearest* (1973, as Court bailiff), *Frankenstein and the Monster from Hell* (1973, as Coach driver)

## Maddern, Victor

Frequently cast as lower rank military types, this busy British supporting actor (1926–1993) broke into films in 1950 with *Morning Departure* following training at RADA. Over eighty films followed, among them *Top Secret* (1952), *Cockleshell Heroes* (1955), *Private's Progress* (1956), *I'm All Right Jack* (1959), *Carry On Spying* (1964), *Carry On Cleo* (1964), *Chitty Chitty Bang Bang* (1968), *Death on the Nile* (1978) and *Sweet Nothing* (1992), plus a minor role in Hammer's *The Lost Continent* (1968). Also busy in the theater and on television, his credits for the latter include an on-going role in *The Dick Emery Show* (1963–1981, TV) in the seventies and an episode of Hammer's *Journey to the Unknown* (1968, TV). In private life, he worked for a number of religious causes. **Hammer credits:** *The Lost Continent* (1968, as Mate), *One on an Island* (1968, TV [episode of *Journey to the Unknown*], as Baker)

### Maddison, John

Maddison (1912–1989) can be seen as a police inspector in Hammer's *The Phantom of the Opera* (1962, as Police Inspector Dawson [uncredited]). **Hammer credits:** *The Phantom of the Opera* (1962, as Police Inspector Dawson [uncredited])

### *Made for Laughs*

GB, 1952, 34m, bw, cert U

Rarely seen these days, this compilation of silent film clips from circa 1912–1914, narrated by Byron Michie, was released by Exclusive in July 1952. Actors featured in the clips include Charlie Chaplin, Billie Reeves, Slim Summerville, Flora Finch, Sidney Drew and his wife, Edgar Kennedy, Oliver Hardy and Lupino Lane (whose cousin Stanley Lupino had filmed his 1934 stage success *Sporting Love* for Hammer in 1936). The film was later re-issued in 1958 by Winart, minus seventeen minutes of footage (possibly the Chaplin sequences, which might well have been too expensive to re-license). Note that Exclusive had previously released the Chaplin compilation short *Chase Me Charlie* (1918) in 1951.

Production company: Hammer. Distributor: Exclusive. Director/screenplay/compiler/editor: James M. Anderson. Music: De Wolfe. Piano improvisation: Rose Treacher. Sound: Rich-Leevers. Commentator: Byron Michie

### *The Madison Equation* see *Journey to the Unknown*

### Madoc, Philip

Following experience as a linguist and television appearances from 1961 with *Amelia*, this intense-looking British (Welsh) actor (1934–2012) went on to appear in such films as *A High Wind in Jamaica* (1965), *Berserk* (1967), *Deadfall* (1968), *Soft Beds, Hard Battles* (1973) and *Bequest to the Nation* (1973). He also appeared in Hammer's *Dr. Jekyll and Sister Hyde* (1971) as the morgue attendant Byker, whose interest in his female charges seems to run to the exotic. Busy on television, he is best known for playing Detective Chief Superintendent Tate in *Target* (1977–1978, TV) and David Lloyd George in *The Life and Times of David Lloyd George* (1981, TV). He was also a memorable Nazi U-boat Captain in an oft-repeated 1973 episode of *Dad's Army* (1968–1977, TV). His second wife was the actress Ruth Madoc (1943–,

maiden name Ruth Llewellyn), to whom he was married between 1961 and 1981. **Hammer credits:** *Dr. Jekyll and Sister Hyde* (1971, as Byker)

### Magee, Patrick

Following stage experience in his homeland and on the London stage (from 1958), this intense-looking Irish actor (1922–1982) began appearing in films in supporting roles, with *The Criminal* (1960). An unmistakable presence, his other credits include *The Boys* (1962), *The Servant* (1963), *Zulu* (1964), *The Masque of the Red Death* (1964), *Marat/Sade* (1967), in which he played the Marquis de Sade (having played the role in the original stage production), *King Lear* (1970), *A Clockwork Orange* (1971), *Young Winston* (1972) and *Chariots of Fire* (1981). He also appeared in Hammer's *Demons of the Mind* (1972) as Dr. Falkenberg. He was also considered for the role of John Verney in Hammer's *To the Devil a Daughter* (1976). A frequent performer on stage in the works of Samuel Beckett and Harold Pinter, his TV appearances include episodes of *Here Lies Miss Sabry* (1960, TV), *The Avengers* (1961–1969, TV), *Play for Today* (1970–1984, TV) and *The Protectors* (1972–1973, TV). **Hammer credits:** *Demons of the Mind* (1972, as Dr. Falkenberg)

### Maharis, George

This American actor (1928–) played the role of Stephen Drake in *Miss Belle*, an episode of Hammer's *Journey to the Unknown* (1968, TV). Working in both Britain and America, his many film credits include *Sylvia* (1964), *The Happening* (1967), *The Sword and the Sorcerer* (1982) and *Doppelganger* (1993), while his other TV work includes episodes of *Marty* (1953, TV), *Naked City* (1958–1963, TV), *Route 66* (1960–1964, TV), which earned him an Emmy nomination, *The Snoop Sisters* (1973–1974, TV), and *Murder, She Wrote* (1984–1996, TV). His brother is the location manager Robert Maharis. **Hammer credits:** *Miss Belle* (1968, TV [episode of *Journey to the Unknown*], as Stephen Drake)

### Mahoney, Janet

This British actress (1938–) can be seen as Stan Butler's girlfriend Susy in Hammer's *Mutiny on the Buses* (1972). Her other credits include *Doctor in Trouble* (1970) and *Carry On Loving* (1970), plus episodes of *Howerd's Hour* (1968, TV), *Dad's Army* (1968–1977, TV), *Up Pompeii* (1969, TV) and *The Jimmy Logan Show* (1969, TV). Also on stage. Her first husband was assistant director Jim McCutcheon, whom she married in 1963. Her second husband is theater producer Duncan C. Weldon (1941–2019), whom she married in 1974. **Hammer credits:** *Mutiny on the Buses* (1972, as Susy)

### Mahoney, Louis

This Gambian actor (1938–) played Squire Hamilton's "Coloured servant" (as he is billed in the credits) in Hammer's *The Plague of the Zombies* (1966). His other credits include *Curse of the Voodoo* (1965), *The Final Conflict* (1981), *Sheena* (1984), *Cry Freedom* (1987), *Shooting Fish* (1997), *Shooting Dogs* (2005) and *Captain Phillips* (2013), plus a return to Hammer for *Slave Girls*

(1968). His TV work includes episodes of *Danger Man* (1964–1966, TV), *Escape* (1980, TV), *Runaway Bay* (1992–1993, TV), *Oscar Charlie* (2001–2002, TV), *Ten Days to War* (2008, TV), *Being Human* (2008–2012, TV) and *River* (2015, TV). **Hammer credits:** *The Plague of the Zombies* (1966, as Colored servant), *Slave Girls* (1968, as Head boy)

### Maiden, Nora

Maiden can be seen as one of two beach blondes in the Hammer short *A Man on the Beach* (1956). **Hammer credits:** *A Man on the Beach* (1956, as Second beach blonde [uncredited])

### Maidment, Kenneth

A long-time executive with Columbia Pictures, Maidment joined the Hammer board (via their subsidiary, Falcon) in 1959 when the Hollywood studio bought a 49 percent stake in Bray, which also led to a new five-year, twenty-five-film production deal with Hammer. By this time, Maidment was already on the board of directors at Bray (between 1958 and 1964).

### Maidment, Terence

Maidment can be seen as First Shell Man in Hammer's *One Million Years B.C.* (1966). His other credits include *The Painted Smile* (1962), *O Lucky Man!* (1973), *The Pink Panther Strikes Again* (1976) and *The Passage* (1979), plus episodes of *Z Cars* (1962–1978, TV), *The Avengers* (1961–1969, TV) and *The Persuaders!* (1971–1972, TV). **Hammer credits:** *One Million Years B.C.* (1966, as First Shell Man)

### Maine, Charles Eric

This British dramatist and novelist (1921–1981, real name David McIlwain, aka Robert Rayner and Robert Wade) had his 1952 radio play *Spaceways—A Story of the Very Near Future* adapted for the screen by Richard Landau and Paul Tabori for Hammer in 1953. His other credits include the screenplay for *Timeslip* (1955), which had already been made for television in 1953 from a script by himself, and which subsequently became the basis for his 1957 novel *The Isotope Man,* and *The Electronic Monster* (1960), which he adapted from his 1957 novel *Escapement*. Other published works include *Timeliner* (1955), which was based on his 1954 radio play *The Einstein Highway*, *Crisis 2000* (1956), *The Mind of Mr. Soames* (1961), which was filmed in 1970, *The Darkest of Night* (1962 [later revised as *The Big Death*, 1978]) and *Alph* (1972). **Hammer credits:** *Spaceways* (1953)

### Mainwaring, Bernard

This British director (1897–1963) began his career in the silent period, though he proved busiest during the thirties, during which he helmed Hammer's very first production, *The Public Life of Henry the Ninth* (1935), which he also co-wrote. His other films include *Realities* (1930), *The New Hotel* (1932), which he also produced, *Old Roses* (1935), which he also produced, *Line Engaged* (1935), *Show Flat* (1936), *Cross My Heart* (1937), *Member of the Jury* (1937) *Jennifer Hale* (1937), which he also wrote, and *The Villiers Diamond* (1938). His other credits as a writer include *Whispering Tongues* (1934), *The Crimson Candle* (1934), which he also produced, and *Women Aren't Angels* (1943). **Hammer credits:** *The Public Life of Henry the Ninth* (1935)

## Maitland, Marne

In films from 1950 with *Cairo Road*, this Anglo-Indian character actor (1914–1992, full name James Marne Maitland) was frequently called upon to play shifty foreigners, usually of Indian or Middle Eastern extraction. In over sixty films, his credits include *Cairo Road* (1950), *Father Brown* (1954), *Bhowani Junction* (1956), *Tiger Bay* (1959), *Sammy Going South* (1963), *Cleopatra* (1963), *Roma* (1972), *The Man with the Golden Gun* (1974), *The Pink Panther Strikes Again* (1976) and *Appointment in Liverpool* (1988). He also made many Hammer films during his career, first appearing in a supporting role in *Break in the Circle* (1955). He was meanwhile cast to type in the likes of *The Camp on Blood Island* (1958), in which he played a Japanese captain, *The Stranglers of Bombay* (1959), *Visa to Canton* (1960) and *The Reptile* (1966), in which he played the evil Malay. He also co-starred in *The Indian Spirit Guide*, an episode of Hammer's *Journey to the Unknown* (1968, TV), which also appeared in the compendium film *Journey to Midnight* (1968, TVM). His other TV credits include episodes of *Armchair Theatre* (1956–1974, TV), *Swizzlewick* (1964, TV), *Department S* (1969–1970, TV), *The Borgias* (1981, TV) and *A Season of Giants* (1991, TV). Also on stage, including work at the Old Vic. **Hammer credits:** *Break in the Circle* (1955, as Third Russian), *The Camp on Blood Island* (1958, as Captain Sakamura), *I Only Arsked!* (1958, as King Fazim), *The Stranglers of Bombay* (1959, as Patel Shari), *Sands of the Desert* (1960, as Adviser), *Visa to Canton* (1960, as Han Po), *The Terror of the Tongs* (1961, as Beggar), *The Phantom of the Opera* (1962, as Xavier), *The Reptile* (1966, as Malay), *The Indian Spirit Guide* (1968, TV [episode of *Journey to the Unknown*], as Chardur [Ted]), *Journey to Midnight* (1968, TVM, as Chardur [Ted])

## Major Films

Formed by producer John Temple-Smith, Major Films was used to finance such program fillers as *The Girl on the Pier* (1953), *Profile* (1954), *One Way Out* (1955), *Find the Lady* (1956), *Account Rendered* (1957) and *The Big Chance* (1957). Temple-Smith and Major also made the pirate yarn *Captain Clegg* (1962) in conjunction with Hammer. **Hammer credits:** *Captain Clegg* (1962)

## Malandrinos, Andreas

This Greek supporting actor (1888–1970) can be seen as the lodgekeeper in the Hammer comedy *A Weekend with Lulu* (1961). His many other credits include *Raise the Roof* (1930), *Secret Agent* (1936), *My Brother Jonathan* (1948), *Ill Met by Moonlight* (1956), *The Boy Who Stole a Million* (1960), *Help!* (1965) and *The Fearless Vampire Killers* (1967), plus a return to Hammer for another minor role in *The Mummy's Shroud* (1967). He also appeared in such series as *Douglas Fairbanks, Jr. Presents* (1953–1957, TV), *Man from Interpol*

(1960–1961, TV) and *Paul Temple* (1969–1971, TV). **Hammer credits:** *A Weekend with Lulu* (1961, as Lodgekeeper), *The Mummy's Shroud* (1967, as Curator)

## Malicz, Mark

Malicz can be seen in a minor supporting role in *Czech Mate* (1984, TVM [episode of *Hammer House of Mystery and Suspense*]). His other credits include *The Desperate Ones* (1968), *Battle of Britain* (1969), *Puppet on a Chain* (1971) and *Fiddler on the Roof* (1971), plus episodes of *An Enemy of the State* (1965, TV), *The Protectors* (1972–1973, TV) and *BBC2 Playhouse* (1974–1983, TV). **Hammer credits:** *Czech Mate* (1984, TVM [episode of *Hammer House of Mystery and Suspense*], as Porter)

## Malin, Diana

This British actress (1957–) had a minor supporting role in *Black Carrion* (1984, TVM [episode of *Hammer House of Mystery and Suspense*]). Her other credits include episodes of *The Gentle Touch* (1980–1984, TV), *The Chinese Detective* (1981–1982, TV) and *Minder* (1979–1994, TV), while her occasional films include *Little Dorrit* (1988). **Hammer credits:** *Black Carrion* (1984, TVM [episode of *Hammer House of Mystery and Suspense*], as Secretary)

## Malin, Eddie (Edward)

Best remembered for playing the aged Walter in the long-running sitcom *Nearest and Dearest* (1968–1973, TV), this British character actor (1894–1977) repeated the role for Hammer's big screen spin-off in 1973. His other big screen credits include *The Greed of William Hart* (1948), *The Two-Headed Spy* (1958), *A Night to Remember* (1958), *Inn for Trouble* (1960), *Operation Cupid* (1960), *A Hard Day's Night* (1964), *How to Steal a Million* (1966) and *The Bed Sitting Room* (1969), while his other TV work includes episodes of *Sixpenny Corner* (1955–1956, TV), *Hotel Imperial* (1958–1960, TV), *The Troubleshooters* (1965–1972, TV) and *Doctor at Sea* (1974, TV). **Additional notes:** Malin also appeared as Walter Tattersall in a 1972 edition of the TV comedy special *All Star Comedy Carnival* (1969–1973, TV). **Hammer credits:** *Nearest and Dearest* (1973, as Walter Tattersall)

## Malleson, Miles

As both an actor and writer, British born Malleson (1888–1969, full name William Miles Malleson) seems to have been associated with all the key moments in UK film history. A playwright from 1916, his many works include *D Company* (1916), *Black 'Ell* (1925) and *Six Men of Dorset* (1937), plus translations of Moliere. He turned to screenwriting in 1930 with *The W Plan*, and went on to pen such classics as *Nell Gwyn* (1934), *Victoria the Great* (1937) and *The Thief of Bagdad* (1940), while as an actor—usually in comic cameos—he can be found in *Bitter Sweet* (1933), *The 39 Steps* (1935), *Dead of Night* (1945), *Kind Hearts and Coronets* (1949), *Stage Fright* (1950), *The Importance of Being Earnest* (1952) and *I'm All Right Jack* (1959). In films from 1921 with *The Headmaster*, Malleson went on to appear in over eighty productions, including Hammer's *Dracula* (1958), in which he

played the undertaker J. Marx, with whom Peter Cushing's Van Helsing and Michael Gough's Arthur Holmwood have a jocular encounter while trying to track down Dracula's coffin. Malleson had equally scene-stealing roles in a further three Hammer productions, most notably in *The Hound of the Baskervilles* (1959), in which he played Bishop Frankland. Commented *Variety* of this performance: "Miles Malleson contributes most of the rare humor with one of his first-class studies, as a bumbling bishop." Critic Derek Conrad agreed, adding, "Dear Miles Malleson [makes] a nice bumbling Bishop even nicer and more bumbling." Note that Terence Fisher directed all of Malleson's films for Hammer. His occasional TV appearances include episodes of *The Terrible Choice* (1960, TV), *If the Crown Fits* (1961, TV) and *Victoria Regina* (1964, TV). Married three times, Malleson's wives included the actresses Colette O'Neil (1895–1975, real name Constance Annesley), to whom he was married between 1915 and 1923, and Tania Lieven (1909–1978, real name Tatiana Lieven). **Hammer credits:** *Dracula* (1958, as J. Marx [undertaker]), *The Hound of the Baskervilles* (1959, as Bishop Frankland), *The Brides of Dracula* (1960, as Dr. Tobler), *The Phantom of the Opera* (1962, as Cabby)

## Malone, Cavan

This British supporting actor (1936–1982) appeared as a signalman in the Hammer comedy *Further Up the Creek* (1958). His other credits include *Captain Boycott* (1947), *Kind Hearts and Coronets* (1949), *Linda* (1960) and *633 Squadron* (1964), plus episodes of *BBC Sunday-Night Theatre* (1950–1959, TV) and *Suspense* (1962–1963, TV). **Hammer credits:** *Further Up the Creek* (1958, as Signalman [uncredited])

## *Man About the House*

GB, 1974, 90m, Technicolor, RCA, cert A

One of several big screen sitcom spin-offs made by Hammer in the seventies, *Man About the House* is perhaps the tamest. Created by Johnnie Mortimer and Brian Cooke, the series clocked up thirty-nine episodes between 1973 to 1976 and was mildly controversial for the time in that it starred Richard O'Sullivan as catering student Robin Tripp who finds himself sharing digs with two pretty young women: Chrissy played by Paula Wilcox and Jo played by Sally Thomsett. Naturally, there was plenty of sexual banter among the three players, but this being a prime-time sitcom, nothing too untoward ever occurred. Into this brew was added the trio's landlords, George and Mildred Roper, played by Brian Murphy and Yootha Joyce, and various peripheral characters, among them Robin's lothario friend Larry Simmonds, played by Doug Fisher. A ratings winner, the show went on to spawn two spin-offs: *George and Mildred* (1976–1979, TV), in which the bickering landlords moved to suburbia, and *Robin's Nest* (1977–1981, TV), which saw Robin open his own bistro. There was also a long-running American version of the original titled *Three's Company* (1977–1984, TV) starring John Ritter in the O'Sullivan role.

Given its popularity and the then-current vogue for spin-offs, it was perhaps inevitable that the show would make its way to the big screen. All the main cast members made the transfer, while the show's scriptwriters concocted a rather bland story involving their attempts to save their terrace from the hands of a ruthless property developer named Spiros, who wants to demolish it to make way for one of several office blocks he is erecting across London. The idea might have made for a good TV half hour, but stretched out to three times that length, it just doesn't have enough plot to sustain itself. Instead, it is padded out with irrelevancies and resolves itself in a chase round the corridors of Thames Television Studios, where Spiros's oily assistant Morris Pluthero and a corrupt MP who has his mistress secreted away in another flat on the terrace are about to be interviewed on a live chat show.

Save for the opening scene, during which it at first seems that Robin, Chrissy and Jo are sharing a bath, and a later sequence in which Robin fails to beat the girls at strip poker, the sexual banter between the three main characters is sadly kept to a minimum, though Robin and Chrissy do share one amusing exchange. "Look, Chrissy. I'm not a male chauvinist pig," Robin tries to assure her. "I think you are," she replies, to which he retorts, "What do you know about it? You're only a woman!" The bickering between George and Mildred, a highlight of the TV show, has also been watered down. Coos Mildred at one point, "George, those cigarettes are going to kill you. Have another one!" which is about as funny as the put-downs get (George later uncharacteristically calls Mildred a "silly bitch" behind her back). However, it is Chrissy who gets perhaps the most telling line. Sitting atop a double-decker bus with Robin, she observes, "Oh, everything's being pulled down, isn't it? The cinema. They're building another office block. It's terrible, I mean, where's everybody going to play bingo?" Of course, this was as much a comment on the redevelopment of London at the time as it was of the decline of the British film industry, which had more or less been reduced to churning out sex comedies and, er, sitcom spin-offs. And indeed, many of the cinemas *had* become bingo halls.

Blandly directed by John Robins on rather tacky sets by Don Picton, the film looks very much of its period (note the gaudy purple wallpaper in the flat mates' living room). The principals try to make the most of the weak material, but it really is an uphill struggle. Still, there are plenty of guest stars to keep things bubbling along, among them Peter Cellier, who comes off best in his role as the conniving Morris Pluthero, Arthur Lowe as his scheming boss Spiros, Patrick Newell as the corrupt MP Sir Edmund Weir, Bill Maynard as a less-than-hygienic chef, Andria Bird as a sex-starved fellow-resident on the terrace, and Doug Fisher as Robin's mate Larry, whose impromptu date with Jo ends with his car floating in a park lake. Other familiar faces along for the ride include the lovely Aimi Macdonald, Michael Ward, Melvyn Hayes, Michael Robbins, Aubrey Morris, Johnny Briggs, Bill Pertwee, Spike Milligan, Norman Mitchell and Julian Orchard—a veritable A–Z of comedy players, many of them with past associations with Hammer. What a shame they are given so little to do.

Perhaps the most amusing cameos are by Jack Smethurst and Rudolph Walker, the stars of the long-running sitcom *Love Thy Neighbour* (1972–1976, TV), which had been filmed by Hammer in 1973. Seen sharing a drink in the bar at Thames Television, they at first seem to be trading racial insults as per their characters in the show. "No, no, no. White will win in the end," says Smethurst to Walker emphatically. However, in a neat, practically post-modern twist, it turns out they're talking about chess. Unfortunately, the effect of this sly bit of business is somewhat spoiled moments later when George Roper runs past. Recognizing Walker from TV, he exclaims, "'Ere, I know you! You're sambo the nig-nog, straight out of the jungle." The seventies really was another country (this isn't the film's only racist moment; earlier outside a shop a black housewife is shown reprimanding her son, who just happens to be called Enoch). At least another chess reference brings things to a reasonable close. Comments Robin, who is trying to coax Chrissy into a game of strip chess, "But you see the whole object of the game is to try to mate!"

On the floor at Elstree between March 16 and 12 April 1974, as well as on location in and around London, *Man About the House* was released in the UK by EMI on 22 December of the same year, and went on to do reasonable business, recouping its budget in the London area alone, where it pulled in a very respectable £90,000. The vogue for big screen sitcoms was beginning to wind down though, but this didn't prevent the film's producer Roy Skeggs from making two more during a hiatus from Hammer. These were *George and Mildred* (1980), featuring the Ropers, and *Rising Damp* (1980). **Additional notes:** For those who know their way about London, the film contains a rather glaring error. Having exited from Spiros' office block headquarters, Morris Pluthero orders his chauffeur to take him to Thames Television on Euston Rd. However, the office block he has just left is actually part of the same complex and very obviously situated on Euston Rd. As well as the film and TV series, O'Sullivan, Wilcox, Thomsett, Murphy and Joyce also appeared as their characters in the 1973 edition of the TV comedy special *All Star Comedy Carnival* (1969–1973, TV), which was penned by Johnnie Mortimer and Brian Cooke.

Production company: Hammer. Distributor: EMI (UK [ABC circuit]). Producer: Roy Skeggs. Director: John Robins. Screenplay: Johnnie Mortimer, Brian Cooke, based upon their television sitcom. Cinematographer: Jimmy Allen. Music: Christopher Gunning. Title song: *Man About the House*, Christopher Gunning (m), Annie Farrow (ly). Vocalist: Jane Christie [uncredited]. Music director: Philip Martell. Editor: Archie Ludski. Art director: Don Picton. Costumes: Laura Nightingale. Make-up: Eddie Knight. Hair: Betty Sherriff. Recording director: Tony Lumkin. Sound: Claude Hitchcock. Sound editor: Roy Hyde. Dubbing mixer: Dennis Whitlock. Boom operator: Keith Batten [uncredited]. Assistant director: Derek Whitehurst. Production manager: Dennis Hall. Construction manager: Jock Lyall. Camera operator: Rodney "Chick" Anstiss. Gaffer: Ted Hallows. Continuity: Renee Glynne. Stills: Albert Clarke

[uncredited]. Processing: Humphries Laboratories. **Cast:** Richard O'Sullivan (Robin Tripp), Paula Wilcox (Chrissy Plummer), Sally Thomsett (Jo), Brian Murphy (George Roper), Yootha Joyce (Mildred Roper), Doug Fisher (Larry Simmonds), Patrick Newell (Sir Edmund Weir), Peter Cellier (Morris Pluthero), Aimi Macdonald (Hazel Lovett), Jack Smethurst (Himself), Rudolph Walker (Himself), Spike Milligan (Himself), Arthur Lowe (Spiros), Michael Ward (Gideon), Melvyn Hayes (Nigel), Bill Grundy (Interviewer), Michael Robbins (Second doorman), Aubrey Morris (Lecturer), Julian Orchard (Producer), Bill Maynard (Chef), Johnny Briggs (Milkman), Bill Pertwee (Postman), Norman Mitchell (Doorman [Arthur Mullgrave]), Berry Cornish (PA), Bill Sawyer (Chauffeur), Andria Lawrence (Miss Bird), Mark Rogers (Boy scout), Pauline Peart (Secretary), Arthur Hewlett (Elderly man), Annie Leake (Tweedy lady), Corinne Skinner (Housewife), Damaris Hayman (Old woman), Robert Dorning (Colonel Manners), Harry Fielder (unnamed role [uncredited]). **DVD availability:** Momentum Pictures (UK R2 PAL). **CD availability:** *The Hammer Comedy Film Music Collection* (GDI Records), which contains the *Title Song* (the vocal for which the liner notes wrongly credit to lyricist Annie Farrow instead of Jane Christie), *Larry and Jo*, *Robin and Chrissy* and *The Chase to Thames Television*

## Man at the Top

GB, 1973, 87m, Technicolor, cert X

Going to the cinema in Britain in the seventies can't have been much different from flicking on the TV, given the proliferation of small to large screen transfers. It was mostly sitcoms that provided the source material, and not being a company to miss a bandwagon, Hammer had naturally churned out its own selection of big screen transfers, among them *On the Buses* (1971), *Nearest and Dearest* (1973) and *Love Thy Neighbour* (1973). It wasn't just the sitcom that provided inspiration, however. The decade would also produce several dramatic TV inspired transfers, among them *Doomwatch* (1972), *Henry VIII and His Six Wives* (1972 [based upon *The Six Wives of Henry VIII*, 1970, TV]), *Callan* (1974) and *Sweeney!* (1976). Naturally, Hammer was in there pitching too, this time with *Man at the Top*.

Based upon the TV series of the same name, the show ran from 1970 to 1972 and followed the further adventures of Joe Lampton, the anti-hero of the 1957 John Braine novel *Room at the Top*, which had been filmed by Jack Clayton in 1958 with Laurence Harvey as Lampton, an ambitious young clerk who manages to marry into a wealthy industrial family and work his way up the ladder of success. A commercial and critical hit thanks to its adult approach to sex and relationships (something of a ground-breaker for the time), the film went on to win Oscars for leading lady Simone Signoret and screenwriter Neil Peterson. It was also nominated for best picture, best director, best actor and best supporting actress, and inspired a sequel, *Life at the Top* (1965), again starring Laurence Harvey, who this time, weary of his loveless marriage, embarks on an affair.

Harvey passed on the small screen spin-off,

which was produced by Thames Television, leaving the door open for Kenneth Haigh to take over the role, which he did with great successes, clocking up 23 fifty-minute episodes over the show's three-year run. By now, Lampton was working as a management consultant and living in Surrey's stockbroker belt, and as before, is not adverse to the ladies when an opportunity presents itself.

The film spin-off features more of the same, with the ever-ambitious Lampton, now divorced, invited by Lord Ackerman to join his pharmaceutical company as managing director. However, Joe becomes suspicious of his appointment when he discovers that his predecessor, Harish Taranath, committed suicide because D50, a wonder drug with the ability to counter the side effects of malnutrition and tropical diseases, had been produced and marketed to five African countries before the lab tests on it were completed, resulting in one-thousand women being made sterile. Given that his name was on the contract, Joe is naturally keen to prove his innocence and discover who is behind the cover up.

During his investigation, Joe has a number of sexual liaisons, among them Lord Ackerman's wife, Lady Alex, who clearly has a predilection for a bit of rough every now and again, Lord Ackerman's haughty daughter Robin, and two girl hitchhikers he picks up on the motorway while driving North to Middleton Grange, Lord Ackerman's country seat, where, after purloining a secret medical report, he eventually discovers that Ackerman himself is behind the cover up.

As in his previous exploits, Lampton is his usual, belligerent self, making no apologies for his unvarnished attitude to life or the chip he all too obviously carries on his shoulder. As he says to Lady Alex before bedding her, "I didn't waste my time cultivating a rough-hewn working class charm, you know. I was the genuine, foul-smelling, nose-picking, graceless article. I was unpleasant, coarse, poor, crude, resentful. I hated the sound of middle class voices, hated the sight of their neatly pressed trousers and their crisp, white shirts. I wanted to piss on them all from a very great height." Lady Alex seems to have him sussed, though. "Do stop thinking everyone's against you," she comments, to which comes the blunt retort, "Stop thinking that and you're dead." However, it is this attitude that ultimately saves Joe's skin, given Lord Ackerman's attitude to him: "I despise him for his cheap self-assurance, his filthy manners and ridiculous vulgarity. Yet because he's a shrewd businessman he's useful to me—useful at the moment, at any rate. How my father would have loathed him. He never would have forgiven me for employing such a man!"

Very much a film of its period, *Man at the Top* revels in the freer attitudes to sex, nudity and bad language prevalent in the cinema of the early seventies ("Lampton's back ... on top of everything," ran the poster's tag line). However, what once must have seemed reasonably fresh and stylish now seems more than a little tarnished. Padded to excess—the story would barely have filled a television episode—the drama is eked out with a number of irrelevancies, among them Joe's drive

Plain and simple British poster for *Man at the Top* (1973) featuring (from left to right) Mary Maude, Kenneth Haigh and Nannette Newman (Hammer/Dufton/MGM-EMI).

North and his frolic with the two girls he picks up on the motorway and later has a three-way with in a motel shower. His dour pontificating also becomes hectoring after a while. For example, take this unprovoked tirade at the two hitchhikers: "Christ, are you in for a rude awakening, all of you—all the soft-skinned, moist-eyed, flaxen-haired brigade. All those feeble, wanking revolutionaries in their bell-bottomed denims, and all those art school Jesus Christs with their pot-smoking, muddle-headed gospels about candy-flossed futures where everybody fucks, nobody fights and human nature changes overnight. Are you in for a rude awakening!"

Joe's self-regard and self-loathing also become wearing by the end. "I think I'm a bastard—and I think I like it," he smugly announces at one point. Meanwhile, of his highly paid job, he comments, "I can afford to buy myself a higher class of misery." Still, the screenplay does come up with one or two relishable exchanges. "I've always distrusted people like you, and I find it hard to change my ways," Joe says to Lord Ackerman, who responds, "Mutual dislike is often the best basis for a business partnership, don't you think?"

In the hands of director Mike Vardy, the proceedings have a small screen look to them, perhaps because Vardy was better used to helming TV episodes as a living (among them seven of *Man at the Top*). That said, there are one or two attempts at style in the opening minutes, among them the well-staged suicide of Taranath in Hyde Park (on the bandstand adjacent to Rotten Row, ironically enough), and a boxing match into which flashy jump cuts, freeze-frames and flashbacks (in which

Joe is offered the job of managing director by Lord Ackerman) are edited. Unfortunately, the results are less a bravura display of technique and more of an irritant by the time the sequence is over. Vardy's handling of some of the lengthier dialogue scenes meanwhile lacks flair, among them Joe's seemingly endless seduction of Lady Alex in his hotel bedroom.

As Joe, Kenneth Haigh's attempts to play up the role's roughness and misogyny never quite convince, while the over-used tic of widening his eyes for dramatic punctuation has a smack of the amateur dramatics to it. One never quite believes the fact that Joe is supposed to be such a dynamic businessman either. Still, Nanette Newman as Lady Alex is a welcome distraction (though her nude scenes clearly feature a body double), while Harry Andrews has some fun as the devious Lord Ackerman. His casual indifference to the fact that one-thousand women have been made sterile because of the faulty D50 provokes him to observe that this may well have been a blessing in disguise, given that they live "in a remote part of Africa where overpopulation is a major problem anyway." Indeed, he seems more concerned about political upset and the possibility of antagonizing "the self-righteous brigade.

Apparently corrupt in more ways than one, it is hinted that the tactile Ackerman's designs on Joe may also be other than business-related, prompting Joe to snipe, "Stop treating my arm like a choir boy's arse," during one heated exchange. Meanwhile, Joe's woodland sexual liaison with Robin (who has inherited her mother's liking for a bit of rough) seems to be hinting that Joe is literally giving one to the aristocracy, even though it was Robin who instigated the tryst, just as her mother did earlier (soon after, when Joe is chased by Lord Ackerman and other members of the hunt in a bid to secure his loyalty over the D50 affair for fear of reprisal, Joe emphasizes this by commenting, "Sod the lot of you—up yours!"). In the end Joe secures his safety—and future—by giving the story to a newspaper friend on the understanding that it won't be published unless something untoward happens to him; and this despite his low opinion of the press, as expressed earlier in the film ("If I had my way, all papers would be printed ready-perforated with a hole in the corner for the nail").

By no means a classic, *Man at the Top* is an adequate if uninspired reminder of a popular TV series of its time. Plainly (sometimes drably) filmed, it is routine in most ways, from the cinematography of Brian Probyn to the score by Roy Budd, which lacks the flair of his other soundtracks of the period, among them *Get Carter* (1971) and *The Stone Killer* (1973). Shot at Elstree and on location between 3 March and 7 April 1973, the film was released in the UK by MGM-EMI later the same year on 16 September. Commented Michael Carreras of the film, "*Man at the Top* was a total disaster…. What audiences accept on television—which are very shadowy characters in very undramatic situations—don't transfer to the cinema."[4] **Additional notes:** Lord Ackerman's country seat—Pyrford Court in Ripley, Surrey—was also used as a location for the *Wish You Were Here* segment of *Tales from the Crypt* (1972), *Son of Dracula* (1974), *The Cat and the Canary* (1978) and, most famously, *The Omen* (1976). The film also went out on a double bill with the Shaw Brothers kung fu actioner *The Chinese Connection* (1971)—originally known as *Quan ji* and also *Duel of Fists*—which starred David Chiang, soon to be seen in Hammer's *The Legend of the 7 Golden Vampires* (1974).

Production companies: Hammer/Dufton. Distributor: MGM-EMI (UK [ABC circuit]). Producers: Peter Charlesworth, Jock Jacobsen. Presenter: Nat Cohen. Production supervisor: Roy Skeggs. Director: Mike Vardy. Screenplay: Hugh Whitemore, John Junkin, based upon characters created by John Braine. Cinematographer: Brian Probyn. Music: Roy Budd. Music director: Philip Martell. Editor: Chris Barnes. Art director: Don Picton. Make-up: George Blackler. Hair: Elaine Bowerbank. Costumes: Laura Nightingale. Sound: Claude Hitchcock. Sound editor: Terry Poulton. Dubbing mixer: Dennis Whitlock. Assistant director: Ken Baker. Production manager: Ron Jackson. Construction manager: Arthur Banks. Camera operator: Rodney "Chick" Anstiss. Boom operator: Keith Batten [uncredited]. Casting: James Liggat. Continuity: Sally Ball. Production secretary: Sally Pardo [uncredited]. Stunts: Alf Joint [uncredited]. **Cast:** Kenneth Haigh (Joe Lampton), Nanette Newman (Lady Alex Ackerman), Harry Andrews (Lord Ackerman), Danny Sewell (Billy Weston), John Quentin (Digby), Mary Maude (Robin Ackerman), Paul Williamson (Tarrant), Margaret Heald (Eileen), Charlie Williams (George Harvey), Angela Bruce (Joyce Harvey), Anne Cun-ningham (Mrs. Harvey), William Lucas (Marshall), John Collin (Wisbech), Norma West (Sarah Tarrant), Clive Swift (Massey), Patrick McCann (Boxer), John Conteh (Boxer), George Francis (Referee), Jaron Yaltan (Harish Taranath), Tim Brinton (Newsreader), Nell Brennan (Waitress), Verne Morgan (Records clerk) **DVD availability:** Warner (UK R2 PAL)

### Man Bait see The Last Page

### The Man in Black

GB, 1950, 75m, bw, United Programmes, cert A

The first of five second features shot by Hammer at Oakley Court—also see *Room to Let* (1950), *Someone at the Door* (1950), *What the Butler Saw* (1950) and *The Lady Craved Excitement* (1950)—this mild thriller was yet another radio adaptation, this time based on the serial *Appointment with Fear* (1943–1955). An account of how two women came to commit murder, the film is narrated by a storyteller (as per the radio series), yet plays no better for using this device (despite the sepulchral tones of Valentine Dyall). Nevertheless, it remains of passing note for marking the first appearance in a Hammer film by future *Carry On* star Sid James (who plays two roles), and for being scripted by John Gilling, who would go on to helm several films for the company, most notably *The Plague of the Zombies* (1966) and *The Reptile* (1966). Filmed in August 1949 (while James Carreras was away in America negotiating a production and distribution deal with Robert L. Lippert), *The Man in Black* was trade shown in January 1950 and released in the UK by Exclusive on 6 March 1950. **Additional notes:** A still by John Jay depicting the making of the film was featured on to the front cover of the 22 September 1949 issue of *Film Industry*, promoting the Vinten Everest camera with which the film was shot. The film was part-financed with a loan from the National Film Finance Corporation. Oakley Court becomes Oakfield Towers in the film.

Production company: Hammer. Distributor: Exclusive (UK). Producer: Anthony Hinds. Director: Francis Searle. Screenplay: Francis Searle, based on the radio serial *Appointment with Fear* by John Dickson Carr. Story: Francis Searle. Cinematographer: Cedric Williams. Music directors: Frank Spencer, Rupert Grayson. Editor: John Ferris, Ray Pitt [uncredited]. Art Director: Denis Wreford. Costumes: Jaeger (housecoat). Sound: Edgar Vetter. Assistant director: Jimmy Sangster. Second assistant director: Jack Causey [uncredited]. Make-up: Phil Leakey. Hair: Monica Hustler. Camera operator: Peter Bryan. Focus puller: Michael Reed [uncredited]. Clapper loader: Harry Oakes [uncredited]. Continuity: Renee Glynne. Casting: Prudence Sykes. Production manager: Arthur Barnes. Chief electrician: Jack Curtis [uncredited]. Electricians: Charles Mullett [uncredited], Charles Stanbridge [uncredited], Richard Jenkins [uncredited], Percy Harms [uncredited]. Boom operator: Percy Britten [uncredited]. Sound assistant: Gordon Everett [uncredited]. Construction: Freddie Ricketts [uncredited], Mick Lyons [uncredited]. Props: Tommy Money [uncredited]. Stills: John Jay [uncredited]. Production assistant: Michael Carreras [uncredited]. **Cast:** Betty Ann Davies (Bertha Clavering), Sidney James (Henry Clavering/Hodson), Anthony Forwood (Victor Harrington), Valentine Dyall (Storyteller), Laurence Baskcombe (Sandford), Hazel Penwarden (Joan), Sheila Burrell (Janice), Courtney Hope (Mrs. Carter), Mollie Palmer (Elsie), Gerald Case (Doctor)

Simplicity is sometimes best. An eye-catching poster for *The Man in Black* (1950). Note that "It's Exclusive!" (Hammer/Exclusive).

### Man in Hiding see Mantrap

### A Man on the Beach

GB, 1956, 29m, Eastmancolor, CinePanoramic, RCA, cert U

This half-hour drama about a crook who hides out with a blind recluse having robbed a casino disguised as a duchess is something of a curio. It was filmed during a hiatus in feature production by Hammer in July 1955. Set in the South of France, it was helmed by the blacklisted American director Joseph Losey, and features location work shot in Ostend and Dover, as well exteriors shot at Down Place (doubling for the Rocville Casino). The film is primarily of interest for marking the screen-writing debut of assistant director/production manager Jimmy Sangster, who based his script on the 1954 short story *Chance at the Wheel* (aka *Menace at the Casino* [1955 American re-print]) by Victor Canning.

Sadly, despite Sangster's assertion that "the picture was better than the story,"[5] the results are only mildly diverting thanks to the unimaginative direction of Losey, who makes very little of the situations and opportunities to hand, although he is well served by his three main actors, Donald Wolfit, Michael Medwin and Michael Ripper, the latter two of whom get to fight it out on the suncracked mud of a quarry in one mildly effective sequence. As for the "twist" ending in which the thief finally discovers that his host is actually blind, even someone with impaired vision could see it coming a mile off, despite the best precautions of Losey and cinematographer Wilkie Cooper to disguise the fact. "I go and tell you everything—and you couldn't have identified me anyway," bleats the thief when it's too late, prompting the blind man to reply, "For a man who lives by his senses, you're not very observant, are you?" Quite! However, despite the general flatness of the handling, there is a nice touch when the thief is exploring the blind man's seemingly deserted beachside shack and finds a mirror covered in dust, the meaning of which he fails to comprehend.

Production on the featurette began on 18 July 1955, while the location filming took place between 3 and 5 August. The finished film was trade shown on 1 March 1956 and released as a support in the UK by Exclusive on 26 March.

Recalled Harry Oakes of the location shoot in Ostend involving a Rolls-Royce: "The first day there, we drove several miles along by these sand dunes, pulled off the road and into the dunes. A big trunk was then pulled out of the back of the Rolls-Royce and, lo and behold, Mickey Delamar starts putting on a chauffeur's uniform and Tony Hinds puts on a woman's frock, glasses, a wig and a hat! And they doubled-up for long shots. Unionism was very strong in those days so we thought we better keep quiet about this or else we'd get the sack from the union."[6]

Recalled Jimmy Sangster: "Most times I forget about this movie. When asked what my first screenplay was I invariably say *X—The Unknown*. In fact, I wrote one little piece before either of them, another short subject which I entitled *The Camera*. Tony Hinds read it, said it was okay, but he didn't want to make it. But it probably took that to convince him it was okay to write *A Man on the Beach*. Which he did. Which I did. Which Joe Losey did and which I imagine cost practically no money at all in spite of a location in France."[7] **Additional notes:** The film carries a 1955 copyright. Footman colour is billed as Eastman Colour in the credits.

Production company: Hammer. Distributor: Exclusive (UK). Producer: Anthony Hinds. Production supervisor: Mickey Delamar. Director: Joseph Losey. Screenplay: Jimmy Sangster, based on the story *Chance at the Wheel* by Victor Canning. Cinematographer: Wilkie Cooper. Music: John Hotchkiss. Editor: Henry Richardson. Art director: Edward Marshall. Sound: W.H. May. Makeup: Phil Leakey. Hair: Monica Hustler. Camera operator/second unit cinematographer: Len Harris [both uncredited]. Focus puller/second unit operator: Harry Oakes [both uncredited]. Second assistant director: Hugh Harlow [uncredited]. Production secretary: Doreen Soan [uncredited]. Processing: Humphries Laboratories. **Cast:** Donald Wolfit (Carter), Michael Medwin (Max), Michael Ripper (Chauffeur), Edward Forsyth (Inspector Clement [uncredited]), Barry Shawzin (American [uncredited]), Alex de Gallier (Casino manager [uncredited]), Corinne Grey (First beach blonde [uncredited]), Nora Maiden (Second beach blonde [uncredited]), Sandra Walden (Little girl [uncredited]), Kirk S. Siegenburg (Little boy [uncredited])

### The Man Who Could Cheat Death

GB, 1959, 83m, Technicolor, widescreen [1.66:1], RCA, cert X

Having filmed the first color versions of *Frankenstein*, *Dracula* and *The Hound of the Baskervilles* (and with a color remake of *The Mummy* already in the works), Hammer continued their policy of re-working proven material with this color version of the 1939 Barre Lyndon play *The Man in Half Moon Street*, which had previously been filmed under its original title by Paramount in 1944. Unfortunately, having struck box office gold with their previous remakes, *The Man Who Could Cheat Death*—as the film was to be more exploitatively titled—was both a commercial and artistic disaster.

In the original film, Swedish matinee idol Nils Asther had starred as Dr. Julian Karell, a Parisian doctor-cum-sculptor who avoids the ravages of time via a series of gland transplants which give him the appearance of being in his mid-thirties rather than his true age, ninety. In the remake, German character star Anton Diffring top lines as Dr. Georges Bonnet, a "thief of time," as the trailer has it, who has similarly been able to disguise his true age—here one-hundred-and-four—via a series of "uter-parathyroid" transplants performed by his longtime colleague Dr. Ludwig Weiss. Unfortunately, while travelling to Paris to perform the latest operation (which has to be carried out every ten years), the eighty-nine-year-old Weiss suffers a stroke and is thus incapable of performing the vital surgery. Luckily, Bonnet has the remains of an elixir that is able to retard the aging process—but only for four weeks, during which period he has to obtain a replacement gland and a surgeon willing to carry out the operation…

The original film had treated its subject in a highly romanticized manner, akin to the style of *The Picture of Dorian Gray* (1945). Consequently, one has a certain sympathy for the doctor and his bid for eternal youth, despite the fact that he has to commit murder to achieve his goals. For the remake, however (which was provisionally titled *The Man in the Rue Noire*, and for which Hammer had hoped to cast Peter Cushing in the leading role), screenwriter Jimmy Sangster concentrated on the story's more grisly elements, thus turning it into a straight horror yarn. Therefore, any sympathy one might have had for Bonnet (originally Bruner in the draft script) is negated—doubly so, given the cold-eyed performance by Diffring, whom audiences were more used to seeing playing ruthless Nazis. Consequently, instead of being the deluded romantic hero of the piece, as Karell had been, Bonnet is transformed into little more than a dyed-in-the-wool villain in a bog standard surgical thriller, hence the trailer's description of him as a "liar, cheat, murderer, offender against Nature and God" (note that Diffring would play a similar role—that of a deranged plastic surgeon—in his very next film, the somewhat livelier *Circus of Horrors* [1960]).

Therefore, when Bonnet persuades the ill Weiss to convince a fellow surgeon—one Dr. Pierre Gerrard—to perform the operation, the assumption is that it won't be too long before the doctor's nefarious scheme is exposed and he is on the receiving end of the expected retribution, especially as he has also imprisoned his model, Janine Dubois, with whom he has fallen in love, his intention being to perform a similar operation on *her* and thus secure a partner for everlasting life.

Indeed, when Weiss discovers that Bonnet has in fact been murdering people to attain the glands required for the operations (where did he *think* they were coming from?), he breaks the vial containing the elixir, thus sowing the seeds for Bonnet's downfall. In the ensuing struggle, the increasingly desperate Bonnet kills the old man, whose absence he now has to explain to the in-

**Arnold Marle (left) and Anton Diffring (right) share a dramatic moment in *The Man Who Could Cheat Death* (1959) (Hammer/Cadogan/Paramount).**

creasingly suspicious Gerrard, along with the disappearance of Janine, for whom Gerrard also harbors desires. Gerrard nevertheless carries out the surgery, after which Bonnet goes to the warehouse where he has imprisoned Janine, taking with him a gland he has harvested from a prostitute. However, he is trailed there by Gerrard and Inspector Legris (who has been investigating the series of gland murders for a number of years), by which time he has begun to age; apparently, Gerrard only made an incision to convince Bonnet that the operation had taken part, thus forcing him to reveal the whereabouts of Janine. In the ensuing fracas, Bonnet gradually reverts to his true age, while a fire started by a lamp thrown by another of his former conquests, also held captive, sees the whole place go up in flames.

Just as Universal had been involved in the remake of *Dracula*, so Paramount helped to finance and distribute *The Man Who Could Cheat Death*, no doubt keen to board the Hammer bandwagon (a loan from the National Film Finance Corporation also helped to bolster finances). Another incentive for Hammer to remake this not entirely well known property seems to have been a television production—aired as part of ABC's *Hour of Mystery* (1957, TV) series on 22 June 1957 as *The Man in Half Moon Street*—which had also starred Anton Diffring (here named Dr. Thackeray) and Hammer regular Arnold Marle as Dr. Weiss (spelled Weisz for the small screen). Hammer was certainly not adverse to remaking successful television programs (witness *The Quatermass Xperiment* [1955] and *The Abominable Snowman* [1957]). Consequently, both Diffring and Marle were recruited for the film version, which went before the cameras the following year on 17 November 1958, though as has already been noted, Peter Cushing had originally been lined up for the role, but pulled out at the last moment (just six days prior to filming), claiming exhaustion following the shooting of *The Hound of the Baskervilles* (1959), which had only just wrapped. This left the door open for Diffring to reprise the role; of course, Diffring had previously stepped into Cushing's shoes by playing Baron Frankenstein in Hammer's ill-fated television series *Tales of Frankenstein* (1958, TV), and so was already known to the company. Cushing's last minute departure prompted understandable worry for Paramount, who had now lost their prime marquee name. It also resulted in a tersely worded letter from Hammer's lawyer being sent to Cushing's agent at the behest of James Carreras, momentarily putting Cushing's relationship with the studio in jeopardy. That a final binding contract had not yet been signed got Cushing off from threatened legal proceedings, though it did result in the dropping of negotiations between Hammer and Cushing's agent for a new five-picture deal. However, in a matter of weeks the incident was all water under the bridge, given that Cushing was back at Hammer for *The Mummy* (1959). Nevertheless, it remains a rather astonishing episode, given Cushing's ranking as a star name for Hammer and his involvement in their two central moneymaking franchises.

While all this was going on, Hammer at least managed to secure a solid supporting cast, among them Hazel Court as Janine and Christopher Lee as the surgeon Pierre Gerrard, while the familiar faces of Francis de Wolff and Charles Lloyd-Pack were also onboard (note that a brief scene featuring Michael Ripper as a morgue attendant was cut from the release print, although Ripper was still mentioned in the press book cast list). As for the crew, the trailer noted that the film was "produced by the team that gave you *The Curse of Frankenstein* and *Dracula*."

Unfortunately, despite the pedigree of its source, the film—set in 1890 Paris—fails to capture the essence of the material, despite its comparatively lengthy shoot, which concluded on 30 December. As always, Bernard Robinson's plush sets provide plenty to catch the eye. Sadly, Terence Fisher's direction, save for a fog-wreathed Jack the Ripper esque opening sequence which plays out under the credits, is curiously unambitious, with many scenes filmed in lengthy, static takes, almost as if from the stalls of a theater. This, combined with the uncharacteristically bright and bland lighting of Jack Asher and the garish Technicolor film stock, make for some visually tedious and unattractive images (it also makes the film drag inordinately, despite its comparatively brief running time). If that weren't enough, the long awaited climax featuring Roy Ashton's all-too-briefly-seen age acceleration make-up is somewhat fudged. Recalled Ashton, "I was told to make Anton Diffring look as though he was falling to pieces. I felt that the final effect should be a cocktail of fatal diseases spreading rapidly across his body. Glandular fever, smallpox, cholera, typhus and typhoid, representing some of the ailments that Bonnet had come into contact with as a crusading physician."[8]

These disappointments aside, the film does have its bonuses. Despite the unattractive nature of his character, one can't help but admire the steely resolve with which Anton Diffring plays Bonnet. "I want to lift the curtain of life and see what lies beyond," he comments at one stage (it was the character's resolve that prompted the poster's tagline: "His terrifying secret—his hideous obsession made him…. *The Man Who Could Cheat Death*"). He also has a way with a sneery put down, observing of his patients that "their money gives them an overblown sense of their own importance." As always, Hazel Court is a delight to look at as Janine, while Arnold Marle's Dr. Weiss strikes the right note of concern as the voice of reason. Unfortunately, the film's innate lack of pace makes it something of an endurance test to sit through, while its lack of atmosphere and genuine *frissons* only compounds matters, despite the trailer's promise that we would endure "fear as old as time."

Recalled Christopher Lee, "This was a very beautifully photographed film. The sets and costumes were among the best in any Hammer production. Unfortunately, the picture is a bit slow … and lacked the excitement found in other Hammer films of this period."[9] As for his own character he added, "He was rather dull, actually! It *was* a change, however, from the villainous characters with whom I was becoming associated."[10] Said Jimmy Sangster of the film, "I think the best word I can come up with to describe the movie is 'leaden.'"[11] However,

as far as Hazel Court was concerned, "It seemed to me that they took greater pains with *The Man Who Could Cheat Death* than with *The Curse of Frankenstein*, and that it was a more elaborate movie."[12]

The critics also found the £84,000 production to be slow and dull. "Invention and embellishment in this field appear to have been exhausted," claimed *Variety*, though it did concede that the film had "good Technicolor" and that it was "well-acted and intelligently conceived." The *Monthly Film Bulletin* was harsher, adding that the film "offers little in the way of entertainment beyond the sets, costumes and props," while *The Times* described the results as "too wooden and stylized." *The Observer* even expressed a note of concern for the film's makers: "What dreary, lifeless work the concoction of these horror pictures must be." On the plus side, *Picturegoer* found the film to be "quite mad and often scarifying," while *Kinematograph Weekly* labeled it "a sure bet." However, *The Man Who Could Cheat Death* did only moderate business when, following a trade show on 4 June 1959, it was released in the UK by Paramount on 30 November on a double bill with *The Evil That Is Eve* (1957), by which time it had already made its U.S. debut in June, also care of Paramount. Commented the press brochure, "Both *The Curse of Frankenstein* and *Dracula*, earlier Hammer productions, are going to be considered by fans of horror films to have been sissy stuff when they see the newest Hammer entry in the scare-sweepstakes, *The Man Who Could Cheat Death*." Time, of course, has proven otherwise. **Additional notes:** For the European cut of the film, Hazel Court went topless for the scene in which she is seen modeling for Bonnet. For this extremely brief sequence the actress was paid the then-staggering sum of £2,000. Recalled the actress of her topless scene: "It was new in those days, but it was a beautiful setting and supposedly I was being sculpted, so it didn't worry me."[13] Jimmy Sangster penned a novelization of the screenplay for Ace/Harborough (Avon in the U.S.) under the pen name John Sansom, a name he later made use of on his screenplays for *To Have and to Hold* (1963), which was made by Merton Park, and Hammer's belated *Dracula* sequel, *Dracula—Prince of Darkness* (1966). Christopher Lee would also play a doctor named Pierre Gerrard in Hammer's *Taste of Fear* (1961); this was likewise scripted by Jimmy Sangster, who clearly liked the name. Composer Richard Rodney Bennett is billed simply as Richard Bennett. Elements of the story later reappeared in *The Night Strangler* (1973, TVM), in which a 144-year-old alchemist strangles women at twenty-one-year intervals for the rejuvenating properties of their blood.

Production companies: Hammer/Cadogan. Distributor: Paramount (UK [ABC circuit], U.S.). Producer: Michael Carreras. Associate producer: Anthony Nelson Keys. Director: Terence Fisher. Screenplay: Jimmy Sangster, based upon the play *The Man in Half Moon Street* by Barre Lyndon. Cinematographer: Jack Asher. Music: Richard Rodney Bennett. Music director: John Hollingsworth. Supervising editor: James Needs. Editor: John Dunsford. Production design: Bernard Robinson. Costumes: Molly Arbuthnot. Make-up: Roy Ashton.

Hair: Henry Montsash. Sound: Jock May. Camera operator: Len Harris. Focus puller: Harry Oakes [uncredited]. Assistant director: John Peverall. Second assistant director: Tom Walls [uncredited]. Third assistant director: Hugh Harlow [uncredited]. Continuity: Shirley Barnes [uncredited]. Production manager: Don Weeks. Studio manager: Arthur Kelly [uncredited]. Construction manager: Mick Lyons [uncredited]. Chief electrician: Jack Curtis [uncredited]. Master plasterer: Arthur Banks [uncredited]. Master carpenter: Charles Davis [uncredited]. Master painter: Lawrence Wren [uncredited]. Props: Tommy Money [uncredited]. Props buyer: Eric Hillier [uncredited]. Cashier: Ken Gordon [uncredited]. **Cast:** Anton Diffring (Dr. Georges Bonnet), Hazel Court (Janine Dubois), Christopher Lee (Dr. Pierre Gerrard), Arnold Marle (Dr. Ludwig Weiss), Francis de Wolff (Inspector Legris), Gerda Larsen (Street girl), Delphi Lawrence (Margo Philippe), Marie Burke (Guest), Charles Lloyd-Pack (Man), Lockwood West (Doctor), Ronald Adam (Doctor), Barry Shawzin (Doctor), Middleton Woods (Little man), Ian Hewitson (Roget), Denis Shaw (Man in tavern), Frederick Rawlings (Footman), John Harrison (Servant). **DVD availability:** Legend (U.S. R1 NTSC). **Blu-ray availability:** Legend Films (A/1), double-billed with the Amicus film *The Skull* (1965); Eureka Entertainment (B/2), extras include the DVD, a booklet with notes by Marcus Hearn, and video interviews with Kim Newman and Jonathan Rigby

## Man with a Dog

GB, 1957, 24m, bw, cert U

This modest featurette was the last such production to be made by Hammer (*Danger List*, though made shortly before with very much the same team, was released after it, however).

The story of a war veteran who refuses to go into hospital for an operation until various parties agree to look after his dog and newsstand, it was also the last big screen production to be helmed by Gainsborough veteran Leslie Arliss. A sentimental yarn, "rich in warmly human true-to-life appeal" (as Exclusive's press release had it), it was filmed between 25 and 29 March, 1957 (*Danger List*, also helmed by Arliss, had finished shooting just six days earlier). It was released in the UK by Exclusive on 3 November 1957.

Production company: Hammer. Distributor: Exclusive (UK). Producer: Anthony Hinds. Executive producer: Michael Carreras. Associate producer: Anthony Nelson Keys. Director: Leslie Arliss. Screenplay: no credit available. Cinematographer: Arthur Grant. Supervising editor: James Needs. Editor: A.E. Cox. Art director: Ted Marshall. Camera operator: Len Harris. Focus puller: Harry Oakes [uncredited]. Sound: Jock May. Production manager: Don Weeks. **Cast:** Maurice Denham (Mr. Keeble), Sarah Lawson (Vicky Alexander), Clifford Evans (Dr. Bennett), Jan Holden (Nurse), Marianne Stone (Mrs. Stephens), John Van Eyssen (Dr. Langham), Margaret Boyd (Mrs. Tidmarsh), Clive Marshall (Jim), Andrew Motte-Harrison (Giles), Anthony Ford (Alf), Malcolm Knight (Bert)

## Manahan, Anna

This Irish actress (1924–2009) appeared briefly in Hammer's *The Viking Queen* (1967), in which she played a shopkeeper's wife. Primarily on stage in both Britain and America, her other credits include *She Didn't Say No!* (1958), *Of Human Bondage* (1964), *Ulysses* (1967), *Clash of the Titans* (1981), *A Man of No Importance* (1994) and *On the Edge* (2004), plus the series *The Irish R.M.* (1983–1985, TV), in which she played Mrs. Cadogan. **Hammer credits:** *The Viking Queen* (1967, as Shop keeper's wife)

## Manchester Studios (The Film Studios [Manchester] Limited)

During a respite in the lease of Down Place, Hammer made a number of films at other facilities, among them the Manchester Studios—officially known as the Film Studios (Manchster) Limited—at which it shot the interiors for *Never Look Back* (1952). Housed in a converted Methodist church in Rusholme, the studios were built in 1948 by producer and cinema magnate John E. "Pop" Blakely at a personal cost of £70,000, and became the home of Mancunian Films, which made such "local" comedies as *Cup-Tie Honeymoon* (1948), *Holidays with Pay* (1948), *Somewhere in Politics* (1949), *Over the Garden Wall* (1950) and *It's a Grand Life* (1953), featuring such popular music hall stars as Frank Randle, Norman Evans, Tessie O'Shea, Sandy Powell and Jimmy Clitheroe. The studios were sold to the BBC in 1954. **Hammer credits:** *Never Look Back* (1952)

## Mander, Charles

This British supporting actor (1924–1999) popped up as PC Smith in Hammer's *Room to Let* (1950). His other appearances include the TV plays *Mile Away Murder* (1949, TV) and *The Angel Who Pawned Her Harp* (1951, TV), plus episodes of *BBC Sunday-Night Theatre* (1950–1959, TV). **Hammer credits:** *Room to Let* (1950, as PC Smith)

## Mander, Kay

One of Hammer's continuity girls, British born Mander (1915–2013, full name Kathleen Molyneux Mander) worked on two featurettes for the company. Her other credits include *Room for Two* (1940), *The List of Adrian Messenger* (1963), *From Russia with Love* (1963), *Fahrenheit 451* (1966), *Mahler* (1974), *The Human Factor* (1979), *Play Me Something* (1989) and *I Was Catherine the Great's Stable Boy* (1994), plus episodes of *Man in a Suitcase* (1967–1968, TV), *The Professionals* (1977–1983, TV) and *Danger UXB* (1979, TV). She began her career by directing shorts and training films, among them *How to File* (1941), *Highland Doctor* (1943), for which she also provided the story and appeared in, *A Plan to Work On* (1948), which she also wrote, *Histoire de Poissons* (1949), which she also edited, and *The New Boat* (1955), which she wrote, directed and edited. She also produced *How, What and Why? No 2* (1948). In 1935, she worked as secretary for the International Film Congress. In 1944 she founded Basic Films with her husband R.K. Neilson-Baxter (1909–1978), whom she married the same year. **Hammer credits:** *Danger List* (1957), *Clean Sweep* (1958)

## Mander, Peter

This British actor (1924–2008) played one of the dancers featured in the Hammer comedy *The Ugly Duckling* (1959). His other credits include an episode of *Tales from Dickens* (1958–1959, TV). **Hammer credits:** *The Ugly Duckling* (1959, as Dancer [uncredited])

## Mandes, Malaika *see* Martin, Malaika

## Mango, Alec

This British actor (1911–1989, full name Alexander Anthony J. Mango) had minor roles in two Hammer films. His other credits include *Fiddlers Three* (1944), *Zarak* (1956), *We Shall See* (1964), *Khartoum* (1966), *Steptoe and Son* (1972) and *Gothic* (1986), plus episodes of *Z Cars* (1962–1978, TV) and *Upstairs, Downstairs* (1971–1975, TV). **Hammer credits:** *Mask of Dust* (1954, as Guido Rosetti), *Frankenstein Created Woman* (1967, as Spokesman)

## *Maniac*

GB, 1963, 86m, bw, MegaScope [2.35:1], Westrex, cert X

Following the unexpected runaway success of the twist-packed thriller *Taste of Fear* (1961), it was perhaps inevitable that writer-producer Jimmy Sangster would be asked to come up with more of the same, of which *Maniac* proved to be the first of several variants. Like *Taste of Fear*, the film is set in the South of France, albeit this time in the Camargue region ("The Camargue … a remote area in Southern France where wild horses roam, fighting bulls are bred, and violence is never far away…," as the opening caption informs us). However, instead of a crippled heiress, the plot sees one Georges Beynat committed to an asylum for murdering a man with an oxyacetylene torch (ouch!) by way of avenging the rape of his daughter. Several years later, Beynat's wife plans to spring her husband from the asylum with the help of George Farrell, an American painter who has fallen in love with her, the understanding being that the Beynats will divorce following his escape, so that she is free to re-marry. But it transpires that Farrell is merely a pawn in an elaborate plot involving Mrs. Beynat's *real* lover, a psychotic male nurse who has some murderous plans of his own….

With Michael Carreras in the director's chair, principal photography on *Maniac* began on location in France on 28 May 1962, for which Kerwin Mathews returned to Hammer to top line as George Farrell following his appearance in *The Pirates of Blood River* (1962). Shot in MegaScope so as to make the most of the eye-catching locations, the film was lensed by Wilkie Cooper who, as well as photographing the Hammer short *A Man on the Beach* (1956), had also worked with Mathews on *The Seventh Voyage of Sinbad* (1958). As for the rest of the comparatively small cast, it was rounded out with Nadia Gray as the duplicitous Eve Beynat, Liliane Brousse as her daughter Annette, and Donald Houston (wearing a rather obvious stick-on moustache) as the torch-wielding George Beynat.

The location shoot went pretty much as expected, despite the news that the film's interiors would have to be shot at the MGM studio at Bore-

stalks
his wife...
his daughter...
their
lover!

starring
KERWIN
MATHEWS · GRAY
NADIA

also starring
DONALD LILIANE
HOUSTON · BROUSSE

Written and Produced by    Directed by
JIMMY SANGSTER · MICHAEL CARRERAS

A HAMMER FILM PRODUCTION
A COLUMBIA PICTURES RELEASE    Megascope

hamwood owing to an overrun on Hammer's troubled remake of *The Old Dark House* (1963) at Bray. This unexpected change of address didn't affect *Maniac*'s schedule too adversely, however, given that there was plenty of time for art director Edward Carrick and his team to erect the sets at the new venue.

By no means as skilled as its predecessor, the plot of *Maniac* never quite convinces, its various twists being a little too heavily engineered to be entirely believable. The very slow-moving narrative doesn't help matters either, while Michael Carreras's direction lacks the Hitchcockian visual flourishes that Seth Holt brought to *Taste of Fear*. Nevertheless, Wilkie Cooper's scope photography provides a few scenic compensations, while the actors try their best to make the most of the various outlandish circumstances their characters find themselves in ("A story that sears the screen with terror!" exclaimed the trailer).

Commented Kerwin Mathews of his experiences on the film, "Michael Carreras was just breaking through my shield of insecurities on *Maniac* and I always wished we could have had another chance on another film, as he found his way as a director and I matured as an actor."[14] Commented

writer-producer Jimmy Sangster of the film: "I have to say that, all in all, Michael didn't take as much advantage of the locations as he could have. The sheer stark emptiness of the area, which made me choose it in the first place, didn't come across. But I guess nobody went to the movie to watch the scenery, so I'm being picky.... The story, I have to admit, was, to say the least, 'derivative,' as were most of my 'psycho' type movies. They were derivative of each other and they all went back to my original inspiration *Les diaboliques*.... The finished product didn't really live up to expectations."[15]

Cut to a tight but tedious eighty-six minutes, *Maniac* was released in the UK by BLC on 20 May 1963 on what must have been a suicidally dull double bill with Hammer's *The Damned* (1963), while for its American release on 31 October 1963 care of Columbia, it was billed with the studio's remake of *The Old Dark House* (1963). In neither case were the reviews particularly outstanding. Commented *Films and Filming*, "The film is finally and decisively trampled into dim mediocrity by the direction of Michael Carreras, with its marked absence of film sense." **Additional notes:** The film had a famous visitor one day. Remembered Jimmy Sangster: "Nadia Gray asked if she could bring a visitor on the set because he was quite interested in movie making.... She duly brought her visitor onto the set. It turned out to be Orson Welles. He was absolutely charming and didn't once tell us what we were doing wrong."[16] Some posters refer to the film as *The Maniac*.

Production company: Hammer. Distributors: BLC (UK), Columbia (U.S.). Producer: Jimmy Sangster. Director: Michael Carreras. Screenplay: Jimmy Sangster. Cinematographer: Wilkie Cooper. Music/conductor: Stanley Black. Supervising editor: James Needs. Editor: Tom Simpson. Art director: Edward Carrick. Assistant art director: Jean Peyre [uncredited]. Costumes: Molly Arbuthnot, Jean Fairlie [uncredited]. Assistant director: Ross MacKenzie. Second assistant director: Terry Lens [uncredited]. Production manager: Bill Hill. Sound: Cyril Swern. Sound editor: Roy Baker. Boom operator: Bill Baldwin [uncredited]. Sound camera operator: Ron Matthews [uncredited]. Sound maintenance: Peter Martingell [uncredited]. Make-up: Basil Newall, Stella Morris (assistant [uncredited]). Hair: Pat McDermott. Camera operator: Harry Gillam. Focus pullers: Tommy Fletcher [uncredited], Trevor Wrenn [uncredited]. Camera grip: L. Kelly [uncredited]. Camera loader/clapper boy: Ray Andrew [uncredited]. Draughtsman: Fred Carter [uncredited]. Scenic artist: Felix Sergejak [uncredited]. Props buyer: Margery Whittington [uncredited]. Props chargehand: Tommy Ibbetson [uncredited]. Standby props: M. Lord [uncredited]. Continuity: Kay Rawlings. Assistant to the producer: Ian Lewis. Production secretary: Margueritte Green [uncredited]. Titles: Chambers & Partners. Electrical supervisor: Bert Chapple [uncredited]. Electrical chargehand: Geoff Hughes [uncredited]. Carpenter: Tommy Westbrook [uncredited]. Painter: A. Smith [uncredited]. Stagehand: E. Power [uncredited]. Rigger: V. Bailey [uncredited]. Stills: James Swarbrick [uncredited]. Unit driver: Ron Warr

*Top:* **Presenting a new thrill: murder by oxyacetylene torch. Donald Houston features in the poster for *Maniac* (1963), which gives the game away somewhat as to the identity of the story's killer.** *Bottom:* **An unsettling British poster for *Maniac* (1963) (both photographs, Hammer/BLC/Columbia).**

[uncredited]. **Cast:** Kerwin Mathews (Geoff Farrell), Nadia Gray (Eve Beynat), Liliane Brousse (Annette Beynat), Donald Houston (Henri), Norman Bird (Gendarme Salon [for which he was dubbed by André Maranne]), George Pastell (Inspector Etienne), Justine Lord (Grace), Jerold Wells (Giles), Arnold Diamond (Janiello), Leon Peers (Blanchard). **DVD availability:** Sony (U.S. R1 NTSC), as part of the *Icons of Suspense* box set, which also includes *The Snorkel* (1958), *Never Take Sweets from a Stranger* (1960), *Cash on Demand* (1961), *The Full Treatment* (1961) and *The Damned* (1963), extras include trailers. **Blu-ray availability:** Powerhouse Films (all regions), as part of the *Hammer, Volume One: Fear Warning* box set.

## Mankowitz, Wolf

A noted author, playwright and intellectual, British born Mankowitz (1924–1998, full name Cyril Wolf Mankowitz) penned such stage hits as the musicals *Expresso Bongo* (1958, recorded for TV in 1958, filmed in 1959, earning him a BAFTA nomination for best screenplay), *Make Me an Offer* (1959, recorded for TV in 1966) and *Pickwick* (1963). His various screenplays include *A Kid for Two Farthings* (1955, based on his 1953 novel), *The Millionairess* (1960), which earned him a BAFTA nomination, *The Day the Earth Caught Fire* (1961), which won him a shared BAFTA, *Dr. No* (1962), from which he had his name removed, *Waltz of the Toreadors* (1962), which earned him a BAFTA nomination, *Casino Royale* (1967) and *The Hireling* (1973). He also penned a biography of Edgar Allan Poe, *The Extraordinary Mr. Poe* (1978), and scripted the TV series *Dickens of London* (1977, TV).

One of his lesser efforts was the screenplay for Hammer's *The Two Faces of Dr. Jekyll* (1960), which presented a variation on the established story, with the middle-aged Jekyll now turning into the handsome young sadist Hyde. Originally intended as a vehicle for Laurence Harvey, the script was much re-worked, while the indifference of director Terence Fisher to the material, and further cuts imposed by the BBFC, resulted in a film that was both a commercial and critical failure. Commented Mankowitz of his concept for the film: "Evil is attractive to all men. Therefore, it is not illogical that the face of evil should be attractive. That is why I made Mr. Hyde handsome instead of repulsive."[17]

Mankowitz's other plays include *The Mighty Hunter* (1955), *Belle, or The Ballad of Dr. Crippen* (1961), *Passion Flower Hotel* (1965), *Jack Shepherd* (1972) and *The Samson Riddle* (1972). He was also a co-owner of the famous Pickwick Club in London, as well as a co-founder of The White Elephant restaurant and an investor in the Partisan Coffee House. His son is the photographer Gered Mankowitz (1946–). **Hammer credits:** *The Two Faces of Dr. Jekyll* (1960)

## Manley, Peter

British born Manley (1924–2009) was brought in to work as an associate producer on Hammer's *The Lost Continent* (1968) to relieve the burden on Michael Carreras who, as well as writing and producing the film, also took over the direction from Leslie Norman. He began his career working as a second assistant director on *Quartet* (1948) and *The Astonished Heart* (1949), and graduated to first assistant on *Hotel Sahara* (1951), *Lost* (1956) and *Carry On Constable* (1960), although he continued to work as a second assistant on bigger films, such as Disney's *The Story of Robin Hood and His Merrie Men* (1952) and *The Sword and the Rose* (1953). The mid-fifties also saw him start working as a production manager, beginning with *The Spanish Gardener* (1956), which he followed with *In Search of the Castaways* (1962), *The Three Lives of Thomasina* (1963), *The Moon-Spinners* (1964), *Monte Carlo or Bust!* (1969), *The Slipper and the Rose* (1976) and *Heat and Dust* (1982), among others, plus episodes of *The Saint* (1962–1969, TV). His other work as an associate producer includes *The Call of the Wild* (1972), *Kim* (1984, TVM) and *The Chain* (1984). **Hammer credits:** *The Lost Continent* (1968)

## Mann, Adrian

Mann can be seen as Tibor, one of the wolf children in *Children of the Full Moon* (1980, TV [episode of *Hammer House of Horror*]). His other credits include *Doctor Faustus* (1982), plus episodes of *Grange Hill* (1978–2008, TV) and *Saturday Night Thriller* (1982, TV). **Hammer credits:** *Children of the Full Moon* (1980, TV [episode of *Hammer House of Horror*], as Tibor)

## Mann, Arthur

Mann worked as the assistant director on Hammer's *Visa to Canton* (1960). His other credits include *The Glen Is Ours* (1946), *English Criminal Justice System* (1946) and *The Hangman Waits* (1947). **Hammer credits:** *Visa to Canton* (1960)

## Mann, John

Mann had a supporting role in Hammer's *The Last Page* (1952). His other credits include *Such Is Life* (1936), *Here Come the Huggetts* (1948) and *Night and the City* (1950), plus an episode of *Douglas Fairbanks, Jr. Presents* (1953–1957, TV). **Hammer credits:** *The Last Page* (1952, as Jack)

## Mann, Norman

Mann can be seen as one of Squire Hamilton's young bloods in Hammer's *The Plague of the Zombies* (1966). His other credits include *Carry On Cowboy* (1965) and *Venom* (1981), plus episodes of *South Riding* (1974, TV), *All Creatures Great and Small* (1978–1990, TV) and *Mansfield Park* (1983, TV). **Hammer credits:** *The Plague of the Zombies* (1966, as Young blood)

## Mann, Pamela

British born Mann (1927–, aka Pamela Mann-Francis [sometimes minus the hyphen]) worked as the continuity supervisor on the Hammer thriller *Taste of Fear* (1961). She began her film career as a production secretary on such films as *The Spider and the Fly* (1949), and went on to become David Lean's secretary, working on such films as *Summertime* (1955), on which she also temped as the continuity girl, filling in for an ill Maggie Shipway (aka Maggie Unsworth), and *The Bridge on the River Kwai* (1957). She also worked as the location secretary on *The Wind Cannot Read* (1958), which was originally to have been a David Lean film, but was ultimately directed by Ralph Thomas. Her other credits as full continuity girl/script supervisor include *Saturday Night and Sunday Morning* (1960), *Two and Two Make Six* (1962), *Billy Liar* (1963), *Night Must Fall* (1964), *The Thirty-Nine Steps* (1978), *The Empire Strikes Back* (1980), *Raiders of the Lost Ark* (1981), *Return of the Jedi* (1983), *Indiana Jones and the Temple of Doom* (1984) and *Who Framed Roger Rabbit* (1988), plus episodes of *The Professionals* (1977–1983, TV) and *Dick Turpin* (1979–1982, TV). Her husband was the cinematographer-turned-director Freddie Francis (1917–2007), whom she married in 1963, and on several of whose films she worked; he photographed one film for Hammer and directed a further five for them, including *Paranoiac* (1963) and *Dracula Has Risen from the Grave* (1968). Her stepson is the producer Kevin Francis (1944–), who worked as a runner on *Dracula Has Risen from the Grave*. **Hammer credits:** *Taste of Fear* (1961)

## Mann, Tommy

This British actor (1925–) can be seen as Jenkins in Hammer's *That's Your Funeral* (1973). His other credits include episodes of *Z Cars* (1962–1978, TV), *Detective* (1964–1969, TV), *The Benny Hill Show* (1969–1989, TV) and *From a Bird's Eye View* (1971, TV). **Hammer credits:** *That's Your Funeral* (1973)

## Manners, Yvonne

This British actress (1918–2001) can be seen as Mason in Hammer's *Women Without Men* (1956), which marked her screen debut. Her other credits include *Up the Junction* (1968), plus episodes of *Out of the Unknown* (1965–1971, TV), *Lillie* (1978, TV) and *The House of Eliott* (1991–1994, TV). **Hammer credits:** *Women Without Men* (1956, as Mason [uncredited])

## Manning, Ambrose

This British actor (1859–1940) had a supporting role in Hammer's *Song of Freedom* (1936). His other credits include *Squibs* (1921), *A Sailor Tramp* (1922) and *Squibs Wins the Calcutta Sweep* (1922). Also much on stage. **Hammer credits:** *Song of Freedom* (1936, as Trader)

## Manning, Hugh

This British actor (1920–2004) played Edgar, the opinionated pub customer in Hammer's *Quatermass and the Pit* (1967). His other credits include *The Dam Busters* (1955), *Our Man in Havana* (1959), *The Mackintosh Man* (1973), *Rogue Male* (1976, TVM) and *The Elephant Man* (1980), plus episodes of *ITV Television Playhouse* (1955–1967, TV), *The Four Just Men* (1959–1960, TV) and *Mrs. Thursday* (1966–1967, TV), in which he co-starred as Richard. Hunter. **Hammer credits:** *Quatermass and the Pit* (1967, as Edgar)

## Mansi, Louis

If you ever had the need to cast a wide-eyed, explosive Italian part, then Mansi (1926–2010, full name John Louis Mansi) was your man. Perhaps best known to TV audiences for playing Herr Engelbert Von Smallhausen in seven series of *'Allo 'Allo!* (1984–1992, TV), he was also a frequent guest player in a variety of one-offs and series, among them an episode of *Hammer House of*

*Horror* (1980, TV), in which he had a minor supporting role. His film credits include *Secret People* (1952), *The Italian Job* (1969), *Tales from the Crypt* (1972), *Ooh ... You Are Awful* (1972) and *Play Me Something* (1989). His other television work includes episodes of *Gideon's Way* (1965–1966, TV), *The Woman in White* (1966, TV), *Tottering Towers* (1971–1972, TV), *The Boy with Two Heads* (1974, TV) and *Robin's Nest* (1977–1981, TV). **Hammer credits:** *The Thirteenth Reunion* (1980, TV [episode of *Hammer House of Horror*], as Luciano Rossi)

## Mantrap

GB, 1953, 78m, bw, RCA, cert A

Based on the 1952 Elleston Trevor novel *Queen in Danger*, this fairly average thriller sees lawyer Hugo Bishop become involved in the case of Mervyn Speight, who is on the run from a mental institution in a bid to prove he was not responsible for the murder that caused him to be placed there. With the police closing in, it looks like Speight is doomed to a life behind bars, yet thanks to Bishop's investigations, he manages to discover the identity of the real killer who, while being chased by the police, falls to his death on the derelict land he committed his crime....

Like many of Hammer's fifties co-features, *Mantrap* is a fairly routine programer, given some distinction by the presence of Hollywood star Paul Henreid, here in his second and final film for Hammer following *Stolen Face* (1952). The supporting cast is also better than the norm, featuring the likes of a pre–Bond Lois Maxwell as Speight's frightened wife Thelma (who thinks that her husband is out to kill her because she now loves another man), the glamorous Kay Kendall as Bishop's assistant Vera, a very young-looking Bill Travers as Thelma's second "husband" Victor (it would seem she hasn't divorced the first), and Hugh Sinclair as the real culprit of the crime, Maurice Jerrard. The film seems to have been inspired by the clichéd notion that a criminal seemingly always returns to the scene of his crime, though credibility is stretched somewhat when Speight—supposedly innocent—visits the scene of the murder, where Bishop just happens to waiting for him (reasons the lawyer, "This is the most important place in your life—I thought it would only be natural for you to come and look at it again, now that you are free"). The film then piles on the irony with a trowel during the climax by having Jerrard inadvertently return to the crime scene while being chased by the rozzers

Filmed at Bray in early 1952 and released in the UK by Exclusive on 10 March 1953, *Mantrap* was the third film to be produced by Michael Carreras, who was helped in this task by Alexander Paal, who had co-authored the story for Henreid's previous Hammer vehicle. The film was re-titled *Man in Hiding* for its U.S. release care of Fox on 2 October, presumably so it would not be mistaken for the similarly titled *Manbait*, which had been the American title for Hammer's *The Last Page* (1952). **Additional notes:** The film marked the Hammer debuts of camera operator Len Harris, actress Barbara Shelley (here working under her maiden name,

Barbara Kowin) and second assistant director Aida Young. The latter would go on to produce a number of successes for the company, among them the 1968 hit *Dracula Has Risen from the Grave*. Behind the scenes footage of the making of *Mantrap* was shot on 16mm (without sound) and was featured in the 1987 TV documentary *Hammer—The Studio That Dripped Blood*. This includes glimpses of camera operator Len Harris and editor James Needs at work. The film's opening credits bill art director J. Elder Wills simply as Elder Wills, the surname of music director Marcus Dods in misspelled Dodds, while James Needs is rather casually billed as Jim Needs. The end credits state that the film was produced at Exclusive Studios, Bray. The film carries a 1952 copyright.

Production companies: Hammer/Lippert. Distributors: Exclusive (UK), Twentieth Century–Fox (U.S.). Producers: Michael Carreras, Alexander Paal. Director: Terence Fisher. Screenplay: Paul Tabori (also adaptation), Terence Fisher, based on the novel *Queen in Danger* by Elleston Trevor. Cinematographer: Reginald Wyer. Music: Doreen Carwithen. Music director: Marcus Dods. Music played by: The Philharmonia Orchestra. Editor: James Needs. Art director: J. Elder Wills. Costumes: Jane Ironside (for Lois Maxwell), Ricci Michaels, Ltd. (fashion show gowns), Molly Arbuthnot (wardrobe mistress [uncredited]). Production manager: Victor Wark. Assistant director: Bill Shore. Second assistant director: Aida Young [uncredited]. Third assistant director: Vernon Nolt [uncredited]. Make-up: D. Bonnor-Moris. Camera operator: Len Harris. Focus puller: Manny Yospa [uncredited]. Sound: Jack Miller. Assistant sound editor: Jim Groom [uncredited]. Continuity: Renee Glynne. Dialogue director: Nora Roberts. Stills: John Jay [uncredited]. **Cast:** Paul Henreid (Hugo Bishop), Lois Maxwell (Thelma Tasman/Speight), Kieron Moore (Mervyn Speight), Anthony Forwood (Rex Willison), Hugh Sinclair (Maurice Jerrard), Lloyd Lamble (Freddie Frisnay), Bill Travers (Victor Tasman), Mary Laura Wood (Susie Martin), John Penrose (Francois Du Vancet), Kay Kendall (Vera), Conrad Phillips (Barker), Liam Gaffney (Douval), John Stuart (Doctor), Barbara Kowin ([later Barbara Shelley], Fashion compère), Arnold Diamond (Alphonse), Geoffrey Murphy (Plain clothes man), Jane Welsh (Laura), Christina Forrest (Joanna), Anna Turner (Marjorie), Terry Carney (Detective), Sally Newland (Receptionist)

## Manuel, José

Manuel can be seen as one of the Rock people in Hammer's *Creatures the World Forgot* (1971). **Hammer credits:** *Creatures the World Forgot* (1971, as Rock man [uncredited])

## M.A.P. International

This company provided the titles for the Fox-Hammer TV series *Journey to the Unknown* (1968, TV). **Hammer credits:** *Journey to the Unknown* (1968, TV)

## Maranne, André

Best known to English-speaking audiences for playing Sergeant Francois Duvall in the Pink Pan-

ther films, this French character actor (1926–) spent the majority of his career in Britain, where he appeared in such films as *Loser Takes All* (1956), *H.M.S. Defiant* (1962), *A Shot in the Dark* (1964), *Thunderball* (1965), *The Return of the Pink Panther* (1975), *Gold* (1974), *The Pink Panther Strikes Again* (1976), *Revenge of the Pink Panther* (1978), *Trail of the Pink Panther* (1982), *Curse of the Pink Panther* (1983) and *Morons from Outer Space* (1985). He also popped up in episodes of *The Third Man* (1959–1965, TV), *Doctor Who* (1963–1989, TV) and *Yes Minister* (1980–1984, TV). In addition to appearing before the cameras, Maranne also occasionally worked as a dubbing artist, and as such dubbed Norman Bird's dialogue for Hammer's Camargue-set thriller *Maniac* (1963), in which Bird played a gendarme. **Hammer credits:** *Maniac* (1963, as Gendarme Salon [vocal only])

## Marchant, James

Marchant worked as the art director on a handful of Hammer low budgeters, including the first and third Dick Barton adventures. He was wrongly credited as James Mordant in the titles for *The Adventures of PC 49—The Case of the Guardian Angel* (1949). His other credits include *Juno and the Paycock* (1930), *Men Like These* (1932), *Royal Cavalcade* (1935), *My Hands Are Clay* (1948), *The Nitwits on Parade* (1948) and *Penny Points to Paradise* (1951). **Hammer credits:** *Dick Barton—Special Agent* (1948), *The Dark Road* (1948 [uncredited]), *Dr. Morelle—The Case of the Missing Heiress* (1949 [uncredited]), *The Adventures of PC 49—The Case of the Guardian Angel* (1949), *Dick Barton at Bay* (1950)

## Marconi Wireless Telegraph Company

Marconi was thanked by the producers in the opening credits of *The Quatermass Xperiment* (1955) for their co-operation in the making of the film. Founded in 1897, the company opened the world's first radio factory in 1898 and went on to become a world leader in the development of radio and television equipment. **Hammer credits:** *The Quatermass Xperiment* (1955)

## Marden, Dick (Richard)

British born Marden (1928–2006) worked as the assistant editor on the "unofficial" Hammer second feature *Jack of Diamonds* (1949). He went on to edit such major productions as *Anne of the Thousand Days* (1969), *Mary, Queen of Scots* (1971), *Sunday Bloody Sunday* (1971), which won him a BAFTA, *Sleuth* (1972), *Evil Under the Sun* (1982), *The Falcon and the Snowman* (1985), *Hellraiser* (1987), *Hamlet* (1990) and *Jane Eyre* (1996), frequently working with such major directors as Stanley Donen, John Schlesinger and Franco Zeffirelli. Earlier in his career, he worked as a sound editor on *The Vicious Circle* (1957), *The Doctor's Dilemma* (1958) and *The Mouse That Roared* (1959). **Hammer credits:** *Jack of Diamonds* (1949)

## Mareno, Lydia

Mareno was a member of the American rock group Stoneground, which was featured in Hammer's *Dracula A.D. 1972* (1972). Her other credits include *Medicine Ball Caravan* (1971), again with

Stoneground. She was formerly a member of the groups The West Coast Natural Gas Story and Indian Puddin' and Pipe. **Hammer credits:** *Dracula A.D. 1972* (1972)

## Margetson, Arthur

Following experience as a stockbroker, this British actor (1897–1951) launched a successful acting career on stage and screen, appearing in such films as *Wolves* (1930), *Other People's Sins* (1931), *His Grace Gives Notice* (1933) and *Little Friend* (1934). He also appeared in Hammer's second film, *The Mystery of the Mary Celeste* (1935), in which he played Captain Briggs. In 1940, Margetson made his way to Hollywood, where he went on to play minor roles in the likes of *Random Harvest* (1943) and *Sherlock Holmes Faces Death* (1944). His first wife (of three) was actress Vera Lennox (1903–1984), to whom he was married between 1926 and 1933; his second wife was actress Shirley Grey (1902–1982, real name Agnes Zetterstrand), whom he married in 1936, and who also appeared in *The Mystery of the Mary Celeste*. **Hammer credits:** *The Mystery of the Mary Celeste* (1935, as Captain Benjamin Briggs)

## Margo, George

This American actor (1915–2002) had a minor supporting role in Hammer's *The Saint's Return* (1953). In Britain following the war, he appeared in such films as *Circle of Danger* (1951), *Lilacs in the Spring* (1954) and *The Mouse That Roared* (1959), plus such series as *BBC Sunday-Night Theatre* (1950–1959, TV), *Wire Service* (1956–1957, TV) and *The Buccaneers* (1956–1957, TV). He later returned to American where he continued his career appearing in episodes of such TV shows as *The Man from U.N.C.L.E.* (1964–1968, TV), *Cannon* (1971–1976, TV) and *The Bionic Woman* (1976–1978, TV). **Hammer credits:** *The Saint's Return* (1953, unnamed role [uncredited])

## Margutti, Vic

This British special effects technician (1913–1980) formed the company Bowie, Margutti and Co. with fellow effects wiz Les Bowie. One of their earliest jobs was to provide the effects for the Hammer low budgeter *Spaceways* (1953). He also worked (either alone or with Bowie) on several other films for Hammer, including their breakthrough production *The Quatermass Xperiment* (1955). His other credits include *Keep It Clean* (1956), *One Wish Too Many* (1956), *Town on Trial* (1957), *Mysterious Island* (1961) and *Dr. Strangelove* (1964). **Hammer credits:** *Spaceways* (1953), *Five Days* (1954 [uncredited]), *Men of Sherwood Forest* (1954 [uncredited]), *The Quatermass Xperiment* (1955 [uncredited]), *X—The Unknown* (1956), *The Full Treatment* (1961 [uncredited])

## Marion-Crawford, Howard

Perhaps best remembered for playing Dr. Walter Petrie in five Fu Manchu films in the sixties, this mustachioed British character actor (1914–1969, sometimes billed minus the hyphen) specialized in slightly dim upper class types. In films from 1935 with *Me and Marlborough*, he went on to appear in over sixty films, among them *Secret Agent* (1936), *The Rake's Progress* (1945), *North West Frontier* (1959), *Lawrence of Arabia* (1962), *The Face of Fu Manchu* (1965) and *The Castle of Fu Manchu* (1969), while on television he played Dr. Watson to Ronald Howard's Sherlock Holmes in *The Adventures of Sherlock Holmes* (1954–1955, TV). In 1954, he briefly appeared in the Hammer second feature *Five Days* as the bluff businessman-cum-archaeologist Cyrus McGowan. Sadly, this proved to be his only work for the studio. He also voiced Sergei Bondarchuk in the title role of the English dub of the Russian version of *Othello* (1956). His other TV work includes episodes of *Wire Service* (1956–1957, TV), *The Avengers* (1961–1969, TV) and *Danger Man* (1964–1966, TV). His second wife (of two) was the actress Mary Wimbush (1924–2005), to whom he was married between 1946 and 1954; she appeared in Hammer's *Vampire Circus* (1972). His grandfather was the novelist Francis Marion Crawford (1854–1909). **Hammer credits:** *Five Days* (1954, as Cyrus McGowan)

## The Mark of Satan see Hammer House of Horror

## Mark of the Devil see Hammer House of Mystery and Suspense

All spiffed up. Dirk Benedict and Jenny Seagrove in *Mark of the Devil*, an episode of *Hammer House of Mystery and Suspense* (1984) (Hammer/Twentieth Century–Fox).

## Markham, Barbara

This British actress (1910–1983, real name Eunice Barbara Francis, aka Barbara Francis) can be seen as Frau Kummer, the character who temporarily replaces Angela Lansbury's nanny-turned-spy Miss Froy in the plot of Hammer's *The Lady Vanishes* (1979). Her other credits include *Airborne* (1962), *Sunday Bloody Sunday* (1971), *House of Whipcord* (1974) and *Got It Made* (1974), plus episodes of *Public Eye* (1965–1975, TV), *Kate* (1970–1972, TV) and *Intimate Strangers* (1974, TV). She also worked as an elocution teacher, especially in the theater (she was frequently used by the producer Binkie Beaumont), as well as an occasional dialogue coach on such films as *Flash Gordon* (1980) and *Five Days One Summer* (1982). Married twice, her husbands were the actors Cyril Chamberlain (1909–1974), whom she married in 1935, and John Stuart (1898–1979, real name John Alfred Louden Croall), whom she married in 1943. Chamberlain appeared in Hammer's *The Dark Road* (1948) and *The Ugly Duckling* (1959), while Stuart appeared in nine films for the company, among them *Mantrap* (1953), *The Mummy* (1959) and *Paranoiac* (1963). **Hammer credits:** *The Lady Vanishes* (1979, as Frau Kummer)

## Markham, David

This British actor (1913–1983, real name Peter Basil Harrison) played the role of Jorgan Jorgensen, who is suspected of being a resistance traitor, in the Hammer featurette *The Right Person* (1956). He later returned to Hammer to play a featured role in *Blood from the Mummy's Tomb* (1971). On stage following training at RADA, his other credits include *Murder in the Family* (1938), *The Stars Look Down* (1940), *The Blakes Slept Here* (1953), *A Place for Gold* (1960), *Two Gentlemen Sharing* (1969), *Zero Population Growth* (1971), *Family Life* (1971), *Tales from the Crypt* (1972), *Tess* (1979) and *Gandhi* (1982), plus appearances in such series as *Pride and Prejudice* (1952, TV), in which he played Mr. Bingley and *The Life and Times of David Lloyd George* (1981, TV), in which he played Herbert Henry Asquith. He was married to the writer Olive Dehn (1914–2007); their daughters are make-up artist Sonia Markham (1938–2016) and actresses Kika Markham (1940–) and Petra Markham (1947–). **Hammer credits:** *The Right Person* (1956, as Jorgan Jorgensen/Toraf), *Blood from the Mummy's Tomb* (1971, as Dr. Burgess)

## Marks, Alfred

Following experience on stage as a comedian just after the war, this British actor and singer (1921–1996, real name Ruchel Kutchinsky) broke into television in 1950 with *Don't Look Now* and into films from 1951 with *Penny Points to Paradise*. His other big screen credits include *Desert Mice* (1959), *She'll Have to Go* (1962), *Scream and Scream Again* (1970), *Our Miss Fred* (1972) and *Valentino* (1977), as well as the Hammer comedy *A Weekend with Lulu* (1961), in which he played the Comte de Grenoble. His many TV credits include *Alfred Marks Time* (1956–1961, TV), *Fire Crackers* (1964–1965, TV) and *Albert and Victoria* (1970–1971, TV), plus many guest appearances. His wife was the comedienne Paddie O'Neil (1926–2010, real name Adalena Lillian Neil), whom he married in 1952. **Hammer credits:** *A Weekend with Lulu* (1961, as Comte de Grenoble)

## Marks, Joe

British born Marks (1929–) worked as an uncredited additional first assistant director on Hammer's *Don't Panic Chaps* (1959), which led to further work for the company in varying capacities.

Prior to this he worked as a third assistant on *Left Right and Centre* (1959), and as a second assistant on *The Pure Hell of St. Trinian's* (1960) and *Gorgo* (1960). He worked as a first assistant on *Take a Girl Like You* (1969) and *Firepower* (1979), and as a production manager on *Follyfoot* (1971–1973, TV). **Hammer credits:** *Don't Panic Chaps* (1959, additional first assistant director [uncredited]), *Paranoiac* (1963, second assistant director [uncredited]), *Frankenstein Created Woman* (1967, second assistant director [uncredited])

### Marks, Leo

This British dramatist (1920–2001, full name Leopold Samuel Marks) penned the play *Cloudburst*, which was subsequently filmed by Hammer in 1951, with Marks himself contributing to the screenplay with the film's director Francis Searle. He also coached the film's star, Robert Preston, in the ways of coding. Remembered Francis Searle, "He [Preston] was given a lavish reception at the Savoy and later on Leo and I would go up to his suite there, and Leo would get the blackboards out and teach him coding and all that. Leo had been very high up in coding analysis at Baker Street during the war, you see."[18] Indeed, Marks was one of Britain's top cryptographers during the Second World War (having already worked as a setter for *The Times* cryptic crossword), and his innovations included the use of coded poems. Marks' other screenwriting credits include the notorious *Peeping Tom* (1960), *Guns at Batasi* (1964), *Sebastian* (1968), *Twisted Nerve* (1968) and *Soft Beds, Hard Battles* (1974). His other plays include *The Girl Who Couldn't Quite* (1947), which was filmed in 1950, and *The Best Damn Lie* (1957). He was also a technical advisor on *Carve Her Name with Pride* (1958), having written the original code poem, *The Life That I Have*, used by the film's main character Violette Szabo. He wrote about his wartime experiences in his memoir, *Between Silk and Cyanide: A Codemaker's Story, 1941–1945* (1998). He was made a MBE in 1945 for his wartime work. His father was Benjamin Marks, the joint owner of the bookshop Marks and Co. which found fame as the focus of Helene Hanff's book *84 Charing Cross Road* (1970), which has subsequently been dramatized for television (1975, TV), stage (1981), film (1987) and radio (2007). **Hammer credits:** *Cloudburst* (1951, play, co-screenplay)

### Marks, Patricia

Marks can be seen as a nurse in Hammer's *Never Take Sweets from a Stranger* (1960). Her other credits include episodes of *The Professionals* (1977–1983, TV), *Enemy at the Door* (1978–1980, TV) and *Anna of the Five Towns* (1985, TV). **Hammer credits:** *Never Take Sweets from a Stranger* (1960, as Nurse [uncredited])

### Marla, Norma

Marla played the role of Angel in Hammer's Jekyll and Hyde spoof *The Ugly Duckling* (1959). Interestingly, she can also be seen as Maria in Hammer's other Jekyll and Hyde variation, *The Two Faces of Dr. Jekyll* (1960). Note that a moment of nudity involving the actress in the latter was subsequently removed from the release print following objections from the BBFC. She was also completely re-voiced for the film. **Hammer credits:** *The Ugly Duckling* (1959, as Angel), *The Two Faces of Dr. Jekyll* (1960, as Maria)

### Marland, Harold

Marland was one of Hammer's many electricians, working under the supervision of chief electrician Jack Curtis. **Hammer credits:** *The Curse of Frankenstein* (1957 [uncredited])

### Marle (Marlé), Arnold

This German character actor (1887–1970) is best remembered by Hammer fans for playing the sage old Lama in Hammer's *The Abominable Snowman* (1957), a role he'd already played in the television version of the story, *The Creature* (1955, TV). In films from 1919 in his home country with *Das Fraulein von Scuderi*, he also worked on two Hammer second features—*Break in the Circle* (1955) and *The Glass Cage* (1955), from the latter of which his scenes were cut from (although he retains his screen credit)—as well as the shocker *The Man Who Could Cheat Death* (1959), the television version of which (*The Man in Half Moon Street*) he had also appeared in two years earlier (playing Dr. Ludwig Weisz in the TV version, amended to Weiss in the Hammer version). Commented screenwriter Jimmy Sangster of Marle's performance in the Hammer take on the story: "[He] was so far over the top as to be practically out of sight."[19]

Marle's other credits include *One of Our Aircraft Is Missing* (1942), *Men of Two Worlds* (1946), *Portrait from Life* (1948), *Little Red Monkey* (1955), *The Snake Woman* (1961) and *The Password Is Courage* (1962), plus episodes of *BBC Sunday-Night Theatre* (1950–1959, TV), *Hour of Mystery* (1957, TV), *The Avengers* (1961–1969, TV) and *Espionage* (1963–1964, TV). His other German credits include *Die Trommeln Asiens* (1921), *Die malayische Dschonke* (1924) and *Dood water* (1934). Also on stage in both Britain and America. **Hammer credits:** *Break in the Circle* (1955, as Paul Kudnic [billed as Arnold Marlé]), *The Glass Cage* (1955, as Pop Maroni [scenes cut]), *The Abominable Snowman* (1957, as Lama), *The Man Who Could Cheat Death* (1959, as Dr. Ludwig Weiss)

### Marlowe, William

This British actor (1930–2003) played the role of Randolph Verdew in *The Killing Bottle*, an episode of Hammer's *Journey to the Unknown* (1968, TV), which also appeared in the compendium film *Journey to Murder* (1972, TVM). Film credits include *The Uncle* (1964), *The Heroes of Telemark* (1965), *Where's Jack?* (1969), *Zeppelin* (1971), *Revolution* (1984) and *Cry Freedom* (1987), while his other small screen work includes *The Gentle Touch* (1980–1984, TV), in which he played DCI Bill Russell. Married twice, his wives were actresses Catherine Schell (1944–, real name Katherina Freiin Schell Von Bauschlott, aka Catherine Von Schell), to whom he was married between 1968 and 1977, and Kismet Delgado (1929–, aka Kismet Shahani), whom he married in 1983. Schell appeared in Hammer's *Moon Zero Two* (1969). **Hammer credits:** *The Killing Bottle* (1968, TV [episode of *Journey to the Unknown*], as Randolph Verdew), *Journey to Murder* (1972, TVM, as Randolph Verdew)

### Marmont, Percy

On stage from 1900 and in films (in South Africa) from 1916 with *De Voortrekkers*, this prolific British actor (1883–1977) appeared in almost one-hundred films in both Britain and Hollywood, first as a silent lead and later as a character support, playing upper crust types in the C. Aubrey Smith manner. His credits (among them three for Hitchcock) include *The Monk and the Woman* (1917), *The Lie* (1918), *The Silver King* (1924), *Rich and Strange* (1932), *Secret Agent* (1936), *Young and Innocent* (1937), *No Orchids for Miss Blandish* (1948), *Lisbon* (1956) and *Hostile Witness* (1968). He also appeared in two Hammer second features: *The Gambler and the Lady* (1953) as Lord Hortland, and *Four Sided Triangle* (1953) as Sir Walter. He also directed one film during his career, *The Captain's Table* (1936), in which he also starred. His television appearances include episodes of *Douglas Fairbanks, Jr. Presents* (1953–1957, TV), *The Count of Monte Cristo* (1956, TV) and *The New Adventures of Charlie Chan* (1957–1958, TV). His daughters are actress-turned-agent Patricia Marmont (1921–) and actress Pam Marmont (1923–1999). His sons-in-law were actors Nigel Green (1924–1972 [via Patricia]), who appeared in two films for Hammer, and Moray Watson (1928–2017 [via Pam]). His granddaughter is actress Emma Vansittart. **Hammer credits:** *The Gambler and the Lady* (1953, as Lord Hortland), *Four Sided Triangle* (1953, as Sir Walter)

### Marner, Richard

Best known for playing Colonel Von Strohm in the long-running sitcom *'Allo 'Allo!* (1982–1992, TV), in which he appeared in all eighty-five episodes (along with the 1988 London Palladium stage production), this Russian born actor (1921–2004, real name Alexander Molchanoff-Sacha) can be seen as Hans Brecht in Hammer's race track drama *Mask of Dust* (1954). In Britain from 1924, he became an actor after being invalided out of the RAF during World War II. His many film credits include *Appointment with Venus* (1951), *The African Queen* (1951), *The Man Who Knew Too Much* (1956), *The Mouse on the Moon* (1963), *The Spy Who Came in from the Cold* (1965), *You Only Live Twice* (1967), *Tiffany Jones* (1973), *The Boys from Brazil* (1978) and *The Sum of All Fears* (2002), plus much stage and television, among the latter episodes of *BBC Sunday-Night Theatre* (1950–1959, TV), *Crane* (1963–1965, TV), *Special Branch* (1969–1974, TV) and *Mackenzie* (1980). His wife was the actress Pauline Farr (aka Pauline Molchanoff), whom he married in 1947. **Hammer credits:** *Mask of Dust* (1954, as Hans Brecht)

### Marr, B.E.

Marr served on the board of directors at Bray Studios between 1965 and 1966.

### Marr, Leslie

This British racing driver (1922–) can be seen as a driver in Hammer's race track drama *Mask of Dust* (1954). He raced briefly in the mid-fifties, notably in national events between 1952 and 1953, in which he drove his Connaught, and later at the New Zealand GP in 1956, where he placed fourth, despite starting at the back of the grid. He also drove in the British Grand Prix of 1954 and 1955, but scored no points, though he did win the non-championship 1955 Cornwall MRC Formula One race. He later became an accomplished artist. **Hammer credits:** *Mask of Dust* (1954, as Driver)

**Marsch, Ernie** *see* **Marsh, Ernie**

**Marsden, Patrick**

British born Marsden (1925–1971) worked as the production manager on the Hammer comedy *Further Up the Creek* (1958). His other credits include *Expresso Bongo* (1959), *Tunes of Glory* (1960), *Clash by Night* (1964) and *The Jokers* (1967). He also worked as an assistant director on such films as *Up in the World* (1956), *Theatre of Death* (1966) and *The Revolutionary* (1970). He began his career as a third assistant on *Welcome, Mr. Washington* (1944), graduated to second assistant on *Malta Story* (1953) and then to first assistant on *Trouble in Store* (1953). **Hammer credits:** *Further Up the Creek* (1958)

**Marsh, Carol**

Best remembered by Hammer fans for playing Lucy Holmwood in Hammer's *Dracula* (1958), this British actress (1926–2010, real name Norma Lilian Simpson) came to note with her first film, *Brighton Rock* (1947), in which she played the naïve waitress Rose. Her other films include *Alice in Wonderland* (1949), in which she played the title role, *Marry Me* (1949), *Scrooge* (1951) and *Man Accused* (1959), while her television work takes in episodes of *BBC Sunday-Night Theatre* (1950–1959, TV), *Douglas Fairbanks, Jr. Presents* (1953–1957, TV), *Dixon of Dock Green* (1955–1976, TV), *The Royalty* (1957–1958, TV), *Lord Raingo* (1966, TV) and *Marked Personal* (1973–1974, TV). **Hammer credits:** *Dracula* (1958, as Lucy Holmwood)

**Marsh, Ernie**

Marsh (sometimes Marsch) worked as the dubbing mixer on all thirteen episodes of *Hammer House of Mystery and Suspense* (1984, TVM). His other credits include *The Kiss: A Tale of Two Lovers* (1977), *Grace of My Heart* (1996) and *Let's Stick Together* (1998). **Hammer credits:** *Hammer House of Mystery and Suspense* (1984, TVM])

**Marsh, Garry**

Often cast in exasperated roles, this balding British character actor (1902–1981, real name Leslie March Geraghty) began his film career in 1922 with *Long Odds*. His other credits include *Night Birds* (1930), *Number Seventeen* (1932), *Bank Holiday* (1938), *Let George Do It* (1940), *Mr. Drake's Duck* (1951), *Camelot* (1967) and *It's the Only Way to Go* (1970). He also played the role of Kapel in the Hammer second feature *Someone at the Door* (1950). His occasional TV credits include episodes of *The Errol Flynn Theatre* (1957, TV), *Don't Tell Father* (1959, TV) and *The Avengers* (1961–1969, TV). His second wife was the actress Muriel Martin-Harvey (1891–1988, full name Margaret Muriel de Melfort Martin-Harvey). **Hammer credits:** *Someone at the Door* (1950, as Kapel)

**Marsh, Keith**

This bald-headed, owl-eyed British supporting player (1926–2013) is perhaps best remembered for playing Jacko Jackson (catchphrase: "I'll 'ave 'alf") in the sitcom *Love Thy Neighbour* (1972–1976, TV). He reprised the role for Hammer's big screen spin-off in 1973 (but didn't get to say his catchphrase). Prior to this he had appeared in the role of Johnson in Hammer's *Quatermass and the Pit* (1967), in which he finds himself subjected to an experiment with Dr. Roney's brain scanner. He also had a minor role in *Taste the Blood of Dracula* (1970). His other credits include *The Gentle Trap* (1960), *Othello* (1965), *Daleks—Invasion Earth 2150 A.D.* (1966), *Scrooge* (1970) and *The Human Factor* (1979). Busiest on television, his many other credits include episodes of *Saber of London* (1954–1960, TV), *George and the Dragon* (1966–1968, TV), *Pennies from Heaven* (1978, TV), *The Beiderbecke Affair* (1985, TV), *Barbara* (1995–2003, TV) and *The Worst Week of My Life* (2004–2005, TV). **Additional notes:** Marsh also appeared as Jacko Jackson in a 1972 edition of the TV comedy special *All Star Comedy Carnival* (1969–1973, TV). **Hammer credits:** *Quatermass and the Pit* (1967, as Johnson), *Taste the Blood of Dracula* (1970, as Father), *Love Thy Neighbour* (1973, as Jacko Jackson)

**Marsh, Reginald**

Best known for his appearances in various sitcoms, in which he usually played authority figures, this British character actor (1926–2001) was a stalwart of such shows as *The Good Life* (1975–1978, TV), in which he played Sir, and *Terry and June* (1979–1987, TV), in which he played Sir Dennis Hodge. His occasional films include Hammer's *The Ugly Duckling* (1959), *Jigsaw* (1962), *Shadow of Fear* (1963), *It Happened Here* (1963) and *Berserk* (1967). He also later appeared as a doctor in an episode of *Hammer House of Mystery and Suspense* (1984, TVM). His many other TV appearances include episodes of *ITV Play of the Week* (1955–1968, TV), *The Plane Makers* (1963–1965, TV), in which he played Arthur Sugden, and *The Setbacks* (1980–1986, TV). His second wife was actress Rosemary Murray. His children are actresses Rebecca Marsh and Alison Marsh. **Hammer credits:** *The Ugly Duckling* (1959, as Reporter), *Mark of the Devil* (1984, TVM [episode of *Hammer House of Mystery and Suspense*], as Dr. Melford)

**Marshall, Bryan**

This RADA-trained British actor (1938–) can be seen as a young tough in Hammer's *Rasputin—The Mad Monk* (1966), which led to appearances in three further films for the company. His other credits include *Alfie* (1966), *I Start Counting* (1969), *The Tamarind Seed* (1974) and *The Spy Who Loved Me* (1977), plus episodes of *United* (1965–1967, TV), *Warship* (1973–1977, TV), *The Professionals* (1977–1983, TV) and *Buccaneer* (1980, TV). He moved to Australia in 1983, and continued his career in episodes of such series as *Prisoner* (1979–1986, TV), *The Flying Doctors* (1986–1991, TV), *Embassy* (1990–1992, TV), *All Saints* (1998–2009, TV) and *A Moody Christmas* (2012, TV). **Hammer credits:** *Rasputin—The Mad Monk* (1966, as Young tough [uncredited]), *The Witches* (1966, as Tom), *The Viking Queen* (1967, as Dominic), *Quatermass and the Pit* (1967, as Captain Potter)

**Marshall, Clive**

Marshall played the role of Jim in the Hammer short *Man with a Dog* (1957). His other credits include *A Night to Remember* (1958) and *Two Left Feet* (1963), plus episodes of *No Hiding Place* (1959–1967, TV), *The Corner Shop* (1960, TV) and *Maigret* (1960–1963, TV). He later moved to Australia and continued his career with *Conman Harry and the Others* (1979), *Far East* (1982) and *The Wild Duck* (1984), plus episodes of *Rush* (1974–1976, TV), *Shannon's Mob* (1975, TV), *The Timeless Land* (1980, TV), *The Harp in the South* (1987, TV), *Poor Man's Orange* (1987, TV) and *The Potato Factory* (2000, TV). **Hammer credits:** *Man with a Dog* (1957, as Jim)

**Marshall, Edward (Ted)**

In films from the early fifties as a junior draughtsman and art department assistant at the Shepherd's Bush Studios (having qualified as an architect), this British art director went on to design the sets for such major sixties productions as *Tom Jones* (1963), which earned him a shared Oscar nomination, *The Pumpkin Eater* (1964), which earned him a BAFTA nomination, *The Spy Who Came in from the Cold* (1965), which earned him another shared Oscar nomination, *Life at the Top* (1965), which brought a second BAFTA nomination, *The Charge of the Light Brigade* (1968), which brought a third BAFTA nomination, and *Charlie Bubbles* (1968).

Earlier in his career, he designed a number of films for Hammer, beginning with several short subjects before graduating to features. Unfortunately, at the behest of associate producer Anthony Nelson Keys, Marshall was demoted on perhaps his most important Hammer film, *The Curse of Frankenstein* (1957). Recalled draughtsman Don Mingaye, "Ted Marshall actually started that [film]. I really don't know what happened in the front office to this day, but there was obviously a need for a change."[20] To this end, production designer Bernard Robinson took over, though his main contribution seems to have been the rooftop set for the film's fiery finale. Explained Marshall of the situation, "Bernard Robinson ... had considerably more experience of the gothic type sets, and I learned much from working with him on that film and, later, *The Abominable Snowman*."[21]

Marshall's other credits include *The Executioner* (1970), *The Triple Echo* (1972), *Brannigan* (1975), *Trial by Combat* (1976), *Silver Bears* (1978) and *The Thief of Bagdad* (1978, TVM), plus episodes of *The Errol Flynn Theatre* (1957, TV). His early credits as a draughtsman include *The Way to the Stars* (1945), *Uncle Silas* (1947) and *Scrooge* (1951). **Hammer credits:** *Eric Winstone's Stagecoach* (1956), *A Man on the Beach* (1956), *The Edmundo Ros Half Hour* (1956), *Dick Turpin—Highwayman* (1956), *X—The Unknown* (1956 [uncredited]), *The Curse of Frankenstein* (1957), *The Steel Bayonet* (1957), *The Abominable Snowman* (1957), *Man* *with a Dog* (1957), *Danger List* (1957), *Clean Sweep* (1958)

## Marshall, Ted  *see*  Marshall, Edward

## Marshall, Tony

Marshall worked as a unit driver on *The Satanic Rites of Dracula* (1974) and *Hammer House of Mystery and Suspense* (1984, TVM). His other credits include *Four Weddings and a Funeral* (1994). **Hammer credits:** *The Satanic Rites of Dracula* (1974 [uncredited]), *Hammer House of Mystery and Suspense* (1984, TVM [uncredited])

## Marshall, Vicki

This British supporting actress played the role of Kitty in Hammer's *The Ugly Duckling* (1959). **Hammer credits:** *The Ugly Duckling* (1959, as Kitten)

## Marshall, Zena

In films from 1945 with *Caesar and Cleopatra*, this Kenyan born actress (1925–2009) went on to appear in such wide-ranging films as *Miranda* (1948), *Dr. No* (1962), in which she played Miss Taro, *Those Magnificent Men in Their Flying Machines* (1965) and *The Terrornauts* (1967). She also played Lisa Colville, the leading lady in the Hammer crime support *Meet Simon Cherry* (1949). Her television credits include episodes of *Saber of London* (1954–1960, TV), *Danger Man* (1960–1962, TV) and *Public Eye* (1965–1975, TV). Married twice, her first husband was bandleader Paul Adam (1914–) whom she married in 1947; her second husband was writer-producer Ivan Foxwell (1914–2002), whom she married in 1991. **Hammer credits:** *Meet Simon Cherry* (1949, as Lisa Colville)

## Marshall-Gardiner, Jessica

In Britain for many years, this American child actress (1978–, aka Jessica Hathaway) can be seen in a handful of flashback sequences in *Black Carrion* (1984, TVM [episode of *Hammer House of Mystery and Suspense*]). Her other credits include episodes of *Ladies in Charge* (1986, TV) and *The Detectives* (1993–1997, TV), while her occasional films take in *The Manor* (1999) and *She and I* (2015). Also on radio and stage, notably as the young Cosette in *Les Miserables*. Now back in America, she sings with the Blue Rose Harlots. **Hammer credits:** *Black Carrion* (1984, TVM [episode of *Hammer House of Mystery and Suspense*], as Little girl)

## Martell, Harry

This British orchestra "fixer" brought together the musicians used in the orchestras for a number of films, among them several for Hammer (albeit without onscreen credit). His credits include *A Test of Violence* (1970) and *Overlord* (1975). His brother was Hammer music director Philip Martell (1915–1993), with whom he often worked in conjunction. **Hammer credits include:** *To the Devil a Daughter* (1976 [uncredited])

## Martell, Philip

This prolific British music director and occasional composer (1907–1993) was active in films from the late forties with *Murder at the Windmill* (1949) following training at London's Guild Hall,

experience as a cinema violinist towards the end of the silent period (he began playing at the age of five), and work as a pit conductor in the West End at such theaters as the Adelphi. Long associated with Hammer, he had his first brush with the company in 1955, when he was brought in to conduct Bruce Campbell's score for *The Lyons in Paris*. Following the death of John Hollingsworth in December 1963, Martell took over as Hammer's music director in residence, maintaining the position until his own death in 1993. His first assignment was to conduct Don Banks' score for *The Evil of Frankenstein* (1964), on which Hollingsworth had been working at the time of his death. Martell then went on to conduct the music for the majority of Hammer's film and television projects, including the seventeen-part television series *Journey to the Unknown* (1968, TV); rare exceptions include *The Vengeance of She* (1968), which was conducted by Franco Ferrara and *Man at the Top* (1973), which was conducted by its composer Roy Budd (although Martell retained a credit as music supervisor for both). He was also involved in the company's brief flirtation with records in the mid-seventies and their later television series. Remembered James Bernard of working with Martell, "We were always very friendly, but he could be somewhat prickly. He used to go on at me because I'd been classically educated. He liked to see what I was doing all the time I was writing, whereas John [Hollingsworth] tended to leave one alone, which I preferred."[22] Commented composer Harry Robinson of Martell upon being assigned to work on Hammer's *Journey to the Unknown*, "I had heard that he could be a little fiery, so I was a little wary of him."[23] Added David Whitaker, who scored three films for Hammer, "Phil was quite serious, and although we hit it off very well, there weren't many light moments with him."[24] There was certainly no doubting Martell's ability, and he was described by Michael Carreras as "the man with a metronome in his head."[25] James Bernard also held Martell's talents on the podium in high esteem: "He's an excellent conductor, and is marvellous at knowing and deciding exactly where on a film the music should be placed. Apart from his profound musicianship, he is also expert at hitting (and holding) an exact tempo; this is essential in many film sequences where the points of synchronization are mathematically planned by the composer, and are absolutely dependent upon the music being played at the marked tempo. When time is pressing, and tension mounting in the studio, you can understand the iron control of the conductor."[26] As for his own abilities on the conductor's stand, Martell observed, "I don't think anyone does a better job than I do,"[27] though he was the first to admit that "there are lots of people who do better scores than I do."[28] Martell's many other credits as a conductor/music supervisor/music director (over onehundred-and-fifty) include *Miss Pilgrim's Progress* (1950), *Albert R.N.* (1953), *No Road Back* (1957), *Master Spy* (1963), *Catacombs* (1964), *Witchcraft* (1964), *Do You Know This Voice?* (1964), *Dr. Terror's House of Horrors* (1965), *A High Wind in Jamaica* (1965), *Theatre of Death* (1966), *The Deadly Bees* (1966), *It!* (1967), *The Oblong Box* (1969),

*Frankenstein: The True Story* (1973, TVM), *Rising Damp* (1980) and *George and Mildred* (1980). He also supervised the music for two Hammer albums: *Dracula* (1974), which was narrated by Christopher Lee, and *The Legend of the 7 Golden Vampires* (1974), which was narrated by Peter Cushing (he produced the latter with Roy Skeggs). A proposed third album, *Frankenstein*, was abandoned following the disappointing performance of the first two LPs (some sources question whether work was actually done on this project). Martell also worked as a music director for Tyburn, and oversaw the music for *Legend of the Werewolf* (1975), *The Ghoul* (1975) and *The Masks of Death* (1984, TVM), along with their documentary, *Peter Cushing—A One-Way Ticket to Hollywood* (1989, TV). His own film scores include *The Man in the Road* (1956). His brother was the orchestra "fixer" Harry Martell, who worked on several films for Hammer. **Hammer credits:** *The Lyons in Paris* (1955), *The Evil of Frankenstein* (1964), *The Curse of the Mummy's Tomb* (1964), *Fanatic* (1965), *She* (1965), *Hysteria* (1965), *The Brigand of Kandahar* (1965), *The Nanny* (1965), *Dracula—Prince of Darkness* (1966), *The Plague of the Zombies* (1966), *Rasputin—The Mad Monk* (1966), *The Reptile* (1966), *The Witches* (1966), *One Million Years B.C.* (1966), *The Viking Queen* (1967), *Frankenstein Created Woman* (1967), *The Mummy's Shroud* (1967), *Quatermass and the Pit* (1967), *A Challenge for Robin Hood* (1967), *The Anniversary* (1968), *The Vengeance of She* (1968), *The Devil Rides Out* (1968), *Slave Girls* (1968), *The Lost Continent* (1968), *Journey to the Unknown* (1968, TV), *Journey into Darkness* (1968, TVM), *Journey to Midnight* (1968, TVM), *Dracula Has Risen from the Grave* (1968), *Journey to the Unknown* (1969, TVM), *Frankenstein Must Be Destroyed* (1969), *Moon Zero Two* (1969), *Crescendo* (1970), *Taste the Blood of Dracula* (1970), *The Vampire Lovers* (1970), *When Dinosaurs Ruled the Earth* (1970), *Scars of Dracula* (1970), *The Horror of Frankenstein* (1970), *Lust for a Vampire* (1971), *Countess Dracula* (1971), *Creatures the World Forgot* (1971), *On the Buses* (1971), *Hands of the Ripper* (1971), *Twins of Evil* (1971), *Dr. Jekyll and Sister Hyde* (1971), *Blood from the Mummy's Tomb* (1971), *Vampire Circus* (1972), *Journey to Murder* (1972, TVM), *Fear in the Night* (1972), *Straight on Till Morning* (1972), *Mutiny on the Buses* (1972), *Dracula A.D. 1972* (1972), *Demons of the Mind* (1972), *Nearest and Dearest* (1973), *That's Your Funeral* (1973), *Love Thy Neighbour* (1973), *Man at the Top* (1973), *Holiday on the Buses* (1973), *The Satanic Rites of Dracula* (1974), *Captain Kronos—Vampire Hunter* (1974), *Frankenstein and the Monster from Hell* (1974), *Dracula* (1974, LP), *The Legend of the 7 Golden Vampires* (1974), *The Legend of the 7 Golden Vampires* (1974, LP, also producer), *Frankenstein* (1974, LP [unreleased]), *Shatter* (1974), *Man About the House* (1974), *To the Devil a Daughter* (1976), *The Lady Vanishes* (1979), *Hammer House of Horror* (1980, TV), *Hammer House of Mystery and Suspense* (1984, TVM)

## Martelli, Carlo

Having scored a handful of non–Hammer films

for music director Philip Martell, among them *Catacombs* (1964), *Witchcraft* (1964) and *Do You Know This Voice?* (1964), this British composer (1935–), born to an Italian father and an English mother (hence the surname), was invited to score Hammer's second Mummy film, *The Curse of the Mummy's Tomb* (1964). Recalled Martelli of his assignment, "In spring 1964 I watched a rough cut and was then given just three weeks to compose a vast amount of music.... I was relieved to hear that Michael Carreras, the film's director, had used an extract of Franz Reizenstein's music from Hammer's previous Mummy film in the flashback sequences. But this still left me with about forty minutes of music to compose."[29] Despite the rush, Martelli made his tight deadline, providing the film with a brassy, strident score featuring six horns, four trumpets, four trombones and two tubas. Recalled the composer, "The orchestration of the score gave it a particularly grand sound. I was encouraged to use a big brass section, and although there were only around fifty musicians we had the benefit of some of the finest players around."[30]

Martelli was consequently invited back to compose the music for *Slave Girls* (1968). He also provided an additional cue for *Quatermass and the Pit* (1967) titled *Poltergeist?* He was commissioned to write this piece after the film had been re-edited during post-production, by which time the film's credited composer, Tristram Cary, had moved on to another project. This cue is available on GDI's *The Quatermass Film Music Collection.* Commented music director Philip Martell of Martelli, "He was dependable and malleable, which is important in this line of work. He had talent and ability.... He always did what I wanted."[31]

Martelli was trained at the Royal College of Music, by which time he had learned the viola and written several orchestral pieces. He subsequently had his work broadcast by the BBC. His other film credits include *Dr. Syn, Alias the Scarecrow* (1963), on which he "ghosted" some music for the film's credited composer, Gerard Schurmann. He also contributed to Schurmann's scores for *The Bedford Incident* (1965), *Attack on the Iron Coast* (1967) and Hammer's *The Lost Continent* (1968), either as an arranger, orchestrator and/or composer; meanwhile, Schurmann conducted Martelli's score for *Who Killed the Cat?* (1966). Martelli's pieces for the concert platform include *Serenade for Strings* (1955), *Fiesta Overture* (1959), *Aubade* (1984) and *Prelude and Fugue for Eighteen Violas* (1993). He also wrote the opera *The Monkey's Paw* (1990). **Additional notes:** As well as being augmented by music by Franz Reizenstein taken from *The Mummy* (1959), Martelli's score for *The Curse of the Mummy's Tomb* also features music by Kenny Graham, who scored *The Belly Dance.* Martelli's score for *It!* (1967), also conducted by Philip Martell, at times bears a striking resemblance to his work for *The Curse of the Mummy's Tomb.* **Hammer credits:** *The Curse of the Mummy's Tomb* (1964, music), *Quatermass and the Pit* (1967, additional music only [uncredited]), *Slave Girls* (1968, music), *The Lost Continent* (1968, unspecified contribution [uncredited])

## Martin, A.E.

This Australian author (1885–1955, full name Archibald Edward Martin) had his 1944 novel *The Outsiders* (first published as *Common People*) adapted into a film by Hammer. This was re-titled *The Glass Cage* (1955) in Britain, and itself re-titled as *The Glass Tomb* for its American release. The co-owner of a newspaper at eighteen, Martin went on to tour Europe with several carnivals (including one with Houdini) and later became an entrepreneur and a publicist, specializing in theater, circuses, vaudeville and cinema. Other published works (among them several stories for *Ellery Queen's Mystery Magazine*) include *The Misplaced Corpse* (1944), *Death in the Limelight* (1946), *The Power of Leaf* (1948), *The Curious Crime* (1952) and *The Chinese Bed Mysteries* (1954). **Hammer credits:** *The Glass Cage* (1955)

## Martin, Derek

This British stuntman-turned actor (1933–, real name Derek William Rapp) played one of the fairground roustabouts in Hammer's *The Evil of Frankenstein* (1964). Best known for playing Charlie Slater in *EastEnders* (1985–, TV) from 2000 to 2016 (during which time he clocked up 793 episodes), his other TV credits include episodes of *No Hiding Place* (1959–1967, TV), *The Borderers* (1968–1970, TV), *Elizabeth R* (1971, TV), *Spy Trap* (1972–1975, TV), *Only Fools and Horses* (1981–2003, TV), *Eldorado* (1991–1992, TV) and *The Detectives* (1993–1997, TV), while his occasional films include *Secrets of a Windmill Girl* (1966), *The Big Switch* (1969), *The Sex Thief* (1973), *Keep It Up, Jack!* (1974), *Eskimo Nell* (1975), *The Sexplorer* (1975), *Dark Water* (1980) and *Boston Kickout* (1995). **Hammer credits:** *The Evil of Frankenstein* (1964, as Roustabout [uncredited])

## Martin, Doris

British born Martin (1906–1993) worked as the continuity girl on two widely contrasting—and widely spaced—films for Hammer. Her many other credits include *The Curse of the Wraydons* (1947), *Over the Garden Wall* (1950), *Mark of the Phoenix* (1958), *Black Joy* (1977), *Superman* (1978), *Superman II* (1980) and *Supergirl* (1984), plus episodes of *The Adventures of Sir Lancelot* (1956–1957, TV), *One Step Beyond* (1959–1961, TV), *Danger Man* (1964–1966, TV), *The Prisoner* (1967–1968, TV) and *The Persuaders!* (1971–1972, TV). **Hammer credits:** *The Dark Light* (1951), *Dracula Has Risen from the Grave* (1968)

## Martin, Edie

Straight out of a Dickens novel, this diminutive British character actress (1880–1964) was the archetypal little old lady, as seen in countless comedies in the forties and fifties, particularly for Ealing. On stage from 1886, she broke into films in 1931 with *M'Blimey*, and went on to appear in over sixty productions, almost always in cameo roles, among them *A Place of One's Own* (1945), *Great Expectations* (1946), *It Always Rains on Sunday* (1947), *The Lavender Hill Mob* (1951), *The Man in the White Suit* (1951), *Genevieve* (1953) and *The Ladykillers* (1955). One of her last appearances was as a lodgekeeper's wife in the Hammer comedy *A*

*Weekend with Lulu* (1961). **Hammer credits:** *A Weekend with Lulu* (1961, as Lodgekeeper's wife [uncredited])

## Martin, Jack

In Britain from 1933, American born Martin (1899–?) worked as the assistant director on Hammer's disastrous space adventure, *Moon Zero Two* (1969). This led to further work on *Crescendo* (1970), following which he was promoted to production manager on *Creatures the World Forgot* (1971). In fact he alternated between the two duties for much of his career, working as a first assistant on *Mr. Reeder in Room 13* (1938), *Sailors Don't Care* (1940), *Stage Fright* (1950), *Ivanhoe* (1952) and *Moby Dick* (1956), and as a production manager on *Royal Cavalcade* (1935), *This Happy Breed* (1944), *Richard III* (1955) and *Alfred the Great* (1969). He began his career in Hollywood in 1923 working for First National. **Hammer credits:** *Moon Zero Two* (1969, assistant director), *Crescendo* (1970, assistant director), *Creatures the World Forgot* (1971, production manager)

## Martin, Laurie

Martin worked as one of Hammer's unit drivers. **Hammer credits include:** *Paranoiac* (1963 [uncredited]), *The Scarlet Blade* (1963 [uncredited]), *The Kiss of the Vampire* (1963 [uncredited]), *The Evil of Frankenstein* (1964 [uncredited])

## Martin, Malaika

Mombassa born Martin (aka Malaika Mandes) played the role of the exotic snake dancer in Hammer's *Taste the Blood of Dracula* (1970). She toured the UK club circuit of the late sixties/early seventies as an exotic dancer, and usually performed under the name of Malaika Mandes, or simply Malaika (though some sources claim her real name was Diana Woodward). Her skills included belly dancing, fire eating and snake dancing (she was reported to have owned three snakes). **Hammer credits:** *Taste the Blood of Dracula* (1970, as Snake girl)

## Martin, Mia

Martin can be seen as one of the vampires in the cellar of Pelham House in Hammer's *The Satanic Rites of Dracula* (1974). Her other credits include *Suburban Wives* (1971), *Commuter Husbands* (1973) and *The Best of Benny Hill* (1974), the latter featuring clips of her work from *The Benny Hill Show* (1969–1989, TV). She also worked as a model and stage actress. **Hammer credits:** *The Satanic Rites of Dracula* (1974, as Vampire)

## Martin, Skip

This diminutive British actor (1928–1984, real name Derek George Horowitz) is best known to Hammer fans for playing Michael, the white-faced circus clown in *Vampire Circus* (1972). His other credits include *The Hellfire Club* (1960), *The Masque of the Red Death* (1964), in which he played Hop Toad, *Circus of Fear* (1966), *Where's Jack?* (1969), *Son of Dracula* (1973) and *Horror Hospital* (1973), in which he had perhaps his most substantial role as Frederick. He also appeared in episodes of *Adam Adamant Lives!* (1966–1967, TV), *Shirley's World* (1971–1972, TV) and *The*

**Killer clown. Skip Martin looks suitably crazed in this shot from** *Vampire Circus* **(1972) (Hammer/Rank/ Twentieth Century–Fox).**

*Goodies* (1970–1981, TV). **Hammer credits:** *Vampire Circus* (1972, as Michael)

### Martin, Tab

Along with Roy Phillips and Trevor Morais, this British born guitarist (1944–, real name Alan Raymond Breary) was a member of the group The Peddlers, which performed the title song for Hammer's *The Lost Continent* (1968). He was formerly a member of The Tornadoes with Phillips. **Hammer credits:** *The Lost Continent* (1968)

### Martingell, Peter

Martingell worked as the sound maintenance technician on the Hammer thriller *Maniac* (1963). His other credits include *The Password Is Courage* (1962), on which he was a sound assistant, *Invasion Quartet* (1961) and *Kill or Cure* (1962), on which he again worked as sound maintenance, and *Unman, Wittering and Zigo* (1971), on which he was the boom operator. **Hammer credits:** *Maniac* (1963 [uncredited])

### Martyn, Larry

This British actor (1934–1994, full name Lawrence Martyn) played one of the unruly Teddy boys in Hammer's *The Damned* (1963). His other credits include *Too Young to Love* (1959), *Never Back Losers* (1961), *Breath of Life* (1962), *Up the Junction* (1968), *Carry On at Your Convenience* (1971), *For the Love of Ada* (1972) and *The Final Conflict* (1981). Busiest on television, his many credits include episodes of *Z Cars* (1962–1978, TV), *Spring and Autumn* (1972–1976, TV), in which he played Brian Reid, and *Are You Being Served?* (1972–1985, TV), in which he played Mr. Mash between 1972 and 1975. **Hammer credits:** *The Damned* (1963, as Teddy boy [uncredited])

### Marylebone Studios

Thanks to a deal made in late 1946 with Henry Halsted—the owner and production supervisor of Marylebone Studios—Hammer/Exclusive agreed to the making and co-financing of a number of low budget second features. They were: *Death in High Heels* (1947), *Dick Barton—Special Agent* (1948), *The Dark Road* (1948) and *Dick Barton at Bay* (1950), all of which were personally produced by Halsted. The studio was actually a disused church,

and Halsted relinquished control of it in 1950, after which production turned to commercials and documentaries. Among the other films that were made at the studio are *Walking on Air* (1946) and a potted, forty-five-minute version of *Othello* (1946), the latter of which was produced by Halsted and distributed by Exclusive. **Hammer credits:** *Death in High Heels* (1947), *Dick Barton—Special Agent* (1948), *The Dark Road* (1948), *Dick Barton at Bay* (1950)

### *Mask of Dust*

GB, 1954, 79m, bw, RCA, cert U

One of Hammer's slightly more unusual second features (in that it doesn't revolve around an innocent man suspected of murder), this racing drama stars Hollywood import Richard Conte as driver Peter Wells, who, having lost his nerve on the grand prix circuit, determines on clawing it back by winning a race— much to the consternation of his worried wife Pat, played by Mari Aldon.

Recalled Jimmy Sangster, who worked as the production manager on the film, "We did locations at Goodwood race track with cars which might have been okay in their time, but nowadays look like clapped-out wrecks.... In spite of the fact that we used some pretty impressive racing drivers on this shoot (Stirling Moss, Reg Parnell, John Cooper), it still turned out to be a pretty boring picture. Let's face it, a dozen or so cars tearing round a race track ain't much to watch unless the drama that surrounds the events is gripping enough to make you really interested in who's driving. Richard Landau's script wasn't."[32]

Based on the 1953 novel *The Last Race* by Jon Manchip White, the film contains some passable racing sequences. Unfortunately, an over-plus of library footage and back projection work mitigate any excitement generated, although Bill Lenny's editing melds the various elements together ably enough. However, as Sangster observed, the track footage is stalled by the domestic dramas, which conform to the expected confrontational clichés between husband and wife. Says Pat to her husband at one point, whom she wants to give up racing so that they can have a baby, "I won't see my child born in some filthy hotel at the edge of the race track." Unfortunately, her argument is somewhat undermined by the fact

that their current "filthy hotel" accommodation is a luxuriously appointed two-room suite complete with a baby grand, allowing Peter to idly tinkle away while his high maintenance wife expresses her concerns dressed in a flowing negligee (ungrateful cow). However, some of the exchanges do ring true. Notes one hardened driver of another who is apt to pray in church before a race: "You don't win races with a bible in your pocket and a prayer on your lips." Meanwhile, back in the hotel bar, a former driver observes of the racers, "It isn't the drivers that count, only the machines. They know that drivers are expendable. You can't salvage a dead driver."

Compared to the present day multi-million pound grand prix scene, the film offers an antique view of the sport, with most of the drivers on the verge of middle age (this is by no means a young man's sport as depicted here). As for the casual pit-stops, complete with extended chats, they compare badly to today's lightning fast equivalents.

Not quite the *métier* of Terence Fisher, the director nevertheless worked diligently through the material according to Jimmy Sangster, who observed, "It was Terry Fisher's eleventh film for Hammer. He was a production manager's dream.

**If only the movie was this dynamic. The American poster for** *Mask of Dust* **(1954), released in the States as** *A Race for Life* **(Hammer/ Lippert/Exclusive/Twentieth Century–Fox).**

If I told him that we had to finish by six pm today because somebody else wanted to use the race track or he had to finish with a certain actor by a certain date, he never kicked up a fuss. 'All right, dear boy,' was his standard response."[33]

Performance-wise, Richard Conte doesn't quite manage to capture his character's determination to make a comeback at all costs, while as his wife, Mari Aldon provides some well-coiffed glamor amongst the axle grease and burning rubber, though her eye make-up unfortunately gives her a perpetually startled look throughout the proceedings. The supporting cast, prime among them George Coulouris and Meredith Edwards, are reliable hands however, and at least help to keep the drama grounded somewhere in reality, while racing buffs will no doubt appreciate the brief glimpses of the track legends of the day.

Executive produced by Michael Carreras, the film was shot in spring 1954 and released in the UK by Exclusive on 27 December the same year. The film was rather unimaginatively re-titled *A Race for Life* for its slightly earlier U.S. release on 10 December, for which ten minutes were trimmed from the running time. *Variety* described this version as being "An OK entry for a minor double bill." **Additional notes:** Racing driver Geoffrey Taylor, who appears in the film, also doubled for Richard Conte during the star's driving scenes. Some sources refer to the film's American title as *Race for Life* as opposed to *A Race for Life*.

Production companies: Hammer/Lippert. Distributors: Exclusive (UK), Twentieth Century–Fox (U.S.). Producer: Mickey Delamar. Executive producer: Michael Carreras. Director: Terence Fisher. Screenplay: Richard Landau, based on the novel by Jon Manchip White. Cinematographer: Walter "Jimmy" Harvey. Music: Leonard Salzedo. Music director: John Hollingsworth. Editor: Bill Lenny. Art director: J. Elder Wills. Costumes: Molly Arbuthnot. Production manager: Jimmy Sangster. Assistant director: Jack Causey. Second assistant director: Aida Young [uncredited]. Sound: Sid Wiles, Ken Cameron. Sound camera operator: Don Alton [uncredited]. Camera operator: Len Harris. Focus puller: Harry Oakes [uncredited]. Make-up: Phil Leakey. Hair: Monica Hustler. Continuity: Renee Glynne. Driver: Coco Epps [uncredited]. Production secretary: Doreen Soan [uncredited]. **Cast:** Richard Conte (Peter Wells), Mari Aldon (Pat Wells), George Coulouris (Dallapiccola), Tim Turner (Alvarez), Peter Illing (Tony Bellario), Meredith Edwards (Larry Lawrence), Jeremy Hawk (Martin), James Copeland (Johnny), Richard Marner (Hans Brecht), Edwin Richfield (Reporter), Stirling Moss (Himself), Reg Parnell (Himself), John Cooper (Himself), Alan Brown (Driver), Alec Mango (Guido Rosetti), Leslie Marr (Driver), Geoffrey Taylor (Driver [also Richard Conte's stunt double]), Raymond Baxter (Commentator [uncredited]), Paul Carpenter (Commentator [uncredited]). **DVD availability:** VCI Entertainment (U.S., all regions), double-billed with *The Stranger Came Home* (1954); Simply Media (UK R2 PAL), extras include newsreel footage of Stirling Moss and other racing drivers of the day in action

## Mason, C.T. (Cecil Tapscott)

British born Mason (1904–1982) worked as the sound recordist on the Hammer comedy *The Lyons in Paris* (1955). Beginning as an assistant sound recordist on *Boots! Boots!* (1934), he went on to record *Blue Smoke* (1935), *Murder in the Family* (1938), *The Way We Live* (1946), *Eight O'Clock Walk* (1954), *Look Back in Anger* (1959), *Only Two Can Play* (1962), *The Great St. Trinian's Train Robbery* (1966) and *The Fiction Makers* (1968), plus episodes of *Fabian of the Yard* (1954–1956, TV), *The Avengers* (1961–1969, TV), *The Saint* (1962–1969, TV) and *Gideon's Way* (1965–1966, TV). **Hammer credits:** *The Lyons in Paris* (1955)

## Mason, E. (Edward/Teddy)

This sound technician recorded the sound for the Hammer thriller *Taste of Fear* (1961), sharing his duties with Leslie Hammond and Len Shilton. His other credits, mostly as a dubbing/sound editor, include *A Kid for Two Farthings* (1955), *Two-Way Stretch* (1960), *It's All Happening* (1963), *Battle of Britain* (1969), which earned him a shared BAFTA nomination, *Diamonds Are Forever* (1971), *Live and Let Die* (1973), *The Dove* (1974), *Absolution* (1978), *Victor/Victoria* (1982), *Turtle Diary* (1985), *Let Him Have It* (1991) and *The General* (1998), plus episodes of *The Martian Chronicles* (1980, TV) and *Dick Turpin* (1979–1982, TV). **Hammer credits:** *Taste of Fear* (1961)

## Mason, Edward J.

While involved in radio in the forties, this British dramatist (1912–1971) worked with Geoffrey Webb as a scriptwriter on one of the most popular post-war radio series, *Dick Barton, Special Agent*, whose daring exploits ran as a day-time serial on the BBC's Light Program between 1946 and 1951, regularly pulling in an impressive fifteen million listeners. Hammer subsequently made three cheap films based on the character, who was actually the creation of the radio producer Norman Collins, who was also the controller of the Light Program. They were *Dick Barton—Special Agent* (1948), *Dick Barton Strikes Back* (1949) and *Dick Barton at Bay* (1950), none of which Mason was personally involved in. However, he did co-write the scripts for *Celia* (1949), *The Lady Craved Excitement* (1950) and *What the Butler Saw* (1950) for Hammer, all of which were likewise based on his radio serials. His other radio credits include *The Archers* (1950–) and *Shadow Man* (1955), while his television work includes episodes of *I'm Not Bothered* (1956, TV), *Dial 999* (1958–1959, TV), *The Days of Vengeance* (1960, TV) and *How to Be an Alien* (1964, TV). **Hammer credits:** *Dick Barton—Special Agent* (1949, original radio serial), *Dick Barton Strikes Back* (1949, original radio serial), *Celia* (1949, original radio serial, co-screenplay), *What the Butler Saw* (1950, original radio serial, co-screenplay), *Dick Barton at Bay* (1950, original radio serial), *The Lady Craved Excitement* (1950, original radio serial, co-screenplay)

## Mason, Max

Mason can be seen in a minor role in *The House That Bled to Death* (1980, TV [episode of *Hammer House of Horror*]). His other credits include episodes of *Dixon of Dock Green* (1955–1976, TV), *Z Cars* (1962–1978, TV), *The Sweeney* (1975–1978, TV), *The Bill* (1984–2010, TV) and *Peak Practice* (1993–2002, TV), while his occasional films take in *Sex and the Other Woman* (1972), *Four Dimensions of Greta* (1972), *Sex Farm* (1973) and *Sweeney 2* (1978). **Hammer credits:** *The House That Bled to Death* (1980, TV [episode of *Hammer House of Horror*], as Journalist)

## Mason, Sydney

This American actor (1905–1976) can be seen as the Police Chief in Hammer's unsuccessful TV pilot *Tales of Frankenstein: The Face in the Tombstone Mirror* (1958, TV). His many other TV credits, among them many westerns, include episodes of *The Lone Ranger* (1949–1957, TV), *The Cisco Kid* (1950–1956, TV), *The Roy Rogers Show* (1951–1957, TV) and *Craig Kennedy, Criminologist* (1952, TV), in which he played Inspector J.J. Burke. His film credits include *I'll See You in My Dreams* (1951), *The War of the Worlds* (1953), *Creature from the Black Lagoon* (1954), *Ada* (1961) and *Wild Ones on Wheels* (1962), also working as the associate producer on the latter. His father was actor Sidney Mason (1886–1923) and his mother actress Marie Mason. His second wife was actress Martha Mason (1908–1994, real name Martha Gowdy), whom he married in 1945. **Hammer credits:** *Tales of Frankenstein: The Face in the Tombstone Mirror* (1958, TV, as Police Chief [uncredited])

## Massie, Paul

Working primarily in Britain, this Canadian actor (1932–2011) won a BAFTA as best newcomer for his second film, *Orders to Kill* (1958), which led to his being cast as both Dr. Jekyll and Mr. Hyde in Hammer's misconceived variation on the story, *The Two Faces of Dr. Jekyll* (1960). The film was originally intended as a vehicle for Laurence Harvey, who instead went on to make *Butterfield 8* (1960) in Hollywood. The idea was then to replace Harvey with Massie, but only in the role of Hyde, here presented as a youthful sadist to Jekyll's middle-aged doctor. However, Massie lobbied for both roles and eventually won the prize assignment, signing his contract on 19 November 1959, just four days before the production went on the floor. Unfortunately, his lackluster performance did much to damage an already deeply flawed film, which was subsequently greeted with indifference by audiences and critics alike. Massie's other films include *High Tide at Noon* (1957), *Sapphire* (1959), *Libel* (1960), *Raising the Wind* (1961), *The Pot Carriers* (1962) and *The Naked Eye* (1995). He has also popped up in episodes of *The Flying Doctor* (1959, TV), *The Avengers* (1961–1969, TV), *The Main Chance* (1969–1975, TV), *The Pathfinders* (1972–1973, TV) and *Hawkeye, the Pathfinder* (1973, TV). **Hammer credits:** *The Two Faces of Dr. Jekyll* (1960, as Dr. Henry Jekyll and Edward Hyde)

## Masters, Tony (Anthony)

A shared BAFTA winner and Oscar nominee for his brilliant work on *2001: A Space Odyssey* (1968), this British production designer and art director

(1919–1990) began his career as a draughtsman on such films as *The Hasty Heart* (1949), *Carrington V.C.* (1954) and *The Constant Husband* (1955). He gained his first credit as an art director with the celebrated short *The Bespoke Overcoat* (1955), and went to design several films for director Val Guest, among them *Expresso Bongo* (1959), Hammer's *The Full Treatment* (1961) and *The Day the Earth Caught Fire* (1961). His other credits include such large-scale films as *The Heroes of Telemark* (1965), *Papillon* (1973), *The Deep* (1977) and *Dune* (1984). He was married to the actress Heather Sears (1935–1994) from 1957; she appeared in Hammer's *The Phantom of the Opera* (1962). Their sons are production designer Giles Masters (1962–), art director Dominic Masters and editor Adam Masters. **Hammer credits:** *The Full Treatment* (1961)

### Matakitas Is Coming see Journey to the Unknown

### Mather, Berkely

A one-time army lieutenant-colonel, British born Mather (1909–1996, real name John Evan Weston-Davies) penned an unused screenplay for Hammer's adaptation of H. Rider Haggard's novel *She* (1965) in late 1963. His other credits include *Information Received* (1961), for which he provided the story, *Dr. No* (1962), *The Long Ships* (1964) and *Genghis Khan* (1965), for which he again provided the story (and penned the novelization). He also wrote episodes for such series as *Douglas Fairbanks, Jr. Presents* (1953–1957, TV) and *Frontier* (1968–1969, TV). His novels include *The Achilles Affair* (1959), *Geth Straker* (1962), *The Terminators* (1971) and *The Hour of the Dog* (1982). **Hammer credits:** *She* (1965 [unused screenplay])

### Matheson, Judy

This British actress (1945–) can be seen as Amanda in Hammer's *Lust for a Vampire* (1971). Her other credits include *Las crueles* (1969), in which she co-starred with Capucine, *Crucible of Terror* (1971), *The Flesh and Blood Show* (1972), *Scream ... and Die!* (1973), *Percy's Progress* (1974) and *Confessions of a Window Cleaner* (1974), plus a return to Hammer for a brief role in *Twins of Evil* (1971). She also appeared in episodes of *Citizen Smith* (1977–1980, TV) and *The Professionals* (1977–1983, TV). Her first husband (of two) was actor Paul Freeman (1943–), whom she married in 1967. **Hammer credits:** *Lust for a Vampire* (1971, as Amanda), *Twins of Evil* (1971, a Woodman's daughter)

### Matheson, Richard

Working as both a novelist and screenwriter, this acclaimed genre writer (1926–2013) adapted both his own work and that of others for the screen. His many screenplay credits (among them several celebrated Poe adaptations for Roger Corman) include *The Incredible Shrinking Man* (1957), *House of Usher* (1960), *Master of the World* (1961), *The Pit and the Pendulum* (1961), *Tales of Terror* (1962), *The Raven* (1963), *The Comedy of Terrors* (1964), *The Legend of Hell House* (1973), which was based on his 1971 novel *Hell House*, *Somewhere in Time* (1980), *Duel* (1971, TVM), *Jaws 3-D* (1983) and *Twilight Zone: The Movie* (1983).

He also had several brushes with Hammer during his career. The first of these was with *The Night Creatures*, an adaptation of his 1954 novel *I Am Legend*. For this he travelled to London for two months on 18 September 1957. Unfortunately, the production was abandoned following objections from the BBFC, which refused to sanction *any* film made from Matheson's script, amendments and alterations notwithstanding. Consequently, Hammer sold the property on to Robert Lippert (with whom they'd made several crime programers in the early fifties), who finally made it in Italy as *The Last Man on Earth* (1964), by which time the script had been re-written by William P. Leicester and Logan Swanson—the latter actually a pen name for Matheson himself (note that a second version of the story, *The Omega Man*, followed in 1971, and a third in 2007 under the original title).

Matheson next adapted Anne Blaisdell's 1962 novel *Nightmare* for Hammer as *Fanatic* (1965). The story of a young American woman who is imprisoned by the mother of her dead fiancé, *Variety* described the script as being "melodramatic," adding that it "echoes with clichés from other stories set in sinister mansions in [the] English countryside." Thankfully, Matheson had rather better luck with his third big screen project for Hammer, a brisk adaptation of Dennis Wheatley's *The Devil Rides Out* (1968). Although by no means the major commercial success it was expected to be, the film is now rightly regarded as one of the company's very best. Matheson was subsequently approached (but not commissioned) to adapt another Wheatley novel for the screen, *The Haunting of Toby Jugg*. He also had his 1963 story *Girl of My Dreams* adapted as an episode of the Hammer TV series *Journey to the Unknown* (1968, TV), the teleplay for which was written by Robert Bloch and Michael J. Bird.

Matheson's other television credits include contributions to such series as *The Twilight Zone* (1959–1964, TV), *Night Gallery* (1970–1973, TV), *Ghost Story* (1972–1973, TV), *Amazing Stories* (1985–1987, TV) and *Masters of Horror* (2005–2006, TV). Films adapted by others from his novels and short stories include *What Dreams May Come* (1998 [novel 1978]), *Stir of Echoes* (1999, from *A Stir of Echoes* [novel 1958]), *My Ambition* (2006, from *Blood Son* [story 1951]) and *The Box* (2009, from *Button, Button* [story 1970], also filmed as a 1986 episode of *The Twilight Zone* [1985–1989, TV]). **Hammer credits:** *The Night Creatures* (1957 [unproduced]), *Fanatic* (1965, screenplay), *The Devil Rides Out* (1968, screenplay), *Girl of My Dreams* (1968, TV [episode of *Journey to the Unknown*], story)

### Mathews, Kerwin

Best remembered for playing Sinbad in the Ray Harryhausen classic *The Seventh Voyage of Sinbad* (1958), this virile American actor (1926–2007) also appeared in such fantasies as *The Three Worlds of Gulliver* (1960), *Jack the Giant Killer* (1962) and *Battle Beneath the Earth* (1968). On television from 1954 and in films from 1955 following experience as a teacher, his other feature credits include *Five Against the House* (1955), *The Waltz King* (1963), *Barquero* (1969), *Octaman* (1971), *The Boy Who Cried Werewolf* (1973) and *Nightmare in Blood* (1977), after which his career seemed to dry up (he subsequently became an antiques dealer). In the sixties Mathews also appeared in two Hammer films, first playing the dashing Jonathan Standing, who attempts to protect his Caribbean Huguenot community from Christopher Lee's plundering pirate Captain La Roche in *The Pirates of Blood River* (1962). This was followed by the twist-packed thriller *Maniac* (1963), in which he played an American painter who finds himself caught up in a complex murder plot in the Camargue. Mathews' television credits include episodes of *Space Patrol* (1950–1955, TV), *Matinee Theatre* (1955–1958, TV), *General Hospital* (1963–, TV) and *Ironside* (1967–1975, TV). **Additional notes:** Mathews was originally to have starred in the Michael Carreras western *The Savage Guns* (1962), but was replaced by Don Taylor. **Hammer credits:** *The Pirates of Blood River* (1962, as Jonathan Standing), *Maniac* (1963, as Geoff Farrell)

### Mathews, Peter

Mathews worked as the sound camera operator on two films for Hammer. **Hammer credits:** *The Gambler and the Lady* (1953 [uncredited]), *Four Sided Triangle* (1953 [uncredited])

### Mathews, Richard

This British actor (1914–1992) can be seen as the corrupt Right Honorable John Porter MP in Hammer's *The Satanic Rites of Dracula* (1974). His other credits include *Bequest to the Nation* (1973) and *It Could Happen to You* (1975), plus episodes of everything from *Dixon of Dock Green* (1955–1976, TV) to *Doctor Who* (1963–1989, TV). His wife was actress Elizabeth Ashley (1920–2001), whom he married in 1951. **Hammer credits:** *The Satanic Rites of Dracula* (1974, as Right Honorable John Porter MP)

### Mathie, Marion

This British actress (1925–2012) played the role of Anna Muller, the mother of Dracula's intended victim Maria Muller, in Hammer's *Dracula Has Risen from the Grave* (1968). Other credits include *No Kidding* (1960), *Lolita* (1962) and *An Honourable Murder* (1960), plus episodes of *Dixon of Dock Green* (1955–1976, TV), *Redcap* (1964–1966, TV), *Angels* (1975–1983, TV) and *Mapp and Lucia* (1985–1986, TV). She is perhaps best known for playing Hilda Rumpole in *Rumpole of the Bailey* (1978–1992, TV) from 1987 onwards, having inherited the role from Peggy Thorpe-Bates. Her husband was actor John Humphry (1927–2007), whom she married in 1963. **Hammer credits:** *Dracula Has Risen from the Grave* (1968, as Anna Muller)

### Mathiesen, Sarah

Mathiesen worked as Valerie Leon's stand in and double during the making of *Blood from the Mummy's Tomb* (1971). **Hammer credits:** *Blood from the Mummy's Tomb* (1971, as stand in for Valerie Leon [uncredited])

### Mathieson, Muir

In films from 1931, this prolific British (Scottish) conductor (1911–1975, full name James Muir

Mathieson) went on to work on literally hundreds of films during his busy career. He began his conducting career at the age of thirteen with the Stirling Boys Orchestra, with whom he made his BBC debut in a concert broadcast from Glasgow Station. He went on to win two music scholarships and to train further at the Royal College of Music. He began his film career as an assistant music director for Alexander Korda at the age of twenty, becoming the music director of Korda's London Films three years later, gaining his first official credit with *The Private Life of Don Juan* (1934), which he followed with such classics as *Catherine the Great* (1934), *The Ghost Goes West* (1935), *Sanders of the River* (1935), *Things to Come* (1936) and *The Thief of Bagdad* (1940).

During the war years Mathieson also conducted the music for a number of documentary units, including the RAF, Army and Crown Film Units. He went on to become the music director for the Rank Organization, and among the many other feature scores he conducted were those for *Dangerous Moonlight* (1941), *Brief Encounter* (1945), *Richard III* (1956), *Vertigo* (1958) and *You Can't Win 'Em All* (1970), while his own scores include *Anoop and the Elephant* (1973). He appeared on screen twice, conducting the London Symphony Orchestra in *The Seventh Veil* (1945) and, briefly, as Sir Arthur Sullivan in *The Magic Box* (1951). He also conducted the music for three Hammer films: *Lady in the Fog* (1952), which had a score by Ivor Slaney, *Four Sided Triangle* (1953), which had a score by Malcolm Arnold, and *The Revenge of Frankenstein* (1958), which had a score by Leonard Salzedo. For the latter film, Mathieson stepped in at the last minute to conduct the recording sessions when Hammer's by-then resident music director John Hollingsworth (who had been his assistant in the mid-forties) was taken ill with tuberculosis. Mathieson's brother was conductor Dock Mathieson (1914–1985, real name John Davie Mathieson). His wife was ballet dancer Hermione Darnborough (1915–2010). **Hammer credits:** *Lady in the Fog* (1952), *Four Sided Triangle* (1953), *The Revenge of Frankenstein* (1958 [uncredited])

## Mattey, Robert A.

Working primarily for Disney in the fifties and sixties, this legendary American effects technician (1910–1993) worked on such films as *20,000 Leagues Under the Sea* (1954), *The Absent-Minded Professor* (1961), which earned him a shared Oscar nomination, *Babes in Toyland* (1961), *Son of Flubber* (1962), *Mary Poppins* (1964), *The Gnome-Mobile* (1967) and *The Love Bug* (1968), though he is perhaps best remembered for creating Bruce the shark for *Jaws* (1975). He also provided the less than convincing monsters for Hammer's *The Lost Continent* (1968), which include a giant cephalopod and a giant scorpion. **Hammer credits:** *The Lost Continent* (1968)

## Matthews, Brendan

Matthews played the role of Nigel in Hammer's *The Viking Queen* (1967). His other credits include *Of Human Bondage* (1964), *Quackser Fortune Has a Cousin in the Bronx* (1970), *Underground* (1970)

and *The McKenzie Break* (1970). **Hammer credits:** *The Viking Queen* (1967, as Nigel)

## Matthews, Christopher

A briefly familiar face in genre pictures in the late sixties and early seventies Matthews was cast as Paul in Hammer's *Scars of Dracula* (1970), finding himself an unwitting guest and victim of the Count (he ends up hanging from a wall on a spike). His other credits include *Some Like It Sexy* (1969), *Scream and Scream Again* (1970) and *Blind Terror* (1971), plus episodes of *Doctor Who* (1963–1989, TV), *Van Der Valk* (1972–1977, TV) and *Space: 1999* (1975–1977, TV). Recalled the actor of his time on *Scars*, "I just remember it being tremendous fun with Dennis [Waterman] ... and all the girls!"[34] **Hammer credits:** *Scars of Dracula* (1970, as Paul)

## Matthews, Eileen

Matthews worked as the production secretary on Hammer's *One Million Years B.C.* (1966). Her other credits include *The Liquidator* (1965) and *Alfred the Great* (1969). **Hammer credits:** *One Million Years B.C.* (1966 [uncredited])

## Matthews, Francis

Familiar to television audiences for such series as *Paul Temple* (1969–1971, TV) and *Don't Forget to Write* (1977–1979, TV), this dapper British leading man (1927–2014) also had a prolific career on stage (beginning as an assistant stage manager at seventeen) and the big screen. On television from 1951 with *At Your Service Ltd.* and in films from 1956 with *Bhowani Junction*, his other credits include *Corridors of Blood* (1958), *The Lamp in Assassin Mews* (1962), *That Riviera Touch* (1966), *Crossplot* (1969), *May We Borrow Your Husband?* (1986, TVM) and *Do Not Disturb* (1999), as well as episodes of *Heartbeat* (1992–2009, TV), *Jonathan Creek* (1997–2009, TV) and *Beautiful People* (2008–2009, TV).

He had four brushes with Hammer, beginning with *The Revenge of Frankenstein* (1958), in which he played Dr. Hans Kleve, Frankenstein's young assistant. Recalled Matthews of his being cast in the film, "They literally phoned my agent one day and offered me a part in *The Revenge of Frankenstein*. I think the producer Tony Hinds had seen me on television in something. Something I think called *St. Ives*, a piece set in the same period. He thought I looked right, so I played Dr. Kleve."[35]

The following year he appeared as an Arab in the comedy *I Only Arsked!* (1959), Hammer's big screen version of the hit TV sitcom *The Army Game* (1957–1962, TV), although he is perhaps best remembered by fans for appearing in the back-to-back productions of *Dracula—Prince of Darkness* (1966) and *Rasputin—The Mad Monk* (1966). Recalled Matthews, "We had a lot of laughs working on *Dracula—Prince of Darkness*. It was all fairly ridiculous. When you were in the middle of it, you did feel a bit of a fool."[36]

As for working with Terence Fisher, he remembered, "Terry smoked cigars a lot and was asleep most of the time! The real director [on *The Revenge of Frankenstein*] was Jack Asher, the cameraman. He lit the scenes and told you what lighting you

were going to get, and Terry would just say, 'Lovely.' He never really directed."[37] Matthews also seemed to blame Fisher for his rather lackluster performance in *Prince of Darkness*: "Some of the scenes I did in *Dracula* I really wish Terry had told me not to do. Some of my acting in that is quite awful."[38]

Of Hammer films in general he observed during one magazine interview, "They were very *tame* for their day, I thought. The fault with Hammer was they thought—and this is Tony Hinds' fault—that horror consisted of blood. Blood isn't horror. Terror is horror, the fear of the unknown. Sounds can be more terrifying than sights. When you see an arm cut off with blood dripping out of it, straight away you know it's not a real arm, so you can't really be horrified. Those horror films never really scared me at all. They still don't. They were horri*ble*. *The Shining*. Now *that* was terrifying! Hammer relied too much on blood and horrible faces. Audiences became more sophisticated. They got indigestion from all the blood and women being strangled and put upon stakes…. They were very repetitive. One tired of seeing Black Park as well! You thought, God, not another shot of Black Park! You know, with the monks walking along going o-o-o-o-e-r, the coffin, then DONG! DONG! and the gallows. It's not frightening, it's pedestrian."[39] In a later interview, Matthews tried to distance himself from these remarks: "I didn't remember being interviewed for that magazine at all. I got it in Inverness. Somebody came to the stage door and had me sign the magazine. I don't remember doing it!"[40] However, make the comments he did—to the author of this book, no less—during a 1988 tour of the stage play *Holmes and the Ripper*. The article was subsequently published in an issue of *Starburst* magazine in 1989.

Matthews' brother is the actor Paul Shelley (1942–, real name Paul Matthews), and his wife was the actress Angela Browne (1938–2001), whom he married in 1963. Their children are the actors Damien Matthews and Paul Rattigan. **Additional notes:** Matthews and his wife used their own cine-camera to photograph several fascinating behind-the-scenes sequences on the back lot set of Castle Dracula during the filming of *Dracula—Prince of Darkness*. These shots have since been used in several documentaries on Hammer, among them Ted Newsom's *Flesh and Blood—The Hammer Heritage of Horror* (1994, TV). **Hammer credits:** *The Revenge of Frankenstein* (1958, as Dr. Hans Kleve), *I Only Arsked!* (1959, as Mahmoud), *Dracula—Prince of Darkness* (1966, as Charles Kent), *Rasputin—The Mad Monk* (1966, as Ivan Kesnikov), *Flesh and Blood—The Hammer Heritage of Horror* (1994, TV, interviewee, special thanks)

## Matthews, H.J.

Matthews worked as a rigger on Hammer's *Vampire Circus* (1972). **Hammer credits:** *Vampire Circus* (1972 [uncredited])

## Matthews, Martin

Matthews played Jose Amadayo in Hammer's *The Curse of the Werewolf* (1961). His other credits include *The Leather Boys* (1963) and *North Sea Hijack* (1979), while his many TV appearances take in episodes of *Armchair Mystery Theatre* (1960–1965, TV), *When the Boat Comes In* (1976–1981, TV), *Brideshead Revisited* (1981, TV) and *Waterfront Beat* (1990–1991, TV). **Hammer credits:** *The Curse of the Werewolf* (1961, as Jose Amadayo)

### Matthews, Ron

Matthews worked as the sound camera operator on the Hammer thriller *Maniac* (1963). His other credits include *Lucky Jim* (1957), *Brothers In Law* (1957), *Kill or Cure* (1962), *The V.I.P.s* (1963), *Alfred the Great* (1969) and *Unman, Wittering and Zigo* (1971). **Hammer credits:** *Maniac* (1963 [uncredited])

### Maude, Gillian

This Irish supporting actress (1918–1988) played Jean Hunter in Hammer's *Dick Barton—Special Agent* (1948). Her other credits include *Lend Me Your Wife* (1935), *Appointment in London* (1952) and *Piccadilly Third Stop* (1960), while her TV appearances include episodes of *The Adventures of the Big Man* (1956, TV) and *Private Investigator* (1968–1969, TV). Her husband was actor Campbell Singer (1909–1976), real name Jacob Kobel Singer), who appeared in four films for Hammer, including *Dick Barton—Special Agent*. **Hammer credits:** *Dick Barton—Special Agent* (1948, as Jean Hunter)

### Maude, Mary

Maude can be seen as the haughty Robin Ackerman in Hammer's *Man at the Top* (1973), the British poster for which prominently features her. Her other credits include *The House That Screamed* (1969), *Crucible of Terror* (1971), *Scorpio* (1973), *Double Exposure* (1976), *The Four Feathers* (1977, TVM) and *Terror* (1978), plus episodes of *Man in a Suitcase* (1967–1968, TV), *Freewheelers* (1968–1973, TV), in which she played Terry Driver, *Angels* (1975–1983, TV), *Dick Turpin* (1979–1982, TV) and *Lovejoy* (1986–1994, TV). **Hammer credits:** *Man at the Top* (1973, as Robin Ackerman)

### Maugham, Cynthia

One of Hammer's many secretaries, British born Maugham (1907–1965) worked as the production secretary on *The Camp on Blood Island* (1958). Other credits include *Cat Girl* (1957), *Friends and Neighbours* (1959), *The Hands of Orlac* (1960) and *Private Potter* (1962). **Hammer credits include:** *The Camp on Blood Island* (1958 [uncredited])

### Maunder, Dennis

This British theater director (1923–2012) assisted Terence Fisher with the staging of the opera scenes (shot at Wimbledon Theater) for Hammer's *The Phantom of the Opera* (1962). He trained at the Central School of Speech and Drama in the early fifties, and gained experience as an assistant stage manager for the English Opera Group and the Royal Ballet (from 1953 with the latter), and as the resident assistant producer at the Royal Opera House (from 1960). He went on to direct plays in Guildford and Windsor (he went freelance in 1962), as well as operas for Glyndebourne (where he began as an assistant producer in 1963), the Barber Institute and the Wexford Festival among others. He also taught in the opera department at the Guildhall School of Music and Drama between 1967 and 1979. **Hammer credits:** *The Phantom of the Opera* (1962 [uncredited])

### Maunsell, Charles

This Irish actor (1883–1968) can be seen playing a janitor in Hammer's *Never Take Sweets from a Stranger* (1960). His other credits include *Seven Days to Noon* (1950), *Dublin Nightmare* (1958) and *Sentenced for Life* (1960), plus such early TV plays as *Youth at the Helm* (1938, TV), *Parnell* (1938, TV) and *Edna's Fruit Hat* (1939, TV). He also appeared in episodes of such series as *Quatermass and the Pit* (1958–1959, TV), *The Citadel* (1960–1961, TV) and *Maigret* (1960–1963, TV). **Hammer credits:** *Never Take Sweets from a Stranger* (1960, as Janitor [uncredited])

### Maur, Meinhart

This Hungarian character actor (1884–1964) appeared in Hammer's third and final Dick Barton adventure *Dick Barton at Bay* (1950) as Serge Volkoff. Commented the film's poster, "Volkoff, Dick Barton's deadliest enemy, played by Meinhart Maur, the man with 100 faces." Maur's other English-speaking films include *Rembrandt* (1936), *Second Bureau* (1937), *Candlelight in Algeria* (1944), *Never Let Me Go* (1953) and *Malaga* (1954). His earlier German films include *Die Toten kehren wieder—Enoch Arden* (1919), *Harakiri* (1919), *Die Stimme des Herzens* (1924) and *Die Koffer des Herrn O.F.* (1931). Meinhart's wife was the actress Annie Arden. **Hammer credits:** *Dick Barton at Bay* (1950, as Serge Volkoff)

### Maureen, Mollie

This Irish actress (1904–1987, real name Elizabeth Mary Campfield) can be seen as an elderly thief at an auction house in an early scene in *The Corvini Inheritance* (1984, TVM [episode of *Hammer House of Mystery and Suspense*]). She had her finest moment playing a diminutive Queen Victoria in *The Private Life of Sherlock Holmes* (1970), a role she repeated in an episode of *The Edwardians* (1972–1973, TV), though she was perhaps best known for playing Granny Fraser in *Crossroads* (1964–1988, TV) between 1964 and 1970. Her other film credits include *Silent Playground* (1963), *The Return of the Pink Panther* (1975), *The Wicked Lady* (1983) and *Little Dorrit* (1987). Her other TV credits include episodes of *BBC Sunday-Night Theatre* (1950–1959, TV), *The Avengers* (1961–1969, TV) and *The Setbacks* (1980–1986, TV). **Hammer credits:** *The Corvini Inheritance* (1984, TVM [episode of *Hammer House of Mystery and Suspense*], as Elderly lady)

### Maxim, John

This Australian actor (1925–1990, aka John Wills) had minor roles in five Hammer films. His other credits include *The Frightened City* (1961) and *Mary Had a Little…* (1961), plus episodes of *William Tell* (1958–1959, TV), *Doctor Who* (1963–1989, TV) and *The Prisoner* (1967–1968, TV). **Hammer credits:** *Dracula* (1958, as Inn patron [uncredited]), *She* (1965, as Captain of the Guard), *The Brigand of Kandahar* (1965, as Prison guard),

*Dracula—Prince of Darkness* (1966, as Coach driver), *Frankenstein Created Woman* (1967, as Sergeant [uncredited])

### Maxwell, James

Long resident in Britain, this American character actor (1929–1995) trained at the Old Vic Theater School in Bristol, after which he devoted the majority of his career to the stage, as an actor, director, playwright and founder member of Manchester's Royal Exchange Theater. In films from 1958 with *Subway in the Sky*, other credits include *Private Potter* (1962), in which he played Lieutenant Colonel Harry Gunyon, *The Traitors* (1962), *One Day in the Life of Ivan Denisovich* (1971) and *Ransom* (1974). He also played Mr. Talbot in Hammer's *The Damned* (1963), which led to a further appearance as a priest in *The Evil of Frankenstein* (1964). Maxwell's many credits on TV include *Twelfth Night* (1957, TV), the original version of *Private Potter* (1961, TV), also as Lieutenant Colonel Harry Gunyon, plus episodes of *Empire* (1962–1964, TV), *The Hidden Truth* (1964, TV), *Father Brown* (1974, TV), *Raffles* (1975–1977, TV) and *Bergerac* (1981–1991, TV). His wife was actress Avril Elgar (1932–) whom he married in 1952. **Hammer credits:** *The Damned* (1963, as Mr. Talbot), *The Evil of Frankenstein* (1964, as Priest)

### Maxwell, Lois

Known the world over for playing Miss Moneypenny in fourteen of the James Bond films, this much-loved RADA-trained Canadian actress (1927–2007, real name Lois Ruth Hooker, aka Robin Wells) began her film career in England in 1946 with *A Matter of Life and Death* following radio experience as a child in her home country from the age of fifteen (under the name of Robin Wells). Her subsequent films include *Spring Song* (1946), *Corridor of Mirrors* (1948), *Women of Twilight* (1952), *Lolita* (1962), *The Haunting* (1963), *Endless Night* (1972), *Rescue Me* (1988) and *The Fourth Angel* (2001) among others, while her Bond career began with *Dr. No* (1962) and ended with *A View to a Kill* (1985). She also worked in Hollywood on *That Hagen Girl* (1947) and *The Dark Past* (1948), and in Italy on such films as *Domani e troppo tardi* (1950), *Amore e veleni* (1951), *La grande speranza* (1954) and the Bond spoof *Operation Kid Brother* (1967). In the early fifties she appeared in two Hammer potboilers: *Lady in the Fog* (1952) and *Mantrap* (1953), co-starring with Cesar Romero in the former and Paul Henreid in the latter. Her TV credits include episodes of *Douglas Fairbanks, Jr. Presents* (1953–1957, TV), *The Avengers* (1961–1969, TV), *The Saint* (1962–1969, TV), *Stingray* (1964, TV), for which she voiced the character of Lieutenant Atlanta Shore, *Adventures in Rainbow Country* (1969, TV), in which she played Nancy Williams, *The Persuaders!* (1971–1972, TV) and *Alfred Hitchcock Presents* (1985–1989, TV). In 1979 she became a newspaper correspondent for the *Toronto Sun*, a position she held until 1994 (writing as Moneypenny). Her husband was the television executive Peter Churchill Marriott (?–1973), to whom she was married from 1957; their daughter is the actress Melinda Maxwell

(1958–, real name Melinda Marriott). **Hammer credits:** *Lady in the Fog* (1952, as Peggy/Margaret Hampden), *Mantrap* (1953, as Thelma Tasman/Speight)

## May, Dinah

This British actress, model and beauty pageant contestant (1954–) can be seen as a "sexy blonde" in *Mark of the Devil* (1984, TVM [episode of *Hammer House of Mystery and Suspense*]). Crowned Miss Great Britain in 1976, her other credits include episodes of *Blakes 7* (1978–1981, TV), *Harry's Game* (1982, TV), *Brookside* (1982–2003, TV) and *The Optimist* (1983–1985, TV), while her feature credits take in *Death Wish 3* (1985), *A Chorus of Disapproval* (1988) and *Bullseye!* (1990), all of which were directed by Michael Winner, whose personal assistant and hairdresser she went on to become. She later wrote about her experiences with him in *Surviving Michael Winner: A Thirty Year Odyssey* (2014). **Hammer credits:** *Mark of the Devil* (1984, TVM [episode of *Hammer House of Mystery and Suspense*], as Sexy blonde)

## May, Gabrielle

May played the role of Genevieve, the ugly butcher's daughter who has her dowry stolen by Dick Turpin in the Hammer featurette *Dick Turpin—Highwayman* (1956). **Hammer credits:** *Dick Turpin—Highwayman* (1956, as Genevieve [uncredited])

## May, Jock *see* May, W.H.

## May, Peter

May had a minor role in Hammer's *Taste the Blood of Dracula* (1970). He can also be seen in *Countess Dracula* (1971) as Janco. His other credits include *Suburban Wives* (1971) and *Bread* (1971). **Hammer credits:** *Taste the Blood of Dracula* (1970, as Son), *Countess Dracula* (1971, as Janco)

## May, W.H. ("Jock")

Known mostly as Jock May, this prolific British sound technician (1905–1991) worked on many Hammer films in the fifties and sixties, primarily as a recordist and mixer. He finally left the company following the completion of *The Old Dark House* (1963), having worked on thirty-two productions. Recalled make-up man Phil Leakey of May, "Jock May, the sound recordist, was a hardy type. Never wore socks. Summer or the depths of winter."[41] May's many other credits include *Fires Were Started* (1943), *The Silent Village* (1943), *A Diary for Timothy* (1945), *Curse of the Fly* (1965), *The Prime of Miss Jean Brodie* (1969) and *Scrooge* (1970), plus episodes of *The Errol Flynn Theatre* (1956–1957, TV), *Danger Man* (1964–1966, TV), *Man in a Suitcase* (1967–1968, TV) and *Strange Report* (1968–1970, TV). **Hammer credits:** *A Man on the Beach* (1956), *X—The Unknown* (1956), *The Curse of Frankenstein* (1957), *The Abominable Snowman* (1957), *Man with a Dog* (1957), *Danger List* (1957 [uncredited]), *The Camp on Blood Island* (1958), *Dracula* (1958), *The Snorkel* (1958), *Clean Sweep* (1958), *The Revenge of Frankenstein* (1958), *Further Up the Creek* (1958), *I Only Arsked!* (1958), *The Hound of the Baskervilles* (1959), *The Ugly Duckling* (1959), *The Mummy* (1959), *The Man Who Could Cheat Death* (1959), *The Stranglers of Bombay* (1959), *Never Take Sweets from a Stranger* (1960), *The Brides of Dracula* (1960), *The Two Faces of Dr. Jekyll* (1960), *Visa to Canton* (1960), *The Curse of the Werewolf* (1961), *The Shadow of the Cat* (1961), *Watch It, Sailor!* (1961), *The Terror of the Tongs* (1961), *Cash on Demand* (1961), *The Pirates of Blood River* (1962), *The Phantom of the Opera* (1962), *Captain Clegg* (1962), *The Damned* (1963), *The Old Dark House* (1963)

## Mayerl, Billy

This British songwriter (music and/or lyrics), pianist and dance band leader (1902–1959, full name Joseph William Mayerl) contributed to the score of Hammer's *Sporting Love* (1936), the film version of the successful 1934 Lupino Lane stage musical on which he'd worked. His other credits as a composer/songwriter include *Blackmail* (1929), *Honeymoon for Three* (1935), *Trust the Navy* (1935), *Cheer Up* (1936), *Over She Goes* (1937), the film version of another Lupino Lane stage musical (from 1936), and *Champagne Charlie* (1944). As a performer, he popped up in *Notes and Notions* (1929), *Odd Numbers* (1929), *We'll Smile Again* (1942), *Billy Mayerl Entertains No 1* (1951), *Billy Mayerl Entertains No 2* (1951) and *One Good Turn* (1951). His many compositions include *Marigold* (1927), which was his best known number, *Miss Up-to-Date* (1929), *Bread and Cheese and Kisses* (1935), *Aquarium Suite* (1937) and *Strolling in the Park* (1944). He was also known for his "School of Syncopation" which taught modern music techniques by correspondence (at its height it is purported to have had 30,000 pupils). **Hammer credits:** *Sporting Love* (1936 [uncredited])

## Mayhew, Ann

This supporting actress played the role of Lucienne in the Hammer comedy *The Ugly Duckling* (1959). **Hammer credits:** *The Ugly Duckling* (1959, as Lucienne)

## Maynard, Bill

A familiar face on television since the fifties, this British comedy character actor (1928–2018, real name Walter Frederick George Williams) appeared in a wide variety of comedy series and dramas, among them *Great Scott, It's Maynard* (1955–1956, TV), *Paper Roses* (1971, TV), *Kisses at Fifty* (1973, TV), *Oh No, It's Selwyn Froggitt* (1976–1978, TV), in which he played the title role, *Heartbeat* (1992–2009, TV), in which he played Claude Greengrass in 155 episodes, and *The Royal* (2003–2009, TV), also as Claude Greengrass. Also in films, his credits here include *Till Death Us Do Part* (1969), *Carry On Loving* (1970), *Carry On Henry* (1971), *Carry On at Your Convenience* (1972), *Carry On Matron* (1972), *Adolf Hitler—My Part in His Downfall* (1972), *Carry On Dick* (1974), *Confessions of a Window Cleaner* (1974), *Confessions of a Pop Performer* (1975), *Confessions of a Driving Instructor* (1976), *Confessions from a Holiday Camp* (1977), in all of which he played Mr. Lea, *It Shouldn't Happen to a Vet* (1976), *Oddball Hall* (1990) and *Speed Love* (2016), the latter of which he also executive produced. He can also be seen as an unhygienic chef in Hammer's *Man About the House* (1974).

His son is the actor Maynard Williams (1951–real name Martin Maynard), and his second wife was the actress Tonia Bern (1936–, aka Tonia Bern-Campbell, whom he married in 1989, and who appeared in Hammer's *The Glass Cage* (1955). **Hammer credits:** *Man About the House* (1974, as Chef)

## Maynard, Pat (Patricia)

This British actress (1942–) can be seen as Jean Evans in *The House That Bled to Death* (1980, TV [episode of *Hammer House of Horror*]). Her other small screen credits include episodes of *Sanctuary* (1967–1968, TV), *Doomwatch* (1970–1972, TV), *This Year Next Year* (1977, TV), *Minder* (1979–1994, TV), *The House of Eliott* (1991–1994, TV) and *Doctors* (2000–, TV). Her occasional films include *Night Train to Paris* (1964). She was formerly married to the actor Dennis Waterman (1948–), whom she married in 1977; he appeared in Hammer's *The Pirates of Blood River* (1962), *Eve* (1968, TV [episode of *Journey to the Unknown*]) and *Scars of Dracula* (1973). Their daughter is the actress Hannah Waterman (1975–). **Hammer credits:** *The House That Bled to Death* (1980, TV [episode of *Hammer House of Horror*], as Jean Evans)

## Mayne, Ferdy

In over one hundred films, this German born actor (1916–1998, real name Ferdinand Philip Mayer-Horckel) was frequently called upon to play villains, though he is perhaps best remembered for playing the vampire Count Von Krolock in *The Fearless Vampire Killers* (1967). In films from 1943 with *The Life and Death of Colonel Blimp*, his other credits include *The Echo Murders* (1945), *Blue Murder at St. Trinian's* (1957), *Innocent Bystanders* (1972), *Barry Lyndon* (1975), *Revenge of the Pink Panther* (1978), *Conan the Destroyer* (1984) and *The Killers Within* (1995). He also appeared in three second features for Hammer and, later, *The Vampire Lovers* (1970). Recalled the actor of working with Ingrid Pitt on the latter, "She used rather provocative language between takes and it was rather delicious being bitten by her. And I had a very nice scene in the picture with the most wonderful of actors, Peter Cushing."[42] Mayne's many television credits include episodes of *Epitaph for a Spy* (1953, TV), *The Persuaders!* (1971–1972, TV) and *Teta* (1987, TV), in which he played Count Dracula. His wife was the actress Deirdre de Peyer (1928–2018), to whom he was married between 1950 and 1976. His daughter is the actress Belinda Mayne (1954–). **Hammer credits:** *Celia* (1949, as Antonio), *Third Party Risk* (1955, as Maxwell Carey), *The Glass Cage* (1955, as Bernie), *The Vampire Lovers* (1970, as Doctor), *Flesh and Blood—The Hammer Heritage of Horror* (1994, TV, interviewee, special thanks)

## Mayo

Born in Egypt of Greco-French parents, this theatrical costumier (1905–1990, real name Antoine Malliarakis) designed the costumes for Hammer's *The Two Faces of Dr. Jekyll* (1960), among his creations being the exotic outfits of the Sphinx Girls. Following experience as a decorator of cabaret bars, he began his film career designing the costumes for *Les Enfants du Paradis* (1945), which led to further work on *Reves d'amour* (1947), *Trois femmes* (1952), *Land of the Pharaohs* (1955), *Gervaise* (1956) and *Du mouron pour les petits oiseaux* (1963). He also worked as a designer on *Les quatre mousquetaires* (1953), *Hiroshima Mon Amour* (1959) and *L'homme de Marrakech* (1966). He later became a painter. **Hammer credits:** *The Two Faces of Dr. Jekyll* (1960)

## Mazzei, Andrew

Working in Britain, this French art director (1887–1975, real name Andre Jean Louis Mazzei) designed the sets for two of Hammer's early fifties programers. In films from 1927 with *Mademoiselle from Armentieres*, his other credits include two versions of *Hindle Wakes* (1927 and 1952), *Alf's Button* (1930), *Rome Express* (1932), *Dusty Ermine* (1936), *They Made Me a Fugitive* (1947) and *The Lost Hours* (1952). **Hammer credits:** *The Last Page* (1952), *Wings of Danger* (1952)

## McAvin, Josie

Along with Roy Taylor, this Irish designer (1919–2005) worked as one of the assistant art directors on Hammer's *Creatures the World Forgot* (1971). Her other credits as an assistant art director include *The Devil's Agent* (1962) and *The Quare Fellow* (1962). Primarily known as a set dresser, her credits in this capacity include *Tom Jones* (1963), which earned her a shared Oscar nomination, *The Spy Who Came in from the Cold* (1965), which earned her a second shared Oscar nomination, *Ryan's Daughter* (1970), *Catholics* (1973, TVM), *Heaven's Gate* (1980), *Out of Africa* (1985), which won her a shared Oscar, *The Field* (1990) and *Evelyn* (2002). Her television work includes episodes of *Return of the Saint* (1978–1979, TV) and *Scarlett* (1994, TV), which won her a shared Emmy. **Hammer credits:** *Creatures the World Forgot* (1971)

## McCabe, John

This British composer (1939–2015) scored the Hammer thriller *Fear in the Night* (1972) and three episodes of *Hammer House of Horror* (1980, TV). He also returned for two episodes of *Hammer House of Mystery and Suspense* (1984, TVM). Commented music director Philip Martell of McCabe, "John is very good.... He's a brilliant musician and a very fine pianist."[43] McCabe's other television credits include such plays and series as *Sam* (1973–1975, TV), *Leeds United* (1974, TV), *Come Back, Little Sheba* (1977, TV) and *These Foolish Things* (1989, TV). Something of a child prodigy, he had written thirteen symphonies by the age of eleven, and he went on to study music at Manchester University and the Royal Manchester College of Music. A gifted pianist, he found himself in demand both for recordings and platform recitals. His own works include *Elegy* (1965), *Notturni ed Alba* (1970), *The Flute Concerto* (1990), a number of ballets and several more symphonies. **Additional notes:** McCabe's choral theme from *Guardian of the Abyss* (1980, TV [episode of *Hammer House of Horror*]) was re-used without credit in *And the Wall Came Tumbling Down* (1984, TVM [episode of *Hammer House of Mystery and Suspense*]), which was otherwise scored by Anthony Payne. **Hammer credits:** *Fear in the Night* (1972), *The Thirteenth Reunion* (1980, TV [episode of *Hammer House of Horror*]), *Guardian of the Abyss* (1980, TV [episode of *Hammer House of Horror*]), *Growing Pains* (1980, TV [episode of *Hammer House of Horror*]), *Czech Mate* (1984, TVM [episode of *Hammer House of Mystery and Suspense*]), *The Sweet Scent of Death* (1984, TVM [episode of *Hammer House of Mystery and Suspense*]), *And the Wall Came Tumbling Down* (1984, TVM [episode of *Hammer House of Mystery and Suspense*], uncredited re-use of chant from *Guardian of the Abyss* 1980, TV [episode of *Hammer House of Horror*])

## McCallin, Clement

This RADA-trained British actor (1913–1977) played the leading role of Peter Rossiter in the Hammer programer *The Rossiter Case* (1951). His other films include *Stolen Life* (1939), *The Queen of Spades* (1949), *Murder in the Cathedral* (1952), *Rough Shoot* (1952) and *Happy Deathday* (1969). His television work includes appearances in such plays and series as *The Wooing of Anne Hathaway* (1938, TV), *The Swiss Family Robinson* (1939, TV), *The Tragedy of Richard II* (1950, TV), *BBC Sunday-Night Theatre* (1950–1959, TV), *The Old Curiosity Shop* (1962–1963, TV) and *Sykes* (1972–1979, TV). His second wife was actress Brenda Bruce (1919–1996), whom he married in 1970, and who appeared in Hammer's *Nightmare* (1964). **Hammer credits:** *The Rossiter Case* (1951, as Peter Rossiter)

## McCallum, David

This eternally youthful-looking British (Scottish) actor (1933–) is perhaps best known for playing Illya Kuryakin in the hit TV series *The Man from U.N.C.L.E.* (1965–1968, TV) and its various feature spin-offs (edited together from episodes of the TV show), which earned him two Emmy nominations, although he has also sustained a healthy film career, which began at Rank in the late fifties following training at RADA. His credits include *The Secret Place* (1957), *Violent Playground* (1957), *Robbery Under Arms* (1957), *A Night to Remember* (1958), *Billy Budd* (1962), *The Great Escape* (1963), *Mosquito Squadron* (1969), *The Watcher in the Woods* (1982), *Hear My Song* (1991) and *Dirty Weekend* (1993), plus much TV on both sides of the Atlantic, including *Teacher, Teacher* (1969, TVM), which earned him a best actor Emmy nomination, *Colditz* (1972, TV), *The Invisible Man* (1975, TV), *Sapphire and Steel* (1979, TV) and *Mother Love* (1989, TV), plus an episode of *Hammer House of Mystery and Suspense* (1984, TVM]), in which he played a surveillance expert turned stalker. He is now best know for playing Dr. Donald "Ducky" Mallard in *NCIS: Naval Criminal Investigative Service* (2003–, TV), a role he also played in episodes of *JAG* (1995–2005, TV), *NCIS: New Orleans* (2014–, TV) and an *NCIS* video game (2011). He has also provided the voice of Alfred Pennyworth for a number of Batman video games, among them *Batman: Gotham Knight* (2008), *Son of Batman* (2014) and *Batman vs. Robin* (2015), as well as that of Professor Paradox for several episodes in the various *Ben 10* cartoon series (2008–2014, TV) as well as a 2009 video game. McCallum's first wife (of two) was the actress Jill Ireland (1936–1990), to whom he was married between 1957 and 1967. His sons (with Ireland) are actor and composer Paul McCallum and composer Vaentine McCallum (1963–, aka Val McCallum). His father was the violinist David McCallum (1897–1972). **Hammer credits:** *The Corvini Inheritance* (1984, TVM [episode of *Hammer House of Mystery and Suspense*], as Frank Lane)

## McCallum, Gordon K. (Keith)

Long in Britain, this prolific American born sound technician (1919–1989) began his film career in 1935 at Elstree. After further experience at Pinewood and Denham (working as a boom operator on *This Happy Breed* [1944] and *A Canterbury Tale* [1944] at the latter), he settled at Pinewood in 1946, where he worked on practically all the studio's films. His many credits (over three-hundred), either as recordist, re-recordist, mixer or dubbing mixer, include *I Know Where I'm Going* (1945), *Great Expectations* (1946), *The Importance of Being Earnest* (1952), *Doctor in the House* (1954), *Carry On Sergeant* (1958), *North West Frontier* (1959), *This Sporting Life* (1963), *Goldfinger* (1964), *Battle of Britain* (1969), *Ryan's Daughter* (1970), which earned him shared Oscar and BAFTA nominations, *Diamonds Are Forever* (1971), which brought him a second shared Oscar nomination, *Fiddler on the Roof* (1971), which won him a shared Oscar and a shared BAFTA nomination, *Frenzy* (1972), *Jesus Christ Superstar* (1973), which won him a shared BAFTA, *Superman* (1978), which earned him shared Oscar and BAFTA nominations, *Victor/Victoria* (1982), *Octopussy* (1983) and *Supergirl* (1984). He also earned additional shared BAFTA nominations for his work on *Gold* (1974), *Rollerball* (1975) and *Greystoke: The Legend of Tarzan, Lord of the Apes* (1984). He also worked as the dubbing mixer on Hammer's *Nearest and Dearest* (1973). **Hammer credits:** *Nearest and Dearest* (1973)

## McCallum, Neil

In Britain from 1949, this Canadian character actor (1929–1976) played the role of Hemmings in Hammer's *The Lost Continent* (1968). If that weren't punishment enough, he also had a supporting role in *Moon Zero Two* (1969). His other film credits include *On the Run* (1958), *The Siege of Pinchgut* (1959), *The War Lover* (1962) and *Quest for Love* (1971), while on TV he appeared in episodes of such series as *Saber of London* (1954–1960, TV), *International Detective* (1959–1961, TV), *Vendetta* (1966–1968, TV) and *Jason King* (1971–1972, TV). He also provided voices for *Captain Scarlet and the Mysterons* (1967–1968, TV). He produced two films with Jack Parsons through his own company, Parroch-McCallum. These were *Catacombs* (1964), in which he also appeared, and *The Eyes of Annie Jones* (1964). His work as a writer includes *Do You Know This Voice?* (1964) and *Walk a Tightrope* (1965), of which he appeared in the latter. Also on stage. **Hammer credits:** *The Lost Continent* (1968, as Hemmings), *Moon Zero Two* (1969, as Space captain)

## McCallum-Tate, Kenneth *see* Tate, Kenneth McCallum

## McCann, Patrick

This British light-heavyweight boxer (1951–)

played a boxer in the opening scenes of Hammer's *Man at the Top* (1973), in which he can be seen fighting John Conteh. **Hammer credits:** *Man at the Top* (1973, as Boxer)

## McCarthy, Danny

McCarthy can be seen as a press photographer in *And the Wall Came Tumbling Down* (1984, TVM [episode of *Hammer House of Mystery and Suspense*]). His other credits include episodes of *Grange Hill* (1978–2008, TV), *Brookside* (1982–2003, TV), *The Bill* (1984–2010, TV), *Killer in Waiting* (1984, TV) and *Christabel* (1988, TV). **Hammer credits:** *And the Wall Came Tumbling Down* (1984, TVM [episode of *Hammer House of Mystery and Suspense*], as Press photographer)

## McCarthy, Neil

Seen primarily in supporting roles, this dour-looking British character actor (1932–1985) came to acting following experience as a teacher. In films from 1959 with *Breakout*, he went on to appear in over thirty more productions, among them *We Joined the Navy* (1962), *Zulu* (1964), *The Hill* (1965), *Operation: Daybreak* (1975), *The Monster Club* (1980) and *Clash of the Titans* (1981), in which he played Calibos. He can also be spotted as Hassan in the Charlie Drake comedy *Sands of the Desert* (1960), which was partially financed by Hammer. His small screen appearances include episodes of *Dial 999* (1958–1959, TV), *Barbara in Black* (1962, TV), *Department S* (1969–1970, TV), *Catweazle* (1970–1971, TV) and *The Gentle Touch* (1980–1984, TV). Also on stage. **Hammer credits:** *Sands of the Desert* (1960, as Hassan)

## McCarthy, W.

McCarthy worked as a standby painter on Hammer's *Blood from the Mummy's Tomb* (1971) and *The Satanic Rites of Dracula* (1974). **Hammer credits:** *Blood from the Mummy's Tomb* (1971 [uncredited]), *The Satanic Rites of Dracula* (1974 [uncredited])

## McClelland, Alan

This British actor (1917–1989) can be seen as Mr. Stewart in Hammer's *The Damned* (1963). His other credits include *Appointment in London* (1952), *West 11* (1963), *The Looking Glass War* (1969) and *On the Game* (1974), plus episodes of *BBC Sunday-Night Theatre* (1950–1959, TV), *Douglas Fairbanks, Jr. Presents* (1953–1957, TV), *The Avengers* (1961–1969, TV), *Budgie* (1971–1972, TV) and *Juliet Bravo* (1980–1985, TV). His son is the former child actor Fergus McClelland (1950–). **Hammer credits:** *The Damned* (1963, as Mr. Stewart)

## McClune, Alex

McClune worked as a standby carpenter on *Hammer House of Mystery and Suspense* (1984, TVM). His other credits include *Hellbound: Hellraiser II* (1988). **Hammer credits:** *Hammer House of Mystery and Suspense* (1984, TVM [uncredited])

## McConnell, Bridget

McConnell (sometimes McConnel) can be seen as a gossip in Hammer's *Rasputin—The Mad Monk* (1966). Her other credits include *Can You Keep It*

---

*Up for a Week?* (1974), *Splitting Heirs* (1993), *Mrs. Brown* (1997), *Shakespeare in Love* (1998), *Quills* (2000) and *Miss Potter* (2006), plus episodes of such series as *London Playhouse* (1955, TV), *Romance* (1977, TV) and *Men Behaving Badly* (1992–1999, TV). **Hammer credits:** *Rasputin—The Mad Monk* (1966, as Gossip [uncredited])

## McCord, Cal

This British actor (1904–1983) played Charles Kalliduke in Hammer's *Never Take Sweets from a Stranger* (1960). His other credits include *Kill Me Tomorrow* (1957), *Too Young to Love* (1959), *I've Gotta Horse* (1965), *Isadora* (1968) and *The Adding Machine* (1969), plus episodes of *Armchair Theatre* (1956–1974, TV), *International Detective* (1959–1961, TV) and *Comedy Playhouse* (1961–1975, TV). **Hammer credits:** *Never Take Sweets from a Stranger* (1960, as Charles Kalliduke [uncredited])

## McCorry, John

Costume designer McCorry (1926–1966) provided the wardrobe for Hammer's Robin Hood romp *Sword of Sherwood Forest* (1960). His other credits include *The Golden Salamander* (1950), *No Time to Die* (1958), *I'm All Right Jack* (1959), *Tom Jones* (1963), *A High Wind in Jamaica* (1965) and *Khartoum* (1966). **Hammer credits:** *Sword of Sherwood Forest* (1960)

## McCowen, Alec

On stage in rep from 1942 following training at RADA, this much-liked British character actor (1925–2017, full name Alexander Duncan McCowen) made his film debut with *The Cruel Sea* (1953). Although he spent much of his career in the theater, he appeared in key supporting roles in a number of films, among them Hammer's *The Witches* (1966), in which he played Alan Bax, *Frenzy* (1972), in which he played Chief Inspector Oxford, *Travels with My Aunt* (1972), in which he played Henry Pulling, *Stevie* (1978), *Never Say Never Again* (1983), in which he played Q, *Personal Services* (1986), *Henry V* (1989), *The Age of Innocence* (1993) and *Gangs of New York* (2002), while his TV appearances include *Angel Pavement* (1958, TV), *Play of the Month* (1965–1983, TV) and *Mr. Palfrey of Westminster* (1984–1985, TV), in which he played the title role. **Hammer credits:** *The Witches* (1966, as Alan Bax)

## McCrath, Maggie *see* Rennie, Maggie

## McCulloch, Ian

This British (Scottish) actor (1939–) can be seen as Charles Henderson in *Witching Time*, an episode of *Hammer House of Horror* (1980, TV). He is perhaps best known for playing Greg Preston in *Survivors* (1975–1977, TV), several episodes of which he also wrote. His big screen credits, among them a number of Italian horror films, include *It!* (1967), *I Monster* (1971), *The Ghoul* (1975), *Zombie Flesh Eaters* (1979), *Zombie Holocaust* (1980), *Contamination* (1980), *Moonlighting* (1982) and *Behind the Scenes of Total Hell* (2013). His other small screen credits include episodes of *The Revenue Men* (1967–1968, TV), *The Borderers* (1968–1970, TV), *The Nearly Man* (1974–1975,

---

TV), *The Professionals* (1977–1983, TV), *Taggart* (1983–, TV) and *The Tales of Para Handy* (1993–1994, TV). His brother is the actor and writer Andrew McCulloch (1945–). **Hammer credits:** *Witching Time* (1980, TV [episode of *Hammer House of Horror*], as Charles Henderson)

## McDermott, Gary

McDermott can be seen as the Baroness Kisling's manservant in Hammer's *The Lady Vanishes* (1979), which sees him thrown from a moving train during a scuffle with Elliott Gould's *Life* photographer Robert Condon. Other credits include episodes of *Crossroads* (1964–1988, TV), *Play for Today* (1970–1984, TV), *Poldark* (1975–1977, TV), *Wings* (1977–1978, TV) and *Blakes 7* (1978–1981, TV). His other film credits include *Voyage of the Damned* (1976). **Hammer credits:** *The Lady Vanishes* (1979, as Baroness's manservant)

## McDermott, Hugh

In films from 1936 with *Well Done, Henry* following experience as a sports writer and golf professional, this British (Scottish) actor (1906–1972) was frequently cast in mid–Atlantic roles. His many screen credits include *The Divorce of Lady X* (1938), *The Saint in London* (1939), *Pimpernel Smith* (1941), *No Orchids for Miss Blandish* (1948), *Lilli Marlene* (1950), *Guns in the Heather* (1968) and *Chato's Land* (1972). He also co-starred in the little-seen Hammer/Luckwell second feature *Delayed Flight* (1964). His small screen credits include episodes of *London Playhouse* (1955, TV), *The Adventures of Robin Hood* (1955–1960, TV) and *Brett* (1971, TV). His first wife (of two) was actress Daphne Courtney (1917–), whom he married in 1936. **Hammer credits:** *Delayed Flight* (1964, as Lieutenant Colonel Gavin Brampton)

## McDermott, Pat (Patricia)

British born McDermott (1930–2015) worked as the hair stylist on the Hammer thriller *Maniac* (1963). Her other credits include *Billy Budd* (1962), *The Blue Max* (1966), *Frenzy* (1972), *The Legend of Hell House* (1973), *The Omen* (1976), *Star Wars* (1977), *The Deep* (1977), *Superman* (1978), *Superman II* (1980), *Raiders of the Lost Ark* (1981), *Return of the Jedi* (1983), *Supergirl* (1984) and *Return to Oz* (1985), plus a handful of return visits to Hammer. She also worked on episodes of such series as *Danger Man* (1964–1966, TV), *The Prisoner* (1967–1968, TV) and *Inspector Morse* (1987–2000, TV). **Hammer credits:** *Maniac* (1963), *The Devil Rides Out* (1968), *Frankenstein Must Be Destroyed* (1969), *Countess Dracula* (1971), *Hands of the Ripper* (1971)

## McDermott, Rory

This British actor (1913–1980, sometimes Rory MacDermot) had a minor role in Hammer's *The Dark Road* (1948). His other credits include *Root of All Evil* (1947), *Against the Wind* (1948), *Watch Your Stern* (1960) and *Spare the Rod* (1961), plus episodes of *The Avengers* (1961–1969, TV), *The Saint* (1962–1969, TV), *Z Cars* (1962–1978, TV) and *Danger Man* (1964–1966, TV). **Hammer credits:** *The Dark Road* (1948, unnamed role)

## McDonald, Aimi *see* MacDonald, Aimi

## McDonald, Alan

British born McDonald (1938–, sometimes MacDonald) worked on the camera crew for several Hammer films in the late fifties/early sixties. His later credits as a focus puller include *The Love Box* (1972) and *The Sex Thief* (1973). He also worked as a camera operator on *Captain Scarlet and the Mysterons* (1967–1968, TV). His brother is focus puller Robin McDonald (1946–). **Hammer credits:** *The Ugly Duckling* (1959, clapper boy, camera loader [both uncredited]), *Yesterday's Enemy* (1959, camera loader, clapper boy [both uncredited]), *The Mummy* (1959, clapper loader [uncredited]), *Never Take Sweets from a Stranger* (1960, camera assistant [uncredited]), *The Curse of the Werewolf* (1961, camera assistant [uncredited]), *The Terror of the Tongs* (1961, clapper boy [uncredited])

## McDonald, Barry

McDonald can be seen as an auctioneer at the top of *Guardian of the Abyss* (1980, TV [episode of *Hammer House of Horror*]). His other credits include *The Little Convict* (1979) and an episode of *A Moment in Time* (1979, TV). **Hammer credits:** *Guardian of the Abyss* (1980, TV [episode of *Hammer House of Horror*], as Auctioneer)

## McDonald, John

This British child actor (sometimes MacDonald) played Jimmy the stable boy in the Hammer short *Dick Turpin—Highwayman* (1956). His other credits include *The Young Ones* (1961), *Summer Holiday* (1963), *Half a Sixpence* (1967), *Les demoiselles de Rochefort* (1967) and *Come Back Baby* (1968), plus an episode of *The Des O'Connor Show* (1963–1968, TV). **Hammer credits:** *Dick Turpin—Highwayman* (1956, as Jimmy the stable boy [uncredited])

## McDonald, Mark

McDonald photographed the first two entries in Hammer's successful series of *On the Buses* spin-offs. His other credits include *Flight of the White Heron* (1954), *Shadow of the Boomerang* (1960), *Headline Hunters* (1968), *Up in the Air* (1969), *Go for a Take* (1972), *Blinker's Spy-Spotter* (1972), *Kadoyng* (1972), *Secrets of a Door-to-Door Salesman* (1973) and *Bedtime with Rosie* (1975), plus episodes of *Theatre 625* (1964–1968, TV), *Talking to a Stranger* (1966, TV) and *Here Come the Double Deckers!* (1970–1971, TV). **Hammer credits:** *On the Buses* (1971), *Mutiny on the Buses* (1972)

## McDonald-Peattie, Rosemarie

This make-up artist worked on Hammer's *Dracula Has Risen from the Grave* (1968), sharing her credit with Heather Nurse. Also known as Rosemarie Peattie, her other credits include *The Blood Beast Terror* (1967). **Hammer credits:** *Dracula Has Risen from the Grave* (1968)

## McDowall, Roddy

In films in Britain from the age of ten with *Murder in the Family* (1938), this continually busy British actor (1928–1998, real name Roderick Andrew Anthony Jude McDowall) went to Hollywood in 1940 following appearances several more films, among them *Convict 99* (1938), *Poison Pen* (1939) and *Just William* (1940). He made his U.S. debut in *Man Hunt* (1941), and went on to make a mark in *How Green Was My Valley* (1941), *My Friend Flicka* (1943) and *Lassie Come Home* (1943). In over one-hundred films in total, his adult appearances include *The Longest Day* (1962), *Cleopatra* (1963), *Planet of the Apes* (1968), in which he had his most famous role as the ape Cornelius, *Escape from the Planet of the Apes* (1971), *The Poseidon Adventure* (1972), *Conquest of the Planet of the Apes* (1972), *Battle for the Planet of the Apes* (1973), *The Legend of Hell House* (1973), *Evil Under the Sun* (1982), *Fright Night* (1985), in which he played horror host Peter Vincent, *Fright Night Part 2* (1988) and *Something to Believe In* (1998). Also much on television, his work here includes countless tele-movies, the series of *Planet of the Apes* (1974–1975, TV), in which he played Galen, and numerous guest shots, including the leading role in *The Killing Bottle*, an episode of Hammer's *Journey to the Unknown* (1968, TV), which also appeared in the compendium film *Journey to Murder* (1972, TVM). His other TV work includes episodes of *Sunday Showcase* (1959–1961, TV), which won him a best supporting actor Emmy, *Arrest and Trial* (1963–1964, TV), which earned him a best actor Emmy nomination, *The Fantastic Journey* (1977, TV) and *The Martian Chronicles* (1980, TV). A noted photographer, McDowall also directed one film, *The Ballad of Tam Lin* (1970). **Hammer credits:** *The Killing Bottle* (1968, TV [episode of *Journey to the Unknown*], as Rollo Verdew), *Journey to Murder* (1972, as Rollo Verdew)

## McDuff, Ewen (Ewan)

This actor (sometimes MacDuff) played Ferrers in the Hammer army comedy *I Only Arsked!* (1958). His other credits include *The Siege of Pinchgut* (1959), *The Bridal Path* (1959) and *Evidence in Concrete* (1960), plus episodes of *Armchair Theatre* (1956–1974, TV), *ITV Television Playhouse* (1955–1967, TV) and *No Hiding Place* (1959–1967, TV). **Hammer credits:** *I Only Arsked!* (1958, as Ferrers)

## McEnery, Peter

On stage from 1958, in television from 1959, and in films from 1960 with *Beat Girl*, this boyish-looking British actor (1940–) has appeared in a wide variety of films, from Disney to horror, among them *Tunes of Glory* (1960), *Victim* (1961), *The Moon-Spinners* (1964), *The Fighting Prince of Donegal* (1966), *Entertaining Mr. Sloane* (1970), *The Adventures of Gerard* (1970), *Tales That Witness Madness* (1973), *The Cat and the Canary* (1978), *Safari* (1991) and *Lucky Punch* (1996). Also on television, his credits here include the lead in *The Mark of Satan*, an episode of *Hammer House of Horror* (1980, TV). His other small screen appearances include episodes of *So It Goes* (1973, TV), *Clayhanger* (1976, TV), *The Collectors* (1986, TV), *All Quiet on the Preston Front* (1996, TV) and *Scalp* (2008, TV). His brothers are the photographer David McEnery (1940–2002) and the actor John McEnery (1943–). His first wife was actress Julie Peasgood (1956–), whom he married in 1978; his second wife is actress Julia St. John (1960–), whom he married in 1997. His daughter (with Peasgood) is actress Kate McEnery (1981–). His former sister-in-law (once married to brother John) is the actress Stephanie Beacham (1947–), who appeared in Hammer's *Dracula A.D. 1972* (1972) and *A Distant Scream* (1984, TVM [episode of *Hammer House of Mystery and Suspense*]). **Hammer credits:** *The Mark of Satan* (1980, TV [episode of *Hammer House of Horror*], as Edwyn Bord)

## McFadyen, Ann (Anne)

McFadyen worked as the hair stylist on Hammer's *Vampire Circus* (1972). Her other credits include *Crooks and Coronets* (1969), *Doomwatch* (1972), *Voices* (1973), *The Brute* (1977), *Excalibur* (1981), *Walter* (1982, TVM) and *Harem* (1986, TVM), plus episodes of *The Professionals* (1977–1983, TV) and *Danger UXB* (1979, TV). **Hammer credits:** *Vampire Circus* (1972)

## McGee, Henry

Much on television, this British comedy actor (1928–2006, full name Henry Marris-McGee) is best known for his role as a straight man to Benny Hill in countless specials and series, primarily in *The Benny Hill Show* (1969–1989, TV). His sitcom work includes *Tell It to the Marines* (1959–1960, TV), *The Worker* (1965–1970, TV), *No, That's Me Over Here!* (1967–1979, TV) and *Let There Be Love* (1982–1983, TV), plus countless guest spots in everything from *The Goodies* (1970–1982, TV) to *Sykes* (1972–1979, TV). He also popped up in bit parts in several films in the sixties and seventies, among them Hammer's *Fanatic* (1965), in which he played a vicar, and *Holiday on the Buses* (1973), in which he played a holiday camp manager. His other big screen credits include *The Italian Job* (1968), *Adventures of a Taxi Driver* (1976), *Revenge of the Pink Panther* (1978) and *Carry On Emmannuelle* (1978). As well as stage work, he also appeared with the Honey Monster in a series of poplar commercials advertising Sugar Puffs from 1976 onwards. **Hammer credits:** *Fanatic* (1965, as Vicar [uncredited]), *Holiday on the Buses* (1973, as Coombs [holiday camp manager])

## McGoohan, Patrick

Known to TV audiences for his leading roles in both *Danger Man* (1960–1962, 1964–1966, TV), in which he played Paul Drake, and *The Prisoner* (1967–1968, TV), in which he played Number Six, this American leading man (1928–2009) also sustained a healthy film career, beginning in Britain with *Passage Home* (1955). His other film credits include *Hell Drivers* (1956), *Escape from Alcatraz* (1979), *Braveheart* (1995) and *A Time to Kill* (1996). Back on TV he also introduced *Journey into Darkness* (1968, TVM), a compendium movie featuring two episodes of Hammer's *Journey to the Unknown* (1968, TV). These were *The New People* and *Paper Dolls*. McGoohan filmed his segments while in Hollywood making *Ice Station Zebra* (1968). He also worked as a director in TV, helming five feature-length episodes of *Columbo* (1968–2003, TVM) between 1975 and 2000; he also guest-starred in the series four times, winning supporting actor/guest actor Emmys for *By Dawn's Early Light* (1974, TVM) and *Agenda for Murder* (1990, TVM) respectively (he also directed the latter). He also directed one theatrical feature, *Catch My Soul* (1973). **Hammer credits:** *Journey into Darkness* (1968, TVM, as Host)

### McGrath, George

McGrath can be seen as a businessman in Hammer's *The Two Faces of Dr. Jekyll* (1960). He also popped up in an episode of *Journey to the Unknown* (1968, TV). His other credits include appearances in *Pit of Darkness* (1961), *One More Time* (1970) and *Games That Lovers Play* (1970), plus episodes of such TV series as *The Strange World of Gurney Slade* (1960, TV), *Elgar* (1962, TV), *Crane* (1963–1965, TV) and *W. Somerset Maugham* (1969–1970, TV). **Hammer credits:** *The Two Faces of Dr. Jekyll* (1960, as Businessman [uncredited]), *Somewhere in a Crowd* (1968, TV [episode of *Journey to the Unknown*], as Watcher)

### McGrath, Jay

McGrath appeared as a dancer in Hammer's *Rasputin—The Mad Monk* (1966). His other credits include episodes of *Doctor Who* (1963–1989, TV), *Adam Adamant Lives!* (1966–1967, TV), *The Two Ronnies* (1971–1987, TV) and *Enemy at the Door* (1978–1980, TV). **Hammer credits:** *Rasputin—The Mad Monk* (1966, as Dancer [uncredited])

### McGuffie, Bill

This British (Scottish) singer and musician (1927–1987) can be seen in the Hammer musical featurette *Cyril Stapleton and the Show Band* (1955). A talented pianist, he appeared as such in *The Challenge* (1960) and *Too Hot to Handle* (1960), both of which he also scored. His other films as a composer include *The Unstoppable Man* (1960), *The Leather Boys* (1964), *Daleks—Invasion Earth: 2150 A.D.* (1966), *Corruption* (1968), *The Cherry Picker* (1972) and *The Asphyx* (1973). He also worked on such series as *More Faces of Jim* (1963, TV) and *Mum's Boys* (1968, TV). **Hammer credits:** *Cyril Stapleton and the Show Band* (1955, as Himself)

### McKay, Ian

McKay can be seen as a villager in Hammer's *Captain Kronos—Vampire Hunter* (1974). His other credits include *Cruel Passion* (1977) and *The Custard Boys* (1979), plus episodes of *Adam Adamant Lives!* (1966–1967, TV) and *Softly Softly* (1966–1976, TV). He also worked as a fight arranger on *Far from the Madding Crowd* (1967) and *Robin and Marian* (1976). **Hammer credits:** *Captain Kronos—Vampire Hunter* (1974, as Villager [uncredited])

### McKechnie, James

This British (Scottish) actor (1911–1964) worked as a commentator on a number of films, among them the Exclusive documentary *Scottish Symphony* (1946), on which he shared his duties with George Strachan. His other credits as a narrator/commentator include *Painted Boats* (1945), *Madeleine* (1950), *A Story of Achievement* (1951) and *A Short Vision* (1956), plus the TV series *Kidnapped* (1952, TV), in which he also appeared in a variety of roles. His other credits as an actor include *The Life and Death of Colonel Blimp* (1943), *Two Thousand Women* (1944), *Caesar and Cleopa-*

*tra* (1945), *Bond Street* (1948) and *Scott of the Antarctic* (1948). **Hammer credits:** *Scottish Symphony* (1946, Commentator)

### McKelvie, Donald

Hammer's solicitor in the fifties, it was McKelvie (?–1959) who suggested that the company go public, an idea that was subsequently nixed by James Carreras, who preferred a more private accountability of funds and, in particular, profits.

### McKenzie, Jacqueline

This British (Scottish) actress (1929–), a former lacrosse player, had a nice cameo as a waitress in *36 Hours* (1953). **Hammer credits:** *36 Hours* (1953, as Waitress [uncredited])

### McKenzie, Nicolette

This New Zealand born actress and voice over artist dubbed the voice of Raquel Welch in Hammer's *One Million Years B.C.* (1966), for whom additional grunts were also provided by Nikki Van Der Zyl. Her credits as an actress include *All the Advantages* (1970), *Feelings* (1974) and *Under Suspicion* (1991), while her TV credits include episodes of *Callan* (1967–1972, TV), *Beyond Belief* (1970, TV), *Crown Court* (1972–1984, TV), *Warship* (1973–1977, TV) and *Triangle* (1981–1983, TV). She has also provided vocals for such video games as *City of Lost Children* (1997), *Kameo: Elements of Power* (2005), *El Shaddai: Ascension of the Metatron* (2011) and *Horizon: Zero Dawn* (2017). **Hammer credits:** *One Million Years B.C.* (1966, as Voice of Raquel Welch [uncredited])

### McKern, Leo

Best known for playing the irascible barrister Horace Rumpole in the long-running television drama series *Rumpole of the Bailey* (1978–1992, TV), a role he had first essayed in a 1975 *Play for Today* (1975–1984, TV), and for which he was nominated for three best actor BAFTAs, this one-eyed Australian character actor (1920–2002, real name Reginald McKern) was also familiar to television audiences for playing Number Two in *The Prisoner* (1967–1968, TV) and Zaharov in *Reilly: Ace of Spies* (1983, TV). On stage from 1942 following experience as an engineer and a commercial artist, McKern came to Britain in 1944, where he joined the Old Vic in 1949. In films from 1952 with *Murder in the Cathedral*, he went on to make over fifty features, among them *A Tale of Two Cities* (1958), *The Day the Earth Caught Fire* (1961), *A Jolly Bad Fellow* (1963), *A Man for All Seasons* (1966), *Ryan's Daughter* (1970), *The Omen* (1976), in which he played Carl Bugenhagen, *Candleshoe* (1977), *Damien: Omen II* (1978), again as Bugenhagen, *The Blue Lagoon* (1980) and *On Our Selection* (1995). His third film was Hammer's *X—The Unknown* (1956) in which he played Inspector McGill. This led to a further appearance for the studio in the war drama *Yesterday's Enemy* (1959). His other TV work includes episodes of *The March of the Peasants* (1952, TV), *The Adventures of Robin Hood* (1955–1960, TV), *The Amazing Dr. Clitterhouse* (1962, TV), in which he played the title role, and *Sunday Night* (1965–1968, TV). He also penned the radio drama *Chain of Events*, which was

filmed in 1958 with a script by Patrick Brawn. **Hammer credits:** *X—The Unknown* (1956, as Inspector McGill), *Yesterday's Enemy* (1959, as Max)

### McLaglen, Clifford

This South African born actor (1892–1978) appeared in a handful of British films in the thirties, among them Hammer's second film *The Mystery of the Mary Celeste* (1935) as Captain Jim Morehead. His other credits include *In the Blood* (1923), *Yvette* (1928), *Villa Falconieri* (1929), *The Alleycat* (1929), *Call of the Sea* (1930), *The Bermondsey Kid* (1933) and *The Marriage of Corbal* (1936). Very much from an acting family, his brothers were the actors Victor McLaglen (1886–1959), Arthur McLaglen (1888–1972), Cyril McLaglen (1899–1987), Kenneth McLaglen (1901–1979) and Leopold McLaglen (1884–1951). His nephew was the director Andrew V. McLaglen (1920–2014). **Hammer credits:** *The Mystery of the Mary Celeste* (1935, as Captain Morehead)

### McLaren, John

This Canadian actor (1911–1970) can be seen in a minor supporting role in Hammer's *I Only Arsked!* (1958). His other credits include *The Way to the Stars* (1945), *No Orchids for Miss Blandish* (1948), *Diplomatic Report* (1954), *A King in New York* (1957), *Goldfinger* (1964) and *The Canterbury Tales* (1972). His small screen work includes episodes of *BBC Sunday-Night Theatre* (1950–1959, TV), *Saber of London* (1954–1960, TV), *The Avengers* (1961–1969, TV) and *The Saint* (1962–1969, TV). His wife was the Swedish opera singer Hella Toros, whom he married in 1943. **Hammer credits:** *I Only Arsked!* (1958, as Olding)

### McLennan, Robert

McLennan appeared as a dancer in Hammer's *Rasputin—The Mad Monk* (1966). **Hammer credits:** *Rasputin—The Mad Monk* (1966, as Dancer [uncredited])

### McLeod, Gordon

Working in both Britain and America, this British supporting actor (1890–1963, full name Charles Gordon McLeod) is perhaps best known for playing Inspector Teal in several of the Saint movies, among them *The Saint in London* (1939), *The Saint's Vacation* (1941) and *The Saint Meets the Tiger* (1943). In films from 1919 with *A Smart Set*, his many other movies include *The Only Way* (1925), *The Squeaker* (1937), *Victoria the Great* (1937), in which he played John Brown, *Sixty Glorious Years* (1938), again as John Brown, *Crook's Tour* (1940), *We'll Smile Again* (1942) and *The Man Who Loved Redheads* (1955). He also appeared in two Hammer second features: *A Case for PC 49* (1951) and *The House Across the Lake* (1954), but surprisingly not *The Saint's Return* (1953), in which Teal was played by Charles Victor. His occasional television appearances include episodes of *Your Favorite Story* (1953–1955, TV), *Douglas Fairbanks, Jr. Presents* (1953–1957, TV) and *Adventure Theater* (1956–1957, TV). **Hammer credits:** *A Case for PC 49* (1951, as Inspector Wilson), *The House Across the Lake* (1954, as Doctor Emery)

## McLoughlin, Bronco

This stuntman, stunt coordinator, horsemaster and bit player worked as a stuntman on a handful of films for Hammer. His many other credits include *Dead Cert* (1974), *Excalibur* (1981), *Krull* (1983), *Indiana Jones and the Temple of Doom* (1984), *A View to a Kill* (1985), *The Mission* (1986), in which he was famously tied to a crucifix and sent backwards over a waterfall (a stunt that was featured in the movie's poster campaign), *Much Ado About Nothing* (1993), *Tomorrow Never Dies* (1997) and *Troy* (2004), plus episodes of *The Last Place on Earth* (1985, TV), *The Young Indiana Jones Chronicles* (1992–1993, TV), *Father Ted* (1995–1998, TV), *Primeval* (2007–2011, TV) and *Vikings* (2013–, TV). **Hammer credits:** *The Viking Queen* (1967 [uncredited]), *The Lost Continent* (1968 [uncredited]), *Creatures the World Forgot* (1971 [uncredited])

## McManus, Babbie

McManus choreographed the Greek dancing as performed by the young ladies at Miss Simpson's finishing school in Hammer's *Lust for a Vampire* (1971). **Hammer credits:** *Lust for a Vampire* (1971)

## McMaster, Anew

This Irish actor (1891–1962) can be seen as the judge in Hammer's take on the Robin Hood legend *Sword of Sherwood Forest* (1960). Also on stage, particularly in Shakespeare. **Hammer credits:** *Sword of Sherwood Forest* (1960, as Judge [uncredited])

## McMullen, Ed

McMullen worked as a stand in for James Villiers during the shooting of Hammer's *Blood from the Mummy's Tomb* (1971). **Hammer credits:** *Blood from the Mummy's Tomb* (1971, as stand in for James Villiers [uncredited])

## McMullins, Mark

McMullins had a minor role in Hammer's *Frankenstein Created Woman* (1967). **Hammer credits:** *Frankenstein Created Woman* (1967, as Villager with Body [uncredited])

## McNaughton, Jack

This British supporting actor (1905–1990) played one of the outlaws in Hammer's *Men of Sherwood Forest* (1954) and one of the many POWs in their brutal war drama *The Camp on Blood Island* (1958). This led to further work on the comedy *Up the Creek* (1958) and the Thuggee shocker *The Stranglers of Bombay* (1959). His other credits include *Cardboard Cavalier* (1949), *Trent's Last Case* (1952), *The Purple Plain* (1954) and *The Court Martial of Major Keller* (1961). His occasional TV credits include episodes of *The Flying Doctor* (1959, TV), *No Hiding Place* (1959–1967, TV) and *The Cheaters* (1960–1962, TV). His wife was actress Kay Callard (1923–2008, real name Kathleen Emmett Callard), whom he married in 1960, and who appeared in Hammer's *The Stranger Came Home* (1954). **Hammer credits:** *Men of Sherwood Forest* (1954, as Outlaw [uncredited]), *The Camp on Blood Island* (1958, as Prisoner), *Up the Creek* 

(1958, as Petty Officer), *The Stranglers of Bombay* (1959, as Corporal Roberts)

## McNee, Patrick *see* Macnee, Patrick

## McPhee, Neil

McPhee (sometimes MacPhee) worked as a draughtsman on Hammer's *Never Take Sweets from a Stranger* (1960). His other credits include *The Day of the Triffids* (1962), *Cleopatra* (1963) and *One Way Pendulum* (1964). **Hammer credits:** *Never Take Sweets from a Stranger* (1960 [uncredited])

## McSharry, Carmel

This Irish actress (1926–2018) is best remembered for playing Mrs. Boswell (later Hennessey) at various points in the long-running sitcom *The Liver Birds* (1969–1979, 1996, TV), and Beryl Humphries in her own series *Beryl's Lot* (1973–1977, TV). Her occasional film credits include *Life in Danger* (1959), *The Day the Earth Caught Fire* (1961), *The Leather Boys* (1963), Hammer's *The Witches* (1966), in which she appeared as Mrs. Dowsett, *The Man Outside* (1967) and *All Coppers Are…* (1972). Her other TV work includes episodes of *Oliver Twist* (1962, TV), in which she played Nancy, *In Loving Memory* (1969–1986, TV), *The Sinners* (1970–1971, TV), *Bluebell* (1986, TV) and *Goodnight Sweetheart* (1993–1999, TV). Also on stage. **Hammer credits:** *The Witches* (1966, as Mrs. Dowsett)

## McStay, Michael

This British actor (1933–) played the young Ra-Antef, as seen in the flashback sequences in Hammer's *The Curse of the Mummy's Tomb* (1964). His other credits include *Psyche 59* (1964), *Robbery* (1967), *Battle Beneath the Earth* (1967), *Bread* (1971), *The Stick Up* (1977) and *Jack & Sarah* (1997). Best known for playing Detective Sergeant Perryman in *No Hiding Place* (1959–1967, TV), his other small screen credits include episodes of *Dixon of Dock Green* (1955–1976, TV), *Paul Temple* (1969–1971, TV), *Supergran* (1985–1987, TV) and *The Inspector Lynley Mysteries* (2001–2007, TV). **Hammer credits:** *The Curse of the Mummy's Tomb* (1964, as Young Ra-Antef [uncredited])

## Meaden, Dan

This British actor (1935–2011) can be seen as the town crier in Hammer's *Dr. Jekyll and Sister Hyde* (1971). His other credits include *Information Received* (1961), *Othello* (1965), *The Prince and the Pauper* (1977), *Absolution* (1978) and *Never Say Never Again* (1983). He also appeared as John Little of Cumberland in *Wolfshead: The Legend of Robin Hood* (1969 [released 1973]), which was not made by, but was subsequently bought by, Hammer. His television credits include episodes of *The Benny Hill Show* (1955–1968, TV), *Softly Softly* (1966–1976, TV), in which he played Detective Constable Box, *The Jensen Code* (1973, TV), *Reilly: Ace of Spies* (1983, TV) and *Rockliffe's Babies* (1987–1988, TV). **Hammer credits:** *Wolfshead: The Legend of Robin Hood* (1969 [released 1973], as John 

Little of Cumberland), *Dr. Jekyll and Sister Hyde* (1971, as Town crier)

## Meadows, Stanley

This British supporting actor (1931–, full name Leonard Stanley Meadows) can be seen as an attendant in Hammer's *The Mummy* (1959), which marked his big screen debut. His other credits include *Payroll* (1961), *The Night Caller* (1965), *The Ipcress File* (1965), *Kaleidoscope* (1966) and *The Fixer* (1968), plus episodes of *Armchair Theatre* (1956–1974, TV), *The Saint* (1962–1969, TV), *The Boy with Two Heads* (1974, TV) and *Widows* (1983, TV), in which he played Eddie Rawlins. **Hammer credits:** *The Mummy* (1959, as Attendant)

## Medak, Peter

Working in Britain, Canada and Hollywood, the films of this Hungarian director (1937–) include *Negatives* (1968), *A Day in the Death of Joe Egg* (1970), *The Ruling Class* (1971), *Ghost in the Noonday Sun* (1973), *The Odd Job* (1978), *The Changeling* (1980), *The Krays* (1990), *Let Him Have It* (1991), *Romeo Is Bleeding* (1993), *Species II* (1998) and *The Ghost of Peter Sellers* (2018). In Britain from 1956 (following the Hungarian uprising), he began working as a second assistant director, among his credits in this capacity being three films for Hammer. He soon graduated to first assistant director, and also worked as a second unit director on such films as *Funeral in Berlin* (1966) and *Fathom* (1967), the latter of which also saw him working as an associate producer. His television credits as a director include a number of one-offs and series episodes, among them *Court Martial* (1966, TV), *Space: 1999* (1975–1977, TV), *Mistress of Paradise* (1981, TVM), *The Twilight Zone* (1985–1989, TV), *The Hunchback* (1997, TVM), *David Copperfield* (2000, TV), *Masters of Horror* (2005–2007, TV), *Breaking Bad* (2008–2013, TV), *Hannibal* (2013–2015, TV) and *The Assets* (2014, TV). He was also considered as a director for Hammer's *To the Devil a Daughter* (1976). Married twice, his first wife was actress Carolyn Seymour (1947–), to whom he was married between 1973 and 1984; his second wife is actress Julia Migenes (1949–) whom he married in 1988; his stepdaughter is the actress Martina Migenes. **Hammer credits:** *The Phantom of the Opera* (1962 [uncredited]), *Captain Clegg* (1962 [uncredited]), *The Pirates of Blood River* (1962 [uncredited])

## Medalie, Mervyn

Medalie (sometimes Merwyn) worked as the hairdresser on Hammer's *The Vengeance of She* (1968). His other credits include *The Breaking Point* (1961), *Naked Evil* (1966), *Can Heironymus Merkin Ever Forget Mercy Humppe and Find True Happiness?* (1966) and *Dad's Army* (1971), plus episodes of *The Baron* (1966–1967, TV). **Hammer credits:** *The Vengeance of She* (1968)

## Meddings, Derek

This much admired British effects technician (1931–1995) first came to attention for his painting and model work on such Gerry Anderson-produced films and TV series as *The Adventures of*

*Twizzle* (1957, TV), *Torchy, the Battery Boy* (1957–1959, TV), *Four Feather Falls* (1960, TV), *Supercar* (1961–1962, TV), *Fireball XL5* (1962–1963, TV), *Stingray* (1964–1965, TV), *Thunderbirds* (1965–1966, TV), *Thunderbirds Are Go* (1966), *Captain Scarlet and the Mysterons* (1967–1968, TV), *Thunderbird 6* (1968), *The Secret Service* (1969, TV), *Journey to the Far Side of the Sun* (1969) and *UFO* (1970–1971, TV). He went on to work on several key Bond films, notably *The Spy Who Loved Me* (1977), *Moonraker* (1979), which earned him a shared Oscar nomination, and *GoldenEye* (1995), which earned him a shared BAFTA nomination. His other film credits include *Live and Let Die* (1973), *The Man with the Golden Gun* (1974), *The Land That Time Forgot* (1975), *Superman* (1978), which won him a shared Oscar and a shared BAFTA, *Krull* (1983), *Spies Like Us* (1985), in which he also appears, *Santa Claus: The Movie* (1985), *High Spirits* (1988), *Batman* (1989), which earned him a shared BAFTA nomination, *Hudson Hawk* (1991) and *Cape Fear* (1991). He began his career as a title artist at Denham Studios in the late forties, and went on to work on such films as *The Red Beret* (1953), following which he became a background painter. He went on to become a matte painter for Les Bowie in the fifties, first at Anglo Scottish Pictures and then at Hammer, where (uncredited) he painted a number of mattes and backgrounds. Meddings' father was a carpenter a Denham studios, and his mother worked as a stand-in (often for Merle Oberon) and as a secretary to Alexander Korda. His children are the effects technicians Mark Meddings (1954–) and Noah Meddings, the make-up artist Chloe Meddings, and the location manager Elliott Meddings. **Hammer credits include:** *Dracula* (1958 [uncredited])

## Media Investments PLC

Media Investments PLC owned and invested in a number of companies, among them Best of British Film and Television (aka Best of British Film), which made *The World of Hammer* (1990 [first broadcast 1994], TV) in conjunction with Hammer. **Hammer credits:** *The World of Hammer* (1990 [first broadcast 1994], TV)

## Medwin, Michael

Best known for such TV roles as Corporal Springer in *The Army Game* (1957–1961, TV) and Don Satchley in *Shoestring* (1979–1980, TV), this perpetually cheerful British actor (1923–) began his film career in 1946 in *Piccadilly Incident*, following which he could be spotted in *Just William's Luck* (1947), *Hindle Wakes* (1952), *Genevieve* (1953), *Carry On Nurse* (1959), *Night Must Fall* (1963), *Scrooge* (1970), *The Sea Wolves* (1980), *Britannia Hospital* (1982), *Just Ask for Diamond* (1988), *Staggered* (1994), *Fanny and Elvis* (1999) and *The Duchess* (2008). In the fifties, he also appeared in a handful of Hammer quickies, beginning with the comedy thriller *Someone at the Door* (1950), in which he starred as Ronnie Martin, who, with his sister, concocts a murder story, which subsequently comes true. His other Hammer appearances include *The Lady Craved Excitement* (1950), which gave him another leading role, and the film version

of *The Army Game*, which was re-titled *I Only Arsked!* (1958). In the sixties, Medwin turned his hand to producing (via Memorial Enterprises, which he founded with fellow actor Albert Finney), among his successes being *Charlie Bubbles* (1968), *If....* (1968), *Gumshoe* (1971) and *O Lucky Man!* (1973). His other television appearances include episodes of *ITV Play of the Week* (1955–1968, TV), *The Love of Mike* (1960, TV), *Three Live Wires* (1961, TV), *Return of the Saint* (1978–1979, TV), *Boon* (1986–1992, TV) and *Doctors* (2000–, TV). Also on stage, he was made an OBE in 2005. **Hammer credits:** *Someone at the Door* (1950, as Ronnie Martin), *The Lady Craved Excitement* (1950, as Johnny), *Spaceways* (1953, as Toby Andrews), *A Man on the Beach* (1956, as Max), *The Steel Bayonet* (1957, as Lieutenant Vernon), *I Only Arsked!* (1958, as Corporal Springer)

## Meet Simon Cherry

GB, 1949, 67m, bw, United Programmes, cert A
The fourth and final film made by Hammer at Dial Close, this mild but just about tolerable mystery follows the adventures of a clergyman named Simon Cherry who, waylaid by bad weather at a remote country house while on his way on holiday, investigates the death of a young woman. The question is: was it suicide, murder, euthanasia or natural causes?

The film was based on yet another popular radio series, *Meet the Rev* (1946), under which title it went before the cameras in May 1949, though it should be noted that the character of Simon Cherry had already appeared in seven segments for the TV series *Kaleidoscope* (1946–1953, TV) in 1948; also titled *Meet the Rev*—albeit with the addition of an exclamation mark—these mini episodes starred future Hammer performer Hugh Morton, who had also played the character in the radio series. The movie version, which was part-funded with a loan from the National Film Finance Corporation, meanwhile introduced Hugh Moxey to the screen as the nosey Father Brown–like reverend who, during his night at Harling Manor, senses "an atmosphere of unrest, a sensation that underneath the charming hospitable surface there were hidden undercurrents, deep and sinister."

The finished film was trade shown in November the same year and released in the UK by Exclusive on 10 May 1950. A passable time filler, complete with two flashbacks telling the same story from different angles, the proceedings are routinely but competently mounted and performed, with some intrigue provided by a series of twist revelations, among them the fact that the kindly butler may have done it with a glass of poisoned milk.

The production team of producer Anthony Hinds, director Godfrey Grayson, cinematographer Cedric Williams and editor Ray Pitt were now becoming practiced hands at this kind of program filler, and soon all would congregate at Oakley Court for the next phase of Hammer's development. However, if further adventures for the Rev were planned, they failed to materialize. **Additional notes:** Zena Marshall appears "By arrangement with the J. Arthur Rank Organization"

while John Bailey appears "By arrangement with ABPC." Though the film's full on-screen title is actually *Meet Simon Cherry "The Rev"* it is generally referred to as *Meet Simon Cherry*, as it is throughout this book. Phil Leakey provided a convincing scar make-up for the story's victim, which no doubt stood him in good stead for the horrors that awaited him a few years further into his career with Hammer.

Production company: Hammer. Distributor: Exclusive (UK). Producer: Anthony Hinds. Director: Godfrey Grayson. Screenplay: Godfrey Grayson, A.R. Rawlinson, Gale Pedrick (additional dialogue [uncredited]), based on the radio series *Meet the Rev* by Gale Pedrick. Story: Godfrey Grayson. Cinematographer: Cedric Williams. Music directors: Frank Spencer, Rupert Grayson. Editor: Ray Pitt. Art director: Denis Wreford. Sound: Edgar Vetter. Boom operator: Percy Britten [uncredited]. Sound camera operator: Gordon Everett [uncredited]. Make-up: Phil Leakey. Hair: Monica Hustler. Camera operator: Peter Bryan. Focus puller: Neil Binney [uncredited]. Clapper boy: Michael Reed [uncredited]. Assistant director: Leon Bijou. Second assistant director: Jimmy Sangster [uncredited]. Continuity: Renee Glynne. Chief electrician: Jack Curtis [uncredited]. Electrician: Charles Mullett [uncredited], Richard Jenkins [uncredited], Percy Harms [uncredited]. Construction: Freddie Ricketts [uncredited], Mick Lyons [uncredited]. Casting: Mary Harris. Production manager: Arthur Barnes. Pre-production assistant: Prudence Sykes [uncredited]. Production assistant: Michael Carreras [uncredited]. Props: Tommy Money [uncredited]. Stills: John Jay [uncredited]. **Cast:** Hugh Moxey (the Reverend Simon Cherry), Zena Marshall (Lisa Colville), John Bailey (Henry Dantry), Anthony Forwood (Alan Colville), Ernest Butcher (Young), Arthur Lovegrove (Charlie), Courtney Hope (Lady Harling), Jeanette Tregarthen (Monica Harling), Gerald Case (Doctor Smails)

## Megahy, Francis

Collaborating with Bernie Cooper, British born Megahy (1937–) penned the teleplay for *Charlie Boy*, an episode of *Hammer House of Horror* (1980, TV). Again with Cooper, he wrote *Carpathian Eagle* (1980, TV), which he also directed. He also directed *Growing Pains* for the series, from a script by Nicholas Palmer. His other credits as a director (among them several documentaries) include *Freelance* (1971), which he also co-wrote (with Bernie Cooper) and produced, *Real Life* (1983), which he also co-wrote (again with Cooper), *Taffin* (1987), *The Disappearance of Kevin Johnson* (1995), which he also wrote, *Late Night Girls* (2006), which he wrote, directed and appeared in, *The Best Government Money Can Buy?* (2009), which he also wrote and appeared in, and *Ayrton Senna: Chequered Flag to Green Light* (2014), which he also wrote. **Hammer credits:** *Charlie Boy* (1980, TV [episode of *Hammer House of Horror*], co-teleplay), *Carpathian Eagle* (1980, TV [episode of *Hammer House of Horror*], director, co-teleplay), *Growing Pains* (1980, TV [episode of *Hammer House of Horror*], director)

## MegaScope

One of many widescreen processes employed by Hammer in the fifties, the impressive sounding MegaScope was a variation on CinemaScope, and was first used on the POW drama *The Camp on Blood Island* (1958). For the Thuggee shocker *The Stranglers of Bombay* (1959), the process was temporarily re-named StrangloScope for publicity purposes. **Hammer credits:** *The Camp on Blood Island* (1958), *Further Up the Creek* (1958), *Yesterday's Enemy* (1959), *The Stranglers of Bombay* (1959 [as StrangloScope]), *Never Take Sweets from a Stranger* (1960), *The Two Faces of Dr. Jekyll* (1960), *Sword of Sherwood Forest* (1960), *The Full Treatment* (1961), *Maniac* (1963)

## Megowan, Don

This strapping (6'6") American supporting actor (1922–1981) can be seen in minor roles in such films as *To Catch a Thief* (1955), *The Werewolf* (1956), *The Devil's Brigade* (1968), *Blazing Saddles* (1974) and *The Great Gundown* (1977). However, he deserves a footnote in history for playing the Frankenstein Monster in *The Face in the Tombstone Mirror*, the pilot episode for Hammer's abandoned Hollywood-filmed television series *Tales of Frankenstein* (1958, TV). A former track and field star, his other small screen credits include episodes of *Death Valley Days* (1952–1975, TV), *Gunsmoke* (1955–1975, TV) and *Fantasy Island* (1978–1984, TV). Married twice, his second wife was actress Alva Marie Lacy (1927–1997), whom he married in 1974. **Hammer credits:** *Tales of Frankenstein: The Face in the Tombstone Mirror* (1958, TV, as the Monster)

## Meillon, John

Working in both Britain (from 1959 to 1965) and his native Australia, Meillon (1934–1989) is best remembered for playing Walter Reilly in the first two *"Crocodile" Dundee* movies (1986 and 1988). In films from 1959 with the Australian-shot *On the Beach*, his other films include *The Sundowners* (1960), *633 Squadron* (1964), *Walkabout* (1970), *The Cars That Ate Paris* (1974), *The Picture Show Man* (1977), *Heatwave* (1981) and *The Everlasting Secret Family* (1987). He also co-starred in the Hammer comedy *Watch It, Sailor!* (1961) in which he played a hapless tar who finds himself accused of fathering a child on the day of his wedding. Known in Australia for his voice-overs for Victoria Bitter commercials, his other TV credits include episodes of *My Name's McGooley, What's Yours?* (1967–1968, TV), in which he played Wally Stiller, *Woobinda, Animal Doctor* (1968–1970, TV) and *A Country Practice* (1981–1993, TV). Married twice, his first wife was actress June Salter (1932–2001), to whom he was married between 1958 and 1971; his second wife was actress Bunny Gibson, whom he married in 1972. His son (with Salter) is actor John Meillon, Jr. He was made an OBE in 1979. **Hammer credits:** *Watch It, Sailor!* (1961, as Albert Tuffnell/Thimble)

## Meineke, Eva Marie

This German actress (1923–2018) can be seen as the Satanist Eveline de Grass in Hammer's *To the Devil a Daughter* (1976). Her other credits include *Mit den Augen einer Frau* (1942), *Heidesommer* (1945), *Jacqueline* (1959), *Le serpent* (1973), *Der Sturz* (1979), *Tierärztin Christine* (1993) and *Afrika—Wohin mein Herz mich tragt* (2006, TVM). **Hammer credits:** *To the Devil a Daughter* (1976, as Eveline de Grass)

## Melachrino, George

Working with James Dyrenforth, this British singer, bandleader, composer and songwriter (1909–1965, real name George Miltiades) provided a couple of numbers for the Hammer programer *The Lady Craved Excitement* (1950). These were *The Lady Craves Excitement* (not *Craved*) and *Ladies of the Gaiety*. The musical director of the Army Radio Unit during World War II (nicknamed the "Orchestra in Khaki"), he toured with a show titled *Stars in Battledress*. He formed his own orchestra after the war, and went on to record many top-selling albums of light music, among them *Music for Relaxation* (1958) and *Our Man in London* (1958). His film scores include *Woman to Woman* (1946), *No Orchids for Miss Blandish* (1948), *Old Mother Riley's New Venture* (1948), *Old Mother Riley, Headmistress* (1950), in which he can also be seen as an orchestra leader, *April in Portugal* (1954) and *The Gamma People* (1956). **Hammer credits:** *The Lady Craved Excitement* (1950)

## Melford, Jack

On stage from 1911 and in films from 1931 with *The Sport of Kings*, this British actor (1899–1972, real name John Kenneth George Smith) appeared in featured roles in a number of films during the thirties and forties, among them *Birds of a Feather* (1935), *Jump for Glory* (1937), *Spare a Copper* (1940) and *The Rake's Progress* (1945). He gradually turned to character parts in *My Brother Jonathan* (1948), *Background* (1953) and *A Shot in the Dark* (1964). His last film was Hammer's *Lust for a Vampire* (1971), in which he plays the bishop who rather handily arrives to help the locals dispatch the vampiric Karnsteins. His television credits include episodes of *Z Cars* (1962–1978, TV) and *Softly Softly* (1966–1976, TV). His parents were stage actors Austin Melford and Alice Gambra, his uncle was writer Mark Melford (1851–1914, real name George Smith), and his brother was director Austin Melford (1884–1971, real name Austin Alfred Smith). His wife was actress Roberta Huby (1913–1995), whom he married in 1959 and their daughter was actress Jill Melford (1931–2018), who appeared in Hammer's *Murder by Proxy* (1955) and *The Vengeance of She* (1968). **Hammer credits:** *Lust for a Vampire* (1971, as Bishop)

## Melford, Jill

This British supporting actress (1931–2018) played the role of Miss Nardis in the Hammer thriller *Murder by Proxy* (1955). On stage in America from 1949 and in London from 1953, her other credits include *Will Any Gentleman…?* (1953), *Murder at Site 3* (1959), *Escort for Hire* (1960), *A Stitch in Time* (1963), *The Servant* (1963), *Bunny Lake Is Missing* (1965), *I Want What I Want* (1972), *The Bitch* (1979) and *Shoreditch* (2003). She later returned to Hammer for *The Vengeance of She* (1968). Her television credits include episodes of *Out of This World* (1962, TV), *The View from Daniel Pike* (1971–1973, TV) and *The House of Eliott* (1991–1994, TV). Her father was the actor Jack Melford (1899–1972, real name John Kenneth George Smith), who appeared in Hammer's *The Vampire Lovers* (1970). She was married to the actor John Standing (1934–, real name John Ronald Leon) between 1961 and 1972. **Hammer credits:** *Murder by Proxy* (1955, as Miss Nardis), *The Vengeance of She* (1968, as Sheila Carter)

## Mellor, James

This British actor (1933–1976) had a minor role in *Miss Belle* (1968, TV [episode of *Journey to the Unknown*]). His other credits include episodes of *No Hiding Place* (1959–1967, TV), *The First Lady* (1968–1969, TV) and *The Regiment* (1972–1973, TV), while his occasional films take in *Great Catherine* (1968), *The Oblong Box* (1969), *Doomwatch* (1972) and *On the Game* (1974). **Hammer credits:** *Miss Belle* (1968, TV [episode of *Journey to the Unknown*], unnamed role [uncredited])

## Melly, Andree

This distinctive-looking British actress (1932–) is best known to Hammer fans for playing the vampire girl Gina in Hammer's *The Brides of Dracula* (1960). Her other credits include *So Little Time* (1952), *The Belles of St. Trinian's* (1954), *The Secret Tent* (1956), *Nowhere to Go* (1958), *The Big Day* (1960), *Beyond the Curtain* (1960) and *The Horror of It All* (1964). Her TV credits include episodes of *Lilli Palmer Theatre* (1955–1956, TV), *Little Women* (1958, TV), in which she played Jo March, *Maigret* (1960–1963, TV), *Spy Trap* (1972–1975, TV), *Turn On to T-Bag* (1988, TV) and *T-Bag and the Pearls of Wisdom* (1990, TV). Her brother was the legendary jazz musician, songwriter and screenwriter George Melly (1926–2007, full name Alan George Heywood Melly), and her husband is actor Oscar Quitak (1926–, full name Morris Oscar Quitak), whom she married in 1964, and who appeared in Hammer's *The Revenge of Frankenstein* (1958) and *Black Carrion* (1984, TVM [episode of *Hammer House of Mystery and Suspense*]).

Recalled Melly of working on *The Brides of Dracula*, "Terence Fisher was not actually a director who was very interested in Stanislavsky or duration or, you know, any kind of profound ideas about acting and one's approach to acting. He was a very professional filmmaker, obviously interested in lighting and cutting and editing, and expected his actors to be professional."[44] **Hammer credits:** *The Brides of Dracula* (1960, as Gina)

## Melrose, Peter

British born Melrose (1930–) provided the matte paintings for Hammer's *Dracula Has Risen from the Grave* (1968), among them several creatively angled rooftop scenes. Recalled Melrose of his work on the film, "Both the budget and the time schedule were very tight…. [Producer Aida Young] kept describing the castles I painted as Gibbs castles—a Gibbs castle being the well-known trademark of the toothpaste manufacturer!"[45] Melrose's other credits, either as a matte painter or scenic artist, include *The Day the Earth Caught Fire* (1961), *The Spy Who Came in from the*

**Andree Melly (left) and Yvonne Monlaur (right) share toast and confidences in Hammer's *The Brides of Dracula* (1960) (Hammer/Hotspur/Rank/Universal-International).**

that everyone felt secure knowing that come hell or high water what had to be done would be done and what had to be there would be there."[46] Remembered Jimmy Sangster of the movie, "We shot on locations quite close to the studio and the weather was kind to us. Val Guest was one of the most efficient directors I'd ever worked with. Every day, when work started, he'd pin on a board an outline of every shot he intended doing that day. Great for the assistant director who could marshal all the technical crew accordingly. And pretty good for the production manager too."[47]

Trade shown in November 1954, the film was released in the UK by Exclusive on 6 December the same year and proved a popular enough success to provoke talk of a possible follow-up simply titled *Friar Tuck*, with Reginald Beckwith set to reprise his role as the portly monk. Unfortunately, the film didn't come to pass, although *Men of Sherwood Forest* was re-released by RFI (Regal Films International) in 1961. The film was meanwhile released in America in 1956 care of the Astor Pictures Corporation. Hammer later returned to the subject of Robin Hood with *Sword of Sherwood Forest* (1960), *A Challenge for Robin Hood* (1967) and the acquired *Wolfshead: The Legend of Robin Hood* (1969 [first shown 1973]).

Production company: Hammer. Distributors: Exclusive (UK), Astor (U.S.). Producer: Michael Carreras. Director: Val Guest. Screenplay: Allan

---

*Cold* (1965), *The Fearless Vampire Killers* (1967), which features another "Gibbs castle," *Frankenstein: The True Story* (1973, TVM), *Superman III* (1983) and *Legend* (1985). He also provided some unused mattes for Hammer's *When Dinosaurs Ruled the Earth* (1970). **Hammer credits:** *Dracula Has Risen from the Grave* (1968), *When Dinosaurs Ruled the Earth* (1970 [unused mattes, uncredited])

### Men of Sherwood Forest

GB, 1954, 77m, Eastmancolor, RCA, cert U

Although by no means the definitive version of the Robin Hood story (it inevitably pales besides the Errol Flynn classic *The Adventures of Robin Hood* [1938]), this reasonably lively swashbuckling romp was nevertheless another important stepping stone for Hammer in that it was the company's first film in color (Eastmancolor to be precise, the process with which the studio would later photograph some of its greatest horrors). Shot on location at Bodiam Castle in Sussex, the production was director Val Guest's second for Hammer following *Life with the Lyons* (1954); it was also his second in color following the Technicolor *Penny Princess* (1952), which had been made for Rank/Conquest.

Set in 1194, the script, provided by Allan Mackinnon, follows the storyline familiar from legend (and Hollywood), and sees Robin and his men fight to return King Richard to his rightful place on the English throne following his return from the Crusades. Hammer's first major historical production, it benefits from several sunny woodland locations, though it must be said that J Elder Wills'

castle interiors look somewhat cramped, no doubt owing to the similarly cramped budget and the equally cramped confines of Bray. Nevertheless, the cast performs with reasonable energy—especially during the fight sequences—even if the mid–Atlantic accent of Hollywood import Don Taylor proves incongruous as Robin. Featuring a supporting cast of Hammer regulars both past and future—among them John Van Eyssen, Douglas Wilmer, John Kerr and, in his first film, Bernard Bresslaw—the film is a breezy enough romp, and comes as a pleasant change from the company's previous glut of murder melodramas which were by now becoming indistinguishable from one another.

Recalled director Val Guest of the production, which was the first of several films produced for him by Michael Carreras, "Mike ... was a quick learner and soon turned into one of the most organized producers for whom I had ever worked. Somehow he managed to deep-think his productions so

**A lively poster for the Robin Hood jape *Men of Sherwood Forest* (1954) (Hammer/ Exclusive).**

Mackinnon. Cinematographer: Walter "Jimmy" Harvey. Music: Doreen Carwithen. Music director: John Hollingsworth. Editor: James Needs. Art director: J. Elder Wills. Costumes: Michael Whittaker, Molly Arbuthnot. Make-up: Phil Leakey. Hair: Monica Hustler. Special effects: Vic Margutti [uncredited]. Sound: Sid Wiles, Ken Cameron. Assistant director: Jack Causey. Production manager: Jimmy Sangster. Camera operator: Len Harris. Focus puller: Harry Oakes [uncredited]. Continuity: Renee Glynne. Stunts: Peter Munt [uncredited]. **Cast:** Don Taylor (Robin Hood), Eileen Moore (Lady Alys), Reginald Beckwith (Friar Tuck), David King-Wood (Sir Guy Belton), Patrick Holt (King Richard), John Van Eyssen (Will Scarlet), Harold Lang (Hubert), Douglas Wilmer (Sir Nigel Saltire), Leslie Linder (Little John), John Kerr (Brian of Eskdale), Vera Pearce (Elvira), Leonard Sachs (Sheriff of Nottingham), Ballard Berkeley (Walter), Wensley Pithey (Hugo), Toke Townley (Father David), Bernard Bresslaw (Gullible castle guard [uncredited]), Raymond Rollett (Abbot St. Jude [uncredited]), Michael Golden (unnamed role), John Stuart (Moraine [uncredited]), Howard Lang (Town crier [uncredited]), Tom Bowman (Outlaw [uncredited]), Michael Godfrey (Outlaw [uncredited]), Dennis Wyndham (Outlaw [uncredited]), Edward Hardwicke (Outlaw [uncredited]), Jack McNaughton (Outlaw [uncredited]), Peter Arne (unnamed role [uncredited]), Robert Hunter (unnamed role [uncredited]). **DVD availability:** Manga (Spanish, R2 PAL)

## Mendez, Julie

Mostly on stage in cabaret (especially at the Raymond Revue Bar), this British exotic dancer (1938–2013)—belly dancing and snake work a specialty—can be spotted in such films as *The Night We Dropped a Clanger* (1959), *Panic* (1963), *Devils of Darkness* (1964), in which she performed with her seven-foot boa constrictor Lulu (one of two snakes she possessed), *Theatre of Death* (1966), *Duffy* (1968) and *The Abominable Dr. Phibes* (1971), again with one of her snakes (in the stag reel watched by Terry-Thomas). She also popped up in episodes of *Virgin of the Secret Service* (1968, TV), as well as a 1970 episode of *On the Buses* (1969–1973, TV) titled *The Snake*, in which she again performed her snake dance. She can also be seen as a nightclub dancer in Hammer's *She* (1965). Her most famous credit is performing as the belly dancer under the credits of *From Russia with Love* (1963). She also worked as a choreographer, occasionally staging numbers for films, among them the nightclub routines performed by the Sphinx Girls in Hammer's *The Two Faces of Dr. Jekyll* (1960). Her other films as a choreographer include *Carry On … Up the Khyber* (1968). Sometimes billed as Julie Mendes or Julia Mendez. **Hammer credits:** *The Two Faces of Dr. Jekyll* (1960, choreographer), *She* (1965, as Nightclub dancer)

## Merchandise

Aside from trading cards, records, CDs, magazines and tie-in novelizations, there have been a number of Hammer-related collectibles produced by a variety of companies down the years. In 1996, The London Postcard Company produced eighteen full-color poster cards, featuring artwork from everything from *The Quatermass Xperiment* (1955) through to *The Vampire Lovers* (1970). There were even three double-bill cards, among them *The Devil Rides Out* (1968) and *Slave Girls* (1968). In June 2008, the Royal Mail issued a series of Carry On and Hammer stamps, among the latter poster images of *The Curse of Frankenstein* (1957), *Dracula* (1958) and *The Mummy* (1959). There have also been character models (care of Creatures Unlimited), posters, calendars, tee shirts, phone cards, model kits and action figures.

## Meredith, Jill Mai

British born Meredith can be seen as Jenny in Hammer's *The Curse of the Mummy's Tomb* (1964). Her other credits include *Carry On Cruising* (1962), *The Cool Mikado* (1963), *The Leather Boys* (1963), *Carry On Spying* (1964), *You Must Be Joking!* (1965), *A Penny for Your Thoughts* (1966) and *Billion Dollar Brain* (1967), plus episodes of *Dixon of Dock Green* (1955–1976, TV), *Z Cars* (1962–1978, TV) and *No, That's Me Over Here!* (1967–1970, TV). **Hammer credits:** *The Curse of the Mummy's Tomb* (1964, as Jenny)

## Meredith, Lu Anne

This American born actress (1913–1998) can be spotted in the role of Nelly Gray in the Hammer comedy *Sporting Love* (1936). A former WAMPAS Baby Star (of 1934), her American films include *Love Detectives* (1934), *George White's Scandals* (1934) and *Night Life of the Gods* (1935), while her other British credits take in *Ball at Savoy* (1936) and *Sing As You Swing* (1937). **Hammer credits:** *Sporting Love* (1936, as Nelly Gray)

## Merlin Film Productions, Ltd.

Specializing in documentary films, this British production company was later bought by Hammer. Explained camera operator Harry Oakes, who worked for both Merlin and Hammer, "They [Hammer] used to make films under different company names for taxation purposes."[48] One of these was the Eastern shocker *The Terror of the Tongs* (1961), which was made in conjunction with Merlin, as was *Captain Clegg* (1962). **Hammer credits:** *The Terror of the Tongs* (1961), *Captain Clegg* (1962)

## Merrall, Mary

On stage from the age of seventeen, this busy British actress (1890–1973, real name Elsie Lloyd) broke into films in the mid-teens with *Fatal Fingers* (1916). She went on to appear in many productions, among them *The Manxman* (1917), *The Duke's Son* (1920), *Love on the Dole* (1941), *The Belles of St. Trinian's* (1954) and *Who Killed the Cat?* (1966). She can also be seen in the Hammer war drama *The Camp on Blood Island* (1958) playing Mrs. Beattie to Walter Fitzgerald's Cyril Beattie. Her television credits include episodes of *The Avengers* (1961–1969, TV), *The Saint* (1962–1969, TV) and *Justice* (1971–1974, TV). Married three times, her second husband was the actor Ian Swinley (1891–1937), to whom she was married between 1916 and 1926. Her third husband was the actor Franklyn Dyall (1870–1950), whom she married in 1929, and with whom she managed the Abbey Theater in Dublin. Her stepson was the actor Valentine Dyall (1908–1985), who appeared in a handful of films for Hammer, among them *Dr. Morelle—The Case of the Missing Heiress* (1949) and *The Man in Black* (1950). **Hammer credits:** *The Camp on Blood Island* (1958, as Mrs. Beattie)

## Merrett, Tony

Merrett had a supporting role in Hammer's *River Patrol* (1948). **Hammer credits:** *River Patrol* (1948, unnamed role)

## Merritt, George

Frequently cast as a representative of the law, this British character actor (1890–1977) can be seen as such in Hammer's *Quatermass 2* (1957) and *Dracula* (1958). On stage from 1909 and in films from 1930 with *Thread O' Scarlet*, his many other credits include *The Clairvoyant* (1934), *Spare a Copper* (1940), *A Canterbury Tale* (1944), *Night of the Full Moon* (1954) and *Crooks and Coronets* (1968), as well as a further film for Hammer. His TV appearances include episodes of *The Adventures of Sir Lancelot* (1956–1957, TV), *Gideon's Way* (1965–1966, TV) and *Fall of Eagles* (1974, TV). **Hammer credits:** *Quatermass 2* (1957, as Superintendent), *Dracula* (1958, as Policeman), *The Full Treatment* (1961, as Dr. Manfield)

## Merrow, Jane

This British actress (1941–, real name Jane Meirowsky) of the English rose variety has sadly made all too few films, among them Hammer's *Hands of the Ripper* (1971), in which she plays the blind Laura. A charming performance, it is more Gainsborough than Hammer, and prompted *Photoplay* to describe her character as "a poignant figure." Her other film credits include *Don't Bother to Knock* (1961), *The System* (1964), *Night of the Big Heat* (1967), *Assignment K* (1968), *The Lion in Winter* (1968), *Adam's Woman* (1970), *The Patricia Neal Story* (1981, TVM), *The Yellow Wallpaper* (2013) and *Almosting It* (2016). She can also be spotted as a chorus girl in Hammer's *The Phantom of the Opera* (1962). Her television work includes episodes of *Oliver Twist* (1962, TV), *Lorna Doone* (1963, TV), in which she played the title role, *Hadleigh* (1969–1976, TV), *Van Der Valk* (1972–1977, TV), *Lovejoy* (1986–1994, TV) and *Accused* (1996, TV). Also on stage. **Hammer credits:** *The Phantom of the Opera* (1962, as Chorus girl [uncredited]), *Hands of the Ripper* (1971, as Laura)

## Merry, Susanna (Sue)

Merry worked as the second unit continuity girl/script supervisor on Hammer's *When Dinosaurs Ruled the Earth* (1970). Her other continuity credits include *Wonderwall* (1968), *Carry On Again Doctor* (1969), *The Boy Friend* (1971), *The Wicker Man* (1973), *The Rocky Horror Picture Show* (1975), *Sextet* (1976) and *The Man Who Fell to Earth* (1976), plus episodes of *Man in a Suitcase* (1967–1968, TV) and *The Comic Strip Presents* (1982–2012, TV). **Hammer credits:** *When Dinosaurs Ruled the Earth* (1970)

## Mertineit, Michael

Mertineit worked as one of the assistant directors on Hammer's *The Lady Vanishes* (1979). His other credits include *Die Hamburger Krankheit* (1979), plus such TV work as *Warnung aus dem Käfig* (1981, TVM) and *Es gibt noch Haselnub-Straucher* (1983, TV). He also worked as an assistant production manager on episodes of *Hamburg Transit* (1973–1974, TV) and *Motiv Liebe* (1975, TV). **Hammer credits:** *The Lady Vanishes* (1979)

## Merton, Zienia

Born in Burma, this Anglo-Burmese actress and dancer (1945–) is best known for playing Sandra Benes in *Space: 1999* (1975–1977, TV). Her other television appearances include episodes of *Doctor Who* (1963–1989, TV), *Beryl's Lot* (1973–1977, TV), *Bergerac* (1981–1991, TV), *EastEnders* (1985–, TV), *Wire in the Blood* (2002–2008, TV), *The Sarah Jane Adventures* (2007–2011, TV) and *Wizards vs. Aliens* (2012–2014, TV). She can also be seen in the role of Nurse Lee in *The Late Nancy Irving* (1984, TVM [episode of *Hammer House of Mystery and Suspense*]). Her occasional films include *Masters of Venus* (1982), *Help!* (1965) and *The Adventurers* (1970). She wrote about her life in her autobiography *Anecdotes and Armadillos* (2005). **Hammer credits:** *The Late Nancy Irving* (1984, TVM [episode of *Hammer House of Mystery and Suspense*], as Nurse Lee)

## Mervyn, William

Best remembered for playing the kindly old gentleman in *The Railway Children* (1970), this portly Kenya born British character actor (1912–1976, full name William Mervyn Pickwood) came to films in 1947 with *The Loves of Joanna Godden* following many years' radio experience. In over forty films, his credits include *That Dangerous Age* (1949), *Carve Her Name with Pride* (1958), *Operation Crossbow* (1965), *Carry On Henry* (1970), *Incense for the Damned* (1972) and *The Bawdy Adventures of Tom Jones* (1976). He also had a brief role as a sea captain in the Hammer comedy *Watch It, Sailor!* (1961). Much on stage, Mervyn was also familiar to television audiences, especially in the sitcom *All Gas and Gaiters* (1967–1971, TV), in which played The Right Reverend Cuthbert Hever. His other small screen credits include episodes of *The Sky Larks* (1958, TV), *Oliver Twist* (1962, TV), *Saki* (1962, TV), *It's Dark Outside* (1964–1965, TV), *Mr. Rose* (1967–1968, TV), in which he played the title role, *Tottering Towers* (1971–1972, TV), in which he played the Duke of Tottering, and *Crown Court* (1972–1984, TV). **Hammer credits:** *Watch It, Sailor!* (1961, as Captain)

## Messenger, Vernon

This sound technician worked as one of the sound editors on Hammer's *She* (1965). He later returned in the same capacity for *Shatter* (1974). His many other credits (which include work as a foley editor, dialogue editor, sound supervisor, sound designer and dubbing editor) include *Loser Takes All* (1956), *Zeppelin* (1971), *Black Beauty* (1971), *The Wicker Man* (1973), *The Cassandra Crossing* (1976), *The Thirty-Nine Steps* (1978), *For Your Eyes Only* (1981), *The Living Daylights* (1987),

*Licence to Kill* (1989) and *A Good Man in Africa* (1994). **Hammer credits:** *She* (1965), *Shatter* (1974)

## Messrs. Siebe Gorman and Co. Ltd. *see* Siebe Gorman and Co. Ltd.

## Metcalfe, Ernie

Metcalfe worked as the second assistant director on Hammer's *Someone at the Door* (1950). His other credits include *Dreaming* (1944), on which he was the first assistant director. **Hammer credits:** *Someone at the Door* (1950 [uncredited])

## Metro-Goldwyn-Mayer

Formed in 1920 with the amalgamation of Loew's Inc. and Metro Pictures (the merger with Mayer followed in 1924), this American studio—a Goliath in the thirties, forties and fifties—also handled its own distribution, as well as that for a number of other lesser companies, which it did through its many offices throughout the world. The company handled the UK release of Hammer's very first production, the bar room comedy *The Public Life of Henry the Ninth* (1935). Returns can't have been too healthy, though, as this was the only early Hammer film MGM handled. However, many years later, Hammer used studio space at MGM's British studio at Borehamwood to shoot the interiors for *Maniac* (1963), *Hysteria* (1965), which MGM also released, *She* (1965) and *Quatermass and the Pit* (1967). MGM displayed fleeting interest in backing a sequel to *She* (this was touted under such titles as *Ayesha—Daughter of She*, *She—Goddess of Love*, *She II* and *She—The Avenger*) but the project stalled and re-surfaced with other backers as *The Vengeance of She* (1968). When EMI bought out Warner Bros./Seven Arts from ABPC in 1969, MGM went into a distribution deal with the company as MGM-EMI, partially financing certain films. These included a handful of Hammer projects, several of which it also helped to distribute in the UK, among them the double bill of *The Horror of Frankenstein* (1970) and *Scars of Dracula* (1970).

Other films made or distributed by MGM include *Ben-Hur* (1925, also 1959 and 2016), *Anna Christie* (1930), *Mutiny on the Bounty* (1935), *A Night at the Opera* (1935), *The Wizard of Oz* (1939), *Gone with the Wind* (1939), *Mrs. Miniver* (1942), *Gaslight* (1944), *The Asphalt Jungle* (1950), *Singin' in the Rain* (1952), *Jailhouse Rock* (1957), *Doctor Zhivago* (1965), *2001: A Space Odyssey* (1968), *Shaft* (1971), *Westworld* (1973), *Fame* (1980 and 2009), *Octopussy* (1983), *A Fish Called Wanda* (1988), *Thelma & Louise* (1991), *Species* (1995), *Die Another Day* (2002), *Quantum of Solace* (2008), *Creed* (2015) and *Going in Style* (2017). **Hammer credits:** *The Public Life of Henry the Ninth* (1935), *Maniac* (1963), *She* (1965), *Hysteria* (1965), *Quatermass and the Pit* (1967), *Wolfshead: The Legend of Robin Hood* (1969 [released 1973]), *The Vampire Lovers* (1970), *Scars of Dracula* (1970), *The Horror of Frankenstein* (1970), *Lust for a Vampire* (1971), *On the Buses* (1971), *Dr. Jekyll and Sister Hyde* (1971), *Blood from the Mummy's Tomb* (1971), *Fear in the Night* (1972), *Mutiny on the Buses* (1972), *Demons of the Mind* (1972), *Near-*

*est and Dearest* (1973), *Love Thy Neighbour* (1973), *Man at the Top* (1973), *Holiday on the Buses* (1973)

## MGM *see* Metro-Goldwyn-Mayer

## Michael, Ralph

In films from 1937 with *False Evidence*, this British character actor (1907–1994, real name Ralph Champion Shotter) tended towards upper class roles. His many other films include *John Halifax* (1938), *Dead of Night* (1945), *The Astonished Heart* (1949), *The Sound Barrier* (1952), *A Night to Remember* (1958), *Murder Most Foul* (1964) and *Empire of the Sun* (1987). He can also be seen in the Hammer prison melodrama *Women Without Men* (1956) as Julian Lord, and an episode of *Hammer House of Mystery and Suspense* (1984, TVM). His other TV appearances include episodes of *The Adventures of Robin Hood* (1955–1960, TV), *The Invisible Man* (1958–1960, TV), *It Happened Like This* (1962–1963, TV), *Doctor in the House* (1960–1979, TV), *Doctor at Large* (1971, TV), *Kessler* (1981, TV) and *Jeeves and Wooster* (1990–1993, TV). Married twice, his first wife was actress Fay Compton (1894–1978, real name Virginia Lilian Emmeline Compton Mackenzie) to whom he was married between 1942 and 1946, and who appeared in *Poor Butterfly*, an episode of the Hammer TV series *Journey to the Unknown* (1968, TV), which also appeared in the compendium film *Journey to Midnight* (1968, TVM). His second wife was actress Joyce Heron (1916–1980, full name Elizabeth Joyce Heron), whom he married in 1947. **Hammer credits:** *Women Without Men* (1956, as Julian Lord), *And the Wall Came Tumbling Down* (1984, TVM [episode of *Hammer House of Mystery and Suspense*], as Father Harris)

## Michael Stainer-Hutchins and Peter Daw, Ltd.

This British "services company" created by Michael Stainer-Hutchins and Peter Daw purchased the screen rights to three Dennis Wheatley novels in 1963. These were *The Devil Rides Out* (1934), *To the Devil a Daughter* (1953) and *The Satanist* (1960), all three of which were subsequently optioned by Hammer, the duo's idea being to get a leg up in the film industry by being associated with the productions themselves. Commented Peter Daw in a February 1964 issue of *Kinematograph Weekly*, "We formed our company recently to explore the field of options on neglected properties and finding financial backing for them, and also to be associated with the productions ourselves." The plan worked, and Michael Stainer-Hutchins went on to pesonally provide the title sequence and the effects for Hammer's production of *The Devil Rides Out* (1968), for which he was also one of the associate producers along with Peter Daw. **Hammer credits:** *The Devil Rides Out* (1968)

## Michaels, Anna

Michaels can be seen as Eileen in Hammer's *On the Buses* (1971). **Hammer credits:** *On the Buses* (1971, as Eileen)

## Michaels, Beverly

Popular for a while in the fifties, this American

actress (1928–2007) took the leading role of Angie Booth in the Hammer prison melodrama *Women Without Men* (1956), which marked her final big screen appearance. Her other credits include *East Side, West Side* (1949), *Pickup* (1951), *The Girl on the Bridge* (1951), *Wicked Woman* (1953), *Betrayed Woman* (1955) and *Crashout* (1955). She also appeared in episodes of *The Adventures of the Falcon* (1954–1956, TV), *Alfred Hitchcock Presents* (1955–1962, TV) and *Cheyene* (1955–1963, TV). Married twice, her first husband was the Russian producer Voldemar Vetluguin (1894–1953), to whom she was married between 1949 and 1952. Her second husband was screenwriter Russell Rouse (1913–1987), whom she married in 1955; their son is editor Christopher Rouse (1958–). **Hammer credits:** *Women Without Men* (1956, as Angie Booth)

### Michaels, Ricci *see* Ricci Michaels, Ltd.

### Michell, Ted

Michell worked as a scenic artist on Hammer's *The Satanic Rites of Dracula* (1974). His other credits include *Flash Gordon* (1980), *Ragtime* (1981), *Return of the Jedi* (1983), *Superman III* (1983), *Indiana Jones and the Temple of Doom* (1984), *Return to Oz* (1985), *Hope and Glory* (1987) and *Carry On Columbus* (1992). **Hammer credits:** *The Satanic Rites of Dracula* (1974 [uncredited])

### Michie, Byron

Michie was the commentator for the silent film compilation *Made for Laughs* (1952) for Hammer. His credits as an actor include *Oriental Evil* (1950), in which he starred, and *Tokyo File 212* (1951). **Hammer credits:** *Made for Laughs* (1952, as Commentator)

### Middlemass, Frank

On stage from 1948 following experience in the army (in which he reached the rank of major), this respected British character actor (1919–2006) is best known for playing Dan Archer in the long-running radio soap *The Archers* (1950–). In television from the late fifties and films from the late sixties, his big screen credits include *Otley* (1968), *Barry Lyndon* (1975), *The Island* (1980) and *Mrs. Caldicot's Cabbage War* (2002), while his many small screen credits include episodes of such series as *Poldark* (1975–1977, TV), *Oliver Twist* (1985, TV), in which he played Mr. Brownlow, *The Bretts* (1987–1988, TV), *Heartbeat* (1992–2009, TV), *As Time Goes By* (1993–2005, TV) and *The 10th Kingdom* (2000, TV). He can also be seen as one of the four guests evicted from Anna Spengler's boarding house in Hammer's *Frankenstein Must Be Destroyed* (1969). **Hammer credits:** *Frankenstein Must Be Destroyed* (1969, as Guest)

### Middleton, Guy

Following experience on the stock exchange, this British comedy character actor (1906–1973, full name Guy Middleton-Powell) broke into acting, making his film debut in 1935 with *Jimmy Boy*. Over fifty films followed, among them *Goodbye, Mr. Chips* (1939), *The Rake's Progress* (1945), *The Happiest Days of Your Life* (1950), *The Belles of St. Trinian's* (1954), *Doctor at Large* (1957), *Oh! What a Lovely War* (1969) and *The Rise and Rise of Michael Rimmer* (1970), with raffish cads and officer types a specialty. He worked for Hammer twice, first appearing as Guy Ransome in *Never Look Back* (1952), and then as Major Hobart in *Break in the Circle* (1955). His television appearances include episodes of *Douglas Fairbanks, Jr. Presents* (1953–1957, TV), *The Errol Flynn Theatre* (1957, TV), *Be Soon* (1957, TV) and *Doctor Who* (1963–1989, TV). **Hammer credits:** *Never Look Back* (1952, as Guy Ransome), *Break in the Circle* (1955, as Major Hobart)

### Middleton, Stuart (Stewart)

This British child actor (1956–) played the role of the young Hans in the opening scene of Hammer's *Frankenstein Created Woman* (1967), in which he sees his father beheaded on the scaffold. Robert Morris played the role as a man. His other credits include *Spaceflight IC-1* (1965). **Hammer credits:** *Frankenstein Created Woman* (1967, as Young Hans [uncredited])

### Midwinter, Clive

This British assistant director (1906–1972) worked on the Hammer/Luckwell programer *The Runaway* (1964). He began his career as a third assistant working on *London Town* (1946). He soon after graduated to second assistant on *The White Unicorn* (1947) and *The Glass Mountain* (1949). His other credits as a first assistant include *The Case of Charles Peace* (1949), *Once a Sinner* (1950), *High Terrace* (1956) and *The Three Lives of Thomasina* (1964), plus episodes of *Colonel March of Scotland Yard* (1954–1956, TV) and *Fabian of the Yard* (1954–1956, TV). He also worked as a production manager on such films as *Bond of Fear* (1956), *West of Suez* (1957), *Inn for Trouble* (1960) and *The Marked One* (1963). **Hammer credits:** *The Runaway* (1964)

### Midwinter, Dulcie

A familiar name in British films in the sixties and seventies, this American born costume designer and wardrobe supervisor (1910–1997, maiden name Dulcie Marjorie Allen) worked on dozens of films, among them a handful for Hammer. Her other credits include *Not So Dusty* (1956), *Booby Trap* (1957), *Rag Doll* (1958), *Tunes of Glory* (1960), *Doctor Blood's Coffin* (1961), *Echo of Diana* (1963), *The Quiller Memorandum* (1966), *The Italian Job* (1969), *Tales of Beatrix Potter* (1971), *Frenzy* (1972), *Madhouse* (1974), *Hardcore* (1977) and *Eskimo Nell* (1979), plus episodes of *The Sentimental Agent* (1963, TV), *The Human Jungle* (1963–1964, TV) and *Star Maidens* (1976, TV). **Hammer credits:** *A Challenge for Robin Hood* (1967), *Mutiny on the Buses* (1972), *Captain Kronos—Vampire Hunter* (1974), *Frankenstein and the Monster from Hell* (1974)

### Mikell, George

This Lithuanian actor (1930–) can be seen as a plain clothes policeman in *Czech Mate* (1984, TVM [episode of *Hammer House of Mystery and Suspense*]). In Britain from 1956, his many film credits include *The One That Got Away* (1957), *Sea of Sand* (1958), *A Circle of Deception* (1960), *The Guns of Navarone* (1961), *Zeppelin* (1970), *Young Winston* (1972), *The Sea Wolves* (1980) and *Escape to Victory* (1981). His other television appearances include episodes of *BBC Sunday-Night Theatre* (1950–1959, TV), *The Third Man* (1959–1965, TV), *Bergerac* (1981–1991, TV) and *The Brack Report* (1982, TV). **Hammer credits:** *Czech Mate* (1984, TVM [episode of *Hammer House of Mystery and Suspense*], as Plain clothes policeman)

### Mikhelson, André

Mikhelson can be seen as El Greco in Hammer's *The Gambler and the Lady* (1953), which marked his film debut. He also had a supporting role in *Break in the Circle* (1955). His other credits include *Desperate Moment* (1953), *I Am a Camera* (1955), *Dangerous Exile* (1957) and *Children of the Damned* (1963), plus episodes of *The Count of Monte Cristo* (1956, TV), *White Hunter* (1957–1958, TV) and *The Four Just Men* (1959–1960, TV). **Hammer credits:** *The Gambler and the Lady* (1953, as El Greco [uncredited]), *Break in the Circle* (1955, as First Russian)

### Miles, Anthony

Miles can be seen in a supporting role in Hammer's *Wings of Danger* (1952). He also popped up in *Women Without Men* (1956). **Hammer credits:** *Wings of Danger* (1952, as Sam), *Women Without Men* (1956, as Civilian [uncredited])

### Miles, Vera

In films from 1950 with *When Willie Comes Marching Home* following experience in commercials and as a beauty queen, this American actress (1929–, real name Vera June Ralston) is perhaps best known for her work for Alfred Hitchcock, which includes *Revenge*, the opening episode of *Alfred Hitchcock Presents* (1955–1962, TV), as well as *The Wrong Man* (1956) and *Psycho* (1960), in which she played Lila Crane. She was also set to star in *Vertigo* (1958), but had to drop out when she became pregnant. Her other films include *The Searchers* (1956), *The Man Who Shot Liberty Valance* (1962), *Castaway Cowboy* (1974), *Psycho II* (1983), now as Lila Loomis, and *Separate Lives* (1995). Back on television, she also guest starred in *Matakitas Is Coming*, an episode of Hammer's *Journey to the Unknown* (1968, TV), which also appeared in the compendium film *Journey to the Unknown* (1969, TVM). Her other TV work includes a 1960 episode of *Star Time* (1959–1961, TV) titled *Incident at a Corner* in which she was again directed by Hitchcock, two episodes of *The Alfred Hitchcock Hour* (1962–1965, TV), which were directed by other hands, and episodes of *The Man from U.N.C.L.E.* (1964–1968, TV), *Ironside* (1967–1975, TV), *Cannon* (1971–1976, TV), *Magnum, P.I.* (1980–1988, TV) and *Murder, She Wrote* (1984–1996, TV). Married four times, her husbands were the actor Bob Miles (1927–2007, full name Robert Jenning Miles, Jr.), to whom she was married between 1948 and 1954, the actor Gordon Scott (1926–2007, real name Gordon Merrill Werschkul), to whom she was married between 1956 and 1960, the director Keith Larsen (1924–2006, full name Keith Larsen Burt), to whom she was married between 1960 and 1971, and the assistant director Robert Jones (aka Bob Jones), whom she married in 1973. Her four children include the associate producer Debra Miles (1950–), the actress Kelley Miles (1952–) and the actor Eric Larsen (1961–). **Hammer credits:** *Matakitas Is Coming* (1968, TV [episode of *Journey to the Unknown*], as June Wiley), *Journey to the Unknown* (1969, TVM, as June Wiley)

### Millan, Tony

Millan can be seen in a supporting role as a caddy in *The Late Nancy Irving* (1984, TVM [episode of *Hammer House of Mystery and Suspense*]). His other credits include episodes of *Citizen Smith* (1977–1980, TV), in which he played Tucker, *Sweet Sixteen* (1983, TV), *Stuff* (1988–1991, TV), *Goodnight Sweetheart* (1993–1999, TV) and *High Hopes* (2002–2008, TV). He has also contributed scripts to *Birds of a Feather* (1989–1998, TV), *Not with a Bang* (1990, TV) and *The Brittas Empire* (1991–1997, TV). **Hammer credits:** *The Late Nancy Irving* (1984, TVM [episode of *Hammer House of Mystery and Suspense*], as Caddy)

### Millard, Oscar

This British writer (1908–1990) worked on three episodes of the Hammer series *Journey to the Unknown* (1968, TV). These were *Paper Dolls*, which also appeared in the compendium film *Journey into Darkness* (1968, TVM), *The New People*, which also appeared in the compendium film *Journey into Darkness* (1968, TVM), and *One on an Island*. Working primarily in America, his screenplays include *The Frogmen* (1951), which earned him an Oscar nomination for best story, *Song Without End* (1960), *Dead Ringer* (1964) and *The Salzburg Connection* (1972). He also wrote for such series as *Four Star Playhouse* (1952–1956, TV), *Markham* (1959–1960, TV) and *The Alfred Hitchcock Hour* (1962–1965, TV). Filmed novels include *Uncensored* (1942 [novel 1937]). His other novels include *Burgomaster Max* (1936) and *A Missing Person* (1972). **Hammer credits:** *The New People* (1968, TV [episode of *Journey to the Unknown*], co-teleplay), *One on an Island* (1968, TV [episode of *Journey to the Unknown*], teleplay), *Paper Dolls* (1968, TV [episode of *Journey to the Unknown*], teleplay), *Journey into Darkness* (1968, TVM, co-teleplay)

### Millard, Tamsin

Millard can be seen as one of the Rock people in Hammer's *Creatures the World Forgot* (1971). **Hammer credits:** *Creatures the World Forgot* (1971, as Rock woman [uncredited])

### Miller, Alex

This British actor and vocalist played a singer in the nightclub scenes of Hammer's *The Two Faces of Dr. Jekyll* (1960). His other credits include *Foreign Exchange* (1970, TVM) and an episode of *An Enemy of the State* (1965, TV). **Hammer credits:** *The Two Faces of Dr. Jekyll* (1960, as Singer [uncredited])

### Miller, Jack

Miller worked as the sound recordist on a couple of Hammer fifties co-features. His other credits include *Silent Dust* (1949), *Forces' Sweetheart* (1953), *The Scarlet Spear* (1954) and *The Blue Peter* (1955). **Hammer credits:** *Whispering Smith Hits London* (1952), *Mantrap* (1953)

### Miller, Magda

This British (Scottish) actress (1935–) and dancer appeared as one of the Sphinx Girls in Hammer's *The Two Faces of Dr. Jekyll* (1960). Her other credits include *Man Behind the Headlines* (1956), *Man-Eater* (1957), *Town on Trial* (1957) and *The Secret Man* (1958), plus episodes of *Saber of London* (1954–1960, TV), *Play of the Month* (1965–1983, TV), *Tottering Towers* (1971–1972, TV), in which she played Mimi, and *The Tripods* (1984–1985, TV). **Hammer credits:** *The Two Faces of Dr. Jekyll* (1960, as Sphinx Girl [uncredited])

### Miller, Mandy

Remembered for her touching performance as the deaf and dumb girl in the Ealing drama *Mandy* (1952), this British child actress (1944–, real name Carmen Isabella Miller) began her film career just one year earlier with a brief appearance in *The Man in the White Suit* (1951), which she followed with another cameo in *I Believe in You* (1952). *Mandy* (which earned her a BAFTA nomination for best newcomer) catapulted her to stardom, but she made only a further eight films, among them *Background* (1953), *Raising a Riot* (1955) and *Child in the House* (1956). She also gave a good account of herself in her last film, Hammer's *The Snorkel* (1958), in which she plays a teenager whose keen observations expose the murderous activities of her stepfather. Recalled the film's screenwriter, Jimmy Sangster, "The girl was played by child star Mandy Miller, who Guy Green [the director] thought was too old for the part. He was probably right. But she had a good name at the time and Jim Carreras worked out that he needed all the help he could get on the posters."[49] Sadly, following appearances in such series as *The Third Man* (1959–1965, TV), *The Avengers* (1961–1969, TV) and *The Saint* (1962–1969, TV), she retired from the screen, though in 1981 she did briefly return as an announcer. She also recorded the novelty record *Nellie the Elephant* (1956) as a child. Her sister is the actress Jan Miller, and her niece is the actress Amanda Pays (1959–). **Hammer credits:** *The Snorkel* (1958, as Candy Brown)

### Miller, Mark

Miller is acknowledged in the credits of *Flesh and Blood—The Hammer Heritage of Horror* (1994, TV). **Hammer credits:** *Flesh and Blood—The Hammer Heritage of Horror* (1994, TV)

### Miller, Martin

In Britain from 1939, this Czech actor (1899–1969, real name Rudolf Muller) broke into films in 1942 with *Squadron Leader X*, prior to which he was at first on stage in his homeland and in London with the Little Viennese Theater, which he founded. His fifty-plus film credits also include *Latin Quarter* (1945), *The Third Man* (1949), *An Alligator Named Daisy* (1955), *Peeping Tom* (1960), *The Pink Panther* (1963) and *Assignment to Kill*

(1968). He can also be seen as Rossi in Hammer's remake of *The Phantom of the Opera* (1962). His small screen appearances include episodes of *Douglas Fairbanks, Jr. Presents* (1953–1957, TV), *Echo Four Two* (1961, TV), *The Saint* (1962–1969, TV) and *The Prisoner* (1967–1968, TV). His wife was the actress Hannah Norbert (1916–1998). **Hammer credits:** *The Phantom of the Opera* (1962, as Rossi)

### Miller, Philip (Pip)

Following training at the Alleyn stage school, this British actor (1947–) began appearing in minor roles in films, going on to play Jessica Van Helsing's boyfriend Bob Tarrant in Hammer's *Dracula A.D. 1972* (1972). His other film credits include *Crossplot* (1969), *Up the Front* (1972), *Return of the Jedi* (1983), *Defence of the Realm* (1985) and *Sliding Doors* (1998), while his TV appearances include *Mrs. Amworth* (1975, TV [which also appeared in the compilation feature *Three Dangerous Ladies* in 1977]), *Poldark* (1975–1977, TV), *Juliet Bravo* (1980–1985, TV) and *September Song* (1993–1995, TV). His father was the singer Gary Miller (1924–1968, real name Neville Williams), and his brother is the actor Jonty Miller. **Hammer credits:** *Dracula A.D. 1972* (1972, as Bob Tarrant)

### Miller, Stanley

Miller penned the teleplay for *Do Me a Favor and Kill Me*, an episode of Hammer's *Journey to the Unknown* (1968, TV), which also appeared in the compendium film *Journey to Murder* (1972, TVM). He also did some uncredited work on *The New People* for the series, which itself appeared in the compendium *Journey into Darkness* (1968, TVM). His many other credits include episodes of *Saber of London* (1954–1960, TV), *Richard the Lionheart* (1962–1963, TV), *Maupassant* (1963, TV), *Out of the Unknown* (1965–1971, TV), *The Devil in the Fog* (1968, TV), *Smith* (1970, TV) and *Do You Remember?* (1978, TV). His occasional film credits include *Son of a Stranger* (1957) and *Symptoms* (1974). **Hammer credits:** *The New People* (1968, TV [episode of *Journey to the Unknown*], co-teleplay [uncredited]), *Do Me a Favor and Kill Me* (1968, TV [episode of *Journey to the Unknown*], teleplay), *Journey into Darkness* (1968, TVM, co-teleplay [uncredited]), *Journey to Murder* (1972, TVM, co-teleplay)

### Miller, Tallulah

Miller can be seen as one of the pub whores in Hammer's *Hands of the Ripper* (1971). Her other credits include *The Hands of Orlac* (1960). **Hammer credits:** *Hands of the Ripper* (1971, as Third pub whore)

### Millett, David

Millett can be seen as a policeman in *Kill Me a Murder* (1984, TVM [episode of *Hammer House of Mystery and Suspense*]). His other TV credits include episodes of *The Rivals of Sherlock Holmes* (1971–1973, TV), *Van Der Valk* (1972–1977, TV), *Oil Strike North* (1975, TV), *Minder* (1979–1994, TV) and *Reilly: Ace of Spies* (1983, TV). His occasional films include *Psychomania* (1972), *The Finishing Line* (1977) and *The Brute* (1977). **Hammer**

**credits:** *Paint Me a Murder* (1984, TVM [episode of *Hammer House of Mystery and Suspense*], as Police Sergeant)

**Milligan, Spike**

A comedy legend as both a writer and performer, Indian born Milligan (1918–2002, real name Terence Alan Patrick Sean Milligan) is best remembered for writing and co-creating the classic radio comedy *The Goon Show* (1951–1960). In films from 1951 with *Penny Points to Paradise*, his other credits include *Let's Go Crazy* (1951), which he also co-wrote, *Down Among the Z Men* (1952), *The Case of the Mukkinese Battlehorn* (1956), which he also co-wrote, *Invasion Quartet* (1961), *The Bed Sitting Room* (1969), which was based upon his play (co-authored with John Antrobus), *Adolf Hitler—My Part in His Downfall* (1972), which was based upon his novel, *The Three Musketeers* (1973), *Monty Python's Life of Brian* (1979) and *The Big Freeze* (1994). His TV appearances were legion, including *Idiot Weekly, Price 2d* (1956, TV), *A Show Called Fred* (1956, TV), *Curry and Chips* (1969, TV) and the various incarnations of the long-running *Q5* (1969–1980, TV). In 1974 he popped up as himself in Hammer's big screen version of *Man About the House*. His first wife (of three) was actress June Marlow, to whom he was married between 1952 and 1960. His children include writer Laura Milligan (aka Laura Tierney) and actress Jane Milligan (1966–). **Hammer credits:** *Man About the House* (1974, as Himself)

**Mills, Guy**

This British bit-part player (1898–1962, real name Louis Miller) can be seen as a coach driver in Hammer's *Dracula* (1958). His other credits include *The Chinese Bungalow* (1926) and *They Can't Hang Me* (1955), plus episodes of *As I Was Saying* (1955, TV) and *Hancock's Half Hour* (1956–1960, TV). **Hammer credits:** *Dracula* (1958, as Coach driver [uncredited])

**Mills, Jack**

This British cinematographer (?–2005) photographed the second unit for the Hammer comedy *A Weekend with Lulu* (1961). He returned to Hammer to film the second unit for *One Million Years B.C.* (1966) and the second unit and effects for *Twins of Evil* (1971). His work as a camera operator includes *Town on Trial* (1957), *Gorgo* (1960) and *Mysterious Island* (1961). He also photographed such films as *The Young Detectives* (1963), *Siege of the Saxons* (1963) and *Smokescreen* (1964). He was also the effects cameraman on *Captain Nemo and the Underwater City* (1969) and *Scrooge* (1970), and the second unit photographer on the TV series *The Invisible Man* (1958–1960, TV). His father was the assistant director and production manager Frank Mills. **Hammer credits:** *A Weekend with Lulu* (1961, second unit photography), *One Million Years B.C.* (1966, second unit photography), *Twins of Evil* (1971, second unit photography, special effects photography)

**Mills, James**

Mills can be seen in a supporting role in two of Hammer's early fifties productions. His other cred-

its include a TV version of *Macbeth* (1949, TV) and an episode of *The Adventures of Long John Silver* (1955–1959, TV). **Hammer credits:** *Cloudburst* (1951, as Thompson), *Death of an Angel* (1952, as Howard)

**Mills, Kim**

Mills had a minor role in Hammer's *The Stranger Came Home* (1954). **Hammer credits:** *The Stranger Came Home* (1954, as Roddy [uncredited])

**Mills, Reginald**

In films from the late thirties with *What Would You Do, Chums?* (1939), this noted British editor (1912–1990) went on to cut a number of important films in the forties and fifties, among them several for Michael Powell, including *A Matter of Life and Death* (1946), *The Red Shoes* (1948), which earned him an Oscar nomination, *The Small Back Room* (1949) and *The Battle of the River Plate* (1956). From 1954, he was also the preferred editor of director Joseph Losey, who used him on such films as *The Sleeping Tiger* (1954), *Blind Date* (1959), *The Criminal* (1960), *The Servant* (1963) and *King and Country* (1964). Losey also requested Mills' services on Hammer's *The Damned* (1963) as part of his agreeing to do the film. Mills' other editing credits include *Ulysses* (1967), *Romeo and Juliet* (1968), *Ring of Bright Water* (1969), *Brother Sun, Sister Moon* (1972) and the TV series *Jesus of Nazareth* (1977, TV), which earned him a second BAFTA nomination. He also directed one film, *Tales of Beatrix Potter* (1971). **Hammer credits:** *The Damned* (1963)

**Mills, Richard (Dickie)**

Mills worked as the assistant to make-up man Roy Ashton on several films for Hammer in the sixties. His many solo credits, among them several for director Michael Winner, include *The Third Alibi* (1961), *The Double Man* (1967), *I'll Never Forget What's'isname* (1967), *Smashing Time* (1967), *Hannibal Brooks* (1968), *Chato's Land* (1972), *Scorpio* (1972), *The Big Sleep* (1978), *Flash Gordon* (1980), *The Keep* (1983), *Death Wish 3* (1983) and *Willow* (1988), plus a return to Hammer for *When Dinosaurs Ruled the Earth* (1970). **Hammer credits:** *Paranoiac* (1963, assistant make-up [uncredited]), *The Scarlet Blade* (1963, assistant make-up [uncredited]), *The Kiss of the Vampire* (1963, assistant make-up [uncredited]), *Nightmare* (1964, assistant make-up [uncredited]), *The Evil of Frankenstein* (1964, assistant make-up [uncredited]), *The Devil-Ship Pirates* (1964, assistant make-up [uncredited]), *The Gorgon* (1964, assistant make-up [uncredited]), *Fanatic* (1965, assistant make-up), *The Brigand of Kandahar* (1965, co-make-up), *The Plague of the Zombies* (1966, assistant make-up [uncredited]), *When Dinosaurs Ruled the Earth* (1970, make-up)

**Mills, Zsuzsanna**

Hungarian born Mills (1958–, real name Zsuzsanna Szemes) worked as a second assistant director on *Hammer House of Horror* (1980, TV). Her other credits include *Love and Death* (1975) and *Lionheart* (1987). Her husband is cameraman Alec Mills (1932–), whom she married in 1977.

Hammer credits; *Hammer House of Horror* (1980, TV [uncredited])

**Milner, Roger**

Best known for playing Wilcox the butler in *Brideshead Revisited* (1981, TV), this British actor (1925–2014, sometimes Millner) can also be seen as a registrar in *Mark of the Devil* (1984, TVM [episode of *Hammer House of Mystery and Suspense*]). His other TV credits include appearances in such series and one-offs *Clementina* (1954, TV), *Rainbow City* (1967, TV), *A Warning to the Curious* (1972, TV), *Tales of the Unexpected* (1979–1988, TV) and *Dombey and Son* (1983, TV). Also a writer, his screenplays include *The Queen's Guards* (1960), while his TV work takes in *Speed King* (1979, TVM), *PQ17* (1981, TVM), *Amy* (1984, TVM) and *Across the Lake* (1988, TVM); his stage plays include *How's the World Treating You?* (1966). His wife was actress Carol Snape (1934–), whom he married in 1959. **Hammer credits:** *Mark of the Devil* (1984, TVM [episode of *Hammer House of Mystery and Suspense*], as Registrar)

**Milovan** *see* **Milovan and Serena**

**Milovan and Serena**

This cabaret act played The Webers in Hammer's *Vampire Circus* (1972), in which they perform an erotic dance number, she as a green tiger in full body paint and he as her tamer. The couple worked as erotic dancers for The Raymond Revue Bar in 1971, and were featured in a photographic spread in *Men Only* magazine in May the same year (the magazine had recently been taken over by Paul Raymond, owner of the Revue Bar). It was presumably this exposure that brought them to the attention of Hammer. This appears to be the only film appearance of Milovan (full name Milovan Vesnitch). However, Serena (1951–, real name Serena Robinson, aka Serena Blacquelord/Blaquelord/Blacklord and Linda Broome), who had also worked as a dancer at the Folies Bergere, went on to appear in several more films, among them *The Lovers!* (1973), *Black Lolita* (1975), *Le corps de mon ennemi* (1976), *Fantasm* (1976), *Dracula Sucks* (1979), *Small Town Girls* (1979), *Olympic Fever* (1979), *Insatiable* (1980), *Night of the Juggler* (1980), *Aunt Peg* (1980) and *Trashi* (1981). The couple was also featured in further issues of *Men Only*. **Hammer credits:** *Vampire Circus* (1972, as The Webers)

**Serena in full body paint for her famous tiger dance in *Vampire Circus* (1972) (Hammer/Rank/Twentieth Century–Fox).**

## Milsome, Douglas (Doug)

This British cinematographer (1939–) is best known for his work for Stanley Kubrick, for whom he photographed *Full Metal Jacket* (1987), prior to which he worked for the director as a focus puller on *A Clockwork Orange* (1971), *Barry Lyndon* (1975) and *The Shining* (1980); he also worked without credit as a focus advisor on *Eyes Wide Shut* (1999). His early credits as a clapper loader include *High Tide at Noon* (1957), Hammer's *The Curse of the Mummy's Tomb* (1964) and *Modesty Blaise* (1966), while his other work as a focus puller includes *Sinful Davey* (1969), *Ryan's Daughter* (1970) and *The Spy Who Loved Me* (1977). His credits as a camera operator take in *Yentl* (1983), for which he was the second unit operator, *King David* (1985) and *Highlander* (1986), while his work as a fully-fledged cinematographer includes *Wild Horses* (1984), *Robin Hood: Prince of Thieves* (1991), *Highlander: Endgame* (2000), *Until Death* (2007) and *Bitter Harvest* (2017), as well as the TV series *Lonesome Dove* (1989, TV), which earned him an Emmy nomination. **Hammer credits:** *The Curse of the Mummy's Tomb* (1964 [uncredited])

## Mingaye, Don

In films from 1945 at Islington Studios as a junior scenic artist following training at the St. Martin's Lane School of Art, and experience as a scenic painter for the stage, this British designer (1929–2017) began working at Hammer in the mid-fifties as a draughtsman. Like many people who worked long-term for the studio, Mingaye gradually rose to fully-fledged art director following years as an assistant to Hammer's chief set designer Bernard Robinson. Recalled Mingaye of his association with Robinson, "I found that I got on well with Bernard Robinson, so much so that we formed a relationship and started to work on a string of pictures—one after the other, and closer and closer. The guy didn't have to tell me what he wanted to do. Just start to say something, or make a gesture, and I knew exactly what it was."[50] Mingaye and Robinson also re-used much of the scenery they designed, often incorporating ideas for future sets into current projects. Revealed Mingaye, "We did accommodate … for the picture we were going to make in, say, six months time in that current set. So in fact we were always dove-tailing and making one thing leading to another."[51] Mingaye was first promoted to assistant art director on the remake of *The Hound of the Baskervilles* (1959) and then to art director on *The Curse of the Werewolf* (1961). His first solo project for the studio, during a rare absence by Bernard Robinson, was *The Evil of Frankenstein* (1964), which contains some notable sets for Frankenstein's lab and his derelict chateau, although he also made use of recycled elements from sets designed by Robinson for other films, among them a staircase already seen in *Dracula* (1958) and *The Revenge of Frankenstein* (1958). His work for *Dracula A.D. 1972* (1972), for which he was credited as production designer, added a touch of visual flair to the proceedings, among his sets being the Cavern coffee bar, with its Plexiglas cobweb décor, and Johnny Alucard's trendy split-level Chelsea pad.

Mingaye's non–Hammer credits as an assistant art director include *Private Potter* (1962), *The Deadly Bees* (1966), *Torture Garden* (1967), *Can Heironymus Merkin Ever Forget Mercy Humppe and Find True Happiness?* (1969) and *The Human Factor* (1979), while his credits as an art director include *Danger Route* (1967), *They Came from Beyond Space* (1967), *Salt & Pepper* (1968), *Scream and Scream Again* (1970), *The Mind of Mr. Soames* (1970), *Our Miss Fred* (1972) and *Tusks* (1988). **Additional notes:** Owing to the vagaries of releasing schedules, *The Terror of the Tongs* (1961), on which he worked an uncredited assistant art director, was made before but released after *The Curse of the Werewolf* (1961), *The Shadow of the Cat* (1961) and *Watch It, Sailor!* (1961), on which he'd graduated to art director. **Hammer credits:** *X—The Unknown* (1956, draughtsman [uncredited]), *The Curse of Frankenstein* (1957, draughtsman [uncredited]), *Quatermass 2* (1957, draughtsman [uncredited]), *The Camp on Blood Island* (1958, draughtsman [uncredited]), *Dracula* (1958, draughtsman [uncredited]), *The Revenge of Frankenstein* (1958, draughtsman [uncredited]), *The Hound of the Baskervilles* (1959, assistant art director [uncredited]), *The Ugly Duckling* (1959, assistant art director), *Yesterday's Enemy* (1959, assistant art director [uncredited]), *The Mummy* (1959, assistant art director [uncredited]), *The Stranglers of Bombay* (1959, assistant art director [uncredited]), *Never Take Sweets from a Stranger* (1960, assistant art director [uncredited]), *The Brides of Dracula* (1960, assistant art director [uncredited]), *The Two Faces of Dr. Jekyll* (1960, assistant art director [uncredited]), *Visa to Canton* (1960, assistant art director [uncredited]), *The Curse of the Werewolf* (1961, art director), *The Shadow of the Cat* (1961, art director), *Watch It, Sailor!* (1961, art director), *The Terror of the Tongs* (1961, assistant art director [uncredited]), *Cash on Demand* (1961, art director), *The Phantom of the Opera* (1962, art director), *Captain Clegg* (1962, art director), *The Pirates of Blood River* (1962, art director), *Paranoiac* (1963, art director), *The Damned* (1963, art director [uncredited]), *The Scarlet Blade* (1963, art director), *The Kiss of the Vampire* (1963, art director), *Nightmare* (1964, art director), *The Evil of Frankenstein* (1964, art director), *The Devil-Ship Pirates* (1964, art director), *The Gorgon* (1964, art director), *The Curse of the Mummy's Tomb* (1964, art director), *The Runaway* (1964, art director), *She* (1965, assistant art director), *The Brigand of Kandahar* (1965, art director), *Dracula—Prince of Darkness* (1966, art director), *The Plague of the Zombies* (1966, art director), *Rasputin—The Mad Monk* (1966, art director), *The Reptile* (1966, art director), *The Witches* (1966, art director), *Frankenstein Created Woman* (1967, art director), *The Mummy's Shroud* (1967, art director), *Lust for a Vampire* (1971, art director), *Dracula A.D. 1972* (1972, production designer)

## Mingaye, R. (Roy) A.

British born Mingaye (1931–2017) worked as the boom assistant on the Hammer thriller *Paranoiac* (1963), which led to work on a handful of other productions for the studio. His other credits

include *Cul-de-Sac* (1966), on which he was a sound assistant, *Battle of Britain* (1969), on which he worked as sound maintenance, and *Let It Be* (1970), on which he was a boom operator. **Hammer credits:** *Paranoiac* (1963 [uncredited]), *The Kiss of the Vampire* (1963 [uncredited]), *Nightmare* (1964 [uncredited]), *The Evil of Frankenstein* (1964 [uncredited]), *The Devil-Ship Pirates* (1964 [uncredited]), *The Gorgon* (1964 [uncredited])

## Mintz, Robert

Mintz worked as the post-production consultant on the Fox-Hammer TV series *Journey to the Unknown* (1968, TV). He also worked in this capacity on such series as *12 O'Clock High* (1964–1967, TV), *Daniel Boone* (1964–1970, TV), *Voyage to the Bottom of the Sea* (1964–1968, TV), *The Green Hornet* (1966–1967, TV), *The Time Tunnel* (1966–1967, TV), *Lost in Space* (1965–1968, TV), *Batman* (1966–1968, TV), two episodes of which he also wrote, and *Land of the Giants* (1968–1970, TV), all of which were produced by Fox. His credits as an associate producer include *Cade's County* (1971–1972, TV), *Matt Helm* (1975, TVM), *The Lindbergh Kidnapping Case* (1976, TVM) and *Never Con a Killer* (1977, TVM). He also worked as a co-producer, associate producer, producer, executive producer and completion guarantor on various films and series, among them *The Ghost and Mrs. Muir* (1968–1970, TV), on which he was an associate producer, and *Tabitha* (1977–1978, TV), on which he was a co-producer. **Hammer credits:** *Journey to the Unknown* (1968, TV)

*Miss Belle see Journey to the Unknown*

**Miss C. Smith** *see* **Smith, Cornelia**

## Mitchell, Andrew

Mitchell served on Hammer's board of directors between 1993 and 1996.

## Mitchell, Bill (William)

Known for his deep basso voice, this Canadian actor and voice over artist (1934–1997, full name William Mitchell McAllister, aka Bill McAllister) can be heard speaking the delightfully hammy prologue and epilogue to Hammer's LP version of *Dracula* (1974, LP). On television from 1959 and in films from 1962, his credits as an actor include *Night of the Eagle* (1962), *You Only Live Twice* (1967), *Billion Dollar Brain* (1967), *The Bitch* (1979) and *Riding High* (1981), plus episodes of *BBC Sunday-Night Theatre* (1950–1959, TV), *Doctor Who* (1963–1989, TV) and *Supergran* (1985–1987, TV), in which he played the Reporter. He also provided the narration for *The Beast Must Die* (1974) and (with Bob Saget) the voice of Wurlitzer for *Outer Touch* (1979). He also provided voiceovers for many film trailers, among them those for *The Creeping Flesh* (1972), *From Beyond the Grave* (1974), *Time Bandits* (1981) and *The Doctor and the Devils* (1986), as well as commercials, among them those for Cadbury's Flake and Carlsberg. **Hammer credits:** *Dracula* (1974, LP)

## Mitchell, Douglas

Mitchell appeared as Will Scarlett in Hammer's *A Challenge for Robin Hood* (1967). His other credits include *Curse of the Crimson Altar* (1968) and episodes of *Sir Arthur Conan Doyle* (1967, TV) and *The Search for the Nile* (1971, TV). **Hammer credits:** *A Challenge for Robin Hood* (1967, as Will Scarlett)

### Mitchell, George *see* The George Mitchell Singers

### Mitchell, Jennifer

Mitchell appeared in the Hammer comedy *I Only Arsked!* (1958) as one of the harem girls. Her other credits include *Lilacs in the Spring* (1954). **Hammer credits:** *I Only Arsked!* (1958, as Harem girl [uncredited])

### Mitchell, John (W.)

This prolific British sound technician (1917–2005, full name John William Mitchell) worked as a sound camera assistant on Hammer's very first production, *The Public Life of Henry the Ninth* (1935). After working as either a sound assistant or boom operator on *The Secret of the Loch* (1934), *Sing As We Go* (1934), *No Limit* (1935), *Elephant Boy* (1937), *Victoria the Great* (1937) and *Contraband* (1940) among others, he went on to record well over one-hundred films, among them *They Made Me a Fugitive* (1947), *Hamlet* (1948), *So Long at the Fair* (1950), *Genevieve* (1953), *Doctor in the House* (1954), *The 39 Steps* (1959), *From Russia with Love* (1963), *The Spy Who Came in from the Cold* (1965), *Arabesque* (1966), *Billion Dollar Brain* (1967), *Casino Royale* (1967), *You Only Live Twice* (1967), *On Her Majesty's Secret Service* (1969), *Diamonds Are Forever* (1971), which earned him a shared Oscar nomination, *Live and Let Die* (1973), *Gold* (1974), which earned him a shared BAFTA nomination, *The Black Windmill* (1974), *Death on the Nile* (1978), *Evil Under the Sun* (1982), *A Passage to India* (1984), which earned him a second shared Oscar nomination, and *Manhunter* (1986). He also won a shared Emmy for his work on *The Scarlet and the Black* (1983, TVM). He also worked as the sound mixer on Hammer's *Sword of Sherwood Forest* (1960). He was made an MBE in 2001. He wrote about his film experiences in *Flickering Shadows—A Lifetime in Film* (1997). **Hammer credits:** *The Public Life of Henry the Ninth* (1935, sound camera assistant [uncredited]), *Sword of Sherwood Forest* (1960, sound mixer)

### Mitchell, June

This British actress (1933–2009, real name Elizabeth June Thornton, aka Elizabeth Shipp) can be seen as one of three busty blondes in the opening scene in Hammer's *Wings of Danger* (1952). She also had a small role as a secretary in *Never Look Back* (1952). Her other credits include *Reluctant Heroes* (1951), *It Started in Paradise* (1952), *Gaby* (1956) and *D–Day the Sixth of June* (1956). Her sister was the actress Christine Norden (1924–1988, real name Mary Lydia Thornton), who appeared in two films for Hammer: *The Black Widow* (1950) and *A Case for PC 49* (1951). **Hammer credits:** *Wings of Danger* (1952, as Blonde), *Never Look Back* (1952, as Secretary)

### Mitchell, Malcolm

This British bandleader and musician (1926–1998) appeared in the Hammer featurette *Parade of the Bands* (1956). He can also be seen (with his trio) in *Star of My Night* (1954). Credits as a composer include *That Kind of Girl* (1963), *The Yellow Teddybears* (1963) and *Revolutions for All* (1967), plus the TV series *Mad Movies* (1966, TV). **Hammer credits:** *Parade of the Bands* (1956, as Himself)

### Mitchell, Norman

This gruff-spoken British supporting actor (1918–2001, full name Norman Mitchell Driver) was frequently cast as villains and crooks, among them the highwayman Rooks in the Hammer featurette *Dick Turpin—Highwayman* (1956). In films from 1954 with *The Seekers* following training in medicine (he subsequently spent six years in the Royal Army Medical Corps during World War two), his many other credits include *The Man Who Wouldn't Talk* (1958), *Carry On Spying* (1964), *Carry On Screaming* (1966), *The Great St. Trinian's Train Robbery* (1966), *Half a Sixpence* (1967), *Oliver!* (1968), *Twisted Nerve* (1968) and *The Pink Panther Strikes Again* (1976), plus six further appearances for Hammer, largest among them the crooked Vernon Smallpiece in *Nearest and Dearest* (1973). Also much on television from 1951, his credits here include episodes of *The Adventures of Sir Lancelot* (1956–1957, TV), *Lorna Doone* (1963, TV), *The Prisoner* (1967–1968, TV), *Up Pompeii* (1969–1970, TV), *The Boy with Two Heads* (1974, TV), *Whatever Happened to the Likely Lads?* (1973–1974, TV), *Beryl's Lot* (1973–1977, TV), in which he played Charlie Mills, *George and Mildred* (1976–1979, TV) and *You Rang, M'Lord?* (1988–1993, TV). Also much on radio. His son was the actor Christopher Mitchell (1947–2001). **Hammer credits:** *Dick Turpin—Highwayman* (1956, as Rooks), *A Challenge for Robin Hood* (1967, as Dray driver), *On the Buses* (1971, as London Transport official), *Nearest and Dearest* (1973, as Vernon Smallpiece), *Frankenstein and the Monster from Hell* (1974, as Police Sergeant), *Man About the House* (1974, as Doorman [Arthur Mullgrave]), *Last Video and Testament* (1984, TVM [episode of *Hammer House of Mystery and Suspense*], as Commissionaire)

### Mitchell, Paul

Mitchell worked as a standby rigger on Hammer's *Scars of Dracula* (1970). His other credits as a rigger include *Lifeforce* (1985), *Who Framed Roger Rabbit* (1988), *Indiana Jones and the Last Crusade* (1989), *The World Is Not Enough* (1999), *Sahara* (2005), *Eastern Promises* (2007), *Elizabeth: The Golden Age* (2007) and *The Wolfman* (2010). **Hammer credits:** *Scars of Dracula* (1970 [uncredited])

### Mitchell, Warren

This admired British character actor (1926–2015, real name Warren Misell) will forever be remembered as the bigoted Alf Garnett, a role he played intermittently from 1966 to 1998 in such television series, films and one-offs as *Till Death Us Do Part* (1966–1968, 1972–1975, TV), *Till Death Us Do Part* (1968), *The Alf Garnett Saga* (1972), *Till Death...* (1981, TV), *In Sickness and in Health* (1985–1992, TV), *A Word with Alf* (1991, TV), *An Audience with Alf Garnett* (1997, TV) and *The Thoughts of Chairman Alf* (1998, TV), the latter of which he'd also performed on stage in 1976 (Mitchell stopped playing the role after the death of its writer and creator Johnny Speight in 1998). He also guested as the character in episodes of such series as *A Christmas Night with the Stars* (1958–1994, TV) in 1967 and 1971, *It's Lulu* (1970–1973, TV) in 1973, *The Ernie Sigley Show* (1974–1976, TV) in 1975, and *The Generation Game* (1971–2001, TV) in 1975 among others.

On stage from the age of seven, Mitchell went on to study physical chemistry at Oxford University in 1944, but left soon after to join the RAF. After the war he went to train at RADA, following which he gained further experience on both stage and radio before breaking into television in the mid-fifties. He began making films in 1954 with a walk-on in Hammer's *Five Days*, and went on to appear in over fifty productions, among them *The Passing Stranger* (1954), *Tommy the Toreador* (1959), *Carry On Cleo* (1964), *The Night Caller* (1965), *Help!* (1965), *The Assassination Bureau* (1968), *The Best House in London* (1969), *All the Way Up* (1970), *Stand Up, Virgin Soldiers* (1977), *Norman Loves Rose* (1982), *The Chain* (1985), *Kokoda Crescent* (1988), *Crackers* (1998) and *The 10th Man* (2010). He also crossed paths with Hammer four more times, at first in small roles, but concluding with a leading role in the misguided space opera *Moon Zero Two* (1969), his performance in which *Variety* described as "tongue in cheek," while *Photoplay* averred that his character was "the type of villain designed to make you hiss and boo every time he appears."

Despite his busy film and television schedules, Mitchell remained active on stage throughout his career, appearing regularly in both Britain and Australia (he held dual UK-Australian citizenship from 1988), most notably in two Arthur Miller plays, *Death of a Salesman* (1949) in 1979 and *The Price* (1968) in 2003, both of which earned him Olivier awards (he also filmed *Death of a Salesman* for television in 1996). His appearances as Alf Garnett aside, his other TV work includes episodes of *The Children of the New Forest* (1955, TV), *Man from Interpol* (1960–1961, TV), *Colonel Trumper's Private War* (1961, TV), *The Avengers* (1961–1969, TV), *Danger Man* (1964–1966, TV), *Men of Affairs* (1973–1974, TV), *The Galton and Simpson Playhouse* (1977, TV), *Tickets for the Titanic* (1987, TV), *Gormenghast* (2000, TV) and *Waking the Dead* (2000–2011, TV). He was married to the actress Constance Wake, whom he wed in 1951; their children include the actor Daniel Mitchell and the actress Georgia Mitchell (1968–). **Additional notes:** The role of Alf Garnett was subsequently played by Simon Day in a 2016 remake of a 1967 episode of *Till Death Us Do Part* titled *A Woman's Place Is in the Home*. **Hammer credits:** *Five Days* (1954, as Man in bar [uncredited]), *The Stranglers of Bombay* (1959, as Merchant), *Hell Is a City* (1960, as Travelling salesman), *The Curse of the Werewolf* (1961, as Pepe Valiente), *Moon Zero Two* (1969, as J.J. Hubbard)

## Mitchell, Yvonne

On stage from the age of fourteen, this respected British actress (1915–1979, real name Yvonne Frances Joseph) made her official film debut in *The Queen of Spades* (1948), though prior to this she had appeared as an extra in *Love on the Dole* (1941). She went on to appear in, among others, *The Divided Heart* (1954), which won her a best actress BAFTA, *Woman in a Dressing Gown* (1957), *Sapphire* (1959), which earned her a BAFTA nomination for best actress, *The Trials of Oscar Wilde* (1960), *The Corpse* (1969) and *The Incredible Sarah* (1976). She also appeared in Hammer's *Demons of the Mind* (1972) as Aunt Hilda. She was also considered for the role of Margaret in Hammer's *To the Devil a Daughter* (1976). Also on television, she appeared in such one-offs and series as *1984* (1954, TV), *Out of the Unknown* (1965–1971, TV), *The Legend of Robin Hood* (1975, TV) and *1900* (1977–1978, TV). She also wrote a number of plays and novels, among them the drama *The Same Sky*, which was filmed for television three times, as episodes of *BBC Sunday-Night Theatre* (1950–1959, TV) in 1952, *Armchair Theatre* (1956–1974, TV) in 1956, and *Thursday Theatre* (1964–1965, TV) in 1964 (she appeared in the first two versions in the role of Esther Brodsky). Her other works include a biography of Colette and her own autobiography, which was published in 1957. Her husband was the critic and novelist Derek Monsey (1921–1979), to whom she was married twice, in 1952 and 1978. Their daughter is actress and assistant stage director Cordelia Monsey (1956–, aka Cordelia Mitchell). **Hammer credits:** *Demons of the Mind* (1972, as Aunt Hilda)

## Mockler, Suzanne

Mockler (1944–) played the role of Susan Redford in *The New People*, an episode of Hammer's *Journey to the Unknown* (1968, TV) which also appeared in the compendium film *Journey into Darkness* (1968, TVM). Her other credits include appearances in *The Villains* (1964–1965, TV), *Pity About the Abbey* (1965, TVM) and *Adam Adamant Lives!* (1966–1967, TV). **Hammer credits:** *The New People* (1968, TV [episode of *Journey to the Unknown*], as Susan Redford), *Journey into Darkness* (1968, TVM, as Susan Redford)

## Mohner, Carl

This Austrian leading man (1921–2005) co-starred with Andre Morrell in Hammer's brutal POW drama *The Camp on Blood Island* (1958). Working in both Britain and Europe, his other credits include *Vagabunden* (1949), *The Key* (1958), *Sink the Bismarck!* (1960), *L'uomo di Toledo* (1965), *Khartoum* (1966), *Hell Is Empty* (1967), *Callan* (1974) and *Scar Tissue* (1975). He also wrote and directed *Istanbul Adventure* (1958) and wrote, directed, scored and appeared in *Inshalla, Razzia am Bosporus* (1962). **Hammer credits:** *The Camp on Blood Island* (1958, as Pierre Van Elst)

## Mohr, George (Georg)

Mohr worked as the production manager on the Berlin-shot thriller *Ten Seconds to Hell* (1959) for Hammer. His other credits include *Zu nuen Ufern* (1937), *Bismarck* (1940), *Die Hexe* (1954), *Stresemann* (1957) and *Fabrik der Offiziere* (1960). **Hammer credits:** *Ten Seconds to Hell* (1959)

## Moir, Gunner

This British heavyweight boxer turned actor (1879–1939, real name James Moir) appeared in Hammer's second film, *The Mystery of the Mary Celeste* (1935), as Ponta Katz. His other credits include *Third Time Lucky* (1930), *Side Streets* (1933), *King of the Damned* (1935) and *Excuse My Glove* (1936). The British champion between 1906 and 1909, he took up boxing while serving in the army in India, becoming the Heavyweight Champion of the British Army in India in 1903. After retiring from the sport in 1913 (after being beaten by Bombardier Billy Wells, who went on to strike the anvil in Hammer's thirties logo), he went on to manage a music hall (London's Canterbury Music Hall) and penned an instructional book, *The Complete Boxer* (1930). **Hammer credits:** *The Mystery of the Mary Celeste* (1935, as Ponta Katz)

## Mole Richardson (Mole-Richardson, the Mole Richardson Company)

This lighting supply company provided the lights for Hammer's location-shot *Creatures the World Forgot* (1971). Founded in Hollywood in 1927 by Sicilian born Peter Mole (1891–1960, real name Pietro Mule) and American born Elmer C. Richardson, the company has supplied lighting equipment to many films and TV shows down the decades (among them many European productions), from *Gone with the Wind* (1939) through to *The Three Musketeers* (1973), *Gold* (1974), *The Four Musketeers* (1975), *Sexy Beast* (2000), *The Artist* (2011) and *American Homestead* (2014). The company has won many awards over the years for its various technical developments, achievements and innovations, among them the invention of the Fresnel Solar Spot unit. During the Second World War, the company helped to develop searchlights for military use. **Hammer credits:** *Creatures the World Forgot* (1971)

## *The Molester* see *Never Take Sweets from a Stranger*

## Molho

This furrier provided pieces for four of Hammer's fifties co-features, including those for the fashion house sequences in *Blood Orange* (1953), as well as those sported by Hollywood star Paulette Goddard in *The Stranger Came Home* (1954). His other credits (all as furrier) include *Calling Paul Temple* (1948), *Paul Temple's Triumph* (1950), *Old Mother Riley's Jungle Treasure* (1951), *Hammer the Toff* (1952), *Doctor in the House* (1954), *To Dorothy a Son* (1954), *Value for Money* (1955), *Simon and Laura* (1955) and *Man of the Moment* (1955). **Hammer credits:** *Blood Orange* (1953), *36 Hours* (1953 [uncredited]), *The Stranger Came Home* (1954), *Murder by Proxy* (1955)

## Mollison, Clifford

On stage from the age of sixteen, this British actor (1897–1986) began appearing in films in the thirties, among his early credits being *Almost a Honeymoon* (1930), *The Lucky Number* (1933) and *Mister Cinders* (1934), taking the lead role in the latter. Following army experience during World War II, he resumed his stage and film career, taking smaller character roles in such movies as *Scrooge* (1951), *The Baby and the Battleship* (1956), *The V.I.P.s* (1963) and *Oh! What a Lovely War* (1969). He rounded out his film career with minor roles in three films for Hammer. His occasional TV credits include appearances in *No Hiding Place* (1959–1967, TV), *Doctor at Large* (1971, TV), *Angels* (1975–1983, TV) and *Keep It in the Family* (1980–1983, TV). His brother was the actor Henry Mollison (1905–1985, real name Evelyn Henry Mollison), who appeared in Hammer's *What the Butler Saw* (1950). **Hammer credits:** *That's Your Funeral* (1973, as Witherspoon), *Love Thy Neighbour* (1973, as Registrar), *Frankenstein and the Monster from Hell* (1974, as Judge)

## Mollison, Henry

On stage from the age of nineteen, this British actor (1905–1985, full name Evelyn Henry Mollison) made his film debut in *Balaclava* (1928), which he followed with the likes of *Knowing Men* (1930), *Third Time Lucky* (1931), *Drake of England* (1935), *The Great Impersonation* (1937) and *The Windmill* (1937). Following military experience during World War II (during which he was held as a POW), he continued his movie career with *Hungry Hill* (1947), *The Loves of Joanna Godden* (1947), *Whisky Galore!* (1949), *The Man in the White Suit* (1951) and *Front Page Story* (1953). He also appeared as Bembridge in the Hammer comedy *What the Butler Saw* (1950). Married twice, his first wife was the actress Jane Welsh (1905–2001, real name Louisa Joyce Tudor-Jones), to whom he was married between 1928 and 1937; she appeared in Hammer's *Mantrap* (1953). His second wife was the actress Linda Basquette (1907–1994, real name Lena Copeland Baskette) to whom he was married between 1938 and 1947. His brother was the actor Clifford Mollison (1897–1986), who appeared in three films for Hammer. **Hammer credits:** *What the Butler Saw* (1950, as Bembridge)

## Money, Tommy (Tom)

As Hammer's head prop man during the company's formative post-war years, British born Money (1917–1974) worked (without screen credit) on such films as *Dr. Morelle—The Case of the Missing Heiress* (1949) and *The Man in Black* (1950). He remained with the company throughout the fifties and early sixties, working on such key productions as *The Quatermass Xperiment* (1955), *The Curse of Frankenstein* (1957) and *Dracula* (1958). Recalled art director Don Mingaye of Money: "[He] was a prop man in the theater originally and then he came to Hammer to become their property master, and it was quite a responsibility."[52] Money's other credits include *Things Happen at Night* (1948) and *Trog* (1970). **Hammer credits include:** *Dr. Morelle—The Case of the Missing Heiress* (1949 [uncredited]), *The Adventures of PC 49—The Case of the Guardian Angel* (1949 [uncredited]), *Celia* (1949 [uncredited]), *Meet Simon Cherry* (1949 [uncredited]),

*The Man in Black* (1950 [uncredited]), *Someone at the Door* (1950 [uncredited]), *What the Butler Saw* (1950 [uncredited]), *The Quatermass Xperiment* (1955 [uncredited]), *X—The Unknown* (1956 [uncredited]), *The Curse of Frankenstein* (1957 [uncredited]), *Quatermass 2* (1957 [uncredited]), *The Abominable Snowman* (1957 [uncredited]), *The Camp on Blood Island* (1958), *Dracula* (1958 [uncredited]), *The Revenge of Frankenstein* (1958 [uncredited]), *The Hound of the Baskervilles* (1959 [uncredited]), *The Ugly Duckling* (1959), *The Mummy* (1959 [uncredited]), *The Man Who Could Cheat Death* (1959 [uncredited]), *The Stranglers of Bombay* (1959 [uncredited]), *Never Take Sweets from a Stranger* (1960 [uncredited]), *The Brides of Dracula* (1960 [uncredited]), *The Two Faces of Dr. Jekyll* (1960 [uncredited]), *The Curse of the Werewolf* (1961 [uncredited]), *The Shadow of the Cat* (1961 [uncredited]), *The Terror of the Tongs* (1961 [uncredited]), *Cash on Demand* (1961 [uncredited]), *The Phantom of the Opera* (1962 [uncredited]), *Captain Clegg* (1962 [uncredited]), *The Pirates of Blood River* (1962 [uncredited]), *Paranoiac* (1963 [uncredited]), *The Damned* (1963 [uncredited]), *The Scarlet Blade* (1963 [uncredited]), *The Kiss of the Vampire* (1963 [uncredited]), *The Old Dark House* (1963 [uncredited]), *Nightmare* (1964 [uncredited]), *The Evil of Frankenstein* (1964 [uncredited]), *The Devil-Ship Pirates* (1964 [uncredited]), *The Gorgon* (1964 [uncredited]))

### Monk, Colin

British born Monk (1945–) worked as a draughtsman on Hammer's *One Million Years B.C.* (1966). His other credits in this capacity include *The Deadly Affair* (1966). His later work as a designer includes episodes of such series as *Within These Walls* (1974–1978, TV), *Mind Your Language* (1977–1979, 1986, TV), *Me and My Girl* (1984–1988, TV), *Dempsey and Makepeace* (1985–1986, TV), *The Knock* (1994–2000, TV) and *Murder in Mind* (2001–2003, TV). **Hammer credits:** *One Million Years B.C.* (1966 [uncredited])

### Monkhouse, Bob

One of the legends of British comedy, this actor, scriptwriter, stand-up comic and game show host (1928–2003, full name Robert Alan Monkhouse) began his career as a comic illustrator and short story writer while still at school. Following experience as an animator, Monkhouse became involved with troop shows during his national service in the RAF, which led to work as a writer and comedian on radio from 1948, among his early successes being the Arthur Askey vehicle *Hello, Playmates* (1938–1949), which he co-wrote and also performed in with his most frequent writing partner, Denis Goodwin. In films from 1952 with *Secret People*, Monkhouse went on to appear in a handful of shorts and features, among them *Carry On Sergeant* (1958), *Dentist in the Chair* (1960), for which he also provided additional script material, *Dentist on the Job* (1961), the script for which he again contributed to, *She'll Have to Go* (1962), *Thunderbirds Are Go* (1966 [vocals only]), *The Bliss of Mrs. Blossom* (1968) and *Simon Simon* (1970). He also starred in the Hammer comedy *A Weekend with Lulu* (1961). On television from the early fifties, Monkhouse's many series include *Fast and Loose* (1954, TV), *The Golden Shot* (1967–1975, TV), *Family Fortunes* (1980–, TV), *Celebrity Squares* (1975–1979, 1993–1995, TV) and *Wipeout* (1995–2003, TV), to name but a few, plus countless guest star appearances and one-off specials. **Hammer credits:** *A Weekend with Lulu* (1961, as Fred Scrutton)

### Monlaur, Yvonne

This French actress (1939–2017) won the role of student teacher Marianne Danielle, who finds herself surrounded by vampires in Hammer's *The Brides of Dracula* (1960), thanks to her appearance in *Circus of Horrors* (1960). Described by Hammer's publicists as "France's latest sex kitten," Monlaur found herself performing opposite such British stalwarts as Peter Cushing, Martita Hunt and Freda Jackson. Nevertheless, she appears to have enjoyed the experience, and later recalled that, "Often strong sequences would be shot in a relaxed atmosphere with jokes and nice cups of tea."[53] However, her performance failed to impress the film's screenwriter Jimmy Sangster, who described her as, "Pretty as a picture, but with very little talent. Or maybe she had talent and Terry Fisher just couldn't bring it out."[54]

Monlaur returned to Hammer to appear in *The Terror of the Tongs* (1961) as Lee, a Tong bond slave who helps the hero uncover the murderous secret sect. Commented the *New York Herald Tribune* somewhat ungentlemanly of her performance in the film: "[She] wears a skirt split the length of her thigh but otherwise is not remarkable."

In films from 1956 with *Treize a table*, Monlaur's other credits include *Mannequins de Paris* (1956), *Les collégniennes* (1957), *Inn for Trouble* (1960), *Time to Remember* (1962), *Le concerto de la peur* (1963), *Nick Carter va tout casser* (1964) and *Le ciel sur la tete* (1965). She also popped up in such series as *The Third Man* (1959–1965, TV), episodes of *Tales of the Vikings* (1959–1960, TV), *Bayard* (1964, TV) and *Der Tod lauft hinterher* (1967, TV). **Additional notes:** Monlaur just missed out on being cast as Domino in *Thunderball* (1965); Claudine Auger instead bagged the role. **Hammer credits:** *The Brides of Dracula* (1960, as Marianne Danielle), *The Terror of the Tongs* (1961, as Lee)

### Monolulu, Prince

Born in the Danish West Indies, Monolulu (1881–1965, real name Peter Karl McKay, aka Ras Prince Monolulu) carved out a career for himself in Britain as a racing tipster, having famously backed the winner of the 1920 Epsom Derby against great odds. Such became his fame (catchphrase: "I gotta horse!") that he subsequently appeared as either himself or a racing tipster in a number of films, among them the Hammer second feature *The Gambler and the Lady* (1953). His other credits include *Dandy Dick* (1935), *Educated Evans* (1936), *Derby Day* (1952), *An Alligator Named Daisy* (1955), *Make Mine a Million* (1959) and *The Criminal* (1960). **Hammer credits:** *The Gambler and the Lady* (1953, as Himself [uncredited])

### *The Monster and the Woman* see *Four Sided Triangle*

**Yvonne Monlaur experiences a nasty moment in this lobby card for *The Brides of Dracula* (1960) (Hammer/Hotspur/Rank/Universal-International).**

### Monster Mag

Although it dealt with horror films from a variety of sources, this seventies poster magazine (seventeen issues between 1973 and 1976) featured a number of Hammer covers and posters, among them *Twins of Evil* (1971), *Vampire Circus* (1972) and *Frankenstein and the Monster from Hell* (1974). Edited in its later life by Dez Skinn, who went on to edit and create *The House of Hammer* (aka *Halls of Horror*), the sixteen-page foldout (tagline: "Open it out if you dare!") featured articles by the likes of John Brosnan, John Baxter and Barry Pattison, and was a must-have at the time in the school playground (despite being "For sale to adults only"). Published by Warner, the magazine originally retailed for 15p. Other films featured on the cover included *Doomwatch* (1972) and *Legend of the Werewolf* (1975). In 2014, the banned #2, which was destroyed by Customs & Excise in 1973 (thus making it the most sought after film magazine ever), was re-printed in by Quality, along with #1 and #18 (the never-printed "double X special").

### Montague, Lee

A familiar face on stage, in films and on television, the big screen credits of this British actor (1927–) include *Moulin Rouge* (1952), *The Savage Innocents* (1960), *Billy Budd* (1962), *The Best Pair of Legs in the Business* (1972), *Mahler* (1974) and *Madame Sousatzka* (1988). He can also be seen as Officer Nangdon in Hammer's POW drama *The Camp on Blood Island* (1958) and as Levy in the unrelated follow-up *The Secret of Blood Island* (1965). Of his many TV credits, he has the distinction of being the fist reader on the children's storybook series *Jackanory* (1965–2006, TV). His other small screen appearances include episodes of everything from *The Count of Monte Cristo* (1956, TV) to *Love Soup* (2005–2008, TV). Also on stage. His wife is the actress Ruth Goring (1927–), whom he married in 1955. **Hammer credits:** *The Camp on Blood Island* (1958, as Officer Nangdon), *The Secret of Blood Island* (1965, as Levy)

### Monteros, Rosenda

Best known for playing Petra in *The Magnificent Seven* (1960), this exotic-looking Mexican actress (1935–2018, aka Rosa Mendez) also played the role of Ustane in Hammer's *She* (1965), using her charms to lure John Richardson's Leo Vincey into the clutches of her mistress, Ayesha, played by Ursula Andress. Commented *Variety* of her performance, "All other players are good in routine roles, particularly Monteros as the competing love interest who loses her man and her life." Her other credits include *The White Orchid* (1954), *Tiara Tahiti* (1962), *The Mighty Jungle* (1965), *The Face of Eve* (1968), *Nazarin* (1968), *Cauldron of Blood* (1970), *La casa de Bernarda Alba* (1974, TVM [also 1987 remake, in different roles]) and *Sexo impostor* (2005), plus episodes of *Captain David Grief* (1957–1959, TV), *Espejismo brillaba* (1966, TV), *Santa* (1978, TV), *Los Pardaillan* (1981, TV) and *Lo que callamos las mujeres* (2007, TV). She was married to actor Julio Brancho (1909–1978, full name Julio Brancho Gavilan) between 1955 and 1957. **Hammer credits:** *She* (1965, as Ustane)

### Montgomery, Andrew

Montgomery worked as one of the assistant directors on Hammer's remake of *The Lady Vanishes* (1979). His other credits include *The Legacy* (1978), *P'Tang, Yang, Kipperbang* (1982, TVM), *Testimony* (1987) and *The Dawning* (1988). He also worked as the second unit second assistant director on *The Empire Strikes Back* (1980) and as the second assistant director on *Excalibur* (1981). He went on to work as the location manager on *Off Limits* (1988) and *Saigon* (1988), following which he turned producer with the TV series *The Good Guys* (1992–1993, TV). **Hammer credits:** *The Lady Vanishes* (1979 [uncredited])

### Montsash, Henry

This British hair stylist (1905–1974) was brought in to work on the Hammer shocker *The Curse of Frankenstein* (1957), for which he provided the cast with suitable mid–19th-century coifs. After this he remained with the company for many more films and featurettes, prime among them *Dracula* (1958). His other credits include *The Gorbals Story* (1950), *The Blue Parrot* (1953), *The Skull* (1965), *Dr. Who and the Daleks* (1965), remembered for the dreadful blonde wigs worn by the Thals, *The Psychopath* (1966), *Witchfinder General* (1968) and *The Fiend* (1971), plus episodes of such cult television series as *Randall and Hopkirk (Deceased)* (1969–1971, TV) and *UFO* (1970, TV), the latter of which is remembered for the dreadful purple wigs sported by certain members of the cast. **Hammer credits:** *The Curse of Frankenstein* (1957), *The Abominable Snowman* (1957), *Danger List* (1957), *The Camp on Blood Island* (1958), *Dracula* (1958), *Clean Sweep* (1958), *The Snorkel* (1958), *The Revenge of Frankenstein* (1958), *I Only Arsked!* (1958), *The Hound of the Baskervilles* (1959), *The Ugly Duckling* (1959), *Yesterday's Enemy* (1959), *The Mummy* (1959), *The Man Who Could Cheat Death* (1959), *The Stranglers of Bombay* (1959), *Never Take Sweets from a Stranger* (1960)

### Moon Zero Two

GB, 1969, 100m, Technicolor, RCA, cert U

*Moon Zero Two*. Now there's a title to make grown men shudder! One of Hammer's biggest missteps, this rather silly sci-fi romp was made in a bid to cash in on Stanley Kubrick's *2001: A Space Odyssey* (1968) and the huge interest generated by the American moon landings. Unfortunately, it was put together by a group of middle-aged men who seem wholly to have misunderstood what would appeal to the tastes of the film's target audience: ten-year-old schoolboys. The result is less a space odyssey and more a space oddity; not so much the *Star Wars* (1977) of its day, more the *Starship Invasions* (1978).

Set in 2021, it sees space pilot Bill Kemp, the first man to have set foot on Mars, hired by a villainous millionaire named J.J. Hubbard to retrieve an asteroid made of solid sapphire from outer space (jokes Kemp, "A six-thousand ton jewel—how would you like to meet the broad who could hang that around her neck!"). This requires landing on the asteroid (hints of *Armageddon* [1998] to come), planting boosters on it and sending it to the far side of the moon where it can be recovered.

Recalled director Roy Ward Baker, "The style was a skit on the old-time Western, with all the action taking place on the Moon."[55] Hence the film being promoted as "the first space western," though visiting the set, journalist Ronnie Cass suggested that *High Moon* might have been a better title! The

A distinct case of the poster being better than the film. Great artwork for the release of *Moon Zero Two* (1969), which failed to take off at both the launching pad and the box office (Hammer/Warner Bros./Seven Arts/Warner Pathé Distributors).

sense of exploring a new frontier is also reflected in the lyrics to the title song, which is belted out by Julie Driscoll over the "hilarious" cartoon credits: "Go find the world you're seeking, Where stars are new in the making, It's time to fly, deep space is calling you."

Unfortunately, the screenplay fails to make the most of its outlandish premise, despite some playful incidental touches of detail (all the in-flight movies seem to be westerns, while the moon-base bar has saloon-style doors). Penned by producer Michael Carreras, it was based upon a story provided by Gavin Lyall, Martin Davison and Frank Hardman, who between them could surely have come up with a better concept ( Jimmy Sangster was considered as both the writer and producer). A rather talky and humorless affair, it is often static when it should be kinetic, though occasionally an interesting line does find its way through the morass ("We're all foreigners here—we always will be," Kemp soberly observes of man's presence on the moon).

The script is by no means the film's only defect. Made on an obviously insufficient budget, Scott MacGregor's Moon City sets, though designed with a certain flair, lack real scale, Roy Ward Baker's direction is generally sluggish and Les Bowie's effects, while just about adequate for an episode of *Thunderbirds* (1965–1966, TV), have a toy model look to them. A strong performance from the leading man in the dashing Flash Gordon/Buck Rogers tradition might have saved the day. Unfortunately, as Kemp, the balding, middle-aged James Olsen is a charisma free zone. Totally miscast, he seems like a disgruntled dad just home from a bad day at the office rather than an interplanetary hero. Meanwhile, the supporting cast, among them Warren Mitchell as the corrupt J.J. Hubbard and, in particular, Bernard Bresslaw as Hubbard's bodyguard Harry, seem a little uncertain as to what they've got themselves into.

The film also seems confused regarding its identity. Or as the review in *Variety* succinctly put it, "[It] never makes up its mind whether it's a spoof or a straightforward space adventure." If that weren't bad enough, it also suffers from a series of ill-advised musical breaks performed by The Gojos and a troupe of dolly-bird dancers, which gives it the air of a Saturday night TV variety show. In fact, what Carreras and his team thought they were up to just beggars belief at times, and prompted the *Monthly Film Bulletin* to describe the film as being "just about bad enough to fill older audiences with nostalgia for the inspired innocence of *Flash Gordon*, or even the good old days of Abbott and Costello in outer space." The *Sunday Mirror* was rather more forthright, quipping, "falls flat on its astronaut." *Photoplay* was somewhat kinder, commenting, "this glorious piece of hokum is a joy to watch from start to finish," though it added that "none of the actors attempt to win awards and director Roy Ward Baker does not attempt to inject any 'art' into the production."

Intriguingly, during pre-production, Roy Ward Baker sought the advice of Stanley Kubrick about the problems of filming the weightless scenes with the actors. Recalled Baker, "I went to see him and he spoke freely about the space problems.... He said he had tried everything and found that there is only one way to shoot an actor floating in space: he must be suspended from the roof of the studio and the camera must be placed immediately underneath him, pointing straight up. In that way the wire is behind the actor and can never be seen. He was right."[56]

On the floor at Elstree from 31 March to 10 June 1968, the resultant mess was, not surprisingly, a box office disaster when, following a trade show on 8 October 1969, it was released by Warner Pathé in the UK on 26 October, and by Warner Bros./Seven Arts in America in March 1970. "See the moon community in the year 2021. See the first space gun battle on the moon," excitedly claimed the poster, which was far more dynamic than the film it promotes.

As always, James Carreras cheered on his product at the press launch, describing it as Hammer's "most exciting and big picture."[57] *The Observer* was less enthusiastic, calling the film "as silly a piece of pseudo-science fiction you could loathe to find," while the *Daily Express* described it as "infantile—even for small children." In fact, following its quick disappearance, Hammer never made another science fiction film again, despite their honorable track record with the genre. Said Roy Ward Baker, "When I read of the budgets of space adventure films today I realize that our budget would have been good for about two minutes screen time. It was truly hard and frustrating work and so much time was spent on solving the production problems that not enough attention was paid to the characters or the story. We turned out a reasonably entertaining picture, but it didn't realize our ambitions for it and never could have done, under the circumstances of those days."[58]

In retrospect, despite its various and obvious faults, *Moon Zero Two* is quite an entertaining picture in the "guilty pleasures" category. Although not knowingly camp—which is perhaps its greatest downfall—it is a reasonably colorful romp and certainly no worse than an average episode of the later *Space: 1999* (1975–1977, TV). Very much of its era, the film is now enjoyable mostly as a museum piece, and as such provides a fair amount of undemanding fun, despite its lapses in pace and logic. **Additional notes:** The film's effects were shot at Hammer's old stomping ground Bray, which the company had vacated on 19 November 1966 for Elstree. Remembered special effects assistant Kit West, "I started to do the model photography long before they even got to the floor."[59] A proposed sequel titled *Disaster in Space*, also scripted by Michael Carreras, was announced in 1970, but was shelved following the film's poor box office performance, as was the idea for a spin-off TV series.

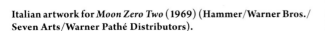

**Italian artwork for *Moon Zero Two* (1969) (Hammer/Warner Bros./Seven Arts/Warner Pathé Distributors).**

The film's screenplay was novelized by John Burke for Pan. The game of "Moonopoly" is used in the film with the permission of game manufacturers John Waddington. Tom Chantrell actually designed two posters for the film. For publicity purposes, James Olson and Catherina Von Schell were photographed on set leafing through a copy of *Film Review* whose cover featured a still of Keir Dullea as astronaut Dave Bowman in *2001*. A behind the scenes "making of" piece recorded for TV at the time can be found on YouTube (type in Making of "Moon Zero Two"); it features interviews with Michael Carreras, Scott MacGregor and Bernard Bresslaw, and depicts Roy Ward Baker directing the Gojos in a dance routine. The film's distinctive spacesuits later popped up in *Invaders from Space*, a 1971 episode of the children's television series *Here Come the Double Deckers!* (1970–1971, TV).

Production companies: Hammer/Warner Bros./Seven Arts. Distributors: Warner Pathé Distributors (UK [ABC circuit]), Warner Bros./Seven Arts (U.S.). Producer: Michael Carreras. Director: Roy Ward Baker. Screenplay: Michael Carreras. Story: Gavin Lyall, Martin Davison, Frank Hardman. Cinematographer: Paul Beeson. Music: Don Ellis. Vocalist: Julie Driscoll. Music director: Philip Martell. Editor: Spencer Reeve. Art director: Scott MacGregor. Assistant art director: John Lageu. Costumes: Carl Toms, Larry Stewart. Make-up: Ernest Taylor. Hair: Ivy Emmerton. Wigs: Leonard. Special effects: Les Bowie, Nick Allder, Kit West, Colin Chilvers (assistant), Peter Lawson (assis-

**Hispanic artwork for *Moon Zero Two* (1969) (Hammer/Warner Bros./Seven Arts/Warner Pathé Distributors).**

tant), Brian Johnson [uncredited], Wally Veevers [uncredited], Terry Schubert [uncredited], Mike Tilley [uncredited]. Recording supervisor: A.W. Lumkin. Sound editor: Roy Hyde. Sound mixer: Claude Hitchcock. Dubbing editor: Len Abbott. Camera operator: John Winbolt. Production manager: Hugh Harlow. Assistant director: Jack Martin. Construction manager: Arthur Banks. Stunt coordinator: Bill Weston (billed as stunt advisor). Stunts: Gerry Crampton [uncredited]. Choreography: Jo Cook. Casting: Susan Whatmough. Continuity: Josie Fulford. Titles: Stokes Cartoons, Ltd.. Poster(s): Tom Chantrell [uncredited]. **Cast:** James Olson (Bill Kemp), Catherina Von Schell (Clementine Taplin), Warren Mitchell (J.J. Hubbard), Bernard Bresslaw (Harry), Adrienne Corri (Liz Murphy), Ori Levy (Karminsky), Dudley Foster (Whitsun), Sam Kydd (Barman), Neil McCallum (Space captain), Joby Blanshard (Smith), Carol Cleveland (Hostess), Leo Britt (Senior customs officer), Michael Ripper (Card player), Robert Tayman (Card player), Roy Evans (Workman), Tom Kempinksi (Officer), Chrissie Shrimpton (Boutique attendant), Simone Silvera (Hubbard's girl), Amber Dean Smith (Hubbard's girl), Claire Shenstone (Hotel clerk), Lew Luton (Immigration officer), The Gojos (Group [Linda Hotchkin, Jane Bartlett, Thelma Bignell, Barbara von der Heyde, Lesley Larbey, Wendy Hillhouse]), Athol Coats (Mercer [uncredited]), Tim Condren (Yellow man [uncredited]), Martin Grace (Red man [uncredited]), Bill Weston (Green man [uncredited]), Robert Lee (Hotel employee [uncredited]), Michelle Barry (Bar dancer [uncredited]), Sue Baumann (Bar dancer [uncredited]), Jane Cunningham (Bar dancer [uncredited]), Irene Gorst (Bar dancer [uncredited]), Sally Graham (Bar dancer [uncredited]), Brenda Krippen (Bar dancer [uncredited]), Freddie Earlle (Little man [uncredited]). **DVD availability:** Warner Bros. (U.S. R1 NTSC), double-billed with *When Dinosaurs Ruled the Earth* (1970); Warner Bros. (U.S. R1 NTSC). **CD availability:** *The Hammer Film Music Collection: Volume One* (GDI Records), which contains the *Title Song*

### Moore, Eileen

In films from 1952 with *Mr. Denning Drives North*, this British actress (1932–) appeared in such productions as *An Inspector Calls* (1954), *A Town Like Alice* (1956), *Devil's Bait* (1959) and *Cry Wolf* (1960). She also co-starred opposite Don Taylor in the Hammer swashbuckler *Men of Sherwood Forest* (1954). Her television credits include episodes of *Douglas Fairbanks, Jr. Presents* (1953–1957, TV), *Colonel March of Scotland Yard* (1954–1956, TV), *Champion*

*House* (1967–1968, TV) and *Catweazle* (1970–1971, TV). She was married to the comedy actor George Cole (1925–2015) between 1954 and 1962; he appeared in two films for Hammer: *Don't Panic Chaps* (1959) and *The Vampire Lovers* (1970). **Hammer credits:** *Men of Sherwood Forest* (1954, as Lady Alys)

### Moore, Irving J. (Joseph)

This American director (1919–1993) helmed additional scenes, shot in the U.S., specifically for the first American telecast of Hammer's *The Kiss of the Vampire* (1963) on NBC in 1966. Following work as an assistant director on such movies as *Charge of the Lancers* (1954), *The Caine Mutiny* (1954), *The Solid Gold Cadillac* (1956) and *The Mountain Road* (1960), Moore went on to become a prolific episode director on such major TV series as *Cheyenne* (1955–1963, TV), *Maverick* (1957–1962, TV), *The Wild Wild West* (1965–1969, TV), *Hawaii Five-O* (1968–1980, TV), *Petrocelli* (1974–1976, TV), *Logan's Run* (1977–1978, TV), *Lou Grant* (1977–1982, TV), *Dallas* (1978–1991, TV) and *Dynasty* (1981–1989, TV). **Hammer credits:** *The Kiss of the Vampire* (1963 [1966 U.S. TV version only])

### Moore, John

This British bit player can be seen as an officer in Hammer's *The Two Faces of Dr. Jekyll* (1960). His other credits include *Hidden Homicide* (1959), *Act of Murder* (1964), *The Frozen Dead* (1966), *Captain Nemo and the Underwater City* (1969), *I Don't Want to Be Born* (1975), *Tess* (1979) and *Empire of the Sun* (1987), plus a return to Hammer for a brief appearance in *Countess Dracula* (1971). His many small screen credits include episodes of *Sword of Freedom* (1957, TV), *Jennings* (1966, TV), *Menace* (1970–1973, TV), *Brideshead Revisited* (1981, TV) and *Doctor Finlay* (1993–1996, TV). **Hammer credits:** *The Two Faces of Dr. Jekyll* (1960, as Officer [uncredited]), *Countess Dracula* (1971, as Priest)

### Moore, Kathleen

Moore worked on the wardrobe for Hammer's *Dr. Jekyll and Sister Hyde* (1971). Her other credits include *The Missing Million* (1942), *Green for Danger* (1946), *Radio Cab Murder* (1954), *The Golden Disc* (1958), *The Projected Man* (1966), *Night of the Big Heat* (1967), *Three Into Two Won't Go* (1969) and *Players* (1979). **Hammer credits:** *Dr. Jekyll and Sister Hyde* (1971)

### Moore, Kieron

On screen from 1946 with *The Voice Within* (the only film he appeared in under his real name), this Irish leading man (1924–2007, real name Kieron O'Hanrahan) went on to appear in films in both Britain and Hollywood, although by the end of his career he had become a featured support. Among his credits are *Mine Own Executioner* (1947), *Anna Karenina* (1948), *The Blue Peter* (1955), *The League of Gentlemen* (1960), *Crack in the World* (1965), *Arabesque* (1966), *Custer of the West* (1967) and *Run Like a Thief* (1968). He also co-starred in the Hammer second feature *Mantrap* (1953) as Mervyn Speight. He returned to Hammer four years later to star with Leo Genn in the war drama *The Steel Bayonet* (1957). Moore later directed and narrated two documentaries: *The Progress of Peoples* (1975) and *The Parched Land* (1979). Note that Moore had been signed to star in Hammer's Spanish Inquisition drama *The Rape of Sabena* (aka *The Inquisitor*) in 1960, but the production was cancelled following objections from co-producers Columbia. His television credits include episodes of *Fabian of the Yard* (1954–1956, TV), *Sir Francis Drake* (1961–1962, TV), *Zero One* (1962–1965, TV), *Department S* (1969–1970, TV), *Ryan International* (1970, TV), which he also created, and *The Zoo Gang* (1974, TV). He also directed two episodes of *The Vise* (1954–1960, TV). He was married to the actress Barbara White (1923–2013, aka Barbara Medin) from 1947. **Hammer credits:** *Mantrap* (1953, as Mervyn Speight), *The Steel Bayonet* (1957, as Captain Mead)

### Moore, Maureen

This glamorous bit part player appeared in the Hammer comedy *I Only Arsked!* (1958) as one of the harem girls. Her other credits include *Life Is a Circus* (1960) and *Carry On Regardless* (1961), plus episodes of *The Third Man* (1959–1965, TV) and *Sir Francis Drake* (1961–1962, TV). **Hammer credits:** *I Only Arsked!* (1958, as Harem girl [uncredited])

### Moore, Pat (Patrick)

Moore worked as an effects assistant to Les Bowie on Hammer's *The Phantom of the Opera* (1962). His credits as a fully-fledged effects technician include *Where the Bullets Fly* (1966), *Rocket to the Moon* (1967), *The Italian Job* (1969), *The Long Day's Dying* (1968), *The Last Valley* (1970), *The Railway Children* (1970), *The Amazing Mr. Blunden* (1972) and *Assassin* (1973). **Hammer credits:** *The Phantom of the Opera* (1962 [uncredited])

### Moore, Robert

Moore had a supporting roles in two of Hammer's fifties second features. His other credits include *Green Fingers* (1947), *Old Mother Riley's New Venture* (1949), *Ghost Ship* (1952), *The Ladykillers* (1955), *Jigsaw* (1962) and *What's So Bad About Feeling Good?* (1968), plus episodes of *Dad's Army* (1968–1977, TV) and *Barlow at Large* (1971–1975, TV). **Hammer credits:** *Lady in the Fog* (1952, unnamed role [uncredited]), *Blood Orange* (1953, as Stevenson [uncredited])

### Moore, William

This British actor (1916–2000) can be seen as Mr. Roberts the farmer in *The Two Faces of Evil* (1980, TV [episode of *Hammer House of Horror*]). His other credits include episodes of *No Hiding Place* (1959–1967, TV), *Coronation Street* (1960, TV), in which he played Cyril Turpin, *Mr. Rose* (1967–1968, TV), *All Creatures Great and Small* (1978–1990, TV), *Sorry!* (1981–1988), in which he played Sydney Lumsden, *My Husband and I* (1987–1988, TV) and *Kavanagh Q.C.* (1995–2001, TV). His occasional films include *Black Jack* (1979), *Enemy* (1998) and *The Runner* (1999). He was married to the actress Mollie Sugden (1922–

2009, real name Isabel Mary Sugden) from 1958. **Hammer credits:** *The Two Faces of Evil* (1980, TV [episode of *Hammer House of Horror*], as Mr. Roberts)

### Morais, Trevor

Along with Roy Phillips and Tab Martin, this British drummer (1944–, aka Morais) was a member of The Peddlers, which performed the title number for the Hammer film *The Lost Continent* (1968). Earlier in his career he was a member of such bands as Faron's Flamingoes and Rory Storm and the Hurricanes. After leaving The Peddlers he later joined Quantum Jump and also worked as a session player for such artists as David Essex and Bjork. He penned the hit single *The Lone Ranger* (1976), which was featured in *The Bitch* (1979), and composed the music for the TV series *ChromiumBlue.com* (2002, TV). **Hammer credits:** *The Lost Continent* (1968)

### Morand, Timothy

Morand can be seen as Collier in *The Corvini Inheritance* (1984, TVM [episode of *Hammer House of Mystery and Suspense*]). Other credits include episodes of *Colditz* (1972–1974, TV), *Secret Army* (1977–1979, TV), *Howards' Way* (1985–1990, TV) and *Inspector Morse* (1987–2000, TV). Occasional film credits include *A Bridge Too Far* (1977), *Les Miserables* (1978, TVM), *Sky Bandits* (1986) and *Fatal Inheritance* (1993). **Hammer credits:** *The Corvini Inheritance* (1984, TVM [episode of *Hammer House of Mystery and Suspense*], as Collier)

### Mordant, James *see* Marchant, James

### Morell, André

A long-standing Hammer favorite, this authoritative British character actor (1909–1978, real name Cecil André Mesritz, aka Cecil Mesritz) began his professional stage career in 1934 following several years of amateur experience, during which he performed under the name Cecil Mesritz. In films from 1938 with *13 Men and a Gun*, he appeared in a handful of other shorts and features before joining the Welsh Fusiliers during World War II. Upon returning from active duty, he resumed his career, appearing in such TV plays as *Death of a Rat* (1946) and such films as *Against the Wind* (1948), which he followed with the likes of *Madeleine* (1950), *Stage Fright* (1950) and *Seven Days to Noon* (1950), working for such major directors as David Lean (for whom he appeared in two further films), Alfred Hitchcock and the Boulting Brothers respectively.

Morell first worked for Hammer in 1952 on the glossy second feature thriller *Stolen Face*, in which he played the supporting role of David. He didn't return to the company again until 1958 for *The Camp on Blood Island*, by which time he'd further established himself in such major films as *Summertime* (1955), *The Man Who Never Was* (1956) and *The Bridge on the River Kwai* (1957), as well as on television with *1984* (1954, TV), in which he co-starred with Peter Cushing. In 1959, he left his mark as Dr. Watson opposite Cushing's Sherlock Holmes in Hammer's much-admired *The Hound of the Baskervilles*. Commented *Variety* of his perform-

ance: "André Morell is also a very good Watson—stolid, dependable and not as stupidly bovine as he is sometimes depicted."

Following *The Hound of the Baskervilles*, Morell returned periodically to the company, starring in *The Shadow of the Cat* (1961), *Cash on Demand* (1961), in which he gave an excellent account of himself as an upper crust bank robber, again opposite Cushing, *She* (1965), *The Mummy's Shroud* (1967) and *The Vengeance of She* (1967), though many regard his best performance for Hammer as Sir James Forbes in *The Plague of the Zombies* (1966). Morell's many other films include *Behemoth the Sea Monster* (1959), *Ben-Hur* (1959), *Judith* (1965), *10 Rillington Place* (1970), *Barry Lyndon* (1975), *The Slipper and the Rose* (1976) and *The First Great Train Robbery* (1978). His many TV appearances include episodes of *BBC Sunday-Night Theatre* (1950–1959, TV), *Douglas Fairbanks, Jr. Presents* (1953–1957, TV), *White Hunter* (1957–1958, TV), *Quatermass and the Pit* (1958–1959, TV), in which he played Professor Bernard Quatermass, *Doctor Who* (1963–1989, TV), *The Caesars* (1968, TV), *Edward the Seventh* (1975, TV) and *The Professionals* (1977–1983, TV). Commented Hammer continuity girl Rene Glynne of Morell, "He was a lovely, wonderful, beautiful man."[60]

Morell was married to the actress Joan Greenwood (1921–1987) from 1959; their son is the actor Jason Morell (1963–). **Additional notes:** Morell's performance as Haumeid in *She* was dubbed by George Pastell. Prior to playing Colonel Gore-Hepburn in Hammer's *Cash on Demand*, Morell had essayed the role on television in *The Gold Inside* (1960, TV). **Hammer credits:** *Stolen Face* (1952, as David), *The Camp on Blood Island* (1958, as Colonel Lambert), *The Hound of the Baskervilles* (1959, as Dr. John Watson), *The Shadow of the Cat* (1961, as Walter Venable), *Cash on Demand* (1961, as Colonel Gore-Hepburn), *She* (1965, as Haumeid), *The Plague of the Zombies* (1966, as Sir James Forbes), *The Mummy's Shroud* (1967, as Sir Basil Walden), *The Vengeance of She* (1968, as Kassim)

### Morelli, Tony

Morelli can be seen as Nicholas in Hammer's *Dick Barton Strikes Back* (1949). **Hammer credits:** *Dick Barton Strikes Back* (1949, as Nicholas)

### Morgan, Charles

Primarily seen in supporting roles, this British (Welsh) actor (1909–2000) can be spotted as Laurie Lovett in the Hammer thriller *Hell Is a City* (1960). He can also be seen in a small role in Hammer's *Cash on Demand* (1961). His other credits include *Train of Events* (1949), *Radio Cab Murder* (1954), *The Day the Earth Caught Fire* (1961), *Au Pair Girls* (1972) and *The Return of the Soldier* (1982). Busiest on television, his many credits here include episodes of *Armchair Theatre* (1956–1974, TV), *Doctor Who* (1963–1989, TV), *Mystery and Imagination* (1966–1970, TV), *The Howerd Confessions* (1976, TV), *Tenko* (1981–1984, TV) and *After Henry* (1988–1992, TV). **Hammer credits:** *Hell Is a City* (1960, as Laurie Lovett), *Cash on Demand* (1961, as Collins)

## Morgan, Dick (Richard)

This bit player and stuntman can be seen briefly as a coach driver's companion in Hammer's *Dracula* (1958). His other credits include *Carry On Cowboy* (1965) and episodes of *Breaking Point* (1966, TV) and *Softly Softly* (1966–1969, TV). **Hammer credits:** *Dracula* (1958, as Coach driver's companion [uncredited])

## Morgan, Elizabeth (Liz)

Morgan played a minor supporting role in Hammer's *Frankenstein Must Be Destroyed* (1969). Busiest on stage and television, her many small screen appearances include episodes of *Finding Out* (1965–1968, TV), which she presented, *Public Eye* (1965–1975, TV), *Terry and June* (1979–1987, TV), *We Are Seven* (1989–1991, TV) and *Hetty Wainthropp Investigates* (1996–1998, TV). She is perhaps best known for providing the voice of Destiny Angel for *Captain Scarlet and the Mysterons* (1967–1968, TV). She also wrote the TV play *The Sisters Three* (1994, TV), in which she also appeared. **Hammer credits:** *Frankenstein Must Be Destroyed* (1969, as Ella's friend [uncredited])

## Morgan, Guy

This British (Welsh) screenwriter (1908–1964) contributed to the script of the Hammer second feature *Never Look Back* (1952). His other credits include *The Captive Heart* (1947), *Anna Karenina* (1948), *Love Pawn* (1953), *The Red Dress* (1954) and *Man in the Road* (1956), plus episodes of *International Detective* (1959, TV) and *No Hiding Place* (1959–1967, TV), on the latter of which he also worked as a script editor. **Hammer credits:** *Never Look Back* (1952)

## Morgan, Robert

This British actor (1964–, aka Robert Craig-Morgan) can be seen in a supporting role in *Black Carrion* (1984, TVM [episode of *Hammer House of Mystery and Suspense*]). Best known for playing Justin Bennett in *Grange Hill* (1978–2008, TV) between 1978 and 1982, his other credits include episodes of *I, Claudius* (1976, TV), *Street Legal* (1987–1994, TV), *Spender* (1991–1993, TV), *Bugs* (1995–1998, TV), *Footballers' Wives* (2000–2006, TV) and *Rellik* (2017, TV). His occasional films include *Pop Pirates* (1984), *Nuns on the Run* (1990), *David Rose* (2010), *Foster* (2011) and *Pride and Prejudice and Zombies* (2016) **Hammer credits:** *Black Carrion* (1984, TVM [episode of *Hammer House of Mystery and Suspense*], as Mate)

## Morgan, Terence

In features from 1948 with *Hamlet* following training at RADA and experience on the stage (he also appeared in the short *It's Just the Way It Is* [1943]), this British leading man (1921–2005) went on to notch up over thirty feature credits, proving particularly popular in the fifties. His big screen appearances include *Mandy* (1952), *Forbidden Cargo* (1954), *The Scamp* (1957), *Piccadilly Third Stop* (1960), *The Penthouse* (1967), *Yesterday's Warriors* (1979) and *The Mystery of Edwin Drood* (1993). He also made a number of films in Europe during his career, among them *L'amante di Paridi* (1954), *I cavalieri dell'illusione* (1954) and *Il grande colpo di Surcouf* (1966). In 1964, he starred as Adam Beauchamp, aka Be, in Hammer's *The Curse of the Mummy's Tomb* (1964). Sadly, his performance was not among his best, just as the film wasn't among Hammer's best. His television work includes the title role in *Sir Francis Drake* (1961–1962, TV), plus episodes of *Out of the Unknown* (1965–1971, TV), *The Persuaders!* (1971–1972, TV) and *King and Castle* (1986–1988, TV). His uncle was the actor Verne Morgan (1900–1984), who appeared in four films for Hammer. **Hammer credits:** *The Curse of the Mummy's Tomb* (1964, as Adam Beauchamp/Be)

## Morgan, Verne

This British supporting actor (1900–1984) appeared in four films for Hammer, beginning with *Women Without Men* (1956), in which he played Barrowman. His other credits include *The Limping Man* (1953) and *The Blazing Caravan* (1954), plus episodes of *The Benny Hill Show* (1955–1968, 1969–1989, TV), *Police Surgeon* (1960, TV), *Seven Faces of Woman* (1974, TV) and *Dick Turpin* (1979–1982, TV). He also worked in the theater as both an actor and producer, and penned the book *English People Speak Like This*. His nephew was the actor Terence Morgan (1921–2005), who appeared in Hammer's *The Curse of the Mummy's Tomb* (1964). **Hammer credits:** *Women Without Men* (1956, as Barrowman [uncredited]), *The Ugly Duckling* (1959, as Barman), *That's Your Funeral* (1973, as Pensioner), *Man at the Top* (1973, as Records clerk)

## Morice, Lola

This British supporting actress and dancer (1912–1998) appeared as a dancer in the Locarno sequences of Hammer's Jekyll and Hyde spoof *The Ugly Duckling* (1959). Her other credits include episodes of *The Wednesday Play* (1964–1970, TV), *The Goodies* (1970–1981, TV), *Some Mothers Do 'Ave 'Em* (1973–1978, TV), *Tales of the Unexpected* (1979–1988, TV) and *Marjorie and Men* (1985, TV). She was married to the actor William Gossling (1912–1982) from 1941. **Hammer credits:** *The Ugly Duckling* (1959, as Dancer [uncredited])

## Morley, Robert

A long-standing audience favorite, this portly British comedy character actor (1908–1992) first made a splash in Hollywood following stage experience in the UK from 1928 and a brief appearance in the British-made *Scrooge* (1935), earning a best supporting actor Oscar nomination for his performance as King Louis XVI in *Marie Antoinette* (1938). Over sixty films followed, with Morley often appearing in scene-stealing supporting roles or cameos, among them *Major Barbara* (1941), *The African Queen* (1951), *Beau Brummell* (1954), *Murder at the Gallop* (1963), *Those Magnificent Men in Their Flying Machines* (1965), *When Eight Bells Toll* (1971), *Theatre of Blood* (1973), *Who Is Killing the Great Chefs of Europe?* (1978) and *Little Dorrit* (1987). In 1963, he appeared as Roderick Femm in Hammer's disappointing remake of *The Old Dark House*. Sadly, the script proved to be beyond even Morley's abilities with sub-standard material. That said, *Kinematograph Weekly* found him to be "quite the most imposing member of the cast." Morley's television credits include episodes of *Tales from Dickens* (1958–1959, TV), *Charge!* (1969, TV), *Lady Killers* (1980–1981, TV) and *War and Remembrance* (1988–1989, TV). His plays include *Goodness, How Sad!* (1938), which was filmed for television in 1938 and for the cinema in 1940 (as *Return to Yesterday*), and *Edward, My Son* (1947 [co-written with Noel Langley]), which was filmed for the cinema in 1949 and for television in 1955 (as an episode of *The United States Steel Hour* [1953–1963, TV]) and 1974 (as *Edouard mon fils*, as an episode of *Au theatre ce soir* [1966–1985, TV]). He was made a CBE in 1957. His children include critic Sheridan Morley (1941–2007), actress Annabel Morley (1946–) and actor Wilton Morley (1951–). His mother-in-law was actress Gladys Cooper (1888–1971). **Hammer credits:** *The Old Dark House* (1963, as Roderick Femm)

## Morley, Ted

British born Morley (1935–2004) worked as the third assistant director on the Hammer comedy *Up the Creek* (1958). He later worked as an assistant director on *One on an Island* (1968, TV [episode of *Journey to the Unknown*]), which led to two further assignments in this capacity for Hammer. He began his career as a third assistant in 1957 on *RX for Murder*, graduated to second assistant on *Idol on Parade* (1959) and became a first assistant on *Davy Jones' Locker* (1966). His other first assistant credits include *The Man Who Haunted Himself* (1970), *Our Miss Fred* (1972) and *Excalibur* (1981). His credits as a production manager include *The Wicker Man* (1973), *Empire of the Sun* (1987), *Braveheart* (1995) and *Felicia's Journey* (1999). He also worked as an associate producer on *Firelight* (1997) and such TV series as *Oktober* (1998, TV) and *The 10th Kingdom* (2000, TV). **Hammer credits:** *Up the Creek* (1958, third assistant director [uncredited]), *One on an Island* (1968, TV [episode of *Journey to the Unknown*], first assistant director), *Fear in the Night* (1972, first assistant director), *Demons of the Mind* (1972, first assistant director)

## Morris, Artro

British born Morris (1926–2014, full name Timothy James Artro-Morris) can be spotted in a brief role in Hammer's *The Witches* (1966). His other credits include *The Strange Affair* (1968), *The Thirty-Nine Steps* (1978) and *The Godsend* (1980), plus a return to Hammer for *Dracula A.D. 1972* (1972). His many TV appearances include episodes of *A Tale of Two Cities* (1965, TV), *Spy Trap* (1972–1975, TV), *Lorna Doone* (1976, TV) and *Howards' Way* (1985–1990, TV). **Hammer credits:** *The Witches* (1966, as Porter [uncredited]), *Dracula A.D. 1972* (1972, as Police Sergeant)

## Morris, Aubrey

This quirky British character actor (1926–2015) popped up in all manner of films and television series. His big screen credits number *The Quare Fellow* (1962), *The Night Caller* (1965), *The Great St. Trinian's Train Robbery* (1966), *A Clockwork Orange* (1971), *The Wicker Man* (1973), *Lisztomania* (1975), *Lifeforce* (1985), *The Rachel Papers* (1989), *Bordello of Blood* (1996) and *Necessary Evil* (2008).

He also had several brushes with Hammer over the years, beginning with an episode of *Journey to the Unknown* (1968, TV), which he followed with two films. The first of these was *Blood from the Mummy's Tomb* (1971), an adaptation of Bram Stoker's *The Jewel of Seven Stars*, the remake of which, *Legend of the Mummy* (1997), he also appeared in (playing Dr. Putnam in the former and Dr. Winchester in the latter). His television credits include episodes of *Ivanhoe* (1958–1959, TV), *The Saint* (1962–1969, TV), *Not on Your Nellie* (1974–1975, TV), *Hot Metal* (1986–1988, TV) and *Deadwood* (2004–2006, TV). Also on stage. **Hammer credits:** *The Madison Equation* (1968, TV [episode of *Journey to the Unknown*], as Frederick Shea), *Blood from the Mummy's Tomb* (1971, as Dr. Putnam), *Man About the House* (1974, as Lecturer)

### Morris, Christopher

This British child actor (1962–) can be spotted as one of the boys who discovers Laura Bellows' body amid the gravestones and rubble of St. Bartolph's in Hammer's *Dracula A.D. 1972* (1972). His other credits include *The Best House in London* (1969), *Battle of Britain* (1969), *The 14* (1973), *The Canterville Ghost* (1974, TVM) and *No Hard Feelings* (1976, TVM), plus episodes of *Never the Twain* (1981–1991, TV), in which he played David Peel (a role previously played by Robin Kermode). **Hammer credits:** *Dracula A.D. 1972* (1972, as Boy [uncredited])

### Morris, Edna

This British supporting actress (1906–1972) can be seen as the unfortunately named charwoman Mrs. Bott in Hammer's *A Case for PC 49* (1951). Her other credits include *The Cure for Love* (1950), *Women of Twilight* (1953), *Saturday Night and Sunday Morning* (1960) and *Rotten to the Core* (1965). Her TV credits include episodes of *BBC Sunday-Night Theatre* (1950–1959, TV), *The History of Mr. Polly* (1959, TV), *Z Cars* (1962–1978, TV) and *Cluff* (1964–1965, TV). **Hammer credits:** *A Case for PC 49* (1951, as Mrs. Bott)

### Morris, Michael

This British make-up artist (1915–) worked on three films for Hammer, among them *Quatermass and the Pit* (1967), one of his tasks for which was to "melt" Julian Glover's Colonel Breen—a feat he pulls off most convincingly. His other credits include *Major Barbara* (1941), *Hamlet* (1948), *The Heart Within* (1957), *Solo for Sparrow* (1962), *She'll Have to Go* (1962), *Ricochet* (1963), *The Magus* (1968), *Otley* (1968), *Three into Two Won't Go* (1969), *The Human Factor* (1979) and *Clockwise* (1986), plus two more for Hammer. Also busy in television, his credits here include episodes of *Stryker of the Yard* (1957, TV), *The Baron* (1966–1967, TV), *Special Branch* (1969–1974, TV), *Shirley's World* (1971–1972, TV) and *The Sweeney* (1974–1978, TV). **Hammer credits:** *Quatermass and the Pit* (1967), *A Challenge for Robin Hood* (1967), *The Vengeance of She* (1968)

### Morris, Robert

Following experience in the army, work as an assistant stage manager and training at RADA, this British actor (1940–) broke into television in 1963 with an episode of *ITV Play of the Week* (1955–1968, TV). In films from 1966 with *A Man for All Seasons*, he went on to play the role of the hapless Hans in Hammer's *Frankenstein Created Woman* (1967), in which his character's soul is transferred into that of his female lover following his execution. He then went on to play the supporting role of Watson in *Quatermass and the Pit* (1967). Recalled the actor of his first brush with Hammer, "Irene Lamb, the casting director, arranged for me to go down to Bray and meet up with Terry Fisher and Tony Nelson Keys…. Not having long left RADA, I was very much into motivations and sub-text and all that. So when they asked me what I thought about the character, I went into this long, involved thing about why my character, Hans, acted the way he did. Irene told me afterwards that, once I'd gone, Terry had turned to Tony and said, 'Bloody hell did we think of all that?!' I think that's one of the reasons I got the part, actually—I seemed to be very much 'into' it."[61] Morris's other film credits include *Promenade* (1968), *Tangiers* (1982) and *My Worst Enemy* (1991), while his other TV work takes in episodes of *The Avengers* (1961–1969, TV), *Z Cars* (1962–1978, TV), *The Guardians* (1971, TV), *Warship* (1973–1977, TV), *Breakaway* (1980, TV) and *Kessler* (1981, TV). **Hammer credits:** *Frankenstein Created Woman* (1967, as Hans), *Quatermass and the Pit* (1967, as Watson)

### Morris, Stella

Morris worked as the assistant to make-up artist Basil Newall on the Hammer thriller *Maniac* (1963). By the time she returned to Hammer to work on *Crescendo* (1970), she had become a fully-fledged make-up artist. Her other credits include *The Mark of Cain* (1947), *Trottie True* (1949), *Gorgo* (1960), *Lolita* (1962), *Naked Evil* (1966), *Father Dear Father* (1973), *The Stud* (1978), *Emmanuelle in Soho* (1981) and *Parker* (1984), plus episodes of *Armchair Theatre* (1956–1974, TV) and *The Pathfinders* (1972–1973, TV). **Hammer credits:** *Maniac* (1963, assistant make-up [uncredited]), *Crescendo* (1969, make-up)

### Morris, Wolfe

This British character actor (1925–1996) played the role of Kusang in Hammer's *The Abominable Snowman* (1957), having already essayed the role in the television original, *The Creature* (1955, TV). This led to work on several other Hammer productions. His other credits include *Ill Met by Moonlight* (1956), *The Best House in London* (1968), *The House That Dripped Blood* (1971), *The Mackintosh Man* (1973) and *Shining Through* (1992), plus episodes of *The Adventures of Robin Hood* (1955–1960, TV), *The Six Proud Walkers* (1962, TV), *Doctor Who* (1963–1989, TV), *The Six Wives of Henry VIII* (1970, TV), in which he played Cromwell, *Beasts* (1976, TV) and *Bergerac* (1981–1991, TV). Also on stage. **Hammer credits:** *The Abominable Snowman* (1957, as Kusang), *The Camp on Blood Island* (1958, as Interpreter), *Further Up the Creek* (1958, as Algeroccan Major), *I Only Arsked!* (1958, as Salesman), *Yesterday's Enemy* (1959, as Informer)

### Morrison, Alan

British born Morrison (1930–2012) worked as the dubbing editor on the Hammer comedy *A Weekend with Lulu* (1961). His other credits as a sound/dubbing editor include *Dentist on the Job* (1961), *Charade* (1963), *The Masque of the Red Death* (1964), *Theatre of Death* (1966), *Rita, Sue and Bob Too!* (1988) and *Vroom* (1990). His credits as an editor include *Behind the Mask* (1958), *The Golden Rabbit* (1962), *The Brides of Fu Manchu* (1966), *The Million Eyes of Sumuru* (1967), *House of 1,000 Dolls* (1967), *Skeleton Coast* (1988) and *Captive Rage* (1988). **Hammer credits:** *A Weekend with Lulu* (1961)

### Morrissey, Neil

This British actor (1962–) is best known for his performances as the dopey biker Rocky Cassidy in *Boon* (1986–1982, TV) and the Stella-guzzling Tony Smart in *Men Behaving Badly* (1993–2002, TV), as well as for voicing the title character of Bob the Builder (1999–2012, TV) for children's television. Less known for his film work, his credits here include *The Bounty* (1984), *Playing Away* (1986), *I Bought a Vampire Motorcycle* (1990), *Staggered* (1994), *Up 'n' Under* (1997), *The Match* (1999), *As One* (2016) and *Crucible of the Vampire* (2017). His other television work includes episodes of *Noel's House Party* (1991–1999, TV), *Happy Birthday Shakespeare* (2000, TV), *Waterloo Road* (2006–2015, TV), in which he played Eddie Lawson, *Line of Duty* (2012–, TV) and *The Night Manager* (2016, TV), plus an episode of *Hammer House of Mystery and Suspense* (1984, TVM]), in which he played a rather young-looking policeman, complete with a non-too-convincing Irish accent. He was married to the actress Amanda Noar (1962–) between 1987 and 1991. **Hammer credits:** *Paint Me a Murder* (1984, TVM [episode of *Hammer House of Mystery and Suspense*], as Policeman)

### Mort, Patricia

This British (Welsh) actress (1933–) can be seen as a maid in an episode of *Hammer House of Horror* (1980, TV). Her other TV work includes episodes of *Starr and Company* (1958, TV), *Ghost Squad* (1961–1964, TV), *The Magnificent Evans* (1984, TV), *Boon* (1986–1992, TV) and *Wales Playhouse* (1990–1996, TV). Her films credits include *Attempt to Kill* (1961), *Time to Remember* (1962) and *That Kind of Girl* (1963). **Hammer credits:** *Rude Awakening* (1980, TV [episode of *Hammer House of Horror*], as Maid)

### Mortimer, Charles

This British actor (1885–1964) can be seen in a supporting role in Hammer's *The Mystery of the Mary Celeste* (1935). His other credits include *Watch Beverly* (1932), *The Small Man* (1935), *Birds of a Feather* (1936), *The Ghost of St. Michael's* (1941), *The Life and Death of Colonel Blimp* (1943) and *The Counterfeit Plan* (1957), plus episodes of *The Warden* (1951, TV) and *Fabian of the Yard* (1954–1956, TV). His wife was the actress Greta Wood (1893–1984, real name Gertrude Sarah Wood), whom he married in 1950. **Hammer credits:** *The Mystery of the Mary Celeste* (1935, as Attorney-General [uncredited])

**Mortimer, Johnnie**

Often working in collaboration with Brian Cooke, this prolific British comedy writer (1931–1992) penned such series as *Father Dear Father* (1968–1973, TV), *Alcock and Gander* (1972, TV) and *Man About the House* (1973–1976, TV), the latter of which spawned two spin-offs, *George and Mildred* (1976–1979, TV) and *Robin's Nest* (1977–1981, TV), plus an American version, *Three's Company* (1977–1984, TV), which was mostly written by other hands (he penned just two episodes), as well as a U.S. version of *George and Mildred* titled *The Ropers* (1979–1980, TV), to which he did contribute several scripts. Mortimer and Cooke also penned the screenplay for Hammer's big-screen transfer of *Man About the House* (1974, TV), but the script for the spin-off of *George and Mildred* (1980), which was produced by Roy Skeggs during a hiatus from Hammer, was written by Dick Sharples. His other credits with Cooke include *Tom, Dick and Harriet* (1982, TV), *Let There Be Love* (1982–1983, TV) and *Full House* (1985–1986, TV). He also worked as a script editor. **Hammer credits:** *Man About the House* (1974)

**Morton, Anthony**

This British actor (1927–2001) can be spotted as a Maitre D' in *In Possession* (1984, TVM [episode of *Hammer House of Mystery and Suspense*]). His other credits include episodes of *No Hiding Place* (1959–1967, TV), *Crossroads* (1964–1988, TV), *Mr. Big* (1977, TV) and *Only Fools and Horses* (1981–2003, TV). His occasional film credits include *Oh! What a Lovely War* (1969), *Performance* (1970), *The Rise and Rise of Michael Rimmer* (1970) and *Confessions of a Driving Instructor* (1976). **Hammer credits:** *In Possession* (1984, TVM [episode of *Hammer House of Mystery and Suspense*], as Maitre D')

**Morton, Hugh**

This prolific British supporting actor (1903–1984) appeared as Mr. Hemingway in the Hammer comedy *Life with the Lyons* (1954). However, in the sequel, *The Lyons in Paris* (1955), he played Colonel Price. He can also be seen briefly in *Quatermass and the Pit* (1967) as an elderly journalist, and in *Mark of the Devil* (1984, TVM [episode of *Hammer House of Mystery and Suspense*]) as a butler. His other credits include *Deadlock* (1943), *Mr. Denning Drives North* (1952), *Payroll* (1961), *Three on a Spree* (1961), *Master Spy* (1961), *The Darwin Adventure* (1972), *The Stud* (1978) and *Oxford Blues* (1984), plus appearances in episodes of many TV series, among them *Kenilworth* (1957, TV), *The Avengers* (1961–1969, TV), *Man at the Top* (1970–1972, TV) and *The New Avengers* (1976–1977, TV). He was also busy on radio, notably as the sleuth Paul Temple in three serials between 1938 and 1939, and as the Reverend Simon Cherry in *Meet the Rev* in 1946; he also went on to play the latter role in seven segments for the TV series *Kaleidoscope* (1946–1953, TV) in 1948, which were also titled *Meet the Rev*, albeit this time with an added exclamation mark (*Meet the Rev!*). However, when it came to Hammer's big screen version of the radio serial, *Meet Simon Cherry*

(1950), the role was instead played by Hugh Moxey. **Hammer credits:** *Life with the Lyons* (1954, as Mr. Hemingway), *The Lyons in Paris* (1955, as Colonel Price), *Adventures with the Lyons* (1957, serial re-issue of *Life with the Lyons*, as Mr. Hemingway), *Quatermass and the Pit* (1967, as Elderly journalist), *Mark of the Devil* (1984, TVM [episode of *Hammer House of Mystery and Suspense*], as Butler)

**The Morton Fraser Harmonica Gang** *see* **Fraser, Morton**

**Moss, Clive**

This child actor had a supporting role in Hammer's *One Million Years B.C.* (1966). His other credits include *Oliver!* (1968) and *Scrooge* (1970). His adult credits include *Let's Get Laid* (1977). His TV appearances include episodes of *Public Eye* (1965–1975, TV), *Till Death Us Do Part* (1965–1975, TV), *Please Sir!* (1968–1972, TV) and *After They Were Famous* (1999–2005, TV), in the latter of which he reminisced about his experiences in *Oliver!* **Hammer credits:** *One Million Years B.C.* (1966, unnamed role [uncredited])

**Moss, Gerald**

This British camera operator (1916–1999) took over from Len Harris on *The Revenge of Frankenstein* (1958) for a brief period when Harris came down with the 'flu. His other credits as an operator include *Welcome, Mr. Washington* (1944), *Dual Alibi* (1946), *Seven Days to Noon* (1950) and *Escapade* (1955). He also photographed the second unit for *Village of the Damned* (1960) and *Naked Evil* (1966), and for such series as *Fabian of the Yard* (1954–1956, TV), *The Adventures of the Big Man* (1956, TV), *Department S* (1969–1970, TV) and *Randall and Hopkirk (Deceased)* (1969–1971, TV). His credits as a cinematographer include *Lisbon Story* (1946), *Invasion Quartet* (1961), *Postman's Knock* (1962) and *Virgin Witch* (1971), plus episodes of *The Adventures of the Big Man* and *Randall and Hopkirk (Deceased)*. **Hammer credits:** *The Revenge of Frankenstein* (1958 [uncredited])

**Moss, Ralph**

This British lightweight boxer (active between 1939 and 1955) had a minor supporting role in Hammer's *The Flanagan Boy* (1953). **Hammer credits:** *The Flanagan Boy* (1953, as Kossov's second)

**Moss, Stirling**

This celebrated British racing driver (1929–) appeared in a handful of films, either as himself or as a racing driver, among them the Hammer drama *Mask of Dust* (1954). His other credits include *The Beauty Jungle* (1964) and *Casino Royale* (1967), as well as the children's TV series *Roary the Racing Car* (2007–2009, TV), which he narrated. Racing between 1948 and 1962, he went on to win sixteen Formula One Grand Prix races. He was made an OBE in 1953 and knighted in 2000 for his services to the motor-racing industry. **Hammer credits:** *Mask of Dust* (1954, as Himself)

**Mossman, George**

British born Mossman (1908–1993) was a spe-

cialist in collecting, renovating and showing horse-drawn coaches. A good deal of his income came from hiring out his vehicles to film companies, and he was frequently on hand to drive them on screen, as he did in Hammer's *Dick Turpin—Highwayman* (1956), in which he played a coachman. His other credits include appearances in *Quentin Durward* (1955), *Dr. Terror's House of Horrors* (1965) and *Carry On Cowboy* (1965). He also provided the coaches and horses for such films as *Carry On Dick* (1974), *Barry Lyndon* (1975), *Jabberwocky* (1977) and *Greystoke: The Legend of Tarzan, Lord of the Apes* (1984), as well as several further Hammer films. His coaches were also a frequent attraction in the annual Lord Mayor's Show in London, and Mossman even provided some carriages for the coronation procession of Queen Elizabeth II in 1953. Many of his carriages are now on display as part of the Mossman Collection in the Stockwood Discovery Center. His family and their coach business were the subject of a Pathé newsreel short in 1961, while in 2014 Mossman was the focus of *The Mossman Legacy—George Mossman's Carriage Collection*, one of the extras on the blu-ray release of *Captain Clegg* (1962). **Hammer credits include:** *Dick Turpin—Highwayman* (1956, as Coachman [uncredited])

**Mossman, John**

Mossman can be seen as a hearse driver in Hammer's *Dracula* (1958). **Hammer credits:** *Dracula* (1958, as Hearse driver [uncredited])

**Mothersill, Donald (Don)**

Mothersill worked as the wardrobe master on *Hammer House of Mystery and Suspense* (1984, TVM), prior to which he had worked for Hammer as a wardrobe assistant on *Scars of Dracula* (1970) and *The Horror of Frankenstein* (1970). His other credits include *The Legacy* (1978), *Sword of the Valiant* (1984), *Lifeforce* (1985), *The Bride* (1985), *The Living Daylights* (1987), *Henry V* (1989), *A Ghost in Monte Carlo* (1990, TVM) and *Duel of Hearts* (1992, TVM). **Hammer credits:** *Scars of Dracula* (1970, wardrobe assistant [uncredited]), *The Horror of Frankenstein* (1970, wardrobe assistant [uncredited]), *Hammer House of Mystery and Suspense* (1984, TVM, wardrobe master)

**Motte-Harrison, Andrew**

This British supporting actor played the role of Giles in the Hammer featurette *Man with a Dog* (1957). His other credits include *Supersonic Saucer* (1956). **Hammer credits:** *Man with a Dog* (1957, as Giles)

**Moulan, Rosita**

Moulan can be seen cavorting about semi-naked as a dancer in Hammer's *Creatures the World Forgot* (1971). **Hammer credits:** *Creatures the World Forgot* (1971, as Dancer)

**Moulder-Brown, John**

Best known to Hammer fans for playing the heroic Anton Kersh in *Vampire Circus* (1972), this British actor (1953–) began his film career as a child, making his debut in *Death Over My Shoulder*

(1958). His other credits include a handful of productions for the Children's Film Foundation, among them *The Missing Note* (1961), the serial *Beware of the Dog* (1964) and *Operation Third Form* (1966), in which he took the lead. His other credits include *Night Train for Inverness* (1960), *Two Living, One Dead* (1961), *The Uncle* (1965), *Deep End* (1970), *King, Queen, Knave* (1972), *Confessions from the David Galaxy Affair* (1979), *Claudia* (1985), *Rumpelstiltskin* (1987) and *Young Alexander the Great* (2010). His television work includes playing the title role in the serial *The Confessions of Felix Krull* (1982, TV), plus episodes of *A Moment in Time* (1979, TV), *Howards' Way* (1985–1990, TV) and *Casualty* (1986–, TV). Recalled the actor of his chance to work on a Hammer film, "I can remember sneaking in through the back doors of the cinema to see the Hammer horrors when I was thirteen or fourteen years old. They were sensational seeing them on the big screen. They were a part of my youth. So when I was offered *Vampire Circus* I was thrilled to be able to do it."[62] **Hammer credits:** *Vampire Circus* (1972, as Anton Kersh)

### The Mound

Built on the back lot at Bray for *The Mummy* (1959), this steep bank, made from old railway sleepers and gravel, went on to appear in a number of Hammer films during the sixties, among them *Dracula—Prince of Darkness* (1966). The site was finally dismantled in 1969, three years after Hammer had vacated Bray for Elstree. **Hammer credits include:** *The Mummy* (1959), *Dracula—Prince of Darkness* (1966)

### Mounteney, Carlisle

This British sound technician (1910–?, real name Carlisle Leonard Mountney, sometimes Mountenay) worked as a recordist on Hammer's *The Snorkel* (1958). His other credits include *Chin Chin Chinaman* (1931), *The Ghost Camera* (1933), *Street Song* (1935), *Mrs. Pym of Scotland Yard* (1940), *London Town* (1946) and *David* (1951). **Hammer credits:** *The Snorkel* (1958 [uncredited])

### Movielab

This American color process was frequently used by American International Pictures in the late sixties and early seventies. Given AIP's financial involvement in the making of Hammer's *The Vampire Lovers* (1970), the process was also used for this production. Other films shot in the Movielab process include *Gentlemen Prefer Nature Girls* (1962), *A Taste of Flesh* (1967), *Count Yorga, Vampire* (1970), *The Return of Count Yorga* (1971), which features a clip of *The Vampire Lovers*, *The Crazies* (1973), *An Unmarried Woman* (1978), *Willie and Phil* (1980) and *Homework* (1982). **Hammer credits:** *The Vampire Lovers* (1970)

### Moving In  see  *Life with the Lyons*

### Mower, Patrick

This debonair, RADA-trained British actor (1938–, real name Patrick Archibald Shaw) made his film debut in Hammer's *The Devil Rides Out* (1968) as the hapless Simon Aron, who finds his life imperiled by the leader of a group of Satanists he has joined (*Variety* described his performance as "adequate"). Mower's subsequent films include *The Smashing Bird I Used to Know* (1969), *Cry of the Banshee* (1970), *Incense for the Damned* (1970), *Percy* (1971), *Carry On England* (1976), *The Asylum* (2000) and *Dream* (2001). Also known for his stage work (including pantomime), Mower has nevertheless been at his busiest on television, where his appearances include episodes of such series as *Mary Barton* (1964, TV), *Swizzlewick* (1964, TV), *Haunted* (1967–1968, TV), in which he played Michael West, *Callan* (1967–1972, TV), in which he played James Cross, *Special Branch* (1969–1974, TV), in which he played Detective Chief Inspector Tom Haggerty, *Target* (1977–1978, TV), in which he played Detective Superintendent Steve Hackett, and *Emmerdale* (1972–, previously *Emmerdale Farm*, TV), which he joined in 2001 as Rodney Blackstock, going on to clock up over 900 episodes. He also appeared in *Czech Mate*, the opening episode of *Hammer House of Mystery and Suspense* (1984, TVM). He was formerly involved with the actress Suzanne Danielle (1957–), who appeared in *Carpathian Eagle* (1980, TV [episode of *Hammer House of Horror*]). **Hammer credits:** *The Devil Rides Out* (1968, as Simon Aron), *Czech Mate* (1984, TVM [episode of *Hammer House of Mystery and Suspense*], as John Patrick Duncan)

### Moxey, Hugh

As the crime solving Reverend Simon Cherry, this British actor (1909–1991) starred in the Hammer programer *Meet Simon Cherry* (1949), which marked his big screen debut. However, if any more films were planned, they failed to materialize, though Moxey himself did return to Hammer for *Spaceways* (1953), in which he played Colonel Daniels. His other credits include *The Franchise Affair* (1951), *Assignment Redhead* (1956), *You Pay Your Money* (1959), *The Snake Woman* (1960), *Mr. Forbush and the Penguins* (1971), *Hennessy* (1975) and *The Final Conflict* (1981). Busy in television, his appearances here include episodes of *The Little Minister* (1950, TV), *BBC Sunday-Night Theatre* (1950–1959, TV), *Danger Man* (1960–1962, TV), *The Main Chance* (1969–1975, TV) and *The Pickwick Papers* (1985, TV). **Hammer credits:** *Meet Simon Cherry* (1949, as the Reverend Simon Cherry), *Spaceways* (1953, as Colonel Daniels)

### Moxey, John Llewellyn

Best known by genre fans for helming the atmospheric shocker *The City of the Dead* (1960), this Argentinean born director (1925–) spent much of his subsequent career in America directing TV movies, among them *The House That Would Not Die* (1970, TVM), *A Taste of Evil* (1971, TVM), *The Night Stalker* (1972, TVM), *Charlie's Angels* (1976, TVM), *Sanctuary of Fear* (1978, TVM), *Killjoy* (1981, TVM) and *Lady Mobster* (1988, TVM), as well as episodes of *Magnum, P.I.* (1980–1988, TV) and *Murder, She Wrote* (1984–1996, TV). He was also set to direct Hammer's remake of *The Lady Vanishes* (1979) when it was intended as a TV movie. His other theatrical features include *Foxhole in Cairo* (1960), *Ricochet* (1963), *Circus of Fear* (1966) and *Strangler's Web* (1966). He began his film career as a third assistant director on *When You Come Home* (1947), graduated to second assistant on *The Hills of Donegal* (1947), and to first assistant on *The Glass Mountain* (1949). His early British television credits include episodes of *London Playhouse* (1955–1956, TV), *The Cheaters* (1960–1962, TV) and *Z Cars* (1962–1978, TV).

### Moyens, Judi (Judy)

This British supporting actress (1941–) played a servant girl in the Hammer remake of *The Hound of the Baskervilles* (1959). **Hammer credits:** *The Hound of the Baskervilles* (1959, as Servant)

### Mozart, George

One of Hammer's early managing directors, British born Mozart (1864–1947, real name David John Gillings) had—like Hammer's founding father, Will Hammer—trodden the boards on the variety circuit as a performer and musician. Never able to resist the temptation to perform, he popped up in several of Hammer's early films, including their very first production, *The Public Life of Henry the Ninth* (1935), in which he played a pub draughts player. He also starred in the Hammer short *Polly's Two Fathers* (1936), which he also scripted. His other films include a series of silent shorts, which he wrote, directed and played the title role. They were *Coney as Peacemaker* (1913), *Coney Gets the Glad Eye* (1913) and *Coney, Ragtimer* (1913). His sound credits include *Mr. George Mozart the Famous Comedian* (1928), which he also wrote, *George Mozart in Domestic Troubles* (1930), which was part of the *Gainsborough Gems* series (1930), *Café Mascot* (1936), *Strange Cargo* (1936), *Overcoat Sam* (1937), *Two on a Doorstep* (1936), *Dr. Sin Fang* (1937) and *Pygmalion* (1938). He also appeared in the early television variety show, *Music-Hall Cavalcade: Stars of Yesterday and Today* (1937, TV). Mozart wrote about his stage experiences in his 1937 autobiography *Limelight*. His granddaughter was the actress, singer and dancer Charmian Innes (1923–2011). His brother, George A. Gillings, was also an early Hammer board member. **Hammer credits:** *The Public Life of Henry the Ninth* (1935, as Draughts player), *The Mystery of the Mary Celeste* (1935, as Tommy Duggan), *Polly's Two Fathers* (1936, as Jack, also screenwriter), *Song of Freedom* (1936, as Bert Puddick), *The Bank Messenger Mystery* (1936, as George Brown)

### Muir, David

This Australian born cinematographer (1935–) photographed one of the flatter-looking episodes of Hammer's *Journey to the Unknown* (1968, TV), which he later followed with far more atmospheric work on *Lust for a Vampire* (1971). He began his career in his home country, photographing the likes of *The Jackeroo* (1960), *Australian Weekend* (1960), *Festival in Adelaide* (1962) and *From the Tropics to the Snow* (1964). His other UK credits include *Scruggs* (1965), *Opus* (1967), *Separation* (1967), which he co-photographed with Aubrey Dewar, *Joanna* (1968), which he co-photographed with Walter Lassally, *Mumsy, Nanny, Sonny & Girly*

(1970), *My Lover My Son* (1970), *And Now for Something Completely Different* (1971) and *Neither the Sea Nor the Sand* (1972). He also photographed *Boesman and Lena* (1974) in South Africa. Back in Australia, he directed, photographed, operated the camera and penned the title song for the short *You Can Have Your Say* (1979). **Hammer credits:** *The Madison Equation* (1968, TV [episode of *Journey to the Unknown*]), *Lust for a Vampire* (1971)

### Muir, Douglas

This British actor (1904–1966) had a supporting role in Hammer's *Wings of Danger* (1952). His other credits include *Laughter in Paradise* (1951), *The Sound Barrier* (1952), *Some Like It Cool* (1962) and *The Double Man* (1967). He also popped up in episodes of *The Appleyards* (1952–1957, TV), *Fabian of the Yard* (1954–1956, TV) and *The Avengers* (1961–1969, TV), in which he played One-Ten in eleven episodes between 1961 and 1963. His wife was the actress and writer Miriam Adams (1907–1987), whom he married in 1931; their daughter is the actress Gillian Muir (1935–). **Hammer credits:** *Wings of Danger* (1952, as Doctor)

### Muir, Jean

This elfin-like British actress (1936–) played Snout, Henry Jekyll's girlfriend, in the Hammer comedy *The Ugly Duckling* (1959). Her other credits include *Strip Tease Murder* (1961) and episodes of *The Benny Hill Show* (1955–1968, TV), *The Man in Room 17* (1965–1966, TV) and *Angel Pavement* (1967, TV). She was formerly a dancer with the girl group The Visionettes. **Hammer credits:** *The Ugly Duckling* (1959, as Snout)

### Mulcaster, Michael

This British supporting actor (1911–1984) played the surly prison warder in Hammer's *The Curse of Frankenstein* (1957). He also appeared in a handful of other films for the company, notable among them *The Hound of the Baskervilles* (1959), in which he played the escaped convict Selden (aka The Notting Hill Ripper), who comes to a sticky end when he is mistaken for Sir Henry Baskerville. He also appeared in *The Brides of Dracula* (1960), in which he played the mysterious man in black Latour, who inexplicably disappears from the plot after just a few minutes. His other credits include *Escape* (1948), *Sea Devils* (1953), *Up to His Neck* (1954) and *The Flesh and the Fiends* (1959), plus episodes of such series as *The Third Man* (1959–1965, TV), *Z Cars* (1962–1978, TV) and *The Rivals of Sherlock Holmes* (1971–1973, TV). His second wife (of two) was the costume designer Joan Ellacott (1920–), whom he married in 1949. **Hammer credits:** *The Curse of Frankenstein* (1957, as Prison warder), *The Revenge of Frankenstein* (1958, as Tattooed man [uncredited]), *The Hound of the Baskervilles* (1959, as Selden/The Notting Hill Ripper), *The Brides of Dracula* (1960, as Latour/man in black [uncredited]), *The Pirates of Blood River* (1962, as William Martin)

### Mulholland, Gordon

This South African born actor (1921–2010) can be seen at the climax of Hammer's *The Lady Craved Excitement* (1950) as an escaped lunatic, complete with phony beard. His other credits include *Treasure Island* (1950) and *Cheer the Brave* (1951). He then continued his career in South Africa with *Coast of Skeletons* (1963), *The Cape Town Affair* (1967), *The Professor and the Beauty Queen* (1968), *Act of Piracy* (1988), *Headhunter* (1989) and *Traitor's Heart* (1999). Also on stage. **Hammer credits:** *The Lady Craved Excitement* (1950, as Lunatic)

### Mullard, Arthur

One of the great characters of British comedy, the hefty frame, rubbery features and cor blimey accent of this British actor (1910–1995, real name Arthur Ernest Mullard) were always a welcome presence, even in the smallest of roles. Following experience as a boxer and bouncer, Mullard began his film career as a stunt man, walk-on and bit player in such films as *Inspector Hornleigh* (1938), *The Silver Fleet* (1943), *Oliver Twist* (1948) and *The Lavender Hill Mob* (1951). He also popped up in Hammer's *Whispering Smith Hits London* (1952) and *Life with the Lyons* (1954). He eventually went on to become a familiar face in such comedies as *Two-Way Stretch* (1960), *The Wrong Arm of the Law* (1962), *The Great St. Trinian's Train Robbery* (1966), *Smashing Time* (1967), *Chitty Chitty Bang Bang* (1968), *Three for All* (1974) and *Adventures of a Plumber's Mate* (1978). In the seventies, he found sitcom fame in *Romany Jones* (1972–1974, TV), in which he and Queenie Watts played the supporting roles of Wally and Lily Briggs, who subsequently went on to appear in their own spin-off series *Yus, My Dear* (1976, TV). Both these shows were created by Ronald Wolfe and Ronald Chesney, the men behind *On the Buses* (1969–1973, TV), and the duo subsequently introduced the Briggses into the action of their third big screen *Buses* spin-off for Hammer, *Holiday on the Buses* (1973), in which they proved to be a comic highlight. Interestingly, Mullard had previously had a bit role in the feature version of *On the Buses* (1971). Mullard's last job was providing a voice for the live-action remake of *101 Dalmatians* (1996). In 1978 he also had an unlikely chart hit with a cover version of *You're the One That I Want* with Hylda Baker, the video of which (shudder) featured the pair dressed as John Travolta and Olivia Newton-John. **Hammer credits:** *Whispering Smith Hits London* (1952, unnamed role [uncredited]), *Life with the Lyons* (1954, unnamed role [uncredited]), *Adventures with the Lyons* (1957, serial re-issue of *Life with the Lyons*, unnamed role [uncredited]), *On the Buses* (1971, unnamed role [uncredited]), *Holiday on the Buses* (1973, as Wally Briggs)

### Muller, Anne

Muller played one of the harem girls in the Hammer comedy *I Only Arsked!* (1958). **Hammer credits:** *I Only Arsked!* (1958, as Harem girl [uncredited])

### Mullett, Charles

Mullett worked as an electrician on a handful of films for Hammer in the late forties/early fifties. **Hammer credits:** *Celia* (1949 [uncredited]), *Meet Simon Cherry* (1949 [uncredited]), *The Man in Black* (1950 [uncredited]), *Someone at the Door* (1950 [uncredited])

### Mullins, Bartlett

With a name like this, this British actor (1904–1992) really should have gone farther than he did. He is best known as the zookeeper shutting up shop in Hammer's *The Quatermass Xperiment* (1955). He was also contracted to play a tramp in *The Curse of Frankenstein* (1957), but failed to appear in the finished film. His other credits include *Dancing with Crime* (1947), *The Three Weird Sisters* (1948), *The Adventures of Hal 5* (1958), *Peeping Tom* (1960), *The Sandwich Man* (1966), *Half a Sixpence* (1967), *Trog* (1970), *Sex and the Other Woman* (1972) and *Tales from the Crypt* (1972), plus three further minor appearances for Hammer. Note that his performance in *Rasputin—The Mad Monk* (1966) was re-voiced by Michael Ripper. His many television appearances include episodes of *Douglas Fairbanks, Jr. Presents* (1953–1957, TV), *Clementina* (1954, TV), *Outbreak of Murder* (1962, TV), *Doctor Who* (1963–1989, TV), *Bright's Boffins* (1970–1972, TV) and *Wings* (1977–1978, TV). **Hammer credits:** *Stolen Face* (1952, as Farmer [uncredited]), *The Quatermass Xperiment* (1955, as Zookeeper [uncredited]), *The Curse of Frankenstein* (1957, as Tramp [role cut prior to filming]), *Rasputin—The Mad Monk* (1966, as Wagoner [uncredited]), *Frankenstein Created Woman* (1967, as Bystander)

### *The Mummy*

GB, 1959, 88m, Eastmancolor [processed by Technicolor], widescreen [1.66:1], RCA, Cert X

Having already tackled color remakes of *Frankenstein* and *Dracula*, it was perhaps inevitable that Hammer would turn their attention that other horror staple *The Mummy*, the remake rights to which (along with several other genre properties) had been turned over to them by Universal, who would release the film in America. Again, rather than a straight remake, Hammer put their own spin on the story, which had previously been filmed in 1932 with Boris Karloff. Like Universal's *Dracula* and *Frankenstein* films, the original production of *The Mummy* had provoked a number of sequels: *The Mummy's Hand* (1940), *The Mummy's Tomb* (1942), *The Mummy's Ghost* (1944) and *The Mummy's Curse* (1945), culminating with the comedy spoof *Abbott and Costello Meet the Mummy* (1955), and it would be from several of these that the Hammer film would draw.

Taking the basic storyline of the original film (that of unrequited love across the millennia), plus various situations and character names from the sequels (as well as certain events from the 1923 Tutankhamun expedition led by Howard Carter and Lord Caenarvon), Jimmy Sangster fashioned a screenplay that sees a group of archaeologists discover the long lost tomb of the High Priestess Ananka in Egypt in 1895, only to find themselves at the mercy of a murderous mummy to avenge the desecration.

Following submissions to the BBFC for approval (which resulted in the usual objections and amendments), the film went onto the floor at Bray on 23 February 1959 for a lengthy eight-week shoot that would last until 16 April, with additional pick-up shots made on the 27 and 28 of April. Again, those with proven track records with the company headed the cast and production team, prime among them actors Peter Cushing and Christopher Lee, director Terence Fisher, designer Bernard Robinson and cinematographer Jack Asher, all of whom would work in tandem to produce one of the studio's most highly regarded productions.

With a budget in excess of £125,000 (which included a loan from the National Film Finance Corporation), the production was also one of the company's most lavish. Indeed, from the opening credits set against a series of richly colored Egyptian murals, the movie is one of Hammer's most opulent. The story opens in Egypt with the discovery of the tomb of Ananka by an archaeological team led by Stephen Banning and his son John. Unfortunately, John has broken his leg, and it is left to his father (who has been searching for the tomb for twenty years) and his uncle Joseph to enter the burial site, much to the consternation of the locals, among them one Mehemet Akhir, who warns that, "He who robs the graves of Egypt dies!" Yet despite

this threat, the two men break the tomb's seal and enter, discovering the place to be laden with riches, among them Ananka's gold-encrusted sarcophagus ("Marvellous absolutely undisturbed!" exclaims Stephen). However, while Joseph rushes back to John's tent to tell him of their remarkable findings, Stephen makes a further discovery—that of the scroll of life ("Said to have been written by the hand of the god Karnak [*sic*] himself," as we later learn), the removal of which from a small recess triggers a door behind which a Mummy lies entombed. Cut to John's tent and a blood-curdling scream is heard. Something has reduced his father to a jabbering wreck—but who or what?

It's now six months later and Stephen Banning has been sent home. Meanwhile, John and his uncle continue their work in the tomb, cataloguing their findings. Yet as John reveals, it's not been a pleasant task: "I've worked in dozens of tombs. I've spent the best part of my life among the dead, but I've never known a place that has such an aura of menace." After this, the tomb is sealed with explosives, much to the anger of the ever-watchful Mehemet Akhir, who vows to Ananka that, "For this desecration you will be avenged," following which he sets his men to work to retrieve the Mummy from the rubble.

The story then moves to England. It is three years later and Stephen Banning is in the Engerfield Nursing Home for the Mentally Disordered, where his son visits him upon his return. Here, Stephen tells John of his encounter in the tomb with the Mummy, which he had inadvertently brought to life by reading the scroll of life ("After 4,000 years, the words of the scroll brought it to life again," he tells his incredulous son). Yet little does he know that the Mummy is not back in Egypt under a pile of rubble, but just a few miles up the road in a crate, awaiting to be transported by two shifters to a house that Mehemet Akhir has taken nearby to extract his promised revenge! Gradually, Stephen Banning's increasing sense of unease alerts him that something is amiss. Indeed, as the two shifters drive by the rest home with their deadly cargo, Banning becomes increasingly unnerved, and in doing so smashes a window, the sound of which itself causes the men on the cart to panic ("Perhaps one of them got out!"), resulting in the

The course of true love never did run smooth. Yvonne Furneaux and Christopher Lee in a scene from *The Mummy* (1959) (Hammer/Rank/Universal International).

crate ending up in the local mire ("I'm not going to have my throat cut by a lunatic, not for all the relics in Egypt").

Yet this proves no deterrent to the seemingly unconcerned Mehemet Akhir when he turns up on the scene. Instead, he simply uses the scroll of life (known as the scroll of Thoth in the Universal films) to raise the Mummy from the swamp, following which he sends him forth to dispatch the first of the desecrators, Stephen Banning, who by now has been placed in a padded cell with a panic button. "It's no use banging on the door or shouting. We won't hear you," warns the orderly, which of course is *exactly* what Banning does when the Mummy pays a deadly visit later that night, crashing through the barred window to strangle him.

Following the enquiry into the murder of his father ("The work of a madman," concludes the coroner), John Banning looks through his father's notes to see if he had any enemies. In doing so, he comes across a portfolio about Ananka, and proceeds to tell her story to his uncle Joseph (who, astonishingly, is unaware of the tale, despite having spent several years in Egypt looking for her tomb!). Banning goes on to relate how the late Ananka's high priest Kharis, who was very much in love with her, had returned to her tomb following her burial in the hope of reviving her with the scroll of life. But Kharis is discovered in this act of desecration, for which he has his tongue cut out, "So the cries that he would utter during the fate that awaited him should not offend the ears of the gods." Following this, he is mummified and incarcerated alive behind a wall by the tomb of his beloved. Comments Banning, "Dad knew all about the legend. Perhaps having discovered that half of it was true, he let his imagination persuade him that the rest of it could have been," he says by way of trying to explain his dead father's delusions.

Meanwhile, Mehemet Akhir sends the Mummy to kill the next desecrator, John's uncle. However, when the Mummy comes crashing through the front door, Banning grabs a gun and fires off six shots, hitting the Mummy twice. Unfortunately,

A classic poster for *The Mummy* (1959). However, the dramatic beam of torchlight through the title character's body caused some concern for Peter Cushing (Hammer/Rank/Universal International).

this is too late to save his uncle. After such a kafuffle, the police are inevitably called in to investigate, and it is now that John tells Inspector Mulrooney, who has been brought up from London, how his father came to be driven mad by his encounter in the tomb with the Mummy and the scroll of life. Naturally, the Inspector is incredulous ("I deal in facts, Mr. Banning. Cold, hard facts"). Later, following the Inspector's departure, Banning notices how much his wife Isobel resembles Ananka (much to her surprise), a coincidence that proves particularly handy when the Mummy returns, crashing through the French windows in its bid to kill him. Despite the fact that Banning defends himself with a spear, which he thrusts through the Mummy's body, it is his wife's plea of "No!" that saves his life, prompting the Mummy to leave.

Upon his inevitable return, Inspector Mulrooney, who has been making his own investigations, tells Banning of the Egyptian who has taken the nearby house. Naturally, John sees this as too much of a coincidence. "Remember, Mr. Banning. No private police work, please," the Inspector warns him, yet this doesn't prevent the archaeologist from paying his new neighbor a call, during which the pair exchange their thoughts about religion ("To me the dead are the dead—clay," Akhir informs an unconvinced Banning).

"Perhaps this man *is* controlling the Mummy," says the Inspector when Banning tells him of his visit. Indeed, soon after, Akhir turns up at Banning's house with the Mummy in tow, his intention being to kill off the final desecrator. Yet the Mummy is again prevented from doing so by the presence of Banning's wife, whom Akhir orders the Mummy to also kill. Unable to carry out this deed, the Mummy instead kills Akhir, breaking his back when the Egyptian tries to stab her himself. The Mummy then takes Isobel to the mire, but she manages to escape at the last moment ("Kharis—put me down!"), following which the Mummy (who luckily understands English and obeys!) is shot to bits by the Inspector and a number of concerned locals, after which it sinks into the depths, clutching the scroll of life.

Hammer's biggest production to date, *The Mummy* was filmed primarily at Bray, where certain sets from *The Man Who Could Cheat Death* (1959) were re-used, although the company also made use of the larger sound stages at Shepperton to film the Egyptian sequences, among them the exterior of the archaeological dig and Ananka's elaborate funeral procession, for which a number of authentic-looking props were built under the supervision of the film's Egyptian advisor, Andrew Low. Among those working on these props was Margaret Carter, the future wife of Hammer production designer Bernard Robinson, to whom the making of the mask of Anubis and other important artifacts for the tomb and funeral procession was entrusted (note that for the funeral sequence, an alternate version was shot for the overseas market, in which the hand maidens went topless, although this apparently went unused). Also for this sequence, a leopard—previously seen in *Cat Girl* (1957)—was loaned from Southport Zoo (although it cannot

*Above:* A later double bill of *The Curse of Frankenstein* (1957) and *The Mummy* (1959). (Hammer/Clarion/Warner Bros./Rank/Universal International) *Below:* Wreaking havoc. George Pastell (in fez), Christopher Lee and Yvonne Furneaux in a scene from *The Mummy* (1959) (Hammer/Rank/Universal International).

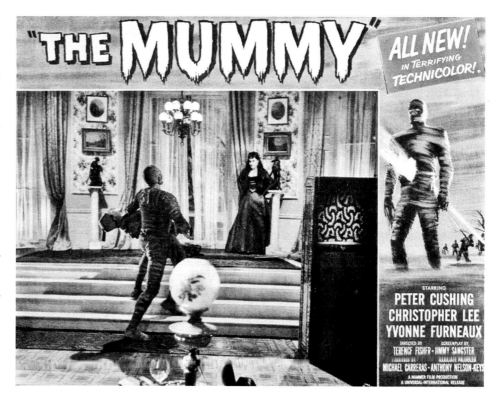

be seen in the sequence), along with two oxen and a pair of Peregrine Wanderer falcons.

The set for the dig, for which pieces from the Shepperton-shot *Yesterday's Enemy* (1959) were recycled, was a fairly expansive affair, complete with tents, palm trees and a length of mine-car track, which handily doubled as dolly rails for the camera for a couple of brief shots. Yet another stage at Shepperton housed the bog set. Meanwhile, back at Bray, Stage 2 played host to Ananka's elaborately appointed tomb interior. As usual, Down Place itself doubled for certain exteriors, among them the outside of John Banning's house, the interior of which was erected on Stage One. Nearby Oakley Court was also briefly used as the exterior of Akhir's rented Engerfield mansion. Additionally, a steep slope (nicknamed The Mound) was built on the back lot, down which the cart carrying the crate trundles, just before it ends up sliding into the bog.

Production-wise, the script is one of Jimmy Sangster's more straightforward efforts, despite its use of flashbacks to explain Stephen Banning's descent into madness (as told by John Banning) and the back-story of Kharis and Ananka (whom Isobel merely resembles, rather than being a direct reincarnation of, as in the original Universal film [in which the character is named Helen Grosvenor]). The dialogue is generally serviceable, though at times merely routine (Banning's encounter with Akhir at his house, during which he insults the Egyptian by describing Karnak as being "a third-rate God," verges on the tedious). The screenplay also contains touches of xenophobia typical of the period in which it was written ("I don't like the cove we're cartin' for. He's a foreigner," says one of the drunken shifters, to which his companion replies, "He can't help that!").

Its suspicions of "Johnny Foreigner" aside, the film also tends to deal in stock characters, among them the local copper ("Now for some particulars, if you don't mind") and the poacher who sees more than he bargained for in the woods ("I've seen the likes tonight that mortal eyes shouldn't look at!"). Luckily, these two roles are played by Hammer stalwarts George Woodbridge and Michael Ripper re-spectively, and so are at least humorously portrayed (ditto the two crate shifters played by Denis Shaw and Harold Goodwin). Less can be said of Eddie Byrne's dull Inspector Mulrooney though, whose character wouldn't seem out of place in one of Exclusive's more routine crime programmers. However, the rest of the cast is generally in fine fettle: Yvonne Furneaux looks stunning as both Isobel and Ananka (though note that her throat and eyes twitch when, as Ananka, she's supposed to be dead), while Felix Aylmer superbly captures Stephen Banning's mounting nervousness as he senses the nearing presence of the Mummy. Meanwhile, George Pastell's Mehemet Ahkir exudes oily evil as the story's true protagonist, though it should be noted that in the credits, his character is referred to as Mehemet Bey!

Admittedly, given his broken leg, Peter Cushing's John Banning is somewhat on the periphery of events to begin with, while later, his limp robs him of the athleticism that he was able to invest in his performance as Van Helsing in *Dracula* (1958). Nevertheless, he pulls off a sprightly jump across the desk in his study when the Mummy comes to call, and manages to thrust a spear straight through its chest when other methods to dispatch it fail. Cushing himself came up with this bit of business by way of explaining the fact the film's poster—already designed—featured the Mummy with a beam of light shining through a hole in its body. Cushing felt this bit of action would satisfy audience expectations. Revealed the star, "When I saw the posters advertising the film, I noticed that Christopher Lee ... had a large hole in his diaphragm with a beam of light passing through it, which was never referred to in the script ... so I asked Terry [Fisher] if I could grab a harpoon hanging on the wall of Banning's study and, during the struggle for survival, drive it clear through my opponent's body. And that's what I did, thus giving some sort of logic to ... the posters."[63]

The film's finest performance, however, comes from Christopher Lee as the towering Kharis (who, it should be noted, is just as guilty of desecration himself as are the members of the expedition 4,000 years later). As in *The Curse of Frankenstein* (1957), Lee remains mute for the majority of the film, save for the flashback, during which he can be heard speaking a certain amount of mumbo jumbo during the incantation sequence ("Thou goest round heaven, thou seest the Being who has knowledge, behold thou art in the Sekhmet boat as it goeth round the horizon of heaven," he intones, managing to keep a straight face throughout!). Yet despite the drawback of being speechless for the remainder of the film, Lee's mastery of mime and body language make his character come across as a genuine threat. No shuffling ragbag of bones and bandages, Lee's Mummy moves with speed and determination, making several explosive entrances during the course of the action, memorable among them his breaking into Stephen Banning's cell and his smashing through the French windows of John Banning's study (note that following the Mummy's strangulation of Stephen Banning, the Mummy turns to make his exit from the cell—however, Lee stops moving when he reaches the wall, just as the camera pans down to the dead man's body on the bed; needless to say, we don't see the Mummy awkwardly clambering back up out of the window!).

Aiding and abetting Lee's magnetic performance is the superbly designed and applied make-up of Roy Ashton, which nevertheless severely limits the actor's facial expressions (his mouth is completely covered by bandages). Yet through the use of his eyes, Lee still manages to convey rage and, more importantly, his anguished love for Ananka/Isobel, investing the character with a certain degree of sympathy. Commented Lee: "As far as I was concerned, when I played the Mummy it was all about redemption. I call it 'the loneliness of evil.' ...The curse of being undead, of being immortal, is actually the source of terrible sorrow."[64] Jimmy Sangster agreed, describing the character as "frightening—and also very sad."[65] Meanwhile, of his make-up Lee said, "Strangely enough, I didn't feel claustrophobic, though I could only act with my eyes and body. Physically, it was immensely demanding. I couldn't see where I was going and kept tripping over. I was swearing like a trooper, but no-one heard because of the bandages over my mouth."[66] As for the laborious make-up application process he recalled, "Roy and I used to sing all the time. I'm a bass baritone and of course, he was a tenor. While working on *The Mummy* we would flit from opera to opera in the morning just to keep ourselves going."[67]

Lee also did the majority of his own stunts for the film, including crashing through various doors and carrying Isobel through the swamp, which resulted in a severe neck strain for the actor. Commented the actor, "Not that Yvonne Furneaux was

**Full throttle. Christopher Lee chokes Peter Cushing in this thrilling moment from *The Mummy* (1959) (Hammer/Rank/Universal International).**

a heavyweight, but when I carried her, she was supposed to be unconscious and couldn't help me by hanging on to my neck. She was a dead weight."[68] However, stuntman Eddie Powell doubled for Lee on occasion, notably in the scene in which the Mummy is shot in Banning's study, for which two small explosive charges were placed on the stuntman's body (which are clearly seen to explode *from* his body rather than actually penetrate it). Interestingly, as well as continuing to double for Lee throughout his career, Powell would himself go on to play the Mummy in Hammer's *The Mummy's Shroud* (1966).

Post-production on the film was a relatively uncomplicated affair, given Hammer's established expediency in such matters. It was during this period that music director John Hollingsworth introduced a new name to Hammer: that of composer Franz Reizenstein. Incredibly, *The Mummy* was Reizenstein's first feature film assignment following several works for the concert platform, along with the first opera specifically commissioned for broadcast on BBC radio. One of the most remarkable scores written for a Hammer production, the music—with its lush, melodic central theme, complete with sepulchral choral embellishments—is infused in equal measure with a sense of both dread and romance. Commented Christopher Lee of Reizenstein's composition, "I think the music of *The Mummy* is greatly superior to all the other music in any other Hammer film. And that's saying a great deal, because there was some *wonderful* music in many of the Hammer films."[69]

Expectations for the film were high, and Hammer's publicists began work on the production in May 1959, commenting in the showman's manual, "The hunt for the Mummy, and his eventual destruction, make for the most grisly, horrific climax since the hounding down and liquidation of the vampire king in Hammer's *Horror of Dracula.*" The film's poster meanwhile warned that, "Its evil look brings madness! Its evil spell enslaves! Its evil touch kills, kills, kills!" The film was subsequently trade shown at Hammer House on 20 August, following which it received its premiere at the London Pavilion on 25 September. However, expectant audiences in the provinces had to wait until 23 October before the film—which was distributed in the UK by Rank—finally went on general release on the ABC circuit, paired with the short *Bed Without Breakfast* (1959). The U.S. release, care of Universal International, followed on 17 December, for which the movie was billed with the low budget western/vampire hybrid *Curse of the Undead* (1959).

As to be expected, not all the reviews were positive. Wrote Paul Dehn in the *News Chronicle*, "The skies are painted; the vegetation potted; and surely Hammer has now wallowed in enough mud to appoint a resident designer of plausible bogs." Meanwhile, Howard Thompson commented in *The New York Times*, "Should have been better … just lumbers." Indeed, the film *does* seem a little halting in its pacing, despite its brief running time, while Terence Fisher's direction occasionally lacks the vigor that distinguished *Dracula*. Nevertheless, there are enough memorable moments peppered throughout the film to more than justify it as a genuine

**The elaborate funeral flashback from *The Mummy* (1959) (Hammer/Rank/Universal International).**

Hammer classic, prime among them the burial sequence and the Mummy's killing sprees in the asylum cell and John Banning's study, all of which are superbly staged. On the down side, the script is a somewhat disjointed collection of elements that don't always fuse together (not surprising, perhaps, given the number of sources), while logic is far from uppermost. For example, John Banning relates the story of his father's encounter with the Mummy in the tomb to Inspector Mulrooney as he *imagines* it to have taken place, including Mehemet Akhir's arrival to steal the scroll of life, while Constable Blake's claims that the bog into which the crate containing the Mummy is "next to bottomless" in parts seems somewhat exaggerated given that the Mummy is able to walk through it twice during the film (in fact the locals can't have been looking very hard for the crate after it has fallen in, given that Kharis rises just next to the bank!).

Yet despite these drawbacks (as well as the occasional technical glitch, such as a shadow cast by the camera as it dollies in for a close-up of the recess in which the scroll of life has been resting), the film contains much to keep one glued, including a handful of minor cinematic flourishes, among them a couple of tilted shots at the asylum by way of emphasizing the state of Stephen Banning's mind, and the placing of the camera atop Ananka's sarcophagus during the funeral procession. Note, too, the build up to the Mummy's entrance through the French windows of Banning's study, which recalls Lucy Holmwood's expectant wait for Dracula in her bedroom. As for Jack Asher's moody lighting, it adds immeasurably to the atmosphere, even if camera movement itself is

fairly limited throughout. His framing, however, is frequently eye-catching.

Despite the critical naysayers, there were some positive notices. *Kinematograph Weekly* described the film as being "extremely well mounted and well acted," while *Variety* averred "Christopher Lee scores as the avenger." The London *Evening Standard* went one better, claiming that, "Hammer films have made the most distinguished of English horror pictures," while *Films and Filming* praised "Hammer's highly organized team" for giving the film "enough gloss to satisfy its undemanding customers and enough thrills to keep them half-way to the edge of their seats." Indeed, audiences (undemanding or otherwise) loved the film, and it went on to be a major commercial success for both Hammer and Universal (in fact it managed to outperform *Dracula* at the box office!). Consequently, three unrelated sequels later appeared: *The Curse of the Mummy's Tomb* (1964), *The Mummy's Shroud* (1966) and *Blood from the Mummy's Tomb* (1971). However, Lee was not involved in any of them. Commented the actor, "Kharis was a part that I'm glad to have played, but not one I wished to repeat—and not just due to the physical aspects. The character is extremely limited and there's nothing more I could have done with him. Terence Fisher, Jimmy Sangster, and I tried to give Kharis a human quality, and I believe we succeeded. He was not just a monster. We showed the man he once was."[70]

**Additional notes:** The name Joseph Whemple hails from the 1932 film, while Stephen (Steve) Banning is taken from *The Mummy's Hand* (1940); this name also features in *The Mummy's Tomb* (1942), as does John Banning, Mehemet Bey, Kharis and Isobel (albeit Evans), while Kharis is also used in *The Mummy's Ghost* (1944) and *The Mummy's Curse* (1944), while Ananka hails from the latter. In 1999, the story was remade by Universal, again as *The Mummy*, the success of which prompted an equally popular sequel, *The Mummy Returns* (2001); both productions were likewise shot at Shepperton. A third film in the franchise, *The Mummy: Tomb of the Dragon Emperor*, appeared in 2008. A reboot starring Tom Cruise followed in 2017.

Production company: Hammer. Distributors: Rank (UK [ABC circuit]), Universal International (U.S.). Producer: Michael Carreras. Associate producer: Anthony Nelson Keys. Director: Terence Fisher. Screenplay: Jimmy Sangster. Cinematographer: Jack Asher. Music: Franz Reizenstein. Music director: John Hollingsworth. Supervising editor: James Needs. Editor: Alfred Cox. Assistant editor: Chris Barnes [uncredited]. Production designer: Bernard Robinson. Assistant art director: Don Mingaye [uncredited]. Costumes: Molly Arbuthnot, Rosemary Burrows (assistant [uncredited]). Make-up: Roy Ashton. Hair: Henry Montsash. Special effects: Bill Warrington, Les Bowie [uncredited]. Camera operator: Len Harris. Focus puller: Harry Oakes [uncredited]. Clapper boy: Alan McDonald [uncredited]. Assistant director: John Peverall [uncredited]. Second assistant director: Tom Walls [uncredited]. Third assistant director: Hugh Harlow [uncredited]. Sound: Jock May. Sound editor: Roy Hyde. Boom operator: Jim Perry [uncredited]. Sound assistant: Claude Hitchcock [uncredited]. Sound camera operator: Al Thorne [uncredited]. Sound maintenance: Charles Bouvet [uncredited]. Production manager: Don

Weeks. Studio manager: Arthur Kelly [uncredited]. Construction manager: Mick Lyons [uncredited]. Chief electrician: Jack Curtis [uncredited]. Master carpenter: Charles Davis [uncredited]. Master plasterer: Arthur Banks [uncredited]. Master painter: Lawrence Wren [uncredited]. Propr Tommy Money [uncredited]. Props buyer: Eric Hillier [uncredited]. Casting: Dorothy Holloway [uncredited]. Continuity: Marjorie Lavelly. Stunts: Eddie Powell [uncredited]. Stills: Tom Edwards [uncredited]. Publicists: Colin Reid [uncredited], Dennison Thornton [uncredited]. Cashier: Ken Gordon [uncredited]. Modelers: Margaret Carter (later Robinson [uncredited]), Arthur Healey [uncredited]. Egyptian advisor: Andrew Low. Poster: Bill Wiggins [uncredited]. **Cast:** Peter Cushing (John Banning), Christopher Lee (Kharis/The Mummy), Yvonne Furneaux (Isobel Banning/High Priestess Ananka), Felix Aylmer (Stephen Banning), Raymond Huntley (Joseph Whemple), John Stuart (Coroner), Eddie Byrne (Inspector Mulrooney), George Pastell (Mehemet Akhir/Bey), Denis Shaw (Mike), Harold Goodwin (Pat), Michael Ripper (Poacher), George Woodbridge (Constable Blake), Gerald Lawson (Irishman in pub), Willoughby Gray (Dr. Reilly), Frank Singuineau (Head Porter), Stanley Meadows (Attendant), David Browning (Sergeant), Frank Sieman (Bill [Red Lion publican]), John Harrison (First priest [uncredited]), James Clarke (Second priest [uncredited]), Fred Rawlings (unnamed role [uncredited]), Eddie Powell (Christopher Lee's stunt double [uncredited]). **DVD availability:** Warner (U.S. R1 NTSC, UK R2 PAL). **Blu-ray availability:** Lionsgate (B/2), extras include the DVD, two documen-

taries, *Unwrapping the Mummy* and *Hammer's Rep Company*, an additional documentary, *The House of Horror: Memories of Bray*, an episode of *The World of Hammer* (1990 [first broadcast 1994], TV) titled *Hammer Stars: Peter Cushing*, a stills gallery, a promo reel and a commentary by Marcus Hearn and Jonathan Rigby, plus *Stolen Face* (1952). **CD availability:** *The Hammer Film Music Collection: Volume One* (GDI Records), which contains the *Main Title*; *The Mummy* (GDI Records), which contains the complete score, plus an introduction by Christopher Lee

### The Mummy's Shroud

GB, 1967, 90m [U.S.], 84m [UK], Technicolor [UK], DeLuxe [U.S.], widescreen [1.85:1], RCA, Cert X

*The Mummy's Shroud* was the last full-length feature made by Hammer at Bray. Sadly, the movie is far from being one of the studio's best, and makes for a rather half-hearted swan song. That said, for those who don't expect too much from it, the film does provide one or two mild thrills and spills amid the clichés.

As well as marking Hammer's last hurrah at Bray, the movie also proved to be writer-director John Gilling's last outing for the company. Based on a story supplied by Anthony Hinds (writing as John Elder, and executive producing without credit), Gilling's script (originally announced as *Shroud of the Mummy*) is almost as dusty as some of the artifacts featured in the movie, and could easily have been written some twenty years earlier for the Universal series (note that Gilling presented his completed script on 6 September—just six days before production began). Like its black and white forebears, it features a revived Mummy that, at the bidding of one Hasmid Ali, goes on a killing spree to avenge those who dared desecrate the burial site of its young master, Kah-to-Bey. Recalled the film's second assistant director Christopher Neame of the screenplay, "It took Gilling five days to complete the script. I know because my job was to take each finished scene along to Pauline, Mr. Keys' secretary, for typing on 'skins,' and then run off the pages on the Gestetner machine. Certainly no great movie came from it, but it was fun to make."[71]

Even Gilling himself later admitted that, "It was a worn-out theme."[72] Therefore, in order to shake a few changes out of the familiar situations, the director latched upon the idea of presenting the Mummy's initial appearances to its various victims via a series of distorted images, which recall his use of a fish-eye lens in *The Shadow of the Cat* (1961), also photographed by Arthur Grant. Consequently, the Mummy is seen through a crystal ball, in a tray of developing fluid and as a shadow, etc., prior to his deadly attacks, which include such means as strangulation and skull crushing (although a decapitation was snipped from the script following its submission to the BBFC).

Unfortunately, in addition to his wheezing script (set in 1920, some three years before the Carter/Caenarvon expedition), Gilling is also scuppered by the film's painfully low budget (some £134,000), which is obvious throughout, never less so than in the interminable opening sequence, which is sup-

Desecrating the tomb of Ananka. Raymond Huntley (left) and Felix Aylmer (right) in a scene from *The Mummy* (1959) (Hammer/Rank/Universal International).

posedly set in Egypt, but clearly shot inside a cramped studio (note the shadows cast by the actors upon the painted cyclorama, which supposedly represents the distant mountains). Indeed, rather like his work for *Frankenstein Created Woman* (1967), Bernard Robinson's sets lack their usual detail and finesse, while Arthur Grant's overly bright lighting lacks atmosphere.

Despite these considerable setbacks, the film does benefit from a stronger cast than usual, led by the always-welcome André Morell as Sir Basil Walden, whose expedition results in so much death and destruction. Michael Ripper, as the manservant Longbarrow, and Catherine Lacey as the mystic Haiti, also donate strong cameos, though the younger, less experienced members of the cast—among them John Phillips, David Buck and Maggie Kimberley—lack personality and appear to be treading water. As for Prem the Mummy, stuntman Eddie Powell is little more than an automaton in an ill-fitting zip-up suit of bandages designed by make-up man George Partleton, despite being based upon the wrappings of an authentic Mummy on display in the British Museum.

The well-staged killings aside, the film also features a highly unusual ending: having completed its task, the Mummy destroys itself by crushing itself to death with its own hands. An impressive sequence, this was achieved by creating a version of the Mummy's head with wax, bandages and fuller's earth by effects man Les Bowie and his team; this was subsequently crushed on camera by the bandaged hands of effects assistant Ian Scoones.

Shot at Bray between 12 September and 21 October 1966, as well as on location at a quarry in Gerrard's Cross (also made use of in *X—The Unknown* [1956]), *The Mummy's Shroud* has the feel of a second feature. In fact it went out as the lower half of a double bill top-lining Hammer's *Frankenstein Created Woman* (1967), and was promoted with the amusing tagline, "Beware the beat of the cloth-wrapped feet." Trade shown at Studio One on 3 May 1967, this bill was subsequently released on the UK's ABC circuit care of Warner Pathé on 18 June, prior to which the same pairing had been released in the U.S. by Fox on 15 March, for which the running time was six minutes longer. Unfortunately, the critics were less than kind on both sides of the Atlantic, with the *Monthly Film Bulletin* best summing up the film as "a stilted rehash," while *Variety* noted that "dialogue, characterizations and plot have little to recommend them." **Additional notes:** Elizabeth Sellars, who plays Barbara Preston, appeared in *Cloudburst* (1951), Hammer's very first film at Bray. Dickie Owen, who played the Mummy in *The Curse of the Mummy's Tomb* (1964), here plays the human incarnation of Prem during the flashback. John Richardson was the original consideration for the role of Paul Preston, eventually played by David Buck. Although *The Mummy's Shroud* was the last feature made by Hammer at Bray, the company did return to film the effects sequences for both *Moon Zero Two* (1969) and *When Dinosaurs Ruled the Earth* (1970).

Production companies: Hammer/Seven Arts/ Associated British Picture Corporation. Distributors: Warner Pathé Distributors (UK [ABC circuit]), Twentieth Century–Fox (U.S.). Executive producer: Anthony Hinds. Producer: Anthony Nelson Keys. Director: John Gilling. Screenplay: John Gilling. Story: John Elder (Anthony Hinds). Cinematographer: Arthur Grant. Music: Don Banks. Music director: Philip Martell. Supervising editor: James Needs. Editor: Chris Barnes. Production design: Bernard Robinson. Art director: Don Mingaye. Costumes: Molly Arbuthnot, Larry Stewart, Rosemary Burrows [uncredited]. Special effects: Bowie Films, Ltd.. Special effects assistant: Ian Scoones [uncredited]. Make-up: George Partleton. Hair: Frieda Steiger. Sound: Ken Rawkins. Sound editor: Roy Hyde. Camera operator: Moray Grant. Focus puller: Bob Jordan [uncredited]. Production manager: Ed Harper. Assistant director: Bluey Hill. Second assistant director: Christopher Neame [uncredited]. Third assistant director: Graham Fowler [uncredited]. Casting: Irene Lamb. Continuity: Eileen Head. Narrator: Tim Turner [uncredited]. Poster: Tom Chantrell [uncredited]. **Cast:** André Morell (Sir Basil Walden), John Phillips (Stanley Preston), Elizabeth Sellars (Barbara Preston), David Buck (Paul Preston), Dickie Owen (Prem [flashback]), Eddie Powell (Prem [The Mummy]), Catherine Lacey (Haiti), Maggie Kimberley (Claire), Michael Ripper (Longbarrow), Tim Barrett (Harry), Roger Delgado (Hasmid Ali), Richard Warner (Inspector Barrani), Bruno Barnabe (Pharaoh), Toni Gilpin (Pharaoh's wife), Toolsie Persaud (Kah-to-Bey), Andreas Malandrinos (Curator), John Garrie (Arab cleaner [uncredited]), Darroll Richards (Sage [uncredited]), George Zenios (Arab reporter [uncredited]), Roy Stephens (Reporter [uncredited]), Pat Gorman (Reporter [uncredited]), Michael Rothwell (Reporter [uncredited]), Terence Sewards (Reporter [uncredited]), Fred Peck (Reporter [uncredited]. **DVD availability:** Anchor Bay (U.S. R1 NTSC), extras include a trailer, TV spots and an episode of *The World of Hammer* (1990 [first broadcast 1994], TV) titled *Mummies, Werewolves and the Living Dead.* **Blu-ray availability:** Studio Canal (B/2), extras include the DVD version, plus trailers, a gallery and two documentaries, *The Beat Goes On: The Making of the Mummy's Shroud* and *Remembering David Buck*

## Mungarvan, Mike

Mungarvan had a minor role in Hammer's *Straight on Till Morning* (1972). His other credits include *Scum* (1977), *American Roulette* (1988), *Young Soul Rebels* (1991) and *Charlie* (2004), plus episodes of *Doctor Who* (1963–1989, TV), in which he played everything from a Time Lord to a Dalek, *Trial* (1971, TV), *Blakes 7* (1978–1981, TV) and *Doctor Who* (2005–, TV). **Hammer credits:** *Straight on Till Morning* (1972, as Client [uncredited])

## Munro, Alex

A long time fixture in summer season at the open air theater in Llandudno's Happy Valley in the fifties, sixties and seventies, this diminutive British (Scottish) entertainer (1911–1986, real name Alexander Horsburgh) made the short hop over to the Pontin's holiday camp near Prestatyn to appear in Hammer's *Holiday on the Buses* (1973). He began his career in an acrobatic act with his brother Archie and his sister June. First known as The Star Trio, and then as The Horsburgh Brothers and Agnes, they toured the variety circuit with Florrie Forde's company, which also featured Flanagan and Allen. During the war years he hosted his own radio series, *The Size of It.* His other credits include *Them Nice Americans* (1958) plus episodes of *Z Cars* (1962–1978, TV) and *Mr. Rose* (1967–1968, TV). He was also the creative controller of Llandudno's Pier Pavilion Theater in the seventies. His second wife was dancer and make-up artist Lilias Munro (1917–2004) whom he married in 1949. His daughter (with first wife Phyllis Robertshaw) was actress Janet Munro (1934–1972, real name Janet Neilson Horsburgh), whose first husband, the actor Tony Wright (1925–1986), to whom she was married between 1956 and 1959, starred in Hammer's boxing melodrama *The Flanagan Boy* (1953); her second husband, the actor Ian Hendry (1931–1984), to whom she was married between 1963 and 1971, had a featured role in Hammer's *Captain Kronos—Vampire Hunter* (1974). In 2014, the road leading up to the Happy Valley was renamed Alex Munro Way, though sadly the open air theater itself is now a children's play area. **Hammer credits:** *Holiday on the Buses* (1973, as Patient)

## Munro, Caroline

A long-standing genre favorite thanks to her striking looks and curvaceous figure, this British actress (1949–) has provided glamorous support in a wide variety of films. Following her debut in the David Bailey–directed short *G.G. Passion* (1966), she went on to appear in *Casino Royale* (1967), *A Talent for Love* (1969), *The Abominable Dr. Phibes* (1971), *The Golden Voyage of Sinbad* (1973), *At the Earth's Core* (1976), *The Spy Who Loved Me* (1977), in which she played the deadly Naomi, *Starcrash* (1979), in which played Stella Starr (1979), *Maniac* (1981), *The Last Horror Film* (1982), *Don't Open Till Christmas* (1983), *Slaughter High* (1986), *The Black Cat* (1991), *Flesh for the Beast* (2003), *Eldorado* (2012) and *Cute Little Buggers* (2017).

She also appeared in two films for Hammer (to whom she was briefly contracted), playing Laura Jane Bellows in *Dracula A.D. 1972* (1972), in which she succumbs to Dracula's bite in a de-sanctified Chelsea church, and *Captain Kronos—Vampire Hunter* (1974), in which she played Carla. Commented *Cinema & TV Today* of her performance in the latter, "Caroline Munro is warmly sensuous and gives more to the role of Carla than she is given." Recalled Munro of her experiences with the studio: "The Hammer films always had a big impact in the States. It was really an invaluable calling card for any actress. Of course, I wasn't with the studio in its heyday, but the important thing is that I did do one of the Dracula films."[73] Recalled Munro's *A.D. 1972* co-star Stephanie Beacham of the actress, "I couldn't believe that anybody so pretty, so beautiful for heaven's sake, could possibly be so nice, but she was. She had no confidence in her acting, but on the other hand she could do that as well…. And she used to look disgustingly good at six o'clock in the morning!"[74]

Also busy as a model, Munro won a "Face of the Year" competition in *The London Evening News* at the age of sixteen and worked for *Vogue* at the age of seventeen, though she is best remembered for a long running campaign for Lamb's Navy Rum in the seventies, a poster of which can be seen on the side of the bus depot in Hammer's *On the Buses* (1971) and *Mutiny on the Buses* (1972). It was this ad campaign that brought her to the attention of Hammer, who put her under contract for a year and hoped to launch her in their ill-fated sci-fi epic *When the Earth Cracked Open* (aka *The Day the Earth Cracked Open*), for which her likeness was featured on promotional artwork. At the time, Munro was described as "The Hammer find of 1971,"[75] though of this initial period with the studio, she revealed that she had "no duties, no official duties."

Also active on television, Munro's credits here include episodes of *The Howerd Confessions* (1976, TV), *The New Avengers* (1976–1977, TV), the quiz show *3-2-1* (1978–1987, TV) on which she was a hostess for a period, *Cue Gary* (1987–1988, TV) and *Sweating Bullets* (1991–1993, TV). Munro's first husband was the actor, writer and producer Judd Hamilton (1942–), to whom she was married between 1970 and 1982. Her second husband is the writer-director George Dugdale, whom she married in 1990. **Additional notes:** Munro was considered for the roles of Sister Hyde in Hammer's *Dr. Jekyll and Sister Hyde* (1971), which went to Martine Beswick, and Sarah (Angel) in *Frankenstein and the Monster from Hell* (1974), which went to Madeline Smith. Michael Carreras also spoke to her about taking on the title role of the unmade

**Caroline Munro looks delectable among the tombstones in this publicity shot for *Dracula A.D. 1972* (1972) (Hammer/Warner/Columbia-Warner/Warner Bros.).**

*Vampirella*. A still of Munro and Christopher Lee, taken from *Dracula A.D. 1972*, is featured on the cover of Hammer's 1974 *Dracula* LP. **Hammer credits:** *Dracula A.D. 1972* (1972, as Laura Jane Bellows), *Captain Kronos—Vampire Hunter* (1974, as Carla), *Flesh and Blood* *The Hammer Heritage of Horror* (1994, TV, interviewee, special thanks)

### Munro, Chris

This British sound technician (1952–) worked as the assistant boom operator on Hammer's *Vampire Circus* (1972). His other credits as a boom operator include *House of Whipcord* (1974). By the time he came to work on *The Satanic Rites of Dracula* (1974), he'd graduated to sound camera operator. He went on to work as a recordist and mixer on many productions, among them *Party Party* (1983), *Runners* (1983), *Pack of Lies* (1987, TVM), *The Bourne Identity* (1988, TVM), *The Russia House* (1990), *Robin Hood: Prince of Thieves* (1991), *Mary Shelley's Frankenstein* (1994), *Backbeat* (1994), which earned him a shared BAFTA nomination, *Judge Dredd* (1995), *Event Horizon* (1997), *The Mummy* (1999), which earned him a shared Oscar nomination, *The World Is Not Enough* (1999), *Lara Croft: Tomb Raider* (2001), *Black Hawk Down* (2001), which won him a shared Oscar and a shared BAFTA nomination, *Van Helsing* (2004), *United 93* (2006), which earned him a shared BAFTA nomination, *Casino Royale* (2006), which won him a shared BAFTA, *Quantum of Solace* (2008), which earned him a shared BAFTA nomination, *The Last Airbender* (2010), *Sherlock Holmes: A Game of Shadows* (2011), *John Carter* (2012), *Captain Phillips* (2013), which earned him a shared Oscar and BAFTA, *Gravity* (2013), which won him a shared Oscar and BAFTA, *Wonder Woman* (2017) and *Ready Player One* (2018), plus episodes of *The Professionals* (1977–1983, TV) and *Georgian Underworld* (2003, TV). **Hammer credits:** *Vampire Circus* (1972, assistant boom operator [uncredited]), *The Satanic Rites of Dracula* (1974, sound camera operator [uncredited])

### Munro, David

British born Munro (1944–1999) worked as the second assistant director on Hammer's *Twins of Evil* (1971) and as the first assistant on four episodes of *Hammer House of Horror* (1980, TV). His other credits as a first assistant include *The Italian Job* (1969), *Soft Beds, Hard Battles* (1974), *The Wild Duck* (1983), *Bush Christmas* (1983) and *Australian Dream* (1987). He has also worked as a writer-director on *Knots* (1975), and as a cinematographer, producer and director on the documentary *Death of a Nation: The Timor Conspiracy* (1994). Married three times, his wives include the actresses Sharon Duce (1950–), whom he married in 1970, and Susan Penhaligon (1949–), to whom he was married between 1974 and 1981. His son (with Penhaligon) is the actor-turned-assistant director Truan Munro (1979–). His father was the actor Hugh Munro (1916–1998), his mother the actress Pamela Barnard (1918–1978), and his grandfather the actor Ivor Barnard (1887–1953). His brother is the actor Tim Munro (1951–). **Hammer credits:** *Twins of Evil* (1971, second assistant

director [uncredited]), *The House That Bled to Death* (1980, TV [episode of *Hammer House of Horror*], assistant director), *The Mark of Satan* (1980, TV [episode of *Hammer House of Horror*], assistant director), *Guardian of the Abyss* (1980, TV [episode of *Hammer House of Horror*], assistant director), *Growing Pains* (1980, TV [episode of *Hammer House of Horror*], assistant director)

### Munt, Peter

This British actor, extra, stuntman and wrangler (1926–2011, real name George Royston Munt) worked on many films for Hammer down the decades, beginning as a stuntman on *Men of Sherwood Forest* (1954), which he followed with appearances in several of their key productions. He can also be seen as Pleasants in *Hands of the Ripper* (1971). His other credits as an actor include *Carry On Cowboy* (1965), *Carry On Henry* (1971), *The House in Nightmare Park* (1973) and *A Room with a View* (1985), while his work as a stuntman takes in *Goldfinger* (1964), *Casino Royale* (1967), *Superman* (1978), *Moonraker* (1979), *Superman II* (1980), *Willow* (1988) and *Braveheart* (1995). His credits as a wrangler take in *Barry Lyndon* (1975) and *Swept from the Sea* (1997). **Hammer credits include:** *Men of Sherwood Forest* (1954, stunts [uncredited]), *The Revenge of Frankenstein* (1958, stunts [uncredited]), *The Hound of the Baskervilles* (1959, stunts [uncredited]), *The Brides of Dracula* (1960, stunts [uncredited]), *The Scarlet Blade* (1963, stunts [uncredited]), *Dracula—Prince of Darkness* (1966, stunts [uncredited]), *The Witches* (1966, stunts [uncredited]), *The Viking Queen* (1967, stunts [uncredited]), *Frankenstein Created Woman* (1967, stunts [uncredited]), *Journey to the Unknown* (1968, TV, stunts [various episodes, uncredited]), *Taste the Blood of Dracula* (1970, stunts [uncredited]), *The Horror of Frankenstein* (1970, stunts [uncredited]), *Countess Dracula* (1971, stunts [uncredited]), *Hands of the Ripper* (1971, as Pleasants), *Twins of Evil* (1971, stunts [uncredited]), *Vampire Circus* (1972, stunts [uncredited]), *Dracula A.D. 1972* (1972, stunts [uncredited]), *Frankenstein and the Monster from Hell* (1974, stunts [uncredited]), *Hammer House of Horror* (1980, TV, stunts [various episodes, uncredited])

### Murcell, George

This Italian born supporting actor (1925–1998) can be seen as Warren in Hammer's *The Steel Bayonet* (1957) and as Meister in *Don't Panic Chaps* (1959). His other credits include *Hell Drivers* (1957), *The Pursuers* (1961), *The Heroes of Telemark* (1965), *Penny Gold* (1973), *Pascali's Island* (1988), *Year of the Gun* (1991) and *CutThroat Island* (1995). He also appeared in episodes of such series as *Supercar* (1961–1962, TV), for which he provided the voice of Masterspy, *Z Cars* (1962–1978, TV), *The Saint* (1962–1969, TV) and *Peter the Great* (1986, TV). Married twice, his wives were actresses Josephine Tweedy (1925–1967), whom he married in 1953, and Elvi Hale (1931–, real name Patricia Elvira Hake), whom he married in 1960. **Hammer credits:** *The Steel Bayonet* (1957, as Warren [uncredited]), *Don't Panic Chaps* (1959, as Meister)

### Murcott, Joel

This American writer (1915–1978) penned the Hammer featurette *Dick Turpin—Highwayman* (1956) while in England working on the television series *The Scarlet Pimpernel* (1955–1956, TV). Initially known for the radio series *The Adventures of Frank Race* (1949–1952) and *Tales of the Texas Rangers* (1950–1952), he went on to work on episodes of such TV series as *The Star and the Story* (1955–1956, TV), *Sheena* (1955–1956, TV), episodes of which he also worked on as a story supervisor and associate producer, *M Squad* (1957–1960, TV), *Alfred Hitchcock Presents* (1955–1962, TV), *Bonanza* (1959–1973, TV), *The Alfred Hitchcock Hour* (1962–1965, TV) and *Barnaby Jones* (1973–1980, TV). His occasional film credits include *Calypso* (1956). Married twice, his second wife was actress Dianne Foster (1928–, real name Olga Helen Laruska), to whom he was married between 1954 and 1959. **Hammer credits:** *Dick Turpin—Highwayman* (1956)

### Murder by Proxy

GB, 1955, 87m, Bw, RCA, Cert A

Although made in late 1953, this rather involved *noir*-style second feature thriller didn't see the light of a projector in the UK until 28 March 1955, when it was released (or possibly allowed to escape) by Exclusive. Known as *Blackout* for its U.S. release, which had occurred a full year earlier on 19 March 1954, the film stars Hollywood import Dane Clark as Casey Morrow, a drunk who, after one particular bender, awakes in a strange apartment only to discover that he has seemingly married a beautiful heiress named Phyllis Brunner and is somehow involved in the murder of her father.

Based on the 1951 novel by Helen Nielsen (aka *Gold Coast Nocturne* and *Dead on the Level*), the plot is a somewhat complex affair, full of red herrings as well as the pre-requisite *femme fatale* played by Belinda Lee, whose Phyllis may or may not be involved in the plot ("I think she did it and she framed me," supposes Morrow at one point). It eventually turns out that Phyllis's devious mother Alicia was responsible for the murder of her husband, after he discovered that she was bleeding him dry financially via a series of property scams and fake charities.

Thanks to its intriguing plot and unexpected developments, the film just about holds one's attention, despite the fact that it is directed in a somewhat pedestrian manner by Terence Fisher via a series of static and often lengthy takes (presumably to keep costs down). Thus the onus is on the actors, who generally come up trumps, particularly Dane Clark as the world-weary Morrow, Belinda Lee as the glamorous Phyllis and, especially, Eleanor Summerfield as Phyllis's former flatmate, the sharp-tongued artist Maggie Doone, who finds her self helping Morrow out of his predicament. Good support is also provided by Andrew Osborn as Lance Gorden, the Brunner's family solicitor and Phyllis's one-time fiancé (Osborn also worked as the film's dialogue director), and the ever reliable Harold Lang as Gorden's slippery assistant Travis, who is involved in the scam. Jazz diva Cleo Laine is also featured belting out a number during the opening nightclub sequence.

Technically, the film is just adequate, with the best contribution coming from art director J. Elder Wills, whose work includes a garret studio for Maggie, complete with angled window, and an eye-catching deco-style nightclub set. **Additional notes:** Actress Nora Gordon is mistakenly billed as Nora Gorden in the credits.

Production companies: Hammer/Lippert. Distributors: Exclusive (UK), Twentieth Century–Fox (U.S.). Producer: Michael Carreras. Director: Terence Fisher. Screenplay: Richard Landau, based on the novel by Helen Nielsen. Cinematographer: Walter "Jimmy" Harvey. Music director: Ivor Slaney. Editor: Maurice Rootes. Art director: J. Elder Wills. Costumes: Molly Arbuthnot, Ben Pearson. Furs: Molho. Sound: Bill Salter, George Burgess. Production manager: Mickey Delamar. Assistant director: Jimmy Sangster. Second assistant director: Aida Young [uncredited]. Dialogue director: Andrew Osborn. Camera operator: Len Harris. Focus puller: Harry Oakes [uncredited]. Make-up: Phil Leakey. Hair: Nina Broe. Continuity: Renee Glynne. **Cast:** Dane Clarke (Casey Morrow), Belinda Lee (Phyllis Brunner), Betty Ann Davies (Alicia Brunner), Andrew Osborn (Lance Gorden), Harold Lang (Travis/Victor Vanno), Eleanor Summerfield (Maggie Doone), Michael Golden (Inspector Johnson), Alfie Bass (Ernie), Delphi Lawrence (Linda), Jill Melford (Miss Nardis), Nora Gordon (Casey's mother), Alvis Maben (Lita Huntley), Cleo Laine (Singer [uncredited]), Ann Gow (unnamed role [uncredited]). **DVD availability:** VCI Entertainment (U.S. all regions), double-billed with *Stolen Face* (1952), extras include a trailer and biographies

### Murison, Margaret

Murison worked as the assistant editor on Hammer's *Blood Orange* (1953). Her other credits include *Three Steps to the Gallows* (1953), on which she worked as a dubbing editor. **Hammer credits:** *Blood Orange* (1953 [uncredited])

### Murphy, Brian

Best remembered for playing the henpecked landlord George Roper in the sitcom *Man About the House* (1973–1976, TV) and its spin-off *George and Mildred* (1976–1979, TV), this RADA-trained British comedy character actor (1932–) was a member of at the Theater Workshop, and made his film debut in the company's big screen transfer of *Sparrows Can't Sing* (1962). His other film credits include appearances in *The Activist* (1969), *The Devils* (1971), *The Boy Friend* (1971), *The Ragman's Daughter* (1972), *I'm Not Feeling Myself Tonight* (1975), *Black Jack* (1980), *Room 36* (2005) and *Grave Tales* (2011), plus Hammer's big screen version of *Man About the House* (1974) and the big screen version of *George and Mildred* (1980), the latter of which was produced by Roy Skeggs during a hiatus from Hammer. Murphy's many other television credits include episodes of *The Avengers* (1961–1969, TV), *Callan* (1967–1972, TV), *Last of the Summer Wine* (1973–2010, TV), in which he played Alvin Smedley between 2003 and 2010, *The Incredible Mr. Tanner* (1981, TV), *L for Lester* (1982, TV), *Lame Ducks* (1984–1985, TV), *Mrs. Merton and Malcolm* (1999, TV), *Benidorm* (2007–2018, TV), *The Café* (2011–2013, TV), *White Van Man* (2011–2012, TV) and *Plebs* (2013–, TV). His second wife is the actress Linda Regan (1949–), whom he wed in 1995; she appeared in Hammer's

A Rorschach-like American ad for *Murder by Proxy* (1954), released in the States as *Blackout* (Hammer/Lippert/Exclusive/Twentieth Century–Fox).

big screen version of *On the Buses* (1971). **Additional notes:** Murphy also appeared as George Roper in a 1973 edition of the TV comedy special *All Star Comedy Carnival* (1969–1973, TV). **Hammer credits:** *Man About the House* (1974, as George Roper)

### Murphy, Geoffrey

Murphy had a minor supporting role in Hammer's *Mantrap* (1953). His other credits include *Poison Pen* (1949, TVM). Also on stage. **Hammer credits:** *Mantrap* (1953, as Plain clothes man)

### Murphy, Paul

Murphy played the supporting role of Dalan in Hammer's *The Viking Queen* (1967). His other credits include *Quackser Fortune Has a Cousin in the Bronx* (1970), *The McKenzie Break* (1970), *Underground* (1970) and *Children in the Crossfire* (1984, TVM), plus episodes of *Pictorial Weekly* (1970–1982, TV). **Hammer credits:** *The Viking Queen* (1967, as Dalan)

### Murr, M. (Mike)

Murr worked as an assistant sound editor on Hammer's *The Horror of Frankenstein* (1970). His other credits, either as a sound editor or dubbing editor, include episodes of *The Sweeney* (1975–1978, TV), *Danger UXB* (1979), *Minder* (1979–1994, TV), *The Flame Trees of Thika* (1981, TV), *Widows* (1983, TV), which earned him a shared BAFTA nomination, *Widows 2* (1985, TV), *Dempsey and Makepeace* (1985–1986, TV) and *Poirot* (1989–2013, TV). **Hammer credits:** *The Horror of Frankenstein* (1970 [uncredited])

### Murray, Don

Best remembered for his Oscar nominated feature debut, in which he played the cowboy who falls for Marilyn's Monroe's café singer in *Bus Stop* (1956), this American leading man (1929–, full name Donald Patrick Murray, aka Don Deer) went on to appear in *The Bachelor Party* (1957), *The Hoodlum Priest* (1961), which he also co-wrote and co-produced, *Advise and Consent* (1962), *The Plainsman* (1966), *Childish Things* (1969), which he also wrote and produced, *Happy Birthday, Wanda June* (1971), *Endless Love* (1981), *Peggy Sue Got Married* (1986), *Made in Heaven* (1987), *Island Prey* (2005) and *Tab Hunter Confidential* (2015), along with countless TV movies, among them *The Borgia Stick* (1967, TVM), *Daughter of the Mind* (1969, TVM) and *Hearts Adrift* (1996, TVM). In 1967 he was invited to play Justinian in Hammer's ill-conceived historical epic *The Viking Queen*, which all but ended his big screen career (Christopher Lee had wisely turned the role down). Remembered producer Paul Temple-Smith of Murray's performance in the film, "[He] was a really nice guy, but he was not a hard man. He could do the dialogue bits with Carita, but as for rallying the Roman soldiers. It was not his scene."[76] Murray's other TV appearances include episodes of *The Outcasts* (1968–1969, TV), *Knots Landing* (1979–1993, TV), in which he played Sid Fairgate, and *A Brand New Life* (1989–1990, TV). His other work as a producer includes *Moving On* (1974), while his work as a director takes in *The Cross and the*

*Switchblade* (1970), which he also co-wrote, *Damien's Island* (1976) and *Elvis Is Alive* (2001), in which he also appeared. Married twice, his first wife was the actress Hope Lange (1933–2003), to whom he was married between 1956 and 1961. His second wife is the actress Bettie Johnson (sometimes Betty Johnson, real name Elizabeth C. Johnson), whom he married in 1962. His children include the actor Christopher Murray (1957–) and the actress Patricia Murray. **Hammer credits:** *The Viking Queen* (1967, as Justinian)

### Murray, Mae

Sharing her credit with Anthony Hinds, Murray worked an associate producer on Hammer's second Dick Barton adventure, *Dick Barton Strikes Back* (1949). Her other credits include *Come Dance with Me* (1950), on which she was the associate producer, and *Shadow of the Past* (1950), which she produced. Both films were directed and produced by Mario Zampi through his own production company, Mario Zampi Productions (Zampi was originally connected to the Barton film). Murray also worked for Gainsborough during her career, gaining experience as an assistant producer on *Caravan* (1946). **Hammer credits:** *Dick Barton Strikes Back* (1949)

### Murray, Michael

Murray worked as the third assistant director on Hammer's *Blood from the Mummy's Tomb* (1971), which he soon after followed with *Straight on Till Morning* (1972). His other credits in this capacity include *All the Right Noises* (1969), *Go Girl* (1970), *Wuthering Heights* (1970), *Tales of Beatrix Potter* (1971), *Straw Dogs* (1971), *For the Love of Ada* (1972), *The Amazing Mr. Blunden* (1972) and *Carry On Girls* (1973), plus episodes of *The Avengers* (1961–1969, TV) and *Catweazle* (1970–1971, TV). His work as a second assistant includes *A Hole Lot of Trouble* (1971), *Confessions of a Driving Instructor* (1976), *Superman* (1978) and *The Corn Is Green* (1978, TVM), while his work as a first assistant takes in *Saturn 3* (1980), *Britannia Hospital* (1982), *Legend* (1985), *Who Framed Roger Rabbit* (1988), *Moll Flanders* (1996) and *Eragon* (2006), plus episodes of *The Sweeney* (1975–1978, TV) and *In Deep* (2001–2003, TV). He has also worked as a production/unit manager on *The Little Drummer Girl* (1984), *Evita* (1996), *The Avengers* (1998), *Batman Begins* (2005), *Fred Claus* (2007), *The Dark Knight* (2008), *Inception* (2010) and *The Dark Knight Rises* (2012), and as an associate producer on *Mrs. Caldicot's Cabbage War* (2002) and episodes of *Boon* (1986–1992, TV). He started out as a runner on *Casino Royale* (1967). **Hammer credits:** *Blood from the Mummy's Tomb* (1971 [uncredited]), *Straight On Till Morning* (1972 [uncredited])

### Murray, Stephen

In films from 1938 with *Pygmalion*, this British actor (1912–1983) went on to make over twenty films, among them *The Next of Kin* (1942), *My Brother Jonathan* (1948), *The End of the Affair* (1955), *A Tale of Two Cities* (1958), *The Nun's Story* (1959) and *Master Spy* (1963). He was best known

for the long-running radio sitcom *The Navy Lark* (1959–1977), in which he played "Number One" from series two onwards between 1959 and 1976, having replaced Dennis Price who played the part in the first series (neither appeared in the subsequent 1959 film). Murray also narrated a number of documentaries, among them *Across Great Waters* (1956) and *Sea Sanctuary* (1960). He starred in one Hammer film, the second feature science fiction drama *Four Sided Triangle* (1953), in which he played a scientist who clones the girlfriend who has rejected him, only to be similarly rejected by her doppelganger (the *Monthly Film Bulletin* described his performance in the film as "unadulterated ham"). His television appearances include *My Friend Charles* (1956, TV), in which he starred as Dr. Howard Latimer, and *The Scarf* (1959, TV), in which he starred as Clifton Morris. Also much on stage. His wife was actress Joan Butterfield. **Hammer credits:** *Four Sided Triangle* (1953, as Bill)

### Murray, William

Murray can be seen as a shop floorwalker in Hammer's *Stolen Face* (1952). His other credits include *The History of Mr. Polly* (1949) and *Laughter in Paradise* (1951). **Hammer credits:** *Stolen Face* (1952, as Floorwalker)

### Murton, Lionel

Born in London but raised in Canada, this busy character actor (1915–2006, full name William Lionel Murton) returned home to make his film debut in *I Live in Grosvenor Square* (1945), as William Murton, which he followed with over fifty other films, among them *The Girl Is Mine* (1950), *The Mouse That Roared* (1959), *Carry On Cowboy* (1965) and *Seven Nights in Japan* (1976). He also appeared in two comedies for Hammer, *Up the Creek* (1958) and its sequel, *Further Up the Creek* (1958), plus an episode of *Journey to the Unknown* (1968, TV). His other television appearances include episodes of *BBC Sunday-Night Theatre* (1950–1959, TV), *O.S.S.* (1957–1958, TV), *Danger Man* (1961–1962, TV), *Strange Report* (1968–1970, TV) and *Yanks Go Home* (1976–1977, TV). **Hammer credits:** *Up the Creek* (1958, as Perkins), *Further Up the Creek* (1958, as Perkins), *The Madison Equation* (1968, TV [episode of *Journey to the Unknown*], as General Wanamaker)

### Musetti, Valentino

Long in Britain, this Italian born stuntman, stunt coordinator and bit player (1943–, aka Val Musetti) came to stunt work via judo, having been the British Junior Champion in 1958 (he became a black belt in 1960). From 1967 onwards, he also pursued an interest in motor racing, and successfully competed in a number of international rallies, including Formula 2. In films and TV from the early sixties with various episodes of *The Avengers* (1961–1969, TV), his other credits include *The Eagle Has Landed* (1976), *A Bridge Too Far* (1977), *Never Say Never Again* (1983), *Wild Geese II* (1985), *Robin Hood: Prince of Thieves* (1991), *Shopping* (1994), *Shiner* (2000) and *Bright Young Things* (2003), plus episodes of *Doctor Who* (1963–1989, TV), *Redcap* (1964–1966, TV), *The New*

*Avengers* (1976–1977, TV), *London's Burning* (1988–2002, TV) and *55 Degrees North* (2004–2005, TV). He also worked on a handful of films for Hammer. **Hammer credits:** *The Plague of the Zombies* (1966 [uncredited]), *Vampire Circus* (1972 [uncredited]), *The Satanic Rites of Dracula* (1974 [uncredited])

### Musgrave, Peter

This British editor (1931–) worked on Hammer's *Vampire Circus* (1972). His other credits include *Silent Playground* (1963), *The Terrornauts* (1967), *They Came from Beyond Space* (1967), *The Girl on a Motorcycle* (1968), *Three for All* (1975) and *Death Train* (1993, TVM). His work as a dubbing/sound editor includes *The Hideout* (1956), *The Grass Is Greener* (1960), *The Innocents* (1961), *Alfie* (1966), *Return to Oz* (1985), *Licence to Kill* (1989), *A Good Man in Africa* (1994) and *GoldenEye* (1995). His earlier credits as an assistant editor and second assistant editor include *The Bosun's Mate* (1953) and *Child's Play* (1954) respectively. **Hammer credits:** *Vampire Circus* (1972)

### Musical Merrytone No. 1

GB, 1936, 11m, Bw, Cert U

Released in the UK by Exclusive in December 1936, this program filler—typical of its period—showcased the talents of Hammer founder Will Hammer in a series of songs, dances and comedy routines. Long unseen, it was the last Hammer production to go before the cameras before the company went into liquidation in 1937. Needless to say, there was no *Musical Merrytone No. 2*.

Production company: Hammer. Distributor: Exclusive (UK). Director: Will Hammer. **Cast:** Will Hammer

### Mutiny on the Buses

GB, 1972, 89m, Technicolor, RCA, cert A

Given the surprise success of *On the Buses* (1971), it was inevitable that Hammer would again return to the goose that had laid the golden egg. Like its predecessor, *Mutiny on the Buses* (1972) was billed as A Hammer Special Comedy Presentation, and saw all of the main cast along with much the same production team re-united.

The set up is pretty much the same as before, with bus driver Stan Butler and his sidekick clippie Jack getting into various scrapes as they attempt to pull various skives on Inspector Blake and the depot's new manager, Mr. Jenkins, whom they treat with equal contempt ("How long will the next bus be?" asks Jenkins of Stan, who doesn't yet know who he is, to which comes the reply, "About thirty-eight feet!"). As well as seeing Stan get engaged to his girlfriend Susy, the story also sees his brother-in-law Arthur made redundant, resulting in Stan giving him some driving lessons on the quiet in a bid to get him a job driving buses (cue lots of grinding gears and mayhem). Meanwhile, Stan's homely sister Olive gets pregnant, which adds to the family's financial woes (it also allows for numerous potty and fart jokes).

Other highlights include the workers' literal interpretation of Jenkins' orders to "only wear the company uniform as supplied—nothing else, right," a series of calamities involving Jenkins' attempts to keep in contact with his work-shy drivers by introducing two-way radios (which Jack duly sabotages by re-tuning them to the local police band), a boozy darts match at which Olive has a fight with one of the clippies, Nymphy Nora, who has been making eyes at Arthur (if you can believe that), the crushing of Blakey's new company van between two buses, and an encounter with an out-of-control foam machine during a fire drill ("Look at him. He looks like the Abominable Snowman," laughs Arthur as Blakey emerges from the mess). After having caught Jenkins in a clinch with Nymphy Nora, Stan also manages to blag a cushy job driving tour buses at Royal Windsor Safari Park, though inevitably things go wrong, with his vehicle invaded with monkeys and a lion.

As before, the script (provided by producers Ronald Wolfe and Ronald Chesney) is a pretty misogynistic affair, with Olive coming in for much of the schtick from Arthur. "Olive, your baby is crying," he says of their son, while as a reprimand he calls her "You stupid great fat lump." He also comments at one point, "Women—they cause all the trouble, you know!" Of course, in this PC world we now live in, this shouldn't be funny, but thanks to the energetic playing of the entire cast, the puns and innuendo keep the titters flowing fairly freely for those prepared to go along with things. "Why can't we get on?" an irate passenger asks Jack of a stationary bus at the start of the film. Knowing full well that Stan is on the upper deck snogging Susy, Jack replies, "Regulations. My driver's carrying out an inspection and we can't leave till he's satisfied," which pretty much sets the tone for the rest of the film.

Things come to a lively climax with Olive announcing that she is pregnant again, Jenkins getting the sack, Blakey being demoted to being Arthur's clippie and Stan losing Susy, the latter development prompting from his mum the classic observation, "Let her go, son. She don't love you. I know that sort of girl. All she thinks about is sex, sex and more sex. What sort of a life would that be?" However, Stan fails to learn his lesson, and ends up inadvertently getting engaged to another of the clippies, Gloria, while snogging her on the upper deck. "Cor blimey, no wait a minute—this is where I come in," he blurts, bringing the film full circle.

Plainly filmed on a low budget by returning director Harry Booth, *Mutiny on the Buses* was before the cameras between 21 February and 1 April 1972, and makes use of most of the sets and locations featured in the first film, save for the addition of Royal Windsor Safari Park, which is heavily promoted. One assumes that Hammer was judicious enough to charge the zoo for the free promotional footage seen in the film; likewise for featuring ads on the buses for Pontin's holidays ("Pontin's—carefree family holidays" and "Go Pontinental to the sun" exhorts the copy). In fact a deal with the latter must surely have taken place at some point, given that the next film in the series, *Holiday on the Buses* (1973), is almost entirely set in a Pontin's holiday camp!

Cheerfully vulgar (for an A certificate) and gamely performed, *Mutiny on the Buses* plays like a lower case *Carry On*, and if taken on that level, it provides a good deal of undemanding fun, as well as an interesting glimpse of what audiences were keen to see at the cinema in the early seventies. Yet despite the film's high quotient of innuendo, Reg Varney felt able to comment, "I think audiences—family audiences—are tired of all the dirt, both visual and verbal, that they've been getting from our permissive society.… They can watch us and have a damn good laugh and never be offended."[77]

Said production manager Christopher Neame of the finished product, "This was a formula film, produced solely to earn money."[78] As indeed it did when released in the UK by MGM-EMI on 30th July 1972 on a double bill with the John Wayne vehicle *The Cowboys* (1972). **Additional notes:** Hammer starlet Caroline Munro can be spotted on the side of the depot in one of her famous Lamb's Navy Rum posters. The film's title was derived from a competition in *The Sun*, which was won by a bus driver called Bob Butler, who earned £1,000 for his efforts. Royal Windsor Safari Park was later featured in *The Omen* (1976).

Production companies: Hammer/EMI. Distributor: MGM-EMI (UK [ABC circuit]). Producers: Ronald Wolfe, Ronald Chesney. Production supervisor: Roy Skeggs. Director: Harry Booth. Screen-

**Action on the side streets. The chase is on in *Mutiny on the Buses* (1972). Note the Pontins ad on the side of the vehicle encouraging vacationers to "Go Pontinental" for their holidays (Hammer/EMI/MGM-EMI/Studio Canal).**

play: Ronald Wolfe, Ronald Chesney, based upon their television series *On the Buses*. Cinematographer: Mark McDonald. Music: Ron Grainer. Music director: Philip Martell. Editor: Archie Ludski. Production designer: Scott MacGregor. Assistant art director: Don Picton. Costumes: Dulcie Midwinter, Mike Jarvis. Hair: Ivy Emmerton. Make-up: Eddie Knight. Assistant director: Ken Baker. Recording director: Tony Lumkin. Sound: John Purchese. Dubbing mixer: Bill Rowe. Sound editor: Roy Baker. Production manager: Christopher Neame. Construction manager: Arthur Banks. Camera operators: Neil Binney, John Howard. Gaffer: Roy Bond. Stunts: Gerry Crampton [uncredited]. Continuity: Doreen Dearnaley. Casting: James Liggat. Publicity: Jean Garioch [uncredited]. **Cast:** Reg Varney (Stan Butler), Doris Hare (Mum/Mrs. Mabel Butler), Anna Karen (Olive Rudge), Michael Robbins (Arthur Rudge), Bob Grant (Jack Harper), Stephen Lewis (Inspector Cyril "Blakey" Blake), Janet Mahoney (Susy), Pat Ashton (Norah), Kevin Brennan (Mr. Jenkins), Damaris Hayman (Mrs. Jenkins), Caroline Dowdeswell (Sandra), Bob Todd (New Inspector), David Lodge (Safari guard), Tex Fuller (Harry), Jan Rennison (Gloria), Juliet Duncan (Gladys), Michael Nightingale (Pilot), Roger Avon (Policeman, Safari Park), David Rowlands (Policeman, on beat), Barry Linehan (Policeman, mobile), Nicolette Chaffey (Nurse), Sally Osborne (Nurse), Dervis Ward (Angry passenger), Wayne Westhorpe (Olive's baby), Shirley English (Passenger [uncredited]), Harry Fielder (Driver [uncredited]). **DVD availability:** DVD Optimum Home Entertainment (UK R2 PAL), as part of a triple bill also containing *On the Buses* (1971) and *Holiday on the Buses* (1973). **CD availability:** *The Hammer Comedy Film Music Collection* (GDI Records), which contains the *Theme*

## Myers, Doug (Douglas)

This British editor (1910–1962) cut the troubled Hammer programer *Who Killed Van Loon?* (1948), after which he returned to work on the comedy *Life with the Lyons* (1954), along with its sequel. His other credits include *The Beloved Vagabond* (1936), *Pimpernel Smith* (1941), *The Adventures of Tartu* (1943), *Corridor of Mirrors* (1948), *Professor Tim* (1957), *Blood of the Vampire* (1958) and *Boyd's Shop* (1960), plus episodes of *Fabian of the Yard* (1954–1956, TV). **Hammer credits:** *Who Killed Van Loon?* (1948), *Life with the Lyons* (1954), *The Lyons in Paris* (1955), *Adventures with the Lyons* (1957, serial re-issue of *Life with the Lyons*)

## Myers, Peter

This British writer and lyricist (1923–1978) wrote the second draft screenplay for the Hammer thriller *The Snorkel* (1958), the first version of which was penned by Jimmy Sangster. His other credits include *Go to Blazes* (1961) and *French Dressing* (1963), plus three popular Cliff Richard musicals, *The Young Ones* (1961), *Summer Holiday* (1963) and *Wonderful Life* (1964), all of which he wrote with Ronald Cass. He also wrote episodes for such series as *No Hiding Place* (1959–1967,

TV), *Cliff!* (1961–1967, TV), *Before the Fringe* (1967, TV) and *Horne A'Plenty* (1968–1969, TV). His many songs include *Toys for Boys* (1955), *Dolly Polka* (1955), *Les Girls* (1963), *Stranger in Town* (1963), *Really Waltzing* (1963) and *Swingin' Affair* (1963), the latter three from *Summer Holiday*. **Hammer credits:** *The Snorkel* (1958)

## The Mystery of the Mary Celeste

GB, 1935, 80m, bw, cert A

Released in the UK by GFD on 14 November 1935, Hammer's second production following *The Public Life of Henry the Ninth* (1935) marked the company's first tentative step into horror territory. Filmed during late July and early August of 1935 at Nettlefold Studios and onboard "the famous 'Q' ship Mary. Mitchell" as the credits have it, it was based on an actual unsolved mystery from 1872, in which the titular ship had been discovered at sea minus its crew, all of whom had unaccountably disappeared (as the opening scroll informs us, "This story was inspired by the findings of the Attorney-General at Gibraltar and portrays the grim sea tragedy of the American brig 'Mary Celeste' found drifting and derelict in Mid-Atlantic on December 5, 1872—one of the strangest and most dramatic chapters in maritime history—"). Originally to have been titled *Secrets of the Mary Celeste* (some sources say *The Secret of the Marie Celeste*), this fictitious solution to the enigma, based on a story by its director Denison Clift, places the blame squarely on Anton Lorenzen, a mad, one-armed sailor who, in an act of revenge for being flogged and thrown overboard many years earlier, murders the entire crew and dumps their bodies in the sea, following which, wracked with guilt, he jumps into the briny to join them.

To play the role of the grizzled Lorenzen, Hammer pushed the boat out financially by securing the services of Bela Lugosi for a whopping $10,000. Lugosi of course had had a major international success with *Dracula* in 1931, since when he had appeared in a number of popular shockers, among them *Murders in the Rue Morgue* (1931), *White Zombie* (1932), *The Black Cat* (1934) and *The Raven* (1935), and following the Broadway premiere of the latter, he sailed to London to make *Mary Celeste*. Indeed, Lugosi's presence in the film enabled it to secure a delayed U.S. release care of Guaranteed Pictures on 15 February 1937 (a prospect denied *The Public Life of Henry the Ninth*), where, trimmed and re-titled *The Phantom Ship*, it was described by *Variety* as "very strong stuff for those who like tragic entertainment," while *Film Daily* praised it

for its "fine sea atmosphere." However, because of the cuts in the American version (which was actually prepared in London), parts of the plot didn't make sense. Consequently, some of Lugosi's dialogue was re-voiced by the British character actor O.B. Clarence (imitating Lugosi) in a bid to explain the omissions. Sadly, only the amended American version of the film—running some 62 minutes—seems presently to survive.

Nevertheless, although very much of its period, complete with wooden performances and creaky dialogue, the film is of archival interest thanks to the Lugosi-Hammer connection, and its early serial killer plot in which the ship's crew are killed one by one by an unseen assailant. As for some of the dialogue, however, it will no longer stand the scrutiny of current sensibilities (and rightly so in this case). For example, observes bar owner Jack Sampson of one of the reluctant sailors he has been coerced into recruiting as crew for the Mary Celeste, "Don't like the look of his face? Then I'll send you a Chink or a nigger."

In addition to Lugosi, the film also features George Mozart, one of Hammer's managing directors, Gibson Gowland, the star of the silent classic *Greed* (1924), and Dennis Hoey, who would later find fame in Hollywood as the dim-witted Inspec-

**Bela Lugosi features in this artwork for *The Mystery of the Mary Celeste* (1935) (Hammer/GFD/Guaranteed Pictures).**

tor Lestrade in the popular Sherlock Holmes films starring Basil Rathbone. Art director J. Elder Wills was also a Hammer board member, and went on to direct two films for the company the following year, as well as design many more.

Lugosi seemingly enjoyed his time working in England. Commented the actor to the *New York World-Telegram* upon his return to the States, "I think in England, if they would have the sense to buy the technicians of Hollywood, they would be very, very keen competition to Hollywood."[79] He also seems to have been impressed by the good manners he encountered, adding, "There is something in England we do not have in the matter of courtesy. Whether they like you or not, they feel if they would not be kind, courteous, they would offend themselves."[80] **Additional notes:** During the storm-swept scenes, the interior cabins of the ship remain perfectly steady. The American release carries a 1936 copyright, and any mention of Hammer has been removed from the credits (the film is listed as a "Guaranteed Pictures" presentation in the opening titles, which feature Warner Bros.-style cameo vignettes of all the featured players, though these are cut from some prints). The credits also list Henry Fraser Passmore as the supervisor rather than its producer. Future Hammer regular John Gilling, who would go on to write and direct several important movies for the company, worked on the film as the assistant to Denison Clift. Recalled Gilling of his experiences, "I didn't get on very well with director Denison Clift; he was an entirely inadequate director who was always blaming me for the mistakes he made himself. So finally I quit. I think that was the only time in my whole career that I ever walked out of a film."[81] While in London, Lugosi continued to promote *The Raven*, attending its British premiere at the Prince Edward Theater on 16 July, during which he made a brief appearance on stage and signed autographs in the foyer, explaining to anyone who asked that his unshaven appearance was necessary for his upcoming film.[82]

Production company: Hammer. Distributors: GFD (UK), Guaranteed Pictures (U.S.). Producer: Henry Fraser Passmore. Director: Denison Clift. Screenplay: Charles Larkworthy, based on a story by Denison Clift. Cinematographers: Geoffrey Faithfull, Eric Cross. Music director: Eric Ansell. Editor: John Seabourne, Sr.. Art director: J. Elder Wills. Continuity: Tilly Day. Assistant director: John Gilling [uncredited]. **Cast:** Bela Lugosi (Anton Lorenzen/Gotlieb), Shirley Grey (Sarah Briggs), Gibson Gowland (Andy Gilling), Edmund Willard (Toby Bilson), George Mozart (Tommy Duggan), Arthur Margetson (Captain Benjamin Briggs), Ben Welden (Boas Hoffman), Dennis Hoey (Tom Goodschard), Clifford McLaglen (Captain Jim Morehead), James Carew (James Winchester), Terence de Marney (Charlie Kaye), Ben Soutten (Jack Samson), Gunner Moir (Ponta Katz), Herbert Cameron (Volkerk Grot), Johnnie Schofield (Peter Tooley), Bruce Gordon (Olly Deveau), J. Edward Pierce (Arian Harbens), Wilfred Essex (Horatio Sprague), Monti De Lyle (Portunato), Alec Fraser (Commodore Mahon), J.B. Williams (Judge [uncredited]), Charles Mor-

timer (Attorney-General [uncredited]). **DVD availability:** Image Entertainment (U.S. R1 NTSC)

---

# N

## N. Kritz Ltd. of Southampton Row

This London-based maker of sartorial wear provided the morning wear for Hammer's *The Gambler and the Lady* (1953). **Hammer credits:** *The Gambler and the Lady* (1953 [uncredited])

## Nadasi, Mia

Nadasi (1944–, real name Myrtill Nadasi, aka Mia Nardi) can be seen as the medium Margaret Tabori in *Visitor from the Grave* (1980, TV [episode of *Hammer House of Horror*]). Born in Hungary, her other acting credits include *Assignment K* (1968) and *Scandal* (1988), plus episodes of *Armchair Theatre* (1956–1974, TV), *Jackanory* (1965–1996, TV), *Special Branch* (1969–1974, TV), *Thomas and Sarah* (1979, TV), *Doctors* (2000–, TV) and *Upstairs, Downstairs* (2010–2012, TV). A noted ballet dancer in her home country (where she partnered Ivan Nagy at the State Ballet Institute), she went on to work as a choreographer on *I Don't Want to Be Born* (1975 [as Mia Nardi]), which was helmed by her husband, the Hungarian director Peter Sasdy (1935–), for whom she defected to England to marry in 1965. He directed a number of productions for Hammer, among them her episode of *Hammer House of Horror*, plus such favorites as *Taste the Blood of Dracula* (1970), *Hands of the Ripper* (1971) and *Countess Dracula* (1971), the latter of which Nadasi again worked on as the choreographer (again as Mia Nardi). Sasdy also directed her in the TV movie *Sherlock Holmes and the Leading Lady* (1990, TVM) and episodes of *Orson Welles' Great Mysteries* (1973–1974, TV) and *Supernatural* (1977, TV). Nadasi's father was the ballet master Ferenc Nadasi (1893–1966), who became the director of the Budapest State Ballet School in 1949. She is the author of the book *Pirouettes and Passions: Growing Up Behind the Curtain* (2006). **Hammer credits:** *Countess Dracula* (1971, choreographer [as Mia Nardi]), *Visitor from the Grave* (1980, TV [episode of *Hammer House of Horror*], as Margaret Tabori)

## Nagy, Bill

This Hungarian supporting actor (1921–1973, full name Paul William Nagy) can be seen as Clarence Olderberry, Jr., in Hammer's controversial child abuse drama *Never Take Sweets from a Stranger* (1960). His other credits include *River Beat* (1953), *Across the Bridge* (1957), *I Was Monty's Double* (1958), *The Long Shadow* (1961), *The Road to Hong Kong* (1962), *The Girl Hunters* (1963), *Goldfinger* (1964), *Where the Spies Are* (1965), *You Only Live Twice* (1967), *The Revolutionary* (1970) and *Scorpio* (1973). His many TV appearances include episodes of *Douglas Fairbanks, Jr. Presents* (1953–1957, TV), *The Saint* (1962–1969, TV) and *Shirley's World* (1971–1972, TV). **Hammer credits:** *Never Take Sweets from a Stranger* (1960, as Clarence Olderberry, Jr.)

## Naismith, Laurence

Best remembered for playing the title character in the children's fantasy *The Amazing Mr. Blunden* (1972), this genial British character actor (1908–1992, real name Lawrence Johnson) began his acting career on stage in 1930 following experience in the Merchant Navy. He returned to the military (the Royal Artillery) during World War II, following which he made his film debut in *Trouble in the Air* (1948). His many subsequent films include *King Hearts and Coronets* (1949), *The Million Pound Note* (1953), *Richard III* (1955), *Greyfriars Bobby* (1961), *Jason and the Argonauts* (1963), in which he played Argos, *The Valley of Gwangi* (1969) and *Diamonds Are Forever* (1971). On the small screen he played Judge Fulton in the cult television series *The Persuaders!* (1971–1972). His other TV credits include episodes of *The Protectors* (1972–1973, TV), *Return of the Saint* (1978–1979, TV) and *I Remember Nelson* (1982, TV). He also appeared in two Hammer supports in the fifties. **Hammer credits:** *Room to Let* (1950, as Editor), *Whispering Smith Hits London* (1951, as Parker)

## *The Nanny*

GB, 1965, 91m, bw, widescreen [1.85:1], RCA, cert X

Of all Hammer's ventures into Hitchcock territory, *The Nanny* is without question the studio's most polished and sophisticated, and certainly worthy of comparison with the Master's best work in this field. Based upon the 1964 novel by Evelyn Piper, it sees a troubled ten-year-old boy named Joey return home after a period at a special school. Joey, it seems, was responsible for the drowning of his younger sister Suzy two years earlier. Yet much to the annoyance of his long-suffering parents, Bill and Virginia Fane, the boy persists in accusing the family's much-loved nanny of the crime, treating her as obnoxiously as possible, despite the woman's best efforts to welcome him back home.

However, as unfolding events reveal, Nanny was indeed responsible for the accidental death of Suzy. Having just been informed that her own daughter has died during a back street abortion, Nanny returns to the Fane home in a distressed state of mind. Going to draw the little girl's bath, she fails to notice that the tot has fallen into the tub while playing with her dolly. Hidden by the drawn shower curtain, she lies unconscious in the rising water, much to Nanny's shock when she soon after pulls back the curtain. Completely unhinged by the experience, Nanny determines on silencing Joey upon his return home from the school. Unfortunately, having cried wolf so consistently, nobody will believe the danger that he is now in, least of all his child-like mother, who still relies on Nanny's ministrations herself (observes Joey's father of the situation, "However much we may all depend on Nanny, the boy doesn't like her. He never did and he never will").

On the floor at Elstree between 5 April and 21 May 1965, as well as on location at Wall Hall College in Aldenham and the nearby Haberdashers' Aske's School, the film proved (retrospectively) to be the first in an eleven-picture deal brokered between Hammer and Seven Arts in June 1965. Like

*Fanatic* (1965), Hammer's previous excursion into psychopathology, which had starred the great Tallulah Bankhead, the studio was keen to employ the services of another Hollywood warhorse to help bolster the film's box office potential. Overtures were initially made to Greer Garson, who had won a best actress Oscar for her performance in *Mrs. Miniver* (1942). The bad news was that Garson turned the picture down over fears that it would harm her reputation, although she would have been more believable in the first part of the story. The good news was that Bette Davis subsequently accepted the role, even though her casting—given her screen history—tends to preclude her character's guilt.

A genuine Hollywood survivor, Davis had begun her film career in the early thirties in a number of unremarkable melodramas before going on to secure front rank stardom after winning two best actress Oscars for *Dangerous* (1935) and *Jezebel* (1938). Over the next fifteen years or so, she proved to be unassailable, yet by the late fifties her career was on the wane. Then she was thrown a lifeline with the camp horror melodrama *What Ever Happened to Baby Jane?* (1962), the success of which not only revived her career, but earned her a much deserved best actress Oscar nomination (her tenth and final), much to the chagrin of her co-star Joan Crawford, with whom she had an on-going feud. The film launched Davis on a series of nut-house melodramas, among them *Dead Ringer* (1964) and *Hush … Hush, Sweet Charlotte* (1964), of which *The Nanny* would prove to be a highlight.

One wouldn't know it from the finished product, but *The Nanny* was a troubled shoot. Although she respected director Seth Holt, who had helmed the Hammer success *Taste of Fear* (1961), Davis, who could be querulous at the best of times, had little time for Holt personally, referring to him behind his back as a "Mountain of Evil."[1] The actress was also suffering from flu for much of the shoot, and filming was frequently held up by the time she took off to recover (given that Davis was in practically every scene, the director quickly ran out of material to shoot in her absence). Holt, meanwhile, in his

Bette Davis gives an eyebrow-raising performance in *The Nanny* (1965) (Hammer/Seven Arts/Associated British Picture/Warner Pathé Distributors/Twentieth Century–Fox/Studio Canal).

only error of judgment, was convinced that Davis was overplaying her role, which led to further confrontation ("She was always telling me how to direct,"[2] he later revealed).

Whatever trouble Davis caused, she was more than worth it, earning sympathy one minute and provoking horror the next in a superbly modulated and controlled performance. In fact the film contains one of the most disturbing scenes to be found in *any* Hammer film: in her bid to permanently silence the troublesome Joey, Nanny plans to suffocate him with a pillow while he sleeps, only to discover that the boy has barricaded himself into his room by placing a chest of drawers against the door, the movement of which wakes the child, who receives the fright of his life when he sees Nanny's grimacing face peering round the door. Shot in extreme close-up, the impact of Davis's pallid features is powerful indeed. The look of resignation on her face when she realizes the error of her ways after trying to drown Joey is also beautifully handled.

As superb as Davis is, *The Nanny* is by no means a one-woman show. As her young charge, William Dix displays a confidence in performance belying his tender years. Just nine at the time of filming, he more than holds his ground opposite the Hollywood legend. Relentlessly obnoxious in his early scenes, his actions manage to generate a good deal of sympathy for Nanny, despite our better judgment. With Greer Garson in the role it's arguable that the cat wouldn't have been let out of the bag quite so soon; with bad Bette in the starched apron, it's a dead cert from the start that she's going to be guilty. Commented *Variety*, "It's not necessary to be an astute student to guess that Bette Davis as a middle-aged Mary Poppins in a fairly fraught household will eventually be up to no good." The journal also noted that the inter-play between Davis and Dix was "skillfully portrayed."

Equally well cast are Wendy Craig as Joey's emotionally weak mother Virginia, and the always welcome James Villiers as his stern father Bill, whose work as a Queen's Messenger means that he is conveniently out of the way abroad for short periods, allowing Nanny to carry out her ill deeds. Jill Bennett as Joey's sophisticated Aunt Pen also leaves a strong mark. This being a thriller, Pen naturally suffers from a weak heart, from which she inevitably succumbs when she belatedly realizes that her nephew has been telling the truth about Nanny all along. In another key sequence, Pen discovers Nanny hovering by Joey's bedroom door with a pillow. Recalling that Nanny doesn't advocate the use of extra pillows for fear of suffocation, she confronts the woman, only to suffer a fatal attack, during which Nanny withholds her medicine. This re-

Tears at teatime. Bette Davis and Wendy Craig in an unsettling moment from *The Nanny* (1965) (Hammer/Seven Arts/Associated British Picture/Warner Pathé Distributors/Twentieth Century–Fox/Studio Canal).

calls a similar scene from one of Davis's earlier classic Hollywood melodramas, *The Little Foxes* (1941), in which she similarly withholds medicine from her dying husband. In addition to Dix, the film also features two other strong performances from youngsters, namely Pamela Franklin as Joey's rebellious teenage neighbor Bobby, and Angharad Aubrey, who is nothing short of delightful as Joey's little sister Suzy.

Visually, the film benefits enormously from Harry Waxman's crisp, almost austere black and white photography, while Holt's assured direction extracts the maximum tension and unease from the central situation while at the same time carefully papering over those inevitable by-products of the psycho genre: the more contrived and convoluted elements of the plot ("Neither the writer nor the director teeters over the edge into hysterics," commended *Variety*). Assisted by a subtle score by Richard Rodney Bennett (effectively centerd on a playground theme) and the sharp cutting of editor Tom Simpson, the film has a real Hollywood sheen to it (inevitably, the film's bathroom sequences have been compared to those in Hitchcock's *Psycho* [1960] by more than one commentator).

Following its trade show on 1 October 1965 and its premiere at the Carlton Haymarket on 7 October, *The Nanny* went on general release in the UK on 7 November on the ABC circuit care of Warner-Pathé. By this time, the film had debuted in America care of Twentieth Century–Fox on 27 October. An immediate box office hit bringing in over $2.25m, it was heralded as something of a triumph for Davis, who must have been doubly pleased given that she was on 9 percent of the gross. Commented the usually hard-to-please Judith Crist in the *Herald Tribune*, "In this, her fourth venture into the Hitchcock-cum-horror *milieu*, Miss Davis is out for character rather than hoax and comes up with a beautifully controlled performance." **Additional notes:** The film's ending, in which Joey makes peace with his mother, was filmed over a two day period *after* post-production. This occurred as a direct result of a complaint from Seymour Poe (head of Fox distribution) who argued that the ending as it then stood (in which Nanny attempts to drown Joey before finally realizing the error of her ways) was much too downbeat. The film has one of the more notable continuity errors to be found in a Hammer film: in the opening credit sequence, Nanny is seen strolling through Regent's Park with her shopping, which includes a box that contains a welcome home cake for Joey. Keep an eye on this obviously empty box when Nanny stops to buy some flowers—she seems to hold it every way but horizontal, yet when she later unpacks it, the cake is in perfect condition. Also note that Bill Fane arranges to be picked up by car one morning at 6:45 a.m. The other members of the household are obviously early risers, as they are all up and about before or just after he leaves.

Production companies: Hammer/Seven Arts/ Associated British Picture. Distributors: Warner Pathé Distributors (UK [ABC circuit]), Twentieth Century–Fox (U.S.). Producer: Jimmy Sangster. Executive producer: Anthony Hinds [uncredited]. Director: Seth Holt. Screenplay: Jimmy Sangster, based upon the novel by Evelyn Piper. Cinematographer: Harry Waxman. Music: Richard Rodney Bennett. Music director: Philip Martell. Supervising editor: James Needs. Editor: Tom Simpson. Production designer: Edward Carrick. Costumes: Rosemary Burrows, Mary Gibson. Make-up: Tom Smith. Hair: A.G. Scott. Production manager: George Fowler. Assistant directors: Christopher Dryhurst, Ariel Levy [uncredited]. Camera operator: Kelvin Pike. Recording supervisor: A.W. Lumkin. Sound: Norman Coggs. Sound editor: Charles Crafford. Continuity: Renee Glynne. Assistant to Miss Davis: Violla Rubber [uncredited]. Painter: Michael Finlay [uncredited]. Poster: Tom Chantrell [uncredited]. **Cast:** Bette Davis (Nanny), William Dix (Joey Fane), Wendy Craig (Virginia Fane), Jill Bennett (Penelope Fane), James Villiers (Bill Fane), Pamela Franklin (Bobby), Maurice Denham (Dr. Beamaster), Alfred Burke (Dr. Wills), Jack Watling (Dr. Medman), Nora Gordon (Mrs. Griggs), Harry Fowler (Milkman), Sandra Power (Sarah), Angharad Aubrey (Suzy Fane), Gary Graham (Boy [uncredited]). **DVD availability:** Optimum Home Entertainment (UK R2 PAL), extras include a commentary by Jimmy Sangster and Renee Glynne; also available as part of Optimum's two box sets *The Best of Hammer Collection* and *Hammer Horror—Ultimate Hammer Horror* (both UK R2 PAL); Twentieth Century–Fox (U.S. R1 NTSC); also available as part of Fox's *Bette Davis Centenary Celebration Collection* (UK R1 PAL). **Blu-ray availability:** Shock Entertainment (B/2, A/1)

## Napier, Russell

In films in Britain since 1947 with *The End of the River*, this Australian actor (1910–1974) racked up over fifty credits during his career, among them *Green Grow the Rushes* (1951), *Little Red Monkey* (1954), *A Night to Remember* (1958), *It!* (1967), *Twisted Nerve* (1968) and *The Black Windmill* (1974). He also appeared in several *Scotland Yard* featurettes (1953–1961) and a handful of Hammer features, including *Death of an Angel* (1952) and *36 Hours* (1954), always cast in authority roles. His TV credits include episodes of *Stryker of the Yard* (1957, TV), *Softly Softly* (1966–1976, TV) and *UFO* (1970–1971, TV). **Hammer credits:** *Death of an Angel* (1952, as Superintendent Walshaw), *Stolen Face* (1952, as Detective Cutler), *The Saint's Return* (1953, as Colonel Stafford [uncredited]), *36 Hours* (1954, as Detective [uncredited]), *The Stranger Came Home* (1954, as Inspector Treherne), *Hell Is a City* (1960, as Superintendent)

## Napper, Pat

Napper composed the theme tune for the TV sitcom *The Army Game* (1957–1961, TV), which was also featured in Hammer's subsequent film version, *I Only Arsked!* (1958). His songs include *Secrets* (1965), which was recorded by Shirley Bassey. **Hammer credits:** *I Only Arsked!* (1958)

## Nappi, Malya

British born Nappi (1915–2003, real name Anastasia Amelia Nappi) can be seen as Tohana in Hammer's prehistoric epic *One Million Years B.C.* (1966). Her other credits include *The Victors* (1963), *Silent Playground* (1963) and *Arabesque* (1966), plus episodes of *Romano the Peasant* (1960), *The Saint* (1962–1969, TV) and *St. Ives* (1967, TV). **Hammer credits:** *One Million Years B.C.* (1966, as Tohana)

## Nardi, Mia *see* Nadasi, Mia

## Narizzano, Silvio

Best known for the Swinging London comedy *Georgy Girl* (1966), this Canadian director (1927–2011) first came to attention in television, working in his homeland, followed by America and then Britain, helming such well-regarded tele-plays as *Death of a Salesman* (1957, TVM) *The Fallen Idol* (1959, TVM) and *Oscar Wilde* (1960, TVM). He made his film debut directing certain scenes for *Under Two Flags* (1960) with Duilio Coletti, but made his official solo debut with Hammer's *Fanatic* (1965) on which he worked with the temperamental Hollywood star Tallulah Bankhead. Commented the director of the film, "I think it's quite not a bad film except for about the last ten minutes."[3] Narizzano's subsequent career took in such films as *Blue* (1968), *Loot* (1970), *Why Shoot the Teacher?* (1978), *The Class of Miss MacMichael* (1978), *Staying On* (1980, TVM) and *The Body in the Library* (1984, TVM) among others. His other TV work includes episodes of *Saki* (1962, TV), *Court Martial* (1965–1966, TV, which won him a shared BAFTA, *Country Matters* (1972–1973, TV) and *Space Precinct* (1994–1995, TV). Note that Narrizano was also considered to helm Hammer's *To the Devil a Daughter* (1976). **Hammer credits:** *Fanatic* (1965)

## Nascimbene, Mario

As well as scores for many homegrown films, the work of this respected Italian composer (1913–2002, full name Mario Ernesto Rosolino Nascimbene) also encompassed the Hollywood epic, the British drama and several of Hammer's prehistoric frolics. Following the study of conducting and composition at the Giuseppe Verdi Conservatory, Nascimbene penned his first score for *L'amore canta* (1941) following a number of works for the concert platform, as well as uncredited contributions to *Solitudine* (1941), which was otherwise scored by Ettore Montanaro. His many subsequent credits include *O.K. Nero* (1951), *The Barefoot Contessa* (1954), *Alexander the Great* (1954), *Room at the Top* (1958), *The Vikings* (1958), *Solomon and Sheba* (1959), *Sons and Lovers* (1960), *Barabbas* (1962), *Where the Spies Are* (1965), *Doctor Faustus* (1967) and *Anno uno* (1974).

In 1966 he scored Hammer's *One Million Years B.C.*, the first of four assignments for the company, for which he made use of a full orchestra complimented by a number of unusual percussion instruments, among them bell sticks, the jawbone of an ass and rocks (this was a *stone*-age picture after all!). He also made use of otherworldly electronic instrumentation, most notably during the opening *Cosmic Sequence*, which presented the formation of the earth. Hence Nascimbene's on screen credit for "music and special musical effects."

Nascimbene returned to Hammer for *The Vengeance of She* (1968), although his overly solemn score was actually recorded in Italy with the Rome Symphony Orchestra under the baton of his regular conductor Franco Ferrara (Philip Martell oversaw the music from the UK). Unfortunately, Nascimbene's music failed to add gravitas to the comic strip proceedings, despite some lively though rather cheesy jazz embellishments care of sax soloist Tubby Hayes, and an ethereal title song performed by Bob Fields ("Oh, who is She?/A misty memo-ree," run the increasingly po-faced lyrics which go on to rhyme "she" with "myster-ee and eternal-ee," etc). Said Nascimbene of the assignment, "I was fascinated by the story, which took part in the ancient era and the modern era, so I wrote a special soundtrack based on two different musical situations."[4]

Nascimbene's other work includes a number of operas and ballets, a television oratorio and the celebrated *Concerto for Four Typewriters and Orchestra*, which was based on his score for the 1952 film *Rome 11 O'Clock*. He was also the Italian table tennis champion!

Commented music director Philip Martell of Nascimbene, "He is the laziest, the greediest man you ever want to work with. He demands a lot of money.... When I found out how much it was, I kicked up hell.,.. He got more money than any British composer I ever engaged and he never did any work."[5] As for Nascimbene's music, Martell commented, "One thing he'd do to save writing notes was to slow the tempo. Where we would write music at 120 or 140 beats per minute, he'd write at 72. It made the music last twice as long. It would take all the speed and emphasis and terror out of the picture."[6] **Hammer credits:** *One Million*

*Years B.C.* (1966), *The Vengeance of She* (1968), *When Dinosaurs Ruled the Earth* (1970), *Creatures the World Forgot* (1971)

## Nash, Michael *see* Carreras, Michael

## Nathan, Jack

This British composer and dance orchestra leader (1910–1990) co-scored an episode of Hammer's *Journey to the Unknown* (1968, TV) with Basil Kirchin. His other film credits, all with Kirchin (either as co-composer or music associate), include *The Shuttered Room* (1967), *The Strange Affair* (1969), *I Start Counting* (1969), *The Abominable Dr. Phibes* (1971) and *The Mutations* (1974). **Hammer credits:** *The Madison Equation* (1968, TV [episode of *Journey to the Unknown*])

## Nation, Oscar

This Swiss actor (1901–?) had a minor supporting role in Hammer's *Women Without Men* (1956). His other credits include *Bedelia* (1946), *Sleeping Car to Trieste* (1948), *The Astonished Heart* (1949) and *Appointment with Venus* (1951). **Hammer credits:** *Women Without Men* (1956, as Mr. Rizzione [uncredited])

## National Film Finance Corporation

Formally incorporated on 1 October 1948 as the National Film Finance Company under the chairmanship of James Haldane Lawrie, this government body was initially financed to the tune of £2.5m to help bolster the ailing British film industry. Renamed the National Film Finance Corporation in April 1949, its finances were bolstered to £5m, and under the chairmanship of Lord (John Charles Walsham) Reith, money was loaned to a number of film companies to help production. The loans to Exclusive were eventually halted in 1951 on the grounds that the company was stable enough to no longer require financial help. The films being produced by Exclusive were also considered as not being "of as high a quality as the Corporation would have wished."[7] However, following a relaxation of the Corporation's terms of reference in 1957, it did later help to finance many Hammer projects. Other companies supported by the Corporation include British Lion, Mancunian, Beaconsfield Films, ACT Films and Group 3.

Recalled Michael Carreras of Hammer's relationship with the NFFC, "We involved ourselves very heavily with the Film Finance Corporation and paid them back in full on the dates required."[8] In fact, despite the NFFC's initially sniffy attitude towards Hammer, it was one of the few companies that actually did pay back the loans. Said Michael Carreras, "A lot of people ended up owing them a great deal of money."[9] **Additional notes:** After he left the corporation in 1953, James Haldane Lawrie went on to form Lawrie Film Productions, Ltd. in 1954, which went on to make *Pacific Destiny* (1956) and *The Scamp* (1957). The company was acquired by Hammer in 1958, through which it made the army comedy *I Only Arsked!* (1958). Lawrie remained on its board of directors, even after the company was re-named Laverstock Productions in 1960. **Hammer films include:** *Dr. Morelle—The Case of the Missing Heiress* (1949), *Celia* (1949),

*Meet Simon Cherry* (1949), *The Man in Black* (1950), *The Dark Light* (1951), *The Curse of Frankenstein* (1957), *The Steel Bayonet* (1957), *The Abominable Snowman* (1957), *The Camp on Blood Island* (1958), *The Snorkel* (1958), *The Hound of the Baskervilles* (1959), *The Ugly Duckling* (1959), *The Mummy* (1959), *The Man Who Could Cheat Death* (1959), *The Stranglers of Bombay* (1959), *Yesterday's Enemy* (1959), *Don't Panic Chaps* (1959), *Never Take Sweets from a Stranger* (1960), *Hell Is a City* (1960), *The Two Faces of Dr. Jekyll* (1960), *Sword of Sherwood Forest* (1960), *The Full Treatment* (1961), *Captain Kronos—Vampire Hunter* (1974), *Frankenstein and the Monster from Hell* (1974)

## National House

Situated at 60 Wardour St., London, National House was Exclusive's first head office when founded in December 1934, from which accounts and publicity were handled. Cinema House, opposite at number 93, handled the company's "logging, barring and sales."[10]

## National Screen

National Screen provided the titles for all thirteen episodes of *Hammer House of Mystery and Suspense* (1984, TVM). Somewhat prone to typos, they seemed unable to decide on the spelling of the first name of the series' production assistant, which is sometimes shown as Sheila Collins and sometimes as Shiela Collins. On the episode titled *Last Video and Testament*, they also managed to misspell the character name of Hugh Dickson (Superintendant instead of Superintendent), and completely missed off the credit for composer Paul Patterson. And to think they did this for a living. Other films that feature credits provided by the company include *The Amorous Prawn* (1962), *The Victors* (1963), *The Omen* (1976), *Circle of Iron* (1978), *Zulu Dawn* (1979), *George and Mildred* (1980), *Rising Damp* (1980), *Enigma* (1983), *Wild Geese II* (1985), *Highlander* (1986) and *84 Charing Cross Road* (1986). Formed in 1920, the company originally made and distributed trailers on behalf of film companies, and went on to handle paper advertising (including posters, front of house stills and campaign books) for many companies, among them Hammer. The company was bought by Carlton Communications in 2000. It ceased to trade in 2007. **Hammer credits:** *Hammer House of Mystery and Suspense* (1984, TVM) **Hammer credits:** *Hammer House of Mystery and Suspense* (1984, TVM)

## Neame, Christopher

After a period as an assistant camera maintenance engineer at Beaconsfield Studios from 1960, and a time working as a junior agent for London Management, this British production manager (1942–2011, aka Anthony Morris) began work as a clapper boy on *Very Important Person* (1961). He joined Hammer in the same capacity on *Dracula—Prince of Darkness* (1966), and gradually worked his way up the rungs of the movie ladder, first at Hammer and then elsewhere, to finally reach the post of producer on such films and TV series as *Emily* (1976), which he also wrote under the name

of Anthony Morris, *The Knowledge* (1979, TVM), *The Flame Trees of Thika* (1981, TV), *The Irish R.M.* (1983–1985, TV), *Monsignor Quixote* (1985, TVM), which he also wrote, and for which he earned a shared BAFTA nomination for best single drama, *Bellman and True* (1987), *Soldier Soldier* (1991–1997, TV) and *Feast of July* (1995), which he also wrote.

Recalled Christopher Lee of Neame, with whom he worked on three films at Hammer, "I well remember him leaping about in an apparent state of perpetual motion. The important thing is that he was never too proud to learn—a quality sadly missing in too many of my colleagues today, who think they know it all after one film."[11] Recalled Neame himself, "The worst part of being a production manager is that if anything goes wrong, it is unquestionably his or her fault, and if it goes right, no credit is ever given. My five years in the job were certainly not my happiest, and I wasn't really cut out for the job."[12]

Neame was the son of cinematographer, producer and director Ronald Neame (1911–2010). His grandmother was the silent screen actress Ivy Close (1890–1968) and his grandfather the director and stills cameraman Elwin Neame (1886–1923, full name Stuart Elwin Neame), while his uncle was the screenwriter Derek Neame (1915–1979). His son is the executive producer Gareth Neame (1967–). His second wife (of three) was production secretary Caroline Langley, whom he married in 1974; she worked on Hammer's *Fear in the Night* (1972) and *Demons of the Mind* (1972). He should not be confused with the British actor of the same name, who also worked for Hammer. **Additional notes:** Neame's name can be seen on a "To Let" sign in *Blood from the Mummy's Tomb* (1971). He was promoted from second assistant to first assistant on the last three days of shooting on *Quatermass and the Pit* (1967), given that first assistant Bert Batt had to leave in order to prepare another film. He also worked on several episodes of the Hammer TV series *Journey to the Unknown* (1968, TV), of which *The New People* appeared in the compilation film *Journey into Darkness* (1968, TVM), *The Indian Spirit Guide* appeared in *Journey to Midnight* (1968, TVM), *The Last Visitor* appeared in *Journey to the Unknown* (1969, TVM) and both *Do Me a Favor and Kill Me* and *The Killing Bottle* appeared in *Journey to Murder* (1972, TVM). For *The Indian Spirit Guide*, he was also required to write a four-minute scene to expand the running time when the original script was found to be too short. He wrote about his experiences at Hammer in a 2003 memoir titled *Rungs on a Ladder—Hammer Films Seen Through a Soft Gauze*. His other books include *A Take on British TV Drama—Stories from the Golden Years* (2004) and *Principal Characters—Film Players Out of Frame* (2005). **Hammer credits:** *Dracula—Prince of Darkness* (1966, clapper boy [uncredited]), *Rasputin—The Mad Monk* (1966, clapper boy [uncredited]), *The Witches* (1966, third assistant director [uncredited]), *Frankenstein Created Woman* (1967, third assistant director, also first assistant director for screen tests, [both uncredited]), *The Mummy's Shroud* (1967, second assistant director [uncredited]), *Quatermass and the Pit* (1967, second assistant director [uncredited], temporary first assistant director [uncredited]), *The Anniversary* (1968, second assistant director [uncredited]), *The Devil Rides Out* (1968, second assistant director [uncredited], second unit director [uncredited]), *Slave Girls* (1968, anamorphic focus assistant [uncredited]), *The Indian Spirit Guide* (1968, TV [episode of *Journey to the Unknown*], unit manager [also penned additional four-minute scene without credit]), *The Last Visitor* (1968, TV [episode of *Journey to the Unknown*], unit manager), *The New People* (1968, TV [episode of *Journey to the Unknown*], unit manager), *Somewhere in a Crowd* (1968, TV [episode of *Journey to the Unknown*], unit manager), *Do Me a Favor and Kill Me* (1968, TV [episode of *Journey to the Unknown*], unit manager), *Girl of My Dreams* (1968, TV [episode of *Journey to the Unknown*], unit manager), *The Killing Bottle* (1968, TV [episode of *Journey to the Unknown*], unit manager), *The Beckoning Fair One* (1968, TV [episode of *Journey to the Unknown*], unit manager), *Journey into Darkness* (1968, TVM, unit manager), *Journey to Midnight* (1968, TVM, unit manager), *Journey to the Unknown* (1969, TVM, unit manager), *Frankenstein Must Be Destroyed* (1969, production manager), *On the Buses* (1971, production manager), *Blood from the Mummy's Tomb* (1971, production manager, second unit director), *Journey to Murder* (1972, TVM, unit manager), *Fear in the Night* (1972, production manager), *Mutiny on the Buses* (1972, production manager), *Demons of the Mind* (1972, production manager), *Frankenstein and the Monster from Hell* (1974, production manager)

## Neame, Christopher

This British actor (1947–) is best remembered by Hammer fans for playing Johnny Alucard in *Dracula A.D. 1972* (1972), about which he recalled, "I was Dracula's disciple, I was twenty-two and enjoyed it enormously."[13] For a short while Hammer seemed to be grooming him for bigger things, which never quite materialized. He can also be seen in a bit part in Hammer's *Lust for a Vampire* (1971). His other film credits include *No Blade of Grass* (1970), *Bloodstone* (1988), *Licence to Kill* (1989), *Edge of Honor* (1991) and *The Prestige* (2006). Busiest in television, especially in America from the mid-eighties, his many credits here include episodes of such wide-ranging series as *Colditz* (1972–1974, TV), in which he played Lieutenant Dick Player, *Secret Army* (1977–1979, TV), in which he played Flight Lieutenant John Curtis, *Dynasty* (1981–1989, TV), *The A-Team* (1983–1987, TV), *Northern Exposure* (1990–1995, TV), *Star Trek: Voyager* (1995–2001, TV) and *Vanished* (2006, TV). He should not be confused with the production manager of the same name, who also worked for Hammer. **Hammer credits:** *Lust for a Vampire* (1971, as Hans), *Dracula A.D. 1972* (1972, as Johnny Alucard/Acolyte), *Flesh and Blood—The Hammer Heritage of Horror* (1994, TV, interviewee, special thanks)

## Nearest and Dearest

GB, 1973, 86m, Technicolor, Westrex, cert A

Another of Hammer's big screen spin-offs, *Nearest and Dearest* was based on a ramshackle but much-liked sitcom that ran between 1968 and 1973. Created and written by Harry Driver and Vince Powell, it featured music hall stars Hylda Baker and Jimmy Jewel as quarrelling siblings Nellie and Eli Pledge, who find themselves having to pull together in order to run the pickle factory they have inherited from their father Joshua. Set in Lancashire, the series' humor was very much in the Northern vein, relishing in lavatory jokes, morbidity and *double entendres*. The scripts also gave Baker free reign with her trademark Malapropisms, catchphrases and flowery insults. Also onboard were Madge Hindle as Lily, Nellie's flaky cousin, and Eddie Malin as Lily's decrepit husband Walter, who always seemed to be in need of the toilet (prompting Nellie's constant query of "Has he been?"). Additional support was provided by Joe Gladwin and Bert Palmer as Stan and Bert, two of the factory's ancient workers.

An audience favorite, the series notched up forty-five episodes during its run, and provoked an American version titled *Thicker Than Water* (1973, TV) starring Julie Harris and Richard Long (this should not be confused with the 1969 British sitcom of the same title, which, coincidentally, also starred Jimmy Jewel, or the 1981 British sitcom of the same title that starred Joss Ackland). Additionally, the show inspired another British sitcom, *Odd Man Out* (1977, TV), also created and written by Vince Powell, which saw a rival brother and sister run a rock candy factory together (this time the stars were Bernard Holley and Helen Keating).

For their big screen version of the sitcom, Hammer went into partnership with Granada, the Manchester-based television company responsible for making the show. Given Powell and Driver's heavy workload as Britain's busiest sitcom writers (they were also contracted to a different studio at the time), scripting duties were instead handed to Tom Brennand and Roy Bottomley, who had contributed scripts to the series, though it should be noted that Powell and Driver subsequently went on to pen the big screen version of one of their other hits, *Love Thy Neighbour* (1972–1976, TV), for Hammer in 1973.

The film's story backtracks to the series' first episode, *It Comes to Us All* (by Powell and Driver), with Eli returning to the family home after a fifteen-year absence so as to visit his father on his deathbed. Confrontations with his sister Nellie inevitably follow, especially when they discover that they have each inherited a half-share of the pickle factory (Pledge's Purer Pickles), with the will stipulating that they have to run it together for a minimum of five years before

they can sell it. In order to cheer themselves up, Nellie and Eli take a holiday in Blackpool for Wakes Week (this inspired by the second episode from series two, *Wish You Were Here*, by Bottomley and Brennand), where Eli bumps into an old friend, a fellow pickle factory owner named Vernon Smallpiece, whom he pairs off with his sister in a bid to boost their ailing business. However, it turns out that Smallpiece is as penurious as the Pledges, and he does a runner on the day of his marriage to Nellie when a court bailiff turns up at the church, revealing that he is bankrupt ("Do you mean to tell me you were only marrying our Nellie for her money?" Eli asks Vernon, to which comes the blunt reply, "Can you think of another reason?"). Consequently, Eli and Nellie head home to make the best of the situation they now find themselves in.

Best described as cheap, albeit far from consistently cheerful, *Nearest and Dearest* is flatly lit and drably set throughout, with Baker and Jewel (who were less than fond of each other in real life) occasionally giving the impression (as they frequently did on the TV show) that they are not entirely sure of their lines. Indeed, the film has the look and feel of the hastily filmed comedies churned out by Mancunian Films in the forties and fifties, a

Hylda Baker and Jimmy Jewel find themselves in a bit of a pickle in this ad for *Nearest and Dearest* (1973), which also features Madge Hindle (top left of jar), Eddie Malin (bottom left) and Pat Ashton (bottom right) (Hammer/Granada/MGM-EMI).

handful of which featured Jewel and his then-comedy-partner Ben Warriss. That said, the film serves as a record of some of Baker's best-known catchphrases and sayings, among them "Thank you very glad," "I've been stood standing at that factory pickling all day," "You big flea's armpit," "You big girl's blouse," and, best of all, "Ooh, look, it's ten past … oh I must get a little hand for this watch." There are also Malapropisms a-plenty. For example, when a man attempts to return a small parcel that Nellie has dropped while getting off the bus, she mistakes him for a stalker, asking him, "How do I know you're not the Boston dangler?" She also refers to the great beyond as "the great behind," wedded bliss as "holy mattress money," and likens Eli to her favorite song in *The Sound of Music*, "Idleswine." Baker also has fun in mispronouncing Vernon's surname, calling him Mr. Smallfry, Mr. Codpiece, Mr. Littlebit and Mr. Bigpiece (she even manages to mangle his Christian name to Vermin).

Baker doesn't get all the best lines, though. John Barrett, who plays her dying father Joshua (as he did in the opening episode), gets some good mileage out of his deathbed scene. When Nellie enquires how she'll know he's died, after having prematurely pulled the bed sheet over his face, he replies, "You'll know when I'm going—I'll take me teeth out." Then, when she expresses disgust at having learned that he's willed the dentures to his friend Stan, he admonishes her, telling her to "Stick 'em in Harpic overnight. There's years in these teeth yet." Indeed, the next time we see them after Joshua has passed away, Stan is proudly wearing them at the graveside (it is Bert who inherits them in the series).

Scenes in the pickle factory itself are sadly all too brief, as are the appearances of Nellie's cousin Lily and her husband Walter, who were more of a fixture in the series. Still, gurning support is given by Joe Gladwin and Bert Palmer as Stan and Bert, while Hammer regular Pat Ashton provides a bit of busty glamor as Eli's girlfriend Freda, whom he attempts to install as his secretary at the factory (when asked if she can type, she replies, "Well I have done a bit with one finger and my last boss said I had a lovely touch"). However, her character isn't above being subjected to some fairly misogynistic behavior from Eli, who constantly leers into her cleavage and at one point gets rid of her by throwing a bag of fish and chips at her. His misogyny isn't solely directed at Freda, though; at one point, Eli calls a barmaid Karma Sutra and later, when asked by a nightclub hostess what he'd like, nods to her breasts and says, "I'll have two of those with chocolate sauce on!"

Given that the film was passed by the censor with an A certificate (making it suitable for accompanied children to watch), it's quite surprising to see a stripper—complete with twirling tassels—featured in the action, as Nellie and Vernon celebrate their engagement at a club. However, her performance at least prompts a couple of relishable comments from Nellie. "Her mother used to do some onion peeling for us. She only lives up the street," she says as the girl begins to dance, adding, "Ooh, she's dropped her glove," before realizing the nature of the performance (this incident, and the

chocolate sauce comment, are actually taken from the fourth episode of season two, *All You Wish Yourself*, by Bottomley and Brennand).

Also featured in the cast are Yootha Joyce as the predatory Blackpool landlady Rhoda Rowbottom (or Mrs. Rockbottom as Nellie calls her), Nosher Powell as a nightclub bouncer, Janie Collinge as the factory's aptly nicknamed Vinegar Vera (Pat Beckett played the role in the series) and Norman Mitchell as the devious Vernon Smallfry, er Smallpiece. Jimmy Jewel's son Kerry meanwhile makes an appearance as the factory's dim-witted tea boy Claude. Sadly, an extended sequence in which the two of them get entangled in a pair of trouser braces as they prepare for Nellie's wedding is excruciating to watch in the extreme. Ditto a sequence featuring Nellie and Vernon dancing in slow motion to the strains of *The Nutcracker Suite* in the countryside, climaxing with Nellie stepping into a cowpat. Admittedly, the film's earthy vulgarity does raise a few mild chuckles, but not nearly as many as can be found in any half-hour episode of the TV show.

Little more than a series of tenuously linked scenes and routines (many of them lifted wholesale from the series), *Nearest and Dearest* was clearly made in a rush. The original schedule was six weeks, but the cast raced through the material in just four (according to Baker, this was because they knew each other so well by this point, though the familiarity of some of the jokes may also have had something to do with it). Flatly directed by John Robins, the film lacks polish throughout. Its location work is also something of a curious mishmash. For example, while the Blackpool scenes do briefly feature action filmed on the promenade (note the grim-faced holidaymakers), the scenes supposedly set in the resort's funfair clearly do not take place in the famous Pleasure Beach.

Billed as "A Hammer/Granada Special Comedy Presentation," the film was on the floor at Pinewood between 10 July to 4 August 1972, and was released in the UK in June 1973 by MGM-EMI following a trade show on 26 April (tagline: "Hylda Baker and Jimmy Jewel will pickle your fancy in *Nearest and Dearest*"). However, when it proved to be less lucrative at the box office than had been hoped for, a planned sequel titled *Nearer and Dearer* was dropped from the schedules, as was *The Godmother*, a spoof of *The Godfather* (1972), which was also to have starred Baker. **Additional notes:** The film carries a 1972 copyright. In addition to appearing in the film, Hylda Baker sings the title song, which has lyrics by herself. A second song by Baker titled *The More You Laugh*, presumably recorded as the B-side for a single release of the title song, was otherwise not used in the film. In the TV show, Bert Palmer was replaced by Freddie Rayner's equally gormless Grenville from the second series onwards, yet it was Palmer who returned for the film. Note the intrusive mic shadow as Nellie finishes her cocoa at Mrs. Rowbottom's boarding house. As well as the film and TV series, Baker, Jewell, Malin and Hindl also played their characters in the 1972 edition of the TV comedy special *All Star Comedy Carnival* (1969–1973, TV), their segment for which was penned by Tom Bren-

nand and Roy Bottomley. John Barrett went on to play Baker's father in the first two (of three) series of *Not On Your Nellie* (1974–1975, TV) even though five years her junior.

Production companies: Hammer/Granada. Distributor: MGM-EMI (UK [ABC circuit]). Producer: Michael Carreras. Associate producer: Roy Skeggs. Director: John Robins. Screenplay: Tom Brennand, Roy Bottomley, based upon the TV series by Vince Powell and Harry Driver. Cinematographer: David Holmes. Music: Derek Hilton. Song: *Nearest and Dearest*, Derek Hilton (music), Hylda Baker (lyrics/vocalist). Music director: Philip Martell. Editor: Chris Barnes. Art director: Scott MacGregor. Costumes: Rosemary Burrows. Makeup: Eddie Knight. Hair: Jeanette Freeman. Camera operator: Rodney "Chick" Anstiss. Assistant art director: Don Picton. Assistant director: Bill Cartlidge. Production manager: Ron Jackson. Construction manager: Arthur Banks. Sound: Les Hammond. Sound editor: Frank Goulding. Dubbing mixer: Gordon K. McCallum. Re-recording mixer: John Hayward. Casting: James Liggat. Continuity: Lorely Farley. **Cast:** Hylda Baker (Nellie Pledge), Jimmy Jewel (Eli Pledge), John Barrett (Joshua Pledge), Madge Hindl (Lily Tattersall), Eddie Malin (Walter Tattersall), Joe Gladwin (Stan), Bert Palmer (Bert Henshaw), Norman Mitchell (Vernon Smallpiece), Pat Ashton (Freda), Peter Madden (Court bailiff), Norman Chappell (Man on bus), Yootha Joyce (Rhoda Rowbottom), Carmel Cryan (Club hostess), Kerry Jewel (Claude), Nosher Powell (Bouncer), Sue Hammer (Scarlet O'Hara), Janie Collinge (Vinegar Vera), Donald Bisset (Vicar), Adele Warren (Mimi La Vere [stripper]). **DVD availability:** DD Home Entertainment (UK R2 PAL). **CD availability:** *The Hammer Comedy Film Music Collection* (GDI Records), which contains the *Title Song* and a second number not featured in the film titled *The More You Laugh*, both of which are performed by Hylda Baker

### Nedeva, Madlena

Nedeva can be seen as Jenny Hartz, the fake nun in Hammer's *The Lady Vanishes* (1979). Her other film credits include *Trail of the Pink Panther* (1982), while her TV credits take in episodes of *The Professionals* (1977–1983, TV), *London Embassy* (1987, TV), *Dangerfield* (1995–1999, TV), *Survivors* (2008–2010, TV), *Stella* (2012–2017, TV) and *Mr. Selfridge* (2013–2016, TV). **Hammer credits:** *The Lady Vanishes* (1979, as Jenny Hartz [nun])

### Needham, Gordon

This British supporting actor (1922–2009) played a male nurse in the poor hospital scenes in Hammer's *The Revenge of Frankenstein* (1958). His other film credits include several installments of *Scotland Yard* (1953–1961), *The Hypnotist* (1957), *No Safety Ahead* (1958) and *Idol on Parade* (1959), plus episodes of *Douglas Fairbanks, Jr. Presents* (1953–1957, TV) and *Saber of London* (1954–1960, TV). **Hammer credits:** *The Revenge of Frankenstein* (1958, as Nurse [uncredited])

## Needs, Colin

Needs worked the second assistant editor on Hammer's *The Witches* (1966) and as the assistant dubbing editor on *Scars of Dracula* (1970). His other credits include work as a sound editor on episodes of *Black Beauty* (1972–1974, TV). **Hammer credits:** *The Witches* (1966, second assistant editor [uncredited]), *Scars of Dracula* (1970, assistant dubbing editor [uncredited])

## Needs, James

One of the longest serving members of Hammer's technical staff, editor James Needs (1919–2003) made his debut with the company in 1950 with *Room to Let*. He began his film career as an assistant in the cutting rooms of Islington Studios in 1935, moving to the Shepherd's Bush Studios (where he worked for Gaumont-British and its subsidiary Gainsborough) following the war. His credits here as an assistant editor/assembly cutter include *Caravan* (1946) and *Jassy* (1947). A fully-fledged editor from 1948 with *Snowbound*, Needs went on to cut such films as *Boys in Brown* (1949), *The Bad Lord Byron* (1949) and *A Boy, a Girl and a Bike* (1949). He gained a foothold at Hammer thanks to stillsman John Jay, who suggested his name to Anthony Hinds, who was looking for an editor at the time. Needs soon became a regular with the company, so much so that in 1957, he was appointed supervising editor. He remained with the company (save for a couple of brief breaks following a disagreement over the company's editing shop) until 1973, making him one of the most prolific contributors to Hammer's history. His other credits include *Girdle of Gold* (1952) and the Children's Film Foundation serial *Professor Popper's Problems* (1975).

Remembered producer John Temple-Smith of Needs, with whom he worked on *Captain Clegg* (1962), "There was one man who was against us and that was James Needs, the supervising editor. We didn't need him. We worked very well with Eric Boyd-Perkins. I liked Eric very much and he was a great enthusiast. He would huddle over the Moviola trimming shots and Jimmy wasn't in on the scene. Jimmy didn't like that at all. He was a malevolent influence."[14] Editor Chris Barnes had better memories of Needs, under whose supervision he worked on many pictures. "I thought Jim was a smashing person. He was very easy going basically. He could get very stroppy when he needed to, but over the years he helped a lot of people. I got on very well with him. As long as you got on and did what was expected of you, he was very loyal to you—a damn fine editor, and a friend."[15] Barnes also recalled that, "As supervising editor, Jim would do all the talking with the producers in their offices, while I would just get on with the work in the cutting rooms."[16]

Despite his profligacy with Hammer, Needs receives but one brief mention in Roy Perkins and Martin Stollery's landmark 2004 BFI study *British Film Editors—The Heart of the Movies*. Comment the authors on page 135 in a section on the advances in editing techniques to denote the passage of time in a narrative over and above the use of fades and dissolves: "Although Hammer produc-

tions acquired a reputation for the occasional startling use of shock cuts, James Needs and Alfred Cox scrupulously follow classical practice when indicating temporal transitions in the company's earlier horror films." Talk about damning with faint praise! **Hammer credits:** *Room to Let* (1950, editor), *What the Butler Saw* (1950, editor), *The Black Widow* (1950, editor), *To Have and to Hold* (1951, editor), *A Case for PC 49* (1951, editor), *Whispering Smith Hits London* (1952, editor), *Wings of Danger* (1952, editor), *Lady in the Fog* (1952, editor), *Mantrap* (1953, editor), *The Flanagan Boy* (1953, editor), *The Saint's Return* (1953, editor), *36 Hours* (1953, editor), *Five Days* (1954, editor), *The House Across the Lake* (1954, editor), *Men of Sherwood Forest* (1954, editor), *Third Party Risk* (1955, editor), *The Quatermass Xperiment* (1955, editor), *The Glass Cage* (1955, editor), *Eric Winstone's Stagecoach* (1956, editor), *The Edmundo Ros Half Hour* (1956, editor), *Women Without Men* (1956, editor), *X—The Unknown* (1956, editor), *Dick Turpin–Highwayman* (1956, editor), *The Curse of Frankenstein* (1957, editor), *Quatermass 2* (1957, editor), *Man with a Dog* (1957, supervising editor), *Danger List* (1957, supervising editor), *The Camp on Blood Island* (1958, supervising editor), *Dracula* (1958, supervising editor), *Clean Sweep* (1958, supervising editor), *The Snorkel* (1958, editor), *The Revenge of Frankenstein* (1958, supervising editor), *Further Up the Creek* (1958, supervising editor), *I Only Arsked!* (1958, supervising editor), *The Hound of the Baskervilles* (1959, supervising editor), *Ten Seconds to Hell* (1959, supervising editor), *The Ugly Duckling* (1959, supervising editor), *Yesterday's Enemy* (1959, supervising editor), *The Mummy* (1959, supervising editor), *The Man Who Could Cheat Death* (1959, supervising editor), *The Stranglers of Bombay* (1959, supervising editor), *Never Take Sweets from a Stranger* (1960, supervising editor), *Hell Is a City* (1960, supervising editor), *The Brides of Dracula* (1960, supervising editor), *The Two Faces of Dr. Jekyll* (1960, supervising editor), *Sword of Sherwood Forest* (1960, supervising editor), *Visa to Canton* (1960, supervising editor), *Taste of Fear* (1961, supervising editor), *A Weekend with Lulu* (1961, supervising editor), *The Curse of the Werewolf* (1961, supervising editor), *The Shadow of the Cat* (1961, supervising editor), *Watch It, Sailor!* (1961, supervising editor), *The Terror of the Tongs* (1961, supervising editor), *Cash on Demand* (1961, supervising editor), *The Phantom of the Opera* (1962, supervising editor), *Captain Clegg* (1962, supervising editor), *The Pirates of Blood River* (1962, supervising editor), *Paranoiac* (1963, supervising editor), *Maniac* (1963, supervising editor), *The Damned* (1963, supervising editor [uncredited]), *The Scarlet Blade* (1963, supervising editor), *The Kiss of the Vampire* (1963, supervising editor), *The Old Dark House* (1963, supervising editor), *Nightmare* (1964, supervising editor), *The Evil of Frankenstein* (1964, supervising editor), *The Devil-Ship Pirates* (1964, supervising editor), *The Gorgon* (1964, supervising editor), *The Curse of the Mummy's Tomb* (1964, supervising editor), *Fanatic* (1965, supervising editor), *She* (1965, supervising editor), *The Secret of Blood Island* (1965, supervising editor), *Hysteria* (1965, supervising editor),

*The Brigand of Kandahar* (1965, supervising editor), *The Nanny* (1965, supervising editor), *Dracula—Prince of Darkness* (1966, supervising editor), *The Plague of the Zombies* (1966, supervising editor), *Rasputin—The Mad Monk* (1966, supervising editor), *The Reptile* (1966, supervising editor), *The Witches* (1966, supervising editor), *One Million Years B.C.* (1966, supervising editor), *The Viking Queen* (1967, supervising editor), *Frankenstein Created Woman* (1967, supervising editor), *The Mummy's Shroud* (1967, supervising editor), *Quatermass and the Pit* (1967, supervising editor), *A Challenge for Robin Hood* (1967, supervising editor), *The Anniversary* (1968, supervising editor), *The Vengeance of She* (1968, supervising editor), *The Devil Rides Out* (1968, supervising editor), *Slave Girls* (1968, supervising editor), *The Lost Continent* (1968, supervising editor), *Dracula Has Risen from the Grave* (1968, supervising editor), *Journey to the Unknown* (1968, TV, supervising editor [all seventeen episodes]), *Journey into Darkness* (1968, TVM, supervising editor), *Journey to Midnight* (1968, TVM, supervising editor), *Journey to the Unknown* (1969, TVM, supervising editor), *Frankenstein Must Be Destroyed* (1969, supervising editor), *The Vampire Lovers* (1970, editor), *Scars of Dracula* (1970, editor), *Dr. Jekyll and Sister Hyde* (1971, editor), *Dracula A.D. 1972* (1972, editor), *Journey to Murder* (1972, TVM, supervising editor), *Love Thy Neighbour* (1973, editor), *Holiday on the Buses* (1973, editor), *Captain Kronos—Vampire Hunter* (1974, editor), *Frankenstein and the Monster from Hell* (1974, editor)

## Neff, Hildegard *see* Knef, Hildegard

## Neil, Peter

Born in Pakistan, Neil (1913–1994) can be seen as Dr. Prichard in Hammer's *To Have and to Hold* (1951). His other credits include *The Stolen Plans* (1952), *Meet Mr. Callaghan* (1954) and *Satellite in the Sky* (1956), plus episodes of *BBC Sunday-Night Theatre* (1950–1959, TV) and *Saber of London* (1954–1960, TV). **Hammer credits:** *To Have and to Hold* (1951, as Dr. Prichard)

## Neilson, Catherine

This British actress (1957–) can be seen as the secret agent Maria Vladekova in *Czech Mate* (1984, TVM [episode of *Hammer House of Mystery and Suspense*]). Her other TV work includes episodes with *Warship* (1973–1977, TV), *Yanks Go Home* (1976–1977, TV), in which she played Doreen Sankey, *Bergerac* (1981–1991, TV), *Yellowthread Street* (1990, TV) and *Thicker Than Water* (1993, TVM). Her occasional films include *Biggles* (1986), *White Mischief* (1987) and *The Trial* (1993). **Hammer credits:** *Czech Mate* (1984, TVM [episode of *Hammer House of Mystery and Suspense*], as Marie Vladekova)

## Neilson, Nigel

This British actor (1919–2000) had a minor supporting role in Hammer's *Wings of Danger* (1952). His other credits include *The Interrupted Journey* (1949), *The Angel with the Trumpet* (1950), *The Story of Robin Hood and His Merrie Men* (1952)

and *Time Is My Enemy* (1954). **Hammer credits:** *Wings of Danger* (1952, as Duty Officer)

### Nelmes, Judith

This British actress(1893–1992)was originally cast in Hammer's *Dracula* (1958) as a coach passenger, but the scene in which she was to have appeared in didn't make the final print (some sources question whether it was filmed at all). Her other credits include *Anna Karenina* (1948), *The Scarlet Web* (1954) and *A Kid for Two Farthings* (1955), plus episodes of *The Quatermass Experiment* (1953, TV) and *Angels* (1975–1983, TV). **Hammer credits:** *Dracula* (1958, as Coach passenger [uncredited, unfilmed])

### Nelson, Julia

This British supporting actress (1924–2010) can be seen in the role of Inga in Hammer's *The Revenge of Frankenstein* (1958). Her other credits include *Three Men in a Boat* (1956), *Spare the Rod* (1961), *Never Put It in Writing* (1964) and *Jane Eyre* (1970, TVM), plus episodes of *Angels* (1975–1983, TV), *The Lost Boys* (1978, TV) and *On the Up* (1990–1992, TV). **Hammer credits:** *The Revenge of Frankenstein* (1958, as Inga [uncredited])

### Nelson, Kenneth

In Britain from the mid-seventies, this American actor (1930–1993) had a minor role in *Last Video and Testament* (1984, TVM [episode of *Hammer House of Mystery and Suspense*]). His film credits include *The Boys in the Band* (1970) in which he played the lead, *Hellraiser* (1987) and *Nightbreed* (1990), while his TV appearances take in episodes of *The Professionals* (1977–1983, TV), *Lost Empires* (1986, TV) and *Hold the Dream* (1986, TV). Also on stage (he was in the original cast of *The Fantasticks*). **Hammer credits:** *Last Video and Testament* (1984, TVM [episode of *Hammer House of Mystery and Suspense*], as Jack)

### Nelson-Keys, Anthony *see* Keys, Anthony Nelson

### Nesbeth, Vernon

In Britain from 1950, this Jamaican actor and singer (?–2017) can be seen in the pre-credits sequence of *Mark of the Devil* (1984, TVM [episode of *Hammer House of Mystery and Suspense*]) as a sick man seemingly cured by a voodoo rite. He is best known as a founder member of the singing group The Southlanders, who had hits with *Earth Angel* (1955), *Alone* (1957), *The Mole in a Hole* (1958) and *Imitation of Love* (1960). His other work as an actor includes episodes of *The Brothers* (1972–1976, TV), *The Cleopatras* (1983, TV) and *Happy Families* (1985, TV). **Hammer credits:** *Mark of the Devil* (1984, TVM [episode of *Hammer House of Mystery and Suspense*], as Sick man)

### Nesbitt, Derren

Adept at menacing roles, this British character actor (1935–, real name Derren Horowitz, aka Derry Nesbitt) broke into films in 1958 with a small part in *A Night to Remember*. His subsequent films include *Room at the Top* (1958), *Victim* (1961), *The Blue Max* (1966), *The Naked Runner* (1967), *Where Eagles Dare* (1969), *Burke and Hare* (1971), in which he played Burke, *Innocent Bystanders* (1972), *Double X: The Name of the Game* (1992), *Flawless* (2007), *Run for Your Wife* (2012) and *Home for Christmas* (2014). He also had a small role as Martin of Eastwood in Hammer's version of the Robin Hood legend *Sword of Sherwood Forest* (1960). In 1975 he wrote, directed and briefly appeared in the sex comedy *The Amorous Milkman*, which was based on his novel of the same name. Also busy on television, his many credits here include *The Adventures of Sir Lancelot* (1956–1957, TV), *William Tell* (1958–1959, TV), in which he played Frederick, *Special Branch* (1969–1974, TV), in which he played Detective Chief Inspector Jordan, and *The Courtroom* (2004, TV), in which he played Judge Arnold Francis. He was married to the actress Anne Aubrey (1937–) between 1961 and 1963. His father was the singing comedian Harry Nesbitt (1905–1968, real name Harry Horowitz) and his uncle was the vaudevillian Max Nesbitt (1903–1966, real name Max Horowitz). His daughter is the actress Kerry Nesbitt. **Hammer credits:** *Sword of Sherwood Forest* (1960, as Martin of Eastwood [uncredited])

### Nesbitt, Frank

British born Nesbitt (1932–2007, aka Francis Nesbitt) worked as the assistant director on Hammer's *The Brigand of Kandahar* (1965). His other credits in this capacity include *Dead Man's Evidence* (1962), *Witchcraft* (1964) and *The Horror of It All* (1964). In 1960 he co-directed the documentary *Search for Oil in Nigeria*. He also directed three films: *Walk a Tightrope* (1963), *Do You Know This Voice?* (1965) and *Dulcima* (1971), the latter of which he also wrote the screenplay for. His other writing credits include episodes of *The Adventures of Robin Hood* (1955–1960, TV), *ITV Play of the Week* (1955–1974, TV) which he co-adapted. He also worked as an associate producer on *The Borrowers* (1973, TVM). **Hammer credits:** *The Brigand of Kandahar* (1965)

### Nesbitt, Sally

Born in India, Nesbitt (1938–, real name Sally Hunt) appeared as a nurse in Hammer's *The Gorgon* (1964). Her other films include *The Class of Miss MacMichael* (1978), *Hopscotch* (1980) and *King Ralph* (1990). Her TV work includes episodes of *The Expert* (1968–1976, TV) and *Crown Prosecutor* (1995, TV). **Hammer credits:** *The Gorgon* (1964, as Nurse [uncredited])

### Neto, Manuel

Neto can be seen as one of the Rock people in Hammer's *Creatures the World Forgot* (1971). **Hammer credits:** *Creatures the World Forgot* (1971, as Rock man [uncredited])

### Nettlefold Studios (Walton Studios/ Hepworth Studios)

This British studio facility, formerly known as the Hepworth Studios, was used to film the interiors for Hammer's *The Mystery of the Mary Celeste* (1935). Other films made at the since demolished site include the later Hammer/ACT comedy *Don't Panic Chaps* (1959), by which time the complex had been renamed Walton Studios (in 1955, following its acquisition by Sapphire Films). For full history see **Walton Studios**. **Hammer credits:** *The Mystery of the Mary Celeste* (1935), *Don't Panic Chaps* (1959)

### Nettleton, Linda

Nettleton worked as a production accountant on all thirteen episodes of *Hammer House of Mystery and Suspense* (1984), sharing her credit with Sheala Daniell. Her credits as a producer's secretary include *Spectre* (1977, TVM) and episodes of *Seagull Island* (1981, TV), while her credits as an accounts secretary include *Britannia Hospital* (1982). **Hammer credits:** *Hammer House of Mystery and Suspense* (1984, TVM])

### *Never Look Back*

GB, 1952, 73m, bw, Gaumont Wales Recording, cert A

During a break in their lease on Down Place, Hammer was forced to make several films at other facilities. Consequently, Hammersmith's Riverside Studios played host to *Wings of Danger* (1952), *Stolen Face* (1952) and *Lady in the Fog* (1952). Meanwhile, this routine thriller about a lady barrister who finds herself providing an alibi for her former fiancé who has been accused of murdering his mistress was bundled off up north to the Manchester Studios—or the Film Studios (Manchester) Limited, as they were officially known. The film was a co-production between Hammer and the Mancunian exhibitor James Brennan, who also worked (without credit) as a producer along with Michael Carreras, whose second official producing credit this was following *The Dark Light* (1951). Remembered director Francis Searle, "We had the entire Old Bailey set in that. It came up from Denham on three low-loaders I think, and it was a bastard to shoot into because of all the different eyelines. Mind you, Connie Willis—one of the ace continuity girls at that time—was a great help on that one."[17]

On the floor from 17 September 1951, the £22,000 production (which included location work on the streets of Manchester) was released in the UK by Exclusive on 26 May 1952, and remains chiefly of note for marking the Hammer debut of Anthony Nelson Keys, who would go on to produce many key films for the company. A rather talkative and static affair, the film benefits chiefly from the performance of Rosamund John as the K.C. who finds her integrity compromised, and a scene-stealing cameo from Brenda de Banzie as a blowsy witness. As to be expected, the courtroom scenes, which feature plenty of cutting and close-ups during the various revelations, prove to be the film's highlight. The rest is a mixed blessing.

Because the film wasn't part of the deal with American producer Robert Lippert, it failed to garner a U.S. release; the lack of a visiting Hollywood star also no doubt hindered its chances in this respect.

Production companies: Hammer/Brennan. Distributor: Exclusive (UK). Producers: Michael Carreras, James Brennan [uncredited]. Associate producers: Thomas Blakeley [uncredited], Anthony Nelson Keys [uncredited]. Director: Francis Searle. Screenplay: Francis Searle, John Hunter, Guy Mor-

gan. Cinematographer: Reg Wyer. Music: Temple
Abady. Music director: John Hollingsworth. Music
played by: The Philharmonia Orchestra. Editor:
John Ferris. Art director: Alec Gray. Costumes:
Molly Arbuthnot. Make-up: Peter Evans. Hair:
Monica Hustler. Sound: Sid Wiles. Production
manager: Anthony Nelson Keys. Assistant direc-
tor: Pat Kelly. Camera operator: Ken Hodges. Con-
tinuity: Connie Willis. Casting: Nora Roberts.
**Cast:** Rosamund John (Anne Maitland, K.C.),
Hugh Sinclair (Nigel Stuart), Guy Middleton (Guy
Ransome), Brenda de Banzie (Molly Wheeler),
Terence Longdon (Alan Whitcomb), Henry Ed-
wards (Geoffrey Whitcomb), John Warwick (In-
spector Raynor), Bill Shine (Willie), Frances Rowe
(Liz), Bruce Belfrage (Judge), Arthur Howard
(Charles Vaughan), H.S. Hills (Lindsell), Helene
Burls (Mrs. Brock), June Mitchell (Secretary), Bar-
bara Shaw (Press woman), David Scase (Camera-
man), Norman Somers (Nigel's junior)

### Never Take Candy from a Stranger see Never Take Sweets from a Stranger

### Never Take Sweets from a Stranger

GB, 1960, 81m, bw, MegaScope [2.35:1], cert
X

Based on the 1954 play *The Pony Cart* by Roger
Garis, this dramatically powerful piece about an
elderly man accused of corrupting two children in
a Canadian township was meant as a heart-felt bid
to further extend Hammer's repertoire. Unfortunately, given the studio's past record, there was a
misconception by some critics that the film was intended as some kind of horrific come-on (the
poster's promise of "A nightmare manhunt for a
maniac prowler!" probably didn't help matters).
Consequently, it was condemned in certain quarters for tackling such a controversial subject (note
that Stanley Kubrick's groundbreaking version of
Vladimir Nabokov's controversial novel *Lolita* was
still two years away).

Loosely based on an incident that took place in
1953 involving the playwright's own daughter ("I
wrote the play to denounce a very serious social
problem,"[18] commented Garis), the film sees the
elderly Clarence Olderberry accused of coercing
two young girls—Jean and Lucille—to dance
naked for him at his house in return for candy (or
as *Variety* rather more bluntly put it, "It deals with
a senile, psychopathic pervert with a yen for little
girls"). When Jean's parents discover what's been
going on, they decide to take the old man to court,
not realizing the power his family wields in the
community, which he helped to establish. Consequently, his counsel uses all means—both fair and
foul—to quash the case against him. Unfortunately, soon after the trial, the old man re-offends,
this time killing one of the girls after chasing them
through the woods...

Paedophilia had never been tackled head on in
the cinema like this before, and the film is astonishingly frank for the time it was made. Indeed,
rather than delicately trip around the subject
through suggestion and insinuation, the script
deals with it without qualms ("We took all our
clothes off," Jean informs her parents when telling

*Above:* A dramatic ad for the controversial *Never Take Sweets from a Stranger* (1960), though the
strapline doesn't quite divulge the true nature of the film's subject matter. *Below:* Another ad for
*Never Take Sweets from a Stranger* (1960). This one at least gives more of a hint of the film's true
nature (both photographs, Hammer/Columbia/Omat).

them about the "game" she
and her friend had been encouraged to play). Inevitably,
the BBFC raised several concerns about John Hunter's
screenplay, which includes
talk of attempted rape and
sexual perversion. However,
via a series of exchanges, producer Anthony Hinds assured
the board that the subject
would be handled as tactfully
as possible by director Cyril
Frankell (whom *Variety*
praised for his "complete sensitivity"), and that Olderberry—as played by the
highly respected character
actor Felix Aylmer—would
not appear too lustful in the
woodland sequences (in fact
Olderberry doesn't speak a
word during the entire film,
apparently at the personal request of Aylmer himself).

On the floor at Bray be-
tween 14 September and 30
October 1959, *Never Take
Sweets* also made use of Oakley Court, Burnham Beaches
and nearby Black Park (commented *Variety*, "Though
filmed in Britain, the Canadian atmosphere is remarkably well conveyed"). Shot in
a fairly straightforward,

The most challenging film
of the decade...

NEVER
TAKE
SWEETS
FROM A
STRANGER

A HAMMER FILM PRODUCTION
*Distributed by* COLUMBIA

almost documentary style by the celebrated cameraman Freddie Francis (who himself would go on to helm several productions for Hammer), the film also benefits from the convincing performances of its cast, prime among them Janina Faye as Jean (Faye had already essayed the role on the West End stage), Gwen Watford and Patrick Allen as her concerned parents, Alison Leggatt as her straightspeaking grandmother Martha, and Felix Aylmer as the lecherous old man, whom *Variety* praised for his "terrifyingly acute study of crumbling evil."

After much debate over the film's certification (Hammer wanted an A, the BBFC insisted on an X), the film was trade shown at the Columbia Theater on 26 February 1960, following which it received its UK premiere at the London Pavilion on 4 March. The film was also to have been released in America by Columbia, but when it was denied a Production Code seal of approval, the studio passed it to the Omat Corporation, through which it received only a handful of bookings as *Never Take Candy from a Stranger* in August the same year, despite the urging of The National Council of Women that, "It should be seen by all parents." The film was again released in America in 1961 care of the Astor Pictures Corporation. Sadly, the movie (which was described by *Kine Weekly* as being "skillfully blended from potent ingredients") quickly disappeared and was infrequently revived, thus preventing Hammer fans for many years from making up their own minds about the studio's honorable intentions and their actual achievements, especially given that the climactic woodland chase, following a perfectly engineered shock encounter with the old man, does in fact resort to well-established genre conventions to generate a sense of peril (indeed, the scene in which the two girls try and escape across a lake in a rowing boat, only to have Olderberry pull them back to shore by the tethering rope, is a genuinely heart-stopping moment).

Commented James Carreras of the film: "The picture was seen by chief constables and by every other society that had anything to do with the subject, and it was acclaimed as the greatest thing ever. But not a soul went to see it. People just don't want messages."[19] Recalled Michael Carreras, "That film was made with the utmost integrity. We knew what the critics would do with it, even before it was filmed. 'Here is Hammer capitalizing on a fiend,' 'A little girl has been molested,' and so on. I know because I lived through it. The picture was never made on that basis…. I think it was very well restrained and very well done."[20] **Additional notes:** The film was part-financed with a loan from the National Film Finance Corporation. The American Omat prints carry the credit, "Howard J. Beck Presents." The credits also announce the film to be "An Omat Release of a Hammer Film Production." The U.S. version substitutes the word "swine" for "bastard" in a line spoken by Patrick Allen, who dubbed himself for the U.S. version. Early in the film, just after Jean's revelation, Martha tries to calm things down by recalling that as a child she and her school friends were often flashed by a middle-aged local suffering from arrested development; unfortunately—and seemingly innocently—the man is named Percy Sanford. Concluding her story, she

comments without any hint of a *double entendre*, "You see, the sight of poor Percy didn't do me any permanent harm." The makers obviously didn't realize that "Percy" is also a British euphemism for penis, as per the phrase "To point Percy at the porcelain." Hence its use as the title for the 1971 movie *Percy* and its sequel *Percy's Progress* (1974), which follow the adventures of a young man who has undergone a penis transplant. Some sources claim that the film is also known as *The Molester*.

Production company: Hammer. Distributors: Columbia (UK), Omat (U.S.), Astor (U.S.). Producer: Anthony Hinds. Executive producer: Michael Carreras. Associate producer: Anthony Nelson Keys. Director: Cyril Frankel. Screenplay: John Hunter, based on the play *The Pony Cart* by Roger Garis. Cinematographer: Freddie Francis. Music: Elisabeth Lutyens. Music director: John Hollingsworth. Supervising editor: James Needs. Editor: Alfred Cox. Assistant editors: Peter Todd [uncredited], Paul Smith [uncredited]. Production designer: Bernard Robinson. Costumes: Molly Arbuthnot. Make-up: Roy Ashton. Hair: Henry Montsash. Sound: Jock May. Sound editor: Arthur Cox. Assistant art director: Don Mingaye [uncredited]. Camera operator: Len Harris. Focus puller: Harry Oakes [uncredited]. Sound camera operators: Al Thorne [uncredited], Michael Sale [uncredited]. Boom operator: Jim Perry [uncredited]. Boom assistant: Maurice Smith [uncredited]. Clapper loader: Les Paul [uncredited]. Camera assistant: Alan McDonald [uncredited]. Assistant director: John Peverall. Second assistant director: Tom Walls [uncredited]. Third assistant director: Dominic Fulford [uncredited]. Production manager: Clifford Parkes. Studio manager: Arthur Kelly [uncredited]. Master carpenter: Charles Davis [uncredited]. Master painter: Lawrence Wren [uncredited]. Chief electrician: Jack Curtis [uncredited]. Casting: Dorothy Holloway [uncredited]. Continuity: Tilly Day, Pauline Wise (trainee [uncredited]). Draughtsman: Neil McPhee [uncredited]. Scenic artist: Gilbert Wood [uncredited]. Stills: Tom Edwards [uncredited]. Special developer/printer: Eric Jones [uncredited]. Props: Tommy Money [uncredited]. Props buyer: Eric Hillier [uncredited]. Production secretary: Pat Green [uncredited]. Stunts: Douglas Robinson [uncredited]. Publicity: Dennis Thornton [uncredited]. **Cast:** Felix Aylmer (Clarence Olderberry), Janina Faye (Jean Carter), Gwen Watford (Sally Carter), Patrick Allen (Peter Carter), Alison Leggatt (Martha), Niall MacGinnis (Defence Counsel), Bill Nagy (Clarence Olderberry, Jr.), Macdonald Parke (Judge), Estelle Brody (Eunice Kalliduke), Robert Arden (Tom Demarest), Vera Cook (Mrs. Demarest), Frances Green (Lucille Demarest), Michael Gwynn (Prosecutor), Helen Horton (Sylvia Kingsley), Budd Knapp (Hammond), Gaylord Cavallaro (Neal Phillips), Michael Hammond (Sammy Nash [uncredited]), Patricia Marks (Nurse [uncredited]), Mark Baker (Clerk [uncredited]), Shirley Butler (Mrs. Nash [uncredited]), Peter Carlisle (Usher [uncredited]), Sonia Fox (Receptionist [uncredited]), Charles Maunsell (Janitor [uncredited]), John Bloomfield (Foreman [uncredited]), Bill Sawyer (Taxi driver [uncred-

ited]), Andre Dakar (Chauffeur [uncredited]), Tom Busby (Policeman [uncredited]), William Abney (Trooper [uncredited]), Jack Lynn (Dr. Montfort [uncredited]), James Dyrenforth (Dr. Stevens [uncredited]), Sheila Robbins (Miss Jackson [uncredited]), Larry O'Connor (Sam Kingsley [uncredited]), Cal McCord (Charles Kalliduke [uncredited]), Hazel Jennings (Mrs. Olderberry [uncredited]), Ray Austin (courtroom onlooker [uncredited]). **DVD availability:** Sony (U.S. R1 NTSC), as part of the *Icons of Suspense* box set, which also includes *The Snorkel* (1958), *Cash on Demand* (1961), *The Full Treatment* (1961), *Maniac* (1963) and *The Damned* (1963), extras include trailers. **Blu-ray availability:** Powerhouse (all regions), as part of the *Hammer, Volume Two* box set

### Neville, Paul

This Australian actor (1888–1963) had a minor role as Harper in Hammer's last pre-war featurette, *The Bank Messenger Mystery* (1936). His other credits include *A Broken Romance* (1929), *Side Streets* (1933), *Danny Boy* (1934), *Passenger to London* (1937) and *Dial 999* (1938). **Hammer credits:** *The Bank Messenger Mystery* (1936, as Harper)

### New Elstree Studios (The Danziger Studios)

Hammer's *The Abominable Snowman* (1957) is credited as having been shot at the New Elstree Studios, although the majority of the film was made at Pinewood and Bray, and on location in the Pyrenees. Also known as the Danziger Studios, the complex also played host to *Quatermass 2* (1957)—which was made after *The Abominable Snowman* but released first—and *Up the Creek* (1958). All three films were directed by Val Guest. Also see **Elstree. Hammer credits:** *Quatermass 2* (1957), *The Abominable Snowman* (1957), *Up the Creek* (1958)

### *The New People* see *Journey to the Unknown*

### The New Symphony Orchestra

This British orchestra performed three scores for Hammer, all of which were composed by Ivor Slaney. The orchestra was best known for its recordings of Gilbert and Sullivan operettas. It should not be confused with the orchestra of the same name that was formed in 1991. **Hammer credits:** *Blood Orange* (1953), *Spaceways* (1953), *The Flanagan Boy* (1953)

### The New Vaudeville Band

This twenties revival combo played the title music for the Hammer comedy *The Anniversary* (1968). The band can also be heard on the soundtrack of *The Bliss of Mrs. Blossom* (1968), and appeared on such TV shows as *Toast of the Town* (1948–1971, TV, later *The Ed Sullivan Show*) and *The London Palladium Show* (1966–1969, TV). They had a U.S. number one hit with *Winchester Cathedral* (1966). Other song releases include *Peek-a-Boo* (1967), which reached number seven in the UK charts. Its members included songwriters Geoff Stephens (1934–) and Alan Klein (1940–), who also billed himself as Tristram—

Seventh Earl of Cricklewood, trumpeter Bob Kerr (1940–), drummer Henri Harrison and singer John Carter (1942–, real name John Nicholas Shakespeare). **Hammer credits:** *The Anniversary* (1968)

## Newall, Basil

This British make-up artist Newall (1924–1991) worked on the Hammer thrillers *Taste of Fear* (1961) and *Maniac* (1963). His many other credits include *Upstairs and Downstairs* (1959), *Kill or Cure* (1962), *From Russia with Love* (1963), *Goldfinger* (1964), *You Only Live Twice* (1967), *Some Girls Do* (1969), *The Slipper and the Rose* (1976), *Superman* (1978), *Clash of the Titans* (1981), *Shirley Valentine* (1989) and *Duel of Hearts* (1992, TVM), plus episodes of *The Protectors* (1972–1973, TV), *Space: 1999* (1975–1977, TV) and *Reilly: Ace of Spies* (1983, TV), which earned him a shared BAFTA nomination. **Hammer credits:** *Taste of Fear* (1961), *Maniac* (1963)

## Newbrook, Peter

This British cinematographer, producer and director (1920–2009) began his film career as a camera assistant in 1934 at Teddington Studios. Following experience with the Army Kinematograph Unit during the war, he resumed his career, working in various capacities behind the camera, including a stint as an operator on Hammer's *Dick Barton Strikes Back* (1949). His career took a step up when he went to work for director David Lean on four prestige productions, beginning on *The Sound Barrier* (1952), on which he was the aerial cameraman, and culminating with *Lawrence of Arabia* (1962), on which he photographed the second unit. His work as a fully-fledged cinematographer includes *That Kind of Girl* (1963), *The Black Torment* (1964) and *Gonks Go Beat* (1965), for which he also co-authored the story. His films as a producer include *The Sandwich Man* (1966), *Press for Time* (1966) and *Corruption* (1967), each of which he also photographed. His other credits include photographing and executive producing *Crucible of Terror* (1971), co-writing and producing *She'll Follow You Anywhere* (1971) and directing *The Asphyx* (1972). **Hammer credits:** *Dick Barton Strikes Back* (1949)

## Newell, Joan

This British supporting actress (1915–2012) can be seen in *The Last Visitor* (1968, TV [episode of *Journey to the Unknown*]), which also appeared in the compendium film *Journey to the Unknown* (1969, TVM). Her many other TV appearances include everything from *Douglas Fairbanks, Jr. Presents* (1953–1957, TV) to *Juliet Bravo* (1980–1985, TV). Her occasional films include *The Last Man to Hang?* (1956), *The Devil's Pass* (1957), *Jigsaw* (1962) and *Stolen Hours* (1963). Her first husband (of two) was the stage director George Ivor. **Hammer credits:** *The Last Visitor* (1968, TV [episode of *Journey to the Unknown*], as Mrs. Plimmer), *Journey to the Unknown* (1969, TVM, as Mrs. Plimmer)

## Newell, Patrick

Best remembered for playing "Mother" in *The Avengers* (1961–1969, TV), this hefty British character actor (1932–1988) was also adept at bluff and pompous types, among them the corrupt MP Sir Edmund Weir in Hammer's big screen version of *Man About the House* (1974). His other film credits include *The Rebel* (1960), *The Dock Brief* (1962), *Father Came Too* (1963), *Every Day's a Holiday* (1964), *The Alphabet Murders* (1965), *Stand Up, Virgin Soldiers* (1977) and *Consuming Passions* (1988), while his small screen work includes episodes of *Room at the Bottom* (1966–1967, TV), *Never Say Die* (1970, TV), *Casanova* (1971, TV), *Wodehouse Playhouse* (1975–1978, TV), *Kinvig* (1981, TV) and *Galloping Galaxies!* (1985–1986, TV). **Hammer credits:** *Man About the House* (1974, as Sir Edmund Weir)

## Newfield, Sam

Working in both Britain and his home country, this prolific American director (1889–1964, real name Samuel Neufeld, aka Sherman Scott and Peter Stewart) helmed over two-hundred shorts and second features during his busy career, including fifteen in 1938 alone! Beginning in 1926 with *Which Is Which?*, his output included such titles as *Sailor George* (1928), *Reform Girl* (1933), *Code of the Mountain* (1935), *The Terror of Tiny Town* (1938), *Lady Chasers* (1946), *Last of the Desperados* (1955) and *Wolf Dog* (1958).

He also directed *Lady in the Fog* (1952) for Hammer/Exclusive, at the request of the American producer Robert Lippert, for whom he had worked many times in Hollywood (several of these Lippert-produced films were released in the UK by Exclusive, among them *Hijacked* [1951] and *The Lost Continent* [1951]). Newfield also helmed scenes for a second Hammer co-feature, *The Gambler and the Lady* (1953), sharing the directing credit with Pat Jenkins. Terence Fisher is also thought to have worked on the film, which Newfield also scripted without credit. His brother was producer Sigmund Neufeld (1896–1979). His wife was continuity girl Violet McComas; their children are actress Jackie Newfield and actor Joel Newfield (1935–). **Hammer credits:** *Lady in the Fog* (1952, director), *The Gambler and the Lady* (1953, screenplay [uncredited], co-director)

## Newland, Sally

Newland can be seen as a receptionist in Hammer's *Mantrap* (1953). Her other credits include *The Elusive Pimpernel* (1950) and an episode of *Strange Experiences* (1955–1956, TV). **Hammer credits:** *Mantrap* (1953, as Receptionist)

## Newlands, Anthony

This British actor (1925–1995) can be seen in the likes of *Room at the Top* (1958), *Beyond This Place* (1959), *Solo for Sparrow* (1962), *Circus of Fear* (1966), *Theatre of Death* (1967), *The Magus* (1968), *Scream and Scream Again* (1970) and *Mata Hari* (1984). He also played the duplicitous psychiatrist Dr. Keller in the Hammer thriller *Hysteria* (1965), in which he attempts to drive a patient mad in an involved plot to murder his wife. His TV appearances include episodes of *The Scarlet Pimpernel* (1956, TV), *Barlow at Large* (1971–1975, TV) and *Lost Empires* (1986, TV). **Hammer credits:** *Hysteria* (1965, as Dr. Keller)

## Newley, Anthony

This multi-talented British actor, singer, writer, director, producer, composer and lyricist (1931–1999, full name George Anthony Newley) began his film career as a child actor *Henry V* (1944), and went on to appear in the serial *Dusty Bates* (1947), *Vice Versa* (1947), *Oliver Twist* (1948), in which he was a memorable Artful Dodger, *The Guinea Pig* (1948) and *A Boy, a Girl and a Bike* (1949). More adult roles followed in the fifties, among them that of Private "Spider" Webb in Hammer's *X—The Unknown* (1956). Newley appeared in over fifty films in total, including *The Good Companions* (1957), *The Small World of Sammy Lee* (1963), *Doctor Dolittle* (1967), *Can Heironymus Merkin Ever Forget Mercy Humppe and Find True Happiness?* (1969), which he also co-wrote, produced, directed and scored, *Mister Quilp* (1975), which he also scored, *It Seemed Like a Good Idea at the Time* (1976) and *The Garbage Pail Kids Movie* (1989). He also directed, but did not appear in, *Summertree* (1971). For the stage, Newley wrote several successful musicals with his friend Leslie Bricusse, among them *Stop the World, I Want to Get Off* (1961), which contained the hit *What Kind of Fool Am I?* Working with Bricusse, Newley also wrote the songs for the musicals *Willy Wonka and the Chocolate Factory* (1971), which earned him a shared Oscar nomination, and *Peter Pan* (1976, TVM), and co-wrote the lyrics for the James Bond title song *Goldfinger* (1964). Newley's TV appearances include episodes of *The Andy Williams Show* (1962–1967, TV), *The Anthony Newley Show* (1971, TV), *Fame* (1982–1987, TV) and *EastEnders* (1985–, TV). Married three times, his wives included the actresses Ann Lynn (1933–, full name Elizabeth Ann Lynn), to whom he was married between 1956 and 1963, and Joan Collins (1933–), to whom he was married between 1963 and 1971. Collins appeared in the Hammer thriller *Fear in the Night* (1972). His children (with Collins) are the actress Tara Newley (1963–) and the actor Alexander Anthony Newley (1965–, aka Sacha Newley). **Hammer credits:** *X—The Unknown* (1956, as Private "Spider" Webb)

## Newman, Jack

Newman worked as a standby painter on *Hammer House of Mystery and Suspense* (1984, TVM). His other credits include *Battle of Britain* (1969) and *A Private Function* (1984). **Hammer credits:** *Hammer House of Mystery and Suspense* (1984, TVM [uncredited])

## Newman, Nanette

In films as a child with the short *Here We Come Gathering: A Story of the Kentish Orchards* (1945), this elegant British actress (1934–) has appeared in over twenty features, including several for her director husband Bryan Forbes (1926–2013, real name John Theobald Clarke), whom she married in 1955, among them *The L-Shaped Room* (1962), *Seance on a Wet Afternoon* (1964), *The Whisperers* (1967), *The Raging Moon* (1970), which earned her a best actress BAFTA nomination, *The Stepford Wives* (1974) and *International Velvet* (1978). Also active in television, her credits here include *Paper*

*Dolls*, an episode of Hammer's *Journey to the Unknown* (1968, TV), which also appeared in the compendium film *Journey into Darkness* (1968, TV). She is also well known for a long-running ad campaign for Fairy Liquid. Her other film credits include *A Personal Affair* (1953), *The League of Gentlemen* (1960), *Captain Nemo and the Underwater City* (1968) and Hammer's film version of the TV series *Man at the Top* (1973), in which she played Lady Alex Ackerman. Of her role in the latter, director Mike Vardy recalled, "Nanette had a certain screen image and was very unhappy with some of the material. We used a body double for one of her scenes because she didn't do nudity. There was a bit of a row about that, but she must have known what the producers were intending to do. Showing a naked breast here and there doesn't really advance the plot but that's what they wanted…. I have to say that in the edit it all worked rather well though, which is why Nanette was so annoyed."[21]

In addition to her work as an actress, Newman also writes cookery and children's books. Her daughters are the former child actress and fashion journalist Sarah Forbes (1959–) and the actress and television presenter Emma Forbes (1965–). Her son-in-law (via marriage to Sarah Forbes) is the actor Sir John Standing (1934–, real name John Ronald Leon). Newman's husband was head of production for EMI between 1969 and 1971, during which period the studio bankrolled several Hammer films, including *The Horror of Frankenstein* (1970) and *Lust for a Vampire* (1970). **Hammer credits:** *Paper Dolls* (1968, TV [episode of *Journey to the Unknown*], as Jill Collins), *Journey into Darkness* (1968, TVM, as Jill Collins), *Man at the Top* (1973, as Lady Alex Ackerman)

### Newman, Peter

This British scriptwriter (1926–1969) penned the screenplay for the Hammer war drama *Yesterday's Enemy* (1959), which itself was based upon his own original 1958 teleplay (Newman also acted as the film's technical advisor, drawing upon his wartime experiences as an RAF pilot and intelligence officer). Newman was subsequently contracted to pen the Spanish Inquisition drama *The Rape of Sabena* (aka *The Inquisitor*) for Hammer, which was to have been made in 1960. However, following objections from the film's co-producers Columbia (as well as the Catholic Church), the project was abandoned. Another script penned by Newman for Hammer—a western titled *The Brutal Land*—also went unmade by Hammer. However, producer Michael Carreras eventually made the project in Spain as *The Savage Guns* (1962) through his own company Capricorn Productions, though by this time the script had been completely re-written by Edmund Morris. Newman's other writing credits include six episodes of *Doctor Who* (1963–1989, TV) in 1964. **Hammer credits:** *Yesterday's Enemy* (1959)

### Newport, Michael

This British actor (1952–) can be seen as Smiler in the Hammer swashbuckler *The Devil-Ship Pirates* (1964). His other credits include *Life at the Top* (1965), *The Naked Runner* (1967), *Decline and Fall … of a Birdwatcher* (1968), *….* (1968) and *Mischief* (1969). His TV work includes episodes of *Dixon of Dock Green* (1955–1976, TV), *Treasure Island* (1968, TV), in which he played Jim Hawkins, and *Doomwatch* (1970–1972, TV). **Hammer credits:** *The Devil-Ship Pirates* (1964, as Smiler)

### Newrick, Bernard

Exclusive's branch manager for the city of Liverpool in the fifties, Newrick remained with the company until its demise in 1959.

### Newth, Jonathan

This busy British actor (1939–) can be seen as MP Harry Dowl in *Tennis Court* (1984, TVM [episode of *Hammer House of Mystery and Suspense*]). His many other TV credits include episodes of *The Six Wives of Henry VIII* (1970, TV), *Ace of Wands* (1970–1972, TV), *The Adventures of Black Beauty* (1972–1974, TV), *The Brothers* (1972–1976, TV), *Tenko* (1981–1984, TV), *After Henry* (1989–1992, TV), in which he played Russell Bryant, *Heartbeat* (1992–2009, TV), *Doctors* (2000–, TV) and *The Crown* (2016–, TV). His occasional films include *Far from the Madding Crowd* (1969), *Yellow Dog* (1973) and *The Affair of the Necklace* (2001). Also much on stage. **Hammer credits:** *Tennis Court* (1984, TVM [episode of *Hammer House of Mystery and Suspense*], as Harry Dowl)

### Neylin, James

This Irish actor (1920–1965) can be seen as Roger in Hammer's Robin Hood adventure *Sword of Sherwood Forest* (1960). His other credits include *Saints and Sinners* (1949), *A Question of Suspense* (1961), *Johnny Nobody* (1961) and *The Running Man* (1963), plus episodes of *BBC Sunday-Night Theatre* (1950–1959, TV) and *Pride and Prejudice* (1952, TV). **Hammer credits:** *Sword of Sherwood Forest* (1960, as Roger [uncredited])

### NFFC (NFFCO) *see* National Film Finance Corporation

### Nichol, Stuart

This Canadian actor (1908–1991) had supporting roles in two of Hammer's fifties second features. His other credits include *No Highway* (1951), *What's Good for the Goose* (1969) and *Leaving Lily* (1975), plus episodes of *BBC Sunday-Night Theatre* (1950–1959, TV), *Quatermass and the Pit* (1958–1959, TV) and *Clouds of Witness* (1972, TV). **Hammer credits:** *Whispering Smith Hits London* (1952, as Martin), *Lady in the Fog* (1952, as Steve)

### Nicholas, Margaret

Nicholas worked as a production assistant on all thirteen episodes of *Hammer House of Horror* (1980, TV). **Hammer credits:** *Hammer House of Horror* (1980, TV)

### Nicholls, Horatio

This prolific British songwriter (1888–1964, real name Lawrence Wright, aka Larry Wright and Gene Williams) provided the music for the chirpy title song for the Hammer comedy *Watch It, Sailor!* (1961). Selling sheet music from 1906, he became the first publisher to open an office in Denmark Street (London's Tin Pan Alley) in 1911, among his successes being the selling of a quarter of a million copies of *The Wright Pianoforte Tutor*. His shows included *Sensations of 1927* (excerpts from which were filmed for a short of the same name in 1927, for which he provided the script and songs), while his many songs (over 600) include *Are We Downhearted? No!* (1914), *Among My Souvenirs* (1927), *The Trail of the Tamarind Tree* (1928), *When the Guards Are on Parade* (1931) and *V Stands for Victory* (1941). **Hammer credits:** *Watch It, Sailor!* (1961)

### Nichols, Dandy

Best remembered for playing Else Garnett, the long-suffering wife of the bigoted Alf Garnett in the sitcom *Till Death Us Do Part* (1966–1975, TV), this British actress (1907–1986, real name Daisy Sander) revived the character for two TV sequels, *Till Death…* (1981, TV) and *In Sickness and in Health* (1985–1992, TV), along with two film spin offs, *Till Death Us Do Part* (1969) and *The Alf Garnett Saga* (1972). In films from 1947 with a bit part in *Hue and Cry*, she went on to appear in minor roles in a number of productions, among them Hammer's *The Glass Cage* (1955), before she found stardom comparatively late in life. Her other feature credits include *The Winslow Boy* (1948), *White Corridors* (1951), *Lost* (1956), *The Vikings* (1958), *Crooks Anonymous* (1962), *The Knack* (1965), *Help!* (1965), *Georgy Girl* (1966), *Carry On Doctor* (1967), *The Birthday Party* (1968), *O Lucky Man!* (1973), *Confessions of a Window Cleaner* (1974), in which she played Mrs. Lea (a role taken over by Doris Hare for the sequels), and *Britannia Hospital* (1982). She also popped up in episodes of such series as *Emergency—Ward 10* (1957–1967, TV), *Mrs. Thursday* (1966–1967, TV), *Late Call* (1975, TV) and *Maybury* (1981–1983, TV). Also much on stage. **Hammer credits:** *The Glass Cage* (1955, as Woman with child [uncredited])

### Nicholson, James H.

With his long-term business partner Samuel Z. Arkoff, this American producer, executive producer and company executive (1916–1972) formed American International Pictures (AIP) in 1955, which went on to make many low budget genre pictures, including a celebrated cycle of films loosely based upon the works of Edgar Allan Poe, among them *House of Usher* (1960) and *The Raven* (1963). In 1970, AIP teamed up with Hammer to make *The Vampire Lovers* (1970). However, though the film was a commercial success, the experiment was not repeated, and Nicholson's involvement in the picture was minimal. His other credits include *I Was a Teenage Frankenstein* (1957), which was made to cash in on Hammer's *The Curse of Frankenstein* (1957), *Tales of Terror* (1962), *The Dunwich Horror* (1969), *Murders in the Rue Morgue* (1971) and *The Legend of Hell House* (1973). **Hammer credits:** *The Vampire Lovers* (1970)

### Nicholson, Kenneth (Ken)

British born Nicholson (1930–) operated the second unit camera for second unit cinematographer Jack Mills on Hammer's *One Million Years B.C.*

(1966). His credits as a clapper loader include *My Brother Jonathan* (1948), *Madness of the Heart* (1949) and *The Story of Robin Hood and His Merrie Men* (1952). His work as a focus puller includes *Murder at 3am* (1953), while his credits as an operator take in *Der Rosenkavalier* (1962) and *All the Way Up* (1970). **Hammer credits:** *One Million Years B.C.* (1966 [uncredited])

### Nicholson, Veronica

This child actress made a brief appearance in Hammer's *Rasputin—The Mad Monk* (1966). **Hammer credits:** *Rasputin—The Mad Monk* (1966, as Young girl [uncredited])

### Nicol, Alex

On stage from the age of nineteen, this American actor (1916–2001, full name Alexander L. Nicol, Jr.) made his film debut in 1950 in *The Sleeping City*. In 1954, he travelled to Britain to appear in two second features for Hammer, the first of which was the thriller *Face the Music*. Nicol's other films include *The Gilded Cage* (1954), *Five Branded Women* (1959), *Bloody Mama* (1969) and *Woman in the Rain* (1976). He also directed several films, among them *The Screaming Skull* (1960) and *Then There Were Three* (1960), in which he also starred. He also directed episodes of such TV series as *Daniel Boone* (1964–1970, TV), *The Legend of Jesse James* (1965–1966, TV), *Tarzan* (1966–1968, TV) and *The D.A.* (1971–1972, TV). Note that Nicol also co-starred in *The Savage Guns* (1962), a western directed by Michael Carreras for his own company Capricorn Productions. This had originally been intended as a Hammer project, but Carreras took the property with him when he temporarily left the studio in the early sixties. **Hammer credits:** *Face the Music* (1954, as James Bradley), *The House Across the Lake* (1954, as Mark Kendrick)

### Nielsen, Helen

This American author and short story writer (1918–2002) had her novel *Murder by Proxy* (1951, aka *Gold Coast Nocturne* and *Dead on the Level*) turned into a film by Hammer in 1955. Her other stories include *Your Witness* and *Death Scene*, which were filmed for television as episodes of *Alfred Hitchcock Presents* (1955–1962, TV) and *The Alfred Hitchcock Hour* (1962–1965, TV) respectively. Her story *Pattern of Guilt* has meanwhile been filmed for both *Alcoa Premiere* (1961–1963, TV) in 1962, and *Tales of the Unexpected* (1979–1988, TV) in 1982. **Hammer credits:** *Murder by Proxy* (1955)

### *Night Creatures* see *Captain Clegg*

### Nightingale, John

This British actor (1942–1980) had a supporting role in *Eve*, an episode of Hammer's *Journey to the Unknown* (1968, TV). His other TV credits include *Coriolanus* (1965, TV), in which he played the title role, and *When the Boat Comes In* (1976–1981, TV), in which he played Tom Seaton, plus appearances in episodes of *Redcap* (1964–1966, TV), *Play for Today* (1970–1984, TV) and *Village Hall* (1974–1975, TV). **Hammer credits:** *Eve* (1968, TV [episode of *Journey to the Unknown*], as First youth)

### Nightingale, Laura

This costume designer and wardrobe mistress worked on several films for Hammer in the seventies, beginning with *The Vampire Lovers* (1970). She also worked on all thirteen episodes of *Hammer House of Horror* (1980, TV) and twelve out of thirteen episodes of *Hammer House of Mystery and Suspense* (1984, TVM), with Janice Wilde providing the costumes for the episode titled *Child's Play*. Her other credits include *Stranger from Venus* (1954), *Another Time, Another Place* (1958), *The Angry Silence* (1960), *The Devil's Daffodil* (1961), *A Kind of Loving* (1962), *Billy Liar* (1963), *The Masque of the Red Death* (1964), *The Comedy Man* (1964), *Innocent Bystanders* (1972), *Rising Damp* (1980) and *George and Mildred* (1980), plus episodes of *The Saint* (1962–1969, TV), *The Baron* (1966–1967, TV), *The Champions* (1968–1969, TV), *Randall and Hopkirk (Deceased)* (1969–1971, TV), *Jason King* (1971–1972, TV), *The Adventurer* (1972–1973, TV), *Get Some In!* (1975–1978, TV), *Rumpole of the Bailey* (1978–1992, TV) and *Widows* (1983, TV). **Hammer credits:** *The Vampire Lovers* (1970), *Scars of Dracula* (1970), *The Horror of Frankenstein* (1970), *Lust for a Vampire* (1971), *Straight on Till Morning* (1972), *Love Thy Neighbour* (1973), *Man at the Top* (1973), *Holiday on the Buses* (1973), *Man About the House* (1974), *To the Devil a Daughter* (1976), *Hammer House of Horror* (1980, TV), *Czech Mate* (1984, TVM [episode of *Hammer House of Mystery and Suspense*]), *The Sweet Scent of Death* (1984, TVM [episode of *Hammer House of Mystery and Suspense*]), *A Distant Scream* (1984, TVM [episode of *Hammer House of Mystery and Suspense*]), *The Late Nancy Irving* (1984, TVM [episode of *Hammer House of Mystery and Suspense*]), *In Possession* (1984, TVM [episode of *Hammer House of Mystery and Suspense*]), *Black Carrion* (1984, TVM [episode of *Hammer House of Mystery and Suspense*]), *Last Video and Testament* (1984, TVM [episode of *Hammer House of Mystery and Suspense*]), *Mark of the Devil* (1984, TVM [episode of *Hammer House of Mystery and Suspense*]), *The Corvini Inheritance* (1984, TVM [episode of *Hammer House of Mystery and Suspense*]), *Paint Me a Murder* (1984, TVM [episode of *Hammer House of Mystery and Suspense*]), *And the Wall Came Tumbling Down* (1984, TVM [episode of *Hammer House of Mystery and Suspense*]), *Tennis Court* (1984, TVM [episode of *Hammer House of Mystery and Suspense*])

### Nightingale, Michael

This British actor (1922–1999, full name Alfred George C. Michael Nightingale) can be seen as Sidney Flood in Hammer's Thuggee shocker *The Stranglers of Bombay* (1959). His other credits include *Ice Cold in Alex* (1958), *Raising the Wind* (1961) *The Iron Maiden* (1962), *Carry On Cabby* (1963), *The Return of the Pink Panther* (1975), *Carry On England* (1976) and *Carry On Emmanuelle* (1978), plus a return to Hammer for a brief role in *Mutiny on the Buses* (1972). His TV work includes *Poor Butterfly*, an episode of Hammer's *Journey to the Unknown* (1968, TV), which also appeared in the compendium film *Journey to Midnight*

(1968, TVM). His other TV appearances include episodes of *Douglas Fairbanks, Jr. Presents* (1953–1957, TV) and *Cadfael* (1994–1996, TV). **Hammer credits:** *The Stranglers of Bombay* (1959, as Sidney Flood), *Poor Butterfly* (1968, TV [episode of *Journey to the Unknown*], as Butler), *Journey to Midnight* (1968, TVM, as Butler), *Mutiny on the Buses* (1972, as Pilot)

### Nightingall, Ken

Nightingall worked as the boom operator on two films for Hammer in the early sixties. His many other credits include *Alfie* (1966), *The Ghoul* (1975), *Star Wars* (1977), *For Your Eyes Only* (1981), *Octopussy* (1983), *A View to a Kill* (1985), *The Living Daylights* (1987) and *Lost in Space* (1998). **Hammer credits:** *Paranoiac* (1963 [uncredited]), *The Kiss of the Vampire* (1963 [uncredited])

### *Nightmare*

GB, 1964, 82m, HammerScope, bw, RCA, cert X

Written and produced by Jimmy Sangster in the wake of the success of *Taste of Fear* (1961), *Nightmare* is easily one of the best of Hammer's "mini Hitchcocks." The plot-packed script may be "highly contrived" as *Variety* put it, yet the enterprise is put across with sufficient style by director Freddie Francis and cinematographer John Wilcox that this barely matters (the film's publicity material described it as "a macabre suspense drama staged in the best Hammer tradition").

The story is the old chestnut of attempting to drive someone insane so that the perpetrators can inherit, or in this case gain control of a young woman's estate (admitted screenwriter Jimmy Sangster of the plot, "*Nightmare* was my fourth psycho-type drama for Hammer and once again the whole thing revolved around a pretty girl in dire peril…. The original storyline was starting to fray a little around the edges by now"[22]). This time the victim is seventeen-year-old Janet, brought home from boarding school to live with her guardian, Henry Baxter, and a new companion, Grace Maddox, following a series of nightmares recalling the time, some years earlier, when her mother went mad and killed her father with a kitchen knife. However, once home, Janet starts to hear noises and has fleeting visions of a phantom-like woman in white. Is she losing her mind, or are Henry and Grace conspiring to drive her to commit murder so that they can wrest control of her inheritance when she is subsequently committed?

Originally to have been titled *Here's the Knife, Dear—Now Use It* (which proved rather *too* revealing), *Nightmare* was on the floor at Bray between 17 December 1962 and 31 January 1963, with a brief hiatus for Christmas. To play the part of the frightened Janet, Freddie Francis and Jimmy Sangster chose a young rep actress named Jennie Linden, who was brought in at the last moment to replace Julie Christie, who had originally signed for the role but subsequently begged off when she was offered the role of Liz in *Billy Liar* (1963), the success of which launched her career. Linden may have been second choice, yet she more than adequately displays Janet's fright and confusion, questioning her sanity as the visions persist ("Three shocking murders ... did she dream them or do them?" questioned the film's poster). Ably supported by David Knight and Moira Redmond as the devious Henry and Grace, the cast also boasts such reliable performers as Brenda Bruce as Janet's teacher Mary Lewis, and Irene Richmond as her adoring housekeeper Mrs. Gibbs. Meanwhile, the striking-looking Clytie Jessop makes a real impact as the fleetingly glimpsed woman in white, who turns out to be Grace disguised as Henry's wife, whom Janet murders when she meets her for real.

Yet as *Variety* put it, the film's "best features" are undoubtedly the direction of Freddie Francis and the atmospheric lighting of cameraman John Wilcox, both of which really crank up the atmosphere of the creepy house where Janet finds herself being driven insane (the carefully framed and angled shots, among them a superb overhead view as the tables are turned on Grace, are impressive indeed). *The Times* agreed and announced that, "Francis can be welcomed to the short roll of British horror specialists." Recalled Jimmy Sangster, "The actual shooting went very smoothly. Locations were done at Oakley Court in six inches of snow, which was a bitch to shoot but looked very good."[23] In fact the film's only letdown proves to be a slackening of pace in the final third as the narrative is tied up and several new twists are added to the plot.

*The stuff of bad dreams. Artwork for* Nightmare (1964) (Hammer/Universal/Rank/Universal International).

**Slick and to the point. An ad for the twist-packed thriller *Nightmare* (1964) (Hammer/Universal/Rank/Universal International).**

The ideal companion to *The Evil of Frankenstein* (1964), also directed by Francis, *Nightmare* proved to be something of a hit with audiences when the double bill was premiered at London's New Victoria cinema on 19 April 1964. The pairing then went on release in the UK on the ABC circuit care of Rank on 31 May, by which time the film had been released in America by Universal International on 8 May. **Additional notes:** The film carries a 1963 copyright.

Production companies: Hammer/Universal. Distributors: Rank (UK [ABC circuit]), Universal International (U.S.). Producer: Jimmy Sangster. Director: Freddie Francis. Screenplay: Jimmy Sangster. Cinematographer: John Wilcox. Music: Don Banks. Music director: John Hollingsworth. Supervising editor: James Needs. Assistant editor: Chris Barnes [uncredited]. Second assistant editor: Alan Willis [uncredited]. Production design: Bernard Robinson. Art director: Don Mingaye. Assistant art director: Ken Ryan [uncredited]. Costumes: Rosemary Burrows, Molly Arbuthnot [uncredited]. Special effects: Les Bowie. Special effects assistants: Ian Scoones [uncredited], Ray Caple [uncredited], Kit West [uncredited]. Make-up: Roy Ashton, Richard Mills (assistant [uncredited]). Hair: Frieda Steiger. Sound: Ken Rawkins. Sound editor: James Groom. Sound camera operator: Al Thorne [uncredited], Michael Sale [uncredited]. Boom operator: Jim Perry [uncredited]. Boom assistant: Roy Mingaye [uncredited]. Production manager: Don Weeks. Studio manager: Arthur Kelly [uncredited]. Construction manager: Arthur Banks [uncredited]. Master carpenter: Charles Davis [uncredited]. Master painter: Lawrence Wrenn [uncredited]. Master electrician: Jack Curtis [uncredited]. Electrician: George Robinson [uncredited]. Master rigger: Ronald Lenoir [un-

credited]. Master plasterer: Stan Banks [uncredited]. Assistant director: Douglas Hermes [uncredited]. Second assistant director: Hugh Harlow [uncredited]. Camera operator: Ronnie Maasz. Focus pullers: Geoff Glover [uncredited], Ronnie Fox Rogers [uncredited]. Camera grip: Albert Cowlard [uncredited]. Camera maintenance: John Kerley [uncredited]. Props: Tommy Money [uncredited]. Proper buyer: Eric Hillier [uncredited]. Stills: Tom Edwards [uncredited]. Publicity: Dennison Thornton [uncredited], Brian Doyle [uncredited]. Continuity: Pauline Wise. Production secretary: Maureen White [uncredited]. **Cast:** Moira Redmond (Grace Maddox), Jennie Linden (Janet), David Knight (Henry Baxter), Brenda Bruce (Mary Lewis), George A. Cooper (John), John Welsh (Doctor), Irene Richmond (Mrs. Gibbs), Timothy Bateson (Barman), Clytie Jessop (Woman in white/Mrs. Baxter), Isla Cameron (Mother), Hedger Wallace (Sir Dudley), Julie Samuel (Anne [Maid]), Frank Forsyth (Waiter), Elizabeth Dear (Young Janet). **DVD availability:** Universal (R1 U.S. NTSC), as part of the *Hammer Horror Series* box set, which also contains *The Brides of Dracula* (1960), *The Curse of the Werewolf* (1961), *The Phantom of the Opera* (1962), *Paranoiac* (1963), *The Kiss of the Vampire* (1963, *Captain Clegg* (1962) and *The Evil of Frankenstein* (1964). **Blu-ray availability:** Final Cut Entertainment (B/2), extras include three documentaries, *Nightmare in the Making*, *Jennie Linden Remembers* and *Madhouse: Inside Hammer's Nightmare*

### Nightmare of Terror see Demons of the Mind

### Nimmo, David

British born Nimmo (1930–1975) worked as an assistant editor on Hammer's *The Gorgon* (1964).

His other credits include *Watch Your Stern* (1960), on which he was an assistant sound editor, *The Terrornauts* (1967), on which he was a sound re-recordist, and *The File of the Golden Goose* (1969), on which he was a sound editor. **Hammer credits:** *The Gorgon* (1964 [uncredited])

## Nixon, Chris

Nixon worked as the publicist on a handful of Hammer productions in the seventies, including their last theatrical feature for thirty years. His other credits include *The Whisperers* (1967), *Carry On … Up the Khyber* (1968), *Side by Side* (1975), *Confessions from a Holiday Camp* (1977), *The Awakening* (1980), *Witness for the Prosecution* (1982, TVM) and *American Gothic* (1988). **Hammer credits:** *Scars of Dracula* (1970 [uncredited]), *The Horror of Frankenstein* (1970 [uncredited]), *The Lady Vanishes* (1979 [uncredited])

## Noble, Larry

This British supporting actor (1914–1993) can be seen as a Chief Petty Officer in the Hammer naval comedy *Up the Creek* (1958). He also appeared in the sequel, though as a different character. His other credits include *Reluctant Heroes* (1951), *The Night We Dropped a Clanger* (1959), *Night Train for Inverness* (1960), and *The Return of the Soldier* (1982), plus an episode of Hammer's *Journey to the Unknown* (1968, TV). His other TV credits include episodes of *The Cheaters* (1960–1962, TV), *Father Brown* (1974, TV) and *Chance in a Million* (1984–1986, TV). **Hammer credits:** *Up the Creek* (1958, as Chief Petty Officer), *Further Up the Creek* (1958, as Postman), *The Beckoning Fair One* (1968, TV [episode of *Journey to the Unknown*], as Mr. Barrett)

## Noel, Daniele

This actress and model played the role of Sharna in Hammer's *The Vengeance of She* (1968). Her other credits include *Return from the Ashes* (1965), *Bedazzled* (1967) and *The Magus* (1968). She was also the subject of a 1965 documentary titled *Daniele*, the commentary for which she also wrote. **Hammer credits:** *The Vengeance of She* (1968, as Sharna)

## Nolf, Vernon

British born Nolf (1920–2009) worked as a third assistant director on two films for Hammer. His other credits include *Stolen Assignment* (1955). **Hammer cedits:** *Mantrap* (1953 [uncredited]), *Four Sided Triangle* (1953 [uncredited]

## Nolte, Charles

This American actor (1923–2010) can be seen as a doctor in Hammer's troubled bomb disposal drama *Ten Seconds to Hell* (1959). A noted acting instructor, his other credits include *War Paint* (1953), *The Steel Cage* (1954), *Under Ten Flags* (1960) and *Armored Command* (1961), plus episodes of *Studio One* (1948–1958, TV), *Cosmopolitan Theatre* (1951, TV), *Schlitz Playhouse of Stars* (1951–1959, TV), *Campbell Playhouse* (1953–1954, TV) and *Tales of the Vikings* (1959–1960, TV). His longtime companion was the actor Terry Kilburn (1926–, real name Terence E. Kilburn). **Hammer** credits: *Ten Seconds to Hell* (1959, as Doctor [uncredited])

## Noonan, Pat

Noonan worked as an electrician on *Hammer House of Mystery and Suspense* (1984, TVM). His other credits include *Confessions of a Window Cleaner* (1974), *Stevie* (1978) and *Biddy* (1983). **Hammer credits:** *Hammer House of Mystery and Suspense* (1984, TVM, [uncredited])

## Noor, Abdul

Noor had a minor role in the Hammer war drama *The Steel Bayonet* (1957). **Hammer credits:** *The Steel Bayonet* (1957, as Arab [uncredited])

## Norden, Christine

Following experience as a singer and dancer (she was the first entertainer to perform for troops in Normandy in 1944), this British actress and post-war sex symbol (1924–1988, real name Mary Lydia Thornton) made her film debut in 1947 with *An Ideal Husband*, which she followed with the likes of *Mine Own Executioner* (1947), *Night Beat* (1947), *Idol of Paris* (1948), *Saints and Sinners* (1949), *The Interrupted Journey* (1949) and *Reluctant Heroes* (1951). She also appeared in two Hammer programers: *The Black Widow* (1950), as a murderous wife, and *A Case for PC 49* (1951). Her occasional TV credits include episodes of *Rooftop Rendezvous* (1948–1950, TV), *Girl Talk* (1962–1970, TV), *Chance in a Million* (1984–1986, TV) and *Inspector Morse* (1987–2000, TV). Married five times, her husbands included the director Jack Clayton (1921–1995), to whom she was married between 1947 and 1953. When her film career dried up, she returned to the stage, making her Broadway debut in 1960 in *Tenderloin*. She was also the first legitimate star to go topless on a Broadway stage in *Scuba Duba* in 1967. Her sister was the actress June Mitchell (1933–2009, real name Elizabeth June Thornton, aka Elizabeth Shipp), who appeared in two films for Hammer: *Wings of Danger* (1952) and *Never Look Back* (1952). **Hammer credits:** *The Black Widow* (1950, Christine Sherwin), *A Case for PC 49* (1951, as Della Dainton)

## Norman, Don

Norman produced Hammer's 1974 album version of *Dracula*, for which he also created the various sound effects. **Hammer credits:** *Dracula* (1974, LP)

## Norman, Keith

Norman worked as the art director on *The Madison Equation* (1968, TV [episode of *Journey to the Unknown*]). His other TV credits include episodes of *R3* (1964, TV), *Detective* (1964–1969, TV), *Gaslight Theatre* (1965, TV), *Thirty-Minute Theatre* (1965–1973, TV) and *ITV Playhouse* (1968–1982, TV). **Hammer credits:** *The Madison Equation* (1968, TV [episode of *Journey to the Unknown*])

## Norman, Leslie

In films from the age of sixteen as a trainee editor, this British director (1911–1993) became a fully-fledged editor just three years later, and went on to cut such pictures as *Compromising Daphne* (1930), *The Old Curiosity Shop* (1934), *The Prime Minister* (1941) and *Nicholas Nickleby* (1947). He first turned to direction in 1939 with *Too Dangerous to Live*, which he co-directed with Anthony Hankey. Following World War II, Norman began writing and producing for Ealing, working as a writer on *A Run for Your Money* (1949) and *Where No Vultures Fly* (1951), and as a producer/associate producer on *Eureka Stockade* (1948), which he also edited, *Mandy* (1952) and *The Cruel Sea* (1953). His first solo film as a director was *The Night My Number Came Up* (1956), which he followed with Hammer's Quatermass clone *X—The Unknown* (1956), the direction of which he took over from Joseph Losey (working as Joseph Walton), who had been removed from the project over fears that the film wouldn't receive a U.S. showing owing to his blacklisting by the House UnAmerican Activities Committee, which had accused him of harbouring communist sympathies (the film's star, the virulently anti-communist Dean Jagger, had also raised objections to Losey).

Norman turned in an efficient enough film, the shooting of which had, however, been beset with problems, among them many nights filming in a freezing gravel pit. Norman was also not liked by the cast or crew. Recalled third assistant director Hugh Harlow, "It was one of the worst pictures I've ever worked on…. Leslie Norman, who was the director, no longer with us, was a bit of a tyrant and was an ex–Ealing director, and the chemistry between people was not gelling very well. It became a very unhappy experience, I remember that."[24] Remembered screenwriter Jimmy Sangster, who also doubled as the film's production manager, "Leslie made his mark right from the off by being a bully from the beginning to the end of the shoot. He took positive pleasure in treating the crew and cast badly. The whole unit had a row with him at one time or another. Anthony Newley christened him 'the Butcher of Ealing' and Michael Ripper, who made over thirty Hammer films during his career, was told by Norman that, if he had been doing the casting, he would have got Victor Maddern instead."[25] Recalled Norman himself of the movie: "It was a sort of science-fiction film. I hated working at Hammer, though, because I never got on with Anthony Hinds. We had Eddie Chapman in the cast, who had a distinct squint in one eye, and Leo McKern, who has only one eye—and I had to play a scene with them looking at each other. I said, 'For Christ's sake, look at each other!' and they said, 'We are!'"[26]

Norman's other directorial credits include *The Shiralee* (1957), *Dunkirk* (1958), *The Long and the Short and the Tall* (1960) and *Mix Me a Person* (1961). In 1968 he returned to Hammer to helm *The Lost Continent*, which was based on the Dennis Wheatley novel *Uncharted Seas*. However, despite having worked the pre-production period, he was removed from the project after just a couple of days' second unit filming and was replaced by the film's writer-producer Michael Carreras, with whom he had disagreed over the film's approach.

Norman's TV credits include episodes of such series as *The Saint* (1962–1969, TV), of which he helmed twenty-one episodes, *Gideon's Way* (1965–1966, TV), *The Baron* (1966–1967, TV), *The Persuaders!* (1971–1972, TV) and *Return of the Saint*

(1978–1979, TV). His son was the film critic Barry Norman (1933–2017). His grandchildren are the actress Samantha Norman (1962–) and the presenter/critic Emma Norman. **Hammer credits:** *X—The Unknown* (1956), *The Lost Continent* (1968 [pre-production only])

### Norman, Monty

Best known for writing the *James Bond Theme*, this British composer (1928–, real name Monty Noserovitch) has spent the majority of his career in the theater, for which he has penned such musicals as *Expresso Bongo* (1958, recorded for TV 1958, filmed in 1959, and recorded again for German television in 1965 as *Bongo Boy*), *Irma La Douce* (1958), which earned him a shared Tony nomination, *Make Me An Offer* (1959, recorded for TV 1966), *Songbook* (1979), which earned him a second Tony nomination, and *Poppy* (1982). His film scores include *Dr. No* (1962) and *Call Me Bwana* (1962), as well as Hammer's *The Two Faces of Dr. Jekyll* (1960), for which he also provided several songs with his most frequent lyricist, David Heneker; his most frequent book collaborator, Wolf Mankowitz, also penned the screenplay. His TV work includes the series *Dickens of London* (1976, TV), which was also scripted by Mankowitz. His first wife (of two) was the actress Diana Coupland (1928–2006). Note that the end credits for *From Russia with Love* (1963) mistakenly bill the composer as Monte Norman. **Hammer credits:** *The Two Faces of Dr. Jekyll* (1960)

### Norman, Roy

British born Norman (1921–1987) worked as an assistant editor on Hammer's *The Curse of Frankenstein* (1957) and *The Camp on Blood Island* (1958), and as the second assistant editor on *The Hound of the Baskervilles* (1959). His other credits include *Diplomatic Passport* (1954), on which he was the second assistant editor, *The Grand Junction Case* (1961), on which he was the assembly editor and the dubbing editor, and *Water in the Bank* (1981), on which he was the editor. He also worked as a sound editor on *Attempt to Kill* (1961), *Invasion* (1966) and *The Adding Machine* (1968), plus episodes of *Scales of Justice* (1962–1967, TV). **Hammer credits:** *The Curse of Frankenstein* (1957, assistant editor, [uncredited]), *The Camp on Blood Island* (1958, assistant editor [uncredited]), *The Hound of the Baskervilles* (1959, second assistant editor [uncredited])

### Novak, Mickell

Working for a period for producer-director Hal Roach in the early forties, Novak (1917–2009) co-authored the screenplay for *One Million B.C.* (1940) which was later remade by Hammer as *One Million Years B.C.* (1966). Her other credits include *Turnabout* (1940) and *Road Show* (1941), again for Roach. She also worked as a publicist and as a celebrity magazine journalist. Her mother was the actress Jane Novak (1896–1990) and her aunt the actress Eva Novak (1898–1988, full name Barbara Eva Novak). Her husband was the producer Walter Seltzer (1914–2011), whom she married in 1938. **Hammer credits:** *One Million Years B.C.* (1966)

**Novelizations** *see* **Publishing**

### Nowag, Lilian

Nowag can be seen in a minor role in Hammer's *Creatures the World Forgot* (1971). **Hammer credits:** *Creatures the World Forgot* (1971, as Old Rock woman [uncredited])

### Nurse, Heather

Nurse worked as a make-up artist on Hammer's *Dracula Has Risen from the Grave* (1968), sharing her credit with Rosemarie McDonald-Peattie. She also assisted Wally Schneiderman on *Scars of Dracula* (1970). Her solo credits include *Steptoe and Son* (1972), *Born to Boogie* (1972), *Madame Sin* (1972), *Ooh ... You Are Awful* (1972) and *Steptoe and Son Ride Again* (1973). **Hammer credits:** *Dracula Has Risen from the Grave* (1968), *Scars of Dracula* (1970 [uncredited])

### Nye, Pat

This RADA-trained British character actress (1908–1994, full name Patricia Nye) played the role of Ma Brady, the kindly greasy spoon proprietress who turns out to be the head of a gang of lorry hijackers in Hammer's *The Adventures of PC 49—The Case of the Guardian Angel* (1949). Much on stage, her other film credits include *Mr. Perrin and Mr. Traill* (1948), *Appointment with Venus* (1951) and *The Mirror Crack'd* (1980). Also busy in television, her credits here include episodes of everything from *Please Sir!* (1968–1972, TV) to *Doctor on the Go* (1975–1977, TV). During World War II, she was the Chief Officer of The Wrens, for which she was made an OBE in 1946. Her father was the actor Ralph Nye. **Hammer credits:** *The Adventures of PC 49—The Case of the Guardian Angel* (1949, as Ma Brady)

# O

### Oakes, Harry

Following his National Service, during which he worked with the Army Photographic Unit, this British cameraman (1921–2012) gained experience working on documentaries for Merlin Films in the late forties. He first worked for Hammer as a loader on the comedy thriller *Celia* (1949), which led to a healthy run of pictures for the company, during which he graduated to focus puller. Oakes briefly returned to Merlin Films in 1952, but was back at Hammer later the same year for the making of *The Saint's Return* (1953). This led to an incredibly busy period with the company, during which he became their resident focus puller.

Collaborating closely with Hammer's in-house camera operator Len Harris, the duo went on to work on all of the studio's major horror productions, providing reliable support for such cinematographers as Walter "Jimmy" Harvey and Jack Asher, and such directors as Val Guest and Terence Fisher. Oakes finally lost his job at Bray following the temporary closure of the studio in 1962, despite having loyally worked on over eighty shorts and features (all without screen credit), although he did briefly

return to Hammer to work on the second unit for *The Brigand of Kandahar* (1965).

Oakes' other credits include episodes of *Jack Hylton Presents* (1955, TV), to which he was farmed out during a slack period at Bray, and *The Errol Flynn Theatre* (1956, TV), which was shot at Bray, plus such films as *The Baby and the Battleship* (1956), *Superman* (1978), *Dracula* (1979), *Flash Gordon* (1980), *Superman III* (1983), *Aliens* (1986) and *Memphis Belle* (1990). He also worked on a number of films and television series for producer Gerry Anderson, including *Thunderbirds Are Go* (1966), *Captain Scarlet and the Mysterons* (1967, TV), *Joe 90* (1968, TV), *Thunderbird 6* (1968), *The Secret Service* (1969, TV), *Journey to the Far Side of the Sun* (1969), *The Investigator* (1973, TV [unscreened]), *Space: 1999* (1975–1977, TV), *Terrahawks* (1983–1986, TV), *Space Police* (1987, TV [unscreened]) and *Space Precinct* (1994–1995, TV). **Hammer credits:** *Celia* (1949, loader [uncredited]), *The Man in Black* (1950, clapper loader [uncredited]), *Someone at the Door* (1950, loader [uncredited]), *What the Butler Saw* (1950, loader [uncredited]), *The Black Widow* (1950, loader [uncredited]), *Dick Barton at Bay* (1950, loader [uncredited]), *The Lady Craved Excitement* (1950, loader [uncredited]), *The Rossiter Case* (1951, loader [uncredited]), *To Have and to Hold* (1951, loader [uncredited]), *The Dark Light* (1951, loader [uncredited]), *A Case for PC 49* (1951, focus puller [uncredited]), *Cloudburst* (1951, focus puller [uncredited]), *Whispering Smith Hits London* (1952, focus puller [uncredited]), *Death of an Angel* (1952, focus puller [uncredited]), *The Last Page* (1952, focus puller [uncredited]), *Wings of Danger* (1952, focus puller [uncredited]), *Lady in the Fog* (1952, focus puller [uncredited]), *The Saint's Return* (1953, focus puller [uncredited]), *Blood Orange* (1953, focus puller [uncredited]), *36 Hours* (1953, focus puller [uncredited]), *Face the Music* (1954, focus puller [uncredited]), *Five Days* (1954, focus puller [uncredited]), *Life with the Lyons* (1954, focus puller [uncredited]), *The House Across the Lake* (1954, focus puller [uncredited]), *The Stranger Came Home* (1954, focus puller [uncredited]), *Men of Sherwood Forest* (1954, focus puller [uncredited]), *Mask of Dust* (1954, focus puller [uncredited]), *The Lyons in Paris* (1955, focus puller [uncredited]), *Break in the Circle* (1955, focus puller [uncredited]), *Murder by Proxy* (1955, focus puller [uncredited]), *Third Party Risk* (1955, focus puller [uncredited]), *Cyril Stapleton and the Show Band* (1955, focus puller [uncredited]), *The Quatermass Xperiment* (1955, focus puller [uncredited]), *The Eric Winstone Bandshow* (1955, focus puller [uncredited]), *The Glass Cage* (1955, focus puller [uncredited]), *The Right Person* (1956, focus puller [uncredited]), *Just for You* (1956, focus puller [uncredited]), *Copenhagen* (1956, focus puller [uncredited]), *Eric Winstone's Stagecoach* (1956, focus puller [uncredited]), *A Man on the Beach* (1956, focus puller [uncredited], second unit operator [uncredited]), *Parade of the Bands* (1956, focus puller [uncredited]), *The Edmundo Ros Half Hour* (1956, focus puller [uncredited]), *Women Without Men* (1956, focus puller [uncredited]), *X—The Unknown* (1956, focus puller [uncredited]), *The*

*Dick Turpin—Highwayman* (1956, focus puller [uncredited]), *The Curse of Frankenstein* (1957, focus puller [uncredited]), *Quatermass 2* (1957, focus puller [uncredited]), *The Steel Bayonet* (1957, focus puller [uncredited]), *Adventures with the Lyons* (1957, serial re-issue of *Life with the Lyons*, focus puller [uncredited]), *The Abominable Snowman* (1957, focus puller [uncredited]), *Man with a Dog* (1957, focus puller [uncredited]), *Danger List* (1957, focus puller [uncredited]), *The Camp on Blood Island* (1958, focus puller [uncredited]), *Dracula* (1958, focus puller [uncredited]), *Clean Sweep* (1958, focus puller [uncredited], second unit operator [uncredited]), *The Snorkel* (1958, focus puller [uncredited]), *The Revenge of Frankenstein* (1958, focus puller [uncredited]), *Further Up the Creek* (1958, focus puller [uncredited]), *I Only Asked!* (1958, focus puller [uncredited]), *The Seven Wonders of Ireland* (1958, focus puller [uncredited]), *The Hound of the Baskervilles* (1959, focus puller [uncredited], second unit camera operator [uncredited]), *Ten Seconds to Hell* (1959, focus puller [uncredited]), *The Ugly Duckling* (1959, focus puller [uncredited]), *Yesterday's Enemy* (1959, focus puller [uncredited]), *The Mummy* (1959, focus puller [uncredited]), *The Man Who Could Cheat Death* (1959, focus puller [uncredited]), *The Stranglers of Bombay* (1959, focus puller [uncredited]), *Never Take Sweets from a Stranger* (1960, focus puller [uncredited]), *The Brides of Dracula* (1960, focus puller [uncredited]), *The Two Faces of Dr. Jekyll* (1960, focus puller [uncredited]), *Taste of Fear* (1961, second unit photography [uncredited]), *The Curse of the Werewolf* (1961, focus puller [uncredited]), *The Shadow of the Cat* (1961, focus puller [uncredited]), *Watch It, Sailor!* (1961, focus puller [uncredited]), *The Terror of the Tongs* (1961, focus puller [uncredited]), *Cash on Demand* (1961, focus puller [uncredited], additional camera operator [uncredited]), *The Phantom of the Opera* (1962, focus puller [uncredited]), *Captain Clegg* (1962, focus puller [uncredited]), *The Pirates of Blood River* (1962, focus puller [uncredited]), *The Damned* (1963, focus puller [uncredited]), *The Brigand of Kandahar* (1965, second unit photography [uncredited])

## Oakley Court

Built in 1859 for Sir Richard Hall Say, Oakley Court was the second of three country house "studios" used by Hammer before their permanent move to Down Place at Bray. Situated on the banks of the River Thames, the turreted Victorian folly was used to film *The Man in Black* (1950), *Room to Let* (1950), *Someone at the Door* (1950), *What the Butler Saw* (1950) and *The Lady Craved Excitement* (1950), during which it was briefly named Exclusive Studios. Now a luxury hotel, the building was also featured in many of Hammer's later horror films, including *The Curse of Frankenstein* (1957), in which it appears as Castle Frankenstein, *The Mummy* (1959), in which it stands in for Mehemet Akhir's Engerfield home, *The Brides of Dracula* (1960), in which it can be seen as the entrance to Chateau Meinster, and *The Old Dark House* (1963), in which it is the manor belonging to the murderous Femm family. It can

also be seen as Squire Hamilton's home in *The Plague of the Zombies* (1966) and Dr. Franklyn's house in *The Reptile* (1966).

Recalled a reporter for the trade paper *The Cinema*, who visited Oakley Court during the production of *The Man in Black*, "The house, I was surprised to discover, is still fully furnished. The owner, too, is still in residence, but keeps himself entirely to his own wing, leaving Exclusive to do as they will in the major part of the building." [1] Remembered Jimmy Sangster of Hammer's filmmaking days at Oakley Court, "We rented the place furnished and weren't allowed to move a stick of it. It was said that you could arrive at a cinema in the middle of a movie and know it was a Hammer film because you'd seen the same set, furnished the same way, in their last three pictures. Only the actors were different. And such was the repertory-type casting that Hammer favored, even they were difficult to distinguish from one movie to the next." [2]

Other films making use of the building as a location include *Half a Sixpence* (1967), *Mumsy, Nanny, Sonny & Girly* (1970), *And Now the Screaming Starts* (1973), *Vampyres* (1974), *Dracula* (1974, TVM), in which it doubled for Carfax Abbey, *The Man from Nowhere* (1975) and *The Rocky Horror Picture Show* (1975). It was also featured in such television series as *Supernatural* (1977, TV), specifically in the episode titled *Lady Sybil*, and *Pie in the Sky* (1994–1997, TV). **Additional notes:** Nearby Water Oakley Farm was used as the rocket crash site in Hammer's *The Quatermass Xperiment* (1955), in which it was referred to as Oakley Green. Also see **Dial Close**, **Gilston Park** and **Hampden House**. **Hammer credits:** *The Man in Black* (1950), *Room to Let* (1950), *Someone at the Door* (1950), *What the Butler Saw* (1950), *The Lady Craved Excitement* (1950), *The Stranger Came Home* (1954), *The Curse of Frankenstein* (1957), *The Mummy* (1959), *Never Take Sweets from a Stranger* (1960), *The Brides of Dracula* (1960), *The Old Dark House* (1963), *Nightmare* (1964), *The Plague of the Zombies* (1966), *The Reptile* (1966)

## Oates, Robert

Oates can be seen in a supporting role in *Mark of the Devil* (1984, TVM [episode of *Hammer House of Mystery and Suspense*]). His many other TV credits include episodes of *Armchair Thriller* (1967–1980, TV), *Boon* (1986–1992, TV) and *Midsomer Murders* (1997–, TV). His occasional film credits include *Withnail & I* (1987), *Paper Mask* (1990), *The Fifth Element* (1997) and *Finding Neverland* (2004). **Hammer credits:** *Mark of the Devil* (1984, TVM [episode of *Hammer House of Mystery and Suspense*], as Hara)

## O'Brien, Glenys

O'Brien can be seen as Maggie in Hammer's *The Horror of Frankenstein* (1970). Her other credits include *A Clockwork Orange* (1971) and episodes of *Crossroads* (1964–1988, TV) and *Six with Rix* (1972, TV). **Hammer credits:** *The Horror of Frankenstein* (1970, as Maggie)

## O'Brien, Maria

O'Brien can be seen as Omah in Hammer's

*When Dinosaurs Ruled the Earth* (1970). Her other film credits include *Toomorrow* (1970), *The Adventures of Barry McKenzie* (1972) and *Escort Girls* (1974), plus episodes of *Z Cars* (1962–1978, TV), *Brett* (1971, TV), *The Persuaders!* (1971–1972, TV), *Van Der Valk* (1972–1992, TV) and *Dickens of London* (1976, TV). **Hammer credits:** *When Dinosaurs Ruled the Earth* (1970, as Omah)

## O'Connell, Maurice

O'Connell (1941–) can be seen as Hanson, the SI7 undercover man who pays with his life for penetrating Pelham House in Hammer's *The Satanic Rites of Dracula* (1974). His other occasional film credits include *The Medusa Touch* (1978), *The Bitch* (1979), *Curse of the Pink Panther* (1983) and *A Prayer for the Dying* (1987), while his TV credits take in episodes of such series as *Crown Court* (1972–1984, TV), *Widows* (1983, TV), in which he played Harry Rawlins, *Widows 2* (1985, TV), again as Harry Rawlins, and *Inspector Morse* (1987–2000, TV). **Hammer credits:** *The Satanic Rites of Dracula* (1974, as Hanson)

## O'Connor, John

O'Connor worked as the assistant director on three episodes of *Hammer House of Mystery and Suspense* (1984, TVM). His other TV credits include episodes of *The Avengers* (1961–1969, TV), *Return of the Saint* (1978–1979, TV) and *Minder* (1979–1994, TV). His film work includes *Journey to the Far Side of the Sun* (1969), *Song of Norway* (1970), *The Great Waltz* (1972), *Biggles* (1986), on which he was also a co-associate producer, and *A Show of Force* (1990). **Hammer credits:** *The Sweet Scent of Death* (1984, TVM [episode of *Hammer House of Mystery and Suspense*]), *The Late Nancy Irving* (1984, TVM [episode of *Hammer House of Mystery and Suspense*]), *And the Wall Came Tumbling Down* (1984, TVM [episode of *Hammer House of Mystery and Suspense*])

## O'Connor, Joseph *see* O'Conor, Joseph

## O'Connor, Larry

O'Connor can be seen as Sam Kingsley in Hammer's *Never Take Sweets from a Stranger* (1960). His other credits include an episode of *ITV Playhouse of the Week* (1955–1974, TV). **Hammer credits:** *Never Take Sweets from a Stranger* (1960, As Sam Kingsley [Uncredited])

## O'Connor, Martin

British born O'Connor (1913–1997) worked as the key grip on Hammer's *One Million Years B.C.* (1966). His other credits in this capacity include *The Yellow Balloon* (1953), *Moby Dick* (1956), *The Key* (1958), *The Guns of Navarone* (1961) and *Billy Budd* (1962). **Hammer credits:** *One Million Years B.C.* (1966 [uncredited])

## O'Conor, Joseph

Best known for playing Mr. Brownlow in the musical *Oliver!* (1968), this Irish character actor (1910–2001, sometimes Joseph O'Connor) began his stage career at the age of twenty-three following training at RADA. In films from 1950 with *Paul Temple's Triumph*, he went on to appear in over twenty films, among them *Stranger at My Door* (1950), *Gorgo* (1960), *Anne of the Thousand Days* (1969), *The Black Windmill* (1974), *Tom & Viv* (1996) and *Elizabeth* (1998), while his TV credits include appearances in *The Forsyte Saga* (1967, TV), in which he played old Jolyon Forsyte, *The Railway Children* (1968, TV), in which he played the kindly old gentleman, *Lost Hearts* (1973, TV), in which he played Mr. Abney, *The Scarlet and the Black* (1993, TV) and *The Glass* (2001, TV). He also played Don Jose in the Hammer swashbuckler *The Devil-Ship Pirates* (1964) and the coroner in *The Gorgon* (1964). However, he spent the majority of his career on stage, particularly at the Bristol Old Vic and The National Theater. His second wife was the actress Lizann Rodger (full name Elizabeth A. Rodger), whom he married in 1979. **Additional notes:** The credits for *The Devil-Ship Pirates* mistakenly bill O'Conor as O'Connor, a fate that also befell him in *A Walk with Love and Death* (1969), *Lost Hearts* (1973, TV) and *Elizabeth* (1998). **Hammer credits:** *The Devil-Ship Pirates* (1964, as Don Pedro), *The Gorgon* (1964, as Coroner)

## O'Dea, Jimmy

This Irish character actor (1899–1965) had a minor supporting role in Hammer's *Dick Barton Strikes Back* (1949). He was best known in his home country for his comedy creation Biddy Mulligan, the Pride of Coombe. His other film credits include *Casey's Millions* (1922), in which he played the lead, *Ireland's Border Line* (1939), *The Rising of the Moon* (1957) and *Darby O'Gill and the Little People* (1959), in which he had his most high profile role, that of King Brian, the mischievous leprechaun. **Hammer credits:** *Dick Barton Strikes Back* (1949, as Thug [uncredited])

## Odeon International Licensing

In 2009, Odeon International Licensing, in addition to their usual selection of Moto GP products, designed and distributed a number of Hammer-related items for sale, including coffee mugs, mouse mats, a coloring set with re-usable stickers and a sixty-piece art pack complete with paints, pens and crayons. The collection was, according to Odeon, "styled with a unique retro feel that will appeal to kids, students and original Hammer addicts alike."

## O'Donnel, P.

O'Donnell worked as the production secretary on Hammer's *The Horror of Frankenstein* (1970). **Hammer credits:** *The Horror of Frankenstein* (1970 [uncredited])

## O'Donnell, Peter

This British writer and cartoonist (1920–2010) is best known for creating (with Jim Holdaway) the *Daily Express* comic strip *Modesty Blaise*, which was filmed (unsuccessfully) by director Joseph Losey in 1966 (the screenplay, by Evan Jones, was based upon a story by O'Donnell and Stanley Dubens). He was also, somewhat curiously, signed by Hammer to pen the screenplay for *The Vengeance of She* (1968), a follow up to the company's 1965 hit *She*. Unfortunately, the film was a commercial disaster of some significance, and

seems to have scuppered any ambitions O'Donnell might have had to carry on as a screenwriter. His other writing credits include the TV series *Take a Pair of Private Eyes* (1966, TV). Other films featuring the Modesty Blaise character include *Modesty Blaise* (1902, TVM) and *My Name Is Modesty: A Modesty Blaise Adventure* (2004), on which O'Donnell was a creative consultant. **Hammer credits:** *The Vengeance of She* (1968)

## O'Dwyer, Patrick

O'Dwyer had a supporting role in *Wolfshead: The Legend of Robin Hood* (1969 [released 1973]), which was bought, but not made, by Hammer. His other credits include an episode of *Scott on...* (1964–1974, TV). **Hammer credits:** *Wolfshead: The Legend of Robin Hood* (1969 [released 1973], as Tom)

## O'Farrell, Bernadette

In films from 1948 with *Captain Boycott*, this Irish actress (1924–1999) had her greatest hit on television playing Maid Marian in *The Adventures of Robin Hood* (1955–1960, TV), though she left the series in 1957 and was replaced by Patricia Driscoll. O'Farrell's other films include *The Happiest Days of Your Life* (1950), *Lady Godiva Rides Again* (1951), *The Story of Gilbert and Sullivan* (1953) and *The Wildcats of St. Trinian's* (1980), all of which were either directed or produced by her husband, Frank Launder (1906–1997), whom she married in 1950. In 1952, O'Farrell played the role of Heather McMara in the Hammer second feature *Lady in the Fog*. When it came to the film version of *The Adventures of Robin Hood*, which was made by Hammer as *Sword of Sherwood Forest* (1960), the role of Maid Marian was played by a third actress, Sarah Branch. Note that her husband's screenplay for Hitchcock's *The Lady Vanishes* (1938), originally co-authored with Sidney Gilliat, was remade by Hammer in 1979. **Hammer credits:** *Lady in the Fog* (1952, as Heather McMara)

## O'Flynn, Philip

This Irish actor (1927–1999, real name Pilib O'Floinn) played a merchant in Hammer's ill-fated *The Viking Queen* (1967). His other credits include *Captain Lightfoot* (1955), *What a Carve Up!* (1961), *The Quare Fellow* (1962), *Young Cassidy* (1964), *The Violent Enemy* (1967) and *Ryan's Daughter* (1970). Also on stage, particularly at the Queen's Theater and Abbey Theater in Dublin. **Hammer credits:** *The Viking Queen* (1967, as Merchant)

## O'Gorman, John

This busy British make-up artist (1911–1977) worked with Roy Ashton on Hammer's *She* (1965), having already worked with its star, Ursula Andress, on *Dr. No* (1962). He would go on to make up Andress again on *Casino Royale* (1967), *The Southern Star* (1969), *Perfect Friday* (1970) and *The Fifth Musketeer* (1979). His other credits include *Mine Own Executioner* (1947), *Betrayed* (1954), *The Vikings* (1958), *Summer Holiday* (1963), *Charade* (1963) and *The Blue Bird* (1976). He also made up Ingrid Bergman on several films, including *Indiscreet* (1958), *The Inn of the Sixth Happiness* (1958), *Goodbye Again* (1961), *The Visit*

(1964), *The Yellow Rolls-Royce* (1964), *Cactus Flower* (1969) and *Murder on the Orient Express* (1974). **Hammer credits:** *She* (1965)

## O'Hara, Gerry

In films from 1941 as an assistant for the documentary unit Verity Films, this British director (1924–, aka Laurence Britten) went on to gain further experience as an assistant director on such films as *Quartet* (1948), *Trio* (1950), *Richard III* (1955), *Term of Trial* (1962) and *Tom Jones* (1963). He turned to direction himself with *That Kind of Girl* (1963), and went on to helm such variable fare as *The Pleasure Girls* (1965), which he also scripted, *Maroc 7* (1966), *The Spy's Wife* (1971), which he also co-scripted, *Leopard in the Snow* (1977), *The Bitch* (1979), which he also scripted, *Fanny Hill* (1983) and *The Mummy Lives* (1993). He also provided the stories for *Hot Target* (1985) and *Incident at Victoria Falls* (1992, TVM). Working as a director in television, his credits here include *Do Me a Favor and Kill Me*, an episode of Hammer's *Journey to the Unknown* (1968, TV), which also appeared in the compendium film *Journey to Murder* (1972, TVM). He also wrote several episodes of *The Professionals* (1977–1983, TV), on which he also worked as a script editor. His screenplay for a suspense thriller titled *Restless*, which was optioned by Hammer in 1973, failed to make it before the cameras. **Hammer credits:** *Do Me a Favor and Kill Me* (1968, TV [episode of *Journey to the Unknown*]), *Journey to Murder* (1972, TVM)

## O'Kelly, Lieutenant Colonel William

O'Kelly worked as the production liaison on Hammer's *The Viking Queen* (1967), which was filmed in Ireland. He worked in similar capacities on *The Blue Max* (1966), *Ryan's Daughter* (1970), *Von Richthofen and Brown* (1971) and *Barry Lyndon* (1975), all of which were filmed in Ireland. He was also the technical advisor on *Shake Hands with the Devil* (1959), which again was filmed in Ireland. **Hammer credits:** *The Viking Queen* (1967)

## *The Old Dark House*

GB, 1963 [U.S. 1963, UK 1966], 86m [UK 77m], Technicolor [U.S. bw], RCA, cert A

A collaboration between Hammer and the American exploitation producer William Castle must have seemed like a sure bet on paper. Unfortunately, the association proved to be something of a disaster for both parties, particularly Hammer, which was going through something of an identity crisis at the time following the temporary shutdown of Bray Studios in early 1962.

Like Hammer, Castle had had his greatest successes with the horror genre, having produced and directed such gimmick-laden items as *Macabre* (1958), *House on Haunted Hill* (1959) and *Homicidal* (1961), the latter an enjoyably cheeky rip-off of *Psycho* (1960) that had been doubled billed with Hammer's *The Terror of the Tongs* (1961) on both sides of the Atlantic. Consequently, when it was suggested that Castle and Hammer officially pool their resources for a remake of Universal's *The Old Dark House* (1932), the omens at first seemed fortuitous.

Hammer's plans to remake *The Old Dark House*

began in 1961, yet when it was learned that Castle was also planning a remake, the idea was temporarily shelved (Castle had actually acquired the rights to J.B. Priestley's 1928 novel *Benighted*—on which *The Old Dark House* was based—in 1960). However, it was while Castle was visiting Bray to promote the *Tongs/Homicidal* double bill that the idea of a collaboration was mooted, no doubt helped by the fact that not only was Columbia backing Castle's version of the project, they also owned 49 percent of Bray, thus being able to supply studio space to boot.

Plans were later formalized between Castle and Anthony Hinds in New York in March 1962, and a screenplay was subsequently commissioned from the American writer Robert Dillon, then best known for *City of Fear* (1958). While the 1932 film adhered reasonably closely to the source material, Dillon's screenplay, either by design or request, was a much broader affair, perhaps because, astonishingly, Hammer wanted a U certificate release. Therefore, instead of a group of travellers finding shelter from a storm in the home of a family of eccentrics while driving through the Welsh hills, we follow the adventures of a London-based American car-salesman named Tom Penderel, who encounters all manner of oddballs when asked by his flatmate, one Casper Femm, to drive his brand new car down to the Femm family seat on his behalf. Here, Tom not only discovers that he may be related to the Femms, but also witnesses various gruesome incidents as the family is bumped off one by one by someone keen to gain control of the family fortune.

In ballyhooing the picture during pre-production, James Carreras confidently announced that, "The days of the straight shocker have just about run their course. The market is shifting and comedy is back in favor."[3] Unfortunately, these were words that he eventually came to repent.

The cast seemed particularly well chosen, among them some of the cream of British comedy, including such audience favorites as Robert Morley, Fenella Fielding, Joyce Grenfell, Janette Scott and Peter Bull (as twins, no less). Meanwhile, the American television comedian Tom Poston was signed to play the hapless Tom Penderel so as to guarantee the film some appeal Stateside. *The Old Dark House* would actually be Poston's second collaboration with Castle following on from *Zotz!* (1962), a comedy about a rare coin with occult powers. Unfortunately, the film all too clearly displayed Castle's lack of affinity with comedy, which would also prove to be the undoing of *The Old Dark House*, which, instead of a finely accentuated study in eccentricity, opts for sub-*Carry On* pratfalls, which prompted the *Monthly Film Bulletin* to comment, "This comedy-shocker is abysmal—repeat abysmal—from beginning to end." As indeed it is.

Shot at Bray between 14 May and 22 June 1962, the movie also made use of nearby Oakley Court, which doubled as the Femms' family seat, while other scenes were filmed on the studio back lot, on which was erected a partially-built ark (don't ask!). However, the shoot was a troubled one, beset by an electricians' strike and Castle's increasing dislike

of Bray. As a consequence, the film overran its allotted schedule, forcing the interiors of Hammer's next production, *Maniac* (1963), to be relocated to Borehamwood.

Once completed, the film's problems were by no means over. For its American release care of Columbia on 31 October 1963, it was stripped of color and put out on the lower half of a double bill with the afore-mentioned *Maniac*. British audiences, however, had to wait until 16 September 1966 to see it. Released on a double bill with *Big Deal at Dodge City* (1966), the film retained its Technicolor photography but was instead stripped of nine minutes of running time in a futile bid to secure the originally-aimed for U certificate. It was finally awarded an A, though not before the studio tested an X version on exhibitors, who passed on the film in this form (*The British Film Catalogue, Volume 1* confirms the existence of this trade show X version, which was eventually made available on DVD in 1996).

"The ghost doesn't walk in this family—it runs riot!" claimed one of the film's posters, while another queried, "House haunting? It's all in good fun, of corpse ... mostly the murderous kind!" Sadly, the film is a disappointment in almost every way. The cast overplay their hand at every turn, particularly the bug-eyed Poston, who irritates more than he amuses, while the flat direction lacks visual flair, as well as any of Castle's customary gimmicks (*Kinematograph Weekly* noted that the film was "inclined to fall between two stools, for the humor is slight and the suspense entirely lacking"). In fact, aside from a minor shock moment involving death by knitting needles, the film's one genuine highlight proves to be its amusingly sketched title sequence, as designed by the celebrated cartoonist Charles Addams, creator of the Addams Family, whose ghoulish images of the film inevitably pales besides (Addams even signs his own signature—as Chas Addams—on screen with a small paint brush, his hand having been covered with monstrous hair for the shot). After that, it's downhill all the way. And quite a way down it is too.

Although a disappointment for all concerned, Hammer and the Hollywood producer didn't sever their links entirely following this debacle, for in 1965 Castle's thriller *The Night Walker* (1965) was

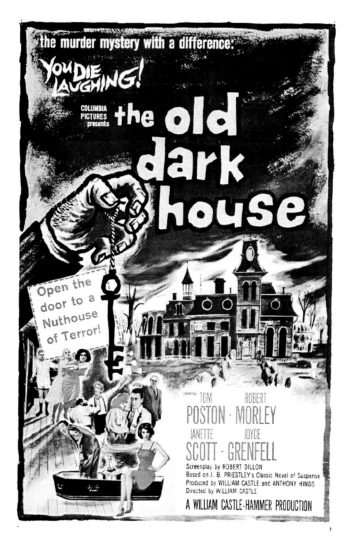

This ad for *The Old Dark House* (1963) actually contains more style than the rather ramshackle film it promotes (Hammer/Castle/British Lion Columbia/Columbia).

put out on a double bill in the UK with Hammer's brutal POW adventure *The Secret of Blood Island* (1965). However, plans for a second Hammer/Castle co-production titled *Too Many Ghosts* fell by the wayside. **Additional notes:** The film carries a 1962 copyright. When Tom drives to the Femm family seat during a thunderstorm, the rain cascades down on his windscreen, but the blue-screen background of the road on which he is travelling is clearly rain free. In another scene, Tom is menaced by a hyena, the close-up of which is very obviously an immobile stuffed animal with drool dripping from its mouth. William Castle gets credited twice in the U.S. cut of the film, which removed Anthony Hinds' producer credit: he thus receives a credit stating that the film is "Produced and Directed by William Castle," following which he gets another credit stating that the film is "Directed by William Castle." Fenella Fielding, meanwhile, does not receive a credit in the opening titles, despite her substantial role (only Poston, Morley, Scott and Grenfell receive up front mentions). Note the use of the Y-shaped staircase from *The Kiss of the Vampire* (1963), which also appeared in *Paranoiac* (1963). Boris Karloff, who had played Morgan the butler in the original 1932 film, was approached by Castle to appear in the remake, but turned the offer down.

Production companies: Hammer/Castle. Distributors: British Lion Columbia (UK [ABC circuit]), Columbia (U.S.). Producers: William Castle, Anthony Hinds [uncredited]. Associate producer: Donna Holloway. Director: William Castle. Screenplay: Robert Dillon, based upon the novel *Benighted* by J.B. Priestley. Cinematographer: Arthur Grant. Music/conductor: Benjamin Frankel. Supervising editor: James Needs. Assistant editor: Chris Barnes [uncredited]. Production design: Bernard Robinson. Assistant art director: Ken Ryan [uncredited]. Costumes: Molly Arbuthnot, Rosemary Burrows. Special effects: Les Bowie. Special effects assistants: Ian Scoones [uncredited], Kit West [uncredited]. Make-up: Roy Ashton. Hair: Frieda Steiger. Sound: Jock May. Sound editor: James Groom. Production manager: John Draper. Assistant director: Douglas Hermes. Second assistant director: Dominic Fulford [uncredited]. Third assistant director: Hugh Harlow [uncredited]. Camera operator: Moray Grant. Camera grip: Albert Cowlard [uncredited]. Camera assistant: Jim Perry [uncredited]. Construction manager: Arthur Banks [uncredited]. Master carpenter: Charles Davis [uncredited]. Master painter: Lawrence Wrenn [uncredited]. Master plasterer: Stan Banks [uncredited]. Master electrician: Jack Curtis [uncredited]. Master rigger: Ronald Lenoir [uncredited]. Props: Tommy Money [uncredited]. Props buyer: Eric Hillier [uncredited]. Title design: Charles Addams. Publicity: Dennison Thornton [uncredited], Brian Doyle [uncredited]. Continuity: Pauline Wise. Production secretary: Maureen White [uncredited]. **Cast:** Tom Poston (Tom Penderel), Robert Morley (Roderick Femm), Fenella Fielding (Morgana Femm), Janette Scott (Cecily Femm), Joyce Grenfell (Agatha Femm), Mervyn Johns (Potiphar Femm), Peter Bull (Casper Femm/Jasper Femm), Danny Green (Morgan Femm), John Harvey (Club receptionist), Amy Dalby (Gambler [uncredited]), Fred Peck (Casino patron [uncredited]), Ernie Rice (Casino patron [uncredited]), Fred Haggerty (Stunt double for Tom Poston [uncredited]) **DVD Availability:** Sony (U.S. R1 NTSC), as part of the *William Castle Horror Collection* which also features *13 Ghosts* (1960) and *Homicidal* (1961), among others

## Oldknow, John

British born Oldknow (1927–1989) worked as the production manager on all seventeen episodes of Hammer's *Journey to the Unknown* (1968, TV), although he doesn't receive an onscreen credit on *The Madison Equation*. Of these programs, *Poor Butterfly* and *The Indian Spirit Guide* appeared in the compendium film *Journey to Midnight* (1968, TVM), *Paper Dolls* and *The New People* appeared in the compendium film *Journey into Darkness* (1968, TVM), *Matakitas Is Coming* and *The Last Visitor* appeared in the compendium film *Journey to the Unknown* (1969, TVM), while *The Killing*

*Bottle* and *Do Me a Favor and Kill Me* appeared in *Journey to Murder* (1972, TVM).

His other credits as a production manager or unit manager include *The Buttercup Chain* (1970), *Lion of the Desert* (1981), *Fanny Hill* (1983) and *Parker* (1984). He began his career as a third assistant director on *Caesar and Cleopatra* (1945), became a second assistant on *Cosh Boy* (1952) and graduated to first assistant on *Murder at 3am* (1953). **Hammer credits:** *Journey to the Unknown* (1968, TV), *Journey into Darkness* (1968, TVM), *Journey to Midnight* (1968, TV), *Journey to the Unknown* (1969, TVM), *Journey to Murder* (1972, TVM)

## Olrich, April

This Tanzanian born actress (1933–2014, real name Edith April Oelrichs) appeared in the Hammer prison melodrama *Women Without Men* (1956). Trained as a ballet dancer, her other credits include *The Battle of the River Plate* (1956), *It's All Over Town* (1965), *The Skull* (1965), *The Intelligence Men* (1965), *Keep It Up Downstairs* (1976), *Hussy* (1980) and *Supergirl* (1984). Her TV credits include episodes of *Saber of London* (1954–1960, TV), *The Avengers* (1961–1969, TV) and *Fresh Fields* (1984–1986, TV). She was married to the actor Nigel Pegram (1940–), whom she wed in 1968. **Hammer credits:** *Women Without Men* (1956, as Margueritte)

## Olsen, Pauline

This British supporting actress (1925–, aka Pauline Olson) played a nurse in the Hammer medical drama *Danger List* (1957). Her other films include *Star of My Night* (1954) and *Johnny on the Spot* (1954), while her TV credits include episodes of *Saber of London* (1954–1960, TV), *The Adventures of Sir Lancelot* (1956–1957, TV) and *Adventures of the Sea Hawk* (1958, TV). **Hammer credits:** *Danger List* (1957, as Nurse [uncredited])

## Olson, James

In films from the mid-fifties with *The Sharkfighters* (1956) following stage experience, this dour-looking American actor (1930–) went on to notch up a handful of leading roles in the sixties and seventies, among them two for Hammer. The first was as a space pilot in the ill-judged space western *Moon Zero Two* (1969), for which the actor unfortunately lacked the required charisma. He fared a little better in his second film for the studio, *Crescendo* (1970), a convoluted thriller in the style of *Taste of Fear* (1961) and its numerous derivatives, in which he played twins, one of whom, not unexpectedly given the plot, turns out to be mad. However, it should be noted that Christopher Lee had originally been cast in the role/s, but when the production company changed from Compton to Hammer, he was unceremoniously given the elbow by the film's American backers Warner Bros., who insisted upon an American name.

Olson's other films include *The Strange One* (1957), *Rachel, Rachel* (1968), *Wild Rovers* (1971), *The Andromeda Strain* (1971), *Ragtime* (1981) and *Amityville II: The Possession* (1982). The majority of his work has been on television, though, where he has guested in episodes of such wide-ranging series as *Harbormaster* (1957, TV), *Route 66* (1960–

1964, TV), *McCloud* (1970–1977, TV), *Barnaby Jones* (1973–1980, TV), *Lou Grant* (1977–1982, TV), *Matt Houston* (1982–1985, TV) and *Murder, She Wrote* (1984–1996, TV). **Hammer credits:** *Moon Zero Two* (1969, as Bill Kemp), *Crescendo* (1970, as Georges/Jacques)

## Olympic Studios

This recording studio and post-production facility (situated in Barnes, just outside London) was used to record the music for Hammer's *The Lost Continent* (1968), the sessions for which were supervised by sound technician Keith Grant. Other film scores recorded or mixed at the complex include *The Italian Job* (1969), *Kidnapped* (1971), *The Rocky Horror Picture Show* (1975), *Saturn 3* (1980), *Yentl* (1983), *The Dresser* (1983), *The Fly* (1986), *Evita* (1996), *Buffalo Soldiers* (2001) and *Flawless* (2007). **Hammer credits:** *The Lost Continent* (1968)

## O'Madden, Lawrence

This British actor (1905–1972) had a minor supporting role in the Hammer second feature *The Last Page* (1952). His other credits include *The Goose Steps Out* (1942), *San Demetrio London* (1943), *Night Boat to Dublin* (1946) and *Guilt Is my Shadow* (1950). Also on stage. **Hammer credits:** *The Last Page* (1952, as First customer)

## O'Mara, Kate

Although she made too few films, this glamorous British actress (1939–2014, real name Frances Meredith Carro, aka Merrie Carroll) remains a Hammer favorite, as much for her smoldering looks and voluptuous figure as for her underrated thesping abilities. Following training at the Ada Foster School, she began her career as a speech therapist, but gradually turned her attention to the stage. She made her film debut in *Home and Away* (1956), in which she appeared under the name of Merrie Carroll, and her Hammer debut in the pirate yarn *Captain Clegg* (1962), in which she played an onlooker in a village tavern. She began to appear in more substantial roles in the late sixties in such films as *Great Catherine* (1967), *The Limbo Line* (1968) and *The Desperados* (1969). However, it was Hammer who gave her her big break in 1970 with the role of Mademoiselle Paradot, the governess who succumbs to the lesbian charms of Carmilla in *The Vampire Lovers* (1970). This in turn led to a featured role in *The Horror of Frankenstein* (1970) as Alys, the servant-lover of Baron Frankenstein.

O'Mara's other film credits include *The Tamarind Seed* (1974) and *Feelings* (1975). Busy in television from the early sixties as a guest in such series as *The Avengers* (1961–1969, TV) and *The Saint* (1962–1969, TV), she later went on to score a major success in *Dynasty* (1985–1987, TV), in which she played the scheming Caress Morell. Her other TV work includes episodes of *Doctor Who* (1963–1989, TV), in which she played The Rani, *The Brothers* (1972–1976, TV), *Howards' Way* (1989–1990, TV), *Absolutely Fabulous* (1992–2012, TV), *Bad Girls* (1999–2006, TV) and *Benidorm* (2007–2018, TV), as well as the notorious North Sea ferry soap *Triangle* (1981–1983, TV), in which she played Katherine Laker. Also much on stage, she formed the British Actors' Theater Company in the eighties, with which she toured for many years.

Recalled Ingrid Pitt of her experiences with O'Mara on *The Vampire Lovers*: "When the time came to kill the Kate O'Mara character, who believed I loved her and was unaware of my vampire tendencies, I first slung her on the floor, knelt to take her in my arms and smiled down at her. As the camera moved in close and I displayed my fangs inches from her neck, suddenly out popped the fangs, straight into her cleavage. Time and again we had to do the scene and the bloody things sprang out like exocet missiles homing in on her breasts.... Kate was helpless with laughter. Roy [Ward Baker, the director] was unbelievably patient but I wanted to get it in the can. I'd seen the clapper boy chewing gum so I called him over, took it out of his mouth, stuck the fangs in with it and killed her—clean, quick—and she laughed no more."[4]

Recalled O'Mara of her time with the studio, "I was nearly under contract to Hammer after I'd done *The Vampire Lovers* and *The Horror of Frankenstein*."[5] However, she turned the offer down because, "I thought that would be my career from then on. My ambitions were more widespread than that.... They were talking about six films over the next three years."[6] Among the films O'Mara was considered for was *Dr. Jekyll and Sister Hyde* (1971), but she eventually lost the role to Martine Beswick when it was decided she didn't look enough like co-star Ralph Bates. Likewise she lost the role as one of the title characters in *Twins of Evil* (1971) when the casting department could not find another actress who looked enough like her to play her sibling. Some sources state that she was also to have played the mischievous witch Lucinda Jessop in *Witching Time*, one of the better episodes of *Hammer House of Horror* (1980, TV), but Patricia Quinn eventually filled the role.

O'Mara was the daughter of actress Hazel Bainbridge (1911–1998) and the sister of actress Belinda Carroll (1945–), who was formerly married to the actor Simon Williams (1946–), who appeared in *The Late Nancy Irving* (1984, TVM [episode of *Hammer House of Mystery and Suspense*]). She was married to the actor Jeremy Young (1934–) between 1961 and 1976; he had a small role in Hammer's *Rasputin—The Mad Monk* (1966). Her second husband was the actor Richard Willis (1957–), to whom she was married between 1993 and 1996. **Hammer credits:** *Captain Clegg* (1962, as Girl at inn [uncredited]), *The Vampire Lovers* (1970, as Mademoiselle Perodot), *The Horror of Frankenstein* (1970, as Alys)

## Omat Corporation

This American distribution company released Hammer's controversial pedophile drama *Never Take Sweets from a Stranger* (1960) in America as *Never Take Candy from a Stranger*. Unfortunately, the film received very few bookings, having been denied a Production Code seal of approval. It was again released in America in 1961 by the Astor Pictures Corporation. **Hammer credits:** *Never Take Sweets from a Stranger* (1960)

## On the Buses

GB, 1971, 88m, Technicolor, RCA, cert A

In the forties and fifties, Hammer frequently turned to radio and television for source material, the result being such hits as *Dick Barton—Special Agent* (1948) and *The Quatermass Xperiment* (1955). At the suggestion of Brian Lawrence, they revived the trend in the seventies with this big screen version of the popular sitcom *On the Buses*, which clocked up seventy-four episodes during its lengthy run between 1969 and 1973, along with a spin-off series, *Don't Drink the Water* (1974–1975, TV), and an American copy, *Lotsa Luck* (1973, TV). The series was the brainchild of Ronald Chesney and Ronald Wolfe, whose previous hits had included *The Rag Trade* (1961–1963, TV), which had starred a Cockney comic named Reg Varney, to whom the two Ronalds again turned to top line their new show.

The series revolved round bus driver Stan Butler and his clippie Jack Harper, who are always getting into scrapes—usually in the pursuit of a bit of "crumpet"—and almost always caught in the act by their miserable jobsworth boss Inspector Blake, known to one and all as Blakey. Meanwhile, back at home, Stan has to contend with his mum, his gormless sister Olive, and her bone-idle husband Arthur. All these main characters were retained for the film version, which sees Stan and Jack having to deal with a new threat at their bus depot: a staff shortage resulting in—get this—the hiring of *women* drivers!

The film may have been made at the dawn of women's lib, but this doesn't seem to have penetrated the film's highly unionized male workforce ("Women? Women bus drivers?" exclaims Jack incredulously upon hearing about the new recruits). Consequently, Stan and Jack attempt to sabotage the new arrivals by putting spiders in their cabins and diuretic tablets in their tea, all of which causes the expected chaos on the roads. In fact, so high are feelings running, that when Stan cops off with one of the new drivers, his mates are quick to lay the law down. "The lads won't stand you fraternizing with a woman bus driver," warns Jack. Meanwhile, back at the depot, an even greater crisis has arisen. The staff shortage has penetrated the canteen, resulting in "No chips!" as one distraught driver puts. Consequently, Olive is brought in to save the day, but her lack of culinary skills only ends up making matters worse. "The

potatoes are going to boil over," she screams amid the chaos, only for Jack to retort, "Leave 'em—it'll put the joint out!" However, the women finally win the day, with Blakey being made Chief Inspector, and the four women drivers who have been the butt of Stan and Jack's pranks promoted to inspectors!

Like many comedy films and sitcoms of the period, the humor in *On the Buses* is very much of the seaside postcard manner, being heavily laced with sexual innuendo ("Do you mean to say he's been using that lady's facilities?" Blakey asks Stan, having caught the duo making a longer than scheduled stop for their break so that Jack can have a bit of hanky-panky, to which comes the reply, "Well, you could say that!"). Indeed, the humor is pretty misogynistic at times. Comments Mum of the heavily pregnant Olive at one point, "I was hours having Olive. She was so long in coming, she was born under two birth signs; her top half's Leo and her bottom half's Virgo!" Even the recruitment poster at the depot manages to be both sexist and filled with innuendo: "Busmen wanted. Good Money. It's a grand life on the buses. Regular rises!"

EMI Film Productions present a Hammer Productions Release

FROM TELLY LAUGHS TO BELLY LAUGHS

Non-stop Laughs

A HAMMER SPECIAL COMEDY PRESENTATION

ON THE BUSES

IS ON THE BIG SCREEN in COLOUR

Starring **REG VARNEY**

Also Starring **DORIS HARE · STEPHEN LEWIS** and **MICHAEL ROBBINS · BOB GRANT · ANNA KARIN**

Written and Produced by **RONALD WOLFE** and **RONALD CHESNEY**

DIRECTED BY *HARRY BOOTH*

**All aboard for the ride of your life. A cheerful ad for the innuendo-pack *On the Buses* (1971). Note that the poster misspells Anna Karen's name (Hammer/EMI/MGM-EMI/Studio Canal).**

Or, as some wag has later defaced it with the aid of a marker pen, "It's a 'randy life' on the buses."

However, if approached with an open-minded post-PC attitude, some of the jokes are undeniably funny, and are certainly expertly put over by a seasoned team of troupers, who know how to get the most out of a good cleavage gag. As the perpetually cheeky Stan, Reg Varney is Cheerfulness personified, except, that is, when the women drivers extract their revenge by shoving an air compressor up his trouser leg (ouch!). As the ever-randy Jack, Bob Grant keeps the sniggers flowing, though how he manages to pull so many "birds" with his gravestone gnashers remains a mystery. As Stan's mum, Doris Hare brings a touch of homely cheer, while as her feckless son-in-law Arthur, Michael Robbins superbly navigates the depths of indolence and indifference. However, the film's real star turn comes from Anna Karen as the dim-witted Olive, blithely riding a tide of frequently cruel jibes and situations, no more so than being jammed in a motorbike sidecar while in the advanced throes of labor. Stephen Lewis also leaves his mark as the continually undermined Blakey. With his Hitler moustache, down-turned mouth and moans of indignation he is—along with Anna Karen's Olive—one of British comedy's great creations.

The supporting cast also makes the most of the lowbrow humor, among them comedy stalwarts Pamela Cundell and Pat Coombs as two of the unfortunate female drivers, Wendy Richard (mistakenly billed Wendy Richards in the credits) as an annoyed housewife whose underwear has been misappropriated from a launderette by Blakey (don't ask!), and Brian Oulton as the depot's short-tempered manager.

Behind the cameras, Harry Booth, who had helmed many of the TV episodes, was in the director's chair, while writers Ronald Wolfe and Ronald Chesney were also onboard as producers, albeit under the watchful eye of Hammer's recently appointed production supervisor Roy Skeggs. Filmed at Elstree in between 8 March and 7 April 1971 in conjunction with EMI, the budget for *On the Buses* was a parsimonious £97,000, given that no expensive gothic sets and period costumes were required. In fact, much use was made of the locations in the surrounding environs of Hertfordshire, allowing Stan and Jack to drive to such glamorous destinations as Canal Walk, Town's End, Station Approach, Docklands and the Gasworks.

However, the big question was: would audiences pay to see what they could already watch for free each week on television? The answer was a resounding yes, and when released in the UK by MGM-EMI on 8 August 1971 the film (which was billed as "A Hammer Special Comedy Presentation") went on to become the most successful home-made British release of the year, raking in £1.4m in its first six weeks in Britain and Australia, where the series was an equally huge hit. "From telly laughs to belly laughs" heralded the poster, which also promoted the film's big screen status and the fact that it was in color (most TV viewers would have been watching the series in black and white, as color sets weren't yet predominant).

Recalled production manager Christopher

Neame, "Within weeks of its release it became Hammer's quickest domestic earner."[7] In fact the film went on to break no less than eighty-eight all-time house records during its first week of release. Commented Michael Carreras of the film's success, "The situation comedy type of television spin-off seemed just about right at the time. Even if the film isn't what could be considered to be a masterpiece, it takes a fortune at the box office. Hammer is a commercial operation and therefore you have got to follow a successful formula with other films that are likely to repeat that success, so you end up with *Love Thy Neighbour*."[8] As for filming, assistant director Derek Whitehurst recalled, "It was great fun, very amusing and Reg Varney was great. The stupid scene on the motorbike, where it goes one direction and the side-car goes the other, was a bit hairy to do, but it worked."[9]

The critics may have carped, but the film re-invigorated Hammer. Consequently, while they continued to make horror films, they also now pursued a path in comedy with equal vigour. In addition to two sequels to *On the Buses—Mutiny on the Buses* (1972) and *Holiday on the Buses* (1973)—they also turned their attention to such spin-offs as *Love Thy Neighbour* (1973), *Nearest and Dearest* (1973) and *Man About the House* (1974), among others. In fact the British film industry in general went a little spin-off crazy during this period, churning out big screen versions of such small screen hits as *Up Pompeii* (1971), *Dad's Army* (1971), *Please Sir!* (1971), *Steptoe and Son* (1972), *For the Love of Ada* (1972), *Father Dear Father* (1972), *Never Mind the Quality, Feel the Width* (1973), *Bless This House* (1973), *Rising Damp* (1980) and *George and Mildred* (1980). And that was just the comedies. **Additional notes:** Future Hammer star Caroline Munro can be seen on a billboard outside the bus depot in one of her famous Lamb's Navy Rum ads ("Join the Lamb's Navy," encourages the tagline). Reg Varney's daughter Jeanne can be spotted in a small role as Mavis. Despite the film's sauciness, these were clearly more innocent times, given one of the lines in the pub singalong-style title song: "There's always gay life on the buses; Make sure you leave your bird at home; You'll see so many on the buses; You won't be sitting on your own," which could be interpreted in a number of ways! Drummer Brian Bennett, of The Shadows fame, can be heard playing on the single release of the title song (though not in the film). The titles mistakenly bill actress Brenda Grogan as Brenda Gogan. As well as the film and TV series, Grant, Lewis, Karen and Hare appeared as their characters in a segment for the 1972 edition of *All Star Comedy Carnival* (1969–1973, TV), which was penned by Grant and Lewis (despite some claims to the contrary, Varney and Robbins did not appear in the sketch). The film was later double-billed with *Up Pompeii* (1971) for a re-release ("Double up with laughter," ran the poster's tagline).

Production companies: Hammer/EMI. Distributor: MGM-EMI (UK [ABC circuit]). Producers: Ronald Wolfe, Ronald Chesney. Production supervisor: Roy Skeggs. Director: Harry Booth. Screenplay: Ronald Wolfe, Ronald Chesney, based upon their television series *On the Buses*. Cinematogra-

pher: Mark McDonald. Music: Max Harris. Music director: Philip Martell. Song: *It's A Great Life on the Buses*, music by Geoff Unwin, lyrics by Roger Ferris. Vocalists: Quinceharmon. Pianist: Frank Horrox [uncredited]. Editor: Archie Ludski. Production designer: Scott MacGregor. Assistant art director: Ron Benton. Costumes: Rosemary Burrows, June Kirby. Make-up: Eddie Knight. Hair: Ivy Emmerton. Recording director: Tony Lumkin. Sound: John Purchese. Sound editor: Peter Keen [uncredited]. Dubbing mixer: Billy Rowe. Camera operator: Neil Binney. Focus puller: Bob Jordan [uncredited]. Camera operator (special unit): John Howard [uncredited]. Assistant director: Derek Whitehurst. Runners: Phil Campbell [uncredited], Brian Reynolds [uncredited]. Production manager: Christopher Neame. Construction manager: Bill Greene. Painter: Michael Finlay [uncredited]. Continuity: Doreen Dearnaley. Promotional artwork: Tom Chantrell [uncredited]. Poster: Arnaldo Putzu [uncredited], Eddie Paul [uncredited]. **Cast:** Reg Varney (Stan Butler), Doris Hare (Mum/Mrs. Mabel Butler), Anna Karen (Olive Rudge), Michael Robbins (Arthur Rudge), Bob Grant (Jack Harper), Stephen Lewis (Inspector Cyril "Blakey" Blake), Brian Oulton (Manager), Pat Ashton (Sally), Pamela Cundell (Ruby), Pat Coombs (Vera), Wendy Richard (Housewife), David Lodge (Busman), Peter Madden (Mr. Brooks), Jeanette Wild (Suzy), Andrea Lawrence (Betty), Nosher Powell (Betty's husband), Jeanne Varney (Mavis), Maggie McGrath (Gladys), Brenda Grogan (Bridget), Caroline Dowdeswell (Sandra), Eunice Black (Ada), Claire Davenport (Peggy), Tex Fuller (Harry), Terry Duggan (Nobby), Anna Michaels (Eileen), Norman Mitchell (London Transport official), Ivor Salter (Fist policeman), George Roderick (Second policeman), David Rowlands (Parson), Hilda Barry (Old woman), Reginald Peters (Medical orderly), Moira Foot (Katy), Linda Regan (Girl on bus), Shirley English (Canteen lady [uncredited]), Arthur Mullard (unnamed role [uncredited]), Harry Fielder (unnamed role [uncredited]). **DVD availability:** Optimum Home Entertainment (UK R2 PAL), as a triple bill also containing *Mutiny on the Buses* (1972) and *Holiday on the Buses* (1973). **CD availability:** *The Hammer Comedy Film Music Collection* (GDI records), which contains the *Title Song* (*It's a Great Life on the Buses*) and *End Credits*, plus a bonus vocal-only version of the *Title Song* (though it's open to question as to how much of a bonus this actually is)

### *One Million Years B.C.*

GB, 1966, 100m [UK], 91m [U.S.], Technicolor [UK], DeLuxe [U.S.], Panamation, widescreen [1.85:1], RCA, cert A

"This is the way it was!" claimed the poster somewhat brazenly for this prehistoric fantasia about love and survival in a barren landscape, which was also advertized as being Hammer's one-hundredth production (it was far in excess of this if all the shorts and featurettes are included). Like *She* (1965) before it, the idea for the movie came from Kenneth Hyman, whose association with Hammer included a handful of production credits in the late fifties/early sixties, as well as closer ties through the American company Seven Arts, for which he now worked, and with which Hammer had recently entered into an eleven-picture deal.

The film was a direct re-working of the 1940 Hal Roach classic *One Million B.C.* (also known as *Man and His Mate* and *The Cave Dwellers*), itself a remake of D.W. Griffith's *Man's Genesis* (1912), the screenplay for which producer Michael Carreras simply adapted (in fact, so cursory was Carreras's update, the original authors receive a full screen credit). The 1940 film had starred Carole Landis, Victor Mature and horror legend Lon Chaney, Jr., whose adventures had included encounters with a number of magnified lizards doubling as dinosaurs (which were, of course, actually extinct by the time man arrived on the scene several million years later). However, like Hammer's remake of *She*, which had starred Ursula Andress, the accent in the retread would be on glamor, this time in the personification of Raquel Welch's Shell Girl Loana, who finds herself drawn to John Richardson's Tumak, a rough-hewn Rock Man who has been banished from his tribe following skirmishes with his father Akhoba and his brother Sakana.

"This is a story of long, long ago when the world was just beginning," we are informed by Robert Beatty's opening narration, following which we are treated to an impressive montage of explosions and molten lava care of effects man Les Bowie (in truth, the sequence was achieved through a mix of porridge, red food coloring and gushing tap water at a cost of £1,200!). This is "a young world, a world early in the morning of time, a hard, unfriendly world," the narration continues, as we're treated to some stunning views of the desolate landscape of Lanzarote, following which we are introduced to the main characters. "This is Akhoba, leader of the Rock tribe, and these are his sons, Sakana and Tumak. There's no love lost between them. And *that* is our story." Well, not quite, given that, following his expulsion from his clan, Tumak goes on a perilous journey across an inhospitable land inhabited by dinosaurs and cannibals before finally being discovered by Loana and the peaceful Shell People, whose ways and customs he is introduced to. In fact, with its warring tribes and star-crossed lovers, the film plays like a stone-age version of *Romeo and Juliet*.

Budgeted at a whopping £367,000, and eventually coming in at over £422,000 (the combined cost of Hammer's previous *four* productions), *One Million Years B.C.* was very much a prestige enterprise for the company, making extensive use of locations in the Canary Islands, where the unit began filming under the direction of Don Chaffey on 18 October 1965 (in addition to the barren island of Lanzarote, the islands of Teneriffe and Gran Canaria were also used).

It was Chaffey's job to work on the sequences featuring the actors, while effects maestro Ray Harryhausen, with whom Chaffey had previously collaborated on *Jason and the Argonauts* (1963), concentrated on the staging of the effects sequences, which he storyboarded in detail via a series of sketches and elaborate paintings so as to better help the actors react to the animated dinosaurs which would be added later during the lengthy post-

*Above:* John Richardson points out the way to Raquel Welch in *One Million Years B.C.* (1966). *Below:* What's that coming over the hill? Raquel Welch and John Richardson look suitably scared in *One Million Years B.C.* (1966) (both photographs, Hammer/Seven Arts/Associated British Pathé/Associated British Picture Corporation/Warner Pathé Distributors/Twentieth Century–Fox/Studio Canal).

production period. Harryhausen was already very much an industry legend, having apprenticed with the great Willis O'Brien on *Mighty Joe Young* (1949) before going on to score solo successes with such fantasies as *The Seventh Voyage of Sinbad* (1958), *The Three Worlds of Gulliver* (1960) and *Mysterious Island* (1961), all of which had been made under the aegis of producer Charles Schneer for Columbia (the latter film had gone out on a double bill with Hammer's *The Pirates of Blood River* [1962] in Britain and America in 1962). However, following *First Men in the Moon* (1964), Schneer decided to pursue a number of live action projects, and so when Harryhausen received the offer from Michael Carreras to become involved in *One Million Years B.C.* he readily accepted the assignment, despite his confessed aversion to remakes.

Harryhausen wasn't the only person who had initially expressed an aversion to working on the film. Having just completed her first leading role in the science

fiction adventure *Fantastic Voyage* (1966), Raquel Welch was less than keen to take on a role that would require little of her, except to utter such made-up lingo as "akeeta" and "neetcha" *ad infinitum* while running about in a doe-skin bikini, a publicity shot of which taken by Pierre Luigi would become one of the most iconographic images of the sixties, and usher in the era of Hammer Glamor, providing the company with a valuable new marketing tool which it would exploit to the full over the next few years. However, Richard Zanuck, the head of Twentieth Century–Fox, which then owned Welch's contract, insisted that she do the film as a loan out, for which the studio received $25,000. The actress eventually capitulated, and the film went on to become one of her biggest hits, eventually taking in a worldwide gross in excess of $9m (£3.6m), though this hasn't prevented her from belittling it ever since, perhaps because what little dialogue she did have was subsequently dubbed by Nicolette McKenzie in post-production (Nikki Van Der Zyl also dubbed in some additional grunts for the actress).

Filming in the Canaries took a whole month, during which the cast and crew encountered the familiar location curse of unseasonal bad weather.

**Slightly disturbing Polish artwork for *One Million Years B.C.* (1966) (Hammer/Seven Arts/Associated British Pathé/Associated British Picture Corporation/Warner Pathé Distributors/Twentieth Century–Fox/Studio Canal).**

Recalled Raquel Welch, "I was out there in my little bikini in the middle of the snow! I was freezing to death through half the movie…. The crews had fires and stuff burning underneath the cameras to keep them from freezing."[10] Welch also recalled having to react to the invisible monsters: "They were very precise about it. They had already choreographed how the monster was going to move, what was supposed to happen. They told us exact eyelines, what we were supposed to do, and how we're supposed to thrust a spear…. When you were doing it, it just seemed so ridiculously silly. You felt like a fool, quite frankly."[11]

These sequences finally in the can, the unit returned to the more controlled climes Elstree studios on 20 November, where the various cave interiors were filmed, along with the scenes at the Shell People's encampment. These sequences were completed by 6 January 1966, following which began the nine-month slog of animating the rubber dinosaurs frame by frame, among them an allosaurus, brontosaurus, triceratops, ceratosaurus and pterandon, the latter of which flies off with Loana at one point in an attempt to feed her to its young! However, a scene involving a phororhacos (a giant bird) was abandoned for budgetary reasons, while a sequence involving a brontosaurus was pared back from its original length, although staged stills featuring the dinosaur attacking the Rock People were created for publicity purposes. For the first and last time in his career, Harryhausen also made use of a live lizard (an iguana filmed in slow motion) by way of introducing the audience to the film's various prehistoric creatures, his reasoning (somewhat flawed) being that, "By using real creatures we might convince the viewers that all of what they were about to see was indeed real."[12] He also made use (albeit briefly) of a magnified tarantula.

Despite its various anachronisms (among them the aforementioned doe-skin bikini, along with the false eye-lashes and modern-day hair-dos sported by the Shell People), *One Million Years B.C.* is, despite a couple of slow patches, an impressively staged production peppered by some memorable effects sequences, prime among them the attack of the allosaurus, which Tomak manages to stake with a branch as it leaps at him! The clash between a triceratops and a ceratosaurus is also impressively staged and animated by Harryhausen. Elsewhere, the rich color photography of Wilkie Cooper (another *Jason and the Argonauts* veteran)

makes excellent use of the desolate locations, as does the second unit camera work of Jack Mills. Less convincing are art director Robert Jones' cave interiors, which look as fake as his work for *She* (note the rubber wall off which one of the cannibals bounces during the fight sequence observed by Loana and Tumak). However, the impressive, other-worldly score by Mario Nascimbene, which makes use of such diverse percussive elements as bell sticks, rocks and the jawbone of an ass, more than compensates, adding immeasurably to the stone-age atmosphere, while the rituals of the Rock People are realistically staged by director Don Chaffey, particularly in the scene in which the hungry clan scrabbles with each other over the freshly roasted boar captured by the men-folk.

Given their lack of dialogue save for the occasional grunt and groan (which saved on the expense of dubbing and sub-titling foreign releases!), the cast manage to convey the feelings and motivations of their characters quite convincingly via mime and body language. Particularly adept in this department are Robert Brown as Tumak's bullying tribal leader father Akhoba, and Percy Herbert as Tumak's jealous brother Sakana. Meanwhile, Raquel Welch (who doesn't appear until almost a third the way through the movie) never looks less than stunning, while John Richardson appears suitably disheveled after his journey across the wastes. Also worth noting is Martine Beswick's strenuous performance as Nupondi—another of the Rock People—particularly when she takes on Loana in a convincing cat fight, seemingly a Beswick pre-requisite following her well-remembered gypsy fight in *From Russia with Love* (1963).

Once the film had completed its lengthy post-production period, it was released on the ABC circuit in the UK by Warner-Pathé on 30 December 1966, having been trade shown on 25 October. The film's American release care of Twentieth Century–Fox (which cut nine minutes from the running time) followed on February 21 1967. The critics greeted the film with mixed feelings. "The picture follows a plot line more primitive than its subject," moaned *Time*, while *Newsweek* averred that it "might have been fun if it had been more foolish," adding that, "Just a bit more stupidity could have turned the trick." The film seemed to do the trick for *Variety*, however, which described it as "good humored, full-of-action commercial nonsense," while the *Los Angeles Times* noted that though the film lacked "the romantic quality of the original" it was "well-directed by Don Chaffey" and had "surprisingly good" special effects. The *Monthly Film Bulletin* agreed, adding that "Hammer production finesse is much in evidence and Don Chaffey has done a competent job of direction." *The Spectator* likewise singled out the director, noting that, "Chaffey directs at a fair clip." *Kinematograph Weekly* meanwhile described the film as being "colorful nonsense with enough impressive and ingenious special effects to fascinate audiences."

The critical carping notwithstanding, the film was an immediate hit on both sides of the Atlantic. At the time, Brian Lawrence described the film, which went on to become Hammer's biggest commercial success, as "The most important film the company has ever produced." Indeed, this Jurassic lark was embraced by young and old alike, and remains a firm favorite of its kind to this day. Given such strong returns, Hammer inevitably returned to the well for several further helpings during the ensuing years, churning out such variations *Slave Girls* (1968), which made use of the same sets, *When Dinosaurs Ruled the Earth* (1970) and *Creatures the World Forgot* (1971). **Additional notes:** Iceland was originally suggested for the film's location work, while plans to shoot in widescreen by Michael Carreras were nixed by Ray Harryhausen, who had previously encountered problems filming his effects in the Panavision process on *First Men in the Moon* (1964). Some sources indicate that Ursula Andress was sought to play Loana. A patronizing narration spoken by David Kossoff was removed from the finished film and replaced by a briefer and more apt one spoken by Robert Beatty. Keep an eye out for the wire that lifts the Shell Man into the air as he is supposedly being lifted off the ground in the mouth of the allosaurus. Certain shots of landscapes and cloudscapes from the film later appeared in the opening sequence of Hammer's *The Lost Continent* (1968). Raquel Welch's appearance in her doeskin bikini was voted in at number eighty-six in Channel Four's *100 Greatest Sexy Moments* (2003, TV), which seems rather far down the list; the number one spot went to Ursula Andress' emergence from the sea as Honey Rider in *Dr. No* (1962). The volcano eruption was later re-used in Hammer's *Creatures the World Forgot* (1971). *One Million Years B.C.* was re-released on 10 August 1969 on a double bill with Hammer's *She* (1965), which brought in a nice windfall of £190,000. Hammer also approached Fox about a possible television series based upon *One Million Years B.C.* in 1967, but instead ended up making *Journey to the Unknown* (1968, TV) with the company. The film's poster, along with that for *The Man in the White Suit* (1951), is featured on the cover of Sim Branaghan's BFI study *British Film Posters: An Illustrated History* (2006). A poster of Raquel Welch's famous doe skin bikini pose meanwhile plays an integral part in the film *The Shawshank Redemption* (1994), though given that the film's protagonist Andy Dufresne (Tim Robbins) escapes from jail in 1966, it wouldn't actually have been available for him to put on his cell wall, as *One Million Years B.C.* wasn't released until the end of December 1966 in the UK and February 1967 in the U.S., following which the poster became popular.

Production companies: Hammer/Seven Arts/ Associated British Pathé/Associated British Picture Corporation. Distributors: Warner Pathé Distributors (UK [ABC circuit]), Twentieth Century–Fox (UK). Producer: Michael Carreras. Associate producer: Aida Young. Director: Don Chaffey. Screenplay: Michael Carreras, based upon the screenplay *One Million B.C.* (1940) by Mickell Novak, George Baker and Joseph Frickert. Cinematographer: Wilkie Cooper. Music/special musical effects: Mario Nascimbene. Music director: Philip Martell. Supervising editor: James Needs. Editor: Tom Simpson. First assistant editor: Robert Dearberg [uncredited]. Assistant editors: Chris

Barnes [uncredited], Anthony Sloman [uncredited]. Art director: Robert Jones. Assistant art director: Kenneth McCallum Tait. Costumes: Carl Toms, Ivy Baker. Special effects: Ray Harryhausen (stop motion effects), Les Bowie (prologue effects), George Blackwell (mechanical and floor effects [uncredited]), Ray Caple (mattes [uncredited]), Bob Cuff (mattes [uncredited]). Special effects assistants: Ian Scoones [uncredited], Kit West [uncredited]. Make-up: Wally Schneiderman. Hair: Olga Angelinetta. Recording supervisor: A.W. Lumkin. Sound: Bill Rowe, Len Shilton. Sound editors: Roy Baker, Alfred Cox. Production manager: John Wilcox. Assistant director: Denis Berterer. Second assistant director: Colin Lord [uncredited]. Third assistant director: Ray Atcheler [uncredited]. Camera operator: David Harcourt. Focus puller: Geoffrey Glover [uncredited]. Second unit photography: Jack Mills. Second unit camera operator: Kenneth Nicholson [uncredited]. Clapper loader: Ted Deason [uncredited]. Gaffer: Steve Birtles [uncredited]. Key grip: Martin O'Connor [uncredited]. Draughtsman: Colin Monk [uncredited]. Scenic

**T**RAVEL BACK THROUGH TIME AND SPACE TO THE EDGE OF MAN'S BEGINNINGS...DISCOVER A SAVAGE WORLD WHOSE ONLY LAW WAS LUST!

Raquel Welch adopts an iconic pose in this classic poster for *One Million Years B.C.* (1966) (Hammer/Seven Arts/Associated British Pathé/Associated British Picture Corporation/Warner Pathé Distributors/Twentieth Century–Fox/Studio Canal).

artist: Bill Beavis [uncredited]. Continuity: Gladys Goldsmith, Marjorie Lavelly. Stunts: Gerry Crampton [uncredited], Peter Pocock [uncredited], Joe Dunne [uncredited], Frank Henson [uncredited]. Animal sculptures: Arthur Hayward [uncredited]. Publicity: Bob Webb [uncredited], Alan Thomson [uncredited]. Stills: Ronnie Pilgrim [uncredited], Pierre Luigi [uncredited], Terry O'Neill [uncredited]. Production secretary: Eileen Matthews [uncredited]. Production accountant: John Trehy [uncredited]. Poster: Tom Chantrell (also 1969 double bill re-issue with *She* [1965], [uncredited]). **Cast:** Raquel Welch (Loana), John Richardson (Tumak), Percy Herbert (Sakana), Martine Beswick (Nupondi), Robert Brown (Akhoba), Jean Wladon (Ahot), Lisa Thomas (Sura), William Lyon Brown (Payto), Malya Nappi (Tohana), Yvonne Horner (Ullah), Richard James (Young Rock Man), Terence Maidment (First Shell Man), Micky De Rauch (First Shell Girl), Frank Hayden (First Rock Man),

James Payne (Caveman), Clive Moss (unnamed role [uncredited]), Robert Beatty (Narrator [uncredited]), Nicolette McKenzie (Voice of Raquel Welch [uncredited], with Nikki Van Der Zyl [uncredited]). **DVD availability:** Twentieth Century–Fox (U.S. R1 NTSC), extras include the trailer; Optimum Home Entertainment (UK R2 PAL), extras include interviews with Ray Harryhausen and Raquel Welch. **Blu-ray availability:** Kino Lorber (A/1), extras include a commentary by Tim Lucas and interviews with Raquel Welch and Ray Harryhausen; Sony (B/2). **CD availability:** *One Million Years B.C.* (Legend), which contains seven cues from the score; *The Hammer Film Music Collection: Volume Two* (GDI Records), which contains *Finale* and *End Credits*; *The Monster Movie Music Album* (Silva Screen), which contains a newly recorded *Hammer Stone-Age Suite*, including eight-minutes of the *One Million Years B.C.* score

*One on an Island* see *Journey to the Unknown*

## O'Neal, Robert

O'Neal can be seen in a bit part in Hammer's *36 Hours* (1953). **Hammer credits:** *36 Hours* (1953, as Driver [uncredited])

## O'Neil, Colette

This busy British (Scottish) actress (1937–, real name Colette McCrossan) can be spotted as the madwoman with a penchant for seeing imaginary spiders in Hammer's *Frankenstein Must Be Destroyed* (1969). Mainly on television, her credits include episodes of *Hancock's Half Hour* (1956–1960, TV), *Kidnapped* (1963, TV), *Adam Adamant Lives!* (1966–1967, TV), *Fraud Squad* (1969–1970, TV), *Maybury* (1981, TV), *Bad Girls* (1999–2006, TV) and *Doctors* (2000–, TV). Her other occasional films include *Mortdecai* (2015). **Hammer credits:** *Frankenstein Must Be Destroyed* (1969, as Madwoman)

## O'Neill, Terence (Terry)

Following experience in the American film industry, British born O'Neill joined Hammer in 1949 as the personal assistant to studio chief James Carreras. His father-in-law was C.J. Latta, one of the founding fathers of The Variety Club of Great Britain, with which Carreras had strong ties from the mid-fifties onwards.

## O'Neill, Terry

This noted British stills and portrait cameraman (1938–, full name Terence Patrick O'Neill) took pictures of many icons of the sixties and seventies, among them Raquel Welch on the set of *One Million Years B.C.* (1966), though it should be noted that the famous image of Welch in her doeskin bikini was actually taken by Pierre Luigi. Recalled O'Neill of Welch, "She was very worried she was going to be typecast after this [film]. What she really wanted was more serious roles. This was a typical sixties creation, with weird animated dinosaurs and lots of grunting. But the shoot with Raquel was great fun. She was a complete natural in front of the camera."[13] Others captured by O'Neill's lens include Queen Elizabeth II, Sandie Shaw, Audrey Hepburn, Jean Shrimpton, Terence Stamp, The Beatles, The Rolling Stones and Twiggy. His first wife was actress Vera Day (1935–), who appeared in four films for Hammer. His second wife was actress Faye Dunaway (1941–), to whom he was married between 1982 and 1987, and for whom he executive produced *Mommie Dearest* (1981) via Dunaway/O'Neill Associates, Inc. His son is the actor Liam Dunaway O'Neill (1980–). **Hammer credits:** *One Million Years B.C.* (1966 [uncredited])

## Onions, Oliver

This British writer (1873–1961, full name George Oliver Onions, aka George Oliver) had his 1911 story *The Beckoning Fair One* adapted for an episode of Hammer's *Journey to the Unknown* (1968, TV). It also formed (albeit without credit) the basis of an Italian film *Un tranquillo posto di campagna* (1968), also known as *A Quiet Place in the Country* (the title was also hijacked for a 2015 episode of *Salem* [2014–2017, TV], but with no connection to the story). Onions' other works include *In Accordance with the Evidence* (1910), *Widdershins* (1911), a collection of ghost stories from which *The Beckoning Fair One* hailed, *The Debit Account* (1913), *Gray Youth—The Story of a Very Modern Courtship and a Very Modern Marriage* (1914), *A Case in Camera* (1921) and *Ghosts in Daylight* (1924). He began his career as a magazine illustrator and designer of book jackets and posters. His wife was the writer Berta Ruck (1878–1978, real name Amy Roberta Ruck), whom he married in 1909; his granddaughter was the television producer and director Jane Oliver (1941–2013) **Additional notes:** Experts on the author are said to "know their Onions." But not really. **Hammer credits:** *The Beckoning Fair One* (1968, TV [episode of *Journey to the Unknown*])

## Onslow, Maud(e)

Onslow worked as the hair stylist on *One on an Island* (1968, TV [episode of *Journey to the Unknown*]), which led to further assignments for Hammer. Her other credits include *The End of the River* (1947), *Mogambo* (1953), *Across the Bridge* (1957), *The Fast Lady* (1962), *Bunny Lake Is Missing* (1965), *Wuthering Heights* (1970), *Barry Lyndon* (1975) and *The Legacy* (1978). **Hammer credits:** *One on an Island* (1968, TV [episode of *Journey to the Unknown*]), *Demons of the Mind* (1972), *Love Thy Neighbour* (1973), *The Satanic Rites of Dracula* (1974), *Frankenstein and the Monster from Hell* (1974)

## The Oobladee Dancers

This troupe of dancers appeared as a group of natives in Hammer's *She* (1965), in which they were choreographed by Cristyne Lawson. Their name is derived from the Afro-Caribbean saying "Oobladee, ooblada, life goes on." Note that the Beatles song *Obladi, Oblada* didn't come along until 1968, though it was actually pre-empted by six months by *another* song of the same title by John Halsey and Mike Patto, itself taken from the saying frequently used by their friend, the African conga player Jimmy Scott. **Hammer credits:** *She* (1965)

## Operation Universe

GB, 1957 [released 1959], 28m, Eastmancolor, HammerScope, RCA, cert U

This documentary short was written, produced and directed by former Hammer camera operator Peter Bryan, who would also go on to script several films for the company, among them *The Hound of the Baskervilles* (1959). Narrated by the Canadian actor Robert Beatty—who had starred in Hammer's *Wings of Danger* (1952), on which Bryan had worked as a camera operator—the film takes a look at Deuce, one of Britain's first computers ("A high-speed calculator, an electronic brain") and also examines the British preparations for space travel ("Man has already mastered the air; now the last great challenge awaits him—the conquest of space"). It also features some amazingly primitive experiments with radioactive substances (Carbon 14). Observes the narrator at this point, during which a lab technician somewhat lumberingly processes the deadly material, "A keen eye and a steady hand is essential here, for every particle is valuable." No shit, Sherlock! As for the comment that "This is an unseen enemy," it could quite easily have come from one of Hammer's science fiction films of the period.

Recalled camera operator Len Harris, who turned cinematographer for the film, "Obviously, all quite dated now."[14] He also revealed that, "The plasterers at Bray made a wonderful plaster reproduction of the surface of the moon, which I had to track up to."[15] At this point the narrator proclaims, "The planets and the stars await us."

Made in late 1957 (the year to which it is copyrighted), the film wasn't released in the UK until 1959 by Columbia. **Additional notes:** The credits thank the following companies for their help with the making of the film: The Radiochemical Center, The National Physical Laboratory, The Central Electricity Authority, The University of Manchester Experimental Station, The RAF Institute of Aviation and The Mount Wilson and Palomar Observatories. Eastmancolor is credited as Eastman Colour. The film's concept and structure is similar to the three *Popular Science* shorts Exclusive distributed in 1952.

Production company: Hammer. Distributor: Columbia (UK). Producer: Peter Bryan. Director: Peter Bryan. Screenplay and story: Peter Bryan. Cinematographer: Len Harris. Editor: Bill Lenny. Narrator: Robert Beatty. Processing: Humphries Laboratories

## Orchard, Julian

Adept at snooty roles, this much-liked British comedy character actor (1930–1979) was a familiar face on television in such series as *The World of the Beachcomber* (1968–1969, TV) and *Whack-O!* (1971–1972, TV). In films from 1959 with *The Great Van Robbery*, his other credits include *Crooks Anonymous* (1962), *Half a Sixpence* (1967), *Carry On Doctor* (1968), *Bless This House* (1972), *The Slipper and the Rose* (1976) and *Revenge of the Pink Panther* (1978). He also appeared in Hammer's big screen version of the TV sitcom *Man About the House* (1974). Also on stage (everything from Shakespeare to dame in pantomime at the London Palladium), he trained at London's Guildhall School of Music and Drama. **Hammer credits:** *Man About the House* (1974, as Producer)

## O'Regan, Terence

This Irish actor (1927–1981) had a supporting role in Hammer's *Stolen Face* (1952). His other credits include *Moulin Rouge* (1952), plus episodes of *The Count of Monte Cristo* (1956, TV) and *Assignment Foreign Legion* (1955, TV). His wife was actress Daphne Elphinstone (1914–), whom he married in 1951. **Hammer credits:** *Stolen Face* (1952, as Pete Snipe)

## O'Rourke, Charles

O'Rourke played a servant in Hammer's *The Vengeance of She* (1968). His TV appearances include episodes of *Z Cars* (1962–1978, TV), *Doctor Who* (1963–1989, TV) and *Adam Adamant Lives!* (1966–1967, TV). **Hammer credits:** *The Vengeance of She* (1968, as Servant)

## Osborn, Andrew

In films from the mid-thirties with the likes of *Who Goes Next?* (1938), *Idol of Paris* (1948), *Dark Interval* (1950), *The Second Mrs. Tanqueray* (1953) and *Beau Brummell* (1954), this British supporting actor (1910–1985) went on to become a successful television producer, notably with *Maigret* (1960–1963, TV), which he executive produced. As an actor, he also appeared in three second features for Hammer, also working as the dialogue director on the third of these. His other credits as a television producer include *R3* (1964–1965, TV) *The Gathering Storm* (1974, TVM) and *The Aphrodite Inheritance* (1979, TV). **Hammer credits:** *Spaceways* (1953, as Philip Crenshaw), *Blood Orange* (1953, as Captain Simpson), *Murder by Proxy* (1955, as Lance Gorden, also dialogue director)

## Osborn, Rupert

This supporting actor (sometimes Osborne) played the role of Gerry in Hammer's *Captain Clegg* (1962). His other credits include *The Witness* (1959), *Konga* (1961) and *The Pumpkin Eater* (1964). **Hammer credits:** *Captain Clegg* (1962, as Gerry)

## Osborne, David

Osborne worked as a focus puller on two films for Hammer, sharing his credit on *Paranoiac* (1963) with Robin Higginson. His other credits as a focus puller include *East of Sudan* (1964) and *2001: A Space Odyssey* (1968). His credits as a clapper loader include *Final Appointment* (1954), while his work as a camera operator takes in *Hunted in Holland* (1960). **Hammer credits:** *Paranoiac* (1963 [uncredited]), *The Kiss of the Vampire* (1963 [uncredited])

## Osborne, Maureen

Osborne rose to the rank of producer's secretary at Hammer following work as a receptionist at Bray in the mid-fifties.

## Osborne, Sally

This British actress (1952–, full name Sally Osborn-Smith, sometimes billed Osborn) can be seen as a nurse in Hammer's *Mutiny on the Buses* (1972). Her other credits include *Sweeney!* (1976) and *Haunted Honeymoon* (1986), plus episodes of *Survivors* (1975–1977, TV), *The Cedar Tree* (1976, TV), in which she played Elizabeth Bourne, *Cribb* (1980–1981, TV), *King's Royal* (1982–1983, TV), in which she played Gwen Hoey, and *Pulaski* (1987, TV). Her sister is the production manager and associate producer Jennie Osborn. **Hammer credits:** *Mutiny on the Buses* (1972, as Nurse)

## Osborne, Tony

This British pianist, songwriter, composer and music director (1922–2009, real name Edward Benjamin Osborne) orchestrated Trevor H. Sandford's theme for the Hammer comedy *A Weekend with Lulu* (1961), and also provided additional music for the movie. His credits as a composer include *The Secret Door* (1964), *The Fiend* (1971), which he co-scored with Richard Kerr, *Nobody Ordered Love* (1972) and *Black Gunn* (1972). He also worked as an arranger, songwriter and conductor

on the musical *Every Day's a Holiday* (1964). He was a pianist with many top orchestras before establishing himself as a composer and orchestra leader (with Tony Osborne and His Dancing Strings). His songs include *The Lights of Lisbon* (1958). His son is the songwriter Gary Osborne (1949–). **Hammer credits:** *A Weekend with Lulu* (1961)

## Oscar, Henry

On stage from the age of twenty, this prolific British character actor (1891–1969, real name Henry Oscar Wale) also worked as a theater director, and was known for touring plays and entertainments to the troops during both World War I and II (during the latter as a drama director for ENSA). In films from 1932 with *After Dark*, he went on to appear in over eighty productions, among them *The Man Who Knew Too Much* (1934), *The Saint in London* (1939), *They Made Me a Fugitive* (1947), *Private's Progress* (1956), *Lawrence of Arabia* (1962) and *The City Under the Sea* (1965). To Hammer fans he is best known for playing the abrupt Herr Lang in *The Brides of Dracula* (1960), whose rude behavior insults both the hero of the piece, Dr. Van Helsing, as well as the villain, Baron Meinster. Oscar holds the distinction of being the first actor ever to be contracted to BBC radio in 1922. **Hammer credits:** *The Brides of Dracula* (1960, as Otto Lang)

## The Oscars *see* Academy Awards

## O'Shannon, Finnuala

O'Shannon (1935–1992) can be seen as one of the vampires in the cellar of Pelham House in Hammer's *The Satanic Rites of Dracula* (1974). Her other credits include *Sally's Irish Rogue* (1958) and *The Playboy of the Western World* (1962), plus episodes of *The Verdict Is Yours* (1958–1963, TV), *The Wednesday Play* (1964–1970, TV) and *BBC2 Playhouse* (1974–1983, TV). **Hammer credits:** *The Satanic Rites of Dracula* (1974, as Vampire)

## O'Shaughnessey, Brian

This British actor (1931–2001) can be seen as Mak in Hammer's *Creatures the World Forgot* (1971). He lived for many years in South Africa, where most of his other films were made. His other credits include *African Gold* (1965), *The Rider in the Night* (1968), *Zulu Dawn* (1979), *The Gods Must Be Crazy* (1980), *Warhead* (1996), *Operation Delta Force 3: Clear Target* (1999) and *Falling Rocks* (2000). **Hammer credits:** *Creatures the World Forgot* (1971, as Mak)

## O'Shea, Milo

On stage from 1935, this Irish character actor (1926–2013) sustained a busy career on stage (including stints at the Abbey Theater), in films and on television in both Britain and America. In films from 1951 with *Talk of a Million* (though some sources claim he had a walk-on role in *Contraband* [1940]), his forty-plus credits include *Carry On Cabby* (1963), *Ulysses* (1967), which earned him a BAFTA nomination, *The Angel Levine* (1970), *Theatre of Blood* (1973), *The Verdict* (1982), *Only the Lonely* (1991), *The Butcher Boy* (1997) and

*Puckoon* (2002). His TV work includes the sitcom *Me Mammy* (1969–1971, TV), in which he played Bunjy Kennefic, *QB VII* (1974, TV), *Ellis Island* (1984, TV) and *The West Wing* (1999–2006, TV). He also appeared in *The New People*, an episode of Hammer's *Journey to the Unknown* (1968, TV), which was also included in the compendium film *Journey into Darkness* (1968, TVM). His wives were actresses Maureen Toal (1930–2012), from 1951 to 1974, and Kitty O'Sullivan, whom he married in 1974. His son is actor Steve O'Shea. **Hammer credits:** *The New People* (1968, TV [episode of *Journey to the Unknown*], as Matt Dystal), *Journey into Darkness* (1968, TVM, as Matt Dystal)

## Osman, Ahmed

Osman can be seen as a priest in Hammer's *Blood from the Mummy's Tomb* (1971). Interestingly, he also appeared in the remake, *The Awakening* (1980), albeit in a different role. His other credits include episodes of *Crown Court* (1972–1984, TV), *Warship* (1973–1977, TV) and *Are You Being Served?* (1972–1985, TV). **Hammer credits:** *Blood from the Mummy's Tomb* (1971, as Priest)

## Osment, Alyssa

Osment (sometimes Osmens) worked as one of the assistant editors on *The World of Hammer* (1990 [first broadcast 1994], TV), sharing her credit with Amanda Jenks. She also worked in the same capacity on twenty-six episodes of *Best of British* (1987–1994, TV) between 1993 and 1994 **Hammer credits:** *The World of Hammer* (1990 [first broadcast 1994], TV)

## Osmond, Hal

This British supporting actor (1903–1959) can be seen as a railway porter in Hammer's *Death of an Angel* (1952). He also had minor supporting roles in three further Hammer productions. In films from 1937 with *Non-Stop New York*, his other credits include *The Rake's Progress* (1945), *Top Secret* (1953), *The Net* (1953), *A Night to Remember* (1958) and *Jack the Ripper* (1959). His occasional TV credits include episodes of *The Adventures of Robin Hood* (1955–1960, TV) and *Saber of London* (1954–1960, TV), of which he appeared in twenty-one episodes in a variety of different roles. **Hammer credits:** *Death of an Angel* (1952, as Railway porter), *Stolen Face* (1952, as Photographer), *The Gambler and the Lady* (1953, as Fred), *Dick Turpin—Highwayman* (1956, as Mac)

## Ostime, Roger

This British actor (1928–) can be seen in a minor supporting role in *The Thirteenth Reunion* (1980, TV [episode of *Hammer House of Horror*]). His many other small screen credits include episodes of *Quatermass and the Pit* (1958–1959, TV), *The Cleopatras* (1983, TV) and *Maid Marian and Her Merry Men* (1989–1993, TV). His occasional film credits include *The Blue Max* (1966) and *84 Charing Cross Road* (1987). He was married to actress Hilary Mason (1917–2006) from 1955. **Hammer credits:** *The Thirteenth Reunion* (1980, TV [episode of *Hammer House of Horror*], as Crenshaw [butler])

## O'Sullivan, Arthur

This Irish actor (1912–1981) had a small role in

Hammer's *The Viking Queen* (1967). His other credits include *The Quare Fellow* (1962), *Mystery Submarine* (1962), *Girl with Green Eyes* (1964) and *Young Cassidy* (1964), plus episodes of *Play for Today* (1970–1984, TV) and *Once Upon a Time* (1973, TV). **Hammer credits:** *The Viking Queen* (1967, as Old man)

### O'Sullivan, Richard

In films as a child before making a successful transition into teenage and adult roles, this much-liked British comedy actor (1944–) is best known for playing catering student Robin Tripp in the hit sitcom *Man About the House* (1973–1976, TV), which in turn spawned a popular spin-off, *Robin's Nest* (1977–1981, TV), in which his character opened his own bistro. O'Sullivan's early film credits include *The Stranger's Hand* (1953), *The Green Scarf* (1954), *It's Great to Be Young!* (1956), *Dangerous Exile* (1957), *Carry On Teacher* (1959) and *Cleopatra* (1963), in which he played Ptolemy. He made the leap into early adulthood with a role in the Cliff Richard musical *Wonderful Life* (1964), which he followed with *Au Pair Girls* (1972), *Can You Keep It Up for a Week?* (1974) and Hammer's big screen version of *Man About the House* (1974). Also busy in television during this period, his credits here include *Foreign Affairs* (1966, TV), *Doctor at Large* (1971, TV), *Now Look Here* (1971–1973, TV), *Alcock and Gander* (1972, TV), *Doctor in Charge* (1972–1973, TV), *Dick Turpin* (1979–1982, TV) and *Me and My Girl* (1984–1988, TV). He was briefly married to the actress Diana Terry in 1971. **Additional notes:** O'Sullivan also appeared as Robin Tripp in a 1973 edition of the TV comedy special *All Star Comedy Carnival* (1969–1973, TV). **Hammer credits:** *Man About the House* (1974, as Robin Tripp)

### Oulton, Brian

A familiar face in British comedies of the sixties, this British actor (1908–1992) began his film career in 1931 with *Sally in Our Alley*, which led to appearances in over fifty further films, among them *This Man Is News* (1938), *Panic at Madame Tussaud's* (1948), *The Huggetts Abroad* (1949), *Carry On Nurse* (1959), *Carry On Constable* (1960), *The Iron Maiden* (1962), *Carry On Camping* (1969), *Ooh ... You Are Awful* (1972) and *Gandhi* (1982). He also played Mr. Dingle in Hammer's *The Damned* (1963), a vampire disciple *The Kiss of the Vampire* (1963), and a short-tempered manager in *On the Buses* (1971). Despite his prolific film and television career, the latter of which took in episodes of everything from *Wire Service* (1956–1957, TV) to *The Young Ones* (1982–1984, TV), Oulton spent much of his working life in the theater, working as an actor, director and occasional playwright. He was married to the actress Peggy Thorpe-Bates (1914–1989). **Hammer credits:** *The Damned* (1963, as Mr. Dingle), *The Kiss of the Vampire* (1963, as Disciple), *On the Buses* (1971, as Manager)

### Owen, Bill

Best known for playing the unkempt William "Compo" Simmonite in the seemingly endless sit-com *Last of the Summer Wine* (1973–2010, TV), of which he appeared in 184 episodes, this much-liked British comedy character actor (1914–1999, real name William John Owen Rowbotham, aka Bill Rowbotham) came to films in 1941 with the short *Song of the People* following experience as a holiday camp entertainer. In over forty films, usually as squaddie or spiv types, his credits include *Holiday Camp* (1947), *Trottie True* (1949), *Davy* (1957), *Carry On Sergeant* (1958), *Carry On Nurse* (1959), *Carry On Regardless* (1960), *Carry On Cabby* (1963), *Georgy Girl* (1966), *O Lucky Man!* (1973) and *Laughterhouse* (1984). He can also be seen as the unfortunate Bludgin in Hammer's *The Secret of Blood Island* (1965), in which he is beaten to death in a Malayan prison camp. His other television credits include episodes of *Taxi!* (1963–1964, TV), *Coppers End* (1971, TV) and *Brideshead Revisited* (1981, TV), while for the theater he worked as an actor, director, playwright and lyricist (he penned the book and lyrics for the 1966 musical *The Match Girls*). He was also long-associated with the National Association of Boys Clubs, his work for which earned him an MBE in 1976. His son is the actor Tom Owen (1949–). **Hammer credits:** *The Secret of Blood Island* (1965, as Bludgin)

### Owen, Cliff

Beginning his career as a third assistant director on *Brighton Rock* (1947), this British director (1919–1994) went on to helm a string of comedies of varying quality in the sixties and seventies, among them such familiar titles as *The Wrong Arm of the Law* (1962), *That Riviera Touch* (1966), *Steptoe and Son* (1972), *Ooh ... You Are Awful* (1972), *No Sex Please—We're British* (1973) and *The Bawdy Adventures of Tom Jones* (1976). He was therefore a somewhat curious choice to helm *The Vengeance of She* (1968) for Hammer, especially given that Sidney Hayers was also considered for the job. Unfortunately, the film was a critical, commercial and artistic disaster, and Owen didn't work for the company again. His other credits include a handful of documentary shorts and episodes of such TV series as *The Third Man* (1959, TV), *On Trial* (1960, TV) and *The Avengers* (1961–1969, TV). His other early credits include *Under Capricorn* (1949), on which he was the second assistant director, and *The Magic Box* (1952), on which he was the assistant director. **Hammer credits:** *The Vengeance of She* (1968)

### Owen, Dickie

Best known for playing the Mummy, Ra-Antef, in Hammer's *The Curse of the Mummy's Tomb* (1964), this British supporting actor (1927–2015) can also be seen minus the bandages as Bragg in the Hammer thriller *Hell Is a City* (1960). His other credits include *The Criminal* (1960), *Zulu* (1964), *Three Hats for Lisa* (1965) and a return to the Mummy genre with Hammer's *The Mummy's Shroud* (1967), in which he this time played Prem in the flashback (the later mummified incarnation of the character was played by stuntman Eddie Powell). His TV credits include episodes of *The Saint* (1962–1969, TV), *Z Cars* (1962–1978, TV) and *Orlando* (1965–1968, TV). Off the radar for many years, to the point where many thought he had died, Owen eventually turned up at a Hammer convention in London's Central Hall Westminster on 8 November 2014, and proved to be one of the most popular guests with the fans. **Additional notes:** Stuntman Eddie Powell replaced Owen for the sewer climax in *The Curse of the Mummy's Tomb* after Owen was invalided by an accident. **Hammer credits:** *Hell Is a City* (1960, as Bragg), *The Curse of the Mummy's Tomb* (1964, as Ra-Antef), *The Mummy's Shroud* (1967, as Prem [flashback])

### Owen, Fred

Owen had a minor role in Hammer's *Dick Barton at Bay* (1950). **Hammer credits:** *Dick Barton at Bay* (1950, as Gangster)

### Owen, Jeff

Owen worked as the music advisor on the Hammer featurette *The Eric Winstone Bandshow* (1955). **Hammer credits:** *The Eric Winstone Bandshow* (1955)

Dickie Owen catches up with the day's news during a break in the filming of *The Curse of the Mummy's Tomb* (1964) (Hammer/Swallow/British Lion Columbia/Columbia).

## Owen, Yvonne

In films from the mid-forties, this British actress (1923–1990) appeared in such notable films of the period as *The Seventh Veil* (1945), *Holiday Camp* (1948) and *Quartet* (1948). She also starred in the Hammer comedy-thriller *Someone at the Door* (1950), in which she and co-star Michael Medwin concoct a fictitious murder, which subsequently comes true. She was long married to the character actor Alan Badel (1923–1982), whom she wed in 1942. Their daughter is the actress Sarah Badel (1943–). **Hammer credits:** *Someone at the Door* (1950, as Sally Martin)

## Owen-Smith, Brian

Owen-Smith (sometimes Brian Owen or, minus the hyphen, Brian Owen Smith) oversaw the wardrobe for Hammer's *Taste the Blood of Dracula* (1970) among others. His other credits include *633 Squadron* (1964), *Funeral in Berlin* (1966), *The Last Safari* (1967), *Dracula* (1973, TVM), *The Last of Sheila* (1973), *Caravans* (1978) and *The Passage* (1979). **Hammer credits:** *Taste the Blood of Dracula* (1970), *When Dinosaurs Ruled the Earth* (1970), *Countess Dracula* (1971), *Vampire Circus* (1972)

## Owens, Margery (Marjorie)

Owens worked as the continuity girl on Hammer's *The Glass Cage* (1955). Her many other credits include *Things Happen at Night* (1947), *Whisky Galore!* (1949), *The Queen of Spades* (1949), *Hindle Wakes* (1952), *Escapement* (1958) and *Invasion* (1965). **Hammer credits:** *The Glass Cage* (1955)

## Owens, Pat (Patricia)

In films in Britain from 1943 with *Miss London Ltd.*, this Canadian actress (1925–2000) went on to make several more films in the UK—among them *Give Us the Moon* (1944), *Panic at Madame Tussaud's* (1948), *The Happiest Days of Your Life* (1950) and Hammer's *The Stranger Came Home* (1954)—before making the move to Hollywood in 1956, where she appeared in *No Down Payment* (1957), *The Fly* (1958), in which she played Helene Delambre, *Sayonara* (1957), *Seven Women from Hell* (1961) and *The Destructors* (1968), shortly after which she retired. Her TV work includes episodes of *Gunsmoke* (1955–1975, TV), *Lassie* (1954–1974, TV) and *Follow the Sun* (1961–1962, TV). Her first husband (of three) was the writer Sy Bartlett (1900–1978, real name Sacha Baraniev), to whom she was married between 1956 and 1958. **Hammer credits:** *The Stranger Came Home* (1954, as Blonde)

## Owens, Richard

This British actor (1931–2015) played the role of Dr. Kersh in Hammer's *Vampire Circus* (1972). Mostly on television, his many credits here include episodes of *No Hiding Place* (1959–1967, TV), *The Champions* (1968–1969, TV), *Upstairs, Downstairs* (1971–1975, TV) and *Inspector Morse* (1987–2000, TV). He was formerly married to actress Polly Adams (1939–, real name Pauline Adams). Their daughters are actresses Susannah Harker (1965–, real name Susannah M. Owens) and Caroline Harker (1966–, real name Caroline Owens). **Hammer credits:** *Vampire Circus* (1972, as Dr. Kersh)

## Oxenford, Daphne

This British actress (1919–2012) had a minor supporting role in Hammer's *Frankenstein Must Be Destroyed* (1969). Much on television, her many credits include episodes of *The Villains* (1964–1965, TV), *Follyfoot* (1971–1973, TV), *Man About the House* (1973–1976, TV), *To the Manor Born* (1979–1981, TV), *Fresh Fields* (1984–1986, TV) and *Land of Hope and Gloria* (1992, TV). She also played the Queen Mother *Prince William* (2002, TVM), and the elderly Dame Agatha Christie in *The Unicorn and the Wasp*, a 2008 episode of *Doctor Who* (2005–, TV), but her scenes were cut (Fenella Woolgar played the younger Christie). She was best known for her radio work, notably the children's program *Listen with Mother* (1950–1982), which she narrated between 1950 and 1971, opening each program with the classic phrase, "Are you sitting comfortably? Then I'll begin." **Hammer credits:** *Frankenstein Must Be Destroyed* (1969, as Lady in garden [uncredited])

## Oxley, David

Remembered for his prologue cameo as the corrupt Sir Hugo Baskerville in Hammer's *The Hound of the Baskervilles* (1959), this British supporting actor (1920–1985) can also be seen as a doctor in the studio's war drama *Yesterday's Enemy* (1959). His other credits include *The Elusive Pimpernel* (1950), in which he made his screen debut, *Ill Met by Moonlight* (1956), *The Black Ice* (1957), *Life at the Top* (1964) and *House of the Living Dead* (1974). His occasional TV credits include episodes of *Sherlock Holmes* (1954–1955, TV), *African Patrol* (1958–1959, TV) and *Zero One* (1962, TV). **Hammer credits:** *The Hound of the Baskervilles* (1959, as Sir Hugo Baskerville), *Yesterday's Enemy* (1959, as Doctor)

---

# P

## Paal, Alexander

A one-time associate of film mogul Alexander Korda, for whom he worked on such Hollywood films as *Lydia* (1941), this Hungarian producer (1910–1972) began his career in Europe as a photo journalist (he helped to chronicle the fall of Nazi Germany for *The New York Times*), an art photographer (his books include the 1938 photo study *Body in Art*) and a World War II combat cameraman, following which he worked in America as a noted stills and portrait photographer (his subjects included such star names as Claudette Colbert, Tyrone Power, Joan Crawford, Gary Cooper, Ronald Colman, Laurence Olivier, Olivia de Havilland and Dolores Del Rio).

Paal came to Britain in 1949 and went on to either produce or associate produce a number of low budget thrillers. This led to several brushes with Hammer, the first of which was with *Cloudburst* (1951), which he helped to finance. He also provided the story for *Stolen Face* (1952) with Richard Landau and Steven Vas, and produced a couple of fifties second features with Michael Carreras. He later produced and co-wrote the story for *Countess Dracula* (1971), and hoped to set up a project about the real Dracula, Vlad Tepes, at Hammer, with Mike Raven in the title role, but James Carreras turned the idea down.

Paal's other credits as a producer or executive producer include *A Tale of Five Cities* (1951), for which he also provided the idea, *Three Cases of Murder* (1955) and *The Golden Head* (1965). He also co-wrote and co-directed *Columbus Discovers Kraehwinkel* (1954). He was married to the actress Eva Bartok (1927–1998, real name Eva Ivanova Szoke) between 1948 and 1950; she appeared in Hammer's *Spaceways* (1953) and *Break in the Circle* (1955).

Recalled Ingrid Pitt, who starred in *Countess Dracula* for Paal, "[He] was a brilliant stills photographer and did sessions with me at his studio in London at weekends. The best photos I possess from my entire career were taken by him."[1] However, Paal's career as a stills man caused problems for director Francis Searle on *Cloudburst*: "Paal was on the set quite a lot and, having been a stills man in America, proved to be a bit of a thorn in the side to my lighting cameraman Jimmy Harvey."[2]

Paal's other credits as a stills cameraman include *Casino Royale* (1967). **Hammer credits:** *Cloudburst* (1951, producer [uncredited]), *Stolen Face* (1952, co-story), *Mantrap* (1953, producer), *Four Sided Triangle* (1953, producer), *Countess Dracula* (1971, producer, co-story)

## Pacific Title

This American post-production facility and optical effects house has provided the titles for literally hundreds of movies and television programs. It provided new end titles for *Journey to Midnight* (1968, TVM), a compendium film featuring two episodes from Hammer's *Journey to the Unknown* (1968, TV). These were *Poor Butterfly* and *The Indian Spirit Guide*. As a consequence, the end credits had to be re-done to take in the cast and crew of both programs. Other series, TV movies and movies with titles and opticals by Pacific include *The Twilight Zone* (1959–1964, TV), *Rawhide* (1959–1966, TV), *Judgment at Nuremberg* (1961), *My Fair Lady* (1964), *The Dunwich Horror* (1970), *The Exorcist* (1973), *The Towering Inferno* (1974), *Innerspace* (1987), *Gremlins 2: The New Batch* (1990), *The Client* (1994), *Lara Croft: Tomb Raider* (2001), *The Simpsons Movie* (2007), *X-Men Origins: Wolverine* (2009), *She's Out of My League* (2010) and *A Million Ways to Die in the West* (2014). **Hammer credits:** *Journey to Midnight* (1968, TVM)

## Paddick, Hugh

Best remembered for playing the highly camp Julian to Kenneth Williams' even camper Sandy in the celebrated sixties radio series *Round the Horne* (1965–1968 [catchphrase: "Hello, I'm Julian and this is my friend Sandy"]), this British comedy actor (1915–2000) sadly made too few films. Mostly on stage and television from the early fifties, his rare film credits include *School for Scoundrels* (1960), *We Shall See* (1964), *San Ferry Ann* (1965),

*The Killing of Sister George* (1968), *Up Pompeii* (1971) and *Up the Chastity Belt* (1971), in which he played an extremely camp Robin Hood opposite Rita Webb's equally unlikely Maid Marion. He also had a minor role in Hammer's *That's Your Funeral* (1973). His many TV appearances include episodes of *Gert and Daisy* (1959, TV), *Beryl Reid Says Good Evening* (1968, TV), *Pardon My Genie* (1972–1973, TV), *Can We Get On Now, Please?* (1980, TV) and *Campion* (1989–1990, TV). **Hammer credits:** *That's Your Funeral* (1973, as Window dresser)

## Page, Alan

British born page (1922–1987) played a customer in Hammer's *The Curse of the Werewolf* (1961). His other credits include *The Lonely Man* (1957) and episodes of *Quatermass and the Pit* (1958–1959, TV) and *Love and Mr. Lewisham* (1959, TV). **Hammer credits:** *The Curse of the Werewolf* (1961, as Customer [uncredited])

## Page, Anthony

Born in India, this stage, film and television director (1935–) came to the cinema following experience in the theater (where he continues to work with great success), including training at the Neighborhood Playhouse in New York. He worked as an assistant director at the Royal Court in London from 1958 and later as its artistic director, making a name for himself directing plays by John Osborne, one of which, *Inadmissible Evidence* (1968), also marked his film debut. Working on both sides of the Atlantic, his other credits for both the large and small screen include *Alpha Beta* (1973), *Pueblo* (1973, TVM), which earned him an Emmy nomination, *The Missiles of October* (1974, TVM), which earned him a second Emmy nomination, *F. Scott Fitzgerald in Hollywood* (1976, TVM), *I Never Promised You a Rose Garden* (1977), *Absolution* (1978), *The Patricia Neal Story* (1981, TVM), for which he helmed the UK sequences (Anthony Harvey directed the U.S. sequences), *Monte Carlo* (1986, TV), *Middlemarch* (1994, TV), *Human Bomb* (1998, TVM) and *My Zinc Bed* (2008). He also helmed Hammer's remake of Hitchcock's *The Lady Vanishes* (1979), for which he inevitably received a number of critical brickbats. In 1997 he won a Tony award as best director for his Broadway revival of *A Doll's House*. **Hammer credits:** *The Lady Vanishes* (1979)

## Page, Lizabeth

Page played one of the harem girls in the Hammer comedy *I Only Arsked!* (1958). Her credits as a dancer include an episode of *Jack Hylton's Monday Show* (1958, TV). **Hammer credits:** *I Only Arsked!* (1958, as Harem girl [uncredited])

## Pagett, Nicola

Best known for playing Elizabeth Bellamy in the television series *Upstairs, Downstairs* (1971–1975, TV), this Egyptian born actress (1945–, real name Nicola Scott) has appeared in only a handful of films, among them Hammer's *The Viking Queen* (1967), in which she played Talia. Her other credits include *Ouch!* (1967), *Anne of the Thousand Days* (1969), *Oliver's Story* (1978), *Privates on Parade*

(1982) and *An Awfully Big Adventure* (1995). She also played the title role in the series *Anna Karenina* (1978, TV). Her many other TV appearances include episodes of *Gideon's Way* (1965–1966, TV), *The Caesars* (1968, TV), *A Woman of Substance* (1984, TV), *A Bit of a Do* (1989, TV) and *Up Rising* (2000, TV). **Hammer credits:** *The Viking Queen* (1967, as Talia)

## *Paid to Kill* see *Five Days*

## *Paint Me a Murder* see *Hammer House of Mystery and Suspense*

## Palance, Jack

A best supporting actor Oscar winner for his role as Curly in *City Slickers* (1991), this American actor (1919–2006, real name Volodymyr Palanyuk, aka Walter Palance and Jack Brazzo) began his film career in 1950 with *Panic in the Streets* following a period as a professional boxer (under the name of Jack Brazzo) and military experience during the war, during which he received severe burns to his face, resulting in reconstructive plastic surgery (he was also awarded the Purple Heart). In over one-hundred films, he is best remembered for playing Jack Wilson, the bad guy in *Shane* (1953). His other credits include *Sign of the Pagan* (1955), *The Professionals* (1966), *Monte Walsh* (1970), *Dracula* (1974, TVM), in which he played the title role, *Welcome to Blood City* (1977), *Hawk the Slayer* (1980), *Young Guns* (1988), *Batman* (1989), in which he played Carl Grissom, *City Slickers II: The Legend of Curly's Gold* (1994), this time as Duke Washburn, *Natural Born Killers* (1994), *Treasure Island* (1999), in which he played Long John Silver, and *Back When We Were Grown Ups* (2004, TVM). He also starred in Hammer's bomb disposal drama *Ten Seconds to Hell* (1959), which also featured his first wife (of two), Virginia Baker (1922–2003), to whom he was married between 1949 and 1968. Commented *Variety* of Palance's character in the film, "Jack Palance, self-styled leader of the unit, is a man of courage and conviction. But he's a moody individual who appears to be continually wrestling with inner problems." He also starred in such TV series as *The Greatest Show on Earth* (1963–1964, TV) and *Bronk* (1975–1976, TV), and guest starred in many more. His children (with Baker) are the actresses Holly Palance (1950–) and Brooke Palance (1952–), and the actor Cody Palance (1955–1998). **Hammer credits:** *Ten Seconds to Hell* (1959, as Eric Koertner)

## The Palladium Cellars

Situated in the cellars of the London Palladium theater, this Tussauds-style waxworks exhibition, produced by Michael Carreras through Presentations Unlimited, featured a number of Hammer exhibits, among them a full-scale wax effigy of Peter Cushing. Other film stars featured included Laurel and Hardy, John Wayne (as Rooster Cogburn), Harry Secombe (as Mr. Bumble) and Faye Dunaway (as Bonnie Parker). "The Palladium Cellars—London's key attraction," boasted the publicity. It also promised, "A journey into fun, fear and fantasy." The £1m enterprise was officially opened by Hollywood star Yul Brynner (then ap-

pearing at the Palladium in a revival of *The King and I*) on 15 May 1980. Commented Michael Carreras, who by this time had actually left Hammer, "What we have aimed at is a participation entertainment that will give the public quality visual and audio excitement, and value for money."[3] Sadly, the venue closed prematurely when its lease ran out.

## Palmer, Bert

Specializing in toothless types, this British comedy character (1900–1980) is best remembered for playing Bert Henshaw in the first season of the sitcom *Nearest and Dearest* (1968–1973, TV), a role he repeated for Hammer's 1973 big screen spin-off, and Uncle Stavely (catchphrase: "I heard that—pardon?") in *I Didn't Know You Cared* (1975–1979, TV). His film credits include *A Kind of Loving* (1962), *Smokescreen* (1964), *That's All We Need* (1971) and *The National Health* (1973), while his other TV appearances include episodes of *Out of This World* (1962, TV), *Softly Softly* (1966–1976, TV) and *Dawson's Weekly* (1975, TV). He was married to actress Lynn Carol (1914–1990) from 1934. **Hammer credits:** *Nearest and Dearest* (1973, as Bert Henshaw)

## Palmer, Bob

Palmer was one of Hammer's many electricians, working under the supervision of chief electrician Jack Curtis. His other credits include *Big Top* (1949). **Hammer credits include:** *The Curse of Frankenstein* (1957 [uncredited])

## Palmer, David

This British actor (1949–) played George in Hammer's *The Damned* (1963). His other credits include *Five Have a Mystery to Solve* (1964), plus episodes of *Compact* (1962–1965, TV) and *The Dickie Henderson Show* (1960–1968, TV). **Hammer credits:** *The Damned* (1963, as George)

## Palmer, Denys

Palmer devised the tribal routines seen in Hammer's *Slave Girls* (1968). He returned to choreograph the climactic sacrificial sequence for *The Witches* (1966), which was made after *Slave Girls*, but released first. His other credits include *Life Is a Circus* (1960) and *The Ghost Goes Gear* (1966), plus episodes of *Doctor in the House* (1969–1970, TV), *The Two Ronnies* (1971–1987, TV) and *Napoleon and Love* (1972, TV). **Hammer credits:** *Slave Girls* (1968), *The Witches* (1966)

## Palmer, June

This busty British actress and model (1940–2004, aka June Powers and Rachel Wells) had a minor supporting role in Hammer's *Taste the Blood of Dracula* (1970). Renowned for her prolific nude modeling work for Harrison Marks in the sixties, she also modeled for photographer and stuntman Arthur Howell (1920–2003), who not only discovered her, but became her second husband between 1993 and 2000. Her other film credits include *The Naked World of Harrison Marks* (1965), *The Nine Ages of Nakedness* (1969), *Games That Lovers Play* (1970), *It's the Only Way to Go* (1971), *Not Tonight, Darling* (1971) and *On the Game*

(1974). **Hammer credits:** *Taste the Blood of Dracula* (1970, as Redheaded prostitute [uncredited])

## Palmer, Maria

Long in America, this Austro-Hungarian actress (1917–1981, real name Maria Pichler) began her career on stage as a child, working with the director Max Reinhardt. She also appeared in the film *Rumpelstilzchen* (1923), under her real name. Following training at the Vienna Conservatory, she moved to American in 1938 and made her U.S. stage debut in 1942. In films there the same year with the short *Nostradamus and the Queen*, she went on to appear in *Mission to Moscow* (1943), *Strictly Dishonorable* (1951), *By the Light of the Silvery Moon* (1953) and *Outcasts of the City* (1958). She can also be seen in sequences shot specifically for the U.S. telecast of Hammer's *The Evil of Frankenstein* (1964), in which she appeared as the mother of the mute girl, here named Rena. Her other TV appearances include episodes of *Your Show Time* (1949, TV), *Hopalong Cassidy* (1952–1954, TV) and *Perry Mason* (1957–1966, TV). **Hammer credits:** *The Evil of Frankenstein* (1964, as Rena's mother)

## Palmer, Mollie

Palmer played supporting roles in two Hammer programers in 1950. Her other credits include *Good-Time Girl* (1948), *The Undefeated* (1949), *The Teckman Mystery* (1954) and *A Kid for Two Farthings* (1955). **Hammer credits:** *The Man in Black* (1950, as Elsie), *What the Butler Saw* (1950, as Maudie)

## Palmer, Nicholas

Mostly working in television, this British writer and producer (1937–1995) penned an episode of *Hammer House of Horror* (1980, TV). His other credits as a writer include episodes of *No Hiding Place* (1959–1967, TV), *New Scotland Yard* (1972–1974, TV), *Heartland* (1979–1980, TV) and *Unnatural Causes* (1986, TV), while his credits as a producer include *Fraud Squad* (1969–1970, TV), *Beasts* (1976, TV), of which he produced the whole series, *The Home Front* (1983, TV) and *Connie* (1985, TV). His occasional films as a producer include *All the Fun of the Fair* (1979), *Facelift* (1984) and *Gentry* (1987). **Hammer credits:** *Growing Pains* (1980, TV [episode of *Hammer House of Horror*])

## Paltenghi, David

This British actor, director and choreographer (1919–1961) helmed the Hammer featurette *Dick Turpin—Highwayman* (1956). His other directorial credits include *Orders Are Orders* (1954), *The Love Match* (1955), *Keep It Clean* (1956), *The Tyburn Case* (1957) and *Escapement* (1957), for the latter of which he directed the dream sequence (the main body of the film was directed by Montgomery Tully). His work as a choreographer includes *Stage Fright* (1950), *The Sword and the Rose* (1953), *Up to His Neck* (1954), *You Know What Sailors Are* (1954), *The Black Knight* (1954), in which he also appeared, *Dance Little Lady* (1954) and *Port Afrique* (1956), while his work as an actor includes appearances in *Sleeping Car to Trieste* (1948), *Hamlet* (1948), *The Queen of Spades* (1948), *Invita-

tion to the Dance* (1953), the 3D musical short *Harmony Lane* (1954) and *Battle of the River Plate* (1956). A principal dancer with Sadler's Wells from 1941 to 1947, he studied ballet with Marie Rambert and Anthony Tudor, and went on to dance for Tudor's London Ballet company in 1939 and—following its amalgamation with London Ballet—Ballet Rambert in 1940, for which he also created a number of dance pieces, among them *Prismatic Variations* and *Scherzi Della Sorte*. **Hammer credits:** *Dick Turpin—Highwayman* (1956)

## Panacoustic

This sound process was used to record two Hammer second features. **Hammer credits:** *The Black Widow* (1950), *The Lady Craved Excitement* (1950)

## Panamation

Presumably because the rights to Dynamation and its derivatives Super Dynamation and Dynarama belonged to Columbia, for whom he usually worked, effects wiz Ray Harryhausen came up with the effects process Panamation for his work on the Hammer epic *One Million Years B.C.* (1966). Like the other processes, however, the name was meaningless, being merely a promotional gimmick, somewhat akin to Gerry Anderson's Supermarionation. Given the subject matter of *One Million Years B.C.*, maybe Dinorama might have been a better moniker. **Hammer credits:** *One Million Years B.C.* (1966)

## Panavision

Along with CinemaScope, this widescreen system is perhaps the best known, thanks to its use in such high profile films *The Magnificent Seven* (1960), *Lawrence of Arabia* (1962), *Thunderball* (1965), *You Only Live Twice* (1967), *Chitty Chitty Bang Bang* (1968), *The Towering Inferno* (1974), *Star Wars* (1977), *Raiders of the Lost Ark* (1981), *Gandhi* (1982), *Titanic* (1997), *Die Another Day* (2002) and *Jupiter Ascending* (2015). Hammer also used the process to film *The Legend of the 7 Golden Vampires* (1974), but sadly too little was made of its framing possibilities thanks to a hurried schedule and lackluster handling. Rather better looking, thanks to the assured lensing of Douglas Slocombe, was the studio's use of the process in their remake of *The Lady Vanishes* (1979). Variations on the process, which was invented by Robert Gottschalk (who was also the president of the company), include Super Panavision, Panavision 70 and Super Panavision 70. The company, which now also provides camera equipment and lenses, has won many awards, plaques and citations for its various developments, including three Academy Awards of merit (bestowed in 1977, 1993 and 2002). **Hammer credits:** *The Legend of the 7 Golden Vampires*

(1974), *The Lady Vanishes* (1979), *Let Me In* (2010)

## Pannicelli, Frank

Based at Pinewood, this model maker and effects technician made the model dog used at the climax of Hammer's *The Hound of the Baskervilles* (1959). **Hammer credits:** *The Hound of the Baskervilles* (1959 [uncredited])

## Paper Dolls  see  *Journey to the Unknown*

Nanette Newman and Michael Tolan pose for the cameras during a break filming the *Paper Dolls* episode of *Journey to the Unknown* (1968) (Hammer/ABC/Twentieth Century–Fox).

## Parade of the Bands

GB, 1956, 28m, Eastmancolor, HammerScope, cert U

Released in the UK by Exclusive on 17 April 1956, *Parade of the Bands* was one of six musical featurettes made by Hammer during a lull in feature production at Bray. Filmed in Eastmancolor and CinemaScope at Elstree Studios, the film contains a succession of dance orchestras popular at the time. Like all the other shorts in this series, the proceedings were supervised by self-confessed jazz nut Michael Carreras. **Additional information:** An early title for the project seems to have been *Contrast in Rhythm*.

Production company: Hammer. Distributor: Exclusive (UK). Producer: Michael Carreras. Director: Michael Carreras. Camera operator: Len Harris. Focus puller: Harry Oakes [uncredited]. **Cast:** Malcolm Mitchell and his Orchestra, Cleo Laine, Johnny Dankworth and his Orchestra, Frank Weir and his Orchestra, Lisa Ashwood, Rusty Hurran, Freddy Randall and His Band, Eric Jupp and his Players, Francisco Cavez and his Latin-American Orchestra

## Paradine Productions

Owned by television broadcaster David Frost, this British production company was behind such productions as *The Rise and Rise of Michael Rimmer* (1970), *Charley One-Eye* (1973) and *The Slipper and the Rose* (1976). It was also set to make *Nessie* with Hammer in 1977, with Bryan Forbes (who had made *The Slipper and the Rose* and had been head of production at EMI during part of Hammer's tenure there) onboard as writer-director. Unfortunately, the project was cancelled when Columbia, which was providing the majority of the finance, pulled out of the proceedings. The company derived its name from Frost's middle name.

## Paramount

The history of Paramount Pictures can be traced back to 1914, when the company, formed by W.W. Hodkinson, distributed films for smaller production outfits. The same year, Paramount merged with Famous Players, a production company formed by the nickelodeon showman Adolph Zukor, and Lasky Productions, which had been formed by Jesse Lasky. This new multi-merger (known primarily as Famous Players Lasky) went on to make several notable silent productions, among them *The Sheik* (1921) and *The Ten Commandments* (1923). In the thirties and forties (by which time it was simply known as Paramount), its successes included *Trouble in Paradise* (1932), the Crosby-Hope-Lamour *Road* series (1940–1962) and *Going My Way* (1944), while the fifties saw such blockbusters as *The Greatest Show on Earth* (1952) and the remake of *The Ten Commandments* (1956). In the sixties the company was taken over by oil giant Gulf and Western, yet the hits kept coming, notable among them *Love Story* (1970), *The Godfather* (1972), *Chinatown* (1974), *Grease* (1978), *Saturday Night Fever* (1979), the *Star Trek* franchise (1979–), the *Indian Jones* series (1981–1989, 2008), *The Addams Family* (1991) and the multi-Oscar winning *Forrest Gump* (1994). More recent successes include *Mission: Impossible* (1996) and its sequels, *Titanic* (1997), which Paramount co-financed with Twentieth Century–Fox, *Lara Croft: Tomb Raider* (2001), *Shrek* (2001) and its sequels, *Interstellar* (2014), *Star Trek Beyond* (2016) and *Transformers: The Last Knight* (2017).

In the late fifties, when Hammer was enjoying its first major brush with success thanks to such box office hits as *The Quatermass Xperiment* (1955), *The Curse of Frankenstein* (1957) and *Dracula* (1958), a number of Hollywood majors began to take an interest in the English studio, investing in and distributing their films. Among the giants catching a ride on the Hammer bandwagon were Universal, Columbia, Warner Bros. and United Artists. Not wishing to miss out on the action, Paramount offered Hammer the remake rights to *The Man in Half Moon Street* (1944) in return for the worldwide distribution. Unfortunately, the resultant film, now titled *The Man Who Could Cheat Death* (1959), was one of Hammer's rare commercial and artistic disappointments of the period.

Of Paramount importance. Dramatic poster artwork for *The Man Who Could Cheat Death* (1959), which Paramount both invested in and distributed (Hammer/Cadogan/Paramount).

Consequently, it was over a decade before the two companies crossed paths again, when Paramount showed interest in a World War II drama scripted by Don Houghton titled *The Savage Jackboot*, but the project failed to materialize. Instead, Paramount financed *Captain Kronos—Vampire Hunter* (1974), which it also released in the U.S. It also handled the U.S. release of *Frankenstein and the Monster from Hell* (1974), putting it out on a double bill with *Captain Kronos*. **Hammer credits:** *The Man Who Could Cheat Death* (1959), *Captain Kronos—Vampire Hunter* (1974), *Frankenstein and the Monster from Hell* (1974)

## *Paranoiac*

GB, 1963, 80m, bw, HammerScope [2.35:1], RCA, cert X

Based upon the 1949 novel *Brat Farrar* by Josephine Tey, *Paranoiac* tells the story of Tony Ashby, a handsome young man who turns up at his family's country home many years after apparently drowning. Naturally, his brother Simon, sister Eleanor and aunt Harriet are somewhat suspicious of his arrival, especially given that a family fortune of some £600,000 is at stake. Indeed, Tony's reappearance triggers some surprising revelations, including an all too real skeleton in the closet.

Hammer bought the rights to *Brat Farrar* way back in 1954, and the project was originally announced for production in 1955, but it never materialized. It then disappeared for several years before being announced again, this time as part of the studio's 1958–1959 program. Tantalizingly, at this stage it was to have been filmed in Technicolor by director Joseph Losey, working from a script by Paul Dehn, with Dirk Bogarde penciled in to star. Unfortunately, Columbia went cold on the project, fearing it wouldn't be commercial enough. Consequently, it was put on the back burner yet again

until the success of *Psycho* (1960) and Hammer's own *Taste of Fear* (1961) prompted renewed interest in the thriller genre. However, by this time the property had been re-packaged. Out were Dehn, Losey and Bogarde, who were replaced by Jimmy Sangster, Freddie Francis and Oliver Reed respectively. The title had also been changed to the far more intriguing *Paranoiac*.

Like the studio's horror films, the script came in for a certain degree of criticism when submitted for approval to the BBFC, among the board's concerns being the story's strong hints of incest (Eleanor falls in love with Tony *before* realizing that he is an impostor, while Aunt Harriet seems to have more than maternal feelings for Simon). The use of the family chapel for the grim *denouement* also raised some eyebrows, given that the body of the real Tony is discovered incarcerated behind the organ pipes, where Simon hid him having murdered him as a boy. Once these concerns had been addressed by Jimmy Sangster, the film was okayed for production, and went on to the floor at Bray on 23 July 1962, making use of sets recycled from the studio's ill-fated remake of *The Old Dark House* (1963).

To helm the production, Hammer called upon cameraman-turned-director Freddie Francis, who had previously photographed *Never Take Sweets from a Stranger* (1960) for the studio. Francis had only recently turned to direction, having taken over (without credit) from Steve Sekley on *The Day of the Triffids* (1962). He'd also helmed the rather tame comedy *Two and Two Make Six* (1962). With *Paranoiac*, however, he would finally get to flex his stylistic muscles, investing the proceedings with a certain Hitchcockian flair, experimenting with lenses and camera angles, and making atmospheric use of light and shadow, so as to help accentuate the film's macabre storyline. Recalled Jimmy Sang-

**Alexander Davion and Janette Scott in a cliffhanging moment from *Paranoiac* (1963) (Hammer/ Rank/Universal International).**

ster, "Freddie was the perfect choice for directing *Paranoiac*. Camerawise he was a master at creating suspense. He could light a set so you would be scared as soon as it appeared on screen."[4]

Ably assisted by cameraman Arthur Grant, Francis delivered a brisk and efficient little thriller, ably performed by a well chosen cast, who turn what are basically little more than ciphers into believable characters, bringing to life what could have been, in other hands, a somewhat mechanically contrived

**A French poster for *Paranoiac* (1963) (Hammer/Rank/Universal International).**

compendium of twists and revelations. Particularly effective is Oliver Reed's performance as the unhinged Simon, which *Variety* described as "blending bits of spoiled brat and sneaky madman for a menacing portrayal." The same source also found that "Alexander Davion makes a fine baddie-turned-hero, thesping with ease and believability." Elsewhere, though, *Monthly Film Bulletin* found the results to be "Bizarre, far-fetched and tasteless." However, *Films and Filming* could barely contain its enthusiasm, particularly regarding the film's direction: "It can go without saying that any film directed by [Freddie] Francis is bound to be eye-catching, but the real pleasure of *Paranoiac*, his best to date, lies in the realization that all the time he spent, from mid-teens to mid-forties, going through the traditional film-making mill that can so easily grind enthusiasts into conformity, has not undermined an individuality which gives this current little effort its lively zing."

Recalled Jimmy Sangster of his screenplay, "I tried to keep as much of the Josephine Tey material in the screenplay as possible but, as usual, budgetary restrictions forced us to drop the showjumping sequences which were a major part of the novel. So basically we ended up with the main framework, which was really excellent, embellished with whatever 'nasties' I could come up with."[5]

Principal photography on the production was completed on 31 August 1962, following which the film was cut and scored by James Needs and Elisabeth Lutyens respectively. However, it wasn't trade shown

in the UK until 7 September 1963 at Hammer House, by which time it had already been released in America care of Universal International on 15 May 1963. In fact UK audiences had to wait until 26 January 1964 to see it, when Rank sent it out as the lower half of a double bill top-lining Hammer's classy vampire yarn *The Kiss of the Vampire* (1963), with which it had also shared its American release. Revealed the publicity pack sent out to cinema managers, "There are no vampires, werewolves or bug-eyed monsters in the film. There is, however, a human monster in the shape of Simon Ashby (Oliver Reed), who will stop at nothing, not even cold-blooded murder, to get his way.... He is, in fact, the paranoiac of the title." With a completely straight face, it then went on to advise, "Do not reveal the ending." **Additional notes:** The film carries a 1962 copyright. A piece of piano music composed by James Bernard for *The Kiss of the Vampire* can be heard playing on a record player in an early scene between Simon and Aunt Harriet. The film also features a Y-shaped staircase also seen in *The Kiss of the Vampire* and *The Old Dark House* (1963), making one wonder whether audiences seeing the *Paranoiac*/*Kiss* double bill noticed these crossovers. The Ashby tomb is actually Dracula's sarcophagus from *Dracula* (1958). The story was later filmed as a six-part television series in 1986 under the original title *Brat Farrar*. Some posters bestow an exclamation mark upon the title: *Paranoiac!*

Production company: Hammer. Distributors: Rank (UK), Universal International (U.S.). Producer: Anthony Hinds. Associate producer: Basil Keys. Director: Freddie Francis. Screenplay: Jimmy Sangster, based upon the novel *Brat Farrar* by Josephine Tey. Cinematographer: Arthur Grant. Music: Elisabeth Lutyens. Music director: John Hollingsworth. Supervising editor: James Needs. Assistant editors: Chris Barnes [uncredited], Alan Willis [uncredited]. Production designer: Bernard Robinson. Art director: Don Mingaye. Assistant art director: Ken Ryan [uncredited]. Costumes: Molly Arbuthnot, Rosemary Burrows. Make-up: Roy Ashton, Richard Mills (assistant [uncredited]). Hair: Frieda Steiger. Special effects: Les Bowie. Special effects assistants: Ian Scoones [uncredited], Kit West [uncredited]. Assistant director: Ross MacKenzie. Second assistant directors: Hugh Harlow [uncredited], Joe Marks [uncredited]. Third assistant director: Ray Corbett [uncredited]. Production manager: John Draper [uncredited]. Construction manager: Arthur Banks [uncredited]. Master carpenter: Charles Davis [uncredited]. Master plasterer: Stan Banks [uncredited]. Master painter: Lawrence Wrenn [uncredited]. Master electrician: Jack Curtis [uncredited]. Master rigger: Ronald Lenoir [uncredited]. Studio manager: Arthur Kelly [uncredited]. Camera operator: Moray Grant. Focus pullers: David Osborne [uncredited], Robin Higginson [uncredited]. Camera grip: Albert Cowlard [uncredited]. Camera loader/clapperboy: Bob Jordan [both uncredited]. Camera maintenance: John Kerley [uncredited]. Sound: Ken Rawkins. Sound editor: James Groom. Sound transfer operator: Al Thorne [uncredited]. Boom operator: Ken Nightingall [uncredited]. Boom assistant: R.A. Mingaye [uncredited]. Sound maintenance: Charles Bouvet [uncredited]. Transcription: H.C. Allen [uncredited]. Props: Tommy Money [uncredited]. Floor props chargehand: W. Smith [uncredited]. Scenic artist: Burt Evans [uncredited]. Electrical chargehands: George Robinson [uncredited], Vic Hemmings [uncredited]. Props buyer: Eric Hillier [uncredited]. Continuity: Pauline Wise. Production secretary: Maureen White [uncredited]. Stills: Curtis Reeks [uncredited]. Publicity: Dennison Thornton [uncredited], Brian Doyle [uncredited]. Drivers: Coco Epps [uncredited], Laurie Martin [uncredited]. Laboratory: Denham Studios [uncredited]. **Cast:** Janette Scott (Eleanor Ashby), Oliver Reed (Simon Ashby), Alexander Davion (Tony Ashby), Liliane Brousse (Francoise), Sheila Burrell (Aunt Harriet), John Bonney (Keith Kossett), Maurice Denham (John Kossett), John Stuart (Williams), Harold Lang (Man at bar), Colin Tapley (Vicar [uncredited]), Sydney Bromley (Tramp [uncredited]), Laurie Leigh (First woman [uncredited]), Marianne Stone (Second woman [uncredited]), Jack Taylor (Sailor [uncredited]), Fred Peck (Man in bar [uncredited]). **DVD availability:** Universal (R1 U.S. NTSC), as part of the *Hammer Horror Series* box set, which also contains *The Brides of Dracula* (1960), *The Curse of the Werewolf* (1961), *The Phantom of the Opera* (1962), *The Kiss of the Vampire* (1963), *Captain Clegg* (1962), *Nightmare* (1964) and *The Evil of Frankenstein* (1964); Eureka Entertainment (R2 UK PAL). **Blu-ray availability:** Eureka Entertainment (B/2), extras include a trailer and stills gallery

## Pardo, Sally

Also known as Sally Hyman (under which name she also worked for Hammer), Pardo was a production secretary on several films for the studio in the early seventies. Her other credits in this capacity include *And Now for Something Completely Different* (1971), *The Fiend* (1971), *Rentadick* (1972), *Bartleby* (1972) and *Sword of the Valiant* (1984). She also worked as a production assistant on *Yellow Submarine* (1968), *The Hiding Place* (1975), *Heaven's Gate* (1980), *Ivanhoe* (1982, TVM) and *Superman III* (1983), plus episodes of *Out* (1978, TV) and *Quatermass* (1979, TV). Meanwhile, her credits as a production manager take in *The Girl in a Swing* (1988), while her work as a production co-ordinator includes *The Bourne Identity* (1988, TVM), *Air America* (1990) and *Cyborg Cop* (1993). She trained as a journalist and went on to form her own media company in the nineties. **Hammer credits:** *Crescendo* (1970 [as Sally Pardo, uncredited]), *Blood from the Mummy's Tomb* (1971 [as Sally Hyman, uncredited]), *Love Thy Neighbour* (1973 [as Sally Pardo, uncredited]), *Man at the Top* (1973 [as Sally Pardo, uncredited]), *The Satanic Rites of Dracula* (1974 [as Sally Pardo, uncredited])

## Pardoe, Peter

Pardoe (1935–2011, sometimes Pardo) operated the boom for the Hammer swashbuckler *The Crimson Blade* (1963). His other credits as a boom operator include *Incense for the Damned* (1970), while his work as a sound recordist includes *Nobody Ordered Love* (1972), *Claudia* (1985) and episodes of *Dick Turpin* (1979–1982, TV). He also worked as the sound mixer on *Biggles* (1986). **Hammer credits:** *The Scarlet Blade* (1963 [uncredited])

## Parély, Mila

This French actress (1917–2012, real name Olga Colette Peszynsky) played the role of Helen Pascal in the Hammer low budgeter *Blood Orange* (1953). She began her film career in 1933 with *Baby*. Her other credits include such classics as *La Regle du Jeu* (1939), *Les anges du péché* (1943) and *La Belle et la Bete* (1946). Married twice, her husbands were actor Jean Marais (1913–1998, real name Jean Alfred Villain-Marais) from 1944 to 1946, and the racing driver Thomas Alastair Sutherland Ogilvy Mathieson (1908–1991, aka Taso) from 1947. **Hammer credits:** *Blood Orange* (1953, as Helen Pascal)

## Parfitt, Judy

Adept at snobbish and superior roles, this admired British character actress (1935–) has spent the majority of her career on stage, beginning in 1954 following training at RADA. Her occasional film roles include *Hamlet* (1969), *Galileo* (1974), *The Chain* (1984), *Maurice* (1987), *Diamond Skulls* (1989), *Wilde* (1997), *Girl with a Pearl Earring* (2003), which earned her a BAFTA nomination for best supporting actress, and *The Moth Diaries* (2011). She is also known to television audiences through her appearances in such series as *Shoulder to Shoulder* (1974, TV), *Jewel in the Crown* (1984, TV), in which she had one of her best roles as the spiteful Mildred Layton (earning herself a best actress BAFTA nomination in the process), *The Charmer* (1987, TV), *The Charmings* (1987–1988, TV), *The Long Firm* (2004, TV), *Little Dorrit* (2008, TV) and *Call the Midwife* (2012–, TV), in which she plays Sister Monica Joan. She also appeared in *Do Me a Favor and Kill Me*, an episode of Hammer's *Journey to the Unknown* (1968, TV), which also appeared in the compendium film *Journey to Murder* (1972, TVM). Her husband, from 1963, was actor Tony Steedman (1927–2001). **Hammer credits:** *Do Me a Favor and Kill Me* (1968, TV [episode of *Journey to the Unknown*], as Faith Wheeler), *Journey to Murder* (1972, as Faith Wheeler)

## Pariss, Andrew

Pariss can be seen in a minor role in an episode of *Hammer House of Horror* (1980, TV), in which he plays William Tell's son in an apple commercial. **Hammer credits:** *Charlie Boy* (1980, TV [episode of *Hammer House of Horror*], as Boy)

## Parke, Macdonald

Long in Britain, this Canadian character actor (1891–1960) played the judge in Hammer's *Never Take Sweets from a Stranger* (1960), which proved to be his last film role. His other credits include *Shipyard Sally* (1939), *Candlelight in Algeria* (1943), *Yellow Canary* (1943), *Teheran* (1948), *I Was Monty's Double* (1958) and *The Battle of the Sexes* (1960), plus episodes of *Douglas Fairbanks, Jr. Presents* (1953–1957, TV) and *The New Adventures of Martin Kane* (1957, TV). **Hammer credits:** *Never Take Sweets from a Stranger* (1960, as Judge)

## Parke, Nurse Yvonne

During the filming of dangerous stunts, Hammer always had a nurse on standby. During the filming of Captain "Jock" Easton's fiery death plunge through a skylight at the climax of *The Curse of Frankenstein* (1957), this task fell to Nurse Parke. **Hammer credits:** *The Curse of Frankenstein* (1957 [uncredited])

## Parker, Alan

This British composer and musician (1944–) played the electric guitar on the soundtrack for Hammer's *Dracula A.D. 1972* (1972). He has played with such groups as Blue Mink and Ugly Custard. His albums include *Afro Rock* (1973), *The Rock Machine* (1974) and *Freedom Road* (1974), for which he also provided tracks. His own film and TV credits (either as composer, conductor, arranger or musician) include *The Adventures of Sir Prancelot* (1972, TV), *Minder* (1979–1994, TV), *One Summer* (1983, TV), *Jaws 3-D* (1983), *The Phoenix and the Magic Carpet* (1995) and *Alex Rider: Stormbreaker* (2006). **Hammer credits:** *Dracula A.D. 1972* (1972)

## Parker, Charles

Working in British films from the early forties, this respected Canadian make-up artist (1910–1977) headed the make-up department at MGM's British studios in the fifties. His countless credits include *The New Lot* (1943), *Under Capricorn* (1949), *Edward, My Son* (1949), *Ivanhoe* (1952), *Knights of the Round Table* (1953), *Beau Brummell* (1954), *Ben-Hur* (1959), *Lawrence of Arabia* (1962), *Zulu* (1964), *Ryan's Daughter* (1970), *The Ruling Class* (1970), *The Devils* (1971), *Murder on the Orient Express* (1974) and *Star Wars* (1977). He also worked on the Hammer potboiler *The Viking Queen* (1967). **Hammer credits:** *The Viking Queen* (1967)

## Parker, Clifton

Following experience as a piano teacher and copyist, and the composition of several classical pieces which had come to the attention of the music director Muir Mathieson, this British composer (1905–1989, full name Edward John Clifton Parker) began to score documentaries in 1942, among them *Battle Is Our Business* (1942), *Western Approaches* (1944) and *Children on Trial* (1946). Following uncredited contributions to *Unpublished Story* (1942) and *In Which We Serve* (1942), he also began scoring fictional films with *Schweik's New Adventures* (1943) and *Yellow Canary* (1943), which led to many further credits, among them *Johnny Frenchman* (1945), *The Blue Lagoon* (1949), *Night of the Demon* (1957), *Sink the Bismarck!* (1960), *The Hellfire Club* (1960) and *The Informers* (1963). He also continued to score documentaries, including several for BTF (British Transport Films), among them *Ocean Terminal* (1952) and *Blue Pullman* (1960), as well as for the stage (*The Silver Curlew* [1950] and *Penny Plain* [1952]) and radio (*The Passing of Crab Village* [1950]).

In 1961, he was invited by John Hollingsworth

to score the Hammer thriller *Taste of Fear* (1961), for which he penned an effectively orchestrated score featuring a piano motif by way of reflecting the protagonists' attempts to drive a young heiress mad by thinking she is hearing music played by a locked piano. Parker eventually quit film and television scoring over royalty issues. His second wife was the ballet dancer Yoma Sasburg (real name Johanna Margaretha Sasburg), whom he married in 1943. His daughter is the writer Julia Stoneham (1933–, real name Julia Clifton Parker). **Hammer credits:** *Taste of Fear* (1961)

### Parker, Graham

British born Parker (1930–1992) worked as the assistant art director on eight episodes of Hammer's *Journey to the Unknown* (1968, TV). Of these, *The Indian Spirit Guide* also appeared in the compendium film *Journey to Midnight* (1968, TVM), *The New People* appeared in the compendium film *Journey into Darkness* (1968, TVM), *The Last Visitor* appeared in the compendium film *Journey to the Unknown* (1969, TVM), and *The Killing Bottle* appeared in the compendium film *Journey to Murder* (1972, TVM). His other credits as an assistant art director include *Connecting Rooms* (1969) and *The McKenzie Break* (1970). **Hammer credits:** *The Killing Bottle* (1968, TV [episode of *Journey to the Unknown*]), *The Indian Spirit Guide* (1968, TV [episode of *Journey to the Unknown*]), *Miss Belle* (1968, TV [episode of *Journey to the Unknown*]), *The Last Visitor* (1968, TV [episode of *Journey to the Unknown*]), *The New People* (1968, TV [episode of *Journey to the Unknown*]), *Somewhere in a Crowd* (1968, TV [episode of *Journey to the Unknown*]), *Girl of My Dreams* (1968, TV [episode of *Journey to the Unknown*]), *The Beckoning Fair One* (1968, TV [episode of *Journey to the Unknown*]), *Journey into Darkness* (1968, TVM), *Journey to Midnight* (1968, TVM), *Journey to the Unknown* (1969, TVM), *Journey to Murder* (1972, TVM)

### Parker, Mary

This British supporting actress (1930–) can be seen in the role of Mrs. Zeissman in the Hammer thriller *Third Party Risk* (1955). Her other credits include *You Lucky People* (1955) and *The Hostage* (1956), plus episodes of *Douglas Fairbanks, Jr. Presents* (1953–1957, TV) and *Saber of London* (1954–1960, TV). **Hammer credits:** *Third Party Risk* (1955, as Mrs. Zeissman)

### Parker, Mibs

This hair stylist worked on seven episodes of Hammer's *Journey to the Unknown* (1968, TV). Of these, *The Indian Spirit Guide* also appeared in the compendium film *Journey to Midnight* (1968, TVM), *The New People* appeared in the compendium film *Journey into Darkness* (1968, TVM), *The Last Visitor* appeared in the compendium film *Journey to the Unknown* (1969, TVM), and both *The Killing Bottle* and *Do Me a Favor and Kill Me* appeared in the compendium film *Journey to Murder* (1972, TVM). Her other credits include *From Beyond the Grave* (1974) and *The Great McGonagall* (1975), plus episodes of *Here Come the Double Deckers!* (1970, TV) and *Jason King* (1971–

1972, TV). She also worked as an assistant hair stylist on *2001: A Space Odyssey* (1968). **Hammer credits:** *The Indian Spirit Guide* (1968, TV [episode of *Journey to the Unknown*]), *The Killing Bottle* (1968, TV [episode of *Journey to the Unknown*]), *The Last Visitor* (1968, TV [episode of *Journey to the Unknown*]), *The New People* (1968, TV [episode of *Journey to the Unknown*]), *Somewhere in a Crowd* (1968, TV [episode of *Journey to the Unknown*]), *Do Me a Favor and Kill Me* (1968, TV [episode of *Journey to the Unknown*]), *Girl of My Dreams* (1968, TV [episode of *Journey to the Unknown*]), *The Beckoning Fair One* (1968, TV [episode of *Journey to the Unknown*]), *Journey to Midnight* (1968, TVM), *Journey into Darkness* (1968, TVM), *Journey to the Unknown* (1969, TVM), *Journey to Murder* (1972, TVM)

### Parkes, Clifford

Working as a production manager, Parkes supervised the making of the Hammer comedy *Don't Panic Chaps* (1959), which was filmed at Walton Studios and on location on Chobham Common. His other credits as a production manager/supervisor include *Hello London* (1958), *Catacombs* (1965), *A Funny Thing Happened on the Way to the Forum* (1966), *Funeral in Berlin* (1966), *Fathom* (1967), *Schizo* (1976) and *Claudia* (1985), plus several more films for Hammer, for whom he also produced *A Challenge for Robin Hood* (1967). His other credits as an associate producer include *A High Wind in Jamaica* (1965), *The Best House in London* (1969), *Crooks and Coronets* (1969), *Cry of the Banshee* (1970) and *Murders in the Rue Morgue* (1971). **Hammer credits:** *Don't Panic Chaps* (1959, production manager), *Never Take Sweets from a Stranger* (1960, production manager), *The Two Faces of Dr. Jekyll* (1960, production manager), *Visa to Canton* (1960, production manager), *The Curse of the Werewolf* (1961, production manager), *Watch It, Sailor!* (1961, production manager), *The Terror of the Tongs* (1961, production manager), *Cash on Demand* (1961, production manager), *The Phantom of the Opera* (1962, production manager), *The Pirates of Blood River* (1962, production manager), *The Scarlet Blade* (1963, production manager), *A Challenge for Robin Hood* (1967, producer)

### Parkes, Timothy

Parkes had a minor supporting role in *The Madison Equation* (1968, TV [episode of *Journey to the Unknown*]). His other credits include *The Blue Max* (1966), *Suburban Wives* (1971) and *Commuter Husbands* (1973), plus episodes of *Z Cars* (1962–1978, TV) and *The Persuaders!* (1971–1972, TV). **Hammer credits:** *The Madison Equation* (1968, TV [episode of *Journey to the Unknown*], as Fire officer)

### Parkhouse, Charles

This British sound technician (1907–1982) worked as the sound recordist on the "unofficial" Hammer second feature *Jack of Diamonds* (1949). His other credits include *The Turners of Prospect Road* (1947), *The Monkey's Paw* (1948), *Down Among the Z Men* (1952) and *The Eternal Question* (1956). **Hammer credits:** *Jack of Diamonds* (1949)

### Parmentier, Richard

In Britain from 1974, this American actor (1946–2013, real name Richard La Parmentier) can be seen in a supporting role in *Paint Me a Murder* (1984, TVM [episode of *Hammer House of Mystery and Suspense*]). His other credits include *Stardust* (1974), *Rollerball* (1975), *Star Wars* (1977), *Superman II* (1980), *Octopussy* (1983), *Who Framed Roger Rabbit* (1988) and *The Berlin Conspiracy* (1992), plus episodes of *Space: 1999* (1975–1977, TV), *Lillie* (1978, TV), *Reilly: Ace of Spies* (1983, TV) and *Capital City* (1989–1990, TV). Also a writer, his credits include episodes of *Boon* (1986–1992, TV) and *Love Hurts* (1992–1994, TV). His second wife was actress Sarah Douglas (1952–), to whom he was married between 1981 and 1984. **Hammer credits:** *Paint Me a Murder* (1984, TVM [episode of *Hammer House of Mystery and Suspense*], as Kates)

### Parnell, Jack

This noted British band leader (with the Jack Parnell Orchestra), conductor and drummer (1923–2010, real name John Russell Parnell) provided the "specialty numbers" for Hammer's *Stolen Face* (1952). Best known for his work as a television conductor, his many credits include contributions to such shows and specials as *Cliff!* (1961, TV), *Frank Ifield Sings* (1965, TV), *It Must Be Dusty* (1968, TV), *This Is Tom Jones* (1969, TV), *Another Evening with Burt Bacharach* (1970, TV), *Barbra Streisand and Other Musical Instruments* (1973), which won him two Emmys, and *The Muppet Show* (1976–1981, TV). Also a composer, he provided music for episodes of such series as *Love Story* (1963–1974, TV), *Two in Clover* (1969–1970, TV) and *Father Brown* (1974, TV). His uncle was the television producer Val Parnell (1894–1972, full name Valentine Charles Parnell) and his grandfather the stage ventriloquist Fred Russell (1862–1957, real name Thomas Frederick Parnell). His son is drummer Ric Parnell (1951–, real name Richard J. Parnell). **Hammer credits:** *Stolen Face* (1952)

### Parnell, Reg

This respected British racing driver (1911–1964) did some track work for the Hammer drama *Mask of Dust* (1954). Racing from 1935, he took part in the first Formula One World Championship Grand Prix at Silverstone in 1950, and went on to win the BRDC Daily Express International Trophy in 1951. He also managed several racing teams, among them the Aston Martin team. **Hammer credits:** *Mask of Dust* (1954, as Himself)

### Parr, Bobby

This British actor (1942–, real name Robert Parrin) had a minor supporting role in Hammer's *Dr. Jekyll and Sister Hyde* (1971). His other credits include *Groupie Girl* (1970), *The Land That Time Forgot* (1975), *Arabian Adventure* (1979) and *Robin Hood: Prince of Thieves* (1991), plus episodes of *Love Story* (1963–1974, TV) and *Adam Adamant Lives!* (1966–1967, TV). **Hammer credits:** *Dr. Jekyll and Sister Hyde* (1971, as Young apprentice)

### Parry, Ken

Much on television in supporting roles, this

British comedy actor (1930–2007) appeared in Hammer's *That's Your Funeral* (1973) as a porter, sharing a few quips with Michael Ripper. His other film credits include *Friends and Neighbours* (1959), *Just for Fun* (1963), *The Taming of the Shrew* (1967), *Otley* (1968), *Lisztomania* (1975), *Lifeforce* (1985) and *The Rainbow Thief* (1990). His many TV credits include episodes of everything from *Tales from Dickens* (1958–1959, TV) to *Oliver Twist* (1999, TV), via *The Avengers* (1961–1969, TV) and *Filthy Rich and Catflap* (1987, TV). Also on stage, especially in Shakespeare. **Hammer credits:** *That's Your Funeral* (1973, as Porter)

### Parsons, Alibe

Long in Britain, American born Parsons (1945–) can be seen as Momma Rose, the proprietress of an illegal gambling den in *Mark of the Devil* (1984, TVM [episode of *Hammer House of Mystery and Suspense*]). Her many other TV credits include episodes of *Gangster* (1976–1978, TV), *Lovejoy* (1986–1994, TV) and *Casualty* (1986–, TV). Her film credits include *Game for Vultures* (1979), *The Bitch* (1979), *The Sender* (1982), *Aliens* (1986), *Waz* (2007) and *Incendiary* (2008). **Hammer credits:** *Mark of the Devil* (1984, TVM [episode of *Hammer House of Mystery and Suspense*], as Momma Rose)

### Partleton, Bill (William)

This British make-up artist (1911–1975, sometimes W.T. Partleton, William Partleton or Billy Partleton) worked on five episodes of Hammer's *Journey to the Unknown* (1968, TV), of which *The Indian Spirit Guide* also appeared in the compendium film *Journey to Midnight* (1968, TVM), *The New People* appeared in the compendium film *Journey into Darkness* (1968, TVM), and *Do Me a Favor and Kill Me* appeared in the compendium film *Journey to Murder* (1972, TVM). His many other credits include *Cottage to Let* (1941), *The Wicked Lady* (1945), *Quartet* (1948), *Trio* (1950), *Encore* (1951), *Hell Drivers* (1957), *Peeping Tom* (1960), *Carry On Spying* (1964), *Those Magnificent Men in Their Flying Machines* (1965), *Arabesque* (1966), *David Copperfield* (1970, TVM), *The Beast in the Cellar* (1970), *Jane Eyre* (1970, TVM) and *The Wicker Man* (1973), plus an episode of *The Avengers* (1961–1969, TV). He also worked on the Hammer feature, *Fear in the Night* (1972). His brother was the make-up artist George Partleton (1909–1992), who also worked on several films for Hammer as well as an episode of *Journey to the Unknown*. **Hammer credits:** *The Indian Spirit Guide* (1968, TV [episode of *Journey to the Unknown*]), *The New People* (1968, TV [episode of *Journey to the Unknown*]), *Do Me a Favor and Kill Me* (1968, TV [episode of *Journey to the Unknown*]), *Girl of My Dreams* (1968, TV [episode of *Journey to the Unknown*]), *One on an Island* (1968, TV [episode of *Journey to the Unknown*]), *Journey into Darkness* (1968, TVM), *Journey to Midnight* (1968, TVM), *Journey to Murder* (1972, TVM), *Fear in the Night* (1972)

### Partleton, George

British born Partleton (1909–1992) worked as the make-up artist on Hammer's *The Witches*

(1966), which led to further assignments with the company, among them *The Mummy's Shroud* (1967), for which he based his make-up for the title character on an actual Mummy found in the British Museum. His other credits include *Journey Together* (1946), *The Wooden Horse* (1950), *The Sound Barrier* (1952), *The Belles of St. Trinian's* (1954), *Hobson's Choice* (1954), *The Amorous Prawn* (1962), *Lolita* (1962), *The Masque of the Red Death* (1964), *The Penthouse* (1967), *The File of the Golden Goose* (1969), *Get Carter* (1971), *A Clockwork Orange* (1971), *Schizo* (1976) and *Pop Pirates* (1984). He also worked on an episode of Hammer's *Journey to the Unknown* (1968, TV) titled *The Killing Bottle*, which also appeared in the compendium film *Journey to Murder* (1972, TVM). His brother was the make-up artist Bill Partleton (1911–1975), who also worked on *Journey to the Unknown* (one of his five episodes, *Do Me a Favor and Kill Me* [1968, TV], also appeared in the compendium film *Journey to Murder*). **Hammer credits:** *The Witches* (1966), *Frankenstein Created Woman* (1967), *The Mummy's Shroud* (1967), *The Anniversary* (1968), *The Lost Continent* (1968), *The Killing Bottle* (1968, TV [episode of *Journey to the Unknown*]), *Journey to Murder* (1972, TVM)

### Pasco, Richard

On stage from 1943, and in films and on television from the mid-fifties, this respected British character actor (1926–2014) is best known for his

work in such television series as *Sorrell and Son* (1984, TV) and *Drummonds* (1985, TV). His film credits include *Kill Me Tomorrow* (1957), *Room at the Top* (1958), *The Watcher in the Woods* (1980) and *Mrs. Brown* (1997). He also appeared in a number of films for Hammer, beginning with the wartime drama *Yesterday's Enemy* (1959), although he is perhaps best remembered by fans for succumbing to the Gorgon's gaze at the climax of *The Gorgon* (1964). He was also considered for the role of Henry Beddows in Hammer's *To the Devil a Daughter* (1976). His other TV appearances include episodes of *ITV Play of the Week* (1955–1968, TV), in which he made an impact playing the lead Jimmy Porter in a production of *Look Back in Anger* (1956, TV), *The Adventures of Robin Hood* (1955–1960, TV), *The Three Musketeers* (1966, TV), *Wagner* (1983, TV) and *Hetty Wainthropp Investigates* (1996–1998, TV). Married twice, Pasco's first wife was actress Greta Watson (1931–2000), to whom he was married between 1956 and 1964; his second wife is actress Barbara Leigh-Hunt (1935–), whom he married in 1967. **Hammer credits:** *Yesterday's Enemy* (1959, as Lieutenant Hastings), *Sword of Sherwood Forest* (1960, as Earl of Newark), *The Gorgon* (1964, as Paul Heitz), *Rasputin—The Mad Monk* (1966, as Dr. Boris Zargo)

### Paskin, Stan

This British supporting actor (1891–1947, full name Frank Stanley Paskin) appeared as a taxi

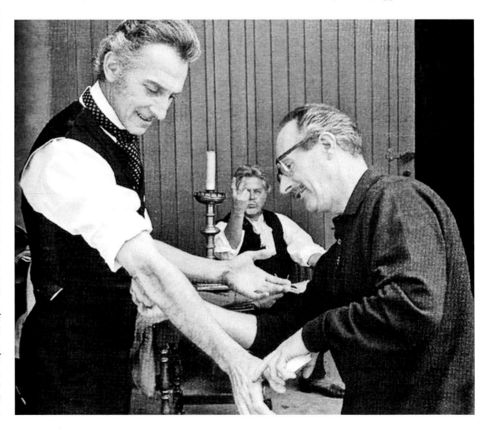

Peter Cushing (left) gets a touch-up from make-up man George Partleton (right) between takes on *Frankenstein Created Woman* (1967). Thorley Walters (center) lets his feelings be known (Hammer/Seven Arts/Associated British Picture Corporation/Warner Pathé Distributors/Twentieth Century–Fox/Studio Canal).

driver in Hammer's first post-war production, *Crime Reporter* (1947). He also popped up in a bit part in *River Patrol* (1948). His other credits include *Pal O'Mine* (1936), *Let the People Sing* (1942), *Old Mother Riley Detective* (1943), *Millions Like Us* (1943), *Give Me the Stars* (1945) and *That's Odd* (1960). **Hammer credits:** *Crime Reporter* (1947, as Taxi driver), *River Patrol* (1948, unnamed role)

### Passmore, Henry Fraser

One of Hammer's first managing directors, British born Passmore (1905–1987) also produced the company's first four features (sometimes credited as production supervisor), beginning with the comedy *The Public Life of Henry the Ninth* in 1935. Perhaps the most notable of these early productions was the Paul Robeson musical *Song of Freedom* (1936). Passmore's other films as a producer include another Paul Robeson vehicle, *Big Fella* (1937), plus *The Last Adventurers* (1937), *Love in Waiting* (1948), *The Delavine Affair* (1954), *Conscience Bay* (1960) and *The Missing Note* (1961). He also worked as a production manager/supervisor on the serial *The Voyage of Peter Joe* (1946) and such Boulting Brothers productions as *Lucky Jim* (1957), *Brothers in Law* (1957), *Happy Is the Bride* (1958) and *Carlton-Browne of the F.O.* (1959). **Hammer credits:** *The Public Life of Henry the Ninth* (1935), *The Mystery of the Mary Celeste* (1935), *Song of Freedom* (1936), *Sporting Love* (1936)

### *Passport to China* see *Visa to Canton*

### Pastell, George

Best remembered for playing the oily Mehemet Akhir (listed as Mehemet Bey in the credits) in Hammer's lavish remake of *The Mummy* (1959), this character actor (1923–1976, real name Nino Pastellides) was frequently called upon to play villains from India and the Middle East. However, as Jimmy Sangster recalled, "He wasn't Indian, Egyptian or French, but he always looked exactly right."[6] Actually, he had been born in Cyprus. In films from 1949 with *Adam and Evelyn*, Pastell's many other films include *Moulin Rouge* (1952), *The Angry Hills* (1959), *From Russia with Love* (1963), *Impact* (1963), *A Man Could Get Killed* (1966), *Licensed to Kill* (1965) and *The Magus* (1968). He also popped up in three more Hammer films, including another of the studio's Mummy sagas, *The Curse of the Mummy's Tomb* (1964), in which he played the unfortunate Hashmi Bey, who finds himself crushed underfoot by the Mummy. Note that Pastell also dubbed André Morell's voice in Hammer's *She* (1965). His many TV appearances include episodes of *The Third Man* (1959–1965, TV), *Maigret* (1960–1963, TV), *Softly Softly* (1966–1976, TV) and *Department S* (1969–1970, TV). **Hammer credits:** *The Gambler and the Lady* (1953, as Jaco Spina), *The Mummy* (1959, as Mehemet Akhir/Bey), *The Stranglers of Bombay* (1959, as High Priest), *Maniac* (1963, as Inspector Etienne), *The Curse of the Mummy's Tomb* (1964, as Hashmi Bey), *She* (1965, as voice of André Morell [uncredited])

### Patch, Wally

This prolific British supporting actor (1888–1970, real name Walter Vinicombe) appeared in well over two-hundred shorts and features from 1927 onwards, beginning with *Boadicea*, prior to which he had been something of a Jack-of-all-trades, working as bookie, sandblaster and boxing promoter, after which he turned his attention to the music halls. Specializing in down-to-earth Cockney types, his many appearances include *The Luck of the Navy* (1927), *The Private Life of Henry VIII* (1933), *The Lady Vanishes* (1938), *The Life and Death of Colonel Blimp* (1943), *Brighton Rock* (1947), *I'm All Right Jack* (1959), *Sparrows Can't Sing* (1962) and *Poor Cow* (1967). He also appeared in Hammer's very first production, *The Public Life of Henry the Ninth* (1935), in which he played a pub landlord. He also played a small role in the 1948 featurette *River Patrol*, one of Hammer's early post-war program fillers. Sadly, he didn't feature in any of the studio's later horror films—which is curious, given Hammer's predilection for Cockney types. Patch's many TV appearances include episodes of *Douglas Fairbanks, Jr. Presents* (1953–1957, TV), *Z Cars* (1962–1978, TV) and *The Wednesday Play* (1964–1970, TV), of which he can be seen in *Up the Junction* (1965, TV) and *Cathy Come Home* (1966, TV). **Hammer credits:** *The Public Life of Henry the Ninth* (1935, as Landlord), *River Patrol* (1948, The Guy)

### Paterson, Paul

This British composer (1947–, sometimes billed as Patterson) scored four episodes of *Hammer House of Horror* (1980, TV) and four episodes of *Hammer House of Mystery and Suspense* (1984, TVM), prior to which he'd made contributions to Paul Glass's score for Hammer's *To the Devil a Daughter* (1976) when the composer was running behind schedule. His other credits include *The Dancing Princesses* (1978, TVM) and *The Exercise* (1984, TVM). Note that his name is missing on the final credit roll for *Last Video and Testament* (1984, TVM [episode of *Hammer House of Mystery and Suspense*]). **Hammer credits:** *To the Devil a Daughter* (1976, additional music [uncredited]), *The Two Faces of Evil* (1980, TV [episode of *Hammer House of Horror*]), *The Mark of Satan* (1980, TV [episode of *Hammer House of Horror*]), *Rude Awakening* (1980, TV [episode of *Hammer House of Horror*]), *Children of the Full Moon* (1980, TV [episode of *Hammer House of Horror*]), *A Distant Scream* (1984, TVM [episode of *Hammer House of Mystery and Suspense*]), *In Possession* (1984, TVM [episode of *Hammer House of Mystery and Suspense*]), *Black Carrion* (1984, TVM [episode of *Hammer House of Mystery and Suspense*]), *Last Video and Testament* (1984, TVM [episode of *Hammer House of Mystery and Suspense*, uncredited])

### Pathé

Pathé processed the Eastmancolor stock for a number of Hammer releases, including *Sword of Sherwood Forest* (1960), *The Phantom of the Opera* (1962) and *The Kiss of the Vampire* (1963). Also see **Associated British-Pathé Hammer credits:** *Sword of Sherwood Forest* (1960), *The Terror of the Tongs* (1961), *The Phantom of the Opera* (1962), *Captain Clegg* (1962), *The Kiss of the Vampire* (1963), *The Brigand of Kandahar* (1965)

### Paton, Charles

This British actor (1874–1970) can be seen as a grocer in Hammer's *Celia* (1949). A former music hall performer, his other credits include *John Citizen's Lament* (1927), *Piccadilly* (1929), *Rynox* (1932), *The Ghost Camera* (1933), *Rembrandt* (1936), *The Saint in London* (1939), *The Goose Steps Out* (1942), *London Town* (1946) and *The Adventurers* (1951). **Hammer credits:** *Celia* (1949, as Grocer)

### Patrick, John

Patrick can be seen in a supporting role in *Black Carrion* (1984, TVM [episode of *Hammer House of Mystery and Suspense*]). His other credits include *Gandhi* (1982), *Revolution* (1986) and *Buster* (1988), plus episodes of *The Professionals* (1977–1983, TV), *Dick Turpin* (1979–1982, TV) and *Inspector Morse* (1987–2000, TV). **Hammer credits:** *Black Carrion* (1984, TVM [episode of *Hammer House of Mystery and Suspense*], as Police Sergeant)

### Patrick, Nigel

Noted for his breezy upper class manner, this British leading man (1912–1981, real name Nigel Dennis Wemyss) made his stage debut at the age of nineteen and broke into films three years later with *Mrs. Pym of Scotland Yard* (1935). Following war service (as a lieutenant-colonel in the infantry) he returned to films with *Uneasy Terms* (1948), which in turn led to notable roles in the likes of *Spring in Park Lane* (1948), *The Browning Version* (1951), *The Sound Barrier* (1952), which earned him a BAFTA nomination for best actor, *Raintree County* (1957), *Sapphire* (1959), *The League of Gentlemen* (1960) and *The Mackintosh Man* (1973). As well as several plays, he also directed two films: *How to Murder a Rich Uncle* (1957) and *Johnny Nobody* (1961), in both of which he appeared. With fellow co-star Cyril Raymond, he also co-scripted the "unofficial" Hammer thriller *Jack of Diamonds* (1949), which was part-financed by Will Hammer, and based upon a story "Binnacle." His TV appearances include episodes of *Zero One* (1962–1965, TV), in which he starred as Alan Garnett, *It Takes a Thief* (1968–1970, TV) and *Sunday Night Thriller* (1981, TV). His wife was the actress Beatrice Campbell (1922–1979), whom he married in 1951. **Hammer credits:** *Jack of Diamonds* (1949, as Alan Butler, also co-screenplay)

### Patten, George

Patten worked as an assistant editor on Hammer's *The Gorgon* (1964). His other credits include the short *Standard Malaysian Rubber* (1969), which he edited. **Hammer credits:** *The Gorgon* (1964 [uncredited])

### Patterson, Lee

In films and television in both Britain and America, this Canadian actor (1929–2007) can be seen in such features as *The Passing Stranger* (1954), *Above Us the Waves* (1955), *Jack the Ripper* (1959), *Chato's Land* (1972), *Bullseye!* (1990) and *Healer*

(1994), while his television credits take in episodes of *Douglas Fairbanks, Jr. Presents* (1953–1957, TV), *Surfside* (1960–1962, TV), in which he played Dave Thorne, the long running soap *One Life to Live* (1968–1978, TV), in which he played Joe Riley, *Department S* (1971–1972, TV) and *Zorro* (1990–1993, TV). In 1953 he appeared as Joe in the Hammer thriller *36 Hours*. **Hammer credits:** *36 Hours* (1953, as Joe)

### Patterson, Paul *see* Paterson, Paul

### Pattillo, Alan

This British editor and director (1929–) edited Hammer's *Straight on Till Morning* (1972). His other credits as an editor include *Walkabout* (1970), *Innocent Bystanders* (1972), *Open Season* (1974), *All Quiet on the Western Front* (1979, TVM), which won him a shared Emmy, *Camille* (1984, TVM) and *Cyborg Cop* (1983). Long associated with producer Gerry Anderson, he also edited episodes of *Four Feather Falls* (1960, TV), worked as a script editor and writer on *Thunderbirds* (1965–1966, TV), penned episodes of *Captain Scarlet and the Mysterons* (1967–1968, TV) and *UFO* (1970–1971, TV), and directed episodes of *Four Feather Falls*, *Supercar* (1961–1962, TV), *Fireball XL5* (1962–1963, TV), *Stingray* (1964–1965, TV), *Thunderbirds* and *Terrahawks* (1983–1986, TV). His other credits include work as a sound effects editor/sound editor on *No Time to Die* (1958), *Secret Ceremony* (1969), *Performance* (1970) and *Britannia Hospital* (1982). **Hammer credits:** *Straight on Till Morning* (1972)

### Pattison, Barry (Barrie)

In Britain for a period in the sixties and early seventies, Australian born Pattison (1945–, aka Robert Aarons) worked as the second assistant editor on Hammer's *Blood from the Mummy's Tomb* (1971). His credits as an editor include *Ten Bob in Winter* (1963) and *Globe of Death* (1972). His credits as a director include *Mandrake Gestures Hypnoticly* (1972), which he also scripted, *Imagine Seeing the Cars Go Past* (1978), *I Am No God* (1982) and *Zombie Brigade* (1988), which he also produced and directed. He also appeared in *It Happened Here* (1965) and worked as an assistant director on *Sweet and Sexy* (1970). His books include *I've Been in Some Big Towns: The Life and Films of Anatole Litvak* (2011). **Hammer credits:** *Blood from the Mummy's Tomb* (1971 [uncredited])

### Patton, Stan

Patton worked as a camera grip on Hammer's *The Satanic Rites of Dracula* (1974). His other credits include *Not Tonight, Darling* (1970) and *In Celebration* (1974). **Hammer credits:** *The Satanic Rites of Dracula* (1974 [uncredited])

### Paul, Christina

This British born actress of Polish descent (1948–, aka Christine Paul-Podlasky and Christine Paul, real name Krystyna Podleska) can be seen as Rosa, the girl who falls in love with the vampiric Emil in Hammer's *Vampire Circus* (1972). Her other credits include *Deep End* (1971) and *Macbeth* (1971), plus episodes of *The Venturers* (1975, TV) and *World's End* (1981, TV). Her Polish credits include *Barwy ochronne* (1977), *Kontrakt* (1980, TVM) and *Zamiana* (2009), plus episodes of *Tygrysy Europy* (2003, TV) and *Ojciec Mateusz* (2010, TV). **Hammer credits:** *Vampire Circus* (1972, as Rosa)

### Paul, Eddie

Paul designed the poster campaign for Hammer's *On the Buses* (1971), which was subsequently illustrated by Arnaldo Patzu, and *Frankenstein and the Monster from Hell* (1974), which was subsequently illustrated by Bill Wiggins. Other campaigns worked on include *From Russia With Love* (1963), *Get Carter* (1971), *Aces High* (1976) and *Warlords of Atlantis* (1978). **Hammer credits include:** *On the Buses* (1971 [uncredited]), *Frankenstein and the Monster from Hell* (1974 [uncredited])

### Paul, Jeremy

Working primarily in television, this British writer (1939–2011, real name Jeremy Paul Roche) penned the teleplay for *Poor Butterfly*, an episode of Hammer's *Journey to the Unknown* (1968, TV), which also appeared in the compendium film *Journey to Midnight* (1968, TVM). He subsequently went on to write the screenplay for the company's *Countess Dracula* (1971). Recalled Ingrid Pitt, who played the title role in the film, "Everything about *Countess Dracula* was perfect. The script by Jeremy Paul was excellent, giving the old Countess a lot of depth, and I was sure I would shine in the role."[7] Noted for his period dramas, Paul's other credits include episodes of such series *The Edwardians* (1972, TV), *Upstairs, Downstairs* (1971–1975, TV), *The Duchess of Duke Street* (1976–1977, TV), *Sorrell and Son* (1984, TV), *The Return of Sherlock Holmes* (1986–1988, TV) and *Campion* (1989–1990, TV). His mother was the actress Joan Haythorne (1915–1987, real name Joan Haythornwaite), who appeared in *Countess Dracula*. His wife was actress Patricia Garwood (1941–). **Hammer credits:** *Poor Butterfly* (1968, TV [episode of *Journey to the Unknown*]), *Journey to Midnight* (1968, TVM), *Countess Dracula* (1971)

### Paul, John

This British supporting actor (1921–1995) played the role of Lieutenant-Colonel Derry in the Hammer war picture *The Steel Bayonet* (1957). He later appeared in *The Curse of the Mummy's Tomb* (1964) as Inspector Mackenzie and in *Mark of the Devil* (1984, TVM [episode of *Hammer House of Mystery and Suspense*]) as millionaire businessman Matt Helston. His other credits include *The Long Arm* (1956), *The Man Who Wouldn't Talk* (1958), *Some Girls Do* (1969), *Cromwell* (1970), *Eye of the Needle* (1981) and *Cry Freedom* (1987). Of his many small screen credits, he is best known for playing Dr. Spencer Quist in *Doomwatch* (1970–1972, TV) and its big screen spin-off (1972). **Hammer credits:** *The Steel Bayonet* (1957, as Lieutenant-Colonel Derry), *The Curse of the Mummy's Tomb* (1964, as Inspector Mackenzie), *Mark of the Devil* (1984, TVM [episode of *Hammer House of Mystery and Suspense*], as Matt Helston)

### Paul, Les

Paul worked as the clapper loader on Hammer's *Never Take Sweets from a Stranger* (1960). His other credits in this capacity include *Life in Danger* (1959), while his work as a focus puller includes *Man from Tangier* (1957). He also worked as a visual effects lighting cameraman on episodes of *Captain Scarlet and the Mysterons* (1967–1968, TV). **Hammer credits:** *Never Take Sweets from a Stranger* (1960 [uncredited])

### Pavlovic, Drina

This British actress and page-three model (1953–) can be spotted as one of the schoolgirls in Hammer's *Vampire Circus* (1972). Her other credits include *Sex Play* (1974) and *Carry On Behind* (1975), plus episodes of *Please Sir!* (1968–1972, TV), *Whatever Happened to the Likely Lads?* (1973–1974, TV) and *Victorian Scandals* (1976, TV). Her husband is actor Stephen Bent (1952–), whom she married in 1984. **Hammer credits:** *Vampire Circus* (1972, as Schoolgirl [uncredited])

### Paxtons (W. Paxton & Co. Ltd./The Paxton Library)

This London-based music publisher provided the soundtrack for the Hammer featurette *River Patrol* (1948). The company began selling recordings circa 1941. Composers providing music for their library included Granville Bantock, Edward Carmer, Peter Yorke, Frederick Charrosin and Dolf van der Linden, the latter of whom conducted the Dutch Metropole Orchestra in many of the recordings (this during the period when the Musicians' Union prevented library music being recorded in Britain). Records produced by the company include performances by such artists as Eric Winstone and His Orchestra (who recorded *Passing Clouds* for the company) and Johnny Dankworth (who recorded *Bugle Call Bop*). **Hammer credits:** *River Patrol* (1948)

### Payne, Anthony

This respected British composer, musicologist and lecturer (1936–) provided the music for two episodes of *Hammer House of Mystery and Suspense* (1984, TVM]). In 1998, Payne was asked to "elaborate" the sketches for Elgar's unfinished *Symphony No. 3* (which can be heard in *An Education* [2009], otherwise scored by Paul Englishby). His own works include the *Phoenix Mass* (1969), *Spirit's Harvest* (1985), *Time's Arrow* (1990), *A Hidden Music* (1992), *Empty Landscape—Heart's Ease* (1995) and *Visions and Journeys* (2002). His wife is the singer Jane Manning (1938–), whom he married in 1966. In 2007, they both received honorary doctorates (their third each) from Durham University, where he had read music as a student. **Hammer credits:** *And the Wall Came Tumbling Down* (1984, TVM [episode of *Hammer House of Mystery and Suspense*]), *Tennis Court* (1984, TVM [episode of *Hammer House of Mystery and Suspense*])

### Payne, Daniel

Payne appeared as one of the wolf children in *Children of the Full Moon* (1980, TV [episode of *Hammer House of Horror*]). **Hammer credits:**

*Children of the Full Moon* (1980, TV [episode of *Hammer House of Horror*], as Small boy)

## Payne, Howard

Responsible for camera maintenance at Hammer, Payne also worked at Elstree for ABPC. It was Payne who found the widescreen lens that was subsequently used for the HammerScope process. Made in Copenhagen, the lens was originally intended for use at ABPC, but a minor flaw saw it passed on to Hammer at a reduced cost.

## Payne, James

Payne can be seen in minor supporting roles in a handful of Hammer films, beginning with *The Scarlet Blade* (1963). His many other credits, several of which make use of his skills as a driver (especially of taxis) include *Summer Holiday* (1963), *Operation Crossbow* (1965), *Kaleidoscope* (1965), *You Only Live Twice* (1967), *Otley* (1968), *Up Pompeii* (1971), *A Touch of Class* (1973), *An American Werewolf in London* (1981), *The Holcroft Covenant* (1985), *Lady Jane* (1986), *London Suite* (1996, TVM), and *102 Dalmatians* (2000). He has also worked as a stand-in. **Hammer credits:** *The Scarlet Blade* (1963, as Man in tavern [uncredited]), *The Brigand of Kandahar* (1965, as Soldier [uncredited]), *One Million Years B.C.* (1966, as Caveman), *Quatermass and the Pit* (1967, as Man running from station [uncredited]), *Love Thy Neighbour* (1973, as Taxi driver [uncredited])

## Payne, Laurence

Although he spent the majority of his career on stage, this British actor (1919–2009) also racked up a number of film appearances, beginning with *A Matter of Life and Death* (1946). His other credits include *Glad Tidings* (1953), *The Trollenberg Terror* (1958), having already appeared in the same role in the 1956 TV series, *Ben-Hur* (1959), *The Singer Not the Song* (1960), *Crosstrap* (1962), in which he played the lead, Hammer's *Vampire Circus* (1972), in which he played the key role of Mueller (a role he inherited from Anton Rodgers, who was taken ill just prior to shooting), and *One Deadly Owner* (1974). His many TV credits include episodes of *The Three Musketeers* (1954, TV), in which he played D'Artagnan, *Moonstrike* (1963, TV), *The Midnight Men* (1964, TV), *Sexton Blake* (1967–1971, TV), in which he played the title character, *Cribb* (1980–1981, TV) and *Airline* (1982, TV). Also a novelist, his 1961 book *The Nose on My Face* (one in a series featuring the character Chief Inspector Sam Birkett) was filmed as *Girl in the Headlines* (1963). Married three times, his first wife was the actress Sheila Burrell (1922–2011), whom he married in 1944, and who appeared in five films for Hammer: *The Man in Black* (1950), *The Rossiter Case* (1950), *Cloudburst* (1951), *Women Without Men* (1956) and *Paranoiac* (1963). His second wife was the actress Pamela Alan (1921–), whom he married in 1955. **Hammer credits:** *Vampire Circus* (1972, as Mueller)

## Payne, Leo

Payne had a supporting role in Hammer's *Creatures the World Forgot* (1971). **Hammer credits:** *Creatures the World Forgot* (1971, as Old tribal artist [uncredited])

## Payne, Natalie

Payne appeared as one of the wolf children in *Children of the Full Moon* (1980, TV [episode of *Hammer House of Horror*]). **Hammer credits:** *Children of the Full Moon* (1980, TV [episode of *Hammer House of Horror*], as Irenya)

## Payne, Sid

Payne acted as the lab contact between Hammer and Technicolor on Hammer's *The Satanic Rites of Dracula* (1974). **Hammer credits:** *The Satanic Rites of Dracula* (1974 [uncredited])

## Payne, Willie (Willy)

This Nigerian actor (1922–2017) had a minor role in Hammer's *The Witches* (1966). His other credits include *Two Gentlemen Sharing* (1969), *The Haunting of M* (1981) and *Great Moments in Aviation* (1993, TVM), plus a return to Hammer for a bit part in *The Devil Rides Out* (1968). His TV appearances include episodes of *The Larkins* (1958–1964, TV), *A for Andromeda* (1961, TV), *Bill Brand* (1976, TV) and *Rumpole of the Bailey* (1978–1992, TV). **Hammer credits:** *The Witches* (1966, as Adam [uncredited]), *The Devil Rides Out* (1968, as Servant [uncredited])

## Payton, Barbara

This glamorous but tragic American film star (1927–1967, real name Barbara Lee Redfield) died at the age of just thirty-nine following years of drug and alcohol abuse and brushes with prostitution. In films from 1949 with the short *Silver Butte*, she went on to appear in just a handful of features, among them *Dallas* (1950), *Bride of the Gorilla* (1951), *The Great Jesse James Raid* (1952) and *Murder Is My Beat* (1955). She starred in two films for Hammer in the fifties: *Four Sided Triangle* (1953), in which she played the dual roles of Lena and Helen (one the clone of the other), and *The Flanagan Boy* (1953), in which her treacherous Lorna Vecchi persuades an up-coming boxer to murder her promoter husband. The *Monthly Film Bulletin* described her work in *Four Sided Triangle* as "seldom convincing," though *Picture Post* was more positive about her appearance, describing her as being "Blonde as Hamlet and blue-eyed as a china doll." The American trailer for *Bad Blonde*, as *The Flanagan Boy* was known in the States, described the actress as "The most sensational woman of two continents."

Recalled continuity girl Renee Glynne of the actress, who was one of several Hollywood personalities who worked for Hammer during this period, "Barbara Payton was a little different from most of these American stars in that she was an 'up and coming' rather than a 'down and going.'"[8] Payton's third husband of four was actor Franchot Tone (1905–1968, real name Stanislas Pascal Franchot Tone), to whom she was married between 1951 and 1952. She recalled the ups and downs of her incident-packed life in the ghost-written memoir *I Am Not Ashamed* (1963). **Hammer credits:** *Four Sided Triangle* (1953, as Lena/Helen), *The Flanagan Boy* (1953, as Lorna Vecchi)

## Peach, Philip

Peach worked as a standby painter on Hammer's *Scars of Dracula* (1970). **Hammer credits:** *Scars of Dracula* (1970 [uncredited])

## Peacock, John

This child actor-turned playwright (1945–2017) found his talents being nurtured at Hammer by Michael Carreras, who had championed his acclaimed 1971 play *Children of the Wolf*, which the studio acquired during its West End run. Peacock worked on the screenplay for a period in 1971 with the film's proposed director, Seth Holt, who tragically died before the script could go before the cameras. Peacock was subsequently asked to work with producer Wilbur Stark on a project about twin vampires, which—no, you've guessed wrongly—eventually became *Vampire Circus* (1972), with which Peacock had no involvement, and which only featured elements from their story (primarily the Helga and Heinrich characters).

Peacock subsequently penned the screenplay for Hammer's *Straight on Till Morning* (1972), for which he also co-authored the lyrics for the title song, which was composed, co-written and performed by Annie Ross, who also appeared in the film, along with Shane Briant, who had likewise come to Hammer's attention via *Children of the Wolf*. Peacock also wrote the first draft screenplay for *To the Devil a Daughter* (1976), for which he was credited for the adaptation of the Dennis Wheatley novel upon which it was based. The script was subsequently re-worked through several further drafts by Christopher Wicking.

Peacock later took over as the story editor on *Hammer House of Mystery and Suspense* (1984, TVM) following the departure of Don Houghton through illness. Schedules were tight, and Peacock had to expand many of the scripts. As he recalled, "It was a terrific challenge, and whenever there's pressure within a crew, it's terrific because everyone was pulling together, and most people who were there had been part of the family—the Hammer family—before, so you knew everybody."[9] He also penned the introductions specifically filmed for the series' U.S. showings, and co-authored *And the Wall Came Tumbling Down* (1984, TVM [episode of *Hammer House of Mystery and Suspense*]) with Dennis Spooner.

Peacock remained on at Hammer as the story editor of a proposed second season of *Hammer House of Mystery and Suspense*, but despite having commissioned thirteen stories, among them *The Housekeeper* by Nigel Kneale, the series was cancelled by Fox following a change of management. Sadly, his long-dormant screenplay for *Children of the Wolf* also failed to get off the ground a second time when revived by director John Hough in the mid-eighties. He also worked on an unfilmed adaptation of Daphne Du Maurier's *The House on the Strand* for Hammer, for which he also scouted locations in Cornwall, and compiled stories for another unmade series, *The Hammer Mystery Theatre*.

His other plays include *Caprice in a Pink Palazzo* (1968), while his radio work includes *Attard in Retirement* (1980), *Basic Magic* (1998) and *Bringing*

*Eddie Home* (2006). His other television credits include episodes of *Armchair Theatre* (1956–1974, TV), *Menace* (1970–1973, TV), *The Shadow of the Tower* (1972, TV) and *Dial M for Murder* (1974, TV), while his occasional film credits include *The Smashing Bird I Used to Know* (1969). **Hammer credits:** *Straight on Till Morning* (1972, screenplay), *To the Devil a Daughter* (1976, adaptation), *Hammer House of Mystery and Suspense* (1984, TVM, story editor, U.S. intros [uncredited]), *In Possession* (1984, TVM [episode of *Hammer House of Mystery and Suspense*], story editor), *Black Carrion* (1984, TVM [episode of *Hammer House of Mystery and Suspense*], story editor), *Last Video and Testament* (1984, TVM [episode of *Hammer House of Mystery and Suspense*], story editor), *Mark of the Devil* (1984, TVM [episode of *Hammer House of Mystery and Suspense*], story editor), *The Corvini Inheritance* (1984, TVM [episode of *Hammer House of Mystery and Suspense*], story editor), *Paint Me a Murder* (1984, TVM [episode of *Hammer House of Mystery and Suspense*], story editor), *Child's Play* (1984, TVM [episode of *Hammer House of Mystery and Suspense*], story editor), *And the Wall Came Tumbling Down* (1984, TVM [episode of *Hammer House of Mystery and Suspense*], co-teleplay, story editor), *Tennis Court* (1984, TVM [episode of *Hammer House of Mystery and Suspense*], story editor)

## Peacock, Keith

This stuntman and actor (1931–1966) played one of the zombies in Hammer's *The Plague of the Zombies* (1966). In addition to appearing in the classic graveyard dream sequence, for which he had to claw his way from a shallow grave, he was also required to go up in flames for the fiery tin mine climax. His other credits as a stuntman include *Carry On Cruising* (1962) and *Casino Royale* (1967), while his work as an actor takes in *Circus of Fear* (1966) and *Our Man in Marrakesh* (1967), plus episodes of *No Hiding Place* (1959–1967, TV), *Out of the Unknown* (1965–1971, TV) and *The Prisoner* (1967–1968, TV). He died while filming a stunt for the television series *Softly Softly* (1966–1976, TV). **Hammer credits:** *The Plague of the Zombies* (1966, as Zombie [uncredited])

## Peake, Lisa

This actress and model (1935–2000) played one of the nightclub dancers seen in the opening scene in Hammer's *She* (1965). Her other credits include *Expresso Bongo* (1959), *A Matter of Choice* (1963) and *Bunny Lake Is Missing* (1965), pus episodes of *The Avengers* (1961–1969, TV) and *Z Cars* (1962–1978, TV). As a model she appeared in such magazines as *Blighty*. **Hammer credits:** *She* (1965, as Nightclub dancer)

## Peake, Michael

This British supporting actor (1918–1967) can be spotted in *The Man Who Never Was* (1956), *Make Mine Mink* (1960), *Strongroom* (1961), *Band of Thieves* (1962), *The Bay of St. Michel* (1963) and *The Intelligence Men* (1965). He also appeared in a handful of minor roles for Hammer in the early sixties. His many TV credits include episodes of *Sword of Freedom* (1957, TV), *Sir Francis Drake*

(1961–1962, TV) and *The Rat Catchers* (1966–1967, TV). **Hammer credits:** *The Curse of the Werewolf* (1961, as Farmer in cantina [uncredited]), *The Terror of the Tongs* (1961, unnamed role [uncredited]), *The Pirates of Blood River* (1962, as Kemp), *The Devil-Ship Pirates* (1964, as Grando), *The Gorgon* (1964, as Policeman)

## Peake RN, (Commander) Peter

Naval Commander Peake provided technical advice for the Hammer comedy *Further Up the Creek* (1958). His other credits as an advisor include *The Key* (1958), *Watch Your Stern* (1960) and *Sink the Bismarck!* (1960). **Hammer credits:** *Further Up the Creek* (1958)

## Pearce, Jacqueline

Best known to horror fans as Anna the snake-woman in Hammer's *The Reptile* (1966), this striking British actress (1943–2018) made just two films for the studio, the other being *The Plague of the Zombies* (1966), in which she played the ill-fated Alice Tompson. In films in small roles from the mid-sixties following training at RADA, Pearce's other credits include *Genghis Khan* (1965), *Sky West and Crooked* (1965), *Don't Lose Your Head* (1966), *The Magnificent Two* (1967) and *Don't Raise the Bridge, Lower the River* (1967). Following further training in America at the Actors' Studio in the seventies, she returned to Britain where she resumed her career, most notably on television, where she played Supreme Commander Servalan in the cult favorite *Blakes 7* (1978–1981, TV). Her other film credits include *White Mischief* (1987), *How to Get Ahead in Advertising* (1989), *Princess Caraboo* (1994) and *Guru in Seven* (1997), plus ap-

pearances in episodes of *Dark Season* (1991, TV), *The Young Indiana Jones Chronicles* (1992–1993, TV) and *Doctors* (2000–, TV).

Recalled the actress of the make-up she had to wear for *The Reptile*: "Dreadful make-up—very claustrophobic—which had to be glued on, fangs, long fingernails which had curled in the heat by the end of the day."[10] Meanwhile, of her role in *The Plague of the Zombies* she added, "I got decapitated in that one. I much preferred being a zombie."[11] Yet despite the inherent silliness of it all she noted, "I took it terribly seriously. I don't think mine were nearly as tongue-in-cheek as [some]."[12] She also had nothing but praise for make-up man Roy Ashton, who made her up for both films. "Roy was a total professional who took it all very seriously. He gave a great deal of thought to the design and application of the make-up and was of course very much an artist in his own field."[13]

Commented *Kinematograph Weekly* of the actress's performance in *The Reptile*, "Jacqueline Pearce is an attractive Anna and a quite horrible cobra," while of her work in *Plague* the *Monthly Film Bulletin* observed, "Jacqueline Pearce is outstanding as the ill-fated Alice, who has her head knocked off to save her from zombiehood."

Pearce was married to the actor Drewe Henley (1940–2017) between 1963 and 1967; he appeared in Hammer's *When Dinosaurs Ruled the Earth* (1970). **Hammer credits:** *The Plague of the Zombies* (1966, as Alice Tompson), *The Reptile* (1966, as Anna Franklyn/The Reptile)

## Pearce, Joe

Pearce (1915–1999) worked for Hammer as a stills man on *Scars of Dracula* (1970) and *The Hor-*

Jacqueline Pearce (left) attempts to put the bite on Jennifer Daniel (right) in *The Reptile* (1966) (Hammer/Seven Arts/Associated British Picture Corporation/Warner Pathé/Twentieth Century–Fox/Studio Canal).

ror of Frankenstein (1970). His other credits include *The Miniver Story* (1950), *The Rough and the Smooth* (1959), *Lolita* (1962), *The V.I.P.s* (1963), *You Only Live Twice* (1967), *There's a Girl in My Soup* (1970), *Murder on the Orient Express* (1974), *Confessions from a Holiday Camp* (1977), *All Quiet on the Western Front* (1979, TVM), *Dragonslayer* (1981) and *Ivanhoe* (1982, TVM). **Hammer credits:** *Scars of Dracula* (1970 [uncredited]), *The Horror of Frankenstein* (1970 [uncredited])

### Pearce, Lennard

Best known for playing Grandad in the sitcom *Only Fools and Horses* (1981–2003, TV) between 1981 and 1983, this British character actor (1915–1984) can also be seen as a rector in *Witching Time*, an episode of *Hammer House of Horror* (1980, TV). His many other TV appearances include episodes of *No Hiding Place* (1959–1967, TV), *Nearest and Dearest* (1968–1973, TV), *Bless Me Father* (1978–1981, TV) and *Shroud for a Nightingale* (1984, TV). His film credits include the featurette *Face of Darkness* (1976), in which he played the lead. **Hammer credits:** *Witching Time* (1980, TV [episode of *Hammer House of Horror*], as Rector)

### Pearce, Terry

British born Pearce (1949–) worked as the third assistant director on Hammer's *Lust for a Vampire* (1971). His other credits in this capacity include *Tales from the Crypt* (1973), *Frankenstein: The True Story* (1973, TVM) and *The Ghoul* (1975). His work as a second assistant includes *The Class of Miss MacMichael* (1978), *The Wildcats of St. Trinian's* (1980), *Nate and Hayes* (1983), *Willow* (1988), *Edge of Sanity* (1989) and *Feast of July* (1995), plus episodes of *Dick Turpin* (1979–1982, TV) and *Press Gang* (1989–1993, TV), while his work as a first assistant includes *The Bitch* (1979). He also worked as a clapper loader on *2001: A Space Odyssey* (1968), *The Great McGonagall* (1975) and *The Odd Job* (1978), and as a focus puller on episodes of *Boon* (1986–1992, TV), *Inspector Morse* (1987–2000, TV) and *Monarch of the Glen* (2000–2005, TV). **Hammer credits:** *Lust for a Vampire* (1971 [uncredited])

### Pearce, Tim

Pearce can be seen in the dual roles of Brinkley and Robert Ford in *And the Wall Came Tumbling Down* (1984, TVM [episode of *Hammer House of Mystery and Suspense*]). His other TV credits include episodes of *United* (1965–1967, TV), *Catweazle* (1970–1971, TV), *Jesus of Nazareth* (1977, TV) and *Dear John* (1986–1987, TV). His occasional films include *Mix Me a Person* (1962), *Layout for Five Models* (1972) and *Arabian Adventure* (1979). **Hammer credits:** *And the Wall Came Tumbling Down* (1984, TVM [episode of *Hammer House of Mystery and Suspense*], as Brinkley/Robert Ford)

### Pearce, Vera

This Australian actress and singer (1895–1966, full name Annie Vera Pearce) played the role of Elvira in Hammer's *Men of Sherwood Forest* (1954). In films from the mid-teens in her own country, her early credits include *The Shepherd of the South-ern Cross* (1915) and *The Martyrdom of Nurse Cavell* (1916). Her later British credits include *Just My Luck* (1933), *Southern Roses* (1937), *Please Teacher* (1937), *Nicholas Nickleby* (1947), *The Night We Got the Bird* (1960) and *Nothing Barred* (1961). **Hammer credits:** *Men of Sherwood Forest* (1954, as Elvira)

### Pearl, Elna

Pearl had a supporting role in *Eve*, an episode of Hammer's *Journey to the Unknown* (1968, TV). Her other TV credits include episodes of *Z Cars* (1962–1978, TV), *Curtain of Fear* (1964, TV), *The Wednesday Play* (1964–1970, TV) and *The Debussy Film* (1965, TVM). Her occasional film credits include *The Password Is Courage* (1962) and *To Sir, with Love* (1967). **Hammer credits:** *Eve* (1968, TV [episode of *Journey to the Unknown*], as Girl in cinema)

### Pearson, Ben

Pearson provided the special gowns for the Hammer second feature *Blood Orange* (1953), which is set in a fashion house. He also provided Belinda Lee's gowns for *Murder by Proxy* (1955). **Hammer credits:** *Blood Orange* (1953), *Murder by Proxy* (1955)

### Pearson, Freda

Pearson worked as the set dresser on Hammer's *Crescendo* (1970). Her other credits as a set decorator/dresser include *They Were Not Divided* (1950), *Scrooge* (1951), *Serious Charge* (1959), *Dr. No* (1962), *From Russia with Love* (1963), *Goldfinger* (1964), *Thunderball* (1965), *The Blood Beast Terror* (1968) and *Carry On … Up the Khyber* (1968). She also worked as the assistant art director on *The Extra Day* (1956). **Hammer credits:** *Crescendo* (1970)

### Pearson, Freddie

Pearson (often billed as "Freddie" Pearson, complete with quotation marks) worked as the assistant to producer Robert Dunbar on the Hammer comedy *Life with the Lyons* (1954), and as the production manager on its sequel, *The Lyons in Paris* (1955), which was also produced by Dunbar. Other credits as a production manager include *Man-Eater* (1957), *That Woman Opposite* (1957), *Heart of a Child* (1958) and *The Man Upstairs* (1958). **Hammer credits:** *Life with the Lyons* (1954, assistant to the producer [uncredited]), *The Lyons in Paris* (1955, production manager), *Adventures with the Lyons* (1957, serial re-issue of *Life with the Lyons*, assistant to the producer [uncredited])

### Pearson, H.C.

This British sound technician (1907–2002) worked on a handful of Hammer films in the fifties. His many other credits include *Little Stranger* (1934), *Glamour Girl* (1938), *Under New Management* (1946), *Badger's Green* (1949), *Mr. Drake's Duck* (1951), *Cosh Boy* (1952), *Suspended Alibi* (1956), *Grip of the Strangler* (1958), *The Pure Hell of St. Trinian's* (1960) and *The Snake Woman* (1961), plus episodes of *The Adventures of Sir Lancelot* (1956–1957, TV), *The Buccaneers* (1956–1957, TV) and *The Adventures of Robin Hood* (1955–1960, TV), working on an incredible 140 episodes of the latter. **Hammer credits:** *Break in the Circle* (1955), *The Quatermass Xperiment* (1955), *The Glass Cage* (1955)

### Pearson, Richard

This much-liked British (Welsh) character actor (1918–2011, full name Richard de Pearsall Pearson) was a familiar face for decades, having made his stage debut in 1937 and his television debut in 1947 following military experience during the war. In films from 1950 with *The Girl Is Mine*, his many other credits include *Scrooge* (1951), *Libel* (1959), *Charlie Bubbles* (1968), *Sunday Bloody Sunday* (1971), *Royal Flash* (1975), *Tess* (1979), *Water* (1985) and *Pirates* (1986). Frequently cast as kindly upper class types, he can also be seen in *The Thirteenth Reunion*, one of the better episodes of *Hammer House of Horror* (1980, TV), in which he plays Sir Humphrey Chesterton, the benign host of a rather unusual dinner party. Much on stage, his many other TV credits include episodes of *Fabian of the Yard* (1955–1956, TV), *Martin Chuzzlewit* (1964, TV), *Out of the Unknown* (1965–1971, TV), *The Duchess of Duke Street* (1976–1977, TV), *Campion* (1989–1990, TV) and *Men Behaving Badly* (1992–1999, TV). His wife was the actress Patricia Dickson, whom he married in 1949. **Hammer credits:** *The Thirteenth Reunion* (1980, TV [episode of *Hammer House of Horror*], as Sir Humphrey Chesterton)

### Pearson, Sydney (Sid/Syd)

Perhaps best known to Hammer fans for his convincing disintegration of Christopher Lee at the climax of *Dracula* (1958), this effects technician (1916–, real name Sidney Charles Pearson) also worked on a number of other productions for the studio, beginning with the wartime drama *The Steel Bayonet* (1957). Recalled Pearson of his celebrated sequence in *Dracula*, "The disintegration interested me immensely…. We decided we would attempt the sequence in a series of cuts."[14] These depicted the disintegration of Dracula's skull (which was made from latex rubber) and hands, the latter of which Pearson achieved by covering his own hands with Fuller's Earth and then dipping them in pink wax which, when cooled, crumbled in a suitably realistic fashion when Pearson flexed his fingers. Said Pearson, "As they moved, the flesh cracked, dropped away and dust fell to the ground."[15] Less impressive was the giant bat Pearson made to menace Peter Cushing's Van Helsing in *The Brides of Dracula* (1960). His other credits include *Black Narcissus* (1947), *Kind Hearts and Coronets* (1949), *In Search of the Castaways* (1961), *The Long Ships* (1964) and *The Heroes of Telemark* (1965), plus episodes of *The Champions* (1968–1969, TV). **Additional notes:** The "export" version of Pearson's Dracula disintegration wasn't seen in the UK until 2012, when it was released on Blu-ray following the discovery of the footage in Japan in 2011; this version was also broadcast on BBC2 in 2013. **Hammer credits:** *The Steel Bayonet* (1957), *Dracula* (1958), *I Only Arsked!* (1958), *The Snorkel* (1958 [uncredited]), *The Hound of the Baskervilles* (1959), *The Brides of Dracula* (1960), *The Gorgon*

(1964), *Fanatic* (1965), *The Secret of Blood Island* (1965), *The Brigand of Kandahar* (1965), *Creatures the World Forgot* (1971)

### Peart, Pauline

Peart (1931–) can be seen as one of the vampires in the cellar of Pelham House in Hammer's *The Satanic Rites of Dracula* (1974). She also had a brief role as a secretary in Hammer's big screen version of *Man About the House* (1974). Her other credits include *Suburban Wives* (1971), *Nobody Ordered Love* (1972), *Carry On Girls* (1973) and *Cuba* (1979). **Hammer credits:** *The Satanic Rites of Dracula* (1974, as Vampire), *Man About the House* (1974, as Secretary)

### Peatfield, Mike (Michael)

Peatfield worked as the online editor on *The World of Hammer* (1990 [first broadcast 1994], TV). His other credits in this capacity include *Raging Planet* (1997, TV), *Glenn Miller's Last Flight* (2000, TV), *Lon Chaney: A Thousand Faces* (2000, TV), *Jamie's Great Escape* (2005, TV) and *ER Baghdad: A Doctor's Story* (2006, TV). **Hammer credits:** *The World of Hammer* (1990 [first broadcast 1994], TV)

### Peattie, Rosemarie *see* McDonald-Peattie, Rosemarie

### Peck, Bob

Peck worked as the sound recordist on *The Madison Equation* (1968, TV [episode of *Journey to the Unknown*]). His film credits include *Love Is a Splendid Illusion* (1970), *The Oblong Box* (1969), *The Last Valley* (1970) and *Venom* (1971). **Hammer credits:** *The Madison Equation* (1968, TV [episode of *Journey to the Unknown*])

### Peck, Brian

This British supporting actor (1930–) played a soldier in the Hammer shocker *X—The Unknown* (1956). His other credits include *The Voyage of Peter Joe* (1946), *Portrait of Clare* (1950), *Tarnished Heroes* (1961), *Echo of Barbara* (1961), *The Pit* (1962), a short version of Poe's *The Pit and the Pendulum* in which he played the lead, *Mystery Submarine* (1963), *The Set-Up* (1963), *The Jokers* (1967), *Twisted Nerve* (1968) and *Run for Your Wife* (2012). He also appeared in Hammer's *Quatermass and the Pit* (1967) as a Technical Officer. Busy in television, his many credits here include episodes of *Tales from Dickens* (1958–1959, TV), *Cluff* (1964–1965, TV), *Codename* (1970, TV), in which he played Culliford, *The Long Chase* (1972, TV), in which he played Bowers, *Break in the Sun* (1981, TV), *London's Burning* (1988–2002, TV), *Merlin* (2008–2012, TV), *Rev* (2010–2014, TV), *A Touch of Cloth* (2012–2014, TV) and *Boomers* (2014–2016, TV). His wife is the actress Jennifer Wilson (1932–), whom he married in 1959. **Hammer credits:** *X—The Unknown* (1956, as Soldier [uncredited]), *Quatermass and the Pit* (1967, as Technical Officer)

### Peck, Fred

This actor worked as an extra and bit part player on a handful of Hammer films at Bray in the sixties, beginning with *The Curse of the Werewolf* (1961), and ending when the company left the studio following the making of *The Mummy's Shroud* (1967). He sometimes even appeared more than once in each film. His wife was the hairdresser Frieda Steiger, whose many Hammer credits include *The Brides of Dracula* (1960), *Nightmare* (1964) and *The Plague of the Zombies* (1966). **Hammer credits include:** *The Curse of the Werewolf* (1961, as Inn patron [uncredited]), *Captain Clegg* (1962, as Villager in congregation [uncredited]), *The Pirates of Blood River* (1962, as Huguenot villager [uncredited]), *The Phantom of the Opera* (1962, as Stage hand and man in audience [both uncredited]), *Paranoiac* (1963, as Man in bar [uncredited]), *The Kiss of the Vampire* (1963, as Disciple [uncredited]), *The Old Dark House* (1963, as Casino patron [uncredited]), *The Evil of Frankenstein* (1964, as Villager [uncredited]), *Dracula—Prince of Darkness* (1966, as Inn patron [uncredited]), *Rasputin—The Mad Monk* (1966, as Inn patron [uncredited]), *The Reptile* (1966, as Inn patron [uncredited]), *The Witches* (1966, as Coven member [uncredited]), *Frankenstein Created Woman* (1967, as Villager and jury member [both uncredited]), *The Mummy's Shroud* (1967, as Reporter [uncredited])

### Peck, Victor

Peck worked as the production manager on two films for Hammer. His other credits include *Third Time Lucky* (1948), *Happy Ever After* (1954), *Billy Budd* (1962), *The Deadly Affair* (1966), *The Magic Christian* (1969) and *The Offence* (1972). **Hammer credits:** *Sands of the Desert* (1960), *The Anniversary* (1968)

### The Peddlers

This British pop group performed the Roy Phillips-penned title song for Hammer's *The Lost Continent* (1968). Note that an alternate version of the song can be found on the CD release of the film's soundtrack (care of GDI Records). Recalled Michael Carreras of the group, "They were friends of mine and I wanted to have that sort of contrast [to the more traditional Hammer sound]."[16] It is likely that Carreras met the group at the Pickwick Club in London in the sixties, where they had a residency; one of the co-owners of the club was the writer Wolf Mankowitz, who had penned *The Two Faces of Dr. Jekyll* (1960) for Hammer.

In addition to Roy Phillips, the band also comprised of Tab Martin and Trevor Morais. The band's albums include *Live at the Pickwick* (1967), *Three in a Cell* (1968) and *Three for All* (1970). Their biggest hit was the 1969 single *Birth*, which reached number seventeen in the UK charts. The group can also be heard performing their single *Tell the World We're Not In* (1970) on the soundtrack for *Goodbye Gemini* (1970). They also appeared in episodes of such music shows as *Colour Me Pop* (1968–1969, TV) and *Lift Off* (1969–1974, TV, later *Lift Off with Ayshea*). **Hammer credits:** *The Lost Continent* (1968)

### Pedrick, Gale

This British dramatist and BBC script editor (1904–1970, real name Harvey Pedrick) created the radio serial *Meet the Rev* (1946), which was filmed by Hammer as *Meet Simon Cherry* (1949), and for which he also provided uncredited additional dialogue. He also contributed to the screenplay for *George in Civvy Street* (1946) and wrote for such series as *On Camera* (1954–1958, TV) and *Armchair Theatre* (1956–1974, TV). His books include *Profitable Script Writing for TV and Radio* (1961). **Hammer credits:** *Meet Simon Cherry* (1949, additional dialogue [uncredited], radio series)

### Peel, David

Best known for playing the handsome, bequiffed Baron Meinster in Hammer's *The Brides of Dracula* (1960), this RADA-trained British stage actor (1920–1981) appeared in plays in both London and New York. Following military experience in World War II, from which he was discharged in 1942, he broke into films the same year with *Squadron Leader X* (1942). However, save for his appearance for Hammer, his resultant big screen career was desultory, taking in *Escape to Danger* (1943), *We Dive at Dawn* (1943), *Gaiety George* (1946), *They Who Dare* (1953) and *The Hands of Orlac* (1960). As well as the stage, Peel was known for his work on radio in the fifties; he also appeared in a television version of *Rope* (1953, TV).

Recalled co-star Yvonne Monlaur of Peel, "[He] was a lovely man. I was amazed by his diction and his wonderful voice."[17] Astonishingly, although playing a man in his early twenties, Peel was pushing forty when he appeared as Meinster. He later retired from the stage to become an antiques shop proprietor. Recalled *Brides* composer Malcolm Williams somewhat ungallantly of the actor, whom he observed during filming, "I watched David Peel at work. David would bring his two poodles onto the set—an extremely sweet actor if you know what I mean."[18] **Hammer credits:** *The Brides of Dracula* (1960, as Baron Meinster)

### Peel, Eda

Peel can be seen in the role of Maude Dane in the Hammer comedy *Sporting Love* (1936). **Hammer credits:** *Sporting Love* (1936, as Maude Dane)

### Peel, Edward

This British actor (1943–) can be seen as a prison officer in *A Distant Scream* (1984, TVM [episode of *Hammer House of Mystery and Suspense*]). A former teacher, his other TV credits include episodes of *Fly into Danger* (1972, TV), *Treasure Island* (1977, TV), *The Gentle Touch* (1980–1984, TV), *Juliet Bravo* (1980–1985, TV), in which he played DCI Mark Perrin, *The Fourth Arm* (1983, TV), *Cracker* (1993–1996, TV), *Doctors* (2000–, TV), *The Royal Today* (2008, TV) and *Ripper Street* (2012–2016, TV). **Hammer credits:** *A Distant Scream* (1984, TVM [episode of *Hammer House of Mystery and Suspense*], as Prison officer)

### Peers, Leon

This British actor (1931–) can be seen as Blanchard in the Hammer thriller *Maniac* (1963). His other credits include *Dead Lucky* (1960) and episodes of *Deadline Midnight* (1960–1961, TV), *Sir Francis Drake* (1961–1962, TV) and *Man of the World* (1962–1963, TV). **Hammer credits:** *Maniac* (1963)

## Pei-Chi, Huang

Pei-Chi (aka Wong Pei Chi, Pui Kei Wong and Pei-Tsi Wong) played Hsi Po-Kwei, one of the seven fighting brothers in Hammer's *The Legend of the 7 Golden Vampires* (1974). He also popped up in *Shatter* (1974), with which it was filmed back to back. His other credits include *Shen dao* (1968), *Chinese Boxer* (1970), *Five Fingers of Death* (1972), *Si qi shi* (1972), *Xing xing wang* (1977), *Shaolin chuan een* (1982) and *Gam yee wai* (1984). He also worked as a stuntman, stunt-co-ordinator and action director on many films, among them *Wu ha dan* (1974), *Kong que wang chao* (1979) and *Lie mo zhie* (1982). **Hammer credits:** *The Legend of the 7 Golden Vampires* (1974, as Hsi Po-Kwei [uncredited]), *Shatter* (1974, as Second bodyguard)

## Pemberton, Charles

This British actor (1939–2007) can be seen in a rather thankless supporting role in *Charlie Boy*, an episode of *Hammer House of Horror* (1980, TV). His many other TV appearances include episodes of *Softly Softly* (1966–1976, TV), *Follyfoot* (1971–1973, TV), *Shoestring* (1979–1980, TV), *Virtual Murder* (1992, TV) and *The Vicar of Dibley* (1994–2007, TV). His occasional films include *Eskimo Nell* (1975), *Brannigan* (1975), *Adventures of a Taxi Driver* (1976), *The Black Panther* (1977), *Porridge* (1979) and *The Four Feathers* (2002). **Hammer credits:** *Charlie Boy* (1980, TV [episode of *Hammer House of Horror*], as Policeman)

## Pemberton, Reece

Following experience as a stage designer, this British production designer (1914–1977, real name George Reice Pemberton) turned to television in the mid-fifties with *Simon's Good Deed* (1955, TVM), and to films two years later with *Time Without Pity* (1957). His other credits include *The Caretaker* (1963), *Nothing but the Best* (1964), *Arabesque* (1967), *Our Mother's House* (1967) and *Spring and Port Wine* (1970). He also designed *The Anniversary* (1968) for Hammer. His other TV credits include episodes of *ITV Play of the Week* (1955–1968, TV), *ITV Television Playhouse* (1955–1967, TV), *Armchair Theatre* (1956–1974, TV), *ITV Playhouse* (1967–1982, TV) and *Orson Welles' Great Mysteries* (1973–1974, TV). **Hammer credits:** *The Anniversary* (1968)

## Pendrell, Anthony

In films in supporting roles, this British actor (1913–1986) can be seen as a Cabinet Minister in Hammer's *The Two Faces of Dr. Jekyll* (1960). His other credits include *I'll Turn to You* (1946), *Blind Man's Bluff* (1952), *The Man Who Wouldn't Talk* (1957) and *Run with the Wind* (1966), plus episodes of *Quatermass and the Pit* (1958–1959, TV), *Private Investigator* (1958–1959, TV) and *No Hiding Place* (1959–1967, TV). He can also be spotted as one of two staff officers in the Hammer programer *The Runaway* (1964). His daughter is the actress Nicolette Pendrell (1941–2003), who appeared in the Hammer second feature *Delayed Flight* (1964). **Hammer credits:** *The Two Faces of Dr. Jekyll* (1960, as Cabinet Minister [uncredited]), *The Runaway* (1964, as Staff officer)

## Pendrell, Nicolette

British born Pendrell (1941–2003) had a supporting role in the Hammer second feature *Delayed Flight* (1964). Her other credits include *He Who Rides a Tiger* (1965), plus episodes of *Z Cars* (1962–1978, TV), *Doctor Who* (1963–1989, TV), *The White Rabbit* (1967, TV) and *The Sextet* (1972, TV). Her father was the actor Anthony Pendrell (1913–1986) who appeared in *The Two Faces of Dr. Jekyll* (1960) and *The Runaway* (1964) for Hammer. **Hammer credits:** *Delayed Flight* (1964, as Air hostess)

## Penn, Robert (Bob)

British born Penn (1925–2002) handled the stills photography for the Hammer comedy *A Weekend with Lulu* (1961). His many other credits include work on such major films as *Kind Hearts and Coronets* (1949), *The Cruel Sea* (1953), *The Dam Busters* (1955), *Cleopatra* (1963), *The Taming of the Shrew* (1967), *Oliver!* (1968), *On Her Majesty's Secret Service* (1969), *The Omen* (1976), *A Bridge Too Far* (1977), *Superman* (1978), *Alien* (1979), *Flash Gordon* (1980), *Return of the Jedi* (1983), *Aliens* (1986), *Alien³* (1992) and *The Secret Garden* (1993). **Hammer credits:** *A Weekend with Lulu* (1961 [uncredited])

## Pennington, Jon

This British producer (1922–1997, real name Kenneth Jon Pennington) formed the production company BHP with writer George Baxt and agent Richard Finlay Hatton. This went on to make the feline shocker *The Shadow of the Cat* (1961) in conjunction with Hammer and ACT Films. His other credits include *The Case of the Mukkinese Battlehorn* (1956), which he also co-wrote, *At the Stroke of Nine* (1957), which he also co-wrote, *Zoo Baby* (1960), *The Case of the 44s* (1965), which he also co-directed, *The Comedy Man* (1964), *The Liquidator* (1965), *The Plank* (1967), *Till Death Us Do Part* (1968) and *Plod* (1972). He also worked as an associate producer on *The Mouse That Roared* (1959) and *Expresso Bongo* (1959), and wrote episodes for such series as *Compact* (1962–1965, TV), *The Mask of Janus* (1965, TV) and *Adam Adamant Lives!* (1966–1967, TV). **Hammer credits:** *The Shadow of the Cat* (1961)

## Pennington-Richards, C.M.

Following experience as a cinematographer on such shorts and documentaries as *William Tindale* (1937), *Canterbury Pilgrimage* (1937), *Builders* (1942), *Fires Were Started* (1943) and *Theirs Is the Glory* (1946), this busy British director (1911–2005, full name Cyril Montague Pennington-Richards) went on to photograph such features as *Blarney* (1938), *Give Us This Day* (1947), *Scrooge* (1951), *The Wooden Horse* (1950), *White Corridors* (1951) and *Tarzan and the Lost Safari* (1956). He turned to direction in 1953 with *The Oracle*, and went on to helm the likes of *Hour of Decision* (1957), *Inn for Trouble* (1959) and *Sky Pirates*

(1976), which he also co-scripted. He also co-scripted a handful of films for other directors, among them *Guns at Batasi* (1964), *Headline Hunters* (1968) and the seven-part serial *The Boy with Two Heads* (1974), for which he additionally provided the story. He directed one film for Hammer, the rather pedestrian *A Challenge for Robin Hood* (1967), for which he is billed as Pennington Richards in the credits. He also directed episodes of *The Buccaneers* (1956–1957, TV), several of which he also produced, *Ivanhoe* (1958–1959, TV), *The Invisible Man* (1958–1960, TV) and *Zero One* (1962–1963, TV). **Hammer credits:** *A Challenge for Robin Hood* (1967)

## Penrose, John

Best remembered for playing the dull and cuckolded Lionel Holland in *Kind Hearts and Coronets* (1949), this British supporting actor (1914–1983) can also be seen as Barney in the Hammer programer *The Adventures of PC 49—The Case of the Guardian Angel* (1949) and Francois Du Vancet in *Mantrap* (1952). His other credits include *The Spy in Black* (1939), *Freedom Radio* (1941), *The Adventures of Tartu* (1943), *Counterspy* (1953) and *Murder Anonymous* (1955). **Hammer credits:** *The Adventures of PC 49—The Case of the Guardian Angel* (1949, as Barney), *Mantrap* (1953, as Francois Du Vancet)

## Pension Fund Securities *see* PFS

## Pentelow, Arthur

This British actor (1924–1991) had a minor role in *Jane Brown's Body*, an episode of Hammer's *Journey to the Unknown* (1968, TV). His many other TV credits include episodes of *Suspense* (1962–1963, TV), *Mr. Rose* (1967–1968, TV), *The Main Chance* (1969–1975, TV) and *The Strauss Family* (1972, TV), though he is best remembered for playing Henry Wilks, the landlord of The Woolpack, in *Emmerdale* (1972–, originally *Emmerdale Farm*), in which he appeared from its beginning until his death. His film credits include *Privilege* (1967), *Charlie Bubbles* (1968) and *The Gladiators* (1969). **Hammer credits:** *Jane Brown's Body* (1968, TV [episode of *Journey to the Unknown*], as Receptionist)

## Pentingell, Frank *see* Pettingell, Frank

## Penwarden, Hazel

This stage actress was officially "introduced" to the screen in the Hammer programer *The Man in Black* (1950), in which she played Joan. Her other film credits include *Now and Forever* (1956), while her TV work takes in episodes of *ITV Television Playhouse* (1955–1967, TV), *Thirteen Against Fate* (1966, TV), *Crown Court* (1972–1984, TV) and *Dramarama* (1983–1989, TV). **Hammer credits:** *The Man in Black* (1950, as Joan)

## Perceval, John

Perceval provided the story for the Hammer programer *The Runaway* (1964), the screenplay for which he then wrote with John Gerrard Sharp. **Hammer credits:** *The Runaway* (1964)

## Percival, Horace

Best known for his work on the radio series *It's That Man Again* (1939–1949), in which he played such characters as Ali Oop and What's'isname, this British comedy actor (1886–1961) can also be seen as Mr. Wimple in the Hammer comedy *Life with the Lyons* (1954), a role he repeated for the sequel *The Lyons in Paris* (1955) and the TV series *Life with the Lyons* (1955–1960, TV). His other credits include the big screen version of *It's That Man Again* (1943), *The Huggetts Abroad* (1949) and *Cuckoo College* (1949, TV). **Hammer credits:** *Life with the Lyons* (1954, as Mr. Wimple), *The Lyons in Paris* (1955, as Mr. Wimple), *Adventures with the Lyons* (1957, serial re-issue of *Life with the Lyons*)

## Percival, Robert

Percival can be seen as a police sergeant in Hammer's *The Rossiter Case* (1951). His other credits include *The Scarlet Web* (1954), *The Trials of Oscar Wilde* (1960), *The Frightened City* (1961) and *The Loneliness of the Long Distance Runner* (1962), plus episodes of *Four Just Men* (1959–1960, TV) and *The Pursuers* (1961–1962, TV). **Hammer credits:** *The Rossiter Case* (1951, as Sergeant)

## Percy, Edward

This British politician (he was the Tory MP for Ashford between 1943 and 1950) and playwright (1891–1968, real name Edward Percy-Smith) penned the hit 1939 thriller *Ladies in Retirement*, which he co-authored with Reginald Denham, with whom he also collaborated (along with Garret Fort) on the screenplay for the 1941 film version. It was also filmed later for television in 1954 (as an episode of *Lux Video Theatre* [1950–1959, TV]) and later remade as *The Mad Room* (1969). It was also adapted for German TV as *Paradies der alten Damen* (1971, TVM).

His other plays include *If Four Walls Told* (1922), which was filmed in 1922, *Slaves All* (1926), *Suspect* (1937, again with Denham), which was filmed for TV in 1939 and 1952 (the latter as an episode of *Broadway Television Theatre* [1952, TV]), *Lost Hat* (1936), *Trunk Crime* (also with Denham), which was filmed in 1939, the 1941 hit *The Shop at Sly Corner*, which was filmed in 1946, *Give Me Yesterday* (1938, with Denham), *Dressing Gown* (1939, which was co-written with Lilian Denham), *Dr. Brent's Household* (1941) and *Sparks Among the Stubble* (1966).

Percy was also called in by Hammer (at the request of Peter Cushing) to revise and polish their troubled script for *The Brides of Dracula* (1960) following work by Jimmy Sangster and Peter Bryan. **Hammer credits:** *The Brides of Dracula* (1960)

## Percy, Esme

On stage from 1904, this distinguished British actor (1887–1957, real name Saville Esme Percy) went on to study with Sarah Bernhardt and at the Brussels Conservatoire, and later became known for his work in the plays of George Bernard Shaw. In films from 1930 with the Hitchcock thriller *Murder* (in which he played the killer, Handel Fane), his many other credits include two Shaw adaptations—*Pygmalion* (1938) and *Caesar and Cleopatra* (1945)—plus *Nell Gwyn* (1934), *Invitation to the Waltz* (1935), in which he played Napoleon, *The Frog* (1936), *Dead of Night* (1945), *The Ghosts of Berkeley Square* (1947) and *Death in the Hand* (1948), plus episodes of *Gravelhanger* (1954, TV) and *The Scarlet Pimpernel* (1955–1956, TV). He also appeared in Hammer's *Song of Freedom* (1936) as Gabriel Donozetti. **Hammer credits:** *Song of Freedom* (1936, as Gabriel Donozetti)

## Perisic, Zoran

Noted for his work with "Zoptic" front projection (for which he holds several patents and has won various technical awards), this Yugoslavian effects technician (1940–) is best known for his work on *Superman* (1978), which won him a shared Oscar and BAFTA. His other credits include work on *2001: A Space Odyssey* (1968), *Gold: Before Woodstock, Beyond Reality* (1968 [released 1972]), *The Devil's Men* (1976), *The Thief of Baghdad* (1978, TVM), *Superman II* (1980), *Superman III* (1983) and *Return to Oz* (1985), which earned him a shared Oscar nomination. He went on to direct *Sky Bandits* (1986), for which he also provided the effects, and *The Phoenix and the Magic Carpet* (1995), which he also produced. Earlier in his career he provided the front projection work for the Whispering Gallery climax in Hammer's *Hands of the Ripper* (1971). He can be seen speaking about his work in the video documentary *You Will Believe: The Cinematic Saga of Superman* (2006) and the TV documentary *Pinewood: 80 Years of Movie Magic* (2015, TV). **Hammer credits:** *Hands of the Ripper* (1971 [uncredited])

## Perkins, Eric Boyd *see* Boyd-Perkins, Eric

## Perkins, Kay

Perkins worked as the continuity girl on *Wolfshead: The Legend of Robin Hood* (1969 [released 1973]), which was acquired by Hammer. Her other credits include *The Pale Faced Girl* (1969) and several episodes of *The Avengers* (1961–1969, TV). **Hammer credits:** *Wolfshead: The Legend of Robin Hood* (1969 [released 1973])

## Permane, Charles

Permane worked as the production manager on Hammer's *The Witches* (1966). His other credits include *Cosh Boy* (1952), *Blood of the Vampire* (1958), *The Trollenberg Terror* (1958), *Mark of the Phoenix* (1958) and *Circus of Horrors* (1960). **Hammer credits:** *The Witches* (1966)

## Perrin, Jacqueline

This British supporting actress played the role of Ursula in Hammer's *The Ugly Duckling* (1959). **Hammer credits:** *The Ugly Duckling* (1959, as Ursula)

## Perry, Anna

Perry had a minor role in *The House That Bled to Death* (1980, TV [episode of *Hammer House of Horror*]). Her other credits include episodes of *Sherlock Holmes* (1965–1968, TV) and *Out of the Unknown* (1965–1971, TV). **Hammer credits:** *The House That Bled to Death* (1980, TV [episode of *Hammer House of Horror*], as Journalist)

## Perry, Jimmy (Jim)

Perry operated the boom for *X—The Unknown* (1956), which led to a run of work for the studio. He also worked as a camera assistant on *The Old Dark House* (1963). His other credits as a boom operator include *The Quiller Memorandum* (1966), *The Island of Adventure* (1982), *On the Third Day* (1983) and *The Emerald Forest* (1985). **Hammer credits include:** *X—The Unknown* (1956, boom operator [uncredited]), *The Curse of Frankenstein* (1957, boom operator [uncredited]), *The Camp on Blood Island* (1958, boom operator [uncredited]), *The Ugly Duckling* (1959, boom operator [uncredited]), *The Mummy* (1959, boom operator [uncredited]), *The Hound of the Baskervilles* (1959, boom operator [uncredited]), *Never Take Sweets from a Stranger* (1960, boom operator [uncredited]), *The Terror of the Tongs* (1961, boom operator [uncredited]), *The Curse of the Werewolf* (1961, boom operator [uncredited]), *The Old Dark House* (1963, camera assistant [uncredited]), *Nightmare* (1964, boom operator [uncredited])

## Persaud, Toolsie

Persaud played the role of the young Kah-to-Bey in the flashback scene in Hammer's *The Mummy's Shroud* (1967). **Hammer credits:** *The Mummy's Shroud* (1967, as Kah-to-Bey)

## Pertwee, Bill

This British comedy actor (1926–2013, full name William Desmond Anthony Pertwee) is best known for playing the Chief ARP Warden William Hodges in the long-running sitcom *Dad's Army* (1968–1977, TV). His many other TV credits include roles in *Two in Clover* (1969–1970, TV), *Chance in a Million* (1984–1986, TV), *Woof* (1989–1997, TV) and *You Rang, M'Lord?* (1990–1993, TV), plus countless guest appearances. His film work was less frequent, among his credits being *Carry On Loving* (1970), *The Magnificent Seven Deadly Sins* (1971), *Carry On at Your Convenience* (1971 [scenes deleted]), *Carry On Girls* (1973), *What's Up Nurse!* (1977) and *What's Up Superdoc!* (1978). He also made an appearance as a nosey postman in Hammer's big screen version of *Love Thy Neighbour* (1973). He also played a postman in Hammer's version of *Man About the House* (1974). Much on stage (especially in pantomime), he was awarded an MBE in 2007 for his charity work. He was played by Shane Richie in *We're Doomed! The Dad's Army Story* (2015, TVM). The role of Mr. Hodges was subsequently played by Martin Savage in *Dad's Army* (2016). Pertwee's wife was singer and dancer Marion MacLeod (1928–2005), whom he married in 1955. His uncle was the writer Roland Pertwee (1885–1963) and his cousins were the writer Michael Pertwee (1916–1991) and the actor Jon Pertwee (1919–1996, full name John Devon Roland Perwee), who appeared in Hammer's *The Ugly Duckling* (1959). **Hammer credits:** *Love Thy Neighbour* (1973, as Postman), *Man About the House* (1974, as Postman)

## Pertwee, Jon

Best remembered for playing the title role in the long running science fiction series *Doctor Who* (1963–1989, TV) between 1970 and 1974, this versatile British character actor (1919–1996, full name

John Devon Roland Pertwee) began his film career in 1938 with a brief appearance in *A Yank at Oxford*. He turned his attention to radio just after the war, where his vocal talents were put to good use in a variety of programs, among them *Waterlogged Spa* (1948) and *The Navy Lark* (1959–1977). He also began appearing on TV, starting with *The Wandering Jew* (1947, TV), and took up films again with the likes of *Mr. Drake's Duck* (1951), *Carry On Cleo* (1964), *Carry On Cowboy* (1965), *Carry On Screaming* (1966), *The House That Dripped Blood* (1970), *The Boys in Blue* (1983) and *Carry On Columbus* (1992). He can also be seen in Hammer's Jekyll and Hyde spoof *The Ugly Duckling* (1959), in which he played Victor Jekyll, whose son experiments with the family formula. His other TV credits include episodes of *The Avengers* (1961–1969, TV), *Beggar My Neighbour* (1966–1968, TV) and *Virtual Murder* (1992, TV). He also played the title role in *Worzel Gummidge* (1979–1981, TV) and its sequel *Worzel Gummidge Down Under* (1986–1989, TV). His first wife (of two) was the actress Jean Marsh (1934–), to whom he was married between 1955 and 1960. His father was the writer Roland Pertwee (1885–1963) and his brother the playwright and screenwriter Michael Pertwee (1916–1991). His children are the actress Dariel Pertwee (1961–) and the actor Sean Pertwee (1964–). His cousin was the actor Bill Pertwee (1926–2013, full name William Desmond Anthony Pertwee), who appeared in Hammer's *Love Thy Neighbour* (1973) and *Man About the House* (1974). **Hammer credits:** *The Ugly Duckling* (1959, as Victor Jekyll)

### *Peter Cushing—A One-Way Ticket to Hollywood*

GB, 1989, 74m, color, TV

Made by Tyburn, one of Hammer's "rivals" in the seventies, this affectionate *This Is Your Life*–style tribute to the horror legend naturally highlights his work for Hammer, as well as Amicus and Tyburn. Executive produced by Tyburn's founder Kevin Francis, and photographed by his father Freddie (who had directed Cushing in many films for Hammer, Amicus and Tyburn), the program features an extended interview with Cushing by Dick Vosburgh, into which clips from his many films are interspersed, among them *The Curse of Frankenstein* (1957), *Dracula* (1958), *The Brides of Dracula* (1960), *She* (1965) and *Frankenstein Must Be Destroyed* (1969). Non-Hammer clips include scenes from *Legend of the Werewolf* (1975) and *The Masks of Death* (1985, TVM).

Production company: Tyburn. Executive producer: Kevin Francis. Producer: Gillian Garrow. Director: Alan Bell. Cinematographer: Freddie Francis. Music: James Bernard, Malcolm Williamson. Music director: Philip Martell. Editor: David Elliott. Make-up: Christine Allsop. Sound: John Murphy, Rupert Scrivener. Music recordist: Eric Tomlinson. Production controller: Jeffrey Broom. Technical supervisor: Annie Walbank. Camera assistant: Graham Ilazard. Gaffer: Gordon Gowing. Accountant: Alan Mabbott. Assistant accountant: Annette Pearse. Assistant to Kevin Francis: Amanda Bond. Assistant to Gillian Garrow: Sara

Gilbert. Props: Bob Martin. Laboratory liaison: David Trezise. Titles: Screen Ent. (title sketch by Don Roberts). Video post-production: Visnews. Re-recording: Anvil Studios. **Cast:** Peter Cushing, Dick Vosburgh

### Peters, Howard *see* Arnatt, John

### Peters, Jo

This actress and glamor model can be glimpsed during the orgy scene in Hammer's *To the Devil a Daughter* (1976). Her other credits include *Big Zapper* (1973) and *I'm Not Feeling Myself Tonight* (1976), plus episodes of *The Benny Hill Show* (1969–1989, TV) and *The Two Ronnies* (1971–1987, TV). **Hammer credits:** *To the Devil a Daughter* (1976, as Third girl)

### Peters, Luan

Following training at the E15 Acting School and experience as a singer, this curvaceous British actress (1946–, real name Carol Hirsch) began appearing on television in such series as *Nana* (1968, TV), *The Caesars* (1968, TV) and *Albert* (1969–1972, TV). She made her film debut in Hammer's *Lust for a Vampire* (1971), in which she played Trudi. This led to further work for the studio in *Twins of Evil* (1971). Her other big screen credits include *Not Tonight, Darling* (1971), *Man of Violence* (1971), *Freelance* (1971), *Go Girl* (1972), *The Flesh and Blood Show* (1972), *Vampira* (1974), *The Devil's Men* (1976), *The Wildcats of St. Trinian's* (1980) and *Pacific Banana* (1981). Her other TV credits include episodes of *Target* (1977–1978, TV), *Robin's Nest* (1977–1981, TV), *The Professionals* (1977–1983, TV) and *The Enigma Files* (1980, TV), though she is perhaps best remembered for playing the busty Australian Raylene Miles in *The Psychiatrist*, the classic 1979 episode of *Fawlty Towers* (1975–1979, TV), in which her character is inadvertently groped by Basil Fawlty. **Additional notes:** Peters was the subject of a magazine tribute care of Tim Greaves' One Shot Publications titled *Luan Peters—Homage to a Seraph* (1994). **Hammer credits:** *Lust for a Vampire* (1971, as Trudi), *Twins of Evil* (1971, as Gerta)

### Peters, Petra

This German actress (1925–2004) can be seen as Sister Helle in Hammer's *To the Devil a Daughter* (1976). In films primarily in her home country (where her scenes for the Hammer film were shot), her other credits include *Das Madchen Christine* (1949), in which she played the title role, *Furioso* (1950), *Gift im Zoo* (1952), *Magdalena, vom Teufel besessen* (1974) and *Banovic Strahinja* (1983). She was once married to the actor Albert Lieven (1906–1971, real name Albert Fritz Lieven-Lieven), who appeared in Hammer's *The Dark Light* (1951). **Hammer credits:** *To the Devil a Daughter* (1976, as Sister Helle)

### Peters, Reginald (Reg)

Peters can be glimpsed as a medical orderly in Hammer's *On the Buses* (1971). His other film credits include *Inadmissible Evidence* (1968), while his TV work takes in episodes of *Paul Temple*

(1969–1971, TV), *Jason King* (1971–1972, TV) and *The Borgias* (1981, TV). **Hammer credits:** *On the Buses* (1971, as Medical orderly)

### Peterson, Simon

Peterson worked as the second assistant director on Hammer's *Creatures the World Forgot* (1971). **Hammer credits:** *Creatures the World Forgot* (1971)

### Petrie, Gordon

This Guyana born actor, extra and stuntman (1922–2015, aka Prince Kumali and The Great Malumba) worked as a stuntman on Hammer's *I Only Arsked!* (1958). His other credits include *Tarzan and the Lost Safari* (1956), *Circus of Fear* (1966), *You Only Live Twice* (1967), *Death Line* (1972) and *Harry Potter and the Goblet of Fire* (2005). He was best known as a wrestler, and appeared under the names of Prince Kumali, The Great Malumba, Ormand Malumba, Big Brutus, Giant Zulu Warrior and Cam Zimba among others. After retiring from the ring, he was the key photographer at the annual British Wrestlers Reunion for many years. **Hammer credits:** *I Only Arsked!* (1958 [uncredited])

### Pettingell, Frank

On stage from 1911, this likeable British character actor (1891–1966) came to films in 1931 with *Jealousy* and *Hobson's Choice*, playing boot-maker-made-good Will Mossup in the latter. More than fifty further films followed, in which he frequently played robust northerners, among them *Sing As We Go* (1934), *Gaslight* (1940), *When We Are Married* (1942), *The Card* (1952), *Value for Money* (1955) and *Becket* (1964). In 1958 he appeared in the Hammer comedy *Up the Creek* (1958) as the Station Master, for which both the opening and closing credits mistakenly list his surname as Pentingell. His TV work includes episodes of *The Gay Cavalier* (1957, TV), *No Hiding Place* (1959–1967, TV), *An Age of Kings* (1960, TV) and *The Spread of the Eagle* (1963). **Hammer credits:** *Up the Creek* (1958, as Station Master)

### Pettitt, Frank

This British actor (1899–1964) can be seen as a policeman in Hammer's *Face the Music* (1954). His other credits include *Night and the City* (1950), *Victim* (1961) and *Impact* (1963), plus episodes of *Navy Log* (1955–1958, TV), *Gert and Daisy* (1959, TV) and *Detective* (1964–1969, TV). Also on stage. **Hammer credits:** *Face the Music* (1954, as Policeman [uncredited])

### Pettitt, Lesley *see* De Pettitt, Lesley

### Petworth, Harriet

This British supporting actress (1889–1982, sometimes Peterworth) can be spotted as Matron in the Hammer programer *Room to Let* (1950). Her other credits include *Warning to Wantons* (1948) and episodes of *No Hiding Place* (1959–1967, TV), *Harpers West One* (1961–1963, TV) and *The Secret Agent* (1967, TV). **Hammer credits:** *Room to Let* (1950, as Matron)

## Peverall, John

One of Hammer's most prolific assistant directors, British born Peverall (1931–2009) began his association with the company with the comedy *Up the Creek* (1958). Prior to this he had worked his way up through the industry, first in the mail room at Rank from 1945 and then as a lowly fourth assistant director, working on such films as Olivier's *Hamlet* (1948). His other credits as a first assistant include *West 11* (1963), *The Traitors* (1963), *The Moon-Spinners* (1964), *Masquerade* (1965), *Khartoum* (1966), *Only When I Larf* (1968), *The Assassination Bureau* (1968) and *From Beyond the Grave* (1973). He also worked as a unit/production manager on *I Could Go On Singing* (1963), *Stolen Hours* (1963), *The Ghost of Monk's Island* (1967) and *Neither the Sea Nor the Sand* (1972). He lost his job at Hammer following the temporary closure of Bray in 1962. Although later asked to return, he turned the offer down. Recalled Peverall, "I think my four years at Hammer were extremely good years to me. They showed me how films could be made—and could still be made without spending all those huge amounts of money."[19]

Peverall later moved up the industry ladder, working as an associate producer on *The Land That Time Forgot* (1975), *The Man Who Fell to Earth* (1976), *Quadrophenia* (1979) and *McVicar* (1980). He went on to win a best picture Oscar for *The Deer Hunter* (1978), which he produced with Michael Cimino, Barry Spikings and Michael Deeley. His TV credits include *Arthur of the Britons* (1972, TV), on which he was an associate producer, and *The Far Pavilions* (1984, TV), which he executive produced. His second wife was actress Hersha Parady (1945–), whom he married in 1994. **Additional notes:** Peverall worked on both Hammer's *Captain Clegg* (1962) and the Disney version of the same story, *Dr. Syn, Alias the Scarecrow* (1963). **Hammer credits:** *Up the Creek* (1958), *Further Up the Creek* (1958), *I Only Arsked!* (1958), *The Hound of the Baskervilles* (1959), *The Ugly Duckling* (1959), *Yesterday's Enemy* (1959), *The Mummy* (1959 [uncredited]), *The Man Who Could Cheat Death* (1959), *The Stranglers of Bombay* (1959), *Never Take Sweets from a Stranger* (1960), *The Brides of Dracula* (1960), *The Two Faces of Dr. Jekyll* (1960), *The Curse of the Werewolf* (1961), *The Shadow of the Cat* (1961), *Watch It, Sailor!* (1961), *The Terror of the Tongs* (1961), *Cash on Demand* (1961), *The Phantom of the Opera* (1962), *Captain Clegg* (1962), *The Pirates of Blood River* (1962), *The Damned* (1963)

## Peyre, Jean

Peyre (1926–2001) worked as the assistant art director (under Edward Carrick) on the Hammer thriller *Maniac* (1963). His credits as a designer include episodes of *R3* (1964–1965, TV), *The Logic Game* (1965, TV) and *Knightmare* (1987–1994, TV). He also designed effects for such series as *Doctor Who* (1963–1989, TV) and *The Hitchhiker's Guide to the Galaxy* (1981, TV). **Hammer credits:** *Maniac* (1963 [uncredited])

## PFS (Pension Fund Securities)

The pension fund subsidiary of ICI (Imperial Chemical Industries), PFS bought Hammer from James Carreras for the sum of £400,000 on 31 January 1973, thus placing the running of the company solely in the hands of his son Michael Carreras. A further £200,000 was also provided to fund a production slate, which included the troubled *To the Devil a Daughter* (1976). However, when PFS began to call in the loan, it effectively killed off Hammer as a going concern. Indeed, the company was eventually declared insolvent, with debts of £800,000. PFS then sold the concern to Roy Skeggs and Brian Lawrence for £100,000 in 1980, thus making them the company's new owners. Note that Hammer board director Euan Lloyd also used PFS to finance films in the seventies. **Hammer credits:** *To the Devil a Daughter* (1976)

## *The Phantom of the Opera*

GB, 1962, 84m, Eastmancolor [processed by Technicolor in the UK and Pathé in the U.S.], widescreen, RCA, cert A

By the time Hammer came to make their version of Gaston Leroux's 1911 horror romance, the studio was going through something of an identity crisis. If this was Hammer Horror, then it was a somewhat subdued affair, as evidenced by the genteel A certificate awarded to it by the usually hard-nosed BBFC. However, this was by no means a case of Hammer watering down its product to satisfy the censor. In fact, the emphasis on romance rather than horror can be blamed—somewhat astonishingly—on Hollywood superstar Cary Grant, who seriously considered appearing in the film on the strict understanding that it would not revel in shock and gore. Somewhat astutely, the film's producer, Anthony Hinds, "Knew he'd never make it, but he was insistent, so I wrote the thing for him."[20]

Hammer had gained the remake rights to *The Phantom of the Opera* from Universal following their success with *Dracula* (1958). Universal had itself already filmed the story twice: first in 1925 with Lon Chaney, and then later in 1943 with Claude Rains (there had also been a silent German version made in 1916 titled *Das Phantom der Oper*, and an Argentine television version made in 1960 titled *El fantasma de la opera*). The 1925 version, noted for its vast sets and Chaney's remarkable make-up, was generally regarded as the definitive version, although the highly romanticized 1943 remake, which had won Oscars for its color cinematography and art direction, also had its admirers, despite its somewhat dogged emphasis on the music. Therefore, in keeping with Cary Grant's wishes, and the need to sustain his image as a matinee idol, Hammer's take on the story was to adhere to the 1943 version. Consequently, it transpires that it is *not* the Phantom who is responsible for a series of murders in and around the opera house under which he hides, but his dwarf assistant ("Terror haunts these dusty corridors, murder waits its call in the dressing rooms, and on cue, death makes his entrance," exclaimed the trailer, effectively playing up the film's backstage setting).

In his adaptation, for which he was paid £200, Anthony Hinds (working as John Elder) relocated the action from the vast Paris Opera House to a rather more humble venue in London. Here, Professor Petrie sells the ruthless impresario Lord Ambrose D'Arcy some of his compositions, only to subsequently discover that D'Arcy is passing them off as his own, among them Petrie's *grand opus*, *Joan of Arc*. Determined to destroy the plates that will be used to print the music stolen by D'Arcy, Petrie breaks into the printing shop to ruin them with acid. Unfortunately, an accident sees Petrie himself covered in the coruscating liquid, which prompts him to dive for relief into the nearby river. Rescued from drowning by a dwarf who becomes his devoted assistant, Petrie now becomes the Phantom and "haunts" D'Arcy's theater from his lair in the cellars, where he observes the production of his opera. However, when the Phantom abducts the theater's new discovery, Christine Charles, so as to coach her to play the leading role, producer Harry Hunter determines on rescuing her from the clutches of her captor. Realizing that the Phantom is basically a benevolent being, Hunter allows the Professor to continue coaching Christine for the opening night, during which the Phantom finally meets his doom while trying to save his protégé from a falling chandelier, on to which the dwarf has climbed while attempting to escape a stage hand who has caught him observing the opera from the rigging.

As Anthony Hinds had always suspected, Cary Grant did indeed pull out of the film, leaving the producer to cast around for a suitable star with whom to replace him. But who on earth could replace a star of Grant's appeal and stature? Hammer had, of course, previously cast many Hollywood stars in their films, particularly in their fifties second features, making use of names whose careers were on the wane. However, instead of trying to find a match for Grant, Hinds instead decided to offer the role of Petrie/The Phantom to the respected character star Herbert Lom, despite Christopher Lee's ambition to appear in a remake of the property, especially as he believed that the film "would give me a chance to prove that I can sing."[21] However, as Lee recalled, "Because I was living in Switzerland when Hammer filmed it, international tax laws barred me from working in England for long periods. Herbert Lom was, of course, excellent. One can't play them all."[22]

Indeed, Lom was by no means a bad catch, being no stranger to the international scene, having already co-starred in such blockbusters as *War and Peace* (1956), *Spartacus* (1960) and *El Cid* (1961). That he'd already appeared for Hammer back in 1952 in *Whispering Smith Hits London*, which had been produced by Hinds, can't have hurt his chances, either. Having read Hinds' treatment, Lom readily accepted the role, and the film moved one step further towards production. Recalled Lom, "When I read the script I jumped straight out of my chair, grabbed the telephone and told producer Anthony Hinds it was a deal."[23]

To play the all-important role of Christine, Hinds cast the pretty Heather Sears, who had already made a mark in such classic British productions as *The Story of Esther Costello* (1957), *Room at the Top* (1958) and *Sons and Lovers* (1960). Meanwhile, Michael Gough, like Herbert Lom, returned to Hammer for his second time as the swindling D'Arcy, while Edward de Souza was cast as

Harry Hunter, the handsome hero of the piece. As for the supporting cast, it featured the usual Hammer *Who's Who*, among them Michael Ripper, Thorley Walters, Miles Malleson, Harold Goodwin and Keith Pyott. Given his genre track record, Terence Fisher was the natural choice to direct (especially given his much-professed liking for stories with a pronounced romantic angle), while Arthur Grant and Bernard Robinson were required to bring their customary skills to the photography and production design respectively.

On the floor at Bray between 21 November 1961 and 26 January 1962, *Phantom* was, with a budget of £171,000, accorded a reasonably lavish production, prime among the settings being Petrie's cavernous lair beneath the theater, which was decorated with the customary Bernard Robinson bric-a-brac. "The most costly and spectacular thriller of its kind ever filmed in Britain," claimed the press book, which bandied the incredible sum of £400,000 as the budget. However, the reality was somewhat different, and to save money, Wimbledon Theater in South London was used for the opera house interiors (which were filmed between 27 November and 12 December), despite the venue's cramped-looking stage and auditorium ("Terence Fisher was at his wits' end to give it some size,"[24] recalled camera operator Len Harris). To film these sequences, Fisher was assisted by the theater director Dennis Maunder, whose experience in staging opera proved to be a great help when it came to the grouping of the singers, among them a number of professionals for added authenticity (Maunder's screen credit noted that he worked on the film "by permission of the General Administrator, Royal Opera House, Covent Garden, Ltd.").

However, when it came to the designs for the Phantom's mask and burns make-up, Roy Ashton found himself in something of a quandary, given Anthony Hinds' inability to make a decision as to which of several proposed designs he should go for. Indeed, Petrie's make-up had still to be finalized two weeks into the shooting schedule, while his mask was allegedly hastily conceived on location at the Wimbledon Theater during the *third* week of shooting. Revealed Ashton, "I got a piece of old rag, tied it round his [Herbert Lom's] face, cut a hole it in, stuck a bit of mesh over one of the eyes, two bits of string around it and tried it."[25] The results proved effective enough, although they ultimately came in for criticism from fans, who had expected more from the Phantom's appearance, which wasn't quite "the figure of terror incarnate" as the poster claimed. Yet given Hammer's intention to achieve an A certificate (*Phantom Lite*, if you will), Ashton and Fisher were both prevented from making Petrie's appearance too shocking or revolting (once revealed, the Phantom's face has a very similar look to that of Baron Meinster's in *The Brides of Dracula* [1960], after Van Helsing has splashed it with corrosive holy water).

Despite its milder content, following the film's completion, a number of cuts were still demanded by the BBFC so as to make it suitable for children accompanied by adults, among them trims to the revelation of the Phantom's face and alterations to a rather gratuitous scene in which the dwarf stabs a rat catcher (played by Patrick Troughton) in the eye. In fact in pursuing an A certificate, Hammer could be seen as being compliant in emasculating their own movie, prompting *The New York Times* unknowingly to comment, "The only shock is that the British, who could have had a field day with this antique, have simply wafted it back with a lick and promise."

Yet despite its failings (which director Terence Fisher rather surprisingly attributed to "the editing, which could have been better"[26]), the film has a look as opulent as any of Hammer's more cherished productions, prompting *The Times* to observe that "There is a nice profusion of plush in the Victorian setting, and the gaslights, always important on these occasions, do their duty admirably." The cast also adds a touch of class to the proceedings. Herbert Lom is more than successful in tapping into the Phantom's more sympathetic qualities (which here are more the result of Fate than malevolence), Heather Sears (whose singing was dubbed by Patricia Clark) looks suitably doe-eyed as the heroine, Edward de Souza cuts a reasonable swash as the hero, while Michael Gough enjoys chewing the scenery as the devious D'Arcy.

Fisher also manages several notable touches, among them a Hitchcockian jump cut to a diva who at first seems to be screaming but is in fact practicing; a shock sequence in which the hanged body of a stagehand tears through a piece of canvas scenery; and a flashback sequence explaining the Phantom's backstory which is filmed entirely in tilted shots. The use of a crane meanwhile adds a little scope to several scenes by the river. One should also note the main title sequence, which plays out over a series of extreme close-ups of the Phantom's face, rather like the opening credits of *The Curse of the Werewolf* (1961), also directed by Fisher, the credits for which likewise play out over an extreme close-up of the werewolf's weeping eyes. However, unlike previous adaptations, the Phantom *himself* removes his own mask in order to improve his sight during his bid to save Christine; in the previous versions, it had been Christine, through sheer curiosity, who removes the mask, leading to the classic shock revelation, here somewhat arbitrarily abandoned.

The film did have its champions, among them *Variety*, which conceded that it had its "fair measure of goose pimples." It also noted that "the atmosphere of brooding evil still works up to some effective highlights." However, *The Observer* described the film as "a very tame remake of the famous original," while *Films and Filming* found it to be "a little short on genuine thrills." Perhaps not surprisingly, following its UK premiere on 7 June 1962 at the Odeon Leicester Square on a double bill with Hammer's own *Captain Clegg* (1962), the film failed to garner much interest at the box office when released by Rank on the ABC circuit (again with *Clegg*) on 25 June, despite the poster's claim that it was "The greatest thrill classic of all time." It fared rather better in America when released by Universal on 15 August, with some of the footage cut from the British print now restored.

By no means one of Hammer's gems, the film is worthy of at least being regarded as a polished rhinestone, despite some rather dull opera sequences. **Additional notes:** During the scene in which Harry Hunter offers to take Christine out to lunch, take a look at the clock on the wall in the background, which declares the time to be seven forty. Leroux's story has subsequently been filmed for both the large and small screen several more times since, notably in 1983 (TVM), 1989, 1991 (twice, TVM), 1998 and 2004 (the latter being based on the long-running 1986 Andrew Lloyd-Webber stage musical, which was also staged for television from the Royal Albert Hall in 2011). There was also an animated version in 1987. Other films making use of the interior of Wimbledon Theater include *Half a Sixpence* (1967). Daniel Nyberg, the stage manager of the Wimbledon Theater, was also an assistant director in his own right on such films as *Konga* (1960), *Alfred the Great* (1969) and, in Canada, *Prom Night* (1980); he would later form Danith Productions in Canada, in which he was joined by Michael Carreras for a period in 1981, when the duo tried to set up a studio complex in Toronto. Following the completion of *The Phantom of the Opera*, Bray Studios temporarily shut down, so that Hammer could better assess where its future lay (this was the result of a lack of funding from America, despite the company's continued ties with Columbia and Universal). As a consequence, several long-serving staff members lost their jobs, prime among them camera operator Len Harris, his focus puller Harry Oakes, continuity girl Tilly Day and assistant director John Peverall.

Production companies: Hammer/Laverstock. Distributors: Rank (UK [ABC circuit]), Universal International (U.S.). Producer: Anthony Hinds. Associate producer: Basil Keys. Director: Terence Fisher. Screenplay: John Elder (Anthony Hinds), "based on the composition by Gaston Leroux". Cinematographer: Arthur Grant. Music/conductor: Edwin Astley. Supervising editor: James Needs. Editor: Alfred Cox. Assistant editor: Chris Barnes [uncredited]. Production design: Bernard Robinson. Art director: Don Mingaye. Costumes: Rosemary Burrows, Molly Arbuthnot. Special effects: Les Bowie. Special effects assistants: Ian Scoones [uncredited], Brian Johncock [uncredited], Pat Moore [uncredited]. Make-up: Roy Ashton, Colin Garde [uncredited]. Hair: Frieda Steiger. Sound: Jock May. Sound editor: James Groom. Production manager: Clifford Parkes. Assistant director: John Peverall. Second assistant director: Peter Medak [uncredited]. Camera operator: Len Harris. Focus puller: Harry Oakes [uncredited]. Camera grip: Albert Cowlard [uncredited]. Construction manager: Arthur Banks [uncredited]. Master carpenter: Charles Davis [uncredited]. Master plasterer: Stan Banks [uncredited]. Master painter: Lawrence Wrenn [uncredited]. Master electrician: Jack Curtis [uncredited]. Master rigger: Ronald Lenoir [uncredited]. Props: Tommy Money [uncredited]. Props buyer: Eric Hillier [uncredited]. Stunts: Gerry Crampton [uncredited], Paddy Hayes [uncredited], Peter Pocock [uncredited]. Continuity: Tilly Day. Opera staging: Dennis Maunder. Stills: Tom Edwards [uncredited]. Processing: Pathé. **Cast:** Herbert Lom (Professor Petrie/The Phantom), Heather Sears (Christine

Charles), Edward de Souza (Harry Hunter), Thorley Walters (Lattimer), Michael Gough (Lord Ambrose D'Arcy), Ian Wilson (Dwarf), Miles Malleson (Cabby), Harold Goodwin (Bill), Miriam Karlin (Charwoman), Martin Miller (Rossi), John Harvey (Sergeant Vickers), Renee Houston (Mrs. Tucker), Marne Maitland (Xavier), Michael Ripper (Cabby), Patrick Troughton (Rat catcher), Sonya Cordeau (Yvonne), Liane Aukin (Maria), Keith Pyott (Weaver), Liam Redmond (Police Inspector [uncredited]), John Maddison (Chief Inspector Dawson [uncredited]), Leila Forde (Teresa [uncredited]), Geoffrey L'Oise (Frenchman [uncredited]), Jane Merrow (Chorus girl [uncredited]), Fred Wood (Stage hand [uncredited]), Fred Peck (Stage hand and man in audience [both uncredited]), Patricia Clark (Heather Sears' vocals [uncredited]), Jackie Cooper (Herbert Lom's stunt double [uncredited]). **DVD availability:** Universal (R1 U.S. NTSC), as part of the *Hammer Horror Series* box set, which also contains *The Brides of Dracula* (1960), *The Curse of the Werewolf* (1961), *Paranoiac* (1963), *The Kiss of the Vampire* (1963), *Captain Clegg* (1962), *Nightmare* (1964) and *The Evil of Frankenstein* (1964). **Blu-ray availability:** Final Cut Entertainment (B/2), extras include interviews and a documentary, *The Making of The Phantom of the Opera*, which is narrated by Edward de Souza. **CD availability:** *The Hammer Film Music Collection: Volume Two* (GDI Records), which contains the *Main Title*.

### *The Phantom Ship* see *The Mystery of the Mary Celeste*

### Phibbs, Giles

Phibbs can be seen in a minor role in Hammer's *Vampire Circus* (1972). His other credits include episodes of *Doctor Who* (1963–1989, TV), *The Troubleshooters* (1965–1972, TV), *Tales of the Unexpected* (1979–1988, TV) and *The Chief* (1990–1995, TV). **Hammer credits:** *Vampire Circus* (1972, as Sexton)

### The Philharmonia Orchestra

The Philharmonia Orchestra (aka The New Philharmonia Orchestra) was used for the recording of Temple Abady's score for Hammer's *Never Look Back* (1952) and Doreen Carwithen's music for *Mantrap* (1953). Founded in 1945 primarily as a recording orchestra, it has over one-thousand releases to its credit, making it the world's most recorded orchestra. Other film scores performed by the orchestra include those for *Scott of the Antarctic* (1948), *Battle of the Bulge* (1965), *The Night of the Generals* (1967), *Nicholas and Alexandra* (1971), *Vanity Fair* (2004) and *Splice* (2009). **Hammer credits:** *Never Look Back* (1952), *Mantrap* (1953)

### Phillips, Bunty

Phillips (?–1993) worked as the make-up artist on Hammer's *Hands of the Ripper* (1971). However, some of the film's gorier make-up effects were provided by an uncredited Roy Ashton. Phillips' other credits include *Gonks Go Beat* (1965), *Daleks—Invasion Earth 2150 A.D.* (1966), *They Came from Beyond Space* (1967), *Spring and Port Wine* (1970),

*Hardcore* (1977), *What's Up Superdoc!* (1978), *Rising Damp* (1980), *George and Mildred* (1980), *Ordeal by Innocence* (1984) and *A View to a Kill* (1985), plus episodes of *The Pathfinders* (1972–1973, TV), *Danger UXB* (1979, TV) and *Widows* (1983, TV). **Hammer credits:** *Hands of the Ripper* (1971)

### Phillips, Conrad

Best remembered for playing the title role in the television series *The Adventures of William Tell* (1958–1959, TV), this British actor (1925–2016, real name Conrad Philip Havord) broke into films in 1948 with *A Song for Tomorrow*, which led to appearances in over forty further films, among them *Lilli Marlene* (1950), *Zarak* (1957), *Circus of Horrors* (1960), *Heavens Above!* (1963), *Impact* (1963), which he also co-wrote, *Who Killed the Cat?* (1966) and *The Ghost of Monk's Island* (1967), after which he concentrated on stage and television work, among his credits being an episode of *Hammer House of Horror* (1980, TV). He also guest starred in a new series about the William Tell legend titled *Crossbow* (1987–1988, TV), playing Stefan for three episodes in season one (Will Lyman assumed the title role). A second feature regular in the fifties and sixties, Phillips worked for Hammer three times during this period, beginning with *The Last Page* (1952), in which he played the supporting role of Sergeant Todd. His other TV credits include episodes of *Douglas Fairbanks, Jr. Presents* (1953–1957, TV), *The Avengers* (1961–1969, TV), *Sutherland's Law* (1973–1976, TV) and *Never the Twain* (1981–1991, TV). **Hammer credits:** *The Last Page* (1952, as Sergeant Todd), *Mantrap* (1953, as Barker), *The Shadow of the Cat* (1961, as Michael Latimer), *The Mark of Satan* (1980, TV [episode of *Hammer House of Horror*], as Dr. Mauders)

### Phillips, Eric

This British supporting actor (1908–1966) played the role of Sergeant Wright in the Hammer programer *The Adventures of PC 49—The Case of the Guardian Angel* (1949). He also played the role in the original radio series upon which the film was based, *The Adventures of PC 49* (1947–1953), but was replaced in the second film, *A Case for PC 49* (1951), by Campbell Singer. His other credits include *Touch and Go* (1955) and episodes of *The Adventures of Clint and Mac* (1957, TV), *Private Investigator* (1958–1959, TV) and *No Hiding Place* (1959–1967, TV). **Hammer credits:** *The Adventures of PC 49—The Case of the Guardian Angel* (1949, as Sergeant Wright)

### Phillips, Frank

This British actor (1901–1980) can be seen as the BBC announcer in Hammer's *The Quatermass Xperiment* (1955). An actual BBC newsreader and announcer, he began his broadcasting career on radio in 1935, turning to television as a compere in 1947. On stage from 1923 as a singer, his other credits include *Passport to Pimlico* (1949), *Mr. Drake's Duck* (1951), *Appointment with Venus* (1951), *The Dam Busters* (1955), *I'm All Right Jack* (1959) and *Triple Cross* (1966), in all of which he played either a television or radio announcer, a role he also played in such series as *Quatermass and the*

*Pit* (1958–1959, TV) and *A Piece of Resistance* (1966, TV), the latter an episode of *The Wednesday Play* (1964–1970, TV). **Hammer credits:** *The Quatermass Xperiment* (1955, as BBC announcer [uncredited])

### Phillips, Gerry (Geremy)

This British supporting actor (1938–) played the role of Tiger in the Hammer comedy *The Ugly Duckling* (1959). He can also be seen as a Teddy boy in *The Damned* (1963). His other credits include episodes of *No Hiding Place* (1959–1967, TV) and *Paradise Walk* (1961, TV). **Hammer credits:** *The Ugly Duckling* (1959, as Tiger), *The Damned* (1963, as Teddy boy [uncredited])

### Phillips, Jennifer

Phillips worked as the continuity girl on *The Madison Equation* (1968, TV [episode of *Journey to the Unknown*]). Her other credits include *The Night Digger* (1971). **Hammer credits:** *The Madison Equation* (1968, TV [episode of *Journey to the Unknown*])

### Phillips, Jeremy see Phillips, Geremy

### Phillips, John

Much on stage, this British character actor (1914–1995, real name William John Phillips) was frequently cast as military types (in real life he was awarded the Military Cross for his services during the Second World War). His various big screen credits include *Angels One Five* (1952), *Village of the Damned* (1960), *A Prize of Arms* (1962), *Becket* (1964), *Torture Garden* (1967), *Quadrophenia* (1979), *Ascendancy* (1982), *The Last of England* (1987) and *Merlin of the Crystal Cave* (1991, TVM). He also had the substantial role of Stanley Preston in Hammer's *The Mummy's Shroud* (1967), prior to which he'd played a guard in *Women Without Men* (1956) for them. His many TV credits include episodes of *Bleak House* (1959, TV), *The Sentimental Agent* (1963, TV), *Jane Eyre* (1973, TV), *Jesus of Nazareth* (1977, TV) and *One by One* (1984–1987, TV). **Hammer credits:** *Women Without Men* (1956, as Guard [uncredited]), *The Mummy's Shroud* (1967, as Stanley Preston)

### Phillips, Leo

Phillips played the role of Sergeant Peterson in the Hammer sci-fi quickie *Spaceways* (1953). He can also be seen as a night watchman in *Blood Orange* (1953) and as a dresser in *Face the Music* (1954). His other credits include *Treasure Island* (1950), *The Cruel Sea* (1953) and *The Scarlet Web* (1954). **Hammer credits:** *Spaceways* (1953, as Sergeant Peterson [uncredited]), *Blood Orange* (1953, as Harry [night watchman, uncredited]), *Face the Music* (1954, as Dresser [uncredited])

### Phillips, Leslie

There are very few comedy performers who could make so much out of such simple catchphrases as "Hel-lo" and "Ding dong," which is why Phillips (1924–) is a British legend. The archetypal ladies' man of British comedy, he began his acting career on stage at the age of five, and later studied at the Italia Conti School of Speech and Drama. In films from 1938 with *Lassie from Lancashire* (1938), he went on to appear in over sixty productions, developing his character as the wolfish man about town. Career highlights include *Les Girls* (1957), *Carry On Nurse* (1959), *Carry On Teacher* (1959), *Carry On Constable* (1960), *Doctor in Love* (1960), *Very Important Person* (1961), *The Fast Lady* (1962), *You Must Be Joking!* (1967), *Out of Africa* (1984), *Empire of the Sun* (1987), *Scandal* (1988), in which he played Lord Astor, *August* (1996), *Venus* (2006), which earned him a BAFTA nomination for best supporting actor, *Late Bloomers* (2011) and *After Death* (2012). Equally busy on radio, he was a familiar voice in *The Navy Lark* (1959–1977) in which he played Sub-Lieutenant Phillips (he also appeared in the 1959 film version), while his television credits include episodes of *The Adventures of Robin Hood* (1955–1960, TV), *Our Man at St. Mark's* (1963–1966, TV), *Chancer* (1990–1991, TV) and *Monarch of the Glen* (2000–2005, TV), plus many guest appearances. Meanwhile, in 2013, he was the subject of the documentary *Hello: A Portrait of Leslie Phillips* (2013, TV). In 1961, Phillips co-starred in the Hammer comedy *A Weekend with Lulu* (1961), in which he played one of a group of hapless Britishers holidaying on the Continent. Married three times, his first wife was actress Penelope Bartley (1925–1981), to whom he was married between 1948 and 1965; his second wife was actress Angela Scoular (1945–2011), whom he married in 1982. He was awarded an OBE in 1998 and a CBE in 2008. **Hammer credits:** *A Weekend with Lulu* (1961, aka Timothy Gray)

### Phillips, Michelle

Formerly a member of The Mamas and the Papas (with whom she had such hits as *Monday, Monday* and *California Dreamin'*), this American singer and actress (1944–, real name Holly Michelle Gilliam) took the starring role in *Paint Me a Murder* (1984, TVM [episode of *Hammer House of Mystery and Suspense*]). In films from 1971 with *The Last Movie*, her other credits include *Dillinger* (1973), *Valentino* (1977), *Bloodline* (1979), *Savage Harvest* (1981), *Scissors* (1991), *The Price of Air* (2000), *Kids in America* (2005) and *Unbeatable Harold* (2006), plus episodes of such series as *Aspen* (1977, TV), *Vegas* (1978–1981, TV), *Knots Landing* (1979–1983, TV), in which she played the villainous Anne W. Matheson, *Hotel* (1983–1988, TV), *Malibu Shores* (1996, TV) and *7th Heaven* (1996–2007, TV). Married four times, her husbands include songwriter John Phillips (1935–2001), to whom she was married between 1962 and 1970, and actor-director Dennis Hopper (1936–2010), to whom she was briefly married in 1970. Her children include actress-singer Chynna Phillips (1968–, real name Gilliam Chynna Phillips) and actor Austin Hines (1982–). **Hammer credits:** *Paint Me a Murder* (1984, TVM [episode of *Hammer House of Mystery and Suspense*], as Sandra Lorenz)

### Phillips, Redmond

In Britain for a period during the fifties and sixties, this New Zealand born actor (1912–1993) appeared in such films as *A Night to Remember* (1958), *The Criminal* (1960), *There Was a Crooked Man* (1960), *Love Is a Ball* (1962) and *Tom Jones* (1963). He also played Hans in Hammer's *The Gorgon* (1964), and popped up in episodes of such TV series as *The Last Chronicle of Barset* (1959, TV), *The Avengers* (1961–1969, TV) and *The Saint* (1962–1969, TV). Later working in Australia, he went on to appear in *Little Boy Lost* (1978), *Phar Lap* (1983), *Razorback* (1984) and *Burke & Wills* (1985), as well as episodes of *The Rovers* (1969, TV), *Barrier Reef* (1971–1972, TV), *A Country Practice* (1981–1993, TV) and *Runaway Island* (1982, TV) and *The Miraculous Mellops* (1991, TV). **Hammer credits:** *The Gorgon* (1964, as Hans)

### Phillips, Roy

This British singer, songwriter, guitarist and keyboard player (1943–) penned the title song for Hammer's *The Lost Continent* (1968). This was performed by himself and The Peddlers (of which he was a member, along with Tab Martin and Trevor Morais) and was arranged by the film's composer Gerard Schurmann. Run the lyrics, "I only know the secret it holds, The fears that it hides and the stories untold…. This forgotten soul that the storm has sent, To the lost continent." During his earlier career, Phillips had also been a member of such bands as The Soundtracks, The Tornadoes (also with Tab Martin) and The Saints (aka Andy Cavell and The Saints), appearing with the latter in *Live It Up!* (1963). **Hammer credits:** *The Lost Continent* (1968)

### Phillips, Sian

This highly respected British (Welsh) actress (1933–, real name Jane Elizabeth Ailwen Phillips), noted for her imperious, aquiline features, began her career on radio as a child of eleven. Following training at RADA, she made her West End debut in 1957, since when she has been a familiar figure in all media. On television her credits include *Shoulder to Shoulder* (1974, TV), *How Green Was My Valley* (1975, TV), *I, Claudius* (1976, TV), which earned her a best actress BAFTA nomination, and an episode of *Hammer House of Horror* (1980, TV), while her film credits take in *Young Cassidy* (1964), *Becket* (1964), *Goodbye, Mr. Chips* (1969), *Murphy's War* (1971), *Clash of the Titans* (1981), *Dune* (1984), *Valmont* (1989), *The Age of Innocence* (1993), *The Gigolos* (2006), *Bella Fleace Gave a Party* (2012), *Under Milk Wood* (2014, TVM) and *La Lune Folle* (2016). She has also continued to appear with regularity on the stage, and was made a CBE in 2000. Her second husband (of three) was the actor Peter O'Toole (1932–2013), to whom she was married between 1959 and 1979. Her third husband was the actor Robin Sachs (1951–2013), to whom she was married between 1979 and 1991; he appeared in Hammer's *Vampire Circus* (1972). Her children are actresses Pat O'Toole and Kate O'Toole (1960–). **Hammer credits:** *Carpathian Eagle* (1980, TV [episode of *Hammer House of Horror*], as Mrs. Henska)

### Phillpotts, Ambrosine

Following training at RADA, this British actress (1912–1980) went on to forge a solid career in the theater, which she augmented with supporting roles in films, often being cast as upper crust types. Her many credits include *This Man Is Mine* (1948), *Room at the Top* (1958), *Doctor in Love* (1960), *Carry On Cabby* (1963), *Life at the Top* (1965) and *The Wildcats of St. Trinian's* (1980). She also played the supporting role of the fur department clerk Miss Patten in Hammer's *Stolen Face* (1952). Also busy on television, she was familiar to seventies audiences as Lady Helen Hadleigh in *Hadleigh* (1969–1976, TV). Her other TV credits include episodes of *The Small House at Allington* (1960, TV), *That's Your Funeral* (1970–1971, TV) and *Follyfoot* (1971–1973, TV). **Hammer credits:** *Stolen Face* (1952, as Miss Patten)

### Phipps, Nicholas

Frequently cast in minor authority roles or as the archetypal English silly ass, this affable British character actor (1913–1980) began his film career in 1940 with a brief appearance in *Contraband*, prior to which he'd appeared in a handful of early TV plays, among them *Hands Across the Sea* (1938, TV) and *First Stop North* (1939, TV). Following wartime experience, he went on to appear in the likes of *You Will Remember* (1946), *Maytime in Mayfair* (1949), *The Pure Hell of St. Trinian's* (1960), *The Amorous Prawn* (1962), *Summer Holiday* (1963) and *The Rise and Rise of Michael Rimmer* (1970). He also appeared in Hammer's wartime comedy *Don't Panic Chaps* (1959) as Major Mortimer, and an episode of *Journey to the Unknown* (1968, TV). Despite his popularity as a supporting name, Phipps' actually had a greater success as a screenwriter, penning (sometimes in collaboration) such successes as *Piccadilly Incident* (1946), *Spring in Park Lane* (1948), *Doctor in the House* (1954), *Doctor at Sea* (1955), *Doctor at Large* (1957), *Doctor in Love* (1960) and *Doctor in Distress* (1963), several of which he also appeared in. **Hammer credits:** *Don't Panic Chaps* (1959, as Major Mortimer), *Eve* (1968, TV [episode of *Journey to the Unknown*], as Laverly-Smith)

### Phipps, William

This prolific American actor (1922–2018, sometimes William Edward Phipps) can be seen in sequences shot specifically for the U.S. telecast of Hammer's *The Evil of Frankenstein* (1964), in which he appeared as the father of the mute girl, here named Rena. His other credits include *Crossfire* (1947), *Cat-Women of the Moon* (1953), *Executive Suite* (1954), *Black Gold* (1963), *Cavalry Command* (1963), *Gunfight in Abilene* (1967), *Eleanor and Franklin* (1976, TVM), in which he played Theodore Roosevelt, *Bogie* (1980, TVM), *Messenger of Death* (1988) and *Sordid Lives* (2000). He also provided the voice of Prince Charming for Disney's *Cinderella* (1950). Extremely busy on television, his countless credits here include episodes of everything from *The Adventures of Wild Bill Hickok* (1951–1958, TV) to *Dallas* (1978–1991, TV). **Hammer credits:** *The Evil of Frankenstein* (1964, as Rena's father)

### Pickering, Donald

Perhaps best known for playing Dolly Longstaffe in the TV series *The Pallisers* (1974, TV) and Dr. Watson in *Sherlock Holmes and Doctor Watson* (1980, TV), this British character actor (1933–

2009) has also appeared in supporting roles in a handful of films, among them *Doctor at Large* (1957), *Fahrenheit 451* (1966), *A Bridge Too Far* (1977), *The Thirty-Nine Steps* (1978), *Zulu Dawn* (1979), *Half Moon Street* (1986) and *The Man Who Knew Too Little* (1997). He can also be seen in Hammer's *A Challenge for Robin Hood* (1967) as Sir Jamyl de Penitone. His many other TV appearances include episodes of *On Trial* (1960, TV), *The Champions* (1968–1969, TV), *Dick Turpin* (1979–1982, TV), *Lovejoy* (1986–1994, TV) and *Holby City* (1999–, TV). **Hammer credits:** *A Challenge for Robin Hood* (1967, as Sir Jamyl de Penitone)

### Picton, Don

British born Picton (1916–1981, full name Gilbert Donald Picton) worked as the assistant art director on Hammer's *The Lost Continent* (1968), liaising closely with the film's credited designer Arthur Lawson, for whom he'd earlier worked as a draughtsman on *A Matter of Life and Death* (1943), *Black Narcissus* (1947), *The Red Shoes* (1948) and *The Elusive Pimpernel* (1950); he also worked for Lawson as an assistant art director on *The Battle of The River Plate* (1956) and as a set dresser on *Peeping Tom* (1960), all of which were directed by Michael Powell. Picton went on to work as the assistant art director on Hammer's *Crescendo* (1970), *The Horror of Frankenstein* (1970), *Scars of Dracula* (1970), *Blood from the Mummy's Tomb* (1971), *Vampire Circus* (1972) and *Mutiny on the Buses* (1972), this time assisting Scott MacGregor. He finally gained fully-fledged art director credits for himself with *Fear in the Night* (1972), *Man at the Top* (1973), *Holiday on the Buses* (1973) and *Man About the House* (1974), but continued to work as an assistant for MacGregor on *Nearest and Dearest* (1973), *That's Your Funeral* (1973) and *Frankenstein and the Monster from Hell* (1974), and also for Lionel Couch on *Love Thy Neighbour* (1973) and *The Satanic Rites of Dracula* (1974). His final credit for Hammer was again as a fully fledged art director on *To the Devil a Daughter* (1976). His other credits as an assistant art director include *Cleopatra* (1963), *Some Will, Some Won't* (1969), *Burke and Hare* (1972) and *For Your Eyes Only* (1981), while his credits as an art director include *Clash of the Titans* (1981). **Hammer credits:** *The Lost Continent* (1968, assistant art director), *Crescendo* (1970, assistant art director), *Scars of Dracula* (1970, assistant art director [uncredited]), *The Horror of Frankenstein* (1970, assistant art director [uncredited]), *Blood from the Mummy's Tomb* (1971, assistant art director), *Vampire Circus* (1972, assistant art director), *Fear in the Night* (1972, art director), *Mutiny on the Buses* (1972, assistant art director), *Nearest and Dearest* (1973, assistant art director), *That's Your Funeral* (1973, assistant art director), *Love Thy Neighbour* (1973, assistant art director), *Man at the Top* (1973, art director), *Holiday on the Buses* (1973, art director), *The Satanic Rites of Dracula* (1974, assistant art director), *Frankenstein and the Monster from Hell* (1974, assistant art director), *Man About the House* (1974, art director), *To the Devil a Daughter* (1976, art director)

### Pidler, J.H. (Lieutenant Commander, R.N.)

The unfortunately named Pidler acted as the technical advisor for the Hammer naval comedy *Up the Creek* (1958). **Hammer credits:** *Up the Creek* (1958)

### Pierce, J. Edward

Pierce (aka Edgar Pierce) can be seen in a supporting role in Hammer's first foray into horror, *The Mystery of the Mary Celeste* (1935). **Hammer credits:** *The Mystery of the Mary Celeste* (1935, as Arian Harbens)

### Pierce, Norman

This British supporting actor (1900–1968) played one of Hammer's archetypal landlords in *The Brides of Dracula* (1960), overseeing the various comings and goings at the Running Boar inn. His other credits include *Number, Please* (1931), *Sweeney Todd: The Demon Barber of Fleet Street* (1936), *Sexton Blake and the Hooded Terror* (1938), *In Which We Serve* (1942), *Escape Route* (1952) and *The Rough and the Smooth* (1959), plus episodes of *Dixon of Dock Green* (1955–1976, TV), *No Hiding Place* (1959–1967, TV) and *The Herries Chronicle* (1960, TV). He also sustained a busy stage career. **Hammer credits:** *The Brides of Dracula* (1960)

### Pike, Kelvin

This Australian cameraman (1929–) operated the camera for Hammer's *The Nanny* (1965). He began his career as a clapper loader on such films as *Mogambo* (1953) and *The Dark Avenger* (1955), following which he graduated to focus puller on *Oh … Rosalinda!!* (1955) and *The Rebel* (1961), and then to camera operator on *Two Weeks in Another Town* (1962), *A Prize of Arms* (1962), *Billy Budd* (1962), *Dr. Strangelove* (1964), *Khartoum* (1966), *2001: A Space Odyssey* (1968), *Puppet on a Chain* (1971), *Valentino* (1977), *The Empire Strikes Back* (1980), *The Shining* (1980), *Heaven's Gate* (1980) and *Krull* (1983). His credits as a fully-fledged cinematographer include *The Dresser* (1983), *Gulag* (1985, TVM), *A Dry White Season* (1989) and *Betsy's Wedding* (1990). **Hammer credits:** *The Nanny* (1965)

### Pilgrim, Ronnie

British born Pilgrim (1915–2003) worked as a stills man on Hammer's *One Million Years B.C.* (1966), though it should be noted that the iconographic portrait of Raquel Welch posing in her doeskin bikini was actually taken by Pierre Luigi (Terry O'Neill also worked on the film). Pilgrim returned to Hammer for further assignments in the seventies. His many other credits include *The Shop at Sly Corner* (1947), *The Dam Busters* (1955), *Summer Holiday* (1963), *The Man Who Haunted Himself* (1970) and *The Railway Children* (1970). **Hammer credits:** *One Million Years B.C.* (1966 [uncredited]), *Blood from the Mummy's Tomb* (1971 [uncredited]), *Straight on Till Morning* (1972 [uncredited]), *Frankenstein and the Monster from Hell* (1974 [uncredited]), *The Satanic Rites of Dracula* (1974 [uncredited])

### Pilgrim, Rosemary

Pilgrim worked as the assistant to casting director James Liggat on Hammer's *The Satanic Rites of Dracula* (1974). **Hammer credits:** *The Satanic Rites of Dracula* (1974 [uncredited])

### Pinewood Studios

The country house of this fabled British studio—Heatherden Hall—has been used as a backdrop in countless films, among them *Reach for the Sky* (1956), *From Russia with Love* (1963), *Carry On … Up the Khyber* (1968), *Chitty Chitty Bang Bang* (1968), *The Great Gatsby* (1974), *Bugsy Malone* (1976) and *Who Dares Wins* (1982). It also doubled for Sir James Forbes' residence in Hammer's *The Plague of the Zombies* (1966). Hammer also filmed the snowscapes for *The Abominable Snowman* (1957) on the larger sound stages at Pinewood. They also made their Robin Hood adventure *A Challenge for Robin Hood* (1967) at Pinewood after they left Bray for Elstree, which was too busy to accommodate them for this particular film. Other Hammer films made at Pinewood include *Hands of the Ripper* (1971), *Vampire Circus* (1971) and their last cinema feature for three decades, *The Lady Vanishes* (1979). The sound post-production for *Creatures the World Forgot* (1971) was handled there, too, and *Nessie* was also set to be shot at Pinewood before its eventual collapse.

Formerly the home of the Canadian born Lieutenant Colonel Grant Morden, the hall was auctioned off in 1934 following his death, and was bought by Charles Boot (of Boots the Chemist fame) for £35,000. The building of the first studio began in December 1935 and it was in operation by September 1936, with the first film on the floor being *London Melody* (1937). The British flour magnate J. Arthur Rank became a prime shareholder in the venue in 1937, and under his stewardship the studio went from strength to strength. Subsequent films made at Pinewood include *Gangway* (1937), *Pygmalion* (1938), *Great Expectations* (1946), *The Importance of Being Earnest* (1952), *Carry On Sergeant* (1958), *The Ipcress File* (1965), *You Only Live Twice* (1967), *Frenzy* (1972), *The Spy Who Loved Me* (1977), *Superman* (1978), *Death on the Nile* (1978), *Clash of the Titans* (1981), *Legend* (1985), *Batman* (1989), *Evita* (1996), *Eyes Wide Shut* (1999), *Quills* (2000), *Casino Royale* (2006), *The Bourne Ultimatum* (2007), *Mama Mia!* (2008), *Skyfall* (2012), *Prometheus* (2012), *Guardians of the Galaxy* (2014), *The Force Awakens* (2015), *Spectre* (2015), *Rogue One: A Star Wars Story* (2016) and *The Last Jedi* (2017), plus countless TV series and one-off episodes. Hammer eventually returned to the studio to film *The Woman in Black* (2012) and its sequel. The studio has been the subject of several books and documentaries, among the former *Movies from the Mansion: A History of Pinewood Studios* (1982), *The Pinewood Story: The Authorised History of the World's Most Famous Film Studio* (2000) and *Pinewood Studios: 70 Years of Fabulous Filmmaking* (2007), while the latter include *Pinewood: 80 Years of Movie Magic* (2015, TV). **Hammer credits:** *The Abominable Snowman* (1957), *The Plague of the Zombies*

(1966), *A Challenge for Robin Hood* (1967), *Dracula Has Risen from the Grave* (1968), *When Dinosaurs Ruled the Earth* (1970 [sound recording only]), *Countess Dracula* (1971), *Creatures the World Forgot* (1971 [sound post-production only]), *Hands of the Ripper* (1971), *Twins of Evil* (1971), *Vampire Circus* (1972), *Nearest and Dearest* (1973), *That's Your Funeral* (1973), *The Lady Vanishes* (1979), *The Woman in Black* (2012), *The Woman in Black 2: Angel of Death* (2015)

### Pinkney, Lynn

Pinkney can be seen in a supporting role in *Matakitas Is Coming*, an episode of Hammer's *Journey to the Unknown* (1968, TV), which also appeared in the compendium film *Journey to the Unknown* (1969, TVM). Her films include *The Marked One* (1963), *Marat/Sade* (1967) and *Sebastian* (1968). **Hammer credits:** *Matakitas Is Coming* (1968, TV [episode of *Journey to the Unknown*], as Tracy), *Journey to the Unknown* (1969, TVM, as Tracy)

### Pinney, Barbara

Pinney played one of the harem girls in the Hammer comedy *I Only Arsked!* (1958). Her other credits include *Fire Maidens from Outer Space* (1956). **Hammer credits:** *I Only Arsked!* (1958, as Harem girl [uncredited])

### Piper, Evelyn

This American writer (1908–1994, real name Marryam Modell) had her 1964 novel *The Nanny* filmed by Hammer in 1965. Writing short stories from 1941, other filmed works include her 1957 novel *Bunny Lake Is Missing* (1965). Her other novels include *The Sound Years* (1946), *The Lady and Her Doctor* (1956), *Hanno's Doll* (1961) and *The Stand-In* (1970). **Hammer credits:** *The Nanny* (1965)

### *The Pirates of Blood River*

GB, 1962, 84m, Eastmancolor, HammerScope, RCA, cert U

According to *What the Censor Saw*, the 1973 autobiography of BBFC secretary John Trevelyan, *The Pirates of Blood River* "is the only film I can remember that started as an X film and went out as a U film." Based on a story by Jimmy Sangster and originally announced in 1960 as *Blood River*, the picture came about after Michael Carreras suggested that it might be fun to make a pirate movie. However, finances being what they usually were at Hammer, the proviso was that the majority of the action had to occur on land (recalled the screenwriter: "A landlocked pirate movie—good old Hammer!"[27]). Consequently, Sangster devised a story and screenplay that sees a nefarious pirate captain force one of his men to reveal the whereabouts of his hometown, a Huguenot community suspected of having a hidden hoard of treasure. John Hunter and the film's director John Gilling subsequently re-wrote the screenplay when it was considered much too bloodthirsty as kiddie matinee fare. Consequently, the action was toned down during this process, and still further during editing, first achieving an A certificate, and finally a U.

Although set in the West Indies, the film was actually shot on the back lot at Bray and in nearby Black Park, which gives the proceedings a curiously English air, despite the fact that everyone is running around in heavy tan make-up. Nevertheless, this is a lively enough romp, thanks to the vivacity of the direction by John Gilling, who by now was a practiced hand at this kind of picture, having previously completed *Fury at Smugglers' Bay* (1960) with Peter Cushing for Regal Films. This time it was the turn of Cushing's frequent co-star Christopher Lee to take the leading role as the ruthless Captain La Roche (Captain Doom in the original script), while the part of the young Huguenot, Jonathan Standing, was essayed by Kerwin Matthews, best known for playing the title role in Ray Harryhausen's *The Seventh Voyage of Sinbad* (1958). Several Hammer familiars peopled the rest of the cast, among them Marla Landi, Michael Ripper, Oliver Reed, Denis Shaw and Marie Devereux, while Anthony Nelson Keys supervised the crew, having made the jump from associate producer to producer for the movie.

Photographed in Eastmancolor and Hammer-Scope between 3 July and 31 August 1961, the production encountered one or two problems during its nine-week shoot, among them the filming of a sequence set in a lake in Black Park, which proved to be something of a quagmire for the cast, who found themselves sinking into the stinking black mud, much to their discomfort and disgust. Recalled Christopher Lee of the lake, "I walked in and went straight up to my chin and I'll never forget the expressions on the faces of my bold buccaneers…. Gilling thought it was very funny; I could see him laughing and that's why I really let him have it."[28] And with good cause, it would seem, for it has since been discovered that the septic tanks from Pinewood Studios drained directly into the lake, which had been condemned for any kind of recreational activity! Remembered fellow Hammer actor Andrew Keir, "That horrible pond! I think it was where people used to throw all their dead dogs. It smelled terrible. It was very, very gruesome."[29]

The muddy lake wasn't the only problem encountered on the film. Oliver Reed recalled that the stuntmen proved reluctant to work on one scene. "The stuntmen wouldn't jump over a bank or something. I went charging over this bank with a sword in my mouth, followed by a medical student, who was one of the crowd—and all the stuntmen

stopped; they wouldn't do it. John Gilling, who was the director, fired them all. And from that time on, he thought I was really quite something, because I'd do things that stuntmen wouldn't do. It was only because I was stupid!"[30]

Meanwhile, a sequence involving a young woman's attempts to escape from a pursuing pirate by swimming across a piranha-infested river, only to be attacked by the man-eating fish, found itself on the cutting room floor, proving to be too strong for the U category that the film now found itself aiming for. Recalled the censor John Trevelyan, "In the X version, a shoal of piranha fish rushed through the water and attacked the girl who struggled and was apparently dragged under the water which then became tinged with blood; in the A version the piranha fish rushed through the water but the scene stopped as they reached the girl; in the U version the piranha fish never appeared at all."[31] Which is a shame, given the low budget ingenuity Les Bowie and his team of effects technicians lavished upon the sequence, which saw piranha fish made out of silver foil flashing their way through the water, accompanied by bubble-jets and lashings

A slightly racy American ad for *The Pirates of Blood River* (1962), given that the film was primarily aimed at kids (Hammer/British Lion Columbia/Columbia).

of fake blood (recalled effects assistant Brian John-cock of Bowie's efforts, "He was just magic about things like that."[32]).

Otherwise, it was business as usual for the cast and crew, who delivered a lively and entertaining film that, following its trade show on 5 May 1962 at the Columbia Theater, proved to be an immediate success with its intended audience when premiered on a double bill with Ray Harryhausen's *Mysterious Island* (1961) at the London Pavilion on 13 July 1962 (the title alone must have appealed to schoolboys across the land). Backed by a lavish £50,000 campaign (Columbia's "biggest ever" according to *Kinematograph Weekly*), this double bill then went on general release in the UK on the ABC circuit care of Columbia on 13 August, the same month the pairing was released in America again by Columbia. By the time the box office receipts had been counted, the duo proved to be Britain's most successful double bill of 1962.

Critical reaction to the film was mixed. *Kinematograph Weekly* described *The Pirates of Blood River* as having a "thrilling story [and] robust characterization," while the *Monthly Film Bulletin* labeled it a "stodgy, two-dimensional costume piece." Recalled Christopher Lee of his role as La Roche (whom one of his men describes as being "as strong as a lion, as cunning as a mongoose, and as vicious as a snake"), "This was my first Hammer picture that no one could call a horror film. It was very nicely done and was a big money maker."[33] Remembered Jimmy Sangster of the film, "The whole cast was first rate, as usual in a Hammer film. Kerwin Mathews, who went on to do *Maniac* for me, was suitably swashbuckling. Christopher Lee gave his usual energetic, menacing, first-rate performance and dear old Michael Ripper was given a part he could get his teeth into. Oliver Reed was there, so too was Glenn Corbett, an American who lent virtually nothing to the box office and very little to the part."[34]

Production company: Hammer. Distributors: British Lion Columbia (UK [ABC circuit]), Columbia (U.S.). Producer: Anthony Nelson Keys. Executive producer: Michael Carreras. Director: John Gilling. Screenplay: John Gilling, John Hunter. Story: Jimmy Sangster. Cinematographer: Arthur Grant. Music: Gary Hughes. Music director: John Hollingsworth. Supervising editor: James Needs. Editor: Eric Boyd-Perkins. Production design: Bernard Robinson. Art director: Don Mingaye. Costumes: Molly Arbuthnot, Rosemary Burrows. Special effects: Les Bowie. Special effects assistants: Ian Scoones [uncredited], Kit West [uncredited], Brian Johncock [uncredited]. Make-up: Roy Ashton. Hair: Frieda Steiger. Sound: Jock May. Sound editor: Alfred Cox. Camera operator: Len Harris. Focus puller: Harry Oakes [uncredited]. Assistant director: John Peverall. Second assistant director: Peter Medak [uncredited]. Production manager: Clifford Parkes. Construction manager: Arthur Banks [uncredited]. Master carpenter: Charles Davis [uncredited]. Master painter: Lawrence Wrenn [uncredited]. Master rigger: Ronald Lenoir [uncredited]. Props: Tommy Money [uncredited]. Props buyer: Eric Hillier [uncredited]. Master electrician: Jack Curtis [uncredited].

Master plasterer: Stan Banks [uncredited]. Casting: Stuart Lyons. Continuity: Tilly Day. Horse master/master of arms: Bob Simmons. Stunts: Gerry Crampton [uncredited], Bernard Barnsley [uncredited], Terry Richards [uncredited], Steve James [uncredited]. **Cast:** Kerwin Mathews (Jonathan Standing), Christopher Lee (Captain La Roche), Peter Arne (Hench), Oliver Reed (Brocaire), Glenn Corbett (Henry), Marla Landi (Bess), David Lodge (Smith), Michael Ripper (Mac), Marie Devereux (Maggie Mason), Andrew Keir (Jason Standing), Jack Stuart (George Mason), Jerold Wells (Commandant), Dennis Waterman (Timothy Blackthorne), Lorraine Clewes (Martha Blackthorne), Diane Aubrey (Margaret Blackthorne), Desmond Llewelyn (Blackthorne), Keith Pyott (Silas), Denis Shaw (Silver), Michael Peake (Kemp), Richard Bennett (Seymour), Michael Mulcaster (William Martin), John Roden (Settler [uncredited]), Ronald Blackman (Pugh [uncredited]), John Collin (Lance [uncredited]), Don Levy (Carlos [uncredited]), John Bennett (Guard at penal colony [uncredited]), Fred Peck (Huguenot villager [uncredited]), Bill Brandon (Pirate [uncredited]), Ernie Rice (Pirate [uncredited]). **DVD availability:** Sony (U.S. R1 NTSC), part of the *Icons of Adventure* box set. **CD availability:** *The Hammer Film Music Collection: Volume Two* (GDI Records), which contains the *Main Title*

## Pitcher, John

Pitcher worked as the third assistant director on Hammer's *The Quatermass Xperiment* (1955). His other credits in this capacity include *Zarak* (1956), while his first assistant credits take in *The Diplomatic Corpse* (1958) and *A Woman Possessed* (1958). **Hammer credits:** *The Quatermass Xperiment* (1955 [uncredited])

## Pithey, Wensley

Wow, what a name! Following experience as a radio announcer in his home country, this South African character actor (1914–1993) came to Britain in 1947, making his screen debut the same year in *The Mark of Cain*. Over fifty films followed, among them *Cardboard Cavalier* (1948), *Blue Murder at St. Trinian's* (1957), *The Pure Hell of St. Trinian's* (1960), *Oliver!* (1968), *White Mischief* (1987) and *American Friends* (1991). He also worked for Hammer twice, first on *Lady in the Fog* (1952), in which he played the supporting role of Sid the barman who mixes an explosive cocktail with leading man Cesar Romero. He followed this with the role of Hugo in the *Men of Sherwood Forest* (1954) two years later. Busy on television, his many credits here include episodes of *Robin Hood* (1953, TV), in which he played Friar Tuck, *Special Branch* (1969–1974, TV), *Return of the Saint* (1978–1979, TV) and *Lipstick on Your Collar* (1993, TV). He also played Winston Churchill four times, appearing as the statesman in *Edward and Mrs. Simpson* (1978, TV), *Ike* (1979, TVM), *Suez 1956* (1979, TV) and *FDR: The Last Year* (1980, TVM), and was well known in Germany for playing a coffee expert in a series of Tchibo coffee ads between 1961 and 1976. **Hammer credits:** *Lady in the Fog* (1952, as Sid [barman]), *Men of Sherwood Forest* (1954, as Hugo)

## Pitt, Ingrid

Following a horrific childhood that saw her interned in the Stutthof Concentration Camp with her mother (about which she wrote with candor in her 1999 autobiography *Life's a Scream*), this glamorous Polish leading lady (1937–2010, real name Ignoushka Petrov) pursued an acting career, first at the prestigious Berliner Ensemble and later (having escaped East Germany by swimming the River Spree and marrying Laud Pitt, the handsome U.S. Lieutenant who rescued her) as a member of the Spanish National Theater. She broke into movies in Spain in the mid-sixties appearing as an extra in such Spanish-shot international productions as *Doctor Zhivago* (1965), *Chimes at Midnight* (1966) and *A Funny Thing Happened on the Way to the Forum* (1966), and went on to play roles in *Un beso en el puerto* (1966), *Barreiros 66* (1966), *Los duendes de Andalucia* (1966) and *El sonido de la muerte* (1966). She then moved to America where she began appearing in minor roles in episodes of such television series as *Dundee and the Culhane* (1967, TV) and *Ironside* (1967–1975, TV), after which she finally got her big international break playing the underground contact Heidi in the wartime blockbuster *Where Eagles Dare* (1969).

Following this, Pitt pursued her career in England, where she went on to marry her second husband, Rank booker George Pinches in 1972. It was while attending a launch party for *Alfred the Great* (1969) that Pitt met James Carreras. "I hadn't a clue who he was and I'm sure he didn't recognize me either,"[35] she later admitted. "Gradually, however, it dawned on me that he was an active producer, a rare species indeed in the British film industry at that time. He hadn't a chance. By the time I left I had his card next to my heart and he had promised to see me in his office the next day."[36] This meeting led directly to her being offered the role of Carmilla in Hammer's *The Vampire Lovers* (1970), despite competition from Shirley Eaton for the part (Eaton was ultimately dismissed as being too old for the role, despite being born the same year as Pitt, who, to her advantage, was claiming to have been born in 1944 at the time). In fact Pitt's casting raised a few eyebrows at the Ministry of Labor, which queried Hammer's choice of a foreign actress over a British one. James Carreras was quick to defend the actress, though, commenting, "This particular role of a female vampire requires special physical characteristics which Miss Pitt does possess and which we have not been able to find in the many British artistes we have considered."[37]

Much was made of Pitt's so-called "physical characteristics" in the film, including a handful of nude scenes. Recalled the actress, "I'd never done the full-frontal before but I was proud of my body and not too reluctant to show it. Madeleine Smith, who played my second victim, had also kept her gear on in front of the cameras so far. She was a little more apprehensive but saw the relevance and agreed to get it off. Nevertheless, we both had reservations, especially as we weren't too familiar with the producers, so I spoke to Jimmy [Carreras] and asked him if we couldn't have a closed set: the producers and other non-essential personnel could go to London and see the rushes. He agreed at once…. I discovered that when you're naked on set everyone is terribly nice to you and looks after you beyond the call of duty. This is particularly the case when you're doing a bath scene, which I seemed to do a lot of at Hammer…. They're terrified you might lose the mood or—God forbid—want to get dressed. Jimmy had sent champagne to the set, and Madeleine and I indulged ourselves."[38]

Pitt's success in *The Vampire Lovers* led to appearances in a number of seventies horror films, including Hammer's *Countess Dracula* (1971), in which she played the title role (and the filming of which prevented her from appearing in the follow up to *The Vampire Lovers*, *Lust for a Vampire* [1971], in which her role was assumed by Yutte Stensgaard), *The House That Dripped Blood* (1971) and *The Wicker Man* (1973). Recalled Pitt, "After *The Vampire Lovers* I considered myself a part of the Hammer stable, not exactly in the same class as Michael Ripper, of course, but a paid-up Hammerite none the less. When I heard that they were setting up a new film I was all ears. I discovered it was to be a film about Elizabeth Bathori, the biggest serial killer of all time and a relative of Vlad Tepes—the Impaler. That was enough for me and I called James Carreras immediately."[39]

Pitt took her preparation for the role very seriously. As she recalled, "I made my mother come and stay, and I studied her way of speaking as she had the kind of voice and intonations I thought the Countess would have had. I gave her the sort of croakiness that Eastern Europeans have when they smoke and drink a lot of vodka. After each take I would rush to the sound man and listen to the playback. I was happy with the result."[40]

Astonishingly, despite doing some of her best work, Pitt had her performance for *Countess Dracula* re-voiced at the insistence of the director, Peter Sasdy (himself Hungarian), who claimed that her accent caused problems in certain scenes—a somewhat curious claim, given that her voice had caused no problems in her previous films (indeed, her European cadences would surely have been perfect for the role). Instead, the actress was dubbed with an English rose accent, much to her consternation. Said Pitt of the incident, "When I found out Sasdy had re-voiced me I asked him why, and he said, 'We couldn't understand what you were saying in the rushes.' But this was total crap! I know—I was there too. I heard it, and nobody is more self-critical than me, believe me. And everyone else thought my different voices as the old and young countess were great…. I'm still sick about it. Every time I think about it I could weep. He took the soul away from my performance."[41]

Sadly, *Countess Dracula* was Pitt's last big screen association with Hammer, though it should be noted that she was offered the role of Lady Durward in *Captain Kronos—Vampire Hunter* (1974), but turned it down owing to its lack of size. The part is certainly little more than a cameo, but integral to the plot, and Pitt would have been perfect for it. Remembered the actress, "The part was so small I didn't do it. By now I was an 'above the title' leading lady—the part was really just a recap of Countess Dracula and far beneath me in my newly

elevated status."[42] Instead, Wanda Ventham played the part. Pitt also tried to interest the studio in a script she had written entitled *Dracula…. Who?*, which she had conceived on the set of *The Wicker Man*. Unfortunately, the project (which sees the Count converting to vegetarianism) languished in development hell, along with several other projects being considered by the company at the time, though this didn't prevent her from trying to launch it elsewhere. Pitt eventually returned to Hammer for a cameo appearance in the online serial *Beyond the Rave* (2008).

Pitt's other credits include *Nobody Ordered Love* (1972), *Where the Action Is* (1975,

*Right:* **A rose by any other name. Ingrid Pitt proves to be the epitome of Hammer glamor as she shows off her legs to the best advantage in this publicity shot taken during the making of *The Vampire Lovers* (1970) (Hammer/AIP/Fantale/MGM-EMI/American International).** *Below:* **There isn't any other stair quite like it. Ingrid Pitt takes a break during the making of *Countess Dracula* (1971) (Hammer/Rank/Twentieth Century–Fox).**

TVM), *Who Dares Wins* (1982), *Parker* (1984), *The House* (1984, TVM), *Wild Geese II* (1985), *Hanna's War* (1988), *The Asylum* (2000), *Green Fingers* (2000), *Minotaur* (2006) and *Sea of Dust* (2008). She also appeared on stage and television in Britain, including guest roles in episodes of *Smiley's People* (1982, TV) and *Doctor Who* (1963–1989, TV), and made films in Argentina, where she lived for a while in the seventies, among them *El lobo* (1975). In addition to her work as an actress, Pitt was also a successful author, writing both fiction and non-fiction, among her works being *Cuckoo Run* (1980), *The Perons* (1984), *Eva's Spell* (1985), *Katarina* (1986), *The Ingrid Pitt Bedside Companion for Vampire Lovers* (1998), *The Ingrid Pitt Bedside Companion for Ghosthunters* (1999) and *The Ingrid Pitt Book of Murder, Torture and Depravity* (2000). She also had her own website, Pitt of Horror, and wrote a regular column for the horror fanzine *Shivers*.

Her third husband was the former racing driver Tony Rudlin, whom she married in 1993 and who managed her later career (which included many film fair and convention appearances), and with whom she formed a production company named Hammer Glamor along with Veronica Carlson.

Said Roy Ward Baker of Pitt, whom he directed in *The Vampire Lovers*, "She's great, and a real lady. Intensely practical and with a sharp mind. She's all right."[43] Recalled effects man Bert Luxford of Pitt, with whom he worked on *Countess Dracula*, "Ingrid was a charming lady and quite the opposite to her character in the film, I'm pleased to say. What amazed me with her was her sheer tenacity and determination to succeed. I later discovered that she had endured awful experiences at the hands of the Nazis in concentration camps that she and her mother were held in. Words cannot describe what she went through, and I admired her, and admire her still, tremendously for it."[44] **Additional notes:** Some of Pitt's lines for *The Vampire Lovers* were revoiced by Olive Gregg. Pitt's daughter, actress Steffanie Pitt (real name Steffanie Blake), attended Hampden House boarding school for girls in the early eighties; this was the location for *Hammer House of Horror* (1980, TV), the cancelled second season of which Pitt was lined up to contribute to as a writer. Pitt was the subject of a magazine tribute care of Tim Greaves' One Shot Publications titled *Ingrid Pitt—Queen of Horror* (1996); she was also featured in the same company's earlier *Daughter of the Night—Carmilla on Screen* (1994), the cover for which was illustrated with a portrait of the actress. **Hammer credits:** *The Vampire Lovers* (1970, as Carmilla/Mircalla/Marcilla Karnstein), *Countess Dracula* (1971, as Countess Elizabeth Nadasdy), *Flesh and Blood—The Hammer Heritage of Horror* (1994, TV, interviewee, special thanks), *Beyond the Rave* (2008, as Tooley's mum)

## Pitt, Norman

This British actor (1911–1986, full name William Norman Pitt) can be seen as a policeman at the climax of the Hammer comedy *What the Butler Saw* (1950), which marked his film debut. His other credits include *Strictly Confidential* (1959), *French Dressing* (1963), *Privilege* (1967), *Oliver!*

(1968), *One More Time* (1969) and *Little Lord Fauntleroy* (1980, TVM), plus episodes of *The Big Pull* (1962, TV), *Sherlock Holmes* (1965–1968, TV) and *The Brothers* (1972–1976, TV). **Hammer credits:** *What the Butler Saw* (1950, as Policeman)

## Pitt, Ray

This editor/supervising editor worked on a handful of low budget Hammer co-features in the late forties/early fifties. His many other credits include *Calling the Tune* (1936), *I Married a Spy* (1938), *Let George Do It* (1940), *Spare a Copper* (1940), *The Next of Kin* (1942), *The Black Sheep of Whitehall* (1942), *Under Secret Orders* (1943) and *A Gunman Has Escaped* (1948). **Hammer credits:** *Dr. Morelle—The Case of the Missing Heiress* (1949), *Dick Barton Strikes Back* (1949), *The Adventures of PC 49—The Case of the Guardian Angel* (1949), *Celia* (1949), *Meet Simon Cherry* (1949), *The Man in Black* (1950 [uncredited]), *Someone at the Door* (1950 [uncredited])

## Pizor, Bill

The business partner of Robert L. Lippert, the American born Pizor (1890–1959, full name William M. Pizor) was one of Hammer's silent U.S. partners, and proved a valuable Stateside asset during the company's burgeoning years in the late forties and early fifties. Specializing in low budget westerns, his own credits as a producer or executive producer include *A Chocolate Cowboy* (1925), *The House of Terror* (1928), *Cowboy Cavalier* (1929),

*The Texan* (1932), *The Lone Rider* (1934), *West of the Law* (1934) and *A Street of Memory* (1937). His son was the producer Irwin Pizor (1917–1997).

## The Plague of the Zombies

GB, 1966, 91m, Technicolor [UK], DeLuxe [U.S.], widescreen [1.85:1], RCA, cert X

The third film in Hammer's quartet of back-to-back productions, *The Plague of the Zombies* followed close on the heels of *Dracula—Prince of Darkness* (1966) and *Rasputin—The Mad Monk* (1966), the latter of which had finished principal photography on 20 July 1965, just one week before *Plague* went on the floor at Bray on 28 July (the fourth film, *The Reptile* [1966] would likewise follow in the footsteps of *Plague*). For *Rasputin*, the exterior of Castle Dracula had been altered to that of a Russian winter palace. Now it became a small Cornish village, with the icy moat on which both Dracula and Rasputin had met their deaths dug out to create a subterranean graveyard. Meanwhile, the castle walls were stripped of their cladding and redressed as quaint Cornish cottages, shops and a small inn, while the wooden drawbridge became a stone bridge.

The screenplay for *Plague* was the work of former Hammer cameraman Peter Bryan, who had already written *The Hound of the Baskervilles* (1959) and *The Brides of Dracula* (1960) for the company. Originally submitted as a synopsis titled *The Zombie* in 1962, this treatment was then worked upon by Anthony Hinds before being announced to the press a year later. Further revisions

**Ben Aris (center), Jacqueline Pearce (body) and Diane Clare (right) in the great shock moment from *The Plague of the Zombies* (1966) (Hammer/Seven Arts/Associated British Picture Corporation/Warner Pathé Distributors/Twentieth Century–Fox/Studio Canal).**

followed before the script was announced again in 1964, first as *Horror of the Zombies* and then as *The Horror of the Zombie* (the promotional artwork for the latter featured a zombie with two holes in its chest with light shining through them, recalling the contentious artwork for *The Mummy* [1959]). The film gained its final title just a month before filming, by which time the script had been amended so as to comply with the demands of the BBFC following the usual reactionary fuss and nonsense. An incident packed affair, it sees medical professor Sir James Forbes and his daughter Sylvia journey to Cornwall after having received a mysterious letter from Dr. Peter Tompson, a former pupil of Sir James's, whose young wife Alice is also a close friend of Sylvia's. "For some time our village has been beset by a number of mysterious and fatal illnesses," reads the note, which is enough enticement to send Sir James and Sylvia off to Cornwall to investigate. Upon their arrival at the village, strange goings-on immediately attract their attention, and eventually lead to the discovery that the local squire, one Clive Hamilton, is in fact using voodoo rituals learned during a trip to Haiti to resurrect the dead so as to work his condemned tin mine!

Certain events in the film recall incidents in Bryan's script for *The Hound of the Baskervilles*, key among them the hunting down of Sylvia in the woods by the squire's drunken cronies, which echoes the opening scene in *Hound* in which a poor servant girl is run to ground by the corrupt Sir Hugo Baskerville ("Come on, little fox, go to ground!" leers one of Hamilton's men somewhat suggestively once Sylvia has been captured). Hamilton's men are also responsible for a shocking incident that occurs upon the arrival of Sir James and his daughter at the village: in pursuit of a fox, the men and their horses career through a funeral procession, knocking over the coffin, out of which tumbles the body of the deceased (Johne Martinus on the coffin lid, plain John Martinus in the credits), much to the distress of Sylvia, who witnesses the whole episode.

Sir James's suspicions are further aroused when he meets Alice, who seems to be in some kind of catatonic state, and learns from Peter that the squire has forbidden him from carrying out autopsies. "This isn't London, sir," explains Peter. "This is a Cornish village inhabited by simple country people, riddled with superstition, and all dominated by a squire. He acts as coroner, magistrate, judge and jury." Consequently, in order to acquire a body on which to perform an autopsy, Sir James simply suggests that, "We'll dig one up!" Unfortunately, while exhuming the corpse of the recently buried Martinus, Sir James and Peter are caught red-handed by the police. However, before being taken to the police station by Sergeant Swift and his young constable, Sir James rips open the coffin lid to reveal that the coffin is actually empty! With Sergeant Swift now on Sir James's side (the copper's son was also a victim of the plague), the professor determines that, "We must find out about the disease. Find out what it is and destroy it!"

An opportunity to do so presents itself all too soon, for while Sir James and Peter have been about

A shocking discovery. From left to right, Brook Williams, Diane Clare, André Morell and Jacqueline Pearce (on ground) in a scene from *The Plague of the Zombies* (1966) (Hammer/Seven Arts/Associated British Picture Corporation/Warner Pathé Distributors/Twentieth Century–Fox/Studio Canal).

their grisly work in the graveyard, Alice has wandered into the night, secretly followed by Sylvia who, after her encounter with the squire's men, comes across a seemingly deserted tin mine, from the head of which she is shocked to see Alice thrown by what appears to be the zombified form of Johne Martinus. At last, Sir James has a body on which to perform an autopsy (much to the distress of Peter), the results of which—along with information gleaned from the vicar's library—lead him to conclude that the dead are being raised by means of voodoo ("Someone in this village is practicing witchcraft. That corpse wandering up on the moors is an undead").

With grim determination, Sir James now sets about rooting out the evil. Indeed, when Alice transforms into a zombie in her coffin before his very eyes following Hamilton's interrupted attempts to exhume her, the professor is quick to behead her with a handy shovel, prompting Peter to faint away, during which he dreams of a mass rising of the dead (from the usual, conveniently shallow graves). Yet reality proves to be even more surprising, for having exhumed the coffins of all the recently deceased, Sir James discovers every grave to be empty! With Sylvia now seemingly in the squire's sights for zombification, Sir James breaks into Hamilton's home, where he discovers a number of blood-covered effigies hidden in a desk drawer. Attacked by one of the squire's acolytes, Sir James manages to stab him to death in the ensuing struggle. However, the body falls into a fireplace, setting the house alight, along with the voodoo dolls and their counterparts in the mine below, fi-

nally bringing to an end the squire's reign of terror.

A minor gem, *The Plague of the Zombies* is the archetypal Hammer horror film in every sense of the term, offering a superb package of chills, shocks and amateur detective work, directed with pace and style by John Gilling, who would go on to helm the fourth film in the back-to-back quartet, *The Reptile* (1966). Working in close conjunction with cinematographer Arthur Grant, Gilling presents the action in a series of inventively framed and tightly edited scenes, with exposition mercifully pared to the bone so as to allow the events to speak for themselves. Undoubtedly, the misty, green-hued dream sequence in which the dead arise from their graves is the film's highlight. Presented in a series of angled shots so as to emphasize the nightmarish imagery, the sequence is a genuine *tour de force* (note that the puddle into which Peter treads is actually blood red). Other notable scenes include the iconographic shot of Alice's body being thrown from the mine by Johne Martinus, Sir James' excitingly-staged fight with the acolyte in Hamilton's study, the pursuit of the local vicar (who has been assisting Sir James) through the streets of the village, the juxtaposition of Alice's funeral with a voodoo ceremony in the mine, and the decapitation of Alice, which is achieved more through suggestive editing than full-on gore.

Cast-wise, the film's main asset is André Morell, who brings a genuine touch of class to the role of Sir James, his character developing from a slightly fusty, gentleman's club type into a man of action and principle during the course of the story. James Mason sound-a-like John Carson also gives good

*Top left:* **That voodoo that you do. Things are about to turn nasty in** *The Plague of the Zombies* **(1966). John Carson is at right under the mask and robe.** *Top right:* **Night of the living dead. Stylish artwork for** *The Plague of the Zombies* **(1966).** *Bottom left:* **Things don't appear to be going well for our heroes in** *The Plague of the Zombies* **(1966). From left to right, Brook Williams, Diane Clare and André Morell (all three photographs, Hammer/Seven Arts/Associated British Picture Corporation/Warner Pathé Distributors/Twentieth Century–Fox/ Studio Canal).**

value for money as the dastardly squire, determined to exploit his tenants in both life *and* death (if he'd had a moustache, he surely would have twirled it!). Meanwhile, Jacqueline Pearce conveys Alice's dishevelment and disorientation with total conviction. Somewhat less effective is Brook Williams' wishy-washy Peter Tompson and Diane Clare's bland, pudgy-faced Sylvia (given the whey-like color of her complexion and the zit on her chin in the early scenes, she's not exactly leading lady material; her acting can't have been much cop either, as she was completely re-voiced during post-production). However, it is the supporting player Ben Aris as the zombified Johne Martinus who remains in the mind.

On the production front, the film benefits enor-mously from Bernard Robin-son's lavish set designs, among the highlights being the squire's baronial hall (a re-configuring of the Castle Dracula set using the same stairway and fireplace), his plush study with its studded blue velvet wall-seats, and the elaborate mine interior, com-plete with sacrificial altar and strategically-placed beams for added visual interest. As for the exterior shots, Oakley Court doubles for the squire's manor, while an insert of Pinewood Studios' Heathe-den Hall stands in for Sir James's London home. Loca-tion work was meanwhile un-dertaken in nearby Black Park (for the woodland scenes) and Chobham Com-mon (for Sir James's journey to Cornwall).

All of the film's other tech-nical elements are also well up to par, among them the tight editing of Chris Barnes and James Needs, and Roy Ashton's flaky-skinned zombie make-up, achieved via a *papier-mache*-like mix of latex and paper tissues (however, it must be said that Alice's decapitated head, with its staring zombie eyes, slightly lets the side down, as does a mask worn by one of the zombies during the fiery climax). Re-called Ashton, who also created the iconic mask worn by the squire, "There were no problems with this make-up; patience and care in its application is the essential factor. As for design I used a handful of my favorite medical text books and a generous helping of imagination."[45] The wardrobe depart-ment also made a key contribution to the look of the zombies, thanks to Rosemary's Burrows' idea to costume them in sack cloth. Remembered Bur-rows, "I can't remember how many sack cloth out-fits we knocked up, but it was a big operation. There was [*sic*] more than thirty outfits. We needed them all at once for the finale, when the mine burns down."[46] Things are meanwhile capped off with a vigorous James Bernard score, which makes use of a thunderous kettledrum motif during the opening voodoo ceremony.

Principal photography on *The Plague of the Zom-bies* was completed by 6 September 1965, and the film was ready for its trade show with *Dracula— Prince of Darkness* just over three months later on 17 December. Released in the UK on the ABC cir-cuit by Warner-Pathé on 9 January 1966 (on the lower half of a double bill with *Dracula—Prince of Darkness*), the film was an immediate hit with au-diences. In its review of the movie, *Films and Filming* noted that, "John Gilling directs with the requisite panache, and the acting is no more wooden than it should be—there is not the usual difficulty in distinguishing the zombies from the other actors," while the *Monthly Film Bulletin* called it "The best Hammer Horror for quite some time, with remarkably few of the lapses into crudity which are usually part and parcel of this company's work." The film's American release care of Twen-tieth Century–Fox (again with *Dracula—Prince of Darkness*) followed on 12 January, and proved equally successful, even if *Variety*'s generally positive review (which described the movie as "a well-made horror programer") mistakenly pointed out that the production had been "filmed at Ire-land's Bray Studios." A television ad campaign meanwhile helped to drum up business, while pa-trons were handed fangs (for the boys) and zombie eyes (for the girls) when they entered the theaters. The poster meanwhile billed the double bill as "The greatest all new fright show in town!" and carried the tag lines "Bloodthirsty vampire lives again" for *Dracula—Prince of Darkness*, and "Only the Lord of the Dead could unleash them!" for *The Plague of the Zombies*.

**Additional notes:** Gaffe spotters should note that as Alice is thrown from the head of the mineshaft by Johne Martinus, she blinks, even though she's supposed to be dead. Also note the two red fire extinguishers in the squire's study during the fight between Sir James and the acolyte, the lack of a possessory apostrophe on the sign for The Gardener's Arms, the use of a mask from *The Kiss of the Vampire* (1963) by one of Hamilton's men during the pursuit of the vicar, the fact that Alice can briefly be seen in long shot in her zombie make-up *before* her graveyard transformation, and the lack of green zombie make-up on the hands of Johne Martinus during the dream sequence. Two pit props in the mine can also be seen to wobble as the actors walk past them in an early scene, while the top of the set can be seen as Peter tells Sylvia to "Come and sit down" after she almost faints. Susan George can be seen watching footage from the graveyard resurrection scene on TV in *Fright* (1971), whose producers, Harry Fine and Michael Style, had just made the three Karnstein films for Hammer, so hopefully they got a good deal on the clips. The film's screenplay was novelized by John Burke for *The Second Hammer Horror Film Omnibus* (1967), which was published by Pan.

Production companies: Hammer/Seven Arts/ Associated British Picture Corporation. Distributors: Warner Pathé Distributors (UK [ABC circuit]), Twentieth Century–Fox (U.S.). Producer: Anthony Nelson Keys. Executive producer: Anthony Hinds. Director: John Gilling. Screenplay: Peter Bryan (and Anthony Hinds [uncredited script development]). Cinematographer: Arthur Grant. Music: James Bernard. Music director: Philip Martell. Supervising editor: James Needs. Editor: Chris Barnes. Production design: Bernard Robinson. Art director: Don Mingaye. Costumes: Rosemary Burrows. Special effects: Bowie Films, Ltd.. Make-up: Roy Ashton, Richard Mills (assistant [uncredited]). Hair: Frieda Steiger. Production manager: George Fowler. Assistant director: Bert Batt. Second assistant director: Hugh Harlow [uncredited]. Camera operator: Moray Grant. Focus puller: Bob Jordan [uncredited]. Sound: Ken Rawkins. Sound editor: Roy Baker. Continuity: Lorna Selwyn. Stunts: Peter Diamond [uncredited], Bernard Barnsley [uncredited], Valentino Musetti [uncredited]. Publicity: Reg Williams [uncredited]. Poster: Tom Chantrell [uncredited]. **Cast:** André Morell (Sir James Forbes), John Carson (Clive Hamilton), Diane Clare (Sylvia Forbes), Alex Davion (Harry Denver [billed as Alex Davion]), Brook Williams (Dr. Peter Tompson), Jacqueline Pearce (Alice Tompson), Michael Ripper (Sergeant Swift), Roy Royston (Vicar), Dennis Chinnery (Constable Christian), Marcus Hammond (Martinus), Louis Mahoney (Coloured servant), Francis Willey (Young blood), Bernard Egan (Young blood), Norman Mann (Young blood), Tim Condron (Young blood), Ben Aris (Johne Martinus), Jerry Verno (Landlord [uncredited]), Jolyon Booth (Coachman [uncredited]), Peter Diamond (Zombie [uncredited]), Keith Peacock (Zombie [uncredited]), Reg Harding (Zombie [uncredited]), Del Watson (Zombie [uncredited]), Ernie Rice (Inn patron [uncredited]), Ann Diley (Jacqueline Pearce's stand-in [uncredited]). **DVD availability:** Studio Canal/Warner (UK R2

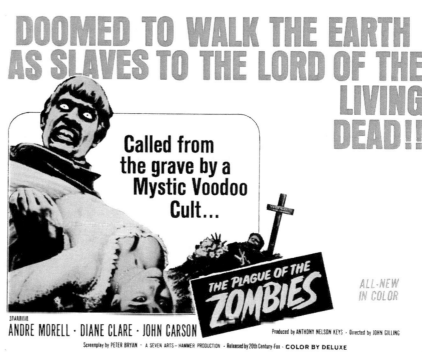

*Top:* **Relaxing between takes during the making of** *The Plague of the Zombies* (1966). **From left to right, André Morell, Brook Williams, Diane Clare and Jacqueline Pearce.** *Bottom:* **American poster for** *The Plague of the Zombies* (1966) **(both photographs, Hammer/Seven Arts/Associated British Picture Corporation/Warner Pathé Distributors/Twentieth Century–Fox/Studio Canal).**

PAL); Anchor Bay (U.S. R1 NTSC), extras include a trailer and TV spot and an episode of *The World of Hammer* (1990 [first broadcast 1994], TV) titled *Mummies, Werewolves and the Living Dead*. **Blu-ray availability:** Studio Canal (B/2), extras include a DVD version, *Raising the Dead* featuring John Carson and Jacqueline Pearce, a restoration comparison, a restored trailer and an episode of *The World of Hammer* (1990 [first broadcast 1994], TV) titled *Mummies, Werewolves and the Living Dead*. **CD availability:** *The Hammer Film Music Collection: Volume Two* (GDI Records), which contains the *Main Title*

### Platt, Victor

This British supporting actor (1920–2017, real name Victor Elphick) played a Sapper sentry in the Hammer wartime drama *The Steel Bayonet* (1957). His other credits include *The History of Mr. Polly* (1948), *Man Detained* (1961), *Playback* (1962), *The Traitors* (1963) and *Hot Millions* (1968), plus episodes of *The Adventures of Robin Hood* (1955–1960, TV), *Quatermass and the Pit* (1958–1959, TV), *The Avengers* (1961–1969, TV), *The Saint* (1962–1969, TV), *Two in Clover* (1968–1969, TV) and *Crown Court* (1972–1984, TV). His wife was the actress Diane Watts (1930–). **Hammer credits:** *The Steel Bayonet* (1957, as Sapper sentry [uncredited])

### Pleasence, Donald

Although he eventually came to be known as a horror star, this always busy British character actor (1919–1995) sadly never made a genre picture for Hammer, although he did appear in the studio's gritty, Manchester-shot thriller *Hell Is a City* (1960), in which he played a bookmaker whose business is robbed by an escaped con. In films from 1954 with *The Beachcomber*, Pleasence went on to appear in over one-hundred-and-twenty productions, among them *1984* (1955), *A Tale of Two Cities* (1958), *Circus of Horrors* (1960), *The Caretaker* (1963), *The Great Escape* (1963), *Fantastic Voyage* (1966), *Cul-de-Sac* (1966), *From Beyond the Grave* (1973), *Dracula* (1979), *Race for the Yankee Zephyr* (1981), *Escape from New York* (1981), *Shadows and Fog* (1991) and *Safe Haven* (1995). He was also considered for the role of John Verney in Hammer's *To the Devil a Daughter* (1976). One of the screen's best villains, he made an excellent Blofeld in *You Only Live Twice* (1967), but is best known for playing Dr. Sam Loomis in the *Halloween* films, of which he appeared in five between 1978 and 1995. Also busy in television on both sides of the Atlantic, his many credits here, beginning with the TV play *The Dybbuk* (1952, TV), include episodes of *The Adventures of Robin Hood* (1955–1960, TV), *The Defenders* (1961–1965, TV), *Hawaii Five-O* (1968–1980, TV), *Jesus of Nazareth* (1977, TV), *Centennial* (1978–1979, TV) and *Lovejoy* (1986–1994, TV). He also narrated the memorable public information film *The Spirit of Dark and Lonely Water* (1973, TV), in which a cowled figured warns against the dangers of playing near water; aimed at children, it haunted a generation. Married four times, his wives included the actresses Miriam Raymond (1916–2009, aka Miriam P. Walker), to whom he was married between 1941 and 1958, Josephine Crombie (1929–1997), to whom he was married between 1959 and 1970, and Miera Shore, to whom he was married between 1970 and 1988. His children include the actresses Angela Pleasence (1941–, full name Daphne Anne Angela Pleasence), Lucy Pleasance (1961–), Polly Jo Pleasence (1963–) and Miranda Pleasence (1970–). His former son-in-law (married to Angela Pleasence) was the actor Michael Cadman, who appeared in Hammer's *Rasputin—The Mad Monk* (1966) and *Countess Dracula* (1971). **Hammer credits:** *Hell Is a City* (1960, as Gus Hawkins)

### Plomley, Roy

Best known for creating and hosting the long-running radio series *Desert Island Discs* (1942–), this British writer and broadcaster (1914–1985) also tried his hand at screenwriting, co-writing the scripts for two early Hammer thrillers: *Dr. Morelle—The Case of the Missing Heiress* (1949) and *Celia* (1949). His other screenwriting credits include *The Blakes Slept Here* (1953). He went on to pen several plays, among them *Murder Without Malice* (1959), *Two Bottles of Relish* (1961), *Curtsey to the King* (1966) and *There's a Fortune In It* (1967). His credits as an actor include *To the Public Danger* (1948) and *Double Confession* (1950), plus episodes of *Kaleidoscope* (1946–1953, TV). He was awarded an OBE in 1975. His wife was the actress Diana Wong (?–2012), whom he married in 1942, and, who appeared in Hammer's *Death in High Heels* (1947). **Hammer credits:** *Dr. Morelle—The Case of the Missing Heiress* (1949), *Celia* (1949)

### Plummer, Terry

This British stuntman, stunt arranger and bit player (1936–2011, full name Terence Plummer) appeared in a handful of films for Hammer in the sixties. His many other credits include *From Russia with Love* (1963), *Goldfinger* (1964), *Where's Jack?* (1969), *The Man with the Golden Gun* (1974), *Superman II* (1980), *My Left Foot* (1989), *GoldenEye* (1995) and *The Calcium Kid* (2004), plus episodes of *The Avengers* (1961–1969, TV), *The Sweeney* (1975–1978, TV), *Boon* (1986–1989, TV) and *Murder in Mind* (2001–2003, TV). **Hammer credits:** *The Scarlet Blade* (1963 [uncredited]), *She* (1965 [uncredited]), *The Brigand of Kandahar* (1965 [uncredited])

### Plytas, Steve

Perhaps best remembered for playing Kurt, the drunken chef who develops a crush on Manuel in *Gourmet Night*, the classic 1975 episode of *Fawlty Towers* (1975–1979, TV), this Turkish actor (1913–1994) was a familiar face on British TV in the seventies and eighties, guesting in a variety of series, among them *Robin's Nest* (1977–1981, TV), *Hazell* (1978–1980, TV) and *Hammer House of Mystery and Suspense* (1984, TVM). He also sustained a busy film career, appearing in the likes of *A Night to Remember* (1958), *Passport to Shame* (1958), *The Spy Who Came in from the Cold* (1965), *Those Magnificent Men in Their Flying Machines* (1965), *Theatre of Death* (1966), *On Her Majesty's Secret Service* (1969), *Carry On Emmannuelle* (1978), *Revenge of the Pink Panther* (1978), *Eleni* (1985) and *Batman* (1989). **Hammer credits:** *Czech Mate* (1984, TVM [episode of *Hammer House of Mystery and Suspense*], as Head waiter)

### Pockett, Christine

Pockett appeared as a dancer in Hammer's *The Vengeance of She* (1968). Her other credits include *Killers of Kilimanjaro* (1959) and *Salt & Pepper* (1968), plus episodes of *Theatre 625* (1964–1968, TV) and *Three of a Kind* (1967, TV). **Hammer credits:** *The Vengeance of She* (1968, as Dancer)

Dancer Christine Pockett makes her move in *The Vengeance of She* (1968) (Hammer/Seven Arts/ABPC/Warner Pathé Distributors/Twentieth Century–Fox).

### Pocock, Peter

This British stuntman and bit player (1934–2007) worked for Hammer consistently from the late fifties onwards. His other credits include *Carry On Cowboy* (1965) and *Superman* (1978), plus episodes of *Doctor Who* (1963–1989, TV), *Marty* (1968–1969, TV) and *Dick Turpin* (1979–1982, TV). **Hammer credits include:** *The Hound of the Baskervilles* (1959 [uncredited]), *The Brides of Dracula* (1960 [uncredited]), *The Curse of the Werewolf* (1961 [uncredited]), *The Phantom of the Opera* (1962 [uncredited]), *The Damned* (1963 [uncredited]), *The Gorgon* (1964 [uncredited]), *The Secret of Blood Island* (1965 [uncredited]), *Dracula—Prince of Darkness* (1966 [uncredited]), *One Million Years B.C.* (1966 [uncredited]), *The Devil Rides Out* (1968 [uncredited], *Dracula Has Risen from the Grave* (1968 [uncredited]), *When*

*Dinosaurs Ruled the Earth* (1970 [uncredited]), *The Horror of Frankenstein* (1970 [uncredited]), *Dr. Jekyll and Sister Hyde* (1971 [uncredited])

## Pohlman, Helen

This British actress can be spotted as Amanda in the Hammer comedy *The Ugly Duckling* (1959). **Hammer credits:** *The Ugly Duckling* (1959, as Amanda)

## Pohlmann, Eric

In British films from 1948 with *Portrait from Life*, this rotund Austro-Hungarian actor (1913–1979, real name Erich Pollak) came to Britain in 1939 just prior to the outbreak of World War II. Frequently cast as an oily villain, he went on to make many films, among them *Blackout* (1950), *The Belles of St. Trinian's* (1954), *Carry On Spying* (1964) and *The Return of the Pink Panther* (1975), in the latter of which he spoofed Sidney Greenstreet. He also provided the voice of Ernst Stavro Blofeld in two James Bond films: *From Russia with Love* (1963) and *Thunderball* (1965), though on-screen the role was played by Anthony Dawson. Pohlmann made several second features for Hammer in the fifties, beginning with *The Gambler and the Lady* (1953), in which he played Arturo Colonna, and *The Glass Cage* (1955), in which he played Henri Sapolio, the World Champion Starving Man. He also appeared in a couple of comedies for the company. Much on stage in Britain, Germany and Austria, his many TV credits include episodes of *Douglas Fairbanks, Jr. Presents* (1953–1957, TV), *The Baron* (1966–1967, TV), *The Champions* (1968–1969, TV), *Department S* (1969–1970, TV) and *Hadleigh* (1969–1976, TV). His wife was the actress Liselotte Goetting (1904–1968), whom he married in 1939. **Hammer credits:** *The Gambler and the Lady* (1953, as Arturo Colonna), *Blood Orange* (1953, as Mercedes), *36 Hours* (1953, as Slossen), *Break in the Circle* (1955, as Emile), *The Glass Cage* (1955, as Henri Sapolio), *Further Up the Creek* (1958, as President), *Sands of the Desert* (1960, as Scrobin), *Visa to Canton* (1961, as Colonel Ivano King)

## Pollock, Ellen

This German actress (1902–1997) played the role of Roberta de Wynter in the Hammer melodrama *To Have and to Hold* (1951). Much on stage, particularly in the works of George Bernard Shaw (she was the president of The Shaw Society), her other film credits include *Moulin Rouge* (1928), *Sons of the Sea* (1939), *Spare a Copper* (1940), *Something in the City* (1950), *The Hypnotist* (1957), *Master Spy* (1962), *Finders Keepers* (1966), *Horror Hospital* (1973) and *The Wicked Lady* (1983). Her television credits include episodes of *Douglas Fairbanks, Jr. Presents* (1953–1957, TV), *Suspense* (1962–1963, TV) and *World's End* (1981, TV). Married twice, her second husband was the artist James Proudfoot (1908–1971), whom she married in 1945. **Hammer credits:** *To Have and to Hold* (1951, as Roberta [Bobby] de Wynter)

## Pollock, George

Best known for helming the highly popular Miss Marple murder-mysteries of the sixties—*Murder She Said* (1961), *Murder at the Gallop* (1963), *Murder Most Foul* (1964), *Murder Ahoy* (1964)—this British director (1907–1979) began his career as a third assistant in 1933. He gradually worked his way up the ladder, becoming a first assistant on *Rhythm in the Air* (1936). He eventually became David Lean's first assistant director in the forties, working on *Blithe Spirit* (1945), *Brief Encounter* (1945), *Great Expectations* (1946), *Oliver Twist* (1948), *The Passionate Friends* (1949) and *Madeleine* (1950). He also worked as a second unit director on *The Third Man* (1949). Pollack began directing his own films in 1957 with *A Stranger in Town*, and went on to helm such films as *Rooney* (1957), *And the Same to You* (1960), *Kill or Cure* (1962) and *Ten Little Indians* (1965). He also directed the Hammer comedy *Don't Panic Chaps* (1959), but it wasn't among his greatest successes. His TV credits include episodes of *Zero One* (1962–1965, TV), *Gideon's Way* (1965–1966, TV) and *Danger Man* (1964–1966, TV). **Hammer credits:** *Don't Panic Chaps* (1959)

## *Polly's Two Fathers*

GB, 1936, 23m, bw, cert U

This brief drama concerns a girl who, having been adopted by a couple of kindly Norfolk fishermen, saves a nobleman from drowning, and later marries a seaman. Produced and directed by Hammer founder Will Hammer, and scripted by Hammer board member George Mozart (both of whom also star), the film has been little seen since it was released in the UK by Exclusive in January 1936.

Production company: Hammer. Distributor: Exclusive (UK). Producer: Will Hammer. Director: Will Hammer. Screenplay: George Mozart. **Cast:** Will Hammer (Bill), George Mozart (Jack), April Vivian (Polly), Pat Aherne (Fred), Ian Wilson (Lord Stockridge)

## Polycarpou, Peter

This British actor is best known for playing Chris Theodopolopodous in the sitcom *Birds of a Feather* (1989–1998, TV). He can also be seen in a supporting role in *Black Carrion* (1984, TVM [episode of *Hammer House of Mystery and Suspense*]). His other TV credits include episodes of *The Professionals* (1977–1983, TV), *Sunburn* (1999–2000, TV), *Mile High* (2003–2005, TV) and *Family Tree* (2013, TV). His occasional films include *Evita* (1996), *Julie and the Cadillacs* (1999), *De-Lovely* (2004), in which he played Louis B Mayer, *O Jerusalem* (2006), *I Could Never Be Your Woman* (2007) and *Blue Iguana* (2018). Also on stage, including musicals, among them the original West End runs of *Les Miserables* and *Miss Saigon*. **Hammer credits:** *Black Carrion* (1984, TVM [episode of *Hammer House of Mystery and Suspense*], as Driver)

## Pomeroy, John

In films from 1946 as an assistant cutter, this British editor (1921–1979) went on to edit such films as *Our Girl Friday* (1953), *Dance Little Lady* (1954), *Carry On Admiral* (1957), *The City of the Dead* (1960), *The Comedy Man* (1963) and *The Plank* (1967). He also edited Hammer's feline shocker *The Shadow of the Cat* (1961). In 1958 he directed his one and only film, *Dublin Nightmare*. His earlier credits as a second assistant editor include *Hamlet* (1948) and *The Weaker Sex* (1948), while his work as an assistant editor includes *Night Was Our Friend* (1951) and *Sea Devils* (1953). **Hammer credits:** *The Shadow of the Cat* (1961)

## Ponting, Roy

Ponting (1918–1973) worked as the costumier on Hammer's *Creatures the World Forgot* (1971). His other credits include *King and Country* (1964), *The Italian Job* (1969), *And Soon the Darkness* (1970), *The Last Grenade* (1970) and *The Magnificent Seven Deadly Sins* (1971). **Hammer credits:** *Creatures the World Forgot* (1971)

## Poole, Anthony

Poole can be seen as one of the fairground roustabouts in Hammer's *The Evil of Frankenstein* (1964). **Hammer credits:** *The Evil of Frankenstein* (1964, as Roustabout [uncredited])

## Poole, Frank

Poole worked as Rank's head of distribution, and was directly involved in the development of *The Lady Vanishes* (1979) between Rank and Hammer. **Hammer credits:** *The Lady Vanishes* (1979)

## Poole, Margie

Poole can be seen as Jackie in Hammer's *Dr. Jekyll and Sister Hyde* (1971). **Hammer credits:** *Dr. Jekyll and Sister Hyde* (1971, as Jackie)

## Poole, Michael

Poole can be seen as a workman in Hammer's *Quatermass and the Pit* (1967). His other credits include *Innocent Bystanders* (1972), *The Mackintosh Man* (1973), *Whoops Apocalypse* (1986) and *The Raven* (2012), plus episodes of *Magnolia Street* (1961, TV), *A Little Princess* (1973, TV), *Jenny's War* (1985, TV) and *Jeeves and Wooster* (1990–1993, TV). Also on stage. **Hammer credits:** *Quatermass and the Pit* (1967, as Workman [uncredited])

## Pooley, Kirstie

Pooley had a minor supporting role in *The Corvini Inheritance* (1984, TVM [episode of *Hammer House of Mystery and Suspense*]), which was directed by her former step-mother, Gabrielle Beaumont (1942–). Her other TV credits include episodes of *The Glittering Prizes* (1976, TV), *The Professionals* (1977–1983, TV), *Bulman* (1985–1987, TV) and *War and Remembrance* (1988, TV), in which she played Eva Braun. Her film credits include *The Johnstown Monster* (1971), which was produced by her step-mother and written and directed by her father, Olaf Pooley (1914–2015, real name Ole Krohn Pooley), who also appeared in the film. Her other films include *White Cargo* (1973) and *The Last Word* (1975). Her mother was the actress Irlin Hall (1923–1991). **Hammer credits:** *The Corvini Inheritance* (1984, TVM [episode of *Hammer House of Mystery and Suspense*], as First female model)

## *Poor Butterfly* see *Journey to the Unknown*

## The Port of London Authority

This London authority was thanked by the producers in the opening credits of *The Quatermass Xperiment* (1955) for their co-operation in making the film, which made use of London's docklands during several key sequences. The authority has been helpful in the making of many films, ranging from *Seven Days to Noon* (1950) to *Battle of Britain* (1969). **Hammer credits:** *The Quatermass Xperiment* (1955)

## Portell, Petula

Portell can be seen as Petra in Hammer's *Dr. Jekyll and Sister Hyde* (1971). **Hammer credits:** *Dr. Jekyll and Sister Hyde* (1971, as Petra)

## Porteous, Emma

Born in India, Porteous (1936–) has designed the costumes for a number of high profile productions, among them *Clash of the Titans* (1981), *Octopussy* (1983), *A View to a Kill* (1985), *Aliens* (1986), *The Living Daylights* (1987) and *Judge Dredd* (1995). Her other credits include *Leo the Last* (1969), *Entertaining Mr. Sloane* (1970), *Performance* (1970), *Steptoe and Son Ride Again* (1973), *The Tamarind Seed* (1974), *The Dogs of War* (1980), *1984* (1984), *No Surrender* (1985), *My Life So Far* (1999) and *All Forgotten* (2001), as well as contributions to such TV series and one-offs as *Dr. Jekyll and Mr. Hyde* (1973, TVM), which earned her an Emmy nomination, *Dick Turpin* (1979–1982, TV), *Space: 1999* (1975–1977, TV) and *Around the World in 80 Days* (1989, TV), which earned her a second Emmy nomination. She also designed the wardrobe for Hammer's *The Lady Vanishes* (1979), which included costumes for tweedy English types as well as a madcap American heiress. Her husband was the actor Peter Porteous (1930–2005), whom she married in 1963. **Hammer credits:** *The Lady Vanishes* (1979)

## Porter, Bob (Robert)

This British assistant director turned producer (1924–) worked as the assistant director on Hammer's Robin Hood romp *Sword of Sherwood Forest* (1960). Following wartime experience in the army, he started his film career as an assistant casting director, a stand-in—notably for Stewart Granger, to whom he was contracted for a period—and a stuntman. Working in a variety of capacities, his other credits went on to include two Stewart Granger vehicles, *The Little Hut* (1957), on which he was the third assistant director, and *Harry Black* (1958), on which he was the second assistant, as well as *H.M.S. Defiant* (1962), on which he was the first assistant and the location manager. He also worked as a second unit director on *Zulu* (1964) and *Golden Rendezvous* (1977), additionally working as an associate producer on the latter. His other credits as an associate producer include *Sands of the Kalahari* (1965), *Where's Jack?* (1969), *The Italian Job* (1969) and *The Last Valley* (1970). He went on to form Oakhurst Film Productions with Stanley Baker and Michael Deeley (which made *Where's Jack?* and *The Italian Job*), and Robert Porter Film Productions. He also worked for a time

in America for Avco Embassy as a production supervisor and associate producer. **Hammer credits:** *Sword of Sherwood Forest* (1960)

## Porter, Eric

This distinguished British stage actor (1928–1995), noted for his Shakespearean roles, had his greatest success on television in *The Forsyte Saga* (1967, TV), in which he played Soames Forsyte, earning himself a best actor BAFTA award for his performance. On stage from 1945 and in films from 1964 with *The Fall of the Roman Empire*, his other credits include *The Pumpkin Eater*, *The Heroes of Telemark* (1965), *Kaleidoscope* (1966), *Antony and Cleopatra* (1972), *The Day of the Jackal* (1973), *The Belstone Fox* (1973), *Hennessy* (1975), *The Thirty-Nine Steps* (1978) and *Little Lord Fauntleroy* (1980, TVM). He also starred in two Hammer films, first playing Captain Lansen in the disappointing *The Lost Continent* (1968). He returned to the studio three years later to play Dr. John Pritchard in the far superior *Hands of the Ripper* (1971), in which his character's use of psychoanalysis to help deal with the mental trauma suffered by Jack the Ripper's daughter leads to a bloodbath. Commented *Photoplay* of his performance, "Eric Porter proves that he would make a more than worthy successor to Vincent Price." High praise indeed! Note that Porter was also offered the role of Baron Friedrich Zorn in Hammer's *Demons of the Mind* (1972). However, when the start date was changed, the actor was instead moved to the Ripper project. His other television appearances include episodes of *Knock on Any Door* (1965–1966, TV), *The Power Game* (1965–1969, TV), *Anna Karenina* (1977, TV) and *Oliver Twist* (1985, TV), in which he played Fagin. **Hammer credits:** *The Lost Continent* (1968, as Captain Lansen), *Hands of the Ripper* (1971, as Dr. John Pritchard)

**After the mayhem. Eric Porter comforts Angharad Rees in *Hands of the Ripper* (1971), one of Hammer's bloodier offerings (Hammer/Rank/Universal).**

## Porter, Sarah

Porter had a minor supporting role in *In Possession* (1984, TVM [episode of *Hammer House of*

*Mystery and Suspense*]). Her other TV credits include episodes of *Thriller* (1973–1976, TV), *Wings* (1977–1978, TV), in which she played Lorna Collins, *A Horseman Riding By* (1978, TV), in which she played Elinor Codsall, *Cover* (1981, TV), *Blott on the Landscape* (1985, TV), in which she played Bessie Williams, and *Boon* (1986–1992, TV). **Hammer credits:** *In Possession* (1984, TVM [episode of *Hammer House of Mystery and Suspense*], as Daughter)

## Posta, Adrienne

Beginning in films as a child under her real name with *No Time for Tears* (1957), this cheeky-faced British comedy actress (1949–, real name Adrienne Poster) went on to enliven a number of films in the sixties and seventies, among them *To Sir, with Love* (1967), *Up the Junction* (1968), *Here We Go Round the Mulberry Bush* (1968), *Spring and Port Wine* (1970), *Up Pompeii* (1971), *The Alf Garnett Saga* (1972), *Adventures of a Taxi Driver* (1975), for which she also performed the theme song *My Cruisin' Casanova*, *Carry On Behind* (1975) and *Adventures of a Private Eye* (1977), in which, as Lisa Moroni, she did an engagingly cruel impersonation of Liza Minnelli's Sally Bowles character from *Cabaret* (1972). Also much on TV, her credits here include appearances in *Top Secret* (1961–1962, TV), *Alexander the Greatest* (1971–1972, TV), *The Bar Mitzvah Boy* (1976, TVM), *Edward the Seventh* (1975, TV), in which she played Marie Lloyd, *Cue Gary* (1987–1988, TV) and *Red Dwarf* (1988–1999, TV), plus the cartoon series *Angelina Ballerina* (2001–2004, TV), for which she provided the voice of Grandma Mouseling. She also appeared in an episode of Hammer's *Journey to the Unknown* (1968, TV). Her first husband (of two) was singer and actor Graham Bonnet (1947–), whom she married in 1974. **Hammer credits:** *Miss Belle* (1968, TV [episode of *Journey to the Unknown*], as Girl)

## Poston, Tom

Popular on television in such series as *The Steve Allen Show* (1956–1959, TV), which won him a best supporting actor Emmy, *Mork and Mindy* (1978–1982, TV), *Newhart* (1982–1990, TV) and *Grace Under Fire* (1995–1998, TV), this American comedy actor (1921–2007, full name Thomas Gordon Poston) also appeared in a handful of films, among them two for producer-director William Castle: *Zotz!* (1962) and Hammer's disappointing remake of *The Old Dark House* (1963), in both of which he played the lead. His other big screen credits include *City That Never Sleeps* (1953), *Cold Turkey* (1970), *Carbon Copy* (1981) and *The Story of Us* (1999). Commented *Kinematograph Weekly* of his performance in *The Old Dark House*, "Tom Poston is passable in the role of the invited one, but his performance doesn't quite warrant his journey from America." Married four times (twice to the same woman, Kay Hudson), Poston's other wives were the actresses Jean Sullivan (1923–2003), to whom he was married between 1955 and 1968, and Suzanne Pleshette (1937–2008), whom he married in 2001. **Hammer credits:** *The Old Dark House* (1963, as Tom Penderel)

### Potter, John

This British sound technician (1949– ) worked as a boom operator on the Hammer series *Journey to the Unknown* (1968, TV). His other credits include *The Limbo Line* (1968), *Assassin* (1973), *Carry On Girls* (1973), *Tiffany Jones* (1973), in which he can be seen playing a boom man, *The Legend of Hell House* (1973) and *Moments* (1974). **Hammer credits:** *Journey to the Unknown* (1968, TV [uncredited])

### Poulton, Raymond

This British editor (1916–1992) worked on Hammer's *The Vengeance of She* (1968). His many other credits include *While I Live* (1947), *Betrayed* (1954), *The Three Worlds of Gulliver* (1960), *Barabbas* (1962), *Berserk* (1967), *Live and Let Die* (1973), *The Man with the Golden Gun* (1974), *Force Ten from Navarone* (1978), *Sergeant Steiner* (1979) and *Danger on Dartmoor* (1980). He was also an associate editor on *The Guns of Navarone* (1961) and *Mackenna's Gold* (1969). **Hammer credits:** *The Vengeance of She* (1968)

### Poulton, Terry

This British sound editor (1930–1993) worked on Hammer's *Captain Clegg* (1962). He returned to the company for *The Horror of Frankenstein* (1970) and several seventies productions. He also worked as a dubbing editor on ten episodes of *Hammer House of Mystery and Suspense* (1984, TVM). His other credits (either as a dubbing editor, sound editor or sound mixer) include *The Colditz Story* (1955), *Greyfriars Bobby* (1961), *And Now for Something Completely Different* (1971), *Sinbad and the Eye of the Tiger* (1977), *The Thirty-Nine Steps* (1978), *The First Great Train Robbery* (1978), *Rising Damp* (1980), *Clash of the Titans* (1981), *The Last Horror Film* (1982) and *Superman IV: The Quest for Peace* (1987). His early credits include work as a second assistant editor on *Dear Murderer* (1947) and *Moulin Rouge* (1952). **Hammer credits:** *Captain Clegg* (1962, sound editor), *The Horror of Frankenstein* (1970, sound editor), *Lust for a Vampire* (1971, sound editor), *Countess Dracula* (1971, sound editor [uncredited]), *Creatures the World Forgot* (1971, sound editor), *Demons of the Mind* (1972, sound editor), *Man at the Top* (1973, sound editor), *The Satanic Rites of Dracula* (1974, sound editor), *Czech Mate* (1984, TVM [episode of *Hammer House of Mystery and Suspense*], dubbing editor), *The Sweet Scent of Death* (1984, TVM [episode of *Hammer House of Mystery and Suspense*], dubbing editor), *A Distant Scream* (1984, TVM [episode of *Hammer House of Mystery and Suspense*], dubbing editor), *In Possession* (1984, TVM [episode of *Hammer House of Mystery and Suspense*], dubbing editor), *Black Carrion* (1984, TVM [episode of *Hammer House of Mystery and Suspense*], dubbing editor), *Last Video and Testa-* *ment* (1984, TVM [episode of *Hammer House of Mystery and Suspense*], dubbing editor), *The Corvini Inheritance* (1984, TVM [episode of *Hammer House of Mystery and Suspense*], dubbing editor), *Child's Play* (1984, TVM [episode of *Hammer House of Horror*], dubbing editor), *And the Wall Came Tumbling Down* (1984, TVM [episode of *Hammer House of Mystery and Suspense*], dubbing editor), *Tennis Court* (1984, TVM [episode of *Hammer House of Mystery and Suspense*], dubbing editor)

### Pound, Toots

This supporting actress had minor roles in two of Hammer's second feature supports of the fifties. Her other credits include *Svengali* (1954). **Hammer credits:** *Third Party Risk* (1955, as Lucy [uncredited]), *Women Without Men* (1956, as Scrubber [uncredited])

### Powell, Anthony (Tony)

Powell worked as the clapper loader on Hammer's *The Revenge of Frankenstein* (1958) and *The Hound of the Baskervilles* (1959). His other credits include *The One That Got Away* (1957). **Hammer credits:** *The Revenge of Frankenstein* (1958 [uncredited]), *The Hound of the Baskervilles* (1959 [uncredited])

### Powell, Eddie

One of *the* great British stuntmen, Powell (1927–2000, full name Edwin Charles Powell) was one of the pioneers of his profession. Perhaps best known for frequently doubling Christopher Lee and Gregory Peck, he came to films in 1948 following wartime experience in the Grenadier Guards, serving as a dispatch rider in Germany (itself a fairly precarious occupation!). His long-time association with Hammer began with *Dracula* (1958), which in turn led to many further appearances. Recalled Christopher Lee of Powell: "He was a double with me on many pictures and a good actor in his own persona."[47] Remembered Powell, "I was always doing falls and things with Chris. Stakes going in, what have you … carrying actresses wherever. Quite nice, actually!"[48]

In addition to stunt work, Powell also portrayed several key characters for Hammer, among them Prem the Mummy in *The Mummy's Shroud* (1967), which was his first credited role, the Goat of Mendes in *The Devil Rides Out* (1968), and the Inquisitor in *The Lost Continent* (1968). Recalled Powell of his appearance as the Goat of Mendes, "It was a bit chilly. I was standing in a hole on top of a rock made out of plaster. I was covered with large bits of skin. Nobody had to worry about the Devil's legs as you never saw them. I had some extremely hairy artificial legs sticking out in front of me. These were jointed so it looked as though I was sitting crossed legged."[49] However, if you want to see Powell *sans* elaborate make-up, he can also be seen as the stranger in the bar in the opening sequence of *She* (1965).

Note that during the filming of *The Mummy's Shroud*, Powell appeared in a photo ad for the Milk Marketing Board, encouraging people to "Drinka pinta milka day." It should also be noted that Powell took over as the Mummy Ra-Antef for the sewer climax of *The Curse of the Mummy's Tomb* (1964) following an accident involving fellow stuntman Dickie Owen, who had been playing the character. Recalled Powell of his work on the sequence, "I was carrying this bird and the scroll of life through the sewer and at a certain point I had to go down and hold my breath under the water. They thought it would take two days to shoot. I did it in one take. Michael Carreras said I'd saved them a lot of time and money and they would double what I was getting on the contract. Hammer was a marvellous company to work for."[50]

In addition to his work for Hammer, Powell was also involved in such wide-ranging films as *From Russia with Love* (1963), *A Place to Go* (1963), *Where Eagles Dare* (1969), *The Omen* (1976), *Alien*

Eddie Powell downs a few pints in this publicity shot taken to help promote the benefits of drinking milk for the Milk Marketing Board during the making of *The Mummy's Shroud* (1967) (Hammer/Seven Arts/Associated British Picture Corporation/Warner Pathé Distributors/Twentieth Century–Fox/Studio Canal).

(1979), in which—uncredited—he played the alien, *The Sea Wolves* (1980), *The Living Daylights* (1987), *Indiana Jones and the Last Crusade* (1989), *Batman* (1989), *Robin Hood: Prince of Thieves* (1991), *Patriot Games* (1992) and *Relative Values* (2000). He also doubled for two other screen Draculas: Jack Palance in *Dracula* (1973, TV) and Frank Langella in *Dracula* (1979).

Recalled Christopher Lee of Powell: "I was very fond of Eddie. He was an outstanding stuntman—always dedicated to his work, very precise and never impatient."[51] Recalled Powell of his first time doubling for Lee, "It was Roy Ashton who suggested that I double Christopher Lee in the first place. I was working on a film called *The Death of Uncle George* [actually *How to Murder a Rich Uncle*]. At the time I didn't know who the hell Christopher Lee was!"[52] Remembered Janina Faye of Powell, "'Speaking was not one of his favorite pastimes! Eddie always said he was better at the action stuff, but he had a never-ending supply of eventful and interesting stories to tell."[53]

Powell's wife was the wardrobe supervisor Rosemary Burrows, whom he married in 1967; like her husband, she also did much work for Hammer. Powell's brother Joe (1922–2016) was also a stuntman, and he appeared in two films for Hammer: *The Abominable Snowman* (1957) and *The Brigand of Kandahar* (1965). **Hammer credits include:** *Dracula* (1958, doubling for Christopher Lee [uncredited]), *The Mummy* (1959, stunts [uncredited], Christopher Lee's stunt double [uncredited]), *The Curse of the Mummy's Tomb* (1964, as Ra-Antef [sewer climax only, uncredited]), *She* (1965, as Stranger in bar [uncredited]), *Dracula—Prince of Darkness* (1966, doubling for Christopher Lee [uncredited]), *The Mummy's Shroud* (1967, as Prem [The Mummy]), *The Devil Rides Out* (1968, as the Goat of Mendes [uncredited]), *The Lost Continent* (1968, as Inquisitor), *Dracula Has Risen from the Grave* (1968, as Christopher Lee's stunt double [uncredited]), *Taste the Blood of Dracula* (1970, stunts [uncredited]), *Scars of Dracula* (1970, as Christopher Lee's stunt double [uncredited]), *Dracula A.D. 1972* (1972, as Christopher Lee's stunt double [uncredited]), *The Satanic Rites of Dracula* (1974, as Christopher Lee's stunt double [uncredited]), *To the Devil a Daughter* (1976, as Christopher Lee and Anthony Valentine's stunt double [uncredited])

### Powell, Greg

A veteran of the James Bond and Harry Potter franchises, this British stuntman, stunt co-ordinator, horsemaster, second unit director and bit part actor (1954–) hails from a family of stuntmen. In films from the early seventies, his many credits include *You Can't Win 'Em All* (1970), *The Spy Who Loved Me* (1977), *For Your Eyes Only* (1981), *Willow* (1988), *Far and Away* (1992), *Mission: Impossible* (1996), *The World Is Not Enough* (1999), *Harry Potter and the Goblet of Fire* (2005), *The Da Vinci Code* (2006), *Harry Potter and the Deathly Hallows: Part 2* (2011), *Fast & Furious 6* (2013), *Avengers: Age of Ultron* (2015) and *The Hitman's Bodyguard* (2017), plus episodes of *Follyfoot* (1971–1973, TV), *We'll Meet Again* (1982, TV), *Supergran*

(1985–1987, TV) and *Band of Brothers* (2001, TV), which earned him a shared Emmy nomination. He also worked on various episodes of *Hammer House of Mystery and Suspense* (1984, TVM). His uncle is the stuntman Dinny Powell (1932–, real name Dennis Powell), his brother the stuntman Gary Powell (1963–) and his father the stuntman and actor Nosher Powell (1928–2013, real name George Frederick Bernard Powell), who appeared in several films for Hammer, including *The Quatermass Xperiment* (1955), *Dracula* (1958) and *On the Buses* (1971). **Hammer credits:** *Hammer House of Mystery and Suspense* (1984, TVM, [uncredited])

### Powell, Joe

In films following the war, this British stuntman and actor (1922–2016) also ran the Soho office of Captain "Jock" Easton's stuntman's agency. His own appearances include Hammer's *The Abominable Snowman* (1957), in which he played one of the title creatures, glimpsed briefly at the climax (the other was played by Jock Easton). He can be spotted *sans* Yeti make-up in Hammer's *The Brigand of Kandahar* (1965), in which he played the Colour Sergeant. His other credits include *The Small Voice* (1948), *Captain Horatio Hornblower R.N.* (1951), *Moby Dick* (1956), Hammer's *The Steel Bayonet* (1957), *Zulu* (1964), *Casino Royale* (1967), *You Only Live Twice* (1967), *Where Eagles Dare* (1969), *On Her Majesty's Secret Service* (1969), in which he doubled for both George Lazenby and Telly Savalas during the bobsled sequence, *The Odessa File* (1974), *The Pink Panther Strikes Again* (1976), *Death on the Nile* (1978), *Flash Gordon* (1980), *Top Secret!* (1984), on which he also helmed the second unit, *A View to a Kill* (1985) and *Half Moon Street* (1986). He was also involved in the casting of extras on such large-scale films as *The Inn of the Sixth Happiness* (1958), *55 Days at Peking* (1963) and *Genghis Khan* (1965). Powell's brother was the stuntman Eddie Powell (1927–2000, full name Edwin Charles Powell), who did much work for Hammer. His sister-in-law is Hammer's longtime wardrobe supervisor Rosemary Burrows. **Hammer credits include:** *The Steel Bayonet* (1957, stunts [uncredited]), *The Abominable Snowman* (1957, as Yeti [uncredited]), *The Brigand of Kandahar* (1965, as Colour Sergeant)

### Powell, Lester

This prolific British dramatist (1912–1993) penned the radio serial *Return from Darkness* (1948), which was adapted by Hammer as *The Black Widow* (1950). His radio series *Lady in a Fog* (1947), which featured the detective Philip Odell, made a similar jump to the screen two years later as *Lady in the Fog*, though for America, it was retitled *Scotland Yard Inspector*. Powell's other radio work featuring Odell includes *The Odd Story of Simon Ode* (1948), *Spot the Lady* (1949), *Love from Leighton Buzzard* (1950), *Lady on the Screen* (1952), *Lady in a Fog* (1958 [remake]), *Test Room Eight* (1958) and *Tea on the Island* (1961). His novels, again all featuring Odell, include *A Count of Six* (1948), *Shadow Play* (1949), *Spot the Lady* (1950

[taken from the radio play]), *Still of Night* (1952) and *The Black Casket* (1953). His screen credits include *Stryker of the Yard* (1953) and *Companions in Crime* (1954), while his TV work takes in episodes of *The Man Who Was Two* (1957, TV), *The Unforeseen* (1960, TV), *The Avengers* (1961–1969, TV) and *The Big M* (1967, TV). Other radio plays include *Natalia* (1966), *The Death Watch* (1975) and *Trotsky in Finland* (1983). **Hammer credits:** *The Black Widow* (1950), *Lady in the Fog* (1952)

### Powell, Nosher

Frequently cast as bruisers, this British actor and stuntman (1928–2013, real name George Frederick Bernard Powell) played such a role in Hammer's *On the Buses* (1971), prior to which he'd worked for the company as a stuntman on *The Quatermass Xperiment* (1955) and *Dracula* (1958) among others. His other stunt credits include *Henry V* (1944), *A Night to Remember* (1958), *Ben-Hur* (1959), *Those Magnificent Men in Their Flying Machines* (1965), on which he was Gert Frobe's stunt double, *Thunderball* (1965), *You Only Live Twice* (1967), *Venom* (1971), *The Mackintosh Man* (1973), *Star Wars* (1977), *The Spy Who Loved Me* (1977), *Superman* (1978), *Moonraker* (1979), *Victor/Victoria* (1982), *Willow* (1988) and *First Knight* (1995). He also returned to Hammer for further hard man roles in *Nearest and Dearest* (1973) and *Love Thy Neighbour* (1973). His other acting credits include *The Sandwich Man* (1966), *Carry On Dick* (1974) and *Eat the Rich* (1987), plus episodes of *The Avengers* (1961–1969, TV), *The Sweeney* (1975–1978, TV) and *The Comic Strip Presents* (1982–2012, TV), most notably *Five Go Mad in Dorset* (1982, TV), in which he played Fingers. His brother is the stuntman Dinny Powell (1932–, real name Dennis Powell), and his sons are the stuntmen Greg Powell (1954–), who worked on *Hammer House of Mystery and Suspense* (1984), and Gary Powell (1963–). **Hammer credits:** *The Quatermass Xperiment* (1955, stunts [uncredited]), *Dracula* (1958, stuntman [uncredited]), *Sword of Sherwood Forest* (1960, stunts [uncredited]), *She* (1965, stunts [uncredited]), *The Secret of Blood Island* (1965, stunts [uncredited]), *On the Buses* (1971, as Betty's husband), *Nearest and Dearest* (1973, as Bouncer), *Love Thy Neighbour* (1973, as Bus driver)

### Powell, Vince

Working in collaboration with Harry Driver, this prolific British comedy writer (1928–2009, real name Vincent Joseph Smith) created and penned such sitcom hits as *George and the Dragon* (1966–1968, TV), *Never Mind the Quality, Feel the Width* (1967–1971, TV), *Nearest and Dearest* (1968–1973, TV), a big screen version of which Hammer released in 1973, albeit with a script by Tom Brennand and Roy Bottomley, *Two in Clover* (1969–1970, TV), *For the Love of Ada* (1970–1971, TV), *Bless This House* (1971–1976, TV) and *Spring and Autumn* (1973–1976, TV). The duo was also responsible for the hugely popular but no longer politically correct race relations sitcom *Love Thy Neighbour* (1972–1976, TV), a big screen version of which Hammer made in 1973, based upon a script by Driver and Powell. Following Driver's death in 1973, Powell went on to write and create *My Son Reuben* (1974, TV), *Young at Heart* (1977–1982, TV) and *Mind Your Language* (1977–1979, 1986, TV). Other big screen versions of Powell-Driver sitcoms include *For the Love of Ada* (1972), penned by Powell and Driver, *Never Mind the Quality, Feel the Width* (1973), also penned by the duo, and *Bless This House* (1972), which was written by Dave Freeman. **Hammer credits:** *Nearest and Dearest* (1973, original series), *Love Thy Neighbour* (1973, co-screenplay)

## Power, E.

British born Power (1942–) worked as a stagehand on the Hammer thriller *Maniac* (1963). **Hammer credits:** *Maniac* (1963 [uncredited])

## Power, Sandra

Power can be seen briefly as Sarah in Hammer's *The Nanny* (1965). Her other credits include *The Sandwich Man* (1966). **Hammer credits:** *The Nanny* (1965, as Sarah)

## Powers, Stefanie

Although best known for such television series as *The Girl from U.N.C.L.E.* (1966, TV) and *Hart to Hart* (1979–1983, TV), the latter of which earned her two Emmy nominations and five Golden Globe nominations, this glamorous American actress (1942–, real name Stefania Zofya Feder-kiewicz) has also had a spasmodic movie career, making her debut in *Tammy Tell Me True* (1961). A former swimming champion, her other big screen credits include *Experiment in Terror* (1962), *The New Interns* (1964), *Warning Shot* (1967), *Herbie Rides Again* (1973), *Escape to Athena* (1979), *Rabbit Fever* (2006), *Jump!* (2008)

**Stefanie Powers poses for the cameras during the making of *Crescendo* (1970) (Hammer/Warner Bros./Seven Arts/Warner Pathé Distributors).**

and *Ring by Spring* (2014). In 1965, she gave a good account of herself as Patricia Carroll, a young woman held captive by the demented mother of her dead fiancé in Hammer's *Fanatic*. Commented continuity girl Renee Glynne of the actress, "Stefanie Powers was a breath of fresh air in *Fanatic*."[54] Powers was subsequently invited back to star in both *Jane Brown's Body*, an episode of *Journey to the Unknown* (1968, TV) and *Crescendo* (1970), in both of which she found herself embroiled in equally tortuous plots. However, it should be noted that the original casting choice for the latter was Susan Hampshire, who lost the role when the film's production company changed from Compton to Hammer. Wed twice, Powers' first husband was the actor Gary Lockwood (1937–, real name John Gary Yurosek), to whom she was wed between 1966 and 1974. **Hammer credits:** *Fanatic* (1965, as Patricia Carroll), *Jane Brown's Body* (1968, TV [episode of *Journey to the Unknown*], as Jane Brown/Glenville), *Crescendo* (1970, as Susan Roberts)

## Prador, Irene

This Austrian actress and singer (1911–1996, real name Irene Peiser) played a supporting role in the Hammer thriller *The Snorkel* (1958). Her other credits include *No Orchids for Miss Blandish* (1948), *Jet Storm* (1959), *The Devil's Daffodil* (1961), *A Nice Girl Like Me* (1969) and *The Hiding Place* (1975), plus a return to Hammer for *To the Devil a Daughter* (1976) and an episode of *Hammer House of Mystery and Suspense* (1984, TVM]). Her other TV credits include episodes of *O.S.S.* (1957–1958, TV), *Jason King* (1971–1972, TV) and *Dear John* (1986–1987, TV), in which she played Mrs. Lemenski. Her sister was the actress Lilli Palmer (1914–1986, real name Lilli Marie Peiser). **Hammer credits:** *The Snorkel* (1958, as Frenchwoman), *To the Devil a Daughter* (1976, as Matron), *Last Video and Testament* (1984, TVM [episode of *Hammer House of Mystery and Suspense*], as Hotel guest)

## Pravda, George

This Austro-Hungarian actor (1918–1985, aka Jiri Pravda) played the mad scientist Dr. Brandt in Hammer's *Frankenstein Must Be Destroyed* (1969), in which he has his brain transplanted into the body of Freddie Jones' Professor Richter. On stage around the world (France, Australia, Britain), Pravda's many other film credits include *Parohy* (1947), *Krizova trojka* (1948), *No Time to Die* (1958), *Thunderball* (1965), *Inspector Clouseau* (1968), *Dracula* (1973, TVM), *Hanover Street* (1979) and *The Man Who Cried* (2000). Prolific in television, his credits here include episodes of *Sailor of Fortune* (1955–1956, TV), *Callan* (1967–1972, TV), *Holocaust* (1978, TV) and *Wagner* (1983, TV). His wife was the actress Hana-Maria Pravda (1916–2008, real name Hana Beck), whom he married in 1946; she appeared in *Czech Mate* (1984, TVM [episode of *Hammer House of Mystery and Suspense*]). **Hammer credits:** *Frankenstein Must Be Destroyed* (1969, as Dr. Brandt)

## Pravda, Hana-Maria

This Austro-Hungarian actress (1916–2008, real name Hana Beck) can be seen in a supporting role in *Czech Mate* (1984, TVM [episode of *Hammer*

*House of Mystery and Suspense*]). Her film credits include *Before Winter Comes* (1968), *The Kremlin Letter* (1970), *Dracula* (1973, TVM), *Death Wish 3* (1985), *Shining Through* (1992), *Bullseye!* (1990) and *Paradise Grove* (2003). Her TV work takes in episodes of *The Men from Room 13* (1959–1961, TV), *Napoleon and Love* (1972, TV) and *Ashenden* (1991, TV). A concentration camp survivor, she was fluent in several languages, including French, German and Russian. Her second husband was the Czech actor George Pravda (1918–1985, aka Jiri Pravda), whom she married in 1946; he appeared in Hammer's *Frankenstein Must Be Destroyed* (1969). **Hammer credits:** *Czech Mate* (1984, TVM [episode of *Hammer House of Mystery and Suspense*], as Mrs. Jiracek)

## *Prehistoric Women* see *Slave Girls*

## Prentice, Bernie

British born Prentice (?–) worked as the gaffer on Hammer's *The Viking Queen* (1967). His other credits, either as gaffer, underwater gaffer or chief electrician, include *Phaedra* (1962), *Sands of the Kalahari* (1965), *Ryan's Daughter* (1970), *The First Great Train Robbery* (1978), *The World Is Not Enough* (1999), *Harry Potter and the Goblet of Fire* (2005), *A Closed Book* (2009), *Captain Phillips* (2013) and *Widow's Walk* (2018). **Hammer credits:** *The Viking Queen* (1967 [uncredited])

## Prentice, Derek

Long in Britain, this South African actor (1904–1977) can be seen as the butler to Marius Goring's Baron Keller in Hammer's *Break in the Circle* (1955). His other credits include *Derby Day* (1952), *You Lucky People* (1955) and *The Treasure of Monte Cristo* (1961), plus episodes of *Douglas Fairbanks, Jr. Presents* (1953–1957, TV), *OSS* (1957–1958, TV) and *Man in a Suitcase* (1967–1968, TV). **Hammer credits:** *Break in the Circle* (1955, as Butler)

## Preston, Robert

In films from 1938 with *King of the Alcatraz*, this personable and dynamic American actor (1918–1987, real name Robert Preston Meservey) came to prominence in such films as *Union Pacific* (1939) and *Beau Geste* (1939). A reliable star or co-star during the forties, his films include *Reap the Wild Wind* (1942) and *The Macomber Affair* (1947), by which time his career was suffering a down turn. Hence his appearance in Hammer's *Cloudburst* (1951), in which he played John Graham, a code breaker who determines on catching the thieves who ran down his wife during a getaway. However, by the end of the decade, Preston's star had been resurrected, thanks to his celebrated performance as Harold Hill in the stage musical *The Music Man* (1957), which he went on to film in 1961. His other movies include *The Dark at the Top of the Stairs* (1960), *All the Way Home* (1963), *Child's Play* (1972), *Mame* (1974), *S.O.B.* (1981) and *Victor/Victoria* (1982), which earned him a best supporting actor Oscar nomination.

Recalled Francis Searle, who directed Preston in *Cloudburst*, and to whom it was left to introduce the Hollywood star to Down Place for the first time: "We arrived at the studio and he seemed a bit subdued, so I said, 'Well, Bob, here we are—this is it.' He said, 'Erm, this is the prop department,' and I said, 'No, mate, this is the studio!'"[55] After his initial doubts, Preston eventually enjoyed working for Hammer, as he recalled in an interview for *Picturegoer* at the time: "Why build phony interiors in a studio when you can film the real thing? It's different and refreshing after Hollywood. I wouldn't have missed it."

Preston was married to the actress Catherine Craig (1915–2004, real name Catherine Jewel Feltus) from 1940. Note that he appeared in *Whispering Smith* (1948), the modern day follow-up to which—minus Preston—Hammer filmed as *Whispering Smith Hits London* (1951). **Hammer credits:** *Cloudburst* (1951, as John Graham)

## Price, Brendan

This British actor (1947–) had a brief scene as a paranormal research scientist in *In Possession* (1984, TVM [episode of *Hammer House of Mystery and Suspense*]). His TV credits include episodes of *The Liver Birds* (1969–1996, TV), *Target* (1977–1978, TV), *Robin of Sherwood* (1984–1986, TV), *Doctors* (2000–, TV) and *The Refugees* (2014–2015, TV). His film credits include *Secrets of a Door-to-Door Salesman* (1973), *The Sleep of Death* (1981), *Savage Grace* (2007), *Exorcismus* (2010), *Google and the World Brain* (2013), in which he played H.G. Wells, and *Angelus* (2014, TVM). **Hammer credits:** *In Possession* (1984, TVM [episode of *Hammer House of Mystery and Suspense*], as Paranormal research scientist)

## Price, Dennis

Best remembered for playing the murderous Louis Mazzini in the cherished *Kind Hearts and Coronets* (1949), this dapper British leading man (1915–1973, real name Dennistoun Franklyn John Rose-Price) began his film career in 1938 as an extra in *No Parking*. Following the war, during which he fought with the Royal Artillery, he resumed his career with a role in Powell and Pressburger's *A Canterbury Tale* (1944), which led to a lengthy career taking in over seventy films, among them *A Place of One's Own* (1945), *Holiday Camp* (1947), *Snowbound* (1948) and *The Bad Lord Byron* (1949). Inevitably, over the years, Price's status as a leading man diminished, and he emerged as a character actor of some distinction, frequently cast in devious or cowardly roles, among them appearances in *Private's Progress* (1956), *I'm All Right Jack* (1959), *Oscar Wilde* (1960), *The Pure Hell of St. Trinian's* (1960), *Victim* (1961) and *The V.I.P.s* (1963). He ended his career appearing mostly in horror films (several of which were clearly beneath him), among them *The Horror of It All* (1964), *The Earth Dies Screaming* (1964), *The Haunted House of Horror* (1969), *Vampyros Lesbos* (1971), *Tower of Evil* (1972), *Dracula contra Frankenstein* (1972), in which he played Frankenstein, *Horror Hospital* (1973), *La maldicion de Frankenstein* (1973), in which he again played Frankenstein, *Theatre of Blood* (1973) and *Son of Dracula* (1974), in which he played Van Helsing.

Price worked for Hammer five times during his career, first starring in the wartime comedy *Don't Panic Chaps* (1959). The parlour farce *Watch It, Sailor!* (1961) followed, along with supporting roles in two horror films and a comedy. Recalled Damien Thomas of Price, with whom he co-starred in *Twins of Evil* (1971), "It was enlightening to work with Dennis Price who, I knew, had had some pretty rough breaks, at a time when he might expect to be able to sit back and rest on his laurels. He had great charm and optimism, and he was very cheerful despite the set-backs in his life, and the illness that was making it difficult for him to walk. You wouldn't know, as a member of the viewing public, that he did the whole thing in carpet slippers because of the pain he was obviously suffering in his legs; and of course one never heard him complain."[56]

Price's TV work includes episodes of *Chelsea at Nine* (1957–1960, TV), *Harry's Girls* (1963, TV), *The World of Wooster* (1965–1967, TV), in which he played Jeeves, *Jason King* (1971–1972, TV) and *The Adventurer* (1972–1973, TV). He was married to the actress Joan Schofield between 1939 and 1950; she had a minor part in Hammer's *Quatermass 2* (1957). **Hammer credits:** *Don't Panic Chaps* (1959, as Captain Edward von Krisling), *Watch It, Sailor!* (1961, as Lieutenant-Commander Hardcastle), *The Horror of Frankenstein* (1970, as Grave robber), *Twins of Evil* (1971, as Dietrich), *That's Your Funeral* (1973, as Eugene Soul)

## Price, Penny

Price had a minor supporting role in Hammer's *Captain Kronos—Vampire Hunter* (1974). Her other credits include an episode of *Armchair Theatre* (1956–1974, TV). **Hammer credits:** *Captain Kronos—Vampire Hunter* (1974, as Whore)

## Price, Peter

British born Price (1930–2015) worked as the assistant director on Hammer's *The Secret of Blood Island* (1965). Beginning as a third assistant director on *Bedelia* (1949), he became a second assistant on *The Green Man* (1956) and a first assistant on *The Two-Headed Spy* (1958). His other credits in this capacity include *Invasion Quartet* (1961), *Sammy Going South* (1963), *The Great St. Trinian's Train Robbery* (1966), *The Executioner* (1970), *The Mechanic* (1972), *Gold* (1974), *Rollerball* (1975), *Ascendancy* (1982) and *Tusks* (1988), plus episodes of *The Saint* (1962–1969, TV), *Danger Man* (1964–1966, TV), *The Persuaders!* (1971–1972, TV) and *The Bill* (1984–2010, TV). **Hammer credits:** *The Secret of Blood Island* (1965)

## Price, Steve

Price was a member of the American rock group Stoneground, which was featured in Hammer's *Dracula A.D. 1972* (1972). He went on to become a member of the band Pablo Cruise. His other film appearances include *Medicine Ball Caravan* (1971), again with Stoneground. **Hammer credits:** *Dracula A.D. 1972* (1972)

## Priestley, J.B.

This celebrated British novelist and playwright (1894–1984, full name John Boynton Priestley)

has had a number of his works filmed for both the cinema and television, among them *The Good Companions* (1933, 1956 and 1980, TV), *Dangerous Corner* (1934, 1965, TV, 1970, TV, 1972, TV [Russian], 1983, TV), *When We Are Married* (1942, 1975, TV, 1987, TV) and *An Inspector Calls* (1954, 1972, TV [French], 1982, TV). His novel *Benighted* has also been filmed twice as *The Old Dark House*, first by Universal in 1932, and later, by Hammer, in 1963 (in conjunction with William Castle). Priestley can be seen introducing *They Came to a City* (1943), and as himself in the documentary *Battle for Music* (1943). His screenplays (either solo or in collaboration) include *Sing As We Go* (1934), *Jamaica Inn* (1939) and *Last Holiday* (1950 [remade 2006]), the latter of which he also produced with Stephen Mitchell and A.D. Peters. **Hammer credits:** *The Old Dark House* (1963)

## Pring, Gerald

This British actor (1888–1970) played the role of Inspector Benson in the Hammer potboiler *The Dark Road* (1948). His other credits include *The Lady of the Photograph* (1917), *The Nut* (1921), *Well Done, Henry* (1936), *Dark Eyes of London* (1939), *Black Memory* (1947) and *Murder in the Cathedral* (1952). Also on stage in Britain and America. **Hammer credits:** *The Dark Road* (1948, as Inspector Benson)

## Pringle, Harry

This British supporting actor can be seen in a minor role in Hammer's *The Brides of Dracula* (1960). His other credits include *Linda* (1960) and *Three Hats for Lisa* (1965) and episodes of *The Younger Generation* (1961, TV), *No Hiding Place* (1959–1967, TV) and *Dr. Finlay's Casebook* (1962–1971, TV). **Hammer credits:** *The Brides of Dracula* (1960, as Karl [uncredited])

## Prizeman, Jim

Prizeman worked as a stagehand on two of Hammer's second features. **Hammer credits:** *Someone at the Door* (1950 [uncredited]), *What the Butler Saw* (1950 [uncredited])

## Probert, Sion

Probert can be seen as a tavern patron in Hammer's *The Vampire Lovers* (1970). His other credits include *Groupie Girl* (1970) and episodes of *The Sweeney* (1975–1978, TV), *Hi-de-Hi!* (1980–1988, TV), *Covington Cross* (1992, TV) and *Our Friends in the North* (1996, TV). **Hammer credits:** *The Vampire Lovers* (1970, as Young man in tavern [uncredited])

## Probyn, Bryan

This British cinematographer (1920–1982) photographed the Hammer psycho-thriller *Straight on Till Morning* (1972), which was one of a handful of films he worked on for director Peter Collinson, among them *The Long Day's Dying* (1968), *Innocent Bystanders* (1972) and *Target of an Assassin* (1976). His other credits include *Poor Cow* (1967), *The Jerusalem File* (1971), for which he photographed additional scenes, *Downhill Racer* (1969), *Badlands* (1973), on which he shared his credit with Stevan Larner and Tak Fujimoto, *Plugg* (1975), *The Mango*

*Tree* (1977) and *Far East* (1982). He also photographed five more films for Hammer, sharing his credit on *Shatter* (1974) with John Wilcox and Roy Ford. His earlier credits include work as a camera assistant on the documentary short *Every Day Except Christmas* (1957). Of all Hammer's cinematographers, he seems to have had the most wildly eclectic career, given that he worked on both *Holiday on the Buses* and *Badlands* in 1973. You can just imagine the conversation on the set of *Badlands* between shots:

Terence Malick: So, what were you working on before you joined us?

Bryan Probyn: *Holiday on the Buses*.

Terence Malick: Brilliant…. Tell me, though. What's Reg Varney *really* like?

**Hammer credits:** *Straight on Till Morning* (1972), *Man at the Top* (1973), *Holiday on the Buses* (1973), *The Satanic Rites of Dracula* (1974), *Frankenstein and the Monster from Hell* (1974), *Shatter* (1974)

### Procter, Maurice

This former Manchester policeman (1906–1973) penned the 1954 crime novel *Hell Is a City*, which was based upon his own experiences in the force. The book was subsequently filmed by Hammer and released in 1960, though a proposed television series failed to materialize. His other novels include *Rich Is the Treasure* (1952), which was filmed as *The Diamond* (1954), and *Two Men in Twenty* (1964), which was filmed for German television as *Flucht aus London* (1981, TV). He also penned a 1963 episode of *No Hiding Place* (1959–1967, TV) titled *Hot Ice*. Further books by him include *No Proud Chivalry* (1947), *The End of the Street* (1949), *The Midnight Plumber* (1957) and *The Dog Man* (1969). **Hammer credits:** *Hell Is a City* (1960)

### Proud, Peter

This British (Scottish) art director and production designer (1913–1989, real name Ralph Priestman Proud) designed the sets for Hammer's *Fanatic* (1965). He began his career as an assistant art director in 1928, working on such films as *Murder* (1930), *Orders Is Orders* (1933) and *Waltzes from Vienna* (1933). His credits as a fully-fledged art director/production designer include *The Man Who Knew Too Much* (1934), *Educated Evans* (1936), *Green for Danger* (1946), *Desert Mice* (1959), *The League of Gentlemen* (1960), *Candidate for Murder* (1962), *Saturday Night Out* (1963), *Theatre of Death* (1966) and *The Naked Runner* (1967), plus episodes of such series as *The Adventures of Sir Lancelot* (1956–1957, TV), *The Buccaneers* (1956–1957, TV), *The Adventures of Robin Hood* (1955–1960, TV), which earned him an Emmy nomination and *The Magnificent Six and ½* (1967, TV). He also co-directed and co-produced *Esther Waters* (1948) with Ian Dalrymple, and co-wrote *The Planter's Wife* (1952). **Hammer credits:** *Fanatic* (1965)

### Provis, George

This British art director and production designer (1908–1989) designed the sets for the Ham-

mer comedy *Further Up the Creek* (1958), for which he built the bridge of a battleship atop the standing set of Castle Dracula on the Bray back lot. His many other credits include *One Good Turn* (1936), *Quartet* (1948), *The Late Edwina Black* (1951), *Venetian Bird* (1952), *Hide and Seek* (1963), *Catacombs* (1964), *Night Train to Paris* (1964), *The File of the Golden Goose* (1969), *The Fiend* (1971) and *Craze* (1974). He also returned to Hammer for *The Viking Queen* (1967). **Hammer credits:** *Further Up the Creek* (1958), *The Viking Queen* (1967)

### Prowse, Dave

In films from 1967 with *Casino Royale*, in which he briefly appears as the Frankenstein Monster, this tall (6'7") and muscular British actor and bodybuilder (1935–) is best known for playing Darth Vader in *Star Wars* (1977), *The Empire Strikes Back* (1980) and *Return of the Jedi* (1983), although the character's voice was provided by James Earl Jones. His many other credits, usually in bit roles, include *Hammerhead* (1968), *A Clockwork Orange* (1971), *Up Pompeii* (1971), *Up the Chastity Belt* (1971), *Carry On Henry* (1971), *Blacksnake* (1973), *White Cargo* (1973), *Callan* (1974), *The People That Time Forgot* (1977) and *Jabberwocky* (1977). He also trained Christopher Reeve for his role in *Superman* (1978). TV-wise he played the Green Cross Code Man in a series of TV ads in the eighties. His other TV work includes appearances in episodes of *The Champions* (1968–1969, TV), *The Tomorrow People* (1973–1979, TV), *The Hitchhiker's Guide to the Galaxy* (1981, TV) and *Crossbow* (1987–1990, TV). His later film credits include *Open Mic'rs* (2006) and *The Kindness of Strangers* (2010). Prior to working in films, Prowse was involved in the bodybuilding scene. He entered the Mr. Universe contest in 1960 and went on to become the British Olympic Heavyweight Weightlifting Champion for three consecutive years, in 1962, 1963 and 1964. He made his stage debut in 1965.

Prowse is also remembered for a number of brushes with Hammer during his career, first appearing as the Monster in *The Horror of Frankenstein* (1970), which made good use of his physique, though not his limited talents as an actor (he can also be briefly seen as a bandit in the same film). He followed this up with an appearance as a circus strongman in *Vampire Circus* (1972), after which he again played Frankenstein's Monster in *Frankenstein and the Monster from Hell* (1974), in which his

**Back lot japes. Dave Prowse in full monster regalia looms over his co-star Madeline Smith (right) and a visiting Veronica Carlson (center) and Julie Ege (left) during a break in the filming of *Frankenstein and the Monster from Hell* (1974) (Hammer/Paramount/Avco Embassy/Paramount).**

few lines as the creature were re-voiced during post-production. For the film, Prowse recalled that he was introduced "to the doyen of the gothic horror directors—Terence Fisher."[57] Meanwhile, of his make-up for *Monster from Hell* he recalled, "It was a very simple make-up job. The body was made up on a wet suit, so I just had to get in and zip it on. The face was done on a mask. They made a couple of masks, some with eyes, others without eyes. And I used to get the whole thing on in about ten minutes flat."[58] Sadly, it shows.

Prowse was awarded a CBE in 2000. He wrote about his movie experiences in his autobiography *Straight from the Force's Mouth* (2011). His brother is the occasional actor Bob Prowse. **Hammer credits:** *The Horror of Frankenstein* (1970, as The Monster/Bandit), *Vampire Circus* (1972, as Strongman), *Frankenstein and the Monster from Hell* (1974, as The Monster)

### *The Public Life of Henry the Ninth*

GB, 1935, 60m, bw, cert U

Hammer's very first production, this long-unseen second feature comedy centers round a pub potman—played by radio and music hall star Leonard Henry—who wins a showbiz contract after having performed a couple of songs in his local. Made at the ATP Studios (Associated Talking Pictures) in Ealing in December 1934, the film was press shown in January 1935 and released in the UK by MGM on 17 June 1935. Among its cast is George Mozart, one of Hammer's managing directors, who, like Will Hammer, had performed on the variety stage. The film was re-issued in 1940 by Exclusive, since when it has disappeared from view. Recalled the production's sound camera assistant John Mitchell, "The film was shot in two weeks…. Editing was completed during the third week, as was the music scoring, and we dubbed the film on the following Saturday and Sunday, taking twenty-four hours of non-stop work…. My salary was £2 per week—no overtime payment, just one shilling and threepence for supper!"[59]

In reviewing the film, *Today's Cinema* believed it to have been "solely fashioned to exploit the gurgling gaieties of Leonard Henry, concert party star and idol to millions of radio fans." *Kinematograph Weekly* noted that the film would be "quite a useful supporting proposition for popular industrial halls," though it went on to add that it made "no attempt to compete seriously with slick American entertainment of the same caliber." That said, the reviewer conceded that, "it does in its modest way fill an hour quite pleasingly." Remembered John Mitchell, "It was a very successful box office draw with cinema patrons."[60]

**Additional notes:** The film's title is a play on the internationally popular Charles Laughton vehicle *The Private Life of Henry VIII* (1933), which had earned its star Britain's first ever best actor Oscar. Wally Patch, who is featured here, also appeared in the Laughton film. Leonard Henry went on to appear in several stage productions presented by Will Hammer, among them *Summer Pierrots*.

Production company: Hammer. Distributor: MGM (UK). Producer: Henry Fraser Passmore. Director: Bernard Mainwaring. Screenplay: Bernard Mainwaring, Herbert Ayres. Sound camera assistant: John Mitchell [uncredited]. **Cast:** Leonard Henry (Henry), Betty Frankiss (Maggie), Dorothy Vernon (Mrs. Fickle), Herbert Langley (Policeman), Mai Bacon (Liz), Wally Patch (Landlord), Aileen Latham (Liz), George Mozart (Draughts Player), Jean Lester (unnamed role [uncredited]), Neal Arden (unnamed role [uncredited]), Dennis Wyndham (unnamed role [uncredited])

## Publishing

A number of Hammer screenplays have been novelized over the years in a bid to boost publicity as well as the coffers. Many of these are now rarities, and much sought after by collectors, more often for their covers than their literary content. In fact Hammer had ties with a number of publishing houses over the years, while in the sixties, by which time they were firmly established as the House of Horror, the company—like the equally merchandisable Alfred Hitchcock—lent its name to a number of horror omnibuses, among them two compendiums published by Pan, the first of which was titled *The Hammer Horror Omnibus* (1966 [later re-printed as *The Hammer Horror Film Omnibus*]). This was written by John Burke and included adaptations of *The Curse of Frankenstein* (1957), *The Revenge of Frankenstein* (1958), *The Gorgon* (1964) and *The Curse of the Mummy's Tomb* (1964). The follow-up, again authored by John Burke and also for Pan, was titled *The Second Hammer Horror Film Omnibus* (1967), and this time included adaptations of *Dracula—Prince of Darkness* (1966), *The Plague of the Zombies* (1966) and *Rasputin—The Mad Monk* (1966) and *The Reptile* (1966).

Other novelizations and tie-in publications include *Spaceways* (by Charles Eric Maine, author of the original radio play, published by Pan), *The Camp on Blood Island* (published by Panther [no author credited on cover]), *Dracula* (by Bram Stoker, published by Perma, with a cover photo from the film), *Yesterday's Enemy* (by Maurice Moiseiwitsch, published by Corgi), *I Only Arsked!* (by Sid Colin and Jack Davies, published by Pan), *The Phoenix* ([filmed as *Ten Seconds to Hell*] by Lawrence Bachmann, published by Fontana), *The Man Who Could Cheat Death* (by Jimmy Sangster, writing as John Sansom, published by Ace/Harborough [note that as well as Sansom, the American paperback print of the book published by Avon also credits Barre Lyndon, author of *The Man in Half Moon Street*, the original 1939 play on which the film is based, and which had previously been filmed in 1944; Lyndon receives first billing]), *The Hound of the Baskervilles* (by Sir Arthur Conan Doyle, published by Dell [U.S. only]), *The Stranglers of Bombay* (by Stuart James, published by Monarch), *The Terror of the Tongs* (by Jimmy Sangster, published by Digit), *The Brides of Dracula* (by Dean Owen, published by Monarch), *The Damned* ([original title *The Children of Light*] by H.L. Lawrence, published by Consul), *The Witches* (by Peter Curtis [Norah Lofts], published by Pan), *The Lost Continent* (by Dennis Wheatley, published by Arrow), *Moon Zero Two* (by John Burke, published by Pan), *The Vampire Lovers* (by J. Sheridan Le Fanu, published by Fontana), *Countess Dracula* (by Michael Parry, published by Sphere [Beagle in the U.S.]), *Scars of Dracula* ([as *The Scars of Dracula*] by Angus Hall, published by Sphere [Beagle in the U.S.]), *Lust for a Vampire* (by William Hughes, published by Sphere [Beagle in the U.S.]), *Hands of the Ripper* (by Spencer Shew, published by Sphere), *Captain Kronos—Vampire Hunter* ([as *Kronos*] by Hugh Enfield, published by Fontana) and *The Lady Vanishes* (by Ethel Lina White, published by Sphere).[61]

In 2010, John Ajvide Lindqvist's 2004 novel *Let the Right One In* was re-printed as *Let Me In* by St. Martin's Griffin as a tie in to coincide with the release of Hammer's U.S. remake of *Lat den ratte komma in* (2008, aka *Let the Right One In*). In 2011, the revived Hammer also began publishing tie-ins, new commissions and re-prints of classic stories via Hammer Books (a division of Arrow, itself a division of Random House), among its first releases being K.A. John's novelization of *Wake Wood* (2009), Francis Cottam's novelization of *The Resident* (2011), and a re-print of *The Witches* by Peter Curtis (Norah Lofts), which had been filmed by the company back in 1966. New novelizations of classic Hammers were also commissioned (as opposed to re-prints of already published tie-ins), among them *Countess Dracula*, *Kronos* and *Hands of the Ripper* by Guy Adams; *X—The Unknown*, *The Revenge of Frankenstein* (for the third time!) and *Twins of Evil* by Shaun Hutson; and *Vampire Circus* by Mark Morris. Intriguingly, several of these

Where it all started. The cast of *The Public Life of Henry the Ninth* (1935) (Hammer/MGM).

titles present fresh takes on the established stories; for example, *Countess Dracula* is set in Hollywood during the transition to sound, while *Vampire Circus* has been updated to present day Britain.

**Additional notes:** The subject was examined in a 2012 documentary short titled *Hammer Novelisations: Brought to Book*. As well as originally being novelized in the seventies, *Captain Kronos—Vampire Hunter* was also presented as a comic strip in *The House of Hammer* (aka *House of Horror* and *Halls of Horror*). Other comic adaptations (same source) include *The Brides of Dracula* (1960), *Dracula—Prince of Darkness* (1966) and *The Mummy's Shroud* (1967).

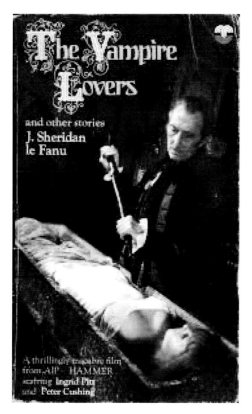

Paperback hero. Peter Cushing dispatches Ingrid Pitt on the cover of this tie-in for *The Vampire Lovers* (1970) (Hammer/AIP/Fantale/MGM-EMI/American International/Fontana).

## Pulford, Eric

This noted British poster designer and illustrator (1915–2005) worked on the ad campaign for Hammer's last theatrical feature for thirty years, *The Lady Vanishes* (1979). Working on film posters from 1944, his other credits include the British campaigns for *Henry V* (1944), *The Invisible Man's Revenge* (1945), *Oliver Twist* (1948), *A Queen Is Crowned* (1953), *The Purple Plain* (1954), *From Russia with Love* (1963), *The War Wagon* (1967), *The Golden Voyage of Sinbad* (1974), *The Island at the Top of the World* (1974) and *The Evil That Men Do* (1984). A major force in British poster design, he worked on over one-thousand campaigns via Pulford Publicity and Britain's main film advertising agency Downton Advertising (aka Down-

tons), a controlling interest in which he bought in 1963. During his career he worked for the Rank, Gaumont and Odeon chains, as well as for such film companies as British Lion, United Artists, Disney, Columbia, Brent Walker and Avco Embassy. **Additional notes:** A copy of Pulford's poster for *The Lady Vanishes* can be seen in *The Last Horror Film* (1982). **Hammer credits:** *The Lady Vanishes* (1979 [uncredited])

## Pullen, Tony (Anthony)

Pullen worked as a sound editor on seven episodes of Hammer's *Journey to the Unknown* (1968, TV), of which *Poor Butterfly* also appeared in the compendium film *Journey to Midnight* (1968, TVM) and *Paper Dolls* appeared in the compendium film *Journey into Darkness* (1968, TVM), while both *The Last Visitor* and *Matakitas Is Coming* appeared in the compendium film *Journey to the Unknown* (1969, TVM). His other credits include *The Mikado* (1967). **Hammer credits:** *Eve* (1968, TV [episode of *Journey to the Unknown*]), *Poor Butterfly* (1968, TV [episode of *Journey to the Unknown*]), *Paper Dolls* (1968, TV [episode of *Journey to the Unknown*]), *Miss Belle* (1968, TV [episode of *Journey to the Unknown*]), *The Last Visitor* (1968, TV [episode of *Journey to the Unknown*]), *Jane Brown's Body* (1968, TV [episode of *Journey to the Unknown*]), *Matakitas Is Coming* (1968, TV [episode of *Journey to the Unknown*]), *Journey into Darkness* (1968, TVM), *Journey to Midnight* (1968, TVM), *Journey to the Unknown* (1969, TVM)

## Purchese, John

Purchese recorded the sound for Hammer's *On the Buses* (1971), which led to further work for the company. His other credits include *The Jokers* (1967), *Bedazzled* (1967), *Hard Contract* (1969), *Song of Norway* (1970) and episodes of *Here Come the Double Deckers!* (1970, TV). **Hammer credits:** *On the Buses* (1971), *Straight on Till Morning* (1972), *Mutiny on the Buses* (1972), *Demons of the Mind* (1972)

## Purdie, Doug

Purdie (sometimes Purdy) worked as the property master on *Hammer House of Mystery and Suspense* (1984, TVM). His other credits include *Mr. Forbush and the Penguins* (1971) and *Return to Oz* (1985). **Hammer credits:** *Hammer House of Mystery and Suspense* (1984, TVM [uncredited])

## Purdie, Ron

Purdie worked as the assistant director on *Wolfshead: The Legend of Robin Hood* (1969 [released 1973]), which was acquired by Hammer. His other credits in this capacity include *No Time to Die* (1958), *Snow* (1965), *The Wicked Lady* (1983), *Dirty Weekend* (1993) and *Parting Shots* (1999), plus episodes of *The Avengers* (1961–1969, TV). His work as a location manager includes *Death on the Nile* (1978) and *The Odd Job* (1978), while his work as a production manager takes in episodes of *The New Avengers* (1976–1977, TV), *The Professionals* (1977–1983, TV) and *Starting Over* (2007, TV), as well as the film *Hidden City* (1988). He also worked as an associate producer on episodes of *Widows 2* (1985, TV) and *Jeeves and Wooster*

(1990–1993, TV), as a line producer on *Circus* (2000), and as a producer on *S.N.U.B.!* (2010) and *The Magnificent Eleven* (2013). **Hammer credits:** *Wolfshead: The Legend of Robin Hood* (1969 [released 1973])

## Putzu, Arnaldo

Italian born Putzu (1927–2012) illustrated a handful of posters for Hammer in the early seventies, among them *On the Buses* (1971), which was based on a design by Eddie Paul. His other work includes the British campaigns for *Cromwell* (1970), *Kidnapped* (1971), *Virgin Witch* (1972), *The Getaway* (1972), *Carry On Dick* (1974) and *The Sea Wolves* (1980). He also designed magazine covers for the likes of *Look-in*. **Hammer credits include:** *Creatures the World Forgot* (1971 [uncredited]), *On the Buses* (1971 [uncredited]), *The Legend of the 7 Golden Vampires* (1974 [uncredited])

## Pyne, Natasha

Best known for playing Anna Glover in the long-running sitcom *Father Dear Father* (1968–1973, TV), this British actress (1946–, full name Primula Mary Natasha Menzies Pyne) also notched up several film credits in the sixties and seventies, among them appearances in *Who Killed the Cat?* (1966), *The Taming of the Shrew* (1967), *The Breaking of Bumbo* (1970), the big screen version of *Father Dear Father* (1972), *Madhouse* (1974) and *One of Our Dinosaurs Is Missing* (1975). She can also be seen as Jane in the Hammer swashbuckler *The Devil-Ship Pirates* (1964). Much on stage, her other TV work includes episodes of *Mystery and Imagination* (1966–1970, TV), *Van Der Valk* (1991–1992, TV) and *Cadfael* (1994–1996, TV). Her husband is the actor Paul Copley (1944–), whom she married in 1972. **Hammer credits:** *The Devil-Ship Pirates* (1964, as Jane)

## Pyott, Keith

In supporting roles, this British actor (1902–1968) can be seen as the count's butler in the Hammer comedy *A Weekend with Lulu* (1961). His many other credits include *The Spider and the Fly* (1949), *Sea Devils* (1953), *Village of the Damned* (1960), *Bluebeard's Ten Honeymoons* (1960), *Masquerade* (1965), *Chimes at Midnight* (1966) and brief appearances three further Hammer productions. His TV appearances take in episodes of *The Quatermass Experiment* (1953, TV), *The Human Jungle* (1963–1964, TV) and *The Caesars* (1968, TV). **Hammer credits:** *A Weekend with Lulu* (1961, as Count's butler), *The Phantom of the Opera* (1962, as Weaver), *The Pirates of Blood River* (1962, as Silas), *The Devil Rides Out* (1968, as Max [uncredited])

# Q

## Quatermass and the Pit

GB, 1967, 98m, Technicolor [UK], DeLuxe [U.S.], widescreen [1.78:1], RCA, cert X

Hammer's plans to film Nigel Kneale's third Quatermass television series, *Quatermass and the*

*Pit* (1958–1959, TV), were put on hold when the studio's second big screen adaptation *Quatermass 2* (1957) failed to match the box office performance of its predecessor, *The Quatermass Xperiment* (1955). However, from 1960, *Pit* was on the cards in one form or another, although it wasn't until April 1961 that the material was finally optioned. Further foot-dragging then followed when Columbia, which had expressed an interest in the project, turned cold on the idea. Consequently, it wasn't until August 1963 that an official announcement was made to the press regarding the film, at which point director Freddie Francis and producer Anthony Hinds were attached to the project, then budgeted at £180,000 and known as either *The Pit* or *Quatermass and "The Pit"* (quotation marks included).

The series (which, as had its predecessor, been helmed by Rudolph Cartier), was broadcast by the BBC between Christmas and New Year of 1958 and 1959, and had proven extremely popular with viewers. This time the good Professor was played by Hammer favorite André Morell, while the story involved the discovery of a five-million-year-old skull and an alien capsule during excavation work to redevelop the final vestiges of war-torn London. Working in close alliance with palaeontologist Matthew Roney, Quatermass comes to the conclusion that Martians had attempted to colonize the Earth many millions of years ago, and that early man had somehow been transmuted in the process, all of which goes some way to help explain such present-day phenomena as extra sensory perception and poltergeist activity. A heady brew of ideas,

the series was Kneale's most intellectually challenging so far.

Despite the announcement in 1963, nothing further was heard from Hammer regarding *Quatermass and the Pit* for some time. Recalled Kneale, "Hammer had tried to make *Quatermass and the Pit* earlier, but it collapsed for the sole reason that they couldn't get the money: not because of purity of mind or anything! The American financiers hadn't come through."[1] Finally, in 1966, the project was taken up by Seven Arts as part of their ongoing program of films with the company, although it wasn't until 1967 that the impending production was again announced to the press, by which time the producer was Anthony Nelson Keys and the director Roy Ward Baker. As for the screenplay, for the first time on a Quatermass film this was solely in the hands of Nigel Kneale himself, whose primary task was to trim the series' epic 180-minute running time down to a more manageable length. Kneale had actually submitted his first draft screenplay as early as March 1964, yet the lack of interest in the project from America meant that it had lain gathering dust for almost three years.

By the time *Quatermass and the Pit* went before the cameras on 27 February 1967, Hammer had left its long-standing home base of Bray (on 19 November 1966). This had been at the urging of one of the company's partners, ABPC, which wanted Hammer to make the move to Elstree. Ironically, the sound stages of Elstree were too busy to accommodate the Quatermass film. Instead, the movie went on the floor at MGM British in Borehamwood, where the £270,000 production bene-

fited from the larger soundstages and a back lot already replete with the kind of standing street sets required for the production, among them leftovers from *Triple Cross* (1967) and *The Dirty Dozen* (1967), hence the rather odd-looking European-style roofs on the buildings.

In Kneale's original tele-script, the story focused on the excavation of a bombsite in Knightbridge. For the film, this was updated to the extension of the Central Line on the London Underground (at the suggestion of Anthony Hinds), during which workmen discover the first of several oversized skulls in the clay-like subsoil. This discovery results in the newspaper headline "Underground ape men," and sees palaeontologist Dr. Matthew Roney and his team brought in to investigate. The story is a big one, and at a press conference on the station platform, Roney informs the gathered journalists that "This is one of the most remarkable finds ever made," adding that, "These fossils prove, I firmly believe, that creatures essentially resembling mankind walked the earth as long ago as five-million years." He even has a reconstruction of one of the ape-like creatures on hand to better explain his theory.

The find is about to become even more exciting with the unearthing of what at first is believed to be a giant pipe. However, when it is suspected that the metallic object may well be an unexploded bomb from the last war, an army disposal unit is called in to investigate ("That's right. Tear it all up," exclaims Roney as the men trudge through his precious excavation site). But even they seem baffled by the object when their magnetic listening device fails to adhere to the smooth, corrosion-free surface. It's at this point that Colonel Breen is brought in to supervise the operation. He is not alone, though, having been accompanied to the site by Professor Bernard Quatermass. There is little love lost between the two, who have recently been forced to work together by the government on a rocket project Quatermass had so far been developing by himself, Breen's idea being to hijack the system so as "to police the earth with ballistic missiles" based on the moon ("The ultimate weapon—it always is!" comes the Professor's wearily sarcastic response).

However, they are distracted from their assignment by further developments on the Underground, where another of the skulls has been discovered, this time *inside* a cavity in the bomb, prompting Roney to observe that, "That's no bomb. Whatever *is* it?" Intrigued by the discovery, Quatermass decides to stay on at the site and do a little investigating of his own, to which end he explores some nearby derelict houses with a local copper and Barbara Judd, Roney's helpful assistant. Having noted a number of curious scratches on a wall, Quatermass learns from the increasingly nervous policeman that the houses were apparently host to a number of mysterious disturbances. "Things got so bad they had to clear out. Noises, bumps, even things being seen," explains the copper before finally rushing outside, having clearly been spooked by the place. The Professor's interest in the area is then further piqued when Barbara notices that the street on which the Underground is

**Examining the evidence. Andrew Keir and friend in *Quatermass and the Pit* (1967) (Hammer/Seven Arts/Associated British Picture Corporation/Warner Pathé Distributors/Twentieth Century–Fox/Studio Canal).**

situated has had its name changed from Hob's Lane to Hobbs Lane, adding that, "Hob was once a sort of nickname for the Devil."

Quatermass next visits Roney's lab, where he observes the Doctor's experiment to record the thoughts of a volunteer via a prototype brain scanner. Raising the subject of the skulls, Quatermass asks Roney, "Were they of this earth?" to which comes the reply, "I'm sorry to disappoint, but the answer's only yes, they were." However, Roney's assistant Barbara has also been doing a little investigating of her own, having discovered a number of newspaper clippings about the Underground site, the original digging of which had caused a "disturbance" back in 1927.

Back at the dig, things are developing apace, for by now the sizable "bomb" has been fully exposed, but not even an oxyacetylene torch can penetrate the impervious substance from which it is made ("It's not even warm," notes Breen after one of his men has given it a sustained blast at three-thousand degrees). Even more intriguing is the discovery of a sealed compartment inside the craft, on the wall of which a pentacle—"one of the cabbalistic signs used in ancient magic"—has been etched. "The Germans didn't make this and then lose the secret!" Quatermass observes.

Accompanied by Barbara, Quatermass next visits the archives of Westminster Abbey, to further investigate the site, learning from the librarian that in 1763 "alarming noises" were heard during the digging of a well, while charcoal burners felling trees in 1341 had provoked similar phenomena. "All disturbances of the ground," notes Barbara. In fact as far back as Roman times the area seems to have been prone to such unexplained occurrences (there is even evidence to be found on cave paintings from 30,000 years ago, as we later learn).

Back at the Underground, the army has brought in a civilian expert to drill through into the craft's secret compartment with a "borazon" drill. "I reckon this little beauty'll cut through anything," boasts the drill's operator, Sladden. But the drill makes no impact. Yet a few moments later, a hole appears in the wall, which then proceeds to disintegrate, revealing on the other side a number of green, locust-like aliens, which immediately begin to corrupt upon being exposed to the "filthy London air." "I think these are old friends we're haven't seen for a while," says Roney of the strange three-legged arthropods, prompting Quatermass to ask, "Was this really a Martian?"

By now the press is having a field day ("Space machine found," boasts the *Evening News*). Quatermass and Roney are meanwhile beginning to fit the pieces together. "The man-apes besides the missile were abnormal," observes the Professor, who then wonders whether they had in fact been taken to Mars to be "altered by selected breeding, atomic surgery—methods we can't even guess—and then returned with new faculties instilled in them." In other words, "a colony by proxy." But the question still remains, *why*? As before, Colonel Breen remains blinkered to the various hypotheses, still preferring to believe the craft to be some kind of experimental V-weapon or propagandist tool.

Further confirmation as to the true origin of the

**Bryan Marshall (in beret), James Donald (center) and Andrew Keir (right) have a close encounter with an alien in *Quatermass and the Pit* (1967) (Hammer/Seven Arts/Associated British Picture Corporation/Warner Pathé Distributors/Twentieth Century–Fox/Studio Canal).**

craft is soon after observed by Barbara, who has returned to the seemingly deserted site to retrieve a microscope and a box of slides. Also present is Sladden, who is dismantling his drill inside the craft. Suddenly, things begin to move within the chamber as if compelled by some unseen force. This, accompanied by a loud pulsating sound, is enough to send Sladden running from the scene, the unseen force seemingly accompanying him, causing everything he passes to fly about as he does so. Sladden eventually finds sanctuary in the grounds of a nearby church, but even here the ground undulates beneath his collapsed body.

"I felt sure he had been in contact with spiritual evil," comments the vicar when Quatermass interviews Sladden about his experience in the clergyman's office sometime later, prompting the Professor to reason that, "Perhaps it was always in him. In all of us. An inheritance of dormant faculties; clairvoyance, telekinesis…" Quizzed further, Sladden describes life under a brown sky amid a seething mass of beings. "They were alive. Hopping like locust, hundreds and hundreds. And I knew *I* was one!" "I think what he gave us just now was a record of life on Mars five-million years ago," comments Quatermass, leading him to conclude that the fusing of the aliens with early man could well explain such phenomena as the unconscious ability to provoke movement and the outbreak of poltergeist activity. "*We're* the Martians now!" concludes Barbara.

Back at Roney's lab, Quatermass mulls over what has happened while the Doctor naps, having

personally attempted again to get a reading on his brain scanner. When images from the scanner start to appear on a nearby monitor as the Doctor sleeps, Quatermass hits upon the idea of using the device in the Underground, so as to get an image of the scene Sladden described. However, during the experiment, it is not Quatermass but Barbara who proves susceptible to the vision ("I can *see*!"), the recording of which the Professor subsequently interprets as "a race purge, a cleansing of the Martian hives."

Amazingly, Colonel Breen remains adamant that the bug-like craft is merely a German bomb (a "Satan," he observes, thus making it a Satan bug). To this end he has allowed television cameras into the Underground to film it. However, during the live broadcast, lights placed inside the craft explode and a technician is burned, and the long-dormant craft itself begins to glow and pulsate ("It's coming alive—it's glowing," observes Barbara). In fact the accompanying low register vibrations become so intense that the station itself begins to collapse, sending the gathered crowd running into the street. But even here they are not safe, for the vibrations cause the local pub (where drinkers have been watching the broadcast) to collapse. As for the blinkered Colonel Breen, he finally gets his comeuppance, and is "melted" by the glowing craft.

"Were they people?" asks Quatermass of Roney as he observes the crowd, by now baying like animals, killing each other, just as the Martians had done all those millions of years earlier. Indeed, Quatermass himself proves susceptible to the mysterious force governing the crowd. "I wanted to kill you, and could have done without moving or trying," he says to Roney as they shelter in the ruins of the pub as further nearby buildings begin to collapse. Luckily, not everyone is susceptible to the force, among them Roney. Consequently, when the ground erupts and a Devil-like apparition appears over the London skyline, it is the Doctor who bids to "earth" it by using the armature of a building crane ("Mass into energy—the Devil's enemy was iron"). The force is finally destroyed by Roney (who pays for doing so with his life) and order restored, leaving Quatermass and Barbara to reflect upon the fantastic events that have unfolded as the credits finally begin to roll (note that this was the second ending filmed; the first, subsequently discarded during additional post-production work, had Quatermass and Barbara walking away, arm in arm, smiling in triumph).

**Spiraling out of control. The American poster *Quatermass and the Pit* (1967), which was re-titled *Five Million Years to Earth* for its U.S. release. Incidentally, at no point in the film does Big Ben collapse (Hammer/Seven Arts/Associated British Picture Corporation/Warner Pathé Distributors/Twentieth Century–Fox/Studio Canal).**

Making *Quatermass and the Pit* was a major enterprise, and there's no doubting that the production would have been too big a proposition for the confines of Bray (the vicar's spacious office looks about as big as the climactic Westminster Abbey set from *The Quatermass Xperiment!*). To this end, it was perhaps fortuitous that the company was forced to film at MGM, and luckier still to acquire the talents of director Roy Ward Baker to helm the enterprise, given that Val Guest—who had directed the two previous installments—was tied up with the James Bond spoof *Casino Royale* (1967), which, coincidentally, was also being shot at MGM.

Baker's credits included such classics as *The October Man* (1947), *Morning Departure* (1950) and *The One That Got Away* (1957). He'd also had a sojourn in Hollywood where, while working for Fox, he had directed Marilyn Monroe in *Don't Bother to Knock* (1952). Yet during the sixties his career had somewhat fizzled out, and so he had taken refuge in television, where he involved himself in the making of episodes of such highly regarded series as *The Avengers* (1961–1969, TV) and *The Saint* (1962–1969, TV). There was no denying that Baker remained a major talent. After all, he had been the man behind the acclaimed Titanic reconstruction *A Night to Remember* (1958), one of the most technically challenging films ever made in Britain. In fact it would be his experience on this film that would prove invaluable while staging the scenes of mass hysteria and destruction to be likewise found in the *Quatermass and the Pit*. Recalled the film's producer Anthony Nelson Keys of his decision to use Baker on the film, "I wanted a director with a very great deal of technical know-how. I knew that Roy had in his day, made these types of pictures—for example the sinking of the Titanic. He'd been to Hollywood and he'd just come back and I thought this is the man I want."[2]

Despite never having directed a fantasy film before, Baker felt reasonably qualified to helm the project. "I'd never made a picture with a science fiction basis before," he admitted, before adding that, "I'd made several dramas in a documentary style, and I think that experience

helped me a lot with *Quatermass and the Pit*—you had to believe it."[3] It also helped having an excellent screenplay. "The first time I read the script I thought, 'This is fireproof—this is an absolute winner,'"[4] he observed.

Given Nigel Kneale's ill-disguised dislike of Brian Donlevy, Hammer sought a new face to play Quatermass, and to this end Anthony Quayle, Trevor Howard, Kenneth More (who had starred in *A Night to Remember*), Van Heflin, Harry Andrews, Peter Finch and Jack Hawkins were all considered for the role, as was Hammer stalwart André Morell, who had essayed the part in the television version. In the end, the choice assignment was handed to another Hammer veteran Andrew Keir, who made the part his own ("I was very happy with Andrew Keir, who they eventually chose,"[5] Kneale later admitted). Meanwhile, respected character star James Donald was hired to play the key role of palaeontologist Dr. Matthew Roney, while Barbara Shelley, Keir's co-star in *Dracula—Prince of Darkness* (1966), was brought onboard to play Roney's assistant Barbara Judd, making this her eighth and final appearance for Hammer.

Another vital piece of casting was Julian Glover (who had worked with Baker on the 1965 *Avengers* episode *Two's a Crowd*) as the tunnel-visioned Colonel Breen, while Duncan Lamont played the hapless Sladden. As for the technical crew, they featured many of the old guard from Bray, among them cinematographer Arthur Grant, supervising editor James Needs, effects wiz Les Bowie, first assistant director Bert Batt and production designer Bernard Robinson (here billed as "supervising art director").

Recalled Roy Ward Baker of his crack team, "Arthur Grant, the lighting cameraman, was a treasure, with long experience of Hammer films, although this was a science-fiction story, not the usual horror. The art director was brilliant, Bernard Robinson, whose genius lay in conjuring up magnificent sets and then putting them up on unmagnificent budgets. The special effects played an important part in the film and Les Bowie, also a Hammer regular, rose to the occasion.... Bert Batt was my first assistant and he drove the shooting on at a good, steady hunting pace. He particularly gloried in managing the live effects on the sets and directing the crowds. He was a tremendous help."[6] Recalled second assistant director Christopher Neame of Robinson's sets, "Bernie Robinson surpassed himself with our underground set.... It could not have been more real, with mountains of soggy clay from the tunnel digging at either end; the circular sides and roof reflecting the workers' arc lights and the very real drip-drip-dripping of seeping water."[7]

Production was a complex affair and carried on until 25 April 1967, during which Baker tackled such effects-heavy sequences as the re-activation of the long dormant spacecraft and the ensuing scenes of chaos and destruction. Yet at no time did he lose sight of the more intimate human drama amid the hubris.

Superbly photographed in rich hues by Arthur Grant, whose fluid work also makes effective use of hand-held cameras during the scenes of mass-panic, *Quatermass and the Pit* is that rare animal: a seamless blend of visual thrills and fertile concepts, artfully relayed by clear but dexterous dialogue. In fact Kneale's screenplay is a model of construction, building to an explosive climax via a series of carefully modulated revelations. In other hands this could have been unspeakably verbose, yet working on the principal that less is more, Kneale creates a sustained air of intrigue, from the unearthing of the first skull to the final earthing of the "Devil" (thus making it one of his most symmetrical narratives). Admittedly, certain ideas are merely window dressing (such as the unexplained claw marks in the derelict house), which prompted *The Sun*'s Anne Pacey to observe that, "The occasional references to witchcraft, devilry, gargoyles and the incarnation of true evil are thrown in probably to make the whole fantasy a lot weightier than it is." But this is to ignore the flair with which these various ingredients have been assembled, and the cumulative impact they have. One should also note the film's rich vein of wit ("I never had a career, only work," says Quatermass to Breen at one point) and the prescience of some of its observations ("If we found that our earth was doomed say by climactic changes, what would we do about it?" wonders Quatermass). As always, though, Kneale himself was less than entirely satisfied with the finished product, despite his solo writing credit. Seemingly unable to differentiate between the needs of a serial, where ideas can be developed at leisure, and a film, in which they have to be relayed within the constraints of a more specific running time, he commented, "Again, it suffered from shrinkage. On that occasion, I did do the script entirely without other hands involved, but I don't think it was as good as the BBC's version."[8]

On the contrary, for a film more than fifty years old, *Quatermass and the Pit* has aged extremely well, unlike the protracted TV series. Admittedly, some of the effects are a little rough around the edges (tumbling masonry is often seen to be bouncing Styrofoam), but such is the sense of alarm during the crisply edited scenes of panic and devastation, this barely seems to matter. In fact the film is packed with thrilling sequences and clever bits of business, such as the rippling floor effect, which carries the same level of impact as the "breathing door" in *The Haunting* (1963), and the use of inanimate objects seemingly brought to life by unseen forces, pre-dating similar scenes in *The Exorcist* (1973) by some six years.

Also note the title sequence—a skull set against a background of red smoke—which helps to build the atmosphere, and the opening optical, which sees a thin strip of the screen open out to reveal the full frame. In fact every department makes its own valuable contribution to the film, from the art department (which was also responsible for the design of the sleek, five-million-year-old bug-like spacecraft) to the costume department (note that Barbara is wearing a green dress in the scene in which she has her vision of long-ago Mars; she also later sports a red dress, again tying her to the planet). These sterling contributions are topped off with a dramatic score by Tristram Cary, which combines atonal orchestral passages with a number

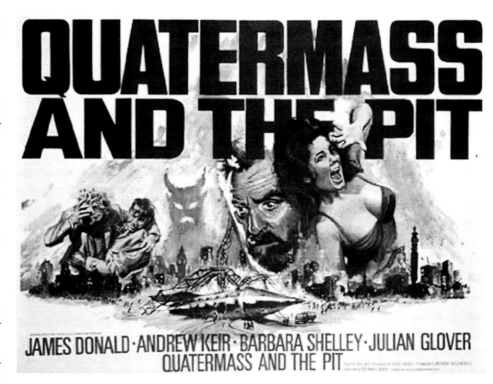

There's no doubting the real focus of this British poster for *Quatermass and the Pit* (1967). Under the circumstances, the Post Office Tower takes on unfortunate phallic connotations (Hammer/Seven Arts/Associated British Picture Corporation/Warner Pathé Distributors/Twentieth Century–Fox/Studio Canal).

of eerie electronic effects, as befitting the film's fantastical scenario. However, it should be noted that Carlo Martelli was brought in at the last moment to score an additional cue for the film titled *Poltergeist*? Stock cues by Armando Sciascia and Dennis Farnon were also used in the film. These were added following additional editing, by which time Cary had moved on to another project (Martelli's cue plays over the scene in which Quatermass, Barbara and the policeman explore the derelict house, hence the cue's question mark; Sciascia's cue [titled *Ultima Ora*] plays over the appearance of the Devil, while Farnon's piece [titled *Deserted Harbour*] plays over the end credits). Further stock music by Frederic Curzon is also featured on the soundtrack.

As Professor Quatermass, Andrew Keir offers a slightly more fatherly interpretation of the role than Brian Donlevy, thanks to his interaction with Barbara. In any case, the barked orders of Donlevy would have been out of tune with the proceedings, given that this time Quatermass is more an observer than an instigator, which could explain why James Donald receives top billing as Roney, who is as much a focus of the action as the Professor. As the boffin-turned-martyr, the actor exudes the right kind of tweedy, schoolmasterly enthusiasm, which perfectly balances Julian Glover's performance as the cold, by-the-book Colonel Breen. The film's true revelation, however, is Barbara Shelley as Roney's assistant Barbara. Seemingly a token role at first, she goes on to become a major player in the unfolding events (akin to the housemaid in *Blithe Spirit*), and gives herself wholeheartedly to

the rigorous demands the proceedings make of her. Simply put, she is without question the best actress Hammer ever had—and gorgeous to look at to boot. Meanwhile, the supporting cast features such able cameo players as Noel Howlett, memorable in his brief scene as the Abbey librarian leafing through the pages of an enormous book, and Edwin Richfield as the short-tempered Minister.

Recalled Roy Ward Baker of his exceptional cast, "Andrew Keir was certainly the best of the Quatermasses and was acknowledged as such by all and sundry. Thirty years later I was astounded to be told that he thought that I wanted Kenneth More for the part—quite untrue—and therefore paid no attention to him. I had no idea he was unhappy while we were shooting. His performance was absolutely right in every detail and I was presenting him as the star of the picture. Perhaps I should have interfered more. James Donald and Barbara Shelley were outstanding. I had met Julian Glover previously on an episode of *The Avengers*. He turned in a tremendous character, forceful, autocratic but never over the top."[9] In fact the only real problem Baker encountered on the film was with parts of the exterior set: "The street set was a great problem because we couldn't build the width of the road. If you look carefully at the set you'll see the road was about ten feet wide; you could barely get two cars past one another, but we managed to make it look different."[10]

One of Hammer's finest productions, *Quatermass and the Pit* is a riveting experience. Promoted with the tagline, "The most terrifying science-fiction film ever made," it was released in the UK on a double bill with *Circus of Fear* (1966) by Warner Pathé on 7 November 1967 to generally good reviews. Indeed, Dylis Powell noted that it was made with "an absolutely straight face," while Penelope Mortimer found that it was "well put together, competently photographed, [and] on the whole sturdily performed." However, *Films and Filming* declared that it "fails to carry one tenth of the unnerving credibility of the Quatermass predecessors," while the *Evening Standard* described it as being a "well-made, but wordy, blob of hokum." For its U.S. release on 16 August care of Twentieth Century–Fox, the film was re-titled *Five Million Years to Earth* and double-billed with Hammer's *The Viking Queen* (1967). Commented the *Motion Picture Exhibitor*, "This starts off on an interesting premise and proceeds along at a suspense-building pace. At times, however, the story tends to become a trifle involved with complications and utterances that may stretch the imaginations of even some science-fiction viewers." Observed Nigel Kneale of the finished film: "It wasn't as good as the BBC series, but it was okay. A lot of detail had to be cut. It's a simpler thing. They had more money for sets and actors, really. Roy Baker did a very good job on it. Andrew Keir was fine. I was very happy with it."[11] **Additional notes:** When Quatermass returns to the station from the Westminster archives, Roy Ward Baker and continuity girl Doreen Dearnaley can very briefly be seen reflected in the window of the professor's departing taxi. In addition to the use of Martian red and green in Barbara Shelley's costumes, these colors are also predominantly featured in certain sets; indeed, Quatermass himself is first seen sitting in an oversized red leather chair. Second assistant director Christopher Neame was promoted to first assistant for the last three days of shooting, as the film's first assistant Bert Batt had to leave to prepare another film. Andrew Keir played Quatermass again in the 1996 BBC radio drama *The Quatermass Memoirs*. Director John Carpenter made playful use of the name Hobbs End in his 1995 film *In the Mouth of Madness*. Following the film's release, Hammer announced *Quatermass 4* in 1969, but the film failed to appear, and the project eventually emerged as *Quatermass* (1979, TV), a TV series made by Euston Films (it was also trimmed and released theatrically in some territories). Note the similarity between Kneale's supposition that the Martians played an integral part in the acceleration of Man's development and the use of the monolith in *2001: A Space Odyssey* (1968). The tube station contains posters of *The Witches* (1966) and *Dracula—Prince of Darkness* (1966), the former with a screenplay by Nigel Kneale, the latter co-starring Barbara Shelley! Effects from the film are used in *The Changes* (1975, TV). One final question: when he climbs the crane to earth the Devil, why does Roney clamber to the end of its boom arm? Surely he should have climbed into the operator's cabin? If the ground underneath the crane hadn't conveniently given way, he'd still be there now!

Production companies: Hammer/Seven Arts/Associated British Picture Corporation. Distributors: Warner Pathé Distributors (UK [ABC circuit]), Twentieth Century–Fox (U.S.). Producer: Anthony Nelson Keys. Director: Roy Ward Baker. Screenplay: Nigel Kneale, based upon his television series. Cinematographer: Arthur Grant. Music: Tristram Cary (and Carlo Martelli [additional music, uncredited]). Stock music: Armando Sciascia [uncredited], Dennis Farnon [uncredited], Frederic Curzon [uncredited]. Music director: Philip Martell. Supervising editor: James Needs. Editor: Spencer Reeve. Supervising art director: Bernard Robinson. Art director: Ken Ryan. Costumes: Rosemary Burrows. Special effects: Bowie Films, Ltd., Bill Warrington [uncredited], Kit West [uncredited], Roy Field [uncredited]. Special effects assistant: Ian Scoones [uncredited]. Makeup: Michael Morris. Hair: Pearl Tipaldi. Sound: Sash Fisher. Sound editor: Roy Hyde. Camera operator: Moray Grant. Focus puller: Bob Jordan [uncredited]. Gaffer: Steve Birtles [uncredited]. Production manager: Ian Lewis. Assistant director: Bert Batt. Second assistant director/temporary first assistant director: Christopher Neame [both uncredited]. Third assistant director: Bill Wesley [uncredited]. Stunts: Gerry Crampton [uncredited], George Leech [uncredited]. Construction manager: Arthur Banks [uncredited]. Second unit photography: Len Harris [uncredited]. Continuity: Doreen Dearnaley. Casting: Irene Lamb. Poster: Tom Chantrell [uncredited]. **Cast:** James Donald (Dr. Matthew Roney), Andrew Keir (Professor Bernard Quatermass), Barbara Shelley (Barbara Judd), Julian Glover (Colonel Breen), Duncan Lamont (Sladden), Maurice Good (Sergeant Cleghorn), Sheila Steafel (Journalist), Bryan Marshall (Captain Potter), Grant Taylor (Sergeant Ellis), Peter Copley (Howell), Edwin Richfield (Minister), Thomas Heathcote (Vicar), Robert Morris (Watson), Hugh Futcher (Sapper West), Hugh Morton (Elderly journalist), Keith Marsh (Johnson), Roger Avon (Electrician), Charles Lamb (Newsvendor), Brian Peck (Technical Officer), John Graham (Inspector), Noel Howlett (Abbey librarian), Hugh Manning (Edgar), June Ellis (Kitty), James Culliford (Corporal Gibson), Bee Duffell (Miss Dobson), Peter Bennett (London Transport Officer [uncredited]), Peter Bourne (Electrician [uncredited]), John Bown (Television interviewer [uncredited]), Simon Brent (Orderly Officer [uncredited]), David Crane (Attendant [uncredited]), Mark Elwes (Technician [uncredited]), Joseph Greig (Pub customer [uncredited]), Walter Horsbrugh (Messenger [uncredited]), Alastair Hunter (Doorkeeper [uncredited]), Michael Poole (Workman [uncredited]), Elroy Josephs (Workman [uncredited]), John Rutland (London Transport Officer [uncredited]), Albert Shepherd (Loader [uncredited]), Gareth Thomas (Workman [uncredited]), Ian White (Television announcer [uncredited]), William Ellis (Journalist [uncredited]), Brian Walton (Journalist [uncredited]), Leslie Southwick (Journalist [uncredited]), Harry Fielder (Possessed man [uncredited]), Anthony Rayner (Soldier [uncredited]), James Payne (Man running from station [uncredited]. **DVD availability:** Anchor Bay (U.S. R1 NTSC), extras include a commentary by Nigel Kneale and Roy Ward Baker, a trailer, TV spots and an episode of *The World of Hammer* (1990 [first broadcast 1994], TV) titled *Sci-Fi*; Studio Canal/Warner (UK R2 PAL). **Blu-ray availability:** Studio Canal (B/2), which includes the DVD and the same extras. **CD availability:** *Quatermass and the Pit* (Cloud Nine Records), which contains eight cues from the original soundtrack; *The Hammer Quatermass Film Music Collection* (GDI Records), which contains the entire score, including the electronic music sections and the additional cue by Carlo Martelli; *The Hammer Film Music Collection: Volume One* (GDI Records), which contains the *Main Title*

### The Quatermass Experiment see The Quatermass Xperiment

### Quatermass 2

GB, 1957, 85m, bw, RCA, cert X

The national release of Hammer's big screen version of *The Quatermass Xperiment* (1955) in November 1955 had rather handily coincided with the broadcast of the second six-part Quatermass television series *Quatermass II*, which began airing on the BBC on October 22. The value of this free publicity was immediate on the film's box office returns, and Quatermass became *the* character of the moment during the following months. Naturally, Hammer was keen to exploit this newfound success, and made it known that they planned to film the second Quatermass series as soon as possible. In fact, so keen were they, they even tried to persuade Nigel Kneale into allowing them to use the character in their Quatermass clone *X—The Unknown* (1956). Quite rightly, Kneale was having none of this!

The theme for the second television series (again helmed by Rudolph Cartier) was alien infiltration, with Professor Quatermass (now played by John Robinson following the death of Reginald Tate just weeks before the series was due on air) called upon to protect mankind from invasion via mind control. A slightly more intellectual proposition than its predecessor, it nevertheless again managed to pull in impressive viewing figures.

Somewhat insultingly, Nigel Kneale had been totally excluded from the first Quatermass film. This time, however, he no longer worked for the BBC and so had to be approached personally about the screen rights, especially given his newly acquired membership to the Screenwriters' Guild. Consequently, he was allowed to adapt his own teleplay, thus giving him a greater interest in (though not necessarily much more control of) the finished product. Indeed, Kneale's initial draft was subsequently sent to the film's director Val Guest for further work. As Guest recalled, "Kneale did his screenplay and sent it to Hammer and was paid by Hammer. Hammer then sent it to me, as the guy who was going to direct it, with one or two of their own notes of what they wanted changed. Then I went ahead and did some squeezing together."[12]

The result is a brisk affair that, like the first film, streamlines events and discards irrelevancies. This time it is to the remote Winnerden Flats that the Professor heads to investigate a shower of meteorites. They are no ordinary meteorites though, given that they turn out to be "some sort of container," as Quatermass puts it, implying "knowledge, mathematics, precise planning, *intelligence*." Indeed, these streamlined objects turn out to be carrying alien parasites able to control the minds of their victims, among them residents of the nearby new town as well as top ranking members of the government. "Who knows how many infected people they've got in high places," muses Quatermass. Hence the secretive rubber-stamping of a giant refinery-like construction on the Flats, outwardly a synthetic food processing plant built by the locals, but in truth an alien acclimatization center based—ironically—on the Professor's own designs for a lunar acclimatization facility.

Working with Inspector Lomax again, Quatermass—seemingly the lone voice of reason amid the conspiracy—eventually manages to join a government inspection party and gain entry into the sinister-looking plant, which is patrolled by "zombie" guards. Once he has ascertained the true nature of the enterprise, he manages to destroy the blancmange-like creatures, which he does by exposing them to lethal doses of oxygen. He also gives the order for his latest rocketship to be launched towards the aliens' base—an asteroid orbiting "the dark side of the earth." Mission accomplished, Lomax ponders, "You know what worries me? How am I going to make a final report about this?" To which Quatermass responds, "What worries me is how final can it be?"

Given the success of the first Quatermass film, *Quatermass 2* was allotted a bigger budget than its predecessor, the majority of which was provided by United Artists, which was also set to release the film worldwide in a non-perpetual distribution deal cleverly brokered by James Carreras (UA had released the first film Stateside). Even so, £92,000 and a six-week schedule beginning on 21 May 1956 were hardly luxurious. Bray was still being used to film *The Errol Flynn Theatre* (1955–1956, TV) by the time *Quatermass 2* was ready to go before the cameras. Consequently, the film's interiors were shot at the Danziger Studios at New Elstree (credited as the New Elstree Studios), while exteriors were filmed on location on Chobham Common, the South Downs, at Hemel Hempstead (doubling as Winnerden Flats) and the Shell Haven Refinery (doubling for the alien acclimatization facility, just as it had done for the television series).

Cast-wise, Brian Donlevy was brought back to reprise the role of Quatermass, much to the consternation of Nigel Kneale, whose newly acquired powers were obviously not extensive enough to influence casting. Commented the writer of the Hollywood star's re-appearance, "Mr. Donlevy had had two more years of soaking up a lot of Scotch every lunchtime. By the afternoon he couldn't remember what the story was, so it had to change to deal with that, which pretty much well sank it as far as I was concerned."[13] Kneale's claim aside, there is little or no evidence of this in this finished film, and Donlevy spits out his lines with conviction and authority, so much so that when he offers an explanation of the aliens' ability to control their victims' minds—"Something is implanted—an instinct, a

blind compulsion to act for them"—one is inclined to accept his statement rather than greet it with incredulity. Sadly, the role of Inspector Lomax was now to be played by John Longden instead of the rather more charismatic (and expensive) Jack Warner, though the technical crew remained very much the same second time round, save for the addition of designer Bernard Robinson, who would go on to be a major influence with Hammer (his superb set for the interior of the Palace of Westminster, where Quatermass has his meeting with MP Vincent Broadhead, is an indication of his work to come, owing to its ingenious use of limited space).

Thanks to the forward planning of director Val Guest, principal photography on *Quatermass 2* was brisk, and concluded on 13 July, following which the film was handed to James Needs for editing and, eventually, James Bernard to score (the composer was again requested to provide a string and percussion composition, just as he had done for *The Quatermass Xperiment* and *X—The Unknown*). The results were trade shown at the Wardour St. Theater on 22 March 1957, with the premier run following two months later at the London Pavilion on 24 May. Billed with the Brigitte Bardot sex drama *And God Created Woman* (1957), *Quatermass 2* finally went on general release in the UK on the ABC circuit on 17 June. For its American release in September the same year, for which it was re-titled *Enemy from Space*, *Variety* observed, "British producers, when they turn to science-fiction, generally are vague in approach and this import does little to dispel the impression."

Perhaps because the film's theme of alien invasion via the mental and physical possession of mankind was a popular device of science fiction at the time—as per *Invaders from Mars* (1953), *Invasion of the Body Snatchers* (1956) and several other films—the reaction to *Quatermass 2* wasn't quite as overwhelming as it had been for the first film, despite the poster's promise of "A nightmare of horror and fear!" No doubt hence *Variety's* observation that, "Val Guest's direction is as uncertain as [the] script on which he collabs with Nigel Kneale," though it did concede that the "special effects are imaginative." The *Daily Express* meanwhile described the film as "eerie, exciting and tense."

But this is to dismiss the film too freely. It does possess faults, among them a surfeit of exposition scenes in the Professor's lab. Yet such is the notion of the central concept ("The mass destruction of

An Italian poster for *Quatermass 2* (1957) (Hammer/Clarion/ United Artists).

men's minds," as Quatermass puts it), this barely seems to matter, especially given that it perfectly tunes into certain paranoias of the day, among them fears of Big Brother–like totalitarianism, nuclear power plants, the Secret State, corruption in high places and infiltration from beyond the Iron Curtain. It also nicely taps into old wartime protocols and sensibilities. For example, when he asks Dawson, the Camp Secretary, of the locals' involvement with the plant, Quatermass is informed that "Our people are working on this project, mister. They're construction workers building it—and getting good money. In return we're asked to keep our mouths shut—same as in wartime, see?" Recalled Nigel Kneale, "It was a period when a lot of mysterious radar establishments and places of that sort had been built across the country, and if anything it was done with even greater secrecy than it would be now, because there was a great nervousness in the country. People were frightened of what might drop from the skies, and they didn't want to ask too much about what was going on. People just hoped everything would be all right, but rumours did circulate: 'What's this thing being put up on the coast?,' 'Who put it there?,' 'Is it really to keep the Russians away, or is it something else?' I decided my story would be about the 'something else.'"[14]

As Kneale pointed out, the film does indeed possesses a pervading sense of dread perfectly complimented by James Bernard's unsettling score. Nevertheless, Brian Donlevy's performance as Quatermass again leaves one in no doubt as to who is in charge of terminating the aliens' plans to colonize earth. The film also contains some potent imagery, among them the strange scars sported by the "possessed" and the death of government minister Vincent Broadhead, who finds himself covered with toxic sludge at the refinery, memorably leaving a smear of goo on the side of a containment tank as he stumbles down a flight of metal stairs ("It burns. This is the food and it burns," he informs Quatermass with his dying breath). This particular scene required four takes from Tom Chatto, the unfortunate actor involved, but the results have since become iconographic (it was no doubt scenes such as this that prompted *Picture Show* to comment, "The X certificate given this film is sheerly for the horror in it. It is sure to satisfy thrill-lovers with strong stomachs").

Some of the dialogue has an equally strong impact: "That pipe has been blocked by human pulp," declares Quatermass during the final battle with the aliens. As always with Kneale, there are also some far-seeing ideas contained in the film. For example, when discussing his new rocket, Quatermass declares that "I'm going to send it up there and bring it back not once but a hundred times," thus pre-empting the space shuttle by some twenty years.

Unfortunately, given its failure to match *The Quatermass Xperiment* in terms of box office, any plans to film Kneale's third Quatermass serial, *Quatermass and the Pit* (which was broadcast between the Christmas and New Year of 1958 and 1959), were subsequently put on hold until 1967, despite various announcements.

**Additional notes:** Though it was by no means the first film sequel, *Quatermass 2* was nevertheless the first sequel to carry a number. The opening credits carry the following statement: "The producers acknowledge the assistance received from the Hemel Hempstead New Town Development Corporation during the shooting of this film." Meanwhile, the closing credits announce that, "The producers wish to acknowledge with thanks the facilities extended to them by "Shell" Refining and Marketing Company for the shooting of many scenes at Shell Haven Refinery, Essex." Actor John Rae played McLeod in both the film and the original 1955 TV series (E.G. McLeod in the series, E.J. McLeod in the film). Sidney James is billed as Sydney James.

Production companies: Hammer/Clarion. Distributor: United Artists (UK [ABC circuit], U.S.). Producer: Anthony Hinds. Executive producer: Michael Carreras. Production supervisor: Anthony Nelson Keys. Director: Val Guest. Screenplay: Nigel Kneale, Val Guest, based upon the television serial by Nigel Kneale. Story: Nigel Kneale. Cinematographer: Gerald Gibbs. Music: James Bernard. Music director: John Hollingsworth. Editor: James Needs. Assistant editor/sound editor: Alfred Cox. Assistant editor: Michael Hart [uncredited]. Art director: Bernard Robinson. Costumes: Rene Coke. Special effects: Bill Warrington, Henry Harris, Frank George, Brian Johncock [uncredited], Les Bowie (mattes [uncredited]). Make-up: Phil Leakey. Camera operator: Len Harris. Focus puller: Harry Oakes [uncredited]. Assistant director: Don Weeks. Second assistant director: Stanley Goulder [uncredited]. Third assistant director: Hugh Harlow [uncredited]. Sound: Cliff Sandell. Boom operator: Claude Hitchcock [uncredited]. Production manager: John Workman. Continuity: June Randall. Production secretary: Angela Taub [uncredited]. Construction manager: Freddie Ricketts [uncredited]. Chief electrician: Jack Curtis [uncredited]. Electrician: Steve Birtles [uncredited]. Clapper loader: Alan Gatward [uncredited]. Master plasterer: Arthur Banks [uncredited]. Props: Tommy Money [uncredited]. Draughts-

men: Don Mingaye [uncredited], David Butcher [uncredited]. Stills: John Jay [uncredited]. Publicist: Bill Batchelor [uncredited]. **Cast:** Brian Donlevy (Professor Bernard Quatermass), John Longden (Inspector Lomax), Sidney James (Jimmy Hall [billed as Sydney James]), William Franklyn (Brand), Bryan Forbes (Marsh), Charles Lloyd-Pack (Dawson [Camp Secretary]), Vera Day (Sheila), Tom Chatto (Vincent [Vinnie] Broadhead), Percy Herbert (Gorman), John Van Eyssen (The P.R.O.), Michael Ripper (Ernie), John Rae (E.J. McLeod), Jane Aird (Miss McLeod), Lloyd Lamble (Inspector), Betty Impey (Kelly), John Stuart (Commissioner), Marianne Stone (Secretary [Miss Bealey]), Gilbert Davis (Banker), Howard Williams (Michaels), Edwin Richfield (Peterson), Joyce Adams (M.P.), Philip Baird (First lab assistant), Robert Raikes (Second lab assistant), George Merritt (Superintendent), Arthur Blake (Constable), John Fabian (Intern), Michael Balfour (Harry), Ronald Wilson (Man in car), Jan Holden (Girl in car [uncredited]), Vernon Greeves (First man [uncredited]), Joan Schofield (Shopper [uncredited]), Barry Lowe (Chris [uncredited]), Henry Rayner (Drunk [uncredited]), Alastair Hunter (MP [uncredited]). **DVD availability:** Anchor Bay (U.S. R1 NTSC), extras include a commentary by Nigel Kneale and Val Guest, the U.S. trailer and an episode of *The World of Hammer* (1990, [first broadcast 1994], TV) titled *Sci-Fi*; DD Home Entertainment (UK R2 PAL), extras include a commentary by Nigel Kneale and Val Guest and a filmed interview with Val Guest; Hammer (UK R2 PAL), double-billed with *The Quatermass Xperiment* (1955). **Blu-ray availability:** Shock (B/2), as an extra with *The Quatermass Xperiment*. **CD availability:** *The Hammer Quatermass Film Music Collection* (GDI), which contains three brief cues from the original score: *Opening Credits*, *Things in Domes* and *End Credits*; *The Hammer Film Music Collection: Volume Two* (GDI), which contains the *Main Title*; *The Devil Rides Out: The Film Music of James Bernard* (Silva Screen), which contains a newly recorded *Quatermass Suite* featuring two cues from Bernard's score, *Defeat of the Aliens* and *Finale*; *The Great British Film Music Album: Sixty Glorious Years 1938–1998* (Silva Screen), which contains a new recording of *Defeat of the Aliens*

### The Quatermass Xperiment

GB, 1955, 82m [U.S. 78m], bw, cert X

When it opened at the London Pavilion in Piccadilly Circus on Friday 26 August 1955, Hammer's *The Quatermass Xperiment* broke the house record for takings. Made on a meager budget of just £42,000, it was the latest in a long line of big screen adaptations of proven radio and television successes made by the company, among them *Dick Barton—Special Agent* (1948) and *Life with the Lyons* (1954). In fact Hammer had somewhat cornered the market in cheaply produced B-features in the early fifties, the quality of which varied from the acceptable to the downright tortuous. However, after almost a decade of learning the ropes from scratch, *The Quatermass Xperiment* hit all of its buttons perfectly thanks a number of key elements, among them its strong source material, its

**Slimetime. Brian Donlevy looks on as Tom Chatto discovers to his cost the true nature of the food in the containment tanks in *Quatermass 2* (1957) (Hammer/Clarion/United Artists).**

vigorous handling by director Val Guest, an eerie score by composer James Bernard and a strong cast, among them several veterans of previous Hammer productions.

The film's enormous success changed the course of Hammer practically overnight. Instead of concentrating on low budget spin-offs and shop-worn programers, the company now turned its attention to science fiction and horror with fervor, *setting* trends rather than following them as it had previously done. Indeed, the impact of the film was wide reaching, and affected not only Hammer's own fortunes, but those of the British and American film industries, which were quick to jump onto the latest bandwagon. As one critic succinctly put it, *The Quatermass Xperiment* "can truly be said to have changed the course of British film history."

The original television version—more conventionally known as *The Quatermass Experiment*—had actually been commissioned by the BBC to fill an unforeseen gap in their schedules. Consequently, staff writer Thomas Nigel Kneale was quickly pressed into service to provide six thirty-minute episodes on a subject of his choosing. As the writer recalled, "It was the middle of the summer and someone said, 'For God's sake, someone write something!'"[15]

The story Kneale devised involved the first manned flight into space, pre-empting the Apollo moon-shot by some sixteen years. But something goes drastically wrong during the experiment, and only one of the mission's three astronauts—Victor Carroon—returns alive, and when he begins to mutate into a creature whose intentions seem to be the destruction of mankind, the genius behind the space program—one Professor Bernard Quatermass—has to step in and help destroy the byproduct of his experiments. As Kneale remembered, "When I was thinking up the story, no one knew if it was safe to fire a rocket in to space. There was a lot of unease about this at the time. People didn't know what you might pick up in space. There was a tremendous worry about contamination. So I thought I'd write a story about a space flight that returns with some very nasty contamination!"[16]

Once Kneale had his premise, he quickly got to work on the scripts, finding the surname of his title character in the London phone directory. The character's Christian name was meanwhile a tribute to Bernard Lovell, the creator of Jodrell Bank, whom Kneale regarded as a pioneer and the "ultimate questing man."[17] In fact, such was the rush of writing and production, the first episode was being broadcast before Kneale had finished work on the final two. However, the impact of the innovative series was immediate, and its six episodes—transmitted live on Wednesday evenings between 18 July and 22 August 1953—cleared the streets and pubs, making this a television event not too far removed from the recent coronation of Elizabeth II.

One of those glued to his set watching the series was Hammer producer Anthony Hinds, and it was he who suggested to James Carreras that the studio enter into negotiations with the BBC to purchase the film rights to the property. Seeing the potential, Carreras proceeded, securing a deal that would see any profits split fifty-fifty between Hammer and the Beeb. However, that said, it should be noted that according to the BBC's Written Archive Center, Hammer pursued the film rights to *The Quatermass Experiment* because of the interest of their American partners in adapting the series into a film.[18] Nigel Kneale has since revealed that producer-director Sidney Gilliat was also interested in making a film version of the series, but backed away because "he was frightened by the new X certificate."[19]

The project was then offered to veteran writer-director Val Guest, who had already helmed four films for Hammer (Austrian émigré Rudolph Cartier had helmed the television version). Yet Guest wasn't immediately taken by the idea, as he later admitted. "Tony Hinds took me to lunch one day and asked me if I'd seen *The Quatermass Experiment* on television. Well, I think I was the only person in England who'd not seen *any* of it! I wasn't a science fiction buff at all. Then Tony said that if somebody offered a job I should take it! So I agreed to have a look at the [television] scripts, which he gave me a few days later at Northolt Airport, just as I was off to Tangiers for a holiday with my wife. So I took this great package of scripts to Tangiers with me and put them by the bed. Well, we'd been there about a week when my wife said, 'Haven't you read these yet?' I said no, and that science fiction wasn't my cup of tea. And she said, 'Since *when* has it not been your cup of tea?' So I thought I'd better read them, so I took them down to the sun beach, read them and was riveted! So I called Tony and said, 'Yes, I'd love to do it!'"[20]

Astonishingly, when it came to writing the screenplay for the film, Nigel Kneale was left out of the loop, given his status as a lowly staff writer (though he did amend some dialogue for a scene featuring a BBC announcer). Commented Kneale, "I would like to have been asked to write the film, but I was never offered the chance. I was not considered important enough!"[21]

Consequently, given his track record, Guest was invited to script the film as well as direct. This meant a good deal of trimming, given that the serial had a total running time of three hours. Inevitably, the required cuts didn't go down too well with Kneale. Recalled Guest, "He rather felt that we had

BRIAN DONLEVY
RICHARD WORDSWORTH
JACK WARNER · MARGIA DEAN

El EXPERIMENTO del Dr. QUATERMASS

DIRECTOR: VAL GUEST

Margia Dean, Brian Donlevy (both top left) and Richard Wordsworth feature in this Spanish poster for *The Quatermass Xperiment* (1955) (Hammer/Concanen/Lippert/Exclusive/United Artists).

butchered his scripts. But you *have* to if you're going to bring six episodes down to the length of one film. He's a brilliant writer—I'm not saying anything bad about his work—but it was too verbose for the screen."[22] Guest subsequently streamlined the narrative. He also hit upon a novel way of filming the proceedings. "I said to Tony Hinds that I would love to do it as a factual film, as though *Panorama* had said, 'Go out and cover this story.' I said I'd like to do it almost *cinema verité* in some places, to give the impression that the events were being covered as they happened, like an old newsreel."[23]

As had been the case with many of Hammer's previous productions, American backing was needed to help finance the making of *The Quatermass Xperiment*, and to this end Robert Lippert's lengthy association with the studio was again brought into service. As always, though, in the case of U.S. involvement, there were some provisos, among them the requirement of an American co-writer and an American star to help sell the film

Stateside. Consequently, Richard Landau, who had already worked on six scripts for Hammer, was brought in to co-script the film with Guest, his prime objective being to make sure that the dialogue didn't contain too many British colloquialisms. Meanwhile, Hollywood star Brian Donlevy was chosen to play the title role, which had been essayed by Reginald Tate in the television version.

Donlevy had been a major star in the thirties and forties, having appeared in such classics as *Beau Geste* (1939), *Destry Rides Again* (1939) and *The Great McGinty* (1940), more often than not in fast-talking, tough-guy roles. However, like many of the Americans who found themselves working for Hammer in the fifties, his star was in the descent, though obviously he was deemed enough of a draw to be cast in the first place. Director Val Guest was more than happy to have the star playing Quatermass. "He told us proudly, ours would be his 57th motion picture—what's more he was a delight to work with."[24] Unfortunately, Nigel Kneale was less than impressed with the star's resultant perform-

The three-handed monster looks slightly comical in this ad for the American release *The Quatermass Xperiment* (1955), for which the film was re-titled *The Creeping Unknown* (1955). Margia Dean's credit perhaps better reflects her relationship with Spyros Skouras than it does the size of her role in the film (Hammer/Concanen/Lippert/Exclusive/United Artists).

ance, famously describing it as "a wet raincoat looking for somewhere to drip."[25]

Save for the odd excised scene or incident, *The Quatermass Xperiment* follows the basic structure of the television show pretty closely, though as Val Guest recalled, "It wasn't easy condensing six weeks' television into a screenplay for a ninety-minute feature film and of necessity a lot of the TV scenes and dialogue had to go."[26] The film opens with two lovers walking down a country lane with cheerful abandon. However, their smooching in a nearby haystack is soon interrupted when an object ("Sounds like a jet," says the boy) crashes into the field from the night sky, partially destroying the farmhouse into which they run for cover (though curiously, *not* the highly combustible haystack!). The approach of the object "was widely observed over the Southern Counties," a BBC announcer informs radio listeners, though the boyfriend's assertion that "It's probably a meteor, isn't it?" is quickly dispelled by the revelation of a rocketship, which has crashed into the ground tip first.

The man responsible for the rocket mission is soon racing to the scene, informing his concerned colleagues (and, of course, *us*) that, "For the first time in the history of the world, man has sent a rocket fifteen hundred miles into space—you can't expect such an experiment to be perfect!" The man is Professor Bernard Quatermass (or Quater*muss*, as Donlevy pronounces it), through whom we also learn that radio contact with the rocketship has been lost for over fifty-seven hours, and that it was through *his* control that it was subsequently brought back to earth. The immediate concern is for the three-man crew inside the craft: Victor Carroon, Charles Green and Ludwig Reichenheim. Yet when the door of the rocketship is finally opened, only one man—Carroon—emerges. The other two, it seems, have completely disappeared, much to the consternation of Quatermass, given that the rocket has remained sealed during its entire journey.

The answer obviously lies with Carroon, who must surely know what went on. Unfortunately, the astronaut has been so traumatized by his experiences that he is unable to speak. Inevitably, the police are called in to investigate the matter. Inspector Lomax leads these proceedings, and it's clear straight away that he and Quatermass are destined to clash. "I'm a plain simple bible man," Lomax informs the increasingly exasperated scientist, adding, "I've a routine mind and I can do routine things." Yet though the inspector agrees to give Qua-

termass some leeway, he does stand his ground over the fact that his men have already finger-printed and attempted to interview the seemingly comatose Carroon (though his prints—little more than splodges—barely seem to be human). He also informs the Professor that as far as the police are concerned, "When three men take off in a rocket and only one comes back, in our reckoning that leaves minus two. And minus two puts us in the embarrassing position of having to investigate plus one, whether he's conscious, unconscious or a gibbering idiot!"

It subsequently transpires that Carroon has not been taken to a public hospital, but to Quatermass's lab instead, where a sick room has been prepared, thus enabling Quatermass and his colleague, Dr. Gordon Briscoe, to better keep an eye on him. And they are right to be concerned, as the astronaut seems to be undergoing some kind of transformation. "There's been a change, I'm convinced of that," Briscoe informs his superior. In fact the mute Carroon seems to have developed a curious interest in plant life, given that he can't take his eyes off the roses that his American wife Judith has brought for him (is Carroon supposed to be American too, one wonders?).

Events now begin to gather momentum when Quatermass's young assistant, who has been giving the crashed rocketship a thorough once-over, discovers a strange jelly-like substance in its casing. "It could be animal—it could be human," says Briscoe. Could the jelly be the remains of the other two astronauts? Quatermass isn't sure: "Something happened in here … something beyond our understanding at the moment." Back at the lab, Carroon continues to transform ("His hand … another change," observes Briscoe). However, Quatermass's lack of compassion for Carroon leaves the astronaut's wife unimpressed. "There's no room for personal feelings in science, Judith," he informs her. Consequently, when her husband is finally moved to the Central Clinic, she hatches a plan to spring him, hiring the services of Christie, a smarmy private eye who disguises himself as a male nurse to accomplish his task ("Wives usually employ me to get them *away* from their husbands," he quips, as he sets off smuggle out Carroon).

Christie obviously doesn't know what he's got himself into, for having helped the stricken Carroon get dressed, he pops down the corridor to call the elevator. While he's doing this, Carroon's obsession with thorned plant life takes a new, rather more shocking turn: he smashes his fist into a small cactus that has been placed in his room for decoration. Having seemingly absorbed the plant's spiky qualities into his arm, Carroon hides it within his jacket, thus raising Christie's curiosity when he returns to escort him to the waiting lift. This proves to be his undoing, for Carroon now uses his arm as a weapon with which to kill Christie, doing so with a single blow, leaving the private eye with a horribly distorted face and hand. "Looks as though the life was drawn right out of him," observes Inspector Lomax when he later turns up on the crime scene. In the meantime Carroon has wandered out to the clinic car park, where his waiting wife helps him to the car. Inevitably, she too is curious about her husband's arm, and pulls over to take a closer look. Yet just when it looks like Carroon is about to kill his wife too, humanity momentarily seems to get the better of him, and he quickly absconds, leaving Judith screaming the place down (she may never recover from the shock, we're soon after informed).

By now the police are on Carroon's trail, searching London for him as far a-field as Piccadilly, the Tower of London and the Docks at Deptford (comments Lomax of his evasive quarry, "He's been seen in Liverpool, Margate, Ostend and the Orkneys!"). At none of these locations, Carroon is instead about to pay a small chemists' shop a visit, seemingly to find a make-shift cure for the pain he is obviously suffering from, dispatching the concerned proprietor with a blow from his deformed "cactus arm" in the process. Again, Lomax and Quatermass turn up on the scene to investigate the aftermath, Briscoe's opinion being that Carroon was not in fact attempting to dull his pain with the various pills and potions scattered about the shop, but to *accelerate* his transformation.

Carroon hides out that night in a disused barge (the Plaudit) at the docks in Deptford, only to be greeted the next morning by the sound of a young girl playing "tea time" with her dollies. Again, the remaining humanity within Carroon prevents him from killing the child, reversing audience expectations given that the scene (newly created for the film) is practically a replay of the well-known scene in *Frankenstein* (1931), in which Boris Karloff's Monster *does* kill a young girl he encounters by a lake. Instead, Carroon shambles off to seek the cover under which he can make his final transformation, eventually finding it at the zoological gardens at Regent's Park Zoo (actually filmed at the more convenient Chessington Zoo), where, the next day, several of the animals are found dead, while the ground is covered with a slug-like trail of slime. "What manner or shape of thing do we look for now?" wonders Lomax. We soon get an idea when a drunken derelict named Rosie calls in at her local police station to inform the boys in blue that she has seen a curious shape while resting in a doorway. However, when asked where she saw the object walking, she replies, "Walking? It was kind of *crawling* ... up on a wall."

When they turn up at the wall in question, Lomax and Quatermass discover the tell-tale trail of slime, leaving them wondering where the creature will turn up next, and in what form, given that at the zoo Briscoe had discovered a piece of shed skin which, back at the lab, begins to grow and spoor, raising fears that, if unchecked, the monster could quickly multiply and prove a threat to the whole of mankind. Consequently, the sewers, underground system and docks are searched again. Yet the creature turns up at the most unlikely of places: Westminster Abbey, where Sir Lionel Dean is about to broadcast a program about the building's architecture and restoration live on the BBC. The alarm is first raised when a man is discovered dead at the scene, much to the annoyance of the program's producer, who insists on going ahead with the broadcast from another part of the abbey. But this idea is soon scotched when the cameras spot the creature—now grown to an enor-

mous size and no longer recognizable as human—clinging to some scaffolding which has been erected for the renovation work.

Having arrived on the scene, Quatermass quickly decides to use the resources at his disposal to destroy the creature, getting one of the television technicians to attach a cable to the scaffolding, through which he electrocutes the monster via a surge in power provided by Battersea Power Station, which has to black out London in order to comply. Yet Quatermass seems unbowed by the whole devastating experience, and the film ends with his announcement of a new mission into space, at which the film cuts to its final image, that of a second rocketship taking off for "the other side of the air" (note that Quatermass actually alludes to this second rocket when discussing the three returning astronauts with Blake on the way to the crash site: "Dead or alive, Blake, they'll be heroes. Let me tell you something. They'll fire the imagination, so there'll be a hundred men begging for the same privilege when we launch the second rocket").

*The Quatermass Xperiment* began principal photography on 18 October 1954 at Bray Studios, although some second unit scenes at Chessington Zoo had been filmed the previous week on 14 October. The main unit shot for five weeks, through towards the end of November, although further crowd scenes were captured as late as 31 December, taking advantage of the New Year celebrations. The shoot also saw scenes recorded as far a-field as Windsor (the exterior of Woods the chemists in Queen Charlotte St. [which can also be spotted in the 1952 short *The Stranger Left No Card*]) and Westminster Bridge, while Down Place and its two studios played host to the film's various interiors, including Lomax's office, Briscoe's lab and the Central Clinic (is that the Hammer staff bus parked outside in the car park?). The nearby village of Bray (note the local garage) was also used extensively for the opening scenes in which the emergency services speed their way to the site of the crashed rocketship, which was filmed in a field at the nearby Water Oakley Farm (Oakley Green in the film), with the rocket apparently nailed to a tree for support.

Although the film's cast is top-lined by a Hollywood star ("Donlevy plays the scientist with a grim and ruthless conviction," commented *Variety*), the remainder of the roles are filled by some of the best British

character actors working at the time, chief among them Jack Warner (who appeared "By arrangement with J. Arthur Rank Organization," to whom he was contracted), whose cheerfully efficient Inspector Lomax provides solid balance to the barked orders of Brian Donlevy's Quatermass (sorry, Quater*muss*). Incredibly popular at the time, Warner was familiar to audiences from his appearances in several film comedies featuring the Huggett family—*Holiday Camp* (1947), *Here Come the Huggetts* (1948), etc.—although he was becoming increasingly known for playing coppers in such films as *The Blue Lamp* (1949), in which he portrayed PC George Dixon, a role that he would later revive for the long-running television series *Dixon of Dock Green* (1955–1976, TV). In fact it was Warner who was the cause of the film's meager budget spiraling from an originally planned £40,000. Recalled Val Guest, "When Jack Warner went into a few pro rata days the figure had rocketed to a reckless £42,000."[27]

In addition to Warner, the cast also includes such stalwarts as David King-Wood, who gets his fair share of juicy lines as Dr. Gordon Briscoe; Gordon Jackson, who perfectly captures the impatience of the television producer keen to transmit his program on architecture, despite the mounting

**Starfish invasions. Polish artwork for *The Quatermass Xperiment* (1955). Note that Margia Dean takes top billing (Hammer/Concanen/Lippert/Exclusive/United Artists).**

problems; and Thora Hird, who is excellent in her two-minute cameo as the shambling Rosie, whose realization that the creature she has seen is not, for once, the result of the gin bottle, causes her to faint with the cry of, "It's me legs!" Hird actually received fourth billing for this brief but memorable role, two places above David King-Wood, who appears throughout the film. However, the prime-supporting role goes to Richard Wordsworth (great-great-grandson of the poet Wordsworth), making his film debut as the doomed Carroon, a role he plays entirely in mime (his one line—a whispered "Help me!" in the ambulance—is actually relayed by Briscoe). Aided and abetted by Phil Leakey's increasingly gruesome make-up (the "cactus arm" is surprisingly effective), he brilliantly captures the pain—both physical and mental—of the transmogrifying astronaut. For his efforts, Wordsworth was billed last.

The Hammer techies also pull their weight, chief among them cinematographer Walter "Jimmy" Harvey, whose stark black and white photography, with its harsh over-head lighting, adds immeasurably to the film's austere atmosphere; editor James Needs, whose sharp cutting makes sure that no scene runs longer than is necessary, thus keeping the running time down to an astonishingly brisk eighty-two minutes; composer James Bernard, whose nervy string and percussion score unsettles as much as it thrills; and veteran art director J. Elder Wills, whose sets are both serviceable and, on occasion, eye-catching, as per the crisp, white, *art deco*-style corridors of the Central Clinic and the equally antiseptic look of Briscoe's lab, with its dentist-like examination chair and its cozy sick room annex.

However, the real hero of the piece is director Val Guest, who keeps the action moving at all times, particularly in the opening scenes of mayhem and panic, during which he makes very effective use of a lengthy dolly track (the collapse of the farmhouse into which the two lovers run for shelter is also spectacular and surprising). Later, he also uses subjective camera work—the staple of stalk-and-slash pics in the seventies and eighties—as the increasingly monstrous Carroon shuffles past the nervous-looking animals in the zoo at night, his deformed body seen only via a few judicious glimpses of shadow and the trailing of a flap of unsightly "skin." Script-wise, Guest makes sure that the proceedings are peppered with a good deal of tension-relieving humor, too. For example, when a disgruntled mother is informed that the zoo has been closed for the day following Carroon's night-time spree, she retorts with a highly indignant, "Closed? But we've come all the way from Epping!" Meanwhile, the shots of London as the police search for the missing astronaut among derelict boats, warehouses and bomb shelters (which were photographed by camera operator Len Harris) add immeasurably to Guest's bid to give the film a sense of *cinema verité*-style immediacy, firmly rooting the proceedings in a rather shabby-looking post-war realism.

Inevitably, given its low budget and brisk shooting schedule, a number of gaffes can be found in the finished product, chief among them the reflection of arc lights in the passing fire engines and ambulances in the opening scenes (though the director later *includes* these lights in the scene, having the army operate them by way of illuminating the disaster site for the emergency services). The shadow of a boom mic can also be seen on the wall during several of the scenes in Briscoe's lab. One also can see over the top of the elevator set in the Central Clinic owing to the low placement of the camera. Though it is pouring down with rain outside the clinic, no rain can be seen outside Carroon's window, either, and when Judith Carroon enters the clinic (completely dry), the noisy rain soundtrack fails to appear as it does when other outside doors are opened. Crew and camera shadows can also be spotted at the crash site, by the canal with the little girl, and at the zoo.

Script-wise, there are also a few irregularities. How, for example, did Quatermass fund the seemingly private enterprise of his rocketship experiment? How did he personally affect its return to earth—radio control? How does the limping Carroon manage to cover so much ground within such a short space of time, given that we see him in Windsor and Deptford, all of which are miles apart? And if Carroon attacks the chemist on a Sunday, how come church bells are ringing first thing the *following* morning when he meets the little girl by the boat? And how *does* the monster sneak into Westminster Abbey without being seen, given that its slime trail goes right past the front door? Also note that the door to the crashed rocket is conveniently accessible (and the wrong way up, given that the rocket crashed nose first). Elsewhere, it should be noted that Margia Dean is dubbed throughout ("In my opinion she couldn't act at all,"[28] commented Nigel Kneale, which perhaps explains why), while Brian Donlevy refers to Reichenheim as Greichenheim when first visiting Lomax in his office. Finally, the frisky medic at the Central Clinic who tries to pick up two nurses by promising them a meal at the local Chinese, which is apparently open till midnight, is destined for disappointment, as a previously seen clock has already revealed the time to be 12:40 a.m.

As far as the screenplay is concerned, it should be noted that some of Kneale's more ingenious ideas didn't make it into the shooting script, the cleverest of these being the revelation that, upon killing his victims, Carroon "absorbs" their memories and knowledge, hence his murder of the chemist, so that he can *learn* how to accelerate his transformation via the mixing of powders and potions (a few brief lines would surely have better explained this than the few vague hints we get). Additional trims were also made to the script prior to filming following its submission for approval to the British Board of Film Censors, the board fearing that audiences might be overly abhorred by some of the story's more extreme scenes and situations (among their concerns were worries about the film's gruesome make-ups, a concern that was reflected in *Variety*'s review of the film, which commented, "There is an occasional over-plus of horror close-ups of the victims"). That said, the script has a welcome leavening sense of humor, particularly in those scenes featuring Inspector Lomax ("Well,

you might almost say we've been given a rocket," he quips after being given a telling off by the Professor).

In a bid to gain publicity from the fact that the finished film would inevitably be stamped with an X certificate (then regarded as death at the box office), James Carreras decided to fully embrace the rating, coming up with the brilliant idea of phonetically modifying the film's title from *The Quatermass Experiment* to *The Quatermass Xperiment* so as to further emphasize—and exploit—the connection. "X is not an unknown quantity—make sure your public know about *The Quatermass Xperiment*" cinema managers were urged via the showman's manual. Midnight showings for brave customers were also suggested ("If properly exploited, this stunt could be of great value and cause much controversy," commented the manual), while another idea suggested that managers place a row of seats with dummies chained to them outside their cinemas, accompanied by a sign asking, "What is the strange force that will keep you chained to your seat while seeing *The Quatermass Xperiment*?" The film was only the twelfth awarded an X following the inception of the category in 1951, though it should be noted that later prints restored the title to *The Quatermass Experiment*, which explains why the main titles, filmed against a backdrop of moving clouds, suddenly freeze for the newly inserted title shot.

Trade shown at Studio One on 25 August 1955, *The Quatermass Xperiment* began its premier UK engagement the following day at the London Pavilion, for which it was double-billed with another Hammer production, a widescreen musical short titled *The Eric Winstone Bandshow* (1955). For its national release on the ABC circuit care of Exclusive on 20 November, it was somewhat curiously programed with the similarly X-rated French thriller *Rififi* (1955), while for its American release in June 1956, care of United Artists, who bought the film outright for $125,000, it was trimmed by four minutes, re-titled *The Creeping Unknown* (apparently because Quatermass had no name recognition in the U.S.), and billed with the Basil Rathbone shocker *The Black Sleep* (1956), whose supporting cast included such genre stalwarts as Lon Chaney, Jr., John Carradine, Tor Johnson and Bela Lugosi, the latter of whom had starred in *The Mystery of the Mary Celeste* for Hammer back in 1935. The double bill went on to earn over $1,600,000 for UA, a whopping take given the outlay. Meanwhile, the film's German release on 11 May 1956 was handled by Robert Lippert, who re-titled it *Shock*.

The box office response to *The Quatermass Xperiment* was overwhelming (the film's pairing with *Rififi* made it the UK's most successful double bill of 1955), and despite the inevitable brickbats about subject matter, critical reaction was generally enthusiastic too. "This is the best and nastiest horror film that I have seen since the war—how jolly that it is also British," raved Paul Dehn in the *News Chronicle*, while *The New Statesman* observed that, "The film does in fact touch the imagination…. What we witness in a number of scenes is much extended by what we don't quite see." The *News of the World* meanwhile predicted that "all earnest addicts of science fiction yarns will undoubtedly love every minute of it." In fact the film became such a success it was ballyhooed on the October 1955 cover of *Today's Cinema* on which an image of Richard Wordsworth's Victor Carroon was accompanied by the clever headline "Get out of your Quotamess with *Quatermass*." Meanwhile, Stateside, *Variety* described the film as, "an extravagant piece of science fiction," adding that it drew "its entertainment from a series of wildly improbable happenings."

*The Quatermass Xperiment* was by no means the first science fiction film, nor was it the first film to deal with space travel or invading aliens, the fifties having already seen such American-made epics as *Rocketship X-M* (1950), which had been distributed in the UK by Exclusive, *Destination Moon* (1950), *The Thing* (1951), *It Came from Outer Space* (1953) and *The War of the Worlds* (1953) among others. Even the Brits had had a go with *Devil Girl from Mars* (1954), which was made by the Danziger brothers Edward J. and Harry Lee, who were Hammer's "rivals" in the second feature market. Yet as an addition to this then-popular trend, *The Quatermass Xperiment* more than stood its ground, particularly given its unpromising start with the two lovers, whose forced laughter is truly cringe making. In fact, in many ways it was a trailblazer: note, for example, that in the retrieved film of the doomed space mission that Quatermass and Lomax view, Carroon is seen to "space walk" up the walls of the rocket, pre-dating very similar scenes in Stanley Kubrick's *2001: A Space Odyssey* (1968) by some thirteen years (though sharp-eyed viewers should keep a look out for the bits of the interior not sufficiently secured for this sequence, which was achieved by tipping the set and the camera over together while the actors playing Green and Reichenheim were strapped into their seats to complete the illusion).

Compared to Hammer's previous second feature product, *The Quatermass Xperiment* represented a gigantic leap, akin to an artist making the jump from clumsy crayons to oil painting. Ironically, it was the usually critical Nigel Kneale who perhaps best summed up the film's appeal. "It has a strong and well-constructed story, it's well directed and it certainly moves. It's not mine any more, but it goes at a cracking pace—and the sort of performances it has fit that pace."[29] In fact so confident was James Carreras that the film would be a hit, he put a halt on all feature production for the time being—save for *Women Without Men* (1956)—so as to better figure out what to do next (among the films given the chop was a second feature thriller titled *The Black Opal*, which was set to have gone before the cameras on 12 September 1955, with Terence Fisher in the director's chair). Instead, to keep things ticking over, the studio concentrated on a number of musical shorts while the "next big thing" was discussed. Of course, this proved to be a *very* big thing indeed: *The Curse of Frankenstein* (1957). **Additional notes:** *The Quatermass Xperiment* provoked two sequels from Hammer, both based upon TV serials penned by Kneale. These were *Quatermass 2* (1957), again starring Brian Donlevy, and *Quatermass and the Pit* (1967), star-

ring Andrew Keir as Quatermass. Kneale also penned a four-part 1979 TV series titled *Quatermass*, which had originally been offered to Hammer as a feature provisionally titled *Quatermass 4*; this starred John Mills as the Professor, and was also released theatrically in some territories in a trimmed down version titled *The Quatermass Conclusion*. Interestingly, in episode one, there is an oblique reference to *The Quatermass Xperiment*, as the Professor's earlier endeavours are briefly mentioned. In 1996, Kneale wrote *The Quatermass Memoirs* for BBC radio, for which Andrew Keir returned as Quatermass, while in 2005, BBC4 transmitted a live version of *The Quatermass Experiment* starring Jason Flemyng, which was based upon a compressed version of Kneale's original scripts. In 1996, Warner Bros. in conjunction with Donner/ Shuler Donner announced plans to remake several Hammer classics, among them *The Quatermass Xperiment*, which was set to get a $30m makeover, with both Sean Connery and Anthony Hopkins mooted to play the Professor. Sadly, neither this nor any of the other proposed projects materialized. The film's opening titles carry the following credit: "The Producers wish to thank the following for their co-operation: BBC Television Service, The Air Ministry, Marconi Wireless Telegraph Company, The British Interplanetary Society, General Radiological Limited." The eye-catching, steeply inclined street by the railway sidings in which Rosie has seen the monster crawl up the wall had previously been used by Hammer as a location in the opening sequence in *The Gambler and the Lady* (1953) and during a night time chase sequence in *Five Days* (1954); it also seems to appear in *Whispering Smith Hits London* (1952). James Bernard was actually the second choice of composer; John Hotchkiss, who would go on to score two shorts for Hammer, was originally assigned the project, but had to pull out owing to illness. Interestingly, some shots in the sequence in which the police and military hunt down Carroon were lifted from similar scenes in the thriller *Seven Days to Noon* (1950), which focuses on the hunt for a scientist who has absconded to London with an atomic device; made by the Boulting Brothers, the film is noted for its Oscar-winning story by Paul Dehn and James Bernard, elements of which are also echoed in the Hammer film. Likewise, footage of the fire engine racing to the crash site in *The Quatermass Xperiment* can also be spotted in *The Day the Earth Caught Fire* (1961), which was also directed by Val Guest (the film's editor, Bill Lenny, who frequently worked with Guest, had also previously worked for Hammer, albeit not on *The Quatermass Xperiment*). Imitations include *Caltiki il mostro immortale* (1959, aka *Caltiki, the Immortal Monster*), which hijacks much of the film's plot, right down to having a victim's arm becoming infected upon contact with the monster.

It should also be noted that Jimmy Sangster worked very briefly on the film one evening as a second unit production manager, overseeing the shot in which the lights at Battersea Power Station are blacked out. Recalled Sangster: "I guess Val Guest and the main unit were off shooting somewhere else, either that, or they didn't want to

involve a large unit in a night location. So there was just me and a three-man camera team. I arranged with the guy in charge of the power station that he would switch off the floodlights at exactly midnight while we photographed it from the other side of the river. We synchronized our watches, I gave him a £25 backhander and joined the crew where we set up the camera. At 30 seconds to midnight we rolled the camera and, exactly on time, the floodlights illuminating the power station went out. I was about to tell the guys to cut the camera and let's go home when other lights started to go out along the river frontage. Obviously I'd overtipped the guy. He blacked out a huge part of London south of the river and didn't switch the power on again until fifteen minutes later. There was a short paragraph about the affair in the newspapers the next day. 'Mysterious blackout south of the river.'"[30]

Production companies: Hammer/Concanen/ Lippert. Distributors: Exclusive (UK [ABC circuit]), United Artists (U.S.). Producer: Anthony Hinds. Director: Val Guest. Screenplay: Richard Landau, Val Guest, Nigel Kneale (amended dialogue [uncredited]), based on the TV series *The Quatermass Experiment* by Nigel Kneale. Cinematographer: Walter "Jimmy" Harvey. Music: James Bernard. Music director: John Hollingsworth. Editor: James Needs. Assistant editor: Henry Richardson [uncredited]. Art director: J. Elder Wills. Costumes: Molly Arbuthnot. Special effects: Les Bowie, Vic Margutti [uncredited], Roy Field [uncredited], Ray Caple [uncredited]. Sound: H.C. Pearson, Ken Cameron (dubbing [uncredited]). Sound camera operator: Don Alton [uncredited]. Sound maintenance: John Woodiwiss [uncredited]. Boom operator: Percy Britten [uncredited]. Camera operator: Len Harris (also second unit cinematographer for dragnet sequence [uncredited]). Second camera operator: Richard Leatherbarrow [uncredited]. Focus puller: Harry Oakes [uncredited]. Clapper loader: Tommy Friswell [uncredited]. Assistant director: Bill Shore. Second assistant director: Aida Young [uncredited]. Third assistant director: John Pitcher [uncredited]. Make-up: Phil Leakey. Hair: Monica Hustler. Continuity: Renee Glynne. Production manager: T.S. Lyndon-Haynes. Second unit production manager: Jimmy Sangster [uncredited]. Stills cameraman: John Jay [uncredited]. Production secretary: Dora Thomas [uncredited]. Construction manager: Freddie Ricketts [uncredited]. Chief electrician: Jack Curtis [uncredited]. Electricians: George Robinson [uncredited], Steve Birtles [uncredited], Charles Stanbridge [uncredited]. Master plasterer: Arthur Banks [uncredited]. Accountant: Larry Edmonds [uncredited]. Cashier: Ken Gordon [uncredited]. Props: Tommy Money [uncredited]. Props buyer: Jim Day [uncredited]. Receptionist: Pauline Wise [uncredited]. Stunts: Nosher Powell [uncredited]. **Cast:** Brian Donlevy (Professor Bernard Quatermass), Jack Warner (Inspector Lomax), Richard Wordsworth (Victor Carroon), Margia Dean (Judith Carroon), David King-Wood (Dr. Gordon Briscoe), Thora Hird (Rosie [Rosemary] Elizabeth Wriggley), Gordon Jackson (Television producer), Lionel Jeffries (Blake), Harold Lang (Christie), Sam Kydd (Station

Sergeant), Maurice Kaufmann (Marsh [uncredited]), Stanley Van Beers (Ludwig Reichenheim [uncredited]), Gron Davies (Charles Green [uncredited]), Frank Phillips (BBC announcer [uncredited]), Donald Gray (TV announcer [uncredited]), Arthur Lovegrove (Sergeant Bromley [uncredited]), Jane Asher (Girl with dolls [uncredited]), Betty Impey (Nurse [uncredited]), Marianne Stone (Second nurse [uncredited]), Basil Dignam (Sir Lionel Dean [uncredited]), Edward Dane (Policeman at station [uncredited]), John Stirling (Major [uncredited]), Margaret Anderson (Maggie [uncredited]), Eric Corrie (Maggie's boyfriend [uncredited]), Henry Longhurst (Maggie's father [uncredited]), Michael Godfrey (Fireman [uncredited]), Ernest Hare (Fire chief [uncredited]), Fred Johnson (Inspector [uncredited]), James Drake (Sound engineer [uncredited]), Arthur Gross (Floor manager [uncredited]), George Roderick (Policeman [uncredited]), John Kerr (Lab assistant [uncredited]), John Wynn (Best [uncredited]), Bartlett Mullins (Zookeeper [uncredited]), Molly Glessing (Annoyed mother at zoo [uncredited]), Mayne Lynton (Zoo official [uncredited]), Harry Brunning (Alf [hospital receptionist, uncredited]), Barry Lowe (Tucker [male nurse, uncredited]), Jane Aird (Mrs. Lomax [uncredited]), Toke Townley (Chemist [uncredited]). **DVD availability:** DD Home Entertainment (UK R2 PAL), extras include a commentary and filmed interview with Val Guest; Hammer (UK R2 PAL), double-billed with *Quatermass 2* (1957); the film is also available in a number of Hammer box sets, such as *Hammer Horror—The Early Classics*. **Blu-ray availability:** Shock (B/2), extras include *Quatermass 2* and *X—The Unknown*. **CD availability:** *The Devil Rides Out: The Film Music of James Bernard* (Silva Screen), which contains a newly recorded *Quatermass Suite* featuring *Introduction* and *Death of the Monster*; *The Hammer Quatermass Film Music Collection* (GDI Records), which contains seven cues from Bernard's original score—*Opening Credits, News Headlines, Examining Carroon, Carroon Is Restless, Cacti, Metamorphosis* and *Another Victim*

### The Queen's Award to Industry

At the suggestion of board member Brian Lawrence, James Carreras put Hammer forward for consideration of the prestigious Queen's Award to Industry on the strength of the company's export earnings, which between 1964 and 1967 were valued at £2,742,797. Hammer went on to win the award—the first film company ever to do so—and news of this was announced to the press on 18 April 1968. The award ceremony itself took place at Pinewood on 29 May 1968 on the church set during a break in the filming of *Dracula Has Risen from the Grave* (1968). The award was presented by Brigadier Sir Henry Floyd, the Lord Lieutenant of the County of Buckinghamshire, and was received on behalf of the company by Hammer's long-standing construction manager Arthur Banks in the presence of James Carreras, Anthony Hinds, Christopher Lee, Peter Cushing and the assembled crew. A celebratory lunch followed, during which, incredibly, Sir Henry praised Hammer for

not including "scenes of actual personal violence" in their films, and for having "a responsibility towards the viewing public." What makes this statement all the more amazing is that it was made after Sir Henry had spent the morning watching Dracula's bloody demise on a giant gold cross!

### Quentin, John

This British actor (1935–, real name Quentin Stevenson) can be seen as Digby in Hammer's *Man at the Top* (1973). His many other credits include *Isadora* (1968), *Ransom* (1975), *Wittgenstein* (1993), *Shadowlands* (1993) and *Cousin Bette* (1998). His many television credits include episodes of *Martin Chuzzlewit* (1964, TV), *Colditz* (1972–1974, TV), *Raffles* (1975–1977, TV), *Lovejoy* (1986–1994, TV) and *Longitude* (2000, TV). However, he is best known for playing Bertie Wooster to Michael Denison's Jeeves in a series of Croft Original sherry ads in the eighties and nineties. **Hammer credits:** *Man at the Top* (1973, as Digby)

### The Quiet Ones

GB, 2014, 98m, color, widescreen [1.78:1], cert 15

Having dealt with the spiritual world with great success with their adaptation of *The Woman in Black* (2012), Hammer next turned their attention to a more modern day encounter with paranormal activity—this time in 1974—in which an Oxford college professor and his students repair to a remote house in order to carry out a series of experiments on a disturbed young woman who appears to be possessed by the tormented soul of a girl named Evey, whose increasingly malevolent powers they fall victim to as they attempt to film and analyze her manifestations.

Directed by John Pogue from a screenplay by himself, Tom de Ville, Oren Moverman and Craig Rosenberg, the story is supposedly based on an actual event, the so-called Philip Experiment, which took place in Toronto in 1972. Shot on location in Oxfordshire between 12 June and 16 July 2012, the film stars Jared Harris as Professor Coupland, and

Sam Claflin, Olivia Cooke and Erin Richards as his young charges. It was released in the UK on 10 April 2014 (its premiere was held at the Odeon West End nine days earlier), and opened in the U.S. two weeks later on 24 April, both care of Lionsgate.

Commented Jared Harris of the film, "I don't love horror movies that are gore fests. What is good about *The Quiet Ones* is that it makes you think,"[31] while of Hammer's revival he noted, "It's a great thing these guys are doing. Hammer is a brand that people have an association with and a good one.... The other brand that hasn't been revived but should be is the old Ealing comedies. They weren't naff romantic comedies, they were socially relevant and had a point."[32]

Commented London's *Evening Standard* of the film (which it awarded two stars), "This supernatural shocker from the Hammer Films stable, directed by John Pogue, actually has some decent moments." However, it went on to balance this initial enthusiasm by noting that, "The horrors of human fallibility give way to more predictable and silly upsets (yes, it's our old friend telekinesis!), and though Harris and Cooke are wonderful together, other cast members—notably Erin Richards as sexy posh girl Kristina—are a problem. I've long had a theory that bad thesps have the ability to neutralize fear. Richards' powers are off the chart." Added *The Independent* (which also awarded the film two stars), "Hammer's latest is an enjoyably half-baked foray into the paranormal which mashes together ideas from *Peeping Tom*, *The Exorcist* and Dennis Wheatley in random fashion.... In case we're in doubt of the early 1970s setting, Erin Richards wears hot pants and miniskirts while the sound of Slade is never far away." Elsewhere, the MailOnline (which likewise awarded the film just two stars) headlined its review with the observation, "A Hammer horror that isn't scary? Shocking!"

The *Financial Times* (which garlanded the film with four stars) offered a more positive view, however, commenting of Jared Harris's performance, "His absolute seriousness, his refusal to camp anything up, puts him in the same league as Peter Cushing, who was early Hammer's greatest asset. There is simply nothing more Hammer than Jared Harris in *The Quiet Ones*." Praise indeed! Yet despite Harris's earnestness, the film failed to find much of an audience, getting lost amid the shuffle of similar shockers thanks to its tried and tested mix of found footage, unexpected loud noises, running about in dark places, unexpected loud noises, jumpy editing, unexpected loud noises, cult revelations and unexpected loud noises, all of which make it seem like little more than a by-the-numbers amalgamation of *Paranormal Activity* (2007), *The Last Exorcism* (2010), *Insidious* (2010) and a bad episode of *Most Haunted* (2002–2011, TV), with Harris in the Derek Acorah role.

**A proud moment. Peter Cushing (left) and Christopher Lee (right) admire The Queen's Award to industry bestowed on Hammer during the making of *Dracula Has Risen from the Grave* (1968) (Hammer/Seven Arts/Warner Pathé Distributors/Warner–Seven Arts).**

**Additional notes:** The film debuted at number five in the UK box office charts, taking £681,000 at the tills; the number one film, *Captain America: The Winter Soldier* (2014), by then in its third week, took £2.76m by comparison. The film's eventual U.S. take was just in excess of $8.5m (it took some $3.8m on its opening weekend, playing at 2,027 screens), plus a further $9.3m internationally, bringing its eventual worldwide take to $17.8m. The song *Bertha Butt Boogie*, which features on the film's soundtrack, wasn't released until 1975.

Production companies: Hammer/The Traveling Picture Show Company. Distributor: Lionsgate (UK, U.S.). Producers: Tobin Armbrust, James Gay-Rees, Ben Holden, Simon Oakes, Steven Chester Prince. Executive producers: Alexander Yves Brunner, Carissa Buffel, Guy East, Jillian Longnecker, Kevin Matusow, Nigel Sinclair. Line producer: Tina Pawlik. Co-producers: Geno Tazioli, Bill Wohlken. Director: John Pogue. Screenplay: Tom de Ville, John Pogue, Oren Moverman, Craig Rosenberg. Cinematographer: Matyas Erdély. Music: Lucas Vidal. Editor: Glenn Garland. Assistant editors: Dennis Thorlaksen, Stewart McAlpine. Assistant conform editor: Michael Williams. Production design: Matt Gant. Art director: Caroline Barclay. Set decorator: Anita Gupta. Costumes: Camile Benda. Costume supervisor: Eleanor Landgrebe. Make-up: Paul Boyce. Special effects supervisors: Scott McIntyre, Gavin J. Whelan. Visual effects: Mark Cramer (producer), Micah Gallo (executive producer). Special effects (Lit Post): Tyler A. Hawes, Gustavo Mendes, Scott Purdy, Geno Tazioli (account executive). Special effects: Travis Baumann, Moises Flores Cabrera, Jamison Scott Goei, Holly Gregory Horter, Stewart McAlpine, Thomas McVay, Chris Reilly, Thomas Tannenberger, Dennis Thorlaksen, Norbert Varga, Vivian Wei. Special effects assistant (dailies): Neil Jenkins. Production manager: Livia Rao. Production co-ordinator: Ella Chaitow. Production assistant: Emily Mayson. Post-production manager: Bill Wohlken. Location manager: Ben O'Farrell. First assistant director: Mark Fenn. Second assistant director: Penny Davies. Third assistant director: Danny Albury. Casting: Sasha Robinson. Sound supervisor: Dan Snow. Sound mixer: Henry Milliner. Mix engineer: Jason Abell. Foley artist: Tara Blume. Foley mixer: Shaun Cunningham. Foley editor: Kyle Lane. Supervising sound editors: Tom Boykin, Eric Lalicata. Sound effects editors: Ryan Gegenheimer, Sergio R. Rocha. ADR mixer: Matt Hovland. Boom operators: Elliott Gilhooly, Ramon Pyndiah. Sound trainee: Miles Croft. Standby art director: Joe Barcham. Graphic designer: Carly Mason. Art department assistant: Chris Peters. Stunts: Andy Bennett, Gary Arthurs, David Newton, Heather Phillips. Gaffer: John Eusden. Key grip: Phil Whittaker. Grip: Frank Hellebrand. Electricians: Rik Durrell, Stefan Mitchell. Steadicam operator/camera operator (camera): James Layton. Dit trainee: Michael Middleton-Downer. First assistant camera (camera): Karl Clarke. Second assistant camera: Robin Webster. Generator operator: Kilian Drury. Gaffer: John Eusden. Costume standby: Jessie Fell. Costume assistant: Bonnie Radcliffe. Music supervisor: Andy Ross. Music co-ordinator: Nate Underkuffler. Music scoring mixer: Steve Kempster. Executive music producer: Steve Dzialowski. Music business and legal executive: Charles M. Barsamian. Music clearance: Chris Piccaro. Drivers: Nick Leishman, Michael Middleton-Downer, Ben Dillon. Script supervisors: Nicoletta Mani, Alexandra Owen (additional), Lizzie Pritchard (second unit). Production accountant: Barbara Chinn. Post-production accountant: Emily Rice. Location assistant: Tom Bott. Floor runners: Jonny Hodgetts, Aylwyn Michel, Alex Reid (dailies). Carpenter: Mark Sutherland. Assistant to John Pogue: Suzy McClintock. Executive assistant to Jillian Longnecker: Jason Tamasco. Legal services: Kami Naghdi, Melissa Fish. Titles: Aaron Becker. Creative executives: Aliza James, Jennifer Ruper. Insurance: David Johnstone (Media Insurance Brokers). **Cast:** Jared Harris (Professor Joseph Coupland), Olivia Cooke (Jane Harper), Sam Claflin (Brian McNeil), Erin Richards (Kristina Dalton), Rory Fleck-Byrne (Harry Abrams), Laurie Calvert (Philip), Richard Cunningham (Provost), Aldo Maland (Young David), Max Pirkis (Older David), Tracy Ray (David's Mother), Richard Cunningham (Provost), Eileen Nicholas (Neighbor), Rebecca Scott (Student), Harman Singh (Student), Max Mackintosh (Student), Aretha Ayeh (Student), Ben Holden (Doctor [voice]), Nick Owenford (Professor [uncredited]), Dean Mitchell (Asylum attendant [uncredited]). **DVD availability:** Lionsgate (UK R2 PAL). **Blu-ray availability:** Lionsgate (B/2). **CD availability:** Varese Sarabande, which contains 20 cues, among them *Evey Burning*, *Jane Gets Electrocuted* and *Bathtub Attack*, plus numbers by Slade, T. Rex and Steve Roth

## Quigley, Joe

Quigley can be seen as a boxer in Hammer's *The Flanagan Boy* (1953). His other credits include episodes of *Dixon of Dock Green* (1955–1976, TV), *King of the River* (1966, TV), *Menace* (1970–1973, TV) and *Adam Smith* (1972, TV). **Hammer credits:** *The Flanagan Boy* (1953, as Lou Kossov)

## Quigley, Margaret

Quigley worked as the production secretary on Hammer's *X—The Unknown* (1956). **Hammer credits:** *X—The Unknown* (1956 [uncredited])

## Quigley, Robert

British born Quigley (1913–1989) provided the story for *Last Video and Testament* (1984, TVM [episode of *Hammer House of Mystery and Suspense*]), which was subsequently scripted by Roy Russell. His other credits include a 1980 episode of *Tales of the Unexpected* (1979–1988, TV) titled *I'll Be Seeing You*, for which he again provided the story. **Hammer credits:** *Last Video and Testament* (1984, TVM [episode of *Hammer House of Mystery and Suspense*])

## Quinceharmon

This British vocal group sang the title song for Hammer's *On the Buses* (1971). Briefly signed to EMI in the seventies, their singles and demos include *Sunshine City*, *Mr. Sun*, *Stubborn As a Mule*, *Suddenly the Whole World's Mine*, *Strange Feeling* and *Birminhgam*. **Hammer credits:** *On the Buses* (1971)

## Quinlan, Siobhan

Quinlan makes a belated appearance as Carol, the sister of Nina Baden-Semper's Barbie Reynolds, in Hammer's big screen version of *Love Thy Neighbour* (1973). Her other film credits include *Assault* (1971) and *Steptoe and Son Ride Again* (1973), while her TV credits include episodes of *Budgie* (1971–1972, TV), *Jason King* (1971–1972, TV), *Doctor in Charge* (1972–1973, TV) and *King of Kensington* (1975–1980, TV). **Hammer credits:** *Love Thy Neighbour* (1973, as Carol)

## Quinn, Mary

This British actress (1924–2003) can be spotted as the innkeeper's wife in Hammer's *Rasputin—The Mad Monk* (1966). Mostly on TV, her other credits include episodes of *Private Investigator* (1958–1959, TV), *Gideon's Way* (1965, TV) and *Softly Softly* (1966–1976, TV). **Hammer credits:** *Rasputin—The Mad Monk* (1966, as Innkeeper's wife [uncredited])

## Quinn, Patricia

This Irish actress (1944–, aka Lady Patricia Stephens) is best known for playing Magenta in the original run of the cult stage musical *The Rocky Horror Show* and its subsequent film version, *The Rocky Horror Picture Show* (1975), in the opening scene of which her lips can be seen singing *Science Fiction Double Feature*. In films from 1971 with *Up the Chastity Belt* following experience as a Playboy bunny girl, her other film credits include *Up the Front* (1972), *The Alf Garnett Saga* (1972), *Hawk the Slayer* (1980), *Shock Treatment* (1981), *Monty Python's The Meaning of Life* (1983), *England, My England* (1995), *Mary Horror* (2011) and *The Lords of Salem* (2012). Her TV work includes appearances in *August for the People* (1963, TVM), *I, Claudius* (1976, TV), in which she played Livilla, *The Professionals* (1977–1983, TV) and *Witching Time*, an episode of *Hammer House of Horror* (1980, TV), in which she played a mischievous witch from the seventeenth century who disturbs the life of a modern day film composer (some sources state that Kate O'Mara was the original choice for the role). In 1995, she was briefly married to the actor Sir Robert Stephens (1931–1995) just before his death. She was formerly married to the actor Don Hawkins (1943–). Her son is the actor Quinn Hawkins (1971–) and her nephew is the musician Johnny Quinn of Snow Patrol fame. **Hammer credits:** *Witching Time* (1980, TV [episode of *Hammer House of Horror*], as Lucinda Jessop)

## Quinn, Tony

This Irish supporting actor (1899–1967) played the role of Professor Hawkley in the Hammer second feature *The Runaway* (1964). On stage from the age of twenty following experience as an office clerk, he went on to appear at the famous Abbey Theater. On the London stage from 1927 and in British films from 1934 with *Lest We Forget*, he went on to appear in over fifty films, among them *Just William* (1939), *Hungry Hill* (1946), *The Secret*

*Tent* (1956), *The Trunk* (1961) and *Rotten to the Core* (1965). He was also an expert on military history. **Hammer credits:** *The Runaway* (1964, as Professor Hawkley)

**Quitak, Oscar**

Best remembered by Hammer fans for playing the disfigured dwarf in *The Revenge of Frankenstein* (1958), this British character actor (1926–, full name Morris Oscar Quitak) can be seen in many other films, among them *The Guinea Pig* (1948), *Top of the Form* (1953), *The Traitor* (1957), *Operation Amsterdam* (1958) and *Brazil* (1985). Also busy in television, his many credits here include episodes of *Interpol Calling* (1959, TV), *Paul Temple* (1969–1971, TV), *Holocaust* (1978, TV) and *Hammer House of Mystery and Suspense* (1984, TVM). His wife is actress Andree Melly (1932–), whom he married in 1964, and who appeared in Hammer's *The Brides of Dracula* (1960). Remembered Quitak of appearing with Peter Cushing on *The Revenge of Frankenstein*, "He was wonderful to work with. He was always prepared for every shot, a complete perfectionist."[33] **Hammer credits:** *The Revenge of Frankenstein* (1958, as Dwarf/Karl), *Black Carrion* (1984, TVM [episode of *Hammer House of Mystery and Suspense*], as Estate manager)

---

# R

---

*A Race for Life* see *Mask of Dust*

**Race, R.**

Race worked as a stagehand on Hammer's *The Satanic Rites of Dracula* (1974). **Hammer credits:** *The Satanic Rites of Dracula* (1974 [uncredited])

**Radd, Ronald**

Best remembered for playing the sadistic POW commandant Colonel Yamamitsu in Hammer's *The Camp on Blood Island*, which marked his big screen debut, this British character actor (1929–1976) can also be seen in such diverse productions as *The Small World of Sammy Lee* (1963), *Where the Spies Are* (1965), *Mister Ten Per Cent* (1966), *The Seagull* (1968), *The Offence* (1972) and *The Spiral Staircase* (1975). He also appeared in an episode of Hammer's *Journey to the Unknown* (1968, TV). His other TV work includes episodes of *Treasure Island* (1957, TV), *HMS Paradise* (1964–1965, TV), in which he played CPO Banyard, *Callan* (1967–1972, TV), *The Main Chance* (1969–1975, TV) and *Hunter's Walk* (1973–1976, TV). Also on stage, he worked in both the West End and on Broadway. **Hammer credits:** *The Camp on Blood Island* (1958, as Colonel Yamamitsu), *Stranger in the Family* (1968, TV [episode of *Journey to the Unknown*], as Wally Gold)

**Rae, John**

This British (Scottish) supporting actor (1895–1977) can be seen as E.J. McLeod, the charge-hand welder of the alien plant in Hammer's *Quatermass 2* (1957), a role he also played in the 1955 TV series (albeit as E.G. McLeod). He also played one of the Yeti in Hammer's *The Abominable Snowman* (1957)—or rather, his eyes were featured in one of the close-ups. On stage from 1918, Rae's other film credits include *Neutral Port* (1940), *The Brave Don't Cry* (1952), *The Bridal Path* (1959), *Morgan: A Suitable Case for Treatment* (1966) and *Oh! What a Lovely War* (1969). His TV work includes episodes of *Count Albany* (1938, TV), *Twelfth Night* (1939, TV), *Quatermass and the Pit* (1958–1959, TV), *Gideon's Way* (1965–1966, TV) and *Bouquet of Barbed Wire* (1976, TV). **Hammer credits:** *Quatermass 2* (1957, as E.J. McLeod), *The Abominable Snowman* (1957), as Yeti [eyes, uncredited])

**Rafat, Soraya**

This Oriental supporting actress played a hostess in Hammer's *Visa to Canton* (1960). Her other credits include *Up to His Neck* (1955) and *Design for Loving* (1962), plus episodes of *The Adventures of Robin Hood* (1955–1960, TV), *Z Cars* (1962–1978, TV), *The Indian Tales of Rudyard Kipling* (1964, TV) and *The Mind of the Enemy* (1965, TV). **Hammer credits:** *Visa to Canton* (1960, as Hostess [uncredited])

**Raffin, Deborah**

This American leading lady (1953–2012) appeared in a handful of reasonably high profile films in the mid-seventies before becoming more of a television staple. Her big screen credits include *Forty Carats* (1973), *The Dove* (1974), *The Sentinel* (1977), *Touched by Love* (1980), *Death Wish 3* (1986) and *Morning Glory* (1993), the latter of which she also co-wrote. Her television work (movies and series) includes *Nightmare in Badham County* (1976, TVM), *Ski Lift to Death* (1978, TVM), *Willa* (1978, TVM), *Lace II* (1985, TV), *Noble House* (1987, TVM), *7th Heaven* (1996–2007, TV) and *The Secret Life of the American Teenager* (2008–2013, TV), plus an episode of *Hammer House of Mystery and Suspense* (1984, TVM), in which she plays a faithless wife out to kill her older husband for his money and business (Raffin was a last minute replacement for Carol Lynley). Her credits as a producer or executive producer include *Home Song* (1996, TVM), *Family Blessings* (1996, TVM), which she also co-directed, *Unwed Father* (1997, TVM), *Wilde* (1997) and *Futuresport* (1998, TVM). Raffin's mother was the actress Trudy Marshall (1920–2004). Her husband was the producer Michael Viner (1944–2009), to whom she was married between 1974 and 2005, and in several of whose films she appeared, and with whom she also founded and ran Dove audio books—named after her 1974 film—between 1985 and 1997. **Hammer credits:** *Last Video and Testament* (1984, TVM [episode of *Hammer House of Mystery and Suspense*], as Selina Frankham)

**Raglan, James**

This British supporting actor (1901–1961) played the role of Lord Armadale in Hammer's second Dick Barton picture, *Dick Barton Strikes Back* (1949). This led to a further three appearances for the company. His other films include *The Forger* (1928), *Rolling Home* (1935), *The Black Rider* (1954) and *Chain of Events* (1958), plus episodes of such TV series as *The Secret Garden* (1952, TV) and *No Hiding Place* (1959–1967, TV). His wife was actress Daphne Raglan (1912–1999, maiden name Daphne Gardner Lewis), whom he married in 1931. **Hammer credits:** *Dick Barton Strikes Back* (1949, as Lord Armadale), *Dr. Morelle—The Case of the Missing Heiress* (1949, unnamed role [uncredited]), *Celia* (1949, as Inspector Parker), *Whispering Smith Hits London* (1952, as Superintendent Meaker)

**Raglan, Robert**

Frequently cast as authority figures (especially policemen and military officers), this British character actor (1909–1985) played the role of Colonel Hammett in Hammer's *Slave Girls* (1968). In films from 1946 with *The Courtneys of Curzon Street*, his other sixty-plus credits include *The Ringer* (1952), *Private's Progress* (1956), *A Night to Remember* (1958), *Jigsaw* (1962), *Loot* (1970), *Catch Me a Spy* (1971) and *The Mirror Crack'd* (1980), plus countless television appearances, among them episodes of *Douglas Fairbanks, Jr. Presents* (1953–1957, TV), *Dad's Army* (1968–1977, TV), in which he played Colonel Pritchard, *The Adventurer* (1972–1973, TV) and *Shelley* (1979–1983, TV). **Hammer credits:** *Slave Girls* (1968, as Colonel Hammett)

**Raikes, Robert**

Raikes played a lab assistant in Hammer's second Quatermass film. His other credits include *That Woman Opposite* (1957), *Account Rendered* (1957), *Battle of the V-1* (1958), *Links of Justice* (1958) and *Top Floor Girl* (1959), plus episodes of *Saber of London* (1954–1960, TV), *As I Was Saying* (1955, TV) and *The Adventures of Robin Hood* (1955–1960, TV). **Hammer credits:** *Quatermass 2* (1957, as Second lab assistant)

**Railton, Douglas**

One of Hammer's publicity directors, Railton joined the company in 1957 and worked on the campaigns for *The Camp on Blood Island* (1958) and *Dracula* (1958) among others. Prior to this, he worked as a journalist on such publications as *Today's Cinema*, for which in 1954 he was responsible for a glowing eight-page feature devoted to Exclusive's 20th anniversary (which no doubt stood him in good stead with his future employers). **Hammer credits include:** *The Camp on Blood Island* (1958 [uncredited]), *Dracula* (1958 [uncredited])

**Rainer, Jean**

Rainer appeared as one of the harem girls in the Hammer comedy *I Only Arsked!* (1958). **Hammer credits:** *I Only Arsked!* (1958, as Harem girl [uncredited])

**Raines, Cristina**

Born in the Philippines, this glamorous actress (1952–, real name Cristina L. Herazo) worked in film and television on both sides of the Atlantic in the seventies and eighties. Her TV work includes *Flamingo Road* (1980–1981, TV), in which she played Lane Ballou, and *The Late Nancy Irving* (1984, TVM [episode of *Hammer House of Mystery and Suspense*]), in which she played the title character. Her big screen credits take in *Hex* (1973), *Russian Roulette* (1975), *Nashville* (1975), *The Duellists* (1977), *Silver Dream Racer* (1980), *Real*

*Life* (1983) and *North Shore* (1987). Her other TV work includes episodes of *Movin' On* (1974–1976, TV), *Simon & Simon* (1981–1988, TV), *Quo Vadis?* (1985, TV) and *Hardball* (1989–1990, TV). Her husband is the writer, producer and director Christopher Crowe (1948–), whom she married in 1986. **Hammer credits:** *The Late Nancy Irving* (1984, TVM [episode of *Hammer House of Mystery and Suspense*], as Nancy Irving)

## Rakoff, Alvin

Long resident in Britain, this Canadian director and producer (1927–) is best known for his television work, which, following brief experience as a journalist, began in the early fifties, first at the CBC (Canadian Broadcasting Company) and then the BBC, where he directed acclaimed versions of *Waiting for Gillian* (1954, TV), which won him the National Television Award, *Requiem for a Heavyweight* (1957, TV) and *The Caine Mutiny Court Martial* (1958, TV). He went on to helm a number of variable big screen productions, among them *Passport to Shame* (1958), *The Comedy Man* (1964), *Crossplot* (1969), *Hoffman* (1970) and *City on Fire* (1979). His other better-regarded TV work includes *Don Quixote* (1972, TV), *Shades of Greene* (1975–1976, TV), which earned him a BAFTA nomination for best single play (the episode *Cheap in August* [1975, TV]), *A Voyage Round My Father* (1982, TVM), which earned him a BAFTA nomination for best single drama, *Mr. Halpern and Mr. Johnson* (1983, TV), *Paradise Postponed* (1986, TV), which earned him a shared BAFTA nomination for best drama series, and *A Dance to the Music of Time* (1997, TV). Also a writer and adapter (either solo or with others), his credits here include *A Flight of Fancy* (1952, TV), *The Troubled Air* (1953, TV), *Say Hello to Yesterday* (1970), which he also directed, plus uncredited contributions to Hammer's *The Curse of the Mummy's Tomb* (1964), which was otherwise penned by Michael Carreras (working as Henry Younger). He began directing Bette Davis in Hammer's adaptation of the stage hit *The Anniversary* (1968), but was replaced by Roy Ward Baker after one week following "artistic differences" with the Hollywood actress. Recalled Rakoff, "I was a very young director, and she was certainly the alpha female—very dominant…. When we first met we got on very well…. She immediately said to me that I reminded her of [her former husband] Gary Merrill…. I should have taken it as an omen…. The producers did say, when we first started to disagree with each other, 'In the event of a row, Alvin, you're not going to be the survivor.' And the row did happen. The megastar and the young director have a row, and the megastar wins. It's not really surprising when you think about it."[1] As for the finished film, he described it as, "a mess of a film built around Davis's foolish, overbaked posturings and camera-hoggings."[2] No sour grapes there, then.

Rakoff's first wife was the actress Jacqueline Hill (1929–1993), whom he married in 1958. His second wife is actress Sally Hughes, whom he married in 2013. **Hammer credits:** *The Curse of the Mummy's Tomb* (1964, co-screenplay [uncredited]), *The Anniversary* (1968, director [removed])

## Rambaut, Richard

This British designer (1938–1974) worked as the chief draughtsman on Hammer's *Vampire Circus* (1972), following which he graduated to assistant art director on *Straight on Till Morning* (1972). His other credits as a draughtsman include *The Charge of the Light Brigade* (1968), *Alfred the Great* (1969) and *O Lucky Man!* (1973), while his credits as an assistant art director include *Rocket to the Moon* (1967), *The Virgin Soldiers* (1969), *The Wicker Man* (1973) and *The Romantic English-woman* (1975). His credits as an art director include *The Touchables* (1968), *Bleak Moments* (1971), *S*P*Y*S* (1974) and *Galileo* (1975). **Hammer credits:** *Vampire Circus* (1972, chief draughtsman [uncredited]), *Straight on Till Morning* (1972, assistant art director)

## Ramsden, Dennis

This British actor (1918–2018) played the role of the fake medium Mrs. Hubbard (in highly convincing drag) in *The Indian Spirit Guide*, an episode of Hammer's *Journey to the Unknown* (1968, TV), which also appeared in the compendium film *Journey to Midnight* (1968, TVM). His other TV work includes episodes of *The Plane Makers* (1963–1965, TV), *Bless This House* (1971–1976, TV) and *As Time Goes By* (1992–2005, TV), while his occasional film credits take in *The Intrepid Mr. Twigg* (1968), *Romance with a Double Bass* (1974), *George and Mildred* (1980) and *Run for Your Wife* (2012). Also on stage. **Hammer credits:** *The Indian Spirit Guide* (1968, TV [episode of *Journey to the Unknown*], as Mrs. Hubbard), *Journey to Midnight* (1968, TVM, as Mrs. Hubbard)

## Ranasinghe, Don

Ranasinghe (1928–1978) worked as the sound editor on Hammer's *Frankenstein Must Be Destroyed* (1969). His other credits in this capacity include *The Tomb of Ligeia* (1964) and *The Guru* (1969). He also worked as an assembly editor on *That Riviera Touch* (1966), as an assistant editor on *Press for Time* (1966), and as a dialogue editor on *Figures in a Landscape* (1970). **Hammer credits:** *Frankenstein Must Be Destroyed* (1969)

## Randall, Freddy

This British bandleader and trumpet player (1921–1999) appeared with his orchestra in the Hammer featurette *Parade of the Bands* (1956). A big name in the fifties on the traditional jazz scene, he also performed with such groups as The Saint Louis Four (which was his own first band, formed in 1939), Albert Bale's Darktown Strutters and Will De Barr's Band. His TV credits include episodes of *Say It with Music* (1957, TV) and *Six-Five Special* (1957–1958, TV). **Hammer credits:** *Parade of the Bands* (1956, as Himself)

## Randall, June

British born Randall (1927–2015) joined Hammer as a continuity girl on *X—The Unknown* (1956), after which she worked for the company periodically over the years. She began as an assistant continuity girl on *Dear Murderer* (1947), *When the Bough Breaks* (1947) and *Miranda* (1948), graduating to full continuity girl/script supervisor on *The Blind Goddess* (1948). Her many other credits, among them five Bond films and three for director Stanley Kubrick, include *Quartet* (1948), *That Woman Opposite* (1957), *Circus of Horrors* (1960), *Where's Jack?* (1969), *Wuthering Heights* (1970), *A Clockwork Orange* (1971), *Barry Lyndon* (1975), *The Spy Who Loved Me* (1977), *The Shining* (1980), *Flash Gordon* (1980), *Outland* (1981), *Gandhi* (1982), *A View to a Kill* (1985), *The Living Daylights* (1987), *Licence to Kill* (1989), *Alien*[3] (1992), *GoldenEye* (1995), *Tom's Midnight Garden* (1999) and *Back to the Secret Garden* (2001), plus thirty-five episodes of *The Avengers* (1961–1969, TV), twenty-four episodes of *The Saint* (1962–1969, TV) and twelve episodes of *Tales from the Crypt* (1989–1996, TV).

Remembered Randall of working with director Robert Young on Hammer's *Vampire Circus* (1972), "Robert Young was very nice. He was the only director I've ever worked with who went out and bought me a sandwich in the lunch hour…. He had a tough time on that because of [producer] Wilbur Stark. It was a hard film because it had such a short schedule and he had to quickly get out all these crowd scenes and so on."[3] Meanwhile, of working with Brian Clemens on *Captain Kronos—Vampire Hunter* (1974), she recalled, "Brian Clemens was brilliant. It was one of the happiest films I've ever worked on…. I enjoyed working on it because Brian Clemens is a very nice man and is a wonderful writer."[4] **Hammer credits:** *X—The Unknown* (1956), *Quatermass 2* (1957), *Sands of the Desert* (1960), *The Anniversary* (1968), *The Devil Rides Out* (1968), *Vampire Circus* (1972), *Captain Kronos—Vampire Hunter* (1974)

## Randall, Stephanie

Born in South Africa, Randall (1942–) played the role of Amyak in Hammer's *Slave Girls* (1968). Her other credits include episodes of *No Hiding Place* (1959–1967, TV), *Riviera Police* (1965, TV), *Legend of Death* (1965, TV) and *The Prisoner* (1967–1968, TV). **Hammer credits:** *Slave Girls* (1968, as Amyak)

## Randall, Walter

Randall (1919–) played a walk-on role in Hammer's *The Terror of the Tongs* (1961). His other credits include *Nudist Paradise* (1958), *The Hand* (1960), *The Secret of Monte Cristo* (1961) and *Tiffany Jones* (1973), plus episodes of *Quatermass and the Pit* (1958–1959, TV), *Doctor Who* (1963–1989, TV), *Go Girl* (1970, TV) and *Yes Minister* (1980–1984, TV). **Hammer credits:** *The Terror of the Tongs* (1961, unnamed role [uncredited])

## Rank Film

Named after the British flour magnate J. (Joseph) Arthur Rank (1888–1972, aka Lord Rank), Rank Film gradually came into being in the late thirties following Rank's initial promotion of religious films in 1933 (he was a devout Methodist) via the Religious Film Society. He subsequently became involved in mainstream cinema in 1935 with the formation of GFD (General Film Distributors), in which he invested substantially. GFD handled the releases of several lower berth British production companies, among them Hammer, for which it released their second film, *The Mystery of the Mary Celeste* (1935).

Further investment by Rank, this time in the General Cinema Finance Corporation (which had a stake in Universal, and with which GFD soon after merged) followed in 1936. By this time, Rank had also entered production with *Turn of the Tide* (1935), which led to the building of Pinewood Studios in 1936 (which, like Bray Studios, was centerd round a country house, Heatherden Hall). In 1937, Rank became chairman of Pinewood following his buyout of other investors. The same year he also acquired Denham Studios, while in 1938 he invested heavily in Oscar Deutsch's Odeon cinema chain, moving on to its board of directors in 1939. Involvement in several other production companies followed, among them Gaumont-British, Cineguild, Wessex and Two Cities. Consequently, by the early forties, to all intents and purposes, Rank *was* the British film industry.

More recently, The Rank Organization (as it is now known) has diversified into hotels, bowling alleys, printing technology (Xerox) and color processing via Rank Film Laboratories. The latter handled the Technicolor processing of Hammer's *Hands of the Ripper* (1971), the Eastmancolor processing of *Twins of Evil* (1971), the color processing of *Vampire Circus* (1972), for which no color brand is listed, and *Hammer House of Mystery and Suspense* (1984, TVM). Subsequently, film production has petered out, although Rank still remains a major name in distribution in the UK.

J. Arthur Rank remained chairman of his company until 1969, following which he became president for life. He was made a Baron in 1957 for his services to the British film industry. Note that Bombadier Billy Wells, the second muscleman to bang Rank's introductory gong was the same muscleman seen hammering the anvil in Hammer's first screen logo.

Hammer's involvement with Rank has mostly been through distribution, beginning with *The Mummy* (1959), which it released on the ABC circuit. *The Brides of Dracula* (1960) was meanwhile released on Rank's own circuit. Following a break between 1965 and 1971, Rank became involved with Hammer again, distributing several of the company's films in the seventies as well as investing in them. Among these titles were *Countess Dracula* (1971) and *Hands of the Ripper* (1971). Unfortunately, a four-picture deal negotiated by Michael Carreras in 1972 failed to yield any results, despite some of the titles being announced; these were *Village of the Vampires* (aka *Vampire Virgins*), a follow-up to *Twins of Evil* (1971), *Mistress of the Seas* and *Vault of Blood*. A later clip film, *That's Hammer*, proposed in 1978, also fell by the wayside owing to complications in acquiring the rights to the clips, given that Hammer's back catalogue was actually owned by a number of other film companies. However, Rank *did* help to finance and distribute Hammer's last theatrical feature for thirty years, *The Lady Vanishes* (1979), the color for which Rank also processed.

In the mid-nineties, Rank announced plans to make a series of new projects with Hammer, but nothing came of the announcement. **Hammer credits:** *The Mystery of the Mary Celeste* (1935 [care of GFD]), *The Mummy* (1959), *The Brides of Dracula* (1960), *Captain Clegg* (1962), *The Phantom of the Opera* (1962), *Paranoiac* (1963), *The Kiss of the Vampire* (1963), *Nightmare* (1964), *The Evil of Frankenstein* (1964), *The Secret of Blood Island* (1965), *Countess Dracula* (1971), *Hands of the Ripper* (1971), *Twins of Evil* (1971), *Vampire Circus* (1972), *That's Your Funeral* (1973), *The Lady Vanishes* (1979), *Hammer House of Mystery and Suspense* (1984, TVM)

## Rank Film Laboratories  *see*  Rank Film

## Ranson, Malcolm

This British child actor (1947– ) can be seen in the Hammer comedy *Up the Creek* (1958). His other credits include *Gideon's Day* (1958) and *The Piper's Tune* (1962), plus episodes of *Formula for Danger* (1960, TV) and *The Adventures of Tom Sawyer* (1960, TV). He later became a fight arranger and worked on such TV and film productions as *By the Sword Divided* (1983–1985, TV), *Macbeth* (1983, TV), *Edward II* (1991), *Feast of July* (1995), *Twelfth Night* (1996) and *Nicholas Nickleby* (2002). Also much stage work as a fight choreographer, especially Shakespeare. **Hammer credits:** *Up the Creek* (1958, as Boy)

## Raphael, Jimmy

This supporting actor played a patrol guard in Hammer's *The Camp on Blood Island* (1958). His other credits include *More Than Robbery* (1958, TV). **Hammer credits:** *The Camp on Blood Island* (1958, as Patrol [uncredited])

## Rasputin—The Mad Monk

GB, 1966, 91m, Technicolor [UK], DeLuxe [U.S.], CinemaScope [2.10:1], RCA, cert X

The second of four films shot back-to-back by Hammer on the same sets, *Rasputin—The Mad Monk* began filming at Bray on 8 June 1965, just a few days after much the same cast and crew had completed principal photography on *Dracula—Prince of Darkness* (1966) on 4 June. Owing to some judicious scheduling by production manager Ross MacKenzie (who worked on both films), the last two weeks of the *Dracula* shoot had taken place on location in nearby Black Park, as did the first few days of *Rasputin*, thus allowing the studio's carpenters enough time to re-vamp both the interior and exterior sets from the first film in readiness for the start date of the second (for example, the exterior of Castle Dracula became a Russian winter palace, while its basement was transformed into a lively street café).

The idea for a film about Rasputin had actually originated with Hammer character actor George Woodbridge. This was subsequently taken up by Anthony Hinds who, writing as John Elder, fashioned a screenplay about how the Russian monk successfully insinuated his way into the court of Tsar Nicholas II with the help of a compliant courtier, only to come to a violent end when murdered by her brother.

However, the studio had to tread carefully, for in the early thirties, MGM had been successfully sued for a whopping $1m by Prince Yousoupoff, who claimed that though he *had* actually murdered Rasputin, his wife had *not* been raped by the monk, as had been insinuated in the studio's lavishly

A glowering Christopher Lee dominates this British poster for *Rasputin—The Mad Monk* (1966) (**Hammer/Associated British Picture Corporation/Seven Arts/Warner Pathé/Twentieth Century–Fox/Studio Canal**).

mounted historical drama *Rasputin and the Empress* (1932). This had starred the celebrated Barrymore clan: Lionel Barrymore as Rasputin, Ethel Barrymore as Empress Alexandra and John Barrymore as Prince Paul Chegodieff (for which read Yousoupoff). Consequently, by the time Hammer came to make their version of events, Hinds wisely decided to revise his screenplay, initially titled *The Mad Monk* (though an earlier Rasputin project dating from 1961 titled *The Sins of Rasputin* seems to have been the true origin of the Woodbridge idea).

Consequently, Hinds, despite basing his screenplay on two of Yousoupoff's own published books, *Rasputin* and *Lost Splendour*, purposefully changed names and fictionalized most of the characters and events, save for Rasputin himself and the royal family. No doubt hence the arse-covering disclaimer at the top of the script (presumably penned at the insistence of the legal department), which emphatically pointed out that, "This is an entertainment, not a documentary. No attempt has been made at historical accuracy … all the characters and incidents may be regarded as fictitious." The completed script was then sent to Yousoupoff and his legal representatives for approval (Yousoupoff was apparently required to sign every page in a bid to guarantee that no legal action would follow). The resultant film is therefore less a historical docudrama and more a costume charade embellished with moments of sex and horror, among the latter that old Hammer standby, a severed hand. Yousoupoff may have passed the script for filming, but the BBFC did not, requesting a number of revisions regarding the story's inherent sadism. Nevertheless, the production retained enough implied sex and violence to make it a marketable commodity.

There was only one Hammer star who could have played Rasputin convincingly, and that was Christopher Lee, who was duly offered the tantalizing role, the only proviso being that he also resurrect the role of Dracula in *Dracula—Prince of Darkness*. Lee had long resisted the studio's pleas to revive the character over fears of being typecast, yet the chance to play Rasputin (along with the added enticement of a percentage of the producer's gross on both films) proved too strong a temptation to resist, and the actor duly signed on the dotted line (Lee had been fascinated by the character since childhood, during which he had been introduced to Rasputin's assassins; he'd also met Rasputin's daughter as well as the troublesome Yousoupoff and his co-conspirator, the Grand Duke Dimitry Pavlovich).

In addition to Lee, a number of his co-stars from the *Dracula* sequel also returned, among them Barbara Shelley as Sonia Vasilivitch (the courtier who helps the monk insinuate his way into the lives of the royal family), Francis Matthews as Ivan Kesnikov (who pushes Rasputin to his death from a window) and Suzan Farmer as Kesnikov's sister Vanessa. New to the cast were Dinsdale Landen as Peter Vasilivitch, Richard Pasco as Dr. Boris Zargo and Renee Asherson as the Tsarina. Meanwhile, behind the cameras, the technical crew remained much the same, save for the director, Terence Fisher, who handed the baton to Don Sharp.

Sadly, production on *Rasputin* was hobbled from the start, given that $25,000 had to be slashed from the already tight budget. This was a direct result of Hammer having to acquire the rights to their original production of *Dracula* (1958), so as to be able to use a lengthy re-cap clip from it in the sequel. Consequently, scenes in *Rasputin* had to be either cut or re-shaped so as to accommodate this financial cutback. Among the losses were a lavish ballroom sequence, and additional café and monastery scenes (note that a clip from the ballroom scene in Fox's *Anastasia* [1956], also shot in the Cinema-Scope format, is briefly featured to give the film a sense of scale). Recalled Don Sharp of the film's injurious cutbacks, "Tony Hinds came to me and said we were running over budget and asked for input on scenes that had to be cut to compensate. So we ended up losing a whole ballroom set and cutting scenes involving the Tzar's court."[5]

Unfortunately, the limited budget is all too obvious in the finished film, which lacks the scope and period opulence required in the telling of such a story. The treatment also falls between two stools, being neither a faithful representation of the facts nor an out-and-out horror film in the Hammer tradition. *Variety* described the movie as "a somewhat fanciful and unbelievable approach to the subject," despite the trailer's erroneous claim that it was at last telling "the real, shocking story," making one wonder if Yousoupoff had seen and signed the script for the trailer. The cramped confines of Bray were also pushed to their limits to accommodate all the sets. Recalled clapper boy Christopher Neame, "A large café set … was built in the converted workshop with its sides standing about six inches from the 'stage' walls. Of course, such a thing would be illegal today, and it probably was then…. The fire risk was greater still for a scene that took place in a barn. The set was put up in the old dining-room stage. Straw was scattered liberally around, and the action called for one of the characters to overturn an oil lamp, thereby starting a fire. It's hardly believable that we could have done that."[6]

In addition to the problems encountered on set, the finished film was further harmed by some rather awkward post-production work, which hurriedly followed the completion of principal photography on 20 July 1965. For example, the climactic fight between Kensikov, Zargo and Rasputin, which took three days to shoot, was trimmed back to its bare bones, resulting in a number of continuity discrepancies in the final cut. A number of emasculating trims were also demanded by the BBFC, which further compromised the narrative flow of the film (a sequence in which Rasputin throws acid into the face of Peter Vasilivitch caused particular problems, as did Sonia's suicide). Yet despite its drawbacks, the finished product still manages to compel for much of its running time, thanks primarily to the mesmerizing performance of Christopher Lee as Rasputin, whom he portrays with his customary authority. With his basso voice, wild hair and commanding presence, the actor dominates every scene he appears in, delivering his lines with relish ("When I go to confession, I don't offer God small sins: petty squabbles, jealousy. I offer Him sins worth forgiving," he informs his bishop after having been caught drinking and wenching). Avoiding ham and pantomime villainy, Lee presents a fully rounded and believable character that remains one of the high points of his career. The film also benefits greatly from Don Sharp's staging, which presents Bernard Robinson's sets to their best advantage, despite the budgetary cutbacks. The supporting cast, in particular Barbara Shelley as the vulnerable Sonia, and Richard Pasco as Rasputin's friend Dr. Zargo, also attack their roles with conviction, while Don Banks' robust score at least provides the film with an epic sound.

Yet the whiff of failure seemed to be in the air, and despite a poster campaign that encouraged audiences to "Scream through every second of them!" *Rasputin—The Mad Monk* met with a less than rapturous reception when it was released in the UK on the ABC circuit by Warner Pathé on 6 March 1966 with *The Reptile* (1966), both of which had been trade shown at Studio One on 14 February. This double bill crossed the Atlantic a month later where it was released on 6 April by Twentieth Century–Fox, which promoted the main feature by giving away free Rasputin beards—blue for the boys, pink for the girls. "Use the beard to get the younger crowd into the theater. Youth nowadays are particularly susceptible to weird hair-dos and the beatnik look," commented the somewhat patronizing pressbook to prospective cinema managers.

Critical reaction was generally mixed, with the majority of the praise being reserved for Lee's performance. "In his best part for ages, Christopher Lee gives his best performance," exclaimed *The Daily Cinema*, an opinion that was reflected in *Kinematograph Weekly*, which claimed that the actor "gives probably his best performance yet in a career spattered with monsters and eccentrics." Director Don Sharp also rated Lee's work in the film: "It was a lovely performance, wasn't it? He was very enthusiastic about it. We had to spend a little time together up front, working out how we were going to do all those hypnosis sequences. But once we'd worked out how to do them, things went fine. He was tremendous, so magnetic in it."[7]

Lee himself was likewise proud of his work. "I felt at the time that Rasputin was my best played role,"[8] he commented, but had some reservations about the film itself: "We only had ninety minutes to tell a story, and a great deal had to be left out. This was also due to the budget. The film gave no sense of court life or of life in the city streets. It did, however, capture something of the peasants in the country. I tried to emphasize Rasputin's power over the people in his circle—both men and women—and the mystery of him."[9] No doubt hence the trailer's description of the character as "History's man of mystery."

A major disappointment for all concerned, *Rasputin—The Mad Monk* failed to exploit its considerable potential, and remains one of Hammer's unsung films from this period. **Additional notes:** Rasputin has also been featured in a number of other films, among them *The Fall of the Romanoffs* (1917), *Rasputin* (1930, 1938, 1996, TVM and 2010), *The Night They Killed Rasputin* (1960), *I Killed Rasputin* (1967), *Nicholas and Alexandra*

(1971), *Anastasia* (1997), *Killing Rasputin* (2003) and *Raspoutine* (2011, TVM). *Rasputin and the Empress* (1932) was known in some territories as *Rasputin the Mad Monk*. As for Prince Yououpoff, he died on 27 September 1967, a year-and-a-half after the UK release of the Hammer film; he was eighty. Litigious to the last, in 1965 he unsuccessfully sued the American television network CBS over yet another Rasputin project, a half-hour play titled *If I Should Die* (1963, TV), the legal wrangling over which Hammer's lawyers and executives—and particularly Anthony Hinds—paid special attention to. Dinsdale Landen is mistakenly credited as Nicholas Pennell in the film's American press book (Pennell never actually worked for Hammer). The film's screenplay was novelized by John Burke for *The Second Hammer Horror Film Omnibus* (1967), which was published by Pan. It also sounds like Bartlett Mullins' wagoner (referred to by Rasputin as "little father") has been re-voiced by Michael Ripper. Coincidentally, not only did George Woodbridge *not* appear in *Rasputin*, following a brief appearance in *The Reptile*, he never worked for Hammer again.

**Ra-Ra-Rasputin. Distinctive American artwork for *Rasputin—The Mad Monk* (1966), complete with beard giveaway promo (Hammer/Associated British Picture Corporation/Seven Arts/Warner Pathé/Twentieth Century–Fox/Studio Canal).**

Production companies: Hammer/Seven Arts/Associated British Picture Corporation. Distributors: Warner Pathé Distributors (UK [ABC circuit]), Twentieth Century–Fox (U.S.). Producer: Anthony Nelson Keys. Director: Don Sharp. Screenplay: John Elder (Anthony Hinds). Cinematographer: Michael Reed. Music: Don Banks. Music director: Philip Martell. Supervising editor: James Needs. Editor: Roy Hyde. Production design: Bernard Robinson. Art director: Don Mingaye. Costumes: Rosemary Burrows. Make-up: Roy Ashton. Hair: Frieda Steiger. Production manager: Ross MacKenzie. Assistant director: Bert Batt. Second assistant director: Hugh Harlow [uncredited]. Camera operator: Cece Cooney. Clapper boy: Christopher Neame [uncredited]. Sound: Ken Rawkins. Sound editor: Roy Baker. Choreographer: Alan Beall [uncredited]. Fight arranger: Peter Diamond [uncredited]. Continuity: Lorna Selwyn. Poster: Tom Chantrell [uncredited]. **Cast:** Christopher Lee (Grigori Rasputin), Barbara Shelley (Sonia Vasilivitch), Francis Matthews (Ivan Kesnikov), Suzan Farmer (Vanessa Kesnikov), Richard Pasco (Dr. Boris Zargo), Dinsdale Landen (Peter Vasilivitch), Renée Asherson (Tsarina), Derek Francis (Landlord), Joss Ackland (Bishop), John Bailey (Dr. Ziglov), Alan Tilvern (Patron), Mary Barclay (Superior lady [uncredited]), Michael Cadman (Michael [uncredited]), Fiona Hartford (Tania [uncredited]), Prudence Hyman (Gossip [uncredited]), Michael Godfrey (Doctor [uncredited]), Robert Duncan (Tsarevitch [uncredited]), Lucy Fleming (Wide Eyes [uncredited]), John Welsh (Abbott [uncredited]), Bryan Marshall (Young tough [uncredited]), Bridget McConnell (Gossip [uncredited]), Cyril Shaps (Foxy Face [uncredited]), Leslie White (Cheeky man [uncredited]), Jeremy Young (Court messenger [uncredited]), Maggie Wright (Tart [uncredited]), Helen Christie (Tart [uncredited]), Bartlett Mullins (Wagoner [uncredited], re-voiced by Michael Ripper [uncredited]), Robert McLennan (Dancer [uncredited]), Jay McGrath (Dancer [uncredited]), Veronica Nicholson (Young girl [uncredited]), Mary Quinn (Innkeeper's wife [uncredited]), Fred Peck (Inn patron [uncredited]), Celia Ryder (Fat woman [uncredited]), Ernie Rice (Barman [uncredited]), Robert Rowland (Bar drunk [uncredited]), Brian Wilde (Brute [uncredited]), Terry Richards (Christopher Lee's stunt double [uncredited]). **DVD availability:** Anchor Bay

(U.S. R1 NTSC), extras include a commentary by Christopher Lee, Barbara Shelley, Francis Matthews and Suzan Farmer, a trailer, two TV spots and an episode of *The World of Hammer* (1990 [first broadcast 1994], TV) titled *Hammer Stars: Christopher Lee*, Studio Canal/Warner (UK R2 PAL). **Blu-ray availability:** Studio Canal (B/2), extras include a DVD version of the film, plus two documentaries, *Tall Stories: The Making of Rasputin the Mad Monk* and *Brought to Book: Hammer Novelisations*, a gallery of stills, a commentary by Christopher Lee, Barbara Shelley, Suzan Farmer and Francis Matthews, and an episode of *The World of Hammer* (1990 [first broadcast 1994], TV) titled *Costumers*. **CD availability:** *The Hammer Film Music Collection: Volume Two* (GDI Records), which contains the *Main Title*

## Raven, Mike

Following experience as a ballet dancer, bit player, theater production manager, author and radio deejay (for Radio Atlanta, Radio Luxembourg and Radio One), this British actor (1924–1997, real name Austin Churton Fairman, aka Churton Fairman) made a bid to become a horror star in the early seventies. As such, he made his debut in Hammer's *Lust for a Vampire* (1971) as Count Karnstein, having arranged an introduction with the film's producers, Harry Fine and Michael Style, via the photographer Philip Stearns, who was a mutual acquaintance. Clearly enthused by the role, Raven even set about re-writing a black magic incantation spoken by his character. Recalled the actor: "I sewed several spells together, so we wouldn't get any unwanted additions to the cast on set!"[10]

Recalled co-star Suzanna Leigh of Raven: "He was sooo *intense*! Oh, God! And he knew everything about the whole occult business and *everything*! For him it was *very* serious—there was no tongue in cheek *there*!"[11] Unfortunately, much to his consternation, Raven was re-voiced by Valentine Dyall, while close-ups of his character's bloodshot eyes were actually stock footage of Christopher Lee's eyes taken from *Dracula Has Risen from the Grave* (1968). Commented the actor of being re-voiced, "That horrified me more than anything in the entire film!"[12] As for his role, he recalled, "I didn't want the character to actually be a vampire; I wanted him to appear as the Devil's emissary—or an agent of evil, if you like. I saw him as a puppet master with Yutte as the puppet."[13]

After Hammer failed to show any interested in *Disciple of Death*, a script he had written about Satanic worship, Raven turned his back on the company. He subsequently went on to appear in *I, Monster* (1971), in which he co-starred with Christopher Lee and Peter Cushing, and *Crucible of Terror* (1971), in which he played the lead. He then personally helped to finance *Disciple of Death* (1972), which, with the film's director Tom Parkinson, he went on to write and produce (as Churton Fairman). He also played the lead role. Sadly, by this time it was clear that Raven was failing to click with audiences, and so he retired from the screen to a hill farm in Cornwall, where he became a sheep farmer. Raven's other screen credits include a bit part in *On Approval* (1943), plus episodes of *Free for All* (1968–1969, TV) and *2Gs and the Pop People* (1972, TV). His mother was the actress Hilda Moore (1890–1929). **Additional notes:** In 1971 the Hungarian producer Alexander Paal tried to interest Hammer in a film about the real Dracula, Vlad Tepes, with Mike Raven in the title role, but the idea was turned down by James Carreras, who didn't want to alienate Christopher Lee. **Hammer credits:** *Lust for a Vampire* (1971, as Count Karnstein)

### Rawkins, Ken

This prolific British sound technician (1918–1971, full name Kenneth George Rawkins) recorded the sound for the Hammer thriller *Paranoiac* (1963), which led to a run of further assignments with the studio. His other credits include work in the dubbing suites for *Caesar and Cleopatra* (1945) and *Men of Two Worlds* (1946), following which he became a sound recordist/sound camera operator on such films as *The Woman in Question* (1950), *The Story of Robin Hood and His Merrie Men* (1952), *Siege of the Saxons* (1963), *The City Under the Sea* (1965), *Die, Monster, Die!* (1965), *Torture Garden* (1967), *The Deadly Bees* (1966), *Journey to the Far Side of the Sun* (1969) and *Some Will, Some Won't* (1969), plus episodes of *The Avengers* (1961–1969, TV) and *UFO* (1970–1971, TV). **Hammer credits:** *Paranoiac* (1963), *The Kiss of the Vampire* (1963), *The Scarlet Blade* (1963), *Nightmare* (1964), *The Devil-Ship Pirates* (1964), *The Evil of Frankenstein* (1964), *The Gorgon* (1964), *The Runaway* (1964), *The Secret of Blood Island* (1965), *Fanatic* (1965), *Dracula—Prince of Darkness* (1966), *Rasputin—The Mad Monk* (1966), *The Plague of the Zombies* (1966), *The Witches* (1966), *Frankenstein Created Woman* (1967), *The Mummy's Shroud* (1967), *The Devil Rides Out* (1968), *Dracula Has Risen from the Grave* (1968), *Frankenstein Must Be Destroyed* (1969)

### Rawle, Jeff

This British actor (1951–) can be seen in a minor supporting role in *Charlie Boy* (1980, TV [episode of *Hammer House of Horror*]). Best known for playing the role of Billy Fisher in the TV sitcom *Billy Liar* (1973–1974, TV), his many other TV credits include episodes of *Bedtime Stories* (1974, TV), *Leave It to Charlie* (1978–1980, TV), *Fortunes of War* (1987, TV), *Wycliffe* (1994–1998, TV), *Hollyoaks* (1995–, TV), in which he played Silas Blissett between 2010 and 2011, *Faith in the Future* (1995–1998, TV), in which he played Paul Cooper, *Drop the Dead Donkey* (1990–1998, TV), in which he played George Dent, *William and Mary* (2003–2005, TV) and *Doc Martin* (2004–, TV), in which he played Roger Fenn. His occasional films include *The Life Story of Baal* (1978), *A Hitch in Time* (1978), *Home Before Midnight* (1979), *Crystal Gazing* (1982), *The Doctor and the Devils* (1985), *Blackball* (2003), *Harry Potter and the Goblet of Fire* (2005), *Trimming Pablo* (2011), *An Adventure in Space and Time* (2013, TVM) and *Redistributors* (2016). He also co-wrote *The Young Poisoner's Handbook* (1995), the short *Mrs. Meitle-*

*meihr* (2002) and the TV series *The Charles Dickens Show* (2012, TV), of which he appeared in the latter. Also much on stage, he is married to the actress Nina Marc, whom he married in 1996. **Hammer credits:** *Charlie Boy* (1980, TV [episode of *Hammer House of Horror*], as Franks)

### Rawlings, Fred (Frederick)

This British supporting actor (1915–2003) appeared in a handful of minor roles for Hammer in the late fifties/early sixties. An occasional writer, he had his story *Do Me a Favor and Kill Me* adapted for an episode of Hammer's *Journey to the Unknown* (1968, TV); this also appeared in the compendium film *Journey to Murder* (1972, TVM). His TV work as an actor meanwhile includes episodes of *The Secret Kingdom* (1960, TV), *Sir Francis Drake* (1961–1962, TV) and *Doctor Who* (1963–1989, TV). **Hammer credits:** *The Mummy* (1959, unnamed role [uncredited]), *The Man Who Could Cheat Death* (1959, as Footman), *Taste of Fear* (1961, as Plainclothesman [uncredited]), *Do Me a Favor and Kill Me* (1968, TV [episode of *Journey to the Unknown*], story), *Journey to Murder* (1972, TVM, story)

### Rawlings, Kay

British born Rawlings (1918–1981, real name Kathleen Muriel Rawlings) worked as the continuity girl on Hammer's Camargue-set thriller *Maniac* (1963), and returned for two later projects. She began her career as a production secretary on *Romeo and Juliet* (1954) and went on to work as a continuity girl on *Zarak* (1956), *Tarzan's Greatest Adventure* (1959), *Born Free* (1966), *You Only Live Twice* (1967 [second unit]), *Venom* (1971), *Endless Night* (1972), *Regan* (1974, TVM), *Superman* (1978), *The Fifth Musketeer* (1979), *The Empire Strikes Back* (1980) and *Venom* (1981). **Hammer credits:** *Maniac* (1963), *Frankenstein and the Monster from Hell* (1974), *The Lady Vanishes* (1979)

### Rawlings, Keith

This British actor (1922–2015) had a supporting role in the Hammer second feature *Delayed Flight* (1964). His other credits include *The Yangtse Incident* (1957) and episodes of *Jennings at School* (1958, TV), *Dixon of Dock Green* (1955–1976, TV), *The Adventures of Robin Hood* (1955–1960, TV) and *Crane* (1963–1965, TV). **Hammer credits:** *Delayed Flight* (1964, as Police Inspector)

### Rawlings, Margaret

Born in Japan, this noted stage actress (1906–1996) spent the majority of her career in the theater, having made her debut in 1927. She did, however, appear in a handful of films, among them Hammer's *Hands of the Ripper* (1971), in which she has a brief but effective scene as the psychic Madame Bullard. Her other film credits include *The Way of Lost Souls* (1929), *Roman Holiday* (1953), *Beautiful Stranger* (1954), *No Road Back* (1956) and *Follow Me* (1972). She also frequently appeared on television from 1947 onwards, her credits include appearances in *Hamlet* (1947, TV), in which she played Gertrude, *ITV Play of the Week* (1955–1968, TV), *Armchair Thriller* (1956–1974,

TV) and *Jekyll & Hyde* (1990, TV). Her first husband (of two) was the actor-manager and poet Gabriel Toyne (1905–1963), to whom she was married between 1927 and 1938. **Hammer credits:** *Hands of the Ripper* (1971, as Madame Bullard)

### Rawlinson, A.R. (Arthur Richard)

The work of this prolific British screenwriter (1894–1984) includes *Leap Year* (1932), *The Third String* (1932), *Aunt Sally* (1933), *The Blarney Stone* (1933), *A Cuckoo in the Nest* (1933), *Jew Suss* (1934), *Lancashire Luck* (1937), *King Solomon's Mines* (1937), *Sexton Blake and the Hooded Terror* (1938), *The Face at the Window* (1939), *The Chinese Bungalow* (1940), *Gaslight* (1940), *This England* (1941) and *Calling Paul Temple* (1948) among others. He also contributed to the script of Hitchcock's original version of *The Man Who Knew Too Much* (1934). He went on to work on a handful of Hammer programers in the late forties/early fifties, among them *Celia* (1949) and *Meet Simon Cherry* (1949). He also provided an unused story synopsis for Hammer's abandoned television series *Tales of Frankenstein* (1958, TV), elements from which later resurfaced in *Frankenstein Created Woman* (1967), which was scripted by Anthony Hinds (working as John Elder). His other credits take in *Paul Temple's Triumph* (1950), *The Black Rider* (1954) and *Goalbreak* (1962), plus episodes of *Douglas Fairbanks, Jr. Presents* (1953–1957, TV), *Amelia* (1961, TV) and *The Indian Tales of Rudyard Kipling* (1963–1964, TV). **Hammer credits:** *Celia* (1949, co-screenplay), *Meet Simon Cherry* (1949, co-screenplay), *Someone at the Door* (1950, screenplay), *What the Butler Saw* (1950, co-screenplay), *Tales of Frankenstein* (1958, TV, unused synopsis, elements from which later resurfaced in Anthony Hinds' script for *Frankenstein Created Woman* [1967]), *Frankenstein Created Woman* (1967, ideas and story elements [uncredited])

### Rawlinson, Brian

This British actor (1931–2000) can be seen as a falconer in Hammer's Robin Hood adventure *Sword of Sherwood Forest* (1960). He began his career on stage in London, following which he went on to appear in such films as *Dangerous Exile* (1957), *No Kidding* (1960), *Carry On Cleo* (1964), *Carry On Cowboy* (1965), *The Big Job* (1965), *Far from the Madding Crowd* (1967), *Blind Terror* (1971) and *Sunday Pursuit* (1990). Also busy on television, he is best known for playing Gaff Guernsay in *The Buccaneers* (1956–1957, TV) and Robert Onedin in *The Onedin Line* (1971–1980, TV). **Hammer credits:** *Sword of Sherwood Forest* (1960, as First falconer [uncredited])

### Ray, Philip (Phil)

This British character actor (1898–1978, real name Roy Edgar Ray) can be seen as the priest who wants to stake the young dead woman before her burial at the beginning of Hammer's *Dracula—Prince of Darkness* (1966). He also played the role of Mayor in *Frankenstein Created Woman* (1967). In films from 1935 following military service and stage experience, his other credits include *Sexton Blake and the Bearded Doctor* (1935), *Jamaica Inn* (1939), *The October Man* (1947), *The Winslow Boy*

(1948), *A Night to Remember* (1958), *Sons and Lovers* (1960) and *The Mind Benders* (1963), plus episodes of *ITV Playhouse* (1955–1967, TV), *Emma* (1960, TV), in which he played Mr. Weston, *Silent Evidence* (1962, TV), *Doctor Who* (1963–1989, TV) and *Public Eye* (1965–1975, TV). He fought in both world wars. **Hammer credits:** *Dracula—Prince of Darkness* (1966, as Priest), *Frankenstein Created Woman* (1967, as Mayor)

### Ray, Raymond

This supporting actor (real name John Raymond Hoole) played Frankenstein's uncle in Hammer's *The Curse of Frankenstein* (1957). His other credits include *The Man Upstairs* (1958), *Mary Had a Little…* (1961), *Nothing Barred* (1961) and *A Jolly Bad Fellow* (1964), plus episodes of *The Buccaneers* (1956–1957, TV), *Z Cars* (1962–1978, TV) and *The Saint* (1962–1969, TV). **Hammer credits:** *The Curse of Frankenstein* (1957, as Uncle)

### The Ray Ellington Quartet *see* Ellington, Ray

### Rayburn, Basil

British born Rayburn (1924–2006) worked as the assistant director on the Hammer thriller *Hysteria* (1965). His other credits include *The Frightened City* (1961), *The Loneliness of the Long Distance Runner* (1962), *The Mind Benders* (1963), *Operation Crossbow* (1965) and *Eye of the Devil* (1966). He went on to become a production and unit supervisor/manager and worked on such films as *The Liquidator* (1965), *Otley* (1968), *The Tamarind Seed* (1974), *The Eagle Has Landed* (1976), *The Watcher in the Woods* (1980) and *Haunted Honeymoon* (1986). He also produced *Dulcima* (1971) and was as an associate producer on *The Belstone Fox* (1973), *The Lords of Discipline* (1983), *Haunted Honeymoon* (1986) and *Bellman and True* (1987). His wife was the agent Joy Jameson. **Hammer credits:** *Hysteria* (1965)

### Raymond, Cyril

Best remembered for playing Celia Johnson's dull husband in *Brief Encounter* (1945), British born Raymond (1899–1973) made his stage debut in 1914 and broke into films two years later with *The Morals of Weybury* (1916). His subsequent films include *While London Sleeps* (1922), *The Shadow* (1933), *The Tunnel* (1935), *Goodbye, Mr. Chips* (1939), *Quartet* (1948), *Angels One Five* (1952), *Dunkirk* (1958) and *Night Train to Paris* (1964), plus episodes of *Saber of London* (1954–1960, TV), *Danger Man* (1960–1962, TV) and *The Plane Makers* (1963–1965, TV). In 1949 he appeared in the "unofficial" Hammer film *Jack of Diamonds*, in which he played Roger Keen, another one of his many dependable husband roles; he also co-wrote the film's screenplay with fellow co-star Nigel Patrick, basing it on a story by "Binnacle." During the war, he was a fighter controller during the Battle of Britain. Married twice, his wives were the actresses Iris Hoey (1885–1979) from 1922 to 1936, and Gillian Lind (1904–1983) from 1937. The latter appeared in Hammer's *Fear in the Night* (1972). **Hammer credits:** *Jack of Diamonds* (1949, as Roger Keen, also co-screenplay)

### Raymond, Gary

In films and television following training at RADA and experience on stage with the RSC, this British actor (1935–) had a handful of high profile screen credits in the late fifties and early sixties, among them *Look Back in Anger* (1959), *Suddenly, Last Summer* (1959), *El Cid* (1961), *The Playboy of the Western World* (1962), *Jason and the Argonauts* (1963) and *The Greatest Story Ever Told* (1965), playing Peter in the latter. His TV work takes in episodes of *Martin Chuzzlewit* (1964, TV), in which he played the title role, *The Rat Patrol* (1966–1968, TV), which he made in America and in which he co-starred as Sergeant Jack Moffitt, *The Persuaders!* (1971–1972, TV), *Scarlett* (1994, TV) and *Victoria & Albert* (2001, TV). He also appeared in *The Two Faces of Evil*, one of the better episodes of *Hammer House of Horror* (1980, TV), in which he played an evil doppelganger to eerie effect (interestingly enough, he has a twin brother himself). His other film credits include *The Foreigner* (2003), *Balzan's Contract* (2011) and *Sex, Marriage and Infidelity* (2014). His wife is the actress Delena Kidd (1935–), whom he married in 1961; their daughter is the actress Emily Raymond (1966–). **Hammer credits:** *The Two Faces of Evil* (1980, TV [episode of *Hammer House of Horror*], as Martin Lewis)

### Raymond, Matthew

Raymond was a board director of Saturn Films, Ltd., which was one of Hammer's many subsidiaries. Raymond held this position for the lifespan of the company (between March 1957 and September 1961), during which it was registered at the MGM Studios in Borehamwood, of which Raymond was the managing director at the time.

### Rayner, Anthony

This British actor (1943–) can be seen as one of the soldiers in Hammer's *Quatermass and the Pit* (1967). His other credits as an actor include *Smashing Time* (1967), *Oliver!* (1968), *Salt & Pepper* (1968), *Mrs. Brown, You've Got a Lovely Daughter* (1968) and *Where Eagles Dare* (1969), plus episodes of *Sat'day While Sunday* (1967, TV) and *Dial M for Murder* (1974, TV). He also worked as an assistant location manager on *Midas Run* (1968). **Hammer credits:** *Quatermass and the Pit* (1967, as Soldier [uncredited])

### Rayner, Henry

This British bit-part player (1915–2005) can be seen as a drunk in Hammer's *Quatermass 2* (1957). His other credits include *The Sex Thief* (1973), plus episodes of *BBC Sunday-Night Theatre* (1950–1959, TV), *On Trial* (1960, TV), *The Avengers* (1961–1969, TV) and *Microbes and Men* (1974, TV). Also on stage. **Hammer credits:** *Quatermass 2* (1957, as Drunk [uncredited])

### Raynor, Sheila

This British actress (1908–1998) had supporting roles in two completely contrasting Hammer productions exactly twenty years apart. Her other credits include *They Knew Mr. Knight* (1946), *Room at the Top* (1958), *October Moth* (1960), *Die, Monster, Die!* (1965), *Dulcima* (1971), *A Clockwork Orange* (1971), *Flame* (1975), *The Omen* (1976) and *Madonna and Child* (1980, TV), plus episodes of *William Tell* (1958–1959, TV), *Lizzie Dripping* (1973–1975, TV) and *Rockliffe's Babies* (1987–1988, TV). **Hammer credits:** *Wings of Danger* (1952, as Nurse), *Demons of the Mind* (1972, as Old crone)

### RCA

RCA has long been an industry staple for the sound recording of motion pictures, and was used on many (though by no means all) Hammer productions. Electronic sound recording dates from 1926, and in 1930, RCA introduced a single track, monaural recording strip on the edge of the optical 35mm filmstrip, which could subsequently be read by the Western Electric 35mm film projector. In 1937, RCA introduced multiple (nine) channel recording for the musical *One Hundred Men and a Girl* (though the film was actually released in mono). In development since 1932, the process was also used on *Fantasia* (1940), on which it was named Fantasound. Further developments followed over the decades, including the introduction of stereo and digital sound. Also see High Fidelity RCA Photophone, which was used to record *Song of Freedom* (1936). **Hammer credits:** *Jack of Diamonds* (1949), *Cloudburst*, (1951), *The Last Page* (1952), *Wings of Danger* (1952), *Whispering Smith Hits London* (1952), *Stolen Face* (1952), *Lady in the Fog* (1952), *Death of an Angel* (1952), *Mantrap* (1953), *Four Sided Triangle* (1953), *The Gambler and the Lady* (1953), *The Saint's Return* (1953), *The Flanagan Boy* (1953), *Spaceways* (1953), *36 Hours* (1953), *Blood Orange* (1953), *Face the Music* (1954), *The House Across the Lake* (1954), *Five Days* (1954), *The Stranger Came Home* (1954), *Life with the Lyons* (1954), *Men of Sherwood Forest* (1954), *Mask of Dust* (1954), *The Lyons in Paris* (1955), *Murder by Proxy* (1955), *The Eric Winstone Bandshow* (1955), *Third Party Risk* (1955), *The Glass Cage* (1955), *Break in the Circle* (1955), *The Right Person* (1956), *A Man on the Beach* (1956), *Women Without Men* (1956), *Copenhagen* (1956), *X—The Unknown* (1956), *Quatermass 2* (1957), *Operation Universe* (1957 [released 1959]), *Adventures with the Lyons* (1957, serial re-issue of *Life with the Lyons*), *The Curse of Frankenstein* (1957), *The Abominable Snowman* (1957), *Danger List* (1957), *The Camp on Blood Island* (1958), *Clean Sweep* (1958), *Dracula* (1958), *The Revenge of Frankenstein* (1958), *Up the Creek* (1958), *Further Up the Creek* (1958), *I Only Arsked!* (1958), *The Snorkel* (1958), *The Hound of the Baskervilles* (1959), *The Man Who Could Cheat Death* (1959), *The Mummy* (1959), *The Stranglers of Bombay* (1959), *Hell Is a City* (1960), *The Two Faces of Dr. Jekyll* (1960), *The Brides of Dracula* (1960), *Sword of Sherwood Forest* (1960), *The Terror of the Tongs* (1960), *Visa to Canton* (1960), *Sands of the Desert* (1960), *Taste of Fear* (1961), *The Curse of the Werewolf* (1961), *Shadow of the Cat* (1961), *Cash of Demand* (1961), *Watch It, Sailor!* (1961), *The Full Treatment* (1961), *The Pirates of Blood River* (1962), *The Phantom of the Opera* (1962), *Captain Clegg* (1962), *Paranoiac* (1963), *The Damned* (1963), *The Kiss of the Vampire* (1963),

*The Old Dark House* (1963), *The Scarlet Blade* (1963), *Nightmare* (1964), *The Devil-Ship Pirates* (1964), *The Evil of Frankenstein* (1964), *The Curse of the Mummy's Tomb* (1964), *The Gorgon* (1964), *The Secret of Blood Island* (1965), *She* (1965), *Fanatic* (1965), *The Nanny* (1965), *The Brigand of Kandahar* (1965), *Dracula—Prince of Darkness* (1966), *Rasputin—The Mad Monk* (1966), *The Plague of the Zombies* (1966), *The Reptile* (1966), *One Million Years B.C.* (1966), *The Witches* (1966), *The Viking Queen* (1967), *The Mummy's Shroud* (1967), *A Challenge for Robin Hood* (1967), *Frankenstein Created Woman* (1967), *Quatermass and the Pit* (1967), *The Vengeance of She* (1968), *Slave Girls* (1968), *The Anniversary* (1968), *The Devil Rides Out* (1968), *The Lost Continent* (1968), *Dracula Has Risen from the Grave* (1968), *Frankenstein Must Be Destroyed* (1969), *Moon Zero Two* (1969), *Crescendo* (1970), *When Dinosaurs Ruled the Earth* (1970), *Taste the Blood of Dracula* (1970), *The Horror of Frankenstein* (1970), *Scars of Dracula* (1970), *Lust for a Vampire* (1970), *Countess Dracula* (1971), *On the Buses* (1971), *Blood from the Mummy's Tomb* (1971), *Dr. Jekyll and Sister Hyde* (1971), *Demons of the Mind* (1972), *Dracula A.D. 1972* (1972), *Fear in the Night* (1972), *Straight on Till Morning* (1972), *Mutiny on the Buses* (1972), *Holiday on the Buses* (1973), *Love Thy Neighbour* (1973), *Captain Kronos—Vampire Hunter* (1974), *The Satanic Rites of Dracula* (1974), *Frankenstein and the Monster from Hell* (1974), *Man About the House* (1974), *To the Devil a Daughter* (1976)

## Rea, Charles

This British actor (1923–1992) can be spotted as a sergeant in Hammer's *The Witches* (1966). His other credits include *The Ipcress File* (1965), plus episodes of *Deadline Midnight* (1960–1961, TV), *Softly Softly* (1966–1976, TV), *Hunter's Walk* (1973–1976, TV), in which he played PC Harry Coombes, and *On the Up* (1990–1992, TV). His wife was actress Felicity Peel (1938–, real name Felicity Marion Peel Corbin), whom he married in 1962. **Hammer credits:** *The Witches* (1966, as Sergeant [uncredited])

## Read, Anthony

A former actor and Fleet Street journalist, this prolific British writer and producer (1935–2015) worked as the story editor on *Hammer House of Horror* (1980, TV). He joined the series on 7 April 1980, and also went on to script one episode, *Witching Time*. His other credits as a story editor include episodes of *The Indian Tales of Rudyard Kipling* (1963–1964, TV), *Doctor Who* (1963–1989, TV), *Detective* (1964–1965, TV) and *The Troubleshooters* (1965–1972), several episodes of the latter of which he also either wrote or produced. His other writing credits include everything from *Z Cars* (1962–1978, TV) to *The Tribe* (1999–2003, TV), while his work as a producer takes in *The Lotus Eaters* (1972–1973, TV) and *The Dragon's Opponent* (1973, TV). He later worked as a historian and author, among his books being *Kristallnacht: The Nazi Night of Terror* (1989) and *The Fall of Berlin* (1993), both written with David Fisher. **Hammer credits:** *Hammer House of Horror*

(1980, TV, story editor), *Witching Time* (1980, TV [episode of *Hammer House of Horror*], teleplay)

## Read, Darryl

This British actor (1951–2013) played the role of El Diablo in Hammer's *The Lost Continent* (1968). His other film credits include *The Young Detectives* (1963), *Five Have a Mystery to Solve* (1964), *River Rivals* (1967), *Great Catherine* (1967) and *Remember a Day* (2002), plus episodes of *Our Man at St. Mark's* (1963–1966, TV), *Rock Follies of '77* (1977, TV) and *Mackenzie* (1980, TV). However, he is better known as a musician, songwriter and recording artist. He appeared in such groups as Krayon Angels and Crushed Butler in the sixties, and went on to become a noted figure in the rock and roll and punk scenes (he is known as the "Modfather of Punk"). His singles include *Play with Fire* (1985) and *Trouble in the House of Love* (1985), while his albums include *Book of the Dead* (1989) and *Beat Existentialist* (1992), the latter with The Hornets. **Hammer credits:** *The Lost Continent* (1968, as El Diablo)

## Read, Dolly

This pretty British actress and model (1944–, aka Margaret Read and Dolly Martin) played one of Dr. Ravna's disciples in Hammer's *The Kiss of the Vampire* (1963). She made a few more minor appearances in Britain, in the likes of *Dixon of Dock Green* (1955–1976, TV) and *Tonite Let's All Make Love in London* (1967), though by the time the latter was released she'd already moved to America where, in addition to becoming a Playboy Playmate of the Month (May 1966), she went on to appear in such movies as *That Tender Touch* (1969) and *Beyond the Valley of the Dolls* (1970), in which she played Kelly MacNamara, and episodes of such TV series as *The Match Game* (1973–1982, 1990–1991,TV), *Tattletales* (1974–1978, TV), *Charlie's Angels* (1976–1981, TV), *Vegas* (1978–1981, TV), *Fantasy Island* (1978–1984, TV) and *TV's Funniest Game Show Moments* (1984, TV). In 1971, she married comedian Dick Martin (1922–2008, full name Thomas Richard Martin) of Rowan and Martin fame; they divorced in 1975, but re-married in 1978, and remained so until his death. **Hammer credits:** *The Kiss of the Vampire* (1963, as Disciple [uncredited])

## Read, Jan

Briefly working in films from 1937 as an assistant on a Paul Rotha documentary for the Great Western Railway in Cornwall, this British (Scottish) screenwriter (1917–2012) resumed his film career in America as an assistant to the producer Louis de Rochemont on the docu-thriller *Boomerang!* (1947) following work as a "boffin" during the war. Back in Britain, he got a job in the scenario department of Gainsborough and contributed to the script of *Helter Skelter* (1949). He then had a major success with *The Blue Lamp* (1949), which was based on a treatment by himself and Ted Willis. This was subsequently sold to Ealing after Gainsborough turned it down, and went on to become one of the best-loved films of its era; it also inspired the long-running television series *Dixon of Dock Green* (1955–1976, TV).

Read's other credits include *White Corridors* (1951), *Grip of the Strangler* (1958), *The Roman Spring of Mrs. Stone* (1961), *That Kind of Girl* (1963), *Jason and the Argonauts* (1963) and *First Men in the Moon* (1964), while for television his work includes episodes of *The Adventures of Robin Hood* (1955–1960 TV), *Man in a Suitcase* (1967–1968, TV) and *Strange Report* (1968–1970, TV), on all which he worked as a both writer and script editor. He also penned the second feature thriller *Blood Orange* (1953) for Hammer. He also wrote a good many books and magazine articles on wine, gastronomy and travel, and was a member of various wine orders, among them the Gran Orden de Caballeros, of which he was a founding member. **Hammer credits:** *Blood Orange* (1953)

## Reardon, Corinna

Reardon can be seen as one of the wolf children in *Children of the Full Moon* (1980, TV [episode of *Hammer House of Horror*]). Her other TV credits include episodes *Play for Tomorrow* (1982, TV) and *Press Gang* (1989–1993, TV). **Hammer credits:** *Children of the Full Moon* (1980, TV [episode of *Hammer House of Horror*], as Small girl)

## Rebel, Bernard

This Polish actor (1901–1964) can be seen as the unfortunate Professor Dubois in Hammer's *The Curse of the Mummy's Tomb* (1964), in which he has his left hand chopped off in an early scene. His other credits include *Crook's Tour* (1941), *The Big Blockade* (1942), *Moulin Rouge* (1952), *Little Red Monkey* (1954), *Top Secret* (1952), *The Young Lovers* (1954), *Orders to Kill* (1958) and *The Rebel* (1961), plus episodes of *The New Adventures of Charlie Chan* (1957–1958, TV), *The Third Man* (1959–1965, TV) and *Espionage* (1963–1964, TV). **Hammer credits:** *The Curse of the Mummy's Tomb* (1964, as Professor Dubois [uncredited])

## Redmond, Liam

Following experience on stage with the Abbey Players from 1935 and in New York in 1939, this Irish character actor (1913–1989) broke into films in Britain in 1946 with *I See a Dark Stranger*, for which he also penned dialogue. Work in both Britain and America followed, including appearances in *High Treason* (1951), *Night of the Demon* (1957), *Kid Galahad* (1962), *The Ghost and Mr. Chicken* (1965) and *Barry Lyndon* (1975). He also appeared in two Hammer productions: the second feature thriller *The Glass Cage* (1955) and the horror film *The Phantom of the Opera* (1962). His TV work includes episodes of *Douglas Fairbanks, Jr. Presents* (1953–1957, TV), *The Alcoa Hour* (1955–1957, TV), *The DuPont Show of the Month* (1957–1961, TV), *Going My Way* (1962–1963, TV), *The Saint* (1962–1969, TV) and *You're Only Young Twice* (1971, TV). **Hammer credits:** *The Glass Cage* (1955, as Inspector Lindley), *The Phantom of the Opera* (1962, as Police Inspector [uncredited])

## Redmond, Moira

This British actress (1928–2006) spent the majority of her career in the theater, both in Britain and Australia, although she made a number of films down the decades, beginning with *Violent Moment*

(1959). Her other credits include *Doctor in Love* (1960), *A Shot in the Dark* (1964) and *The Limbo Line* (1968). She also left her mark as the devious companion Grace Maddox in the Hammer thriller *Nightmare* (1964), in which she attempts to drive her young charge out of her mind. Her television work includes episodes of *Edward the King* (1975, TV), *I, Claudius* (1976, TV), *Return of the Saint* (1978–1979, TV), *Nanny* (1981–1983, TV) and *The Wingless Bird* (1997, TV). Her mother was the actress Molly Redmond. Her second husband was the director Herbert Wise (1924–2015, real name Herbert Weisz), to whom she was married between 1963 and 1972, and who directed her in several television productions. **Hammer credits:** *Nightmare* (1964, as Grace Maddox)

### Redstone, Elizabeth

Redstone worked as the first assistant editor on Hammer's *Frankenstein Created Woman* (1967). Her other credits include *Captain Apache* (1971), on which she was an editorial assistant. **Hammer credits:** *Frankenstein Created Woman* (1967 [uncredited])

### Redway, John (John Redway, Ltd.)

The agency of this respected British agent and casting director (?–1990) is acknowledged in the credits of *Flesh and Blood—The Hammer Heritage of Horror* (1994, TV). Among Redway's clients were the Hammer stars Peter Cushing and Christopher Lee, and the Hammer director Don Sharp. His credits as a casting director include *Private Angelo* (1949), *Last Holiday* (1950), *The Magic Box* (1951), *Valley of Song* (1953) and *The Good Beginning* (1953). He also worked as a production assistant on *Inquest* (1939), as a third assistant director on *Brighton Rock* (1947) and as a second assistant director on *Fame Is the Spur* (1947). **Hammer credits:** *Flesh and Blood—The Hammer Heritage of Horror* (1994, TV)

### Reece, Brian

This British actor (1913–1962) made only a handful of films, preferring to spend his career on stage, where he began working in 1931. He is best known for originating the role of Archibald Berkeley-Willoughby (aka PC 49) in the long running BBC radio serial *The Adventures of PC 49* (1947–1953), though surprisingly, he wasn't asked to play the part in the first of the two films made by Hammer, *The Adventures of PC 49—The Case of the Guardian Angel* (1949), in which the part was played by Hugh Latimer. However, he *was* invited to play the part in the sequel, *A Case for PC 49* (1951). Reece's other screen credits include *Fast and Loose* (1954), *Orders Are Orders* (1955), *Geordie* (1955), *Carry On Admiral* (1958) and the Hammer comedy *Watch It, Sailor!* (1961), in which he had a cameo as a solicitor. His TV credits include episodes of *Paging You* (1946–1948, TV), *The New Adventures of Martin Kane* (1957–1958, TV) and *Don't Do It Dempsey* (1960, TV). **Hammer credits:** *A Case for PC 49* (1951, as Archibald Berkeley-Willoughby, aka PC 49), *Watch It, Sailor* (1961, as Solicitor)

### Reed, Barry

Reed worked on sound maintenance on Hammer's *Scars of Dracula* (1970). He went on to become a sound recordist and mixer on such productions as *God's Outlaw* (1986), *Tank Malling* (1989), *The Dreyfuss Boys* (1998), *Vigo* (1998) and *Bodywork* (1999). **Hammer credits:** *Scars of Dracula* (1970 [uncredited])

### Reed, Clive

British born Reed (1932–) worked as the assistant director on Hammer's *Straight on Till Morning* (1972). His other credits, among them four for director Richard Lester, include *Tarzan the Magnificent* (1960), *Dr. No* (1962), *Call Me Bwana* (1963), *Help!* (1965), *Those Magnificent Men in Their Flying Machines* (1965), *The Quiller Memorandum* (1966), *Innocent Bystanders* (1972), *The Amazing Mr. Blunden* (1972), *The Three Musketeers* (1973), *The Four Musketeers* (1974), *Heavenly Pursuits* (1985) and *The Return of the Musketeers* (1989). His earlier credits as a second assistant include *Behind the Headlines* (1956) and *Left Right and Centre* (1959). He also worked as a production or unit manager/supervisor on *In Search of the Castaways* (1961), *Georgy Girl* (1966), *Absolution* (1978) and *Escape from Sobibor* (1987, TVM), and as an associate producer on *Catch-22* (1970), *Carnal Knowledge* (1971) and *The Dirty Dozen: The Deadly Mission* (1987, TVM). **Hammer credits:** *Straight on Till Morning* (1972)

### Reed, Laurie

Reed worked as the sound camera operator on Hammer's *Vampire Circus* (1972). **Hammer credits:** *Vampire Circus* (1972 [uncredited])

### Reed, Les

This British composer, conductor, arranger, pianist, orchestra leader and songwriter (1935–, full name Leslie David Reed) provided the all-important "secret code" tune that Angela Lansbury's Miss Froy attempts to get out of Germany in Hammer's *The Lady Vanishes* (1979). The film's main composer Richard Hartley subsequently worked this theme into his score for the film. A former member of The John Barry Seven, for whom he played the piano, Reed performed with the group on many tracks and singles, among them the original *James Bond Theme* used in *Dr. No* (1962). He also appeared with the group in *A Matter of WHO* (1961), *Girl on a Roof* (1961) and many television pop shows of the day. His other film scores (either whole or contributions to) include *Les Bicyclettes de Belsize* (1969), *The Girl on a Motorcycle* (1968), *The Bush Baby* (1969), *Crosspolot* (1969), *George and Mildred* (1980), *Creepshow 2* (1987) and *Parting Shots* (1999). He is best known for writing such singles as *It's Not Unusual* (1965) and *Delilah* (1967), both of which went on to become international hits for Tom Jones, and which have featured on the soundtracks of many movies. His other songs include *Baby I Don't Care* (1964), *There's a Kind of Hush All Over the World* (1966) and *The Last Waltz* (1967). Artists who have performed his songs include Engelbert Humperdinck, Cleo Laine, Petula Clarke, Gene Pitney, The Carpenters, Herman's Hermits, The Fortunes and

Elvis Presley. Reed was made an OBE in 1998. **Hammer credits:** *The Lady Vanishes* (1979)

### Reed, Michael

Following experience as an assistant at the Studio Film Laboratories and as a clapper boy on such low budgeters as *Dancing with Crime* (1947), *Just William's Luck* (1947) and the Hammer second feature *The Adventures of PC 49—The Case of the Guardian Angel* (1949), this British cinematographer (1929–) went on to specialize in photographing large scale action films, among them *On Her Majesty's Secret Service* (1969), *Shout at the Devil* (1976) and *Wild Geese II* (1985), all of which were directed by Peter Hunt. Reed returned to Hammer in 1959 for the Jekyll and Hyde spoof *The Ugly Duckling*, which he followed with several visually atmospheric films for the company in the sixties, most notably *Dracula—Prince of Darkness* (1966), which he shot back-to-back with *Rasputin—The Mad Monk* (1966).

Recalled the cinematographer of his early work for the company, "I worked with Hammer way, way back when they were Exclusive. They were doing quickies—basically talking radio plays and putting the scripts on film."[14] As for the *Prince of Darkness/ Rasputin* double bill, he remembered, "Shooting those films back-to-back didn't pose any particular problems. It was left to the art department to revamp things. We shot the first film from beginning to end and then, for the second, we went onto the revamped sets. But everyone was in tune to a working system and it cut costs down…. The schedule for each film was four or five weeks. Michael Carreras and Tony Hinds had it well organized. They had a formula for it and, of course, Tony Keys was the great associate producer and kept everything moving along…. I was encouraged by Tony Keys to use my imagination and go for something, even if it was going to take just that bit longer."[15]

Reed's other credits include, *Guns in the Heather* (1968), *Von Richthofen and Brown* (1971), *Diamonds on Wheels* (1974), *The Hiding Place* (1975), *Leopard in the Snow* (1978), *The Passage* (1979), *Loophole* (1981) and *Kim* (1984, TVM), plus episodes of such series as *The Adventures of Robin Hood* (1955–1960, TV), *The Avengers* (1961–1969, TV), *The Saint* (1962–1969, TV), *The New Avengers* (1976–1977, TV), *Paradise Postponed* (1986, TV), which earned him a BAFTA nomination, and *Press Gang* (1989–1993, TV). In addition to his two Hammer films with Don Sharp—*The Devil-Ship Pirates* (1964) and *Rasputin—The Mad Monk* (1966)—Reed also photographed *The Professionals* (1960), *Linda* (1960) and *Our Man in Marrakesh* (1966) for the director. **Hammer credits:** *The Adventures of PC 49—The Case of the Guardian Angel* (1949, clapper boy [uncredited]), *Celia* (1949, clapper boy [uncredited]), *Meet Simon Cherry* (1949, clapper boy [uncredited]), *The Man in Black* (1950, focus puller [uncredited]), *Someone at the Door* (1950, focus puller [uncredited]), *What the Butler Saw* (1950, focus puller [uncredited]), *The Ugly Duckling* (1959, cinematographer), *The Devil-Ship Pirates* (1964, cinematographer), *The Gorgon* (1964, cinematographer), *Dracula—Prince of Darkness* (1966, cinematographer), *Rasputin—*

*The Mad Monk* (1966, cinematographer), *Slave Girls* (1968, cinematographer)

## Reed, Oliver

One of the bad boys of British cinema, this talented but hell-raising leading man (1938–1999, real name Robert Oliver Reed) was the nephew of the celebrated film director Carol Reed (1906–1976), for whom he played Bill Sikes in the Oscarwinning musical *Oliver!* (1968). Working as an extra and bit-player in films from 1955, his early credits include *Value for Money* (1955), *The Square Peg* (1958), *The League of Gentlemen* (1960) and *The Angry Silence* (1960). In 1960, he made a brief appearance as a nightclub pimp in Hammer's *The Two Faces of Dr. Jekyll*, and such was his presence in the scene, he was brought back for *Sword of Sherwood Forest* (1960), in which he was called upon to assassinate Peter Cushing's dastardly Sheriff of Nottingham.

Clearly marked for stardom, Hammer took a gamble with Reed and, at the suggestion of make-up artist Roy Ashton, cast him in the leading role of their 1961 film *The Curse of the Werewolf*, which helped to establish his name with the public. Re-

called Ashton, "Tony Hinds asked me: 'Who do you suppose we can get [for the role]?' I suggested Oliver Reed, since he seemed exactly right…. His powerful bone structure was just right for the appearance and his gifts as an actor were perfect for the part."[16] Indeed, commented director Terence Fisher in the press book for the film, "Were I invited to predict sure stardom for an unknown young actor today, and asked to back that prediction with a heavy bet, the youngster I'd pick would be 22-year-old Mr. Reed."

Producer Anthony Hinds also praised Reed's enthusiasm during this stage of his career, commenting, "He was a marvelous chap with us."[17] Roy Ashton agreed: "He was most co-operative, I must say. He was a real professional chap and very ambitious at the time, as this film was his big chance. He would do anything. Nothing was too much trouble…. He put everything he had into that role, it was a great performance."[18] Said Reed of his hairy get-up, "No one would sit next to me in the studio canteen. Even the waitress used to eye me strangely and keep a distance. I am not surprised. I was scared myself when I saw the rush shots with blood trickling from my mouth and down my clothes and my nostrils plugged up to make them enlarged, and my face made up in a terrifying fashion. I looked a gory mess."[19] Meanwhile, of one particular scene, he recalled, "I frightened the life out of little Michael Ripper in the prison scene, but I frightened Dennis Shaw even more, when I picked up that door and threw it at him. It wasn't a balsawood door—it was a real door (I was fitter in those days). And Dennis shat himself … literally. He shat himself."[20]

Reed went on to appear in several more productions for Hammer, among them the swashbuckling adventure *The Pirates of Blood River* (1962), although it was as the menacing gang leader King in *The Damned* (1963) that he next left his mark. He also proved effective in the fake-heir thriller *Paranoiac* (1963), prompting *Variety* to comment, "Oliver Reed plays the scheming brother with demonic skill." His last film for the company was *The Brigand of Kandahar* (1965), one of the studio's lesser productions, and prompted the actor to take action regarding his career. Commented Reed, "I had heard that things were falling to pieces, and I saw what was happening to Peter and Christopher … in terms of being cast in those sort of roles all

the time. So I called it a day."[21] It would be over twenty-five years before Reed returned to Hammer to narrate the compilation series *The World of Hammer* (1990 [first broadcast 1994], TV), though Michael Carreras had hoped to sign the star for a remake of *Lorna Doone* in 1972 (when Reed proved unavailable, the project was cancelled).

Reed's other films, of which he made over ninety, include *The Bulldog Breed* (1960), *The System* (1964), *The Trap* (1966), *The Jokers* (1967), *Women in Love* (1969), *The Devils* (1970), *The Three Musketeers* (1973), *The Four Musketeers* (1974), *Dr. Heckyl and Mr. Hype* (1980), *Venom* (1981), *The Return of the Musketeers* (1989), *The Adventures of Baron Munchausen* (1988) and *Gladiator* (2000), during the making of which he died from a heart attack brought on by one of his legendary drinking binges (he earned a posthumous best supporting actor BAFTA nomination for the film). His half-brother Simon Reed (1947–) became Reed's press agent. His step-cousin was the actress Tracy Reed (1941–2012, real name Clare Tracy Compton Pelissier), who appeared in an episode of Hammer's *Journey to the Unknown* (1968, TV). **Hammer credits:** *The Two Faces of Dr. Jekyll* (1960, as Pimp [uncredited]), *Sword of Sherwood Forest* (1960, as Melton [uncredited]), *The Curse of the Werewolf* (1961, as Leon), *The Pirates of Blood River* (1962, as Brocaire), *Captain Clegg* (1962, as Harry Crabtree), *The Damned* (1963, as King), *Paranoiac* (1963, as Simon Ashby), *The Scarlet Blade* (1963, as Captain Sylvester), *The Brigand of Kandahar* (1965, as Eli Khan), *The World of Hammer* (1990 [first broadcast 1994], TV, narrator)

## Reed, Robert

This American actor (1932–1992, real name John Robert Rietz) is best known for playing Mike Brady in the long running sitcom *The Brady Bunch* (1969–1974, TV) and its various follow-ups, among them *The Brady Bunch Hour* (1977, TV), *A Very Brady Christmas* (1988, TVM) and *The Bradys* (1990, TV). His other television work includes appearances in *The Defenders* (1961–1965, TV), *Mannix* (1969–1975, TV), in which he played Lieutenant Adam Tobias, *Haunts of the Very Rich* (1972, TVM), *The Boy in the Plastic Bubble* (1976, TVM), *Death of a Centerfold* (1981, TVM) and *Nurse* (1981–1982, TV), plus several guest shots, among them the lead role in *The New People*, an episode of Hammer's *Journey to the Unknown* (1968, TV), which also appeared in the compendium film *Journey into Darkness* (1968, TVM). Also in films, Reed's credits here include *Pal Joey* (1957), *Torpedo Run* (1958), *Star!* (1968), *The Love Bug* (1968), *The Maltese Bippy* (1969) and *Prime Target* (1991). Also on stage, including Broadway. **Hammer credits:** *The New People* (1968, TV [episode of *Journey to the Unknown*], as Hank Prentiss), *Journey into Darkness* (1968, TVM, as Hank Prentiss)

## Reed, Tracy

This British actress (1941–2012, real name Clare Tracy Compton Pelissier) played the role of Joyce in *The Indian Spirit Guide*, an episode of Hammer's *Journey to the Unknown* (1968, TV) which

Oliver Reed looks both disturbed and disturbing in this ad for *Paranoiac* (1963) (Hammer/Rank/Universal International).

also appeared in the compendium film *Journey to Midnight* (1968, TVM). In films as a child from 1944 with *The Way Ahead* (which was directed by her stepfather, Carol Reed), she went on to appear in *Dr. Strangelove* (1964), *Devils of Darkness* (1964), *Casino Royale* (1967), *Hammerhead* (1968), *Percy* (1971) and *Melody* (1971), plus episodes of *Dixon of Dock Green* (1955–1976, TV), *Dr. Finlay's Casebook* (1962–1971, TV), *Detective* (1964–1969, TV) and *Barlow at Large* (1971–1975, TV). Her first husband (of three) was the actor Edward Fox (1937–), to whom she was married between 1958 and 1961; he likewise performed in an episode of *Journey to the Unknown* (1968, TV). This was *Poor Butterfly*, which, like *The Indian Spirit Guide*, also appeared in the compendium film *Journey to Midnight* (1968, TVM). Her second husband was the actor Neil Hallett (1924–2004), to whom she was married between 1970 and 1973; he appeared in Hammer's *X—The Unknown* (1956). Her third husband was the actor Bill Simpson (1931–1986, full name William Nicholson Simpson), to whom she was married between 1974 and 1982. Reed's mother was the actress Penelope Dudley-Ward (1914–1982) and her father the director Anthony Pelissier (1912–1988, full name Harry Anthony Compton Pelissier); her paternal grandmother was the actress Fay Compton (1894–1978, real name Virginia Lilian Emeline Compton Mackenzie), who also appeared in *Poor Butterfly*. Reed's paternal great grandfather was the actor-manager Edward Compton (1954–1918), her paternal great grandmother was the actress Virginia Frances Bateman (1853–1940), her paternal great uncle was the novelist Sir Compton Mackenzie (1883–1972) and her stepfather was the director Sir Carol Reed (1906–1976), thus making her a step-cousin to Oliver Reed (1938–1999), who appeared in several Hammer films. **Hammer credits:** *The Indian Spirit Guide* (1968, TV [episode of *Journey to the Unknown*], as Joyce), *Journey to Midnight* (1968, TVM, as Joyce)

### Reeks, Curtis

Reeks worked as the stills cameraman on two films for Hammer. His other credits include *The Interrupted Journey* (1949), *Murder at the Windmill* (1949), *Something in the City* (1950) and *Shadow of the Eagle* (1950). **Hammer credits:** *Paranoiac* (1963 [uncredited]), *The Kiss of the Vampire* (1963 [uncredited])

### Reents, Claus Dieter

This German actor (1943–1996, first names sometimes hyphenated) can be seen in a minor supporting role in Hammer's *The Lady Vanishes* (1979). His other credits include *La femme qui se poudre* (1972), *De Hauptdarsteller* (1977), *Kalt wie Eis* (1981) and *Der Angriff* (1988), plus episodes of *Tatort* (1970–, TV), *Ein Fall für zwei* (1981–, TV) and *Marienhof* (1992–2011, TV). **Hammer credits:** *The Lady Vanishes* (1979, as First killer)

### Rees, Angharad

Best known for playing Demelza Poldark (née Carne) in the period drama *Poldark* (1975–1977, TV), this British (Welsh) actress (1944–2012) is also known to Hammer fans for playing Jack the

Ripper's murderous daughter Anna in *Hands of the Ripper* (1971). Commented *Variety* of her performance: "Angharad Rees makes the pretty killer entirely believable," while the *LA Times* described the actress as "exquisite but properly terrifying." Back home, *Photoplay* hailed her performance as being "beautifully and cleverly played." Remembered Rees of her character, "I saw Anna as a straight, innocent girl who had been through hard times. She is totally normal to all outward appearances and to herself, and that was what made her all the more horribly sad for me."[22]

The actress's other film credits include *Jane Eyre* (1970, TVM), *Under Milk Wood* (1971), *Baffled!* (1973, TVM), *The Love Ban* (1973), *Moments* (1974), *The Curse of King Tut's Tomb* (1980, TVM) and *The Wolves of Kromer* (1998). She also appeared in episodes of such TV series as *Doctor in the House* (1969–1970, TV), *Doctor in Charge* (1972–1973, TV), *Close to Home* (1989–1990, TV), in which she played Helen De Angelo, and *Trainer* (1991–1992, TV). Her first husband (of two) was the actor Christopher Cazenove (1945–2010), to whom she was married between 1973 and 1994; he appeared in *Children of the Full Moon* (1980, TV [episode of *Hammer House of Horror*]) and *In Possession* (1984, TVM [episode of *Hammer House of Mystery and Suspense*]). She also designed jewelry, some of which (from her Qing Dynasty Collection) was used in *Elizabeth: The Golden Age* (2007). **Hammer credits:** *Hands of the Ripper* (1971, as Anna)

### Rees, Graham

Rees can be seen as one of the guards in Hammer's *The Satanic Rites of Dracula* (1974). Mostly on TV, his credits here include episodes of *Crossroads* (1964–1988, TV), *Airline* (1982, TV), *Shadow of the Noose* (1989, TV) and *Martin Chuzzlewit* (1994, TV). **Hammer credits:** *The Satanic Rites of Dracula* (1974, as Guard 4)

### Reeve, Gladys

Reeve worked as the continuity girl on Hammer's *Up the Creek* (1958). Her other credits include *The Silver Darlings* (1947), *Street of Shadows* (1953), *Count Five and Die* (1957), *Violent Moment* (1959) and *Doctor Blood's Coffin* (1961). **Hammer credits:** *Up the Creek* (1958)

### Reeve, Spencer

This British editor (1923–1973) began his association with Hammer in the mid-fifties as a second assistant editor to Maurice Rootes on *Face the Music* (1954), and as an assistant editor to Bill Lenny on *Break in the Circle* (1955). After cutting the short *The Right Person* (1956), he went on to gain experience elsewhere, but later returned to edit a number of important pictures for Hammer, prime among them *Quatermass and the Pit* (1967) and *The Devil Rides Out* (1968). His other credits include *To Be a Woman* (1951), *Transatlantic* (1960), *Night Train for Inverness* (1960), *The Nudist Story* (1960), *Fate Takes a Hand* (1962) and *Big Zapper* (1973), plus episodes of *The Invisible Man* (1958–1960, TV), *The Saint* (1962–1969, TV) and *The Prisoner* (1967–1968, TV). He also worked as the sound editor on *A King in New York* (1957),

*Witchcraft* (1964) and *The Earth Dies Screaming* (1964), and as a supervising editor on *The Day of the Triffids* (1962). **Hammer credits:** *Face the Music* (1954, second assistant editor [uncredited]), *Break in the Circle* (1955, assistant editor [uncredited]), *The Right Person* (1956, editor), *Frankenstein Created Woman* (1967, editor), *Quatermass and the Pit* (1967, editor), *The Devil Rides Out* (1968, editor), *Dracula Has Risen from the Grave* (1968, editor), *Moon Zero Two* (1969, editor), *Lust for a Vampire* (1971, editor), *Twins of Evil* (1971, editor)

### Reeves, Kynaston

This busy British character actor (1893–1971, real name Philip Arthur Reeves) made his film debut in 1919 with *Many Waters* following experience in the army during World War I and training at RADA. Seventy-plus films followed, among them *The Lodger* (1932), *The Sign of Four* (1932), *The Stars Look Down* (1939), *The Rake's Progress* (1945), *Fiend Without a Face* (1958) and *The Private Life of Sherlock Holmes* (1970), in which he increasingly played doddery authoritative types. He also worked for Hammer twice, first appearing as Lord Grant in *Four Sided Triangle* (1953), and later as Grandfather in *The Shadow of the Cat* (1961). Also busy on television, his credits here include episodes of *Leave It to Todhunter* (1959, TV), *The Jazz Age* (1968, TV) and *The Forsyte Saga* (1967, TV), in which he played Uncle Nicholas Forsyte. Also on stage. **Hammer credits:** *Four Sided Triangle* (1954, as Lord Grant), *The Shadow of the Cat* (1961, as Grandfather)

### Reeves, Michael

This cult British writer and director (1943–1969, full name Michael Leith Reeves, aka Michael Byron) remains best known for his final film, *Witchfinder General* (1968). Following efforts as an amateur filmmaker, the movie-obsessed Reeves began gaining experience in the industry in a number of menial capacities, working as the dialogue director for the screen tests of *Fun in Acapulco* (1963), as a runner on *The Long Ships* (1964), as an assistant director on *Castle of the Living Dead* (1964), in which he also briefly appeared, and as a runner on *Genghis Khan* (1965). He directed his first film in 1965. This was the low budget horror *The She Beast*, which he also co-wrote under the name of Michael Byron (again, he also briefly appeared in the film). He then went on to co-write and direct *The Sorcerers* (1967), which he soon after followed with *Witchfinder General*, which he again co-wrote and directed.

In 1966, Reeves co-authored a thriller titled *Crescendo* with Alfred Shaughnessy, which was to have been made by Compton Films. Unfortunately, money problems saw the project abandoned. However, Michael Carreras soon after picked the screenplay up for Hammer, for whom it was revised by Jimmy Sangster, who went on to share the screen credit with Shaughnessy, leaving Reeves, who had hoped to direct the film, uncredited.

It should also be noted that Reeves was offered an episode of Hammer's TV series *Journey to the Unknown* (1968, TV) to direct, but he turned the offer down. Reeves' other screenplay work includes

*The Oblong Box* (1969), which he re-wrote when signed to direct the film. Tragically, he died before shooting began. **Hammer credits:** *Crescendo* (1970 [uncredited])

### Regal Films International

This British distribution company handled the re-issue of Hammer's *Men of Sherwood Forest* (1954), *The Curse of Frankenstein* (1957), *The Camp on Blood Island* (1958) and *Up the Creek* (1958), all of which were re-released in 1961. Other films handled by the company include *Jack the Ripper* (1959), *Murder at Site 3* (1959 [1961 re-issue, the original 1959 release having been care of Exclusive]), *The Siege of Sidney Street* (1960), *The Treasure of Monte Cristo* (1961), *What a Carve Up!* (1961), *Doctor Who and the Daleks* (1965) and *Dr. Terror's House of Horrors* (1965). **Hammer credits:** *Men of Sherwood Forest* (1954), *The Curse of Frankenstein* (1957), *The Camp on Blood Island* (1958), *Up the Creek* (1958)

### RegalScope

A variation on CinemaScope, this widescreen process—one of several used by Hammer in the fifties—was used for the U.S. release of *The Abominable Snowman* (1957). However, it should be noted that the UK release of the film was in HammerScope. **Hammer credits:** *The Abominable Snowman* (1957 [U.S. only])

### Regan, Joan

Popular in the fifties and sixties, this British singer and recording artist (1928–2013) guest starred in the Hammer musical featurette *Just for You* (1956). Her other film credits include *Six-Five Special* (1958) and *London Calling* (1960), plus countless TV guest shots. She got her first big break singing with the military dance band The Squadronaires, with whom she recorded a cover version of the single *Ricochet* (1953). Her other hits, mostly cover versions, include *Wait for Me, Darling* (1954), *Prize of Gold* (which was used in the 1955 film of the same name) and *Papa Loves Mama* (1960), while her albums include *Just Joan* (1957) and *Remember I Love You* (1996). **Hammer credits:** *Just for You* (1956, as herself)

### Regan, Linda

This British actress (1949–, real name Linda Mary Drinkwater) had a minor role in Hammer's *On the Buses* (1971). Her credits include *Adolf Hitler—My Part in His Downfall* (1972), *Keep It Up, Jack!* (1974), *Confessions of a Pop Performer* (1975), *Carry On England* (1976), *Hardcore* (1977) and *Run for Your Wife* (2012), plus episodes of *Special Branch* (1969–1974, TV), *Doctor at Large* (1971, TV), *Minder* (1979–1994, TV), *Hi-de-Hi!* (1980–1988, TV), in which she played April, and *Doctors* (2000–, TV). Also a crime novelist, her published works include *Behind You* (2006), *Passion Killers* (2007) and *Brotherhood of Blades* (2011). She is married to the actor Brian Murphy (1932–), whom she wed in 1995; he appeared in Hammer's big screen version of *Man About the House* (1974). Her father is the bandleader and agent Peter Regan (real name Peter Albert Drinkwater) and her sister is the actress and writer Carol

Drinkwater (1948–). **Hammer credits:** *On the Buses* (1971, as Girl on bus)

### Regin, Nadja

This glamorous Yugoslavian actress (1931–2019, real name Nadja Poderegin, under which she appeared in several of her early films) played the female interest in Hammer's wartime comedy *Don't Panic Chaps* (1959). In films in Europe from the late forties, her other credits include *Prica o fabrici* (1949), *Cudotvorni mac* (1950), *Der Frontgockel* (1955), *The Man Without a Body* (1957), *Solo for Sparrow* (1962), *From Russia with Love* (1963) and *Goldfinger* (1964), while on TV she appeared in episodes of *International Detective* (1959–1961, TV), *The Saint* (1962–1969, TV) and *Danger Man* (1964–1966, TV). She later worked as a script reader/editor for Hammer, assessing the content of screenplays and making suggestions for their improvement. **Hammer credits:** *Don't Panic Chaps* (1959, as Elsa), *The Vampire Lovers* (1970, script editor [uncredited]), *Vampire Circus* (1972, script editor [uncredited]), *Demons of the Mind* (1972, script editor [uncredited])

### Reid, Colin

One of Hammer's publicists in the late fifties/early sixties, Reid worked on such diverse productions as *Yesterday's Enemy* (1959) and *The Mummy* (1959). His other credits include *The Girl on the Boat* (1962). **Hammer credits include:** *The Revenge of Frankenstein* (1958 [uncredited]), *The Stranglers of Bombay* (1959 [uncredited]), *Yesterday's Enemy* (1959 [uncredited]), *The Ugly Duckling* (1959 [uncredited]), *The Mummy* (1959 [uncredited]), *Taste of Fear* (1961 [uncredited]), *The Terror of the Tongs* (1961 [uncredited])

### Reid, David

Reid worked as an executive producer on *Hammer House of Horror* (1980, TV), sharing his credit with Brian Lawrence. At the time he was the Head of Drama at ATV. His other credits as a producer or executive producer include *The Strauss Family* (1972, TV), episodes of which he also wrote and directed, *Diamonds* (1981, TV), *Sapphire and Steel* (1979–1982, TV) and *On the Line* (1982, TV). His other work as a director takes in episodes of *The Power Game* (1965–1969, TV), *Catweazle* (1970–1971, TV) and *Clayhanger* (1976, TV), while his work as a writer includes *Cold Warrior* (1984, TV), *The English Wife* (1995, TVM) and *Mortimer's Law* (1998, TVM). **Hammer credits:** *Hammer House of Horror* (1980, TV)

### Reid, Gordon

This British (Scottish) actor (1939–2003) had a supporting role in *Visitor from the Grave*, one of the poorer episodes of *Hammer House of Horror* (180, TV). His other TV credits include episodes of *Dr. Finlay's Casebook* (1962–1971, TV), *Sat'day While Sunday* (1967, TV), in which he played Mike Lewis, *Rock Follies* (1976, TV), *Doctor Finlay* (1993–1996, TV), in which he played Angus Livingstone, and *Peak Practice* (1993–2002, TV). Also on stage and radio, his occasional film credits include *Leon the Pig Farmer* (1992), *Mansfield Park*

(1999) and *The Others* (2001). **Hammer credits:** *Visitor from the Grave* (1980, TV [episode of Hammer House of Horror], as Max [uncredited])

### Reid, John

Reid worked as a second camera operator on Hammer's *Face the Music* (1954) and *X—The Unknown* (1956). He spent much of his career photographing shorts and documentaries, among them *Trunk Conveyor* (1952), *The Wall of Death* (1956), *Manriding at Eppleton* (1967), which he also directed, *Training for Safety* (1972) and *Airstream* (1979), which he also directed. **Hammer credits:** *Face the Music* (1956 [uncredited]), *X—The Unknown* (1956 [uncredited])

### Reid, Mike

This British comedian-turned-actor (1940–2007, full name Michael Reid) is best known for playing Frank Butcher in the long-running soap *EastEnders* (1985–, TV), in which he appeared between 1985 and 2005. He began his television career in 1965 playing a small role in *Doctor Who* (1963–1989, TV), which led to further bit parts in such series as *The Saint* (1962–1969, TV), *The Champions* (1968–1969, TV) and *Department S* (1969–1970, TV). He also worked as a stunt driver on such films as *Casino Royale* (1967), *The Dirty Dozen* (1967), *Chitty Chitty Bang Bang* (1968) and Hammer's *The Devil Rides Out* (1968). By this time he had started working the club circuit as a comedian, and went on to become a highly popular stand-up thanks to his exposure on *The Comedians* (1971–1985, TV). Subsequently, he began appearing as a guest star in TV variety shows, and had a co-starring role appositive Queenie Watts and Arthur Mullard in the popular sitcom *Yus, My Dear* (1976, TV), in which he played Benny Briggs. He also presented the children's series *Runaround* (1975–1981, TV) between 1975 and 1977, and had his first major dramatic role in the series *Noah's Castle* (1979–1980, TV), in which he played Vince Holloway. He went on to become something of a national institution, known for his broad Cockney accent and catchphrase of "Triffic." His other film credits include *Dr. Who and the Daleks* (1965), in which he played one of the Thals, *Up the Junction* (1968), *The Adding Machine* (1969), *Steptoe and Son* (1972), *Snatch* (2000) and *Jack Says* (2008), while his other TV appearances include episodes of *Worzel Gummidge* (1979–1981, TV), *The Bob Monkhouse Show* (1983–1986, TV) and *Underworld* (1997, TV). **Hammer credits:** *The Devil Rides Out* (1968 [uncredited])

### Reid, Milton

In Britain from 1936, this hulking Indian born supporting actor (1917–1987, aka Milton Gaylord Reid) began his career as a wrestler under the name of The Mighty Chang. He went on to become a familiar face in British cinema in strongman, body-guard or henchman roles, having made his debut in *The Way Ahead* (1944) following wartime experience as a cavalry trooper. An unmistakable presence, his forty-plus credits include *Ivanhoe* (1952), *Blood of the Vampire* (1958), *Deadlier Than the Male* (1966), *Dr. Phibes Rises Again* (1972), *Au Pair Girls* (1972), *The Return of the Pink Panther*

(1975) and *The People That Time Forgot* (1977), as well as three Bond films: *Dr. No* (1962), *Casino Royale* (1967) and, most memorably, as Sandor in *The Spy Who Loved Me* (1977), in which he had a deadly rooftop fight with James Bond. He also appeared in four Hammer films, beginning with *The Camp on Blood Island* (1958). His TV work includes episodes of *Sir Francis Drake* (1961–1962, TV), *Virgin of the Secret Service* (1968, TV), *Jason King* (1971–1972, TV) and *West Country Tales* (1982–1983, TV). **Hammer credits:** *The Camp on Blood Island* (1958, as Executioner [uncredited]), *Visa to Canton* (1960, as Bodyguard [uncredited]), *The Terror of the Tongs* (1961, as Guardian [uncredited]), *Captain Clegg* (1962, as Mulatto)

Lobby card featuring Milton Reid in a bloody moment from *Captain Clegg* (1962) (Hammer/Merlin/Major/Rank/Universal International).

### Reilly, Christopher

Reilly can be seen as William Morton, the young boy who returns from the grave to wreak vengeance on his uncaring parents in *Growing Pains* (1980, TV [episode of *Hammer House of Horror*]). His other TV credits include episodes of *The Story of the Treasure Seekers* (1982, TV), *Beau Geste* (1982, TV), *Goodbye, Mr. Chips* (1984, TV) and *Dramarama* (1983–1989, TV). **Hammer credits:** *Growing Pains* (1980, TV [episode of *Hammer House of Horror*], as William Morton)

### Reilly, Tommy

This Canadian harmonica player (1919–2000) provided the mouth organ solos in the title song and score for the Hammer comedy *Watch It, Sailor!* (1961). His other film credits as a soloist include *Street of Shadows* (1953), *It's a Great Day* (1955), *The Sundowners* (1960), *Wonderwall* (1968), *The Night Digger* (1971), *Tarka the Otter* (1979) and *The Kitchen Toto* (1987), plus episodes of *Fabian of the Yard* (1954–1956, TV) and *Out of the Unknown* (1965–1971, TV). He also scored such films as *The Navy Lark* (1959), *The Password Is Courage* (1962) and *Tanker* (1971). In London from 1935, he was a prisoner of war during World War II, having been arrested while studying at Leipzig University. Back in London in 1945, he went on to become a recognized soloist on record, radio and the concert platform. He received an MBE in 1992. His son is the writer and composer David T. Reilly. **Hammer credits:** *Watch It, Sailor!* (1961)

### Reizenstein, Franz

A child prodigy, this German composer (1911–1968) began to play the piano and compose short pieces of music from the age of just four. He went on to study composition in Berlin under Paul Hindemith in 1928. He made the move to Britain two years later, continuing his studies at the Royal College of Music under the tutelage of Ralph Vaughan Williams. He then went on to compose a number

of *concerti* as well as two acclaimed choral works: *Voices of Night* (1951) and *Genesis* (1958). In 1952, he was commissioned by the BBC to write *Anna Kraus*, the first opera specifically for broadcast on radio. It was this work, along with the two choral pieces, that brought Reizenstein to the attention of Hammer's music director John Hollingsworth, who subsequently commissioned him to write his first film score for the studio's remake of *The Mummy* (1959). A richly textured work, it exudes an air of both romance and dread, and benefits enormously from Reizenstein's trademark choral embellishments. Reizenstein's subsequent work includes scores for a number of radio dramas and documentaries, as well as further pieces for the concert hall platform, among them *Concerto Popolare* (1956) and *Let's Fake an Opera* (1958), both of them for the famous Hoffnung Concerts. His other feature film scores include *Jessy* (1959), *The White Trap* (1959) and *Circus of Horrors* (1960). He also worked as an arranger on *Once More with Feeling* (1960). **Additional notes:** Parts of Reizenstein's score for *The Mummy* were re-used in the flashback sequences for *The Curse of the Mummy's Tomb* (1964). **Hammer credits:** *The Mummy* (1959), *The Curse of the Mummy's Tomb* (1964 [extracts from *The Mummy* only, uncredited])

### Rennie, Maggie

This British actress (1919–2017, aka Margaret McGrath) can be seen as Gladys in Hammer's *On the Buses* (1971). Her other film credits include *English Without Tears* (1944), *Intent to Kill* (1958), *The V.I.P.s* (1963), *The Great St. Trinian's Train Robbery* (1966), *Hostile Witness* (1968), *Fraulein Doktor* (1968), *The Wicked Lady* (1983) and *Under the Bed* (1988). She also popped up as Mrs. Perkins in *Mark of the Devil* (1984, TVM [episode of *Hammer House of Mystery and Suspense*]). Her other TV work includes episodes of *The Somerset Maugham Hour* (1960–1963, TV), *Thriller* (1973–1979, TV) and *From the Top* (1985–1986, TV). **Hammer credits:** *On the Buses* (1971, as Gladys), *Mark of the Devil* (1984, TVM [episode of *Hammer House*

of *Mystery and Suspense*], as Mrs. Perkins)

### Rennison, Jan

This actress and model can be seen as Gloria in Hammer's *Mutiny on the Buses* (1972). Her other credits include episodes of *Adventures of the Seaspray* (1965–1967, TV), *The Persuaders!* (1971–1972, TV) and *Space: 1999* (1975–1977, TV). She was also a co-host on *Quick on the Draw* (1974–1979, TV). **Hammer credits:** *Mutiny on the Buses* (1972, as Gloria)

### Renown

This British distribution company handled Hammer's last pre-war featurette, *The Bank Messenger Mystery* (1936). Tending to operate at the low budget/second feature/re-issue end of the market, the company also handled films for the likes of Tudor, Sun, Ealing and Empire. Founded by George Minter, it also began producing films in 1948 with the notorious *No Orchids for Miss Blandish*. Other films distributed by Renown include *Lorna Doone* (1934 [1945 re-issue]), *Eye Witness* (1939), *Operation Diamond* (1948), *The Glass Mountain* (1949), *Old Mother Riley's Jungle Treasure* (1951), *Old Mother Riley Meets the Vampire* (1952), *Carry On Admiral* (1957) and *Beat Girl* (1960). **Hammer credits:** *The Bank Messenger Mystery* (1936)

### *The Reptile*

GB, 1966, 91m, Technicolor [UK], DeLuxe [U.S.], widescreen [1.85:1], RCA, cert X

Having wrapped principal photography on *The Plague of the Zombies* (1966) on 6 September 1965, director John Gilling and his crew took a week's break in order to re-group and prepare for the start date of *The Reptile* (1966) on 13 September. *The Reptile* was in fact the fourth film in a series of back-to-back productions that had been shot on much the same sets ("This involved more than usual liaison with the art director, careful re-vamping, re-dressing and so on,"[23] revealed Gilling). The first two films in the series had been *Dracula—Prince of Darkness* (1966) and *Rasputin—The Mad Monk* (1966), which had been helmed by Terence Fisher and Don Sharp respectively. Gilling then took over the megaphone for the two supporting features, of which *The Plague of the Zombies* had been first.

A prime example of a solid, low budget horror film of the period, its premise is fairly straightforward if slightly more far-fetched than usual. It transpires that the daughter of a Cornish doctor periodically turns into a murderous reptile, having been cursed by a Malayan sect while they were researching primitive religions in India, Java, Borneo and Sumatra. Having attacked and killed a number of villagers, she is eventually tracked down by the brother of one of her victims, who has arrived from London with his wife to live in the cottage that he has inherited.

To play the title creature, Hammer turned to Jacqueline Pearce, who had appeared as the unfortunate Alice Tompson in the recently finished *The Plague of the Zombies*. Recalled the actress, "Before we finished shooting on *The Plague of the Zombies* the producer called me into his office and said, 'You've got a marvellous face for films. I'd like you to play the Reptile. I never quite understood that!"[24] Pearce approached the role with relish, first appearing as the creature's nervous human *alter ego* Anna Franklyn before transforming into the venomous snake woman, care of Roy Ashton's elaborate make-up. To play her father, the cold-hearted theologian Dr. Franklyn, reliable character actor Noel Willman was brought back to Hammer, having previously essayed the role of Dr. Ravna in *The Kiss of the Vampire* (1963). Given top billing, Willman heads a cast that also includes Ray Barrett as Harry Spalding, the death of whose brother Charles sparks the plot, Jennifer Daniel (one of Willman's *Kiss* co-stars) as Spalding's wife Valerie, and Michael Ripper (another *Plague* holdover) as Tom Bailey, the landlord of the White Tor public house, who finds himself drawn into in the case. Also onboard were studio regulars Charles Lloyd-Pack as the local vicar and, in his last film for the company, George Woodbridge as White Tor regular Old Garnsey.

The script by Anthony Hinds (writing as John Elder) is little more than the usual collection of mysterious incidents, veiled warnings and something nasty up at the manor house. The project was originally announced in 1963 as *The Reptiles* and, a year later, as *The Curse of the Reptiles*, the promotional artwork for the latter of which proudly announced, "From Hammer—'The Kings of Horror'—the story of a hideous evil…!" The film was intended as a Universal co-production; however, when the Hollywood major turned the idea down, the project went on to become part of Hammer's eleven-picture deal with Seven Arts.

The film makes much use of the standing village set left over from *Plague*. Indeed, save for the renaming of the pub (from The Gardener's Arms to the White Tor) and the addition of a few rowing boats to suggest a seaside environ (save for some seagulls on the soundtrack, we never actually see the coastline), the outdoor set remains much the same, with particular use made of the sunken graveyard, where Harry and Tom disinter the victims so as to determine the cause of death. The interior of the doctor's mansion, Well House, is the usual Bernard Robinson concoction of *objects d'art* and bric-a-brac, plus re-cycled elements from the previous three films, among them colored glass windows and the "Dracula" staircase. However, the exterior is again Oakley Court, which had doubled for Squire Hamilton's home in *Plague* (even the same camera angles are used, including a familiar shot by an ornate fountain). Also like *Plague*, nearby Chobham Common and Frensham Ponds proved handy locations for the moorland sequences, while Grainger's Farm in Woking, Surrey doubled as Larkrise, the Spaldings' picturesque cottage, complete with "roses round the door," as Harry exclaims when he first sees the place.

At ninety-one minutes, the running time of *The Reptile* is perhaps a shade on the generous side, while its simple plot contains a little too much toing and froing by the characters between the village, Larkrise and Well House. Nevertheless, the premise just about holds one's attention thanks to the accumulation of mysterious events and two particularly well-staged shock cuts involving the

revelation of the title creature, the second of which is a genuine seat jolter! As always, Arthur Grant's cinematography is suitably atmospheric (particularly during the day for night scenes), while John

Gilling always chooses the right angle from which to shoot the action, among the film's most effective sequences being those by the convenient sulphur pit in the cave underneath Dr. Franklyn's house,

*Top, from left to right*, Noel Willman, Jacqueline Pearce, Jennifer Daniel and Ray Barrett (knees only) enjoy a musical evening in this scene from *The Reptile* (1966). *Bottom:* Jennifer Daniel (left) and Jacqueline Pearce (right) in a moment from *The Reptile* (1966) (both photographs, Hammer/Seven Arts/Associated British Picture Corporation/Warner Pathé/Twentieth Century–Fox/Studio Canal).

*Top, left:* **From left to right, Jennifer Daniel, Ray Barrett and Michael Ripper manage to ignore the somewhat large microphone while filming a scene for** *The Reptile* **(1966).** *Bottom:* **From left to right, Jennifer Daniel, Ray Barrett and John Laurie in a scene from** *The Reptile* **(1966).** *Top, right:* **Noel Willman (left) and Marne Maitland (right) in a scene from** *The Reptile* **(1966) (all three photographs, Hammer/Seven Arts/Associated British Picture Corporation/Warner Pathé/Twentieth Century–Fox/Studio Canal).**

the warmth from which keeps Anna alive during her annual transformation ("Every winter Anna sheds her skin like a reptile and goes into a deep sleep," we are informed by Franklyn).

The Reptile's appearance is also augmented by some careful costuming by Rosemary Burrows, who recalled, "We wanted something rather special for the Snake Woman to wear, which complemented Roy's fabulous design. It was Hammer's custom to rent frocks as required, or make do and

mend. However, on this one occasion, they actually gave me some money to buy fabric! I found this lovely, silky fabric, which was just right. The look and feel of it was highly suggestive of the sensuality of a snake. I can't remember another time when they allowed me to go out and buy what I wanted. I was bowled over!"[25]

Unlike *Plague*, which suffered from a couple of weak performances, the cast enters into the spirit of the proceedings with gusto. Particularly effective is Noel Willman as Dr. Franklyn, torn between his love for his daughter and his fear of what the Ourang Sancto cult—better known as the Snake People of Borneo—has done to her. Also giving a good account of themselves are Marne Maitland as the evil Malay, whose grip on Franklyn and his daughter is total; Michael Ripper as the helpful publican Tom Bailey (he even gets to utter the clichéd warning, "They don't like strangers in these parts"); John Laurie in an amusing cameo as Mad Peter; and of course Jacqueline Pearce as Anna Franklyn, her body taking on a suitably writhing motion when she transforms into the title creature. Technically, the film is also well up to par, with Roy Ashton providing some convincing victim make-ups, while effective touches include the revelation of Anna's sloughed skin upon her bed by her father, the death of Mad Peter, whose contorted face we see grimacing at the Spaldings' cottage window, Anna's frenzied sitar recital, and the Reptile's failed bid to put the bite on Harry, which is thwarted by his starched collar!

Billed with *Rasputin—The Mad Monk*, with which was trade shown at Studio One on 14 February 1966, *The Reptile* was released in the UK on the ABC circuit by Warner Pathé on 6 March to a lukewarm reception (*Dracula—Prince of Darkness* and *The Plague of the Zombies* had taken all the glory). Commented *Kinematograph Weekly* of the film, "This is utter nonsense but it is directed with

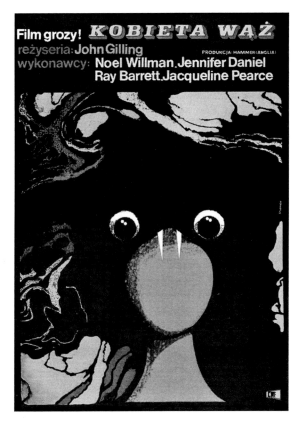

*Above, left:* **A somewhat disconcerting Polish poster for *The Reptile* (1966). It probably made sense to the artist.** *Above, right:* **Marne Maitland gets a hosing down during the making of *The Reptile* (1966).** *Right:* **Noel Willman makes a grab for Jennifer Daniel in *The Reptile* (1966) (all three photographs: Hammer/Seven Arts/Associated British Picture Corporation/Warner Pathé/Twentieth Century–Fox/Studio Canal).**

intelligence and very well acted." It also noted that "the snake metamorphosis is an interesting and effective variant on the werewolf theme." A month later Twentieth Century–Fox released the double bill in America on 6 April. The four back-to-back productions—a snip at £402,000 for the lot—had nevertheless left all at Bray exhausted by the time filming on *The Reptile* had been completed on 22 October 1965, itself coming in at a cost of just over £100,000. Indeed, the experience was not without its casualties: Roy Ashton left Hammer upon the completion of *The Reptile*, bringing to an end his lengthy and fruitful association with the company, save for a couple of pieces of uncredited work. In fact Hammer's golden era at Bray was finally coming to a close. **Additional notes:** Gaffe spotters should note the shadow of the camera crew in the opening shot, as Charles Spalding makes his way across Cragmoor. And where *is* the mysterious music that precedes each killing coming from? We never do find out! Also note the black plastic bucket with which Tom Bailey washes down his pub stoop, the car driving across the background as Harry and Valerie walk up the steps of the graveyard upon their arrival, and the shadow of the rain machine during Harry and Tom's grave digging ad-

venture. And if Anna can't go out into the cold while she is in reptile form—a broken window proves fatal during the climax—how is she able to go out on the chilly common at night and kill the likes of Charles and Mad Peter? The film's screen-

play was novelized by John Burke for *The Second Hammer Horror Film Omnibus* (1967), which was published by Pan.

Production companies: Hammer/Seven Arts/ Associated British Picture Corporation. Distribu-

*Top:* Lobby card for *The Reptile* (1966) featuring Ray Barrett (left) and Michael Ripper (right). *Bottom:* The end is nigh for John Laurie (left) as Ray Barrett (right) looks on in *The Reptile* (1966) (both photographs, Hammer/Seven Arts/Associated British Picture Corporation/Warner Pathé/Twentieth Century–Fox/Studio Canal).

tors: Warner Pathé Distributors (UK [ABC circuit]), Twentieth Century–Fox (U.S.). Producer: Anthony Nelson Keys. Executive producer: Anthony Hinds [uncredited]. Director: John Gilling. Screenplay: John Elder (Anthony Hinds). Cinematographer: Arthur Grant. Music: Don Banks. Music director: Philip Martell. Supervising editor:

James Needs. Editor: Roy Hyde. Production design: Bernard Robinson. Art director: Don Mingaye. Costumes: Rosemary Burrows. Special effects: Bowie Films, Ltd.. Make-up: Roy Ashton. Hair: Frieda Steiger. Sound: William Bulkley. Sound editor: Roy Baker. Production manager: George Fowler. Assistant director: Bill Cartlidge.

Camera operator: Moray Grant. Focus puller: Bob Jordan [uncredited]. Second unit photography: Len Harris [uncredited]. Stunts: Peter Diamond [uncredited]. Continuity: Lorna Selwyn. Poster: Tom Chantrell [uncredited]. **Cast:** Noel Willman (Dr. Franklyn), Ray Barrett (Harry George Spalding), Jennifer Daniel (Valerie Spalding), Jacqueline Pearce (Anna Franklyn/The Reptile), Michael Ripper (Tom Bailey), Marne Maitland (Malay), John Laurie (Mad Peter), David Baron (Charles Edward Spalding), Charles Lloyd-Pack (Vicar), George Woodbridge (Old Garnsey), Harold Goldblatt (Solicitor), Fred Peck (Inn patron [uncredited]), Ernie Rice (Inn patron [uncredited]). **DVD availability:** Anchor Bay (U.S. R1 NTSC), extras include a trailer, TV spots and an episode of *The World of Hammer* (1990 [first broadcast 1994], TV) titled *Vamp*; Anchor Bay (U.S. R1 NTSC), double-billed with *The Lost Continent*; Optimum Home Releasing (UK R2 PAL), extras include a documentary titled *The Serpent's Tale*, a trailer and an episode of *The World of Hammer* (1990 [first broadcast 1994], TV) titled *Wicked Women*. **Blu-ray availability:** Studio Canal (B/2), extras include the DVD version, a documentary titled *The Serpent's Tale*, a restoration comparison featurette and an episode of *The World of Hammer* (1990 [first broadcast 1994], TV) titled *Wicked Women*

### The Resident

U.S./GB, 2010, 91m, color, widescreen [2.35:1], Dolby

While before the cameras, *The Resident* was hailed as Hammer's first "official" return to feature production in thirty years—despite being preceded by *Wake Wood* (2009), the release of which was however delayed until 2011, and *Let Me In* (2010), which, though made after *The Resident*, actually beat it into cinemas. A modern day thriller about a young surgeon who suspects that she may not be alone in her Brooklyn apartment ("This year fear comes home" boasted the trailer), it was described by Hammer itself as being a mix of *Fatal Attraction* (1987) and *Disturbia* (2007). They might also have mentioned that it also borrows from *Rear Window* (1954), *Psycho* (1960) and *Inferno* (1980). Nevertheless, the omens initially appeared to be good, given that Hammer legend Christopher Lee was among the cast, offering (albeit brief) support to leading lady Hilary Swank, whose double-Oscar pedigree certainly adds a touch of class to the production (Lee's knighthood was announced during filming, which was duly celebrated on set). No stranger to horror films, Swank had previously appeared in *The Reaping* (2007) and *The Gift* (2000). She was also directly involved in the production as an executive producer, as she had been on a number of her other films.

Co-starring Jeffrey Dean Morgan and Lee Pace, the film (briefly also known as *Invasion of Privacy* and *Resident*) was based upon an idea by its director, Antti J. Jokinen (best known for his stylish music videos), who also penned the resultant screenplay with Robert Orr and Erin Cressida Wilson. This revolves round Swank as New York surgeon Dr. Juliet Devereau, who rents an apartment by herself following a split from her other half.

However, her handsome landlord isn't quite what he seems, and Devereau finds herself in mortal danger when things start to unaccountably go bump in the night.

Filmed at the Albuquerque Studios in New Mexico between 21 May and 11 July 2009, other key technical personnel involved in its making included cinematographer Guillermo Navarra (known for his work for director Guillermo del Toro), respected production designer J. Dennis Washington, composer John Ottman (known for his scores for director Bryan Singer) and, in a sign of the times, product placement liaison Dana Wilkey (no doubt hence the strategically placed bottles of Stella Artois in Devereau's fridge).

Unfortunately, despite a heavy promotional campaign, the £6.3m film failed to make much headway when released in America on 3 November 2010, and later in Britain on 11 March 2011, where it pulled in just £320,000 from 150 screens (commented *The Standard* of the film's insistent UK campaign, "At one stage there were more ads for *The Resident* at Heathrow Airport than there were planes"). The reviews were also on the tepid side, with *The Guardian* describing the proceedings as "generic and intermittently silly," which indeed they are, while *The Daily Mail* noted that it was "the kind of exercise of mildly salacious voyeurism that has been attempted many times before, in movies such as *Sliver* and *Hider in the House*." However, *Woman's Own* advised its readers that they'd "be leaving the light on for weeks," while *The Standard* acknowledged that the production was a "competently made film by Antti J. Jokinen" that "winds to a bloody conclusion." Indeed, this involves the judicious use of a nail gun and much running about in dusty crawlspaces, while elsewhere we are treated to Swank being injected under her toenail and being sexually molested as she sleeps, which doesn't always make for entirely comfortable viewing. **Additional notes:** Jessica Alba and Maggie Gyllenhaal were apparently attached to the leading role at various stages. Re-shoots occurred in April 2010. Some scenes seem to have ended up on the editing room floor, among them those featuring Peggy Miley as Mrs. Rosenbaum. The camera is briefly reflected in a kitchen window when Lee Pace brings over the groceries to make dinner. The cyclorama outside the apartment Max is renovating when we first see him isn't exactly convincing. Several personnel involved with making *The Resident* stayed on at the Albuquerque Studios to work on Hammer's next Stateside production, *Let Me In* (2010), which was actually released first. The screenplay was novelized by Francis Cottam and published by Hammer Books (via Arrow and Random House).

Production companies: Hammer/Exclusive Media Group. Distributors: Icon (UK), Image Entertainment (U.S.). Producers: Guy East, Simon Oakes, Cary Brokaw. Executive producers: Tobin Armbrust, Alex Brunner, Nigel Sinclair, Tom Lassally, Hilary Swank, Renny Harlin. Co-producers: Jillian Longnecker, Vicki Dee Rock. Creative executive: Ben Holden. Screenplay: Antti J. Jokinen, Robert Orr, Erin Cressida Wilson. Idea: Antti J. Jokinen. Director: Antti J. Jokinen. Cinematographer: Guillermo Navarro. Music: John Ottman. Editors: Stuart Levy, Bob Murawski. First assistant editor: Christine Park. Additional editor: Tony Bacigalupi. On-line editor: Philip Beckner. Production designer: J. Dennis Washington. Art director: Guy Barnes. Additional art director: Jesse Benson. Set designer: Amahl Lovato. Set decoration: Wendy Ozols-Barnes. Make-up artist to Hilary Swank: Vivian Baker. Make-up department head: Blair Leonard. Assistant make-up artist: Ashlynne Padilla. Additional make-up artist: Patricia Greer. Special make-up design: Tony Gardner. Special make-up effects artist: Scott Wheeler, Koji Ohmura (care of W.M. Creations). Hair stylist to Hilary Swank: Anne Morgan. Assistant hair stylist: Elizabeth Gallegos. Music supervisor: Michelle Belcher. Special effects co-ordinators: Werner Hahnlein, Ciril Koshyk. Senior visual effects producer: Amy Hollywood Wixson. Digital post-production manager: Paul Lavoie. Digital intermediate executive: Bill Schultz. Casting: Matthew Barry, Nancy Green-Keyes, Judy Cook, Elizabeth Gabel. Art department co-ordinators: Libbe Green, Loren Schoel. Set dressers: Linda R. Gore, Graham Robertson. Set decoration buyers: Wilhelm Pfau, Billy Ray. Set production assistants: Joann Connolly, Daniel Fisch. Draper: Dennis Riewerts. Costumes: Ann Roth, Yulia Gershenzon, Brandy Marrs, Kortney Lawlor, Daniela Moore, Lauren Warkentien. Construction foreman: Ronald O. Jaynes. Key rigging grip: Mark Steinig. Labor foreman: Leonard Sanchez. Painters: Nichole Miller, Cisco Whitson-Brown, Jon de Pabon. Property master: Ben Lowney. Props: Amy Giedraitis, Mike Biskupski, Denise Ciarcia. Assistant prop master: Brett Andrews. Lead man: R.A. Arancio-Parrain, Bret Ross. Assistant to Tobin Armbrust: Ashley Elizabeth Davis. Assistant to Antti J. Jokinen: Sara Jo Fischer. Assistant to Hilary Swank: Shannon Walker. Production supervisor: Tiffany Tiesiera. Unit production manager: Anne Johns. Production manager, New York: Lucille Smith. Location assistant, New York: Michael McGrail. Production co-ordinator: Rob Corlew. Production co-ordinator, New York unit: Pamela Bertini. Location manager: Hilton Clay Peres. Assistant location managers: Steve Aguino, Loren Schoel. Location manager, New York: Ellen Athena Catsikeas. Location assistant: James Wilkerson. Location unit assistant, New York: Dimitris Soukos. Assistant production co-ordinator: Jennifer Mancuso. Assistant production co-ordinator, New York unit: Gary Martyn. Post facilities manager: Zoe Bower. Post facilities co-ordinator: Tana David. Travel co-ordinator: Kristen Blodget. Second second [*sic*] assistant directors: Trish Stanard, Jane Chase Wells. DGA trainee: X. Sydney Ng. On-set dresser: Lisa Corradino. Sound Designers: Will Riley, David Esparza. Supervising Sound Editor: Will Riley. Sound editor: Paul P. Soucek. Assistant sound editors: Ryan Collins, Callie Thurman. Sound production mixer: Matthew Nicolay. Re-recording mixers: Chris David, Gabriel J. Serrano. ADR supervisor: Robert Jackson. ADR mixers: Travis McKay, Michael Miller. ADR recordist: Jan Petrov. Recordist: Tim Limer. Dialogue editor: Tom Marks. Foley editor: Brian Dunlop. Foley mixer: A. Josh Reinhardt. Sound utility: Edwardo Santiago. Utility sound technician: Miles J.D. Vedder. Dolby sound consultant: James Wright. Camera operator: Paige Thomas. Camera assistants: Timothy James Kane, Liza Bambenek, Chip Byrd, Joe Chess. Camera loader: Erick Castillo. Grips/dolly grips: Kurt Kornemann, Harland Espeset, Lamont Crawford, David Jaxx Nagro, Morgan Davis, David Midthunder, Mark Steinig, Rick Stribling. Best Boy Electric: Greg Argarin. Electrician: Andrew Engert. Dimmer operator: Jacob Cottrell. Video assist: Scott Wetzel. Video Assist Operator: Tyler Fletcher. Rigging best boy: Nikki LeBlanc. Gaffers: David Lee, Jeremy Antonio Oliver. Lighting Technicians: John Gorman, Jason Linebaugh. Chief rigging electrician: Mark Mele. Music editor: Joseph Bonn. Conductors/orchestrators: Jason Lievsay, Nolan Lievsay. Executive music producer: Philip Moross. Additional arrangements: Edwin Wendler. Carpenter: Richard Hurff. Storyboard artists: Ted Boonthanakit, Dan Fitzgerald. Production assistants: Lucas Francy, Stefan Kende, J. Tom Pogue, Robert Vertrees, Cristal Calderon, Joann Connolly, Daniel Fisch, Brandon Leonard, Mollie Kimball Whitson. Post-production assistant: Christos Voutsinas. Studio Stage Manager: Jason Hariton. Colorists: John Daro, Kay Sievert. Production legal counsel: Glenn D. Feig, Susan Kaufman. Transportation co-ordinator: Patrick P.J. Reynolds. Transportation captain: Mark Dometrovich. Driver: James William Ray. Product placement: Dana Wilkey. Production Accountants: Barbara Long, Theresa Marsh. Payroll accountant: Jean E. Jacobson. Accounting assistant: Adrienne L. Graves. Accounting assistant, New York Unit: Katherine Dejesus. Post-production accountant: Emily Rice. Stunt co-ordinator: John Robotham. Utility stunts: Trina Siopy, Stephen Mann. Key craft service: Allison Jandreau-Heil. Additional epk: Monika Agorelius. System support (Foto-Kem): Mitch Spacone. Dog Drainer: Claire Doré. Stills: Lorey Sebastian. Thanks: Christopher Lee, Paavo Jokinen, Lance Hool. Publicity: Davidson Dalling Associates (as D.D.A.). **Cast:** Hilary Swank (Dr. Juliet "Bliss" Devereau), Jeffrey Dean Morgan (Max), Christopher Lee (August), Lee Pace (Jack), Eliezer Meyer (Rabbi Elli), Michael Massee (Security technician), Michael Showers (Doctor), Steven Ray Bryrd (Paramedic), Kisha Sierra (Girl), Aunjanue Ellis (Sydney), Sean Rosales (Carlos), Deborah Martinez (Mrs. Portes), Sheila Traister (Nurse), Nana Visitor (Real estate agent), Arron Shiver (Architect), Michael Badalucco (Moving man), Mark Vincent Morocco (Surgeon), Veronica Hool (Nurse girl), Cliff Gravel (Patient), Sandi K. Shelby (Doctor), Alexandria Morrow (Art model), Penny Balfour (Drug addict), Deborah L. Mazor (stunt double for Hilary Swank), Jacob Chambers (stunt double for Lee Pace), Leandro di Salvo (stand-in for Jeffrey Dean Morgan), Peggy Miley (Mrs. Rosenbaum [scenes cut]), Skippy the Dog (Amelie). **DVD availability:** Icon Home Entertainment (R2 UK PAL), extras include a trailer and a commentary by Antti J. Jokinen. **Blu-ray availability:** Icon Home Entertainment (B/2). **CD availability:** Pale Blue, which contains 17 cues, among them *Bad Wine*, *Erection Dejection* and *Nailing Max*

### Retief, Dani (Danie)

Retief can be seen as the shroud moving about the graveyard in Hammer's *The Vampire Lovers* (1970). His other credits include an episode of *The Strauss Family* (1972, TV). **Hammer credits:** *The Vampire Lovers* (1970, as Shroud [uncredited])

### The Revenge of Frankenstein

GB, 1958, 89m, Technicolor, widescreen [1.85:1], RCA, cert X

Following the international success of *The Curse of Frankenstein* (1957), it was inevitable that Hammer, like Universal before them, would wish to further exploit this Gothic cash cow (they had already entered the sequel market with the Dick Barton films and *Quatermass 2* [1957], among others). To this end, it was quickly announced that *The Blood of Frankenstein* would soon be going into production. But there was one slight problem: Baron Frankenstein had been sent to the guillotine at the end of *The Curse of Frankenstein*. James Carreras's solution was simple: "We sew his head back on again," he told an incredulous Milton Shulman when questioned about this in the *Sunday Express*. The resolution was, in fact, much more ingenious, though it did cause some initial problems for screenwriter Jimmy Sangster. As he later recalled, James Carreras went to America to get funding for the film, following which, "James returned to Lon-

**Artwork for the German release of *The Revenge of Frankenstein* (1958) (Hammer/Cadogan/Columbia).**

don and presented me with the poster. 'We start shooting in ten weeks,' he told me. 'When can you deliver a script?' 'But I killed Frankenstein off in the last picture,' I reminded him. 'You're a writer. You'll think of something,' he said."[26]

Thus Jimmy Sangster was put to work on *The Revenge of Frankenstein*—as the film was now to be called—on 24 July 1957, barely three months following the release of *The Curse of Frankenstein* (note that Sangster was also working on various drafts of *Dracula* during this period). And indeed, his first task was to find an acceptable way around the death of the Baron, alluded to, but not actually *seen* at the climax of the previous film (unlike Universal, which had continually revived the Monster for each successive sequel, Hammer decided to revive the Baron himself).

Sangster's solution was fairly simple: Frankenstein manages to coerce the priest to whom he has been confessing his life story in his cell to take his stead at the guillotine, aided in the deception by the executioner and a fellow prisoner, a crippled dwarf, whom he has promised a new body by way of compensation. Consequently, this enables Frankenstein to carry on his work, which he now does at a poor hospital in Carlsbruck under the name of Dr. Victor Stein ("They will never be rid of me!" exclaims the Baron). Aided and abetted by a young assistant, Dr. Kleve, the Baron harvests the body parts of the patients to produce a new super being. Inevitably, though, things start to go wrong when the supposedly perfect being begins to deteriorate and display signs of cannibalism following a beating from the hospital janitor. Frankenstein, meanwhile, is bludgeoned to death by his patients, only to have his brain transplanted by Dr. Kleve into a second "standby" body, thus enabling him to escape detection and set up a new practice in London's Harley Street under the name of Dr. Franck.

As expected, the script came in for criticism when submitted to the BBFC in November, which resulted in the inevitable objections and suggestions, particularly regarding the cannibalism theme. Various compromises followed, after which the film went on to the floor on 6 January 1958 with pretty much the same crew as *Dracula*, which had completed principal photography just two weeks earlier on Christmas Eve (save for a handful of pick-up shots, which would be made during the production of *Revenge*). Back as Frankenstein was Peter Cushing, fresh from his stint as Van Helsing in the vampire saga, while joining him in the cast was Hammer newcomer Francis Matthews as Stein's assistant, Dr. Hans Kleve, the one person who knows his mentor's true identity. Providing the female interest was Eu-

nice Gayson as Margaret. Also featured in the cast were Hammer regulars Richard Wordsworth, Charles Lloyd-Pack, George Woodbridge and Michael Ripper, while Michael Gwynne, who had appeared in *The Camp on Blood Island* (1958), was cast as the unfortunate Creature.

In designing the film, Bernard Robinson proved a major asset, for not only did his beautifully decorated period sets add great production value to the film, they also recycled a number of sets from *Dracula*. For example, Dracula's crypt became Frankenstein's study at the hospital, as well as part of a graveyard set, while Dracula's library became a hospital ward and the laboratory set, thus saving the production vital financial outlay which could be made use of elsewhere.

As with *The Camp on Blood Island* and *The Snorkel* (both 1958), *The Revenge of Frankenstein* was financed and distributed by Columbia Pictures, who had shown a keen interest in Hammer following the worldwide success of the first Frankenstein film (which had been distributed by Warner Bros.). Principal photography on the much-anticipated sequel was completed by 3 March, with pick-ups and inserts finished off the following day, making this, at eight weeks, one of Hammer's most lavishly scheduled productions. The film wasn't without its casualties, however. Having tired of Hammer's increasing emphasis on horror, make-up artist Phil Leakey decided to jump ship, thus leaving the door open for Roy Ashton to take up the mantle of monster maker in chief.

Having been edited, the film was submitted to the BBFC for approval, and following the deletion of a handful of shots (among them those of certain body parts and a close-up of Frankenstein's swollen face following his beating), the film was duly issued an X certificate. *The Revenge of Frankenstein* received its UK premiere at a midnight showing at the Plaza Cinema, Piccadilly Circus on 27 August 1958, by which time it had already been playing in America for a over month—from 1 June—on a double bill with the classic supernatural thriller *Night of the Demon* (1957 [released Stateside as *Curse of the Demon*]). Some of the reviews were fairly positive, with *Variety* describing it as, "A high grade horror film, gory enough to give adults a squeamish second thought." Inevitably, however, there were those to whom the latest installment was an affront, among them C.A. Lejeune, who described it as "a crude sort of entertainment for a crude sort of audience." If that weren't enough, the critic went on to add, "Films of this kind are the last refuge of unimaginative producers who have lost the art of communicating individually with human beings and have fallen back on the appeal of mass hysteria." Audiences nevertheless embraced the film, and Hammer (and Columbia) had yet another hit on their hands when it went on general release in the UK on 17 November (the poster described the film as "The world's greatest horrorama!").

Technically, *The Revenge of Frankenstein* is a much more polished and assured film than its slightly rough-around-the-edges predecessor (commented *Variety*: "The production is a rich one. The screenplay is well-plotted [and] peopled with interesting characters"). The lighting is much more subtle, while the color ravishes with its richness, though it should be noted that camera movement is somewhat unadventurous, as, indeed, is Terence Fisher's direction, which relies a little too heavily on statically staged *tableaux*, a stylistic whim that would make one of his future films for Hammer, *The Man Who Could Cheat Death* (1959), something of a chore to sit through. The sets, however, are full of inventive flourishes and have much to take the eye. Performance-wise, Peter Cushing is now totally at one with the role of Frankenstein, fully dominating the proceedings. That said, Eunice Gayson's token role is something of an irritation ("Interfering women!" exclaims the Baron after she has stuck her nose into his business one time too often), whist Francis Matthews' Dr. Kleve lacks personality—as indeed does Michael Gwynn's rather plain Creature, though it should be noted that the character is both intelligent and articulate prior to his decline, as per the original Shelley novel.

As for the plot (for which Hurford Janes provided "additional dialogue"), above and beyond the cleverness of reprieving the Baron, it does contain quite a few inconsistencies. For example, the Baron's execution is somewhat conveniently carried out without the presence of any officials, thus enabling Frankenstein to easily pull off the deception (there is also no sign of Paul and Elizabeth, who had visited the Baron at the end of the previous film). And like the death of the Creature, the beheading of the priest takes place off screen. As for the controversial subject of cannibalism, it is so subtly alluded to that it is barely noticeable, while the second Creature into which Dr. Kleve transplants the Baron's brain—thus making him both crea*tor* and creat*ed*—just happens to look like Peter Cushing! Ironically, Kleve's transplant work is a complete success—unlike Frankenstein's own persistent failures with the scalpel throughout the series! The film also features some rather unfortunate comic business (written by an uncredited George Baxt) with two gravediggers played by Michael Ripper and Lionel Jeffries. As for the Baron's penchant for locking up his equipment in the hospital cellar, this would seem normal if he didn't also lock up his assistant Karl with it! Its deficiencies aside, though, the film has enough going for it elsewhere to make it a more than honorable addition the series.

Recalled Francis Matthews of its making, "The seriousness of the material meant that between shots, we all behaved in a ludicrously infantile manner—games, practical jokes and running gags."[27] Meanwhile, of Peter Cushing he remembered, "He made me feel at home instantly…. It was one of the happiest working relationships I have ever enjoyed."[28] As for screenwriter Jimmy Sangster, he opined that, "It turned out to be a pretty good movie, even if I do say so myself…. It certainly had its drawbacks; the terrible woman's part bravely played by Eunice Gayson and a definite slowdown in Act Two as if Terry Fisher (or, more likely, the script) had temporarily lost its way. But there was plenty to outweigh these weaknesses…. The sets were designed by the brilliant Bernard Robinson

Tantalizing artwork for the edited 8mm home release of *The Revenge of Frankenstein* (1958) (Hammer/Cadogan/Columbia).

and beautifully photographed by Jack Asher. The mixture very much as before, which was what Hammer and the American money were aiming for."[29]

Heavily promoted, the film's trailer warned that, "Your blood will congeal when you see this brand new billion-volt shocker!" **Additional notes:** Although he worked with composer Leonard Salzedo in preparing the score for *The Revenge of Frankenstein*, music director John Hollingsworth was taken ill with tuberculosis a few days prior to the recording sessions; consequently, the orchestra was conducted by Muir Mathieson, who worked without screen credit. The film's screenplay was novelized twice, first by Jimmy Sangster for Panther, and later by John Burke for *The Hammer Horror Omnibus* (1966), which was published by Pan

Production companies: Hammer/Cadogan. Distributor: Columbia (UK, U.S.). Producer: Anthony Hinds. Executive producer: Michael Carreras. Associate producer: Anthony Nelson Keys. Director: Terence Fisher. Screenplay: Jimmy Sangster, Hurford Janes, George Baxt [uncredited]. Cinematographer: Jack Asher. Music: Leonard Salzedo. Music director: John Hollingsworth (and

Muir Mathieson [uncredited]). Supervising editor: James Needs. Editor/sound editor: Alfred Cox. Assistant editor: Peter Todd [uncredited]. Second assistant editor: Alan Corder [uncredited]. Production designer: Bernard Robinson. Costumes: Rosemary Burrows, Molly Arbuthnot [uncredited]. Make-up: Phil Leakey. Make-up assistant: Roy Ashton [uncredited]. Hair: Henry Montsash. Camera operators: Len Harris, Gerald Moss [uncredited]. Focus puller: Harry Oakes [uncredited]. Camera grip: Albert Cowlard [uncredited]. Clapper loader: Anthony Powell [uncredited]. Assistant director: Robert Lynn. Second assistant director: Tom Walls [uncredited]. Third assistant director: Hugh Harlow [uncredited]. Special effects: Les Bowie [uncredited]. Sound: Jock May. Production manager: Don Weeks. Continuity: Doreen Dearnaley. Production secretary: Pat Green [uncredited]. Props: Tommy Money [uncredited]. Props buyer: Eric Hillier [uncredited]. Studio manager: Arthur Kelly [uncredited]. Construction manager: Mick Lyons [uncredited]. Chief electrician: Jack Curtis [uncredited]. Master painter: Lawrence Wren [uncredited]. Master plasterer: Arthur Banks [uncredited]. Master carpenter: Charles Davis [uncredited]. Draughtsman: Don Mingaye [uncredited]. Casting: Dorothy Holloway [uncredited]. Cashier: Ken Gordon [uncredited]. Animal trainer: Molly Badham [uncredited]. Stills: Tom Edwards [uncredited]. Stunts: Peter Munt [uncredited]. Publicity: Colin Reid [uncredited]. Poster: John Stockle [uncredited]. **Cast:** Peter Cushing (Baron Victor Frankenstein/Dr. Victor Stein/Dr. Franck), Eunice Gayson (Margaret), Francis Matthews (Dr. Hans Kleve), Michael Gwynne (Karl), Lionel Jeffries (Fritz), John Welsh (Bergman), Oscar Quitak (Dwarf/Karl), Richard Wordsworth (Up Patient), Margery Gresley (Countess Barscynska), John Stuart (Inspector), Charles Lloyd-Pack (President), Arnold Diamond (Molke), Anna Walmsley (Vera Barscynska), George Woodbridge (Janitor), Michael Ripper (Kurt), Avril Leslie (Girl), Middleton Woods (Patient [uncredited]), Gerald Lawson (Patient [uncredited]), Freddie Watts (Patient [uncredited]), Ian Whittaker (Boy [uncredited]), Robert Brooks Taylor (Groom [uncredited]), George Hirste (Dirty patient [uncredited]), Raymond Hodge (Official [uncredited]), John Gayford (Footman [uncredited]), Eugene Leahy (Klein [uncredited]), Michael Mulcaster (Tattooed man [uncredited]), Gordon Needham (Nurse [uncredited]), Alex Gallier (Priest [uncredited]), Julia Nelson (Inga [uncredited]). **DVD availability:** Columbia (UK R2 PAL), extras include a trailer and a stills gallery. **CD availability:** *The Hammer Frankenstein Album* (GDI Records), which contains three brief cues from the film: *Opening Titles*, *Opening Credits* and *End Credits*

### Re-Voicing

Many actors and actresses found their performances re-voiced by Hammer, among them several European starlets in supporting roles. However, even top names such as Ingrid Pitt found themselves dubbed, much to their inevitable chagrin. For the record, those who had their voices dubbed are as follows:

Margia Dean in *The Quatermass Xperiment* (1955)

David Hoffman in *Tales of Frankenstein* (1958, TV)

Norma Marla in *The Two Faces of Dr. Jekyll* (1960)

John Stuart (by Robert Rietti) in *The Scarlet Blade* (1963)

Norman Bird (by André Maranne) in *Maniac* (1963)

Jeanne Roland in *The Curse of the Mummy's Tomb* (1964)

Lelia Goldoni in *Hysteria* (1965)

Ursula Andress (by Nikki Van Der Zyl) in *She* (1965)

André Morell (by George Pastell) in *She* (1965)

Barbara Shelley (screams only) in *Dracula— Prince of Darkness* (1966)

Bartlett Mullins (by Michael Ripper) in *Rasputin—The Mad Monk* (1966)

Diane Clare in *The Plague of the Zombies* (1966)

Raquel Welch (by Nicolette McKenzie) in

*One Million Years B.C.* (1966 [with additional grunts provided by Nikki Van Der Zyl])

Susan Denberg (by Nikki Van der Zyl) in *Frankenstein Created Woman* (1967)

Jenny Till in *A Challenge for Robin Hood* (1967)

John Richardson (by David de Keyser) in *The Vengeance of She* (1968)

Sally-Jane Spencer in *The Anniversary* (1968)

Ewan Hooper in *Dracula Has Risen from the Grave* (1968)

Leon Greene (by Patrick Allen) in *The Devil Rides Out* (1968)

Christopher Lee (screams only) in *Taste the Blood of Dracula* (1970)

Ingrid Pitt (partial dialogue only, by Olive Gregg) in *The Vampire Lovers* (1970)

Madeline Smith in *The Vampire Lovers* (1970)

Jenny Hanley (by Nikki Van Der Zyl) in *Scars of Dracula* (1970)

Mike Raven (by Valentine Dyall) in *Lust for a Vampire* (1970)

Yutte Stensgaard in *Lust for a Vampire* (1970)

Ingrid Pitt in *Countess Dracula* (1970)

Madeleine and Mary Collinson in *Twins of Evil* (1971)

Valerie Leon in *Blood from the Mummy's Tomb* (1971)

Robert Tayman (by David de Keyser) in *Vampire Circus* (1972)

Horst Janson (by Julian Holloway) in *Captain Kronos—Vampire Hunter* (1974)

John Forbes-Robertson (by David de Keyser) in *The Legend of the 7 Golden Vampires* (1974)

Dave Prowse (by David de Keyser) in *Frankenstein and the Monster from Hell* (1974)

Nastassja Kinski in *To the Devil a Daughter* (1976)

Marcus Gilbert (by Peter Graves) in *Tennis Court* (1984, TVM [episode of *Hammer House of Mystery and Suspense*])

### Reynolds, Brian

Having worked as an office boy at Hammer's Wardour Street headquarters in the late sixties (during which time he attended the Queen's Award for Industry presentation in 1968), Reynolds went on to work as a runner on number of films for the company in the early seventies, among them *The Vampire Lovers* (1970) and *Blood from the Mummy's Tomb* (1971). Along with fellow runner Phil Campbell, he wrote about his experiences at the studio in *Running Scared* (2014). **Hammer credits:** *The Vampire Lovers* (1970 [uncredited]), *Scars of Dracula* (1970 [uncredited]), *The Horror of Frankenstein* (1970 [uncredited]), *Lust for a Vampire* (1971 [uncredited]), *Blood from the Mummy's Tomb* (1971 [uncredited]), *Dr. Jekyll and Sister Hyde* (1971 [uncredited]), *On the Buses* (1971 [uncredited]), *Demons of the Mind* (1972 [uncredited]), *Dracula A.D. 1972* (1972 [uncredited]), *Fear in the Night* (1972 [uncredited]), *That's Your Funeral* (1973 [uncredited]), *Captain Kronos—Vampire Hunter* (1974 [uncredited])

### Reynolds, Clarke

American born Reynolds (1917–1994) penned the screenplay for Hammer's dismal historical epic *The Viking Queen* (1967), which he based upon a story by the film's producer, John Temple-Smith. Something of a western specialist (which would explain the anachronistic dialogue in *The Viking Queen*), his other credits, often in collaboration, include *Son of a Gunfighter* (1964), *Genghis Khan* (1964), *Gunfighters of Casa Grande* (1965) and *The Viscount* (1967). He also provided the stories for *Shalako* (1968) and *The Desperados* (1969). **Hammer credits:** *The Viking Queen* (1967)

### Reynolds, Peter

In films from the mid-forties, this British supporting actor (1925–1975, real name Peter Horrocks) appeared in such varied and variable films as *The Captive Heart* (1946), *Devil Girl from Mars* (1954), *Shake Hands with the Devil* (1959) and *Nobody Runs Forever* (1968). He can also be seen in the role of Jeff Hart in the Hammer second feature *The Last Page* (1952), prior to which he'd had a bit part in *The Dark Road* (1948). He also appeared in episodes of such TV series as *Douglas Fairbanks, Jr. Presents* (1953–1957, TV), *Ivanhoe* (1958–1959, TV) and *Department S* (1969–1970, TV). In 1969 he moved to Australia, where he appeared in such films as *Private Collection* (1972), which gave him a rare leading role, and episodes of *Homicide* (1964–1976, TV), *Riptide* (1969, TV), *The Long Arm* (1970, TV), *Elephant Boy* (1973, TV) and *Boney* (1972–1973, TV). He also appeared in a series of cigarette commercials in Australia. **Hammer credits:** *The Dark Road* (1948, unnamed role), *The Last Page* (1952, as Jeff Hart)

### RFI *see* Regal Films International

### Rhodes, Adam

Rhodes can be seen as Little Arthur in Hammer's *Holiday on the Buses* (1973), a role that Wayne Westhorpe had previously played in *Mutiny on the Buses* (1972). His other film credits include the serial *The Boy with Two Heads* (1974) and *The Mine and the Minotaur* (1980), while his TV work takes in an appearance in *Reg Varney* (1973–1974, TV), the latter with his *Holiday on the Buses* co-star Reg Varney. **Hammer credits:** *Holiday on the Buses* (1973, as Little Arthur)

### Rhodes, Marjorie

Frequently cast as harridans, this British comedy actress (1897–1979, real name Marjorie Rhodes Wise) played such a role—that of Emma "Ma" Hornett—in the Hammer comedy *Watch It, Sailor!* (1961). Rhodes actually inherited the part from Peggy Mount, who had previously essayed the role in the film's predecessor *Sailor Beware* (1956), as well as the original stage run on which it was based. In films from 1939 with *Poison Pen* (1939), her other credits include *Just William* (1939), *Old Mother Riley Detective* (1943), *The Weak and the Wicked* (1953), *Yield to the Night* (1956), *A Tale of Two Cities* (1958), *The Family Way* (1966) and *Spring and Port Wine* (1969). Her final film appearance was as the kindly housekeeper Mrs. Bryant in

Hammer's *Hands of the Ripper* (1971). Also busy on stage and television, her small screen appearances include such early TV plays as *The Ringer* (1938, TV) and *Lonesome Like* (1939, TV), plus episodes of *The Grove Family* (1954–1957, TV), *The Ugliest Girl in Town* (1968–1969, TV) and *Softly Softly* (1966–1976, TV). Also on stage in both Britain and America, she earned herself a Tony nomination for her appearance in *All in Good Time* on Broadway in 1965. **Hammer credits:** *Watch It, Sailor!* (1961, as Emma "Ma" Hornett), *Hands of the Ripper* (1971, as Mrs. Bryant)

### Ricci Michaels, Ltd.

This London–based (Mayfair) fashion house designed the fashion show gowns seen in the Hammer thriller *Mantrap* (1953). Noted for its evening wear, the company was incorporated in 1947 and dissolved in 1983. **Hammer credits:** *Mantrap* (1953)

### Rice, Ernie

This bit player and extra can be spotted in several Hammer films, usually as either a villager or inn patron. His many other films include appearances in *Keep Fit* (1937), *All Over the Town* (1947), *The Lavender Hill Mob* (1951), *Hell Below Zero* (1954), *The Naked Truth* (1957), *Lawrence of Arabia* (1962), *From Russia with Love* (1963), *Carry On Cabby* (1963), *Island of Terror* (1966), *Casino Royale* (1967) and *Scrooge* (1970). **Hammer credits include:** *The Pirates of Blood River* (1962, as Pirate [uncredited]), *The Old Dark House* (1963, as Casino patron [uncredited]), *The Evil of Frankenstein* (1964, as Villager [uncredited]), *The Gorgon* (1964, as Villager [uncredited]), *Rasputin—The Mad Monk* (1966, as Barman [uncredited]), *The Plague of the Zombies* (1966, as Inn patron [uncredited]), *The Reptile* (1966, as Inn patron [uncredited]), *Dr. Jekyll and Sister Hyde* (1971, as Pub patron [uncredited])

### Rice, Joan

In films from 1951 with *Blackmailed* following experience as a waitress and beauty queen, this British actress (1930–1997) went on to appear in *Curtain Up* (1952), *The Story of Robin Hood and His Merrie Men* (1952), *One Good Turn* (1954), *The Long Knife* (1958) and *Payroll* (1961), plus episodes of *The New Adventures of Charlie Chan* (1957–1958, TV), *Ivanhoe* (1958–1959, TV) and *Zero One* (1962–1965, TV). She also worked for Hammer twice, first appearing in the prison melodrama *Women Without Men* (1956). She later returned for a supporting role in *The Horror of Frankenstein* (1970). **Hammer credits:** *Women Without Men* (1956, as Cleo Thompson), *The Horror of Frankenstein* (1970, as Grave robber's wife)

### Rich, Gary

Rich had a minor role in Hammer's *Countess Dracula* (1971). His other credits include *Mahler* (1974) and *Tommy* (1975), plus episodes of *Catweazle* (1970–1971, TV) and *Jude the Obscure* (1971, TV). **Hammer credits:** *Countess Dracula* (1971, as Second boy)

### Richard, Wendy

First known for playing the glamorous Miss Brahms in the long-running sitcom *Are You Being Served?* (1973–1985, TV), this British actress (1943–2009, real name Wendy Emerton) went on to appear in the series' 1977 big screen spin-off and its small-screen follow-up, *Grace and Favour* (1992–1993, TV). She subsequently became known for playing the rather less glamorous Pauline Fowler in the soap *EastEnders* (1985–, TV), in which she appeared between 1985 and 2006. In films from 1963 with *Contact*, her other credits include *Help!*, from which her scenes were deleted, *Doctor in Clover* (1966), *No Blade of Grass* (1970), *Gumshoe* (1971), *Carry On Matron* (1972), *Bless This House* (1972) and *Carry On Girls* (1973). She can also be seen in Hammer's *On the Buses* (1971), in which she plays an irate housewife whose underwear has been mistakenly taken from a launderette by Inspector Blake (don't ask!). Unfortunately, the credits misspell her surname as Richards. In addition to her work as an actress, Richard can also be heard as a vocalist on the 1962 single *Come Outside*. Her many other television appearances include episodes of *Harpers West One* (1961–1963, TV), *The Newcomers* (1965–1969, TV) and *Not on Your Nellie* (1974–1975, TV), plus several episodes of *On the Buses* (1969–1973, TV), in which she played a clippie. Her first husband (of four) was music publisher Leonard Black, to whom she was married between 1972 and 1974. She was made an MBE in 2000. **Additional notes:** The role of Miss Brahms was subsequently played by Niky Wardley in the 2016 reboot of *Are You Being Served?* (2016, TV). **Hammer credits:** *On the Buses* (1971, as Housewife)

### Richards, Darroll

British born Richards (1888–1971) played the sage in Hammer's *The Mummy's Shroud* (1967). His other credits include *Facing the Music* (1933), plus episodes of *No Hiding Place* (1959–1967, TV), *Doctor Who* (1963–1989, TV), *Haunted* (1967–1968, TV) and *Nicholas Nickleby* (1968, TV). Also on stage. He married actress Gertrude Kaye in 1930. **Hammer credits:** *The Mummy's Shroud* (1967, as Sage [uncredited])

### Richards, Hugh

This British (Welsh) make-up artist worked on Hammer's *The Anniversary* (1968), assisting George Partleton. His other credits include *Half a Sixpence* (1967), *Oliver!* (1968), *2001: A Space Odyssey* (1968), *Scrooge* (1970), *The Music Lovers* (1970), *Follow Me* (1972), *The Mackintosh Man* (1973) and *Yanks* (1979). His daughter is the make-up artist Sian Richards (1968–). **Hammer credits:** *The Anniversary* (1968 [uncredited])

### Richards, Lee

Richards can be seen in a minor supporting role in *Charlie Boy* (1980, TV [episode of *Hammer House of Horror*]). Often cast as barmaids (including a stint in a Guinness commercial in 1969), her many other TV credits include episodes of *Are You Being Served?* (1972–1985, TV), *Within These Walls* (1974–1978, TV), *Chalk and Cheese* (1977–1979,

TV), *Minder* (1979–1994, TV), *In Sickness and in Health* (1985–1992, TV) and *Hale and Pace* (1988–1998, TV). Her occasional film credits include *Indiana Jones and the Last Crusade* (1989). **Hammer credits:** *Charlie Boy* (1980, TV [episode of *Hammer House of Horror*], as Actress)

### Richards, Pennington *see* Pennington-Richards, C.M.

### Richards, Susan

This British (Welsh) actress (1898–1986) played the role of Mrs. Loker in *Poor Butterfly*, an episode of Hammer's *Journey to the Unknown* (1968, TV) which also appeared in the compendium film *Journey to Midnight* (1968, TVM). Her film credits include *The Rocking Horse Winner* (1950), *Village of the Damned* (1960), *Part-Time Wife* (1961), *The Haunting* (1963), *Never Put It in Writing* (1963) and *I Don't Want to Be Born* (1975), while her many TV credits include episodes of everything from *The Adventures of Robin Hood* (1955–1960, TV) to *Angels* (1975–1983, TV). **Hammer credits:** *Poor Butterfly* (1968, TV [episode of *Journey to the Unknown*], as Mrs. Loker), *Journey to Midnight* (1968, TVM, as Mrs. Loker)

### Richards, Terry

Best remembered for his turn as the sword-wielding Arab who is shot by Indiana Jones in *Raiders of the Lost Ark* (1981), this British stuntman, stunt double and bit player (1932–2014, full name David Terence Richards) also worked on several films for Hammer in the sixties, among them *Rasputin—The Mad Monk* (1966), in which he doubled for Christopher Lee during his climactic fall from a window onto the ice. In films from 1960 with *The Flesh and the Fiends*, his many other credits include *From Russia with Love* (1963), *On Her Majesty's Secret Service* (1969), *The Pink Panther Strikes Again* (1976), *The Empire Strikes Back* (1980), *Superman II* (1980), *Krull* (1983), *The Princess Bride* (1987), *Willow* (1988), *Total Recall* (1990), *Tomorrow Never Dies* (1997) and *The World Is Not Enough* (1999). **Hammer credits:** *The Pirates of Blood River* (1962, stunts [uncredited]), *Captain Clegg* (1962, stunts [uncredited]), *The Scarlet Blade* (1963, stunts [uncredited]), *She* (1965, stunts [uncredited]), *The Brigand of Kandahar* (1965, stunts [uncredited]), *Rasputin—The Mad Monk* (1966, as Christopher Lee's stunt double [uncredited]), *The Viking Queen* (1967, stunts [uncredited]), *The Lost Continent* (1968, stunts [uncredited])

### Richards, Ward

This British art director (1905–1967) designed the sets for Hammer's *Up the Creek* (1958), sharing his credit with Elven Webb. His other credits, either as art director or production designer, include *English Without Tears* (1944), *London Town* (1946), *Swiss Honeymoon* (1947), *The Eternal Question* (1950) and *The Naked Heart* (1950). He also worked as an assistant art director on *Let the People Sing* (1942), *I Know Where I'm Going* (1945) and *They Can't Hang Me* (1955). **Hammer credits:** *Up the Creek* (1958)

### Richardson, Adam

Richardson can be seen as Minton in *Last Video and Testament* (1984, TVM [episode of *Hammer House of Mystery and Suspense*]). His other TV credits include episodes of *Romance* (1977, TV), *Wings* (1977–1978, TV), *Lillie* (1978, TV), *Cribb* (1980–1981, TV) and *Casualty* (1986–, TV). His occasional film credits include *Secret Places* (1984). **Hammer credits:** *Last Video and Testament* (1984, TVM [episode of *Hammer House of Mystery and Suspense*], as Minton)

### Richardson, Beryl

Mostly on stage, Richardson played the role of Rhoda in *The New People*, an episode of Hammer's *Journey to the Unknown* (1968, TV), which also appeared in the compendium film *Journey into Darkness* (1968, TVM). **Hammer credits:** *The New People* (1968, TV [episode of *Journey to the Unknown*], as Rhoda), *Journey into Darkness* (1968, TVM, as Rhoda)

### Richardson, Cliff

This pioneering British effects technician (1905–1985) began his film career in 1924. He worked at Ealing in the forties on such films as *The Big Blockade* (1940), *Ships with Wings* (1941), *San Demetrio London* (1943) and *Dead of Night* (1945). In 1947 he moved to London Films, where he worked on *Mine Own Executioner* (1947) and *Anna Karenina* (1948) among others. Freelance from the early fifties onwards, his other credits include *Dance Little Lady* (1954), *Lawrence of Arabia* (1962), *Casino Royale* (1967), *Battle of Britain* (1969), *The Private Life of Sherlock Holmes* (1970) and *Juggernaut* (1974). He also worked on the effects for Hammer's *The Lost Continent* (1968) with Robert A. Mattey. Richardson's son is the effects technician John Richardson (1946–), and his grandson is the effects technician Marcus Richardson. **Hammer credits:** *The Lost Continent* (1968)

### Richardson, David

Richardson can be seen in a minor role in Hammer's *Lust for a Vampire* (1971). He began his film career as an extra on *Around the World in 80 Days* (1955), though spent most of his career on the small screen, appearing in episodes of such series as *Z Cars* (1962–1978, TV), *On the Buses* (1969–1973, TV) and *Follyfoot* (1971–1973, TV). **Hammer credits:** *Lust for a Vampire* (1971, as Second villager)

### Richardson, Gordon

This British (Scottish) actor (1911–1994) can be seen as Aggressive in Hammer's *Frankenstein and the Monster from Hell* (1974). His other credits incluе *Carry On Loving* (1970) and *Tess* (1979), plus episodes of *Paul of Tarsus* (1960, TV) and *The Expert* (1968–1976, TV). **Hammer credits:** *Frankenstein and the Monster from Hell* (1974, as Aggressive [uncredited])

### Richardson, Henry

This British editor (1936–) gained experience as an assistant working with Hammer's chief editor James Needs in the mid-fifties. As such, one of his jobs was to make notes and timings for music dur-

ing a film's "spotting." Recalled composer James Bernard, "At our music breakdowns for those early films, there were usually just John Hollingsworth, Anthony Hinds, myself, the editor of the film, James Needs, and his assistant the sound editor, who would tell us where the thunderstorms and sound effects were going to be."[30] Richardson's later credits include *Shadow of Fear* (1963), *A Study in Terror* (1965), *The Valley of Gwangi* (1969), a return to Hammer for *Countess Dracula* (1971), *Legend of the Werewolf* (1975), *The Ghoul* (1975), *Octopussy* (1983), *Runaway Train* (1985), which earned him an Oscar nomination, *Mata Hari* (1985), *A Show of Force* (1990), *Shoreditch* (2003), *Moscow Chill* (2007) and *The Payback* (2009). **Hammer credits:** *The House Across the Lake* (1954, assembly cutter [uncredited]), *The Glass Cage* (1955, assembly cutter), *The Quatermass Xperiment* (1955, assistant editor [uncredited]), *X—The Unknown* (1956, assistant editor [uncredited]), *A Man on the Beach* (1956, editor), *I Only Arsked!* (1958, assistant editor [uncredited]), *Ten Seconds to Hell* (1959, editor), *Countess Dracula* (1971, editor)

### Richardson, Jo

Richardson (1936–1976) had a minor role in Hammer's *Dracula A.D. 1972* (1972). She was best known for playing Mrs. Witton in *Crossroads* (1964–1988, TV). **Hammer credits:** *Dracula A.D. 1972* (1972, as Crying matron)

### Richardson, John

In vogue in from the mid-sixties to the early seventies, this handsome British leading man (1934–) is best remembered for playing the hapless Leo Vincey, who falls for the charms or Ursula Andress's Ayesha in Hammer's *She* (1965), and Tumak to Raquel Welch's Loana in *One Million Years B.C.* (1966). In films from the late fifties with

A hirsute John Richardson looks off into the middle distance in this publicity shot for *One Million Years B.C.* (1966) (Hammer/Seven Arts/Associated British Pathé/Associated British Picture Corporation/Warner Pathé Distributors/Twentieth Century–Fox/Studio Canal).

*A Night to Remember* (1958), his other credits (among them many films in Italy) include *The 39 Steps* (1959), *Black Sunday* (1960), *John the Bastard* (1967), *On a Clear Day You Can See Forever* (1970), *Frankenstein 80* (1972), *Torso* (1973), *Eyeball* (1975), *Murder Obsession* (1981) and *The Church* (1989). He was also originally cast as Paul Preston in Hammer's *The Mummy's Shroud* (1967), but the part eventually went to David Buck. However, he did appear in Hammer's *She* sequel, *The Vengeance of She* (1968), as Killikrates. He was married to (and subsequently divorced from) actress Martine Beswick (1941–) from 1967. She likewise appeared in three films for Hammer: *One Million Years B.C.* (1966), *Slave Girls* (1968) and *Dr. Jekyll and Sister Hyde* (1971).

Commented *Kinematograph Weekly* of the actor's performance in *One Million Years B.C.*, "John Richardson is a finely built Tumak and manages to convey some of the fierce incomprehension of this primitive character." Remembered his *B.C.* leading lady Raquel Welch of the actor, "[He] was to die for. When I first saw him, he was the most beautiful man I've ever seen. I was dumbstruck. I thought, 'Man, look at this guy. He's the pretty one. I look butch next to him.'"[31] **Hammer credits:** *She* (1965, as Leo Vincey), *One Million Years B.C.* (1966, as Tumak), *The Vengeance of She* (1968, as Killikrates)

### Richardson, Larry

Richardson worked as the assistant editor on a handful of Hammer films, among them *Creatures the World Forgot* (1971) and *The Legend of the 7 Golden Vampires* (1974), both of which required him to go on location with editor Chris Barnes to South West Africa and Hong Kong respectively. Richardson's other work as an assistant editor includes *All Creatures Great and Small* (1974), *The Seven-Per-Cent Solution* (1976) and *Sense and Sensibility* (1995). His work as an assistant sound editor includes *The Border* (1979)and *The Saint* (1997), while his work as a sound mixer include *Almonds and Raisins* (1985). **Hammer credits:** *The Horror of Frankenstein* (1970 [uncredited]), *Creatures the World Forgot* (1971 [uncredited]), *The Satanic Rites of Dracula* (1974 [uncredited]), *The Legend of the 7 Golden Vampires* (1974)

### Richardson, Laurence

This actor and vocalist can be seen as a singer in the Sphinx nightclub in Hammer's *The Two Faces of Dr. Jekyll* (1960). **Hammer credits:** *The Two Faces of Dr. Jekyll* (1960, as Singer [uncredited])

### Richardson, Mole *see* Mole Richardson

### Richens, F.E.

Richens was Hammer's prints manager in the fifties, as well as the branch managers' representative for Exclusive.

### Richfield, Edwin

In films from the late forties, this busy British character actor (1921–1990) appeared in such titles as *The Blue Parrot* (1953), *Ben-Hur* (1959), *Tommy the Toreador* (1959), *Diamonds on Wheels* (1974) and *Champions* (1984), as well as episodes of *The Buccaneers* (1956–1957, TV), *White Hunter*

(1957–1958, TV), *The Avengers* (1961–1969, TV), *The Man in the Iron Mask* (1968, TV) and *All Creatures Great and Small* (1978–1990, TV). He crossed paths with Hammer several times during his career, first appearing in the "unofficial" Hammer film *Jack of Diamonds* (1949), which marked his big screen debut. His other Hammer credits include comedies, swashbucklers, prisoner of war dramas and horror films. Richfield also penned one screenplay, *Calculated Risk* (1963), and two episodes of *Marked Personal* (1973–1974, TV). His wife was the actress Jan Holden (1931–2005, real name Valerie Jeanne Wilkinson), to whom he was married between 1952 and 1973; she appeared in four films and a TV episode for Hammer, among them *Quatermass 2* (1957), in which they both had roles. **Hammer credits:** *Jack of Diamonds* (1949, as George Paxton), *Mask of Dust* (1954, as Reporter), *X—The Unknown* (1956, as Old Soldier), *Quatermass 2* (1957, as Peterson), *Up the Creek* (1958, as Bennett), *Further Up the Creek* (1958, as Bennett), *The Camp on Blood Island* (1958, as Sergeant-Major), *Sword of Sherwood Forest* (1960, as Sheriff's Lieutenant), *The Secret of Blood Island* (1965, as O'Reilly), *Quatermass and the Pit* (1967, as Minister)

### Richmond, Anthony

Busy in the mid- to late fifties, this British child actor can be seen as Peter Pelham in the Hammer second feature *The Glass Cage* (1955), in which his parents are played by John Ireland and Honor Blackman. His other credits include *Bang! You're Dead* (1954), *Devil Girl from Mars* (1954), *The Divided Heart* (1954), *One Wish Too Many* (1956), *Night of the Demon* (1957), *Violent Playground* (1958) and *No Trees in the Street* (1959), plus the TV series *The Honey Siege* (1959, TV), in which he played Riquet. **Hammer credits:** *The Glass Cage* (1955, as Peter Pelham [uncredited])

### Richmond, Anthony B. *see* Richmond, Tony

### Richmond, H.E.

Richmond worked as the make-up artist on Hammer's *The Glass Cage* (1955). **Hammer credits:** *The Glass Cage* (1955)

### Richmond, Irene

This British (Welsh) actress (1911–2009) can be seen as the caring housekeeper Mrs. Gibbs in the Hammer thriller *Nightmare* (1964), prior to which she had appeared in a minor role in *Women Without Men* (1956) for the company. Her other credits (among them three more for her *Nightmare* director Freddie Francis, who also photographed her in *Saturday Night and Sunday Morning* [1960]) include *The Brain* (1962), *Dr. Terror's House of Horrors* (1965), Hammer's *Hysteria* (1965), *Darling* (1965) and *O Lucky Man!* (1973). Her TV credits include episodes of *Dixon of Dock Green* (1955–1976, TV), *The Secret Kingdom* (1960, TV), *Z Cars* (1962–1978, TV) and *ITV Playhouse* (1967–1980, TV). Her daughter is the actress Penelope Goddard, and her granddaughter is the actress Francesca Button. **Hammer credits:** *Women Without Men* (1956, as Guard [uncredited]), *Nightmare* (1964, as Mrs. Gibbs), *Hysteria* (1965, as Mrs. Kelly)

### Richmond, Tony (Anthony.)

This British cinematographer (1942–) is best known for his work on such Nicolas Roeg films as *Don't Look Now* (1973), which won him a BAFTA, *The Man Who Fell to Earth* (1976) and *Bad Timing* (1980). He began his career as a loader and clapper boy, and as such he worked on a couple of films for Hammer, as well as *Doctor Zhivago* (1965), parts of which were photographed by Roeg. He worked as a focus puller on *Casino Royale* (1967) and *Far from the Madding Crowd* (1969), both of which were photographed by Roeg (the former additional cinematography only), and had his first solo credit as a cinematographer on the documentary *A Cathedral in Our Time* (1967), which led to such films as *Sympathy for the Devil* (1968), *Only When I Larf* (1968), *Vampira* (1974), *The Eagle Has Landed* (1976), *That's Life* (1986), *Sunset* (1988), *Candyman* (1992), *Ravenous* (1999), *Legally Blonde* (2001), *The Rocker* (2008), *Diary of a Wimpy Kid: Dog Days* (2012) and *Coffee Town* (2013), plus episodes of *Audrey* (2012, TV) and *The Assets* (2014, TV). He has directed one film, *Déjà Vu* (1985). His children include the camera operator and cinematographer George Richmond, the first assistant cameraman Jonathan "Chunky" Richmond and the second assistant cameraman Gaston Richmond (1982–). He was married to the actress Jaclyn Smith (1945–) between 1981 and 1989. **Hammer credits:** *The Evil of Frankenstein* (1964 [uncredited]), *The Gorgon* (1964 [uncredited])

### Rickerby, Ricky

Rickerby (sometimes Rickaby) worked as the make-up artist on Hammer's *Holiday on the Buses* (1973). His other credits include *There's Always a Thursday* (1957), *The Last Shot You Hear* (1970) and *Burke and Hare* (1971). **Hammer credits:** *Holiday on the Buses* (1973)

### Rickerby, Steve

Rickerby worked as one of the film archivists on *The World of Hammer* (1990 [first broadcast 1994], TV). **Hammer credits:** *The World of Hammer* (1990 [first shown 1994], TV)

### Ricketts, Freddie (Fred)

British born Ricketts (1913–1968) began working for Hammer in the late forties as a construction carpenter and chief carpenter. He soon after graduated to the position of construction manager and later became studio manager during the company's Bray years. In 1955 Ricketts was joined at Bray by Arthur Kelly, with whom he subsequently split his duties as studio manager. **Hammer credits include:** *Meet Simon Cherry* (1949, construction [uncredited]), *Dr. Morelle—The Case of the Missing Heiress* (1949, chief carpenter [uncredited]), *The Adventures of PC 49—The Case of the Guardian Angel* (1949, chief carpenter [uncredited]), *The Man in Black* (1950, construction [uncredited]), *What the Butler Saw* (1950, construction [uncredited]), *Someone at the Door* (1950, chief carpenter [uncredited]), *The Quatermass Xperiment* (1955, construction manager [uncredited]), *X—The Unknown* (1956, construction manager [uncredited]), *Quatermass 2* (1957, construction manager [un-

credited]), *The Curse of Frankenstein* (1957, construction manager [uncredited]), *The Abominable Snowman* (1957, construction manager [uncredited])

### Ridge, Marilyn

Ridge can be spotted as one of the Sphinx Girls in Hammer's *The Two Faces of Dr. Jekyll* (1960). Her other credits include *West End Jungle* (1964) and an episode of *BBC Sunday Night Theatre* (1950–1959, TV). **Hammer credits:** *The Two Faces of Dr. Jekyll* (1960, as Sphinx Girl [uncredited])

### Ridler, Anne

This British actress (1930–2011) played one of several female prisoners of war in Hammer's *The Camp on Blood Island* (1958). Her other credits include *Person Unknown* (1956), *The Man in My Shoes* (1962), *633 Squadron* (1964) and *Up at the Villa* (1999), plus much television, including episodes of *Dixon of Dock Green* (1955–1976, TV), in which she played Woman Police Sergeant Chris Freeman, *Tom's Midnight Garden* (1974, TV), *Kizzy* (1976, TV) and *Terrahawks* (1983–1986, TV), for which she provided the voices of Kate Kestrel, Cy-Star and It-Star. **Hammer credits:** *The Camp on Blood Island* (1958, as Prisoner)

### Ridley, Arnold

Much loved for his role as Private Charles Godfrey in the long-running sitcom *Dad's Army* (1968–1977, TV), this British character actor (1896–1984, full name William Arnold Ridley) was also a successful playwright, his biggest hit being *The Ghost Train* (1923), which was first performed in 1924, and which has been filmed many times, notably in 1927 (German), 1931 (British), 1933 (twice, Romania and Hungary), 1937 (British, TV), 1939 (Dutch), 1941 (British), 1957 (German, TV), 1963 (German, TV) and 1976 (Danish). Other filmed works include *The Wrecker* (1929 [play 1926]), *Seven Sinners* (1936 [based on *The Wrecker*]), *Easy Money* (1948 [play 1934]) and *Who Killed the Cat?* (1966 [based on *Tabitha*, 1956]). His other plays include *The Great Burnett Mystery* (1925), *The Flying Fool* (1929), *Headline* (1933), *Murder Happens* (1944), *Beggar My Neighbour* (1951), *Amongst Those Present* (1959) and *High Fidelity* (1963). On stage from 1913, he went on to serve in both World Wars, first with the Somerset Light Infantry during World War I, during which he fought in the Battle of the Somme, then later as an intelligence officer with the British Expeditionary Force during World War II. His film appearances take in Hammer's *Stolen Face* (1952), in which he played the supporting role of Dr. Russell, *Wings of Mystery* (1963), the big screen version of *Dad's Army* (1971), *Carry On Girls* (1973) and *The Amorous Milkman* (1975). He also co-directed one film, *Royal Eagle* (1936) with George A. Cooper. His other TV appearances include episodes of *The Human Jungle* (1963–1964, TV), *Mrs. Thursday* (1966–1967, TV) and *Thriller* (1973–1976, TV). He was played by Michael Cochrane in *We're Doomed! The Dad's Army Story* (2015, TVM). The role of Private Godfrey was subsequently played by Michael Gambon in *Dad's Army* (2016). Ridley's second wife was the actress Isola Strong (1911–1997), whom he married in 1939. His third and final wife was the actress Althea Parker (1911–2001). His son (with Parker) is writer Nicolas Ridley. His great-niece is the actress Daisy Ridley (1992–). He was made an OBE in 1982. **Hammer credits:** *Stolen Face* (1952, as Dr. Russell)

### Ridley, Emma

This British actress (1972–) can be seen as the young Sophie Peters in *The House That Bled to Death* (1980, TV [episode of *Hammer House of Horror*]). Joanna White played the older version of the character. Ridley's film credits include *The World Is Full of Married Men* (1979) and *Return to Oz* (1985), in which she played Ozma. Known for being something of a wild child in her youth, she married three times; her first husband was the actor Robert Pereno (1957–), to whom she was married between 1987 and 1989, and her second was the music producer Philip Ehrlich, to whom she was married between 1997 and 1998. Her sister is the actress Joanne Ridley (1970–). She went on to run Goddess Fitness Dance. **Hammer credits:** *The House That Bled to Death* (1980, TV [episode of *Hammer House of Horror*], as Sophie Peters)

### Ridley, Walter

This British composer (1913–2007) penned the song *Alone Together* for the Hammer comedy *I Only Arsked!* (1958). This had lyrics by one of the film's scriptwriters, Sid Colin. Involved in the record industry, Ridley ran the HMV label for EMI, and produced records for such artists as Alma Cogan, Johnny Kidd and The Swinging Blue Jeans. He also contributed songs to such films as *We'll Meet Again* (1943 [*Be Like the Kettle and Sing* and *I'm Yours Sincerely*]), *Circle of Danger* (1951 [*Buttonhole for Baby*]) and *An Alligator Named Daisy* (1955 [*I'm in Love for the Very First Time*]). **Hammer credits:** *I Only Arsked!* (1958)

### Ridoutt, William

Ridoutt played a minor supporting role in Hammer's *To the Devil a Daughter* (1976). His other credits include *Big Zapper* (1973) and *Zapper's Blade of Vengeance* (1974), plus episodes of *Z Cars* (1962–1978, TV), *Play of the Month* (1965–1983, TV) and *The Legend of Robin Hood* (1975, TV). **Hammer credits:** *To the Devil a Daughter* (1976, as Airport porter)

### Rietti, Robert

Long in Britain, this busy Italian character actor (1923–2015, real name Lucio Rietti, sometimes billed Robert Rietty, aka Bobby Rietti) began his career as a child in *Heads We Go* (1933), which he followed with the likes of *The Private Life of Don Juan* (1934), *My Song Goes Round the World* (1934), *The Scarlet Pimpernel* (1934), *Emil and the Detectives* (1935) and *Runaway Ladies* (1938). Following training at RADA and experience with ENSA during the war, he continued his career with *A Matter of Life and Death* (1946), *Call of the Blood* (1948), *Stock Car* (1955), *I Could Go On Singing* (1963), *Zulu* (1964), *The Crooked Road* (1964), *On Her Majesty's Secret Service* (1969), *Sunday Bloody Sunday* (1971), *The Hiding Place* (1975), *The Omen*

(1976), *Never Say Never Again* (1983), *Madame Sousatzka* (1988), *The March* (1990) and *Hannibal* (2001). He can also be seen in minor roles in three Hammer productions: *The Snorkel* (1958), in which he played a Station Sergeant, *The Scarlet Blade* (1963), in which he can briefly be seen as Charles I, and *Last Video and Testament* (1984, TVM [episode of *Hammer House of Mystery and Suspense*]), in which he appeared on a monitor as an Italian executive during a video conference.

In addition to his work as an actor (which includes much stage and radio work), the distinctively voiced Rietti was one of the film industry's most prolific dubbing artists. As such, he is perhaps best known for dubbing Adolfo Celi (Emilio Largo) in *Thunderball* (1965), Tetsuro Tamba (Tiger Tanaka) in *You Only Live Twice* (1967) and ninety-eight separate roles in *Waterloo* (1970). He also provided the voice for the partially seen Blofeld in *For Your Eyes Only* (1981), and it sounds like he dubbed John Stuart (Colonel Beverley) in *The Scarlet Blade*. He also directed the dialogue for the dubbing sessions for many films, among them *The Bird with the Crystal Plumage* (1970), *Opera* (1987) and *Quicker Than the Eye* (1990). His many TV credits include episodes of *The New Adventures of Martin Kane* (1957–1958, TV), *Man of the World* (1962–1963, TV), *From a Bird's Eye View* (1971, TV), *Call Me Mister* (1986, TV) and *Beehive* (2008, TV). He also wrote scripts for episodes of *ITV Play of the Week* (1955–1968, TV) and *Armchair Theatre* (1956–1974, TV), as well as for the theater (including many translations). He even found time to found and edit the drama quarterly *Gambit*. Rietti's father was the actor Victor Rietti (1888–1963, aka Vittorio Rietti) and his brother was the producer Ronald Rietti. His granddaughter is the actress Zoe Rietti. **Hammer credits:** *The Snorkel* (1958, as Station Sergeant), *The Scarlet Blade* (1963, as Charles I, also dubbed John Stuart [both uncredited]), *Last Video and Testament* (1984, TVM [episode of *Hammer House of Mystery and Suspense*], as Marcello)

### Rigal, Phil

Rigal worked as an assistant director on Hammer's *The Gambler and the Lady* (1953), sharing his duties with Ted Holliday. His other credits include *Those Kids from Town* (1942), *Old Mother Riley Detective* (1943) and *Fuel for Battle* (1944). He also worked as a third assistant on *On Approval* (1944) and as a second assistant on *Let the People Sing* (1942), *They Knew Mr. Knight* (1946) and *The Final Test* (1953). **Hammer credits:** *The Gambler and the Lady* (1953 [uncredited])

### Rigby, Edward

This much-liked British comedy character actor (1879–1951, real name Edward Coke) turned to acting following experience as a farmer. In films from 1910 with *The Blue Bird*, he went on to appear in such favorites as *No Limit* (1935), *Young and Innocent* (1937), *A Yank at Oxford* (1938), *A Canterbury Tale* (1944), *Don't Take It to Heart* (1944) and *The Happiest Days of Your Life* (1950). In 1950, he starred as the Earl in the Hammer comedy *What the Butler Saw*, which gave him a rare leading role.

Sadly, it was one of his last films. His son was the director Cyril Coke (1914–1993), and his daughter-in-law was the actress, television presenter and producer Muriel Young (1923–2001), who appeared in Hammer's *Women Without Men* (1956). **Hammer credits:** *What the Butler Saw* (1950, as The Earl)

### Rigg, Carl

This British actor (1942–) had a few brief scenes as a Brighton hotel manager in *In Possession* (1984, TVM [episode of *Hammer House of Mystery and Suspense*]). His other TV credits include episodes of *Softly Softly* (1966–1976, TV), *Marked Personal* (1974, TV), in which he played Gordon Marsh, *Rockliffe's Babies* (1987–1988, TV) and *Doctors* (2000–, TV). His film credits include *Submarine X-1* (1968), *Song of Norway* (1970), *Made* (1972), *The Holcroft Covenant* (1985), *The Living Daylights* (1987) and *The Great Dome Robbery* (2002). **Hammer credits:** *In Possession* (1984, TVM [episode of *Hammer House of Mystery and Suspense*], as Hotel manager)

### *The Right Person*

GB, 1956, 30m, Eastmancolor, CinemaScope, RCA, cert A

One of several widescreen shorts made during a slack period in feature production while Hammer awaited the box office outcome of *The Quatermass Xperiment* (1955), this Copenhagen-set drama—already broadcast as a half hour piece by the BBC the year before—sees a newlywed woman visited in her hotel by a businessman named Rasmussen who believes that her husband, one Jorgan Jorgensen, could well be a long lost wartime comrade from the resistance. "In those days I was Robbie, leader of a little band of saboteurs, experts in throwing high explosive bombs and strangling men from behind," he reveals. He also informs her that he believes her husband to be the traitor who stole funds from the group, as a consequence of which ten of the twelve-man band were shot by the Gestapo. Rasmussen is now here to see if Jorgensen is "the right person" who disappeared all that time ago, and if so, to kill him....

Shot at Bray in March 1955 by director Peter Cotes from a screenplay by Philip Mackie, the film necessitated a trip to Denmark by producer Michael Carreras, camera operator Len Harris and focus puller Harry Oakes to shoot background material of Copenhagen for the film's opening and closing credits. Recalled Harry Oakes, "There being no library material in 'scope, Michael Carreras took Len and myself to Copenhagen for the exteriors."[32] Given the cost of sending a unit to Denmark—albeit a small one—it was also decided to film a short travelogue of the city, which was eventually released as *Copenhagen* (1956), footage from which is also featured in *The Right Person*, including a shot of Michael Carreras and his son Christopher looking at a statue of Hans Christian Andersen (this shot is nicely timed to appear as Carreras' producer credit comes up in screen).

A set-bound affair, *The Right Person* is one of the studio's lesser efforts, given the tedious unraveling of the plot, which is mostly divulged as Rasmussen sits on a sofa with Mrs. Jorgensen (a rather long sofa, of course, thing being a CinemaScope production). There is also the matter of the somewhat tentative quality of the acting (as the wife, Margo Lorenz inadvertently interrupts Douglas Wilmer's Rasmussen at one point, while at another, Wilmer himself is clearly about to say Copenhagen only to change his mind and say Denmark). That said, the credit sequence looks very handsome, and there is some nice camera movement in the opening moments in the Jorgensen's attractively appointed hotel room (though the art director receives no credit). Otherwise, this is a slow-moving half-hour that heads inevitably to an expected twist ending; after Rasmussen has left, not having been able to positively identify Jorgensen as the right man owing to wartime injuries, Jorgensen informs his wife that he has just inherited 100,000 krone from the estate of his recently deceased uncle—the exact amount that went missing all those years ago. Trade shown in December 1955, *The Right Person* was released in the UK by Exclusive on 9 January 1956. **Additional notes:** Eastmancolor is misspelled Eastmancolour in the credits (as it often was). Keep an eye out for the lady cyclist who spots the camera and points it out to her male riding companion during the opening credits. The BBC version of the story, which was broadcast on 29 November 1954, was also scripted by Philip Mackie (it marked his TV debut, just as the Hammer version marked his big screen debut); this presentation featured Noelle Middleton as Martha Jorgensen, John Stone as Jorgen Jorgensen and Walter Rilla as Rasmussen. The story was remade for Australian and German television in 1957 (in separate productions), the latter as *Der Mann, den ich suche* (1957). All told, this must have proved a nice little earner for Mackie.

Production company: Hammer. Distributor: Exclusive (UK). Producer: Michael Carreras. Associate producer: Mickey Delamar. Director: Peter Cotes. Screenplay: Philip Mackie. Cinematographer: Walter "Jimmy" Harvey. Music: Eric Winstone. Editor: Spencer Reeve. Camera operator: Len Harris. Focus puller: Harry Oakes [uncredited]. Sound: Bill Sweeney, J.J.Y. Scarlett. Processing: Humphries Laboratories. **Cast:** Douglas Wilmer (Hans Rasmussen/Robbie), Margo Lorenz (Martha Jorgensen), David Markham (Jorgan Jorgensen/Toraf), Man looking at Statue (Michael Carreras [uncredited]), Boy looking at statue (Christopher Carreras [uncredited]). **DVD availability:** DD Home Entertainment (UK R2 PAL), released on a double bill with *Four Sided Triangle* (1953), extras include a booklet and galleries featuring press book covers, behind-the-scenes shots and fifties Hammer glamor

### Rilla, Wolf

The son of German actor Walter Rilla (1894–1980), this German producer, writer and director (1920–2005) is best known for helming the classic science fiction shocker *Village of the Damned* (1960), which he also co-scripted. In Britain from 1935, he began his career writing for radio in 1942. He made his directorial debut in 1953 with *Noose*

*for a Lady* and went on to make over twenty features, among them *The Blue Peter* (1955), *The Scamp* (1957), *Cairo* (1962), *Secrets of a Door-to-Door Salesman* (1973) and *Bedtime with Rosie* (1974), the latter of which he also produced. He also directed the Hammer comedy *Watch It, Sailor!* (1961). Equally busy in television, his credits here include episodes of *The Scarlet Pimpernel* (1955–1956, TV), *Armchair Theatre* (1956–1974, TV) and *Zero One* (1962–1965, TV). He eventually retired to run a restaurant in France. **Hammer credits:** *Watch It, Sailor!* (1961)

### Rima

This couturier provided the "model clothes" for Hammer's two "Lyons" comedies. **Hammer credits:** *Life with the Lyons* (1954), *The Lyons in Paris* (1955), *Adventures with the Lyons* (1957, serial reissue of *Life with the Lyons*)

### Rimmer, Shane

This busy Canadian supporting actor (1929–2019) has popped up in all manner of British-made films, often as a token American. His many credits take in several Bonds—*You Only Live Twice* (1967), *Diamonds Are Forever* (1971), *Live and Let Die* (1973 [vocal work only]) and *The Spy Who Loved Me* (1977)—and three fantasy adventures for the producer-director team of John Dark and Kevin Connor: *The People That Time Forgot* (1977), *Warlords of Atlantis* (1978) and *Arabian Adventure* (1979). Other credits include *S*P*Y*S* (1974), *Twilight's Last Gleaming* (1977), *Superman* (1978), *Superman II* (1980), *Reds* (1981), *Superman III* (1983), *Morons from Outer Space* (1985), *The Year of the Comet* (1992), *Space Truckers* (1996), *Alien Autopsy* (2006), *Lovelorn* (2010), *Dark Shadows* (2012) and *Darkwave: Edge of the Storm* (2016). However, he is probably best known for his TV work for producer Gerry Anderson, which includes voicing Scott Tracy (and other characters) for *Thunderbirds* (1965–1966, TV) and its two big screen spin-offs, *Thunderbirds Are Go* (1966) and *Thunderbird 6* (1968). He also provided scripts for such Anderson series as *Captain Scarlet and the Mysterons* (1967–1968, TV), *Joe 90* (1968–1969, TV), *The Secret Service* (1969, TV) and *The Protectors* (1972–1973, TV), in addition to vocal performances for the first two, and appeared in *UFO* (1971, TV) and *Space: 1999* (1975–1976, TV), also providing vocals for the latter. He also appeared in such Anderson-related TV documentaries as *Mr. Thunderbird: The Gerry Anderson Story* (2000, TV) and *All About Thunderbirds* (2008, TV). His many other TV guest spots include an episode of *Hammer House of Mystery and Suspense* (1984, TVM). He recalled his career in his autobiography *From Thunderbirds to Pterodactyls* (2012). **Hammer credits:** *Last Video and Testament* (1984, TVM [episode of *Hammer House of Mystery and Suspense*], as Hersh)

### Ripper, Michael

At a gala screening of *Dracula* (1958) at The Barbican Center on Sunday 4 August 1996, Christopher Lee made a few comments to the audience before the film commenced, revealing that, "Whenever I'm asked about Hammer, people always ask me about two people. First they ask me

about Peter Cushing. Secondly, they ask me about Michael Ripper. Well, I'm glad to say that Michael is here with us tonight. Stand up, Michael, and take a bow." At this, a frail Michael Ripper stood from his seat near the back of the auditorium and took a quick bow. The applause was thunderous, and as the actor sat back down, the entire audience rose to its feet. To say that Michael Ripper was one of the best-loved stars in the Hammer rep company is something of an understatement. Indeed, Ripper was not the only person to shed a tear during this memorable and touching moment.

British born Ripper (1913–2000) began his acting career on stage in repertory in 1924. He broke into films in 1936 with *Father and Son*, and went on to play supporting roles in such films as *The Heirloom Mystery* (1936), *His Lordship Regrets* (1938) and *Blind Folly* (1939). Following military service during the war, he returned to films with *Captain Boycott* (1947). He made his first appearance for Hammer in 1948, playing the minor role of Andy Anderson in the low budget crime filler *The Dark Road*, for which he was chosen at an audition by James Carreras himself. By no means a classic, the film was quickly forgotten by the public. Ripper, however, was not forgotten by Hammer (and in particular by producer Anthony Hinds, who became a close friend), and was asked back with increasing regularity. Recalled Ripper of that first audition for Hammer, "I went into the room where they all were, and one of them started to ask me questions—when Jim Carreras said, 'No, it's alright—he's fine—he'll do it…. Goodbye.' And that was it. I was in."[33]

Following appearances in the two PC 49 films and a supporting role in *Blood Orange* (1953), Ripper finally made his first shocker for the company, *X—The Unknown* (1956). An adept character actor, he was much more than monster fodder, however, and played a Japanese driver in *The Camp on Blood Island* (1958), an Arab in *I Only Arsed!* (1958) and a Spanish gypsy in *The Scarlet Blade* (1963). His role as a morgue attendant was unfortunately cut from the release print of *The Man Who Could Cheat Death* (1959), but amendments were made with continuing cameos in such classics as *The Mummy* (1959), *The Brides of Dracula* (1960) and *The Curse of the Werewolf* (1961).

Ripper then went on to have one of his largest roles in Hammer's *The Reptile* (1966), in which, as Tom Bailey, the landlord of the White Tor public house, he helps the hero track down the title creature. However, it was in scene-stealing cameos that the actor truly left his mark, among his best being the myopic manservant Longbarrow in *The Mummy's Shroud* (1967), a role that was described by critic Cecil Wilson as containing "a pathos rarely achieved in the impersonal and well-nigh inhuman world of horror cinema." Even in drab comedy spin-offs like *That's Your Funeral* (1973), he was able to inject some brightness (as well as a fully-rounded character) into his a few brief scenes as a flustered railway porter.

Remembered the actor of his time with the studio, "I did seem to get cast as the same types of people, but I always tried to give them different characters. Tony Hinds was a great friend of mine, and I do miss Hammer."[34] Remembered Jimmy Sangster, "Michael could play anything.... He was utterly reliable on set, a director's delight in that he always added an extra dimension to the part he was playing. He was also a very nice and generous man."[35] The final word on Ripper goes to frequent co-star Christopher Lee: "If anybody represented Hammer more than anybody else it was Michael Ripper. More than Peter or me really, because he was probably in more Hammer films than we were! And there was always a distinctive character and performance from him. He always used to reduce me to helpless streams of laughter. I often couldn't look at him during a take, because he used to play all sorts of tricks on me. We used to laugh so much."[36]

Also busy in television, Ripper's credits here include episodes of *Quatermass and the Pit* (1958–1959, TV), *The Adventures of Robin Hood* (1955–1960, TV), *William Tell* (1958–1959, TV), *Sir Francis Drake* (1961–1962, TV) and *Paper Dolls*, an episode of Hammer's *Journey to the Unknown* (1968, TV), which also appeared in the compendium film *Journey into Darkness* (1968, TVM). His other films include *The Creeping Flesh* (1972), *Legend of the Werewolf* (1975), *The Prince and the Pauper* (1977), *Danger on Dartmoor* (1980), *No Surrender* (1985) and *Revenge of Billy the Kid* (1992). Married three times, his second wife was the actress Catherine Finn (1915–1980), to whom he was married between 1972 and 1978. She appeared in *The Witches* (1966) and an episode of *Journey to the Unknown* (1968, TV) for Hammer. His third wife was the costume designer Cecilia Doidge (1943–2010), whom he married in 1995.
**Additional notes:** Ripper appears to have re-voiced Bartlett Mullins' role as a wagoner in *Rasputin—The Mad Monk* (1966). In 1999, Midnight Marquee published Derek Pykett's biography about the actor, *Michael Ripper Unmasked*, which has seen a number of re-prints. **Hammer credits:** *The Dark Road* (1948, as Andy Anderson), *The Adventures of PC 49—The Case of the Guardian Angel* (1949, as Fingers), *A Case for PC 49* (1951, as George Steele), *Blood Orange* (1953, as Eddie [uncredited]), *X—The Unknown* (1956, as Sergeant Grimsdyke), *A Man on the Beach* (1956, as Chauffeur), *Quatermass 2* (1957, as Ernie), *The Steel Bayonet* (1957, as Private Middleditch), *The Camp on Blood Island* (1958, as Japanese driver), *Up the Creek* (1958, as Decorator), *The Revenge of Frankenstein* (1958, as Kurt), *Further Up the Creek* (1958, as Ticket collector), *I Only Arsked!* (1958, as Azim), *The Man Who Could Cheat Death* (1959, as Morgue attendant [scene cut from print]), *The Ugly Duckling* (1959, as Fish), *The Mummy* (1959, as Poacher), *The Brides of Dracula* (1960, as Coachman), *The Curse of the Werewolf* (1961, as Old soak), *The Pirates of Blood River* (1962, as Mac), *Captain Clegg* (1962, as Jeremiah Mipps), *The Phantom of the Opera* (1962, as Cabby), *The Scarlet Blade* (1963, as Pablo), *The Devil-Ship Pirates* (1964, as Pepe), *The Curse of the Mummy's Tomb* (1964, as Achmed), *The Secret of Blood Island* (1965, as Lieutenant Tojoko), *The Plague of the Zombies* (1966, as Sergeant Smith), *Rasputin—The Mad Monk* (1966, re-voicing of Bartlett Mullins only [uncredited]), *The Reptile* (1966, as Tom Bailey), *The Mummy's*

*Shroud* (1967, as Longbarrow), *Paper Dolls* (1968, TV [episode of *Journey to the Unknown*], as Albert Cole), *Journey into Darkness* (1968, TVM, as Albert Cole), *Dracula Has Risen from the Grave* (1968, as Max), *The Lost Continent* (1968, Sea Lawyer), *Moon Zero Two* (1969, as Card player), *Taste the Blood of Dracula* (1970, as Cob), *Scars of Dracula* (1970, as Landlord), *That's Your Funeral* (1973, as Arthur [railway])

### Ritch, David
This South African supporting actor (1932–) played Mahomet in the Hammer war drama *The Steel Bayonet* (1957). He can also be seen as a hotel clerk in *The Snorkel* (1958). His other credits include *Strangers' Meeting* (1957) and episodes of *Sword of Freedom* (1957, TV), *Kenilworth* (1957, TV), *The Invisible Man* (1958–1960, TV) and *Danger Man* (1964–1966, TV). **Hammer credits:** *The Steel Bayonet* (1957, as Mahomet), *The Snorkel* (1958, as Hotel clerk)

### Ritchie, Barbara
British born Ritchie (1928–1990) worked as the hair stylist on Hammer's *Dracula A.D. 1972* (1972), which led to a further assignment for the company. Her other credits include *Stranger from Venus* (1954), *Expresso Bongo* (1959), *Dr. Strangelove* (1964), *The Ipcress File* (1965), *Kaleidoscope* (1966), *Revenge* (1971), *Young Winston* (1972), *The Pink Panther Strikes Again* (1976), *International Velvet* (1978), *The Empire Strikes Back* (1980), *Krull* (1983), *Legend* (1985), *Willow* (1988) and *Bullseye!* (1990), plus episodes of *The Zoo Gang* (1974, TV) and *The Professionals* (1977–1983, TV). **Hammer credits:** *Dracula A.D. 1972* (1972), *Captain Kronos—Vampire Hunter* (1974)

### *River Patrol*
GB, 1948, 43m, cert A
The second of two low budget featurettes produced by Hammer in association with Knightsbridge, this Thames-set crime drama follows the adventures of a customs agent as he attempts to catch a gang of nylon smugglers (or as the poster has it: "The inside story of the constant battle between the smuggling gangs and the secret dept. of the customs").
Released in the UK by Exclusive in March 1948, the production re-united many of those who had worked on the previous Hammer/Knightsbridge film, *Crime Reporter* (1947), including producer Hal Wilson, director Ben R. Hart, cinematographer Brooks-Carrington and actor John Blythe (the affiliation who ran Knightsbridge). Screenwriter James Corbett and actor Stan Paskin were also back onboard.

Long unseen, the film was finally made available for viewing on Hammer's YouTube site in 2012, though not everyone was grateful. Posted one disgruntled viewer: "A truly appalling film. Zero production values, actors that can't act with a script not worth a penny. How Hammer survived after films like this is unbelievable." Indeed, the film is amateurishly staged and performed throughout, the script is trite and the action one notch down from substandard, though a final punch up in which our hero takes out one of the villains is surprisingly violent for its time (the film actually ends with the camera closing in on Blythe's bandaged hands, which have The End written on them).

**Additional notes:** According the BFI's database, some scenes for the film were shot at Windsor Studios. The noted sketch artist George Lane makes a cameo in the film as a nightclub cartoonist. The film's poster bills John Blythe as "Your Crime Reporter," thus linking the film with its predecessor. Cinematographer Brooks-Carrington is credited as Brookes-Carrington. An earlier Knightsbridge film, a documentary short titled *Old Father Thames* (1946), had been released by Exclusive.

Production companies: Hammer/Knightsbridge. Distributor: Exclusive (UK). Producer: Hal Wilson. Director: Ben R. Hart. Screenplay: James Corbett. Photography: Brooks-Carrington. Music: Paxtons. Editor: James Corbett. Sound: Leevers-

Stylish artwork for *River Patrol* (1948). The film was less so. Note the boxes of nylons bottom left (Hammer/Knightsbridge/Exclusive).

Rich. **Cast:** John Blythe (Robby), Lorna Dean (Jean), Wally Patch (The Guy), George Lane (Cartoonist), Stan Paskin (unnamed role), Wilton West (unnamed role), George Kane (erroneously billed as cartoonist), Fred Collins (unnamed role), Douglas Lee (unnamed role), George Crowther (unnamed role), Dolly Gwynne (unnamed role), Tony Merrett (unnamed role), Johnny Doherty (unnamed role), Andrew Sterne (unnamed role [uncredited]), Iris Keen (unnamed role [uncredited])

### Riverside Studios

Located on the banks of the River Thames in the London Borough of Hammersmith, this busy studio played host to three Hammer films during a break in the company's lease on Down Place. They were *Wings of Danger* (1952), *Stolen Face* (1952) and *Lady in the Fog* (1952). A former tyre depot, the studios were originally owned by singing star Jack Buchanan (from 1933, via the Triumph Film Company); he later sold them to the mogul Alf Shipman (who also owned Twickenham and Southall Studios). The facility housed a number of quota quickies in the thirties, forties and fifties, among them several made by producer Reginald Smith's Producers' Distributing Company. It also played host to such British classics as *The Happiest Days of Your Life* (1950) and *Father Brown* (1954). The BBC acquired the studios in 1954, and used the facilities to make such programs as *Hancock's Half Hour* (1956–1960, TV), *Quatermass and the Pit* (1958–1959, TV) and *Playschool* (1964–1988, TV). The BBC sold the studios in 1975, since when they have been used for all manner of stage, film, music, dance and television productions, as well as such events as the launch party for Channel Four's opening night in 1982. In the nineties, the studios were best known for the television series *TFI Friday* (1996–2000, 2015, TV). The complex also hosts exhibitions. **Additional notes:** The dubbing for Hammer's *The House Across the Lake* (1954) also took place at the studio. **Hammer credits:** *Wings of Danger* (1952), *Stolen Face* (1952), *Lady in the Fog* (1952), *The House Across the Lake* (1954 [dubbing only])

### Rixon, Bob

Rixon worked for many years as Hammer's projectionist at their Wardour Street headquarters, where his duties included showing rushes, screen tests and finished films.

### RKO

Formed in 1921 by the Keith Orpheum cinema circuit and the Radio Corporation of America, RKO Radio Pictures Inc. became known in the thirties as the home to Fred Astaire and Ginger Rogers, who made such hit musicals as *Flying Down to Rio* (1933), *Top Hat* (1935) and *Swing Time* (1936) there. Other hits for the company included *King Kong* (1933), which Hammer later hoped to remake, and *The Informer* (1935), as well as such Orson Welles classics as *Citizen Kane* (1940) and *The Magnificent Ambersons* (1942). It also made the horror films of producer Val Lewton, among them *Cat People* (1942) and *The Body Snatcher* (1945), the latter of which Hammer proposed to remake as part of a later (unmade) television series

titled *The Haunted House of Hammer*. The studio also released films for independent production companies, among them Disney and Goldwyn.

In 1952, RKO handled the American release of the Hammer second feature *Whispering Smith Hits London*, which was re-titled *Whispering Smith vs. Scotland Yard* for its U.S. showings. The film was co-financed by Sol Lesser, who had a long association with RKO, having produced several Tarzan pictures for the studio. In 1953, the RKO lot was sold to Lucille Ball's Desilu Productions. RKO also released Hammer's *Return of the Saint* (1953), another Lesser co-production, which it re-titled as *The Saint's Girl Friday* for its American showings, and the comedy featurette *Clean Sweep* (1958), which only saw a UK release. RKO was also set to handle the U.S. release of Hammer's *X—The Unknown* (1956), which also had money invested in it by Sol Lesser, but the film was eventually sold on to Warner Bros., who billed it with Hammer's *The Curse of Frankenstein* (1957) for its initial U.S. showings. However, it should be noted that the film's trailer carries an RKO distribution credit, and that RKO did eventually release the movie on a double bill with *The Cyclops* (1957). **Hammer credits:** *Whispering Smith Hits London* (1952), *The Saint's Return* (1953), *X—The Unknown* (1956), *Clean Sweep* (1958)

### Robb, David

This British actor (1947–) can be seen as art dealer Vincent Rhodes in *Paint Me a Murder* (1984, TVM [episode of *Hammer House of Mystery and Suspense*]). His many other TV appearances include episodes of *I, Claudius* (1976, TV), *Supernatural* (1977, TV), *First Among Equals* (1986, TV), *Up the Garden Path* (1990–1993, TV), *Strathblair* (1992–1993, TV), in which he played Andrew Menzies, and *The Courtroom* (2004, TV), though he is best known for playing Dr. Clarkson in *Downton Abbey* (2010–2015, TV). His films include *Zapper's Blade of Vengeance* (1974), *The Deceivers* (1988), *Swing Kids* (1993), *Elizabeth: The Golden Age* (2007) and *The Young Victoria* (2009). His wife was the actress Briony McRoberts (1957–2013), whom he married in 1978. **Hammer credits:** *Paint Me a Murder* (1984, TVM [episode of *Hammer House of Mystery and Suspense*], as Vincent Rhodes)

### Robb-King, Peter

This noted British make-up artist (1950–) worked as the assistant make-up artist (under Eddie Knight) on Hammer's *Blood from the Mummy's Tomb* (1971). His other credits include *Doctor in Trouble* (1970), *Young Winston* (1972), *Mahler* (1974), *The Rocky Horror Picture Show* (1975), *Dracula* (1979), *Outland* (1981), *Return of the Jedi* (1983), *Legend* (1985), which earned him Oscar and BAFTA nominations (both shared with Rob Bottin), *Aliens* (1986), which earned him a BAFTA nomination, *The Last of the Mohicans* (1992), which won him a BAFTA, *The Fugitive* (1993), *The Rock* (1996), *Lost in Space* (1998), *The Matrix Reloaded* (2003), *Batman Begins* (2005), *The Dark Knight* (2008), which earned him a further BAFTA nomination, *Scream 4* (2011) and *The*

*Five-Year Engagement* (2012), while his TV work includes episodes of *The Grinder* (2015–2016, TV) and *Fresh Off the Boat* (2015–, TV). **Hammer credits:** *Blood from the Mummy's Tomb* (1971 [uncredited])

### Robbie, Christopher

British born Robbie (1938–) can be seen as General Neruda, the Head of Internal Security in *Czech Mate* (1984, TVM [episode of *Hammer House of Mystery and Suspense*]). He also had a role in *Wolfshead: The Legend of Robin Hood* (1969 [released 1973]), which was made by other hands, but later acquired by Hammer. Trained at RADA, his other credits include *Where Has Poor Mickey Gone?* (1964), *Eyewitness* (1970), *Biggles* (1986), *Rabbit Fever* (2006) and *Enemies Closer* (2013), plus episodes of *The Avengers* (1961–1969, TV), *The House of Eliott* (1991–1993, TV) and *Holby City* (1999–, TV). **Hammer credits:** *Wolfshead: The Legend of Robin Hood* (1969 [released 1973], as Roger of Doncaster), *Czech Mate* (1984, TVM [episode of *Hammer House of Mystery and Suspense*], as General Neruda)

### Robbins, Michael

Best remembered for playing the work-shy Arthur Rudge in the long-running sitcom *On the Buses* (1969–1973, TV), of which he appeared in 61 of the 74 episodes, this British comedy actor (1930–1992) went on to revive the character for Hammer's three big screen spin offs. He also had brief roles in two other TV spin-offs for the company. His other film credits include *Lunch Hour* (1962), *Rattle of a Simple Man* (1964), *The Whisperers* (1967), *Up the Junction* (1968), *The Looking Glass War* (1969), *Zeppelin* (1971), *The Pink Panther Strikes Again* (1976) and *Victor/Victoria* (1982), while on TV he appeared in episodes of such series as *Thick as Thieves* (1974, TV), *Fairly Secret Army* (1984–1986, TV) and *The New Statesman* (1987–1992, TV). A former bank clerk, he was married to the actress Hal Dyer (1935–2011) from 1960; she also appeared in *Holiday on the Buses* (1973). **Additional notes:** Contrary to some sources, Robbins did not appear as Arthur Rudge in a 1972 edition of the TV comedy special *All Star Comedy Carnival* (1969–1973, TV). **Hammer credits:** *On the Buses* (1971, as Arthur Rudge), *Mutiny on the Buses* (1972, as Arthur Rudge), *That's Your Funeral* (1973, as Second funeral director), *Holiday on the Buses* (1973, as Arthur Rudge), *Man About the House* (1974, as Second doorman)

### Robbins, Sheila

This supporting actress (aka Sheila Davis) played the role of Miss Jackson in Hammer's *Never Take Sweets from a Stranger* (1960). Her other credits include *Suddenly, Last Summer* (1959) and a 1960 ad campaign for Persil washing powder. **Hammer credits:** *Never Take Sweets from a Stranger* (1960, as Miss Jackson [uncredited])

### Roberts, Annette

Roberts can be seen as one of the schoolgirls in Hammer's *Twins of Evil* (1971). **Hammer credits:** *Twins of Evil* (1971, as Schoolgirl [uncredited])

## Roberts, Christian

This RADA-trained British actor (1944–) is best remembered for playing Tom Taggart in Hammer's *The Anniversary* (1968), in which he trades insults with his waspish, one-eyed mother, played by Hollywood legend Bette Davis, who even plants an open-mouthed kiss on him in the course of the action. His other credits include *To Sir, with Love* (1967), *The Desperados* (1968), *Twisted Nerve* (1968), *The Last Valley* (1970) and *Short Ends* (1976), plus episodes of *Haunted* (1967–1968, TV), *Clochemerle* (1972, TV) and *Feet First* (1979, TV). Also in the theater, where he has worked as both an actor and a producer. He now works as a hotelier and restaurateur in Barbados. **Hammer credits:** *The Anniversary* (1968, as Tom Taggart)

## Roberts, Clarissa

This British actress (1938–) appeared as one of the harem girls in the Hammer comedy *I Only Arsked!* (1958). Her other credits include an episode of *The Two Charleys* (1959, TV). Her husband was actor Joe Baker (1928–2001), whom she married in 1960 but later divorced. **Hammer credits:** *I Only Arsked!* (1958, as Harem girl [uncredited])

## Roberts, Leslie

Roberts provided the choreography for the nightclub scenes in Hammer's *The Lady Craved Excitement* (1950). His other screen credits include *Honeymoon for Three* (1935), *Cheer Up* (1936) and *Queen of Hearts* (1936), on all of which he worked in conjunction with Carl Hyson, and *Down Among the Z Men* (1952) and *Forces' Sweetheart* (1954). He also appeared as a dance instructor in *O.H.M.S.* (1937). Busiest on television, his many credits here take in episodes of *The Ted Ray Show* (1955–1959, TV), *The Wakey Wakey Tavern* (1956–1968, TV) and *Vera Lynn Sings* (1957, TV), on each of which he also worked as an associate producer as well as the choreographer. Other TV shows worked on include *Rooftop Rendezvous* (1948–1950, TV), *Top Hat* (1950–1952, TV) and *The Saturday Show* (1955–1962, TV), while his various dance troupes included The Leslie Roberts Silhouettes, The Blonde Toppers and The Television Toppers. **Hammer credits:** *The Lady Craved Excitement* (1950)

## Roberts, Mike (Michael)

This prolific British cameraman (1939–2000) worked as the focus puller on Hammer's *Slave Girls* (1968). In films from 1958 with *Battle of the V-1* as a clapper loader, his other credits in this capacity include *I Was Monty's Double* (1958), *School for Scoundrels* (1960) and *The Naked Edge* (1961). His credits as a focus puller include *His and Hers* (1961), *Theatre of Death* (1966), *The Prime of Miss Jean Brodie* (1969), *Diamonds Are Forever* (1971), *Live and Let Die* (1973), *The Man with the Golden Gun* (1974) and *Sinbad and the Eye of the Tiger* (1977). He then became an operator with *Silver Bears* (1977), *Dominique* (1978), *Clash of the Titans* (1981), *The Killing Fields* (1984), *Empire of the Sun* (1987), *City of Joy* (1992), *Notting Hill* (1999) and *Chocolat* (2000). He most often worked in conjunction with the cinematographer Ted Moore. **Hammer credits:** *Slave Girls* (1968)

## Roberts, Nora

This casting director and dialogue director (?–1968) worked on a handful of Hammer second features in the fifties. Her other credits as a casting director include *William Comes to Town* (1948), *Laughter in Paradise* (1951), *Safari* (1956), *The Inn of the Sixth Happiness* (1958), *Sons and Lovers* (1960) and *Lisa* (1962), plus episodes of *Fabian of the Yard* (1954–1956, TV). **Hammer credits:** *Cloudburst* (1951, casting [uncredited]), *Stolen Face* (1952, casting), *Never Look Back* (1952, casting), *Four Sided Triangle* (1953, dialogue director), *Spaceways* (1953, dialogue director), *Mantrap* (1953, dialogue director)

## Robertson, Ben

Robertson can be seen in a supporting role in *The Late Nancy Irving* (1984, TVM [episode of *Hammer House of Mystery and Suspense*]). His other TV credits include *An Affair in Mind* (1988, TVM), *A Woman at War* (1991, TVM) and *The Stretch* (2000, TVM), while his occasional film credits take in *The Little Drummer Girl* (1984), *Whoops Apocalypse* (1986) and *Robinson Crusoe* (1997). **Hammer credits:** *The Late Nancy Irving* (1984, TVM [episode of *Hammer House of Mystery and Suspense*], as Nurse Baines)

## Robertson, Dennis

Robertson worked as the assistant director on Hammer's *Dracula Has Risen from the Grave* (1968). His other credits include *Bindle* (1966), *Ulysses* (1967), *The Killing of Sister George* (1968) and *A Story of Tutankhamun* (1973), plus episodes of *Gideon's Way* (1965–1966, TV). **Hammer credits:** *Dracula Has Risen from the Grave* (1968)

## Robertson, Harry *see* Robinson, Harry

## Robertson, John Forbes *see* Forbes-Robertson, John

## Robeson, Paul

Of imposing presence, this massive American actor and singer (1898–1976) is perhaps best remembered for playing the role of Joe in the 1928 London stage production of *Showboat* and also in the 1936 film version, in which he delivers a powerful rendition of *Ol' Man River*. A former college football player and graduate of Rutgers, he went on to study law, but instead turned to the stage at the request of playwright Eugene O'Neill, for whom he performed in both *All God's Chillun' Got Wings* (1924) and the 1924 revival of *The Emperor Jones* (1920). Acclaimed concert performances and recordings followed, while in 1925 he made his screen debut it *Body and Soul*. Unfortunately, his passion for Leftist ideology—he made the first of several visits to the Soviet Union in 1934—and black activism made him an increasingly controversial figure, despite his continued success on stage (in *Othello* in 1930) and screen. In fact his passport was revoked by the State Department in 1950, despite his denials that he was actually a member of the Communist party, thus curtailing his career in Europe for several years (it also meant that he wasn't able to receive the Stalin Peace Prize, awarded to him in 1952, until 1958, by which time he was again free to travel). He subsequently resumed his European career, but increasing ill health gradually ended his stage appearances.

His other films, mostly made in Britain, include *Sanders of the River* (1935), *Big Fella* (1937), *King Solomon's Mines* (1937), *Jericho* (1937), *The Proud Valley* (1940) and *Tales of Manhattan* (1942). He also starred in Hammer's third production, *Song of Freedom* (1936), in which he played John Zinga, a dockworker turned opera singer who discovers that he is actually the head of an African tribe. The star was pleased with the film's approach to race, and noted in an interview with *Film Weekly* at the time that it was the first "To give a true picture of many aspects of the life of the colored man in the West. Hitherto, on screen, he has been caricatured or presented only as a comedy character. This film shows him as a real man, with problems to be solved, difficulties to be overcome."[37] Indeed, writing about the film in *The Spectator*, the noted author and critic Graham Greene picked up on the film's relaxed attitudes to race, observing that, "The best scenes are the dockland scenes, the men returning from work, black and white in an easy companionship." **Hammer credits:** *Song of Freedom* (1936, as John Zinga)

## Robillard, Elizabeth

This Canadian child actress (1958–) appeared as one of the five "watchers" in *Somewhere in a Crowd*, an episode of Hammer's *Journey to the Unknown* (1968, TV). Her other TV credits include episodes of *The Avengers* (1961–1969, TV), *The Pretenders* (1972, TV) and *Angels* (1975–1983, TV), while her films credits include *A Day in the Death of Joe Egg* (1972). **Hammer credits:** *Somewhere in a Crowd* (1968, TV [episode of *Journey to the Unknown*], as Watcher)

## Robins, John

Robins helmed four big screen sitcom spin-offs for Hammer, among them *That's Your Funeral* (1973), in which he can also be seen briefly as a vicar during the opening credits. Although made first, *That's Your Funeral* was released after *Nearest and Dearest* (1973), with which it was more or less shot back-to-back. His TV work includes directing episodes of such shows as *Mr. Aitch* (1967, TV) and *The Best Things in Life* (1969–1970, TV), though he is best known for his work on *The Benny Hill Show* (1969–1989, TV), which won him a shared BAFTA in 1972, as well as nominations in 1971 and 1975 (the latter shared), plus shared Emmy nominations in 1980 and 1981. His other work with Hill includes the TV short *Eddie in August* (1970, TV), which he co-directed with the comedian. He also produced (with Roy Skeggs) and directed the Benny Hill compilation film, *The Best of Benny Hill* (1974). Robins' other work as a television producer includes episodes of such series as *Swallows and Amazons* (1963, TV), *Thorndyke* (1964, TV) and *R3* (1964, TV). He is also acknowledged in the credits of *Flesh and Blood—The Hammer Heritage of Horror* (1994, TV). **Hammer credits:** *Nearest and Dearest* (1973, director), *That's Your Funeral* (1973, director, also cameo appearance as vicar [uncredited]), *Love Thy Neighbour* (1973, director), *Man About the House* (1974, director), *Flesh and Blood—The Hammer Heritage of Horror* (1994, TV, acknowledgment)

## Robinson, Bernard

As Hammer's long-serving designer in chief, British born Robinson (1912–1970) had a hand in the art direction of many of the company's key horror films, creating lavish-looking sets that belied both their minimum budgets and the cramped studios in which they were erected. Commented associate producer Anthony Nelson Keys of Robinson's abilities, "He was one of the greatest, he really was. Built sets out of nothing."[38] Robinson began his film career as a draughtsman at Teddington Studios in 1935 following his education at the Liverpool School of Art. He graduated to art director in 1939 at British Lion, and worked for director George King on such films as *The Case of the Frightened Lady* (1940) and *Crimes at the Dark House* (1940). During the war, he became a camouflage and decoy expert for the Air Ministry, after which he returned to films, designing such productions as *The Shop at Sly Corner* (1946), *While I Live* (1947), *Forbidden* (1948), *Murder at the Windmill* (1949), *Emergency Call* (1952), one of eight films he designed for director Lewis Gilbert, *Cash Boy* (1952), *Old Mother Riley Meets the Vampire* (1952), *The Sea Shall Not Have Them* (1954) and *Reach for the Sky* (1956).

Robinson joined Hammer in 1956 following further experience at Apollo Films and Pinnacle Productions. At Pinnacle, Robinson had worked with associate producer Anthony Nelson Keys, and when Keys was asked to join Hammer for the filming of *Quatermass 2* (1957), he invited Robinson to join him. Robinson's impact was immediate, and he was soon after asked to take over the art direction of *The Curse of Frankenstein* (1957) from Ted Marshall.

Following this, he went on to design such major gothic productions as *Dracula* (1958), the sets for which were noted for their visual flair ("Lavish setting and the magnificent use of backgrounds give the production a commanding appearance," noted *The Daily Cinema*). However, it should be noted that Robinson's elegantly dressed interiors for Castle Dracula were deemed such a radical departure from the cobwebbed ruins seen in the 1931 Universal film, he was almost removed from the project. Nevertheless, he redeemed himself by re-dressing several of the sets for use elsewhere in the film, thus saving the studio a great deal of money. In fact this ingenious re-cycling policy saw many sets revamped and re-used in both the films they were designed for, as well as other completely different productions. For example, certain sets constructed for *Dracula* were re-dressed and re-used in *The Revenge of Frankenstein* (1958), which went into production immediately following *Dracula*. Consequently, sharp-eyed viewers will be able to spot certain staircases, columned archways and fireplaces which went on to appear in film after film.

Other key productions designed by Robinson include *The Hound of the Baskervilles* (1959), noted for the impressive interiors of Baskerville Hall, and

*The Mummy* (1959), which features many eye-catching Egyptian artefacts, several of them made by his future (second) wife, Margaret Carter (1920–2016), whom he married in 1960 and who went on to work on several Hammer films. *The Mummy* also continued Robinson's money-saving re-cycling policy, given that sets from both *The Man Who Could Cheat Death* (1959) and *Yesterday's Enemy* (1959) were re-worked for the production. As for his work on the exotic, India-set *The Stranglers of Bombay* (1960), critic Paul Dehn observed, "We are almost totally won over by the production designer and his assistant art director to the belief that the film is being shot in India when in reality it was shot at Bray. Extraordinary pains have been taken to deceive experts, and experts will, I think, admit its preponderant authenticity."

Robinson excelled himself with his work for *The Brides of Dracula* (1960), which contained another of his signature grand halls. Commented Margaret Robinson of her husband's eye for detail, "He had the reputation of being one of the few art directors who dressed his own sets. He liked things to be precisely where he wanted them."[39] Cinematographer Jack Asher agreed, commenting, "Bernard's attention to detail was amazing. The *objects d'art* that dotted the sets were always first class."[40] He also observed that Robinson's period sets "exuded grace and style."[41]

Robinson's re-cycling policy meanwhile was taken to its next logical step with *Visa to Canton* (1960) and *The Terror of the Tongs* (1961). These were filmed back-to-back on the same sets, which were suitably re-dressed, beginning with 1910 Hong Kong for *Tongs* (which was made first but released second) and 1960s China for *Visa*. Similarly, sets for the abandoned Spanish Inquisition drama *The Rape of Sabena* (aka *The Inquisitor*) were also expected to double for *The Curse of the Werewolf* (1961). Again, these were originally planned as back-to-back productions before *Sabena* was unceremoniously pulled from the schedule at the last moment following objections about the project from the film's chief investors, Columbia.

It was to the French Riviera for Robinson's next assignment, *Taste of Fear* (1961), for which he created the interiors *and* exteriors of a cliff-top villa, among them a spacious terrace and a spectacular but all-too-briefly-seen kitchen set (however, note the size of the minute swimming pool in the villa's garden, which seems to grow in size underwater when the chauffeur dives in to retrieve a body!). These sets were built on the larger soundstages of Elstree, given that *The Shadow of the Cat* (1961), which was also designed by Robinson, was shooting at Bray simultaneously. Said writer-producer Jimmy Sangster of Robinson's work on *Taste of Fear*, "Once again Bernie Robinson came up trumps. Not this time a medieval castle or village inn, but a perfect interior to fit the Villa de la Garoupe which I'd found at Cap d'Antibes. It was a huge composite set, taking in the entrance hall, living room, the girl's bedroom, leading out onto the patio with garage, chauffeur's quarters and pool house, then some rocks climbing to a small promontory which was supposed to overlook the

Window of opportunity. The cast of *The Kiss of the Vampire* (1963) congregate in front of an impressive piece of set design by Bernard Robinson. Left to right: Jacquie Wallis, Barry Warren, Isobel Black, Noel Willman, Jennifer Daniel, Edward de Souza and Stan Simmons (Hammer/Universal/Rank/Universal International).

sea. If we'd done the movie at Bray it would have involved at least five separate sets."[42]

If there was one thing that Robinson truly excelled at, it was baronial hallways, and his set for the interior of Chateau Ravna in *The Kiss of the Vampire* (1963) is one of his most lavish. However, his re-cycling policy meant that keen-eyed viewers would be able to spot a Y-shaped staircase which was also used in *The Old Dark House* (1963) and *Paranoiac* (1963).

Following the completion of *The Devil-Ship Pirates* (1964), during which the boat the *Diablo* capsized during filming, Robinson began to take an increasing number of breaks (he tended to avoid the films made by Hammer at Elstree). Consequently, his art director Don Mingaye designed the sets for *The Evil of Frankenstein* (1964) and *The Runaway* (1964), both of which were shot at Bray. Meanwhile, working out of Elstree, Edward Carrick designed *Hysteria* (1965) and *The Nanny* (1965), Robert Jones designed *She* (1965), *One Million Years B.C.* (1966) and *Slave Girls* (1968), Peter Proud designed *Fanatic* (1965), Reece Pemberton designed *The Anniversary* (1968), Lionel Couch designed *The Vengeance of She* (1968) and Arthur Lawson designed *The Lost Continent* (1968). Working out of Pinewood, Maurice Carter designed *A Challenge for Robin Hood* (1967). However, Robinson was back at his drawing board for *The Gorgon* (1964) and several other projects, prime among them four films shot back-to-back at Bray, ingeniously using the same sets, suitably redressed. These were *Dracula—Prince of Darkness*

(1966), for which Robinson created a new baronial hall for Castle Dracula, *Rasputin—The Mad Monk* (1966), for which the exterior of Castle Dracula became a Russian winter palace, *The Plague of the Zombies* (1966), which included a sunken graveyard exterior, and *The Reptile* (1966). Recalled clapper boy Christopher Neame of this hectic period of back-to-back filming, "One finished on the Friday evening at exactly five-twenty and the other started at eight-thirty on the Monday morning.... The art department only had a weekend to convert Transylvanian interiors into Russian. This was where Bernie came into his own."[43]

When Hammer finally vacated Bray on 19 November 1966, Robinson went with them, working on such major assignments as *Quatermass and the Pit* (1967) and *The Devil Rides Out* (1968), both of which benefited from the larger sound stages available at MGM Borehamwood and ABPC Elstree respectively. Robinson may well have missed the close-knit community at Bray, but his work on subsequent productions for Hammer was every bit as inventive as his best work at Bray. Indeed, his work for *The Devil Rides Out* is easily among his best (the richly appointed interiors for Simon Aron's country home, particularly the attic observatory, retain the established Bray style).

Following his rather disappointing work for *Dracula Has Risen from the Grave* (1968), which features some of his least eye-catching designs, Robinson concluded his career at Hammer on another high note with *Frankenstein Must Be Destroyed* (1969), which has the look and feel of a

Bray production, despite being filmed at Elstree. Robinson died the following year, and with him went some of the Hammer magic. Indeed, once with Hammer, he spent the majority of his remaining career with the company, helping to create its distinctive look, and only occasionally worked elsewhere, among his other non–Hammer credits being *Carve Her Name with Pride* (1958), which was his final film for director Lewis Gilbert, *Run a Crooked Mile* (1969, TVM) and *Destiny of a Spy* (1969, TVM).

Said Michael Carreras of Robinson, "[He] was a man of absolutely implicit faith in his own technique and who knew instinctively that quality didn't necessarily cost money to achieve. The man had quality and taste. He would not, even if you gave him only four pence for a set, let you photograph it until he was personally satisfied that it met with his own high standards."[44] Remembered director Terence Fisher, "Although his sets looked ravishing, they never even cost the little amount of money he had at his disposal. They were very well dressed.... With Bernie the low budget never showed. On the contrary."[45] Anthony Hinds agreed, describing Robinson as, "A very clever man at making a lot out of not very much."[46] Commented Christopher Lee of the designer, "Bernie was the real star of Hammer films."[47] **Additional notes:** On some of his later credits, Robinson was billed as supervising art director (as noted below). **Hammer credits:** *Quatermass 2* (1957), *The Curse of Frankenstein* (1957), *Day of Grace* (1957), *The Abominable Snowman* (1957), *Dracula* (1958), *The Revenge of Frankenstein* (1958), *The Hound of the Baskervilles* (1959), *The Man Who Could Cheat Death* (1959), *Yesterday's Enemy* (1959), *The Ugly Duckling* (1959), *The Mummy* (1959), *The Stranglers of Bombay* (1959), *Never Take Sweets from a Stranger* (1960), *The Two Faces of Dr. Jekyll* (1960), *The Brides of Dracula* (1960), *Visa to Canton* (1960), *The Curse of the Werewolf* (1961), *The Shadow of the Cat* (1961), *Watch It, Sailor!* (1961), *Cash on Demand* (1961), *The Pirates of Blood River* (1962), *Captain Clegg* (1962), *The Phantom of the Opera* (1962), *The Damned* (1963 [uncredited]), *The Old Dark House* (1963), *Paranoiac* (1963), *The Kiss of the Vampire* (1963), *The Scarlet Blade* (1963), *Nightmare* (1964), *The Devil-Ship Pirates* (1964), *The Gorgon* (1964), *The Curse of the Mummy's Tomb* (1964), *The Secret of Blood Island* (1965), *The Brigand of Kandahar* (1965), *Dracula—Prince of Darkness* (1966), *Rasputin—The Mad Monk* (1966), *The Plague of the Zombies* (1966), *The Reptile* (1966), *The Witches* (1966), *Frankenstein Created Woman* (1967), *The Mummy's Shroud* (1967), *Quatermass and the Pit* (1967 [billed as supervising art director]), *The Devil Rides Out* (1968 [billed as supervising art director]), *Dracula Has Risen from the Grave* (1968 [billed as supervising art director]), *Frankenstein Must Be Destroyed* (1969 [billed as supervising art director])

### Robinson, Douglas (Doug)

This burly British boxer, supporting player and stuntman (1930–) can be seen as a boxer in Hammer's *The Two Faces of Dr. Jekyll* (1960), prior to which he'd worked as a stuntman on *The Glass*

**Putting things into perspective. Peter Cushing stands on the stairs in one of Bernard Robinson's immaculate sets for *The Brides of Dracula* (1960) (Hammer/Hotspur/Rank/Universal-International).**

*Cage* (1955) and *Never Take Sweets from a Stranger* (1960). His other credits as an actor include *Port of Escape* (1956), *Piccadilly Third Stop* (1960), *The Frightened City* (1961), *Jason and the Argonauts* (1963), *Outland* (1981) and *The Boy Who Saved Christmas* (1998), while his credits as a stunt man/stunt arranger take in *You Only Live Twice* (1967), *Where Eagles Dare* (1969), *Diamonds Are Forever* (1971), *Live and Let Die* (1973), *The Man with the Golden Gun* (1974), *The Spy Who Loved Me* (1977), *Superman* (1978), *For Your Eyes Only* (1981), *Victor/Victoria* (1982), *Never Say Never Again* (1983), *A View to a Kill* (1985), *The Living Daylights* (1987), *Batman* (1989) and *Son of the Pink Panther* (1993). He also worked on episodes of such action-centric TV series as *The Avengers* (1961–1969, TV) and *Dempsey and Makepeace* (1985–1986, TV). His brother was the boxer/actor/stuntman "Tiger" Joe Robinson (1927–2017, full name Joseph William Robinson), who also appears in *The Two Faces of Dr. Jekyll*. Their father was the world champion wrestler Joseph Robinson. **Hammer credits:** *The Glass Cage* (1955, stunts [uncredited]), *Never Take Sweets from a Stranger* (1960, stunts [uncredited]), *The Two Faces of Dr. Jekyll* (1960, as Boxer [uncredited])

## Robinson, Ernie *see* Robinson, Urnee

## Robinson, George

Robinson worked as an electrician on Hammer's *The Quatermass Xperiment* (1955). He went on to be one of the electrical chargehands on *Paranoiac* (1963) and *The Kiss of the Vampire* (1963), sharing his duties with Vic Hemmings, and the electrical supervisor for *The Scarlet Blade* (1963) and *The Evil of Frankenstein* (1964). His other credits include *Young Winston* (1972), *The Beast Must Die* (1974) and *The Land That Time Forgot* (1975). **Hammer credits include:** *The Quatermass Xperiment* (1955, electrician [uncredited]), *Paranoiac* (1963, electrical chargehand [uncredited]), *The Kiss of the Vampire* (1963, electrical chargehand [uncredited]), *The Scarlet Blade* (1963 [uncredited]), *Nightmare* (1964 [uncredited]), *The Evil of Frankenstein* (1964, [uncredited])

## Robinson, Harry

This British (Scottish) composer (1932–1996, real name Henry McLeod Robertson, aka Lord Rockingham) had a fruitful relationship with Hammer, beginning with the television series *Journey to the Unknown* (1968, TV), for which he supplied the memorable title theme featuring an eerie whistling solo. He also penned scores for four of the show's episodes. Recalled Robinson of this assignment, "Joan Harrison [the executive producer] had thrown out all the themes she'd already heard, and she was badgering Philip Martell to come up with someone new. I believe she'd said she didn't want any of the usual Hammer composers. In the end, I wrote a tune [and] made a crazy demo of it…. She liked it and asked to see me."[48]

Prior to *Journey to the Unknown*, Robinson had worked as an arranger for theater, radio and television. His TV credits included work for the pop series *Six-Five Special* (1957–1958, TV) and *Oh Boy!* (1958–1959, TV), while his stage credits in-

cluded the arrangements for two Lionel Bart musicals, *Fings Ain't Wot They Used T'be* (1960) and *Maggie May* (1964). He had also worked as a music director for EMI and Decca (his name change to Robinson was seemingly the result of an erroneous spelling on his first paycheck). Using the pseudonym Lord Rockingham he'd also penned the song *Hoots Mon*, which had been a number one hit in 1958. He began his film career by arranging songs for such features as *Light Up the Sky* (1960), *Don't Bother to Knock* (1961) and *It's Trad, Dad!* (1962), and began scoring with *Valley of the Kings* (1964), which he followed with several Children's Film Foundation films, among them *Operation Third Form* (1966), *The Sky Bike* (1967), *Danny the Dragon* (1967) and *The Great Pony Raid* (1968). In the seventies, following his horror debut with AIP's *The Oblong Box* (1969), he went on to provide the music for a number of key films for Hammer, among them the "Karnstein trilogy" of *The Vampire Lovers* (1970), *Lust for a Vampire* (1971), the score for which includes the much-derided song *Strange Love* (lyrics by Frank Godwin), and *Twins of Evil* (1971).

Given his pop music background, Robinson admitted being worried at being asked to score features for the studio: "After all, Hammer had a reputation for using respected composers who were classically trained—James Bernard, Benjamin Frankell and also Malcolm Williamson. I felt a bit like the odd man out."[49] Yet despite his initial misgivings, Robinson's work for Hammer is among the most highly regarded of the studio's later output. Said Robinson of his work for *The Vampire Lovers*, which was made in conjunction with AIP, "The assignment was a happy one for me and I think that everybody was pleased with the end result. I had always admired the Hammer gothic horrors, and likewise had always been a fan of the AIP pictures. I especially liked the Edgar Allan Poe stories they brought to the screen—really scary stuff. *The Vampire Lovers* was my homage to both companies and also to the composers that they regularly used, like James Barnard and Les Baxter."[50] Following *The Vampire Lovers*, Robinson went on to score its sequel, *Lust for a Vampire*, which also made use of certain cues from its predecessor. Recalled the composer, "I basically worked the same sort of formula on *Lust* as I had done on *The Vampire Lovers*, although I did attempt to make *Lust* sound more romantic."[51]

Meanwhile, for *Countess Dracula* (1971), which he penned in just twelve days, Robinson accentuated the film's East European setting by featuring a cimbalom in his score, which added immeasurably to the film's atmosphere. Robinson remembered that the film's producer and director—both Hungarian—"wanted me to do a historically correct score. And I followed their instructions by steeping myself in ethnic Hungarian music and using certain instruments like the cimbalom."[52] The composer next started to work on *Dr. Jekyll and Sister Hyde* (1971), but following "artistic differences" with the film's producer, Albert Fennell, Robinson asked Hammer's music director Philip Martell to remove him from the project. Recalled Robinson, "I started doing some work on *Dr. Jekyll and Sister*

*Hyde*. This entailed barrel organ themes and songs. I then found myself overstretched on other scores and, candidly, didn't think I was going to get on with Albert Fennell who'd always worked with another good composer, Laurie Johnson…. I felt like the second wife to Laurie's Rebecca…. So I asked Philip to convey my regrets to all and extricate me from that contract. I don't think Albert Fennell lost much sleep over that."[53]

Consequently, Robinson was asked to work on *Twins of Evil*, the conclusion of the "Karnstein trilogy." Said Robinson of his experiences on the film, "I personally thought that *Twins of Evil* was a fairly good movie and I did enjoy writing the score. There was a lot of action in it, and I remember going to the spotting sessions and watching the film and thinking more or less straight away 'western.' This was because of the large amount of dashing around on horseback that Peter Cushing and his merry band of Puritans did in the film. But not the normal sort of western; maybe something along the lines of, say, the Italian western scores that had been so successful. And to my surprise, the idea actually worked."[54] But not everything was straightforward, as the composer later admitted: "The problem with *Twins of Evil* was that I had no idea when it was day, when it was night. Was it the night before or was it the morning afterwards? If you've got a sequence when you're bridging all that and you're attempting to help the time change it's very difficult. There was one bit where I thought it was the same sequence, and when I saw the picture I suddenly realized afterwards that it was supposed to be three days later!"[55] Which goes some ways to explaining the film's sometimes disjointed sense of narrative!

Robinson didn't usually visit the sets of the films he scored, but recalled that, "I remember visiting the set of *Twins*. I had to because I was playing the harpsichord offstage for the hero."[56] Robinson's last assignment for Hammer proved to be for *Demons of the Mind* (1972), which he rates as "my best score."[57] He also recalled that "The original title *Blood Will Have Blood* had to be changed because the British censor objected to the double use of blood."[58]

Robinson's other credits include *The File of the Golden Goose* (1969), *Fright* (1971), *Legend of the Werewolf* (1975), *The Ghoul* (1975), *Not Now, Comrade* (1976), *Why Not Stay for Breakfast?* (1979), *Hawk the Slayer* (1980), which he also produced and co-wrote (as Harry Robertson) and *Jane and the Lost City* (1987), which he also produced and co-wrote the story for (again as Robertson). He also worked on many Children's Film Foundation adventures, among them the serial *The Boy with Two Heads* (1974), plus *The Johnstown Monster* (1971), *Blinker's Spy-Spotter* (1972), *Wreck Raisers* (1972), *The Flying Sorcerer* (1973), *The Battle of Billy's Pond* (1976), *Sky Pirates* (1977), *Sammy's Super T-Shirt* (1978), *Electric Eskimo* (1979), *Deep Waters* (1979), *A Hitch in Time* (1979), *The Boy Who Never Was* (1980), which he also produced (as H. MacLeod Robinson), *A Horse Called Jester* (1980) and *Terry on the Fence* (1985).

Sniped Philp Martell of Robinson's film work, "He's a dance band composer. Obviously, he didn't find his right métier in the dance music, or he would have stayed there. Those two producers, Harry Fine and Michael Style came aboard and they thought Robinson was great. They expected he would score every Hammer film they made"[59] He did.

Robinson's wife was the actress Ziki Arnot (1934–2000, real name Myrtle Olive Felix Arbuthnot), whom he married in 1958. **Hammer credits:** *Journey to the Unknown* (1968, TV, theme), *Eve* (1968, TV [episode of *Journey to the Unknown*]), *Miss Belle* (1968, TV [episode of *Journey to the Unknown*]), *Somewhere in a Crowd* (1968, TV [episode of *Journey to the Unknown*]), *The Beckoning Fair One* (1968, TV [episode of *Journey to the Unknown*]), *The Vampire Lovers* (1970), *Lust for a Vampire* (1971), *Countess Dracula* (1971), *Twins of Evil* (1971), *Demons of the Mind* (1972)

### Robinson, Joe ("Tiger" Joe)

This burly British wrestler (winner of the 1952 European Heavyweight Championship), RADA-trained actor and stunt man (1927–2017, full name Joseph William Robinson) can be seen as a Corinthian in Hammer's *The Two Faces of Dr. Jekyll* (1960). A judo champion and black belt at karate, his other credits include *Fit as a Fiddle* (1952), *A Kid for Two Farthings* (1955), *The Bulldog Breed* (1960), *Carry On Regardless* (1961), *The Loneliness of the Long Distance Runner* (1962), *Barabbas* (1962), *Doctor in Distress* (1963) and *Diamonds Are Forever* (1971), in which he had his most high profile role as Peter Franks, with whom Sean Connery's James Bond has a memorable fight in a glass-paneled elevator. He also appeared in episodes of such TV series as *The Avengers* (1961–1969, TV) and *The Saint* (1962–1969, TV). His brother is the boxer/actor/stuntman Douglas Robinson (1930–), who also appears in *The Two Faces of Dr. Jekyll* (as well as two other Hammer films), and with whom he co-authored *Honor Blackman's Book of Self Defence* (1965). They also ran a gym together just off London's Leicester Square, among their clients being Christopher Lee. In the fifties, Robinson was offered the role of Rank gong man, but turned the offer down (Ken Richmond took over the part). **Hammer credits:** *The Two Faces of Dr. Jekyll* (1960, as Corinthian [uncredited])

### Robinson (née Carter), Margaret

Following experience as a mask maker for the theatrical costumiers Theater Zoo from 1957, this British prop maker (1920–2016, maiden name Margaret Carter) was invited by Hammer's production designer Bernard Robinson to make a mask for the Great Dane playing the "Hound from Hell" in Hammer's *The Hound of the Baskervilles* (1959). Unfortunately, the mask, made from rubber and rabbit skin, wasn't entirely convincing. Recalled Robinson, "I was the one who was responsible for the mask for *The Hound of the Baskervilles*. I was rather ashamed of the mask I made—it was the worst one I ever made, and the only one people know about!"[60] Nevertheless, despite this inauspicious debut, Carter (as she was then known) was asked back by Robinson to work as a prop maker on a number of subsequent productions for

the studio, prime among them *The Mummy* (1959), on which she more than redeemed herself by making many of the film's impressive Egyptian artifacts, among them the mask of Anubis.

Other pieces built by her include the statue of Kali for *The Stranglers of Bombay* (1959), which was also used as part of a foyer display during the film's premiere run at the London Pavilion. She also made two pythons for *The Two Faces of Dr. Jekyll* (1960), but unfortunately, the scene for which they were intended was cut. The giant griffins seen in Castle Meinster in *The Brides of Dracula* (1960) were also her work, as was a Kuan Lin fertility goddess made for *Visa to Canton* (1961) and the gargoyle seen during the Christening scene in *The Curse of the Werewolf* (1961).

Carter went on to become Robinson's second wife (his first wife died following a long illness), marrying him on 5 November 1960. She gave birth to their son Peter (1961–1999) the following year. Robinson was later invited back to provide the mask for the title character in *The Phantom of the Opera* (1962), but turned the assignment down, given that she was too busy looking after her baby. She later painted two portraits for use in Hammer films. These were of Count Mitterhaus for *Vampire Circus* (1972) and Peter Cushing for *Fear in the Night* (1972). **Additional notes:** The smaller griffins Robinson made for *The Brides of Dracula* re-appeared in *The Kiss of the Vampire* (1963), *Dracula—Prince of Darkness* (1966) and *Lust for a Vampire* (1971). She reminisced with self-deprecating charm about her experiences on *The Hound of the Baskervilles* in the *Timeshift* documentary *How to Be Sherlock Holmes—The Many Faces of a Master Detective* (2013, TV), which was first broadcast on BBC4 in January 2014. **Hammer credits:** *The Hound of the Baskervilles* (1959 [uncredited]), *The Mummy* (1959 [uncredited]), *The Stranglers of Bombay* (1959 [uncredited]), *The Two Faces of Dr. Jekyll* (1960 [uncredited]), *Visa to Canton* (1960, modeller [uncredited]), *The Brides of Dracula* (1960 [uncredited]), *The Curse of the Werewolf* (1961 [uncredited]), *The Kiss of the Vampire* (1963 [uncredited]), *Dracula—Prince of Darkness* (1966 [uncredited]), *Lust for a Vampire* (1971 [uncredited]), *Vampire Circus* (1972 [uncredited]), *Fear in the Night* (1972 [uncredited])

### Robinson, Urnee (Ernie/Urnie)

Robinson worked as the camera operator on *Wolfshead: The Legend of Robin Hood* (1969 [released 1973]), which was acquired by Hammer, as well as Hammer's *Creatures the World Forgot* (1971), for which he is credited as Ernie Robinson. His other credits include *Thursday the Fourteenth* (1966), *Eyewitness* (1970), *Venom* (1971), *Treasure Island* (1972), *Charley One-Eye* (1973) and *Persecution* (1974), plus episodes of *The Avengers* (1961–1969, TV), *Catweazle* (1970–1971, TV) and *The Pathfinders* (1972–1973, TV). His credits as a photographer include *Someone Special* (1966) and *Go Girl* (1972). He also worked as a second unit director on *Promise Her Anything* (1965). **Hammer credits:** *Wolfshead: The Legend of Robin Hood* (1969 [released 1973]), *Creatures the World Forgot* (1971)

### Robson, Dorothy

This British actress (1909–1994, real name Dorothy Mary Shackleton) can be seen as a seamstress in the Hammer thriller *Blood Orange* (1953). Her other credits include episodes of *Quatermass and the Pit* (1958–1959, TV), *The History of Mr. Polly* (1959, TV), *The Bergonzi Hand* (1963, TV) and *No Cloak—No Dagger* (1963, TV). **Hammer credits:** *Blood Orange* (1953, as Seamstress [uncredited])

### Robson, Ken (Kenny)

Robson appeared as a dancer in Hammer's *The Witches* (1966). His other credits include *Melody* (1971) and *Fiddler on the Roof* (1971), plus episodes of *Tales of the Unexpected* (1979–1988, TV) and *Marjorie and Men* (1985, TV). **Hammer credits:** *The Witches* (1966, as Dancer [uncredited])

### Robson, Ron

British born Robson (1926–1991) worked as the camera operator on Hammer's *To the Devil a Daughter* (1976). His other credits include *The Brain Machine* (1955), *The Bespoke Overcoat* (1956), *Up the Junction* (1968), *That'll Be the Day* (1973) and *The Ritz* (1976). His earlier credits as a focus puller include *Ha'penny Breeze* (1950) and *Crow Hollow* (1951). He also worked as a camera assistant on *The Case of Charles Peace* (1949). His work as a cinematographer includes *Whoops Apocalypse* (1986). **Hammer credits:** *To the Devil a Daughter* (1976)

### Roden, John

Roden played one of the Huguenot settlers in the Hammer swashbuckler *The Pirates of Blood River* (1962). Mostly on television, his credits include episodes of *Quatermass II* (1955, TV), *Z Cars* (1962–1978, TV), *The Wednesday Play* (1964–1970, TV), *Softly Softly* (1966–1976, TV) and *Angels* (1975–1983, TV). His other films include *Hunted in Holland* (1961) and *The Never Never Murder* (1961). **Hammer credits:** *The Pirates of Blood River* (1962, as Settler [uncredited])

### Roderick, George

This British supporting actor (1913–1976) played one of the many policemen seen in Hammer's *The Quatermass Xperiment* (1955), a role he also played in the studio's *Women Without Men* (1956). His other credits include *Serious Charge* (1959), *Operation Third Form* (1966), *Finders Keepers* (1966), *Press for Time* (1966) and *Carry On Again Doctor* (1969), plus a return to Hammer to play minor roles in three big screen sitcom spin offs. His TV work includes episodes of *The Larkins* (1958–1964, TV), *Three Live Wires* (1961, TV), *Codename* (1970, TV) and *The Persuaders!* (1971–1972, TV). **Hammer credits:** *The Quatermass Xperiment* (1955, as Policeman [uncredited]), *Women Without Men* (1956, as Policeman [uncredited]), *On the Buses* (1971, as Second policeman), *That's Your Funeral* (1973, as Butler), *Love Thy Neighbour* (1973, as Man at bus stop)

### Rodger, Struan

This British actor (1946–) can be seen as Detective Constable Gray in *The Sweet Scent of Death*

(1984, TVM [episode of *Hammer House of Mystery and Suspense*]). In television from the late sixties with *Hobson's Choice* (1967, TV), his other credits include appearances in such tele-movies and series as *Les Miserables* (1978, TVM), *Boys from the Blackstuff* (1982, TV), *Edge of Darkness* (1985, TV), *Prime Suspect 3* (1993, TV), *Chandler & Co.* (1994–1995, TV), *Doctor Who* (2005–, TV), *Game of Thrones* (2011–2019, TV) and *The Enfield Haunting* (2015, TV). His film credits include *Who Is Killing the Great Chefs of Europe?* (1978), *Chariots of Fire* (1981), *Diamond Skulls* (1989), *Four Weddings and a Funeral* (1994), *Young Adam* (2003), *Stardust* (2007), *Kill List* (2011) and *The World We Knew* (2018). **Hammer credits:** *The Sweet Scent of Death* (1984, TVM [episode of *Hammer House of Mystery and Suspense*])

### Rodgers, Suzanne

Rodgers worked as Veronica Carlson's stand-in on Hammer's *Frankenstein Must Be Destroyed* (1969). Recalled Carlson of Rodgers, "She was professional, diligent and good company. For the fireplace scene, when I had simply to sit gazing forlornly into the flames dreaming of what might have been, I elected to sit, as the lighting was to take only moments. Suzanne took a well-earned break (those lights can be so hot). During those brief moments, maybe ten or fifteen minutes, I was unaware that the stills photographer took a picture. This was the picture my future husband would later fall in love with—as soon as he saw it he said, 'I'm going to marry that girl.' We married in 1974."[61] **Hammer credits:** *Frankenstein Must Be Destroyed* (1969, as Veronica Carlson's stand-in [uncredited])

### Rodney, Jack

This supporting actor (1916–1967) played Mandrake in the Hammer swashbuckler *The Devil-Ship Pirates* (1964). His other credits include *The Cure for Love* (1950), *The Criminal* (1960) and *The Share Out* (1962). He can also be seen as Boniface in Hammer's *The Viking Queen* (1967). His TV work includes episodes of *The Quatermass Experiment* (1953, TV), *Steptoe and Son* (1962–1974, TV) and *Public Eye* (1965–1975, TV). **Hammer credits:** *The Devil-Ship Pirates* (1964, as Mandrake), *The Viking Queen* (1967, as Boniface)

### Rodrigo, Edward G. (Roddy)

Rodrigo (1910–2003) worked as the production/props buyer on a handful of Hammer films in the early seventies. His other credits include *Anna Karenina* (1948), *Once a Sinner* (1950), *The Late Edwina Black* (1951), *Lawrence of Arabia* (1962), *The Empire Strikes Back* (1980), *The Shining* (1980), *Priest of Love* (1981) and *The Dark Crystal* (1982). **Hammer credits:** *Scars of Dracula* (1970 [uncredited]), *Blood from the Mummy's Tomb* (1971 [uncredited]), *Vampire Circus* (1972 [uncredited]), *Fear in the Night* (1972 [uncredited]), *The Satanic Rites of Dracula* (1974 [uncredited])

### Rodrigo, Roddy *see* Rodrigo, Edward G.

### Rodwel, S.

One of Shepperton's master plasterers, Rodwel worked on *Yesterday's Enemy* (1959) for Hammer, which was primarily shot at the studio because of an over-crowded schedule at Bray. **Hammer credits:** *Yesterday's Enemy* (1959 [uncredited])

### Rogers, Doris

Known for playing nosey neighbor Florrie Wainwright in the radio and television series *Life with the Lyons* (1950–1954 and 1955–1960, TV, respectively), this British comedy actress (1895–1975) also appeared in the role in the two film spin-offs produced by Hammer. Her other film credits include *The Love Race* (1931), *Honeymoon for Three* (1935), *Gangway* (1937), *Maytime in Mayfair* (1949) and *Madame Louise* (1951), while her TV work takes in episodes of *The Avengers* (1961–1969, TV), *Mrs. Thursday* (1966–1967, TV) and *The Pallisers* (1974, TV). **Hammer credits:** *Life with the Lyons* (1954, as Florrie Wainwright), *The Lyons in Paris* (1955, as Florrie Wainwright), *Adventures with the Lyons* (1957, serial re-issue of *Life with the Lyons*, as Florrie Wainwright)

### Rogers, Eric

This British composer, arranger and orchestra leader (1921–1981) is best known for providing the music for twenty-two of the *Carry On* comedies (twenty-three if one counts uncredited contributions to *Carry On Cruising* [1962]). All the films were produced by Peter Rogers (no relation), for whom Rogers also scored *The Iron Maiden* (1962), *Nurse on Wheels* (1963), *The Big Job* (1965), *Revenge* (1971), *Assault* (1971), *Quest for Love* (1971) and *Bless This House* (1972) among others. A noted orchestrator and conductor, he transcribed Lionel Bart's score for the original stage production of *Oliver!* (1960) and conducted Monty Norman's score for the first James Bond film *Dr. No* (1962). He also made a number of uncredited contributions to a variety of films, among them *Night and the City* (1950), on which he worked as an orchestrator, *Doctor in the House* (1954), for which he provided additional music, and Hammer's *The Stranger Came Home* (1954), for which he provided source music. His other films (not always credited) include *Painted Boats* (1945), *Gaiety George* (1946), *The Wooden Horse* (1950), *Meet Mr. Lucifer* (1953), *This Is My Street* (1963), *Three Hats for Lisa* (1965) and *Hoverbug* (1969). He also worked as an additional orchestrator and associate music supervisor on the film version of *Oliver!* (1968). **Hammer credits:** *The Stranger Came Home* (1954 [uncredited])

### Rogers, Maclean

In films from the dawn of the sound era with script work for *God's Clay* (1928), this British director (1899–1962, full name Percy Miller Maclean Rogers) went on to helm over eighty shorts and features, most of them low budget comedies. Beginning with *The Third Eye* (1929), which he also wrote, his other credits include *The Right Age to Marry* (1935), *Easy Riches* (1938), *Old Mother Riley Joins Up* (1939), *Calling Paul Temple* (1948) and *Not a Hope in Hell* (1960). He also helmed the Hammer comedy featurette *Clean Sweep* (1958). His credits as a producer include *The Crime at Blossoms* (1933), *The Scoop* (1934), which he also directed, *Facing the Music* (1941), which he also wrote and directed, and *The Love Match* (1955). He also edited *A Warm Corner* (1930), *Rookery Nook* (1930) and *Carnival* (1931), among others. His TV credits as a director include episodes of *Love and Kisses* (1955, TV) and *White Hunter* (1957–1958, TV). **Hammer credits:** *Clean Sweep* (1958)

### Rogers, Mark

Rogers can be seen briefly as a bob-a-jobbing boy scout in Hammer's *Man About the House* (1974). His other credits include episodes of *Tom Brown's Schooldays* (1971, TV), *The Adventures of Black Beauty* (1972–1974, TV), *Jubilee* (1977, TV) and *Nicholas Nickleby* (1977, TV). **Hammer credits:** *Man About the House* (1974, as Boy scout)

### Rogers, Ronnie Fox

British born Rogers (1932–2008) worked as a camera operator on Hammer's *When Dinosaurs Ruled the Earth* (1970), prior to which he'd worked as a focus puller on *Nightmare* (1964). His other credits as an operator include *Joanna* (1968), *Le Mans* (1971), *Superman* (1978), *The Bride* (1985) and *The Kitchen Toto* (1987). His earlier credits include *The Inn of the Sixth Happiness* (1958), on which he was the clapper loader, *The City of the Dead* (1960), on which he was a camera assistant, and *H.M.S. Defiant* (1962), on which he was the focus puller. **Hammer credits:** *Nightmare* (1964, focus puller [uncredited]), *When Dinosaurs Ruled the Earth* (1970)

### Roland, Jeanne

This Burmese born actress (1937–, real name Myrna Jean Rollins) played the role of Annette Dubois in Hammer's *The Curse of the Mummy's Tomb* (1964), a part she secured after meeting the film's writer-producer-director Michael Carreras

**Jeanne Roland looks contemplative in this still taken during the making of *The Curse of the Mummy's Tomb* (1964) (Hammer/Swallow/British Lion Columbia/Columbia).**

at a party. However, it should be noted that her performance was subsequently dubbed with what has to be one of the most irritating French accents ever heard. Her other films include *Casino Royale* (1967), *You Only Live Twice* (1967), *Sebastian* (1968) and *Salt & Pepper* (1968), while her TV work includes episodes of *The Avengers* (1961–1969, TV), *The Saint* (1962–1969, TV) and *Take a Pair of Private Eyes* (1966, TV). Married twice, her second husband is the producer Barry J. Kulick (1942–), whom she married in 1967. **Hammer credits:** *The Curse of the Mummy's Tomb* (1964, as Annette Dubois)

**Roland, Pamela**

Roland played Adele in *Wolfshead: The Legend of Robin Hood* (1969 [released 1973]), which was bought—but not originally made—by Hammer. Her other credits include *The Stud* (1978) and episodes of *Judge Dee* (1969, TV), *Doctor in Charge* (1972–1973, TV) and *The Lotus Eaters* (1972–1973, TV). **Hammer credits:** *Wolfshead: The Legend of Robin Hood* (1969 [released 1973], as Adele)

**Rolfe, Alan**

This British actor (1908–2005) had a supporting role in Hammer's *Blood Orange* (1953). A member of ENSA during World War II, his other credits include *Gift Horse* (1952), *Park Plaza 605* (1953), *The Battle of the River Plate* (1956) and *Peeping Tom* (1960), plus episodes of *O.S.S.* (1957–1958, TV), *Dial 999* (1958–1959, TV) and *The Wednesday Play* (1964–1970, TV). **Hammer credits:** *Blood Orange* (1953, as Inspector [uncredited])

**Rolfe, Guy**

In films from 1937 with *Knight Without Armour*, this gaunt British leading character actor (1911–2003, real name Edwin Arthur Rolfe) turned to performing following experience as a boxer and racing-car driver. His early films include *The Drum* (1938) and, following a hiatus for the war, *Odd Man Out* (1947), *Nicholas Nickleby* (1947) and *The Spider and the Fly* (1949). From the fifties onwards, he also appeared in a number of Hollywood films, among them *King of the Khyber Rifles* (1953), *King of Kings* (1961) and *The Fall of the Roman Empire* (1963), while in the nineties he emerged from retirement to appear as Toulon the puppet master (a role he inherited from William Hickey) in a handful of the *Puppet Master* films, beginning with *Puppet Master III: Toulon's Revenge* (1991). In the fifties, Rolfe appeared in two films for Hammer, the first of which was the wartime drama *Yesterday's Enemy* (1959), in which he played the padre who witnesses the brutalities of war. This led to his being cast as the heroic British army officer Captain Lewis in *The Stranglers of Bombay* (1959), in which he infiltrates the deadly Thuggee cult. His TV work includes episodes of *The Champions* (1968–1969, TV), *Kessler* (1981, TV) and *Crossbow* (1988, TV). Rolfe's first wife was the actress Jane Aird (1926–1993), who appeared in three Hammer films: *The Quatermass Xperiment* (1955), *X—The Unknown* (1956) and *Quatermass 2* (1957). His second wife was the actress Margaret Allworthy. **Hammer credits:** *Yesterday's Enemy* (1959, as Padre), *The Stranglers of Bombay* (1959, as Captain Lewis)

**Rollet, Raymond**

This British character actor (1907–1961) appeared in a handful of films from 1940, beginning with *Pastor Hall*. His other credits include *Thunder Rock* (1942), *They Can't Hang Me* (1955), *Blue Murder at St. Trinian's* (1957), *Part-Time Wife* (1961) and *The Golden Rabbit* (1962), plus episodes of *Whirligig* (1950–1956, TV), *Dixon of Dock Green* (1955–1976, TV) and *The Cheaters* (1960–1962, TV). He also played minor parts in two Hammer films, but failed to appear in a third, *The Curse of Frankenstein* (1957), despite being contracted to play Father Felix. **Hammer credits:** *Men of Sherwood Forest* (1954, as Abbot St. Jude), *Dick Turpin—Highwayman* (1956, as Hawkins), *The Curse of Frankenstein* (1957, as Father Felix [role cut prior to filming])

**Rollings, Gordon**

In supporting roles, this British actor (1926–1985) can be seen as Humper in the Hammer comedy *A Weekend with Lulu* (1961), which marked his film debut. Best known for his appearances in a series of adverts for John Smith's Yorkshire Bitter in the eighties, his other film credits include Hammer's *Captain Clegg* (1962), *The Valiant* (1962), *Just for Fun* (1963), *Great Catherine* (1968), *The Bed Sitting Room* (1969), *The Pink Panther Strikes Again* (1976), *Superman II* (1980) and *Superman III* (1983), while his TV work includes episodes of *No Hiding Place* (1959–1967, TV), *Coronation Street* (1960–, TV), *Play School* (1964–1988, TV), *The Adventures of Parsley* (1970, TV), which he narrated, *Black Arrow* (1972–1975, TV) and *Bootle Saddles* (1984, TV). He also worked as a radio broadcaster in Israel and as a clown in Paris. **Hammer credits:** *A Weekend with Lulu* (1961, as Humper [uncredited]), *Captain Clegg* (1962, as Wurzel)

**Romain, Yvonne**

One of the great beauties of the British cinema, this sadly underused British actress (1938–, real name Yvonne Warren, sometimes Yvonne Romaine) turned to films following work as a photographic model. Initially appearing under her real name, Yvonne Warren, her first film was *The Baby and the Battleship* (1956). Her other films include *Action of the Tiger* (1957), *The Silent Enemy* (1958), *Corridors of Blood* (1958), *Circus of Horrors* (1960) and Hammer's *The Curse of the Werewolf* (1961), in which she played the mute servant girl who gives birth to a lycanthrope after being raped by a ravening beggar. Interestingly, her cousin Loraine Carvana played the same character as a child earlier in the film. Recalled the actress of her role, "I played a deaf mute! I said send me the script and there were no lines! But in fact it was a very telling little part."[62]

Romain went on to appear in two further films for Hammer: *Captain Clegg* (1962) and *The Brigand of Kandahar* (1965), both of which, like *The Curse of the Werewolf*, featured Oliver Reed. Romain's other credits include *The Frightened City* (1961), *Village of Daughters* (1961), *Return to Sender* (1963), *Devil Doll* (1964), *Smokescreen* (1964), *The Swinger* (1966), the Elvis Presley ve-

hicle *Double Trouble* (1966) and *The Last of Sheila* (1973), in which she is briefly glimpsed at the top of the film as the title character before being killed by a hit and run driver. Sadly, this proved to be her last big screen appearance. Her TV work includes episodes of *The Adventures of Sir Lancelot* (1956–1957, TV), *Danger Man* (1960–1962, TV), *Miss Adventure* (1964, TV) and *T.H.E. Cat* (1966–1967, TV). Her husband is the composer, lyricist and screenwriter Leslie Bricusse (1931–), whom she married in 1958. **Hammer credits:** *The Curse of the Werewolf* (1961, as Jailer's daughter), *Captain Clegg* (1962, as Imogene), *The Brigand of Kandahar* (1965, as Ratina)

**Roman, Guy**

Roman had a supporting role in the "unofficial" Hammer second feature *Jack of Diamonds* (1949). This appears to be his only credit, despite receiving fourth billing in the film (in which he is listed as Guy Roman, contrary to the claim on IMDb that his surname is Romano). **Hammer credits:** *Jack of Diamonds* (1949, Douamier)

**Romanoff, Liz**

Romanoff can be seen as Emma in Hammer's *Dr. Jekyll and Sister Hyde* (1971). Her other credits include *Love Is a Splendid Illusion* (1970). **Hammer credits:** *Dr. Jekyll and Sister Hyde* (1971, as Emma)

**The Rome Symphony Orchestra (Orchestra Di Roma)**

This renowned orchestra played Mario Nascimbene's score for Hammer's *The Vengeance of She* (1968), which was conducted by Franco Ferrara. Other film scores played by the orchestra include *The Golden Voyage of Sinbad* (1973), *The Postman* (1994), *Life Is Beautiful* (1997), *Tea with Mussolini* (1999) and *Callas Forever* (2002). **Hammer credits:** *The Vengeance of She* (1968)

**Romero, Cesar**

Beginning in 1933 with *The Shadow Laughs*, this handsome American leading man (1907–1994) clocked up well over one-hundred film appearances, including *The Thin Man* (1934), *Wee Willie Winkie* (1937), *Return of the Cisco Kid* (1939), *The Cisco Kid and the Lady* (1939), which marked the first of six appearances as the Cisco Kid (Warner Baxter played the Kid in *Return*, in which Romero appeared as Lopez), *Captain from Castile* (1947), *Vera Cruz* (1954), *Ocean's 11* (1960), *Lust in the Dust* (1984) and *The Player* (1992), though to TV audiences he is best remembered for playing The Joker in *Batman* (1966–1968, TV) and its subsequent film spin-off in 1966. In 1952 he travelled to Britain to star in the Hammer second feature *Lady in the Fog*, in which he played an American journalist who, while visiting London, helps to solve the murder of a young woman's brother, at first believed to have been the victim of a hit and run accident. Romero's many other TV appearances include episodes of *Passport to Danger* (1954–1956, TV), in which he starred as Steve McQuinn, *Zorro* (1957–1959, TV), *77 Sunset Strip* (1958–1964, TV), *Burke's Law* (1963–1966, TV), *Night Gallery* (1970–1973, TV), *Falcon Crest* (1981–1990, TV), in which he played Peter Stavros, *Matt*

*Houston* (1982–1985, TV) and *The Golden Girls* (1985–1992, TV), plus countless chat show appearances. **Hammer credits:** *Lady in the Fog* (1952, as Philip Odell)

### Ronane, John

This British actor (1933–) appeared as Preston in *One on an Island*, an episode of Hammer's *Journey to the Unknown* (1968, TV). His film credits include supporting roles in *Doctor Blood's Coffin* (1960), *A Kind of Loving* (1962), *King Rat* (1965), *How I Won the War* (1967), *Sebastian* (1968), *Charlie Bubbles* (1968), a return to Hammer for *That's Your Funeral* (1973), *The Spiral Staircase* (1975), *The London Conspiracy* (1976), *Most High* (2012) and *College Debts* (2015). His other TV work includes episodes of *On Trial* (1960, TV), *The Six Wives of Henry VIII* (1970, TV), *Strangers* (1978–1982, TV), in which he played Detective Inspector David Singer, and *Press Gang* (1989–1993, TV). **Hammer credits:** *One on an Island* (1968, TV [episode of *Journey to the Unknown*], as Preston), *That's Your Funeral* (1973, as Roland Smallbody)

### Ronay, Edina

The daughter of food critic Egon Ronay (1915–2010), this voluptuous Hungarian actress (1943–) can be seen in the role of Saria in Hammer's slice of flesh and hokum, *Slave Girls* (1968). Now a respected fashion designer, her other credits include *The Pure Hell of St. Trinian's* (1960), *The Black Torment* (1964), *Night Train to Paris* (1964), *The Big Job* (1965), *Carry On Cowboy* (1965), *A Study in Terror* (1965), *He Who Rides a Tiger* (1965), *Our Mother's House* (1967), *The Window Cleaner* (1968) and *Three* (1969). She also appeared in episodes of such TV series as *The Avengers* (1961–1969, TV), *Sherlock Holmes* (1965–1968,

**Hammer glamor. Edina Ronay pouts up a storm in this publicity shot for *Slave Girls* (1968) (Hammer/Seven Arts/Associated British Picture Corporation/Warner Pathé/Twentieth Century-Fox).**

TV) and *Shades of Greene* (1975, TV). Her sister is editor Esther Ronay. Her husband is assistant cameraman Dick Polak, whom she married in 1971; their daughter is actress Shebah Ronay (1972–). **Hammer credits:** *Slave Girls* (1968, as Saria)

### Ronay, Gabriel

Ronay conceived the idea for Hammer's *Countess Dracula* (1971). This was then worked into a story by the film's producer and director, Alexander Paal and Peter Sasdy, and subsequently turned into a screenplay by Jeremy Paul. **Hammer credits:** *Countess Dracula* (1971)

### Rooker, Richard

British born Rooker (1944–) worked as an assistant art director on all thirteen episodes of *Hammer House of Horror* (1980, TV), sharing his credit with Bob Bell. His other credits as an assistant art director include *The Monster Club* (1980), while his work as a production designer includes *Frenchman's Farm* (1987) and *Contagion* (1987), the latter of which also saw him receive a credit as an associate producer. **Hammer credits:** *Hammer House of Horror* (1980, TV)

### *Room to Let*

GB, 1950, 68m, bw, United Programmes, cert A

The second Hammer film to be made at Oakley Court, and yet another in their long line of radio adaptations (this time dating from 1947), this tame thriller is little more than a variation on the classic Alfred Hitchcock silent *The Lodger* (1926), which had already been remade twice under its original title in 1932 and 1944 (yet another remake titled *Man in the Attic* would follow in 1953). Here the action is set in 1904, some sixteen years after Jack the Ripper's supposed incarceration in an asylum. Following a fire at the institution during which one of the inmates escapes, the mysterious Dr. Fell arrives from Leipzig to take up residence in an Edwardian household whose owner has hit hard times. However, it isn't long before Dr. Fell has raised the suspicions of his crippled landlady and her daughter into thinking that he is Jack the Ripper, a suspicion shared by their friend Curley Minter, an eager cub reporter who had reported the asylum fire.

The film is told as a flashback by the now elderly Minter, who recalls the case to a couple of friends. "It all began on the night of a terrible fire in a small private mental home called The Towers," he begins, soon after which we witness the arrival of the be-cloaked Dr. Fell, whose dress and demeanour soon has the household fearing for their lives, especially given the good doctor's odd actions and pronouncements. Preferring the curtains kept closed at all times, he explains that this way, "The night seems closer to us," adding that, "It never comes soon enough for me. Quite soon you'll understand what I mean."

Sadly, the ensuing drama is uninventively handled by director Godfrey Grayson, who is certainly no Hitchcock when it comes to generating tension; in any case he is somewhat hobbled by a rather silly screenplay that has Fell marked as a villain from the start (his ominous pronouncements aside, a search of his room reveals that his wardrobes and

drawers are empty, save for some surgical instruments and a torn street map marked with crosses). In fact the only moment of genuine note comes towards the end of the film when, having shot Fell through the heart, the crippled landlady makes her escape down the stairs in her wheelchair, holding onto the banister as she bumps herself down step by step, during which we are treated to some effective point-of-view shots.

As the cub reporter Curley Minter, Jimmy Hanley provides the requisite eagerness and enthusiasm, though as Fell, the velvety-voiced Valentine Dyall is required to do little more than look sepulchral and act in an increasingly suspicious manner. The supporting cast merely goes through the motions, save for Christine Silver as the crippled Mrs. Musgrave and Merle Tottenham as the jittery maidservant Alice, whose chirpy presence adds a small measure of humor to the proceedings. Otherwise, this is a disappointingly flat affair, despite its potentially intriguing subject matter, which also includes a locked room finale: having shot Fell, the landlady locks his dead body in his room, sliding the key under the door; when Curly climbs through the bedroom window to see what has happened, he pretends that the door has also been bolted from the inside, giving the lie that Fell committed suicide, thus letting the landlady off the crime (even though the gun was never found).

Filmed in October 1949, *Room to Let* was trade shown in March 1950 and released in the UK by Exclusive on 15 May the same year. **Additional notes:** Future Hammer director John Gilling contributed to the screenplay, following his work on *The Man in Black* (1950). *That* film had co-starred future *Carry On* favorite Sid James in the first of several appearances for Hammer; *this* film features future *Carry On* star Charles Hawtrey in a rare serious role as Mike Atkinson. The film also introduced actress Constance Smith to the screen as Molly Musgrave, despite it being her tenth film (interestingly, the actress would soon after go to America, where she appeared in the afore-mentioned *Man in the Attic*). The film also marked the Hammer debut of editor James Needs (who, in 1957, would become the studio's in-house supervising editor). The original radio drama proved to be Margery Allingham's only radio play.

Production company: Hammer. Distributor: Exclusive (UK). Producer: Anthony Hinds. Director: Godfrey Grayson. Screenplay: John Gilling, Godfrey Grayson, based on the radio play by Margery Allingham. Cinematographer: Cedric Williams. Music/conductor: Frank Spencer. Editor: James Needs. Cutter: Alfred Cox. Art director: Denis Wreford. Costumes: Myra Cullimore. Sound: Edgar Vetter. Assistant director: Jimmy Sangster. Camera operator: Peter Bryan. Production manager: Arthur Barnes. Continuity: Renee Glynne. Make-up: Phil Leakey. Hair: Monica Hustler. Casting: Prudence Sykes. Electrician: Percy Harms [uncredited]. Production assistant: Michael Carreras [uncredited]. **Cast:** Jimmy Hanley (Curley Minter), Valentine Dyall (Dr. Fell), Christine Silver (Mrs. Musgrave), Laurence Naismith (Editor), Reginald Dyson (Sergeant Cranbourne), Constance Smith (Molly Musgrave), Charles

Hawtrey (Mike Atkinson), Merle Tottenham (Alice), J.A. La Penna (J.J.), Charles Mander (PC Smith), Cyril Conway (Dr. Mansfield), John Clifford (Atkinson), Stuart Saunders (Porter), Charles Houston (Tom), Harriet Petworth (Matron), F A Williams (Butler), Aubrey Dexter (Harding), H. Hamilton Earle (Orderly), Archie Callum (Night watchman)

## Rootes, Maurice

This British editor (1917–1997) cut the Hammer second feature *The Last Page* (1952), which led to a handful of further assignments for the company. His other credits include *The Last Days of Dolwyn* (1949), *Maria Chapdelaine* (1950), *Reluctant Bride* (1955), *The Great Van Robbery* (1963), *Jason and the Argonauts* (1963), *First Men in the Moon* (1964), *Clash by Night* (1965), *Custer of the West* (1967) and *Krakatoa, East of Java* (1969), plus episodes of *The Adventures of Robin Hood* (1955–1960, TV), *The Adventures of Sir Lancelot* (1956–1957, TV) and *The Forest Rangers* (1963–1966, TV). **Hammer credits:** *The Last Page* (1952), *Stolen Face* (1952), *The Gambler and the Lady* (1953), *Four Sided Triangle* (1953), *Spaceways* (1953), *Blood Orange* (1953), *Face the Music* (1954), *Murder by Proxy* (1955)

## Ros, Edmundo

Hugely popular in the fifties and sixties, this Trinidadian dance band leader (1910–2011) introduced the infectious samba rhythms of Latin-American music to Britain. A frequent guest on both radio and television, he also toured Britain's theaters and made the occasional film appearance between recording albums (he was with Decca between 1944 and 1974), among them the Hammer musical featurette *The Edmundo Ros Half Hour* (1956). His other films include guest shots in *What Do We Do Now?* (1945), *Here Come the Huggetts* (1948), *Judgment Deferred* (1952) and *The Primitives* (1962). His many albums include *Ros Mambos* (1956), *Rhythms of the South* (1958), *Hollywood Cha Cha Cha* (1959), *Dance Again* (1962) and *This Is My World* (1972). In 2000, he was the subject of a television biopic, *I Sold My Cadillac to Diana Dors: The Edmundo Ros Story*, which featured clips from *The Edmundo Ros Half Hour*. He was made an OBE the same year. **Hammer credits:** *The Edmundo Ros Half Hour* (1956, as Himself)

## Rosay, Francoise

Working in her home country as well as in Britain and America, this noted French actress and singer (1891–1974, real name Francoise Bandy de Naleche) began her film career in the silent era with an appearance in *Falstaff* (1911). Her many other credits include *Le frere de lait* (1917), *Gribiche* (1925), *The grand jeu* (1933), *The Halfway House* (1944), *September Affair* (1950), *The Red Inn* (1951), *The Seventh Sin* (1957), *Up from the Beach* (1965) and *Troi millards sans ascenseur* (1972). She also co-starred in the Hammer thriller *The Full Treatment* (1961), playing opposite fellow-French actor Claude Dauphin. She was married to the director Jacques Feyder (1885–1948, real name Jacques Leon Louis Frederix) from 1917, and with whom she co-wrote one film, *Visages d'enfants*

(1925), which he directed, and on which she worked as an assistant director. Their son was the actor-turned-producer Bernard Farrel (1926–1999). **Hammer credits:** *The Full Treatment* (1961, as Madame Prade)

## Rose, Cleo

Rose appeared in supporting roles in three of Hammer's fifties co-features. Her other credits include *Radio Cab Murder* (1954), *Up to His Neck* (1954) and an episode of *Sherlock Holmes* (1954–1955, TV). **Hammer credits:** *Blood Orange* (1953, as Vivien [uncredited]), *36 Hours* (1953, as Wren [uncredited]), *The House Across the Lake* (1954, as Abigail)

## Rose, Clifford

This British actor (1929–) can be seen in a supporting role in *Last Video and Testament* (1984, TVM [episode of *Hammer House of Mystery and Suspense*]). His other TV work includes appearances in such series and one-offs as *As You Like It* (1963, TV), *Roads to Freedom* (1970, TV), *Victorian Scandals* (1976, TV), *Secret Army* (1977–1979, TV), in which he played Sturmbannfuhrer Ludwig Kessler, *Buccaneer* (1980, TV), *One by One* (1984–1987, TV) and *Wallis and Edward* (2005, TVM), in which he played King George V. His occasional feature credits include *Tell Me Lies* (1968), *Work Is a Four-Letter Word* (1968), *Callan* (1974), *The Good Father* (1985), *Pirates of the Caribbean: On Stranger Tides* (2011) and *The Iron Lady* (2011). Also much on stage, especially in Shakespeare. His brother was the actor David Rose (1931–2004), who appeared in *The Late Nancy Irving* (1984, TVM [episode of *Hammer House of Mystery and Suspense*]). His wife was actress Celia Ryder (1928–2012), whom he married in 1957 and who appeared in Hammer's *Rasputin—The Mad Monk* (1966). **Hammer credits:** *Last Video and Testament* (1984, TVM [episode of *Hammer House of Mystery and Suspense*], as Bennet)

## Rose, David

This British actor (1931–2004) can be seen as a policeman in the climactic scene of *The Late Nancy Irving* (1984, TVM [episode of *Hammer House of Mystery and Suspense*]), in which he turns up to rescue the title character. His other TV credits include episodes of *The Indian Tales of Rudyard Kipling* (1963–1964, TV), *Callan* (1967–1972, TV) and *Hannay* (1988–1989, TV), while his occasional film appearances take in *80,000 Suspects* (1963), *Confessions of a Window Cleaner* (1974) and *1871* (1990). His brother is the actor Clifford Rose (1929–), who appeared in *Last Video and Testament* (1984, TVM [episode of *Hammer House of Mystery and Suspense*]). His sister-in-law was actress Celia Ryder (1928–2012), who appeared in Hammer's *Rasputin—The Mad Monk* (1966). **Hammer credits:** *The Late Nancy Irving* (1984, TVM [episode of *Hammer House of Mystery and Suspense*], as Policeman)

## Rose, Harry

Along with Thomas Glover, Rose (1902–1955) photographed a handful of scenes for Hammer's *Song of Freedom* (1936), whose main cinematog-

rapher was Eric Cross. Rose's other credits as a cinematographer include *Gay Love* (1934), *It's You I Want* (1936) and *There'll Always be an England* (1945), while his work as a camera operator includes *Crimes at the Dark House* (1940), *On Approval* (1944), *Madonna of the Seven Moons* (1945) and *The Wicked Lady* (1945). **Hammer credits:** *Song of Freedom* (1936)

## Rose, Jack

Rose worked as the camera operator on Hammer's *Dick Barton at Bay* (1950). His other credits as an operator include *My Hands Are Clay* (1948), while his work as a cinematographer takes in *Dry Dock* (1936), *Strange to Relate* (1943), *The Way of the World* (1947) and *The Adventures of Jane* (1949). **Hammer credits:** *Dick Barton at Bay* (1950)

## Rose, Veronica

In films from the early thirties with *Just Smith* (1933), this British (Scottish) actress (1911–1968) played the role of Agnes Gregory in the Hammer programmer *Death in High Heels* (1947), while the following year she appeared in *The Dark Road* (1948) as Mother, which marked her final film appearance. Her other credits include *A Cuckoo in the Nest* (1933), *Fighting Stock* (1935), *For Valour* (1937) and *Warn That Man* (1943). **Hammer credits:** *Death in High Heels* (1947, as Agnes Gregory), *The Dark Road* (1948, as Mother)

## Rosenberg, Max J.

This American producer (1914–2004) is best remembered for forming Amicus Productions with his long time partner, writer and producer Milton Subotsky, with whom he made such fondly regarded genre pictures as *Dr. Terror's House of Horrors* (1965), *The Skull* (1965), *Torture Garden* (1967), *Asylum* (1972) and *Vault of Horror* (1974). Rosenberg met Subotsky while working on the children's television series *Junior Science* (1953, TV), and they went on to make their feature debut with the exploitation musical *Rock, Rock, Rock!* (1956). The same year they approached Eliot Hyman, who had connections with Warner Bros., about a remake of *Frankenstein* (1931). Hyman subsequently set up a deal with Hammer, but when Subotsky's script proved less than satisfactory, Hyman removed both him and Rosenberg from the project. However, they received a $5,000 payoff for their pains, along with a 15 percent share of the profits (after deductions) from Hyman's half of the deal.

Rosenberg's other films include *Jamboree* (1957), *The City of the Dead* (1960), *The Deadly Bees* (1966), *Scream and Scream Again* (1970), *Madhouse* (1974), *The Land That Time Forgot* (1974), *Bloody Birthday* (1981) and *Perdita Durango* (1997). In the seventies, Subotsky and Rosenberg planned to make a 3D version of *Frankenstein*, but eventually abandoned the project over fears of being sued by Hammer. Also in the seventies, Rosenberg formed a distribution company known as Dynamite Entertainment, which handled the U.S. releases of Hammer's *The Satanic Rites of Dracula* (1974) and *The Legend of the 7 Golden Vampires* (1974). He is also acknowledged in the credits of *Flesh and Blood—The Hammer Heritage of Horror*

(1994, TV). **Hammer credits:** *The Satanic Rites of Dracula* (1974, distributor), *The Legend of the 7 Golden Vampires* (1974, distributor), *Flesh and Blood—The Hammer Heritage of Horror* (1994, TV, acknowledgment)

### Rosmer, Milton

In films from 1915 with *The Mystery of a Hansom Cab*, this British leading man (1881–1971, real name Arthur Milton Lunt) became a reliable character support in later years, appearing in the likes of *South Riding* (1938), *Goodbye, Mr. Chips* (1939), *Hatter's Castle* (1942) and *The Small Back Room* (1949). Between 1930 and 1938, he also directed or co-directed several films, among them *Balaclava* (1930), which he also co-wrote, *Maria Marten, or The Murder in the Red Barn* (1935) and *The Challenge* (1938), which he also co-wrote. In 1948 he played the role of Simmonds in the Hammer quickie *Who Killed Van Loon?* (1948), but the film was beset with money problems. His occasional TV credits include episodes of *Pride and Prejudice* (1952, TV), in which he played Mr. Bennet, *The Count of Monte Cristo* (1956, TV) and *The Scarlet Pimpernel* (1955–1956, TV). Also on stage, his wife was the actress Irene Rooke (1874–1958), whom he married in 1919. **Hammer credits:** *Who Killed Van Loon?* (1948, as Simmonds)

### Ross, Alec

This British supporting actor (1922–1971) played the role of Tony in Hammer's first Dick Barton adventure, *Dick Barton—Special Agent* (1948). He began appearing in films after wartime experience in the RAF. His other film credits include *Jim the Penman* (1947) and *Diamond City* (1949), while his TV work takes in episodes of *The Escape of R.D.7* (1961, TV), *Harry Worth* (1966–1970, TV) and *Softly Softly* (1966–1976, TV). He was married to the actress Sheila Hancock (1933–) from 1955; she appeared in Hammer's *The Anniversary* (1968). His daughter is the actress Melanie Thaw (1964–, real name Melanie Jane Ross). **Hammer credits:** *Dick Barton—Special Agent* (1948, as Tony [uncredited])

### Ross, Annie

A noted jazz singer and occasional actress, British born Ross (1930–, real name Annabelle Short, aka Annabelle Logan) was raised in America, where she began performing as a child, appearing in such films as *Our Gang Follies of 1938* (1937), *Cinderella's Feller* (1940) and *Presenting Lily Mars* (1943), all under the name of Annabelle Logan. After studying drama in New York, she returned to Britain, where she launched her singing career. Back in America she became a member of the jazz trio Lambert, Hendricks and Ross. In the seventies, she pursued a solo career as both a singer and actress, working on both sides of the Atlantic in such films as *Alfie Darling* (1975), *Superman III* (1983), *Throw Momma from the Train* (1987), *Pump Up the Volume* (1990), *Short Cuts* (1993) and *Blue Sky* (1994). She also appeared in Hammer's *Straight on Till Morning* (1972), in which she played Liza. In addition to appearing in the film, she also composed, performed and co-wrote the lyrics (with screenwriter Michael Peacock) for the title song.

She also worked as a dubbing artist, among her credits being the re-voicing of Britt Ekland in *The Wicker Man* (1973), Marlene Clark in *The Beast Must Die* (1974) and the singing vocals of Ingrid Thulin in *Salon Kitty* (1976). Her albums include *Annie Ross Sings a Handful of Songs* (1963), which was produced by John Barry, and *Annie By Candlelight* (1965). Her brother was actor and comedian Jimmy Logan (1928–2001, real name James Allan Short), her aunt was actress and singer Ella Logan (1910–1969, real name Ina Allan) and her nephew is singer Domenick Allen (1958–, full name Domenick Allen Capaldi). She was married to actor Sean Lynch (1934–1979) between 1963 and 1977; he appeared in Hammer's *The Brigand of Kandahar* (1965). **Hammer credits:** *Straight on Till Morning* (1972, as Liza)

### Ross, Bert

This prolific British sound technician (1904–1972) recorded the sound for the Hammer thriller *The Full Treatment* (1961). His many other credits include *Harmony Heaven* (1929), *Mister Cinders* (1934), *Quiet Weekend* (1946), *The Third Man* (1949), *The Sound Barrier* (1952), *Tunes of Glory* (1960), *Thunderball* (1965) and *Scream and Scream Again* (1970). **Hammer credits:** *The Full Treatment* (1961)

### Ross, Beth

Ross had a minor role in Hammer's *Who Killed Van Loon?* (1948). Her other credits include *Operation Diamond* (1948), *Trottie True* (1949) and *Old Mother Riley, Headmistress* (1950). **Hammer credits:** *Who Killed Van Loon?* (1948, unnamed role [uncredited])

### Ross, Hector

This British (Scottish) actor (1912–1980) had a supporting role in the Hammer second feature *Delayed Flight* (1964). Other credits include *Night Beat* (1947), *Bonnie Prince Charlie* (1948), *Happy Go Lovely* (1951) and *Ben-Hur* (1959), plus episodes of *The Adventures of Sir Lancelot* (1956–1957, TV), *Out of the Unknown* (1965–1971, TV) and *Trial* (1971, TV). His second wife was actress June Sylvaine (1928–1980), whom he married in 1952. **Hammer credits:** *Delayed Flight* (1964, as Styles)

### Ross, Joanna

Ross can be seen in a supporting role in Hammer's *Captain Kronos—Vampire Hunter* (1974). Her other credits include episodes of *Doctor Who* (1963–1989, TV), *Up Pompeii* (1969–1970, TV), *Moonbase 3* (1973, TV) and *Doctor on the Go* (1975–1977, TV). **Hammer credits:** *Captain Kronos—Vampire Hunter* (1974, as Myra)

### Rossington, Norman

Following experience as a carpenter and training at the Bristol Old Vic Theater School, this stocky British character player (1928–1999) began appearing in films in 1953 with *Street of Shadows*. However, it was his performance as Private Cupcake Cook in the sitcom *The Army Game* (1957–1961, TV) that shot him to fame. This in turn led to his appearing in Hammer's subsequent film version, *I Only Arsked!* (1958). Rossington's other

films include *A Night to Remember* (1958), *Carry On Sergeant* (1958), *Saturday Night and Sunday Morning* (1960), *Lawrence of Arabia* (1962), *A Hard Day's Night* (1964), *Young Winston* (1972), *Digby, the Biggest Dog in the World* (1973) and *The Krays* (1990), while on television he appeared in such series as *Our House* (1960–1962, TV), *Curry and Chips* (1969, TV), *Follow That Dog* (1974, TV) and *And the Beat Goes On* (1996, TV). He also did much stage work, including appearances for the Royal Shakespeare Company and the National Theater. **Hammer credits:** *I Only Arsked!* (1958, as Private Cupcake Cook)

### Rossini, Jan

Rossini can be seen as a Rock girl in Hammer's *When Dinosaurs Ruled the Earth* (1970). Her other credits include *The Oblong Box* (1969), *The File of the Golden Goose* (1969) and *Cry of the Banshee* (1970), plus episodes of *R3* (1964–1965, TV), *Randall and Hopkirk (Deceased)* (1969–1971, TV) and *Doctor in the House* (1969–1970, TV). **Hammer credits:** *When Dinosaurs Ruled the Earth* (1970, as Rock girl)

### Rossiter, Leonard

Best known for playing the conniving landlord Rupert Rigsby in the classic sitcom *Rising Damp* (1974–1978, TV), this British character actor (1926–1984) also sustained a reasonably busy film career in supporting roles, beginning with *A Kind of Loving* (1962). His other credits include *Billy Liar* (1963), *King Rat* (1965), *Oliver!* (1968), *Otley* (1968), *2001: A Space Odyssey* (1968), *Barry Lyndon* (1975) and the big screen version of *Rising Damp* (1980). He can also be seen as Dr. Wallis in Hammer's *The Witches* (1966). His many other television credits include the cult sitcom *The Fall and Rise of Reginald Perrin* (1977–1980, TV) and *Tripper's Day* (1984, TV), plus a highly popular series of Cinzano commercials, in which he appeared with Joan Collins. Much on stage, he died during the interval of the West End revival of *Loot*. Married twice, his wives were the actresses Josephine Tewson (1931–), to whom he was married between 1959 and 1961, and Gillian Raine (1926–2018), whom he married in 1972. **Hammer credits:** *The Witches* (1966, as Dr. Wallis)

### *The Rossiter Case*

GB, 1951, 75m, bw, cert A

One of four films made by Hammer at Gilston Park, this unremarkable melodrama finds one Peter Rossiter accused of murdering his mistress (ironically named Honor), although the genuine culprit is actually his apparently disabled wife Liz, who hasn't walked since they some while ago. Indeed, it would seem that hysteria brought on by the news that her husband's paramour is with child prompts her momentary recovery, during which she shoots the woman dead with her husband's gun ("You don't deserve to live!" cries the wronged wife at one point). Adapted from the hoary 1949 play *The Rossiters* by Kenneth Hyde (itself taken from a 1948 television drama of the same name), the film went before the cameras in May 1950 and was released in the UK by Exclusive to a less than expectant world on 29 January 1951.

A routine production in every way, it is very hesitantly directed by Francis Searle, with much padding in evidence. To this end, many shots are held far longer than is necessary, seemingly to bulk out the running time, while at one point the family gather around a piano to sing songs to each other, including—get this—*Ba Ba Black Sheep*. The genteel acting, meanwhile, seems of another age (all the characters are frightful sticks with received pronunciation), while the dialogue is liberally peppered with "darlings" as the cast stand around sipping their cocktails (the wife's final line, as she walks towards the police, about to confess, is a toe curling, "Oh, Peter—aren't I tall?"). There is just one minor Hitchcockian moment: when the maid discovers the victim's body, she makes to let out a scream, at which we cut to the telephone ringing at the local doctor's surgery. Otherwise, this is an irritating little trifle set in musty-looking surroundings, of passing interest only for an early blink-and-you'll-miss-him appearance by Stanley Baker (seen in a country pub), who would later star in two films for Hammer: *Yesterday's Enemy* (1959) and *Hell Is a City* (1960). **Additional notes:** The play was later recorded for television under its original title in 1958 as part of *ITV Play of the Week* (1955–1968, TV), and later for radio in 1967. Jimmy Sangster is billed as James Sangster.

Production company: Hammer. Distributor: Exclusive (UK). Producer: Anthony Hinds. Director: Francis Searle. Screenplay: Kenneth Hyde, John Gilling, Francis Searle, John Hunter, based on the play *The Rossiters* by Kenneth Hyde. Cinematographer: Walter "Jimmy" Harvey. Music director: Frank Spencer. Editor: John Ferris. Assistant director: Jimmy Sangster. Camera operator: Peter Bryan. Loader: Harry Oakes [uncredited]. Sound: Edgar Vetter. Production manager: Arthur Barnes. Continuity: Renee Glynne. Make-up: Phil Leakey. Hair: Monica Hustler. Casting: Prudence Sykes. Production assistant: Michael Carreras [uncredited]. **Cast:** Helen Shingler (Liz Rossiter), Clement McCallin (Peter Rossiter), Sheila Burrell (Honor Christopher), Henry Edwards (Dr. Bendix), Frederick Leister (Sir James Ferguson), Ann Codrington (Marty Rossiter), Dorothy Batley (Nurse West), Stanley Baker (Joe), Gabrielle Blunt (Alice), Ewen Solon (Inspector), Dennis Castle (Constable), Robert Percival (Sergeant), Eleanore Bryan (Agnes), Fredric Steger (Hobson), Anthony Allen (Arthur)

## Rothwell, Michael

Rothwell (?–2009) played a reporter in Hammer's *The Mummy's Shroud* (1967). His other credits include *The Sandwich Man* (1966), *Fragment of Fear* (1970), *Start the Revolution Without Me* (1970) and *Rentadick* (1972), plus episodes of *Thirty-Minute Theatre* (1965–1973, TV), *Vanity Fair* (1967, TV), *Jude the Obscure* (1971, TV) and *The Innes Book of Records* (1979–1981, TV). Also on stage. **Hammer credits:** *The Mummy's Shroud* (1967, as Reporter [uncredited])

### *The Round-Up* see *Life with the Lyons*

## Rowe, Bill (Billy)

This prolific British sound technician (1931–1992, full name William Oliver Rowe) has credits as both a recordist and dubbing mixer, among the former Hammer's *One Million Years B.C.* (1966). His other credits include *The Rebel* (1961), *Wonderful Life* (1964), *A Touch of Class* (1973), *The Legend of Hell House* (1973), *Tommy* (1975), *Barry Lyndon* (1975), *Julia* (1977), *Rising Damp* (1980), *Krull* (1983), *F/X* (1986), *A Summer Story* (1988) and *Bitter Moon* (1992), plus a return to Hammer for further work, often as a dubbing mixer. He won shared BAFTAs for his work on *Alien* (1979), *The French Lieutenant's Woman* (1981) and *The Killing Fields* (1984), and a shared Oscar for *The Last Emperor* (1987). He was also nominated (all shared) for BAFTAs for his work on *A Clockwork Orange* (1971), *Chariots of Fire* (1981), *The Mission* (1986), *The Last Emperor* (1987) and *Batman* (1989). He also worked on such series as *The Avengers* (1961–1969, TV), *Department S* (1969–1970, TV), *The Protectors* (1972–1973, TV) and *All You Need Is Love* (1977, TV). For many years he was the director of the post-production sound department at Elstree, hence his many credits. **Hammer credits:** *One Million Years B.C.* (1966, sound), *The Vengeance of She* (1968, sound), *The Horror of Frankenstein* (1970, dubbing mixer), *On the Buses* (1971, dubbing mixer), *Dr. Jekyll and Sister Hyde* (1971, sound), *Dracula A.D. 1972* (1972, dubbing mixer), *Mutiny on the Buses* (1972, dubbing mixer), *Holiday on the Buses* (1973, dubbing mixer), *Captain Kronos—Vampire Hunter* (1974, dubbing mixer), *To the Devil a Daughter* (1976, dubbing mixer)

## Rowe, Frances (Fanny)

This British supporting actress (1913–1988, aka Frances Morton) can be seen in the role of Liz in the Hammer quickie *Never Look Back* (1952). In films from 1944 with *They Came to a City* following stage experience (from 1936), her other screen credits include *Street Corner* (1953), *The Teckman Mystery* (1954), *Jane Eyre* (1970, TVM) and *Lady Caroline Lamb* (1972). Her TV work includes episodes of *Gideon's Way* (1965–1966, TV), *Rising Damp* (1974–1978, TV) and *Fresh Fields* (1984–1986, TV). She was married to the actor Clive Morton (1904–1975), whose second wife she was. **Hammer credits:** *Never Look Back* (1952, as Liz)

## Rowland, Noel

British born Rowland (1907–1996) worked as the camera operator on Hammer's *The Glass Cage* (1955). His other credits include *The Cumberland Story* (1947), *The Oracle* (1953) and *The Big Day* (1960), plus episodes of *The Buccaneers* (1956–1957, TV), *The Adventures of Sir Lancelot* (1956–1957, TV), *The Adventures of Robin Hood* (1955–1960, TV) and *Captain Scarlet and the Mysterons* (1967–1968, TV). He also photographed the documentary short *The Eighty Days* (1944). **Hammer credits:** *The Glass Cage* (1955)

## Rowland, Robert

This British bit player (1928–2010) had a minor role in Hammer's *Rasputin—The Mad Monk* (1966). A former boxer, his other credits include *Arabesque* (1966), *The Deadly Affair* (1966), *Casino Royale* (1967) and *Berserk* (1967), plus episodes of *Doctor Who* (1963–1989, TV) and *Gideon's Way* (1965–1966, TV). **Hammer credits:** *Rasputin—The Mad Monk* (1966, as Bar drunk [uncredited])

## Rowlands, David

This British (Welsh) actor (1944–) can be spotted as a parson in Hammer's *On the Buses* (1971), in which, from his seat atop a double-decker, he espies a lady bus driver relieving herself in some bushes. And who said family entertainment is dead? He also popped up in *Mutiny on the Buses* (1972), this time as a policeman. His other credits include *Bless This House* (1972), *Assassin* (1973), *Vampira* (1974) and *11 Harrowhouse* (1974), plus episodes of *Counterstrike* (1969, TV), *Citizen Smith* (1977–1980, TV) and *'Allo 'Allo!* (1982–1992, TV). He has also worked as a radio reporter. **Hammer credits:** *On the Buses* (1971, as Parson), *Mutiny on the Buses* (1972, as Policeman, on beat)

## Rowsell, Janette

Rowsell (aka Jannette Rousell) played one of the Lulubelles in the Hammer comedy *A Weekend with Lulu* (1961). Her other credits include *Goldfinger* (1964) and *Chitty Chitty Bang Bang* (1968), plus episodes of *BBC Sunday-Night Theatre* (1959, TV) and *It's a Square World* (1960–1964, TV). **Hammer credits:** *A Weekend with Lulu* (1961, as Lulubelle [uncredited])

## The Royal Philharmonic Orchestra

This celebrated British orchestra performed four scores for Hammer: Frank Spencer's music for *Cloudburst* (1951), *Whispering Smith Hits London* (1952) and *The Last Page* (1952), and Malcolm Arnold's score for *Four Sided Triangle* (1953), the latter of which was conducted by the prolific Muir Mathieson. Founded in 1946 by Sir Thomas Beecham, the London-based RPO has also performed a number of other film scores, among them *The Red Shoes* (1948), *The Tales of Hoffmann* (1951) and *Saturn 3* (1980). In 1981 they had a chart hit with the single *Hooked on Classics*. **Hammer credits:** *Cloudburst* (1951), *The Last Page* (1952), *Whispering Smith Hits London* (1952), *Four Sided Triangle* (1953)

## Royal Productions

This American production company helped to finance *The Saint's Return* (1953) for Hammer. **Hammer credits:** *The Saint's Return* (1953)

## The Royal School of Military Music

Twelve brass players from the Royal School of Military Music (home base Kneller Hall in Twickenham) can be heard on the soundtrack of Hammer's *She* (1965), for which they play the various trumpet fanfares for the imperious Ayesha, as composed by James Bernard, and conducted by their own director of music. **Hammer credits:** *She* (1965)

## Royle, Carol

This British actress (1954–) can be seen in the dual roles of Kim and Catherine Parkes in *And the Wall Came Tumbling Down* (1984, TVM [episode of *Hammer House of Mystery and Suspense*]). Her other TV credits include episodes of *The Cedar Tree* (1976, TV), *The Outsider* (1983, TV) and *Doctors* (2000–, TV), while her occasional films include *The Greek Tycoon* (1978), *Tuxedo Warrior* (1982) and *Miss in Her Teens* (2014). Her father was the actor Derek Royle (1928–1990) and her mother the make-up artist Jane Royle (1932–2010); her sister is the actress Amanda Royle (1962–). **Hammer credits:** *And the Wall Came Tumbling Down* (1984, TVM [episode of *Hammer House of Mystery and Suspense*], as Kim/Catherine Parkes)

## Royston, Roy

This British actor (1899–1976) can be seen as the vicar in Hammer's *The Plague of the Zombies* (1966), which was his last big screen appearance. His other credits date back to the silent era and include *A Double Life* (1912), *Mr. Wu* (1919), *The Magistrate* (1921), *Just for a Song* (1929) and *The Big Splash* (1935). **Hammer credits:** *The Plague of the Zombies* (1966, as Vicar)

## Roza, Lita

Popular in the fifties, this British singer (1926–2008, full name Lilian Patricia Lita Roza) guest starred in the Hammer musical featurette *Cyril Stapleton and the Show Band* (1955). Her other film credits include *Cast a Dark Shadow* (1955) and *My Way Home* (1978). She was also a regular on radio and television during her career, guest starring on such TV series as *Val Parnell's Startime* (1956–1960, TV), *The Dickie Valentine Show* (1966–1967, TV) and *Looks Familiar* (1970–1987, TV), and was once a vocalist with the Ted Heath Orchestra. Her albums include *Love Songs for Night People* (1963). **Hammer credits:** *Cyril Stapleton and the Show Band* (1955, as Herself)

## Rozendo, Jose

Rozendo can be seen as one of the Rock people in Hammer's *Creatures the World Forgot* (1971). **Hammer credits:** *Creatures the World Forgot* (1971, as Rock man [uncredited])

## Rozycki, Christopher

This Polish actor (1943–2015, real name Krzysztof Rozycki, aka Christopher Rodzioki) can be seen in a supporting role in *Czech Mate* (1984, TVM [episode of *Hammer House of Mystery and Suspense*]). In films from 1971 in his homeland, where his credits include *Wiktoryna czyli czy Pan pochodzi z Beauvais?* (1971), he moved to Britain in the early eighties and went on to appear in such films as *Local Hero* (1983), *Truly Madly Deeply* (1990), *The Saint* (1997), *Zbigniev's Cupboard* (2010 [voice only, as Zbigniev]) and *The Honourable Rebel* (2015), in which he played Sir Alexander Korda, as well as such TV series as *Bergerac* (1981–1991, TV), *Casualty* (1986–, TV), in which he played Kuba Trzcinski between 1986 and 1989 and *Downton Abbey* (2010–2015, TV). His second wife (of two) was actress Joanna Hole (1955–), whom he married in 1991. **Hammer credits:** *Czech Mate* (1984, TVM [episode of *Hammer House of Mystery and Suspense*], as Immigration officer)

## Ruane, Claire

Ruane had a minor role in the Hammer comedy *That's Your Funeral* (1973). Her other credits include *Quatermass* (1979), plus episodes of *The Budds of Paragon Row* (1959, TV), *The Dickie Henderson Show* (1960–1968, TV), *The Benny Hill Show* (1969–1989, TV) and *The Marty Feldman Comedy Machine* (1971–1972, TV). **Hammer credits:** *That's Your Funeral* (1973, as Partner)

## Rubber, Violla

Described by Jimmy Sangster as "a rather strange lady companion/gofer-type person,"[63] Rubber worked as the personal assistant to Hollywood star Bette Davis during the production of her two films for Hammer. She was also the vice-president of BD (Bette Davis) Productions. Christopher Neame recalled of Rubber that she was "an extraordinary American woman, with a big floppy bag, floppy shoes, and a harsh tongue."[64] Recalled director Alvin Rakoff upon first meeting with Davis and her companion, "Violla was very much her [Davis's] protector; that's what she was there for. Every time I said something that she thought Bette would disagree with, Violla would kick me under the table. I left that evening with a lot of bruises."[65] She clearly made an impression on those who met her. **Hammer credits:** *The Nanny* (1965 [uncredited]), *The Anniversary* (1968 [uncredited])

## Ruddock, John

This Peruvian actor (1897–1981) had a minor role in Hammer's *Women Without Men* (1956). His many other credits *Escape to Danger* (1943), *Quo Vadis* (1951), *Martin Luther* (1953), *Lust for Life* (1956) and *Lawrence of Arabia* (1962), as well as appearances on television in such plays and series as *The Seventh Man* (1937, TV), *The Spies* (1966, TV) and *Survivors* (1975–1977, TV). Also much on stage, particularly in Shakespeare, he went on to become a drama coach at the Guildford School of Acting **Hammer credits:** *Women Without Men* (1956, as Policeman [uncredited])

## *Rude Awakening* see *Hammer House of Horror*

## Rudley, Sarett

Rudley penned the teleplay for *Miss Belle* (based on the 1957 short story *Miss Gentibelle* by Charles Beaumont), which proved to be one of the odder episodes of Hammer's *Journey to the Unknown* (1968, TV). His other TV work includes episodes of *Suspicion* (1957–1959, TV) and *Alfred Hitchcock Presents* (1955–1962, TV), both of which, like *Journey to the Unknown*, were produced by Joan Harison, no doubt hence his involvement. **Hammer credits:** *Miss Belle* (1968, TV [episode of *Journey to the Unknown*])

## Rudling, John

This British actor (1907–1983) played the role of Hodgson in *The Killing Bottle*, an episode of Hammer's *Journey to the Unknown* (1968, TV) which also appeared in the compendium film *Journey to Murder* (1972, TVM). Best known for playing Brabinger in the sitcom *To the Manor Born* (1979–1981, TV), his other TV work includes episodes of *Leave It to Todhunter* (1958, TV), *Porridge* (1974–1977, TV) and *Sorry!* (1981–1988, TV), and such early TV plays as *Capital Punishment* (1937, TV) and *Who Killed Cock Robin?* (1938, TV). His occasional film credits number *Night and the City* (1950), *The Man in the White Suit* (1951), *The Titfield Thunderbolt* (1953), *The Ladykillers* (1955) and *Law and Disorder* (1958). **Hammer credits:** *The Killing Bottle* (1968, TV [episode of *Journey to the Unknown*], as Hodgson), *Journey to Murder* (1972, TVM, as Hodgson)

## Rule, Janice

In films from 1951 with *Fourteen Hours*, this American actress (1931–2003, full name Mary Janice Rule) also appeared in the likes of *Gun for a Coward* (1956), *The Chase* (1966), *The Swimmer* (1968), *Gumshoe* (1971), *Missing* (1982) and *American Flyers* (1985). Also much on television, her credits here include a starring role in *Stranger in the Family*, an episode of Hammer's *Journey to the Unknown* (1968, TV). Her other small screen credits include episodes of *Campbell Playhouse* (1952–1954, TV), *Route 66* (1960–1964, TV), *Banyon* (1972–1973, TV) and *Murder, She Wrote* (1984–1996, TV). Rule eventually retired from acting to take up a career as a psychoanalyst. Married three times, her husbands were the writer N. Richard Nash (1913–2000, real name Nathan Richard Nusbaum), to whom she was married for a period in 1955, the writer Robert Thom (1929–1979), to whom she was married between 1956 and 1961, and the actor Ben Gazzara (1930–2012, real name Biagio Anthony Gazzara), to whom she was married between 1961 and 1982; her daughter is the editor Elizabeth Gazzara. **Hammer credits:** *Stranger in the Family* (1968, TV [episode of *Journey to the Unknown*], as Paula Wyatt)

## Rule, Martin

Rule worked as the second assistant editor on Hammer's *Vampire Circus* (1972). **Hammer credits:** *Vampire Circus* (1972 [uncredited])

## Rumney, Peter

Rumney can be seen in a minor role in *The Corvini Inheritance* (1984, TVM [episode of *Hammer House of Mystery and Suspense*]). His other TV credits include an episode of *Grange Hill* (1978–2008, TV). **Hammer credits:** *The Corvini Inheritance* (1984, TVM [episode of *Hammer House of Mystery and Suspense*], as Jogger)

## Runacre, Jenny

In British films from 1969 with the musical remake of *Goodbye, Mr. Chips*, this South African born actress (1946–) went on to appear in an interesting selection of seventies productions, among them *The Creeping Flesh* (1972), *The Mackintosh Man* (1973), *Son of Dracula* (1974), *The Passenger* (1975), *Joseph Andrews* (1976), *The Duellists* (1977), *Jubilee* (1978), in which she played Queen Elizabeth I, and Hammer's remake of *The Lady Vanishes* (1979), in which she played Mrs. Todhunter. Her other credits include *Shadey* (1985), *Restoration* (1995), *Boogie Woogie* (2009) and *Perfect Piece* (2016), while her TV credits take in episodes of *The New Avengers* (1976–1977, TV),

*Taggart* (1983–2010, TV) and *Brideshead Revisited* (1985, TV), in which she played Brenda Champion. **Hammer credits:** *The Lady Vanishes* (1979, as Mrs. Todhunter)

## The Runaway
GB, 1964, 62m, bw, cert U

This little seen crime support was made by Hammer as a low-budget co-production with producer Bill Luckwell (working via his own production company). Shot back-to-back at Bray with another Hammer/Luckwell co-production titled *Delayed Flight* (1964), it follows the MI5 investigation of a Polish chemist who may have had access to a top secret formula during World War II, during which he was working as a Russian agent.

Very much a hark back to Hammer's black and white second feature days, the film remains of passing interest for being the last film of its leading lady, Greta Gynt, who had previously co-starred in Hammer's *Whispering Smith Hits London* (1952). The film also marked the fleeting return of cinematographer Walter "Jimmy" Harvey, who had photographed many of the company's programers in the fifties, among them the Whispering Smith film (he also stayed on for *Delayed Flight*). Hammer's in-house art director Don Mingaye and sound recordist Ken Rawkins were also involved in the production, along with one or two faces familiar from previous Hammer productions, among them Alex Gallier and Denis Shaw.

Released in the UK by Columbia in November 1964, the film also (somewhat surprisingly) managed a Stateside showing, again care of Columbia.

Production companies: Hammer/Luckwell. Distributor: Columbia (UK, U.S.). Producers: Bill Luckwell, David Vigo. Director: Tony Young. Screenplay: John Perceval, John Gerrard Sharp (additional dialogue). Story: John Perceval. Cinematographer: Walter "Jimmy" Harvey. Music: Wilfred Burns. Editor: Norman Cohen. Art director: Don Mingaye. Sound: Ken Rawkins. Assistant director: Clive Midwinter. Production manager: Ronnie Bear. **Cast:** Greta Gynt (Anita Peshkin), Alex Gallier (Adrian Peshkin), Tony Quinn (Professor Hawkley), Paul Williamson (Thomas), Michael Trubshawe (Sir Roger Clements), Wendy Varnals (Tania), Denis Shaw (Agent), Howard Lang (Norring), Ross Hutchinson (Leopold Cleaver), Stuart Saunders (Conway Brockfield), Anthony Pendrell (Staff officer), Arnold Bell (Staff officer), John Dearth (Sergeant Hardwick), Leonard Dixon (Constable), John Watson (Hazleton), Ian Wilson (Caretaker)

### Russell, Grace Denbeigh
This British supporting actress (1890–1969, sometimes Denbigh-Russell, sometimes minus the hyphen, real name Grace Winifred Russell) had minor roles in two Hammer films. Her other credits include *Great Expectations* (1946), *The Mudlark* (1950), *A Night to Remember* (1958), *Trouble with Eve* (1959) and *The Night We Got the Bird* (1961), plus episodes of *Abigail and Roger* (1956, TV) and *No Hiding Place* (1959–1967, TV). **Hammer credits:** *Celia* (1949, as Woman in shop), *The Camp on Blood Island* (1958, as Prisoner)

### Russell, Graham
Russell had a minor role in Hammer's *Who Killed Van Loon?* (1948). His other credits include *The Way of the World* (1947). **Hammer credits:** *Who Killed Van Loon?* (1948, unnamed role [uncredited])

### Russell, Mark
Russell can be seen as one of the Rock people in Hammer's *Creatures the World Forgot* (1971). **Hammer credits:** *Creatures the World Forgot* (1971, as Rock man [uncredited])

### Russell, Mike
Russell worked as the publicist on Hammer's *To the Devil a Daughter* (1976). His other credits in this capacity include *Confessions of a Pop Performer* (1975), *Stand Up, Virgin Soldiers* (1977), *The Man in the Iron Mask* (1977, TVM), *Hanover Street* (1979), *The Dogs of War* (1980) and *Red Sonja* (1985). **Hammer credits:** *To the Devil a Daughter* (1976)

### Russell, Robert
Russell (1936–2008, aka Bob Russell) can be seen in a supporting role in *Czech Mate* (1984, TVM [episode of *Hammer House of Mystery and Suspense*]). His many other TV credits include episodes of *Police Surgeon* (1960, TV), *Department S* (1969–1970, TV) and *The Chinese Detective* (1981–1982, TV), while his films take in *Witchfinder General* (1968), in which he played John Stearne, *Carry On Loving* (1970), *Silver Dream Racer* (1980) and *Strange Horizons* (1993). **Hammer credits:** *Czech Mate* (1984, TVM [episode of *Hammer House of Mystery and Suspense*], as Security Guard 1)

### Russell, Roy
This British actor can be seen in a minor role in Hammer's *The Dark Road* (1948). His other credits include *Fire Over England* (1937), *Hindle Wakes* (1950), *Richard III* (1955) and *Grip of the Strangler* (1958), while his TV credits take in episodes of *The Adventures of Robin Hood* (1955–1960, TV) and *Nom-de-Plume* (1956, TV). Also on stage, especially in reviews and musicals, including the London run of *Brigadoon* (1949). **Hammer credits:** *The Dark Road* (1948, unnamed role)

### Russell, Roy
This British writer (1918–2015) penned the teleplay for *Last Video and Testament* (1984, TVM [episode of *Hammer House of Mystery and Suspense*]), which was based on a story by Robert Quigley. His many other TV credits include episodes of *The Saint* (1962–1969, TV), *The Queen Street Gang* (1968), *The Onedin Line* (1971–1980, TV) and *Tales of the Unexpected* (1979–1988, TV). **Hammer credits:** *Last Video and Testament* (1984, TVM [episode of *Hammer House of Mystery and Suspense*])

### Russell, William *see* Enoch, Russell

### Russo, Donald
Russo worked as the art director on Hammer's *Cloudburst* (1951) and *Death of an Angel* (1952). **Hammer credits:** *Cloudburst* (1951), *Death of an Angel* (1952)

### Rutland, John
This British bit player (1916–2013) appeared as a London Transport Officer in Hammer's *Quatermass and the Pit* (1967). His other credits include *Calculated Risk* (1963), *Take Me Over* (1963), *A Little of What You Fancy* (1968) and *Chariots of Fire* (1981), plus episodes of everything from *The Adventures of Robin Hood* (1955–1960, TV) to *One Foot in the Grave* (1990–2000, TV). **Hammer credits:** *Quatermass and the Pit* (1967, as London Transport Officer [uncredited])

### Rutter, Mike (Michael)
Rutter worked as the clapper loader on Hammer's *X—The Unknown* (1956). He later returned as a senior camera assistant on *Dracula—Prince of Darkness* (1966), and as a focus puller on *Hammer House of Mystery and Suspense* (1984, TVM). His other credits as a focus puller include *Billy Liar* (1963), *The Blood on Satan's Claw* (1971), *Summer Wishes, Winter Dreams* (1973) and *Space Raiders* (1983), while his work as a camera operator takes in *The Squeeze* (1977), *The Holcroft Covenant* (1985), *Highlander* (1986) and *Fatal Sky* (1990). **Hammer credits:** *X—The Unknown* (1956, clapper loader [uncredited]), *Dracula—Prince of Darkness* (1966, senior camera assistant [uncredited]), *Hammer House of Mystery and Suspense* (1984, TVM, focus puller [uncredited])

### Ryan, Ken (Kenneth)
Ryan (1934–) worked in Hammer's art department as a draughtsman and assistant art director in the sixties before becoming a fully-fledged designer on *Quatermass and the Pit* (1967). His other credits as an art director include *Ring of Bright Water* (1969), *Up in the Air* (1969), *Sammy's Super T-Shirt* (1978) and *Bear Island* (1979), plus episodes of *The Professionals* (1977–1983, TV) and *Spitting Image* (1984–1996, TV). **Hammer credits:** *The Curse of the Werewolf* (1961, draughtsman [uncredited]), *Paranoiac* (1963, assistant art director [uncredited]), *The Scarlet Blade* (1963, assistant art director [uncredited]), *The Kiss of the Vampire* (1963, assistant art director [uncredited]), *The Old Dark House* (1964, draughtsman [uncredited]), *Nightmare* (1964, assistant art director [uncredited]), *The Gorgon* (1964, draughtsman [uncredited]), *The Witches* (1966, draughtsman [uncredited]), *Quatermass and the Pit* (1967, art director)

### Ryan, Madge
In Britain from 1957, this Australian character actress (1919–1994) spent much of her career on stage at the National Theater, but made occasional ventures into films, often playing memorable supporting roles, most notably in *Summer Holiday* (1963), as Stella, the showbusiness mother from hell, and Hitchcock's *Frenzy* (1972), as a dragon-like marriage bureau client. She also appeared in Hammer's remake of Hitchcock's *The Lady Vanishes* (1979) in which she played one of two tweedy English ladies caught onboard a train full of spies and intrigue. Her other credits include *Upstairs and Downstairs* (1959), *The Strange Affair* (1968), *I Start Counting* (1969), *A Clockwork Orange* (1971), *Endless Night* (1971) and *Who Is Killing the Great Chefs of Europe?* (1978), plus episodes of *The Flying*

*Doctor* (1959, TV), her only Australian television work, *The Saint* (1962–1969, TV), *The Protectors* (1972–1974, TV), *Nanny* (1981–1983, TV) and *Alleyn Mysteries* (1990–1994, TV). **Hammer credits:** *The Lady Vanishes* (1979, as Rose Flood Porter)

### Ryan, Marion

This British singer (1931–1999, real name Marion Sapherson) appeared in the Hammer musical short *Eric Winstone's Stagecoach* (1956). Her other film appearances include *It's All Happening* (1963), while her TV appearances take in guest shots on the likes of *Oh Boy!* (1958–1959, TV), *Find the Singer* (1959, TV) and *The Bing Crosby Show* (1961, TV). Her singles include *Love Me Forever*, which reached number five in the charts in 1958. Her second husband was the American impresario and producer Harold Davison (1922–2011), whom she married in 1968. Her (twin) sons are the singers Paul Ryan (1948–1992) and Barry Ryan (1948–). **Hammer credits:** *Eric Winstone's Stagecoach* (1956, as herself)

### Ryan, Paddy

This British bit player and stunt man (1911–1990) had minor roles in three films for Hammer, beginning with *Dick Barton at Bay* (1950), in which he played the three-fingered gangster Fingers. His other credits include *The Sword and the Rose* (1953), *Undercover Girl* (1958) and *An American Werewolf in London* (1981), plus episodes of *The Adventurer* (1972–1973, TV) and *Danger UXB* (1979, TV). His stunt work includes *Captain Boycott* (1947), *Cardboard Cavalier* (1949), *Ivanhoe* (1950), *You Only Live Twice* (1967) and *The Keep* (1983). **Hammer credits:** *Dick Barton at Bay* (1950, Fingers)

### Ryan, Philip

Ryan can briefly be seen as a police constable in Hammer's *Hands of the Ripper* (1971). His other credits include *The Hands of Orlac* (1960), *The Strange Affair* (1968) and *The World Is Full of Married Men* (1979), plus episodes of *Adam Adamant Lives!* (1966–1967, TV), *Paul Temple* (1969–1971, TV) and *The Life and Loves of a She-Devil* (1986, TV). **Hammer credits:** *Hands of the Ripper* (1971, as Police Constable)

### Ryder, Celia

This British actress (1928–2012) had a supporting role in Hammer's *Rasputin—The Mad Monk* (1966). Her TV credits include appearances in *The Castiglione Brothers* (1958, TVM), *Z Cars* (1962–1978, TV) and *Miss Marple: The Mirror Crack'd* (1992, TVM). She was married to actor Clifford Rose (1929–) who appeared in *Last Video and Testament* (1984, TVM [episode of *Hammer House of Mystery and Suspense*]). **Hammer credits:** *Rasputin—The Mad Monk* (1966, as Fat woman [uncredited])

---

# S

### Sabine, Winifred

This British (Scottish) actress (1900–1984, full name Winifred Sabine-Pasley) can be seen as Mouse in Hammer's *Frankenstein and the Monster from Hell* (1974). Her other credits include *The House That Dripped Blood* (1970) and *For the Love of Ada* (1972), plus episodes of *No Hiding Place* (1959–1967, TV), *Upstairs, Downstairs* (1971–1975, TV), *Within These Walls* (1974–1978, TV) and *Angels* (1975–1983, TV). She was married to the actor and stand-in Alfred Wright (1888–1963) from 1953. **Hammer credits:** *Frankenstein and the Monster from Hell* (1974, as Mouse)

### Sachs, Leonard

Best-remembered as the gavel-smashing master of ceremonies in the long-running variety series *The Good Old Days* (1953–1983, TV), which he compared between 1955 and 1983, this South African born actor (1909–1990) also performed in a number of television dramas, among them *1984* (1954, TV), *Elizabeth R* (1971, TV) and *The Glittering Prizes* (1976, TV). His film roles were less frequent, however, among them two for Hammer: *Men of Sherwood Forest* (1954), in which he played the Sheriff of Nottingham, and *Taste of Fear* (1961), in which he played Spratt the solicitor. His other screen credits include *Man from Tangier* (1957), *The Siege of Sidney Street* (1960), *Pit of Darkness* (1961) and *Thunderball* (1965). Also on stage, notably with The Players' Theater in London, which he established in 1936 with Peter Ridgeway, and for which they founded the extremely popular *Old Time Music Hall* in 1937 (aka *Ridgeway's Late Joys*). His wife was actress Eleanor Summerfield (1921–2001), whom he wed in 1947. She appeared in four Hammer productions: *The Last Page* (1952), *Face the Music* (1954), *Murder by Proxy* (1955) and *Rude Awakening* (1980, TV [episode of *Hammer House of Horror*]). Their son was the actor Robin Sachs (1951–2013), who appeared in Hammer's *Vampire Circus* (1972). **Hammer credits:** *Men of Sherwood Forest* (1954, as The Sheriff of Nottingham), *Taste of Fear* (1961, as Spratt)

### Sachs, Robin

Mostly on stage and television (especially in America from the early nineties), this RADA-trained British actor (1951–2013) is best known to Hammer fans for playing the acrobat Heinrich in *Vampire Circus* (1972). His other film credits include *Henry VIII and His Six Wives* (1972), *The Lost World: Jurassic Park* (1997), *Galaxy Quest* (1999), *Ocean's Eleven* (2001) and *Northfork* (2003), while his TV work takes in episodes of *Murder, She Wrote* (1984–1996, TV), *Nash Bridges* (1996–2001, TV), *Babylon 5* (1994–1998, TV), *Star Trek: Voyager* (1995–2001, TV) and *Castle* (2009–2016, TV). He also provided vocals for a number of video games, among them *Stars Wars: Knights of the Old Republic* (2003), *Rainbow Six: Lockdown* (2005), *Mass Effect 2* (2010) and *Biohazard: Damnation* (2013). His father was the actor Leonard Sachs (1909–1990), who appeared in two films for Hammer: *Men of Sherwood Forest* (1954) and *Taste of Fear* (1961). His mother was the actress Eleanor Summerfield (1921–2001), who appeared in four productions for Hammer: *The*

*Last Page* (1952), *Face the Music* (1954), *Murder by Proxy* (1955) and *Rude Awakening* (1980, TV [episode of *Hammer House of Horror*]). Sachs was married to the actress Sian Phillips (1933–, real name Jane Elizabeth Ailwen Phillips) between 1979 and 1991; she appeared in *Carpathian Eagle* (1980, TV [episode of *Hammer House of Horror*]). His second wife was the actress Casey DeFranco, to whom he was married between 1995 and 2006. **Hammer credits:** *Vampire Circus* (1972, as Heinrich)

### Sachs, Tom

In films from 1951 as an assistant in the art department at Pinewood Studios, this British producer (1929–) subsequently turned his hand to production management, in which capacity he worked on a handful of films for Hammer, beginning with *The Vampire Lovers* (1970), though his association with the company can actually be traced back to 1952 when he worked as a lowly third assistant director on *The Flanagan Boy* (1953). His other credits as production manager include episodes of *Espionage* (1963, TV) and such films as *The Liquidator* (1965) and *Nothing but the Night* (1972). Sachs also began working as an associate producer in the mid-sixties, among his credits being *The Frozen Dead* (1966), *It!* (1967), *The Amorous Milkman* (1975), *The Spiral Staircase* (1975), *The Sellout* (1976), the screenplay for which he had originally brought to Hammer, who couldn't get it off the ground, and *The Holcroft Covenant* (1985). He also worked as the production supervisor on *Half Moon Street* (1986), *Spies Inc.* (1988), on which he was also the second unit director, and *Taffin* (1988). In the seventies, he periodically tried to launch the likes of *Vlad the Impaler*, *Death Rattle*, *The Dracula Odyssey* and *The Scavengers* with Hammer, but none of them made it to the screen. He was subsequently offered a place on Hammer's board of directors by Michael Carreras, but turned it down. Commented Sachs, "Michael felt it would be beneficial if I became a director, but I didn't want to do it. It was a very uncertain situation and I didn't feel I wanted to get involved."[1] However, Sachs did go on to produce Hammer's last theatrical feature for thirty years, *The Lady Vanishes* (1979). **Hammer credits:** *The Flanagan Boy* (1953, third assistant director [uncredited]), *The Vampire Lovers* (1970, production manager), *Scars of Dracula* (1970, production manager), *The Horror of Frankenstein* (1970, production manager), *Lust for a Vampire* (1971, production manager), *Twins of Evil* (1971, production manager), *Vampire Circus* (1972, production manager), *Straight on Till Morning* (1972, production manager), *The Lady Vanishes* (1979, producer)

### Sagar, Anthony

This British supporting actor (1920–1973) played a gateman in Hammer's *X—The Unknown* (1956). His other feature credits, among them eight *Carry Ons*, include *Sailor Beware* (1956), *Miracle in Soho* (1957), *Carry On Sergeant* (1958), *Carry On Nurse* (1959), *The Early Bird* (1965), *Carry On Henry* (1970), from which his scenes were deleted, *Villain* (1971) and *The Offence*

(1972), plus a return to Hammer for *That's Your Funeral* (1973). His many TV credits include episodes of *The Moonstone* (1959, TV), *Dixon of Dock Green* (1955–1976, TV) and *New Scotland Yard* (1972–1974, TV). **Hammer credits:** *X—The Unknown* (1956, as Gateman [uncredited]), *That's Your Funeral* (1973, as Policeman [crematorium])

### St. Clement, Pam

This British actress (1942–, full name Pamela Ann St. Clement) is best known for playing Pat Butcher/Evans in the long-running British soap *EastEnders* (1985–, TV), in which she appeared between 1986 and 2012 (plus a 2016 ghostly comeback), notching up more than 2,500 episodes. Her other television credits include episodes of *Follyfoot* (1971–1973, TV), *Within These Walls* (1974–1978, TV), *A Horseman Riding By* (1978), *Thomas and Sarah* (1979, TV) and *Leonardo* (2011–2012, TV), plus a brief appearance as a doctor at the end of *Czech Mate* (1984, TVM [episode of *Hammer House of Mystery and Suspense*]). Her occasional film credits include *Doomwatch* (1972), *Hedda* (1975), *Scrubbers* (1982) and *Biggles* (1986). **Hammer credits:** *Czech Mate* (1984, TVM [episode of *Hammer House of Mystery and Suspense*], as Doctor)

### St. John, Betta

In films from the late thirties as a youngster with *Destry Rides Again* (1939) following experience on stage, this American actress (1929–, real name Betty Jean Striegler) appeared in such films as *Lydia* (1941), *Jane Eyre* (1943), *All the Brothers Were Valiant* (1953), *The Robe* (1953), *The Student Prince* (1954) and *The Naked Dawn* (1956). In 1956 she moved to Britain (following previous work engagements in the UK), where she continued her career with *High Tide at Noon* (1957), *Tarzan and the Lost Safari* (1957), *The City of the Dead* (1960) and *Tarzan the Magnificent* (1960). She also co-starred in the Hammer thriller *The Snorkel* (1958), in which her psychotic husband, played by Peter Van Eyck, gasses her to death. Her small screen work includes appearances in *Douglas Fairbanks, Jr. Presents* (1953–1957, TV), *The Count of Monte Cristo* (1956, TV), *Rendezvous* (1957–1960, TV) and *The Third Man* (1959–1965, TV). Also on stage, notably in the original Broadway productions of *Carousel* (1945) and *South Pacific* (1949). Her husband was the actor Peter Grant (?–1992), whom she married in 1952. **Hammer credits:** *The Snorkel* (1958, as Jean Edwards)

### St. John, Vera *see* Carreras, (Lady) Vera

### St. Leger, Alecia

This dancer and bit-part player can be spotted in the Hammer comedy *The Ugly Duckling* (1959). Her husband is actor Jack Armstrong, who also appeared in the same film. **Hammer credits:** *The Ugly Duckling* (1959, as Dancer [uncredited])

### *The Saint's Girl Friday* see *The Saint's Return*

### *The Saint's Return*

GB, 1953, 73m [UK], 68m [U.S.], bw, RCA, cert U

Having briefly dabbled with science fiction in *Spaceways* (1953), it was back to the more mundane world of crime for this, Hammer's following second feature production. One of a handful of films part-financed by the American mogul Sol Lesser, it was produced by his son Julian and Hammer's own Anthony Hinds. Released in the States by RKO as *The Saint's Girl Friday*, it was an attempt to continue the popular Saint series in Britain ("The Saint hits London and mixes blondes, bullets and blackmail!" exclaimed the American poster, though it should be noted that the series had already visited Britain with *The Saint in London* [1939], which had been shot in the UK).

For this latest installment, Louis Hayward returned to the role of Simon Templar following a fifteen-year absence. The star had first essayed the part in the first film in the series, *The Saint in New York* (1938). Since then, Templar had been portrayed by George Sanders in five films, and by Hugh Sinclair in two. Interestingly, Sinclair wasn't asked to continue in the role for Hammer, despite having already appeared in a couple of films for the studio: *Never Look Back* (1952) and *Mantrap* (1953). Indeed, it must have been galling to Sinclair to know that the new Saint film was in preparation at Bray while he was shooting *Mantrap*.

A fairly routine entry in the series, the film sees Templar track down a gang of crooked gamblers known as the River Mob, whose activities have been responsible for the death of a former girlfriend who found herself in debt to them. To helm it, Lesser Sr. brought in a fast-working second feature director named Seymour Friedman, who had previously worked with Hayward in Hollywood on

*The Son of Dr. Jekyll* (1951); interestingly, he'd also worked for Hammer's other American financier Robert Lippert on *Loan Shark* (1952), which had been released in the UK by Exclusive. However, while Friedman may well have been efficient at churning out the shots, he failed to add any visual flair to the proceedings, which, although by no means intolerable, don't exactly grip. Recalled Jimmy Sangster, "I remember we shot in midwinter, the weather was foul, we went way over schedule and wound up with a fairly boring picture."[2]

Made in late 1952 (during which period it was known as *The Saint Returns*), the film was trade shown in July 1953 and released in the UK by Exclusive on 12 October the same year; its American release followed on 15 April 1954. An adequate pot boiler, it is well enough served by leading man Hayward, Naomi Chance as the elegant Lady Carol Denby, who is also caught up with the River Mob, and Fred Johnson as the Saint's artist friend Irish Cassidy, who in a twist ending, turns out to be the chief of the River Mob ("Cross 'em once and a man's wife is as good as a widow," Irish warns the unsuspecting Templar at one point). Good support is also provided by the always-reliable Harold Lang in one of his many scene-stealing cameos for Hammer as the manager of the Mob's riverboat gambling den, and Charles Victor as Scotland Yard's flustered Inspector Teal. **Additional notes:** Five minutes were trimmed from the running time of the film for its American release, the titles for which misspell the name of art director J. Elder Wills as J. Elderwills and composer Ivor Slaney as Ivor Slanley (camera operator Len Harris is also billed more

An attractive lobby card for the American release of *The Saint's Return* (1953), for which the film was re-titled *The Saint's Girl Friday* (Hammer/Lesser/Royal Productions/Exclusive/RKO).

formally as Leonard Harris). The name of Hammer director Terence Fisher (not involved with this particular production) can be seen on some plans Templar discovers in a drawer while rifling through a flat (Fisher is actually listed as Lord Terence Fisher!). The theme tune penned by Leslie Charteris for the series is incorporated into Slaney's score at various points (it was also later used for the TV series [1962–1969] starring Roger Moore). If any further entries in the series were intended (as has been mooted), they failed to materialize.

Production companies: Hammer/Lesser/Royal Productions. Distributors: Exclusive (UK), RKO (U.S.). Producers: Anthony Hinds, Julian Lesser. Director: Seymour Friedman. Screenplay: Allan Mackinnon, based on characters created by Leslie Charteris. Cinematographer: Walter "Jimmy" Harvey. Music: Ivor Slaney. Theme: Leslie Charteris. Editor: James Needs. Art director: J. Elder Wills. Sound: Bill Salter. Production manager: John (Pinky) Green. Assistant director: Jimmy Sangster [uncredited]. Second assistant director: Aida Young [uncredited]. Camera operator: Len Harris. Focus puller: Harry Oakes [uncredited]. Chief electrician: Jack Curtis [uncredited]. Clapper boy: Tommy Friswell [uncredited]. Make-up: Phil Leakey [uncredited]. Hair: Nina Broe [uncredited]. Dialogue director: Patrick Jenkins [uncredited]. Continuity: Renee Glynne [uncredited]. **Cast:** Louis Hayward (Simon Templar/The Saint), Sydney Tafler (Max Lennar), Naomi Chance (Lady Carol Denby), Harold Lang (Jarvis), Charles Victor (Inspector Claude Eustace Teal), Thomas Gallagher (Hoppy Uniatz), Jane Carr (Kate French), Russell Enoch (Keith Merton), Fred Johnson (Irish Cassidy), Diana Dors (Girl), Russell Napier (Colonel Stafford [uncredited]), Sam Kydd (Joe Podd/Barclay [uncredited]), Ian Fleming (unnamed role [uncredited]), Ian Wilson (unnamed role [uncredited]), Eric Chitty (unnamed role [uncredited]), John Wynn (unnamed role [uncredited]), George Margo (unnamed role [uncredited])

### Saire, David

Saire can be seen as the KEMPI Chief in Hammer's *The Secret of Blood Island* (1965). His other credits include *Man in the Shadow* (1957), *Operation Cupid* (1960), *The Greengage Summer* (1961) and *Rattle of a Simple Man* (1964), plus episodes of *Assignment Foreign Legion* (1956–1957, TV) and *The Andromeda Breakthrough* (1962, TV). He also directed episodes of such series as *Thirty-Minute Theatre* (1965–1973, TV), *Sherlock Holmes* (1965–1968, TV) and *ITV Saturday Night Theatre* (1969–1974, TV). He also worked on stage. **Hammer credits:** *The Secret of Blood Island* (1965, as KEMPI Chief)

### Sale, Michael

This sound technician operated the sound camera for a handful of films for Hammer, beginning with *X—The Unknown* (1956). He also worked as the sound transfer operator on *The Scarlet Blade* (1963) and *The Evil of Frankenstein* (1964). His other credits as a recordist include *Scream Baby Scream* (1969), *The Engagement* (1970), *Romance* *of a Horse Thief* (1971) and *The Thief of Baghdad* (1978, TVM), plus episodes of *The Professionals* (1977–1983, TV). **Hammer credits:** *X—The Unknown* (1956, sound camera operator [uncredited]), *The Curse of Frankenstein* (1957, sound camera operator [uncredited]), *The Camp on Blood Island* (1958, sound camera operator [uncredited]), *The Ugly Duckling* (1959, sound camera operator [uncredited]), *Never Take Sweets from a Stranger* (1960, sound camera operator [uncredited]), *The Terror of the Tongs* (1961, sound camera operator [uncredited]), *The Scarlet Blade* (1963, sound transfer operator [uncredited]), *Nightmare* (1964, sound camera operator [uncredited]), *The Evil of Frankenstein* (1964, sound transfer operator [uncredited]), *The Gorgon* (1964, sound camera operator [uncredited])

### Salew, John

In films from 1938 with *It's in the Air* following extensive stage experience, this portly Irish actor (1902–1961) went on to rack up over one-hundred appearances, among them *The Briggs Family* (1940), *The Rake's Progress* (1945), *It Always Rains on Sunday* (1947), *Kind Hearts and Coronets* (1949), *The Good Companions* (1956) and *Three on a Spree* (1961). He can also be seen in the Hammer thriller *Face the Music* (1954) as Max Margulis. His TV work includes appearances in such plays and series as *Thread O' Scarlet* (1938, TV), *L'avare* (1939, TV), *Douglas Fairbanks, Jr. Presents* (1953–1957, TV), *The New Adventures of Charlie Chan* (1957–1958, TV) and *Maigret* (1960–1963, TV). **Hammer credits:** *Face the Music* (1954, as Max Margulis)

### Sallis, Peter

Best known for playing Norman Clegg for over thirty years in the long-running (some would say interminable) sitcom *Last of the Summer Wine* (1973–2010, TV), of which he appeared in all 295 episodes, this much-liked British character actor (1921–2017) turned to acting after experience as a clerk prior to World War II, during which he served in the RAF. He went on to train at RADA after the war, which led to stage work. He made his film debut in 1954 with *Stranger from Venus* (prior to which he began to appear on television in 1947), and went on to appear in supporting roles (usually as meek characters) in over thirty further productions, among them *Anastasia* (1956), *A Night to Remember* (1958), *The V.I.P.s* (1963), *Scream and Scream Again* (1970), *Full Circle* (1976) and *Who Is Killing the Great Chefs of Europe?* (1979). He also provided the voice of Wallace for the hugely successful series of animated adventures featuring Wallace and Gromit: *A Grand Day Out* (1991), *The Wrong Trousers* (1993), *A Close Shave* (1995) and *Wallace and Gromit: The Curse of the Were-Rabbit* (2005), plus the TV series *Wallace and Gromit's World of Invention* (2010, TV). Sallis appeared twice for Hammer, first in the minor role of Don Enrique in *The Curse of the Werewolf* (1961), and later in the more substantial role of Samuel Paxton in *Taste the Blood of Dracula* (1970). Revealed the actor of his association with Hammer: "I'm not a fan. I mean I must admit they're probably the only two Hammer films that I've ever seen."[3] Sallis was made an OBE in 2007. His wife was the actress Elaine Usher (1932–2014), whom he married in 1957; his son is the set decorator and production designer Crispian Sallis (1959–, full name Timothy Crispian Sallis). **Hammer credits:** *The Curse of the Werewolf* (1961, as Don Enrique), *Taste the Blood of Dracula* (1970, as Samuel Paxton)

### Salter, Bill (William)

This sound recordist (?–1983) worked on the Hammer second feature *The Last Page* (1952). This led to further work for the company, culminating with *A Weekend with Lulu* (1961). Recalled Jimmy Sangster of Salter, "Bill [was] the original grumpy old man. He could hear aeroplanes through his headphones before the bloody things had even taken off from Heathrow, fifteen miles away. And he'd interrupt the scene in the middle to tell us about it."[4] Salter's other credits include *Rome Express* (1932), *The Good Companions* (1933), *Boys Will Be Boys* (1935), *The Frozen Limits* (1939), *Quartet* (1948), *Geordie* (1955), *The Silent Enemy* (1958), *On the Fiddle* (1961) and *Life in Danger* (1964), plus episodes of *London Playhouse* (1955–1956, TV). His son is the sound technician John Salter. **Hammer credits:** *The Last Page* (1952), *Wings of Danger* (1952), *Stolen Face* (1952), *Lady in the Fog* (1952), *The Gambler and the Lady* (1953), *Four Sided Triangle* (1953), *The Flanagan Boy* (1953), *The Saint's Return* (1953), *Spaceways* (1953), *Blood Orange* (1953), *36 Hours* (1953), *Face the Music* (1954), *Five Days* (1954), *Life with the Lyons* (1954), *The House Across the Lake* (1954), *The Stranger Came Home* (1954), *Murder by Proxy* (1955), *Adventures with the Lyons* (1957, serial re-issue of *Life with the Lyons*), *A Weekend with Lulu* (1961)

### Salter, Ivor

This British actor (1925–1991) can be seen as a policeman in Hammer's *On the Buses* (1971), settling a dispute over some misappropriated underwear. His other credits include *The Heart Within* (1953), *When Strangers Meet* (1963), *Murder Ahoy* (1964), *Be My Guest* (1965), *The Ghost of Monk's Island* (1967), *Lady Caroline Lamb* (1972) and *House of Mortal Sin* (1976). Busiest on television, his many credits here include episodes of everything from *White Hunter* (1957–1958, TV) to *In Loving Memory* (1979–1986, TV). **Hammer credits:** *On the Buses* (1971, as First policeman)

### Salzedo, Leonard

Beginning with the fifties second feature drama *The Stranger Came Home* (1954), this British composer (1921–2000, full name Leonard Lopes-Salzedo) went on to score a total of six films for Hammer, plus one belated television episode. He began his career by studying music at the Royal College of Music, and went on to compose several concert works and ballets, notably for Ballet Rambert, for whom he was also their musical director between 1967 and 1972. He also played for the London Philharmonic Orchestra (1947–1950) and the Royal Philharmonic Orchestra (1950–1966), while his work as a musical director took in stints with Balletts Negres (1946, and about which he was interviewed in the 1986 documentary *Ballet Black*), Royal Scottish Ballet (1972–1974) and London City Ballet (1982–1986).

His other screen credits include *Before I Wake* (1954) and *Sea Wife* (1957). He also arranged the song *Anononio's Zapateado* for *Honeymoon* (1959). Some sources claim that stock music by Salzedo was used in *The Curse of the Werewolf* (1961). His platform pieces include *Divertimento for Three Trumpets and Three Trombones* (1959), which was later used at the theme tune for the BBC's *Open University* (1969–, TV) from the seventies to the nineties. His ballets include *The Fugitive* (1944), *Market Day* (1946) and *The Witch Boy* (1955). **Hammer credits:** *The Stranger Came Home* (1954), *Mask of Dust* (1954), *The Glass Cage* (1955), *Women Without Men* (1956), *The Steel Bayonet* (1957), *The Revenge of Frankenstein* (1958), *The Curse of the Werewolf* (1961 [stock music only, uncredited]), *The Silent Scream* (1980, TV [episode of *Hammer House of Horror*])

## Sam, Poing Ping

This Oriental actor had a bit part in Hammer's *The Terror of the Tongs* (1961). His other credits include *Marco Polo* (1961) and *The Sinister Man* (1961). **Hammer credits:** *The Terror of the Tongs* (1961, unnamed role [uncredited])

## Sampson, Annie

Sampson was the lead singer of the American rock group Stoneground, which was featured in Hammer's *Dracula A.D. 1972* (1972). Her other credits include *Medicine Ball Caravan* (1971), again with Stoneground. She has recorded with the likes of Elvin Bishop, Eddie Money and Maria Muldaur, and has performed with Jerry Garcia and Elvis Costello. Her own albums include *Under the Moon* (1996). **Hammer credits:** *Dracula A.D. 1972* (1972)

## Samson, Hugh

Samson worked as the publicist on Hammer's *Blood from the Mummy's Tomb* (1971). His other credits include *The Hasty Heart* (1949), *Stage Fright* (1950), *No Place for Jennifer* (1950), *Last Holiday* (1950) and *The Flesh Is Weak* (1957). **Hammer credits:** *Blood from the Mummy's Tomb* (1971 [uncredited])

## Samuel, Julie

This British supporting actress (1944–) can be spotted as a maid in the Hammer thriller *Nightmare* (1964). Her other credits include *Jigsaw* (1962), *Ferry Cross the Mersey* (1964) and *The Magnificent Seven Deadly Sins* (1971), as well as episodes of such series as *Z Cars* (1962–1978, TV), *Love Story* (1963–1974, TV), *Honey Lane* (1967–1969, TV) and *Crown Court* (1972–1984, TV). She was married to the assistant director Derek Cracknell (1935–1991). **Hammer credits:** *Nightmare* (1964, as Anne [Maid])

## Samworth, Stan

Samworth worked as the sound camera operator on Hammer's *Twins of Evil* (1971). His other credits include *Kill Me Tomorrow* (1957), *The Rebel* (1960), *Night of the Prowler* (1963) and *Hennessy*

(1975). **Hammer credits:** *Twins of Evil* (1971 [uncredited])

## Sandall, Cliff *see* Sandell, Cliff

## Sandell, Cliff

This sound technician (sometimes billed Sandall) recorded the sound for a handful of Hammer films in the fifties. His other credits, either as recordist or mixer, include *The Glass Mountain* (1949), *My Death Is a Mockery* (1952), *To Dorothy a Son* (1954) and *The Traitor* (1957). He also did the sound maintenance for *The Dock Brief* (1962). **Hammer credits:** *X—The Unknown* (1956 [uncredited]), *Quatermass 2* (1957), *The Steel Bayonet* (1957), *Day of Grace* (1957)

## Sanders, George

Ideally cast as world-weary bounders (his autobiography was titled *Memoirs of a Professional Cad* [1960]), this Russian-born leading man (1906–1972) broke into films in Britain in 1934 with a small part in the Gracie Fields musical *Love, Life and Laughter*, following experience in the textile industry and as a tobacco salesman in South America, as well as an actor on stage (in revue) and on radio. He made the move to Hollywood in the mid-thirties, making his screen debut there with *Lloyds of London* (1937). He became a star in 1939 when he took over the role of Simon Templar (The Saint) from Louis Hayward, appearing in five subsequent films, among them *The Saint Strikes Back* (1939) and *The Saint in Palm Springs* (1941). Sanders then switched to playing The Falcon (four times), a role that his real-life brother Tom Conway (1904–1967, real name Thomas Charles Sanders) then took over, playing the character a total of ten times (note that Conway appeared in the Hammer second feature *Blood Orange* [1953], while Hayward returned to the role of The Saint in Hammer's *The Saint's Return* [1953]).

In more than one-hundred films, Sanders' other credits include *Foreign Correspondent* (1940), *The Moon and Sixpence* (1942), *The Picture of Dorian Gray* (1945), *Forever Amber* (1947), *All About Eve* (1950), which won him a best supporting actor Oscar, *Village of the Damned* (1960), *The Quiller Memorandum* (1966) and *Psychomania* (1972). He also presented the television series *George Sanders' Mystery Theatre* (1956–1957, TV), guested in such shows as *The Man from U.N.C.L.E.* (1964–1968, TV) and *Batman* (1966–1968, TV), in which he played Mr. Freeze, and penned two novels, *Crime on My Hands* (1944), which some sources claim was ghost written by Craig Rice, and *Stranger at Home* (1946), which was filmed by Hammer in 1954 as *The Stranger Came Home*, and which some sources claim was also ghost written, this time by Leigh Brackett. Married four times, Sanders' wives included the actresses Zsa Zsa Gabor (1917–2016, real name Sari Gabor), to whom he was married between 1949 and 1954, Benita Hume (1906–1967), to whom he was married between 1959 and her death, and Magda Gabor (1915–1997, full name Magdolna Gabor), to whom he was married between 1970 and 1971. Bored with life, Sanders committed suicide. **Hammer credits:** *The Stranger Came Home* (1954)

## Sands of the Desert

GB, 1960, 92m, Technicolor, RCA, cert U

Although not ostensibly a Hammer film, this footling comedy about a travel agent who flies out to the Middle East to investigate a sabotaged holiday camp (Bossom's Bedouin Holiday Camp) is included here for completeness primarily because Hammer invested in the project. Shot at Elstree and released in the UK by Warner-Pathé on 8 September 1960, it was one of a handful of vehicles created for (and co-scripted by) the diminutive television comic Charlie Drake during this period, but (like the rest of them) it failed to establish his persona on the big screen.

Despite being photographed by the great Gilbert Taylor, the film is rather cheap looking, while the comedic situations fail to take flight (it transpires that the holiday camp is being sabotaged because it is sitting on top of a priceless oil field). Meanwhile, the star's performance is as resistible as usual, while the supporting cast—among them several Hammer familiars—look suitably lost. Sadly, it's not all a mirage, and turns up with reasonable regularity on television. **Additional notes:** The title seems to be a play on the Laurel and Hardy classic *Sons of the Desert* (1933). The movie introduces Sarah Branch to the screen, who appeared in two further Hammer films released the same year: *Hell Is a City* (1960) and *Sword of Sherwood Forest* (1960), in which she played Lady Marian Fitzwalter. The film's unit driver, Eddie Frewin, makes a brief appearance in the film as an Arab driver. A clip from the movie was featured in the comedy compilation featurette *Laughter and Life* (1961), which failed to achieve a cinema release.

Production company: Associated British Picture Corporation. Distributor: Warner-Pathé (UK). Producer: Gordon L.T. Scott. Director: John Paddy Carstairs. Screenplay: John Paddy Carstairs, Charlie Drake (additional dialogue). Story: Stafford Byrne (original story), Anne Burnaby, Robert Hall (film story). Scenario editor: Frederick Gotfurt. Cinematographer: Gilbert Taylor. Music/conductor: Stanley Black. Music played by: The Associated British Orchestra. Song: *The Old Shadow* by Max Diamond (music and lyrics). Editor: Richard Best. Art director: Robert Jones. Costumes: Eileen Sullivan. Make-up: L.V. Olark. Hair: Polly Young. Assistant director: Ross MacKenzie. Production manager: Victor Peck. Camera operator: Val Stewart. Sound: Len Shilton, H.L. Bird. Dubbing editor: Arthur Southgate. Recording director: A.W. Lumkin. Choreography: Malcolm Clare. Casting: Robert Lennard. Continuity: June Randall. Unit driver: Eddie Frewin [uncredited]. **Cast:** Charlie Drake (Charlie Sands), Sarah Branch (Janet Brown), Peter Arne (Sheikh El Jabez), Rebecca Dignam (Nerima), Raymond Huntley (Bossom), Peter Illing (Sheikh Ibrahim), Harold Kasket (Abdulla), Neil McCarthy (Hassan), Marne Maitland (Adviser), Derek Sydney (Mamud), Inia Te Wiata (Fahid), William Kendall (Consul), Martin Benson (Selim), Alan Tilvern (Mustafa), Paul Stassino (Pilot), Eric Pohlmann (Scrobin), Charles Carson (Philpots), Judith Furse (Yasmin), Robert Brown (Tourist [uncredited]), Sally Douglas (Harem girl [uncredited]), Eddie Frewin (Arab driver [uncredited]), Steven Counterman (Boy on bus [uncredited]), Irene Barrie (unnamed role [uncredited]), Mia Karam (unnamed role [uncredited]). **DVD availability:** Network (UK R2 PAL), extras include the trailer, a stills gallery and a pdf of the press brook. **CD availability:** *The Film Music of Stanley Black* (Chandos), which contains four newly recorded movements from the score

## Sangster, Jimmy ( James)

From his debut with Hammer in 1949 as a second assistant director on their second Dick Barton adventure *Dick Barton Strikes Back*, Welsh born Sangster (1927–2011, full name James Henry Kinmel Sangster) went on to become the company's most reliable writer, tackling such classic horror subjects as Frankenstein, Dracula and the Mummy (Christopher Neame described him as being "quintessentially Hammer"[5]).

Following his National Service in the Royal Air Force (prior to which he'd gained a little film-related experience as an assistant projectionist for National Film Services in 1943, as well as a general dogsbody for the likes of Carlton Hill Studios and Ealing), Sangster entered the film industry as a lowly third assistant director to producer Mario Zampi, making his debut with *Third Time Lucky* (1949). When Zampi was asked to produce *Dick Barton Strikes Back* for Hammer, he took many of his regular crew to work on the film with him, including Sangster, who was now a second assistant director. However, when Zampi left the project, Sangster stayed on with Hammer to finish the film, which in turn led to further job offers, *Dr. Morelle—The Case of the Missing Heiress* (1949) being the next (though made after the Barton film, *Morelle* actually went on national release first).

By the time he made *The Man in Black* (1950), his sixth film for the company, Sangster had been promoted to first assistant director (which, at just twenty-one, made him Britain's youngest first assistant director). Recalled Sangster of the Hammer work ethic during this period: "Monday, Tuesday and Thursday we worked until six pm, Wednesday and Friday until 5:30. The unions were very strong in those days. We had the ACT which covered the camera crew, sound and production staff, NATKE which covered the hairdressers, wardrobe staff and make-up, along with the chippies, painters and plasterers, and the ETU, the electricians' trade union. There was also Equity, which covered actors, and a fifth union I can't even remember which was supposed to take care of crowd players. And all these unions were as tough as old boots. They'd worked hard for their agreements and, by Christ, we'd better stick to them."[6]

Sangster's first wife was the Hammer hair stylist Monica Hustler (1926–), whom he married in 1950. They immigrated to Canada together in 1952, though it wasn't long before they returned home, given that the only job Sangster could get was selling insurance. Following a short period as a bookmaker's clerk for his father-in-law, Sangster was back at Hammer for *The Flanagan Boy* (1953), resuming his post as assistant director following a call from Tony Hinds (remembered Sangster: "I found out later that he wanted somebody else but

the guy wasn't available, and he acted under the assumption that the devil you know is better than the one you don't"[7]). He was then promoted again to production manager for *The Stranger Came Home* (1954), while in 1955 he penned his first produced screenplay (following a trial run with a short subject that he titled *The Camera*, which Anthony Hinds read but declined to make); this was for the dramatic short *A Man on the Beach* (1956), which Sangster adapted from the 1954 Victor Canning story *Chance at the Wheel* (aka *Menace at the Casino* [1955 American re-print]). Learning on the job, he later admitted, "I never read a book on how to write a screenplay. I just sat down and wrote a screenplay. To this day I haven't read a book on scriptwriting. I've read the anecdotal-type books like *Adventures in the Screen Trade* that William Goldman wrote…. But an actual 'how to' book complete with graphs and diagrams? Forget it!"[8]

Sangster's first feature screenplay came the same year. This was for *X—The Unknown* (1956), which also marked the last time he worked as a production manager. He was paid £450 to fulfill both roles. At first, Sangster was not keen to take on the job of screenwriter, and needed a certain degree of persuasion by Anthony Hinds and Michael Carreras, with whom he thrashed out the film's story. Revealed Sangster of his relationship with Hinds and Carreras, "I was extremely lucky in the guys I was working for. Tony Hinds and Michael Carreras. Tony, as well as a producer, was a writer himself, said he liked to employ me as a writer because apart from being a good friend, I always did what he told me to. Obviously, he told me to do the right things."[9]

Sangster quickly adapted to his new job, and when a screenplay by Milton Subotsky for a proposed new version of *Frankenstein* proved unusable, Sangster was the first person Anthony Hinds turned to for a new one. Recalled Sangster on what eventually became his screenplay for *The Curse of Frankenstein*: "They paid me just £450 for that script, and even in those days that was not considered a lot! But if I hadn't written it, somebody else would have. And I knew what I was doing by then, more or less, and as far as Hammer were concerned, I always wrote to budget. I'd been budgeting pictures for them for the previous six or seven years, so I was left to my own devices."[10] However, as Sangster revealed, "At the time I wasn't even aware that there had been another script. It wasn't until quite recently, when I'd been reading some of the books written about Hammer, that I discovered it existed."[11]

Following his work on *The Curse of Frankenstein*, Sangster went through something of a fallow period, which finally came to an end when he began work on a television series titled *Motive for Murder* (1957, TV), which he had submitted to ITV. However, he was back at Hammer soon after to begin work on the screenplay adaptation of Bram Stoker's *Dracula*, which remains one of his best pieces. Reported *Film Comment* of his work, "The scenes are smoothly meshed, the dialogue crisp enough, the plotting done with a deft hand at creating a sense of mystery." Sangster's biggest task in writing this particular screenplay was whittling down a lengthy and complex narrative told via diary entries, letters

and the perspectives of various characters (Sangster himself described the novel as being "told in the first person by around six different people"[12]). As he later revealed, "The main problem up front was to simplify the storyline. Remember, I had to deliver the whole story in ninety minutes. In fact the final screen version ran only eighty-two. I did this by eliminating a lot of the subsidiary characters. Anybody who saw the movie will no doubt remember that I didn't bring the Count to England either. No way was Hammer Films going to go with a ship, at sea, at night, in a storm … forget it. Sure, have Dracula leave the country. He can cross a border between Transylvania and Ruritania by horse and carriage as long as it can all be shot at Bray Studios…."[13] No doubt hence the astute observation in his fulsome *Times* obituary: "Sangster's experience as a production manager gave him a valuable insight into what was achievable on Hammer's limited budgets, and the company soon came to rely on his artfully reductive adaptations of horror classics."

This proved to be a busy period for Sangster, who as well as writing *Dracula* (1958), also penned *The Revenge of Frankenstein* (1958) for Hammer (for which he ingeniously saved Baron Frankenstein from the guillotine), as well as *The Trollenberg Terror* (1958) for Tempean, *Blood of the Vampire* (1958) for Berman and Baker, *Jack the Ripper* (1958), again for Berman and Baker, and an unproduced adaptation of *The Day of the Triffids* for Warwick. In addition to these scripting duties, he also provided a pilot script titled *The Single-Minded Blackmailer* for Hammer's television series *Tales of Frankenstein* (1958, TV), along with several story synopses. He also worked on an ongoing story arc for three thirteen-episode series of the show. Unfortunately, Sangster's pilot script was rejected by Columbia in lieu of *The Face in the Tombstone Mirror*, which was scripted by Catherine and Henry Kuttner—all to no avail, however, as the series was subsequently cancelled.

Recalled Sangster of this astonishingly busy period, "I truly believe that one of the reasons Tony Hinds employed me as much as he did at the off was because he knew I was aware of Hammer's way of working and I wasn't going to write anything into my scripts that they couldn't afford to shoot."[14] Sangster was also mindful to keep his scripts brief and to the point: "Remember, way back then, a program consisted of two features, along with news and trailers, so the idea was to keep 'em short. The final running time [of *Dracula*] was eighty-two minutes. Add that to another eighty-minute picture, plus fifteen minutes of other stuff, and you had a program of under three hours…. In those days, when writing a script, by the time you reached page 110 you'd better be thinking of ending it pretty soon."[15]

The busy workload continued during this period, resulting in *The Man Who Could Cheat Death* (1959), which was a rare flop, and *The Mummy* (1959), which managed to out-gross *Dracula* at the box office. Sangster also wrote the novelization for *The Man Who Could Cheat Death* under the pseudonym of John Sansom, a name he would later reuse on his scripts for the Edgar Wallace programers

*To Have and to Hold* (1963), *Face of a Stranger* (1964) and *Traitor's Gate* (1964), as well as Hammer's *Dracula—Prince of Darkness* (1966). He also novelized (under his own name) *The Revenge of Frankenstein* and *The Terror of the Tongs* (1961).

In March 1959, Sangster delivered his script for Hammer's much-anticipated *Dracula* sequel, *Disciple of Dracula*. However, when Christopher Lee refused to revive the Count, the screenplay was re-worked by Peter Bryan, Edward Percy and producer Anthony Hinds, who removed Dracula from the proceedings altogether. The film finally emerged as *The Brides of Dracula* (1960), for which Sangster received a co-screenplay credit with Bryan and Percy. Despite some flaws in the narrative owing to the various tamperings, the film was a major commercial success, and is regarded by many Hammer fans to be one of the studio's very best productions (note that Sangster began work on *Disciple of Dracula* under the title *The Revenge of Dracula* in 1958; this version of the script was subsequently discarded, but later resurfaced as the basis for the official *Dracula* sequel, *Dracula—Prince of Darkness*).

Following an adaptation of the John Brooks boardroom novel *The Big Wheel*, which failed to make it before the cameras, it was back to more routine sadism next with *The Terror of the Tongs* (1961), which exposed the brutalities of a secret but powerful Hong Kong sect. Originally to have been titled *The Hatchet Men*, it covered similar territory as *The Stranglers of Bombay* (1959), though this time the victims were hacked to death rather than strangled. Prior to this, Sangster had scripted a gangster thriller titled *The Criminal*, which was originally intended as a Hammer production. Unfortunately, despite having interested Stanley Baker in the script, Michael Carreras sold the property on to producer Jack Greenwood at Merton Park when the star demanded that Joseph Losey direct the film, which was subsequently re-written by Alun Owen. Released in 1960, the film was re-titled *The Concrete Jungle* for America (despite Owen's re-write, Sangster nevertheless went on to pen two of his Edgar Wallace adaptations for Greenwood).

In 1960, Sangster got his first opportunity to produce at Hammer, thanks to his friend Michael Carreras, who was impressed by a script the writer had been hawking around variably titled *See No Evil* and *Hell Hath No Fury*, but which finally went on the floor at Elstree as *Taste of Fear* (1961). Written by Sangster in a bid to escape being typecast as a writer purely of gothic horrors, this convoluted thriller about an heiress who finds herself in peril while visiting her father on the French Riviera was originally to have been produced by Sydney Box. However, when Box suffered a heart scare, the project was passed on to his brother-in-law Peter Rogers, from whom Sangster subsequently bought it back. He then offered it to Berman & Baker, for whom he'd already penned a number of films, but when they balked at his request to also produce the film, he finally admitted defeat and took it to Hammer, for whom it became a major commercial hit, launching Sansgter on a new career as a writer of psycho-thrillers.

1961 also saw Sangster produce (with José Maesso) *The Savage Guns* (1962) for Michael Carreras's company Capricorn Productions. The project had originally been slated to be made by Hammer as *The Brutal Land*, but following Carreras's temporary departure from the studio—a direct result of the plug being pulled on *The Rape of Sabena* (aka *The Inquisitor*)—Carreras took the project with him, along with Sangster (the film was made in Spain, where it was known as *Tierra brutal*). However, the writer was back working for Hammer once production had been completed, providing the story and original screenplay for the swashbuckling yarn *The Pirates of Blood River* (1962), which was subsequently re-written by John Hunter and the film's director, John Gilling, following concerns that it was too bloodthirsty for a children's movie (remembered Sangster, who simply received a story credit on the film, "They didn't ask me to do the rewrites, probably because I was long gone on some other project"[16]). He also wrote and produced *Maniac* (1963), the first of several twist-packed psychological thrillers made by Hammer following the success of *Taste of Fear*. Described as "mini Hitchcocks" by James Carreras, they included *Paranoiac* (1963), *Nightmare* (1964) *Hysteria* (1965) and *The Nanny* (1965), although the latter is, according to Jimmy Sangster, more of a "psychological thriller in which, while we might end up with a couple of bodies … nobody actually takes a knife or gun to anyone."[17]

*The Nanny* was the first of two films Sangster made with the redoubtable Bette Davis (it was followed by *The Anniversary* [1968], which Sangster also wrote and produced). Sangster described the Hollywood legend as being, "Tough. Demanding. A perfectionist. She was all these things. Awkward bitch too, on occasion. But she never asked for anything that she didn't consider was to the benefit of the movie as a whole. If it could be proved otherwise, fine, she'd withdraw her demand."[18] Davis was seemingly worth the trouble, as Sangster regards *The Nanny* as "the best film I ever made for Hammer."[19]

Sangster continued to write and produce for Hammer throughout the sixties (he was originally set to write and produce *Moon Zero Two* [1969], which was eventually made by other hands), while in 1970 he finally made his directorial debut with *The Horror of Frankenstein*, an ill-advised semi-comic remake of *The Curse of Frankenstein* (1957), which he also co-wrote (with Jeremy Burnham) and produced. A major misfire, the production remains one of the low points of Sangster's career. Recalled Sangster, "*The Horror of Frankenstein* came to me out of left field. I was living in Los Angeles, just having done a *Movie of the Week* script…. I told my agent that I wanted to stay in Los Angeles and he was busy looking around for work, out of the blue, I got this call from Hammer…. They'd had a script written by a guy named Jeremy Burnham…. Hammer had obviously committed to the project … but they told me the script needed some work done on it. Would I be interested in doing the rewrite? I told them I wasn't. What if they let me produce it? Still not interested. Been there, done that. Then I had an idea.

I'd rewrite their script and produce it providing they let me direct as well…. Deal!"[20]

Shortly afterwards, he was approached by Anthony Hinds who, though he had by now left Hammer, had been commissioned to write a new Mummy film. In a letter to Sangster, Hinds proposed that he join him to co-write the film with him and also direct. "I gather that Hammer is pleased with your performance as a director,"[21] wrote Hinds, going on to add, "If you have been bitten by the bug and fancy doing some more of it, maybe you'd like to work on the script with me."[22] He concluded, somewhat tellingly: "You will appreciate I have no influence at Hammer anymore, so this is not a contract."[23] However, the project was abandoned by James Carreras on 22 April 1970 after potential distributors failed to show much interest in the untitled film.

Consequently, Sangster's next official directing chore for the company was *Lust for a Vampire* (1971). Though by no means a classic, this was nevertheless a much better production than *The Horror of Frankenstein*, despite Sangster's own low opinion of it, thanks primarily to the inclusion of a "pop song" titled *Strange Love* on the soundtrack and several glaring continuity errors that made it to the release print (commented Sangster of the song, "I have never been so embarrassed in my life when that song came on!"[24]).

Sangster then worked on the script for an unproduced thriller titled *The Goldfish Bowl*. He was also considered as a director for *Dr. Jekyll and Sister Hyde* (1971), but the job finally went to Roy Ward Baker. He eventually returned with *Fear in the Night* (1972), one of his trademark Hitchckockian twist-in-the-tail thrillers, which he produced, directed and co-wrote with Michael Syson (Sangster's original script had actually been hanging around since 1963, when it was first announced as *Brainstorm* and later, in 1967, as *The Claw*). Some sources indicate that he also worked on an early treatment for *The Satanic Rites of Dracula* (1974), when it was originally announced as *Dracula Is Dead … And Well and Living in London*, though it seems that none of his work made it into the final Don Houghton script (that said, the BFI database does list him as an uncredited story consultant on the film).

*Fear in the Night* proved to be Sangster's last screen credit for Hammer, though by no means the last time he worked for them. Following the cancellation of the Mike Raven project *The Disciple* (which he was set to produce and direct for Hammer), his next project for the company was to write a treatment for *Vampirella*, Hammer's proposed screen version of James Warren's popular comic strip, in early 1976. Unfortunately, nothing came of the project, the script for which was subsequently worked on by Lew Davidson, Christopher Wicking, John Starr and Michael Carreras (writing as Henry Younger). Likewise, Sangster was also set to work as the associate producer on *Death Rattle*, a $1.3m western based on a script by Bima Stagg, but again the project floundered. Other scripts penned by Sangster that failed to make it to the screen over the years include *The Bride of Newgate Goal* (aka *Midnight Jones* and *The Reluctant Virgin*), an adaptation of the John Blackburn novel *Bury Him Darkly*, a proposed TV series titled *The Hallowe'en House of Horror*, and a Faustian comedy called *The Fairytale Man*, which was eventually made by Disney as *The Devil and Max Devlin* (1981). He was also penciled in for involvement in a proposed TV series, *The Hammer Mystery Theatre*, as late as 1989/1990.

After leaving Hammer, Sangster went on to pen such films and series as *Ghost Story* (1972–1973, TV), on which he was also the story consultant, *Maneater* (1973, TVM), *The Legacy* (1978), *Ebony, Ivory and Jade* (1979, TVM), which he also produced, *Phobia* (1980), which was directed by John Huston no less, *The Toughest Man in the World* (1984, TVM), *Beyond Belief* (1992, TV) and *Flashback—Morderische Ferien* (2000). He also wrote a total of eight novels. Said Sangster of this period: "I suppose one could say that after I left Hammer the good times continued to roll. They certainly paid better."[25] He also re-married—he and Monica Hustler had divorced in 1968–his second wife being the actress Mary Peach (1934–), whom he married in 1995.

Recalled Sangster of his years with Hammer, "When I originally wrote *Dracula* and *The Curse of Frankenstein* they were classified as horror films. X certificate in UK cinemas, nobody under the age of sixteen allowed in. Then came what I call the 'slasher' movies, more and more blood and guts. I'm not knocking them, I hasten to say. I don't particularly *enjoy* them, but most of them are well made and, to vast audiences of young people, entertaining. But what it has done is to force us to re-classify those early Gothic horrors that Hammer made. I now describe them as 'fairy stories.'"[26]

With regards to his recognition as a writer of horror films, he was somewhat philosophical: "If the first film I'd written had been a comedy, I would have probably been writing the *Carry On*s. It just so happened that the first film I wrote was a horror film, so the films I was being asked to write were all horror films. And a horror film is no different from any other film; you have to tell a story. I'm a great believer in films having a story—a beginning, a middle and an end.... People say, 'Why did you do *this*?' Or, 'Why did you approach it *that* way?' And, 'What was the inner meaning of *this*?' The reason I did that was for *wages*, or because we couldn't afford to do it any other way."[27] He also noted that, "Most of us who worked for Hammer were just reasonably competent technicians who were lucky enough to find an employer who was three times as busy than any other production company of the time.... There was nothing special about what we did. Anybody else in the business could have done the same. Except Hammer decided to go Gothic and we all got lucky. Especially Terry Fisher and me. We just happened to be in the right place at the right time."[28]

Meanwhile, of Hammer's subsequent years in the wilderness before their recent revival, he noted at the time, "In my opinion, Hammer is a ship that lost its rudder a long time ago. Since then it has been wallowing around under very little control while various people and/or corporations try to get it back on course without actually knowing the course they want it on. A lot of talk from a lot of people, and nothing happens. The only people keeping Hammer alive are the fans."[29] **Additional notes:** Sangster worked as the second unit production manager for a very brief scene involving the turning off of the lights at Battersea Power Station for *The Quatermass Xperiment* (1955). Sangster's books on cinema include *Do You Want It Good or Tuesday?* (1997), *Inside Hammer* (2001) and *Screenwriting—Techniques for Success* (2003). He also served as a board director on the Hammer subsidiary Saturn Films, Ltd. between 1957 and 1961. He was interviewed about his career with Hammer in *A History of Horror with Mark Gatiss* (2010, TV). **Hammer credits:** *Dr. Morelle—The Case of the Missing Heiress* (1949, second assistant director [uncredited]), *Dick Barton Strikes Back* (1949, second assistant director [uncredited]), *The Adventures of PC 49—The Case of the Guardian Angel* (1949, second assistant director [uncredited]), *Celia* (1949, second assistant director [uncredited]), *Meet Simon Cherry* (1949, second assistant director [uncredited]), *The Man in Black* (1950, assistant director), *Room to Let* (1950, assistant director), *Someone at the Door* (1950, assistant director), *What the Butler Saw* (1950, assistant director), *The Black Widow* (1950, assistant director), *The Lady Craved Excitement* (1950, assistant director [billed as James Sangster]), *The Rossiter Case* (1951, assistant director [billed as James Sangster]), *To Have and to Hold* (1951, assistant director), *A Case for PC 49* (1951, assistant director), *Cloudburst* (1951, assistant director), *Whispering Smith Hits London* (1952, assistant director), *Death of an Angel* (1952, assistant director), *The Last Page* (1952, assistant director), *Wings of Danger* (1952, assistant director), *Stolen Face* (1952, assistant director), *The Flanagan Boy* (1953, assistant director), *The Saint's Return* (1953, assistant director [uncredited]), *Spaceways* (1953, assistant director), *Blood Orange* (1953, assistant director), *36 Hours* (1953, assistant director), *Face the Music* (1954, assistant director), *Five Days* (1954, assistant director), *The House Across the Lake* (1954, assistant director), *The Stranger Came Home* (1954, production manager), *Men of Sherwood Forest* (1954, production manager), *Mask of Dust* (1954, production manager), *Break in the Circle* (1955, production manager), *Murder by Proxy* (1955, assistant director), *Third Party Risk* (1955, production manager), *The Quatermass Xperiment* (1955, second unit production manager [uncredited]), *A Man on the Beach* (1956, screenplay), *Women Without Men* (1956, production manager), *X—The Unknown* (1956, screenplay, production manager), *Dick Turpin—Highwayman* (1956, production manager [uncredited]), *The Curse of Frankenstein* (1957, screenplay), *The Snorkel* (1958, co-screenplay), *Tales of Frankenstein* (1958, TV, unused synopses and unused teleplay, *The Single-Minded Blackmailer*), *Dracula* (1958, screenplay), *The Revenge of Frankenstein* (1958, co-screenplay [plus novelization]), *The Mummy* (1959, screenplay), *The Man Who Could Cheat Death* (1959, screenplay [plus novelization, as John Sansom]), *The Brides of Dracula* (1960, co-screenplay), *Taste of Fear* (1961, producer, screenplay), *The Terror of the Tongs* (1961, screenplay [plus novelization]), *The Pirates of Blood River* (1962, story), *Paranoiac* (1963, screenplay), *Maniac* (1963, producer, screenplay), *Nightmare* (1964, producer, screenplay), *The Devil-Ship Pirates* (1964, screenplay), *Hysteria* (1965, producer, screenplay), *The Nanny* (1965, producer, screenplay), *Dracula—Prince of Darkness* (1966, screenplay [as John Sansom]), *The Anniversary* (1968, producer, screenplay), *Crescendo* (1970, co-screenplay), *The Horror of Frankenstein* (1970, director, producer, co-screenplay), *Lust for a Vampire* (1971, director), *Fear in the Night* (1972, producer, director, co-screenplay), *The Satanic Rites of Dracula* (1974, story consultant [uncredited]), *Flesh and Blood—The Hammer Heritage of Horror* (1994, TV, interviewee, special thanks)

### Sangster, Monica *see* Hustler, Monica

### Sansom, John *see* Sangster, Jimmy

### Sansom, Robert

This British actor (1903–1979, full name Stanley Robert Sansom) can be seen as a doctor in Hammer's *Face the Music* (1954). His other credits include *He Found a Star* (1941), *In Which We Serve* (1942), *The Hypnotist* (1957), *The Shakedown* (1959) and *The Trunk* (1960). Prolific on television, his many credits here include episodes of *Private Investigator* (1958–1959, TV), *Champion House* (1967–1968, TV), *The Edwardians* (1972, TV) and *1990* (1977, TV). **Hammer credits:** *Face the Music* (1954, as Doctor [uncredited])

### Sarafian, Mike

Sarafian worked as the focus puller on the Hammer swashbuckler *The Scarlet Blade* (1963). His other credits include work as camera assistant on *The Whisperers* (1967) and *Deadfall* (1968), and as an operator on *Hoffman* (1970). **Hammer credits:** *The Scarlet Blade* (1963 [uncredited])

### Sargent, Gundel

This actress, dancer and model can be seen as one of the Sphinx Girls in Hammer's *The Two Faces of Dr. Jekyll* (1960). Her other credits include *The Devil's Daffodil* (1961) and *It's Magic* (1962), plus an episode of *Man in a Suitcase* (1967–1968, TV). **Hammer credits:** *The Two Faces of Dr. Jekyll* (1960, as Sphinx Girl [uncredited])

### Sasdy, Peter

Equally at home working in film or television, this Hungarian director (1935–) trained at the BBC and began directing for TV in the late fifties, helming episodes of *Emergency—Ward 10* (1957–1967, TV) between 1959 and 1960. This led to work on such series as *Ghost Squad* (1961–1964, TV), *The Plane Makers* (1963–1965, TV) and *Out of the Unknown* (1965–1971, TV). In 1968 he directed two episodes of Hammer's *Journey to the Unknown* (1968, TV). These were *The New People*, which also appeared in the compendium film *Journey into Darkness* (1968, TVM) and *Girl of My Dreams*, the visual impact of which directly led to his helming his first feature film. A prime assignment, this was Hammer's *Taste the Blood of Dracula* (1970), to which he brought a certain directorial savvy above and beyond most Hammer films of the period. This in turn led to his being assigned *Countess Dracula* (1971), for which he also co-authored the story, and, best of all, *Hands of the Ripper* (1971), which remains his most polished production. Indeed, *Variety* described it as being "Well-directed by Peter Sasdy," adding that, "the tension is skillfully developed." It also noted that the "murders are particularly gruesome and there are shocks that will have the most hardened film-goer sitting up."

According to Ingrid Pitt, who starred in *Countess Dracula*, filming went far from smoothly, with Sasdy constantly in conflict with his producer, Alexander Paal. "They had terrible rows in Hungarian on the set,"[30] she recalled. "The atmosphere was almost unbearable at times. In the end I couldn't stand the constant bickering any more so I got a friend of mine, a fellow countryman of theirs, to teach me some Hungarian swearwords. The next time they rowed I appeared at the top of the stairs. In colloquial Hungarian I shouted: 'Do be quiet, you carry on like shitty little gnomes. We're losing time here...' They were shocked. They thought I had understood what they had been saying all the time."[31]

Sasdy's other films include *Nothing but the Night* (1972), *Doomwatch* (1972), *The Stone Tape* (1972, TVM), *I Don't Want to Be Born* (1975), *Welcome to Blood City* (1977) and *The Lonely Lady* (1982), while his other TV credits take in *The Spoils of Poynton* (1970, TV), *Murder at the Wedding* (1979, TV), *The Secret Diary of Adrian Mole Aged 13¾* (1985, TV), *The Growing Pains of Adrian Mole* (1987, TV) and *Covington Cross* (1992, TV), plus a return to Hammer for three episodes each of *Hammer House of Horror* (1980, TV) and *Hammer House of Mystery and Suspense* (1984, TVM). He was also one of several directors considered for Hammer's *Dr. Jekyll and Sister Hyde* (1971), but the job eventually went to Roy Ward Baker. He was also considered for Hammer's *To the Devil a Daughter* (1976), which was helmed by Peter Sykes.

Recalled Sasdy of his time with the studio that dripped blood, "I loved it at Hammer. I enjoyed it a lot and gained a lot of self-confidence. Looking back, some of it was pretty good. I looked at *Hands of the Ripper* recently, on TV in America, and I thought, 'That's not bad!' I was quite pleased."[32]

Sasdy's wife is actress and ballet dancer Mia Nadasi (1944–, real name Myrtill Nadasi, aka Mia Nardi), whom he married in 1965, and who appeared in *Visitor from the Grave* (1980, TV [episode of *Hammer House of Horror*]), which he directed. She also worked as the choreographer on *Countess Dracula* (as Mia Nardi). **Hammer credits:** *The New People* (1968, TV [episode of *Journey to the Unknown*], director), *Girl of My Dreams* (1968, TV [episode of *Journey to the Unknown*], director), *Journey into Darkness* (1968, TVM, director), *Taste the Blood of Dracula* (1970, director), *Countess Dracula* (1971, director, co-story), *Hands of the Ripper* (1971, director), *Visitor from the Grave* (1980, TV [episode of *Hammer House of Horror*], director), *Rude Awakening* (1980, TV [episode of *Hammer House of Horror*], director), *The Thirteenth Reunion* (1980, TV [episode of *Hammer House of Horror*], director), *The Sweet Scent of Death* (1984, TVM [episode of *Hammer House of Mystery and Suspense*], director), *The Late Nancy Irving* (1984, TVM [episode of *Hammer House of Mystery and Suspense*], director), *Last Video and Testament* (1984, TVM [episode of *Hammer House of Mystery and Suspense*], director)

### The Satanic Rites of Dracula

GB, 1974, 88m, Technicolor, widescreen [1.85:1], RCA, cert X

Given the less than favorable reaction to the modern-dress *Dracula A.D. 1972* (1972) from both audiences and critics (not to mention backers and distributors), it seems somewhat surprising that Hammer would again return to the same well for this direct sequel, originally announced as *Dracula Is Dead ... And Well and Living in London*. However, Warner Bros. had commissioned the film before *A.D. 1972* had been completed, and so were honor bound to take it. Nevertheless, the finished film received only a limited release in the UK by Columbia-Warner, while in America it was sold on to an independent distributor, Dynamite Entertainment, which didn't release it until 1978 under the title *Count Dracula and His Vampire Bride*. All of this is a great shame, as *Satanic Rites* is a vast improvement on its predecessor.

Instead of a de-sanctified church, the action this time centers round Pelham House, a remote country retreat in Croxted Heath that plays host to the Psychical Examination and Research Group, whose activities have been infiltrated by Hanson, an undercover SI7 officer on a mission to discover the group's true purpose. His cover blown, Hanson is being held captive by one of the building's security guards, whom he manages to kill and make his escape to a waiting SI7 car. Once back at headquarters, the badly beaten agent reveals to his superiors, Peter Torrence and Colonel Matthews, that the group is actually a front for Satanists in the thrall of an Oriental high priestess. "They have filthy obscene rites," he informs them. "They call on the name of the Devil. They seem to take strength from their own blasphemy!" What's more, Hanson discloses that a number of the country's elite are members of the sect, among them Professor Julian Keeley, a Nobel Prize winner who specializes in bacteriology, germ warfare and diseases of the blood; Lord Carradine, whose property portfolio seemingly includes half of London; General Sir Arthur Freeborne; and the Right Honorable John Porter MP, a minister of the crown with special responsibilities for the security services ("A nod from him and a dozen civil service pensions go out of the window—including mine!" observes Colonel Matthews, whose department has been operating without official sanction).

Hanson dies from his injuries shortly after making his statement. However, the photographs he was able to take with the miniature camera hidden inside his wristwatch confirm the identities of the four men involved in the group. A fifth photo curiously lacks the presence of another man Hanson also mentioned.

In order to further investigate Hanson's findings, Colonel Matthews orders that Inspector Murray from Scotland Yard's Special Branch be brought onto the case. Given that the sect's activities include blood rituals, Murray likewise calls upon his friend Professor Lorrimer Van Helsing to join the investigation. "Hobgoblins and witches and things that go bump in the night?" jokes a skeptical Torrence after Murray has played a recording of Hanson's revelations for Van Helsing in his study.

Christopher Lee faces a thorny situation in this attention-grabbing ad for *The Satanic Rites of Dracula* (1974) (Hammer/Warner/Columbia-Warner/Dynamite Entertainment).

But the Professor is quite earnest: "Yes, well hob-goblins are fantasy creatures of the nursery, Mr. Torrence. As for witches, they certainly exist, although ninety per cent of them are charlatans. Things *do* go bump in the night—quite often!"

Van Helsing, whose granddaughter Jessica now works as his assistant, also discloses that he knows one of the men involved in the group, Professor Julian Keeley, having met him while at Oxford. Thus Van Helsing agrees to pay Keeley a visit at his Foundation for Science. Observed entering the seemingly deserted building by one of the Pelham House guards, Van Helsing discovers his friend in an agitated state, having just completed an assignment: the creation of a new, ultra virulent strain of the bubonic plague. Keeley also freely admits to worshipping the Devil ("You need to feel the thrill of disgust, the beauty of obscenity"). But before Van Helsing can persuade his friend to destroy the results of his deadly experiment, the Pelham House guard slips into the room and shoots Van Helsing. Luckily, the bullet merely grazes his forehead, but upon coming to, he discovers Keeley hanging from a beam and the Petrie dishes containing the virus gone.

Prior to these developments, Torrence's secretary Jane has been kidnapped by two of the guards as she drives home from SI7. Imprisoned in a room at Pelham House, she is soon visited by the true sect leader, none other than Dracula himself, who proceeds to make her his latest victim. Ironically, it is to Pelham House that Torrence and Inspector Murray now head to further their investigations. Accompanied on the trip by Jessica Van Helsing, the men insist that she stay in the car while they question Chin Yang, the high priestess whom Hanson had told them about. Being a liberated girl, Jessica is having none of this and sneaks after them, breaking into the basement so as to snoop about. However, she gets more than she bargained for when she discovers Jane's apparently dead body chained to a wall. But Jane isn't dead, she's become a vampire like the other girls held captive in the cellar. Hearing Jessica's screams as the vampire girls attack, Torrence and Murray rush to the basement, where Torrence is shocked to discover Jane, who begs her boss to set her free before attempting to put the bite on him. Acting quickly, Murray kills her with a makeshift stake, after which the trio flee the premises.

By now it has been discovered that a wealthy businessman named D.D. Denham had been financing Professor Keeley's deadly experiment, which had to be ready for 23 November, which Van Helsing reveals to be the Sabat of the Undead (hence the tag line, "Evil begets evil on the Sabbath of the undead!"). More intriguingly, all the men in the Pelham House sect are on Denham's board, whose worldwide interests include chemicals, oil and banks. Naturally, Van Helsing is more concerned that Pelham House is home to a plague of vampires. "My family has fought this corruption for generations. Each time it was destroyed, so it has risen again like a Phoenix, but hell bent on revenge. Only this time I believe it's not only a personal vendetta, but something infinitely more far-reaching. The plague basilus, Pelham House, the

The double bill poster for *The Satanic Rites of Dracula* (1974) and *Blacula* (1972) (Hammer/Warner/Columbia-Warner/Dynamite Entertainment/American International Pictures/Power Productions).

mental destruction of intellectuals such as Professor Keeley and the others, it is all an integral part of a means to a definite end."

Indeed, Van Helsing goes on to recall that, on his way home from his meeting with Professor Keeley, he noted that a tower block belonging to Denham had been built on the former site of the de-sanctified church of St. Bartolph's where he killed Dracula more than two years ago, and so begins to wonder if the Count and Denham could be one and the same. Yet as Inspector Murray points out, "With only diseased dead bodies to feed on surely even a vampire himself would perish." Replies the Professor, "Perhaps deep in his subconscious, that is what he really wants." As far-fetched as this analogy might first appear, one has to remember that as far back as *Dracula* (1931), the Count had wistfully reflected that, "To die, to be really dead, that must be glorious."

Consequently, Murray, Torrence, the Colonel and Jessica head off to Pelham House to observe the comings and goings. "It all seems so unbelievable in the light of day," comments Murray. However, when the Colonel and Torrence are killed by the guards, and he and Jessica are chased by a sniper and end up being held captive, he quickly re-assesses his opinion.

Meanwhile, armed with a small gun loaded with a silver bullet he has fashioned from a crucifix, Van Helsing heads for Denham's Chelsea tower block where, having requested a meeting with the reclusive businessman (who has observed his arrival on CCTV), he discovers that Denham and Dracula are indeed one and the same when he gets the desired reaction after he tricks the businessman into touching a bible he has surreptitiously placed on his desk ("You *are* Count Dracula!"). But before

Van Helsing can use his gun, two of the Count's acolytes prevent him from doing so and move to kill him. However, the Count stops them from doing so. "It cannot be made so simple for him—not Van Helsing. Nor for his granddaughter."

Back at Pelham House, Inspector Murray is being held captive in the cellar, where the high priestess attempts to seduce and bite him, but he manages to fight her off with the aid of a net and stakes her through the heart. When the other cellar dwellers then make their move on him, he simply turns on the sprinkler system, the running water from which kills them, thus allowing him to make his escape. Meanwhile, Dracula, Van Helsing and the remaining three sect members arrive at Pelham House, where the Count intends to make Jessica, who has been lain out on an altar, his vampire bride ("Van Helsing, I choose the spawn of your blood to be my consort"). By now, Murray is in the building's control room, where he observes the ceremony on CCTV, which, however, fails to relay Dracula's image (as Van Helsing had pointed out earlier, once he figured out that Dracula must have been in the fifth photo that Hanson took, "Vampires are spectral creatures; their image casts no reflection in a mirror, nor can the lens of a camera record their likeness").

Before the Count makes Jessica his consort, he reveals his ultimate plan: "I have chosen four messengers of death, four horsemen of my created apocalypse, four carriers of the plague who will infect their miserable brethren. You, Van Helsing, are now one of the four." Then, on the stroke of midnight, Dracula wills one of his acolytes to crush the phial of plague that he is holding in his hand, resulting in his immediate infection. It seems that Dracula has won the day. Above, Inspector Murray has been discovered by one of the guards, who attacks him with a metal bar. However, after a struggle, Murray manages to see the goon off by using the bar to electrocute him on the surveillance equipment, which consequently blows the floor out and conveniently starts a fire below in the altar room.

In the ensuing chaos, in which Jessica is rescued by Murray, Van Helsing breaks a window with a chair and runs into the nearby woods, hotly pursued by Dracula ("My revenge is spread over centuries and has just begun," he rages). As he makes his escape, Van Helsing scrambles through a patch of hawthorn bushes and coerces the Count to follow. Van Helsing had earlier revealed that the hawthorn is one of the many means by which a vampire can be killed, and this proves to be the case, as Dracula now struggles, caught amid the thorns. Not wanting to take a chance, the Professor determines to finish the job properly, and so grabs a post from a nearby fence with which he stakes the vampire, who in time honored tradition dissolves to dust. Weak but triumphant, Van Helsing bends down to retrieve Dracula's gold ring, and as he does so, the action freeze-frames and the credits finally roll.

*Satanic Rites* is an improvement on *A.D. 1972* in many ways. The screenplay by Don Houghton, who was also elevated to associate producer on the film, is much more confident in its plotting, and frequently cross cuts between the action (slickly handled by editor Chris Barnes), all of which helps to build suspense and maintain narrative drive (some sources indicate that Jimmy Sangster worked on an early treatment, but it seems unlikely that any of his work made it into the finished script, though the BFI database does list him as an uncredited story consultant). The quality of the dialogue is also far better (no dated seventies slang this time), with Houghton even making a sly reference to the previous film. Comments Torrence of the sect's activities: "I can understand young kids taking a fly at it for kicks, but we're talking about sophisticated, mature adults." He also recycles some lines. "Thus by the six thousand terrors of hell are you anointed," declares Chin Yang during the opening rite, recalling Johnny Alucard's similar declaration of "By the six thousand terrors of hell I baptize thee" to Laura in *A.D. 1972*. And at least Dracula plays an active role in the modern world this time round, rather than being holed up away from it as in the previous movie.

The film also plays like a cross between an episode of *The Avengers* and a James Bond film, with Dracula the ultimate Bond villain (and like a Bond villain, he insists on disclosing his master plan before he has carried it out to the full). Of course, Christopher Lee, coaxed back to play the Count one last time by James Carreras, would go on to play Francisco Scaramanga in the James Bond film *The Man with the Golden Gun* (1974), while Joanna Lumley, who had replaced Stephanie Beacham as Jessica Van Helsing, was not only a former Bond girl (she'd appeared in *On Her Majesty's Secret Service* [1969]), but would also go on to play Purdey in *The New Avengers* (1976–1977, TV), so the analogy isn't entirely unwarranted, especially

when one considers the high tech gadgetry Dracula and his acolytes make use of (light sensors, CCTV, computers, laboratory equipment). The Count also plans to destroy the world (a favorite hobby of Bond villains), carries out his plans from atop a specially built tower block lair (albeit in Chelsea), has a team of sheepskin-clad henchmen to do his bidding, and is hunted down by secret government agents. It should also perhaps be noted that the reclusive, Howard Hughes–like Denham recalls the reclusive Willard Whyte in another Bond epic, *Diamonds Are Forever* (1971). In fact Lee himself described the role as "a cross between Dr. No and Howard Hughes."[33]

The film's visual look is also more assured, with director Alan Gibson and cinematographer Bryan Probyn framing the action—even the dialogue scenes—from a wide variety of exciting angles. They also make use of several devices to enhance the excitement. For example, Hanson's struggle with the guard, in which he manages to strangle his captor with the rope that he was bound with, is presented in slow motion, while a grainy filter is used during the sprinkler scene in which the vampire girls are killed. Distorting lenses are also used, along with point of view shots. For example, when Jane is being terrified in her car by the guards, one of them smashes the windscreen with an iron bar and puts his gloved hands through the broken glass to grab her; however, it is the POV camera he grabs and shakes, adding visual panache to an already brutal and exciting scene (though how the two guards then get Jane to Pelham House unnoticed through the streets of London is conveniently glossed over).

The film also makes better use of London locations than its predecessor, beginning with a montage of shots during the credits, in which a silhouette of Dracula grows in size as the sequence progresses (these location shots are now of historical interest, presenting a valuable picture of London in the early seventies, including the building of St. Thomas's Hospital, a shot of which opens the film). And while Dracula again isn't shown wandering the streets of the modern metropolis (he is primarily confined to Pelham House and his tower block), he seemingly does make use of modern day transport (when he, Van Helsing and the two acolytes arrive at Pelham House towards the end of the film, a car door is heard to slam just before they make their entrance).

The score by John Cacavas also has a Bondian flavor to it (Bond guitarist Vic Flick even plays on the soundtrack), and like Mike Vickers' work for *A.D. 1972*, it blends traditional orchestral sounds with electric guitars and driving beats to good effect (the *Main Title* cue is especially well orchestrated, and contains a James Bernard–like three-note *Dra*-cu-la motif of its own). Like Vickers, Cacavas also makes judicious use of a spooky sounding organ for extra effect. Meanwhile, the sets by Lionel Couch, particularly those of the SI7 offices and Dracula's penthouse lair, have a slick, modern appearance (note the cobweb motif on the hallway floor of Pelham House).

As with most Hammer films of this period, *Satanic Rites* has its fair share of nudity and violence

(which caused its American release some problems, resulting in some not always judicious editing). In this case, the nudity includes several shots of a naked woman on an altar during the opening rite, in which she is covered with the blood of a cockerel and stabbed with a knife, the wound from which miraculously heals before the onlookers ("Death is no prison to those who have given their souls to the Prince of Darkness," assures Chin Yang). Later, Jane is staked through her naked breast in the cellar by Inspector Murray (a shot usually trimmed for television screenings). The film also features a number of realistic shootings (during Hanson's escape, one of the motorcycle guards is shot through his visor), while Hanson's injuries look pretty gruesome once back at SI7. Of course, things climax with the pre-requisite disintegration of Dracula, which is handled with reasonable panache by Les Bowie (even if the deflating of one of Dracula's hands looks like it was achieved with the help of a punctured Marigold glove). Remembered Christopher Lee of this particular disintegration sequence, which proved to be the worst for him to film: "They discovered that vampires cannot abide hawthorns. I thought the religious connotation in dubious taste, but a film studio is not the ideal setting to thrash out a theological issue. I had to crash through a tangle of hawthorn bushes with a crown of thorns on my head, with Peter Cushing on the further side waiting to impale me with a stake snatched from a fence. They lacked the foresight to provide a dummy tree and I had to tear a way through the vegetation with spines two inches long, emerging for the *coup de grace* shedding genuine Lee blood like a garden sprinkler."[34]

The cast, meanwhile, remains one of the best assembled for a later Hammer production. As always, Peter Cushing gives the film a solid center as Van Helsing (when he says of vampirism, "This evil is more potent and addictive than heroin, I assure you—and the end result is just as fatal," one is inclined to take him at his word). Christopher Lee, working opposite Cushing for the last time for Hammer, even allows himself a little sly fun in his interpretation of D.D. Denham, whom he invests with a Bela Lugosi–like Transylvanian accent for his brief scene, before resuming his normal voice once unmasked. Personally, though, Lee was less than impressed with the direction the film took, revealing, "The producers were desperately trying to update Dracula. He was made the head of a corporation…. Oh, how I fought that. It was very sad for me to see the role deteriorate from film to film."[35]

Elsewhere, Freddie Jones invests the misguided Professor Keeley with both a sweaty fervor and a tragic pathos, a balancing act few others could surpass. On the side of the law, William Franklyn brings an air of casual charm and sarcasm to Torrence, Richard Vernon adds a touch of the old school tie attitude to Colonel Matthews, while Michael Coles is even better than he was in *A.D. 1972* as the steely Inspector Murray (it would have been nice to see the character develop in further adventures). Needless to say, Joanna Lumley looks stunning throughout as Jessica Van Helsing, whose

Nancy Drew–like determination to be involved in the action with the men adds some spark to the proceedings (even if Jess finds herself in some fairly predictable girl-in-peril situations as a consequence).

A brisk, action packed, stylishly directed and solidly written shocker, *Satanic Rites* brings Hammer's Dracula cycle to an exciting (if not quite complete) close. Sadly, at the time, it was not what the public wanted, and the critics tarred the film with the same brush as *A.D. 1972*. "Shot with the kind of flashy anonymity that one expects of a TV series," sniffed David Pirie in the *Monthly Film Bulletin*. The *Daily Mirror* was more upbeat, describing it as "a horror movie with a touch of class, as you would expect from those specialists, Hammer Productions," while the *Daily Express* noted that, "Alan Gibson directs with more style than the nonsense deserves." However, the *Financial Times* was less enamoured with the results: "From what inspirational abyss Hammer dredged up the script for their latest Dracula film one trembles to think," it sniped. *People Weekly* agreed: "Hammer Films have by now about drained the life out of the genre."

On the floor at Elstree between 13 November and 27 December 1972, the £223,000 film was a last hurrah for Sir James Carreras just before his retirement from Hammer on 31 January 1973, though the film wasn't actually released in the UK by Columbia-Warner until almost a year later on 13 January 1974, when it went out on a double bill with another modern day variation on the *Dracula* story, *Blacula* (1972). It didn't make its American debut until November 1978 care of Dynamite Entertainment, whom Warners had sold it on to (in 1979, Dynamite double-billed the film with *The Seven Brothers Meet Dracula*, the disastrous U.S. cut of Hammer's *The Legend of the 7 Golden Vampires* [1974] and sent it out on the drive-in circuit).

Observed Christopher Lee of his last appearance as the Count: "I was fifty years old and no longer interested in playing a character that had been good to me in an increasingly worsening series of films…. I think the fans were as unhappy as I was about what happened, and it was best for all concerned to end it. The time was right for me to move on, and I did. The Bond film … the Musketeers films. I moved on and didn't look back. I'll always be grateful for Dracula and what he did for my career, but everything comes to an end."[36] **Additional notes:** Although released in 1974, the film carries a 1973 copyright. When Torrence, Jess and Inspector Murray arrive at Pelham House, they are buzzed through the main gate—which must have been repaired fairly quickly given that a motorcyclist had smashed it from its hinges the night before. At one point, Van Helsing claims that, "I destroyed Count Dracula once. It was more than two years ago in St. Bartolph's churchyard," which makes a mockery of the timeline, given that *Satanic Rites* takes place less than two years after *A.D. 1972*; this also seems rather a short time during which to have designed and built an office block on the site of St. Bartolph's and for Dracula to have established his business empire, though it should be noted that

in *A.D. 1972*, Johnny Alucard does say of St. Bartolph's, "It's a church due for demolition," so who knows—maybe the building plans were already well in hand. Then again, Van Helsing observes of the block, "That new building is about two years old," which really does throw a spanner into the works. Though *Satanic Rites* marked Christopher Lee's final appearance as Dracula for Hammer, he did go on to narrate their 1974 *Dracula* LP. Meanwhile, John Forbes Robertson went on to appear (albeit briefly) as the Count in Hammer's *The Legend of the 7 Golden Vampires* (1974). Peter Cushing went on to guest star in *The Eagle's Nest* (1976, TV), the debut episode of *The New Avengers* (1976–1977, TV), which re-united him with his *Satanic Rites* co-star Joanna Lumley. Pelham House is actually High Canons, a country house previously seen as Mocata's house in *The Devil Rides Out* (1968); it would also go on to feature briefly in Hammer's *To the Devil a Daughter* (1976). It would seem that Joanna Lumley replaced Stephanie Beacham because Beacham refused to sign a long-term contract with Hammer, as well as several other studios ("I turned them all down,"[37] the actress later admitted). Like its direct predecessor, *Satanic Rites* eschews the use of rubber bats, which would have looked out of place in a contemporary setting. Director Dan Curtis filmed scenes for his 1974 TV movie *Dracula*, starring Jack Palance as the Count, in Hammer's old stomping ground Oakley Court, which doubled for Carfax Abbey; the film was shown on American television on 8 February 1974, and could possibly have been a contributing factor to the delayed U.S. release *Satanic Rites*. The film's UK co-feature *Blacula* contains a brief appearance by Dracula, here played by Charles Macaulay. Finally, note that in the American trailer for *Satanic Rites*, the narrator intones, "The king of the undead marries the queen of the zombies!" Eh?

Production companies: Hammer/Warner. Distributors: Columbia-Warner (UK), Dynamite Entertainment (U.S.). Producer: Roy Skeggs. Associate producer: Don Houghton. Director: Alan Gibson. Screenplay: Don Houghton. Story consultant: Jimmy Sangster [uncredited]. Cinematographer: Bryan Probyn. Music: John Cacavas. Music director: Philip Martell. Editor: Chris Barnes. Art director: Lionel Couch. Assistant art director: Don Picton. Costumes: Rebecca Breed, Freddie MacManus [uncredited]. Special effects: Les Bowie. Make-up: George Blackler, Cliff Sharpe (assistant [uncredited]). Hair: Maude Onslow. Sound: Claude Hitchcock. Sound editor: Terry Poulton. Dubbing mixer: Dennis Whitlock. Boom operator: Keith Batten [uncredited]. Sound camera operator: Chris Munro [uncredited]. Sound maintenance: Eric Chotan [uncredited]. Camera operator: Rodney "Chick" Anstiss. Focus puller: Malcolm Vinson [uncredited]. Clapper boy/loader: Peter Carmody [uncredited]. Camera grip: Stan Patton [uncredited]. Electrical supervisor: Sid Wainwright [uncredited]. Chargehand electrician: Mick Harkin [uncredited]. Assistant editor: Larry Richardson [uncredited]. Production manager: Ron Jackson. Construction manager: Ken Softley. Assistant director: Derek Whitehurst. Second assistant direc-

tor: Christopher Carreras [uncredited]. Third assistant director: Graham Easton [uncredited]. Draughtsman: Bill Bennison [uncredited]. Production buyer: Edward Rodrigo [uncredited]. Chargehand props: Rex Hobbs [uncredited]. Props: Wilf France [uncredited]. Chargehand dresser: Arthur Jacobs [uncredited]. Scenic artist: Ted Michell [uncredited]. Standby carpenter: D. Clarke [uncredited]. Stagehand: R. Race [uncredited]. Standby rigger: J. Fleetwood [uncredited]. Standby painter: W. McCarthy [uncredited]. Continuity: Elizabeth Wilcox. Casting: James Liggat. Assistant to casting director: Rosemary Pilgrim [uncredited]. Stunts: Valentino Musetti [uncredited]. Runner: Nicholas Baker [uncredited]. Stills: Ronnie Pilgrim [uncredited]. Publicity: Jean Garioch [uncredited]. Publicity secretary: Sue Edwards [uncredited]. Production secretary: Sally Pardo [uncredited]. Producer's secretary: Katy Arnold [uncredited]. Production accountant: Ken Gordon [uncredited]. Accounts assistant: Georgina Grout [uncredited]. Driver: Tony Marshall [uncredited]. Lab contact: Sid Payne [uncredited]. Processing: Humphries Laboratories. Poster: Tom Chantrell [uncredited]. **Cast:** Christopher Lee (Count Dracula/D.D. Denham), Peter Cushing (Professor Lorrimer Van Helsing), Michael Coles (Inspector Murray), William Franklyn (Peter Torrence), Joanna Lumley (Jessica Van Helsing), Freddie Jones (Professor Julian Keeley), Richard Vernon (Colonel Matthews), Patrick Barr (Lord Carradine), Richard Mathews (The Right Honorable John Porter MP), Barbara Yu Ling (Chin Yang), Lockwood West (General Sir Arthur Freeborne), Valerie Van Ost (Jane), Maurice O'Connell (Hanson), Peter Adair (Doctor), John Harvey (Commissionaire), Marc Zuber (Guard 1), Paul Weston (Guard 2), Ian Dewar (Guard 3), Graham Rees (Guard 4), Maggie Fitzgerald (Vampire), Finnuala O'Shannon (Vampire), Pauline Peart (Vampire), Mia Martin (Vampire), Eddie Powell (Christopher Lee's stunt double [uncredited]). **DVD availability:** Anchor Bay (U.S. R1 NTSC), extras include two trailers and an episode of *The World of Hammer* (1990 [first broadcast 1994], TV) titled *Dracula and the Undead*; Cleopatra (U.S. R0 NTSC), extras include a rather pointless bonus CD featuring music "inspired" by *The Satanic Rites of Dracula*, including cues by Icarus Witch, Gravediggaz and Electric Hellfire Club. **CD availability:** *The Hammer Film Music Collection: Volume Two* (GDI Records), which contains the *Main Title*; *The Satanic Rites of Dracula* (GDI Records/Buysoundtrax Records), which contains the complete score, plus one unused track

## Saturn Films, LTD.

Registered at MGM, Borehamwood, Hertfordshire, Saturn was one of Hammer's many subsidiaries. Its lifespan lasted from March 1957 to September 1961, and its directors were James Carreras, Michael Carreras and Matthew Raymond (who was the managing director of MGM British Studios at the time).

## Saunders, Charles

Following experience as an editor from 1927,

this British director (1904–1997) went on to helm a variety of second features, beginning with *No Exit* (1930), which he also wrote and produced. His other credits include *The Tawny Pipit* (1944), which he also co-wrote and co-directed with Bernard Miles, *Dark Interval* (1951), *Come Back Peter* (1952), which he also wrote, *Kill Her Gently* (1958), *Womaneater* (1958) and *Danger by My Side* (1962). He also helmed one Hammer film, *Death of an Angel* (1952). His TV work includes episodes of *Douglas Fairbanks, Jr. Presents* (1953–1957, TV), *Fabian of the Yard* (1954–1956, TV) and *Dial 999* (1958–1959, TV), while his earlier work as an editor includes *Immediate Possession* (1931), *We Dine at Seven* (1931), *Maria Marten, or The Murder in the Red Barn* (1935), *Sweet Devil* (1938) and *The Gentle Sex* (1943). He also worked as an assistant director on *The Laughter of Fools* (1933), as a second unit director on *The Way to the Stars* (1945) and as a location manager on *The White Unicorn* (1947). **Hammer credits:** *Death of an Angel* (1952)

### Saunders, Doreen

Saunders worked as the continuity girl on Hammer's *Dick Barton—Special Agent* (1948). Her other credits include *My Hands Are Clay* (1948) and *The Gorbals Story* (1950). **Hammer credits:** *Dick Barton—Special Agent* (1948)

### Saunders, Stuart

This British supporting actor (1909–1988) played the role of Porter in the Hammer thriller *Room to Let* (1950) and later turned up as a policeman in both *Lady in the Fog* (1952) and *Miss Belle* (1968, TV [episode of *Journey to the Unknown*]). He also popped up in the Hammer/Luckwell second feature *The Runaway* (1964). His other credits include *Dentist in the Chair* (1960), *Lawrence of Arabia* (1962), *Licensed to Kill* (1965) and *Octopussy* (1983), plus episodes of *Douglas Fairbanks, Jr. Presents* (1953–1957, TV), *Sixpenny Corner* (1955–1956, TV), *Softly Softly* (1966–1976, TV) and *Robin's Nest* (1977–1981, TV). His daughter was the actress Elizabeth Saunders (1940–1981). **Hammer credits:** *Room to Let* (1950, as Porter), *Lady in the Fog* (1952, as Policeman [uncredited]), *The Runaway* (1964, as Conway Brockfield), *Miss Belle* (1968, TV [episode of *Journey to the Unknown*], as Sergeant Williams)

### Savage, Mike

A familiar face on British TV from the mid-seventies onwards, this Irish supporting player (1943–) can be seen as a policeman in *The Two Faces of Evil* (1980, TV [episode of *Hammer House of Horror*]). His other TV work includes episodes of *Dixon of Dock Green* (1955–1976, TV), *The Crezz* (1976, TV), *The Fuzz* (1977, TV), *The Deceivers* (1980–1981, TV), *Andy Capp* (1988, TV) and *Harbour Lights* (1999–2000, TV). His occasional film credits include *Confessions from a Holiday Camp* (1977) and *Linen White* (2013). He also runs the production company XED Film and Television Associates with his writing partner Allan Bardsley. Also much on stage. **Hammer credits:** *The Two Faces of Evil* (1980, TV [episode of *Hammer House of Horror*], PC Jenkins)

### Saville, Edith

This British character actress (1894–1987, sometimes Savile, real name Edith Spiegel) played the role of Lady Grant to Kynaston Reeves' Lord Grant in the Hammer second feature *Four Sided Triangle* (1953). Her other credits include *The Greek Interpreter* (1922), *Carnival* (1931), *Forging Ahead* (1933), *A Woman Possessed* (1958) and *Help!* (1965), plus episodes of *No Hiding Place* (1959–1967, TV), *The Saint* (1962–1969, TV) and *Taxi!* (1963–1964, TV). Her husband was writer J. Sabben-Clare (1878–1968), whom she married in 1937. **Hammer credits:** *Four Sided Triangle* (1953, as Lady Grant)

### Savory, Gerald

This prolific British dramatist (1909–1996) is noted for such plays as *It Pays to Advertise* (1931), *George and Margaret* (1937), which was filmed in 1940, *A Likely Tale* (1957) and *Hand in Glove* (1944), which he co-wrote with Charles Freeman, and which was based upon his 1942 novel *Hughie Roddis*, and which was later filmed as *Urge to Kill* (1960). His screenplays include uncredited contributions to Hitchcock's *Young and Innocent* (1937) plus *The Girl Downstairs* (1938), although he is best known for his television work (he was made head of plays at the BBC in 1965). This includes adaptations of *Count Dracula* (1977, TVM), *Dr. Jekyll and Mr. Hyde* (1980, TVM) and *Mapp and Lucia* (1985–1986, TV), plus fourteen episodes of *ITV Play of the Week* (1955–1968, TV), among them versions of *Blithe Spirit* and *The Vortex* (both 1964). His other credits include *Take Three Girls* (1969–1971, TV), which he devised and produced, *The Six Wives of Henry VIII* (1970, TV), which he devised, and *Elizabeth R* (1971, TV), which he likewise devised. He also penned one of the better episodes of *Hammer House of Horror* (1980, TV), the labyrinthine *Rude Awakening*. **Hammer credits:** *Rude Awakening* (1980, TV [episode of *Hammer House of Horror*])

### Sawday, Diana

Sawday can be spotted as a gypsy dancer in Hammer's *Countess Dracula* (1971). **Hammer credits:** *Countess Dracula* (1971, as Gypsy dancer)

### Sawyer, Bill

This British bit-player can be seen as a taxi driver in Hammer's *Never Take Sweets from a Stranger* (1960). He later popped up in *Twins of Evil* (1971) as one of the Puritans and in *Man About the House* (1974) as a chauffeur. His other credits include *Crossroads to Crime* (1960). **Hammer credits:** *Never Take Sweets from a Stranger* (1960, as Taxi driver [uncredited]), *Twins of Evil* (1971, as Puritan [uncredited]), *Man About the House* (1974, as Chauffeur)

### Saxon, Sybil

Some sources note that Saxon had her scene as a bank clerk deleted from the Hammer second feature *The Last Page* (1952). Which is a shame, given that this appears to be her only screen credit. **Hammer credits:** *The Last Page* (1952, as Bank clerk [scene deleted, uncredited])

### Sayers, Patricia

Sayers played one of the Sphinx Girls in Hammer's *The Two Faces of Dr. Jekyll* (1960). **Hammer credits:** *The Two Faces of Dr. Jekyll* (1960, as Sphinx Girl [uncredited])

### Saynor, Charles

British born Saynor (1902–1979) can be seen as a policeman in Hammer's *Cloudburst* (1951). He also had a bit part in *Women Without Men* (1956). His other credits include *Blanche Fury* (1948), *The Blue Lamp* (1949), *I Am a Camera* (1955) and *Look Back in Anger* (1959), plus episodes of *Saber of London* (1954–1960, TV), *The Black Tulip* (1956, TV) and *Softly Softly* (1966–1976, TV). **Hammer credits:** *Cloudburst* (1951, as Constable), *Women Without Men* (1956, as Man at doorway [uncredited])

### Scammell, Roy

This British stuntman, stunt arranger and bit player (1932–, sometimes Scammel) worked as a stuntman on Hammer's *The Vampire Lovers* (1970). His many other credits include *Circus of Fear* (1966), *Monte Carlo or Bust!* (1969), in which he doubled for Susan Hampshire, *A Clockwork Orange* (1971), for which he stunt doubled for Malcolm McDowell, *Rollerball* (1975), *Golden Rendezvous* (1977), *Alien* (1979), *Sheena* (1984), *Nuns on the Run* (1990), *GoldenEye* (1995), *Tell Him Next Year* (2010) and *Seize the Night* (2015), plus episodes of *Doctor Who* (1963–1989, TV), *Space: 1999* (1975–1977, TV) and *The New Statesman* (1987–1992, TV). **Hammer credits:** *The Vampire Lovers* (1970 [uncredited])

### Scarf, Donna

Scarf can be seen in a minor role in *In Possession* (1984, TVM [episode of *Hammer House of Mystery and Suspense*]). Her other credits include episodes of *The Benny Hill Show* (1969–1989, TV), *The Upchat Line* (1977, TV) and *Blakes 7* (1978–1981, TV), plus the film *Let's Get Laid* (1977). **Hammer credits:** *In Possession* (1984, TVM [episode of *Hammer House of Mystery and Suspense*], as Hotel receptionist)

### *The Scarlet Blade*

GB, 1963, 82m, Technicolor, HammerScope [2.35:1], RCA, cert U

Said to be the favorite film of its writer-director John Gilling, this widescreen 1648-set period adventure follows the exploits of a Royalist avenger named The Scarlet Blade, who, with the help of his followers, aims to bring to an end the activities of the ruthless Colonel Judd, a Royalist-turned-Ironside determined on hanging everyone whom he perceives to be a traitor to the cause of Oliver Cromwell ("This is the story of a band of freemen who destroyed a tyrant," heralds the opening caption, pre-empting the ending somewhat). Unfortunately, in addition to The Scarlet Blade—in actuality the nobleman Edward Beverley, out to avenge the death of his father—Judd has to contend with the Royalist sympathies of his own daughter, Clare, who has fallen in love with Beverley, whom she has been helping. Meanwhile, Judd's right hand man, Captain Sylvester, who himself has unreciprocated feelings for the Colonel's daughter, also begins to display signs of having sympathies with the other side ("Every man has a reason for switching his allegiance").

Originally announced back in 1955 as *King Charles and the Roundheads* (since when it had been substantially re-written), *The Scarlet Blade* was shot in Black Park and on the back lot at Bray between 1 March and 17 April 1963. However, given that it was aimed at the kiddie matinee market (hence the U certificate), it is a surprisingly slow-moving and talkative affair. Much too serious and far from the fun it could have been, the film suffers from perfunctory dialogue, over-lit interiors, unconvincing studio work (soundstage exteriors) and the use of overly-familiar back lot sets (the standing village set and the remains of the entrance to Castle Dracula). The lack of greenery in the sequences shot in Black Park meanwhile gives the film a harsh, austere look, while on a more minor note, the leading lady's hairdo gives the distinct impression of having just been set in a sixties salon. Even the action sequences—several of which involve an impressive number of horses and men—aren't as well staged as they could have been, having the look of a muddy Sunday re-enactment (the main battle sequence, arranged by stunt supervisor Peter Diamond, was apparently shot in half a day—and looks it!).

On the plus side, Lionel Jeffries gives a good account of himself as the ruthless Colonel Judd, while Oliver Reed lends solid support as the not entirely sympathetic Captain Sylvester (his death scene, in which he is shot by Judd and collapses against a refectory table is perhaps the film's most vivid moment). Duncan Lamont also gives a good account of himself as the self-important Major Bell (the scene in which he gives his orders to Captain Sylvester while eating his breakfast is particularly well-handled by the actor). Less impressive is June Thorburn as the priggish heroine Clare Judd, while Jack Hedley's Scarlet Blade—absent from the action for much of the running time, despite being the title character—lacks any noticeable charisma (Oliver Reed would surely have been a better choice for the role).

Rush-released onto the ABC circuit by Warner-Pathé in time for the school holidays on 11 August 1963, the film was double-billed with the Continental swashbuckler *Son of Captain Blood* (1962) and proved to be a solid box office success. The film's American release care of Columbia followed in March 1964, for which it was re-titled *The Crimson Blade* and double billed with another Hammer swashbuckler, *The Devil-Ship Pirates* (1964). **Additional notes:** Despite the film's rather drab look, Jack Asher's cinematography (perhaps his least impressive for Hammer) was nominated for a BAFTA (the award ultimately went to Ted Moore for his work on the James Bond adventure *From Russia with Love* [1963]). First assistant director Douglas Hermes walked off the film in mid-production following an altercation with director John Gilling over the shooting of a sequence involving a noose. He was subsequently replaced by the film's second assistant director Hugh Harlow for the remainder of principal photography.

Production companies: Hammer/Associated

Inn for trouble. From left to right, Jack Hedley, Oliver Reed, June Thorburn, Michael Ripper and Suzan Farmer in *The Scarlet Blade* (1963) (Hammer/Associated British Picture Corporation/Warner Pathé/Columbia).

British Picture Corporation. Distributors: Warner Pathé (UK [ABC circuit]), Columbia (U.S.). Producer: Anthony Nelson Keys. Director: John Gilling. Screenplay: John Gilling. Cinematographer: Jack Asher. Music: Gary Hughes. Music director: John Hollingsworth. Supervising editor: James Needs. Editor: John Dunsford. Assistant editor: Martyn K.E. Green [uncredited]. Production design: Bernard Robinson. Art director: Don Mingaye. Assistant art director: Ken Ryan [uncredited]. Costumes: Rosemary Burrows, Molly Arbuthnot [uncredited], Gloria Barnes (assistant [uncredited]). Special effects: Les Bowie. Special effects assistants: Bill Warrington [uncredited], Ian Scoones [uncredited], Kit West [uncredited]. Make-up: Roy Ashton, Richard Mills (assistant [uncredited]). Hair: Frieda Steiger. Sound: Ken Rawkins. Sound camera operator: Al Thorne [uncredited]. Sound transfer operator: Michael Sale [uncredited]. Sound editor: James Groom. Sound maintenance: Charles Bouvet [uncredited]. Boom operator: Peter Pardoe [uncredited]. Production manager: Clifford Parkes. Studio manager: Arthur Kelly [uncredited]. Assistant director: Douglas Hermes. Second assistant director: Hugh Harlow ([uncredited] promoted to first assistant director during production following the departure of Douglas Hermes). Third assistant director: Stephen Victor [uncredited]. Stunt supervisor: Peter Diamond [uncredited]. Stunts: Gerry Crampton [uncredited], Frank Henson [uncredited], Terry Richards [uncredited], Peter Munt [uncredited], Terry Plummer [uncredited]. Camera operator: Cece Cooney. Focus pullers: Mike

Sarafian [uncredited], Peter Hurst [uncredited]. Camera grip: Albert Cowlard [uncredited]. Camera loader/clapper boy: David Kelly [uncredited]. Camera maintenance: John Kerley [uncredited]. Construction manager: Arthur Banks [uncredited]. Master carpenter: Charles Davis [uncredited]. Master plasterer: Stan Banks [uncredited]. Master painter: Lawrence Wrenn [uncredited]. Master electrician: Jack Curtis [uncredited]. Electrical supervisor: George Robinson [uncredited]. Electrical chargehand: Vic Hemmings [uncredited]. Master rigger: Ronald Lenoir [uncredited]. Props: Tommy Money [uncredited]. Floor props: John Goddard [uncredited]. Props buyer: Eric Hillier [uncredited]. Publicity: Dennison Thornton [uncredited], Brian Doyle [uncredited]. Stills: Tom Edwards [uncredited]. Continuity: Pauline Wise (also production secretary [uncredited]). Production secretary: Barbara Allen [uncredited]. Drivers: Coco Epps [uncredited], Laurie Martin [uncredited]. **Cast:** Lionel Jeffries (Colonel Judd), Oliver Reed (Captain Sylvester), June Thorburn (Clare Judd), Jack Hedley (Edward Beverley/The Scarlet Blade), Clifford Elkin (Philip Beverley), Suzan Farmer (Constance Beverley), Harold Goldblatt (Jacob), Michael Ripper (Pablo), Duncan Lamont (Major Bell), Charles Houston (Drury), John Harvey (Sergeant Grey), John Stuart (Colonel Beverley [uncredited]), Robert Rietti (Charles I [uncredited]), Michael Byrne (Lieutenant Hawkins [uncredited]), Harry Towb (Cobb [uncredited]), John H. Watson (Fitzroy [uncredited]), Douglas Blackwell (Blake [uncredited]), Denis Holmes (Chaplain [uncredited]), Eric Corrie

(Duncannon [uncredited]), John Woodnutt (Lieutenant Wyatt [uncredited]), Leslie Glazer (Gonzales [uncredited]), George Woodbridge (Town Crier [uncredited]), James Payne (Man in tavern [uncredited]), Bill Brandon (Roundhead guard [uncredited]), Peter Diamond (Trooper [uncredited]), Fred Haggerty (Guard [uncredited]). **DVD availability:** Optimum Home Entertainment (UK R2 PAL), Sony (U.S. R1 NTSC), as *The Scarlet Blade* (as opposed to its established U.S. title)

### Scarlett, J.J.Y. *see* Scarlett, York

### Scarlett, York (Yorke)

Scarlett (aka J.J.Y. Scarlett) worked as a sound recordist on the Hammer comedy musical *Sporting Love* (1936). His other credits include *Housing Problems* (1935), *Spare Time* (1939), *The Devil's Hand* (1943), *Chance of a Lifetime* (1950), *The Door In the Wall* (1956), *The Chaplin Revue* (1959) and *Heavens Above!* (1963), plus a return to Hammer for *The Eric Winstone Bandshow* (1955) and *The Right Person* (1956), on both of which he was credited as J.J.Y. Scarlett. **Hammer credits:** *Sporting Love* (1936 [as York Scarlett]), *The Eric Winstone Bandshow* (1955 [as J.J.Y. Scarlett]), *The Right Person* (1956 [as J.J.Y. Scarlett])

### *Scars of Dracula*

GB, 1970, 96m, Technicolor, widescreen [1.85:1], RCA, cert X

There was a good deal of belt-tightening going on at Hammer in the early seventies following the virtual disappearance of their American backers. Consequently, budgets and shooting schedules were slashed, sets were increasingly re-cycled and quality took a noticeable downturn. One of the victims of this new production policy was the studio's fifth Dracula outing, which was paired with the even worse *The Horror of Frankenstein* (1970), several sets from which it re-used, a scam that audiences seeing the double bill must surely have noticed.

Anthony Hinds' screenplay for *Scars of Dracula* had originally been penned as a direct follow up to *Dracula Has Risen from the Grave* (1968). However, when Christopher Lee stated that he would no longer play the character, Hinds was persuaded to write a new script, much to his chagrin. This was *Taste the Blood of Dracula* (1970), which originally eschewed Dracula entirely. When Lee was eventually persuaded to play the Count again by James Carreras (at the insistence of Warner Bros.), this second script was subsequently amended to include Dracula. Then, when it came to make the follow up to *Taste the Blood of Dracula*, the original *Scars of Dracula* script was simply dusted off and put into production with little in the way of restructuring—hence the lack of series continuity at the top of the film, though why Hinds didn't simply revert to the *Scars* script as a direct follow up to *Risen from the Grave* seems curious, unless he felt the second script was better (which it undoubtedly is). Consequently, at the climax of *Taste*, Dracula is destroyed in a disused church in London, while at the beginning of *Scars*, his remains have somehow made it back to his crypt in Castle Dracula.

Presumably, the front office thought audiences would neither mind nor care about such discrepancies. That said, Christopher Lee had his own theory as to the lack of series continuity, as he revealed in a letter to his fan club president Gloria Lillibridge: "The reason they have brought this character back without accounting for his sudden appearance is, I'm quite certain, deliberately contrived in case I should say no and they can put in another actor (which they're always telling me they're going to do or will do one day), in which case there is no need for any further continuity."[38] Indeed, Lee went on to point out that "The new Frankenstein they're making now is being made without Peter Cushing. I suppose they feel they can do without us now."[39] In fact, actor John Forbes-Robertson, who would eventually take over the role of Dracula in *The Legend of the 7 Golden Vampires* (1974), was seemingly approached by director Roy Ward Baker during the film's protracted contractual negotiations as a replacement for Lee.

This time Dracula is revived with the aid of a bat that vomits blood onto his ashes, which subsequently re-form, allowing him to go on yet another killing spree—though given the film's tight budget, he is something of a stay-at-home, carrying out his foul deeds within the confines of his half-ruined castle, preying on those who just happen to call by within the context of the narrative. Among these is a young man named Paul, who, having gone on the run after being caught with the Burgomaster's daughter, takes refuge in the castle, only to find himself the guest of Dracula and his consort Tania. When Paul fails to return home, his brother Simon, accompanied by his girlfriend Sarah, decide to go and look for the missing young man, and likewise find themselves taking refuge at the castle. During their time there, Simon becomes certain that Dracula is somehow involved in Paul's disappearance, especially having discovered a cracked miniature portrait of Sarah that his brother intended giving her for her birthday. Shortly after, he and Sarah flee the castle, Simon having learned that her food has been drugged. Following this Simon learns how to destroy a vampire from a local priest, after which he returns to the castle to confront Dracula, during the course of which he finally discovers his brother's body, hung on a hook in the Count's crypt....

Routine in every way, the story is simply a reworking of ideas that had already been tried and tested several times too often in the previous episodes, while the much-delayed climax in which Dracula is struck by a somewhat convenient bolt of lightening as he removes an iron railing that Simon has staked him with, javelin-style, almost beggars belief (Lee's stunt double, Eddie Powell, became a human torch for the sequence, and it's clearly not Lee in some of the shots). The dialogue is equally risible, and seems even more so when spoken by some of the film's younger, more inexperienced cast members, among them Dennis Waterman and Christopher Matthews, as brothers Simon and Paul respectively, and Jenny Hanley as Sarah, whose performance was subsequently revoiced by Monica Van Der Zyl. According to director Roy Ward Baker, producer Aida Young cast the film herself to save the expense of hiring a casting director. Of her endeavours, Baker later commented, "The cast was extraordinarily cheap."[40] Even Christopher Lee seems to squirm a little at having to deliver idle parlor chatter to Paul during their initial encounter ("Before the castle was destroyed, strangers were always welcome," he informs his barely interested guest).

**CHRISTOPHER LEE**

**DRACULA – Nächte des Entsetzens**

**Draculas Blutrausch**

Christopher Lee swipes the bed curtains in this German lobby card for *Scars of Dracula* (1970) (Hammer/EMI/MGM-EMI/Continental/Studio Canal).

Equally, Hammer regular Michael Ripper as a tavern landlord is also unable to make much of such hackneyed lines as "We know where the evil lies—we must free ourselves—now!" following which he and the other villagers head off to burn down Castle Dracula, leaving the womenfolk behind in the safety of the church. However, it must be admitted that this leads to the film's one true moment of invention: when the men return from their fiery task, they discover that their spouses and children have all been torn to shreds by a horde of bats (cue some effectively gory make-ups by Wally Schneiderman and his assistant Heather Nurse). Otherwise, this is very much the mixture as before, further compromised by flat lighting, fake rubber bats, traffic cop direction and some cheap-looking sets, among them the less-than-convincing ramparts of Castle Dracula and the obvious re-use of Baron Frankenstein's baronial hall from *The Horror of Frankenstein*, which here (barely re-dressed) doubles as the Burgomaster's residence. Commented assistant director Derek Whitehurst of this obvious re-usage, "*Horror of Frankenstein* and *Scars of Dracula* went out as a double bill—it looks awful."

You are very aware of what's going on actually … [The] sets just look familiar, you can't avoid it."[41] Even Dracula's resurrection scene was lifted from the climactic disintegration scene of *Taste the Blood of Dracula*, but here shown in reverse.

The film's few pluses include James Bernard's frequently energetic music, which helps to gee along what action there is (the composer provides the Count with a new, more aggressive theme to accompany his familiar three-note *Dra*-cu-la motif, while the love scenes between Simon and Sarah are accompanied by a touching *romanza*). Commendably, there is also an attempt to link the film to Stoker's novel by including previously unused incidents, such as Dracula's ability to scale the walls of his castle. This brief episode was inserted at the insistence of director Roy Ward Baker, who described its inclusion as "the only contribution I felt I had made to the Dracula cycle."[42] However, there was the question of how the scene should be achieved. Recalled Baker, "I talked it over with Scott MacGregor, the art director…. This was my fifth picture with Scott. He was keen to realize the idea but it would need a specially built set, which was certainly not in the budget. There was a lot of humming and ha'ing in the production department but eventually they managed it."[43] Yet despite the efforts of all concerned, Baker admitted to not being entirely pleased with the set he was given for the scene: "It was pretty crappy, but I made my point."[44] Another point he wanted to achieve was to make Dracula more the focus of the proceedings: "Christopher Lee had made Count Dracula into a character of his own; the best there was, no doubt of that. During the last two or three of these pictures Dracula's presence in the stories had gradually waned, becoming a coat hanger, so Christopher was not displeased to see that this new script was clearly Dracula's story."[45]

Baker also attempted to introduce an element of magic into the proceedings: "One thing happened by accident. Christopher had to pick up a girl and carry her from one place to another in the castle. They were in this room, a large bedroom I think. We were rehearsing and he suddenly stopped and looked at me and said: 'I've picked up the lady but how do I open the door?' So I said, 'Dracula doesn't open his own

doors.' I got a props man and a piece of string, so that when Dracula walks towards the door, it swings open and shuts behind him. That was a special effect you got for nothing. But it was that element, and the scene in which Dracula climbs down the castle wall, which were taken from the book, which nobody had done before."[46] (Note that a door does in fact mysteriously open for Dracula in the early scenes of the original *Dracula* [1931] when the Count is showing Mr. Harker to his room, but little attention is paid to the effect; however, in the Spanish language version of the same film, much more is made of this eerie phenomenon, particularly by Harker).

Performance-wise, Patrick Troughton momentarily enlivens the mostly tiresome proceedings with his turn as Dracula's put upon manservant Klove (a role previously played by Philip Latham in *Dracula—Prince of Darkness* [1966]), while Anouska Hempel certainly looks eye-catching in her black wig and purple velvet dress as Tania. Content-wise, the film has more sadism in it than its predecessors. For example, Dracula stabs his consort Tania to death with a (somewhat rubbery-looking) dagger, though a shot of him drinking from the wound was trimmed from the release print at the insistence of the BBFC, as were shots of Tania's dismembered limbs, cut up and dissolved in a bath of acid by Klove (however, shots of Jenny Hanley's bloodied breasts—a previous no-no with the censor—were allowed to pass in the scene in which a bat attacks her and removes a crucifix from around her neck). Dracula also brands his poor manservant with a sword (and not for the first time judging from the scars on his back). This shot was achieved by placing reflective strips onto the sword onto which was then shone a faint red light. Less effective is the superimposition of red eyes upon Dracula's closed lids when Simon attempts to stake him in his coffin. However, the best shot comes early in the proceedings, when the men return to the church for their kinfolk after having torched Castle Dracula: when they discover the bloodied bodies of their wives and children, there is a shot of blood dripping down onto a sconce of white candles, at which the screen goes red and we cross-fade to Sarah's birthday cake, which is covered in red candles. These minor instances aside, however, there is, overall, very little to get excited about here.

Financed to the tune of £200,000 by EMI, *Scars of Dracula* went onto the floor at MGM-EMI Elstree on 11 May 1970, just eight days after the completion of *The Horror of Frankenstein*, with which it also shared a number of technical crew as well as the afore-mentioned re-vamped sets. The film was in the can by and 19 June and ready for its premiere engagement at London's New Victoria cinema on 23 October care of MGM-EMI. It then went on general release in the UK on the ABC circuit on 8 November. Needless to say, critical reaction was mostly subdued. Commented *Films and Filming*, "Despite the impressive presence of Christopher Lee as a passionate and sadistic Dracula, this is run of the mill vampire material for addicts, with the customary castle hung with yards of red plush, the uncouth retainer, taciturn villagers and a humorous clergyman."

**Distinctive artwork for *Scars of Dracula* (1970) (Hammer/EMI/MGM-EMI/Continental/Studio Canal).**

Reaction to the American release care of Continental on 13 January 1971, again with *The Horror of Frankenstein*, was likewise muted (Warner Bros. actually turned down the offer to release the films). Summing things up in a nutshell in *Cinefantastique*, John R. Duvoli commented, "Roy Ward Baker's direction is not as atmospheric as it was in, say, *The Vampire Lovers*, and the film suffers from cheap set design and the obvious low budget." Elsewhere, *Today's Cinema* observed that "the Count must have been drinking blood of the wrong group; otherwise, he would never stoop so low as to stab a woman to death or burn a disobedient servant with a red hot sword," while the *New York Daily News* advised its readers to "skip this one." Even its star averred that "This was the worst of the Hammer series in all departments. It has nothing to recommend it—a bad, bad film that is just about as far from Bram Stoker or Hammer's first Dracula as it's possible to get."[47] **Additional notes:** In the trailer, the film is actually referred to as *The Scars of Dracula*, as it also was in Tom Chantrell's early promotional artwork and Angus Hall's novelization, published by Sphere in the UK and Beagle in the U.S. The trailer has the gall to hail the movie as "Hammer's masterpiece of macabre." The poster for the double bill of *Scars of Dracula* and *The Horror of Frankenstein* can be seen in a cinema foyer in the British horror film *The Fiend* (1971). The strapline on one of the double-bill posters described Dracula and Frankenstein as "The blood-brothers of horror and terror!" Clips from *Scars of Dracula* can be found in the 1975 Swedish documentary *In Search of Dracula*, which is presented by Christopher Lee.

Shots of Castle Dracula can meanwhile be spotted in *Dorabella*, the final episode of the BBC series *Supernatural* (1977, TV). Continuity-wise, note the crumpled cyclorama surrounding the ramparts of Castle Dracula, the top of which can be seen when a giant bat swoops around one of the turrets when Simon and Sarah arrive. The crack in the miniature portrait Paul has made as a gift for Sarah changes throughout the film, from diagonal to vertical. While staying at Castle Dracula, Paul is clearly seen to be wearing a pair of bright red seventies-style underpants, the color of which at least matches the tacky furnishings of the bedroom he is staying in (red curtains, bed sheets and furniture upholstery, all of which look as if they've been purchased from the nearest furniture shop). According to the IMDb, the film also played some solo engagements Stateside from 23 December 1970, which were handled by the distributors Levitt-Pickman.

Production companies: Hammer/EMI. Distributors: MGM-EMI (UK [ABC circuit]), Continental (U.S.). Producer: Aida Young. Director: Roy Ward Baker. Screenplay: John Elder (Anthony Hinds). Cinematographer: Moray Grant. Music: James Bernard. Music director: Philip Martell. Editor: James Needs. Assistant editors: Adrian MacDonald (first assistant [uncredited]), Stephen Hyde (second assistant [uncredited]). Art director: Scott MacGregor. Assistant art director: Don Picton [uncredited]. Costumes: Laura Nightingale, Donald Mothersilll (assistant [uncredited]). Special effects: Roger Dicken, Brian Johnson [uncredited], Ray Caple (mattes [uncredited]). Makeup: Wally Schneiderman, Heather Nurse (assis-

tant). Hair: Pearl Tipaldi. Recording supervisor: Tony Lumkin. Sound: Ron Barron. Dubbing mixer: Dennis Whitlock. Sound editor: Roy Hyde. Boom operator: David Crozier [uncredited]. Sound camera operator: David Tappenden [uncredited]. Sound maintenance: Barry Reed [uncredited]. Assistant dubbing editor: Colin Needs [uncredited]. Camera operator: Neil Binney [uncredited]. Clapper boy/loader: Roderick Barron [uncredited]. Focus puller: Bob Stilwell [uncredited]. Camera grip: Peter Woods [uncredited]. Gaffer: Sid Wainwright [uncredited]. Assistant director: Derek Whitehurst. Second assistant director: Nick Granby [uncredited]. Third assistant director: Lindsey C. Vickers [uncredited]. Runners: Phil Campbell [uncredited], Brian Reynolds [uncredited]. Laborer: Dennis Barr [uncredited]. Production manager: Tom Sachs. Construction manager: Arthur Banks. Draughtsman: Tony Baines [uncredited]. Scenic artist: Bob White [uncredited]. Production buyer: Roddy Rodrigo [uncredited]. Standby props: Wally Hockings [uncredited]. Standby carpenter: Richard Slattery [uncredited]. Standby stagehand: F. Keoghan [uncredited]. Standby rigger: Paul Mitchell [uncredited]. Standby painter: Philip Peach [uncredited]. Standby plasterer: Lambeth Slobart [uncredited]. Chargehand electrician: Jack Collins [uncredited]. Continuity: Betty Harley. Stills: Joe Pearce [uncredited]. Production accountant: Ken Gordon [uncredited]. Assistant production accountant: Stuart King [uncredited]. Publicist: Chris Nixon [uncredited]. Drivers: George Andrews [uncredited], John Bevan [uncredited]. Poster: Mike Vaughan [uncredited]. Promotional artwork: Tom Chantrell [uncredited]. **Cast:** Christopher Lee (Count Dracula), Dennis Waterman (Simon), Jenny Hanley (Sarah Framsen), Christopher Matthews (Paul), Patrick Troughton (Klove), Delia Lindsay (Alice), Anouska Hempel (Tania), Michael Gwynn (Priest), Wendy Hamilton (Julie), Bob Todd (Burgomaster), Michael Ripper (Landlord), Margo Boht (Maria [landlord's wife]), George Innes (Servant), Toke Townley (Waggoner), Morris Bush (Farmer), David Leland (First officer), Richard Durden (Second officer), Clive Barrie (Fat young man), Olga Anthony (Girl at party [uncredited]), Eddie Powell (Christopher Lee's stunt double [uncredited]), Nikki Van Der Zyl (voice of Jenny Hanley [uncredited]). **DVD availability:** Anchor Bay (U.S. R1 NTSC), extras include a commentary by Christopher Lee and Roy Ward Baker, biographies, two trailers, a stills gallery and a 1996 documentary titled *The Many Faces of Christopher Lee*; Warner (UK R2 PAL). **CD availability:** *Scars of Dracula* (GDI Records), which contains the complete score; *The Devil Rides Out: The Film Music of James Bernard* (Silva Screen), which contains a new recording of the *Love Theme*; *The Great British Film Music Album: Sixty Glorious Years 1938–1998* (Silva Screen), which contains a new recording of *Romanza* (under the title *The Scars of Dracula*)

## Scase, David

This British actor (1919–2003) can be seen as a cameraman in Hammer's *Never Look Back* (1952). His other credits include *Billy Liar* (1963)

British poster for the double bill of *Scars of Dracula* (1970) and *The Horror of Frankenstein* (1970). As well as sharing artwork similarities (the castle seems to be the same in each poster), the two films also shared some of the same sets (Hammer/EMI/MGM-EMI/Continental/Studio Canal).

and episodes of *Z Cars* (1962–1978, TV), *The XYY Man* (1976–1977, TV), *Till We Meet Again* (1989, TV) and *Truckers* (1992, TV). He also directed a number of stage plays, notably at Manchester's Library Theater in the mid-fifties. **Hammer credits:** *Never Look Back* (1952, as Cameraman)

### Schell, Catherine

This Hungarian actress (1944–, real name Katherina Freiin Schell Von Bauschlott, aka Catherina Von Schell) began appearing in films in her homeland as Catherina Von Schell with *Lana—Konigin der Amazonen* (1964), in which she played the title role. In British films from the late sixties, her early English-speaking credits include *Amsterdam Affair* (1968), *On Her Majesty's Secret Service* (1969) and Hammer's *Moon Zero Two* (1969), in which she played the female lead, Clementine Taplin. Her other credits include *Madame Sin* (1972), *The Return of the Pink Panther* (1975), *The Prisoner of Zenda* (1979), *The Island of Adventure* (1982) and *On the Black* Hill (1987). Also on television, she is best known for playing Maya in *Space: 1999* (1975–1977, TV). Her other TV work includes episodes of *The Adventurer* (1972–1973, TV), *Mog* (1985–1986, TV), *One by One* (1985–1987, TV) and *The Knock* (1994–2000, TV). Married twice, her husbands were the actor William Marlowe (1932–2003), to whom she was married between 1968 and 1977, and the director Bill Hays (1932–2006, full name William Hays), whom she married in 1982. Marlowe appeared *The Killing Bottle* (1968, TV [episode of *Journey to the Unknown*]), which also appeared in the compendium film *Journey to Murder* (1972, TVM).

**Hammer credits:** *Moon Zero Two* (1969, as Clementine Taplin)

**Publicity shot of Catherina Von Schell (later Catherine Schell) taken during the making of *Moon Zero Two* (1969) (Hammer/Warner Bros./Seven Arts/Warner Pathé Distributors).**

Catherina Von Schell (later Catherine Schell) gets a nasty surprise in *Moon Zero Two* (1969) (Hammer/Warner Bros./Seven Arts/Warner Pathé Distributors).

### Schlockoff, Alain

French born Schlockoff (1948–) is best known for founding the genre magazine *L'Ecran Fantastique* in 1969, and for running the annual Paris International Science Fiction and Fantasy Film Festival (the Convention Française du Cinéma Fantastique), which was founded in 1972 and frequently held at the 2,800-seat Rex Theater (the event ran until 1989, and had a one-off revival in 2000). Schlockoff worked as an extra on Hammer's *The Horror of Frankenstein* (1970), presumably during a set visit. His other credits include the documentary *J'étais* (2004) and the TV series *Cinéphiles de notre temps* (2012, TV). Prior to his work on *L'Ecran Fantastique*, he also contributed to *Horizons du Fantastique*. **Additional notes**: Hammer's *Frankenstein and the Monster from Hell* (1974) received its world premiere at the Paris festival in April 1974. Guests at the festival during its lifetime included such Hammer names as Terence Fisher, Christopher Lee, Caroline Munro, Peter Cushing and Roy Ward Baker. **Hammer credits:** *The Horror of Frankenstein* (1970, unnamed role [uncredited])

### Schneiderman, Wally (Walter)

Schneiderman (1922–, sometimes Schneidermann) worked as the make-up artist on Hammer's *One Million Years B.C.* (1966). His other credits include *Corridors of Blood* (1958), *Inspector Clouseau* (1968), *Where's Jack?* (1969), *Bear Island* (1979), *Eye of the Needle* (1981), *The Holcroft Covenant* (1985), *Labyrinth* (1986), *The Trouble with Spies* (1987) and *Chaplin* (1992), which earned him a shared BAFTA nomination. He also returned to Hammer for *Slave Girls* (1968) and *Scars of Dracula* (1970). **Hammer credits:** *One Million Years B.C.* (1966), *Slave Girls* (1968), *Scars of Dracula* (1970)

### Schofield, Joan

Schofield can be seen as a shopper in Hammer's second Quatermass film. Her other credits include *The Angel with the Trumpet* (1950), *Trio* (1950) and *The Weapon* (1956, TV), plus episodes of *Saber of London* (1954–1960, TV). She was married to the actor Dennis Price (1915–1973, real name Dennistoun Franklyn John Rose-Price) between 1939 and 1950. He appeared in five films for Hammer: *Don't Panic Chaps* (1959), *Watch It, Sailor!* (1961), *The Horror of Frankenstein* (1970), *Twins of Evil* (1971) and *That's Your Funeral* (1973). **Hammer credits:** *Quatermass 2* (1957, as Shopper [uncredited])

### Schofield, Johnnie

This prolific British character actor (1889–1955, full name John William Schofield) played a wide variety of small roles during his busy career, but only took a leading role once, in *Down Melody Lane* (1943). In films from the early thirties with *The Pride of the Force* (1933), his other credits include *Hawley's of High Street* (1933), *The Outcast* (1934), *The Spy in Black* (1939), *Contraband* (1940), *Went the Day Well?* (1942), *Waterloo Road* (1944), *The Way Ahead* (1944), *The Way to the Stars* (1945), *Train of Events* (1949), *The Net* (1953) and *Carrington V.C.* (1954). He also notched up two appearances for Hammer during their first flourish of life in the mid-thirties. Also on stage as a song and dance man in revue and pantomime, his father was the comedian John Orlando Schofield, and his grandson is the actor John Altman (1952–). **Hammer credits:** *The Mystery of the Mary Celeste* (1935, as Peter Tooley), *Song of Freedom* (1936, unnamed role)

## Schratt, Peter

This Austrian actor (1932–1996) had a minor role in Hammer's *The Lady Vanishes* (1979). His other credits include *Der Vater* (1969, TVM) and *Traumnovelle* (1969, TVM). **Hammer credits:** *The Lady Vanishes* (1979, as German officer)

## Schrecker, Frederick

This Austrian actor (1892–1976, real name Friedrich Schrecker, aka Fritz Schrecker) played one of several plainclothesmen seen in the Hammer thriller *Taste of Fear* (1961). In films in his homeland from 1926 with *Der Feldherrnhugel*, his other credits include *Innocents in Paris* (1953), *The Master Plan* (1955), *Billion Dollar Brain* (1967) and *Deviation* (1971), plus episodes of *International Detective* (1959–1961, TV), *Dial M for Murder* (1974, TV) and *The Glittering Prizes* (1976, TV). **Hammer credits:** *Taste of Fear* (1961, as Plainclothesman [uncredited])

## Schubert, Terry

British born Schubert (1938–) contributed to the effects for Hammer's *Moon Zero Two* (1969) and *Taste the Blood of Dracula* (1970). He went on to work on such projects as *Superman* (1978), *Saturn 3* (1980), *Raiders of the Lost Ark* (1981), *Krull* (1983), *Indiana Jones and the Last Crusade* (1989), *Some Mother's Son* (1996), *Highlander: Endgame* (2000) and *Shanghai Knights* (2003). **Hammer credits:** *Moon Zero Two* (1969 [uncredited]), *Taste the Blood of Dracula* (1970 [uncredited])

## Schulz, Clive D.

Schulz (aka Uwe Schulz) provided and supervised the animals for Hammer's *Creatures the World Forgot* (1971). **Hammer credits:** *Creatures the World Forgot* (1971)

## Schurmann, Gerard

Although best known for his horror scores, among them those for *Horrors of the Black Museum* (1959) and *Konga* (1960), this Dutch-Indonesian born composer (1924–, aka Gerbrand Schurmann) was surprisingly never a mainstay at Hammer. He did, however, write two atonal scores for the company a decade apart: *The Camp on Blood Island* (1958) and *The Lost Continent* (1968). Brought up in the Dutch East Indies, Schurmann eventually settled in Britain, where he became an assistant to the composer Alan Rawsthorne, for whom he orchestrated such film scores as *The Cruel Sea* (1953). Schurmann's other work as an orchestrator includes *The Vikings* (1958) for Mario Nascimbene, *Exodus* (1960) for Ernest Gold, and, most importantly, *Lawrence of Arabia* (1962) for Maurice Jarre. By this time, Schurmann had himself become a composer with a Dutch docu-drama *Broken Dykes* (1955). His first feature score was for *But Not in Vain* (1948), which he followed with *The*

*Long Arm* (1956), *Cone of Silence* (1960), *Dr. Syn—Alias the Scarecrow* (1963), *The Bedford Incident* (1965), *Attack on the Iron Coast* (1967), his music for which is augmented by cues from Ron Goodwin's score for *633 Squadron* (1964), *Claretta* (1984) and *The Gambler* (1997) among others. Meanwhile, his many concert works include *Variants* (1970), *The Double Heart* (1976) and *The Gardens of Exile* (1990).

Recalled Schurmann of his work on *The Lost Continent*: "[Michael Carreras] made a particular point of telling me it was Hammer Film's most lavish and expensive production to date, and that the score would need special care. Unfortunately, I was not free at the time owing to other musical commitments for concerts, and suggested therefore that in the circumstances he should ask another composer. However, after a little while, and for whatever reasons, he came back to me, having apparently decided not to go elsewhere, but to wait about six months until I was free. Well, this was truly amazing—a generous and most flattering offer, and I could of course do no less than graciously accept."[48] However, as the composer went on to reveal, "It was not until considerably later that I discovered that another score had already been written and recorded for the film and rejected."[49] As for his finished score he added, "The final mix in the film is indeed without doubt the worst overall it has ever been my misfortune to encounter as a composer!"[50] **Additional notes:** Schurmann also arranged the title song for *The Lost Continent*. This was composed by Roy Phillips and performed by The Peddlers. Elements of Schurmann's score for *The Lost Continent*, along with *Horrors of the Black Museum*, were re-used for his concert piece *Six Studies of Francis Bacon* (1968). **Hammer credits:** *The Camp on Blood Island* (1958), *The Lost Continent* (1968)

## Schuster, Hugo

British born Schuster (1908–1992) can be seen in a supporting role in Hammer's *Five Days* (1954). His other credits include *Hotel Reserve* (1944), *The Third Man* (1949), *Father Brown* (1954) and *The Blue Max* (1966), plus episodes of *Show Me a Spy* (1951, TV), *Out of the Unknown* (1965–1971, TV) and *The Prisoner* (1967–1968, TV). **Hammer credits:** *Five Days* (1954, as Professor)

## Schwinges, Albert

Schwinges worked as one of the production supervisors on Hammer's *The Lady Vanishes* (1979). His other credits in this capacity (usually as production manager) include *Ein Zug nach Manhattan* (1981), *Murder East—Murder West* (1990, TVM), on which he was also the line producer, *Sternzeichen* (2003), *Der Hafenpastor* (2013, TVM) and *Der Hafenpastor und das graue Kind* (2015, TVM). His credits as a producer include *B-52* (2001) and *Manner im gefahrlichen Alter* (2004, TVM). He also executive produced the TV series *Zur Sache, Lena!* (2008, TV) and line produced *Arnes Nachlass* (2013, TVM). **Hammer credits:** *The Lady Vanishes* (1979)

## Sciascia, Armando

Stock music by this Italian composer (1920–

2017, aka H. Tical), taken from a piece titled *Ultima Ora*, was used in Hammer's *Quatermass and the Pit* (1967). Sciascia's own film credits (among them a curious mix of sex documentaries, spaghetti westerns and horror films) include *Tropico di notte* (1961), *Sexy* (1962), *Metempsyco* (1963), *Per un dollaro a Tuscon si muore* (1964), *Europa: operazione streep-tease* (1964), *The Kinky Darlings* (1964), *L'uomo che brucio il suo cadavere* (1964) and *3 colpi di Winchester per Ringo* (1966). He also composed the theme tunes for such TV series as *Gli eroi di ieri, oggo, domani* (1964, TV) and *The Liars* (1966, TV). **Hammer credits:** *Quatermass and the Pit* (1967 [uncredited])

## Scoones, Ian

Long associated with Hammer, this British special effects technician (1940–2010) began his career (on the recommendation of Peter Cushing) as an assistant to Les Bowie, with whom he first worked on the Val Guest classic *The Day the Earth Caught Fire* (1961). He made his debut with Hammer (again as an assistant to Bowie) on *Taste of Fear* (1961), which led to a long run of films with the company. After his last feature for Hammer, *Quatermass and the Pit* (1967), Scoones returned to the company after a thirteen-year absence, this time as the head of effects for all thirteen episodes of *Hammer House of Horror* (1980, TV). His other credits include *1984* (1984), *Car Trouble* (1985), *Haunted Honeymoon* (1986), *A Prayer for the Dying* (1987) and *The Mystery of Edwin Drood* (1993), plus episodes of *Doctor Who* (1963–1989, TV), *Ripping Yarns* (1976–1979, TV), *Blakes 7* (1978–1981, TV) and *GBH* (1991, TV).

Recalled Scoones of his apprenticeship with the legendary Bowie, "Les would do most of his designing in the pub, thinking aloud and drawing on the bar with a finger dipped in spilt beer. I had to make a mental note of all these bar squiggles, translating them onto the back of Players cigarette packets."[51] Meanwhile, of Scoones himself, a *Sunday Times* reporter visiting the set of *Hammer House of Horror* observed that he was, "Dressed entirely in black except for a blood red shirt, he talks in a cultured drawl worthy of Boris Karloff, through a permanent veil of cigarette smoke. His sinister elegance upstages the lumpy human shape straining through the body bag behind him."[52] **Hammer credits:** *Taste of Fear* (1961, special effects assistant [uncredited]), *The Shadow of the Cat* (1961, special effects assistant [uncredited]), *The Phantom of the Opera* (1962, special effects assistant [uncredited]), *Captain Clegg* (1962, special effects assistant [uncredited]), *The Pirates of Blood River* (1962, special effects assistant [uncredited]), *Paranoiac* (1963, special effects assistant [uncredited]), *The Damned* (1963, special effects assistant [uncredited]), *The Scarlet Blade* (1963, special effects assistant [uncredited]), *The Kiss of the Vampire* (1963, special effects assistant [uncredited]), *The Old Dark House* (1963, special effects assistant [uncredited]), *Nightmare* (1964, special effects assistant [uncredited]), *The Evil of Frankenstein* (1964, special effects assistant [uncredited]), *The Devil-Ship Pirates* (1964, special effects assistant [uncredited]), *She* (1965, special effects assistant [uncredited]), *One Million Years B.C.* (1966, special effects assistant [uncredited]), *Frankenstein Created Woman* (1967, special effects assistant [uncredited]), *The Mummy's Shroud* (1967, special effects assistant [uncredited]), *Quatermass and the Pit* (1967, special effects assistant [uncredited]), *Hammer House of Horror* (1980, TV, special effects)

*Scotland Yard Inspector* see *Lady in the Fog*

### Scott, A.G.

Scott (full name Alfred G. Scott) worked as the hair stylist on Hammer's *The Nanny* (1965), on which he coiffed the film's legendary Hollywood star, Bette Davis. He obviously did a good job, as he was invited back to perform the same duties on *The Anniversary* (1968). His other credits include *The Ghosts of Berkeley Square* (1947), *Yield to the Night* (1956), *Exodus* (1960), *Lawrence of Arabia* (1962), *The Lion in Winter* (1968), *Ryan's Daughter* (1970) and *The Mackintosh Man* (1973). **Hammer credits:** *The Nanny* (1965), *The Anniversary* (1968)

### Scott, Alex

This British actor (1929–2015) played the role of Hermann in Hammer's *Twins of Evil* (1971). His other credits include *Ricochet* (1963), *The Sicilians* (1964), *Darling* (1965), *Fahrenheit 451* (1966), *The Abominable Dr. Phibes* (1971), *The Asphyx* (1973) and *A Shocking Accident* (1982), plus much television work, including episodes of *London Playhouse* (1955–1956, TV), *Martin Chuzzlewit* (1964, TV) and *Hazell* (1978–1979, TV). He moved to Australia in the eighties where he continued his career with *Now and Forever* (1983), *Sky Pirates* (1983) and *Romper Stomper* (1992). **Hammer credits:** *Twins of Evil* (1971, as Hermann)

### Scott, Ann

Scott played a bit role in Hammer's *The Terror of the Tongs* (1961). **Hammer credits:** *The Terror of the Tongs* (1961, as Girl [uncredited])

### Scott, Avis

This British actress (1918–2010, real name Avis Scutt) played the leading role of June Harding in the Hammer romantic melodrama *To Have and to Hold* (1951), in which her dying husband attempts to secure her future happiness by matchmaking her with his divorced friend. She also had a supporting role in *Five Days* (1954). Her other credits include *Millions Like Us* (1943), *Brief Encounter* (1945), *Waterfront* (1950), *Emergency Call* (1952) and *Storm Over the Nile* (1955), plus episodes of *Douglas Fairbanks, Jr. Presents* (1953–1957, TV) and *Saber of London* (1954–1960, TV). **Hammer credits:** *To Have and to Hold* (1951, as June Harding), *Five Days* (1954, as Eileen)

### Scott, Carolyn

Scott worked as the designer on all thirteen episodes of *Hammer House of Horror* (1980, TV), making frequent use of the series' production base, Hampden Hall, for both interior and exterior locations. She also worked on ten episodes of *Hammer House of Mystery and Suspense* (1984, TVM).

Her other credits as an art director include *George and Mildred* (1980), *Killer's Moon* (1982), *Claudia* (1985) and *The I Inside* (2004), while her work as an assistant art director/designer includes *Rising Damp* (1980) and *God's Outlaw* (1986). She also worked as a set decorator on *The Scarlett Pimpernel* (1982, TVM), which earned her a shared Emmy nomination, *The Madness of King George* (1994), which won her a shared Oscar, *Some Mother's Son* (1996) and *Face* (1997). **Hammer credits:** *Hammer House of Horror* (1980, TV), *Czech Mate* (1984, TVM [episode of *Hammer House of Mystery and Suspense*]), *The Sweet Scent of Death* (1984, TVM [episode of *Hammer House of Mystery and Suspense*]), *A Distant Scream* (1984, TVM [episode of *Hammer House of Mystery and Suspense*]), *The Late Nancy Irving* (1984, TVM [episode of *Hammer House of Mystery and Suspense*]), *In Possession* (1984, TVM [episode of *Hammer House of Mystery and Suspense*]), *Black Carrion* (1984, TVM [episode of *Hammer House of Mystery and Suspense*]), *Last Video and Testament* (1984, TVM [episode of *Hammer House of Mystery and Suspense*]), *Mark of the Devil* (1984, TVM [episode of *Hammer House of Mystery and Suspense*]), *The Corvini Inheritance* (1984, TVM [episode of *Hammer House of Mystery and Suspense*]), *Paint Me a Murder* (1984, TVM [episode of *Hammer House of Mystery and Suspense*])

### Scott, Gordon L.T.

Following experience as a production manager on *The Weak and the Wicked* (1955), *The Dam Busters* (1955) and *It's Great to Be Young!* (1956), British (Scottish) Scott (1920–1991) turned his hand to producing. Among his credits are *Look Back in Anger* (1959), *The Pot Carriers* (1963), *Crooks in Cloisters* (1963), *Friend or Foe* (1982) and *Out of the Darkness* (1985). He also produced two Charlie Drake vehicles: *Sands of the Desert* (1960) and *Petticoat Pirates* (1961), the first of which was partially financed by Hammer. His work as an associate producer includes *Mr. Forbush and the Penguins* (1971), *The Maids* (1974) and *Nasty Habits* (1976), while his work as an executive producer includes *Hanover Street* (1979). He began his career as a second assistant director on *Frieda* (1947), and worked his way up to first assistant on the likes of *Passport to Pimlico* (1949), *Laughter in Paradise* (1951) and *Rob Roy: The Highland Rogue* (1953). He was also the executive in charge of production on thirty-three episodes of *The Avengers* (1961–1969, TV) between 1968 and 1969. **Hammer credits:** *Sands of the Desert* (1960)

### Scott, Harold

This British character actor (1891–1964) can be seen as the Lang School's stableman Severin in Hammer's *The Brides of Dracula* (1960), in which he spends a couple of minutes whittering on about horse brasses. No wonder Marianne Danielle is keen to get rid of him. His other credits include *The Water Gypsies* (1932), *Return of a Stranger* (1937), *Edward, My Son* (1949), *The Spanish Gardener* (1956), *The Hand* (1960), *The Young Ones* (1961), *The Man Who Finally Died* (1962) and *The Yellow Rolls-Royce* (1964), plus episodes of *The*

*Children of the New Forest* (1955, TV), *Dixon of Dock Green* (1955–1976, TV) and *Maigret* (1960–1963, TV). Also on stage. **Hammer credits:** *The Brides of Dracula* (1960, as Severin [uncredited])

### Scott, Janette

In films from the age of four with *Went the Day Well?* (1942), this British child star (1938–, full name Thora Janette Scott) had her greatest success with the divorce drama *No Place for Jennifer* (1949). Her career as a teenager and adult includes appearances in *The Magic Box* (1951), *The Good Companions* (1956), *School for Scoundrels* (1959), *The Day of the Triffids* (1962), *The Beauty Jungle* (1964), *Crack in the World* (1965) and *Bikini Paradise* (1967), after which she retired from the screen following her marriage to the second of her three husbands, the American singer-actor Mel Tormé (1925–1999, full name Melvin Howard Tormé), to whom she was married between 1966 and 1977.

Scott starred in two films for Hammer: their long-delayed thriller *Paranoiac* (1963) and their ill-fated remake of *The Old Dark House* (1963), the latter of which was made first but released second. Recalled the actress of her work in *The Old Dark House*, "[It] came along when I was getting absolutely sugary-sweet in the parts I was playing. I absolutely loved it. Even though I was sweet and charming again, in the end, everyone was going to find out that I did it! To all of them!"[53] However, the actress admitted that, "The original version of *The Old Dark House* was a much better film than our remake. Ours wasn't funny enough. It fell between two stools."[54]

According to the actress, she and her leading man got pretty close during the making of her second film for Hammer. Said Scott, "When we were making *Paranoiac* together, Oliver Reed, as my mother would say, got it bad and he decided I was the only woman for him. So he was rather sweet, and would come to visit me at home on the weekends."[55] Of Scott's performance in *Paranoiac* (1963), *Variety* commented, "Janette Scott is pretty and disarming as the sister and emotes credibly."

Scott's mother was the actress Thora Hird (1911–2003), who appeared in four films for Hammer: *The Quatermass Xperiment* (1955), *Women Without Men* (1956), *Clean Sweep* (1958) and *Further Up the Creek* (1958). Her first husband was the television host and songwriter Jackie Ray (1922–2006, real name John Arthur Rae), to whom she was married between 1959 and 1965. Her children (with Tormé) are the actress and singer Daisy Tormé (1969–) and the songwriter James Tormé (1973–); her former step-children are the actor Steve March (1953–, real name Steve Michael Tormé), the actress Melissa Tormé-March (1955–) and the writer Tracy Tormé (1959–).

Scott returned to television in 1997 for an uncredited cameo in an episode of *Last of the Summer Wine* (1973–2010, TV), in which her mother was appearing at the time; she also later had a small role in *How to Lose Friends & Alienate People* (2008). **Hammer credits:** *Paranoiac* (1963, as Eleanor Ashby), *The Old Dark House* (1963, as Cecily Femm)

## Scott, J.D.

Scott penned the screenplay for the Hammer medical short *Danger List* (1957). **Hammer credits:** *Danger List* (1957)

## Scott, John

Following experience as a music arranger for a number of pop groups and top solo artists in the sixties (among them The Hollies, Tom Jones and Cilla Black), this prolific British composer and conductor (1930–, real name Patrick John O'Hara Scott) began writing film music in 1965 with *A Study in Terror*. He went on to score a wide variety of productions in both Britain and America during his career, among them *Rocket to the Moon* (1967), *Trog* (1970), *Antony and Cleopatra* (1972), *Billy Two Hats* (1973), *Symptoms* (1974), *The People That Time Forgot* (1977), *The Final Countdown* (1980), *King Kong Lives* (1986), *Black Rainbow* (1989) *The Scarlet Tunic* (1998), *Shergar* (1999), *Time of the Wolf* (2002) and *The Wicker Tree* (2011). Also busy in television, his many credits here include two episodes of Hammer's *Journey to the Unknown* (1968, TV). These were *The New People*, which also appeared in the compendium film *Journey into Darkness* (1968, TVM), and *Do Me a Favor and Kill Me*, which also appeared in the compendium film *Journey to Murder* (1972, TVM). **Hammer credits:** *The New People* (1968, TV [episode of *Journey to the Unknown*]), *Do Me a Favor and Kill Me* (1968, TV [episode of *Journey to the Unknown*]), *Journey into Darkness* (1968, TVM), *Journey to Murder* (1972, TVM)

## Scott, John Patrick *see* Scott, John

## Scott, Karin

This Australian actress (1957–, aka Anna Scott, Anna Simone Scott and Kerry Anne Scott) can be seen in a minor supporting role in *Growing Pains* (1980, TV [episode of *Hammer House of Horror*]). Her early credits in her homeland include *The Golden Cage* (1975) and *Scobie Malone* (1975). On stage and in films and television in both Britain and America, her other credits include periods in the U.S. soaps *Another World* (1964–1999, TV) in 1988 and *Days of Our Lives* (1965–, TV) in 1992. Her film credits include *The Last Marxist* (1994), *Philosophy in the Bedroom* (1995) and *Late Night Girls* (2006). Her credits as a writer include *The Red Scarf* (2006) and *Chasing Chekhov* (2008), in both of which she appeared, the latter being based upon her play. She also produced *Coming into Money* (1998), which she also wrote and appeared in. Her husband is the actor, writer, producer, director and location manager Peter Sands. **Hammer credits:** *Growing Pains* (1980, TV [episode of *Hammer House of Horror*], as Nurse)

## Scott, Kathryn Leigh

Familiar to U.S. television viewers for the series *Dark Shadows* (1966–1971, TV), in which she played Maggie Evans, this prolific American actress (1943–, real name Kathryn Kringstad) also guested in such series as *Marked Personal* (1973–1974, TV), *Space: 1999* (1975–1979, TV), *Hammer House of Horror* (1980, TV), *Dallas* (1978–1991, TV), *Philip Marlowe, Private Eye* (1983–1984, TV), *Paradise* (1988–1990, TV) and *Huff* (2004–2006, TV). Her films include *House of Dark Shadows* (1970), in which she again played Maggie Evans, *The Great Gatsby* (1974), *Brannigan* (1975), *Witches' Brew* (1980), *Assassination* (1987), *One Eight Seven* (1997), *Parasomnia* (2008), *Dark Shadows* (2012), in which she had a cameo, and *Three Christs* (2017). **Hammer credits:** *Visitor from the Grave* (1980, TV [episode of *Hammer House of Horror*], as Penny Van Bruten)

## Scott, Kevin

Long in Britain, this American supporting actor (1928–) played had a minor role in the Hammer thriller *Visa to Canton* (1960). His other credits include *Floods of Fear* (1959), *Call Me Bwana* (1962), *The Cool Mikado* (1963), *The Mouse on the Moon* (1963), *2001: A Space Odyssey* (1968), *The Pink Panther Strikes Again* (1976), *Supergirl* (1984) and *Little Shop of Horrors* (1986), plus episodes of *International Detective* (1959–1961, TV), *The Saint* (1962–1969, TV) and *The Troubleshooters* (1965–1972, TV). Also on stage. **Hammer credits:** *Visa to Canton* (1960, unnamed role [uncredited])

## Scott, Lizabeth

In films from 1945 with *You Came Along*, this glamorous American actress (1922–2015, real name Emma Matzo) began her career on stage, and at one point understudied Tallulah Bankhead in the Broadway run of *The Skin of Our Teeth* before eventually taking over the role herself. She went on to make more than twenty movies during her career, among them *The Strange Case of Martha Ivers* (1946), *Scared Stiff* (1953), *Loving You* (1957) and *Pulp* (1972). One of her best performances was in the Hammer second feature *Stolen Face* (1952), in which she played both a glamorous concert pianist and a convict whose features are altered by a plastic surgeon to resemble those of the pianist's. Commented *Variety* of her performance, "Miss Scott has a dual assignment ... and she is capable enough in both, considering the heavy-handed, slow direction by Terence Fisher." Recalled Jimmy Sangster of Scott: "[She] astounded me on the first day of shooting by telling me she wouldn't be available Wednesday or Thursday because she was due for a period. I remember asking her 'A period of what?' I was very naïve in those days."[56] Scott's television appearances include episodes of *Lux Video Theatre* (1950–1959, TV), *Studio 57* (1954–1956, TV) and *Burke's Law* (1963–1966, TV). **Hammer credits:** *Stolen Face* (1952, as Alice Brent/Lily Conover)

## Scott, Margaretta

On stage from 1929 following training at RADA, this distinguished British actress (1912–2005) began her film career in 1934 with *The Private Life of Don Juan*. Although she spent the majority of her career in the theater, her film credits include a number of choice titles, among them *Things to Come* (1936), *The Return of the Scarlet Pimpernel* (1937), *Fanny by Gaslight* (1944), *Where's Charley?* (1952) and *The Scamp* (1957), while her television credits include episodes of *Elizabeth R* (1971, TV) and *All Creatures Great and Small* (1978–1980, TV), in which she played Mrs. Pumphrey. She also appeared in the Hammer thriller *Crescendo* (1970) as Danielle Ryman. However, it should be noted that the original casting choice was Flora Robson, who lost the role when the film's production company changed from Compton to Hammer. Scott's husband was the composer-conductor John Wooldridge (1919–1958), whom she married in 1948. Her daughter is the actress Susan Wooldridge (1950–) and her son is the theater director Hugh Wooldridge (1952–). **Hammer credits:** *Crescendo* (1970, as Danielle Ryman)

## Scott, Michelle

Scott played the girl terrorized by a body snatcher and Baron Frankenstein in the pre-credits sequence of *The Evil of Frankenstein* (1964). Her other credits include *Dr. Who and the Daleks* (1965) and episodes of *The First Lady* (1968–1969, TV), *The Basil Brush Show* (1968–1980, TV) and *Churchill's People* (1975, TV). **Hammer credits:** *The Evil of Frankenstein* (1964, as Girl [uncredited])

## Scott, Peter Graham

Following experience as a child actor in such films as *Young and Innocent* (1937) and *Pastor Hall* (1940), this British director (1923–2007) turned to the technical side of filmmaking, first training as an editor. Among the films he cut were *It Began on the Clyde* (1946), *Brighton Rock* (1947), *The Perfect Woman* (1949), *Landfall* (1949), *Shadow of the Eagle* (1950) and *Never Take No for an Answer* (1952). He made his directorial debut in 1948 with *Panic at Madame Tussaud's*, which was distributed by Exclusive, and which led to such projects as *Sudan Dispute* (1947), which he also produced, *Sing Along with Me* (1952) and *Escape Route* (1952), the latter of which he co-directed with Seymour Friedman. In television from 1953 as a director with *Our Marie*, he went on to become a noted producer, working on such series and one-offs as *The Citadel* (1960, TV), *The Onedin Line* (1970–1973, TV), which earned him a BAFTA nomination for best drama series, and *The Canterville Ghost* (1986, TV), while his directorial credits took in episodes of *The Avengers* (1961–1969, TV) and *Danger Man* (1960–1968, TV).

In the fifties he also helmed a number of low budget second features for the producer Paul Temple-Smith, among them *The Hideout* (1956), *Account Rendered* (1957) and *The Big Chance* (1957). Scott also directed the Hammer pirate yarn *Captain Clegg* (1962) for Temple-Smith, to which he brought several brisk visual touches. Recalled Scott of the film's involved pre-production, "John Temple-Smith turned up with the script of *Dr. Syn* as made in 1936 with George Arliss. We'd signed Peter Cushing and Oliver Reed when all of a sudden Disney announced they had bought the rights to the *novel* of *Dr. Syn* and we realized we'd only bought the rights to the Gaumont-British script of *Dr. Syn*. But we had acquired it in good faith, so Disney said, 'Call it something else,' and we called it *Captain Clegg*. We made it in five weeks and it's one of the best films I ever made."[57] Remembered Temple-Smith of Scott, "I made four films with Peter and enjoyed working with him more than any other director. I learned a tremendous amount from him. We worked very closely together. When we were making *Captain Clegg* we pushed the boundaries out beyond what people thought we would be able to do. We got much more into that film than anybody thought we could with the time and money available."[58]

Scott's many other credits as a director include *Devil's Bait* (1959), *The Big Day* (1960), *Father Came Too* (1963), *The Cracksman* (1963) and *Subterfuge* (1968), plus episodes of *The Avengers* (1961–1969, TV) and *Follow Me* (1977, TV), both of which he produced. **Hammer credits:** *Captain Clegg* (1962)

### Scott, Richard

Scott can be seen as a Satanist in Hammer's *The Devil Rides Out* (1968). His other credits include episodes of *ITV Play of the Week* (1955–1958, TV), *Deadline Midnight* (1960–1961, TV) and *The Morecambe and Wise Show* (1968–1977, TV). **Hammer credits:** *The Devil Rides Out* (1968 [uncredited])

### Scott, Sherman *see* Newfield, Sam

### Scott, Stephen W. (Walter)

This British bit player (1928–) can be spotted as a farmer in Hammer's *The Curse of the Werewolf* (1961). His other credits include *The Flesh and the Fiends* (1960), plus episodes of *BBC Sunday-Night Theatre* (1950–1959, TV), *Quatermass II* (1955, TV), *The Infamous John Friend* (1959, TV) and *The Scarf* (1959, TV). **Hammer credits:** *The Curse of the Werewolf* (1961, as Farmer [uncredited])

### Scott, Steven

This British supporting actor (1920–1981) played Walters in the Hammer shocker *The Stranglers of Bombay* (1959). His other credits include *Look Back in Anger* (1959), *Make Mine Mink* (1960), *Guns of Darkness* (1962), *Sammy Going South* (1963), *That Riviera Touch* (1966) and *Carry On ... Up the Khyber* (1968), plus a walk-on role in Hammer's *The Terror of the Tongs* (1961). Also busy in television, his credits here include episodes of *Ivanhoe* (1958 -1959, TV), *The Avengers* (1961–1969, TV), *The Jazz Age* (1968, TV) and *Churchill's People* (1975, TV). **Hammer credits:** *The Stranglers of Bombay* (1959, as Walters), *The Terror of the Tongs* (1961, unnamed role [uncredited])

### Scott, Zachary

This American actor (1914–1965) actually began his career on stage in Britain, though it was back home in America that he found stardom on the screen, where villainous roles became something of a standby, among them his memorable turn as Monty Beragon in *Mildred Pierce* (1945). He made his film debut in 1944 with *The Mask of Dimitrios*, and went on to appear in over thirty films before he was struck down with a brain tumour, among them *The Southerner* (1945), *Flamingo Road* (1949) and *It's Only Money* (1962). In 1952, he was contracted to appear in the Hammer thriller *Wings of Danger*, in which he played Richard Van Ness, a pilot who investigates a smuggling ring. Recalled continuity girl Renee Glynne of the visiting

Hollywood star, "I adored Zachary Scott; velvet voice, velvet personality."[59] Scott's TV work includes episodes of *Pulitzer Prize Playhouse* (1950–1952, TV), *Your Show of Shows* (1950–1954, TV) and *The Rogues* (1964–1965, TV). Married twice, his wives were the actresses Elaine Anderson (1914–2003), to whom he was married between 1935 and 1950, and Ruth Ford (1911–2009), whom he married in 1952. **Hammer credits:** *Wings of Danger* (1952, as Richard Van Ness)

### *Scottish Symphony*

GB, 1946, 38m, bw, cert U

Little information is available about this documentary short, apparently a travelogue about the beauties of Scotland, which was distributed in the UK by Exclusive, who also co-financed the film with the Federated Film Corporation.

Production companies: Exclusive/Federated Film Corporation. Distributor: Exclusive (UK). Producer: Harold Baim. Director: Harold Baim. Screenplay: Edward Eve. Cinematographer: Lou Burger. **Cast:** James McKechnie (Commentator), George Strachan (Commentator)

### Scott-James, Shirli

Scott-James can be seen as one of the Sphinx Girls in Hammer's *The Two Faces of Dr. Jekyll* (1960). Her other credits include *The Entertainer* (1960). **Hammer credits:** *The Two Faces of Dr. Jekyll* (1960, as Sphinx Girl [uncredited])

### Scoular, Christopher

This British (Scottish) actor (1945–2014) can be seen as Truscott in *Last Video and Testament* (1984, TVM [episode of *Hammer House of Mystery and Suspense*]). His other TV credits include episodes of *Softly Softly* (1966–1976, TV), *Maggie and Her* (1976–1979, TV), *Hannay* (1988–1989, TV), *The Knock* (1994–2000, TV) and *Ladies of Letters* (2009–2010, TV), while his occasional films include *An American Werewolf in London* (1981) and *Until Death* (2002). Also on stage. **Hammer credits:** *Last Video and Testament* (1984, TVM [episode of *Hammer House of Mystery and Suspense*], as Truscott)

### Screen Gems

A subsidiary of Columbia Pictures, Screen Gems was behind Hammer's aborted television series *Tales of Frankenstein* (1958, TV), of which only the pilot episode, *The Face in the Tombstone Mirror*, was filmed. Despite the failure of this series, it didn't prevent Hammer from pitching further ideas to Screen Gems. These were the Africa-set *Safari* in 1961 (for which Michael Carreras scouted locations), and, in 1967, *Hell Is a City*, which was to have been based on the studio's 1960 film. Other series produced by the company include *Father Knows Best* (1954–1960, TV), *Dennis the Menace* (1959–1963, TV), *Route 66* (1960–1964, TV) and *I Dream of Jeannie* (1965–1970, TV). The company is also involved in distribution and, since the late nineties, feature production, among its credits being such films as *Arlington Road* (1999), *The Cave* (2005), *Not Easily Broken* (2009) and *The Wedding Ringer* (2015). **Hammer credits:** *Tales of*

*Frankenstein: The Face in the Tombstone Mirror* (1958, TV)

### Scrivener, Ken

Born in India, Scrivener (1919–2006) worked as the dubbing mixer two episodes of *Hammer House of Horror* (1980, TV). His other TV credits, either as recordist or mixer, include episodes of *The Professionals* (1977–1983, TV), *Return of the Saint* (1978–1979, TV), *Reilly: Ace of Spies* (1983, TV), which earned him a shared BAFTA nomination, and *Robin of Sherwood* (1984–1986, TV), while his many film credits include *The Eighty Days* (1944), *Life in Her Hands* (1951), *Privilege* (1967), *Run Wild, Run Free* (1969), *Conduct Unbecoming* (1975), *It Lives Again* (1978), *Savage Hunt* (1980), *Xtro* (1983) and *Prisoners of the Lost Universe* (1983). His son is the dubbing mixer Rupert Scrivener and his grandson is re-recording mixer Adam Scrivener (1981–). **Hammer credits:** *Witching Time* (1980, TV [episode of *Hammer House of Horror*]), *The Thirteenth Reunion* (1980, TV [episode of *Hammer House of Horror*])

### Scully, Terry

This British actor (1932–2001) can be seen as Dick Tate in Hammer's *Captain Clegg* (1962). His other credits include *The Projected Man* (1966), *Night After Night After Night* (1969), *Goodbye Gemini* (1970) and *The Asphyx* (1973). Busy in television, his many credits here include episodes of *An Age of Kings* (1960, TV), in which he played Henry VI, *Softly Softly* (1966–1976, TV), *Survivors* (1975–1977, TV), in which he played Vic Thatcher, and *Angels* (1975–1983, TV). Also on stage. **Hammer credits:** *Captain Clegg* (1962, as Dick Tate)

### Seabourne John, Sr.

This British editor (1890–?) cut the early Hammer shocker *The Mystery of the Mary Celeste* (1936). His other credits include *The Man Without a Face* (1935), *Sweeney Todd: The Demon Barber of Fleet Street* (1936), *The Crimes of Stephen Hawke* (1936), *Under a Cloud* (1937), *The Volunteer* (1943), *The Wooden Horse* (1950), *A King in New York* (1957) and *In the Wake of a Stranger* (1959), plus several for Powell and Pressburger, among them *Contraband* (1940), *The Life and Death of Colonel Blimp* (1943), *A Canterbury Tale* (1944) and *I Know Where I'm Going* (1945). He also worked as the associate director on *One of Our Aircraft Is Missing* (1942), again for Powell and Pressburger. His sons are editor, producer and director John Seabourne, Jr., and editor, director and producer Peter Seabourne (1923–2005). **Hammer credits:** *The Mystery of the Mary Celeste* (1936)

### Seagrove, Jenny

Born in Malaya (now Malaysia), this actress (1957–) came to attention as the scullery maid turned-businesswoman Emma Harte in the blockbusting mini series *A Woman of Substance* (1985, TV) and its sequel, *Hold the Dream* (1986, TV). Her film credits (among them several for her former partner, director Michael Winner) include *Moonlighting* (1982), *Local Hero* (1983), *Appointment with Death* (1988), *A Chorus of Disapproval* (1989), *Bullseye!* (1990), *The Guardian* (1990),

*Don't Go Breaking My Heart* (1998), *Zoe* (2001) and *Run for Your Wife* (2012). A frequent guest star on television, her credits here include an episode of *Hammer House of Mystery and Suspense* (1984, TVM). She is more recently known for playing Jo Mills in *Judge John Deed* (2001–2007, TV). Also much on stage, including tours and the West End. She was married to the actor Madhav Sharma between 1984 and 1988. Her partner is theater producer Bill Kenwright (1945–). **Hammer credits:** *Mark of the Devil* (1984, TVM [episode of *Hammer House of Mystery and Suspense*], as Sarah Helston)

### Seal, Elizabeth

Following training at the Royal Academy of Dancing, this Italian born actress (1933–) made her London stage debut in 1951. In films from 1954 with *Radio Cab Murder*, her other credits include *Town on Trial* (1956), in which she was officially introduced, *Cone of Silence* (1960), Hammer's *Vampire Circus* (1972), in which she played Gerta Hauser, *Mack the Knife* (1990) and *Lara Croft Tomb Raider: The Cradle of Life* (2003). Her television work includes episodes of *Z Cars* (1962–1978, TV), *Softly Softly* (1966–1976, TV), *Trelawney of the Wells* (1971, TV) and *Doctors* (2000–, TV), though it is on stage that she has had her greatest triumphs, among them the title role in the musical *Irma La Douce*, which she played in London in 1958 and on Broadway in 1960, winning a Tony in the process. Her husband was the photographer Michael Ward (1929–2011), whom she married in 1976, and who, as Lawrence Ward, appeared in Hammer's *The Last Page* (1952). **Hammer credits:** *Vampire Circus* (1972, as Gerta Hauser)

### Searle, Francis

Working almost exclusively in second features, this prolific British writer, director and producer (1909–2002) began his film career in 1935 following experience in advertising as a layout artist. Working as a set dresser, editor, assistant director and prop buyer at Highbury Studios, he went on to make shorts for the *Cinemagazine* series in 1936. He began making documentaries in 1939 with *War Without End* and made his feature debut with *Girl in a Million* in 1946. Following his second feature length film, *Things Happen at Night* (1949), Searle became a resident director for Hammer, helming nine films within the space of three years for the company, beginning with the comedy thriller *Celia* (1949), which he also co-scripted. Like most Hammer product of this period, the films were mostly routine program fillers, though some, such as *Cloudburst* (1951), were more tolerable than most, and featured imported American stars such as Robert Preston.

Recalled Searle of his period with Hammer, "They'd seen my stuff and, as they were on the up, wanting to do better, I was invited to join them. That was my first experience of shooting in houses rather than in a studio, and that was a real problem to me—no floating walls and staircases here. We coped, but it was a real challenge."[60] Given the circumstances of shooting in somewhere like Oakley Court, the trade paper *The Cinema Studio* noted that Searle had a "scale plan showing each individ-

ual set up and camera plot; this is exhibited on the set for all to see and facilitates rapid change-overs." He also insisted on read-throughs prior to shooting: "So as not to meet up cold on the set, we had read-throughs for the artists at Hammer House. You had to instill a feeling of professionalism into the thing, rather than having people just walk into rooms at Cookham or Bray and say to themselves, 'Oh, Christ—is this a picture or what?' Sometimes the read-throughs were very useful: if somebody turned out not to be right, I'd change the artist."[61]

During his tenure with Hammer, Searle never actually signed a contract. "There was a gentlemen's understanding and it wasn't until the horror films got going, which I couldn't take to, that the pace slowed for me."[62] As for his dealings with James Carreras and Tony Hinds, Searle remembered, "He was a great salesman, was Jim, bit of a villain but I loved him. He very seldom came to the studio—he didn't want to get involved as long as the stuff on the screen looked all right. Tony Hinds didn't interfere either. He was very sympathetic—a clever bloke and very easy to work with. He was particularly good at vetting scripts and so on."[63]

Searle's many other credits as a director include *Love's a Luxury* (1952), *One Way Out* (1955), which he shot at Bray for producer John Temple-Smith's film company Major, *The Gelignite Gang* (1956), *Emergency* (1962), which he also produced, *Night of the Prowler* (1962) and *The Marked One* (1963), while in the mid-sixties/early seventies he made a number of shorts, among them *Miss MacTaggart Won't Lie Down* (1966), *It All Goes to Show* (1969), *The Pale Faced Girl* (1969), *A Hole Lot of Trouble* (1970) and *A Couple of Beauties* (1973), all of which he also produced. His other work as a producer includes *Stolen Assignment* (1955), which he produced for director Terence Fisher and ACT Films at Bray, and *The Diplomatic Corpse* (1958). Searle also made a dramatic short, *Day of Grace* (1957), for Hammer, while his thriller *Murder at Site 3* (1959) was the last feature to be distributed by Exclusive for fifty years. **Hammer credits:** *Celia* (1949, director, co-screenplay), *The Man in Black* (1950, director, story), *Someone at the Door* (1950, director), *The Lady Craved Excitement* (1950, director, co-screenplay), *The Rossiter Case* (1951, director, co-screenplay), *A Case for PC 49* (1951, director), *Cloudburst* (1951, director, co-screenplay), *Whispering Smith Hits London* (1952, director), *Never Look Back* (1952, director, co-screenplay), *Day of Grace* (1957, producer, director, co-screenplay)

### Searle, Humphrey

Best known for scoring *The Haunting* (1963), this British composer (1915–1982) was brought in by Hammer's music director John Hollingsworth to write the music for *The Abominable Snowman* (1957), which makes atmospheric use of a variety of gongs and bells in the *Main Title* cue. Trained in London and Vienna, Searle's other film scores include *The Baby and the Battleship* (1956), *Action of the Tiger* (1957), *Left Right and Centre* (1959), *October Moth* (1960) and *The Tide of Traffic* (1972). He also penned scores for episodes of *Doctor Who* (1963–1989, TV), *Theatre 625* (1964–

1968, TV) and *Oresteia* (1979, TV). He also wrote operas, among them *Diary of a Madman* (1958), ballets and pieces for the concert platform, including symphonies and piano concertos. **Hammer credits:** *The Abominable Snowman* (1957)

### Searle, Pamela

This British actress and pageant queen (1943–) played one of the many harem girls in the Hammer comedy *I Only Arsked!* (1958). Her other credits include *Operation Bullshine* (1959) plus episodes of *Dial 999* (1958–1959, TV) and *Glencannon* (1959, TV). She was Miss England in 1959, and went on to be the third runner up in the subsequent Miss Universe contest, in which she was also named Miss Photogenic. She went on to appear in a couple of films in America—*Bells Are Ringing* (1960) and *If a Man Answers* (1962)—as well as episodes of *Bachelor Father* (1957–1962, TV), *Thriller* (1960–1962, TV), *Route 66* (1960–1964, TV) and *Ensign O'Toole* (1962–1963, TV). Her magazine covers include *Blighty Parade* (in April 1959). **Hammer credits:** *I Only Arsked!* (1958, as Harem girl [uncredited])

### Sears, Heather

A best actress BAFTA winner for her performance in *The Story of Esther Costello* (1957), this British leading lady (1935–1994) began her film career in the mid-fifties with *Touch and Go* (1955) following stage experience in rep. In 1962 she played Christine Charles, the female lead in Hammer's remake of *The Phantom of the Opera* (1962), although her singing was dubbed by Patricia Clark. Her other credits include *Dry Rot* (1956), *Room at the Top* (1958), *Sons and Lovers* (1960), *The Black Torment* (1964) and *Great Expectations* (1975, TVM), plus episodes of *The Informer* (1966–1967, TV), *The Main Chance* (1969–1975, TV) and *Tales of the Unexpected* (1979–1988, TV), following which she spent the remainder of her career on stage. Her sister was the actress Ann Sears (1933–1992). Her husband was art director Tony Masters (1919–1990), whom she married in 1957, and who designed Hammer's *The Full Treatment* (1961). **Hammer credits:** *The Phantom of the Opera* (1962, as Christine Charles)

### *The Secret of Blood Island*

GB, 1965, 84m, Eastmancolor, RCA, cert X

In this somewhat belated (not to mention unrelated) follow up to *The Camp on Blood Island* (1958), British prisoners of war at the notorious Malayan detention camp attempt to hide a female British agent who has inadvertently parachuted into the place after her plane has been shot down. Once inside the camp, she has to convince the guards that she is just another of the many male prisoners, who meanwhile conspire to smuggle her away….

As with its predecessor, *The Secret of Blood Island* offers a potent blend of action and sadism, with Bill Owen's George Bludgin living up to his name by being bludgeoned to death at one point. Elsewhere, the cast features a number of names from the previous film—albeit in different roles—among them Lee Montague, Michael Ripper, Edwin Richfield and Barbara Shelley, the latter of whom plays the role of Elaine, the secret agent. Jack Hedley meanwhile takes top billing as Sergeant Crewe, who leads the effort to keep her presence hidden from the Japanese guards, among them the ruthless commandant Major Jacomo, played by Patrick Wymark. As with the previous film, all the main Japanese characters are played by British actors sporting epicanthic folds above their eyes, prompting *Variety* to comment, "Among the Japanese roles … there isn't a convincing performance in the group. Particularly bad is Patrick Wymark, with ludicrous make-up that is of no help"

Shot between 23 July and 7 September 1964 at Pinewood and on "location" at Black Park (where the camp was erected), the movie saw the final return to Hammer of legendary lighting cameraman Jack Asher, whose painstaking methods were now at distinct odds with the company's increasingly cost-conscious approach to filming. Based on an original screenplay by Hammer regular John Gilling, the production was helmed by Quentin Lawrence, who'd previously directed the well-regarded character piece *Cash on Demand* (1961) for the studio. Unfortunately, his handling of the material here is disappointingly routine, despite the brutalities ("The most savage drama of the world's most savage war!" exclaimed the poster). In fact, the film is more often sluggish when it should be nail biting.

The movie was trade shown at the Rank Theater on 13 May 1965. Although a popular enough attraction in Britain when released by Rank on the ABC circuit on a double bill with *The Night Walker* (1965) on 14 June, the film had proved to be a hard sell for Universal upon its earlier Stateside release in April of the same year. International sales also proved difficult. This apparently had something to do with the fact that the Japanese government, not happy with the film's content, had managed to instigate a series of embargoes on the film in certain territories, just as it had done on its predecessor in 1958. Astonishingly, despite their track record with Universal—remember, *Dracula* (1958) had apparently saved the Hollywood giant—*The Secret of Blood Island* consequently brought an end to Hammer's association with the company. So much for gratitude! **Additional notes:** The credits mistakenly bill Marcus Dods as Marcus Dodds.

Production company: Hammer. Distributors: Rank (UK [ABC circuit]), Universal International (U.S.). Producer: Anthony Nelson Keys. Director: Quentin Lawrence. Screenplay: John Gilling. Cinematographer: Jack Asher. Music: James Bernard. Music director: Marcus Dods. Supervising editor: James Needs. Editor: Tom Simpson. Production design: Bernard Robinson. Costumes: Jean Fairlie. Special effects: Sydney Pearson, Gordon Baber [uncredited]. Sound: Ken Rawkins. Sound editor: James Groom. Make-up: Roy Ashton. Hair: Frieda Steiger. Production manager: Don Weeks. Assistant director: Peter Price. Second assistant director: Hugh Harlow [uncredited]. Camera operator: Harry Gillam. Stunt co-ordinator: Peter Diamond [uncredited]. Stunts: Nosher Powell [uncredited], Peter Pocock [uncredited], Gerry Crampton [uncredited]. Continuity: Pauline Harlow. Stills: Tom Edwards [uncredited]. Technical advisor: Freddy

Bradshaw. **Cast:** Jack Hedley (Sergeant Crewe), Barbara Shelley (Elaine), Patrick Wymark (Major Jocomo), Charles Tingwell (Major Dryden), Peter Welch (Richardson), Bill Owen (Bludgin), Edwin Richfield (O'Reilly), Lee Montague (Levy), Michael Ripper (Lieutenant Tojoko), Philip Latham (Captain Drake), Glyn Houston (Berry), Ian Whittaker (Mills), David Saire (KEMPI Chief), Henry Davies (Taffy), Peter Craze (Red), John Southworth (Leonard)

### Seddon, Joy

Seddon (aka Joy Cuff) worked as a model prop maker on Hammer's *She* (1965) and as a model maker on its sequel, *The Vengeance of She* (1968). Her other credits as a model maker include *2001: A Space Odyssey* (1968), plus episodes of *Thunderbirds* (1965–1966, TV), on which she began her career sculpting puppet heads. She also worked as a matte painter on *Mackenna's Gold* (1969), *The Adventures of Baron Munchausen* (1988) and *Erik the Viking* (1989). Her father-in-law (with whom she frequently worked) was the matte painter Bob Cuff (1922–2010), who also worked for Hammer (she married his son in 1969). **Hammer credits:** *She* (1965, model prop maker [uncredited]), *The Vengeance of She* (1968, model maker [uncredited])

### Seear, Andrew

This British actor (1951–) had a supporting role in *Sweet Scent of Death* (1984, TVM [episode of *Hammer House of Mystery and Suspense*]). His other TV credits include episodes of *Enemy at the Door* (1978–1980, TV), *Flickers* (1980, TV), *Between the Lines* (1992–1994, TV), *The Final Cut* (1995, TV) and *Supply and Demand* (1998, TV), while his occasional films include *From a Far Country* (1981), *Plenty* (1985), *Half Moon Street* (1986), *Shadowlands* (1993) and *Simply Irresistible* (1999). Also on radio. **Hammer credits:** *Sweet Scent of Death* (1984, TVM [episode of *Hammer House of Mystery and Suspense*], as Michael Patson)

### Seely, Wendy

Seely can be seen in a minor role in *Last Video and Testament* (1984, TVM [episode of *Hammer House of Mystery and Suspense*]). Her other small screen credits include episodes of *Breakaway Girls* (1978, TV), *Premiere* (1977–1980, TV) and *Starlings* (1988, TV). **Hammer credits:** *Last Video and Testament* (1984, TVM [episode of *Hammer House of Mystery and Suspense*], as Linda)

### Segal, Michael

This British actor (1924–1996) had a minor role in Hammer's *That's Your Funeral* (1973). His other credits include *Hide and Seek* (1963), *Witchfinder General* (1968), *The Black Windmill* (1974) and *Candleshoe* (1977), plus much television, including episodes of *The Prisoner* (1967–1968, TV), *Father Dear Father* (1968–1973, TV), *Man About the House* (1973–1976, TV) and *Lovejoy* (1986–1994, TV). **Hammer credits:** *That's Your Funeral* (1973, as Council chairman)

### Segal, Zohra

This Indian actress and dancer (1912–2014, real name Zohra Begum Mumtaz-Ullah Khan, aka

Zohra Sehgal) can be seen as Putri in Hammer's *The Vengeance of She* (1968). Her other credits include *Dharti Ke Lal* (1946), *Heer* (1956), *The Long Duel* (1967), *The Guru* (1969), *Tales That Witness Madness* (1973), *The Honorary Consul* (1983), *Caravaggio* (1986), *Masala* (1991), *Landmark* (2001), *Anita and Me* (2002), *Bend It Like Beckham* (2002), *Chicken Tikka Masala* (2005) and *Saawaria* (2007), plus episodes of *The Indian Tales of Rudyard Kipling* (1964, TV), *It Ain't Half Hot Mum* (1974–1981, TV) and *Khwahish* (1999, TV). Her husband was the dancer Kameshwar Sehgal (1920–1959), whom she married in 1942 (he committed suicide). She wrote about her experiences in *Close-Up: Memoirs of a Life on Stage and Screen* (2010). **Hammer credits:** *The Vengeance of She* (1968, as Putri)

### Sehgal, Zohra *see* Segal, Zohra

### Seiler, Neil

On stage from 1948, this British actor (1925–2003) can be seen briefly in Hammer's *Captain Kronos—Vampire Hunter* (1974) as a priest. His small screen credits include episodes of *The Villains* (1964–1965, TV), *Softly Softly* (1966–1976, TV), *Crown Court* (1972–1984, TV) and *Days of Hope* (1975, TV). **Hammer credits:** *Captain Kronos—Vampire Hunter* (1974, as Priest)

### Self, William

This American producer and production executive (1921–2010) was in charge of distribution for Twentieth Century–Fox TV at the time it was involved in the making of the Hammer series *Journey to the Unknown* (1968, TV). Following experience in advertising and as an actor in such films as *The Story of G.I. Joe* (1945), *Monsieur Verdoux* (1947), *The Great Gatsby* (1949), *The Thing from Another World* (1951) and *Destination Gobi* (1953), Self started working as a producer on the television series *Schlitz Playhouse of Stars* (1951–1959, TV), four episodes of which he also directed. This led to work as a producer on *The Frank Sinatra Show* (1957–1958, TV) and *Adventures in Paradise* (1959–1962, TV), following which he became an executive in charge of production. His credits in this capacity, among them several series for producer Irwin Allen, include *12 O'Clock High* (1964–1967, TV), *Daniel Boone* (1964–1970, TV), *Voyage to the Bottom of the Sea* (1964–1968, TV), *Lost in Space* (1965–1968, TV), *Batman* (1966–1968, TV), *The Time Tunnel* (1966–1967, TV) and *Land of the Giants* (1968–1970, TV). His work as a film producer meanwhile includes *Ride the High Iron* (1956), *The Shootist* (1976) and *From Noon Till Three* (1976), plus, as executive producer, such tele-features as *The Tenth Man* (1988, TVM), *Sarah, Plain and Tall* (1991, TVM), which earned him a shared Emmy nomination, and *Sarah, Plain and Tall: Winter's End* (1999, TVM). Among his various positions at Fox, he was Vice President in Charge of Production Fox Television, President Fox Television and Vice President Fox Corporation. In 1975, he formed Frankovich/Self Productions with producer Mike Frankovich. He also worked for CBS as Vice President Head of the West Coast, Vice President in Charge of Movies and Mini Series and President of CBS Theatrical Film Division. **Hammer credits:** *Journey to the Unknown* (1968, TV), *Journey* into Darkness (1968, TVM), Journey to Midnight (1968, TVM), Journey to the Unknown (1969, TVM), Journey to Murder (1972, TVM)

### Sellar, Maurice

British born Sellar (1930– ) created the Best of British format with Robert Sidaway, Ashley Sidaway and Lou Jones. This format was applied to the clip shows Best of British (1987–1994, TV) and The World of Hammer (1990 [first broadcast 1994], TV), the latter of which was made by the group's Best of British Film and Television Productions in conjunction with Hammer. His other credits include Swinging UK (1964), on which he was an associate producer. He also wrote scripts and sketches for such comedy series as The Jimmy Tarbuck Show (1968–1975, TV), Milligan in... (1972–1973, TV), The Two Ronnies (1971–1987, TV), Whoops Baghdad! (1973, TV), Down the Gate (1975–1976, TV) and Then Churchill Said to Me (1993, TV). He also contributed additional material to Up the Front (1972). **Hammer credits:** The World of Hammer (1990 [first broadcast 1994], TV)

### Sellars, Elizabeth

In films from 1949 with Floodtide, this beautiful British (Scottish) leading lady (1921– ) appeared in both the first and final film to be made at Bray by Hammer. They were Cloudburst (1951), in which she co-starred with Robert Preston as a woman who is run down by a car of escaping thieves, and The Mummy's Shroud (1967), in which she played Barbara Preston. Her other films include Madeleine (1950), The Barefoot Contessa (1954), 55 Days at Peking (1963), The Hireling (1973) and A Ghost in Monte Carlo (1990, TVM). She has also appeared in many stage plays, while her television work includes episodes of Douglas Fairbanks, Jr. Presents (1953–1957, TV), ITV Play of the Week (1955–1968, TV), Shades of Greene (1975, TV) and Made in Heaven (1990, TV). **Hammer credits:** Cloudburst (1951, as Carol Graham), The Mummy's Shroud (1967, as Barbara Preston)

### Sellers, Arlene

Sellers (1921–2004) worked as an executive producer on Hammer's The Lady Vanishes (1979), along with Michael Carerras and her most frequent producing partner Alex Winitsky. Her other credits as an executive producer (all with Winitsky) include The Seven-Per-Cent Solution (1976), Swing Shift (1984) and You Ruined My Life (1987, TVM), while her credits as a producer (again, all with Winitsky) include Cross of Iron (1977), House Calls (1978), Cuba (1979), Irreconcilable Differences (1984), Stanley and Iris (1990) and Circle of Friends (1995). She also formed Alex Winitsky/Arlene Sellers Productions through which they made the TV series of House Calls (1979–1982, TV). **Hammer credits:** The Lady Vanishes (1979)

### Sellers, Peter

One of the all-time comedy greats, this much troubled and much-married British comedy star (1925–1980, real name Richard Henry Sellers) came to films in 1951 with Penny Points to Paradise following experience on stage with ENSA during the war, and on radio in such shows as Ray's a Laugh (1949–1961), Crazy People (1951) and, of course, The Goon Show (1951–1960). The son of music hall artists, Sellers began his career as a mimic, and during his early years in film made something of a name for himself in comic character roles, among them notable appearances in The Ladykillers (1955), The Smallest Show on Earth (1957), tom thumb (1958) and I'm All Right Jack (1959), which won him a BAFTA for best actor. Having lost weight, he made the leap to leading man status in the early sixties, breaking the American market thanks to his performances in the likes of Waltz of the Toreadors (1962), The Pink Panther (1963), which provoked several sequels, among them A Shot in the Dark (1964) and The Return of the Pink Panther (1975), and Dr. Strangelove (1964), which earned him a best actor Oscar nomination. Sellers' other films include Lolita (1962), Casino Royale (1967), Murder by Death (1976) and Being There (1979), which earned him a second best actor Oscar nomination. He also appeared in the Hammer naval comedy Up the Creek (1958), having been cast in the role of black marketeer CPO Bosun Docherty by director Val Guest, against the initial wishes of James Carreras. Recalled Guest of Sellers' casting, "I had decided he should be put into a starring role in Up the Creek, but I had a terrible job selling him to the people at Wardour Street because no one had heard much of him other than as a radio comic. I finally had to go to my old friend Jimmy Carreras, who pointed out that Hammer didn't do comedies but that, if I really wanted to do this one, they would back me as long as I had someone well known alongside Sellers. I suggested David Tomlinson and Jimmy okayed that. It was a big hit; it made Hammer a lot of money and Sellers went on to great things."[64] In fact the film was such a commercial success it provoked a sequel, Further Up the Creek (1958), though by this time Sellers had moved on, and his part was re-written for Frankie Howerd. In addition to performing, Sellers also directed one film, Mr. Topaze (1961), and took over the direction of The Fiendish Plot of Dr. Fu Manchu (1980) from Piers Haggard (interestingly, the film also features David Tomlinson in a supporting role). During the early years of his career, he also used his vocal talents to dub voices for a number of films, among them The Black Rose (1950), Our Girl Friday (1953), for which he played a parrot, and The Man Who Never Was (1956), for which he provided the voice of Winston Churchill. Married four times, Sellers' wives included the actresses Anne Hayes (1930– ), to whom he was married between 1951 and 1963, Britt Ekland (1942–, real name Britt-Marie Eklund), to whom he was married between 1964 and 1968, and Lynne Fredrick (1954–1994), to whom he was married from 1977 to his death. Frederick appeared in Hammer's Vampire Circus (1972). His daughter (with Eklund) is the actress Victoria Sellers (1965–). Sellers was played by Geoffrey Rush in the biopic The Life and Death of Peter Sellers (2004). **Hammer credits:** Up the Creek (1958, as CPO Bosun Docherty)

### Selley, Reg

Selley worked as the camera operator on Hammer's The Dark Road (1948). His other credits in this capacity include The Adventures of Jane (1949), while his work as a cinematographer includes the documentaries Roc Bomb Power Indicator and Ground Zero Indicator (1966) and Golborne—One Man's Answer (1967). He also directed a documentary short, The Healing Spirit (1964). **Hammer credits:** The Dark Road (1948 [uncredited])

### Selmer, Ltd.

This company is credited as having provided the musical instruments for the Hammer featurette The Eric Winstone Bandshow (1955). A division of Conn-Selmer Inc., it specializes in the manufacture of student and professional instruments, notably such wind instruments as flutes, clarinets, saxophones and oboes. **Hammer credits:** The Eric Winstone Bandshow (1955)

### Selwyn, Clarissa see Clarissa Selwynne

### Selwyn, Lorna

British born Selwyn (1908–2002, full name Lorna Selwyn-Shore) worked as the continuity girl on Hammer's famous quartet of back-to-back productions in the mid-sixties, beginning with Dracula—Prince of Darkness (1966). Her other credits include The Surgeon's Knife (1957), Naked Evil (1966), Witchfinder General (1968), Come Play with Me (1977) and The Playbirds (1978), plus episodes of The Buccaneers (1956–1957, TV) and The Avengers (1961–1969, TV). Recalled Selwyn of her duties, "Continuity is present during all the time the film is being made, whether in the studio or out of doors, whether during the daytime or during the night. She must keep fairly close to the director, who may wish to check with her some previous scene or other detail. This means that her script must always be kept up to the minute so that the required information is quickly to hand."[65] **Hammer credits:** Dracula—Prince of Darkness (1966), Rasputin—The Mad Monk (1966), The Plague of the Zombies (1966), The Reptile (1966)

### Selwynne, Clarissa

In films from the silent period, this British actress (1886–1948, real name Clarissa Schultz, aka Clarissa Selwyn) played Aunty Fanny in the Stanley Lupino comedy Sporting Love (1936), which was Hammer's fourth film. Her many other films include The Grit of a Dandy (1914), The Curse of Eve (1917), The Cup of Fury (1920), Dangerous Days (1920), Black Oxen (1923), The Heart of a Follies Girl (1928), Slightly Married (1932), Jane Eyre (1934) and Call It a Day (1937). **Hammer credits:** Sporting Love (1936, as Aunty Fanny)

### Serena see Milovan and Serena

### Sergejak, Felix (Feliks)

Sergejak (1906–1982) worked as a scenic artist on the Hammer thriller Maniac (1963), a job he repeated for The Witches (1966) and Frankenstein Created Woman (1967). His other credits include Your Money or Your Wife (1959), King and Country (1964) and The Great St. Trinian's Train Robbery (1966). **Hammer credits:** Maniac (1963 [uncredited]), The Witches (1966 [uncredited]), Frankenstein Created Woman (1967 [uncredited])

### Serret, John

This French actor (1917–1997) played Inspector Legrand in the Hammer thriller *Taste of Fear* (1961). His other credits include *Bedelia* (1946), *Sleeping Car to Trieste* (1948), *A Circle of Deception* (1960), *The Mercenaries* (1968), *A Nice Girl Like Me* (1969), *Plenty* (1985) and *Strike It Rich* (1990), plus episodes of *Douglas Fairbanks, Jr. Presents* (1953–1957, TV), *Man from Interpol* (1960–1961, TV), *The Brothers* (1972–1976, TV) and *Bergerac* (1981–1991, TV). **Hammer credits:** *Taste of Fear* (1961, as Inspector Legrand)

### Sessions, Robert (Bob)

This British actor (1940–1998) appeared in *One On an Island*, an episode of Hammer's *Journey to the Unknown* (1968, TV). His other credits include *Permission to Kill* (1975), *Water* (1985), *Nightbreed* (1990), *Funny Man* (1994) and *Wilde* (1997), plus episodes of *Colditz* (1972–1974, TV) and *Rumpole of the Bailey* (1978–1992, TV). His wife was actress Sarah Taunton, whom he married in 1967. **Hammer credits:** *One On an Island* (1968, TV [episode of *Journey to the Unknown*], as Joe Hallum)

### Seton, Joan

This British actress (1922–1985) can be seen in the supporting role of Elsie Steele, the wife of Michael Ripper's ex-con George Steele, in Hammer's *A Case for PC 49* (1951). Her other credits include *Latin Quarter* (1945), *Lisbon Story* (1946), *The Monkey's Paw* (1948), *A Boy, a Girl and a Bike* (1949) and *Riders in the Sky* (1968). **Hammer credits:** *A Case for PC 49* (1951, as Elsie Steele)

### Settelen, Peter

This British actor (1951–) can be seen as a policeman investigating the murder of a tattooist in *Mark of the Devil* (1984, TVM [episode of *Hammer House of Mystery and Suspense*]). His many other TV credits include episodes of *Hunter's Walk* (1973–1976, TV), *Devenish* (1977–1978, TV) and *Bulman* (1985–1987, TV), while his occasional film credits include *A Bridge Too Far* (1977) and *Schwarzwald* (2014). A noted public speaking coach, he worked for a period as a speech writer and vocal coach for Diana, Princess of Wales in 1992, and later sold several of the tapes from the sessions to NBC, which broadcast them in America; however, a BBC documentary also featuring material from the tapes was subsequently pulled. The tapes were finally aired in the UK on Channel 4 in 2017. He is also the author of *Just Talk to Me: From Private Voice to Public Speaker* (2011). **Hammer credits:** *Mark of the Devil* (1984, TVM [episode of *Hammer House of Mystery and Suspense*], as Detective Sergeant Kirby)

### Seven Arts

Formed in 1957 by legendary Hollywood producer Ray Stark, Seven Arts co-financed a number of Hammer films, beginning with the 1959 bomb disposal thriller *Ten Seconds to Hell*. In June 1965, Seven Arts signed an eleven-picture deal with Hammer, which went on to produce such box office hits as *Dracula—Prince of Darkness* (1966) and *One Million Years B.C.* (1966). In 1967, Seven Arts bought out Warner Bros. at a cost of $125m.

Kenneth Hyman—whose own ties with Hammer included a brief period as a producer with the company in the late fifties/early sixties—now became the Vice President of Worldwide Production for the newly titled Warner Bros./Seven-Arts, which subsequently announced a further five-picture deal with Hammer, which led to the making of such films as *Dracula Has Risen from the Grave* (1968) and *When Dinosaurs Ruled the Earth* (1970). Recalled Michael Carerras of the company's close association with Seven Arts, "It led to the 'Americanization' of Hammer."[66] **Hammer credits:** *Ten Seconds to Hell* (1959), *Fanatic* (1965), *She* (1965), *The Nanny* (1965), *Dracula—Prince of Darkness* (1966), *The Plague of the Zombies* (1966), *Rasputin—The Mad Monk* (1966), *The Reptile* (1966), *The Witches* (1966), *One Million Years B.C.* (1966), *The Viking Queen* (1967), *Frankenstein Created Woman* (1967), *The Mummy's Shroud* (1967), *Quatermass and the Pit* (1967), *A Challenge for Robin Hood* (1967), *The Anniversary* (1968), *The Vengeance of She* (1968), *The Devil Rides Out* (1968), *Slave Girls* (1968), *The Lost Continent* (1968), *Dracula Has Risen from the Grave* (1968), *Frankenstein Must Be Destroyed* (1969), *Moon Zero Two* (1969), *Crescendo* (1970), *Taste the Blood of Dracula* (1970) and *When Dinosaurs Ruled the Earth* (1970)

### The Seven Brothers Meet Dracula see The Legend of the 7 Golden Vampires

### The Seven Wonders of Ireland

GB, 1958, 10m, Eastmancolor, HammerScope, cert U

This travelogue short about the beauties of Ireland was filmed in March 1957 by director Peter Bryan while in Ireland to shoot second unit footage of the Irish Sweep Stakes draw for the comedy featurette *Clean Sweep* (1958). Long out of circulation, it was released in the UK by Exclusive as a program filler in 1958.

Production company: Hammer. Distributor: Exclusive (UK). Producer: Peter Bryan. Director: Peter Bryan. Cinematographer/camera operator: Len Harris. Focus puller: Harry Oakes [uncredited]

### Sewards, Terence

This British actor (1938–) played a reporter in Hammer's *The Mummy's Shroud* (1967). His other credits include *Where the Bullets Fly* (1966), *Hannibal Brooks* (1968) and *Royal Flash* (1975 [scenes deleted]), plus a return to Hammer for *Captain Kronos—Vampire Hunter* (1974). His small screen appearances include episodes of *The Avengers* (1961–1969, TV), *Thriller* (1973–1976, TV) and *Dick Barton: Special Agent* (1979, TV). **Hammer credits:** *The Mummy's Shroud* (1967, as Reporter [uncredited]), *Captain Kronos—Vampire Hunter* (1974, as Tom)

### Sewell, Danny

This British light-heavyweight boxer (1930–2001) turned to acting following a bout of polio. He can be seen as Billy Weston in Hammer's *Man at the Top* (1973). His other credits include episodes of *Nick of the River* (1959, TV), *Z Cars* (1962–1978, TV) and *Rogue's Gallery* (1968–1969,

TV). Also on stage, he played Bill Sykes in the original London production of *Oliver!* (1960), and later took the role to Broadway and on tour in America. His brother was the actor George Sewell (1924–2007), who appeared in Hammer's *The Vengeance of She* (1968), plus an episode of *Hammer House of Mystery and Suspense* (1984, TVM). **Hammer credits:** *Man at the Top* (1973, as Billy Weston)

### Sewell, George

A familiar face on television care of such series as *Spindoe* (1968, TV) and *The Detectives* (1993–1997, TV), this reliable British character actor (1924–2007) also appeared in a handful of films, among them Hammer's *The Vengeance of She* (1968), in which he played Harry. His other big screen credits include *Sparrows Can't Sing* (1962), *This Sporting Life* (1963), *Kaleidoscope* (1966), *Get Carter* (1971) and *Barry Lyndon* (1975). He was also considered for the role of George de Grass in Hammer's *To the Devil a Daughter* (1976). His other TV credits include an episode of *Hammer House of Mystery and Suspense* (1984, TVM), plus appearances in *The Power Game* (1965–1969, TV), *Paul Temple* (1969–1971, TV), *Special Branch* (1969–1974, TV), *UFO* (1970–1971, TV), *Tinker Tailor Soldier Spy* (1979, TV), *The Upper Hand* (1990–1996, TV) and *Harry and the Wrinklies* (1999, TV). Also much on stage, particularly with Joan Littlewood's Theater Workshop (for whom he made his professional debut in *Fings Ain't Wot They Used T'be* in 1960). His brother was the boxer-turned-actor Danny Sewell (1930–2001) who appeared in Hammer's *Man at the Top* (1973). **Hammer credits:** *The Vengeance of She* (1968, as Harry), *Mark of the Devil* (1984, TVM [episode of *Hammer House of Mystery and Suspense*], as Detective Inspector Grant)

### Sewell, Vernon

Prolific as a writer, producer and director in the forties and fifties, British born Sewell (1903–2001) began his film career as a camera assistant in 1930 on *Kissing Cup's Race*. He started directing in 1933 with the German-made *Morgenrot*, which he co-directed with Gustav Ucicky, which he followed with the featurette *The Medium* (1934), which began an association with producer-director Michael Powell (with whom he co-wrote the film). This led to work as a production assistant on Powell's *The Edge of the World* (1938) and as a second unit director on *The Spy in Black* (1939). It also led to Sewell's British feature debut, *The Silver Fleet* (1943), which he co-wrote and co-directed with Gordon Wellesley, while Powell produced without credit (this following work by Sewell as a director on a handful of documentary shorts).

After military service during the war, Sewell continued his career with such films as *The World Owes Me a Living* (1945), *Latin Quarter* (1945), which he also wrote, *Ghost Ship* (1952), which he also wrote and produced, *The Floating Dutchman* (1952), *Soho Incident* (1956), *Battle of the V-1* (1958), *House of Mystery* (1961), which he also wrote, *The Blood Beast Terror* (1968) and *Burke and Hare* (1971). In 1949, he formed V.S. (Vernon

Sewell) Productions, through which he made the yachting adventure *Jack of Diamonds*, which was part financed by Will Hammer (the film also had a crew of mostly Hammer technicians and was released by Exclusive). This eventually led to two "official" Hammer productions: *The Black Widow* (1950) and *The Dark Light* (1951).

A keen yachtsman, Sewell's boat the *Gelert* featured in several of his films, including *Jack of Diamonds*, *The Dark Light*, *Ghost Ship*, *The Floating Dutchman* and *Dangerous Voyage* (1953). Revealed Sewell, "[It] was a wonderful prop, and it would have cost a lot of money to hire a yacht of that size. I only kept it going because I was able to push it into movies. In the end people used to say, 'Vernon, your yacht again!'"[67] Meanwhile, of his career in general he commented, "I always finished my films on budget and on time, and I really did only the films I wanted to."[68]

His wife was actress Joan Carol (1906–1986; real name Joan Roscoe Catt), whom he married in 1950, and who appeared almost exclusively in his films, including his three for Hammer. **Hammer credits:** *Jack of Diamonds* (1949, producer [through V.S. Productions], director), *The Black Widow* (1950, director), *The Dark Light* (1951, director, screenplay)

## Seyler, Athene

On stage from 1909, this highly respected British comedy character actress (1889–1990) also sustained a healthy film career, notching up over seventy productions, beginning with *The Adventures of Mr. Pickwick* (1921), the first of many Dickens adaptations she subsequently appeared in. The archetypal British old dear in later years, her many credits include *Scrooge* (1935), *Quiet Wedding* (1941), *Nicholas Nickleby* (1947), *The Queen of Spades* (1949), *The Pickwick Papers* (1952), *Night of the Demon* (1957), *Make Mine Mink* (1960) and *Nurse on Wheels* (1963). She also appeared in Hammer's *Visa to Canton* (1963), in which she was somewhat unconvincingly cast as the Chinese Mao Tai Tai. Her TV credits include episodes of *Tales from Dickens* (1958–1959, TV), *The Avengers* (1961–1969, TV) and *Play of the Month* (1969–1973, TV). She was made a CBE in 1959. Her second husband was the actor Nicholas Hannen (1881–1972), whom she married in 1960. **Hammer credits:** *Visa to Canton* (1960, as Mao Tai Tai)

## Sforzini, Tony

Sforzini worked as the make-up artist on the Hammer thriller *The Full Treatment* (1961), one of several films he worked on for director Val Guest. His many other credits, among them several key films for Laurence Olivier, include *In Which We Serve* (1942), *Henry V* (1944), *Blithe Spirit* (1945), *Hamlet* (1948), *Treasure Island* (1950), *Richard III* (1955), *The Prince and the Showgirl* (1957), *The Entertainer* (1960), *The Naked Edge* (1961), *The Day the Earth Caught Fire* (1961), *Jigsaw* (1962), *80,000 Suspects* (1963), *Stolen Hours* (1963), *Where the Spies Are* (1965), *The Mikado* (1967), *Where Eagles Dare* (1969), *A Touch of Class* (1973) and *Confessions of a Window Cleaner* (1974). **Hammer credits:** *The Full Treatment* (1961)

## *The Shadow of the Cat*

GB, 1961, 79m, bw, RCA, cert X

Although some sources dictate otherwise, *The Shadow of the Cat* is a genuine Hammer film, despite being credited as a BHP production. Formed in February 1960 by screenwriter George Baxt, agent Richard Finlay Hatton and director Jon Pennington, BHP (Baxt-Hatton-Pennington) was created in order to take advantage of production sponsorship by ACT Films, the producing branch of the Association of Cine and Allied Technicians union, which had already been involved in the Hammer comedy *Don't Panic Chaps* (1959) and several other British films of the period, among them *Dangerous Cargo* (1954), *The Diplomatic Corpse* (1958) and *Dead Lucky* (1960). Hammer's involvement was primarily as a provider of production facilities and technical staff, the costs of which were to be covered on a nominal "for hire" basis.[69] However, given the number of key Hammer technicians involved in the project, there's no doubting the film's pedigree (if further proof were needed, Hammer's own documentation refers to it as being their seventy-third production[70]).

Filmed at Bray between 14 November and 22 December 1960 on an eventual budget of £81,000, the film (which was also backed by Universal, as well as ACT) is a fairly standard creepy house thriller about a vengeful cat that seemingly kills the greedy relatives responsible for the murder of its wealthy old mistress ("She saw … she *knows*," comments one of the plot's frightened participants). The screenplay by George Baxt runs through the expected clichés, among them much prowling around in dark rooms and corridors during the pre-requisite thunderstorms. Nevertheless, the film is directed with a certain degree of finesse by John Gilling, here making his directorial debut for Hammer following the scripting of a number of second features for them in the early fifties, among them *The Man in Black* (1950) and *Wings of Danger* (1952). The delay in Gilling directing for Hammer was apparently the result of a falling out between the writer and the studio over his screenplay for *Whispering Smith Hits London* (1952), the story for which had been credited to Whispering Smith creator Frank H. Spearman, when in fact it had been based on an original short story by Gilling titled *Where Is Sylvia?* Gilling, whose directorial career was by now firmly established, was eventually invited to helm the Spanish Inquisition drama *The Rape of Sabena* (aka *The Inquisitor*) for Hammer in late 1960. However, when this project was abandoned, his contract was simply moved over to *The Shadow of the Cat*.

Before making the film, Gilling did a quick rewrite of Baxt's script, which originally had the cat as a purely imaginary creature whose shadow is only ever seen (hence the title), as per Val Lewton's *Cat People* (1944). Perhaps ceding that this concept might have been a little too subtle for audiences out for a few shocks and jolts, Gilling instead decided to have the cat as an all-too-real presence in the house, which enabled him to photograph a good deal of the feline action sequences from the cat's point of view, using an effectively disconcerting fish-eye (cat's-eye?) lens. He also filmed the first murder from the perspective of the old lady, cleverly blurring the face of her attacker when she takes off her glasses.

In addition to Gilling's Bava-esque flair for staging, which is a triumph of technique over the plot's absurdity, the film also contains some eye-catching art direction care of Bernard Robinson and his team (the exterior of the creepy mansion has an effectively austere look to it), while Arthur Grant's roving camera gives the proceedings a real sense of style and movement (he also makes use of a number of disconcerting tilted shots to add to the visual drama at key points). Meanwhile, Greek composer Mikis Theodorakis (still three years away from his international breakthrough with *Zorba the Greek* [1964]) adds to the musty atmosphere with his offbeat score, complete with a driving *Jaws*-like motif. As for the cast, how can you go wrong with such stalwarts as André Morell, Barbara Shelley, Freda Jackson and Catherine Lacey? The real star of the film, however, is the title creature, as played by Tabitha, who was provided and trained by John Holmes, whose patient encouragement, assisted by some clever photography and cutting, effectively helps to convey the feline's malevolence, such as it is. After all, how truly scary can a moggy actually be? Indeed, Barbara Shelley's Beth Venable seems to acknowledge this fundamental flaw when she comments, "Do you seriously mean to tell me that an ordinary domestic cat is terrorizing three grown ups?"

Premiered on 12 April 1961 on a double bill with Hammer's *The Curse of the Werewolf* (1961), *The Shadow of the Cat* went on general release in the UK (again with *Werewolf*) on 1 May care of Universal-International. "Stare into these eyes if you dare," goaded the poster, which also described the movie as "The most shocking suspense-thriller of the year!" The trailer meanwhile pondered, "What strange power changed this harmless household pet into an instrument of death?" The double bill's American release, also care of Universal-International, followed on 7 June. Upon its British release, *Kinematograph Weekly* praised the film for "Having clearly proved that 'horrific' melodrama need not be served with tomato sauce." Consequently, it claimed that the film "should have been given an A not an X certificate." **Additional notes:** Keep an eye out for the boom shadow reflected in a mirror about 8½ minutes into the film as André Morell escorts Conrad Phillips and Alan Wheatley to the front door. The film cleverly features nine players in the house. As the trailer has it, "One cat, nine lives. Nine lives: Walter, Clara, Andrew, Beth, Michael, Jacob, Edgar, Louise, Ella. Nine lives on the edge of terror. Nine lives in the shadow of the cat."

Production companies: BHP/ACT Films/ Hammer. Distributor: Universal International (UK, U.S.). Producer: Jon Pennington. Director: John Gilling. Screenplay: George Baxt (and John Gilling [uncredited]). Cinematographer: Arthur Grant. Music/conductor: Mikis Theodorakis. Supervising editor: James Needs. Editor: John Pomeroy. Production design: Bernard Robinson. Art director: Don Mingaye. Costumes: Molly Arbuthnot. Special effects: Les Bowie. Special effects assistants: Ian Scoones [uncredited], Kit West [uncredited]. Make-up: Roy Ashton. Hair: Frieda Steiger. Sound: Jock May, Ken Cameron. Sound editor: Alban Streeter. Camera operator: Len Harris. Focus puller: Harry Oakes [uncredited]. Assistant director: John Peverall. Second assistant director: Dominic Fulford [uncredited]. Production manager: Don Weeks. Construction manager: Arthur Banks [uncredited]. Master carpenter: Charles Davis [uncredited]. Master painter: Laurence Wrenn [uncredited]. Master plasterer: Stan Banks [uncredited]. Master electrician: Jack Curtis [uncredited]. Master rigger: Ronald Lenoir [uncredited]. Props: Tommy Money [uncredited]. Props buyer: Eric Hillier [uncredited]. Stills: Tom Edwards [uncredited]. Stunts: Jackie Cooper [uncredited]. Casting: Stuart Lyons. Continuity: Tilly Day. Cat trainer: John Holmes. **Cast:** André Morell (Walter Venable), Barbara Shelley (Beth Venable), William Lucas (Jacob), Conrad Phillips (Michael Latimer), Freda Jackson (Clara), Catherine Lacey (Ella Venable), Vanda Godsell (Louise), Richard Warner (Edgar), Andrew Crawford (Andrew), Alan Wheatley (Inspector Rowles), Kynaston Reeves (Grandfather), Henry Kendall (Doctor [uncredited]), Charles Stanley (Dobbins [uncredited]), Vera Cook (Mother [uncredited]), Kevin Stoney (Father [uncredited]), Howard Knight (Boy [uncredited]), Angela Crow (Girl [uncredited]), John Dearth (Constable Hamer [uncredited]), Rodney Burke (Workman [uncredited]), George Doonan (Ambulance man [uncredited]), Fred Stone (Ambulance man [uncredited]), Tabitha (Cat). **DVD availability:** Final Cut (UK R2 PAL), extras include a documentary, *Shadowplay: Inside The Shadow of the Cat*, a trailer, a stills gallery and an audio track featuring special effects assistant Ian Scoones titled *Catastrophy*

### Shall We Sing see *Getting Together with Reginald Foort*

### Shaps, Cyril

This RADA-trained British character actor (1923–2003) began appearing in films in the late fifties following experience on radio (from the age of twelve) and the stage. His credits include *The Silent Enemy* (1958), *Never Let Go* (1960), *The Pursuers* (1961), in which he had the lead role, *11 Harrowhouse* (1974), *The Odessa File* (1974), on which he dubbed Towje Kleiner, *The Barmitzvah Boy* (1976, TVM), *The Spy Who Loved Me* (1977), *The Madness of King George* (1994), *The Man Who Cried* (2000) and *The Pianist* (2002), while on television he was familiar as Rabbi Levi in the sitcom *Never Mind the Quality, Feel the Width* (1967–1968, TV). He can also be spotted in a minor role in Hammer's *The Terror of the Tongs* (1961) and as Foxy Face in *Rasputin—The Mad Monk* (1966). He later appeared in an episode of *Hammer House of Mystery and Suspense* (1984, TVM), coming to a sticky end in a haunted indoor tennis court. His many other television appearances include episodes of *Quatermass II* (1955, TV), *Theatre 625* (1964–1968, TV), *Holocaust* (1978, TV), *Private Schulz* (1981, TV) and *Anna Karenina* (2000, TV). **Hammer credits:** *The Terror of the Tongs* (1961,

unnamed role [uncredited]), *Rasputin—The Mad Monk* (1966, as Foxy Face [uncredited]), *Tennis Court* (1984, TVM [episode of *Hammer House of Mystery and Suspense*], as Dr. Magnusson)

### Sharman, Bruce

British born Sharman (1929–) worked as the assistant director on Hammer's *She* (1965). During filming in Israel, a local effects technician lost two fingers when a grenade unexpectedly exploded. Recalled the film's associate producer Aida Young, "The first assistant went berserk. It was terribly hot and he couldn't stand the sight of the blood and somebody had to knock him out."[71] Sharman's other credits as an assistant director include episodes of *The Saint* (1962–1969, TV), while his work as a unit/production manager or supervisor includes *Catch Us If You Can* (1965), *Smashing Time* (1967), *The Raging Moon* (1971), *The Amazing Mr. Blunden* (1972), *Star Wars* (1977), *The Empire Strikes Back* (1980) and *Return to Oz* (1985). He also worked as an assistant producer on *The Rescue Squad* (1963), as an associate producer on *The Four Feathers* (1977, TVM), *The Great Muppet Caper* (1981) and *The Dark Crystal* (1982), as a producer on *Henry V* (1989), and as an executive producer on *Darkness Falls* (1999). He began his career as an actor on stage and television, and his credits for the latter include episodes of *The Snow Queen* (1955, TV), *The Adventures of Robin Hood* (1955–1960, TV), *Kidnapped* (1956, TV) and *Sword of Freedom* (1957–1958, TV). In 1993 he co-founded Bloomsbury Films with Chris Parkinson, which went on to make *Bathtime* (1996), *So This Is Romance?* (1997) and *Darkness Falls* (1998). His former wife was the actress Perlita Neilson (1933–2014, real name Margaret Philippa Sowden), whom he married in 1956. **Hammer credits:** *She* (1965)

### Sharp, Don

In Britain from 1948 following experience as an actor in his home country, this busy Tasmanian born director (1921–2011) began his film career with *Ha'penny Breeze* (1949), which he co-wrote, co-produced, co-directed (without credit) and starred in. He went on to act in such films as *Appointment in London* (1952) and *The Cruel Sea* (1953), while his screenplays included *Background* (1953) and *The Blue Peter* (1955), on which he again directed some scenes without credit. His first official screen credit as a director was for the children's film *The Stolen Airliner* (1955), which he also wrote. He followed this with a number of low budget second features, children's films and documentaries, among them *The Golden Disc* (1968), which he co-wrote, *The Adventures of Hal 5* (1958), which he again also wrote, and a documentary, *The Changing Years* (1958). A number of low budget second features followed, among them *The Golden Disc* (1958), which he co-wrote, *Keeping the Peace* (1959), *The Professionals* (1960) and *Linda* (1960), all which brought him to the attention of Hammer producer Anthony Hinds, who subsequently offered Sharp his first horror film, the much-admired *The Kiss of the Vampire* (1963), despite the fact that he'd never made a horror film before.

Recalled Sharp, "What happened was my agent

at the time, John Redway, said he wanted to meet up with me. He said, 'I think you ought to do a film for Hammer,' and I said, 'But they make horror movies! I can't do that—I've never even seen one!' Then I asked, 'Why me, anyway?' and he told me that Hammer producer Tony Hinds was looking for new directors, and he'd sent him *The Professionals* to look at, so he could see how I measured up. Well, I was invited down to see Tony Hinds, who liked *The Professionals*, and we got on very well indeed, and he offered me *Kiss of the Vampire*. Though I'd never seen a horror film, I liked the script, plus the challenge of making something as way out as vampires and garlic believable for an audience."[72] Sharp subsequently viewed a handful of Hammer's films, including *The Curse of Frankenstein* (1957) and *Dracula* (1958), and despite initial reservations, quickly found himself a convert. "What intrigued me about them was that after about twenty minutes I was fully hooked despite a totally absurd situation,"[73] he admitted.

*Kiss* was a commercial and critical success. Commented *Films and Filming* of Sharp's contribution: "All credit to Don Sharp for tuning what could have been a creaking, monotonously predictable story into an exceptionally well-made (with some beautifully framed shots) and entertaining film … the production standard is extraordinarily high, and most remarkably he has handled it with buoyant freshness."

Consequently, *Kiss* led to several further genre assignments for Sharp, among them *Witchcraft* (1964), *The Face of Fu Manchu* (1965), *Curse of the Fly* (1965), *The Brides of Fu Manchu* (1966), *Psychomania* (1972) and *Dark Places* (1973). It also led to two more films for Hammer: the lively swashbuckling yarn *The Devil-Ship Pirates* (1964), remembered by the crew for the capsizing of the title craft the *Diablo* during filming, and the historical shocker *Rasputin—The Mad Monk* (1966), noted for Christopher Lee's full-blooded performance in the leading role. However, as Sharp recalled of the latter, "We had to cut corners…. It wasn't an entirely happy movie, though it was great from a performance point of view."[74]

Sharp was very much in control of his films. Recalled first assistant director Bert Batt, who worked on *The Devil-Ship Pirates*, "He [Don] came to work with a rigid shot list and to an inch knew where the camera would be for every set-up."[75] This was no doubt because of the tight schedules and budgets he frequently had to work with. Said the director of *The Devil-Ship Pirates*, "That was a difficult one…. It had a lot of physical action in it, which I loved, but it was difficult to do on a tight schedule. Action has to look dangerous, and it is dangerous unless it is well rehearsed and lots of precautions are taken. That takes time. The demands of the producer to keep you going mean that you can't do as well as you want to."[76] Said actor Andrew Keir of working with Sharp on the film: "He's a good workman. He knows exactly what he wants and he makes very clean films."[77]

Sharp's many other credits include *It's All Happening* (1963), *Our Man in Marrakesh* (1966), *Rocket to the Moon* (1967), *Callan* (1974), *The Four Feathers* (1978, TVM), *The Thirty-Nine Steps*

(1978), *Bear Island* (1979) and *Secrets of the Phantom Caverns* (1984). He also directed the second unit for such films as *The Fast Lady* (1962), *Those Magnificent Men in Their Flying Machines* (1965) and *Puppet on a Chain* (1970), while for television his credits include *A Woman of Substance* (1983, TV), *Hold the Dream* (1986, TV), *Tears in the Rain* (1988, TVM) and *Act of Will* (1989, TV), plus *Guardian of the Abyss*, one of the best episodes of *Hammer House of Horror* (1980, TV). Recalled Sharp of the latter: "Roy Skeggs rang me up and said, 'We've got this series going and we're going to use as many of the old Hammer directors as possible. Are you interested?' He sent me a story of Devil worship—'Guardian of the Abyss'—and after a few rewrites away we went. It was a bit more ambitious than making your regular television episode and was like making a mini Hammer feature. It was a joy to do."[78] This was Sharp's last brush with Hammer, though he revealed that, "I was offered other features, but I didn't want to get stuck with horror movies, just as I later didn't want to get stuck just doing action movies. One likes a varied menu!"[79] **Additional notes:** Sharp was offered *The Vengeance of She* (1968) to direct by producer Aida Young, but he turned the project down owing to his commitment to direct *Taste of Excitement* (1969). He was also approached by Michael Carreras to take over the direction of *Blood from the Mummy's Tomb* (1971) following the death of Seth Holt, but he turned the project down owing to commitments elsewhere. In October 1974, Sharp looked set to direct Hammer's *To the Devil a Daughter* (1976), but the convoluted pre-production period saw him make an exit after three months to pursue other projects. Sharp's first wife was the Australian actress Gwenda Wilson (1922–1977), whom he married in 1945. His second wife was the British actress Mary Steele (1933–), whom he married in 1956; one of their children (of four) was the music producer and songwriter Jonny Dollar (1964–2009, real name Jonathan Peter Sharp). **Hammer credits:** *The Kiss of the Vampire* (1963), *The Devil-Ship Pirates* (1964), *Rasputin—The Mad Monk* (1966), *Guardian of the Abyss* (1980, TV [episode of *Hammer House of Horror*])

### Sharp, Jack

This British composer, arranger and conductor (1921–1994, real name Dennis Berry, aka Peter Dennis) wrote the music for *Wolfshead: The Legend of Robin Hood* (1969 [released 1973]), which was acquired by Hammer, and for which he shared his credit with Jack Sprague. The founder and conductor of the Peter Dennis Band and the Peter Dennis Orchestra, his songs include *Apple Honey* and *You Couldn't Be Sweeter*, while his albums include *No Waiting* (1971) and *Pretty Pose* (1980). He began his career as a copyist and went on to arrange for the Squadronaires and Ted Heath. He contributed to the music scores for *And Now for Something Completely Different* (1971), *The Beastmaster* (1982) and *Neverending Story II: The Next Chapter* (1990). He also managed the Peer International Library (aka the Peer-Southern music library). **Hammer credits:** *Wolfshead: The Legend of Robin Hood* (1969 [released 1973])

### Sharp, John

This rotund British actor (1920–1992, sometimes Sharpe) played supporting roles in five films for Hammer, among them that of Detective Sergeant Jackson in the thriller *Dr. Morelle—The Case of the Missing Heiress* (1949). His other films include *The Golden Rabbit* (1962), *Bunny Lake Is Missing* (1965), *Three Bites of the Apple* (1967), *Mrs. Brown, You've Got a Lovely Daughter* (1968), *Top Secret!* (1984) and *The Bride* (1985). His small screen credits include episodes of *The Onedin Line* (1971–1980, TV) and *All Creatures Great and Small* (1978–1990, TV), in which he played Mr. Biggins. **Hammer credits:** *Dr. Morelle—The Case of the Missing Heiress* (1949, as Detective Sergeant Jackson), *Celia* (1949, as Mr Haldane), *A Case for PC 49* (1951, as Desk Sergeant), *The House Across the Lake* (1954, as Mr. Hardcastle), *That's Your Funeral* (1973, as Mayor)

### Sharp, John Gerrard

Sharp provided additional dialogue for the Hammer/Luckwell second feature *The Runaway* (1964), which otherwise had a story and screenplay by John Perceval. **Hammer credits:** *The Runaway* (1964)

### Sharpe, Cliff

British born Sharpe (1914–) worked as the assistant make-up artist (under George Blackler) on Hammer's *The Satanic Rites of Dracula* (1974). His other credits as a fully-fledged make-up artist include *Shadow of a Man* (1956), *Pop Gear* (1965), *The Haunted House of Horror* (1969) and *Julius Caesar* (1969), plus two episodes of *UFO* (1970–1971, TV). **Hammer credits:** *The Satanic Rites of Dracula* (1974 [uncredited])

### Sharpe, Edith

On stage from 1919, this British character actress (1894–1984) spent the majority of her career treading the boards. However, she found time to appear in a handful of films, among them two thrillers for Hammer: *Cloudburst* (1951), in which she played Mrs. Reece, and *Cash on Demand* (1961) in which she played Miss Pringle. Her other screen credits include *The Education of Elizabeth* (1921), *Music Hath Charms* (1935), *The Guinea Pig* (1948), *Brothers in Law* (1956) and *The Devil Never Sleeps* (1962). She also appeared in episodes of *Douglas Fairbanks, Jr. Presents* (1953–1957, TV), *Dixon of Dock Green* (1955–1976, TV) and *War and Peace* (1972–1974, TV). **Hammer credits:** *Cloudburst* (1951, Mrs. Reece), *Cash on Demand* (1961, as Miss Pringle)

### Sharvell-Martin, Michael

This British actor (1944–2010, real name Michael Ernest Martin) can be seen as a policeman in two Hammer TV spin-offs. His other credits include *Rentadick* (1972), *The Love Ban* (1973) and *Not Now, Comrade* (1976), plus much television, including episodes of *The Benny Hill Show* (1969–1989, TV), *Here Come the Double Deckers!* (1970–1971, TV), *Are You Being Served?* (1972–198, TV), *Terry and June* (1979–1987, TV), *Close Relations* (1998, TV) and *Doctors* (2000–, TV). **Hammer credits:** *That's Your Funeral* (1973, as First Police-

man [motorway]), *Love Thy Neighbour* (1973, Constable)

### Sharwin, Moyna

Sharwin appeared as one of the Sphinx Girls in Hammer's *The Two Faces of Dr. Jekyll* (1960). **Hammer credits:** *The Two Faces of Dr. Jekyll* (1960, as Sphinx Girl [uncredited])

### *Shatter*

GB/Hong Kong, 1974, 90m, Technicolor, cert X

While in Hong Kong to make the horror/martial arts hybrid *The Legend of the 7 Golden Vampires* (1974), Michael Carreras hit upon the idea of making a second film utilizing much the same production team. The Shaw Brothers, who were backing the vampire film, quickly agreed, and pre-production was hastily put into motion on a modern day thriller making extensive use of Hong Kong locations. Unfortunately, *Legend* was plagued by production problems, including poor communication and poor facilities, which did little to auger well for the forthcoming *Shatter*, into which Carreras was now locked. If anything, the second film proved to be even more of a nightmare than the first.

Don Houghton, who was in Hong Kong as a producer on *Legend*, was quickly put to work on the screenplay, while Carreras started looking for a suitable director. The project would have been ideal for such Hammer veterans as Don Sharp and Val Guest, but instead Carreras rather surprisingly opted for the American director Monte Hellman, known then, as now, for his westerns *The Shooting* (1966) and *Ride in the Whirlwind* (1966), and the cult road movie *Two-Lane Blacktop* (1971). Hellman was a fast worker and used to dealing with low budgets, which can't have escaped Carreras's attention. He had also been in Hong Kong recently to prep a film that subsequently fell through, and so his knowledge of the area proved a valuable asset.

Hellman's pre-production period was short to say the least: just two weeks, with filming commencing on 17 December 1973 (*Legend* had only just finished principal photography on 11 December). The rush was too much and the script suffered as a consequence. Commented Hellman, "If you have a script that doesn't work, all the doctoring in the world can't really make anything out of it…. If I'd had more creative control I wouldn't have shot this script. It would have been a better script."[80] However, given the commitment to start filming, Hellman had to proceed as best he could.

To star in the film, the American actor Stuart Whitman was cast as assassin Shatter, who has been hired by a Hong Kong–based German banker named Hans Leber to kill General Ansabi M'Goya, the dictator of the East African Republic of Badawi. However, when Shatter returns to Hong Kong to collect his $100,000 payment for the assignment, he is himself the subject of a number of attempts on his life, all of them seemingly authorized by Leber. Determined to get his money, Shatter decides to take Leber on, which only adds to his troubles ("You're finished. You are bad news. It is like you're dead," Leber informs him). Even Rattwood, the local police inspector, seems indifferent to his plight ("You're marked, Shatter," he warns him after two of his men have roughed him up in an alleyway). But help is at hand in the guise of a young barman named Tai Pah, whose deadly martial arts skills Shatter makes extensive use of as he attempts to bring Leber to book, discovering along the way that the banker is part of an international opium syndicate involving M'Goya's brother, Colonel Dabula M'Goya, who sanctioned the death of his sibling so as to take over the country and secure the connection with Hong Kong.

Familiar to audiences via such films as *The Mark* (1961), *The Comancheros* (1962) and *Those Magnificent Men in Their Flying Machines* (1965), Whitman seemed ideal casting as the world-weary assassin. The supporting cast was meanwhile truly international, among them Anton Diffring as Hans Leber, Peter Cushing (billed as "guest star") as Rattwood, and local martial arts star Ti Lung as Tai Pah. Crew-wise, making the jump from *Legend* were cinematographers John Wilcox and Roy Ford (who were also joined by Hammer regular Brian Probyn), art director Johnson Tsau (simply billed as Johnson), continuity girl Renee Glynne and several members of the sound department.

Suffering from the same communication problems and differing approaches to production that had beleaguered *Legend*, *Shatter* was a troubled shoot from the start. As filming proceeded, the tension mounted between Carreras and Hellman. This conflict finally erupted over a seemingly trivial incident involving a shirt to be worn by the actor playing Ansabi M'Goya for a bedroom scene (Hellman wanted him to be wearing a shirt under his jacket, Carreras didn't, so as to speed up the action as he undresses to seduce a young woman). As the various arguments escalated, Hellman decided to jump ship after three hectic weeks of shooting. Consequently, as he had done so on occasion in the past, Carreras decided to complete the film himself. Revealed Hellman, "Michael didn't fire me until we'd finished with all the European actors; when we finished all those scenes, our only thing left to do was the kung-fu with the Chinese actors."[81] Hellman thus returned to America, where he went on to direct another cult film, *Cockfighter* (1974), for producer Roger Corman, with whom he'd begun his career in the late fifties, directing *Beast from Haunted Cave* (1959).

Needless to say, the resultant film is something of a hotchpotch, though much of what Hellman shot remains in the final print. Interestingly, Michael Carreras actually had high hopes for the finished product, his ambition being that if it were successful, he would use it as a launch pad for a TV series starring Whitman and Cushing. Indeed, the film actually has the look of a seventies cop show, and might have made a good(ish) pilot had it been cut down to fill a one-hour slot. At ninety minutes, however, it is clearly padded and becomes a chore to watch as a consequence. Commented Monte Hellman of the finished film, "It's too short a script…. Consequently, everything is paced too slowly to add time, and I think that's one of the reasons why it's hard to watch."[82]

A rather grotty-looking slice of thick ear that fo-

All smiles for the cameras, though it was a different matter behind the scenes. From left to right, Michael Carreras, Peter Cushing, Run Run Shaw and Stuart Whitman between scenes on the set of *Shatter* (1974) (Hammer/Shaw Brothers/EMI/ Avco Embassy).

cuses on the seedier side of Hong Kong, this is by no means a picture postcard view of the province. "Filmed in Hong Kong, where the action is!" boasted the trailer, though Michael Carreras put it more aptly in a note to Brian Lawrence at the time: "The action sequences lack excitement, the dialogue scenes are dull and Hong Kong looks like a slum."[83] For the most part, the staging is fairly perfunctory, while in terms of plotting and dialogue exchanges, Houghton's script is routine at best. When Shatter is asked his name by Tai Pah's friend Mai-Ling, who becomes involved in his plight, she responds, "That's not a name," to which comes the thudding reply, "Yeah, more like a way of life." Later, as Shatter, Tai Pah and Mai Ling dine at a street stall, Houghton's script inevitably mocks the local cuisine. "The snake here is excellent. You should try some," Pah urges Shatter (Houghton had already proffered a typically xenophobic view of the local food in *The Legend of the 7 Golden Vampires* by showing the head of a frog being chopped off in preparation for consumption).

Whitman's performance as Shatter is perhaps just a little too hang dog given the fact that his life is supposed to be in the balance for much of the film (the actor has since admitted to having partied fairly hard during production), while as the corrupt Hans Leber, the heavy-lidded Anton Diffring looks like he's about to fall asleep at times (but who can blame him given the dialogue?). As the hardnosed Rattwood, Peter Cushing fares better, despite a rather curious accent that tends to come and go. As usual, he adds various bits of business so as to make the most of his brief appearances, during which he always seems to be popping a piece of candy into his mouth by way of emphasizing a point (his casual disposal of a sweet wrapper in a trash can as he walks away after their alleyway en-

counter perfectly sums up his indifference to Shatter). Commented Stuart Whitman, "Peter Cushing, he was loaded with all sorts of little gimmicks that just made his performance very fluid and easy. I picked up a few tricks from him, no question about it."[84]

The film's real find, though, is local martial arts star Ti Lung, a slender, muscle-bound Bruce Lee look-alike with plenty of personality and bags of energy in the fight sequences (the trailer describes him as "The master of man's deadliest weapon: the human body"). His best sequence is the finale in a casino penthouse suite in which he and Shatter use everything at hand to defeat Leber and his goons. A fast-paced and reasonably well-edited slice of chop socky, it gives the film a belated boost of excitement, culminating in the deaths of Leber and Dabula M'Goya who, having both been shot by Shatter, fall backwards though the windows to their deaths below (unfortunately, the falling bodies are very clearly dummies, which slightly dissipates the effect). "That evens the score a little," says Shatter, after which he meets Rattwood at the docks, handing him a list of Leber's associates that he earlier managed to purloin from Ansabi M'Goya's hotel room, for which the inspector pays him $10,000HK. "It'll help you buy that bar in Won Chai," says Rattwood. "There'll be a heavy mortgage, so perhaps it's just as well you're here for life. Be time to pay it off—if you live that long. Once in a while you might even find yourself smiling."

A major disappointment for Michael Carreras (who can't have been smiling much himself during this period), *Shatter* sat on the shelf for three years before finally limping out in the UK care of EMI in September 1977. Predictably, amid the glut of kung fu and exploitation flicks also showing at the time, it was met with indifference. For its American release care of Avco-Embassy in March 1975 the film was re-titled *Call Him Mr. Shatter* (presumably in a nod to *They Call Me Mr. Tibbs!* [1970]). However, it met with much the same reaction, despite some heavy drumming in the trailer. "It's the most ferocious martial arts thriller of them all," exclaimed the excited voiceover, while of Shatter himself it warned, "Cross him and he'll put you in a box!" **Additional notes:** Keep and eye out for the Hitchcock-like cameo by Michael Carreras, who can be spotted being served a drink in the foyer of a hotel as Ansabi M'Goya and his entourage walk through at the top of the film. As for the camera-gun that Shatter uses to assassinate M'Goya, this idea seems to have been purloined from Hitchcock's *Foreign Correspondent* (1940). The actor Yemi Ajibade plays both General Ansabi M'Goya and his brother Colonel Dabula M'Goya. Lily Li's character clearly introduces herself as Mai-Ling during the course of proceedings, yet in the end credits she is listed as Mai-Mee (and as May-Ling in the German subtitles). Burt Reynolds was considered for the lead role, but was discounted when his salary demands rose after the release of *Deliverance* (1972).

Production companies: Hammer/Shaw Brothers. Distributors: EMI (UK), Avco Embassy (U.S.). Producers: Michael Carreras, Vee King Shaw. Director: Michael Carreras, Monte Hellman [uncredited]. Screenplay: Don Houghton. Cinematographers: Brian Probyn, John Wilcox, Roy Ford. Music: David Lindup. Music director: Philip Martell. Editor: Eric Boyd-Perkins. Assistant editor: Denis Whitehouse. Art director: Johnson Tsau (credited simply as Johnson). Special effects: Les Bowie. Assistant director: Godfrey Ho. Production manager: Chua Lam. Camera operator: Roy Ford. Focus puller: Keith Jones. Sound: Les Hammond. Dubbing mixer: Dennis Whitlock. Sound editors: Vernon Messenger, Jim Groom. Sound maintenance: Dan Grimmel. Boom operator: Tommy Staples. Assistant to the producer: Christopher Carreras. Continuity: Renee Glynne. Production secretary: Jean Walter. **Cast:** Stuart Whitman (Shatter), Ti Lung (Tai Pah), Lily Li (Mai-Ling), Peter Cushing (Rattwood), Anton Diffring (Hans Leber), Yemi Ajibade (General Ansabi M'Goya/Colonel Dabula M'Goya), Lo Wei (Howe), Liu Ya Ying (Leber's girl), Liu Ka Yong (First bodyguard), Huang Pei Chih (Second bodyguard), James Ma (Thai boxer), Chiang Han (Korean boxer), Kao Hsiung (Japanese boxer), Ho Ki-Chiong (Rattwood's thug [uncredited]), Hark-On Fung (Kung-fu student [uncredited]), Hoi Sang Lee (Referee [uncredited]). **DVD availability:** Anchor Bay (U.S. R1 NTSC), extras include a commentary by Stuart Whitman and Monte Hellman, plus a trailer, TV spots and an episode of *The World of Hammer* (1990 [first broadcast 1994], TV) titled *Thriller*

## Shaughnessy, Alfred

Following experience as a playwright and as an apprentice at Ealing (prior to which he had attended the Royal Military College Sandhurst and worked briefly on the London Stock Exchange), this British writer, producer and director (1916–2005) broke into films and television in the early fifties, and divided his time between the two for much the remainder of his career. Working as a producer, his early credits include *Laxdale Hall* (1952), which he also co-wrote, *Room in the House* (1955), which he also wrote, *Heart of a Child* (1958) and *Lunch Hour* (1962). He also directed a handful of films, among them *Cat Girl* (1957), *Suspended Alibi* (1956), *Six-Five Special* (1958) and *The Impersonator* (1961), which he also co-wrote. Meanwhile, his work as a screenwriter, either alone or in collaboration, includes *High Terrace* (1956), *Just My Luck* (1957) and *Tiffany Jones* (1973). However, he had his most enduring success on television, earning acclaim for the much-loved and admired series *Upstairs, Downstairs* (1970–1975, TV), for which he penned fifteen episodes (earning two Emmy nominations); he also worked as the series' script editor (Shaughnessy's family was a pillar of British high society, and he was able to use his own personal experiences, which included encounters with royalty, as research).

His other television credits as a writer include *Our Marie* (1953, TV), *The Cedar Tree* (1976–1978, TV), which he also created, *The Adventures of Sherlock Holmes* (1984–1985, TV) and *Ladies in Charge* (1985, TV). He also penned the script for *The Last Visitor*, an episode of Hammer's *Journey to the Unknown* (1968, TV), which also appeared in the compendium film *Journey to the Unknown* (1969, TVM). Prior to this he co-authored a screenplay titled *Crescendo* with Michael Reeves, which was subsequently bought by Hammer in 1966 after its production fell through at Compton Films. However, it lay on the shelf until 1969, when it was overhauled by Jimmy Sangster, with whom Shaughnessy shares the screen credit (the film was released in 1970).

Shaughnessy's books and memoirs include *Both Ends of the Candle* (1978), *Sarah* (1989), *Hugo* (1994) and *A Confession in Writing* (1997). He was married to the actress Jean Lodge (1927–) from 1948; she appeared in Hammer's *Dr. Morelle—The Case of the Missing Heiress* (1949), *Dick Barton Strikes Back* (1949) and *Death of an Angel* (1952). Their sons are the actors Charles Shaughnessy (1955–) and David Shaughnessy. **Hammer credits:** *The Last Visitor* (1968, TV [episode of *Journey to the Unknown*], teleplay), *Journey to the Unknown* (1969, TVM, teleplay), *Crescendo* (1970, co-screenplay)

## Shaw, Barbara

Shaw can be seen as a press woman in the opening night club scene in Hammer's *Never Look Back* (1952). Her other credits include *The Woman in the Hall* (1947), *Esther Waters* (1948), *Blind Man's Bluff* (1952) and *No Haunt for a Gentleman* (1952). **Hammer credits:** *Never Look Back* (1952, as Press woman)

## Shaw, Barnaby

Along with his brother Roderick (1958–1996), this British actor (1960–) played quadruplets in *Paper Dolls*, an episode of Hammer's *Journey to the Unknown* (1968, TV), which also appeared in the compendium film *Journey into Darkness* (1968, TVM). He can also be seen in Hammer's *Vampire Circus* (1972), again with his brother Roderick. His other credits include *House of Cards* (1968) and episodes of *UFO* (1970–1971, TV), *War and Peace* (1972–1974, TV), *The Pallisers* (1974, TV) and *Edward the Seventh* (1975, TV). His father was the actor Lauriston Shaw and his mother the singer Davina Dundas. **Hammer credits:** *Paper Dolls* (1968, TV [episode of *Journey to the Unknown*], as Stephen), *Journey into Darkness* (1968, TVM, as Stephen), *Vampire Circus* (1972, as Gustav Hauser)

## Shaw, Denis

In minor roles in eight Hammer films, this British character actor (1921–1971) is perhaps best remembered by fans for playing Mike, one of the drunken crate shifters in *The Mummy* (1959). His other credits include *The Long Memory* (1952), *The Colditz Story* (1955), *Jack the Ripper* (1958), *The Deadly Affair* (1966) and *The File of the Golden Goose* (1969), while his television appearances include episodes of *The Adventures of Robin Hood* (1955–1960, TV), *Saber of London* (1954–1960, TV) and *Here Come the Double Deckers!* (1970–1971, TV). **Hammer credits:** *The Mummy* (1959, as Mike), *The Man Who Could Cheat Death* (1959, as Man in tavern), *The Two Faces of Dr. Jekyll* (1960, as Tavern patron [uncredited]), *A Weekend with Lulu* (1961, as Bar patron), *The Curse of the Werewolf* (1961, as Gaoler), *The Pirates of Blood River* (1962, as Silver), *The Runaway* (1964, as Agent), *The Viking Queen* (1967, as Osiris)

## Shaw, Don

This prolific writer (1934–) toshed out *The Mark of Satan*, one of the more tedious episodes of *Hammer House of Horror* (1980, TV). His many other credits include episodes of *The First Lady* (1968–1969, TV), *Doomwatch* (1970–1972, TV), *Survivors* (1975–1977, TV), *Danger UXB* (1979, TV), *The Citadel* (1983, TV), *Bad Company* (1993, TV) and *Dangerfield* (1995–1999, TV), as well as such one-offs as *Bomber Harris* (1989, TVM), which earned him a shared BAFTA nomination for best single drama. **Hammer credits:** *The Mark of Satan* (1980, TV [episode of *Hammer House of Horror*])

## Shaw, Francis

This British composer (1942–) wrote the score for *Paint Me a Murder* (1984, TVM [episode of *Hammer House of Mystery and Suspense*]). His other credits include *The Barretts of Wimpole Street* (1982, TVM), *Jamaica Inn* (1983, TV), *And a Nightingale Sang* (1989, TVM), *Vendetta* (1995), *A Loving Act* (2001) and *Evil* (2003), plus episodes of *A Family Affair* (1979, TV) and *Crime and Punishment* (1979, TV). He also orchestrated and conducted *A Room with a View* (1985), composed additional music for *The Fourth Protocol* (1987), and was a music associate on *Ladies in Lavender* (2004). Other works include *Fanfare for Four Trumpets* (2007). **Hammer credits:** *Paint Me a Murder* (1984, TVM [episode of *Hammer House of Mystery and Suspense*])

## Shaw, Jack

This British actor (?–1970) played the role of Dick Barton's sidekick Jock Anderson in Hammer's first Dick Barton adventure, *Dick Barton—Special*

*Agent* (1948). However, he failed to appear in either of the sequels. **Hammer credits:** *Dick Barton—Special Agent* (1948, as Jock Anderson)

### Shaw, Ralph

Exclusive's branch manager for the city of Birmingham in the fifties, Shaw remained with the company until its demise at the end of the decade.

### Shaw, Richard

This British actor (1920–2010) had a minor role in Hammer's *The Gambler and the Lady* (1953). In films from 1946 with *Johnny Comes Flying Home*, his many other credits include *Three Little Girls in Blue* (1946), *The Crooked Sky* (1957), *Bottoms Up* (1960), *633 Squadron* (1964), *Give Us Tomorrow* (1978) and *Young Toscanini* (1988), plus episodes of *ITV Play of the Week* (1955–1968, TV), *Quatermass and the Pit* (1958–1959, TV), in which he played Sladden, *No Hiding Place* (1959–1967, TV) and *George and Mildred* (1976–1979, TV). **Hammer credits:** *The Gambler and the Lady* (1953, as Louis)

### Shaw, Roderick

Along with his brother Barnaby (1960–), this British actor (1958–1996) played quadruplets in *Paper Dolls*, an episode of Hammer's *Journey to the Unknown* (1968, TV), which also appeared in the compendium film *Journey into Darkness* (1968, TVM). He later appeared in *Vampire Circus* (1972), again alongside his brother Barnaby. His other credits include *The Adventures of Black Beauty* (1972–1974, TV), in which he played Kevin Gordon, and an episode of *The Pallisers* (1974, TV). His father was the actor Lauriston Shaw and his mother the singer Davina Dundas. **Hammer credits:** *Paper Dolls* (1968, TV [episode of *Journey to the Unknown*], as Rodney Blake), *Journey into Darkness* (1968, TVM, as Rodney Blake), *Vampire Circus* (1972, as Jon Hauser)

### Shaw, Roland

British born Shaw (1920–2012) composed the score for Hammer's *Straight on Till Morning* (1972). His other credits, mostly as an arranger or conductor, include *Dance Hall* (1950), *Konga* (1960), *Summer Holiday* (1963), *The Secret of My Success* (1965), *Song of Norway* (1970) and *The Great Waltz* (1972). **Hammer credits:** *Straight on Till Morning* (1972)

### Shaw, Run Run (Sir)

This prolific Chinese producer (1907–2014) formed the Shaw Brothers production company in 1958 with his brother Runme Shaw (1901–1985, real name Renmei Shao), which was based at the Shaw Brothers Studios in Clear Water Bay in the Kowloon district of Hong Kong (prior to this they had run a releasing company in Singapore and a production company named Unique Productions in Shanghai from 1924). Noted for cornering the martial arts market, Shaw's many films (either as producer, presenter or studio executive) include *Madame White Snake* (1963), *The One-Armed Swordsman* (1967), *The Bells of Death* (1968), *Golden Swallow* (1968), which went out in the UK as *The Girl with the Thunderbolt Kick* on a double bill with Hammer's *Captain Kronos—Vampire*

*Hunter* (1974), *Quan ji* (1971), which went out as *The Chinese Connection* on a double bill with Hammer's *Man at the Top* (1973) in some UK cinemas, *King Boxer* (1971), *Fists of Vengeance* (1972), which was double-billed in the UK with Hammer's *Frankenstein and the Monster from Hell* (1974), *Blood Money* (1974), *Cannonball* (1976), *Master Killer* (1978), *Fist of the White Lotus* (1982) and *8-Diagram Pole Fighter* (1984).

After being introduced to Michael Carreras by Don Houghton's Malaysian wife Pik Sen Lim, Shaw agreed to co-finance two films for Hammer: *The Legend of the 7 Golden Vampires* (1974), which he executive produced with Carreras, and *Shatter* (1974), with his nephew Vee King Shaw (1944–2017) involved as a producer on both films, neither of which managed to revive Hammer's flagging fortunes.

Recalled Michael Carreras of his association with Shaw, "I was excited by what I saw as a potentially lucrative partner in Run Run Shaw; I mean, here was a man who had the resources and market to make a hundred films a year if he wanted to."[85] However, the failure of *The Legend of the 7 Golden Vampires* to take off mystified Carreras: "It opened well here in the West End, but the fact that it made more money outside the Orient than it did inside seemed to defeat the purpose as far as I was concerned. It should've worked, and to this day I'm still puzzled about what went wrong."[86]

Commented *Shatter* star Stuart Whitman, who was less than impressed by the studio's facilities and Shaw himself, "I couldn't believe the restaurant there at Run Run Shaw's studio. It was on the top floor and the dishes were piled up and the dogs were walking in and out and pissing on the plates. It was disgusting and I kicked up my heels. Run Run Shaw wanted to kill me. The man would appear—he was like invisible—then all of a sudden he would appear. And he had parties and all that, but he would never invite me to any of them because I was an outcast. I couldn't go along with this idiot. I suppose he's still alive, because only the good guys die early."[87] Amazingly, thanks to ginseng and sheer bloody-mindedness, he lived to the ripe old age of 106!

Shaw went on to form Hong Kong's biggest local TV station TVB in 1967, remaining its chairman until 2011. He also later became involved with international productions, among them *Inseminoid* (1981), which he presented, and *Blade Runner* (1982), which he co-executive produced without credit. He directed only one film, *Xiangxialao Tan Qinjia* (1936). He was made a CBE in 1974, and knighted in 1977. His second wife was the singer, producer and production executive Mona Shaw (1934–2017, real name Meng-Lan Li, aka Fong Yat-Wa), whom he married in 1997. **Hammer credits:** *The Legend of the 7 Golden Vampires* (1974, presenter), *Shatter* (1974, production company)

### Shaw, Runme

The brother of Sir Run Run Shaw (1907–2014), Chinese born Runme Shaw (1901–1985, real name Renmei Shao) worked on Hammer's *The Legend of the 7 Golden Vampires* (1974) without credit as an executive producer. His many other credits (ei-

ther as a producer, presenter or studio executive) include *Nujum pak belalang* (1959), *Xi xiang ji* (1965), *Golden Swallow* (1968), which went out in the UK as *The Girl with the Thunderbolt Kick* on a double bill with Hammer's *Captain Kronos—Vampire Hunter* (1974), *San xiao* (1969), *Quan ji* (1971), which went out as *The Chinese Connection* on a double bill with Hammer's *Man at the Top* (1973) in some UK cinemas, *Tai yin zhi* (1972), *Fists of Vengeance* (1972), which was double-billed in the UK with Hammer's *Frankenstein and the Monster from Hell* (1974), *Qing suo* (1975), *Cobra Girl* (1977) and *Dai e qun ci* (1984). **Hammer credits:** *The Legend of the 7 Golden Vampires* (1974, executive producer [uncredited]), *Shatter* (1971, production company)

### Shaw, Vee King

This Hong Kong–based producer (1944–2017) shared his credit with Don Houghton on Hammer's *The Legend of the 7 Golden Vampires* (1974). This was shot back-to-back with the thriller *Shatter* (1974), on which he shared his credit with Michael Carreras. His other credits include *Gerak kilat* (1966) and *Xing xing wang* (1977). His uncle was producer Sir Run Run Shaw (1907–2014). **Hammer credits:** *The Legend of the 7 Golden Vampires* (1974), *Shatter* (1974)

### Shaw Brothers

In 1924, brothers Runme and Run Run Shaw set up Unique Productions in Shanghai. Later moving to Singapore, they founded a releasing company named Shaw Brothers. This in turn became a giant production facility in Clear Water Bay in Hong Kong's Kowloon district in 1958, and was run by various members of the Shaw clan (think of its as a sort of Easternized Warner Bros.). Noted for its martial arts films, the company was churning out as many as forty films per year by the mid-sixties, among them *The Love Eternal* (1963), *The Story of Sue San* (1964), *Come Drink with Me* (1966) and *The One-Armed Swordsman* (1967) and its sequels. The pace was kept up in the seventies with the likes of *King Boxer* (1971), *Death Kick* (1973) and *Cleopatra Jones and the Casino of Gold* (1976). During this period, the company also made two films in conjunction with Hammer: *The Legend of the 7 Golden Vampires* (1974) and the action thriller *Shatter* (1974), both of which were filmed in Hong Kong. Note that the Shaw-produced *Golden Swallow* (1968) was double-billed with Hammer's *Captain Kronos—Vampire Hunter* (1974) in the UK, albeit under the alternative title of *The Girl with the Thunderbolt Kick*, while *Quan ji* (1971) went out as *The Chinese Connection* on a double bill with Hammer's *Man at the Top* (1973) in some UK cinemas; *Fists of Vengeance* (1972) was meanwhile double-billed with *Frankenstein and the Monster from Hell* (1974) in the UK. **Hammer credits:** *The Legend of the 7 Golden Vampires* (1974), *Shatter* (1974)

### Shaw Brothers Studios

Established in 1958 and located in Clear Water Bay in Hong Kong's Kowloon district, this studio facility was used to film Hammer's *The Legend of the 7 Golden Vampires* (1974) and *Shatter* (1974).

Other films made at the studio include *Five Golden Dragons* (1967), which had co-starred Christopher Lee, *Valley of the Fangs* (1971), *Blood Money* (1974), *Cannonball* (1976) and *The 36th Chamber of Shaolin* (1978). By the mid–1980s, the Shaw Brothers had ceased to make films in Hong Kong, and were instead focusing on TVB, Hong Kong's fist terrestrial commercial TV station, which they had founded in 1973. The studio re-opened two decades later after a $130m refurb, this time run by the next generation of the family and their colleagues. New productions included *Drunken Monkey* (2003), *Turning Point* (2009), *The Fortune Buddies* (2011) and *I Love Hong Kong* (2012). **Hammer credits:** *The Legend of the 7 Golden Vampires* (1974), *Shatter* (1974)

### Shawzin, Barry

This French supporting actor (1930–1968) played the "American" in the Hammer featurette *A Man on the Beach* (1956). His other credits include *Guns of Darkness* (1962), *The Spanish Sword* (1962) and *Duffy* (1968), as well as an appearance as a doctor in Hammer's *The Man Who Could Cheat Death* (1959). He also produced, directed and co-wrote the short film *The Day the Sky Fell In* (1961). His television appearances include episodes of *The Adventures of Robin Hood* (1955–1960, TV), *Sir Francis Drake* (1961–1962, TV) and *Man in a Suitcase* (1967–1968, TV). **Hammer credits:** *A Man on the Beach* (1956, as American [uncredited]), *The Man Who Could Cheat Death* (1959, as Doctor)

### She

GB, 1965, 105m, Technicolor, HammerScope [2.35:1], RCA, cert A

The origins of Hammer's adaptation of the famous 1887 novel by H. Rider Haggard can be traced back to 1962, when it was suggested by Kenneth Hyman that the book would be an ideal subject for the company (the story had already been filmed seven times during the silent period and, most famously, in 1935 by producer Merian C. Cooper). At this stage in his career, Hyman was vice president in charge of production for Seven Arts, but had previously had several brushes with Hammer as a producer, and so any suggestions he might have to make were obviously taken seriously.

The story had everything grist to its mill for a bloodthirsty adventure in its tale of three friends who journey across Africa in search of the lost city of Kor, where they encounter its two-thousand-year-old ruler Ayesha, who has retained her beauty by periodically bathing in the blue flame of eternal life. Originally announced as a co-production between Seven Arts and ABPC (with whom Hammer had entered into a business partnership in 1963), the film was to have been based upon a screenplay by John Temple-Smith who had produced *Captain Clegg* (1962) for the studio. Universal was also to have been involved in the project at this point, but their cooling relationship with Hammer saw them withdraw from the proceedings early on. MGM would eventually provide funds for the film in return for U.S. distribution, but not before Hammer had also approached Paramount, AIP and the independent producer Joseph E. Levine for backing.

Unfortunately, Temple-Smith's screenplay was deemed unsatisfactory, and so it was re-worked by Berkely Mather, by which time Ursula Andress (hailed by publicists as "The world's most beautiful woman") had been signed for a fee of $50,000 to play the title character of Ayesha in what was a two-picture deal with Seven Arts. Andress had of course recently scored an international hit as Honey Rider in the first James Bond film *Dr. No* (1962), which, coincidentally, had also been co-scripted by Mather. However, Mather's screenplay was similarly rejected—as was a re-working of the original John Temple-Smith material by the film's director, Robert Day. The problem, it would seem, was the bloodthirsty nature of the original story, which contained numerous stabbings and beatings, along with the sadistic nature of Ayesha herself, who clearly takes pleasure in killing and immolation. Ironically, given their reputation, Hammer actually wanted to step back from the book's more horrific elements and present a family-oriented adventure on a grand scale, accentuating the central love story between Ayesha and the English adventurer whom she believes to be the reincarnation of her faithless lover, Killikrates, the High Priest of Isis, whom she murdered centuries earlier.

It was the eventual return to Hammer of Michael Carreras—who had been pursuing a series of personal projects through his own production company—that eventually rescued *She* from development hell. Coming onboard as producer (pre-production had hitherto been in the hands of Anthony Hinds), Carreras started from scratch by commissioning a new screenplay by David T. Chantler, who had co-written the screenplay for Hammer's *Cash on Demand* (1961). Chantler was ruthless with the novel, pruning back the more gruesome elements, as well as excising several extraneous characters and altering certain relationships. Instead he accentuated the romance and spectacle of the piece.

Setting the film in 1918 Palestine just after the end of World War I, Chantler's adaptation sees three Englishmen—a Cambridge don named Major Horace Holly, his young friend Leo Vincey and their manservant Job—in search of fresh adventure by way of avoiding returning home (comments Holly over a drink in a disreputable nightclub they have found, "I've no desire to go back to Cambridge to teach a lot of pimply-faced undergraduates the mysteries of the ancient civilizations"). Their adventure comes soon enough when Leo is kidnapped and taken to a palatial house after being enticed by the charms of a mysterious young woman named Ustane. Once at the house, Leo meets the beautiful Ayesha, who provides him with a map and ring, urging him to trek "across the Desert of Lost Souls and through the Mountains of the Moon" so as to be with her again, for it transpires that he bears a remarkable resemblance to her long-dead lover ("The likeness is exact," comments Billali, Ayesha's faithful high priest).

However, Leo has trouble convincing his friends what has happened to him (when he returns with Holly and Job to the house where he was held captive, they find the place deserted, prompting Holly to comment, "You really should take more water with it, old chap!"). Yet Holly and Job are persuaded to join Leo on his perilous journey after having seen the map, which contains the location of the lost city of Kuma (as it is now named), the whereabouts of which Holly has always longed to discover.

With the screenplay problems no longer an issue and the cast now in place—among them Peter Cushing as Major Holly, John Richardson as Leo, Bernard Cribbins as Job and Christopher Lee as Billali—*She* finally went into production on 24 August 1964, backed by a healthy budget of £250,000 (the final tally, including Andress's paycheque, eventually came in at £323,778). The shoot began with two weeks' location work to cover the friends' perilous trek, which was filmed in the Negev and Danago deserts in Israel. Upon completion of these scenes (which also required the presence of Ursula Andress for a brief oasis sequence), the unit returned to England and the soundstages of Elstree Studios, where principal photography continued until 17 October.

No doubt thanks to the exotic charms of the then-in vogue Andress (who posed nude in the June 1965 issue of *Playboy* to help promote the film), *She* proved to be a major box office success in both Britain and America. "Director Robert Day's overall excellent work brings out heretofore unknown depths in Andress's acting," praised *Variety*, seemingly unaware of the fact that the star had been dubbed by Nikki Van Der Zyl, just as she had been in *Dr. No* (it should also be noted that André Morell, who plays the tribal leader Haumeid, was also dubbed by Hammer regular George Pastell, presumably because his upper crust English accent was at odds with the role he was playing, making one wonder why he was cast in the first place).

Yet despite the undeniable appeal of Miss Andress, resplendent in a series of diaphanous gowns by Carl Toms, the film as a whole is a curiously lackluster affair, thanks primarily to Robert Jones' curiously cloistered and claustrophobic art direction, which reduces the lost city of Kuma to a series of rather unconvincing studio sets, wholly unworthy of Holly's awe when he first sees them. The trials of the friends' journey across the desert are efficiently enough handled via a series of dissolves, yet could just as effectively have been filmed on Camber Sands, thus saving the production the added expense of travelling to Israel (note that the distant shots of the Mountains of the Moon were lifted directly from MGM's *King Solomon's Mines* [1950], also based upon a novel by H. Rider Haggard). Unfortunately, the remainder of the film is very much studio-bound (including the early scenes in the streets of Palestine), with only an unconvincing matte painting of the ruined city of Kuma to give the film the sense of scale it very much needs but sadly lacks throughout.

No doubt owing to the extensive pruning (the book's vital Cambridge prologue is missing), the central characters lack background and come across as somewhat ill conceived. Cushing's stoical

Major Holly, for example, actually begins the film as something of a letch (he uses his empty brandy glass to accentuate the charms of a belly dancer in the opening nightclub sequence), while Job's captipping devotion to both Holly and Leo lacks feasibility. As written, John Richardson's Leo just doesn't possess the fevered state of mind that compels him to cross a vast desert to be with a woman he has only briefly met, while Christopher Lee's Billali seems to be missing the scenes which would explain his blinkered devotion to Ayesha (a scene in which the character was to be heard chanting at a religious ceremony was recorded for playback but sadly went unfilmed owing to the demands of the tight schedule). In the face of such shallow writing, the actors are left floundering, their performances as cardboard as the sets through which they pass. Unfortunately, the script's problems are further compounded by the plodding direction of Robert Day, while the unatmospheric lighting of Harry Waxman's widescreen photography accentuates rather than diminishes the fairground fakery of the art direction.

On the plus side, the scene in which Ayesha has fifteen of Haumeid's men thrown into a fiery pit gives the film a fleeting sense of what it could have been, while the climax in which Ayesha bathes in the blue flame of eternal life is truly fantastical, and is given additional impact by Roy Ashton's aging of Ursula Andress. Remembered Aida Young, "That took us all day to shoot. We put aside a Saturday, so that we could concentrate on it. We called in only the people who needed to be involved with the aging. Today, of course, her face would get old on a computer. It could be done in twenty minutes. Roy was so innovative and so technically excellent."[88] The real star of the film, however, is James Bernard's music (written and orchestrated in just five weeks), which provides the proceedings with a much-needed air of magic, mystery and majesty. The haunting central theme, built around the phrase "She who must be obeyed," is one of the composer's finest, and is augmented by a subsidiary military-style "Journey" theme that perfectly evokes the friends' arduous trek across the desert.

Recalled Christopher Lee of his work on the film, "Billali wasn't much of a challenge in the acting department, except physically. My sword fight with John Richardson was very demanding. He bashed me around quite a bit. I was, quite literally, nearly decapitated, all accidentally, mind you. You can't make a screen fight look real unless some actual fighting is done."[89] Nevertheless, there were compensations, chief among them the chance to work again with Peter Cushing. "I'm afraid we were occasionally a bit silly on this one—more so than usual. We always had great fun off camera, but never more so than on *She*. It was a good looking picture that, I believe, gave the audience its money's worth."[90]

Launched on a massive wave of publicity, *She*, despite its deficiencies, caught the imagination of the public when, following its trade show at Studio One on 12 March 1965, it was released on the ABC circuit in the UK by Warner-Pathé on 18 April on a double bill with *Pop Gear* (1965). *Monthly Film Bulletin* greeted the film as "a flat and uninspired

affair." Despite some similarly negative reviews ("Lacks style, sophistication, humor, sense and above all, a reason for being," sniped Bosley Crowther in the *New York Times*), the film's American release care of MGM on 1 September proved to be equally popular, prompting the *Independent Film Review* to comment, "MGM has come up with one of the most potently exploitable films of the year." Indeed, Hammer and its backers took out a series of ads ballyhooing the film's success ("*She* is the biggest box office news in England since *Goldfinger*," boasted one ad in *Variety*, while another claimed that "*She*-ing is believing!"). With box office like this, it was perhaps inevitable that *She* would go the way of Dracula, Frankenstein and the Mummy and provoke a sequel. Unfortunately, bringing *The Vengeance of She* (1968) to the screen proved to be equally as arduous as the production problems encountered on *She* itself. **Additional notes:** A promotional short titled *The She Story* was shown in cinemas prior to the film's release. This featured clips from the movie as well as footage shot in both the studio and abroad on location. Among those seen in the behind the scenes footage were Raquel Welch, Peter Cushing, Bernard Cribbins, producer Michael Carreras, director Robert Day and cinematographer Harry Waxman. The shields carried by Ayesha's guards later re-appeared in Hammer's *The Viking Queen* (1967). *She* was re-released on 10 August 1969 on a double bill with Hammer's *One Million Years B.C.* (1966), which brought in an extra £190,000 of revenue. A chant from James Bernard's soundtrack later turned up uncredited in a voodoo scene in *Mark of the Devil* (1984, TVM [episode of *Hammer House of Mystery and Suspense*]). The story was remade in 1982 with Sandahl Bergman, and in 2001 with Ophélie Winter; neither version set the world on fire.

Production companies: Hammer/Seven Arts/ Associated British Picture Corporation/Seven Arts. Distributors: Warner-Pathé (UK [ABC circuit]), MGM (U.S.). Producer: Michael Carreras. Associate producer: Aida Young. Director: Robert Day. Screenplay: David T. Chantler, based upon the novel by H. Rider Haggard. Cinematographer: Harry Waxman. Music: James Bernard. Music director: Philip Martell. Supervising editor: James Needs. Editor: Eric Boyd-Perkins. Art director: Robert Jones. Assistant art director: Don Mingaye. Costumes: Jackie Cummins, Carl Toms. Special effects: Bowie Films, Ltd., George Blackwell, Special effects assistants: Ian Scoones [uncredited], Kit West [uncredited], Ray Caple [mattes [uncredited]], Bob Cuff [mattes [uncredited]]. Opticals: Paul De Burg [uncredited]. Make-up: Roy Ashton, John O'Gorman. Hair: Eileen Warwick. Recording director: A.W. Lumkin. Sound: Claude Hitchcock. Sound editors: James Groom, Vernon Messenger,

**Christopher Lee sneers for the cameras in this publicity shot for *She* (1965) (Hammer/Associated British Picture Corporation/Seven Arts/Warner-Pathé/MGM/Studio Canal).**

Roy Hyde [uncredited]. Production manager: R.L.M. Davidson. Location manager: Yoski Hausdorf. Construction manager: Arthur Banks. Gaffer: Steve Birtles [uncredited]. Assistant director: Bruce Sharman. Camera operator: Ernest Day. Choreography: Cristyne Lawson. Continuity: Eileen Head. Assistant to producer: Ian Lewis. Stunts: Gerry Crampton [uncredited], Joe Dunne [uncredited], Terry Plummer [uncredited], Terry Richards [uncredited], Nosher Powell [uncredited]. Research: Andrew Low. Prop maker: Joy Seddon (later Cuff [uncredited]). Poster: Tom Chantrell (also 1969 double bill re-issue with *One Million Years B.C.* [1966]) [uncredited]. **Cast:** Ursula Andress (Ayesha), Peter Cushing (Major Horace Holly), John Richardson (Leo Vincey), Bernard Cribbins (Job), Christopher Lee (Billali), André Morell (Haumeid), Rosenda Monteros (Ustane), John Maxim (Captain of the Guard), Soraya (Nightclub dancer), Julie Mendez (Nightclub dancer), Lisa Peake (Nightclub dancer), Cherry Larman (Handmaiden), Bula Coleman (Handmaiden), The Oobladee Dancers (Native dancers), Roy Stewart (Black Guard [uncredited]), Eddie Powell (Stranger in bar [uncredited]), Nikki Van Der Zyl (voice of Ursula Andress [uncredited]), George Pastell (voice of André Morell [uncredited]). **DVD availability:** Warner Bros. (UK R2 PAL); Optimum (UK R2 PAL); Warner Archive (U.S. R1 NTSC). **CD availability:** *She* (GDI Records), which contains the entire score, plus *The Vengeance of She* and an interview with Mario Nascimbene; *The Devil Rides Out: The Film Music of James Bernard* (Silva Screen), which contains new recordings of *Ayesha—She Who Must Be Obeyed*, *Desert Quest*, *Bedouin Attack*, *In the Kingdom of She—Processional*, *In the Kingdom of She—The Cruelty of She*, *The Eternal Flame* and *The Destruction of She*; *The Hammer Film Music Collection: Volume One* (GDI Records), which contains the Main Title

### Sheard, Michael

This British (Scottish) actor (1938–2005, real name Donald Marriot Perkins) is best remembered for playing the bad tempered Mr. Bronson in the long-running children's series *Grange Hill* (1978–2008, TV) between 1985 and 1989. He also had a brief but memorable cameo as Hitler in *Indiana Jones and the Last Crusade* (1989), a role he also played in *Rogue Male* (1976, TVM), *The Dirty Dozen: Next Mission* (1985, TVM), *Hitler of the Andes* (2003, TV) and a two-part story titled *Hitler's Last Secret* (1978, TV) for *The Tomorrow People* (1973–1979, TV). His other film credits include *England Made Me* (1972), *Force Ten from Navarone* (1978), *The Riddle of the Sands* (1978), *All Quiet on the Western Front* (1979, TVM), *The Empire Strikes Back* (1980), in which he played Admiral Ozzel, and *Green Ice* (1981), plus a brief role in Hammer's *Holiday on the Buses* (1973) as a bus depot manager. His other small screen appearances include episodes of *Suspense* (1962–1963, TV), *The Main Chance* (1969–1975, TV), *Hannay* (1988–1989, TV) and *'Allo 'Allo!* (1982–1992, TV). His second wife was actress Rosalind Allaway (1940–), whom he married in 1961. His son is the actor Simon Sheard. **Hammer credits:** *Holiday on the Buses* (1973, as Depot manager)

### Shearing, Julie

This glamorous actress and model played one of the harem girls in the Hammer comedy *I Only Arsked!* (1958). Her other credits include *Cover Girl Killer* (1959), *The Bulldog Breed* (1960), *Jungle Street* (1961), *The Frightened City* (1961) and *The Share Out* (1962), plus a return to Hammer for *The Terror of the Tongs* (1961), in which she played a Tong room girl. **Hammer credits:** *I Only Arsked!* (1958, as Harem girl [uncredited]), *The Terror of the Tongs* (1961, as Tong room girl [uncredited])

### Sheehan, J.

Sheehan worked as a standby rigger on Hammer's *Blood from the Mummy's Tomb* (1971). **Hammer credits:** *Blood from the Mummy's Tomb* (1971 [uncredited])

### Sheffield, Jean

Sheffield worked as the first assistant dubbing editor on *Hammer House of Mystery and Suspense* (1984, TVM). Her other credits as a foley artist include *Salome's Last Dance* (1988), *In the Name of the Father* (1993), *Twin Town* (1997), *The Beach* (2000), *The Nine Lives of Tomas Katz* (2000) and *School for Seduction* (2004). **Hammer credits:** *Hammer House of Mystery and Suspense* (1984, TVM [uncredited])

### Sheldon, Caroline

This British actress (1950–) can be seen as Elizabeth in Hammer's *The Damned* (1963). Her other credits include episodes of *Tales from Dickens* (1958–1959, TV) and *Badger's Bend* (1963–1964, TV). **Hammer credits:** *The Damned* (1963, as Elizabeth)

### Shelley, Barbara

Following experience as a model, this elegant British leading actress (1932–, real name Barbara Kowin) broke into films with a bit part in the Hammer second feature *Mantrap* (1953), in which she appeared under her maiden name, Barbara Kowin. Shelley soon after moved to Italy, where she made several more films, among them *Ballata tragica* (1954), *The Barefoot Contessa* (1954), *Lacrime di sposa* (1955), *Luna nova* (1955) and *Mio figlio Nerone* (1956). Back in Britain, she resumed her career with the low budget horror film *Cat Girl* (1957), which led to a string of further shockers, among them *Blood of the Vampire* (1958), *Village of the Damned* (1960) and *Ghost Story* (1974).

Her second film for Hammer was the brutal POW saga *The Secret of Blood Island* (1958), which led to work on several key films for the company, among them *The Gorgon* (1964), in which she shared the title role with Prudence Hyman. Commented *Variety* of Shelley's performance in the latter, "Barbara Shelley, as Peter Cushing's assistant, is a redheaded beauty with considerable thesping intelligence and charm." *The Gorgon* was followed by a major role in *Dracula—Prince of Darkness* (1966), in which she proved memorable as the repressed Helen Kent. She also featured prominently in *Rasputin—The Mad Monk* (1966) as Sonia Vasilivitch and, most importantly, played the pivotal role of Barbara Judd in *Quatermass and the Pit* (1967), her performance in which prompted the *Sunday Telegraph* to describe her as "the best frightened lady in the business."

Remembered the actress of one particular sequence in *Prince of Darkness*, "In the scene before Dracula has appeared when we're in the big dining hall, and the moment before Philip Latham appears and mentions the words 'My master is Count Dracula,' the wind machines start up and the candles flicker and the banners blow, and of course these don't stay on the soundtrack, but on the first take of that particular shot, one of the wind machines started far too forcefully, and all the candles, instead of flickering went out, and all four of us, Charles Tingwell, Suzan Farmer, Francis Matthews and myself, automatically burst into 'Happy birthday, dear Dracula, happy birthday to you.' And Terry Fisher, being the sort of man he was, fell into laughing with all the rest of the crew."[91] She also admitted that in the middle of her violent staking scene, "I swallowed one of my fangs."[92]

Recalled Roy Ward Baker, who directed Shelly

**Barbara Shelley comes over all ethereal in this charming publicity shot taken during the making of *Dracula–Prince of Darkness* (1966) (Hammer/Associated British Picture Corporation/Seven Arts/Warner Pathé Distributors/Twentieth Century–Fox/Studio Canal).**

in *Quatermass and the Pit*, "[She was] a marvellous looking woman, and she was very good. She knew exactly what to do and how to do it. I never knew her before *Quatermass*, but she was lovely, very nice."[93]

Shelley's non-genre films include *The End of the Line* (1957), *The Story of David* (1960), *Postman's Knock* (1962), *Blind Corner* (1963) and *More Than a Messiah* (1992), while her television work includes episodes of *White Hunter* (1957–1958, TV), *Doctor Who* (1963–1989, TV), *Justice* (1971–1974, TV), *Oil Strike North* (1975, TV) and *EastEnders* (1985–, TV). She was also interviewed about her career at Hammer in *A History of Horror with Mark Gatiss* (2010, TV). **Hammer credits:** *Mantrap* (1953, as Fashion compere [as Barbara Kownin]), *The Camp on Blood Island* (1958, as Kate Keiller), *The Shadow of the Cat* (1961, as Beth Venable), *The Gorgon* (1964, as Carla Hoffman), *The Secret of Blood Island* (1965, as Elaine), *Dracula—Prince of Darkness* (1966, as Helen Kent), *Rasputin—The Mad Monk* (1966, as Sonia Vasilivitch), *Quatermass and the Pit* (1967, as Barbara Judd)

### Shelley, Elizabeth

This singer appeared in the Hammer musical short *The Edmundo Ros Half Hour* (1956). Her other credits include an episode of *Kaleidoscope* (1946–1952, TV). **Hammer credits:** *The Edmundo Ros Half Hour* (1956, as Herself)

## Shelley, Joanna

Shelley can be seen as a woodsman's daughter in Hammer's *The Vampire Lovers* (1970). Her other credits include episodes of *Doctor at Large* (1971, TV), *The Silver Sword* (1971, TV), *Justice* (1971–1974, TV) and *Country Matters* (1972–1973, TV). **Hammer credits:** *The Vampire Lovers* (1970, as Woodsman's daughter)

## Shelley, Mary Wollstonecraft

This celebrated British authoress (1797–1851, maiden name Mary Wollstonecraft Godwin) is best known for her 1818 novel *Frankenstein; or, The Modern Prometheus*, which has been staged and filmed many times (the first stage production, *Frankenstein; or, The Man and the Monster* appeared in 1826, while Thomas Edison made a potted film version in 1910). Classic versions of the tale include Universal's *Frankenstein* (1931) and its sequel, *Bride of Frankenstein* (1935). The story was remade by Hammer as *The Curse of Frankenstein* in 1957. A major commercial success, it was the first color version of the story, as well as Britain's first color horror film. Six sequels followed, including a loose remake, *The Horror of Frankenstein* (1970). More recent versions of the story include *Mary Shelley's Frankenstein* (1994), *I, Frankenstein* (2014) and *Victor Frankenstein* (2015). Married to the poet Percy Bysshe Shelley (1792–1822) from 1816, her other works include *Mathilda* (1819) and *The Last Man* (1826). She has been portrayed on film several times, notably by Elsa Lanchester in *Bride of Frankenstein* (1935), by Natasha Richardson in *Gothic* (1986), by Alice Krige in *Haunted Summer* (1988) and by Bridget Fonda in *Frankenstein Unbound* (1990). **Hammer credits:** *The Curse of Frankenstein* (1957), *Tales of Frankenstein: The Face in the Tombstone Mirror* (1958, TV), *The Revenge of Frankenstein* (1958), *The Evil of Frankenstein* (1964), *Frankenstein Created Woman* (1967), *Frankenstein Must Be Destroyed* (1969), *The Horror of Frankenstein* (1970), *Frankenstein and the Monster from Hell* (1974), *Frankenstein* (1974, LP [unreleased])

## Shelley, Norman

This British actor (1903–1980) plays one of the four guests evicted from Anna Spengler's boarding house in Hammer's *Frankenstein Must Be Destroyed* (1969). His other credits include *Thread O' Scarlet* (1930), *Went the Day Well?* (1942), *The Monkey's Paw* (1948), *The Angry Silence* (1960), *A Place to Go* (1963), *Otley* (1968) and *Oh! What a Lovely War* (1969), while his television appearances take in episodes of *The Railway Children* (1957, TV), *The Main Chance* (1969–1975, TV) and *To Serve Them All My Days* (1980–1981, TV). A radio stalwart, he played Colonel Danby in *The Archers* (1950–) for many years, and Dr. Watson in *Sherlock Holmes* (1952–1969). It is also claimed that he was Winston Churchill's "voice" in a number of radio broadcasts. **Hammer credits:** *Frankenstein Must Be Destroyed* (1969, as Guest)

## Shelton, Joy

In films from 1943 with *Millions Like Us*, this RADA trained British leading lady (1922–2000) was familiar to radio audiences in the forties and fifties for playing the role of Joan Carr, the girlfriend of PC 49 in *The Adventures of PC 49* (1947–1953), a part she reprised for the second Hammer movie based on the serial, *A Case for PC 49* (1951), the character having been absent from the first film, *The Adventures of PC 49—The Case of the Guardian Angel* (1949). Her other credits include *Waterloo Road* (1944), *Impulse* (1955), *The Greengage Summer* (1961) and *H.M.S. Defiant* (1962), plus episodes of *My Wife Jacqueline* (1952, TV), in which she played Jacqueline Bridger, *Z Cars* (1962–1978, TV) and *The Darling Buds of May* (1991–1993, TV). She was married to the actor Sydney Tafler (1916–1979) from 1944. He appeared in three Hammer films: *The Saint's Return* (1953), *The Glass Cage* (1954) and *A Weekend with Lulu* (1961). Their children are the actors Jennifer Tafler (1945–) and Jonathan Tafler. **Hammer credits:** *A Case for PC 49* (1951, as Joan Carr)

## Shen, Chan

This Taiwanese actor (1940–1984, real name Chan Yi-Cheng) can be seen as Kah, The High Priest of the 7 Golden Vampires, whose body Dracula commandeers so as to better go about his business in Hammer's *The Legend of the 7 Golden Vampires* (1974). His many other credits, which number over 160 films, include *Shi man qing nian shi wan jun* (1967), *Five Fingers of Death* (1972), *Cleopatra Jones and the Casino of Gold* (1975), *Die xian* (1980) and *Di ze ye feng kuang* (1985). His wife was the actress Shirley Yu, to whom he was briefly married in 1976. **Hammer credits:** *The Legend of the 7 Golden Vampires* (1974, as Kah)

## Shenstone, Claire

This British actress (1948–) can be seen as a hotel clerk in Hammer's *Moon Zero Two* (1969). Her other credits include *The Pale Faced Girl* (1969) and *The Best Pair of Legs in the Business* (1972), plus episodes of *Out of the Unknown* (1965–1971, TV), *Doctor in the House* (1969–1970, TV) and *Please Sir!* (1968–1972, TV). **Hammer credits:** *Moon Zero Two* (1969, as Hotel clerk)

## Shepherd, Albert

Shepherd can be spotted as a "loader" in Hammer's *Quatermass and the Pit* (1967). His other credits include *Charlie Bubbles* (1968) and *Before Winter Comes* (1969), plus a return to Hammer for *The Anniversary* (1968), while his small screen work includes episodes of *Danger Man* (1964–1966, TV), *Department S* (1969–1970, TV), *The Growing Pains of PC Penrose* (1975, TV), *Rosie* (1977–1981, TV) and *God's Wonderful Railway* (1980, TV). **Hammer credits:** *Quatermass and the Pit* (1967, as Loader [uncredited]), *The Anniversary* (1968, as Construction worker)

## Shepherd, Cybill

Following experience as a beauty queen (Miss Congeniality) and model, this American actress and singer (1950–) broke into films, making a major impact with her debut in *The Last Picture Show* (1971). She went on to appear in two more films for its director, Peter Bogdanovich, with whom she had a relationship for a period. These were *Daisy Miller* (1974) and *At Long Last Love* (1975), both of which were commercial disasters, following which her career faltered. Her other credits during this period include *The Heartbreak Kid* (1972), *Taxi Driver* (1976) and *Silver Bears* (1977). She was also cast as madcap heiress Amanda Kelly in Hammer's remake of *The Lady Vanishes* (1979), though she hadn't been the first choice (Faye Dunaway and Diane Keaton had also been considered). Shepherd revived her career in the eighties with the hit sleuth series *Moonlighting* (1985–1989, TV), which earned her an Emmy nomination and won her two Golden Globes plus a third nomination, but her film career was still in the doldrums thanks to such titles as *Chances Are* (1989), *Texasville* (1990), which re-united her with Bogdanovich, and *Married to It* (1991). TV again came to the rescue with the hit sitcom *Cybill* (1995–1998, TV), which earned her three Emmy nominations and won her a third Golden Globe plus another nomination, since which she has divided her time between singing engagements and generally unworthy film assignments. Her more recent credits include *The Muse* (1999), *Marine Life* (2000), *Open Window* (2006), *Expecting Mary* (2010) and *Rose* (2017), plus appearances in such series as *I'm with Her* (2003–2004, TV), *The L Word* (2004–2009, TV), *Eastwick* (2009–2010, TV) and *The Client List* (2012–2013, TV), in which she played Linette Montgomery. Her children include actress Clementine Ford (1979–) and writer Ariel Shepherd-Oppenheim (1987–). **Hammer credits:** *The Lady Vanishes* (1979, as Amanda Kelly)

## Shepherd, Pauline

This British supporting player (1938–) can be seen as a tavern girl in Hammer's *The Two Faces of Dr. Jekyll* (1960). Her other credits include *Friends and Neighbours* (1959), *The Pure Hell of St. Trinian's* (1960), *Operation Cupid* (1960) and *Mr. Topaze* (1961), plus episodes of *No Hiding Place* (1959–1967, TV), *Home Tonight* (1961, TV) and *The Avengers* (1961–1969, TV). **Hammer credits:** *The Two Faces of Dr. Jekyll* (1960, as Tavern girl [uncredited])

## Sheppard, Morgan

This British actor (1932–2019, aka William Morgan Sheppard) had a brief role at the conclusion of *Carpathian Eagle* (1980, TV [episode of *Hammer House of Horror*]) and also cropped up in a supporting role as an artist in *Paint Me a Murder* (1984, TVM [episode of *Hammer House of Mystery and Suspense*]). Following stage experience, he made his film debut with *Strongroom* (1962). His other credits include *Marat/Sade* (1967), *Tell Me Lies* (1968), *The Duellists* (1977), *The Sea Wolves* (1980), *Cry Freedom* (1987), *Over Her Dead Body* (2008), *Mysterious Island* (2010), in which he played Captain Nemo, *April Apocalypse* (2013) and *Last Man Club* (2016), plus episodes of *Crown Court* (1972–1984, TV), *The Day of the Triffids* (1981, TV), *Gargoyles* (1994–1996, TV), *Timecop* (1997–1998, TV) and *Biker Mice from Mars* (2006–2007, TV). His son is the actor, producer and director Mark Sheppard (1964–). **Hammer credits:** *Carpathian Eagle* (1980, TV [episode of

*Hammer House of Horror*], as Hospital gardener), *Paint Me a Murder* (1984, TVM [episode of *Hammer House of Mystery and Suspense*], as Mahaffy)

## Shepperton Studios

Filmmaking at Shepperton dates back to 1931 when Scottish businessman Norman Loudon acquired the country house Littleton Park and its sixty acres of grounds. In 1932 the complex was named the Sound City Film Producing and Recording Studios, and among the first films shot there were *Watch Beverly* (1932) and *Reunion* (1932). Other production companies, among them MGM and Argyle Talking Pictures, were soon making use of the facilities, and by 1935, floor space was in big demand, so much so that a program of expansion was undertaken in 1936 which resulted in the addition of several new soundstages. Over the following decades, the studio played host to such films as *French Without Tears* (1939), *Richard III* (1955), *Room at the Top* (1958), *Becket* (1964), *Oliver!* (1968), *Alien* (1979), *Robin Hood: Prince of Thieves* (1990), *Billy Elliot* (1999), *The Golden Compass* (2007), *Hugo* (2011), *Gravity* (2013) and *Avengers: Age of Ultron* (2015). In February 1995, director brothers Ridley and Tony Scott led a consortium to buy the studios. Hammer's connection with the facility includes the shooting of scenes for the wartime drama *Yesterday's Enemy* (1959), along with sequences for *When Dinosaurs Ruled the Earth* (1970). The comedy *A Weekend with Lulu* (1961) was also shot there. **Hammer credits:** *Yesterday's Enemy* (1959), *A Weekend with Lulu* (1961), *When Dinosaurs Ruled the Earth* (1970)

## Sheridan, Cecil

This Irish actor (1909–1980) played the minor role of a shopkeeper in Hammer's *The Viking Queen* (1967). His other credits include *Ulysses* (1967), *Catholics* (1973, TVM) and *Farmers* (1978, TVM). **Hammer credits:** *The Viking Queen* (1967, as Shopkeeper)

## Sheridan, Dinah

Best remembered for her roles in both *Genevieve* (1953) and *The Railway Children* (1970), this charming, always welcome British actress (1920–2012, real name Dinah Nadyejda Ginsburg [some sources say Mec]) made her film debut in 1936 in *Irish and Proud of It* following training at the Italia Conti School. Other early films include *Landslide* (1937), *For You Alone* (1945), *Murder in Reverse* (1945) and *29 Acacia Avenue* (1945), in all of which she co-starred with the first of her four husbands, Jimmy Hanley (1918–1970), to whom she was married between 1942 and 1952, and who went on to appear in Hammer's *Room to Let* (1950) and *The Lost Continent* (1968). Sheridan's other films include *The Huggetts Abroad* (1949), *Blackout* (1950), *Where No Vultures Fly* (1951), *The Sound Barrier* (1952) and *The Story of Gilbert and Sullivan* (1953). Following her second marriage to Rank's managing director John Davis (1906–1993), to whom she was married between 1954 and 1965, Sheridan effectively retired from the screen, but later returned in triumph following her divorce in *The Railway Children*, in which she played the mother. Subsequent appearances include *The Mir-*

*ror Crack'd* (1980) and such series as *Don't Wait Up* (1983, TV) and *All Night Long* (1994, TV). She also popped up in an episode of *Hammer House of Horror* (1980, TV), in which she can be seen as a newspaper editor. Sheridan's third husband was the actor John Merivale (1917–1990), to whom she was married from 1986 until his death. Her son is the one-time Tory party chairman Sir Jeremy Hanley (1945–) and her daughter is the actress and TV presenter Jenny Hanley (1947–), who appeared in Hammer's *Scars of Dracula* (1970). **Hammer credits:** *The Thirteenth Reunion* (1980, TV [episode of *Hammer House of Horror*], as Gwen Cox)

## Sheridan, Gale

Sheridan appeared as one of the harem girls in the Hammer comedy *I Only Arsked!* (1958). Her other credits include *She Always Gets Their Man* (1962) and *Three Spare Wives* (1962), plus an episode of *Rendezvous* (1957–1961, TV). **Hammer credits:** *I Only Arsked!* (1958, as Harem girl [uncredited])

## Sheridan, Paul

This British actor (1897–1973) had a minor role in Hammer's *Who Killed Van Loon?* (1948), and later popped up as a croupier in *The Gambler and the Lady* (1953). His other credits include *Two Wives for Henry* (1933), *It Happened in Paris* (1935), *The Rat* (1937), *Candlelight in Algeria* (1944), *My Brother Jonathan* (1948), *Penny Princess* (1952) and *A French Mistress* (1960), plus episodes of *Douglas Fairbanks, Jr. Presents* (1953–1957, TV). **Hammer credits:** *Who Killed Van Loon?* (1948, unnamed role [uncredited]), *The Gambler and the Lady* (1953, as Croupier [uncredited])

## Sherie, Fenn

Often teamed with Ingram d'Abbes, this British screenwriter (1896–1953) was one of six writers to work on the script for Hammer's Paul Robeson vehicle *Song of Freedom* (1936). With d'Abbes, he also co-authored the Hammer comedy *Sporting Love* (1936), and penned a further Robeson vehicle, *Big Fella* (1937), this time for British Lion. His other credits, all with d'Abbes, include *Blue Smoke* (1935), *Late Extra* (1935), *Terror on Tiptoe* (1936 [which was based on the duo's play *Shadowman*]), *Leave It to Me* (1937), *I've Got a Horse* (1938), *Around the Town* (1938) and *Home from Home* (1939). He began writing for the screen with *Two of a Trade* (1928). **Hammer credits:** *Song of Freedom* (1936), *Sporting Love* (1936)

## Sherman, Marianne

Sherman can be seen as a punk getting a tattoo in *Mark of the Devil* (1984, TVM [episode of *Hammer House of Mystery and Suspense*]). She has also appeared on stage. **Hammer credits:** *Mark of the Devil* (1984, TVM [episode of *Hammer House of Mystery and Suspense*], as Butch girl)

## Sherman, Teddi

This American screenwriter (1921–2019, real name Theodora Sherman, aka Lois Sherman) co-authored the screenplay for Hammer's *Ten Seconds to Hell* (1959) with the film's director, Robert

Aldrich, with whom she re-worked an original script by Lawrence P. Bachmann, upon whose book *The Phoenix* the film was based. Sherman's other credits include *Four Faces West* (1948), *Tennessee's Partner* (1955), *Four for Texas* (1964), again for Aldrich, and *Rage* (1966). She also contributed scripts to such series as *Highway Patrol* (1955–1959, TV), *Tombstone Territory* (1957–1960, TV), *Wagon Train* (1957–1965, TV) and *Mannix* (1967–1975, TV). Her father was the producer Harry Sherman (1884–1952), her sister is the actress Lynn Sherman, and her daughter is the actress Sherman Baylin. **Hammer credits:** *Ten Seconds to Hell* (1959)

## Sherrier, Julian

This Indian born actor (1929–2012) played the role of Bright Arrow in *The Indian Spirit Guide*, an episode of Hammer's *Journey to the Unknown* (1968, TV), which also appeared in the compendium film *Journey to Midnight* (1968, TVM). His film credits include *Laughing Anne* (1953), *The Road to Hong Kong* (1962), *Nine Hours to Rama* (1962), *Stopover Forever* (1964), *633 Squadron* (1964) and *The Deadly Affair* (1966), while his other small screen appearances include episodes of *Saber of London* (1954–1960, TV), *Z Cars* (1962–1978, TV), *The Saint* (1962–1969, TV) and *The Onedin Line* (1971–1980, TV). **Hammer credits:** *The Indian Spirit Guide* (1968, TV [episode of *Journey to the Unknown*], as Bright Arrow), *Journey to Midnight* (1968, TVM, as Bright Arrow)

## Sherriff, Betty

British born Sherriff (1925–2000) worked as the hair stylist on Hammer's *Man About the House* (1974). She later returned for four episodes of *Hammer House of Horror* (1980, TV) and five episodes of *Hammer House of Mystery and Suspense* (1984, TVM). Her many other credits include *The Happiest Days of Your Life* (1950), *Time Lock* (1957), *Emergency* (1962), *The Birthday Party* (1968), *Carry On Emmannuelle* (1978), *Hawk the Slayer* (1980) and *The Second Victory* (1986), plus episodes of such series as *Danger Man* (1964–1966, TV), *The Pathfinders* (1972–1973, TV) and *The Protectors* (1972–1974, TV). **Hammer credits:** *Man About the House* (1974), *The House That Bled to Death* (1980, TV [episode of *Hammer House of Horror*]), *The Mark of Satan* (1980, TV [episode of *Hammer House of Horror*]), *Guardian of the Abyss* (1980, TV [episode of *Hammer House of Horror*]), *Growing Pains* (1980, TV [episode of *Hammer House of Horror*]), *The Corvini Inheritance* (1984, TVM [episode of *Hammer House of Mystery and Suspense*]), *Paint Me a Murder* (1984, TVM [episode of *Hammer House of Mystery and Suspense*]), *Child's Play* (1984, TVM [episode of *Hammer House of Horror*]), *And the Wall Came Tumbling Down* (1984, TVM [episode of *Hammer House of Mystery and Suspense*]), *Tennis Court* (1984, TVM [episode of *Hammer House of Mystery and Suspense*])

## Sherwin, Derrick

This British actor, writer and producer (1936–2018) played Number One in Hammer's *The Vengeance of She* (1968). His other credits include *The Spanish Sword* (1962) and *Accidental Death* (1963), plus episodes of such series as *William Tell* (1958–

1959, TV) and *Scales of Justice* (1962–1967, TV). He also wrote and produced for such series as *Doctor Who* (1963–1989, TV), in which he also appeared, and *Paul Temple* (1969–1971, TV). His wife was the actress Jane Sherwin, to whom he was married between 1956 and 1982. **Hammer credits:** *The Vengeance of She* (1968, as Number One)

### Sherwood, William

This Irish bit player (1898–1986) was originally cast as a priest on a coach in Hammer's *Dracula* (1958), but was sadly robbed of his moment of glory when his scene didn't make it to the final print (some sources query whether it was actually filmed in the first place). He can, however, be seen in *The Man Without a Body* (1957), *Intent to Kill* (1958), *The Girl on the Boat* (1962) and *Operation Third Form* (1966), as well as episodes of *Starr and Company* (1958, TV), in which he played the title role, *Hancock* (1961, TV) and *Quick Before They Catch Us* (1966, TV). Also on stage. **Hammer credits:** *Dracula* (1958, as priest [scene excised])

### Shevaloff, Valerie

Shevaloff can be seen as one of the fourteen Tong room girls in Hammer's *The Terror of the Tongs* (1961). Her other credits include *The Counterfeit Plan* (1957). **Hammer credits:** *The Terror of the Tongs* (1961, as Tong room girl [uncredited])

### Shew, Edward Spencer

A former crime correspondent for the *Daily Express*, Shew (1908–1977) provided the story for Hammer's *Hands of the Ripper* (1971). This was subsequently turned into a screenplay by L.W. Davidson. Shew also novelized the screenplay, which was published by Sphere. His other books include the true crime compendium *A Companion to Murder* (1960), which carried the subtitle *A Dictionary of Death by Poison, Death by Shooting, Death by Suffocation and Drowning, Death by the Strangler's Hand, 1900–1950*; it was followed by *A Second Companion to Murder* (1961). Stories from these books (*The Mass Poisoner* and *Murder Cries Out*) also appeared in issues of the *John Creasey Mystery Magazine* in 1961. His novels include *Miss Proutie or, The Lady Who Rode on a Tiger* (1952). **Hammer credits:** *Hands of the Ripper* (1971)

### Shewring, Sally

British born Shewring worked as a production assistant on Hammer's remake of *The Lady Vanishes* (1979). Her other credits in this capacity include *Flame* (1974), *Sinbad and the Eye of the Tiger* (1977), *Holocaust 2000* (1977), *The Four Feathers* (1978, TVM) and *The Long Good Friday* (1980), as well as the TV series *Dick Turpin* (1979–1982, TV), prior to which she was a production secretary on *10 Rillington Place* (1970). She went on to work as a production co ordinator on *Pink Floyd The Wall* (1982), a unit manager on *She'll Be Wearing Pink Pyjamas* (1984), a location manager on *Runners* (1984) and a production manager on *Biggles* (1986). **Hammer credits:** *The Lady Vanishes* (1979 [uncredited])

### Sheybal, Vladek

Best known for his work for director Ken Russell, which includes *The Debussy Film* (1965, TV), *Billion Dollar Brain* (1967), *Women in Love* (1969), *The Music Lovers* (1970) and *The Boy Friend* (1971), this intense-looking Polish character actor (1923–1992, real name Wladyslaw Sheybal) began his film career in his home country, appearing in the likes of *Trzy kobiety* (1956) and *Kanal* (1957). Once in Britain, he began working as a television director on such series as *ITV Play of the Week* (1955–1968, TV), for which he directed *The Visitors* (1961, TV), and *ITV Television Playhouse* (1955–1967, TV), for which he directed *A Choice of Weapons* (1962, TV), but he soon after returned to acting. Frequently cast as villainous types, his film career includes supporting roles and cameos in *From Russia with Love* (1963), *Casino Royale* (1967), *Deadfall* (1968), *Puppet on a Chain* (1970), *Funny Money* (1982) and *Strike It Rich* (1990). He can also be seen in Hammer's remake of *The Lady Vanishes* (1979), somewhat underused as the Trainmaster. His TV work as an actor includes episodes of *The Saint* (1962–1969, TV), *Z Cars* (1962–1978, TV), *Callan* (1967–1972, TV) and *UFO* (1970–1973, TV), in which he played Dr. Doug Jackson. His brother was the assistant director Kazimierz Sheybal (1920–2003). **Hammer credits:** *The Lady Vanishes* (1979, as Trainmaster)

### Shilton, Len

This British sound technician worked on a handful of Hammer assignments during his prolific career, notable among them *Hell Is a City* (1960), which featured much location work. His many other credits, over one-hundred of them, include *Tank Patrol* (1941), *Lisbon Story* (1946), *Oh … Rosalinda!!* (1955), *It's Great to Be Young!* (1956), *I Was Monty's Double* (1958), *Summer Holiday* (1963), *Theatre of Death* (1966) and *Some Will, Some Won't* (1969), plus episodes of *The Avengers* (1961–1969, TV), *Department S* (1969–1970, TV) and *Randall and Hopkirk (Deceased)* (1969–1971, TV). **Hammer credits:** *Hell Is a City* (1960, sound), *Sands of the Desert* (1960, sound), *Taste of Fear* (1961, sound), *One Million Years B.C.* (1966, sound), *Slave Girls* (1968, sound mixer), *Lust for a Vampire* (1971, dubbing mixer [uncredited])

### Shima, Yvonne

This Canadian-Japanese actress can be seen as Liang Ti in Hammer's Cold War thriller *Visa to Canton* (1960). Her other credits include *The Savage Innocents* (1960), *The World of Suzie Wong* (1960), *The Road to Hong Kong* (1962), *Dr. No* (1962), *The Cool Mikado* (1963) and *Genghis Khan* (1964). **Hammer credits:** *Visa to Canton* (1960, as Liang Ti [uncredited])

### Shine, Bill

Specializing in upper-class types, this British supporting actor (1911–1997, real name Wilfred William Dennis Shine, Jr.) made his film debut in 1929 with *The Flying Scotsman*, which he followed with such eclectic fare as *Rich and Strange* (1932), *Waltzes from Vienna* (1933), *The Scarlet Pimpernel* (1934), *Let George Do It* (1940), *The Red Shoes* (1948), *Blue Murder at St. Trinian's* (1957), *The Yel-*

low *Rolls-Royce* (1964) and *The Jigsaw Man* (1983), among around one-hundred others. Inevitably, he worked for Hammer, but surprisingly only twice. His TV work includes episodes of *The Avengers* (1961–1969, TV) and *Supergran* (1985–1987, TV), in which he played Inventor Black. His father was the actor Wilfred Shine (1863–1939). His first wife (of two) was actress Julia Lang (1921–2010), to whom he was married from 1942 to 1949, and who appeared in Hammer's *Dr. Morelle—The Case of the Missing Heiress* (1949). **Hammer credits:** *Never Look Back* (1952, as Willie), *Women Without Men* (1956, as Reveller)

### Shinerock, John

British born Shinerock (1933–) worked as the focus puller on Hammer's *The Gorgon* (1964). Following experience as a clapper loader on such films as *The Colditz Story* (1955), he graduated to focus puller on *The Golden Disc* (1958), and to camera operator on *The Third Alibi* (1961). His other credits as focus puller include *Dr. No* (1962), *From Russia with Love* (1963) and *The Quiller Memorandum* (1966), while his other credits as a camera operator include *Poppies Are Also Flowers* (1966) and *The Mackenzie Break* (1970). **Hammer credits:** *The Gorgon* (1964 [uncredited])

### Shingler, Helen

This British actress (1919–) played the leading role of Liz Rossiter in the Hammer programer *The Rossiter Case* (1951). Her other films include *Quiet Weekend* (1946), *Judgment Deferred* (1951) and *The Lady with the Lamp* (1951). Also busy on television, her work here includes appearances in *Maigret* (1960–1963, TV), in which she played Madame Maigret, *Love Story* (1963–1974, TV) and *Oscar* (1985, TV). Her husband was the producer Seafield Head (1919–2009), whom she married in 1944; their sons are the actors Murray Head (1946–) and Anthony Head (1954–). **Hammer credits:** *The Rossiter Case* (1951, as Liz Rossiter)

### Shingleton, Wilfred (Wilfrid)

In films from 1932 as an assistant to Edward Carrick, this prolific British art director and production designer (1914–1983) went on to work with a number of major directors (among them David Lean, John Huston, Ronald Neame, Jack Clayton and Roman Polanski) on a series of high profile productions, among them *Great Expectations* (1946), which won him an Oscar, *The African Queen* (1951), *Hobson's Choice* (1953), *Tunes of Glory* (1960), *The Innocents* (1961), *The Blue Max* (1966), which won him a BAFTA, *The Fearless Vampire Killers* (1967), *Macbeth* (1971), *Eye of the Needle* (1981) and *Heat and Dust* (1982). He also designed Hammer's remake of *The Lady Vanishes* (1979), on which he is credited as Wilfred Shingleton (on many films he is listed as Wilfrid Shingleton). His many other credits, among them several George Formby vehicles, include *Keep Fit* (1937), *I See Ice* (1938), *Come On George* (1939), *Let George Do It* (1940), *Turned Out Nice Again* (1941), *Blanche Fury* (1948), *I Could Go On Singing* (1963), *Sebastian* (1968) and *Voyage of the Damned* (1976), plus the TV series *Holocaust* (1978, TV), which earned him a shared Emmy nomination, and

*Gaugin the Savage* (1980, TV), which won him a shared Emmy. **Hammer credits:** *The Lady Vanishes* (1979)

## Shipway, Philip

This British assistant director (1912–1968) worked on Hammer's Manchester-shot thriller *Hell Is a City* (1960). In films from the mid-forties as a second assistant director on such productions as *Caesar and Cleopatra* (1945) and *Great Expectations* (1946), his other credits include a first assistant include *The Woman in the Hall* (1947), *The Wooden Horse* (1950), *Private's Progress* (1956), *Expresso Bongo* (1959) and *The Day the Earth Caught Fire* (1961). He went on to become a production manager on *A French Mistress* (1960), *Sammy Going South* (1963) and *The Collector* (1965). He also worked as an associate producer on *Rotten to the Core* (1965). His credits as a production administrator include *The Family Way* (1966) and *Twisted Nerve* (1968). **Hammer credits:** *Hell Is a City* (1960)

## Shiu, Paula Lee

This Chinese actress (1929–, aka Paula Li Shiu) appeared as a croupier in Hammer's *Visa to Canton* (1960). Her other credits include *Some May Live* (1967) and *Battle Beneath the Earth* (1967), plus episodes of *The Man in Room 17* (1965, TV), *Danger Man* (1964–1966) and *UFO* (1970–1971, TV). Also on stage. **Hammer credits:** *Visa to Canton* (1960, as Croupier [uncredited])

## Shoberova, Olga *see* Berova, Olinka

## Shore, Bill (William)

This assistant director first worked for Hammer as a second assistant on *What the Butler Saw* (1950). Following further work as a second assistant on *Stolen Face* (1952), he graduated to first assistant on several other Hammer productions, including *The Quatermass Xperiment* (1955). His other credits include *Lisbon Story* (1946) and *The Ghosts of Berkeley Square* (1947), both as second assistant, and, as first assistant, *Stolen Assignment* (1955), *The Hypnotist* (1957) and *Horrors of the Black Museum* (1959). His work as a production manager includes *The Key Man* (1957), *The Strange Awakening* (1958), *The Criminal* (1960) and *Konga* (1961). **Hammer credits:** *What the Butler Saw* (1950, second assistant director [uncredited]), *Stolen Face* (1952, second assistant director [uncredited]), *Mantrap* (1953, assistant director), *Four Sided Triangle* (1953, assistant director), *Break in the Circle* (1955, assistant director), *The Quatermass Xperiment* (1955, assistant director), *Women Without Men* (1956, assistant director)

## Shrimpton, Chrissie

This British model and occasional actress (1945–) can be seen in a brief but amusing cameo as a boutique attendant in Hammer's *Moon Zero Two* (1969). Playing with her silver hair and shuffling forward with complete disinterest, she enquires, "Welcome to the Galaxy Boutique. Can I help you? Jupiter jump suits?" Between 1963 and 1966, Shrimpton was the girlfriend of Mick Jagger, and is said to be the inspiration of such songs as *Under My Thumb*, *Stupid Girl* and *19th Nervous*

*Breakdown*. Her other film credits include *All the Right Noises* (1969), *My Lover My Son* (1970) and *Universal Soldier* (1971). Her sister is the sixties supermodel Jean Shrimpton (1942–). **Hammer credits:** *Moon Zero Two* (1969, as Boutique attendant)

## Shuler Donner, Lauren *see* Donner/Shuler Donner

## Sibbald, Tony

This Canadian actor (1936–2011, full name Anthony Dominic Sibbald) can be seen in a minor supporting role in *Mark of the Devil* (1984, TVM [episode of *Hammer House of Mystery and Suspense*]). His other credits include *Cry of the Banshee* (1970), *Hanover Street* (1979), *Superman II* (1980) and *Hackers* (1995), plus episodes of *Doomwatch* (1970–1972, TV), *BBC2 Playhouse* (1973–1982, TV) and *One Foot in the Grave* (1990–2000, TV). **Hammer credits:** *Mark of the Devil* (1984, TVM [episode of *Hammer House of Mystery and Suspense*], as Wilson)

## Sidaway, Ashley

Along with Robert Sidaway (1942–), Maurice Sellar and Lou Jones, Sidaway created the Best of British format, which chronicled the best that British cinema had to offer via a series of clip shows that ran on television between 1987 and 1994. This format was also applied to *The World of Hammer* (1990 [first broadcast 1994], TV), which Sidaway co-wrote and co-created with Robert Sidaway, and on which he also worked as the series' editor. The programs were made by Best of British Film and Television Productions in conjunction with Hammer. Sidaway's credits as an executive producer include *School for Seduction* (2004), *Nouvelle-France* (2004) and *Joy Division* (2006), while his work as a writer includes *The Wonder* (2015), which he also co-produced, plus episodes of *Dark Knight* (2000–2002, TV) and *Chuck the Eco Duck* (2009, TV), the latter of which he also directed. **Hammer credits:** *The World of Hammer* (1990 [first broadcast 1994], TV)

## Sidaway, Robert

Sidaway (1942–) created the Best of British format along with Ashley Sidaway, Maurice Sellar and Lou Jones. As the series of the same title, it ran from 1987 until 1994, and chronicled via a series of clips the best that British cinema had to offer down the decades. The format was also applied to *The World of Hammer* (1990 [first broadcast 1994], TV), which he produced and which he also co-wrote and co-created with Ashley Sidaway. Their production company, Best of British Film and Television Productions, also made the programs in conjunction with Hammer. His credits as an executive producer include *Forests of the Gods* (2005), *Day of Wrath* (2006) and *Joy Division* (2006). He has also produced such series as *The Optimist* (1983–1985, TV) and *Chuck the Eco Duck* (2009, TV). His writing credits include *The Wonder* (2015), which he also produced. His wife is actress Maggie Don (1942–, full name Margaret E. Don), whom he married in 1964, and who appeared in *Poor Butterfly*, an episode of *Hammer's Journey to*

*the Unknown* (1968, TV), which also appeared in the compendium film *Journey to Midnight* (1968, TVM). **Hammer credits:** *The World of Hammer* (1990 [first broadcast 1994], TV)

## (Messers) Siebe Gorman & Co. Ltd.

This company is credited as having provided the diving equipment for Hammer's *Jack of Diamonds* (1949). They are also thanked in the credits of *The Secret of the Loch* (1934). The company was headed by Sir Robert Davis, inventor of the DSEA (the Davis Submerged Escape Apparatus) and author of *Deep Diving and Submarine Operations* (1934). **Hammer credits:** *Jack of Diamonds* (1949)

## Siegenburg, Kirk S.

Siegenburg appeared in the Hammer short *A Man on the Beach* (1956). His other credits include *Windom's Way* (1957) and episodes of *The Four Just Men* (1959–1960, TV). **Hammer credits:** *A Man on the Beach* (1956, as Little boy [uncredited])

## Sieman, Frank

This British supporting actor (1908–1992, sometimes billed as Frank Siemon), played Bill, the publican of the Red Lion in Hammer's remake of *The Mummy* (1959). His other credits include *The Titfield Thunderbolt* (1953), *Dead Man's Evidence* (1962), *Smashing Time* (1967) and *Confessions of a Window Cleaner* (1974), plus another appearance for Hammer in *The Curse of the Werewolf* (1961). His small screen work includes episodes of *Dixon of Dock Green* (1955–1976, TV) and *Shoulder to Shoulder* (1974, TV). **Hammer credits:** *The Mummy* (1959, as Bill [Red Lion publican]), *The Curse of the Werewolf* (1961, as Gardner [uncredited])

## Siemon, Frank *see* Sieman, Frank

## *The Silent Scream see Hammer House of Horror*

## Silk, Geoff

Silk worked as one of the stunt drivers on Hammer's *The Devil Rides Out* (1968), one of his jobs being to double for Nike Arrighi. His brother Jack (1922–2005) also worked on the film as a stunt driver. His credits as an actor include *Circus of Fear* (1966) and episodes of *No Hiding Place* (1959–1967, TV) and *New Scotland Yard* (1972–1973, TV). **Hammer credits:** *The Devil Rides Out* (1968 [uncredited])

## Silk, Jack

This British stunt driver (1922–2005) worked on Hammer's *The Devil Rides Out* (1968), along with his brother Geoff. His other credits include *A Night to Remember* (1958), *The Fast Lady* (1962), *Thunderball* (1965) and *Psychomania* (1972), plus episodes of *The Champions* (1968–1969, TV) and *UFO* (1970–1971, TV). His credits as an actor include *The Wrong Arm of the Law* (1963), *Frenzy* (1972), *Callan* (1974) and *McVicar* (1980). **Hammer credits:** *The Devil Rides Out* (1968 [uncredited])

## Silva, Simone

Born in Egypt of Greek-French parents, this curvaceous actress and singer (1928–1957, real name Martha Simone de Bouillard, aka Simone Sylva) played the role of Mitzi in the Hammer thriller *Third Party Risk* (1955). Her other credits include two French films, *Le tampon du capiston* (1950) and *Boniface somnabule* (1951), plus supporting appearances in several British productions, among them *Lady Godiva Rides Again* (1951), *Escape by Night* (1953), *Street of Shadows* (1953), *The Weak and the Wicked* (1953) and *The Gelignite Gang* (1956). In 1954, she scandalized the Cannes Film Festival by gate crashing a photo-shoot with Robert Mitchum on the Ile de Lerins during which she went topless. Unfortunately, the resultant worldwide publicity failed to launch her career, and, after trying and failing to make it in Hollywood, she was found dead in her Mayfair flat two years later. Her television credits include two episodes of *The Gay Cavalier* (1957, TV). **Hammer credits:** *Third Party Risk* (1955, as Mitzi Molnaur)

### Silva Screen

Founded in 1986 by the appropriately named Reynold D'Silva, this British music label is noted not only for the release of current film soundtracks, but also for its impressive work in preserving past classics via re-issues and new recordings, primarily with The City Prague Philharmonic Orchestra. Among these new recordings have been a number of horror scores, including several Hammer-centric compilations. The first of these was *Dracula: Classic Scores from Hammer Horror*, which featured cues from *Dracula Has Risen from the Grave* (1968), *Dracula* (1958), *Taste the Blood of Dracula* (1970), *Hands of the Ripper* (1971) and *Vampire Circus* (1972). Released in 1989, it was re-issued again in 1993. This was followed by *The Devil Rides Out—Horror, Adventure and Romance*, which presented a selection of cues from the scores of James Bernard, who personally re-orchestrated several of the pieces, among them tracks from *The Kiss of the Vampire* (1963) *She* (1965), *Frankenstein Created Woman* (1967), *The Devil Rides Out* (1968) and *Scars of Dracula* (1970). There was also a *Quatermass Suite*. Released in 1996, the album was soon joined by *Horror!* (1996), which featured cues from *The Abominable Snowman* (1957), *The Curse of the Werewolf* (1961) and *The Curse of the Mummy's Tomb* (1964) among others. The company had also previously re-issued a re-mixed version of *Hammer Horror—A Rock Tribute to the Studio That Dripped Blood* by the rock band Warfare. Originally released by Hammer Film Music, Ltd. in 1989, the new disc reappeared in 1991. Hammer music has also been featured on a number of other compilation albums by Silva Screen, including *Vampire Circus—The Essential Vampire Theme Collection* (1993) and *The Great British Film Music Album: Sixty Glorious Years 1938–1998* (1999).

### Silver, Christine

This British actress (1884–1960) played the role of Mrs. Musgrave in the Hammer thriller *Room to Let* (1950) and Mrs. Penston in *Whispering Smith Hits London* (1952). Her other credits include *The Pleydell Mystery* (1916), *The Labour Leader* (1917), *Judge Not* (1920), *Salute John Citizen* (1942), *Stop Press* (1949), *Mystery Junction* (1951) and *The Hor-*

net's *Nest* (1955), plus episodes of *BBC Sunday-Night Theatre* (1950–1959, TV), *Saber of London* (1954–1960, TV) and *Stryker of the Yard* (1957, TV). **Hammer credits:** *Room to Let* (1950, as Mrs. Musgrave), *Whispering Smith Hits London* (1952, as Mrs. Penston)

### Silver, Pat

This American actress and writer (real name Barbara J. Carleton, aka Barbara Hayden and Pat Silver Lasky) co-wrote the teleplay for *Paint Me a Murder* (1984, TVM [episode of *Hammer House of Mystery and Suspense*]) with her second husband, Jesse Lasky, Jr. (1910–1988), to whom she was married between 1959 and his death, and with whom she frequently collaborated (the couple was also penciled in for involvement in another TV series, *The Hammer Mystery Theatre*). Her other work as a writer includes episodes of *Rescue 8* (1958–1960, TV), *The New Breed* (1961–1962, TV), *Space: 1999* (1975–1977, TV) and *Philip Marlowe, Private Eye* (1983–1986, TV), on which she also worked as a story editor, while her occasional film credits include *The Wizard of Baghdad* (1960), *Pirates of Tortuga* (1961), *Ace Up My Sleeve* (1976) and *Forbidden Sun* (1989). Her books include *The Offer* (1982), *Screenwriting for the 21st Century* (2003) and *Ride the Tiger* (2010). She also penned lyrics for the films *Radio Stars on Parade* (1945) and *Robbers' Roost* (1955), and for such songs as *While You're Young* (1960). Her work as an actress, billed as Barbara Hayden when credited, includes appearances in *The Loves of Carmen* (1948), *A Perilous Journey* (1953) and *The Crimson Kimono* (1959), plus episodes of *Rescue 8* (1958–1960, TV) and *Have Gun—Will Travel* (1957–1963, TV). Her first husband was the actor, singer and vocal coach Tony Romano (1915–2005), whom she married in 1946. Her children (with Romano) are the composer and arranger Richard Niles (1951–, full name Richard Niles Romano) and the singer, cookery writer and restaurateur Lisa Hayden Miller (real name Lisa Romano). Her third husband is the cartoonist Peter Betts (aka Peeby), whom she married in 1997. **Hammer credits:** *Paint Me a Murder* (1984, TVM [episode of *Hammer House of Mystery and Suspense*])

### Silvera, Simone

Silvera can be seen as one of Hubbard's girls in Hammer's *Moon Zero Two* (1969). Her other credits include the unfinished *Crepa padrone, crepa tranquillo* (1970). **Hammer credits:** *Moon Zero Two* (1969, as Hubbard's girl)

### Silverlock, Mike

British born Silverlock (1943–1989) worked as the boom operator on Hammer's *Blood from the Mummy's Tomb* (1971). His other credits include *All the Way Up* (1970), *The Zoo Robbery* (1973), *Sweeney 2* (1978) and *McVicar* (1980), plus episodes of *Van Der Valk* (1972–1977, TV), *The Sweeney* (1975–1978, TV), *Dick Turpin* (1979–1982, TV) and *Young Charlie Chaplin* (1989, TV). His credits as a sound camera operator include *The Wild Affair* (1963), *A Hard Day's Night* (1964), *Alfie* (1966) and *The Deadly Affair* (1966), while

his work as a sound recordist takes in *Somewhere to Run* (1989, TVM) and episodes of *Young Charlie Chaplin* (1989, TV). **Hammer credits:** *Blood from the Mummy's Tomb* (1971 [uncredited])

### Sim, Gerald

In films from 1947 with *Fame Is the Spur*, this British character actor (1925–2014) made a specialty of flawed authority figures. A favorite of directors Bryan Forbes and Richard Attenborough, his many credits include *Seven Days to Noon* (1950), *Whistle Down the Wind* (1961), *Seance on a Wet Afternoon* (1964), *Ryan's Daughter* (1970), *Frenzy* (1972), *The Slipper and the Rose* (1976), *A Bridge Too Far* (1977), *Gandhi* (1982), *Chaplin* (1992) and *Shadowlands* (1993). Also much on television, his credits include the sitcom *To the Manor Born* (1929–1981 and 2007, TV), in which he played the rector, plus many guest appearances, among them episodes of Hammer's *Journey to the Unknown* (1968, TV) and *Hammer House of Mystery and Suspense* (1984, TVM). He also made one film for Hammer, *Dr. Jekyll and Sister Hyde* (1971), in which he played Professor Robertson. His sister was the actress Sheila Sim (1922–2016); his brother-in-law was the director Sir Richard Attenborough (1923–2014). **Hammer credits:** *Stranger in the Family* (1968, TV [episode of *Journey to the Unknown*], as Dr. Evans), *Dr. Jekyll and Sister Hyde* (1971, as Professor Robertson), *Paint Me a Murder* (1984, TVM [episode of *Hammer House of Mystery and Suspense*], as Vicar)

### Simmonds, Annette

This British supporting actress (1917–1959, real name Nancy Doughty O'Hara) played the role of Carrots in the Hammer programer *The Adventures of PC 49—The Case of the Guardian Angel* (1949). Her other credits include *The Trojan Brothers* (1946), *No Orchids for Miss Blandish* (1948), *Blackout* (1950), *The Smart Aleck* (1951) and *The Frightened Man* (1952). **Hammer credits:** *The Adventures of PC 49—The Case of the Guardian Angel* (1949, as Carrots)

### Simmonds, Stan

Simmonds worked as a stuntman on Hammer's *A Challenge for Robin Hood* (1967). Remembered the film's fight arranger Peter Diamond of one sequence involving Simmonds, "I remember the scene where they storm the castle at the end. Big Stan Simmonds hits the table, slips, and you can see his foot go up in the air. That was done in one take, so you couldn't mess about, but he obviously did slip as he jumps across the table."[94] Simmonds' other credits include episodes of *Hancock's Half Hour* (1956–1960, TV), *The Arthur Haynes Show* (1956–1966, TV), *No Hiding Place* (1959–1967, TV) and *Citizen James* (1960–1962, TV). **Hammer credits:** *A Challenge for Robin Hood* (1967 [uncredited])

### Simmons, Bob

This noted British stuntman, action arranger, horse master and master of arms (1922–1988) is best known for his work on the James Bond films, on which he originally doubled for Sean Connery before advancing to the role of action arranger (it is also Simmons instead of Connery who can be seen in the iconic gunbarrel logo at the beginning of the first three films in the series). His credits for the franchise include *Dr. No* (1962), *Goldfinger* (1964), *Thunderball* (1965), *You Only Live Twice* (1968), *Diamonds Are Forever* (1971), *Live and Let Die* (1973), *The Spy Who Loved Me* (1977), *Moonraker* (1979), *For Your Eyes Only* (1981), *Octopussy* (1983) and *A View to a Kill* (1985). His other credits include *Jamaica Inn* (1939), *Ivanhoe* (1952), *The Guns of Navarone* (1961), on which he stunt doubled for Gregory Peck, *The Great Van Robbery* (1963), *Shalako* (1968), *Paper Tiger* (1975), *The Wild Geese* (1978), *The Sea Wolves* (1980) and *Who Dares Wins* (1982). He was also the horse master for two of Hammer's sixties pirate films, prior to which he had a small role in *The Flanagan Boy* (1953). **Hammer credits:** *The Flanagan Boy* (1953, as Booth man), *Captain Clegg* (1962, horse master, fight sequence supervisor), *The Pirates of Blood River* (1962, horse master, master of arms)

### Simmons, Stan

This British actor (1927–2000, full name Stanley Alfred Simmons) can be seen as the servant Hans in Hammer's *The Kiss of the Vampire* (1963). His other credits include *The Secret Man* (1958) and *Curse of the Fly* (1965), plus episodes of *ITV Television Playhouse* (1955–1967, TV), *Armchair Theatre* (1956–1974, TV), *The Six Proud Walkers* (1962, TV) and *The Wednesday Play* (1964–1970, TV). **Hammer credits:** *The Kiss of the Vampire* (1963, as Hans [uncredited])

### Simpson, Etta

This British editor (1902–1983, real name Henrietta Simon, aka Henrietta Booth) cut Hammer's first Dick Barton adventure, *Dick Barton— Special Agent* (1948). Her other credits include *The Body Vanished* (1939) and *The Devil's Jest* (1954). **Hammer credits:** *Dick Barton—Special Agent* (1948)

### Simpson, Ronald

This British actor (1896–1957) can be spotted as Blane in Hammer's third film, the Paul Robeson vehicle *Song of Freedom* (1936). His other credits include *No Escape* (1936), *Mine Own Executioner* (1947) and *The Cruel Sea* (1953), plus episodes of *BBC Sunday-Night Theatre* (1950–1959, TV) and *As I Was Saying* (1955, TV). Also on stage, his wife was the stage actress Lila Maravan (?–1950, real name Doris Lila Muschamp), whom he married in 1923. **Hammer credits:** *Song of Freedom* (1936)

### Simpson, Tom

Simpson was assigned by Hammer's supervising editor James Needs to cut the comedy *A Weekend with Lulu* (1961). His other credits include *Private Information* (1951), *Account Rendered* (1957), *Bluebeard's Ten Honeymoons* (1960) and *The Frozen Dead* (1966), plus five more Hammer films, prime among them *The Nanny* (1965) and *One Million Years B.C.* (1966). He also worked on episodes of *Douglas Fairbanks, Jr. Presents* (1953–1957, TV), *The Avengers* (1961–1969, TV) and *Randall and Hopkirk (Deceased)* (1969–1970, TV). His earlier credits as an assistant editor include *Anna Karenina* (1948) and *The Small Back Room* (1949). **Hammer credits:** *A Weekend with Lulu* (1961), *Maniac* (1963), *The Secret of Blood Island* (1965), *The Brigand of Kandahar* (1965), *The Nanny* (1965), *One Million Years B.C.* (1966)

### Sims, Pat

Sims worked as the production secretary on Hammer's *Frankenstein Created Woman* (1967). Her other credits include *Doctor in Clover* (1966), *Fragment of Fear* (1970), *Dulcima* (1971), *Universal Soldier* (1971), *Young Winston* (1972) and *A Doll's House* (1973). **Hammer credits:** *Frankenstein Created Woman* (1967 [uncredited])

### Sinclair, Andrew

This British writer (1935–) penned an adaptation of Michael Hastings' short story *Tennis Court* for Hammer, which was originally intended as a theatrical feature by the company but instead ended up as an episode of *Hammer House of Mystery and Suspense* (1984, TVM). His other writing credits include *Before Winter Comes* (1969), *The Breaking of Bumbo* (1970), which was based upon his 1959 novel (and for which he also provided the lyrics to the songs *Red Is London* and *Waterloo Station*), *Under Milk Wood* (1972), *Blue Blood* (1973) and *Tuxedo Warrior* (1982), all of which he also directed save for the first title. He also wrote episodes of *Armchair Theatre* (1956–1974, TV) and *Martin Eden* (1979, TV), while his work as a producer includes *Malachi's Cove* (1974). **Hammer credits:** *Tennis Court* (1984, TVM [episode of *Hammer House of Mystery and Suspense*])

### Sinclair, Hugh

On stage from 1922 and in films from the early thirties with *Our Betters* (1933), this RADA-trained British leading actor (1903–1962) co-starred opposite Rosamund John in the Hammer second feature thriller *Never Look Back* (1952), which led to further work, albeit as a supporting actor, on *Mantrap* (1953). His other films include *Escape Me Never* (1935), *Alibi* (1941), *The Rocking Horse Winner* (1949), *Trottie True* (1949) and *The Second Mrs. Tanqueray* (1952), plus episodes of *Douglas Fairbanks, Jr. Presents* (1953–1957, TV) and *A Life of Bliss* (1960, TV). Oddly enough, despite having played the Saint in two American second features—*The Saint's Vacation* (1941) and *The Saint Meets the Tiger* (1943)—Sinclair was not asked to reprise the role for Hammer's take on the series, *The Saint's Return* (1953). Instead, the part of Simon Templar was offered to Louis Hayward, who had essayed the role in the first film in the series, *The Saint in New York* (1938). Sinclair's first wife (of two) was the actress Valerie Taylor (1902–1988), whom he married in 1930. **Hammer credits:** *Never Look Back* (1952, as Nigel Stuart), *Mantrap* (1953, as Maurice Jerrard)

### Sinclair, Peggy

This British actress (1946–) can be seen in a minor role in *Tennis Court* (1984, TVM [episode of *Hammer House of Mystery and Suspense*]). Best known for playing Detective Sergeant Barbara Allin in *Softly Softly* (1966–1977, TV), her other TV credits include episodes of *Armchair Theatre* (1956–1974, TV), *Thriller* (1973–1976, TV), *Let There Be Love* (1982–1983, TV) and *Don't Wait Up* (1983–1990, TV). Her occasional films include *Escape from the Sea* (1968) and *Permission to Kill* (1975). Her husband was the actor Richard Coleman (1930–2008, real name Ronald Coleman). **Hammer credits:** *Tennis Court* (1984, TVM [episode of *Hammer House of Mystery and Suspense*], as Matron)

### Singer, Campbell

This busy British character actor (1909–1976, real name Jacob Kobel Singer) actually made his stage debut in South Africa in 1928. In films from 1938 with *Premiere*, he went on to appear in over fifty productions, among them *Rover and Me* (1949), *The Blue Lamp* (1949), *The Titfield Thunderbolt* (1952), *The Square Peg* (1958) and *The Fast Lady* (1962). He also appeared in several second features for Hammer in the late forties and early fifties, among them two of their Dick Barton films, in both of which he played Sir George Cavendish, and *A Case for PC 49* (1951), in which he played Sergeant Wright (replacing Eric Phillips, who had played the role in the radio series, *The Adventures of PC 49* [1947–1953] as well in the first film Hammer derived from it, *The Adventures of PC 49—The Case of the Guardian Angel* [1949]). Much on television, Singer's work here includes episodes of *ITV Television Playhouse* (1955–1967, TV), *Private Investigator* (1958–1959, TV), in which he starred, *Armchair Theatre* (1956–1974, TV), *The Avengers* (1961–1969, TV) and *Nearest and Dearest* (1968–1973, TV). His wife was the actress Gillian Maude (1918–1988), who also appeared in his first Dick Barton film. **Hammer credits:** *Dick Barton—Special Agent* (1948, as Sir George Cavendish [uncredited]), *Dick Barton at Bay* (1950, as Sir George Cavendish), *A Case for PC 49* (1951, as Sergeant Wright), *Lady in the Fog* (1952, as Inspector Rigby)

### Singer, John

This British supporting actor (1923–1987) played a photographer in Hammer's *Whispering Smith Hits London* (1952) and a dispatch rider in the comedy *Further Up the Creek* (1958). His other credits include *High Treason* (1929), *Love on the Spot* (1932), *Dandy Dick* (1935), *Sweeney Todd: The Demon Barber of Fleet Street* (1936), *Somewhere in England* (1940), *In Which We Serve* (1942), *The Dark Man* (1951), *Betrayed* (1954) and *Track the Man Down* (1955). **Hammer credits:** *Whispering Smith Hits London* (1952, as Photographer), *Further Up the Creek* (1958, as Dispatch rider)

### Singh, Mohan

Singh can be seen as Mocata's servant in Hammer's *The Devil Rides Out* (1968). His television credits include episodes of *No Hiding Place* (1959–1967, TV), *The Troubleshooters* (1965–1972, TV), *Budgie* (1971–1972, TV) and *Fly into Danger* (1972, TV). **Hammer credits:** *The Devil Rides Out* (1968, as Mocata's servant [uncredited])

## Singleton, Mark

This British actor (1919–1986) can be seen as a waiter in two of Hammer's fifties co-features. His other credits include *Take a Powder* (1953), *Top Floor Girl* (1959), *Murder in Eden* (1961), *Salt & Pepper* (1968), *Can You Keep It Up for a Week?* (1975), *Keep It Up Downstairs* (1976) and *Game for Vultures* (1979), plus episodes of *Hancock's Half Hour* (1956–1960, TV), *The Worker* (1965–1970, TV) and *Department S* (1969–1970, TV). **Hammer credits:** *The Gambler and the Lady* (1953, as Waiter [uncredited]), *Face the Music* (1954, as Waiter [uncredited])

## Singuineau, Frank

This Trinidadian supporting actor (1913–1992, full name Francis Ethelbert Singuineau) can be seen as Head Porter in Hammer's remake of *The Mummy* (1959). His other credits include *Simba* (1955), *Peeping Tom* (1960), *Night of the Eagle* (1961), *The Pumpkin Eater* (1964), *Hot Millions* (1968), *Carry On Again Doctor* (1969), *Baxter!* (1973), *Biggles* (1986) and *An American Werewolf in London* (1981), while his TV work takes in episodes of *The Cheaters* (1960–1962, TV), *Love Thy Neighbour* (1972–1976, TV) and *Angels* (1975–1983, TV). **Hammer credits:** *The Mummy* (1959, as Head Porter)

## Sinha, Shivendra

Sinha played Hurri Curri, the hapless steward of the *Corita* in Hammer's *The Lost Continent* (1968), in which he gets dragged to his death by carnivorous kelp (no, really!). His other credits include *The Long Duel* (1967) and *Staying On* (1980, TVM), plus episodes of *Z Cars* (1962–1978, TV), *Frontier* (1968–1969, TV) and *Strange Report* (1968–1970, TV). He also directed and produced one film, *Phir Bhi* (1971), wrote another, *Uranchoo* (1976), and co-directed an episode of *Theatre 625* (1964–1968, TV). **Hammer credits:** *The Lost Continent* (1968, as Hurri Curri)

## Siodmak, Curt

Best known for penning *The Wolf Man* (1941) and the much-filmed 1943 novel *Donovan's Brain*, this German novelist, screenwriter, producer and director (1902–2000, real name Kurt Siodmak) began his career in his home country writing pulp fiction. He turned to films in 1929, writing the screenplay for *Mascottchen*. However, it was his work on the influential *Menschen am Sonntag* (1929) that helped to secure his reputation (Siodmak co-wrote the film with Billy Wilder, which was co-directed by Edgar G. Ulmer, Fred Zinnemann and Siodmak's brother Robert). This success led to writing assignments on such films as *The Shot in the Talker Studio* (1930), *Le bal* (1931), *F.P.1 Fails to Reply* (1933), which was based on his novel, *La crise est finie* (1934), again based on his own novel, and *The Tunnel* (1935).

Following the rise of the Nazis, Siodmak moved to France, Britain and then America, arriving in Hollywood in 1937, having worked on several books and screenplays along the way to help finance the journey. Once in the States, he went on to pen several key genre pictures for Universal, notably *The Wolf Man* (1941), *Frankenstein Meets the Wolf Man* (1942) and *Son of Dracula* (1943). His other credits as a writer include *Non-Stop New York* (1937), *The Ape* (1940), *Invisible Agent* (1942), *I Walked with a Zombie* (1943), *The Climax* (1944) and *The Beast with Five Fingers* (1946). He began directing in 1951 with *Bride of the Gorilla*, and went on to helm *The Magnetic Monster* (1953), *Curucu, Beast of the Amazon* (1956), *Love Slaves of the Amazon* (1957) and *Ski Fever* (1959). In 1958, he directed and associate produced *The Face in the Tombstone Mirror*, the pilot for Hammer's abandoned television series *Tales of Frankenstein* (1958, TV), for which he also provided the story. Considered a disaster by all concerned, Siodmak didn't even mention the half-hour program in his otherwise meticulously detailed 2001 biography, *Wolf Man's Maker*. Siodmak's brother was the director Robert Siodmak (1900–1973). **Hammer credits:** *Tales of Frankenstein: The Face in the Tombstone Mirror* (1958, TV)

## Sirs, Jayne

This child actress had a minor role in Hammer's *The Anniversary* (1968). **Hammer credits:** *The Anniversary* (1968, as Child [uncredited])

## Skeaping, Colin

Best known for being Mark Hamill's stunt double in all three original *Star Wars* films (1977–1983), this British stuntman and occasional bit player (1944–) also worked as the stunt double for Aubrey Morris in Hammer's *Blood from the Mummy's Tomb* (1971). His many other credits (over ninety) include *Live and Let Die* (1973), *Horror Hospital* (1973), *Superman* (1978), *The Thirty-Nine Steps* (1978), *Superman II* (1980), *Condorman* (1981), *Car Trouble* (1985), *A Prayer for the Dying* (1987), *Let Him Have It* (1991), *GoldenEye* (1995) and *28 Days Later...* (2002), plus episodes of *Tales of the Unexpected* (1979–1988, TV), *Hannay* (1988–1989, TV), *Woof!* (1989–1997, TV), *Midsomer Murders* (1997–, TV) and *Ultimate Force* (2002–2006, TV). **Hammer credits:** *Blood from the Mummy's Tomb* (1971, as stunt double for Aubrey Morris [uncredited])

## Skeggs, Graham

The son of Roy Skeggs (1934–2018), Graham Skeggs joined his father in the running of Hammer some time after the departure of Brian Lawrence in May 1985. He worked on the series *The World of Hammer* (1990 [first broadcast 1994], TV), on which he is credited as "for Hammer Films" along with Karen Woods and Wendy Smith. He became a board director in 1996, and went on to become Hammer's legal and business affairs director between 1997 and 2000. Following the sale of Hammer to an investment consortium in January 2000, he remained with the company until 2005, working as the website manager and brand consultant. He has since worked as a communications and marketing manager for various companies, including Ofsted (2006–2009), The Community Development Foundation (2009–2013) and Buckingham County Council (2013–). **Hammer credits:** *The World of Hammer* (1990 [first broadcast 1994], TV)

## Skeggs, Roy R.

Following national service in the army and three years of studies to become an accountant, future Hammer boss Skeggs (1934–2018) entered the film industry in 1956 as an assistant account working for Douglas Fairbanks Productions, while in 1959 he went to work for ABPC. Following expe-

**Producer Roy Skeggs (left) confers with director Terence Fisher (right) on the set of *Frankenstein and the Monster from Hell* (1974) (Hammer/Paramount/Avco Embassy/Paramount).**

rience as a fully-fledged accountant on such films as *Zulu* (1964), Skeggs joined Hammer as a production accountant in October 1963 during the filming of *The Evil of Frankenstein* (1964), initially for a four-week period. He became a production supervisor for the company in January 1971, having been appointed to the role by Michael Carreras, who had been named as the company's new Managing Director by his father on 3 January. Skegg's first job was to oversee the troubled *Blood from the Mummy's Tomb* (1971), which was closely followed by *Dr. Jekyll and Sister Hyde* (1971) and the comedy spin-off *On the Buses* (1971), the latter of which proved to be a major commercial success for the company, resulting in several further comedy spin-offs from the small screen. Recalled Skeggs of *On the Buses*, "Jimmy [Carreras] called me into his office and said, 'This film is being made for pennies, so I want you to produce it.' I said, 'Do you mind if I don't? I can't stand the thing on television.' He said, 'Produce it or go,' and pointed to the door. So I produced it. We made it for £97,000 and it took £1.4 million in its first six weeks in Britain and Australia alone. And it's still making money."[95]

It should be noted that the credited producers of *On the Buses* were actually Ronald Woolfe and Ronald Chesney, while Skeggs is listed as production supervisor. However, it was inevitable that he would graduate to credited producer status within the company at some stage. With this in mind, Michael Carreras made Skeggs the associate producer on *Nearest and Dearest* (1973). He then made the jump to fully-fledged producer with *Frankenstein and the Monster from Hell* (1974). However, owing to the delayed release of some films, he was still occasionally credited as a production supervisor following his rise to producer status, though he did occasionally return to work in this capacity, as he did with *Man at the Top* (1973), which was produced by Peter Charlesworth and Jock Jacobsen, and *Holiday on the Buses* (1973), which was again produced by Ronald Wolfe and Ronald Chesney (and in which he can be spotted a couple of times as a holidaymaker). Meanwhile, in 1974, Skeggs produced, with John Robins, the Benny Hill compilation film *The Best of Benny Hill* (1974). This was released through EMI, with which Hammer had ties at the time, although Hammer itself had no involvement in the project (at the time, Robins had directed several of Hammer's big screen sitcom transfers, as well as the original episodes of *The Benny Hill Show* [1969–1989, TV] from which the clips were taken).

By January 1975, owing to various cost-cutting measures that had seen the exit of various personnel, Skeggs also found himself working as a company director, as well as a producer, a role he took over from Anthony Nelson Keys during the troubled pre-production on *To the Devil a Daughter* (1976). However, in early 1976, Skeggs also found himself going the way of Keys and the others, to be replaced on the board by Euan Lloyd. Remembered Skeggs: "Michael [Carreras] wrote me a very sweet letter when I said I wanted to leave. He said I was one of the few professionals he had worked with. I think he must have been very upset at what

was happening around him but it never came through in conversation."[96] However, three years later, Skeggs returned to work for Hammer following its insolvency in April 1979, collecting residuals on behalf of Pension Film Securities. He did this through Cinema Arts International, a company he formed in 1975 with Brian Lawrence (who had previously collected Hammer's residuals through his own company, Tintern Productions). Ironically, both Skeggs and Lawrence were reinstated as board directors following the departure of Michael Carreras.

Lawrence and Skeggs subsequently went on to make a number of productions through Cinema Arts International, among them the (non–Hammer) big screen versions of *George and Mildred* (1980) and *Rising Damp* (1980), both of which Skeggs produced and Lawrence executive produced. They also made the television series *Hammer House of Horror* (1980, TV), which was made in conjunction with ITC and Chips Productions, with Skeggs producing and Lawrence executive producing with David Reid. This was followed by *Hammer House of Mystery and Suspense* (1984, TVM). The duo subsequently used their profits from the sale of these programs to buy Hammer from Pension Film Securities for just £100,000.

It was during this period that veteran director Val Guest returned to helm three episodes of *Hammer House of Mystery and Suspense* at Skeggs' personal invitation. Of course, Skeggs had come a long way in the company since Guest had first encountered him in the sixties. "He and Brian Lawrence, who was his partner in the new Hammer, they were both accountants, and when I worked there they wrote out the weekly cheques and things for everybody. So I was rather surprised to find that they were now in charge of production."[97]

Brian Lawrence retired in May 1985, following which Skeggs at first ran Hammer by himself (hoping to launch a new feature program), and then in conjunction with his son Graham. Skeggs received a number of offers to sell Hammer during this period, two of which came from director John Hough. However, both eventually fell by the wayside. The second deal, which involved a consortium headed by Dodi Fayed, was particularly structured towards the benefit of Skeggs, who would have been kept on as managing director, and guaranteed finance for two features a year. Recalled Hough, "It was a real sweetheart deal, and had Roy signed it, we would have gone on to make a whole lot more films."[98] However, at the last moment, Skeggs changed his mind, seemingly fearful of allowing the power base to switch to Fayed and the consortium. As Hough put it, "He wanted to continue to be Mr. Hammer."[99]

Unfortunately, because of this decision, there was little left in the pipeline by now, save for a nostalgic television series trading on former glories. Titled *The World of Hammer*, it was made in 1990, but not shown until four years later. Then, after years of inactivity, there was finally some good news in August 1993, when Hammer signed a deal with Warner Bros. and Donner/Shuler-Donner for a series of remakes, among them a $30m version of *The Quatermass Xperiment*. A number of fresh

titles were also announced, along with co-production deals with several other companies, including Rank and Grundy International. Sadly, nothing came of the various deals, and Skeggs eventually sold Hammer in January 2000 to an investment consortium, but retained his links with the company for a period as a consultant.

When asked to compare Roy Skeggs with Michael Carreras, with both of whom he had worked, John Hough commented, "They were totally different. Michael was a swashbuckling impresario tycoon-type of character, who could stand up at the board meetings … and hold forth and captivate the whole audience. And he excelled at that. Roy was shy. He was not shy when he was one on one, and he was a very capable person in terms of producing the shows. But he operated on a very low key basis as against Michael's open, charismatic-type approach."[100] **Additional notes:** Skeggs' name appears on a "To Let" sign in *Blood from the Mummy's Tomb*. In addition to his appearances in *Holiday on the Buses*, he can also be seen as a mourner during the opening credits of *That's Your Funeral*. **Hammer credits:** *The Evil of Frankenstein* (1964, production accountant [uncredited]), *On the Buses* (1971, production supervisor), *Twins of Evil* (1971, production supervisor), *Dr. Jekyll and Sister Hyde* (1971, production supervisor), *Blood from the Mummy's Tomb* (1971, production supervisor), *Vampire Circus* (1972, production supervisor), *Fear in the Night* (1972, production supervisor), *Straight on Till Morning* (1972, production supervisor), *Mutiny on the Buses* (1972, production supervisor), *Dracula A.D. 1972* (1972, production supervisor), *Demons of the Mind* (1972, production supervisor), *Nearest and Dearest* (1973, associate producer), *That's Your Funeral* (1973, production supervisor, also uncredited appearance as mourner), *Love Thy Neighbour* (1973, producer), *Man at the Top* (1973, production supervisor), *Holiday on the Buses* (1973, production supervisor, also cameo appearances as holidaymaker [uncredited]), *The Satanic Rites of Dracula* (1974, producer), *Captain Kronos—Vampire Hunter* (1974, production supervisor), *Frankenstein and the Monster from Hell* (1974, producer), *The Legend of the 7 Golden Vampires* (1974, LP, producer), *Man About the House* (1974, producer), *To the Devil a Daughter* (1976, producer), *Hammer House of Horror* (1980, TV, producer), *Hammer House of Mystery and Suspense* (1984, TVM, producer), *The World of Hammer* (1990 [first broadcast 1994], TV, "Presented by"), *Flesh and Blood—The Hammer Heritage of Horror* (1994, TV, associate producer, also mentioned in acknowledgments)

## Skene, Anthony

British born Skene (1924–2000) penned the teleplay for *Jane Brown's Body*, an episode of Hammer's *Journey to the Unknown* (1968, TV). His other credits include episodes of *Armchair Mystery Theatre* (1960–1965, TV), *Haunted* (1967–1968, TV), *The Prisoner* (1967–1968, TV), *Wicked Women* (1970, TV), *Upstairs, Downstairs* (1971–1975, TV) and *The Adventures of Sherlock Holmes* (1984–1985, TV). **Hammer credits:** *Jane Brown's Body* (1968, TV [episode of *Journey to the Unknown*])

## Skidmore, Alan

This British musician (1942–) played tenor/soprano sax on the soundtrack for Hammer's *Dracula A.D. 1972* (1972). He frequently performs with his own band, The Alan Skidmore Quartet, and has also played with such artists as Georgie Fame, Herbie Hancock, The Nice and Kate Bush. His albums include *Once Upon a Time* (1969), *Tribute to 'trane* (1988) and *After the Rain* (1998). His father was saxophonist Jimmy Skidmore (1916–1988). **Hammer credits:** *Dracula A.D. 1972* (1972)

## Skinner, Ann

British born Skinner (1937–) worked as the production secretary on Hammer's *The Terror of the Tongs* (1961). Her other credits in this capacity include *Whistle Down the Wind* (1961) and *A Kind of Loving* (1962). She became a continuity girl on *Billy Liar* (1963), and went on to work on such films as *Darling* (1965), *Far from the Madding Crowd* (1967), Hammer's *The Viking Queen* (1967), *The Devils* (1970), *Sunday Bloody Sunday* (1971), *The Three Musketeers* (1973), *Star Wars* (1977) and *Magic* (1978), working most frequently for the directors John Schlesinger and Richard Lester. She later turned producer/executive producer with such films as *The Return of the Soldier* (1982), *Heavenly Pursuits* (1985) and *The Slab Boys* (1997), as well as such series as *A Very British Coup* (1988, TV), which won her a shared BAFTA for best drama series, *Chandler & Co.* (1994–1995, TV) and *Birdsong* (2012, TV). **Hammer credits:** *The Terror of the Tongs* (1961, production secretary [uncredited]), *The Viking Queen* (1967, continuity)

## Skinner, Corinne

This Trinidadian actress (1931–, aka Corinne Skinner-Carter) can be seen briefly in Hammer's *Love Thy Neighbour* (1973). She also popped up in *Man About the House* (1974) as a housewife. Her other credits include *Flame in the Streets* (1961), *Up Pompeii* (1971), *Pressure* (1976), *The Godsend* (1980), *Hidden Fears* (1993), *Resonant Frequency* (2014) and *Gholam* (2017). Also busy on television, her work here includes episodes of *Dixon of Dock Green* (1955–1976, TV), *The Bill* (1984–2010, TV), *EastEnders* (1985–, TV) and *Medics* (1990–1995, TV). **Hammer credits:** *Love Thy Neighbour* (1973, as Black bride), *Man About the House* (1974, as Housewife)

## Skundric, Danny

Born in Yugoslavia, Skundric (1928–2014) worked as the floor props chargehand on Hammer's *The Evil of Frankenstein* (1964), a capacity he also held on *Vampire Circus* (1972). His other credits include *Superman* (1978), *Outland* (1981), *Little Shop of Horrors* (1986), *Batman* (1989) and *The Madness of King George* (1994). **Hammer credits:** *The Evil of Frankenstein* (1964 [uncredited]), *Vampire Circus* (1972 [uncredited])

## Slaney, Ivor

Educated at the Royal College of Music, this prolific British composer and conductor (1921–1998) took over as Hammer's resident music director following the departure of Frank Spencer. His first film for the company was *Lady in the Fog* (1952), which led to many further assignments, among them *Spaceways* (1953) and *Murder by Proxy* (1954), while on the 1954 thriller *Face the Music*, he worked on the soundtrack with jazz trumpeter Kenny Baker. Slaney's other credits include *The Scarlet Spear* (1954), *A King's Story* (1965), *Prey* (1977), *Terror* (1979) and *Death Ship* (1980), while his TV work includes episodes of *The Third Man* (1959–1965, TV), *Here's Harry* (1960–1965, TV), *Sir Francis Drake* (1961–1962, TV) and *Here Come the Double Deckers!* (1970–1971, TV). Note that in the credits for the U.S. release of *The Saint's Return* (1953), Slaney's surname is misspelled Slanley. His wife was the pianist Dolores Ventura. **Hammer credits:** *Lady in the Fog* (1952, music), *The Gambler and the Lady* (1953, music), *The Flanagan Boy* (1953, music, conductor), *The Saint's Return* (1953, music), *Spaceways* (1953, music director), *Blood Orange* (1953, music director), *36 Hours* (1953, music), *Face the Music* (1954, co-music), *Five Days* (1954, music director), *The House Across the Lake* (1954, music), *The Stranger Came Home* (1954, stock music only [uncredited]), *Murder by Proxy* (1955, music director)

## Slark, Fred

Slark (1922–1988) worked as a second assistant director on three of Hammer's fifties second features (though some sources actually credit the latter two of them to Aida Young). He began his career as a third assistant on *The Sound Barrier* (1952), and was promoted to second assistant by Hammer. He then went on to become a first assistant (often for Sidney J. Furie), among his credits being *1984* (1956), *I Was Monty's Double* (1958), *Three on a Spree* (1961), *The Young Ones* (1961), *Wonderful Life* (1964), *The Ipcress File* (1965) and *The Boys in Company C* (1978), plus episodes of *Walking Tall* (1981, TV). He also worked as a production manager (again many times for Furie) on *During One Night* (1960), *The Boys* (1962), *The Leather Boys* (1963), *Devil Doll* (1964), *The Naked Runner* (1967), *Song of Norway* (1970), *Gable and Lombard* (1976) and *The Ice Pirates* (1984), plus episodes of *Time Express* (1979, TV) and *Scruples* (1980, TV). **Hammer credits:** *Blood Orange* (1953 [uncredited]), *Face the Music* (1954 [uncredited]), *The House Across the Lake* (1954 [uncredited])

## Slater, John

Frequently cast in Cockney roles, this British character actor (1916–1975) made his film debut in 1938 in *Alf's Button Afloat*, which led to a busy career on both the large and small screen, among his many credits being *Gert and Daisy's Weekend* (1941), *We Dive at Dawn* (1943), *The Million Pound Note* (1953) and *Three on a Spree* (1961). He also made one film for Hammer, the boxing melodrama *The Flanagan Boy* (1953). His TV credits include the long-running series *Z Cars* (1962–1968, TV), in which he played Sergeant Stone in a staggering 421 episodes. **Hammer credits:** *The Flanagan Boy* (1953, as Charlie)

## Slattery, Lotte (Lottie)

Slattery worked on the costumes for Hammer's *Frankenstein Must Be Destroyed* (1969) with Rosemary Burrows. Her other credits include *Negatives* (1968) and *A Severed Head* (1970). **Hammer credits:** *Frankenstein Must Be Destroyed* (1969)

## Slattery, Richard

Slattery worked as a standby carpenter on Hammer's *Scars of Dracula* (1970). **Hammer credits:** *Scars of Dracula* (1970 [uncredited])

## *Slave Girls*

GB, 1968, 74m [UK], 95m [U.S.], Technicolor [UK], DeLuxe [U.S.], CinemaScope, RCA, cert A

Originally titled *Slave Girls of the White Rhino* before being announced as *Prehistoric Women*, this rather silly potboiler about a game hunter who discovers a hidden valley in Africa ruled by women went in to production at Elstree on 22 January 1966, just sixteen days after the completion of principal photography on *One Million Years B.C.* (1966), the sets and costumes from which it makes use of. However, despite the speed with which the film was made (shooting wrapped on 18 February), it wasn't released in the UK until 7 July 1968, when it went out on the lower half of a double bill top lining Hammer's own *The Devil Rides Out* (1968) care of Warner Pathé, though according to *The British Film Catalogue, Volume 1*, it was trade shown as early as March 1966 and was later considered for double billing with *Frankenstein Created Woman* (1967).

The film was the idea of producer-director Michael Carreras, who also penned the screenplay under the pseudonym Henry Younger (commented Christopher Neame of the slapdash script, "The problem was that Michael didn't have quite good enough storytelling qualities, however spirited he was on set"[101]). The story, such as it is, sees Martine Beswick's Queen Kari rule over the not entirely harmonious Amazonian populous, for whom cat fights and hair pulling are an every day occurrence. Comments one of Kari's less-than-happy slaves, "Look at her—she eats upon a throne while we grovel in the dust; we are not beasts of the field, we are women equal to her," only to be impaled on the turning handle of a roasting spit for her defiance. Beswick had appeared in a supporting role in *One Million Years B.C.*, and is here elevated to star status, though upon reflection, she may well have wondered whether this was a good career move, given the cheapness of the enterprise, which climaxes with her own impalement on the horn of a plastic white rhino (clearly being trundled along on wheels). Also returning from *One Million Years B.C.* were a number of production personnel, among them art director Robert Jones and associate producer Aida Young.

With its lack of animated dinosaurs and its fake-looking sets (the film features no exteriors save for some grainy library footage and poor blue screen work), the movie has a rushed feel to it. Flatly directed by Carreras and performed with indifference by the cast (who surprisingly manage to keep their faces straight), this is Hammer at its cheapest and most pedantic, a fact that did not escape the attention of the film's American distributors, Twentieth Century–Fox, which, via a telegram, noted that the film was "exceedingly slow, draggy and boring,"[102] and that "direction is very poor and principals not very active."[103] This could well be the reason why twenty-one minutes of footage were wisely slashed from the running time of the UK release. Yet despite the concerns of Fox, in America—where it was known as *Prehistoric Women*—audiences had to endure the tedium of the full ninety-five-minute cut when it was released there by the studio on 18 December 1968, again with *The Devil Rides Out*, prior to which it had also played as a solo engagement as early as 25 January 1967 ("A legend as evil as black witchcraft, as savage as the primeval jungle!" ballyhooed the trailer for the American version). Sadly, this was not the last Hammer film to treat its audience with such contempt, though teenage boys no doubt enjoyed the amount of bare flesh on display.

Remembered Michael Carreras of the film, "Frankly, I don't know how any of us got through *Prehistoric Women*. If we hadn't had a certain amount of humor, we would never have been able to complete it. I realize now that I should have gone much further with the humor, and turned it into a *total* send-up. It might have been boffo box office if I had."[104] Recalled cinematographer Michael Reed, "*Slave Girls* was a bit of a tongue-in-cheek script…. It was all filmed in the studio. The only problem this caused was to our health more than anything, because we were working in dust all the time. The earth and stuff they used to dress the set

A sultry-looking Martine Beswick gets the point in *Slave Girls* (1968) (Hammer/Seven Arts/Associated British Picture Corporation/Warner Pathé/Twentieth Century–Fox).

dried out after so many weeks, and both Michael and I got a bronchial problem." [105]**Additional notes:** When the captured game hunter first meets the seemingly naked Queen Kari bathing at her waterhole, the skin-colored panties she is wearing to cover her modesty are visible in the rear angle shot. To help with the drawing of his poster for the film—which features a busty Amazonian sat atop a white rhino—artist Tom Chantrell took photos of a rhino at London zoo, and photographed a model astride a large drum wielding a coat hanger in lieu of a whip. *Prehistoric Women* should not be confused with the 1950 American film of the same title, which starred Laurette Luez and Allan Nixon, and was directed by Gregory T. Tallas. The film carries a 1966 copyright.

Production companies: Hammer/Seven Arts/Associated British Picture Corporation. Distributors: Warner Pathé Distributors (UK [ABC circuit]), Twentieth Century–Fox (U.S.). Producer: Michael Carreras. Executive producer: Anthony Hinds. Associate producer: Aida Young. Director: Michael Carreras. Screenplay: Henry Younger (Michael Carreras). Cinematographer: Michael Reed. Music: Carlo Martelli. Music director: Philip Martell. Supervising editor: James Needs. Editor: Roy Hyde. Art director: Robert Jones. Costumes: Carl Toms, Jackie Breed. Special effects: George Blackwell. Make-up: Wally Schneiderman. Hair: Olga Angelinetta. Sound director: A.W. Lumkin. Sound mixers: Sash Fisher, Len Shilton. Dubbing editor: Charles Crafford. Sound editor: Roy Baker. Production manager: Ross Mackenzie. Assistant director: David Tringham. Third assistant director: Nigel Wooll [uncredited]. Camera operator: Robert Thomson. Focus puller: Mike Roberts. Anamorphic focus assistant: Christopher Neame [uncredited]. Choreography: Denys Palmer, Boscoe Holder [uncredited]. Continuity: Eileen Head. Poster: Tom Chantrell [uncredited]. **Cast:** Martine Beswick (Queen Kari), Michael Latimer (David Marchant), Edina Ronay (Saria), Stephanie Randall (Amyak), Carol White (Gido), Yvonne Horner (Amazon), Sydney Bromley (Ullo), Alexandra Stevenson (Luri), Robert Raglan (Colonel Hammett), Mary Hignett (Mrs. Hammond), Steven Berkoff (John), Frank Hayden (Arja), Bari Jonson (High Priest), Louis Mahoney (Head boy), Danny Daniels (Jakara), Sally Caclough (Amazon [uncredited]), Jeanette Wild (unnamed role [uncredited]), Nikki Van Der Zyl (dubbing of various voices [uncredited]). **DVD availability:** Anchor Bay (U.S. R1

NTSC), as *Prehistoric Women*, double-billed with *The Witches* (1966), extras include a trailer and an episode of *The World of Hammer* (1990 [first broadcast 1994], TV) titled *Lands Before Time*; Optimum (UK R2 PAL), extras include trailers, TV spots and an episode of *The World of Hammer* (1990 [first broadcast 1994], TV) titled *Lands Before Time*. **CD availability:** *The Hammer Film Music Collection: Volume Two* (GDI Records), which contains the *Main Title*

### Slawson, Ruth

Slawson worked as the Fox producer on the Hammer series *Hammer House of Mystery and Suspense* (1984, TVM). Her other credits include *Terror in the Family* (1996, TVM), which she executive produced, and, as co-executive producer, *The Great Mom Swap* (1995, TVM), *Annie: A Royal Adventure* (1995, TVM) and *Ellen Foster* (1997, TVM). **Hammer credits:** *Hammer House of Mystery and Suspense* (1984, TVM [uncredited])

### Slimon, Scott

British born Slimon (1915–1980) worked as the set decorator on the Hammer thriller *The Full Treatment* (1961), collaborating with art director Tony Masters and assistant art director Geoff Tozar. His other credits include *The Elusive Pimpernel* (1950), *Suddenly, Last Summer* (1959), which earned him a shared Oscar nomination, *Salt & Pepper* (1968) and *The Fiend* (1972). His work as an art director includes *The Terrornauts* (1967), *They Came from Beyond Space* (1967) and *Torture Garden* (1967), all for Amicus. His earlier credits as a fabric designer include *An Ideal Husband* (1947) and *The Queen of Spades* (1949). **Hammer credits:** *The Full Treatment* (1961)

### Slobart, Lambeth

Slobart worked as a standby painter on Hammer's *Scars of Dracula* (1970). **Hammer credits:** *Scars of Dracula* (1970 [uncredited])

### Slocombe, Douglas

Following experience as a photo-journalist and newsreel cameraman, this highly respected British cinematographer (1913–2016) broke into films in the late thirties as a cameraman on documentaries, newsreels—for which he filmed the invasions of Poland and Holland—and propaganda films for the Ministry of Information and Fleet Air Arm. His Polish footage was featured in the documentary *Lights Out in Europe* (1940), while Ealing used some of his Atlantic convoy footage in their films *The Big Blockade* (1941) and *San Demetrio London* (1943), and, on the strength of this he was offered work at the studio, first as a reporting cameraman on *Went the Day Well?* (1942), and then as an operator on *Champagne Charlie* (1944). Slocombe next photographed the sunny, location-shot romance *Painted Boats* (1945), which led to his photographing several sequences for the acclaimed horror portmanteau *Dead of Night* (1945), among them the connecting thread and the celebrated haunted mirror scene.

Over the following years, Slocombe became Ealing's leading cinematographer, and, working in both black and white and color, lent his visual flair to such acclaimed productions as *Hue and Cry* (1946), *It Always Rains on Sunday* (1947), *Kind Hearts and Coronets* (1949), *The Lavender Hill Mob* (1951), *The Man in the White Suit* (1951), *Mandy* (1952) and *The Titfield Thunderbolt* (1953). Following *Barnacle Bill* (1957), Slocombe left Ealing and went freelance, having already photographed a handful of films for other companies by this time, among them a German production of *Ludwig II* (1955). During the following three decades he worked on many major productions, among them *The Servant* (1963), which won him a BAFTA, *Guns at Batasi* (1964), which earned him a BAFTA nomination, *The Blue Max* (1966), which earned him a BAFTA nomination, *The Lion in Winter* (1968), which earned him a BAFTA nomination, *The Italian Job* (1969), *The Music Lovers* (1970), *Travels with My Aunt* (1972), which earned him both Oscar and BAFTA nominations, *Jesus Christ Superstar* (1973), which earned him a BAFTA nomination, *The Great Gatsby* (1974), which won him a BAFTA, *Rollerball* (1975), which earned him a BAFTA nomination, *Julia* (1977), which earned him a second Oscar nomination and won him a BAFTA, *Nijinsky* (1980), *Raiders of the Lost Ark* (1981), which earned him a third Oscar nomination and a further BAFTA nomination, *Never Say Never Again* (1983), *Indiana Jones and the Temple of Doom* (1984), which earned him a final BAFTA nomination, and *Indiana Jones and the Last Crusade* (1989).

In 1960, Slocombe was invited to photograph the Hammer thriller *Taste of Fear* (1961), which was being helmed by fellow Ealing *alumni* Seth Holt, who had either edited or worked as an associate producer on several films photographed by Slocombe. Their teaming was fortuitous, resulting in an atmospherically shot shocker full of subtle lighting effects and starling images. Sadly, it would be almost twenty years before Slocombe returned to Hammer, to photograph their remake of Hitchcock's *The Lady Vanishes* (1979). Although a commercial disappointment, the film nevertheless benefits enormously from Slocombe's superb Panavision photography, which makes the very most of the breath-taking alpine scenery and the elegant train interiors. **Hammer credits:** *Taste of Fear* (1961), *The Lady Vanishes* (1979)

### Sloman, Anthony

This British editor (1945–) worked as one of the assistant editors on Hammer's *One Million Years B.C.* (1966). His credits as an editor include *San Francisco* (1968), *Rhubarb* (1969), *Radio On* (1980), *The Last Emperor* (1987) and *Souli* (2004). Also a sound editor, his credits in this capacity include *The Class of Miss MacMichael* (1978), *Ascendancy* (1982) and *Shadey* (1985), plus episodes of *Strange Report* (1968–1970, TV) and *Orson Welles' Great Mysteries* (1973–1974, TV). His work as a director includes *Not Tonight, Darling* (1971) and *Foursome* (1972), the latter of which he also wrote, while his work as a producer includes *Vol-au-vent* (1996). Also a critic and film historian, he has served as a governor of the British Film Institute. His son is the assistant editor, production assistant and film critic Jonathan Sloman (1981–). **Hammer**

credits: *One Million Years B.C.* (1966 [uncredited])

### Smallwood, Neville

British born Smallwood (1922–2004) worked as the make-up artist on Hammer's *The Lady Vanishes* (1979). His other credits include *Rough Shoot* (1953), *Footsteps in the Fog* (1955), *The Main Attraction* (1962), *Tamahine* (1962), *Genghis Khan* (1964), *The Heroes of Telemark* (1965), *Modesty Blaise* (1966), *Casino Royale* (1967), *The Last Safari* (1967), *Sinful Davey* (1968), *Zeppelin* (1971), *Dr. Jekyll and Mr. Hyde* (1973, TVM), which earned him an Emmy nomination, *The Sea Wolves* (1980), *Who Dares Wins* (1982) and *White Nights* (1985). **Hammer credits:** *The Lady Vanishes* (1979)

### Smart, Billy (Jr.)

This fairground showman and circus impresario (1934–2005) provided some of the animals for Hammer's *Vampire Circus* (1972). Hailing from a circus/fairground background, both Smart's father (1894–1966) and grandfather were in the business, his father having formed the family circus in 1946. This began touring the UK with his funfair, and quickly established itself as Britain's top circus attraction, especially when the show began appearing on television at Easter and Christmas. The circus stopped touring in 1971, and the television specials, which had been produced by Billy Jr.'s brother David (1929–2007) ended in 1983. In 1990 *Billy Smart's Quality Big Top Show* made its debut, while in 2003 the circus began to tour again, albeit without animals. Previous to its brush with Hammer, Billy Smart's Circus also provided co-operation and facilities for Lynx Films' *Circus of Horrors* (1960). **Hammer credits:** *Vampire Circus* (1972)

### Smart, Stan

Smart worked as the sound recordist on eight episodes of Hammer's *Journey to the Unknown* (1968, TV). Of these, *The Indian Spirit Guide* also appeared in the compendium film *Journey to Midnight* (1968, TVM), *The New People* also appeared in the compendium film *Journey into Darkness* (1968, TVM), *The Last Visitor* also appeared in the compendium film *Journey to the Unknown* (1969, TVM), while both *The Killing Bottle* and *Do Me a Favor and Kill Me* also appeared in the compendium film *Journey to Murder* (1972, TVM). His film credits include *Avalanche* (1969), on which he was the dubbing mixer. **Hammer credits:** *The Killing Bottle* (1968, TV [episode of *Journey to the Unknown*]), *The Indian Spirit Guide* (1968, TV [episode of *Journey to the Unknown*]), *The Last Visitor* (1968, TV [episode of *Journey to the Unknown*]), *The New People* (1968, TV [episode of *Journey to the Unknown*]), *Somewhere in a Crowd* (1968, TV [episode of *Journey to the Unknown*]), *Do Me a Favor and Kill Me* (1968, TV [episode of *Journey to the Unknown*]), *Girl of My Dreams* (1968, TV [episode of *Journey to the Unknown*]), *The Beckoning Fair One* (1968, TV [episode of *Journey to the Unknown*]), *Journey into Darkness* (1968, TVM), *Journey to Midnight* (1968, TVM), *Journey to the Unknown* (1969, TVM), *Journey to Murder* (1972, TVM)

### Smethurst, Jack

This British actor (1932–) is best remembered for playing the bigot Eddie Booth in the hit TV sitcom *Love Thy Neighbour* (1972–1976, TV), a role he repeated in Hammer's big screen spin-off in 1973, and an Australian revival titled *Love Thy Neighbour in Australia* (1980, TV). Prior to playing Eddie Booth, Smethurst was best known for playing Leslie Pollitt in another sitcom, *For the Love of Ada* (1970–1971, TV), the 1972 feature version of which he also appeared in (note that both series were created by Vince Powell and Harry Diver). In films from the late fifties, Smethurst's credits include *Carry On Sergeant* (1958), which marked his debut, *A Kind of Loving* (1962), *Run with the Wind* (1966), another TV spin-off, *Please Sir!* (1971), *Chariots of Fire* (1981) and *La passione* (1996). He also popped up as himself in a gag cameo in Hammer's big screen version of *Man About the House* (1974). His other TV work includes episodes of *No Hiding Place* (1959–1967, TV), *Z Cars* (1962–1978, TV), *Softly Softly* (1966–1976, TV), *Hilary* (1984–1986, TV), *Keeping Up Appearances* (1990–1995, TV) and *Doctors* (2000–, TV). His son is the actor Adam Smethurst (1966–). **Additional notes:** Smethurst also appeared as Eddie Booth in a 1972 edition of the TV comedy special *All Star Comedy Carnival* (1969–1973, TV). **Hammer credits:** *Love Thy Neighbour* (1973, as Eddie Booth), *Man About the House* (1974, as Himself)

### Smith, A.

Smith worked as a painter on the Hammer thriller *Maniac* (1963). **Hammer credits:** *Maniac* (1963 [uncredited])

### Smith, Amber Dean

Smith can be seen as one of Hubbard's girls in Hammer's *Moon Zero Two* (1969). Her other credits include *School for Sex* (1968) and *One More Time* (1970). She also worked as a model for such magazines as *Mayfair* and *Penthouse*. **Hammer credits:** *Moon Zero Two* (1969, as Hubbard's girl)

### Smith, Barbara

Smith played one of the Tong room girls in Hammer's *The Terror of the Tongs* (1961). Her other credits include *Too Hot to Handle* (1960) and *Echo of Barbara* (1960). **Hammer credits:** *The Terror of the Tongs* (1961, as Tong room girl [uncredited])

### Smith, Barry

Smith can be seen as a villager in Hammer's *Captain Kronos—Vampire Hunter* (1974). His other credits include episodes of *Doctor Who* (1963–1989, TV) and *The Chinese Detective* (1981–1982, TV). **Hammer credits:** *Captain Kronos—Vampire Hunter* (1974, as Villager [uncredited])

### Smith, Bob

Smith (?–2012) worked as the focus puller on Hammer's *Lust for a Vampire* (1971) and *Vampire Circus* (1972). His other credits in this capacity include *Neither the Sea Nor the Sand* (1972). He later graduated to camera operator on such films as *The Human Factor* (1979), *The Empire Strikes Back* (1980), on which he was the second unit operator,

*Excalibur* (1981), *Withnail & I* (1987), *White Squall* (1996) and *Sleepy Hollow* (1999). His work as a cinematographer includes *Outside In* (1981) and *Shadow from Light* (1983). **Hammer credits:** *Lust for a Vampire* (1971 [uncredited]), *Vampire Circus* (1972 [uncredited])

### Smith, Bobbie

Smith worked as the hair stylist on Hammer's *The Viking Queen* (1967). Her other credits include *The Intimate Stranger* (1956), *Serena* (1962), *Oliver!* (1968), *The File of the Golden Goose* (1967), *Dracula* (1973, TVM), *Revenge of the Pink Panther* (1978), *Superman II* (1980), *Victor/Victoria* (1982), *Superman III* (1983), *The Trouble with Spies* (1987) and *The Lonely Passion of Judith Hearne* (1987). **Hammer credits:** *The Viking Queen* (1967)

### Smith, Brian John

Smith can be seen as a hippie in the opening party sequence in Hammer's *Dracula A.D. 1972* (1972). **Hammer credits:** *Dracula A.D. 1972* (1972, as Hippie boy)

### Smith, Brian Owen *see* Owen-Smith, Brian

### Smith, Christine

Smith can be seen as one of the schoolgirls in Hammer's *Lust for a Vampire* (1971). Her other credits include an episode of *The Persuaders!* (1971–1972, TV). **Hammer credits:** *Lust for a Vampire* (1971, as Schoolgirl [uncredited])

### Smith, Constance

This Irish actress (1928–2003) played the role of Molly Musgrave in the Hammer thriller *Room to Let* (1950), which officially "introduced" her to the screen, despite the fact that she had already appeared in several films. Her other credits include *Jassy* (1947), *Murder at the Windmill* (1949), *Taxi* (1953) and *La conjiura dei Borgia* (1959), the latter one of several films she made in Europe. Her TV appearances include episodes of *Douglas Fairbanks, Jr. Presents* (1953–1957, TV) and *ITV Television Playhouse* (1955–1967, TV). She was married to the actor-director Bryan Forbes (1926–2013, real name John Theobald Clarke) between 1951 and 1955; he appeared in Hammer's *Quatermass 2* (1957) and, as head of production for EMI in the late sixties/early seventies, green-lit several Hammer productions. He was also set to helm their version of *Nessie* in 1977. **Hammer credits:** *Room to Let* (1950, as Molly Musgrave)

### Smith, Cornelia

This African actress, living in Britain, played Zinga, the Mandingo tribal queen in Hammer's third film, *Song of Freedom* (1936). She is credited on the titles as Miss C. Smith. **Hammer credits:** *Song of Freedom* (1936, as Queen Zinga)

### Smith, Cyril

On stage from the age of eight, this busy British (Scottish) actor (1892–1963, real name Cyril Bruce-Smith) is best remembered for playing the henpecked Henry Hornett in the stage and film versions of both *Sailor Beware* (1956) and *Watch It, Sailor!* (1961), the latter of which was filmed by Hammer. He made his film debut at the age of sixteen in *The Great Fire of London* (1908) and went on to make over one-hundred more, including *Old St. Paul's* (1914), *A Little Bet* (1920), *Fires of Fate* (1923), *The Good Companions* (1933), *Waltzes from Vienna* (1933), *One of Our Aircraft Is Missing* (1942) and *She Knows Y'Know* (1962). He also appeared as the friendly innkeeper Alf Bixby in Hammer's *Stolen Face* (1952). His small screen work includes such series as *Sir Lancelot* (1956–1957, TV), in which he played Merlin, and *Hugh and I* (1962–1967, TV), in which he played Arthur Wormold. **Hammer credits:** *Stolen Face* (1952, as Alf Bixby), *Watch It, Sailor!* (1961, as Henry Hornett)

### Smith, Dorothy

The Scottish Smith (1914–1995) can be spotted in a minor role in Hammer's *Frankenstein Must Be Destroyed* (1969). Her television work includes episodes of *Emergency—Ward 10* (1957–1967, TV), *Dr. Finlay's Casebook* (1962–1971, TV) and *Softly Softly* (1966–1976, TV). **Hammer credits:** *Frankenstein Must Be Destroyed* (1969, as Neighbor [uncredited])

### Smith, Jack

Smith worked as the make-up artist on Hammer's *Dick Barton Strikes Back* (1949). His other credits include *The Trial of Madame X* (1948), *Around the World in 80 Days* (1956), *Suspended Alibi* (1957) and *Private Potter* (1962). **Hammer credits:** *Dick Barton Strikes Back* (1949)

### Smith, Joe

As a member of The Dallas Boys, Smith performed the title song for the Hammer comedy *Watch It, Sailor!* (1961). The group's other credits include appearances on such TV shows as *Six-Five Special* (1957–1958, TV), *All That Jazz* (1962, TV), *Showtime* (1968, TV) and *Saturday Variety* (1972, TV). **Hammer credits:** *Watch It, Sailor!* (1961)

### Smith, Julie

Smith worked as a publicity secretary on Hammer's *Vampire Circus* (1972). Her other credits in this capacity include *Carry On ... Up the Khyber* (1968) and *Carry On Again Doctor* (1969). Her later credits as a unit publicist include *Spice World* (1997), *My Kingdom* (2001), *Song for a Raggy Boy* (2003) and *Octane* (2003). **Hammer credits:** *Vampire Circus* (1972 [uncredited])

### Smith, Keith

This British supporting actor (1926–2008) played the role of Figures in the Hammer comedy *The Ugly Duckling* (1959). His other credits include *I'm All Right Jack* (1959), *The Concrete Jungle* (1960), *Face of a Stranger* (1964), *One Brief Summer* (1970), *The Right Hand Man* (1987), *Splitting Heirs* (1993) and *Captain Jack* (1999). Prolific on television, his credits here include episodes of everything from *Z Cars* (1962–1978, TV) to *The Beiderbecke Affair* (1985, TV). He was once the fencing instructor at LAMDA. **Hammer credits:** *The Ugly Duckling* (1959, as Figures)

### Smith, Madeline (Maddy)

This British actress (1949–, sometimes billed as Maddy or Madeleine Smith) is perhaps best remembered for her brief role as Miss Caruso in the James Bond film *Live and Let Die* (1973), in which Bond unzips her dress with the aid of a magnetic wristwatch. In films from the late sixties with *The Mini Affair* (1967), her credits include a number of comedies and horror films, among the latter three appearances for Hammer, beginning with *Taste the Blood of Dracula* (1970). Recalled Smith of this first role for the studio, "[It was] a tiny, tiny part.... The name of the character was Dolly, a little popsy, but I think if you blinked you missed me. But it was very sweet and I remember being ecstatic to get the part. I always wanted to do a Hammer film."[106]

In *The Vampire Lovers* (1970) she played one of the victims of the vampire Carmilla (the *Sunday Times* described her performance as "round-eyed and no wonder"). Remembered Smith of her experiences on the film, "Our glorious paper moon would never keep still when the cue for 'Action!' was called. The fetid breath of a dozen film-crew members was enough to keep it bouncing about above our heads. It frequently stole the scene.... With my face painted green as a prelude to death, I lay limp in the arms of the slavering female vampire. I was asked to simulate an orgasm and cry and moan in a frenzy of lesbian delight. But I had never heard either word and had no idea what was required.... How we ever came to conclude the scene to everybody's satisfaction, I cannot say."[107]

Unfortunately, Smith's voice was dubbed during post-production. Interestingly, her character was mute for much of *Frankenstein and the Monster from Hell* (1974) too. Recalled the actress of her appearance in the film, "I look at that film now and wonder who the girl is. With her very dark hair, a bit podgy in the fizzog, nothing like me at all!"[108] And of working with Terence Fisher she remembered, "He was one of the kindest, most easy-going directors I've ever worked with. He would always ask you what *you* wanted, how *you* felt about something, and that's very rare in a director. It was the same with Peter Cushing. No matter what you wanted, he was willing to listen."[109] Meanwhile, of the film's supporting players she recalled, "The inmates in the asylum were the *crème de la crème* of acting talent. They were just amazing and their faces shone and I just reacted off them. If you're in a scene with someone like Bernard Lee you can't help but take a little bit of that onto yourself."[110]

As for Peter Cushing, she recalled, "He was a lovely man, a gentle creature. He hardly ever raised his voice above a whisper, and I did not see much of him. I had nothing to say, my role in the film was that of a mute, so we had no scenes to rehearse, Peter and me. However, I do remember him and Shane Briant going off into little huddles together to get their scenes together absolutely right, for they did have dialogue. Peter would be writing little meticulous notes about the scene, and he and Shane would be discussing the scenes, rehearsing them and rehearsing them. That is why Peter Cushing is so renowned, famed and loved, for his utter dedication to the craft."[111]

Recalled production manager Christopher Neame of Smith, "[She] was, in my view, the prettiest of all the [Hammer] leading ladies. Soft-spoken and of gentle mien, she was remarkably easy to work with."[112]

Smith's other credits include *Some Like It Sexy* (1969), *The Ballad of Tam Lin* (1970), *Up Pompeii* (1971), *Up the Front* (1972), *Carry On Matron* (1972), *The Amazing Mr. Blunden* (1972), *Theatre of Blood* (1973), *Galileo* (1974) and *The Bawdy Adventures of Tom Jones* (1976). She also popped up in episodes of *The Adventures of Don Quick* (1970, TV), *Doctor at Large* (1971, TV), *The Two Ronnies* (1971–1987, TV), *The Deceivers* (1980–1981, TV), *The Pickwick Papers* (1985, TV) and *Doctors* (2000–, TV), plus various ad campaigns (among them Super Soft Shampoo).

She recalled her career in the affectionate documentary *Crumpet! A Very British Sex Symbol* (2005, TV) and narrated the documentary *Sex and the Sitcom* (2011, TV). She was also the subject of a magazine tribute care of Tim Greaves' One Shot Publications titled *Madeline Smith—A Celluloid Retrospective* (1992), and the video documentary *Madeline Smith: Vampire Lover* (2013). She was married to the actor David Buck (1936–1989), who appeared in Hammer's *The Mummy's Shroud* (1967) and *Jane Brown's Body* (1968, TV [episode of *Journey to the Unknown*]). **Hammer credits:** *Taste the Blood of Dracula* (1970, as Dolly), *The Vampire Lovers* (1970, as Emma Morton), *Frankenstein and the Monster from Hell* (1974, as Sarah [Angel])

### Smith, Maurice

Smith worked as a sound crew assistant on a handful of films for Hammer in the late fifties/early sixties. His other credits include *Across the Bridge* (1957), *The One That Got Away* (1957), *A Night to Remember* (1958) and *The Heroes of Telemark* (1965). **Hammer credits:** *The Ugly Duckling* (1959, sound assistant [uncredited]), *Never Take Sweets from a Stranger* (1960, boom assistant [uncredited]), *The Terror of the Tongs* (1961, sound assistant [uncredited])

### Smith, Murray

This British writer (1940–2003) penned *Children of the Full Moon*, the fondly remembered werewolf episode of *Hammer House of Horror* (1980, TV). His other credits include episodes of *The Sweeney* (1975–1978, TV), *Hazell* (1978–1979, TV), *Bulman* (1985–1987, TV), *Dempsey and Makepeace* (1985–1986, TV), *The Paradise Club* (1989–1990, TV), *Frederick Forsyth Presents* (1989–1990, TV) and *Extremely Dangerous* (1999, TV), also working as an executive producer on the latter two. His film credits include *Cool It, Carol!* (1970), *Die Screaming Marianne* (1971), *Four Dimensions of Greta* (1972), *Schizo* (1976) and *The Comeback* (1978), all of which were directed by Pete Walker. His novels include *Devil's Juggler* (1993), *Stone Dancer* (1994), *Killing Time* (1995) and *Legacy* (1998). **Hammer credits:** *Children of the Full Moon* (1980, TV [episode of *Hammer House of Horror*])

### Smith, Nicholas

This British actor (1934–2015) can be seen in a minor role in Hammer's *Frankenstein and the Monster from Hell* (1974). Best known for playing Mr. Cuthbert Rumbold in the sitcom *Are You Being Served?* (1972–1985, TV), he also appeared in the big screen spin-off (1977) and its small screen sequel *Grace and Favour* (1992–1993, TV). In films from 1961 with *Partners in Crime*, his other credits include *Those Magnificent Men in Their Flying Machines* (1965), *Salt & Pepper* (1968), *The Twelve Chairs* (1970), *The Curse of the Were-Rabbit* (2005), for which he provided the voice of the Reverend Clement Hedges, and *Every Hidden Thing* (2006). Busiest on television, his other credits here include episodes of *Doctor Who* (1963–1989, TV), *Softly Softly* (1966–1976, TV), *If It Moves, File It* (1970, TV), *Martin Chuzzlewit* (1994, TV), *Doctors* (2000–, TV) and *M.I. High* (2007–2014, TV), in which he played Professor Quakermass in a 2010 episode titled *Quakermass*. His daughter is the actress Catherine Russell (1965–). **Additional notes:** The role of Mr. Rumbold was subsequently played by Justin Edwards in the 2016 reboot of *Are You Being Served?* (2016, TV). **Hammer credits:** *Frankenstein and the Monster from Hell* (1974, as Death Wish [uncredited])

### Smith, Paddy

Smith worked as Peter Cushing's stand in on many of his films, among them several for Hammer. His own credits as an actor include *I Am a Camera* (1955), *Murder at the Gallop* (1963) and *Murder Ahoy* (1964), plus an episode of *The Avengers* (1961–1969, TV).

### Smith, Paul

Smith worked as an assistant editor on Hammer's *Never Take Sweets from a Stranger* (1960) and *The Terror of the Tongs* (1961). His other credits as an assistant editor include *Whistle Down the Wind* (1961) and *Carry On Screaming* (1966), while his credits as a sound editor, among them several for director Richard Lester, include *Royal Flash* (1975), *Robin and Marian* (1976), *Cuba* (1979), *Superman II* (1980), *Superman III* (1983) and *Sheena* (1984). His credits as a dialogue editor take in *The Emerald Forest* (1985), *Hope and Glory* (1987), *Batman* (1989) and *The Sheltering Sky* (1990). **Hammer credits:** *Never Take Sweets from a Stranger* (1960 [uncredited]), *The Terror of the Tongs* (1961 [uncredited])

### Smith, Ricky

Smith worked as the stills cameraman on Hammer's *Vampire Circus* (1972). His other credits include *The Flesh Is Weak* (1957), *Your Money or Your Wife* (1959), *Naked Fury* (1959), *Pit of Darkness* (1961), *Rocket to the Moon* (1967), *Monsieur Lecoq* (1967 [unfinished]) and *The Flesh and Blood Show* (1972), plus episodes of *Shirley's World* (1971, TV). **Hammer credits:** *Vampire Circus* (1972 [uncredited])

### Smith, Roy

This British designer (1929–2017, aka Roy Forge Smith) worked as the art director on Hammer's *One on an Island* (1968, TV [episode of *Journey to the Unknown*]). An up-and-coming designer at the time, he went on to work as an art director/production designer on such films as *The Assassination Bureau* (1968), *Au Pair Girls* (1972), *Monty Python and the Holy Grail* (1975), *Jabberwocky* (1977), *Bill and Ted's Excellent Adventure* (1988), *Teenage Mutant Ninja Turtles* (1990), *Robin Hood: Men in Tights* (1993) and *Dracula: Dead and Loving It* (1995). He also worked on such TV movies and series as *Attila* (2001, TV), *Young Arthur* (2002, TVM), *Martin and Lewis* (2002, TVM) and *Ghost Whisperer* (2005–2010, TV). **Hammer credits:** *One on an Island* (1968, TV [episode of *Journey to the Unknown*])

### Smith, S.W. (Samuel Woolf)

As the managing director of British Lion, British born Smith (1888–1945) received a credit on several of the company's productions, among them the Hammer comedy *Sporting Love* (1936). A producer in his own right, his credits include *A Royal Divorce* (1923), *Valley of the Ghosts* (1928), *The Squeaker* (1930), *Calling All Stars* (1937) and *Tomorrow We Live* (1943). In the late twenties, he moved to Canada for a period to oversee the installation of sound equipment in cinemas ready for the first wave of talkies, following which he returned home and went on to form British Lion in 1927, which was based at Beaconsfield. His brother was the producer, director and executive Herbert Smith (1901–1986). **Hammer credits:** *Sporting Love* (1936)

### Smith, Stanley (Stan)

Working with Bill Lenny, Smith edited the Hammer short *Day of Grace* (1957). His other credits, all as sound editor, include *The Angry Hills* (1959), *The Terrornauts* (1967), *Battle Beneath the Earth* (1967) and *Twisted Nerve* (1968), plus episodes of *The Prisoner* (1967–1968, TV). He also worked as the sound editor on Hammer's *The Viking Queen* (1967). His earlier credits as an assembly cutter include *The Black Knight* (1954) and *The Spaniard's Curse* (1958). **Hammer credits:** *Day of Grace* (1957, editor), *The Viking Queen* (1967, sound editor)

### Smith, Tom

Following experience as an assistant make-up man on the likes of *The Happiest Days of Your Life* (1950) and *The Tales of Hoffmann* (1951), this highly respected British make-up artist (1920–2009) went on to gain credits on such films as *Cover Girl Killer* (1959), *Light in the Piazza* (1962), *The V.I.P.s* (1963), *The Yellow Rolls-Royce* (1964), *A Study in Terror* (1965), *The Fearless Vampire Killers* (1967), *Sleuth* (1972), *A Bridge Too Far* (1977), *The Shining* (1980), *Raiders of the Lost Ark* (1981), *Gandhi* (1982), which earned him BAFTA and Oscar nominations, and *Return of the Jedi* (1983). He also worked intermittently on a handful of films for Hammer, beginning with *The Camp on Blood Island* (1958). His best work for the company can be found in *Countess Dracula* (1971), for which he convincingly aged the otherwise glamorous Ingrid Pitt into the decrepit Countess Elizabeth Nadasdy. His occasional TV credits include episodes of *The Saint* (1962–1969, TV), *A Woman of Substance* (1984, TV) and *Hold the Dream* (1986, TV).

Recalled actor Dave Prowse, who was made up by Smith as the Frankenstein monster for *The Horror of Frankenstein* (1970), "He used to rule the make-up room with an iron fist. I was in the make-up chair for two and a half hours and if I nodded off he would wake me and say, 'Stay awake, I can't work on you if you fall asleep!' He was a real tyrant."[113] Smith won a special BAFTA award in 1992. **Hammer credits:** *The Camp on Blood Island* (1958), *The Nanny* (1965), *The Vampire Lovers* (1970), *The Horror of Frankenstein* (1970), *Countess Dracula* (1971)

## Smith, Vic

Smith worked as the electrical supervisor on Hammer's *Vampire Circus* (1972). His other credits, in various electrical capacities, include *The Astonished Heart* (1950), *Peeping Tom* (1960), *The Day of the Jackal* (1973), *Bugsy Malone* (1976), *Absolution* (1978) and *Hawk the Slayer* (1980). **Hammer credits:** *Vampire Circus* (1972 [uncredited])

## Smith, W.

Smith worked as the floor props chargehand on the Hammer thriller *Paranoiac* (1963). **Hammer credits:** *Paranoiac* (1963 [uncredited])

## Smith, Wendy

Smith worked on the series *The World of Hammer* (1990 [first broadcast 1994], TV), on which she is credited as being "for Hammer Films" along with Graham Skeggs and Karen Woods. **Hammer credits:** *The World of Hammer* (1990 [first broadcast 1994], TV)

## Smith-Whittaker, Albert *see* Whittaker, Albert Smith

## Smythe, Vernon

Smythe can be seen as the butler Jessop in Hammer's *The Curse of the Mummy's Tomb* (1964). His other credits include *The Smart Aleck* (1951), *Sentenced for Life* (1960) and *Date at Midnight* (1960), plus episodes of *Saber of London* (1954–1960, TV), *No Hiding Place* (1959–1967, TV) and *It Happened Like This* (1962–1962, TV). **Hammer credits:** *The Curse of the Mummy's Tomb* (1964, as Jessop)

## Snel, Otto

Born in the Netherlands, Snel (1937–) worked as the dubbing mixer on eleven episodes of *Hammer House of Horror* (1980, TV). The only episodes he didn't work on were *Witching Time* and *The Thirteenth Reunion*, on which Ken Scrivener handled the duties. Prior to this he'd worked as a recording mixer a handful of films for the company. His many other credits, among them many *Carry Ons*, include *55 Days at Peking* (1963), *Carry On Spying* (1964), *Goldfinger* (1964), *You Only Live Twice* (1967), *Carry On Camping* (1969), *Carry On Abroad* (1972), *Superman* (1978), *Aliens* (1986), *Robin Hood: Prince of Thieves* (1991), *Carry On Columbus* (1992) and *The Saint* (1997). **Hammer credits:** *Countess Dracula* (1971 [uncredited]), *Hands of the Ripper* (1971 [uncredited]), *Twins of Evil* (1971 [uncredited]), *That's Your Funeral* (1973 [uncredited]), *The House That Bled to Death* (1980, TV [episode of *Hammer House of*

*Horror*]), *The Silent Scream* (1980, TV [episode of *Hammer House of Horror*]), *The Two Faces of Evil* (1980, TV [episode of *Hammer House of Horror*]), *The Mark of Satan* (1980, TV [episode of *Hammer House of Horror*]), *Visitor from the Grave* (1980, TV [episode of *Hammer House of Horror*]), *Rude Awakening* (1980, TV [episode of *Hammer House of Horror*]), *Charlie Boy* (1980, TV [episode of *Hammer House of Horror*]), *Children of the Full Moon* (1980, TV [episode of *Hammer House of Horror*]), *Carpathian Eagle* (1980, TV [episode of *Hammer House of Horror*]), *Guardian of the Abyss* (1980, TV [episode of *Hammer House of Horror*]), *Growing Pains* (1980, TV [episode of *Hammer House of Horror*])

## *The Snorkel*

GB, 1958, 90m [UK], 74m [U.S.], bw, widescreen [1.66:1], RCA, cert A

Very much a precursor of the "mini Hitchcocks" made by Hammer in the sixties, this intriguingly plotted but rather slackly paced thriller was produced amid the company's initial rush of gothic horrors. Based on a story by the actor Anthony Dawson, who would go on to appear in Hammer's *The Curse of the Werewolf* (1961), it sees a psychopath named Paul Decker murder his wife by gassing her to death in an apparently sealed room; however, his bid to pass the death off as suicide is undermined by the keen observations of his young step-daughter Candy, who surmises that he somehow managed to stage the murder by use of the titular equipment—which, indeed, he did, by crawling underneath the floorboards and breathing in air through tubes connected to the outside of the house ("Where's Paul? You must find him. I know he killed my mother," Candy pleads to the police, not realizing he is still under their feet, waiting to make his escape).

Set in Alassio, Italy, location filming on *The Snorkel* began on 7 September 1957, with much use made of the Villa Pergola, where the exteriors and several interiors were filmed by director Guy Green, a Hammer newcomer best known for his work as a cinematographer on such David Lean classics as *Great Expectations* (1946), which had won him an Oscar, and *Oliver Twist* (1948). Jimmy Sangster had penned the original script before being sidelined by his work on *The Revenge of Frankenstein* (1958) and *Dracula* (1958). Thus, when Green suggested a few minor alterations to the narrative, Peter Myers was brought onboard to quickly carry them out, though Sangster did return to pen a new ending for the film following concerns that the original—in which the villain is left to die after having tried and failed to kill his step-daughter—was too bleak.

Green aside, the remainder of the crew were pretty much Hammer stalwarts, from producer Michael Carreras down to focus puller Harry Oakes. The cast, meanwhile, had a somewhat international flavor: German born Peter Van Eyck top-lined as the deranged killer, Hollywood starlet Betta St. Jean featured as family friend Jean Edwards, while British child sensation Mandy Miller played the canny young girl (her character's dog, Toto, is meanwhile credited as being portrayed by

John Holmes' dog Flush). At the time, Van Eyck was hot to trot thanks to his success in the French thriller *The Wages of Fear* (1953), while Miller had won raves for her touching performance as the deaf and dumb child in *Mandy* (1952).

Given the expense of location filming—something that would remain a rarity throughout Hammer's history—the Italian shoot was completed briskly, following which the unit returned to Bray, where the movie was the first production to grace the new soundstage. This had been erected on the studio's old car park, and work on it had been completed while the unit was in Italy. Filming on the spacious new Stage One continued until 22 October, where designer John Stoll created the Villa Pergola's somewhat baronial looking interiors, which include a staircase that wouldn't have disgraced Castle Dracula and the floorboard crawlspace through which Van Eyck hefts himself to commit his crimes.

*The Snorkel*—which was part-financed with a loan from the National Film Finance Corporation—received its premiere onboard the *Queen Elizabeth* in May 1958. Its UK release on the ABC circuit care of Columbia followed on 7 July, while its American release, also care of Columbia, came on 8 September, for which it was shorn of a whopping sixteen minutes and paired with Hammer's *The Camp on Blood Island* (1958). "Is any bathing beauty safe from the snorkel-killer?" posed one of the film's posters somewhat erroneously, as no bathing beauties are actually threatened in the picture. The double bill was an immediate success, thanks primarily to the lure of the "Jap war crimes" featured in *Blood Island*. In fact the film met with a fairly favorable critical reception at the time, with the *New York Herald Tribune* describing it as "a first class specimen of its kind," while *The Daily Cinema* labeled it "a tense murder thriller." Interestingly, neither film is much revived today, *Blood Island* because it is no longer politically correct, and *The Snorkel*, despite its central conceit, because it is a rather protracted and flatly directed affair, lacking the visual finesse one associates with the better examples the genre has to offer (this despite being photographed by the great Jack Asher). Said director Guy Green of the film, "I liked *The Snorkel* …. It didn't exactly set the Thames on fire but I thought it rather neat. It was Jimmy Sangster's script. Peter Van Eyck was perhaps not a big enough star to carry it but he was good; Mandy Miller was perhaps a bit too old for it."[114] She was.

Recalled Jimmy Sangster of the assignment, "*The Snorkel* was a good story and a good movie as well. I shared the screenplay credit with Peter Myers. 'So how did you get on with Mr. Myers?' somebody once asked me. In fact I've never met the man to this day…. I have shared screenplay credits on at least half a dozen of my movies and never have I worked with any of my supposedly co-writers. Either he has re-written me or, as was the case generally with Hammer, I re-wrote them."[115] **Additional notes:** Footage for the travelogue short *Italian Holiday* (1958) was shot during the location shoot.

Production companies: Hammer/Clarion. Distributor: Columbia (UK [ABC circuit], U.S.). Producer: Michael Carreras. Associate producer: Anthony Nelson Keys. Director: Guy Green. Screenplay: Jimmy Sangster, Peter Myers, based on the story by Anthony Dawson. Cinematographer: Jack Asher. Music: Francis Chagrin. Music director: John Hollingsworth. Editors: James Needs, Bill Lenny [uncredited]. Art director: John Stoll. Costumes: Molly Arbuthnot. Special effects: Sydney Pearson [uncredited]. Camera operator: Len Harris. Focus puller: Harry Oakes [uncredited]. Assistant director: Tom Walls. Sound: Jock May, Ken Cameron, Carlisle Mounteney [uncredited]. Make-up: Phil Leakey. Hair: Henry Montsash. Production manager: Don Weeks. Location manager: Renzo Lucidi. Dog trainer: John Holmes. Continuity: Doreen Dearnaley. **Cast:** Peter Van Eyck (Paul Decker), Betta St. John (Jean Edwards), Mandy Miller (Candy Brown), William Franklyn (Wilson), Grégoire Aslan (Inspector), Henry Vidon (Gardener), Marie Burke (Gardener's wife), David Ritch (Hotel clerk), Armand Guinle (Waiter), Robert Rietti (Station Sergeant), Irene Prador (Frenchwoman), Mary Chapman (unnamed role [uncredited]). **DVD availability:** Sony (U.S. R1 NTSC), as part of the *Icons of Suspense* box set. **Blu-ray availability:** Powerhouse Films (all regions), as part of the *Hammer, Volume Two: Criminal Intent* box set

## Snow, Jimmy (James A.)

British born Snow (1903–1986) worked on the effects crew for Hammer's *Dracula Has Risen from the Grave* (1968). His other credits include *The October Man* (1947), *Hamlet* (1948), *The Battle of the River Plate* (1957) and *You Only Live Twice* (1967). **Hammer credits:** *Dracula Has Risen from the Grave* (1968 [uncredited])

## Soan, Doreen

British born Soan (1926–) worked as one of Hammer's many continuity girls. Her credits for the company include *The Curse of Frankenstein* (1957), prior to which she had worked as a production secretary for them on three films. Her other credits include *They're a Weird Mob* (1966), *The Sorcerers* (1967), *Mosquito Squadron* (1969), *At the Earth's Core* (1976), *Warlords of Atlantis* (1978), *The Scarlet Pimpernel* (1982, TVM), *Trail of the Pink Panther* (1982), *Pack of Lies* (1987, TVM) and *The Lady and the Highwayman* (1989, TVM), plus episodes of *The Avengers* (1961–1969, TV) and *The Sweeney* (1975–1978, TV). Her other earlier credits as a production secretary include *The Frightened Man* (1952). **Hammer credits:** *Face the Music* (1954, production secretary [uncredited]), *Mask of Dust* (1954, production secretary [uncredited]), *A Man on the Beach* (1956, production secretary [uncredited]), *The Curse of Frankenstein* (1957, continuity), *The Abominable Snowman* (1957, continuity), *The Lost Continent* (1968, continuity)

## Soblosky, Perry

Soblosky can be seen in a supporting role in Hammer's *Captain Kronos—Vampire Hunter* (1974). His other credits include episodes of *On the Buses* (1969–1973, TV), *The Adventurer* (1972–

1973, TV) and *Moonbase 3* (1973, TV). **Hammer credits:** *Captain Kronos—Vampire Hunter* (1974, as Barlow)

## Softley, Ken

British born Softley (1930–2000) worked as the construction manager on Hammer's big screen version of *Love Thy Neighbour* (1973) and one of their modern-day Dracula pictures. His other credits include *Billion Dollar Brain* (1967), *The Beast in the Cellar* (1970), *Bear Island* (1979) and *Eye of the Needle* (1981). He began his career as a supervising carpenter on *The Beachcomber* (1954), and also went on to work as a third assistant director on *Spare the Rod* (1961), *Play It Cool* (1962) and *This Sporting Life* (1963), as well as a first assistant on *Give a Dog a Bone* (1965), *The Jokers* (1967) and *Love Is a Splendid Illusion* (1970), as well as episodes of *The Champions* (1968–1969, TV). **Hammer credits:** *Love Thy Neighbour* (1973), *The Satanic Rites of Dracula* (1974)

## Sokolova, Natasha

This exotically named Brazilian born actress (1917–1969, real name Natalia Kremneff) can be seen as one of three busty blondes in the opening scene of Hammer's *Wings of Danger* (1952). She appeared in a handful of other British films during this period, including *The Passionate Friends* (1949), *The Spider and the Fly* (1949) and *So Long at the Fair* (1950). She made her film debut as a child in the Russian film *Veter* (1926), while her British debut followed in 1936 with the advertising featurette *Crowning Glory*, which extolled the virtues of Amami hair products. Also on stage in America and Britain, in ballet and revue. **Hammer credits:** *Wings of Danger* (1952, as Blonde)

## Solomon, Claude

Solomon was the Birmingham branch manager for Exclusive in the early fifties, prior to which he had been a branch manager for Associated British.

## Solomon, James

Solomon played one of the African tribesmen in Hammer's Paul Robeson vehicle *Song of Freedom* (1936). His other credits include *Sanders of the River* (1935), also with Robeson. **Hammer credits:** *Song of Freedom* (1936, as Mandingo)

## Solon, Ewen

Best known to sixties television audiences for playing Lucas in the crime series *Maigret* (1960–1963, TV), this New Zealand born supporting actor (1917–1985) is also known to Hammer fans for playing Stapleton, the illegitimate heir to the Baskerville estate in *The Hound of the Baskervilles* (1959), prior to which he'd played the Inspector in *The Rossiter Case* (1951) for the studio. In British films from 1948 with *London Belongs to Me*, he went on to appear in over fifty productions, including *The Sword and the Rose* (1953), *Robbery Under Arms* (1957), *Jack the Ripper* (1959), *The Message* (1976) and *The Wicked Lady* (1983). There were also appearances in a further three films for Hammer, along with an episode of *Journey to the Unknown* (1968, TV). His other TV work includes episodes of *The Three Musketeers* (1954, TV), in

which he played Rochefort, *Fabian of the Yard* (1954–1956, TV), *The Cabin in the Clearing* (1959, TV), *The Revenue Men* (1967–1968, TV), in which he starred as Caesar Smith, *The Doombolt Chase* (1978, TV), *Kidnapped* (1978, TV) and *Into the Labyrinth* (1981–1982, TV). **Hammer credits:** *The Rossiter Case* (1951, as Inspector), *The Hound of the Baskervilles* (1959, as Stapleton), *The Stranglers of Bombay* (1959, as Camel trader), *The Curse of the Werewolf* (1961, as Don Fernando), *The Terror of the Tongs* (1961, as Tang How), *Somewhere in a Crowd* (1968, TV [episode of *Journey to the Unknown*], as Douglas Bishop)

## Someone at the Door

GB, 1950, 65m, bw, United Programmes, cert U

The third film shot by Hammer at Oakley Court, this rather desperate comedy-thriller (based on a play previously filmed for the big screen in 1936 and for television in 1939 under the same title) follows the schemes of Ronnie and Sally Martin, a newspaper journalist and his sister who, having inherited a supposedly haunted house, decide to make up a story about a murder, so as to sell the story and make some money ("Anything to do with murder and you hit the front page—and that means big money," reasons Ronnie).

In the unfolding drama however, nothing is quite what it seems, which might explain the quirky opening title sequence, which sees the cast pass through an ornate door, which is then removed by two stage hands, revealing it to be a piece of scenery in a field, behind which the crew is standing! Indeed, it turns out that not only is the Martins' murder plot a fake, so is their retainer Price, who has been trying to "haunt" them out of the property so that he and the Martins' neighbor, the seemingly jovial Kapel (played by the jovial Garry Marsh) can search the property for some stolen diamonds. When a real body does turn up, it turns out to be that of the former caretaker Soames, though the inspector investigating the case proves to be bogus too, given that he's also searching for the missing jewels.

Very much a conveyor belt production, the film is somewhat overplayed by its cast, particularly Michael Medwin as the madcap Ronnie, who is labeled a "clumsy idiot" by Sally, though his behavior frequently verges on the retarded. The film remains of passing interest for marking the official Hammer debut of cinematographer Walter "Jimmy" Harvey, who had previously done some uncredited second unit filming on *Celia* (1949), though his work here is rather gloomy looking. As for the content, it occasionally raises an eyebrow given the film's U certificate (Kapel threatens to burn Sally's eyes with his cigar at one point, while the climactic action includes some rough house and a fatal shooting). Still, there are one or two mildly amusing moments along the way. For example, when Ronnie tries to explain away the ghostly sounds he and his sister have been hearing as wind, Sally dismisses the idea, only to be told, "Darling, you'd be surprised what wind can do!"

Made in November 1949 (which helps to explain the cast's almost constant cold breath, both indoors and out), *Someone at the Door* was trade shown in April 1950 and released in the UK by Exclusive on 21 August the same year. The making of the film was reported in the trade paper *The Cinema Studio*, which provided a week-by-week diary of progress. Noted the paragraph detailing the third week of production: "This being the third picture made at Oakley Court, the unit is now functioning at peak efficiency; producer Tony Hinds says that this is due entirely to the collective experience gained with the various time and labor-saving devices in use and the whole-hearted co-operation of unit and artists." **Additional notes:** Some sources claim that Irish actress Marie O'Neill has an uncredited role in the film, but they seem to be confusing this film with *Stranger at My Door*, which was also released in 1950.

Production company: Hammer. Distributor: Exclusive (UK). Producer: Anthony Hinds. Director: Francis Searle. Screenplay: A.R. Rawlinson, based on the play by Major Campbell Christie and Dorothy Christie. Cinematographer: Walter "Jimmy" Harvey. Music director: Frank Spencer. Editor: John Ferris, Ray Pitt [uncredited]. Art director: Denis Wreford. Make-up: Phil Leakey. Hair: Monica Hustler. Assistant director: Jimmy Sangster. Second assistant director: Ernie Metcalfe [uncredited]. Production manager: Arthur Barnes. Second unit cameraman: Billy Williams [uncredited]. Camera operator: Peter Bryan. Loader: Harry Oakes [uncredited]. Sound: Edgar Vetter. Sound mixer: Gordon Everett [uncredited]. Boom operator: Percy Britten [uncredited]. Focus pullers: Michael Reed [uncredited], Jack Howard [uncredited]. Chief carpenter: Freddie Ricketts [uncredited]. Chief electrician: Jack Curtis [uncredited]. Electricians: Charles Mullett [uncredited], Charles Stanbridge [uncredited], Richard Jenkins [uncredited], Percy Harms [uncredited]. Carpenters: Mick Lyons [uncredited], Alf Higgs [uncredited]. Stagehand: Jim Prizeman [uncredited]. Casting: Prudence Sykes. Props: Tommy Money [uncredited]. Stills: John Jay [uncredited]. Continuity: Renee Glynne. Production assistant: Michael Carreras [uncredited]. **Cast:** Michael Medwin (Ronnie Martin), Yvonne Owen (Sally Martin), Garry Marsh (Kapel), Hugh Latimer (Bill Reid), Danny Green (Price), Campbell Singer (Inspector Spedding), John Kelly (PC O'Brien)

### Somers, Julian

This British actor (1903–1976) played the role of Licasi (can that name be a joke?) in the Hammer second feature *The Gambler and the Lady* (1953). His other credits include *Hunted* (1952), *Gibraltar Adventure* (1953), *Missile from Hell* (1958) and *Far from the Madding Crowd* (1967), plus episodes of *Sailor of Fortune* (1956, TV), *Object Z* (1965, TV) and *Van Der Valk* (1972–1977, TV). **Hammer credits:** *The Gambler and the Lady* (1953, as Licasi)

### Somers, Julie

This British actress (1928–2013) played the role of the young Judy Welling in the Hammer second feature *Death of an Angel* (1952), which officially "introduced" her to cinema audiences. Her other credits include episodes of *BBC Sunday-Night Theatre* (1950–1959, TV), *Lilli Palmer Theatre* (1955–1956, TV) and *The Count of Monte Cristo* (1956, TV). Also on stage. **Hammer credits:** *Death of an Angel* (1952, as Judy Welling)

### Somers, Norman

Somers can be seen in a minor supporting role in Hammer's *Never Look Back* (1952). **Hammer credits:** *Never Look Back* (1952, as Nigel's junior)

### *Somewhere in a Crowd* see *Journey to the Unknown*

### Sommers, Russell

Sommers had a minor supporting role in *The Sweet Scent of Death* (1984, TVM [episode of *Hammer House of Mystery and Suspense*]). His other credits include *Top Secret!* (1984), *Supergirl* (1984), *The Razor's Edge* (1984), *The Dirty Dozen: Next Mission* (1985, TVM) and *Lifeforce* (1985). **Hammer credits:** *The Sweet Scent of Death* (1984, TVM [episode of *Hammer House of Mystery and Suspense*], as Young man)

### *Song of Freedom*

GB, 1936, 80m, bw, High Fidelity RCA Photophone, cert U

The third and most distinguished of Hammer's early feature productions, this slightly convoluted drama with music concerns John Zinga, a dock worker who becomes a successful opera singer, only to discover that he is in fact the king of an African tribe on the island of Casanga, to which he returns in a bid to secure their freedom from outmoded tribal customs ("What wouldn't I give to know our people, the people we belong to?" he ponders before his desire comes to pass).

To star in the film, Hammer managed to secure the services of the acclaimed American singer Paul Robeson, who had recently had a film hit with *Sanders of the River* (1935), which he nevertheless went on to disown, thanks to its clichéd depiction of tribal Africans as both savage and childish. Robeson's co-star was the equally admired American born singer Elisabeth Welch, who had settled in Britain. Recalled Welch of her first encounter with Robeson on the set, "Arriving to play opposite that great man—and it being my first speaking part in a film—I was overwhelmed and as nervous as a kitten. The nerves were soon calmed, however, when I saw that huge smile light up his face, and felt the warmth of a friendly giant when he pressed my hand in both of his, and welcomed me."[116]

The handling of the film was very much an internal affair, with Hammer board director Henry Fraser Passmore in charge of production, while fellow board member J. Elder Wills handled the direction, which varies from brisk and inventive (as per some nicely tilted shots during Zinga's *Song of Freedom* number) to borderline amateur (several of the tribal sequences). Meanwhile, two further board members—George Mozart and Hammer founder Will Hammer—played a couple of supporting roles. The most important outside contributor seems to have been the American editor Arthur Tavares, who keeps the action moving at a generally brisk pace. His work also includes a number of striking montage sequences, which make use of library footage from other films.

**A publicity shot taken during the unexpectedly realistic slave ship sequence in *Song of Freedom* (1936) (Hammer/Exclusive/British Lion/Treo Film Exchanges).**

Thanks to the presence of its leading man, who gets to perform such numbers as *Sleepy River*, *Lonely Road* and *Stepping Stones*, the result was a reasonable success, and even earned some begrudging praise from author-critic Graham Greene who, writing in *The Spectator*, commented, "Apart from the profound beauty of Miss Elisabeth Welch and Mr. Robeson's magnificent singing of inferior songs, I find it hard to say in what the charm of this imperfect picture lies. The direction is distinguished but not above reproach, the story is sentimental and absurd, and yet a sense stays in the memory of an unsophisticated mind fumbling on the edge of simple and popular poetry." Greene also picked up on the film's relaxed attitudes to race; blacks and whites intermingle without any prejudice, while blacks are portrayed naturally rather than stereotypically. Zinga and his wife are also seen to be in a loving and trusting relationship. In fact few if any reviewers picked up on the fact that the film was the first British movie to contain a kiss between two black people—something that would have been frowned upon in Britain, and especially America, at the time, yet which passed without comment or incident given the warm relationship in which it is framed (Robeson seemingly had final cut, which may well explain some of the movie's forward-looking attitudes).

The film is also notable for its depiction of the cramped and treacherous living conditions inside slave ships, and this some forty years before similar scenes depicted in the 1977 TV series *Roots* shocked the world (in a brief prologue set in 1700, Zinga's forbears are shown escaping from the island of Casanga and the grip of is hereditary ruler Queen Zinga, whom the opening scrawl describes as "tyrant, despot, mistress of cruelty").

Made at Beaconsfield Studios, the film received its premiere at the Plaza Cinema on London's Lower Regent St on 17 August 1936, and was subsequently released in the UK by British Lion in September the same year (though it should be noted that the opening credits begin with a card claiming "Exclusive Films Present"). It was later re-issued by Exclusive in 1946. According to IMDb, for its American release via Treo Film Exchanges in 1938, the film was "re-edited." **Additional notes:** Screenwriters Fenn Sherie and Ingram D'Abbes, stars Paul Robeson and Elisabeth Welch, and director J. Elder Wills re-united in 1937 for the film *Big Fella*, though this time the producing company was Fortune Films (via British Lion). Composer Eric Ansell had previously worked with Wills on *Tiger Bay* (1934), for which he also co-authored the story with the director; they would also go on to work together on Hammer's *Sporting Love* (1936), as well as *Big Fella*. The screenplay for *Song of Freedom* was actually based upon a story titled *The Kingdom of Zinga* by Claude Wallace and Dorothy Holloway. Some sources claim that Wills worked uncredited as the assistant art director on *Song of Freedom*. Note the shadow of the camera crew on some rocks in the prologue as Zinga's forbears make their escape. The film's American poster boasted that it had "a cast of thousands." It also claimed that it was "a $500,000 epic!" Hmm.... In 1950, the film was selected to open a convention for the People's Party of Ghana, the ceremonies for which were overseen by the country's future president Kwame Nkrumah, who had long been a friend of Robeson's.

Production companies: Hammer/Exclusive (as presenter). Distributors: British Lion (UK), Treo Film Exchanges (U.S.). Production supervisor: Henry Fraser Passmore. Director: J. Elder Wills. Screenplay: Fenn Sherie, Ingram d'Abbes, Michael Barringer [uncredited], Philip Lindsay [uncredited]. Story: Claude Wallace, Dorothy Holloway (*The Kingdom of Zinga*). Photography: Eric Cross. Music: Eric Ansell. Additional music: Jack Beaver [uncredited]. Lyrics: Henrik Ege. Editor: Arthur Tavares. Art director: Norman Arnold. Sound: Harold King. Assistant director: Arthur Allcott. Additional photography: Harry Rose, Thomas Glover. **Cast:** Paul Robeson (John Zinga), Elisabeth Welch (Ruth Zinga), Esme Percy (Gabriel Donozetti), Robert Adams (Monty), Ronald Simpson (Blane), George Mozart (Bert Puddick), Jenny Dean (Marian), Ambrose Manning (Trader), James Solomon (Mandingo tribesman), Ecce Homo Toto (Mandingo), Joan Fred Emney (Nell Puddick), Arthur Eliot (unnamed role [billed as Hon. Arthur Eliot]), Johnnie Schofield (unnamed role), Bernerd Ansell (Sir James Pirrie), Cornelia Smith (Queen Zinga [billed as Miss C. Smith]), Arthur Williams (Endobo [witch doctor, uncredited]), Will Hammer (Potman [uncredited]), Alf Goddard (Alf [uncredited]), Sydney Benson (Gate keeper [uncredited]), Cathleen Cavanagh (unnamed role [uncredited]), Frank Crawshaw (unnamed role [uncredited]), Joe Delmonte (unnamed role [uncredited]). **DVD availability:** Kino Video (U.S. R1 NTSC), double-billed with *Big Fella* (1937); Network (UK R2 PAL), as part of *The Paul Robeson Collection* box set

## Soraya (Princess Soraya)

This Iranian exotic dancer (1932–2001, real name Princess Soraya Esfandiary Bakhtiari) can be spotted as one of the nightclub dancers in Hammer's adaptation of *She* (1965). She went on to star in one film, playing three roles in the episodic drama *I tre volti* (1965). She was married to Shah Mohammed Reza Pahlavi (1919–1980) between 1951 and 1958. Her life story was told in the Italian TV movie *Soraya* (2003, TVM), in which she was portrayed by Anna Valle. **Hammer credits:** *She* (1965, as Nightclub dancer)

## Soskin, Paul

This Russian born producer (1905–1975) began his film career as an art director with the British European Film Corporation following training as an architect, his experience as which saw him involved in the construction of Elstree's Amalgamated Studios in 1937 (the complex was later acquired by MGM). Soskin's films as a producer include *While Parents Sleep* (1935), *Two's Company* (1936), *Quiet Wedding* (1941), *The Weaker Sex* (1948), which he also co-scripted, *Waterfront* (1950), which he again co-scripted, and *Happy Is the Bride* (1957). He made many of his films through his own production companies, which included Soskin Productions, Conqueror Productions and Hotspur Films, Ltd., the latter of which was formed in the mid-fifties. In 1959, Hammer acquired Hotspur (which Soskin remained with) and used it as a subsidiary through which it made *The Brides of Dracula* (1960) and *The Curse of the Werewolf* (1961). **Hammer credits:** *The Brides of Dracula* (1960), *The Curse of the Werewolf* (1961)

## Sottane, Liliane (Lillian, Lillianne)

This glamorous supporting actress and model (1934–2015, first name varies between Liliane, Lillian and Lillianne) played the role of Mala in Hammer's POW saga *The Camp on Blood Island* (1958). She returned shortly after to play Suzanne in the naval comedy *Up the Creek* (1958), which introduced her to the screen (despite its being made and released second). Both her Hammer films were directed by Val Guest. Her other credits include *The Headless Ghost* (1959) and an episode of *Rendezvous* (1957–1961, TV), while her work as a model takes in appearances in such magazines as *Spick* and *Beautiful Britons*. **Hammer credits:** *The Camp on Blood Island* (1958, as Mala [as Lillian Sottane]), *Up the Creek* (1958, as Suzanne [as Liliane Sottane])

## Sound Development Studios

This post-production facility worked on the series *The World of Hammer* (1990 [first broadcast 1994], TV), along with Fountain Television and TVi. **Hammer credits:** *The World of Hammer* (1990 [first broadcast 1994], TV)

## Soutar, John

Soutar (sometimes Souter) worked as a sound cameraman/operator for Hammer on *The Lyons in Paris* (1955) and *Frankenstein Created Woman* (1967). His other credits include *William Comes to Town* (1948) and *The Magic Box* (1951). **Hammer credits:** *The Lyons in Paris* (1955, sound cameraman [uncredited]), *Frankenstein Created Woman* (1967, sound camera operator [uncredited])

## Southall Studios

Hammer used this production facility to film the interiors for their big screen version of *Life with the Lyons* (1954) and its sequel, *The Lyons in Paris* (1955). Situated in Ealing and built by G.B. Samuelson in 1924 from a converted aircraft hangar, it played host to such productions as *Dodging the Dole* (1934) and *Children of the Fog* (1935). Following World War II, the facility was acquired by Alliance Film Studios Limited, which also owned Riverside and Twickenham. During this period it played host to such companies as Group 3 (between 1946 and 1954). By 1954, the sound stages were also being used to make television programs, among them *Colonel March of Scotland Yard* (1954–1956, TV). Other films made at Southall include *Dancing with Crime* (1947), *Things Happen at Night* (1948), *Time, Gentlemen, Please!* (1952) and *Behind the Headlines* (1956). **Hammer credits:** *Life with the Lyons* (1954), *The Lyons in Paris* (1955), *Adventures with the Lyons* (1957, serial re-issue of *Life with the Lyons*)

## Southgate, Arthur

Southgate worked as the dubbing editor on the Charlie Drake comedy *Sands of the Desert* (1960).

His other credits include *Captain Boycott* (1947), *1984* (1956), *Tarzan and the Lost Safari* (1957), *The Moonraker* (1958) and *The Rebel* (1961). **Hammer credits:** *Sands of the Desert* (1960)

### Southwick, Leslie

Southwick (1942–) played one of the journalists in Hammer's *Quatermass and the Pit* (1967). His other credits include episodes of *Z Cars* (1962–1978, TV), *The Man in Room 17* (1965–1966, TV), *Public Eye* (1965–1975, TV), *Fortunes of War* (1987, TV) and *A Perfect Hero* (1991, TV). **Hammer credits:** *Quatermass and the Pit* (1967, as Journalist [uncredited])

### Southworth, John

This British actor (1929–2004) can be seen as Leonard in Hammer's *The Secret of Blood Island* (1965) and Barlowe in *The Brigand of Kandahar* (1965). His other credits include episodes of *Sara Crewe* (1951, TV), *Z Cars* (1962–1978, TV), *The Mallens* (1979, TV) and *The Famous Five* (1996–1997, TV). Also on stage. **Hammer credits:** *The Secret of Blood Island* (1965, as Leonard), *The Brigand of Kandahar* (1965, as Barlowe)

### Soutten, Ben

This one-legged British bit-part player (1891–1969, full name Benjamin Graham Soutten, aka Graham Soutten) appeared in Hammer's second feature, *The Mystery of the Mary Celeste* (1935), as Jack Samson. His other credits include *Hindle Wakes* (1927), *Tiger Bay* (1933), *Sweeney Todd: The Demon Barber of Fleet Street* (1936), *The Crimes of Stephen Hawke* (1936), *Under the Red Robe* (1937) and *Convict 99* (1938). He also worked as an assistant director on *The Secret of the Loch* (1934). He lost his limb during World War I. **Hammer credits:** *The Mystery of the Mary Celeste* (1935, as Jack Samson)

### Soutten, Graham *see* Soutten, Ben

### *Spaceways*

GB, 1953, 76m [U.S. 74m], bw, RCA, cert U

Although *Spaceways* marked another tentative dip into science fiction territory for Hammer following *Stolen Face* (1953) and *Four Sided Triangle* (1953), the results are far from spectacular. As producer Michael Carreras himself later admitted, "The budget was the same as it would have been if it was about two people in bed."[117] Jimmy Sangster agreed: "It was pretty dire, mainly due to the budget restrictions. These days they spend more money on ten seconds of special effects than Hammer spent on an entire movie."[118]

Little more than a routine murder mystery with sci-fi trimmings, the film revolves around the launch of a space rocket and the murder of the wife of Stephen Mitchell, one of the scientists involved. Initially suspected of the crime and of hiding the body in the fuel tank of the rocket, Mitchell fights to clear his name (it transpires that his wife ran away with one of his colleagues, who later shoots her dead). Based on a 1952 radio play by Charles Eric Maine titled *Spaceways—A Story of the Very Near Future* (it was set in 1955), the film not only suffers from its uncomfortable meld of science fic-

tion and a B-feature murder plot, but also from lackluster performances from Howard Duff as Mitchell and the beautiful Eva Bartok as fellow scientist Lisa Frank. A paucity of imagination in both direction and production, which looks more cheese sparing than usual, doesn't help matters either.

The film remains of passing interest for introducing special effects wizard Les Bowie to Hammer (whose work includes some of his trademark matte shots), while some of its scientific predictions (such as the assertion that a manned space station would be orbiting the earth by the following decade) provide some momentary amusement. Otherwise, this is a somewhat dispiriting affair, despite Hammer's publicity claim that the film was "Even greater than *Rocketship X-M*," the Lippert-produced flick that Exclusive had successfully distributed in 1950, and from which a brief effects scene is borrowed.

Filmed between November 1952 and January 1953, *Spaceways* was trade shown in July 1953 and released in the UK by Exclusive on 21 December the same year. The film's running time was trimmed by two minutes for its earlier U.S. release on 7 August by Fox. "The screen's first story of space islands in the sky!" erroneously exclaimed one of the film's posters. *Variety* described it as "a mild, talky and overlengthy melodrama," though it did concede that "Terence Fisher's direction is extremely methodical, as is the playing." However, back home, the *Monthly Film Bulletin* accused it of being "a dull and shoddy affair." Remembered camera operator Len Harris of the main launch sequence in the film, "We had to make it look as if the rocket had actually fired. So I put my hands on

the side of the camera and shook it sideways during the shot, gradually reducing the vibrations until the camera was steady again, as if the rocket was moving. I guess it worked because nobody ever told me later that it was 'bloody silly.'"[119] **Additional notes:** The film carries a 1952 copyright, and is credited as having been "Produced at Exclusive Studios, Bray." Charles Eric Maine novelized his play in 1953, which was published by Pan. Location footage was filmed on Chobham Common, soon to become a feature in several Hammer films.

Production companies: Hammer/Lippert. Distributors: Exclusive (UK), Twentieth Century–Fox (U.S.). Producer: Michael Carreras. Director: Terence Fisher. Screenplay: Richard Landau, Paul Tabori, based on the radio play by Charles Eric Maine. Cinematographer: Reg Wyer. Music director: Ivor Slaney. Music played by: The New Symphony Orchestra. Editor: Maurice Rootes. Art director: J. Elder Wills. Sound: Bill Salter. Camera operator: Len Harris. Special effects: The Trading Post, Ltd., Bowie, Margutti and Co. (Les Bowie, Vic Margutti). Production manager: Victor Wark. Assistant director: Jimmy Sangster. Continuity: Renee Glynne. Make-up: Dick Bonnor-Moris. Hair: Polly Young. Dialogue director: Nora Roberts. Boom operator: Percy Britten [uncredited]. **Cast:** Howard Duff (Stephen Mitchell), Eva Bartok (Lisa Frank), Cecile Chevreau (Vanessa Mitchell), Anthony Ireland (General Hays), Andrew Osborn (Philip Crenshaw), Alan Wheatley (Dr. Smith), Michael Medwin (Toby Andrews), Philip Leaver (Dr. Keppler), Hugh Moxey (Colonel Daniels), David Horne (Minister), Marianne Stone (Mrs. Rogers [uncredited]), Leo Phillips

Rockets galore. Slick artwork for *Spaceways* (1953). If only the film was this exciting. Needless to say, no space islands in the sky are featured (Hammer/Lippert/Exclusive/Twentieth Century–Fox).

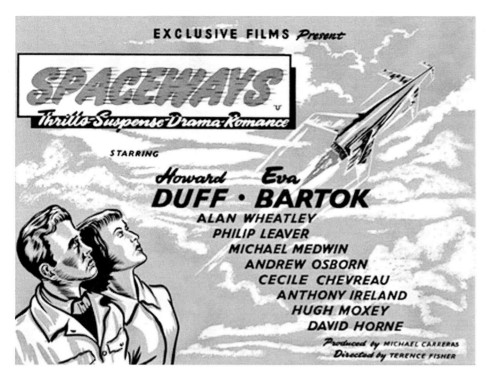

A simple but effective British poster for *Spaceways* (1953) (Hammer/Lippert/Exclusive/Twentieth Century–Fox).

(Sergeant Peterson [uncredited]), Jean Webster-Brough (Mrs. Daniels [uncredited]). **DVD availability:** Simply Home Entertainment (UK R2 PAL), extras include the short *Operation Universe* (1957 [released 1959])

### Sparrow Film Productions

Sparrow was one of Hammer's many subsidiary companies.

### Sparrow, Bobby

Along with soft-core starlets Zoe Hendry, Lindy Benson and Jo Peters, Sparrow can be seen during the orgy scene in Hammer's *To the Devil a Daughter* (1976). Her other credits include *The Man Who Couldn't Get Enough* (1974), *Stardust* (1974), *Confessions of a Pop Performer* (1975), *I'm Not Feeling Myself Tonight* (1976) and *Secrets of a Superstud* (1976). **Hammer credits:** *To the Devil a Daughter* (1976, as Fourth girl)

### Spearman, Frank H. (Hamilton)

This American author (1859–1937) penned the western detective novel *Whispering Smith* (1906), which was filmed in 1916, 1917 (as *Money Madness*), 1926 and 1948. Hammer made a follow-up to the 1948 version titled *Whispering Smith Hits London* in 1952. However, the film's story was actually the work of screenwriter John Gilling, being based on his short story *Where Is Sylvia?* Hammer did, however, acquire a number of other Whispering Smith stories, though none of them made it to the screen, despite an announcement that *Whispering Smith Hits London* would be followed by *Whispering Smith Investigates*. Other films featuring Smith include *Medicine Bend* (1916), *Whispering Smith Rides* (1927), *The Lightning Express* (1930

[a remake of *Whispering Smith Rides*]) and *Whispering Smith Speaks* (1935), while an American TV series titled *Whispering Smith* appeared in 1961 starring Audie Murphy. Other films derived from Spearman's books and stories include *The Girl and the Game* (1915), *Midnight* (1917) and *The Night Flyer* (1928). Other published works include *Doctor Bryson* (1902), *Merrillie Dawes* (1913), *The Marriage Verdict* (1925) and *Hell's Desert* (1932). **Hammer credits:** *Whispering Smith Hits London* (1952)

### Speed, Doris

This British actress (1899–1994) is best known for playing the imperious pub landlady Annie Walker in the long-running soap *Coronation Street* (1960–, TV), in which she appeared between 1960 and 1983. On stage as a child, she later worked as a clerk before returning to the stage as an adult. Just prior to joining *Coronation Street*, she appeared briefly in Hammer's Manchester-shot thriller *Hell Is a City* (1960), in which she can be seen as a hospital sister. Her other TV credits include episodes of *Armchair Theatre* (1956–1974, TV), *Knight Errant Limited* (1959–1961, TV) and *Kipps* (1960, TV), plus such *Street*-related programs as *Annie and Betty's Coronation Street Memories* (1975, TV), *Happy Birthday, Coronation Street!* (1990, TV) and *Classic Coronation Street* (1993, TV). She was made an MBE in 1977, and was played by Celia Imrie in the TV drama *The Road to Coronation Street* (2010, TVM). **Hammer credits:** *Hell Is a City* (1960, as Hospital sister [uncredited])

### Spencer, Frank

Hammer's first resident music director, this British (Scottish) composer and conductor (1911–

1975) supervised the music for the burgeoning company from 1949 to 1952, beginning with the "unofficial" Hammer second feature *Jack of Diamonds* (1949), which he co-scored with Rupert Grayson, who was his most frequent collaborator. His other credits include *Two on the Tiles* (1951), *Laxdale Hall* (1952) and *Continental Nights* (1958). Stock music composed by Spencer was also featured in *Night of the Silvery Moon* (1954), *Cat Girl* (1957) and *Blitz on Britain* (1960). He also wrote the theme tune for the TV series *Tonight* (1957–1965, TV). **Hammer credits:** *Jack of Diamonds* (1949, co-music), *Dr. Morelle—The Case of the Missing Heiress* (1949, co-music director), *Dick Barton Strikes Back* (1949, co-music), *The Adventures of PC 49—The Case of the Guardian Angel* (1949, co-musical director), *Celia* (1949, co-music director), *Meet Simon Cherry* (1949, co-music director), *The Man in Black* (1950, co-music director), *Room to Let* (1950, music, conductor), *Someone at the Door* (1950, music director), *What the Butler Saw* (1950, music director), *The Black Widow* (1950, musical director), *Dick Barton at Bay* (1950, conductor, arranger), *The Lady Craved Excitement* (1950, music director), *The Rossiter Case* (1951, music director), *To Have and to Hold* (1951, music director, song), *The Dark Light* (1951, music director), *A Case for PC 49* (1951, music director), *Cloudburst* (1951, music, conductor), *Whispering Smith Hits London* (1952, music, conductor), *Death of an Angel* (1952, music director), *The Last Page* (1952, music)

### Spencer, Sally-Jane

This British actress (1945–) can be seen as the florist in Hammer's *The Anniversary* (1968), in which her dialogue seems to have been dubbed. Her other credits include *The Great St. Trinian's Train Robbery* (1966), plus episodes of *The Newcomers* (1965–1969, TV), *Department S* (1969–1970, TV) and *The New Avengers* (1976–1977, TV). She is best known for playing Linda Patterson in *The Fall and Rise of Reginald Perrin* (1976–1979, TV) and Linda Perrin in *The Legacy of Reginald Perrin* (1996, TV). **Hammer credits:** *The Anniversary* (1968, as Florist)

### Spenser, David

Born in Ceylon, Spenser (1934–2013, real name David de Saram) can be seen as Gopali in the Hammer shocker *The Stranglers of Bombay* (1959). His other credits include *In Search of the Castaways* (1961), *The Earth Dies Screaming* (1964) and *Some May Live* (1967), plus episodes of *Billy Bunter of Greyfriars School* (1952–1961, TV), in which he played Hurree Jamset Ram Singh, *Z Cars* (1962–1978, TV) and *Play of the Month* (1965–1973, TV). He later formed Saffron Productions with his partner Victor Pemberton (1931–2017) to make television documentaries, among them *Benny Hill: Laughter and Controversy* (1991, TV) and *Benny Hill: The World's Favourite Clown* (1991, TV), both of which he directed. His brother is the actor Jeremy Spenser (1937–, real name Jeremy John Dornhurst de Sarem). **Hammer credits:** *The Stranglers of Bombay* (1959, as Gopali)

**Spooner, Dennis**

This prolific British television writer (1932–1986) contributed scripts to a wide variety of series (many of them for ITC), among them *No Hiding Place* (1959–1967, TV), *The Avengers* (1961–1969, TV), *Fireball XL5* (1962–1963, TV), *The Protectors* (1972–1973, TV), *The New Avengers* (1976–1977, TV), *The Professionals* (1977–1983, TV) and *Bergerac* (1981–1991, TV). He also created such cult series as *Man in a Suitcase* (1967–1968, TV) with Richard Harris, and, with Monty Berman, *The Champions* (1968–1969, TV), *Department S* (1969–1970, TV) and *Jason King* (1971–1972, TV) while solo creations included *Randall and Hopkirk (Deceased)* (1969–1970, TV). He also penned an episode of *Hammer House of Mystery and Suspense*, (1984, TVM), sharing his screen credit with the series' story editor John Peacock, who had to considerably revise Spooner's teleplay. **Hammer credits:** *And the Wall Came Tumbling Down* (1984, TVM [episode of *Hammer House of Mystery and Suspense*])

**Sporting Love**

GB, 1936, 67m, bw, cert U

Based on a successful 1934 play by its star Stanley Lupino (which had run for 302 performances at the Gaiety Theater in London), this frantic comedy with music focuses on the exploits of Percy and Peter Brace, two bankrupt racehorse owners who pretend to have acquired wives so as to please their rich aunt, whom they hope will bail them out of trouble, which follows them thick and fast (as the opening narration informs us, horse racing is, "Known to most as the sport of kings—and to everyone else as a mug's game!").

The fourth of Hammer's early features, it was, like its predecessor *Song of Freedom* (1936), very much an in-house affair, with production and direction again in the hands of board members Henry Fraser Passmore and J. Elder Wills respectively (with the latter also working as an art director under his nickname, Bunty Wills). Cinematographer Eric Cross and writers Fenn Sherrie and Ingram d'Abbes, who had likewise worked on *Song of Freedom*, also made a comeback for this vehicle, whose brash mix of shtick, chases, slapstick, exaggerated double takes, convoluted plot complications and anything-for-a-gag inanity ultimately exhausts more than it entertains. That said, Wills handles the proceedings briskly enough, with plenty of fast cutting and visual wipes to help disguise the film's theatrical origins, while the cast go through their well-honed motions with cheerful brio (they'd certainly played the scenes often enough on stage, and milk them for all they're worth). However, the numbers—jaunty but superfluous—are somewhat awkwardly shoehorned into the proceedings, though they are typical of their period, among them a rendition of the timeless Charles Harris classic *After the Ball*.

Like *Song of Freedom*, *Sporting Love* was made at Beaconsfield Studios ("A Beaconsfield Musical!" exclaimed the ads). As with its predecessor, it was also released in the UK by British Lion. Press shown on 24 May 1936, it made its London debut on 24 November the same year, and was released nationally in December, and proved a modest success, thanks to the presence of its music hall stars Stanley Lupino (father of Ida) and Laddie Cliff, who mug their way through the corn with reckless abandon. Sample gag: "I know one woman who put everything she had on a horse." "Who?" "Lady Godiva!" Boom, boom! **Additional notes:** Exclusive reissued the film in 1941. Stanley Lupino's brother Barry has a bit part in the film. S.W. Smith, who was the managing director of British Lion, also receives a credit in the titles. Actress Clarissa Selwyn is billed as Clarissa Selwynne. Some sources indicate that Will Hammer had been financially involved with the stage show on which the film was based.

Production company: Hammer. Distributor: British Lion (UK). Producer (credited as production supervisor): Henry Fraser Passmore. Director: J. Elder Wills. Screenplay: Fenn Sherie, Ingram d'Abbes, based on the play by Stanley Lupino. Photography: Eric Cross. Music: Eric Ansell [uncredited], Jack Beaver (additional music [uncredited]). Songs: Charles Harris [uncredited], Billy Mayerl [uncredited] and others. Editor: Hugh Stewart. Art directors: Norman Arnold, Bunty Wills (J. Elder Wills). Assistant director: Parry Davis. Sound: Harold King, York Scarlett. Choreographer: Fred Leslie [uncredited]. **Cast:** Stanley Lupino (Percy Brace), Laddie Cliff (Peter Brace), Eda Peel (Maude Dane), Clarissa Selwynne (Aunty Fanny), Wyn Weaver (Wilfred Wimple), Lu Anne Meredith (Nelly Gray), Bobbie Comber (Gerald Dane [uncredited]), Henry Carlisle (Lord Dimsdale [uncredited]), Merle Tottenham (Maid [uncredited]), Syd Crossley (Temperance man [uncredited]), Barry Lupino (unnamed role [uncredited]), Arty Ash (unnamed role [uncredited]), Joe Delmonte (unnamed role [uncredited]), Jeanne Macintyre (unnamed role [uncredited]), Davina Craig (unnamed role [uncredited])

**Sprague, Jack**

Sprague composed the music for *Wolfshead: The Legend of Robin Hood* (1969 [released 1973]), which was acquired by Hammer, and for which he shared his credit with Bernie Sharp. **Hammer credits:** *Wolfshead: The Legend of Robin Hood* (1969 [released 1973])

**Spratling, Jack**

Though barely mentioned in the history of Hammer, British born Spratling was nevertheless one of Exclusive's first managing directors, joining the company at its outset in 1934. He also worked as the company's circuit manager, but left in 1945 following a management re-shuffle.

**Spurling, Leslie**

Spurling played the role of Sergeant Bedd in the Hammer programer *Death in High Heels* (1947). His other credits include *Piccadilly Playtime* (1936) and *Carry On London* (1937), plus an episode of *BBC Sunday-Night Theatre* (1950–1959, TV) and *The Passing By Show* (1951–1953, TV). **Hammer credits:** *Death in High Heels* (1947, as Sergeant Bedd)

**Squire, William**

On stage from 1945 following training at RADA, this British (Welsh) character actor (1916–1989) played the role of the aged Sir John de Courtenay in the early scenes of Hammer's *A Challenge for Robin Hood* (1967), pegging it about ten minutes in. In films from 1951 with *The Long Dark Hall*, his other credits include *Dunkirk* (1958), *Where Eagles Dare* (1969), *The Lord of the Rings* (1978), for which he provided the voice of Gandalf, *The Thirty-Nine Steps* (1978) and *Testimony* (1987). Although busiest on stage, he also appeared in many television series, among them episodes of *How Green Was My Valley* (1960, TV), *Callan* (1967–1972, TV) and *The XYY Man* (1976–1977, TV). He was also familiar to TV audiences as Hunter in the spy series *Callan* (1970–1972, TV). His wife (subsequently divorced) was the actress Juliet Harmer (1941–), whom he married in 1967. **Hammer credits:** *A Challenge for Robin Hood* (1967, as Sir John de Courtenay)

**Squires, Sid**

Squires worked as the sound mixer on *Wolfshead: The Legend of Robin Hood* (1969 [released 1973]), which was acquired by Hammer. His other credits include *The Master Plan* (1955), *Battle of the V-1* (1958), *Danger Route* (1967) and *The Caribbean Fox* (1970), plus episodes of *The Capone Investment* (1974, TV), *Bouquet of Barbed Wire* (1976, TV) and *Mitch* (1984, TV). **Hammer credits:** *Wolfshead: The Legend of Robin Hood* (1969 [released 1973])

**Stack, Brian**

Stack worked as a driver on Hammer's *Blood from the Mummy's Tomb* (1971). **Hammer credits:** *Blood from the Mummy's Tomb* (1971 [uncredited])

**Stack, Roger**

Stack worked as the third assistant director on Hammer's *Demons of the Mind* (1972). His earlier credits as a runner include *Carry On Again Doctor* (1969) and *Carry On Up the Jungle* (1970). **Hammer credits:** *Demons of the Mind* (1972 [uncredited])

**Stainer-Hutchins, Michael**

Stainer-Hutchins (1922–1983) provided the title sequence and the (not always convincing) effects for Hammer's *The Devil Rides Out* (1968), for which he was also one of the associate producers with Peter Daw. Indeed, through their "services company" Michael Stainer-Hutchins and Peter Daw Ltd., the two men had purchased the rights to three Dennis Wheatley novels in September 1963. These were *The Devil Rides Out*, *The Satanist* and *To the Devil a Daughter*, all three of which were then optioned by Hammer two months later, the duo's idea being to get a leg up in the film industry by being associated with the productions themselves. Stainer-Hutchins' other effects credits include *The Day the Earth Caught Fire* (1961) and *Work Is a Four-Letter Word* (1968), as well as the ad *Horlicks: Guards Against Night Starvation* (1960), for which he provided the animation. He also provided the "story conception" for the Oscar-nominated short *The Story of Time* (1951). Commented Christopher Lee of the effects work in *The Devil Rides Out*, "The problems that we had were the problems of the special effects."[120] **Hammer credits:** *The Devil Rides Out* (1968 [uncredited])

### Stallybrass, Anne

This RADA-trained British actress (1938–) can be seen as a pregnant woman in Hammer's *Countess Dracula* (1971). She is perhaps best known for playing Jane Seymour in the TV serial *The Six Wives of Henry VIII* (1970, TV) and Anne Webster in *The Onedin Line* (1971–1980, TV), the latter of which earned her a joint best actress BAFTA nomination, along with her performance in *The Strauss Family* (1972, TV), in which she played Anna Strauss. In films and television following experience in rep, her other TV credits include *Wuthering Heights* (1967, TV), *The Mayor of Casterbridge* (1978, TV), *Knights of God* (1987, TV), *Heartbeat* (1992–2009, TV), in which she played Eileen Reynolds between 1993 and 1998, *Diana: Her True Story* (1993, TVM), in which she played Queen Elizabeth II, *Murder in Mind* (2001–2003, TV) and *A Song for Jenny* (2015, TVM). Her first husband was the actor Roger Rowland (1935–2011), to whom she was married between 1963 and 1972. Her second husband was the actor Peter Gilmore (1931–2013), whom she married in 1987, and with whom she co-starred in *The Onedin Line*. **Hammer credits:** *Countess Dracula* (1971, as Pregnant woman)

### Stampe, Will

This British actor (1920–1981, real name Bernard Stamp) can be seen in a supporting role in Hammer's *Dr. Jekyll and Sister Hyde* (1971). His other credits include *The Greengage Summer* (1961), *The Main Chance* (1964), *Poor Cow* (1967), *Smashing Time* (1967), *Inspector Clouseau* (1968), *The Alf Garnett Saga* (1972) and *Cream in My Coffee* (1980, TVM), plus episodes of *Sir Francis Drake* (1961–1962, TV), *The Wednesday Play* (1964–1970, TV) and *Till Death Us Do Part* (1965–1975, TV). **Hammer credits:** *Dr. Jekyll and Sister Hyde* (1971, as Mine host)

### Stanbridge, Charles

Stanbridge worked as an electrician for Hammer on a handful of films, among his credits being their breakthrough film *The Quatermass Xperiment* (1955). **Hammer credits:** *The Man in Black* (1950 [uncredited]), *Someone at the Door* (1950 [uncredited]), *What the Butler Saw* (1950 [uncredited]), *The Quatermass Xperiment* (1955 [uncredited])

### Stanford, Trevor H. *see* Conway, Russ

### Stanislav, Jiri

This Czech actor (1946–) can be seen as Ivan in *Czech Mate* (1984, TVM [episode of *Hammer House of Mystery and Suspense*]).Other credits include *White Nights* (1985), *Superman IV: The Quest for Peace* (1987) and *The Unbearable Lightness of Being* (1988), plus episodes of *Strangers* (1978–1982, TV), *The Last Place on Earth* (1985, TV), *Maigret* (1991–2005, TV) and *Aféry* (2011, TV). **Hammer credits:** *Czech Mate* (1984, TVM [episode of *Hammer House of Mystery and Suspense*], as Ivan)

### Stanley, Charles

Stanley can be seen as Dobbins in Hammer's

*The Shadow of the Cat* (1961). His other credits include *23 Paces to Baker Street* (1956), *Carry On Nurse* (1959), *Raising the Wind* (1961) and *Carry On Cabby* (1963), plus episodes of *Ivanhoe* (1958–1959, TV) and *No Hiding Place* (1959–1967, TV). Also on stage. **Hammer credits:** *The Shadow of the Cat* (1961, as Dobbins [uncredited])

### Stannard, Don

An important name in Hammer's early post-war films, this British actor (1916–1949, full name Donald Gordon Stannard) began his association with the company with the featurette *Death in High Heels* (1947), a murder mystery in which he took the leading role of Detective Inspector Charlesworth. He obviously made an impression on the top brass, as he was invited back to star as Dick Barton in a series of cheap but popular films. Unfortunately, he died in a car crash on Saturday 9 July 1949 while returning home from a garden party at Dial Close (the country house being used as a "studio" by Hammer at the time), following a celebration to mark the completion of a number of Hammer films, among them *Dick Barton at Bay* (1950). A proposed fourth Barton film—tentatively titled *Dick Barton in Darkest Africa*—was subsequently cancelled, while the third was released posthumously. Commented *Kinematograph Weekly* of the fatal accident in its 14 July issue, "Stannard was killed instantly.... Mrs. Stannard was unhurt, but the other passengers [music director Frank Spencer and actor Sebastian Cabot] all suffered severe shock and lacerations." Recalled Jimmy Sangster of the accident, "I was in the car behind Don's and watched as it went out of control, off the road, and down a steep hill. I was the only person around a couple of days later when the police called and asked if I'd identify the body."[121] Stannard's other credits include *Hold That Kiss* (1938), *Bridal Suite* (1939), *Don Chicago* (1945), *Caesar and Cleopatra* (1945), *Pink String and Sealing Wax* (1946), *I'll Turn to You* (1946) and *The Temptress* (1949). **Hammer credits:** *Death in High Heels* (1947, as Detective Inspector Charlesworth), *Dick Barton—Special Agent* (1948, as Dick Barton), *Dick Barton Strikes Back* (1949, as Dick Barton), *Dick Barton at Bay* (1950, as Dick Barton)

### Stannard, Roy

This British art director and production designer (1931–2008) worked on eight episodes of the Hammer TV series *Journey to the Unknown* (1968, TV), of which four also appeared in compendium films: *The Indian Spirit Guide* in *Journey to Midnight* (1968, TVM), *The Last Visitor* in *Journey to the Unknown* (1969, TVM), *The New People* in *Journey into Darkness* (1968, TVM), and *The Killing Bottle* in *Journey to Murder* (1972, TVM). This led to Stannard designing the sumptuous sets for Hammer's *Hands of the Ripper* (1971), though it should be noted that a number of these, among them a Victorian street, had previously been used in *The Private Life of Sherlock Holmes* (1970), which had been designed by Alexandre Trauner. He also designed Hammer's *Twins of Evil* (1971). Stannard's other credits include *The Spanish Sword* (1962), *The Trygon Factor* (1966), *The Games*

(1970), *A Bridge Too Far* (1977), *Never Say Never Again* (1983) and *Feast of July* (1995), plus episodes of *The Zoo Gang* (1974, TV), *Orson Welles' Great Mysteries* (1973–1974, TV), *The Flame Trees of Thika* (1981, TV) and *A Woman of Substance* (1984, TV). His early credits as a draughtsman include *The Million Pound Note* (1953), *Forbidden Cargo* (1954), *As Long As They're Happy* (1955) and *Lawrence of Arabia* (1962). **Hammer credits:** *The Killing Bottle* (1968, TV [episode of *Journey to the Unknown*), *The Indian Spirit Guide* (1968, TV [episode of *Journey to the Unknown*]), *Miss Belle* (1968, TV [episode of *Journey to the Unknown*]), *The Last Visitor* (1968, TV [episode of *Journey to the Unknown*]), *The New People* (1968, TV [episode of *Journey to the Unknown*]), *Somewhere in a Crowd* (1968, TV [episode of *Journey to the Unknown*]), *Girl of My Dreams* (1968, TV [episode of *Journey to the Unknown*]), *The Beckoning Fair One* (1968, TV [episode of *Journey to the Unknown*]), *Journey into Darkness* (1968, TVM), *Journey to Midnight* (1968, TVM), *Journey to the Unknown* (1969, TVM), *Hands of the Ripper* (1971), *Twins of Evil* (1971), *Journey to Murder* (1972, TVM)

### Stanton, Barry

British born Stanton (1940–) can be seen as Ernst in Hammer's *Demons of the Mind* (1972) and as Tony in *Carpathian Eagle* (1980, TV [episode of *Hammer House of Horror*]). His other credits include *Robbery* (1967), *Tell Me Lies* (1968), *Sweeney 2* (1978), *Leon the Pig Farmer* (1992), *The Madness of King George* (1994) and *Shanghai Knights* (2003), plus episodes of *The Plane Makers* (1963–1965, TV), *Upstairs, Downstairs* (1971–1975, TV), *Now and Then* (1983–1984, TV) and *Holby City* (1999–, TV). **Hammer credits:** *Demons of the Mind* (1972, as Ernst)

### Staples, Tommy

Staples worked as the boom operator on Hammer's *The Legend of the 7 Golden Vampires* (1974) and *Shatter* (1974), both of which were made in Hong Kong. His other credits include *Fedora* (1978), *Who Is Killing the Great Chefs of Europe?* (1978), *Ashanti* (1979), *Yentl* (1983), *Old Gringo* (1989), *Black Beauty* (1994) and *Deadmeat* (2007), plus episodes of *Canterbury Tales* (2003, TV), *Keen Eddie* (2003–2004, TV) and *Bleak House* (2005, TV). **Hammer credits:** *The Legend of the 7 Golden Vampires* (1974), *Shatter* (1974)

### Stapleton, Cyril

Popular in the fifties and sixties, this British musician and conductor (1914–1974) recorded many albums of light music. He and his orchestra, the Show Band, also starred in two musical featurettes for Hammer in the mid-fifties and were frequent guest performers on BBC radio from 1939 onwards, appearing on such shows as *Hit Parade* (1948) and *Golden Slipper* (1948). Prior to this he had played and recorded with such orchestras as The Henry Hall Dance Band and The Jack Payne Orchestra. His other screen credits include *Top of the Bill* (1971) and *Raising the Roof* (1972), for both of which he provided the music. He also provided additional music for *Lionheart* (1968). In 1965 he became the Artists and Repertoire manager at Pye Records, for whom he also recorded. His albums and singles include *Blue Star* (1955), which reached number two in the charts, *The Children's Marching Song* (1959), better known as *Nick-Nack Paddy Wack*, and *Polynesian Melody* (1961). **Hammer credits:** *Cyril Stapleton and the Show Band* (1955, as Himself), *Just for You* (1956, as Himself)

### Stark, Graham

Frequently seen in the films of Peter Sellers, one of whose closest friends he was, this much-liked British comedy actor (1922–2013) began his film career as a teenager in *The Spy in Black* (1939). Following wartime experience in the RAF, during which he became a Gang Show staple, he went on to make a name for himself, first on radio with *Ray's a Laugh* (1949–1961) and *Educating Archie* (1950–1958), and then in films and television. Among his seventy-plus big screen appearances (which include several films for director Blake Edwards) are *Emergency Call* (1952), *The Running Jumping and Standing Still Film* (1960), *A Shot in the Dark* (1964), *The Return of the Pink Panther* (1975), *The Prince and the Pauper* (1977), *Victor/Victoria* (1982), *Blind Date* (1987) and *Son of the Pink Panther* (1993). A noted stills photographer, he also directed two films: the short comedy *Simon Simon* (1970), which he also scripted and appeared in, and *The Magnificent Seven Deadly Sins* (1971), which he also produced. He had only two brushes with Hammer (and both of them comedies), appearing as Chiron in *A Weekend with Lulu* (1961) and as Carnoustie Bligh in the *Watch It, Sailor!* (1961). His many television credits include episodes of *Benny Hill* (1962–1963, TV), *Here Come the Double Deckers!* (1970–1971, TV), *Boon* (1986–1992, TV) and *Comedy Lab* (1999–2001, TV). His books include *Remembering Peter Sellers* (1991) and *Stark Naked* (2003). **Hammer credits:** *A Weekend with Lulu* (1961, as Chiron), *Watch It, Sailor!* (1961, as Carnoustie Bligh)

### Stark, Ray

A legend in Hollywood, this wily American producer (1914–2004) began his showbusiness career after World War II as a literary agent following experience as a journalist and publicity writer. He later switched to being an acting agent, and represented such major stars as Kirk Douglas and Marilyn Monroe. In 1957 he formed the independent production company Seven Arts, bringing in producer Eliot Hyman—who had invested in a number of Hammer films—as a silent partner. Seven Arts subsequently helped to finance a number of films, including Hammer's *Ten Seconds to Hell* (1959), but the production was a troubled one in which Stark overruled the film's credited producer, Michael Carreras, in favor of its director, Robert Aldrich. In 1966 Stark resigned from Seven Arts, which went on to buy out Warner Bros. the following year for $125m, becoming Warner Bros./Seven Arts, which continued to invest in Hammer productions. Stark's personal credits as a producer include *The World of Suzie Wong* (1960), *The Way We Were* (1973), *The Goodbye Girl* (1977), which

earned him a best picture Oscar nomination, *Annie* (1982), *Brighton Beach Memoirs* (1985) and *Steel Magnolias* (1989). His greatest success, however, was the musical *Funny Girl* (1968), which was based on the life story of his mother-in-law, Fanny Brice (1891–1951), the stage version of which he had also been involved with. The film earned Stark a Best Picture Oscar nomination and led to a sequel, *Funny Lady* (1975). Stark went on to form another production company, Rastar (geddit?), in the mid-seventies, which had strong ties with Columbia Pictures, for whom Stark had produced some of his biggest hits. In 1980, he received the Irving G. Thalberg Award. **Hammer credits:** *Ten Seconds to Hell* (1959)

### Stark, Wilbur

This American writer and producer (1912–1995, aka Billy White) produced Hammer's *Vampire Circus* (1972), which was based upon a story co-authored (without screen credit) by himself and George Baxt. The story also featured elements from an abandoned project about twin vampires (Helga and Heinrich in the finished film) which Stark had been developing with writer John Peacock (who had no involvement in the finished film). Stark's other credits as a producer include *My Lover, My Son* (1970), *All I Want Is You … and You … and You…* (1974), which he also scored, and *The Thing* (1982), the latter of which he executive produced. Working as Billy White, he also wrote, produced and directed *The Love Box* (1972) and *The Stud* (1974). His small screen credits as a producer include *Spin the Picture* (1949–1950, TV), *True Story* (1957–1961, TV) and *The Brothers Brannagan* (1960, TV). He was married to (and subsequently divorced from) the broadcaster Kathi Norris (1919–2005); their daughter is the actress Koo Stark (1956–, real name Kathleen Dee-Anne Stark). **Hammer credits:** *Vampire Circus* (1972 [uncredited])

### Starr, John

Starr contributed to Hammer's unproduced screenplay for *Vampirella* in 1976. He also provided a treatment for *Nessie*, based upon a story provided by Michael Carreras and Euan Lloyd. This was subsequently turned into a screenplay by Christopher Wicking, which itself was re-written by Bryan Forbes.

### Starr, Zoe

Starr played the "Indian girl" in Hammer's *The Devil Rides Out* (1968). Her other credits include episodes of *Crane* (1963–1965, TV) and *The First Lady* (1968–1969, TV). **Hammer credits:** *The Devil Rides Out* (1968, as Indian girl [uncredited])

### Stassino, Paul

This RADA-trained Cypriot actor (1930–2012, real name Phaedros Stassinos) can be seen as Silver in Hammer's Thuggee shocker *The Stranglers of Bombay* (1959) and as a pilot in the Charlie Drake comedy *Sands of the Desert* (1960), which was partially financed by Hammer. His other credits include *Ill Met By Moonlight* (1956), *Ice Cold in Alex* (1958), *Thunderball* (1965), *Where the Spies Are* (1965), *The Private Life of Sherlock Holmes* (1970)

and *Die Screaming Marianne* (1971). His television credits include episodes of *Dixon of Dock Green* (1955–1976, TV), *The Saint* (1962–1969, TV) and *The Protectors* (1972–1973, TV). He retired from acting for a period to run a casino in Greece in the early eighties before returning to Cyprus as a stage actor and director. **Hammer credits:** *The Stranglers of Bombay* (1959, as Silver), *Sands of the Desert* (1960, as Pilot)

### Statman, Richard

This British actor (1928–1967) played a reporter in the Hammer comedy *The Ugly Duckling* (1959). His other credits include episodes of *Dixon of Dock Green* (1955–1976, TV), *The Black Tulip* (1956, TV), *Hancock's Half Hour* (1956–1960, TV) and *Kipps* (1960, TV). He was married to the actress Kristin Helga (1928–1991, real name Kristin Finnbogadottir) from 1954. **Hammer credits:** *The Ugly Duckling* (1959, as Reporter)

### Steadman, Tony

Steadman can be seen in a supporting role in *Paint Me a Murder* (1984, TVM [episode of *Hammer House of Mystery and Suspense*]). His other credits include *For the Love of Egypt* (1982, TVM) and *Cold War Killers* (1986, TVM). **Hammer credits:** *Paint Me a Murder* (1984, TVM [episode of *Hammer House of Mystery and Suspense*], as Chief Inspector)

### Steafel, Sheila

A familiar face on television in the sixties and seventies, this South African born comedy actress (1935–) first came to attention as a member of the team on *The Frost Report* (1966–1967, TV). In films from the mid-sixties with *Daleks—Invasion Earth 2150 A.D.* (1966), her credits include supporting roles in *Baby Love* (1968), *Otley* (1968), *Catch Me a Spy* (1971), *Bloodbath at the House of Death* (1983) and *Parting Shots* (1998). She can also be seen as an inquisitive journalist in the early scenes of Hammer's *Quatermass and the Pit* (1967). Her other television work includes episodes of *No Hiding Place* (1959–1967, TV), *Sykes* (1972–1979, TV), *Keep It in the Family* (1980–1983, TV), *You Must Be the Husband* (1987–1988, TV), *Doctors* (2000–, TV) and *Grease Monkeys* (2003–2004, TV). Also on stage and radio. She was married to the actor Harry H. Corbett (1925–1982) between 1958 and 1964, about which she wrote in her autobiography *When Harry Met Sheila* (2010). She was portrayed by Zoe Tapper in the TV play *The Curse of Steptoe* (2008, TVM). **Hammer credits:** *Quatermass and the Pit* (1967, as Journalist)

### *The Steel Bayonet*

GB, 1957, 85m, bw, HammerScope, Western Electric, cert A

Following the success of *The Quatermass Xperiment* (1955), Hammer turned its back on second feature production and instead began to concentrate "on films for global consumption,"[122] as chief executive James Carreras would have it. To this end, in addition to its enthusiastic embracing of the science fiction and horror genres (*The Curse of Frankenstein* [1957] was already being prepped), the studio also turned its attention to other types of film, among them war films, of which it would make several over the following years. The first of these was *The Steel Bayonet*. Originally to have been titled *Observation Post*, it began principal photography on 13 August 1956 with producer Michael Carreras also in the director's chair for the first time on a feature production.

Set in Tunisia in 1943, the story follows the exploits of a rag-tag company of battle-weary soldiers who hold a farmhouse observation post against attack from a German tank unit. Based on a screenplay by Howard Clewes (who also worked as the dialogue director), the film was mostly financed by United Artists, and shot on location on Chobham Common and at the army training grounds at Long Valley, Aldershot, which enabled Hammer to make use of some of the troops and vehicles. Like its previous co-productions with American producer Robert Lippert, the company also brought in an actor with Hollywood credentials to help sales Stateside. This time the star of choice was the British actor Leo Genn, who had had several successes in America, among them *The Snake Pit* (1948) and *Quo Vadis* (1951), the latter of which had earned him an Oscar nomination for best supporting actor. Here he plays troop leader Major Gerrard, and is supported by such Hammer stalwarts as Michael Medwin and Michael Ripper. Captain "Jock" Easton was meanwhile in charge of the many and various stunts, which were performed by the likes of Joe Powell.

A workmanlike effort, the film is plainly but adequately staged by Carreras, who was aided and abetted by the noted cinematographer Jack Asher, who was making his Hammer debut. Together they make the most of the film's limited and limiting budget, part of it care of a loan from the National Film Finance Corporation, managing in the process to make an area of Surrey heath land look like the dusty plains of Tunisia. That said, the story itself is rather mechanical, and the characters little more than a collection of overly familiar British army types exchanging routine dialogue in a not unfamiliar wartime situation (Michael Ripper's Private Middleditch actually dies while bringing Leo Genn's Major Gerrard a cup of tea—in the middle of battle). Consequently, given these flaws, critical and commercial reaction was tepid at best following the film's premier run at London's Leicester Square Odeon, which began on 3 June 1957 care of United Artists, prior to which the film had been trade shown on 14 May. Its American release followed in February 1958, again care of UA. However, given that Hammer had minimum funds invested in the production, and was in any case by then riding the wave of success with *The Curse of Frankenstein*—which had been released the month before, even though made after *The Steel Bayonet*—this hardly seemed to matter. Indeed, the company would soon have larger fish to fry. **Additional notes:** Some of the film's dialogue is no longer politically correct. Having taken over the farm from a local who doesn't wish to leave, Kieron Moore's Captain Mead observes, "They hang on, these wog farmers, don't they?" Some sources claim that Michael Caine appears in the film as a bit player.

Production companies: Hammer/Clarion. Distributor: United Artists (UK, U.S.). Producer: Michael Carreras. Associate producer: Anthony Nelson Keys. Director: Michael Carreras. Screenplay: Howard Clewes. Cinematographer: Jack Asher. Music: Leonard Salzedo. Music director: John Hollingsworth. Editor: Bill Lenny. Art director: Ted Marshall. Costumes: Molly Arbuthnot. Special effects: Sid Pearson, Frank George. Camera operator: Len Harris. Focus puller: Harry Oakes [uncredited]. Sound: Cliff Sandell, Maurice Askew. Sound editor: Alfred Cox. Assistant director: Don Weeks. Make-up: Phil Leakey. Production manager: John Workman. Continuity: Renee Glynne. Stunt arranger: Captain "Jock" Easton. Stunts: Joe Powell [uncredited]. Dialogue director: Howard Clewes. **Cast:** Leo Genn (Major Gerrard), Kieron Moore (Captain Mead), Robert Brown (Sergeant Gill), Michael Medwin (Lieutenant Vernon), Michael Ripper (Private Middleditch), Shay Gorman (Sergeant Gates), Tom Bowman (Sergeant Nicholls), John Paul (Lieutenant-Colonel Derry), Bernard Horsfall (Private Livingstone), Arthur Lovegrove (Private Jarvis), John H. Watson (Corporal Bean), Percy Herbert (Private Clark), Paddy Joyce (Private Ames), Dave Crowley (Private Harris), Jack Stewart (Private Wentworth), Barry Lowe (Private Ferguson), Michael Dear (Private Tweedle), Michael Balfour (Private Thomas), Ian Whittaker (Private Wilson), Raymond Francis (General), Garard Green (Company Commander), Wolf Frees (Divisional Commander), Jeremy Longhurst (German sniper), David Ritch (Mahomet), Michael Collins (First stretcher bearer), David Brown (Second stretcher bearer), William Abney (Artillery Officer), Guy Deghy (Artillery NCO), Abdul Noor (Arab [uncredited]), John Trevor (Sapper Captain [uncredited]), Victor Platt (Sapper sentry [uncredited]), Anthony Warren (German [uncredited]), George Murcell (Warren [uncredited]), Rolf Carston (German NCO [uncredited]), Jack Watson (unnamed role [unconfirmed, uncredited]), Michael Caine (unnamed role [unconfirmed, uncredited])

### Steele, Barry

This British supporting actor (1921–1982, real name Peter John Henry Gardiner Steele) played a soldier in Hammer's *X—The Unknown* (1956). He can also be spotted as Brown in *Yesterday's Enemy* (1959). His other credits include *Millions Like Us* (1943), *The Cruel Sea* (1953), *The Secret Place* (1957), *Tunes of Glory* (1960) and *The V.I.P.s* (1963), plus episodes of *BBC Sunday-Night Theatre* (1950–1959, TV), *Armchair Theatre* (1956–1974, TV) and *The Secret Kingdom* (1960, TV). **Hammer credits:** *X—The Unknown* (1956, as Soldier [uncredited]), *Yesterday's Enemy* (1959, as Brown [uncredited])

### Steele, James

Steele had a supporting role in Hammer's *Wings of Danger* (1952). **Hammer credits:** *Wings of Danger* (1952, as First Flying Officer [uncredited])

### Steele, Pippa

This German actress (1948–1992, sometimes billed as Pippa Steel) is best remembered by Hammer fans for playing the doomed Laura Spielsdorf in *The Vampire Lovers* (1970). She also appeared in the film's sequel, *Lust for a Vampire* (1971), as the equally doomed Susan Pelly. On TV from 1962, her other film credits include *Stranger in the House* (1967), *Oh! What a Lovely War* (1969) and *Young Winston* (1972), while her other TV work takes in episodes of *Z Cars* (1962–1978, TV), *Department S* (1969–1970, TV) and *Dear John* (1986–1987, TV). Recalled Steele of working on *The Vampire Lovers* for director Roy Ward Baker, "He was very, very good, very professional. Very experienced and quite classy. He knew exactly what he wanted. He's a fine director and I was very happy to work with him."[123] **Hammer credits:** *The Vampire Lovers* (1970, as Laura Spielsdorf), *Lust for a Vampire* (1971, as Susan Pelly)

### Steen, Derek

Steen had a minor role in Hammer's *Dr. Jekyll and Sister Hyde* (1971). His other credits include *Mosquito Squadron* (1969) and *Twinky* (1969), plus episodes of *Love Story* (1963–1974, TV), *Wicked Women* (1970, TV) and *UFO* (1970–1971, TV). **Hammer credits:** *Dr. Jekyll and Sister Hyde* (1971, as First sailor)

### Steger, Frederic (Fredric)

This Welsh actor (1894–1975) can be seen as Hobson in Hammer's *The Rossiter Case* (1951). He also had a small role in *Cloudburst* (1951). His other credits include *The Small Voice* (1948), *The Spider and the Fly* (1949) and *The Intimate Stranger* (1956), plus an episode of *Armchair Theatre* (1956–1974, TV). **Hammer credits:** *The Rossiter Case* (1951, as Hobson), *Cloudburst* (1951, as Porter)

### Steigberg, Uli

This German actor (1923–1987) can be seen as a porter in Hammer's remake of *The Lady Vanishes* (1979). His many other credits include *Die Martinsklause* (1951), *Verruckt und zugenaht* (1962), *Deep End* (1971) and *Berlinger* (1975), as well as much television, including episodes of *Koniglich Bayerisches Amtsgericht* (1969–1971, TV) and *Derrick* (1974–1998, TV). **Hammer credits:** *The Lady Vanishes* (1979, as Porter)

### Steiger, Frieda

Steiger worked as the hair stylist on many films for Hammer in the sixties, beginning with *The Brides of Dracula* (1960), the opening credits for which mistakenly bill her as Freda Steiger. Her other credits include *The Seventh Veil* (1945), *Please Turn Over* (1959) and *Dr. Terror's House of Horrors* (1965), plus episodes of *Man in a Suitcase* (1967–1968, TV) and *Strange Report* (1968–1970, TV). Her husband, Fred Peck, also worked for Hammer as an extra and bit part player, popping up in a variety of films at Bray in the sixties, from *The Curse of the Werewolf* (1961) through to *The Mummy's Shroud* (1967). **Hammer credits:** *The Brides of Dracula* (1960), *Visa to Canton* (1960), *The Curse of the Werewolf* (1961), *The Shadow of the Cat* (1961), *Watch It, Sailor!* (1961), *The Terror of the Tongs* (1961), *Cash on Demand* (1961), *The Phantom of the Opera* (1962), *Captain Clegg* (1962), *The Pirates of Blood River* (1962), *Paranoiac* (1963), *The Damned* (1963), *The Scarlet*

*Blade* (1963), *The Kiss of the Vampire* (1963), *The Old Dark House* (1963), *Nightmare* (1964), *The Evil of Frankenstein* (1964), *The Devil-Ship Pirates* (1964), *The Gorgon* (1964), *The Secret of Blood Island* (1965), *The Brigand of Kandahar* (1965), *Dracula—Prince of Darkness* (1966), *The Plague of the Zombies* (1966), *Rasputin—The Mad Monk* (1966), *The Reptile* (1966), *The Witches* (1966), *Frankenstein Created Woman* (1967), *The Mummy's Shroud* (1967)

## Stensgaard, Yutte

In Britain from 1963 to work as an *au pair*, this pretty Danish actress (1946–, real name Jytte Stensgaard) did much television work in the sixties and early seventies, popping up in such shows as *The Saint* (1962–1969, TV), *The Golden Shot* (1967–1975, TV), on which she was one of the hostesses, *On the Buses* (1969–1973, TV), *Jason King* (1971–1972, TV), *The Persuaders!* (1971–1972, TV) and *Dead of Night* (1972, TV). In films from 1967 with the Italian-made *Girl with a Pistol*, her other credits include *Some Girls Do* (1969), *A Promise of Bed* (1969), *Carry On Again Doctor* (1969), *Zeta One* (1969), *Scream and Scream Again* (1970), *Doctor in Trouble* (1970), *Carry On Loving* (1970 [scenes deleted]), *The Buttercup Chain* (1970) and *Burke and Hare* (1971).

However, she is best known for playing Carmilla Karnstein in Hammer's *Lust for a Vampire* (1971), a role she inherited from Ingrid Pitt, who had previously essayed it in *The Vampire Lovers* (1970). Given that she was a virtual unknown at the time, the actress had to audition for the role, recalling, "I remember being interviewed by producers Harry Fine and Michael Style in their office. Large photos of Raquel Welch were on the wall behind them, and I thought I would never match up to her. It was pretty intimidating, but I managed to fake self-confidence!"[124]

She was nevertheless treated like a star once she had secured the role. "When you have a good part in a movie you are given special treatment and perks that you wouldn't normally receive in an ordinary job. Hammer put me up in a beautiful hotel and took me to and from the shoot in a chauffeur-driven limousine. I was also given my own personal dressing room, but what really made me feel 'important' was the provision of my own personal director's chair with my name printed on it!"[125]

Remembered Stensgaard of her brief time in the spotlight with Hammer, "I really enjoyed doing the film and always wished I had more scenes. Doing the filming is the most fun and the most nerve-wracking."[126] Much to her disappointment, Stensgaard had her performance re-voiced for *Lust for a Vampire*. Recalled the actress, "I didn't find out until I saw the film and was quite upset by it. They at least could have told me they were going to do it. They must have decided that they didn't like my accent."[127]

Now living in America, she has at various times worked in a boutique and at selling airtime for a radio station in Oregon. Her first husband (of three) was art director Tony Curtis, to whom she was married between 1967 and 1972, and who did much work for Hammer's "rival" Amicus (his father, Ronnie Curtis [1902–1980], also managed her career). **Additional notes:** The role of Carmilla/Mircalla was subsequently played by Katya Wyeth in *Twins of Evil* (1971). Stensgaard was the subject of two magazine tributes care of Tim Greaves' One Shot Publications: *Yutte Stensgaard—A Pictorial Souvenir* (1992) and *Yutte Stensgaard—Memories of a Vampire* (1992). **Hammer credits:** *Lust for a Vampire* (1971, as Carmilla/Mircalla/Marcilla Heritzen/Karnstein), *Flesh and Blood—The Hammer Heritage of Horror* (1994, TV, special thanks)

## Stephen, Susan

In films from 1951 with *His Excellency*, this British actress (1931–2000) went on to appear in over twenty films, including *Treasure Hunt* (1952), *It's Never Too Late* (1956), *Carry On Nurse* (1959) and *Three Spare Wives* (1962), after which she retired from the big screen. She also appeared in two Hammer films: *Stolen Face* (1952), in which she played the escaped convict Lily, who is transformed into the glamorous Lizabeth Scott by Paul Henreid's plastic surgeon, and *The House Across the Lake* (1954), in which she appeared as Andrea Forrest. Her occasional TV appearances include episodes of *Little Women* (1950, TV) and *The Adventures of Robin Hood* (1955–1960, TV). She was married to the actor and photographer Lawrence Ward (1929–2011, real name Michael Ronald Ward) between 1952 and 1956; he appeared in Hammer's *The Last Page* (1952). Her second husband was the cinematographer-turned-director Nicolas Roeg (1928–2018), to whom she was married between 1957 and 1977. **Hammer credits:** *Stolen Face* (1952, as Lily), *The House Across the Lake* (1954 as Andrea Forrest)

## Stephens, Martin

This British child actor (1949–) is best remembered for playing David Zellaby, one of the alien children in *Village of the Damned* (1960), and Miles in *The Innocents* (1961), in which he shared a disturbing screen kiss with the film's leading lady, Deborah Kerr. His other credits include *The Divided Heart* (1954), *Another Time, Another Place* (1958), *Passionate Summer* (1958), *Harry Black* (1958), *The Hellfire Club* (1960), *The Battle of the Villa Fiorita* (1965) and Hammer's *The Witches* (1966), in which he played Ronnie Dowsett. He also dubbed fellow child actor Ronnie Raymond in the Miss Marple thriller *Murder She Said* (1961). His TV work includes *Tales from Dickens* (1958–1959, TV), in which he played David Copperfield. He gave up acting for a career as an architect, but has since been a convention guest. **Hammer credits:** *The Witches* (1966, as Ronnie Dowsett)

## Stephens, Peter

This British actor (1920–1972) can be seen as an abbot in *Wolfshead: The Legend of Robin Hood* (1969 [released 1973]), which was bought, but not originally made, by Hammer. His other credits include *Private's Progress* (1956), *Kill Her Gently* (1957), *Herostratus* (1967) and *Say Hello to Yesterday* (1971). He can also be spotted as a member of the brotherhood in Hammer's *Twins of Evil* (1971). His television work includes episodes of *Oliver Twist* (1962, TV), *Doctor Who* (1963–1989, TV) and *Arthur of the Britons* (1972–1973, TV). **Hammer credits:** *Wolfshead: The Legend of Robin Hood* (1969 [released 1973], as Abbot of St. Mary's), *Twins of Evil* (1971, as Member of brotherhood [uncredited])

## Stephens, Roy

Stephens can be seen as one of a group of reporters in Hammer's *The Mummy's Shroud* (1967). His other credits include *During One Night* (1961), *Dr. Strangelove* (1964), *The Bedford Incident* (1964), *Up from the Beach* (1965), *Where the Bullets Fly* (1966) and *Isadora* (1968), plus episodes of *The Saint* (1962–1969, TV), *The Troubleshooters* (1965–1972, TV) and *Brett* (1971, TV). **Hammer credits:** *The Mummy's Shroud* (1967, as Reporter [uncredited])

## Stephenson, George

This prolific British sound technician (1920–2001) recorded the sound for Hammer's *A Challenge for Robin Hood* (1967). His many other credits include *The Small Back Room* (1949), *Richard III* (1955), *The Guns of Navarone* (1961), *The Fearless Vampire Killers* (1967), *The Golden Voyage of Sinbad* (1974), *Sinbad and the Eye of the Tiger* (1977), *Warlords of Atlantis* (1978), *Lassiter* (1984) and *Lifeforce* (1985). He earned a shared Emmy nomination for his work on the mini-series *Mussolini: The Untold Story* (1985, TV). **Hammer credits:** *A Challenge for Robin Hood* (1967)

## Sternbach, Bert

Sternbach (1887–1974) worked as the production manager on the additional U.S. scenes shot for Hammer's *Women Without Men* (1956). His many other credits (over one-hundred of them, many of them second feature westerns) include *Better Behave* (1928), *Ghost Patrol* (1936), *Frontier Crusader* (1940), *The Mad Monster* (1942), *Western Cyclone* (1943), *Stagecoach Outlaws* (1945), *Lost Continent* (1951) and *Wolf Dog* (1958). He also worked as an assistant director on *Lightning Carson Rides Again* (1938) and *Trigger Fingers* (1939), and as a producer/supervising producer/associate producer on *Inside Information* (1934), *Million Dollar Haul* (1935) and *The Terror of Tiny Town* (1938), among others. **Hammer credits:** *Women Without Men* (1956)

## Sterne, Andrew

Sterne had a supporting role in Hammer's *River Patrol* (1948). **Hammer credits:** *River Patrol* (1948, unnamed role [uncredited])

## Sterne, Gordon

This British actor (1923–2017) played a policeman in the Hammer thriller *Taste of Fear* (1961). His many other credits include *The Millionairess* (1960), *The V.I.P.s* (1963), *The Vulture* (1966), *The Assassination Bureau* (1968), *The Adding Machine* (1968), *The Chairman* (1969), *Sex Play* (1974), *The Razor's Edge* (1984), *Highlander* (1986), *Merlin* (1993), *Screaming Blue Murder* (2006) and *Penny's Sweet Demise* (2009), plus episodes of *No Hiding Place* (1959–1967, TV), *The Saint* (1962–

1969, TV), *Reilly: Ace of Spies* (1983, TV) and *The Tudors* (2007–2010, TV). **Hammer credits:** *Taste of Fear* (1961, as Policeman [uncredited])

## Stevens, Christine *see* Addaway, Christine

## Stevens, Dorinda

This British actress (1932–2012, real name Dorothy May Stevens) had a minor supporting role in Hammer's *Lady in the Fog* (1952). Her other credits include *It Started in Paradise* (1952), *The Shakedown* (1959), *Carry On Constable* (1960), *Raising the Wind* (1961) and *Night Train to Paris* (1964), plus episodes of *Fabian of the Yard* (1954, TV), *The Avengers* (1961–1969, TV) and *Danger Man* (1964–1966, TV). Her husband was the cinematographer Michael Boultbee, whom she married in 1957. **Hammer credits:** *Lady in the Fog* (1952, unnamed role [uncredited])

## Stevens, Robert

Although he helmed five theatrical features, beginning with *The Big Caper* (1957) and ending with *Change of Mind* (1969), this American director (1920–1989) is better known for his prolific work on television, which includes forty-four episodes of *Alfred Hitchcock Presents* (1955–1962, TV), for which he won an Emmy (for the episode *The Glass Eye* [1957, TV]), and five episodes of *The Alfred Hitchcock Hour* (1962–1965, TV). He also helmed two episodes of Hammer's *Journey to the Unknown* (1968, TV), which, like the Hitchcock programs, were executive produced by Joan Harrison and Norman Lloyd. His many other small screen credits include episodes of *Talent Scouts* (1948–1949, TV), *Suspense* (1949–1954, TV), *The Nurses* (1962–1965, TV) and *The Best of Families* (1977, TV). **Hammer credits:** *Eve* (1968, TV [episode of *Journey to the Unknown*]), *Miss Belle* (1968, TV [episode of *Journey to the Unknown*])

## Stevens, Roy

British born Stevens (1949–2009) worked as the second assistant director on Hammer's *X—The Unknown* (1956) and as the third assistant director on *Frankenstein and the Monster from Hell* (1974) and *To the Devil a Daughter* (1976). His many other credits include work as an assistant director on *The Sundowners* (1960), *Lawrence of Arabia* (1962), *Doctor Zhivago* (1965), *The Thirty-Nine Steps* (1978), *Bear Island* (1979), *Mr. Love* (1985), *Fierce Creatures* (1997) and *School for Seduction* (2004). He also worked as a production manager on *The Mikado* (1966) and *Juggernaut* (1974), an associate producer on *Ryan's Daughter* (1970), for which he also directed the second unit, as a production supervisor on *Pirates* (1986), as a line producer on *Evil Angels* (1988), and as a production controller on *Bye Bye Baby* (1992, TVM). **Hammer credits:** *X—The Unknown* (1956, second assistant director [uncredited]), *Frankenstein and the Monster from Hell* (1974, third assistant director [uncredited]), *To the Devil a Daughter* (1976, third assistant director [uncredited])

## Stevens, Vi

This British actress (1891–1967, full name Violet Stevens) had a minor role in Hammer's *Women Without Men* (1956). In films from 1943 with *We Dive at Dawn*, her other credits include *The Mudlark* (1950), *A Cry from the Streets* (1958) and *The Inspector* (1961), plus episodes of *Bleak House* (1959, TV), *Here's Harry* (1960–1965, TV) and *Hugh and I* (1962–1967, TV), in which she played Mrs. Scott. **Hammer credits:** *Women Without Men* (1956, as Scrubber [uncredited])

## Stevenson, Alexandra

Stevenson can be seen as Luri in Hammer's *Slave Girls* (1968). Her other credits include *You Must Be Joking!* (1965), plus episodes of *Dixon of Dock Green* (1955–1976, TV), *Pardon the Expression* (1965–1966, TV) and *Man in a Suitcase* (1967–1968, TV). **Hammer credits:** *Slave Girls* (1968, as Luri)

## Stevenson, Robert Louis

Acclaimed for penning such frequently-filmed adventure classics as *Treasure Island* (1883) and *Kidnapped* (1886), this much-admired British novelist and short story writer (1850–1894) is perhaps best known for writing the 1885 novella *The Strange Case of Dr. Jekyll and Mr. Hyde*, which has also been filmed many times, beginning with an American production in 1908 (although a stage dramatization by T.R. Sullivan starring Richard Mansfield had appeared as early 1887). Hammer tackled the subject no less than three times, though none of these could be deemed straight versions of the story. The first of these was the comedy *The Ugly Duckling* (1959), which sees the dopey Henry Jekyll turn into the thuggish Teddy boy Teddy Hide. Meanwhile, *The Two Faces of Dr. Jekyll* (1960) sees the dull Jekyll turn into the ladykilling Mr. Hyde, while *Dr. Jekyll and Sister Hyde* (1971) puts a transgender spin on the tale by having the doctor turn into a woman.

The best versions of the story were filmed in 1921 (starring John Barrymore), 1931 (starring Fredric March, who won an Oscar for his efforts) and 1941 (with Spencer Tracy). Other variations on the tale include *The Son of Dr. Jekyll* (1951), *Daughter of Dr. Jekyll* (1957), *The Nutty Professor* (1963 and 1996), *I, Monster* (1970), *Dr. Black and Mr. Hyde* (1975), *Dr. Heckyl and Mr. Hype* (1980), *Jekyll and Hyde … Together Again* (1982) and *Dr. Jekyll and Ms. Hyde* (1995). Serious versions are legion. Other Stevenson works that have gone before the cameras include *The Ebb Tide* (1937 [novel 1894, co-written with Lloyd Osbourne]), *The Body Snatcher* (1945 [story 1884]), *The Master of Ballantrae* (1953 [novel 1889]) and *The Wrong Box* (1966 [novel 1889, co-written with Lloyd Osbourne]). Note that Hammer planned a TV remake of *The Body Snatcher* for their unmade series *The Haunted House of Hammer*. **Hammer credits:** *The Ugly Duckling* (1959), *The Two Faces of Dr. Jekyll* (1960), *Dr. Jekyll and Sister Hyde* (1971)

## Stewardson, Cheryl

Stewardson can be seen as a Rock girl in Hammer's *Creatures the World Forgot* (1971). **Hammer credits:** *Creatures the World Forgot* (1971, as Rock girl [uncredited])

## Stewart, Duncan

Stewart worked as the production account on Hammer remake of *The Lady Vanishes* (1979). His other credits include *Loophole* (1980), *The Neverending Story* (1984), *Castaway* (1986) and *American Roulette* (1988), plus episodes of *Jack the Ripper* (1988, TV), *The Locksmith* (1997, TV) and *Maisie Raine* (1998–1999, TV). **Hammer credits:** *The Lady Vanishes* (1979 [uncredited])

## Stewart, Estelle

Stewart worked as the continuity girl on eight episodes of Hammer's *Journey to the Unknown* (1968, TV). Of these, *The Indian Spirit Guide* also appeared in the compendium film *Journey to Midnight* (1968, TVM), *The New People* appeared in the compendium film *Journey into Darkness* (1968, TVM), *The Last Visitor* appeared in the compendium film *Journey to the Unknown* (1969, TVM), while both *The Killing Bottle* and *Do Me a Favor and Kill Me* also appeared in the compendium film *Journey to Murder* (1972). Her other TV credits include episodes of *The Human Jungle* (1963–1964, TV) and *Gideon's Way* (1964–1967, TV), while her film credits take in *Girl On Approval* (1960), *Conscience Bay* (1960), *The Third Alibi* (1961), *Sparrows Can't Sing* (1962) and *Unearthly Stranger* (1963). **Hammer credits:** *The Killing Bottle* (1968, TV [episode of *Journey to the Unknown*]), *The Indian Spirit Guide* (1968, TV [episode of *Journey to the Unknown*]), *The Last Visitor* (1968, TV [episode of *Journey to the Unknown*]), *The New People* (1968, TV [episode of *Journey to the Unknown*]), *Somewhere in a Crowd* (1968, TV [episode of *Journey to the Unknown*]), *Do Me a Favor and Kill Me* (1968, TV [episode of *Journey to the Unknown*]), *Girl of My Dreams* (1968, TV [episode of *Journey to the Unknown*]), *The Beckoning Fair One* (1968, TV [episode of *Journey to the Unknown*]), *Journey into Darkness* (1968, TVM), *Journey to Midnight* (1968, TVM), *Journey to the Unknown* (1969, TVM), *Journey to Murder* (1972, TVM)

## Stewart, Ewan

This British (Scottish) actor (1957–, full name Andrew Ewan Stewart) can be seen as the childlike Robin Kemble, one of several red herrings in *A Distant Scream* (1984, TVM [episode of *Hammer House of Mystery and Suspense*]), the end credits for which mistakenly bill him as Ewan Stuart. In films from 1979 with *That Summer!*, his other credits include *All Quiet on the Western Front* (1979, TVM), *Remembrance* (1982), *Who Dares Wins* (1982), *Not Quite Jerusalem* (1985), *Rob Roy* (1995), *Titanic* (1997), *Young Adam* (2003), *Alpha Male* (2006), *Valhalla Rising* (2009), *David Rose* (2011) and *Florence Foster Jenkins* (2016). Also busy on television, his other credits here include episodes of *Play for Today* (1970–1984, TV), *Only Fools and Horses* (1981–2003, TV) and *POW* (2003, TV). His father was the singer Andy Stewart (1933–1993). His wife is the actress Clare Byam-Shaw. **Hammer credits:** *A Distant Scream* (1984, TVM [episode of *Hammer House of Mystery and Suspense*], as Robin Kemble)

## Stewart, Hugh

This British producer (1910–2011, full name Hugh St. Clair Stewart, aka H. St. C. Stewart) is best remembered for producing a successful series of Norman Widsom comedies, among them *Man of the Moment* (1955), *Up in the World* (1956), *The Square Peg* (1958), *On the Beat* (1962) and *The Early Bird* (1965), though he began his career as an editor, working on such films as *Marry Me* (1932), on which he was an assistant editor, *Evergreen* (1934), Hitchcock's *The Man Who Knew Too Much* (1934), Hammer's *Sporting Love* (1936), *South Riding* (1938) and *Gaiety George* (1943). His other films as a producer include *An Ideal Husband* (1947), on which he was an associate producer, *Trottie True* (1949), *The Long Memory* (1953), *The Intelligence Men* (1965), *The Flying Sorcerer* (1973) and *High Rise Donkey* (1980). He also co-directed the wartime documentary *Tunisian Victory* (1944) **Hammer credits:** *Sporting Love* (1936)

## Stewart, Jack

This British (Scottish) actor (1913–1966) played the supporting role of Matt in the Hammer quickie *The Dark Light* (1951), which he followed with three further appearances for the studio. His other credits include *Kidnapped* (1959), *Strongroom* (1961), *The Frightened City* (1961), *The Amorous Prawn* (1962) and *The Three Lives of Thomasina* (1963), plus episodes of *The Flying Doctor* (1959, TV), *Interpol Calling* (1959–1960, TV) and *Dr. Finlay's Casebook* (1962–1971, TV). **Hammer credits:** *The Dark Light* (1951, as Matt), *A Case for PC 49* (1951, as Cutler), *The Steel Bayonet* (1957, as Private Wentworth), *The Pirates of Blood River* (1962, as George Mason)

## Stewart, Larry

Stewart worked in wardrobe on a handful of Hammer films in the sixties, beginning with *Frankenstein Created Woman* (1967). His other credits include *The Wooden Horse* (1950), *A Cry from the Streets* (1958), *The Password Is Courage* (1962) and *A Study in Terror* (1965). **Hammer credits:** *Frankenstein Created Woman* (1967), *The Mummy's Shroud* (1967), *Moon Zero Two* (1969)

## Stewart, Peter *see* Newfield, Sam

## Stewart, Robin

Born in India, this handsome actor (1946–2015) is best remembered for playing Mike Abbott in the long-running sitcom *Bless This House* (1971–1976, TV), though it was Robin Askwith who played the role in the 1972 feature film spin off (Stewart had already signed to do a play—*The Man Most Likely To*—and the schedules conflicted). His film credits include *H.M.S. Defiant* (1962), *Tamahine* (1962), *Be My Guest* (1965), *The Haunted House of Horror* (1969), *Get Crazy* (1983) and *The Blue Villa* (1995). He also played Leyland Van Helsing, the son of vampire hunter Professor Lawrence Van Helsing, in Hammer's *The Legend of the 7 Golden Vampires* (1974). His other small screen work includes episodes of *Sons and Daughters* (1982–1987, TV), in which he played Ross Newman, and *Welcher & Welcher* (2003, TV), while his stage work includes a stint on Broadway

in 1960 in the original run of *Camelot* (1960–1963), in which he played Tom of Warwick. **Hammer credits:** *The Legend of the 7 Golden Vampires* (1974, as Leyland Van Helsing)

## Stewart, Roy

This hulking Jamaican actor (1925–2008) played the role of Joachim, Count Karnstein's devoted manservant in Hammer's *Twins of Evil* (1971), prior to which he'd popped up as a bearer in *The Curse of the Mummy's Tomb* (1964) and as a guard in *She* (1965). His other credits include *Games That Lovers Play* (1970), *Carry On Up the Jungle* (1970), *Live and Let Die* (1973), in which he played Quarrel, Jr., *Stand Up, Virgin Soldiers* (1977) and *Arabian Adventure* (1979), plus episodes of *Doctor Who* (1963–1989, TV) and *Space: 1999* (1975–1977, TV). **Hammer credits:** *The Curse of the Mummy's Tomb* (1964, as Bearer in museum [uncredited]), *She* (1965, as Black Guard [uncredited]), *Twins of Evil* (1971, as Joachim)

## Stewart, Val

This British (Scottish) cameraman (1914–1975) worked as the camera operator on the Charlie Drake comedy *Sands of the Desert* (1960). His other credits include *Brighton Rock* (1947), on which he was the focus puller, and, as operator, *Bond Street* (1948), *Last Holiday* (1950), *Tommy the Toreador* (1959) and *The Bargee* (1964), plus episodes of *The Avengers* (1961–1969, TV), *The Saint* (1962–1969, TV) and *Randall and Hopkirk (Deceased)* (1969–1971, TV). **Hammer credits:** *Sands of the Desert* (1960)

## Stilwell (Stillwell), Bob

This British cameraman (1937–2006, sometimes credited as Stillwell) worked as the clapper boy on the Hammer comedy *A Weekend with Lulu* (1961), a role he also fulfilled on *Lawrence of Arabia* (1962). He later returned to Hammer as a focus puller on two films. His other credits include *Doctor Zhivago* (1965), *Swallows and Amazons* (1974), *Time Bandits* (1981), *Raiders of the Lost Ark* (1981), *Who Framed Roger Rabbit* (1988), *Chaplin* (1992), *Waking Ned* (1998) and *Last Orders* (2001). **Hammer credits:** *A Weekend with Lulu* (1961, clapper boy [uncredited]), *Scars of Dracula* (1970, focus puller [uncredited]), *The Horror of Frankenstein* (1970, focus puller [uncredited])

## Stirling, John

Stirling played the role of Major in Hammer's *The Quatermass Xperiment* (1955). He can also be spotted as a police driver in *X—The Unknown* (1956). **Hammer credits:** *The Quatermass Xperiment* (1955, as Major [uncredited]), *X—The Unknown* (1956, as Police driver [uncredited])

## Stock, Michael

Stock can be seen in a minor supporting role in an episode of *Hammer House of Horror* (1980, TV). His other TV credits include episodes of *Father Brown* (1974, TV), *Second Time Around* (1974, TV), *Get Some In!* (1975–1978, TV) and *I, Claudius* (1976, TV), while his film appearances include *A Bridge Too Far* (1977) and *The Golden

Lady* (1979). **Hammer credits:** *Charlie Boy* (1980, TV [episode of *Hammer House of Horror*], as Armourer)

## Stock, Nigel

On stage from the age of twelve, this Maltese born actor (1919–1986) made his film debut in *The Man Who Could Work Miracles* (1936). Over thirty films followed, among them *Lancashire Luck* (1937), *Goodbye, Mr. Chips* (1939), *It Always Rains on Sunday* (1947), *Victim* (1961), *The Lion in Winter* (1968), *Operation: Daybreak* (1975) and *Young Sherlock Holmes* (1985). He also appeared in Hammer's *The Lost Continent* (1968), in which he played Dr. Webster. His television credits include *Sherlock Holmes* (1965–1968, TV), in which he played Dr. Watson to two different Holmeses: Douglas Wilmer and Peter Cushing. He also appeared in episodes of *Van Der Valk* (1972–1977, TV), *Triangle* (1981–1983, TV) and *The Pickwick Papers* (1985, TV) as Mr. Pickwick. Married three times, his second wife was actress Sonia Williams (1926–), whom he was married in 1951; his third wife was actress Richenda Carey (1948–), whom he married in 1979. **Hammer credits:** *The Lost Continent* (1968, as Dr. Webster)

## Stockle, John

This British poster designer (1928–2000) worked on the posters for a handful of Hammer films, including *The Camp on Blood Island* (1958), the controversial imagery of which caused it to be banned by London Transport. Other campaigns designed by Stockle include *Footsteps in the Fog* (1955), *Heaven Fell That Night* (1958), *The Cardinal* (1963), *The Virgin Soldiers* (1969), *White Mischief* (1987) and *House of Games* (1987). He began his career as a lettering artist, cartoonist and greetings card designer before joining the Dixons design agency as a general artist in 1955, and went on to work on many high profile campaigns for Disney and Columbia. **Hammer credits:** *The Camp on Blood Island* (1958 [uncredited]), *The Revenge of Frankenstein* (1958 [uncredited]), *Further Up the Creek* (1958 [uncredited]), *I Only Arsked!* (1958 [uncredited]), *The Terror of the Tongs* (1960 [uncredited]), *Watch It, Sailor!* (1961 [uncredited]), *The Damned* (1963 [uncredited])

## Stockwell, Dean

Perhaps best known for playing Al Calavicci in the hit sci-fi TV series *Quantum Leap* (1989–1993, TV), which earned him four best supporting actor Emmy nominations, this American actor (1936–, full name Robert Dean Stockwell) first came to attention as a child performer in such films as *The Valley of Decision* (1945), which marked his debut, *Anchors Aweigh* (1945), *The Green Years* (1946) and *The Boy with Green Hair* (1948). He matured via such films as *Compulsion* (1959) and *Sons and Lovers* (1960), and went on to appear in such wide-ranging productions as *Long Day's Journey into Night* (1962), *Psych-Out* (1968), *The Dunwich Horror* (1970), *Werewolf of Washington* (1973), *Paris, Texas* (1984), *Dune* (1984), *Blue Velvet* (1986), *Married to the Mob* (1988), which earned him an Oscar nomination as best supporting actor, *Midnight Blue* (1996), *Air Force One* (1997), *Buffalo

*Soldiers* (2001), *Face to Face* (2001), the remake of *The Dunwich Horror* (2009, TVM), *Max Rose* (2013) and *Entertainment* (2015). A frequent guest star on TV, his work here includes an episode of *Hammer House of Mystery and Suspense* (1984, TVM), in which he played a U.S. diplomat in London who plans to do away with his wife. His many other TV appearances include episodes of everything from *Playhouse 90* (1956–1961, TV) to *The A-Team* (1983–1987, TV). He also co-wrote and co-directed one film, *Human Highway* (1982), in which he also appeared, and worked as an associate producer on *Rites of Passage* (1999), in which he again appeared. His brother was the actor Guy Stockwell (1933–2002), and their parents were the actor Harry Stockwell (1902–1984) and the actress Nina Olivette (1910–1993, real name Elizabeth Margaret Veronica, aka Betty Veronica). Married twice, Stockwell's first wife was the actress Millie Perkins (1936–), to whom he was married between 1960 and 1962. **Hammer credits:** *The Sweet Scent of Death* (1984, TVM [episode of *Hammer House of Mystery and Suspense*], as Greg Denver)

## Stoke Court

This effects studio was used by Les Bowie and Vic Margutti to film the effects scenes for Hammer's *The Quatermass Xperiment* (1955) and *Moon Zero Two* (1969). Matte paintings for many other films and television series were also created at the studio. **Hammer credits include:** *The Quatermass Xperiment* (1955), *Moon Zero Two* (1969)

## Stoker, Bram

Celebrated for his gothic grand opus *Dracula*, this Irish novelist (1847–1912, full name Abraham Stoker) worked on the novel while employed as the manager of the actor Henry Irving, prior to which he had worked as a civil servant. First published in 1897, the book has been adapted for the screen many times, beginning with the unofficial *Nosferatu* (1922), which was subject to legal action by Stoker's widow, Florence. Universal released a sanctioned version of the story in 1931 starring Bela Lugosi, which spawned a number of sequels, among them *Dracula's Daughter* (1936), *House of Frankenstein* (1944), *House of Dracula* (1945) and *Abbott and Costello Meet Frankenstein* (1948). Hammer released the first color version of the story in 1958 (known in America as *Horror of Dracula*), and the success of this again led to various sequels (see below) in which the link with Stoker became increasingly tenuous. Further versions of the novel appeared in 1970 (as *Count Dracula*), 1973 (TVM), 1977 (TVM), 1979, 1992 (as *Bram Stoker's Dracula*), 2006 (TVM), 2013 (TV) and 2014, while imitations and spin-offs have been legion. Stoker's other works include *The Jewel of Seven Stars* (1903), which was filmed by Hammer as *Blood from the Mummy's Tomb* (1971), *The Judge's House* (1891), which was proposed for adaptation as part of the unmade TV series *The Haunted House of Hammer*, and *The Lair of the White Worm* (1911), which was filmed by Ken Russell in 1988. In 1974 Hammer also released an album version of *Dracula*, which was narrated by Christopher Lee. This was followed by an album version of *The Legend of the 7 Golden Vampires* (1974), which also featured the Count, narrated by Peter Cushing. **Hammer credits:** *Dracula* (1958), *The Brides of Dracula* (1960), *Dracula—Prince of Darkness* (1965), *Dracula Has Risen from the Grave* (1968), *Taste the Blood of Dracula* (1970), *Scars of Dracula* (1970), *Blood from the Mummy's Tomb* (1971), *Dracula A.D. 1972* (1972), *The Satanic Rites of Dracula* (1974), *The Legend of the 7 Golden Vampires* (1974), *Dracula* (1974, LP version), *The Legend of the 7 Golden Vampires* (1974, LP version)

## Stokes, Barry

Stokes can be seen as the first victim of a serial killer in *Carpathian Eagle* (1980, TV [episode of *Hammer House of Horror*]). His other credits include *Prey* (1978), *Fanny Hill* (1983), *Romance on the Orient Express* (1985, TVM) and *Enemy Mine* (1985), plus episodes of *Softly Softly* (1966–1976, TV), *Survivors* (1975–1977, TV) and *Reilly: Ace of Spies* (1983, TV). His wife is actress Gay Soper and their son was actor Matthew Stokes (1976–2009). **Hammer credits:** *Carpathian Eagle* (1980, TV [episode of *Hammer House of Horror*], as First victim)

## Stokes Cartoons, Ltd.

This animation facility provided the "zany" titles for Hammer's *Moon Zero Two* (1969). The company's other credits include the titles and opticals for *Wonderwall* (1968). **Hammer credits:** *Moon Zero Two* (1969)

## *Stolen Face*

GB, 1952, 72m, bw, RCA, cert A

Like *Wings of Danger* (1952) and *Lady in the Fog* (1952), *Stolen Face* was filmed at the Riverside Studios in Hammersmith during a break in Hammer's lease on Down Place. One of the most brisk and professional of the company's second features, it stars Hollywood import Paul Henreid as Dr. Philip Ritter, an eminent plastic surgeon who alters the face of a due-to-be-released female convict to resemble that of Alice Brent, a concert pianist with whom he has fallen in love but cannot have (observes the scarred girl before her operation, "Nobody wants someone like me around. Would you? Pretty, aren't I? What sort of job could I get with a face like this, eh? Modelling?"). It's Ritter's hope that the girl's new face will lead her away from her life of crime, to which end he also marries her, thus fulfilling his own fantasy. But the girl soon resorts to her true form, and goes on a spree of shoplifting and drinking. However, there is a happy ending of sorts when the concert pianist re-appears in the doctor's life and his drunken wife falls to her death from a train during an argument.

The story, with its vestiges of *Vertigo* to come, not to mention Hammer's similarly-themed *Four Sided Triangle* (1953), teeters on the edge of fantasy, with the surgeon's creation—like Frankenstein's creature—eventually turning against him ("To capture love he cheated nature," observed one of the film's tag-lines). It's all pure hokum, of course, yet benefits from some persuasive acting from Henreid as the lovelorn surgeon, and Lizabeth Scott, who is excellent as both Alice Brent, the glamorous pianist he has fallen for, as well as Lily, the scarred and embittered convict whose features he re-arranges to resemble those of the object of his obsession ("Why don't you stop trying to make me something I'm not," Lily argues during one of the story's key moments).

The film also benefits from slick work from director Terence Fisher and cameraman Walter "Jimmy" Harvey, who give the proceedings a glossy sheen, while the supporting cast contains such reliable names as André Morell as Alice's fiancé David, Everley Gregg as Lady Haringay (who, much to her dismay, is told that she has left it too late to go under the knife), and Arnold Ridley as the kindly prison doctor who explains Lily's plight to Dr. Ritter ("We can blame the war for her condition—she got badly smashed up in the blitz, and it so embittered her she turned criminal").

Make-up man Phil Leakey meanwhile expertly contends with the facial scars required prior to Lily's transformation, experience that no doubt

**Tinsel Town imports Lizabeth Scott and Paul Henried add a touch of Hollywood-style Hammer glamor to *Stolen Face* (1952) (Hammer/Lippert/Exclusive/Twentieth Century–Fox).**

later came in handy when he was required to perform even more extravagant feats on Christopher Lee for *The Curse of Frankenstein* (1957). Hollywood costume designer Edith Head was on also hand to provide Lizabeth Scott's glamorous wardrobe, while Malcolm Arnold penned a solid score for the film, the highlight of which plays over the montage sequence in which Philip and Alice fall in love; this includes a number of brief motifs that reflect the couple's pursuits, which include a drive in the country (accompanied by busy strings), horse riding (accompanied by a hunting horn motif) and a ride in a pony and trap (accompanied by what can best be described as "clip-clop" music). The approach may verge on the obvious, but it all works

beautifully, and the sequence is the highlight of the film. Arnold deployed a similar idea a year later in *Hobson's Choice* (1953), in which he used a series of brief motifs to aurally describe the various uses of a variety of shoes and boots on display in a cobbler's shop.

Made between 22 October and early December 1951 (over-running it's intended 30 November deadline by several days), the film was a modest box office hit when—following a trade show on 24 April 1952 at the Rialto Theater and a premiere London run at The Plaza from 25 April—it went on general released in the UK on 23 June care of Exclusive on a double bill with Lippert's *The Fighting Seventh* (1951). *Today's Cinema* described the

film as "Fair popular entertainment," but added that "None of it should be taken too seriously." Meanwhile, *Picture Show* observed that "The stars make the best of their roles and the settings are good, but the film often lacks conviction," while in America, where it had been released a week earlier care of Fox on 16 June, *Variety* found that the "pacing is laborious, though Paul Henried and Lizabeth Scott supply some substance." **Additional notes:** Despite the better care than usual with which the film was made, note that the crew can be seen reflected in the windscreen of a car as it pulls up outside Dr. Ritter's surgery in the opening scene! Also one wonders how Lily loses her Cockney accent after the surgery, given that she hasn't had any elocution lessons. The actress Maureen Glynne (the niece of continuity girl Renee Glynne's theatrical agent sister-in-law Valery Glynne) was hired as Lizabeth Scott's double for the film. A remake, which failed to materialize, was announced in 1993 by Hammer in conjunction with Warner Bros. and Donner/Shuler Donner. The cover and onscreen menu for VCI Entertainment's *Hammer Film Noir Double Feature Collector's Set* mistakenly lists the film's title as *A Stolen Face*.

Production companies: Hammer/Lippert. Distributors: Exclusive (UK), Twentieth Century–Fox (U.S.). Producer: Anthony Hinds. Director: Terence Fisher. Screenplay: Martin Berkeley, Richard Landau. Story: Alexander Paal, Steven Vas. Cinematographer: Walter "Jimmy" Harvey. Music: Malcolm Arnold. Music played by: The London Philharmonic Orchestra. Specialty numbers: Jack Parnell. Solo pianist: Bronwyn Jones (billed as Miss Bronwyn Jones). Editor: Maurice Rootes. Assembly editor: Bill Lenny [uncredited]. Art director: Wilfred Arnold. Costumes: Edith Head. Furs: Deanfield of London and Paris. Sound: Bill Salter. Sound camera operator: Gordon Everett [uncredited]. Boom operator: Percy Britten [uncredited]. Make-up: Phil Leakey. Hair: Bill Griffiths. Assistant director: Jimmy Sangster. Second assistant director: Bill Shore [uncredited]. Third assistant director: Len Lee [uncredited]. Production manager: Arthur Barnes. Draughtsman: Alec Gray [uncredited]. Camera operators: Peter Bryan, E. Ford [uncredited]. Focus puller: Neil Binney [uncredited]. Clapper loader: Tom Friswell [uncredited]. Stills: John Jay [uncredited], Tom Edwards [uncredited]. Casting: Nora Roberts, Michael Carreras [uncredited]. Continuity: Renee Glynne [uncredited]. **Cast:** Paul Henried (Dr. Philip Ritter), Lizabeth Scott (Alice Brent/Lily Conover), André Morell (David), John Wood (Dr. Jack Wilson), Susan Stephen (Betty), Mary Mackenzie (Lily), Diana Beaumont (May), Terence O'Regan (Pete Snipe), Cyril Smith (Alf Bixby), Everley Gregg (Lady Millicent Haringay), Arnold Ridley (Dr. Russell), Richard Wattis (Wentworth), Russell Napier (Detective Cutler), William Murray (Floorwalker), Ambrosine Phillpotts (Miss Patten), Dorothy Bramhall (Miss Simpson [receptionist]), John Bull (Charles Emmett), Alexis France (Mrs. Emmett), Janet Burnell (Maggie Bixby), Anna Turner (Maid), Howard Douglas (Farmer), Robert Brooks Turner (Farmer), Grace Gavin (Presurgical nurse), John Warren (Railway guard), Hal

Exclusive goes up a gear. British poster for *Stolen Face* (1952) (Hammer/Lippert/Exclusive/Twentieth Century–Fox).

Osmond (Photographer), James Valentine (Sailor), Philip Vickers (Soldier), Frank Hawkins (Commercial traveller [uncredited]), Bartlett Mullins (Farmer [uncredited]), Ben Williams (unnamed role [uncredited]), Maureen Glynne (Lizabeth Scott's double [uncredited]). **DVD availability:** VCI Entertainment (U.S. R1 NTSC), double-billed with *Murder by Proxy* (1955), extras include a trailer and biographies; DD Home Entertainment (UK R2 PAL), double-billed with *Danger List* (1957). **Blu-ray availability:** Icon Entertainment (B/2), as an extra to *The Mummy* (1959)

### Stoll, David

This British actor (1922–) had a minor supporting role in the Hammer second feature *Death of an Angel* (1952). His other credits include *The Night We Dropped a Clanger* (1959), *Little Dorrit* (1988), *King Ralph* (1991) and *The Secret Garden* (1993), plus episodes of *Mystery and Imagination* (1966–1970, TV) and *Tottering Towers* (1971–1972, TV). His grandfather was the impresario Sir Oswald Stoll (1866–1942, real name Oswald Gray). His wife is actress Lyndall Goodman (1937–), whom he married in 1963. **Hammer credits:** *Death of an Angel* (1952, as Plain clothes man)

### Stoll, John

An Oscar winner for his art direction on *Lawrence of Arabia* (1962), an award he shared with production designer John Box and set dresser Dario Simoni, this British designer (1913–1990) began his career by working on such low budgeters as *Secret Venture* (1955), *Assignment Redhead* (1956) and *Cloak without Dagger* (1957), prior to which he'd worked as a draughtsman on *The Courtneys of Curzon Street* (1947), *Maytime in Mayfair* (1949) and *Odette* (1950), as well as a sketch artist on *No Highway* (1951). He went on to design five diverse films for Hammer, beginning with *The Camp on Blood Island* (1958), the art direction for which consisted mostly of a few bamboo huts and some judiciously placed palm trees. Stoll's many subsequent credits include *A Terrible Beauty* (1960), *The Running Man* (1963), *The Seventh Dawn* (1964), *The Collector* (1965), *How I Won the War* (1967), *Hannibal Brooks* (1969), *Shaft in Africa* (1973), *Not Quite Jerusalem* (1984) and *Shirley Valentine* (1989), plus episodes of *Return of the Saint* (1978–1979, TV) and *Master of the Game* (1984, TV). He also received a shared Emmy nomination for his work on the TV remake of *All Quiet on the Western Front* (1979, TVM). **Hammer credits:** *The Camp on Blood Island* (1958), *The Snorkel* (1958), *I Only Arsked!* (1958), *Sword of Sherwood Forest* (1960), *Creatures the World Forgot* (1971)

### Stone, Fred

This British supporting actor (1908–1995) played a Cabinet Minister in Hammer's *The Two Faces of Dr. Jekyll* (1960). His other credits include *The Wild Affair* (1963) and *Dracula* (1973, TVM), plus two more appearances for Hammer. His TV work includes episodes of *Musical Playhouse* (1959, TV), *The Dickie Henderson Show* (1960–1968, TV) and *Haunted* (1967–1968, TV). Also on stage. **Hammer credits:** *The Two Faces of Dr. Jekyll*

(1960, as Cabinet Minister [uncredited]), *The Shadow of the Cat* (1961, as Ambulance man [uncredited]), *Cash on Demand* (1961, as Window cleaner [uncredited])

### Stone, John

This British (Welsh) supporting actor (1924–2007) played Gerry in Hammer's Quatermass clone *X—The Unknown* (1956). His other credits include *Johnny Frenchman* (1945), *Reach for the Sky* (1956), *The Frightened City* (1961), *You Only Live Twice* (1967), *Deadlier Than the Male* (1967) and *Assault* (1971), plus episodes of *The Quatermass Experiment* (1953, TV), *Quatermass II* (1955, TV), *The Avengers* (1961–1969, TV), *Justice* (1971–1974, TV), in which he played Dr. Ian Moody, *Flesh and Blood* (1980–1982, TV), in which he played Max Brassington, and *Strike It Rich* (1986–1987, TV), in which he played Jack Kingsley. **Hammer credits:** *X—The Unknown* (1956, as Gerry [uncredited])

### Stone, Marianne

This prolific British actress (1922–2009, sometimes billed as Mary Stone, real name Mary Haydon Stone) appeared in leading, supporting and character roles during her career, notching up in excess of two-hundred film and television appearances along the way (she was a particular favorite of producer Peter Rogers and director Val Guest, who both used her many times). Beginning in 1943 with *Miss London, Ltd.*, other credits include *Brighton Rock* (1947), *A Run for Your Money* (1949), *Charley Moon* (1956), *Carry On Nurse* (1959), *The Day the Earth Caught Fire* (1961), *Lolita* (1962), *Carry On Screaming* (1966), *Carry On Doctor* (1967), *Au Pair Girls* (1972), *Confessions of a Window Cleaner* (1974), *Confessions from a Holiday Camp* (1977) and *Terry on the Fence* (1985). Inevitably, she crossed paths with Hammer several times during her career, first appearing in *Spaceways* (1953), in which she had the minor role of Mrs. Rogers. Her many TV appearances include episodes of *Public Eye* (1965–1975, TV), *Return of the Saint* (1978–1979, TV) and *The Nineteenth Hole* (1989, TV). She was married to the actor-turned-showbusiness columnist Peter Noble (1917–1997) from 1947. Her daughter is the actress Kara Noble. **Hammer credits:** *Spaceways* (1953, as Mrs. Rogers [uncredited]), *36 Hours* (1953, as Pam Palmer), *The Quatermass Xperiment* (1955, as Second nurse [uncredited]), *Quatermass 2* (1957, as Secretary [Miss Bealey]), *Man with a Dog* (1957, as Mrs. Stephens), *Hell Is a City* (1960, unnamed role [uncredited]), *Watch It, Sailor!* (1961, as Woman), *Paranoiac* (1963, as Second woman [uncredited]), *The Curse of the Mummy's Tomb* (1964, as Landlady), *Hysteria* (1965, as Secretary), *Countess Dracula* (197, as Kitchen maid), *In Possession* (1984, TVM [episode of *Hammer House of Mystery and Suspense*], as Woman downstairs)

### Stone, Sid

Stone (1915–1981) edited four episodes of Hammer's *Journey to the Unknown* (1968, TV), of which *The New People* also appeared in the compendium film *Journey into Darkness* (1968, TVM), while *Do Me a Favor and Kill Me* appeared in the

compendium film *Journey to Murder* (1972, TVM). His other TV credits include episodes of *Saber of London* (1954–1960, TV) and *Catweazle* (1970–1971, TV), while his film credits include *Hearts of Humanity* (1936), *The Arsenal Stadium Mystery* (1939), *Great Day* (1945), *Night and the City* (1950), *The Night We Dropped a Clanger* (1959) and *Dateline Diamonds* (1965). He also produced one film, *Alias John Preston* (1955). **Hammer credits:** *The New People* (1968, TV [episode of *Journey to the Unknown*]), *Somewhere in a Crowd* (1968, TV [episode of *Journey to the Unknown*]), *Do Me a Favor and Kill Me* (1968, TV [episode of *Journey to the Unknown*]), *One on an Island* (1968, TV [episode of *Journey to the Unknown*]), *Journey into Darkness* (1968, TVM), *Journey to Murder* (1972, TVM)

### Stoneground

This American rock group—formed in 1970 in San Francisco—can be seen playing at the opening party in Hammer's *Dracula A.D. 1972* (1972), in which they perform two numbers: *Alligator Man* and *You Better Come Through*. Astonishingly, they got the gig after Rod Stewart's group Faces had been signed for the film and then ditched. At the time, the group's members included songwriters/performers Tim Barnes and Sal Valentino, plus Annie Sampson (who was lead singer), Steve Price, Lydia Mareno, Cory Lerios, Deirdre La Porte, Lynne Hughes, Brian Godula and John Blakeley. The group's albums include *Stoneground* (1971), *Family Album* (1971), *Flat Out* (1976), *Play It Loud* (1980), *Last Dance* (2001) and *Back with a Vengeance* (2004). They can also be seen in the film *Medicine Ball Caravan* (1971). **Hammer credits:** *Dracula A.D. 1972* (1972, as Rockgroup)

### Stoneman, John

British born Stoneman (1939–) worked as the assistant director on Hammer's *When Dinosaurs Ruled the Earth* (1970). His other credits include *Jigsaw* (1962), *Casino Royale* (1967), *Assignment K* (1968), *Toomorrow* (1970) and *Au Pair Girls* (1972), all of which, like his Hammer film, were directed by Val Guest. **Hammer credits:** *When Dinosaurs Ruled the Earth* (1970)

### Stoney, Kevin

Born in India, this supporting actor (1921–2008, full name Thomas Kevin Harvest Stoney) played Father in Hammer's *The Shadow of the Cat* (1961). His many other credits include *Interpol* (1957), *Strongroom* (1961), *The Blood Beast Terror* (1967), *Murder at the Gallop* (1963), *Guns in the Heather* (1968) and *Ordeal by Innocence* (1984), plus two further appearances for Hammer. Busy on television, his many credits here include episodes of *BBC Sunday-Night Theatre* (1950–1959, TV), *The Caesars* (1968, TV), *Spy Trap* (1972–1975, TV), *I, Claudius* (1976, TV) and *Call Me Mister* (1986, TV). He was married to the actress Rosalie Westwater (1922–1985) from 1953; she appeared in Hammer's *Women without Men* (1956). **Hammer credits:** *The Shadow of the Cat* (1961, as Father [uncredited]), *Cash on Demand* (1961, as Detective Inspector Mason), *The Thirteenth Reunion* (1980, TV [episode of *Hammer House of Horror*], as Jack Rothwell)

**Stop Me Before I Kill** see *The Full Treatment*

### Stossel, Ludwig

In films in his home country from 1926 with *In der Heimat, da gibt's ein Wiedersehn!*, this Austrian character actor (1883–1973) moved to Britain in 1938 where he appeared in a handful of films, among them *Return to Yesterday* (1940) and *Dead Man's Shoes* (1940). He soon after moved to America, where he continued his career with *Four Sons* (1940). He went on to appear in many films and TV shows, among them *The Face in the Tombstone Mirror*, the pilot episode of Hammer's aborted television series *Tales of Frankenstein* (1958, TV). His many other credits include *Casablanca* (1942), *Hitler's Madmen* (1943), *Call Me Madam* (1953) and *G.I. Blues* (1960), plus episodes of *Father Knows Best* (1954–1960, TV) and *Man with a Camera* (1958–1960, TV), as well as commercials, among them a long-running ad for the Italian Swiss Colony wine company in the sixties. **Hammer credits:** *Tales of Frankenstein: The Face in the Tombstone Mirror* (1958, TV, as Wilhem)

### Stott, Wally

This British composer, conductor and orchestrator (1924–2009, aka Angela Morley and Walter Stott) provided some of the musical arrangements for the Hammer featurette *The Eric Winstone Bandshow* (1955). His other credits as an arranger include *Dance Hall* (1950), *Charley Moon* (1956) and *The Victors* (1963), plus the anarchic radio series *The Goon Show* (1951–1960 [as *Crazy People* in 1951]). In 1972 he had a sex reassignment operation and became Angela Morley, as whom she worked as an arranger on *The Little Prince* (1974) and *The Slipper and the Rose* (1976), both of which brought shared Oscar nominations, *Star Wars* (1977), *Home Alone* (1990) and *Schindler's List* (1993). She also contributed scores to such films as *Watership Down* (1978) and such TV series as *Dynasty* (1981–1989, TV), *Falcon Crest* (1981–1990, TV) and *The Colbys* (1985–1987, TV). She won three Emmys and a further seven nominations for her TV work. **Hammer credits:** *The Eric Winstone Bandshow* (1955)

### Strachan, George

Strachan worked as a commentator on the Exclusive documentary *Scottish Symphony* (1946), sharing his duties with James McKechnie. **Hammer credits:** *Scottish Symphony* (1946, Commentator)

### Straight on Till Morning

GB, 1972, 96m, Technicolor, widescreen [1.85:1], RCA, cert X

An odd blend of kitchen sink drama and psycho thriller (and not particularly satisfying as either), this curious but generally unappealing film sees Brenda Thompson, a naïve young woman from Liverpool, move to London where, after working briefly in a fashion boutique, she falls in love with a ne'er-do-well named Peter Price. However, after having moved in with him and becoming pregnant, Brenda gradually comes to realize that he is psychotic, and responsible not only for the killing of his dog Tinker, whose death cries he has recorded on tape, but also for the murder of her former flatmate and co-worker Caroline, who had come looking for her.

A rather tired collection of clichés, directed with a sledgehammer by Peter Collinson—better known for the cult classic *The Italian Job* (1969)—the production certainly has an eclectic cast. This is headed by sixties icon Rita Tushingham as Brenda, who is supported by Hammer star-in-waiting Shane Briant as the unbalanced Peter, and jazz legend Annie Ross as one of Peter's former girlfriends, each of whom it would seem has come to a grisly end after he has tired of them.

According to screenwriter John Peacock, the story is a variation on *Peter Pan*, with Brenda as Wendy (as Peter nicknames her) and Peter (whose real name we learn is Clive) as Peter. Hence the film's title, taken from Peter's answer to Wendy's query as to where Never Never Land is situated: "Second [star] to the right and straight on till morning," a line that the film's Peter uses when giving Brenda/Wendy directions to his bedroom, though here he paraphrases "first star to the right," for some reason. Peter also uses the *Pan* line, "An awfully big adventure," when playing with his dog, which is of course named after the fairy Tinkerbell. But as the trailer has it, "This is no fairy tale, as you'll see." It also describes the film as "A love story from Hammer that will make the heart beat faster—and faster yet."

"It's obviously a dated film,"[128] commented Rita Tushingham some thirty years after its release. Indeed, the frantic cross cutting between scenes in the opening twenty minutes, along with the crash shots, zooms and overlapping sound, seems like a rather desperate ploy to grab attention for what basically becomes a two-hander, with Brenda held captive by the increasingly erratic Peter, who eventually forces her to listen to the recording of his killing of Tinker and Caroline on his bedroom stereo system. With its echoes of the infamous Moors murders, this is perhaps the most genuinely uncomfortable and disturbing scene to be found in any Hammer film. Its sheer tastelessness aside, however, one has to note the power with which it is performed by Tushingham, whose distress is a real *tour de force*, and Briant, who quietly but tearfully listens to her reaction out on the stairs. As for the ending, one assumes that Peter has killed Wendy, as he listens alone to one of the stories she made up on his tape recorder. The clue lies in his undarned socks, out of which his toes noticeably stick. Earlier, Peter had stated to Brenda that "cleaning up's a woman's job," hence her coming to live with him to look after, mend and clean for him in return for him giving her the baby she craves.

Its faults aside, among them gross over-length, it should be noted that the film, made just after *Dracula A.D. 1972* (1972) but released before it, provides a far more realistic presentation of London in the early seventies, complete with scenes on the streets of Earl's Court, at a trendy party and in a fashion boutique (where Caroline rather cruelly informs the plain looking Brenda, "You haven't got an awful lot to offer a man, and what you *do* have ... well let's face it."). The dialogue also has far more street-cred, including a number of rare expletives for a Hammer film, though nothing worse than the occasional "piss" or "shit."

On the floor at Elstree between 1 November and 17 December 1971, the finished film was released in the UK by MGM-EMI on 9 July 1972 on the upper half of a double with Hammer's last "mini Hitchcock" *Fear in the Night* (1972). Somewhat tactlessly, the program was promoted with the tagline "Women in Terror." The film's American

**Shane Briant and Rita Tushingham feature in this stark ad for the psychological thriller *Straight on Till Morning* (1972) (Hammer/ EMI/Anglo-EMI/International Co-Productions/Studio Canal).**

release in August 1974, care of International Co-Productions, proved to be a limited one. **Additional notes:** The opening shot of a railway line, which pans over to Brenda's home in Liverpool, was actually shot near Clapham Junction in South London. The exterior shots of Brenda's Liverpool home, where she says goodbye to her mother, were shot in Earl's Court, where Brenda eventually ends up once in London. In the opening scene, Peter is shown driving away from a newsagent's; having driven some distance from the shop, he almost runs down a young woman. However, this accident clearly takes place at the T-junction opposite the newsagent's he's just left. In Brenda's final shot, as she breaks down by the locked front door as Peter approaches her, the sound of her anguished cries don't quite match her lips in the last few seconds, and at the very end of the scene, Tushingham seems suddenly to relax out of character, as if the director has just cried cut, yet the editor hasn't quite trimmed the shot in time. The title song was released as a single by EMI-Columbia (the B-side was a version of *God Bless the Child*). The film is alternatively known as *Dressed for Death*, *The Victim* and *Till Dawn Us Do Part*. Peter's dog is both called and credited as Tinker.

Production companies: Hammer/EMI. Distributors: Anglo-EMI (UK [ABC circuit]), International Co-Productions (U.S.). Producer: Michael Carreras. Production supervisor: Roy Skeggs. Presenter: Nat Cohen. Director: Peter Collinson. Screenplay: John Peacock. Cinematographer: Bryan Probyn. Music: Roland Shaw. Song: *Straight on Till Morning*, Annie Ross (music, co-lyrics, vocalist), John Peacock (co-lyrics). Music director: Philip Martell. Editor: Alan Pattillo. Art director: Scott MacGregor. Assistant art director: Richard Rambaut. Costumes: Laura Nightingale. Make-up: George Blackler. Hair: Pearl Tipaldi. Recording director: Tony Lumkin. Sound: John Purchese. Sound editor: Alan Bell. Dubbing mixer: Dennis Whitlock. Assistant director: Clive Reed. Third assistant director: Michael Murray [uncredited]. Production manager: Tom Sachs. Construction manager: Bill Greene. Camera operators: Roy Ford, Keith Jones. Focus puller: Keith Blake [uncredited]. Stills: Ronnie Pilgrim [uncredited]. Continuity: Betty Harley. Casting: James Liggat. **Cast:** Rita Tushingham (Brenda Thompson), Shane Briant (Peter Price), Annie Ross (Liza), Katya Wyeth (Caroline), Harold Berens (Mr. Harris), James Bolam (Joey), Claire Kelly (Margo Thompson), Tom Bell (Jimmy Lindsay), John Clive (Newsagent), Tommy Godfrey (Customer), Lola Willard (Customer), Mavis Villiers (Indian Princess), Paul Brooke (Uneasy man at bus stop [uncredited]), Mike Mungarvan (Client [uncredited]). **DVD availability:** Anchor Bay (U.S. R1 NTSC), extras include a commentary by Rita Tushingham, a trailer and a text biography of Peter Collinson; Optimum (UK R2 PAL), extras include a commentary by Rita Tushingham, a trailer and a text biography of Peter Collinson. **Blu-ray availability:** Studio Canal (B/2)

## Strange, Eric

Strange worked as "dressing props" on *Hammer*

*House of Mystery and Suspense* (1984, TVM). His many other credits as a propsman include *Sword of the Valiant* (1984), *Mona Lisa* (1986), *Batman* (1989), *Tomorrow Never Dies* (1997), *Lara Croft: Tomb Raider* (2001), *Troy* (2004) and *Jack the Giant Slayer* (2013). **Hammer credits:** *Hammer House of Mystery and Suspense* (1984, TVM [uncredited])

## The Stranger Came Home

GB, 1954, 80m, bw, RCA, cert A

One of the slightly more interesting second features churned out by Hammer in the fifties, this melodrama centers on an amnesiac who returns home after four years—having been presumed dead—only to find himself suspected for a murder he did not commit. Based on the novel *Stranger at Home* (1946) by dapper Hollywood star George Sanders, the film marked the first screenplay effort of its producer, Michael Carreras, who doesn't quite capture the Wildean, epigrammatic nature of the book's dialogue. It also saw first assistant director Jimmy Sangster promoted to production manager, and features exteriors filmed at Oakley Court. However, it is notable chiefly for the presence of its leading lady, Paulette Goddard, for whom it must have been something of a comedown, given that she had starred in such Hollywood classics as *Modern Times* (1936), *The Cat and the Canary* (1939) and *The Great Dictator* (1940).

Filmed at Bray in early 1954, the film was trade shown in July and released in the UK by Exclusive on 9 August the same year. For its American release care of Fox/Lippert it was re-titled *The Unholy Four*. A just about acceptable potboiler, it might have worked better as one of Hammer's sixties psychodramas. As it is, it's a somewhat typical high society murder mystery, with the added intrigue of

guessing who hit the nominal hero, Philip Vickers, over the head so as to produce his amnesia. Also, like Hammer's *Death of an Angel* (1952), several people find themselves accused of committing the first murder, prompting Vickers to comment, "Start covering up tracks and rehearsing alibis. Somebody's going to need a good one." Performance-wise, Goddard brings a touch of Tinseltown glamor to the proceedings as the hero's wife, Angie Vickers, while William Sylvester as her husband makes for a nicely nonchalant leading man. The action is meanwhile adequately handled by Terence Fisher, whose best touch sees the hero's return reflected in a mirror, much to the shock of his wife's devoted secretary, Joan, who also finds herself accused of foul deeds.

Recalled Jimmy Sangster of the movie, "I don't know whether the novel was a success, but the picture certainly wasn't. Indifferently directed by Terry Fisher, it starred Paulette Goddard who, unlike some of the people Hollywood had sent us, had been a real star in her time, an Academy Award nominee and an ex–Mrs. Charlie Chaplin…. This picture marked the end of her career. She returned to Hollywood and packed it in. It should have marked the end of a couple of other careers too."[129] The press shared Sangster's view of the film, with *The New York Times* describing it as "A third rate British who-dunit." **Additional notes:** When Inspector Treherne's car drives through the gates and up to the house, the crew is reflected in its windows. The dog featured in the film was called Coolin. Some sources claim that Sanders' novel was actually ghost written by Hollywood screenwriter Leigh Brackett. Despite her experiences at Bray, Paulette Goddard actually returned to the studio to film *Mademoiselle Fifi*, a 1956

American artwork for *The Stranger Came Home* (1954), released in the States as *The Unholy Four* (Hammer/Lippert/Exclusive/Twentieth Century–Fox/Lippert Pictures, Inc.).

episode of *The Errol Flynn Theatre* (1956–1957, TV).

Production companies: Hammer/Lippert. Distributors: Exclusive (UK), Twentieth Century–Fox/Lippert Pictures, Inc. (U.S.). Producer: Michael Carreras. Director: Terence Fisher. Screenplay: Michael Carreras, based on the novel *Stranger at Home* by George Sanders. Cinematographer: Walter "Jimmy" Harvey (billed as James Harvey). Music: Leonard Salzedo, Ivor Slaney (stock music [uncredited]), Eric Rogers (source music [uncredited]). Music director: John Hollingsworth. Editor: Bill Lenny. Art director: J. Elder Wills. Costumes: Molly Arbuthnot. Furs: Molho. Sound: Bill Salter. Production manager: Jimmy Sangster. Assistant director: Jack Causey. Second assistant director: Aida Young [uncredited]. Camera operator: Len Harris. Focus puller: Harry Oakes [uncredited]. Sound: Sid Wiles, Ken Cameron. Sound camera operator: Don Alton [uncredited]. Make-up: Phil Leakey. Hair: Eileen Bates. Continuity: Renee Glynne. Publicity: Jack Dawe [uncredited]. **Cast:** Paulette Goddard (Angie Vickers), William Sylvester (Philip Vickers), Patrick Holt (Job Crandall), Alvys Maben (Joan Merrill), Russell Napier (Inspector Treherne), Paul Carpenter (Bill Saul), Pat Owens (Blonde), David King-Wood (Sessions), Jeremy Hawk (Sergeant Johnson), Kay Callard (Jenny), Jack Taylor (Brownie [uncredited]), Kim Mills (Roddy [uncredited]), Owen Evans (Redhead [uncredited]), Philip Lennard (Medical examiner [uncredited]). **DVD availability:** VCI Entertainment (U.S., all regions), double-billed with *Mask of Dust* (1954)

### Stranger in the Family  see  Journey to the Unknown

### The Stranglers of Bombay

GB, 1959, 80m, bw, MegaScope/StrangloScope, RCA, cert A

Originally to have been titled *The Horror of the Thugee*, *The Stranglers of Bombay* was a pet project of the American producer Kenneth Hyman, who was effectively serving an internship at Hammer in the late fifties, having already associate produced (without credit) *The Hound of the Baskervilles* (1959), the rights to which he had personally acquired. As announced to the trade papers in 1958, it was Hyman's intent to film John Masters' 1952 novel *The Deceivers*, with John Huston tentatively onboard as director. Set in British East India in 1824, the novel offers a fictitious account of an actual incident in which Major General Sir William Sleeman, an English army officer, discovers and subsequently infiltrates the hitherto secret Kali-worshipping Thuggee cult, whose centuries-old activities of robbery and ritual strangulation he aims to curtail.

Unfortunately, the rights to the novel belonged to Rank, and their managing director John Davis wanted an astonishing $250,000 for the property, a sum large enough to fund two or possibly three Hammer films at the time. Consequently, Hyman declined Davis's offer and decided to film his own version of the story, which, given that it was based on a historical event, was actually in the public do-main. Thus Hyman put to work fellow American David Zelag Goodman on the script, which was now to be titled *The Stranglers of Bengal*. Hyman then pitched the property to James Carreras and Tony Hinds, who agreed to make the film as part of Hammer's ongoing production deal with Columbia, with additional funds coming from a loan from the National Film Finance Corporation.

The original intention had been to shoot in color, yet by the time the film went on the floor at Bray on 6 July 1959, it had been downgraded to a black and white production, albeit in the widescreen MegaScope process, here re-named StrangloScope for publicity purposes. The film, which would shoot until 27 August, had also undergone yet another title change, this time to *The Stranglers of Bombay*. According to Terence Fisher, the reason why *Stranglers* was robbed of color was because, "The producers felt it was better in black and white because it was a documentary story rather than a myth."[130]

As had been the case with *The Hound of the Baskervilles*, Anthony Hinds was the film's listed producer, with Hyman onboard as an associate producer, a result of strict British union rules (the opening credits cite the movie as "A Hammer Film Production in Association with Kenneth Hyman"). Commented Hinds of the subject matter, "This is the first film to deal at length with Thuggee. We went all out to make it as authentic as possible. Why nobody thought of this before is beyond me. The cinema could hardly find a more exciting subject."[131]

In addition to Hinds and Hyman, other *Hound* holdovers include director Terence Fisher, executive producer Michael Carreras, composer James Bernard and art director Bernard Robinson, who re-cycled the exterior of castle Dracula as an Indian village. However, Arthur Grant, who was deemed a faster worker, replaced lighting cameraman Jack Asher, whose perfectionism would soon see him ousted as the studio's cinematographer-in-chief. The cast is meanwhile headed by Guy Rolfe—a holdover from *Yesterday's Enemy* (1959)—as Captain Lewis, the heroic English officer who tracks down the cult, only to find himself tortured as a consequence.

Other cast members include George Pastell as the cult's High Priest, who ends up being burned alive on a pyre, a mongoose named Toki, seen in a deadly fight with a cobra, and Marie Devereux as Karim, a particularly sadistic cult member who takes special pleasure in taunting Captain Lewis with the promise of water while he is pegged out in the blistering sun. Devereux had previously appeared as a harem girl in the Hammer comedy *I Only Arsked!* (1958); she obviously caught someone's eye, and was promoted to featured (albeit non-speaking) status.

Astonishingly, despite initial reservations expressed by the BBFC and the MPAA at the script stage, both of which cautioned restraint, the BBFC awarded the finished film an A certificate, in spite of its frequently gruesome nature, which includes scenes of strangulation, eye-gouging, hanging, stomach slitting and stabbing, though it should be noted that a good deal of this activity is implied through careful framing and editing.

The film premiered at the London Pavilion on 4 December 1959, for which it was advertised with the slogan, "Murder—their religion!" Handled by Columbia, it subsequently went on general release in the UK on the ABC circuit on 18 January 1960, accompanied by the thriller *Kill Her Gently* (1958). The U.S. release, again handled by Columbia, followed in May 1960. Commented *Variety* of the production, "With sharper dialogue and swifter direction this could have been a much better film than it is. But, within its limits, it provides a measure of suspense and interest. Arthur Grant with his camera contributes rather more than screenplay writer David Z. Goodman to the total effect." *Films and Filming* meanwhile criticized the movie for being "a particularly bestial contribution to the Hammer horror cycle." It also noted that it relied on "visual outrages—blindings, evisceration, human heads being thrown on to dinner tables, and so forth." However, in the latter observation, the reviewer was quite wrong, it being a servant's severed hand wrapped in cloth that is thrown onto Captain Lewis's dinner table for his wife to discover.

Reveals the opening legend: "For hundreds of years there existed in India a perverted religious sect, dedicated to the wanton destruction of human life … so secret was this savage cult that even the British East India Company, rulers of the country at that time, was unaware of its existence…." Naturally, the film proceeds to set this unawareness to rights, even if, historically, the claim is inaccurate, given that both the Indian Raj and the British government knew of the existence of the cult, actually known as the Phansigars, or the "strangling ones."

Seen today, *The Stranglers of Bombay* seems surprisingly sadistic for the time at which it was made. Arthur Grant's stark black and white widescreen photography is indeed the production's main asset, thanks to some nicely judged movement in the early scenes. Unfortunately, Terence Fisher's direction is rather listless, and the pace tends to flag between the brutalities (admitted Fisher, "*The Stranglers of Bombay* went wrong. It was too crude"[132]). Meanwhile, Guy Rolfe's Captain Lewis is little more than a two-dimensional cut-out, though good support is provided by George Pastell as the High Priest and Allan Cuthbertson as the gloriously vain and supercilious Captain Connaught-Smith. Yet despite its various plusses and minuses, the film seems somewhat out of character when compared to the studio's cozier gothic horrors. Consequently, it remains something of a curiosity, especially given that it is rarely revived on British television. **Additional notes:** *The Deceivers* was eventually filmed in 1988 by director Nicholas Meyer, with a pre–James Bond Pierce Brosnan in the leading role. Produced by Merchant Ivory, it was not a commercial success. A follow-up production to *Stranglers* titled *The Black Hole of Calcutta* was announced in 1960, but failed to materialize. For its 1996 UK video release, the film was awarded a 15 certificate, but only after seven seconds' worth of cuts had been trimmed from the original A certificate negative! The film's screenplay was novelized by Stuart James for Monarch. Construction manager Mick Lyons died two weeks before filming began.

Production company: Hammer. Distributor: Columbia (UK [ABC circuit], U.S.). Producer: Anthony Hinds. Executive producer: Michael Carreras. Associate producers: Anthony Nelson Keys, Kenneth Hyman [credited as "in association with"]. Director: Terence Fisher. Screenplay: David Zelag Goodman. Cinematographer: Arthur Grant. Music: James Bernard. Music director: John Hollingsworth. Supervising editor: James Needs. Editor/second unit inserts: Alfred Cox. Assistant editor: Chris Barnes [uncredited]. Art director: Bernard Robinson. Costumes: Molly Arbuthnot. Costume suppliers: Bermans [uncredited]. Make-up: Roy Ashton. Sound: Jock May. Sound editor: Arthur Cox. Assistant art director: Don Mingaye [uncredited]. Assistant director: John Peverall. Second assistant director: Tom Walls [uncredited]. Third assistant director: Hugh Harlow [uncredited]. Camera operator: Len Harris. Focus puller: Harry Oakes [uncredited]. Hair: Henry Montsash. Production manager: Don Weeks. Studio manager: Arthur Kelly [uncredited]. Construction manager: Mick Lyons [uncredited]. Chief electrician: Jack Curtis [uncredited]. Master plasterer: Arthur Banks [uncredited]. Master painter: Lawrence Wren [uncredited]. Master carpenter: Charles Davis [uncredited]. Continuity: Tilly Day, Pauline Wise (trainee [uncredited]). Historical advisor: Michael Edwards. Personnel advisor: Jimmy Vaughn [uncredited]. Casting: Dorothy Holloway [uncredited]. Props: Tommy Money [uncredited]. Props buyer: Eric Hillier [uncredited]. Stills: Tom Edwards [uncredited]. Publicists: Dennison Thornton [uncredited], Colin Reid [uncredited]. Modeller: Margaret Carter (later Robinson [uncredited]). **Cast:** Guy Rolfe (Captain Lewis), Allan Cuthbertson (Captain Christopher Connaught-Smith), Andrew Cruickshank (Colonel Henderson), Marne Maitland (Patel Shari), George Pastell (High Priest), Marie Devereux (Karim), Jan Holden (Mary), Tutte Lemkow (Ram Das), David Spenser (Gopali), Paul Stassino (Silver), John Harvey (Burns), Roger Delgado (Bundar), Ewen Solon (Camel trader), Jack McNaughton (Corporal Roberts), Steven Scott (Walters), Michael Nightingale (Sidney Flood), Margaret Gordon (Dorothy Flood), Warren Mitchell (Merchant). **DVD availability:** Sony (U.S. R1 NTSC), as part of the *Icons of Adventure* box set

## StrangloScope

This widescreen process was in fact MegaScope under a different name, concocted by Hammer's publicists to promote their Thuggee thriller *The Stranglers of Bombay* (1959). **Hammer credits:** *The Stranglers of Bombay* (1959)

## Stranks, Alan

This British screenwriter and lyricist (?–1959) created the story and co-authored the screenplay (with director Alfred Goulding) for Hammer's first Dick Barton adventure, *Dick Barton—Special Agent* (1948). He also co-authored (with Vernon Harris) the screenplays for *The Adventures of PC 49—The Case of the Guardian Angel* (1949) and its sequel,

*A Case for PC 49* (1951), both of which were based on his popular radio serial *The Adventures of PC 49*, which ran over one-hundred episodes between 1947 and 1953 (and which Harris had produced). His other films include *Candlelight in Algeria* (1944), for which he wrote the English lyrics for the song *Flamme d'Amour* (music by Hans May, French lyrics by G. Arbib), *The Wicked Lady* (1945), for which he wrote the lyrics for *Love Steals Your Heart* (music by Hans May), and the musical *Waltz Time* (1945), for which he penned the lyrics to such songs as *The Heavenly Waltz, Little White Horse, This Land of Mine* and *Only You* (music again by Hans May). **Hammer credits:** *Dick Barton—Special Agent* (1948, story, co-screenplay), *The Adventures of PC 49—The Case of the Guardian Angel* (1949, source, co-screenplay), *A Case for PC 49* (1951, source, co-screenplay)

## Strasberg, Susan

The daughter of Method guru Lee Strasberg (1901–1982, full name Israel Lee Strassberg) and acting coach Paula Strasberg (1909–1966, maiden name Paula Miller), this talented American leading actress (1938–1999) began her career on stage as a teenager in *The Diary of Anne Frank*, which earned her a Tony nomination. She broke into films in 1955 with *The Cobweb*, which led to over forty further screen credits, among them *Picnic* (1956), *Stage Struck* (1957), *Hemingway's Adventures of a Young Man* (1962), *The Trip* (1967), *The Manitou* (1978), *The Delta Force* (1986) and *The Cherry Orchard* (1992). She also took the leading role(s) of Penny Appleby/Maggie in the Hammer shocker *Taste of Fear* (1961), in which she gave an excellent account of herself as a crippled heiress who discovers a bizarre murder plot. Remembered writer-producer Jimmy Sangster of Strasberg, "I'm sure her career was helped along by her family.... I figured with antecedents like those she would turn out to be a bit of a problem on set, keeping the crew waiting while she searched for an inner motivation before screaming her head off at finding her father's dead body all over the place. In fact, she turned out to be a pussy cat from start to finish."[133] Strasberg's many television credits include episodes of *Goodyear Television Playhouse* (1951–1957, TV), *General Electric Theater* (1953–1962, TV), *Dr. Kildare* (1961–1966, TV), *The Virginian* (1962–1971, TV), *McCloud* (1970–1977, TV), *Mike Hammer* (1984–1987, TV) and *Murder, She Wrote* (1984–1996, TV). She also took part in a number of documentaries about her friend Marilyn Monroe, among them *Remembering Marilyn* (1987), *Marilyn Monroe: Beyond the Legend* (1987), *Marilyn Monroe: Life After Death* (1994), *Marilyn Monroe: The Mortal Goddess* (1994 [*Biography* segment], TV) and *Marilyn in Manhattan* (1998, TV). Her brother is actor and acting coach John Strasberg (1941–). She was married to the actor Christopher Jones (1941–2014, real name William Frank Jones) between 1965 and 1968. **Hammer credits:** *Taste of Fear* (1961, as Penny Appleby/Maggie Frencham)

## Stratford, Tracy

This American child actress (1955–, aka Tracy Stratford Shaw) appeared in sequences shot spe-

cifically for the American telecast of Hammer's *The Evil of Frankenstein* (1964), in which she played Rena, the mute girl as a child. Her other credits include *The Miracle of the Hills* (1959), *Bachelor in Paradise* (1961) and *The Second Time Around* (1961), plus episodes of *Bonanza* (1959–1973, TV), *Ben Casey* (1961–1966, TV) and *The Fugitive* (1963–1967, TV). She is best known for providing the voice of Lucy Van Pelt for the first two Charlie Brown cartoons, *A Boy Named Charlie Brown* (1965, TV) and *A Charlie Brown Christmas* (1965, TV). **Hammer credits:** *The Evil of Frankenstein* (1964, as Rena/Mute as child)

## Stratton, John

Best known to Hammer fans for playing the oily asylum director Adolf Klauss, who comes to a sticky end in *Frankenstein and the Monster from Hell* (1974), this British actor (1925–1991) began appearing on stage in 1943. His burgeoning career was interrupted by wartime experience in the Royal Navy between 1944 and 1947, following which he resumed his stage career, making his West End debut in 1948. In films the following year with *The Small Back Room* (1949), his other big screen credits include *The Cure for Love* (1949), *Seven Days to Noon* (1950), *The Cruel Sea* (1952), *The Challenge* (1959) and *The Love Pill* (1971). Also busy on television, his credits here include *Trinity Tales* (1975, TV), *Just William* (1976–1978, TV), in which he played Mr. Bott, and *The Good Companions* (1980, TV). **Hammer credits:** *Frankenstein and the Monster from Hell* (1974, as Adolf Klauss [Asylum director])

## Street, Roy

This stuntman, stunt co-ordinator and horse-master (?–2015) can count among his many credits several Bond films, from *Goldfinger* (1964) through to *Skyfall* (2012), plus such big budget fare as *Superman* (1978), *Highlander* (1986), *Willow* (1988), *Robin Hood: Prince of Thieves* (1991), *Wrath of the Titans* (2012) and *Avengers: Age of Ultron* (2015). He also worked on a couple of Hammer films. His TV work (which also takes in bit roles) includes episodes of *Doctor Who* (1963–1989, TV), *Red-gauntlet* (1970, TV), *Hart to Hart* (1979–1984, TV) and *Brideshead Revisited* (1981, TV). **Hammer credits:** *The Viking Queen* (1967 [uncredited]), *The Vampire Lovers* (1970 [uncredited])

## Streeter, Alban (Al)

Streeter worked as the sound editor on Hammer's Robin Hood romp *Sword of Sherwood Forest* (1960). This led to work on several further films for the studio. His other credits include *Light Up the Sky* (1960), *Petticoat Pirates* (1961), *Battle of the Bulge* (1965), *Waterloo* (1970), *Starship Invasions* (1977), *Screwballs* (1983) and *Expect No Mercy* (1996), plus episodes of such series as *Dial 999* (1958–1959, TV), *The Littlest Hobo* (1979–1985, TV) and *Friday the 13th: The Series* (1987–1990, TV). **Hammer credits:** *Sword of Sherwood Forest* (1960), *The Curse of the Werewolf* (1961), *The Shadow of the Cat* (1961), *Watch It, Sailor!* (1961), *The Terror of the Tongs* (1961), *Cash on Demand* (1961), *Countess Dracula* (1971)

## Streeter, John

British born Streeter (1925–2012) worked as the sound recordist on seven episodes of Hammer's *Journey to the Unknown* (1968, TV). Of these, *Poor Butterfly* also appeared in the compendium film *Journey to Midnight* (1968, TVM), *Paper Dolls* appeared in the compendium film *Journey into Darkness* (1968, TVM) and *Matakitas Is Coming* appeared in the compendium film *Journey to the Unknown* (1969, TVM). He also worked on Hammer's *Creatures the World Forgot* (1971). He began his career as an assistant boom operator on *Uncle Silas* (1947), became a boom operator with *Port Afrique* (1956) and a sound camera operator with *Night and the City* (1950). His other credits as a recordist include *Private Potter* (1962), *Gonks Go Beat* (1965) *Operation Third Form* (1966) and episodes of *UFO* (1970–1971, TV). **Hammer credits:** *Eve* (1968, TV [episode of *Journey to the Unknown*]), *Poor Butterfly* (1968, TV [episode of *Journey to the Unknown*]), *Paper Dolls* (1968, TV [episode of *Journey to the Unknown*]), *Miss Belle* (1968, TV [episode of *Journey to the Unknown*]), *Jane Brown's Body* (1968, TV [episode of *Journey to the Unknown*]), *Matakitas Is Coming* (1968, TV [episode of *Journey to the Unknown*]), *Stranger in the Family* (1968, TV [episode of *Journey to the Unknown*]), *Journey into Darkness* (1968, TVM), *Journey to Midnight* (1968, TVM), *Journey to the Unknown* (1969, TVM), *Creatures the World Forgot* (1971)

## Stribling, Melissa

Best known for playing Mina Holmwood in Hammer's *Dracula* (1958), this British (Scottish) actress (1926–1992, full name Melissa Stribling Smith) actually began her career as an assistant cutter (editor) at Ealing Studios, where she met her future husband, the director Basil Dearden (1911–1971, real name basil Clive Dear), whom she married in 1947. In films as an actress from 1948 following training at RADA, her twenty-plus shorts and features (several of which were directed by her husband) include *Wide Boy* (1952), *The League of Gentlemen* (1960), *The Secret Partner* (1961), *Only When I Larf* (1968) and *Paris by Night* (1988). Also on television, her credits here include episodes of *Fabian of the Yard* (1954–1956, TV), *Ivanhoe* (1958–1959, TV) and *The Avengers* (1961–1969, TV). She also co-starred in *The New People*, an episode of Hammer's *Journey to the Unknown* (1968, TV), which also appeared in the compendium film *Journey into Darkness* (1968, TVM). Her sons are writer-director James Dearden (1949–) and editor Torquil Dearden (1959–). Recalled the actress of her wardrobe for *Dracula*, "All my costumes were second hand. They had been used in other films, except for my nightdresses, and they spent a great deal of money on them. It was about three weeks before I noticed that everywhere I stood, they had a light behind me."[134] **Hammer credits:** *Dracula* (1958, as Mina Holmwood), *The New People* (1968, TV [episode of *Journey to the Unknown*], as Helen Ames), *Journey into Darkness* (1968, TVM, as Helen Ames)

## Stringer, Michael

This British art director (1924–2004, full name John Michael Stringer) worked as the production designer on Hammer's *Demons of the Mind* (1972). His other credits include *An Alligator Named Daisy* (1955), *Return from the Ashes* (1965), *Casino Royale* (1967), *Inspector Clouseau* (1968), *Alfred the Great* (1969), *Fiddler on the Roof* (1971), which earned him a shared Oscar nomination, *Alice's Adventures in Wonderland* (1972), *One of Our Dinosaurs Is Missing* (1975), *The Jigsaw Man* (1984) and *Hired to Kill* (1990), plus episodes of *The First Olympics: Athens 1896* (1984, TV), which earned him a shared Emmy nomination, and *Paradise Postponed* (1986, TV). He began his career working as an assistant art director on *The White Unicorn* (1947) and as a draughtsman on *Quartet* (1948). **Hammer credits:** *Demons of the Mind* (1972)

## Struthers, Penny

British born Struthers (1946–) worked as the set dresser on Hammer's *The Horror of Frankenstein* (1970) and *Fear in the Night* (1972). Her other credits include work as an art department assistant on *2001: A Space Odyssey* (1968). **Hammer credits:** *The Horror of Frankenstein* (1970 [uncredited]), *Fear in the Night* (1972)

## Strutt, Lionel

This prolific British sound technician (1936–) worked as the sound re-recording mixer on Hammer's *Frankenstein and the Monster from Hell* (1974). His many other credits (over 200) include *The Chalk Garden* (1964), *Repulsion* (1965), *Thunderball* (1965), *The Music Lovers* (1970), *The Empire Strikes Back* (1980), *Excalibur* (1981), *Raiders of the Lost Ark* (1981), *Return of the Jedi* (1983), *A Passage to India* (1984), *Aliens* (1986), *The Russia House* (1990), *Chaplin* (1992), *Jurassic Park* (1993), *Tomorrow Never Dies* (1997), *The King's Speech* (2010), *Brighton Rock* (2010) and *Angel* (2015), plus episodes of *Stingray* (1964–1965, TV), *Thunderbirds* (1965–1966, TV), *Moses the Lawgiver* (1976, TV) and *Jesus of Nazareth* (1977, TV). He later returned as the ADR co-ordinator on Hammer's *Wake Wood* (2009), making him one of the few people to have dealings with both the old and the new Hammer. **Hammer credits:** *Frankenstein and the Monster from Hell* (1974, sound re-recording mixer), *Wake Wood* (2009, ADR co-ordinator)

## Stuart, Alan

This British stuntman and occasional bit part actor (1931–2016) can be seen as a frogman in *Black Carrion* (1984, TVM [episode of *Hammer House of Mystery and Suspense*]), dragging a lake for a missing woman, presumed to have been killed by a pop star. His many other credits as either a stuntman or stunt co-ordinator include *Deadly Strangers* (1975), *The Bride* (1985), *Willow* (1988), *Blue Ice* (1992), *Billy Elliot* (2002) and *Alex Rider: Stormbreaker* (2006), plus episodes of *Band of Brothers* (2001, TV) and *Foyle's War* (2002–2015, TV). His wife was actress Margaret Stuart, whom he married in 1956. **Hammer credits:** *Black Carrion* (1984, TVM [episode of *Hammer House of Mystery and Suspense*], as Frogman)

## Stuart, Charles

Stuart played the minor role of Sidney Robinson in the Hammer thriller *The Dark Road* (1948). Some sources (among them IMBd) claim that Charles Stuart was actually the acting name of a notorious jewel thief known as Stanley Thurston, under which name the BFI database lists him as a performer in *There Is No Escape*, the film's American release title (he is listed as Charles Stuart in the UK release); it also claims the film to be based upon his career. His other credits include *Things to Come* (1936) and *Ships with Wings* (1941). **Hammer credits:** *The Dark Road* (1948, as Sidney Robinson)

## Stuart, Ewan *see* Stewart, Ewan

## Stuart, John

On stage from 1919 and in films from 1920 with *Her Son*, this British (Scottish) leading man and, later in life, character actor (1898–1979, real name John Alfred Louden Croall) went on to appear in well over one-hundred movies, including *The Loves of Mary, Queen of Scots* (1924), *The Pleasure Garden* (1925), *Number Seventeen* (1932), *The Show Goes On* (1937), *Candles at Nine* (1944), *The Ringer* (1952), *Blood of the Vampire* (1958), *Too Many Crooks* (1959) and *Superman* (1978). He worked for Hammer several times during his career, first appearing in as a doctor in *Mantrap* (1953). He later went on to meet Professor Quatermass, Frankenstein and the Mummy in several of the studio's key genre pictures. His many television appearances include episodes of *The Railway Children* (1951, TV), *Douglas Fairbanks, Jr. Presents* (1953–1957, TV), *Saber of London* (1954–1960, TV), in which he played George Hilton in twenty-four episodes, *Doctor Who* (1963–1989, TV) and *Supernatural* (1977, TV). Married three times, his second wife was the actress Muriel Angelus (1909–2004, full name Muriel Angelus Findlay), whom he married in 1933; his third wife was the actress and acting teacher Barbara Markham (1910–1983, real name Eunice Barbara Francis, aka Barbara Francis), whom he married in 1943, and who appeared in Hammer's *The Lady Vanishes* (1979). **Hammer credits:** *Mantrap* (1953, as Doctor), *Four Sided Triangle* (1953, as Solicitor), *Men of Sherwood Forest* (1954, as Moraine [uncredited]), *Quatermass 2* (1957, as Commissioner), *The Revenge of Frankenstein* (1958, as Inspector), *Further Up the Creek* (1958, as Admiral), *The Mummy* (1959, as Coroner), *Paranoiac* (1963, as Williams), *The Scarlet Blade* (1963, as Colonel Beverley [uncredited])

## Stuart, Kathleen

This British actress (1925–1972, real name Kathleen Mary Binder) can be seen in a minor supporting role in Hammer's *Wings of Danger* (1952). Her other credits include *Just William's Luck* (1947), *William Comes to Town* (1948), in both of which she played Ethel Brown, and *Love in Pawn* (1953). She was married to the actor Michael Balfour (1918–1997) from 1950. He appeared in three films for Hammer: *A Case for PC 49* (1951), *Quatermass 2* (1957) and *The Steel Bayonet* (1957). **Hammer credits:** *Wings of Danger* (1952, as Receptionist)

## Studio Film Laboratories

Hammer occasionally used this utilities supplier to film title sequences for their productions, among them those for *Dracula* (1958), which were designed by Les Bowie (note that the credits misspell the surname of make-up artist Phil Leakey, here spelled Leaky). Other films with title sequences provided by the company include *Thunderbirds Are Go* (1966), *Up the Chastity Belt* (1971) and *Up the Front* (1972). They also handled the processing for the cartoon features *The Lion, the Witch and the Wardrobe* (1979, TVM) and *Heavy Metal* (1981).

In 1971, Hammer began negotiations with the company about a possible merger (both companies were in financial crisis at the time, and a merger would have given them some much needed strength, given the perilous state of the British film industry). Sir James Carreras was the first to open negotiations, but these eventually fell through when SFL found an answer to its problems elsewhere. Subsequently, Carreras began negotiations with Tigon Films about a possible merger with Hammer. However, he did this behind the back of his son Michael, who was by this time Hammer's managing director. When Michael discovered what had been going on, he in turn made plans to buy the company himself. He did this by re-opening talks with SFL, with whom he eventually agreed terms. However, before the contracts could be signed, Michael managed to broker a better deal with PFS (Pension Funds Securities), a subsidiary of ICI (Imperial Chemical Industries). Unfortunately, this last minute about-face incurred a five-figure financial penalty with SFL (who were no doubt grateful for the windfall). **Hammer credits include:** *Dracula* (1958 [uncredited])

## Studio Locations Limited

This British special effects house provided the effects for Hammer's *Frankenstein Must Be Destroyed* (1969). **Hammer credits:** *Frankenstein Must Be Destroyed* (1969)

## *The Studio That Dripped Blood*

GB, 1987, 50m, color, TV

Billed as a fortieth anniversary tribute, this nostalgic documentary (first broadcast on BBC2 at 9:30 p.m. on Friday 26 June 1987) features interviews with a number of Hammer stalwarts, among them Anthony Hinds, Jimmy Sangster, Michael Carreras (in an archive interview from 1974), Aida Young, James Bernard, Don Sharp, Ingrid Pitt, Peter Cushing and Christopher Lee, each of whom proffers anecdotes about their time with the company. There are also additional contributions from the likes of Martin Scorsese and David Pirie. The program also features a good many clips from such films as *The Curse of the Werewolf* (1961), *The Evil of Frankenstein* (1964), *The Nanny* (1965), *She* (1965), *Dracula—Prince of Darkness* (1966), *Rasputin—The Mad Monk* (1966), *Quatermass and the Pit* (1967) and *The Devil Rides Out* (1968), along with archive footage of Bray Studios in the fifties and director Terence Fisher working on the set of *Frankenstein Must Be Destroyed* (1969) with Peter Cushing and Veronica Carlson (this clip was taken from a 1969 TV piece filmed by the BBC ti-

tled *Made in Britain: Dracula and Frankenstein Make Money for England*). However, although the program has moments of undeniable interest for fans (including a narration by Mocata himself, Charles Gray), much more could and should have been made of the opportunity at hand, the fifty-minute running time not being merely long enough to do justice to the studio's back catalogue. Indeed, a series would surely have been a better format. Still, one is grateful to see the old guard reminiscing about the good old days.

Production company: BBC. Producers: Nick Jones, David Thompson. Editor: Paul Willey. Thanks: Len Harris, Christopher Wicking. Narrator: Charles Gray

## Sturgess, Mary

Sturgess worked as the assistant hair stylist (under A.G. Scott) on Hammer's *The Anniversary* (1968). Her own credits as a stylist include *African Gold* (1965), *Sweeney 2* (1978), *Sword of the Valiant* (1984) and *Drowning by Numbers* (1988), plus episodes of *The Avengers* (1961–1969, TV), *Van Der Valk* (1972–1977, TV) and *Dick Turpin* (1979–1982, TV). **Hammer credits:** *The Anniversary* (1968 [uncredited])

## Sturgess, Ray

This British cameraman (1910–2000) worked as the operator on Hammer's *The Vengeance of She* (1968). He went on to photograph the second unit for *Creatures the World Forgot* (1971). His early credits as a focus puller include *In Which We Serve* (1942) and *Thunder Rock* (1942), following which he graduated to operator on the likes of *The Gentle Sex* (1943), *Hamlet* (1948), *Seven Days to Noon* (1950), *Carlton-Browne of the F.O.* (1958), *The Vulture* (1967), *The Spaceman and King Arthur* (1979) and *Murder Elite* (1985), plus episodes of *Assignment Foreign Legion* (1956–1957, TV), *The Saint* (1962–1969, TV) and *The Protectors* (1972–1974, TV). He also provided additional photography for such films as *Tawny Pipit* (1944), *Josephine and Men* (1955) and *Guns in the Heather* (1969), and co-photographed *The Johnstown Monster* (1971). **Hammer credits:** *The Vengeance of She* (1968, camera operator), *Creatures the World Forgot* (1971, second unit cameraman)

## Style, Michael

In British television as a sports producer for ATV from 1958 following an eight-year period in Canada from 1950 where he worked for the Canadian Broadcasting Company in a variety of jobs (including holiday relief carpenter and, eventually, a producer of children's programs), this British producer (1933–1983) went on to oversee a number of television dramas, including a version of *Luther* (1968, TVM), which earned him a shared Emmy nomination. In the mid-sixties he formed a television facilities rental company called Intertel Studios, which became involved in the making of *The Madison Equation*, an episode of Hammer's *Journey to the Unknown* (1968, TV), on which his future partner Harry Fine worked as a production associate. In 1969 Style formed Fantale Films with Fine, which went on to make the "Karnstein trilogy" in conjunction with Hammer, all of which were

scripted by Tudor Gates. These were *The Vampire Lovers* (1970), for which Style also worked on the screenplay, *Lust for a Vampire* (1971) and *Twins of Evil* (1971). Fantale's other credits include *Fright* (1971), which Gates again wrote. Style's other credits as a producer include *Monique* (1970) and *The Sex Thief* (1973), the latter of which he produced with Gates (working under the name Teddy White).

Recalled Jimmy Sangster, who directed *Lust for a Vampire* for Style and Fine, "I didn't get on with them at all."[135] This was the result of Style having criticized Sangster in front of the crew. Said Sangster, "A producer is perfectly entitled to criticize the director. After all, he hired him and is responsible for paying his salary. But you don't do it in front of the entire crew on the first day of shooting. Also it helps if he knows what he's talking about, which Michael Style didn't. I don't think Harry Fine did either, but at least he stayed off set."[136]

Style's daughter was the casting director Emma Style (1962–2012). **Additional notes:** It is generally thought that Bernard Delfont came up with the title *Lust for a Vampire* after the film's original title, *To Love a Vampire*, was deemed insufficiently exploitable, though the film's writer Tudor Gates disputed this, claiming that the idea belonged to Style. **Hammer credits:** *The Madison Equation* (1968, TV [episode of *Journey to the Unknown*], facilities rental via Intertel Studios), *The Vampire Lovers* (1970, co-adaptation [uncredited], producer), *Lust for a Vampire* (1971, producer), *Twins of Evil* (1971, producer)

## Styles, Edwin

This British supporting actor (1899–1960) played the role of Dr. Roberts in the Hammer thriller *The Full Treatment* (1961). His other credits include *Hell Below* (1933), *Patricia Gets Her Man* (1937), *Derby Day* (1952), *Top Secret* (1952), *The Dam Busters* (1955) and *Up in the World* (1956), plus episodes of *Douglas Fairbanks, Jr. Presents* (1953–1957, TV) and *Enemy Enterprises* (1954–1957, TV). Also a variety artiste and a radio compere, he appeared as himself in the radio-variety musical *On the Air* (1934). **Hammer credits:** *The Full Treatment* (1961, as Dr. Roberts)

## Subotsky, Milton

This American writer and producer (1921–1991) is best remembered for forming Amicus Productions with his partner Max J. Rosenberg, with whom he made such genre pictures as *Dr. Terror's House of Horrors* (1965), *The Skull* (1965), *The House That Dripped Blood* (1970), *Asylum* (1972) and *Vault of Horror* (1973), although their first films under the name were the youth musicals *It's Trad, Dad!* (1962) and *Just for Fun* (1963). He began his career making documentaries and industrial films, which he wrote, directed and edited. Following experience as an editor with the U.S. Army's Signal Corps during World War II, Subotsky went on to become and ideas man for impresario Billy Rose, and then worked for a while as a sales manager for a distribution company. He began writing for television in 1949, meeting Rosenberg in 1953, with whom he went on to work on a children's series titled *Junior Science* (1954, TV), which he wrote and produced and which Rosenberg financed. They made their first film together in 1956. This was the low budget exploitation musical *Rock, Rock, Rock!*

It was also in 1956 that Subotsky and Rosenberg approached Eliot Hyman about a remake of *Frankenstein* (1931). Hyman had connections with Warner Bros. and suggested that a deal be struck with Hammer to make the film. However, Subotsky's resultant screenplay was deemed insufficiently original. There were also concerns that the script was too short (it was subsequently expanded). Worries that it would be too costly to shoot also raised alarms. "In the end, they decided our script was too expensive to make,"[137] revealed Subotsky. Consequently, Hyman removed the duo from the project, though they didn't go away empty-handed, receiving a $5,000 payoff and a 15 percent share of profits (after deductions) from Hyman's own half of the deal. Observed Subotsky of the finished film, "I didn't like [it] at all 'cause I don't like the Hammer type of film. First of all they talk too much and also they were too gruesome for me. Anyway we wound up only getting a payment and a percentage but that began Hammer as a horror film company."[138]

Subotsky's other credits include *The City of the Dead* (1960), *The Beast Must Die* (1974), *The Uncanny* (1977), *The Monster Club* (1980) and *Lawnmower Man* (1992). **Additional notes:** In the seventies, Subotsky and Rosenberg planned their own 3D remake of *Frankenstein*, but abandoned the project over fears of being sued by Hammer.

### Subsidiary Companies

Over the course of its life, Hammer either bought or created a number of subsidiary companies through which it financed its films and operated its facilities. These companies were also used as a means of protecting Hammer's profits from the taxman. A good many of them were, for some reason, named after birds, and for the record, they were as follows: Atalanta, Cadogan, Clarion, Cloister Productions, Concanen, Concanen Recordings, Cormorant, Falcon, Hammer Television, Hawfinch, Hotspur, Jackdaw, Key, Key Distributors, Kingfisher, Lawrie, Laverstock, Merlin, Saturn Films, Sparrow, Swallow, Travel and Woodpecker. Each has its own entry within the text.

### Sullivan, Eileen

Sullivan provided the wardrobe for the Charlie Drake comedy *Sands of the Desert* (1960). She also worked in the wardrobe department with Rosemary Burrows on Hammer's *Hands of the Ripper* (1971) and *Demons of the Mind* (1972). Her other credits, among them the first five Bond films, include *Small Hotel* (1957), *Village of the Damned* (1960), *Dr. No* (1962), *From Russia with Love* (1963), *Goldfinger* (1964), *Thunderball* (1965), *You Only Live Twice* (1967), *2001: A Space Odyssey* (1968), *The Slipper and the Rose* (1976), *The Monster Club* (1980) and *The Empire Strikes Back* (1980), plus episodes of *Space: 1999* (1975–1977, TV) and *Return of the Saint* (1978–1979, TV). **Hammer credits:** *Sands of the Desert* (1960),

*Hands of the Ripper* (1971), *Demons of the Mind* (1972)

### Sullivan, Hugh

Sullivan can be seen in a brief scene as a company director in *In Possession* (1984, TVM [episode of *Hammer House of Mystery and Suspense*]). His other credits include *Tell Me Lies* (1968), *Homer* (1970) and *Yellow Dog* (1973), plus episodes of *Paul Temple* (1969–1971, TV), *The Shadow of the Tower* (1972, TV), *The Brothers* (1972–1976, TV) and *Fairly Secret Army* (1984–1986, TV). **Hammer credits:** *In Possession* (1984, TVM [episode of *Hammer House of Mystery and Suspense*], as Director)

### Sulzmann, Stan

This British born musician and composer (1938–) played the tenor/soprano sax on the soundtrack for Hammer's *Dracula A.D. 1972* (1972). He toured for many years with his own orchestra, The Stan Sulzmann Big Band (one of several bands he has fronted). His albums include *Feudal Rabbits* (1991), *Birthdays, Birthdays* (2002) and *Jigsaw* (2004). He has played on the soundtracks for such films and TV series as *The Beiderbecke Affair* (1985, TV), *Midnight Movie* (1994, TVM) and *The Old Lady Who Walked into the Sea* (1991). **Hammer credits:** *Dracula A.D. 1972* (1972)

### Summerfield, Eleanor

On stage from 1939 and in films from 1947 with *Take My Life*, this RADA-trained British comedy character actress (1921–2001) tended to play chatterboxes and gossips. Her forty-plus films include *London Belongs to Me* (1948), *Mandy* (1952), *Dentist in the Chair* (1960), *Guns of Darkness* (1962), *Some Will, Some Won't* (1969) and *The Watcher in the Woods* (1981), although her best role was as a glamorous policewoman playing opposite Norman Wisdom in the comedy *On the Beat* (1962). She also worked for Hammer four times, beginning with *The Last Page* (1952) and ending with an amusing turn as Lady Strudwick in *Rude Awakening*, an episode of *Hammer House of Horror* (1980, TV). Her other TV credits include episodes of *London Playhouse* (1955, TV), *Haunted* (1967–1968, TV), *UFO* (1970–1971, TV), *Jake's Progress* (1995, TV) and *Midsomer Murders* (1997–, TV). From 1947 she was married to the actor Leonard Sachs (1909–1990), who appeared in two Hammer films: *Men of Sherwood Forest* (1954) and *Taste of Fear* (1961). Their son was the actor Robin Sachs (1951–2013) who appeared in Hammer's *Vampire Circus* (1972). **Hammer credits:** *The Last Page* (1952, as Vi), *Face the Music* (1954, as Barbara Quigley), *Murder by Proxy* (1955, as Maggie Doone), *Rude Awakening* (1980, TV [episode of *Hammer House of Horror*], as Lady Strudwick)

### Sumner, Geoffrey

Best known for playing Major Upshot-Bagley in the fifties sitcom *The Army Game* (1957–1961, TV), this British comedy character actor (1908–1989) specialized in upper crust types. He turned to acting following experience as a newsreel commentator, making his film debut in 1938 with *Premiere*. Over thirty further credits followed, among

them *Law and Disorder* (1940), *Mine Own Executioner* (1947), *Cul-de-Sac* (1966) and *Side by Side* (1975). He also appeared in three films for Hammer, among them *I Only Arsked!* (1958), the big screen version of *The Army Game*. His other small screen work includes episodes of *BBC Sunday-Night Theatre* (1950–1959, TV), *Dixon of Dock Green* (1955–1976, TV) and *Hadleigh* (1969–1976, TV). Sumner also produced a number of documentaries through his own company, among them *Jet Provost* (1958) and *Listen to Steel* (1963), both of which he commentated. He also continued to commentate for many other shorts, information films and newsreels. **Hammer credits:** *Five Days* (1954, as Chapter), *I Only Arsked!* (1958, as Major Upshot-Bagley), *That's Your Funeral* (1973, as Lord Lieutenant)

### Sumpter, Donald

This busy British actor (1943–) played Sparks in Hammer's *The Lost Continent* (1968). His other credits include *The Window Cleaner* (1968), in which he played the title role, *Night After Night After Night* (1970), *The Black Panther* (1977), in which he played killer Donald Neilson, *Meetings with Remarkable Men* (1979), *Curse of the Pink Panther* (1983), *Rosencrantz and Guildenstern Are Dead* (1990), *Richard III* (1995), *The Constant Gardener* (2005), *The Girl with the Dragon Tattoo* (2011), *Coalition* (2015, TVM), in which he played Paddy Ashdown, *In the Heart of the Sea* (2015) and *The Man Who Invented Christmas* (2017). He has also appeared in such series as *The First Churchills* (1969, TV), *Barlow at Large* (1971–1975, TV), *Bleak House* (1985, TV), *Our Friends in the North* (1996, TV), *The Last Detective* (2003–2007, TV), *Game of Thrones* (2011–2019, TV), *The Secret of Crickley Hall* (2012, TV), *The Mill* (2013, TV) and *Jekyll & Hyde* (2015, TV). **Hammer credits:** *The Lost Continent* (1968, as Sparks)

### Sun Safaris

This travel company handled the location management for Hammer's *Creatures the World Forgot* (1971). **Hammer credits:** *Creatures the World Forgot* (1971)

### Sunbronze Danny Boy

This memorably named Devon Rex cat (1969–?) appeared as Tod Browning's pet in Hammer's *Blood from the Mummy's Tomb* (1971). He was born at the Sunbronze cattery, hence the curious forename (consequently, his siblings included Sunbronze Holy Smoke, Sunbronze Red Dragon, Sunbronze My Way and Sunbronze Softly). For the record, his mother was Hesperian Butterfly Kiss and his father Hassan Truffles. **Hammer credits:** *Blood from the Mummy's Tomb* (1971, as Tod's cat)

### Surtees, Alan

This British supporting player (1924–2000) appears as a police sergeant in Hammer's *Frankenstein Must Be Destroyed* (1969). His other credits include *The Adding Machine* (1968), *Eye of the Needle* (1981) and *Erik the Viking* (1989), plus episodes of *Dixon of Dock Green* (1955–1976, TV), *The Professionals* (1977–1983, TV) and *Peak Practice*

(1993–2002, TV). **Hammer credits:** *Frankenstein Must Be Destroyed* (1969, as Sergeant)

## Suschitzky, Wolfgang

This Austrian cinematographer (1912–2016) came to Britain in 1934, and went on to become a documentary cameraman on such films as *Life Begins Again* (1942), *World of Plenty* (1943) and *Children of the City* (1944), prior to which he'd worked as an assistant photographer on *Animal Kingdom: Zoo Babies* (1938). Many training and public information films followed. He photographed his first feature, *No Resting Place*, in 1951. This led to work on such diverse films as *The Oracle* (1953), *The Bespoke Overcoat* (1955), *Ulysses* (1967), which earned him a BAFTA nomination, *Ring of Bright Water* (1969), *Get Carter* (1971), *Theatre of Blood* (1973), *The Chain* (1984) and *Riders of the Sea* (1987). He also photographed one film for Hammer, *The Vengeance of She* (1968), but it wasn't among his best work. His television credits include twenty-two episodes of *Worzel Gummidge* (1978–1981, TV), *Staying On* (1980, TVM), both of which earned him BAFTA nominations, and *Good and Bad at Games* (1983, TVM). His children are the cinematographer Peter Suschitzky (1941–) and the composer Misha Donat, and his grandson is the cinematographer Adam Suschitzky. **Hammer credits:** *The Vengeance of She* (1968)

## Sutherland, Donald

This internationally admired Canadian leading man (1935–) is best known for his dynamic performances in such diverse films as *M*A*S*H* (1970), *Klute* (1971), *Don't Look Now* (1973), *Ordinary People* (1980), *JFK* (1991) and *Six Degrees of Separation* (1994), as well as for playing Patrick "Tripp" Darling III in the TV series *Dirty Sexy Money* (2007–2009, TV), though he actually launched his film career in Britain, first appearing in *The World Ten Times Over* (1963), following which he cropped up in minor roles in a number of horror films, among them *Castle of the Living Dead* (1964), in which he played both a soldier and a witch, *Dr. Terror's House of Horrors* (1965) and Hammer's *Fanatic* (1965), in which he played the dim-witted Joseph. "He was absolutely gorgeous,"[139] remembered continuity girl Renee Glynne of Sutherland's time on the film. Even at this stage in his career, Sutherland was catching the eye of the critics, with *Variety* describing his performance as a "vivid portrayal." His many other credits include *The Dirty Dozen* (1967), *Billion Dollar Brain* (1967), in which he not only briefly appeared but also provided the voice of The Brain, *Kelly's Heroes* (1970), *The Day of the Locust* (1975), *1900* (1976), *Casanova* (1976), *Invasion of the Body Snatchers* (1978), *Eye of the Needle* (1981), *Backdraft* (1991), *Cold Mountain* (2003), *The Hunger Games* (2012) and its sequels, in which he plays President Snow, *The Best Offer* (2013) and *Ad Astra* (2019). Married three times, his wives include actresses Shirley Douglas (1934–), to whom he was married between 1966 and 1971, and Francine Racette (1947–), whom he married in 1990. His children (with Douglas) are actor Kiefer Sutherland (1966–) and post-production supervisor Rachel Sutherland (1966–). His other children (with Racette) are CAA representative Roeg Sutherland (1974–), actor Rossif Sutherland (1978–) and actor Angus Sutherland (1982–). His granddaughter is actress Sarah Sutherland (1988–). **Hammer credits:** *Fanatic* (1965, as Joseph)

## Sutton, Christopher

Sutton occasionally worked as an assistant director for Hammer in the fifties and early sixties, among his credits being *X—The Unknown* (1956). He later graduated to the post of production manager, and as such returned to Hammer for *Dracula Has Risen from the Grave* (1968) and several others. Of the Hammer product Sutton noted, "The budgets were not large. But all of the money went onto the screen. You saw it all on the screen, with good artists, good sets, good costumes."[140] His early credits as a third assistant include *The Clouded Yellow* (1951) and *The Story of Robin Hood and His Merrie Men* (1952), while his other work as a production manager includes *No Time for Tears* (1957), *The Plank* (1967), *Steptoe and Son* (1972), *I Don't Want to Be Born* (1975) and *The Thief of Baghdad* (1978, TVM). He also worked as a producer on *The Rise and Fall of Idi Amin* (1981), *Indian Summer* (1987) and *Playing Away* (1987). **Hammer credits:** *X—The Unknown* (1956, assistant director), *A Weekend with Lulu* (1961, assistant director), *Dracula Has Risen from the Grave* (1968, production manager), *Taste the Blood of Dracula* (1970, production manager), *When Dinosaurs Ruled the Earth* (1970, production manager), *Countess Dracula* (1971, production manager), *Hands of the Ripper* (1971, production manager)

## Sutton, Hazel

Sutton had a supporting role in Hammer's *Lady in the Fog* (1952). Some sources claim that she also appears in *Up the Creek* (1958). Other credits include *Room at the Top* (1958) and *The Flesh and the Fiends* (1960), plus an episode of *Dial 999* (1958–1959, TV) and *The Larkins* (1958–1964, TV). **Hammer credits:** *Lady in the Fog* (1952, unnamed role [uncredited]), *Up the Creek* (1958, unnamed role [unconfirmed, uncredited])

## Sutton, Kevin

Sutton worked as the sound mixer on Hammer's *When Dinosaurs Ruled the Earth* (1970) and the recordist on *Countess Dracula* (1970) and *Hands of the Ripper* (1971). He began his career in the late forties as a sound assistant on such films as *Maytime in Mayfair* (1949) and *Night and the City* (1950), following which he worked as an assistant boom operator on *Trouble in Store* (1953), *The Beachcomber* (1954) and *A French Mistress* (1960). He soon after became a recordist and (from the mid-sixties) mixer, working on such films as *The Sicilians* (1964), *The Frozen Dead* (1966), *Poor Cow* (1967), *Steptoe and Son* (1972) and *The Class of Miss MacMichael* (1978). **Hammer credits:** *When Dinosaurs Ruled the Earth* (1970, sound mixer), *Countess Dracula* (1971, sound), *Hands of the Ripper* (1971, sound)

## Sutton, Simon

Sutton can be seen in a minor role in *And the Wall Came Tumbling Down* (1984, TVM [episode of *Hammer House of Mystery and Suspense*]). His other TV credits include episodes of *Doctor Who* (1963–1989, TV), *BBC2 Playhouse* (1974–1982, TV) and *Chance in a Million* (1984–1986, TV). **Hammer credits:** *And the Wall Came Tumbling Down* (1984, TVM [episode of *Hammer House of Mystery and Suspense*], as Male nurse)

## Swain, Dick

Swain can be seen as one of the Rock people in Hammer's *Creatures the World Forgot* (1971). **Hammer credits:** *Creatures the World Forgot* (1971, as Rock man [uncredited])

## Swales, Robert

Swales can be seen in a minor supporting role in *The Corvini Inheritance* (1984, TVM [episode of *Hammer House of Mystery and Suspense*]). His other TV work includes episodes of *Within These Walls* (1974–1978, TV), *The Fourth Arm* (1983, TV), in which he played Captain Nigel "Mesange" Macauley, *Galloping Galaxies!* (1985–1986, TV), in which he played Captain Pettifer, and *Birds of a Feather* (1989–1998, TV). **Hammer credits:** *The Corvini Inheritance* (1984, TVM [episode of *Hammer House of Mystery and Suspense*], as Brophy)

## Swallow Productions, Ltd.

One of Hammer's many subsidiary companies, Swallow was originally created to help finance the Cold War thriller *Visa to Canton* (1960), and was used for a further two films. Based at Hammer House and registered at 235–241, Regent St., London, W1, its directors were James Carreras, Michael Carreras and Anthony Hinds. **Hammer credits:** *Visa to Canton* (1960), *The Damned* (1963), *The Curse of the Mummy's Tomb* (1964)

## Swann, Fred A.

Swann worked as the production manager on Hammer's *Up the Creek* (1958) and its sequel. His many other credits include *The Agitator* (1945), *Old Mother Riley at Home* (1945), *Naked Fury* (1959) and *She'll Have to Go* (1962). **Hammer credits:** *Up the Creek* (1958), *Further Up the Creek* (1958)

## Swanson, Maureen

In films from the early fifties with *Moulin Rouge* (1952), this British (Scottish) actress (1932–2011) appeared in both second features and more high profile fare before retiring in the early sixties after marrying William Humble David Ward, the Fourth Earl of Dudley in 1961. Other credits include *Knights of the Round Table* (1953), *A Town Like Alice* (1956), *The Spanish Gardener* (1956) and *The Malpas Mystery* (1963), plus episodes of *Douglas Fairbanks, Jr. Presents* (1953–1957, TV), *Saber of London* (1954–1960, TV) and *No Hiding Place* (1959–1967, TV). She also co-starred in the Hammer quickie *Third Party Risk* (1955). Her son is the cameraman, producer and director Leander Ward (1971–), and her nieces (by marriage) are the actresses Rachel Ward (1957–) and Tracy-Louise Ward (1958–). **Hammer credits:** *Third Party Risk* (1955, as Lolita)

## Swanwick, Peter

This British actor (1922–1968) can be seen as Smithers in Hammer's *Lady in the Fog* (1952). He can also be spotted as the "Teuton" in *The Devil*

*Rides Out* (1968). His many other credits include *The African Queen* (1951), *Betrayed* (1954), *Assignment Redhead* (1956), *The Two-Headed Spy* (1958), *Operation Amsterdam* (1958), *Circus of Horrors* (1960) and *The Looking Glass War* (1969), plus episodes of *Fabian of the Yard* (1954–1956, TV), *Stryker of the Yard* (1957, TV) and *The Prisoner* (1967–1968, TV), in which he played the Supervisor. **Hammer credits:** *Lady in the Fog* (1952, as Smithers), *The Devil Rides Out* (1968, as Teuton [uncredited])

### Swarbrick, James

Swarbrick worked as the stills photographer on the Hammer thriller *Maniac* (1963). His other credits include *Trent's Last Case* (1952), *Our Girl Friday* (1953), *Around the World in 80 Days* (1956) and *The Prince and the Showgirl* (1957). **Hammer credits:** *Maniac* (1963 [uncredited])

### Swart, Fred

Swart can be seen as a tribal chief in Hammer's *Creatures the World Forgot* (1971). His other credits include *Burning Rubber* (1981) and *Gor* (1988), on the latter of which he was also the location manager. He also worked as a location manager on *Zulu Dawn* (1979) and *I'm for the Hippopotamus* (1979). **Hammer credits:** *Creatures the World Forgot* (1971, as Chief)

### Sweden, Morris

This British actor (1911–1979) played supporting roles in the first two installments of Hammer's Dick Barton trilogy. His other credits include *Dreaming* (1945) and *The Fake* (1953), plus episodes of *Douglas Fairbanks, Jr. Presents* (1953–1957, TV), *O.S.S.* (1957–1958, TV) and *The Invisible Man* (1958–1960, TV). Also on stage. **Hammer credits:** *Dick Barton—Special Agent* (1948, as Regan [uncredited]), *Dick Barton Strikes Back* (1949, as Robert Creston)

### Sweeney, Bill (William/W.H.O. Sweeney)

Sweeney recorded the sound for the Hammer featurette *The Right Person* (1956) and the prison melodrama *Women Without Men* (1956). His other credits include *One Good Turn* (1936), *The Edge of the World* (1937), *Mine Own Executioner* (1947), *The Small Back Room* (1949) and *Your Witness* (1950). **Hammer credits:** *The Right Person* (1956), *Women Without Men* (1956)

### Sweeney, Maureen

Sweeney played one of Stan Butler's girlfriends in Hammer's *Holiday on the Buses* (1973). Her other credits include *The Squeeze* (1977) and *Sorted* (2000), plus episodes of *Romany Jones* (1972–1975, TV), *Within These Walls* (1974–1978, TV), *She's Out* (1995, TV) and *Believe Nothing* (2002, TV). **Hammer credits:** *Holiday on the Buses* (1973, as Mavis)

### The Sweet Smell of Death see Hammer House of Mystery and Suspense

### Swern, Cyril

One of the British film industry's busiest sound technicians, Swern (1921–1987, full name Isadore

Cyril Swern) recorded the sound for the Hammer thrillers *Maniac* (1963) and *Hysteria* (1965). His early credits as a boom operator, among them several for Ealing, include *Portrait from Life* (1948), *Good-Time Girl* (1948), *The Lavender Hill Mob* (1951), *The Man in the White Suit* (1951), *The Titfield Thunderbolt* (1953) and *The Night My Number Came Up* (1950). His other credits as a recordist include *The Long Arm* (1956), *The Day They Robbed the Bank of England* (1960), *Village of the Damned* (1960), *The Liquidator* (1965), *Alfred the Great* (1969), *Sitting Target* (1972), *Operation: Daybreak* (1975), *Nijinsky* (1980) and *Starship* (1985), plus episodes of *Espionage* (1963–1964, TV), *Danger Man* (1964–1966, TV) and *The Prisoner* (1967–1968, TV). **Hammer credits:** *Maniac* (1963), *Hysteria* (1965)

### Swift, Clive

Best known for playing the brow-beaten Richard Bucket in the sitcom *Keeping Up Appearances* (1990–1995, TV), this British character actor (1936–2019) has also appeared in such series as *War of the Roses* (1965, TV), *South Riding* (1974, TV), *The Barchester Chronicles* (1982, TV), *Born and Bred* (2002–2005, TV), in which he played the Reverend Brewer, *The Old Guys* (2009–2010, TV) and *Valentine's Kiss* (2015, TV). On stage from 1959, his film credits include *Catch Us if You Can* (1965), *Frenzy* (1972), *The National Health* (1973), *A Passage to India* (1984) and *Memed My Hawk* (1984). He can also be seen in Hammer's *Man at the Top* (1973) as Massey. He was married to the novelist Margaret Drabble (1939–) between 1960 and 1975. His son is the gardener and broadcaster Joe Swift (1965–), his brother was the actor David Swift (1931–2016) and his niece is the actress Julia Swift. **Hammer credits:** *Man at the Top* (1973, as Massey)

### Swires, Steve

As an entertainment journalist, Swires (1951–2006) contributed to such magazines as *Starlog* and *Fangoria*. He is also acknowledged in the credits of such TV and video documentaries as *Flesh and Blood—The Hammer Heritage of Horror* (1994, TV), *100 Years of Horror: Zombies* (1996, TV), *100 Years of Horror: Scream Queens* (1996, TV), *100 Years of Horror: Aliens* (1996, TV) and *Flesh for the Beast* (2003). **Hammer credits:** *Flesh and Blood—The Hammer Heritage of Horror* (1994, TV)

### Sword of Sherwood Forest

GB, 1960, 80m, Eastmancolor, MegaScope [2.35:1], RCA, cert U

The long-running television series *The Adventures of Robin Hood* (1955–1960, TV) had been the first commission for ITC (the Incorporated Television Program Co.), which had been formed in 1954 to help feed the new ITV (Independent Television) network with product. ITC became part of the ATV network (which broadcast the program) in 1957, and went from strength to strength making and broadcasting such popular fare as *William Tell* (1958–1959, TV), *The Saint* (1962–1969, TV) and *The Baron* (1966–1967, TV), all of which proved popular in America.

Following the conclusion of *The Adventures of Robin Hood*, which by 1960 had clocked up a

**Making an ass of themselves. Sarah Branch, Niall MacGinnis and friend are featured in this German lobby card for *Sword of Sherwood Forest* (1960) (Hammer/Yeoman/Columbia).**

healthy 144 episodes, its star Richard Greene saw the potential for a film version. Consequently, he formed a production company—Yeoman Films—with his TV producer Sidney Cole, and pitched the project to Hammer as a co-production. No stranger by this time to television and radio spin-offs, Hammer accepted the offer. The studio had of course already had a brush with the Robin Hood legend with *Men of Sherwood Forest* (1954) six years earlier, while the new film's nominated director Terence Fisher had actually helmed eleven episodes of the series' first season. Fisher had recently finished filming *The Brides of Dracula* (1960) for Hammer, and that film's star, Peter Cushing, was signed up to play the villainous Sheriff of Nottingham, whose plot to have the Archbishop of Canterbury assassinated propels the screenplay by Alan Hackney, who had also worked on the series. Consequently, with Greene and Cole onboard as producers (overseen by executive producer Michael Carreras), the project, originally known as *Death in Sherwood Forest*, was fast-tracked into production, going before the cameras on 23 May 1960.

Shot on location in Ireland and based at Ardmore Studios in County Wicklow, the film benefits enormously from Ken Hodges' MegaScope photography, which makes the most of the leafy green backdrops. By now well versed in the role of Robin Hood, Richard Greene invests the part with a certain degree of vigour, while Peter Cushing is as wily as to be expected as the devious Sheriff (the actor replaced Alan Wheatley, who had played the role on television). Also giving good value for money are Niall MacGinnis as Friar Tuck (replacing Alexander Gauge) and the always-reliable Nigel Green as Little John (previously played by Archie Duncan and Rufus Cruickshank on TV). Sarah Branch meanwhile adds a touch of glamor to the proceedings as Maid Marion (a role previously essayed by Bernadette O'Farrell and Patricia Driscoll in the TV series). Otherwise, the film is rather routinely directed by Fisher, who always seemed to work better within the confines of a studio. However, while his staging of the action is strictly of the Saturday matinee variety, and certainly in no way comparable to the classic Errol Flynn version of 1938, there is a sufficiency of hearty hands-on-hips jollity and swishing of arrows on the soundtrack to keep one watching.

Principal photography in Ireland concluded on 8 July, following which a few insert shots were made back at Bray on 17 August, by which time the post-production process was well underway. This included the recording of a musical prologue and epilogue to the film sung by Denis Lotis, who appears as Alan A'Dale in the film (reveals the opening verse: "Now Robin Hood's in Greenshire Wood, With all his outlaw band, He hunts the fallow deer for food, The Sheriff hunts a man").

The finished film—which was part-financed with a loan from the National Film Finance Corporation—was trade shown on 20 November 1960, following which it went on general release in the UK on the ABC circuit on 26 December care of Columbia on a double bill with the Hammer thriller *Visa to Canton* (1960). *Kinematograph*

*Weekly* described the film as being a "jolly, disarmingly naïve adventure comedy melodrama." However, while *Visa to Canton* secured a U.S. release the following February, *Sword of Sherwood Forest* had only limited engagements Stateside, sometimes playing with Hammer's *The Terror of the Tongs* (1961), which seems like an odd combo (some sources claim *Sword* played in Brooklyn on 18 January 1961). **Additional notes:** Hammer would return to the Robin Hood legend again with *A Challenge for Robin Hood* (1967) and the acquired *Wolfshead: The Legend of Robin Hood* (1969 [first shown 1973]).

Production companies: Hammer/Yeoman. Distributor: Columbia (UK [ABC circuit], U.S. [limited]). Producer: Richard Greene, Sidney Cole. Executive producer: Michael Carreras. Director: Terence Fisher. Screenplay: Alan Hackney. Cinematographer: Ken Hodges. Music: Alun Hoddinott. Songs: Stanley Black. Singer: Denis Lotis. Music director: John Hollingsworth. Supervising editor: James Needs. Editor: Lee Doig. Art director: John Stoll. Costumes: John McCorry, Rachel Austin. Make-up: Gerald Flecther. Hair: Hilda Fox. Sound: Harry Tate. Sound mixer: John W. Mitchell. Sound editor: Alban Streeter. Camera operator: Richard Bayley. Main title design: Chambers & Partners. Production managers: Don Weeks, Ronald Liles. Assistant director: Bob Porter. Casting: Stuart Lyons. Master of archery: Jack Cooper. Master of arms: Patrick Crean. Master of horse: Ivor Collin. Stunts: Paddy Ryan [uncredited], Nosher Powell [uncredited], Jack Cooper [uncredited]. Continuity: Pauline Wise, Dot Foreman. Processing: Pathé. **Cast:** Richard Greene (Robin Hood), Peter Cushing (Sheriff of Nottingham), Sarah Branch (Lady Marian Fitzwalter), Niall MacGinnis (Friar Tuck), Richard Pasco (Earl of Newark), Jack Gwillim (Hubert Walter, Archbishop of Canterbury), Denis Lotis (Alan A'Dale), Nigel Green (Little John), Vanda Godsell (Prioress), Charles Lamb (Old bowyer), Edwin Richfield (Sheriff's Lieutenant), Oliver Reed (Melton [uncredited]), Derren Nesbitt (Martin of Eastwood [uncredited]), Brian Rawlinson (First falconer [uncredited]), Patrick Crean (Lord Ollerton [uncredited]), Reginald Hearne (First man at arms [uncredited]), Adam Kean (Retford [uncredited]), Aiden Grennell (First veteran outlaw [uncredited]), Desmond Llewelyn (Wounded traveller [uncredited]), Maureen Halligan (Portress [uncredited]), John Franklyn (Archbishop's secretary [uncredited]), Anew McMaster (Judge [uncredited]), James Neylin (Roger [uncredited]), Barry de Boulay (Officer [uncredited]), John Hoey (Old Jack [uncredited]), Paddy Ryan (Merry man in tree [uncredited]). **DVD availability:** Sony (U.S. R1 NTSC, UK R2 PAL)

**A cheerful poster for *Sword of Sherwood Forest* (1960) (Hammer/Yeoman/Columbia).**

## Sydney, Derek

This British supporting actor (1920–2000) played Mamud in the Charlie Drake comedy *Sands of the Desert* (1960), which was partially financed by Hammer. His other credits include *Malaga* (1954), *The Treasure of San Teresa* (1959), *Make Mine Mink* (1960), *Carry On Spying* (1964) and *Carry On... Up the Khyber* (1968), plus episodes of *BBC Sunday-Night Theatre* (1950–1959, TV), *Sword of Freedom* (1957, TV), in which he played Captain Rodrigo, *The Saint* (1962–1969, TV) and *Timeslip* (1970–1971, TV). Also on stage. **Hammer credits:** *Sands of the Desert* (1960, as Mamud)

## Sykes, Peter

Working primarily in Britain, this Australian born director (1939–2006) began his career as an assistant for ATV in 1963. He broke into films as a production assistant on *Herostratus* (1967), following which he executive produced *Tell Me Lies* (1968). He made his directorial debut with the featurette *The Committee* (1968), which he also co-wrote. He followed this with *Venom* (1971), which led to Hammer's *Demons of the Mind* (1972). This was followed by the likes of *The House in Nightmare Park* (1973), plus a return to Hammer for their last genre feature for over thirty years, the undervalued *To the Devil a Daughter* (1976). His other credits include *Jesus* (1979) and the musical featurette *The Blues Band* (1981), which he also produced. Like *The Committee* and *Demons of the Mind*, the latter starred singer-turned-actor Paul Jones. Recalled Christopher Lee of working with Sykes on *To the Devil a Daughter* and its botched climax, "He was okay. Very enthusiastic, willing to listen, prepared. To his credit, he was out-voted on the ending, along with me. But he had to go along with his producers—the old story."[141] Note that Sykes can be seen in *To the Devil a Daughter* as a man at the airport. **Hammer credits:** *Demons of the Mind* (1972), *To the Devil a Daughter* (1976, director, also Man at airport [uncredited])

## Sykes, Prudence

Sykes worked as the casting director on several Hammer films in the late forties/early fifties. She was also involved in the pre-production of a handful of films for the company during this period, and even worked as a continuity girl on a couple of occasions. Her other credits as a continuity girl include *Eyes That Kill* (1947). **Hammer credits:** *Dick Barton Strikes Back* (1949, continuity), *The Adventures of PC 49—The Case of the Guardian Angel* (1949, pre-production assistant [uncredited]), *Celia* (1949, pre-production assistant [uncredited]), *Meet Simon Cherry* (1949, pre-production assistant [uncredited]), *The Man in Black* (1950, casting), *Room to Let* (1950, casting), *Someone at the Door* (1950, casting), *What the Butler Saw* (1950, casting), *The Black Widow* (1950, casting), *Dick Barton at Bay* (1950, continuity), *The Lady Craved Excitement* (1950, casting), *The Rossiter Case* (1951, casting), *To Have and to Hold* (1951, casting), *The Dark Light* (1951, casting)

## Sylvester, William

Best remembered for playing Dr. Heywood Floyd in *2001: A Space Odyssey* (1968), this American actor (1922–1995) came to Britain in 1946 to study drama. He made his film debut three years later in *Give Us This Day* (1949), and went on to make over thirty films, among them *They Were Not Divided* (1950), *High Tide at Noon* (1957), *Gorgo* (1960), *Devils of Darkness* (1964), *The Hand of Night* (1968) and—back in America—*Busting* (1973), *The Hindenberg* (1975), *Heaven Can Wait* (1978) and *First Family* (1980). Sylvester was also the male lead opposite Hollywood star Paulette Goddard in the Hammer thriller *The Stranger Came Home* (1954), in which he played amnesiac Philip Vickers. He also appeared in episodes of such series as *Ghost Squad* (1961–1964, TV), *San Francisco International Airport* (1970–1971, TV) and *Quincy M.E.* (1976–1983), following which he retired from the screen. The role of Dr. Heywood Floyd was subsequently played by Roy Scheider in *2010: Odyssey Two* (1984). Married twice, his wives were actresses Sheila Sweet (1927–2003), from 1949 to 1955, and Veronica Hurst (1931–, real name Patricia Veronica Wilmshurst), from 1955 to 1966. **Hammer credits:** *The Stranger Came Home* (1954, as Philip Vickers)

## Symonds, Dusty

Symonds worked as one of the location managers on Hammer's *The Lady Vanishes* (1979). His other credits as a unit/production/location manager include *Robin and Marian* (1976), *Superman* (1978), *Event Horizon* (1997), *Sleepy Hollow* (1999) and *The Phantom of the Opera* (2004). His other credits include work as an assistant director on *A Clockwork Orange* (1971), *Royal Flash* (1975), *Superman II* (1980), *Little Shop of Horrors* (1986) and *Catherine the Great* (2000, TVM). His occasional credits as a producer include *Finders Keepers* (1984), on which he was an associate producer, *The Witches* (1990), on which he was the line producer, and the television series *Dynotopia* (2002, TV), on which he was a producer, and which earned him a shared Emmy nomination. **Hammer credits:** *The Lady Vanishes* (1979)

## Syson, Michael

Syson (1924–1992) worked with Jimmy Sangster on the screenplay for *Fear in the Night* (1972), which Sangster had originally penned back in the early sixties (the project was first announced as *Brainstorm* in 1963 and later as *The Claw* in 1968). His other writing credits include *Conquista* (1971), which he also directed and produced, and *Eagle's Wing* (1979), for which he provided the story. He also produced *Sudden Summer* (1966) and *Bronco Bullfrog* (1970), the latter as associate producer. **Hammer credits:** *Fear in the Night* (1972)

## Szu, Shih

This Taiwanese actress (1953–, aka Si Si and Shy Si) played Mai Kwei, the spunky sister of the vampire hunting brothers in Hammer's *The Legend of the 7 Golden Vampires* (1974), a role subsequently played by Pik Sen Lim on Hammer's 1974 LP version of the story. Her many other credits include *Xue fu men* (1970), *Tao wang* (1975), *Jin jian can gu ling* (1979), *Wang pai da lao qian* (1981) and *Xie hua jie* (1983). **Hammer credits:** *The Legend of the 7 Golden Vampires* (1974, as Mai Kwei)

---

# T

## Tabitha

Tabitha was the cat provided and trained by John Holmes for Hammer's *The Shadow of the Cat* (1961). **Hammer credits:** *The Shadow of the Cat* (1961)

## Tabori, Paul

In Britain from 1937, this Hungarian screenwriter (1908–1974, real name Pal Tabori) worked as a contract writer for Alexander Korda in the forties following experience as a film critic for the *Daily Mail*. He later penned a number of second feature scripts for Hammer, among them *Mantrap* (1953), which he adapted from the Elleston Trevor novel *Queen in Danger*, and then co-wrote with director Terence Fisher. Scripts for *Four Sided Triangle* (1953), again with Fisher (which he this time adapted from the novel by William F. Temple), and *Spaceways* (1953), with Richard Landau, followed. Working solo, Tabori also provided an original screenplay for *Five Days* (1954). Tabori's other credits include *Valley of Eagles* (1951), *Alias John Preston* (1955), *The Malpas Mystery* (1960) and *Doomsday at Eleven* (1963), plus the Children's Film Foundation serial *Beware of the Dog* (1964). He also wrote episodes for such series as *Saber of London* (1954–1960, TV), *Sir Francis Drake* (1961–1962, TV) and *Richard the Lionheart* (1962–1963, TV). **Hammer credits:** *Mantrap* (1953, adaptation, co-screenplay), *Four Sided Triangle* (1953, adaptation, co-screenplay), *Spaceways* (1953, co-screenplay), *Five Days* (1954, screenplay)

## Tafler, Sydney

On stage from 1936 and in films from 1939 with *The Gang's All Here*, this British character actor (1916–1979) was best known for playing spivs and barrow boys. In films from 1941 with *Cottage to Let*, his credits include *I See a Dark Stranger* (1946), *It Always Rains on Sunday* (1947), *Passport to Pimlico* (1949), *Wide Boy* (1952), *Carve Her Name with Pride* (1958), *Carry On Regardless* (1961) and *The Spy Who Loved Me* (1977). He also appeared in a handful of Hammer films, beginning with *The Saint's Return* (1953) in which he played Lenar. Tafler was married to the actress Joy Shelton (1922–2000) from 1944; she appeared in Hammer's *A Case for PC 49* (1949). Their children are the actors Jennifer Tafler (1945–) and Jonathan Tafler. Tafler's sister was the actress and model Hylda Tafler (?–2005, aka Hylda Lawrence, married name Hylda Gilbert) and his brother-in-law the director Lewis Gilbert (1920–2018), in several of whose films he appeared. His sister was actress Sheila Aza (1924–2006, real name Sheila June Tafler). **Hammer credits:** *The Saint's Return* (1953, as Max Lennar), *The Glass Cage* (1955, as Rorke), *A Weekend with Lulu* (1961, as Stationmaster)

## Tait, Kenneth McCallum

This British assistant art director (1915–1985, sometimes credited as K. McCallum Tait, Kenneth McCullum Tait and Kenneth Tait) has credits on such diverse films as *Uncle Silas* (1947), *Under Capricorn* (1949), *State Secret* (1950), *Innocents in Paris* (1952), *The Best Pair of Legs in the Business* (1972) and *The Legend of Hell House* (1973). He also worked for Hammer on two films: *One Million Years B.C.* (1966) and *Captain Kronos—Vampire Hunter* (1974), on both of which he assisted Kenneth Jones, with whom he had already worked as an associate art director on many episodes of *The Avengers* (1961–1969, TV), following which he graduated to fully-fledged art director on several episodes himself. His credits as a set dresser include *Shadow of the Eagle* (1950), *Theatre of Death* (1966) and *Carry On Girls* (1973). **Hammer credits:** *One Million Years B.C.* (1966), *Captain Kronos—Vampire Hunter* (1974)

## Takaki, Kenji

This Japanese actor (1894–1984, aka Kenji Takagi) appeared as a patrol guard in Hammer's *The Camp on Blood Island* (1958). Other credits include *A Town Like Alice* (1956), *55 Days at Peking* (1963), *A High Wind in Jamaica* (1965) and *The Last Grenade* (1970). His TV credits include episodes of *Champion House* (1967–1968, TV). **Hammer credits:** *The Camp on Blood Island* (1958, as Patrol [uncredited])

## Talbot, Ken (Kenneth)

This British cinematographer (1920–1993) photographed seven episodes of Hammer's *Journey to the Unknown* (1968, TV). Of these *The Indian Spirit Guide* appeared in the compendium film *Journey to Midnight* (1968, TVM), *The Last Visitor* appeared in the compendium film *Journey to the Unknown* (1969, TVM), *The New People* appeared in the compendium film *Journey into Darkness* (1968, TVM), while both *The Killing Bottle* and *Do Me a Favor and Kill Me* appeared in the compendium film *Journey to Murder* (1972, TVM). Talbot then went on to photograph *Countess Dracula* (1971) and *Hands of the Ripper* (1971) for Hammer, both of which were helmed by Peter Sasdy, who had also directed *The New People* and *Girl of My Dreams*, and for whom he would also photograph *Nothing but the Night* (1972), *Doomwatch* (1972) and *I Don't Want to Be Born* (1975). Talbot's other credits include *Old Mother Riley, Headmistress* (1950), *Double Cross* (1956), *The Girl Hunters* (1963), *Born Free* (1966), *Battle Beneath the Earth* (1967), *Maroc 7* (1967), *Hammerhead* (1968) and *Underground* (1970), plus episodes of *Douglas Fairbanks, Jr. Presents* (1953–1957, TV), *The New Adventures of Charlie Chan* (1957–1958, TV) and *Tarzan* (1966–1968, TV). He also co-wrote the screenplay for *Depth Charge* (1960) with the film's director Jeremy Summers (he also photographed the film and worked as its associate producer). His earlier credits as a camera operator include *Things Happen at Night* (1947), *The Monkey's Paw* (1948) and *Penny Points to Paradise* (1951). **Hammer credits:** *The Killing Bottle* (1968, TV [episode of *Journey to the Unknown*]), *The Indian Spirit Guide* (1968, TV [episode of *Journey to the Unknown*]), *The Last Visitor* (1968, TV [episode of *Journey to the Unknown*]), *The New People* (1968, TV [episode of *Journey to the Unknown*]), *Do Me a Favor and Kill Me* (1968, TV [episode of *Journey to the Unknown*]), *Girl of My Dreams* (1968, TV [episode of *Journey to the Unknown*]), *The Beckoning Fair One* (1968, TV [episode of *Journey to the Unknown*]), *Journey into Darkness* (1968, TVM), *Journey to Midnight* (1968, TVM), *Journey to the Unknown* (1969, TVM), *Countess Dracula* (1971), *Hands of the Ripper* (1971), *Journey to Murder* (1972, TVM)

## Tales of Frankenstein

U.S., 1958, 26m, bw, Westrex, TV

In 1957, Columbia agreed to help finance Hammer's brutal Japanese POW drama *The Camp on Blood Island* (1958). This was originally to have been part-financed by the American producer Eliot Hyman, who backed out at the last moment. Ironically, the film proved to be a major commercial success and led to further ties with the American studio—ostensibly a three year, nine picture deal, with *The Snorkel* (1958) and *The Revenge of Frankenstein* (1958) first out of the slips, both of which Columbia released in addition to providing funds for. Also part of this package was this proposed weekly half-hour television series based around the further exploits of Baron Frankenstein.

To this end, a pilot episode titled *The Face in the Tombstone Mirror* was made in Hollywood in February 1958 for Columbia's television arm, Screen Gems, at a cost of $80,000 (James Carreras baulked at this figure, claiming that the program could have been made at Bray under British quota for $45,000). Although the program was produced by Michael Carreras, Hammer in fact had very little to do with the project, given that none of the company's regular staff were employed behind the cameras, though it should be noted that the original pilot script for the series—*The Single-Minded Blackmailer*—was penned by Jimmy Sangster, but turned down by Columbia. Nor was Peter Cushing contracted to play the Baron. Instead, for a fee of £500, the role went to the German character actor Anton Diffring, soon to appear in Hammer's *The Man Who Could Cheat Death* (1959).

In fact, the production had something of a Teutonic flavor all round, given that the director, Curt Siodmak, and several of his colleagues also hailed from Germany. Siodmak, of course, had something of a pedigree when it came to horror, having penned the screenplays for *The Wolf Man* (1941) and *Son of Dracula* (1943), as well as helming *The Magnetic Monster* (1953). Unfortunately, the pilot was deemed of such low quality that it failed to make it to air save for a handful of late night spots, while the projected series was subsequently scrapped (six programs were originally planned; this number later grew to twenty-six, half of which were supposedly to have been shot in Britain in the summer of 1958, presumably at Bray).

In the pilot, which opens with a narration promising "a story so weird, so dark, so harrowing," the Baron is working on his latest experiment, but lacks a suitable brain with which to complete it satisfactorily. Says the Baron to his Creature, which he has had to subdue after it has gone on the rampage in his lab, "Your brain came from the skull of a murderer. It still wanted to kill. But with the right brain—the brain of an intelligent man, a good man…. But where to find it?" Enter a potential donor: one Max Halpert, a sculptor whose wife is keen to find a cure for the terminal illness from which he is suffering. Having made their way to the Baron's castle during a violent thunderstorm, Frankenstein professes that he is unable to help the couple, yet following Halpert's death, he determines to make use of the man's brain. To which end, having attended the sculptor's funeral, he pays the gravedigger to leave the grave open so that he can rob it under the cover of darkness. However, when Mrs. Halpert visits the cemetery with flowers the next day, not only does she find the grave still open, she discovers a locket that she had placed around her husband's neck on the earth beside it.

Having discovered what has been going on from the gravedigger, whom she finds drunk at the inn at which she is staying, Mrs. Halpert makes her way to the Baron's castle, where she finds that he has transplanted her husband's brain into the Creature. Recognizing his former wife, the Creature attempts to abduct her, and in so doing, catches sight of his hideous new self in a mirror, which sends him into a frenzy (though it should be noted that the mirror is in the Baron's hall, not in a tombstone, as per the show's title). Following a fight with Frankenstein, the Creature chases the Baron back to the graveyard, with Mrs. Halpert in hot pursuit. "Don't destroy everything now because of a hideous face and a grotesque body that aren't yours," she pleads. But the Creature doesn't heed her and hurls itself into Halpert's open grave. The episode concludes with the Baron's arrest for grave robbing as he attempts to recover the Creature from the earth. But as he exclaims, "There's always tomorrow."

Despite its undeservedly earned reputation, for a half-hour TV show, the black and white production is a reasonably extravagant affair, redolent in style to the later entries in the Universal film series rather than Hammer's more recent full-color reimagining (thus negating the point of the exercise somewhat). Carl Anderson's sets include Frankenstein's lab, his baronial hall and the village graveyard, all of which are quite lavish in scale (this is by no means a hole in the wall production). Given the time restraint, the story also races along, packing a fair degree of incident into its straightforward plot, which quickly moves from one occurrence to the next. In fact, given the brevity of the running time and the fact that the show was quickly banged out, it isn't too much of a stretch to imagine this as how Hammer's proposed big screen *Frankenstein* remake—originally intended as a black and white quota quickie based on a Milton Subotsky script—might have appeared, though had it done so, it's doubtful whether it would have been such a world-beating box office success resulting in a new and profitable future for the studio.

Owing to the brief running time, there is little scope for the actors to portray their roles with any degree of depth, though Anton Diffring is his usual, steely self as the Baron, while Helen Westcott provides a little humanity as Halpert's devoted wife Christine. Don Megowan's Creature/Monster is little more than an aggressive automaton, however, resorting to type at every moment possible (no retort stand or test tube is safe in his presence). Interestingly, Clay Campbell's make-up for the Creature, complete with its square-shaped forehead, closely resembles the classic Jack Pierce make-up from the Universal films, which is surprising, given that Hammer had to avoid any resemblance to it in *The Curse of Frankenstein* (1957) for fear of litigation. That said, the Creature is not referred to by name in the program, either as the Creature or the Monster.

Unfortunately, while undeniably watchable, the format for the series betrayed its inherent weakness, which would have resulted in a basic repetition of the same story each week. Consequently, plans to film a second episode titled *Frankenstein Meets Dr. Varno* (already scripted by Jerome Bixby) were quickly shelved, as were several synopses for further episodes provided by A.R. Rawlinson, Hugh Woodhouse, Edward Dryhurst, Peter Bryan, Cyril Kersh and Jimmy Sangster. Among them were stories revolving around hypnotism, voodoo and cryogenics (some sources claim that Sangster had also worked out a story arc for a total of three thirteen-episode series, to be narrated as flashbacks by the Baron's great-great grandson from notes discovered in his old laboratory[1]). Elements from Peter Bryan's hypnosis synopsis later resurfaced in Anthony Hind's screenplay for *The Evil of*

*Frankenstein* (1964), while elements of A.R. Rawlinson's cryogenics synopsis were featured in *Frankenstein Created Woman* (1967), again scripted by Anthony Hinds. The idea of the Creature recognizing his former wife would be echoed in Bert Batt's script for *Frankenstein Must Be Destroyed* (1969), albeit seemingly unintentionally this time.

Although Hammer had successfully broken into the American film market, in this instance they singularly failed to break into U.S. network television. Obviously scarred by the experience, it would be a decade before they tried again with the anthology series *Journey to the Unknown* (1968, TV), which was produced in association with ABC and Fox, and made in England. Commented Michael Carreras of the experience of making *Tales of Frankenstein*, "It was a total conceptual cock-up. They wanted to do a series nothing like our films—so why should we be involved? The pilot was a dismal failure."[2] **Additional notes:** *Tales of Frankenstein* was finally released on DVD in 2001. The opening narration montage for the program contains a clip from Universal's *Dracula* (1931) featuring the Count's three brides as they walk through the crypt. The narrator—a disembodied head in a crystal ball—is meanwhile lifted from the opening of Universal's *Inner Sanctum* series (1943–1946), hence the fact that the lip movements aren't in synch. The original talking head was played by David Hoffman, who is here dubbed by an uncredited actor. Finally, if the TV series had been a success, one wonders what impact this would have had on Hammer's theatrical cycle of Frankenstein films; as it was, the next of these didn't appear until 1964 in any case.

Production companies: Columbia/Screen Gems/Hammer. Producer: Michael Carreras. Director/associate producer/story: Curt Siodmak. Teleplay: Catherine Kuttner, Henry Kuttner (and Jerome Bixby [uncredited]). Cinematographer: Gert Andersen. Music: no credit given. Supervising editor: Richard Fantl. Editor: Tony DiMarco. Art director: Carl Anderson. Set decorator: James M. Crowe. Make-up: Clay Campbell. Hair: Helen Hunt. Assistant director: Floyd Joyer. Production assistant: Seymour Friedman. **Cast:** Anton Diffring (Baron Victor Von Frankenstein), Helen Westcott (Christine Halpert), Richard Bull (Max Halpert), Don Megowan (The Monster), Ludwig Stossel (Wilhelm), Raymond Greenleaf (Doctor), Peter Brocco (Gottfried), Sydney Mason (Police Chief [uncredited]), David Hoffman (Head in crystal ball [uncredited]). **DVD availability:** Image Entertainment (U.S. R1 NTSC); Alpha Video (U.S. R1 NTSC), double-billed with the Boris Karloff film *The Terror* (1963)

## Talfrey, Hira

This New Zealand born actress (1926–2011, real name Hira Makarini Tohi Tauwhere) played the role of Teresa in Hammer's *The Curse of the Werewolf* (1961). Her other credits include *Sky West and Crooked* (1965), *Witchfinder General* (1968) and *The Oblong Box* (1969), plus episodes of *International Detective* (1959–1961, TV), *Man of the World* (1962–1963, TV), *Jane Eyre* (1963, TV) and *The Runaway Summer* (1971, TV). **Hammer credits:** *The Curse of the Werewolf* (1961, as Teresa)

## Tamara, Princess

This exotic dancer appeared as a stripper in Hammer's big screen version of *Love Thy Neighbour* (1973), in which she is announced as, "Swinging Susie, the girl with the syncopated Bristols." **Hammer credits:** *Love Thy Neighbour* (1973, as Susie)

## Tandy, Donald

This British supporting actor (1918–2014) played a plainclothes policeman in Hammer's *The Two Faces of Dr. Jekyll* (1960). His other credits include *Chance of a Lifetime* (1950), *Crossroads to Crime* (1960), *The Wrong Box* (1966), *11 Harrowhouse* (1974) and *Twenty-One* (1991), plus episodes of *Man from Interpol* (1960–1961, TV), *UFO* (1970–1971, TV), *Escape* (1980, TV) and *EastEnders* (1985–, TV). He was married to actress Diana Buckland (1922–) from 1947. **Hammer credits:** *The Two Faces of Dr. Jekyll* (1960, as Plainclothes policeman [uncredited])

## Tandy, Gareth

British child actor Tandy (1949–) played Tommy in the Hammer thriller *Cash on Demand* (1961). His other credits include *The Secret Tent* (1956), *The Door in the Wall* (1956) and *The Rescue Squad* (1963), plus episodes of *Danger Man* (1960–1962, TV), *Oliver Twist* (1962, TV) and *Dr. Finlay's Casebook* (1962–1971, TV). He went on to become an assistant director, beginning as a third assistant on *Digby: The Biggest Dog in the World* (1973), graduating to second assistant on *The Ritz* (1976) and to first assistant on *Saturn 3* (1980), *Superman II* (1980), *Carry On Columbus* (1992), *The Borrowers* (1997), *Nanny McPhee* (2005), *The Escort* (2008), *Jadoo* (2013) and *Urban Hymn* (2015). He has also worked in this capacity on episodes of such series as *Jeeves and Wooster* (1990–1993, TV), *The Young Indiana Jones Chronicles* (1992–1993, TV) and *Primeval* (2007–2011, TV), and on the second units of such films as *Who Framed Roger Rabbit* (1988), *Indiana Jones and the Last Crusade* (1989), *The Bourne Identity* (2002) and *Charlie and the Chocolate Factory* (2005). His aunt was the actress Jessica Tandy (1909–1994). His wife is the production accountant/financial controller Michelle Tandy (maiden name Michelle Ford), whom he married in 1979. **Hammer credits:** *Cash on Demand* (1961, as Tommy)

## Tanner, Nicholas

Born in India (1901–?) Tanner can be seen as a Commissionaire in the Hammer comedy *The Ugly Duckling* (1959). His other credits include *The Constant Husband* (1955), *One Way Out* (1955) and *The Trunk* (1960), plus episodes of *Fabian of the Yard* (1954–1956, TV) and *Dial 999* (1958–1959, TV). **Hammer credits:** *The Ugly Duckling* (1959, as Commissionaire)

## Tapley, Colin

In films in both Britain and America, this New Zealand born character actor (1907–1995) appeared in a wide variety of productions, beginning with a part in *Search for Beauty* (1934), a role he won following a Paramount talent contest in 1933. He went on to appear in over fifty films, among them *The Black Room* (1935), *Lives of a Bengal Lancer* (1935), *Becky Sharp* (1935), *North West Mounted Police* (1940), *Samson and Delilah* (1949), *The Dam Busters* (1954), *Blood of the Vampire* (1958), *Strongroom* (1961) and *Fraulein Doktor* (1968). He also represented the law in two Hammer crime dramas: *Cloudburst* (1951) and *Wings of Danger* (1952). He can also be seen in *Paranoiac* (1963) as the vicar. Also busy in television, he was best known for playing Inspector Parker in seventy-two episodes of *Saber of London* (1954–1960, TV). He also guested in such series as *White Hunter* (1957–1958, TV), *Man from Interpol* (1960–1961, TV) and *The Cheaters* (1960–1962, TV). Before his first sojourn in Hollywood in 1933, he spent some time in Britain (from 1930), during which period he joined the RAF. **Hammer credits:** *Cloudburst* (1951, as Inspector Davis), *Wings of Danger* (1952, as Inspector Maxwell), *Paranoiac* (1963, as Vicar [uncredited])

## Tappenden, David

Tappenden worked as the sound camera operator on Hammer's *Scars of Dracula* (1970). **Hammer credits:** *Scars of Dracula* (1970 [uncredited])

## Taste of Fear

GB, 1961, 82m, bw, RCA, widescreen [1.85:1], cert X

Although Hammer had frequently dabbled in the thriller genre, particularly during their second feature days, *Taste of Fear* came to be recognized as the launching pad for what were dubbed by James Carreras as their "mini Hitchcocks" of the sixties. In truth, this twist-packed piece has more in common with Henri-Georges Clouzots' *Les diaboliques* (1954) than it does with Hitchcock's *Psycho* (1960), despite a handful of shocks in the style of the latter. Intriguingly, *Les diaboliques* had gone out in the UK on a double bill with Hammer's *X— The Unknown* (1956), which had been scripted by none other than Jimmy Sangster, who was also responsible for the all-important corkscrew plot of *Taste of Fear*. Yet as the writer later revealed, the film, which was initially titled *See No Evil* and then *Hell Hath No Fury*, was not originally intended as a Hammer production and almost went unmade.

Having grown tired of penning scripts for science fiction and horror films (of which he'd also written a number for other companies, among them Tempean and Berman & Baker), Sangster decided to turn his hand to the psychological thriller instead. Hoping to interest a top producer in the property, he wrote the script on spec between other assignments, and managed to get it to producer Sydney Box, who not only took the bait, but also signed him to a three-picture deal as a writer-producer. Ralph Thomas was set to direct the project and Box's sister Betty was onboard as a line producer (she was best known for producing the popular *Doctor* comedies [1954–1970]). Unfortunately, Sydney Box suffered a heart scare not long after and decided to quit the film business altogether. Consequently, all of his properties were passed on to his brother-in-law, *Carry On* producer Peter Rogers, who was married to Betty Box.

Rogers' own schedule was much too busy to include *Taste of Fear*, and so Sangster bought the property back, after which he tried to tempt Berman & Baker with it. However, when they balked at his request to also produce the film, he finally admitted defeat and offered it to his old friend Michael Carreras at Hammer. Impressed with what he read, Carreras offered the project to Columbia, who agreed to help finance the project as well as to Sangster's request to produce the film, their one proviso being that Michael Carreras would be on hand to oversee matters, which he was happy to do in his usual capacity as executive producer.

As it begins to unfold, *Taste of Fear* seems to follow the conventions of its genre fairly strictly. After a brief pre-credits sequence in which the body of a drowned girl is recovered from a lake in Switzerland, the action shifts to the South of France, where a crippled heiress—Penny Appleby—has gone to visit her estranged father, whom she hasn't seen for ten years. However, upon arriving at his cliff-top house, Penny is greeted by her stepmother Jane, whom she's never met, and from whom she learns that her father is away on urgent business. Over the days that follow, Penny comes to suspect that her father isn't actually away on business, but has been murdered by her stepmother and her friend, the sinister Dr. Pierre Gerrard, who is called in to tend to the girl after she apparently has a vision of her seemingly dead father in the summerhouse. Despite a phone call from her father the next day, the visions persist, along with other strange occurrences. Fearing that she is losing her sanity, Penny confides in the chauffeur, Bob, who not only believes her stories, but also agrees with her that something fishy seems to be going on (says Penny of her father's call, "I haven't talked to my father for nine years—it could have been anyone").

But everything is not what it seems, and the twists now come thick and fast, for it transpires (plot spoilers ahead) that it is actually Bob who is in cahoots with Jane and not the sinister doctor. Not only that, but Penny's father really *is* dead, and the duo have been using his body (which they've kept "fresh" at the bottom of the weed-strewn swimming pool) to try and drive Penny insane, so that Jane can take control of her inheritance. Having failed in this bid, Bob—pretending to have "discovered" the body in the pool—drives Penny to the police station to report the murder. On the way, however, they encounter Jane on the road. Stopping to speak to her Bob gets out of the car, which now begins to roll towards the edge of the cliff. Penny attempts to get out, but is unable to do so, and just before the vehicle takes the plunge, she sees her father's dead body slumped down in the front seat. Bob and Jane's plan seems to come off after all ("It worked, Bob!" exclaims Jane).

But Sangster isn't through with the twists yet, for Penny turns up at the house a few days later, much to the surprise of Jane, whose visiting solicitor spots her sitting in her wheelchair at the cliff-top end of the garden. Not only did the girl manage to escape from the back of the car, she is also now able to walk! But as Penny informs the now incredulous Jane, Penny isn't Penny at all, but her best friend Maggie Frencham. The *real* Penny committed suicide in Switzerland three weeks earlier. Not only this, but Penny's father *knew* about his daughter's death, but didn't tell Jane because, as he had already revealed in a letter to his daughter, which Maggie had also read, he was suspicious about his wife's behavior. Consequently, when another letter arrived for Penny from her father inviting her to the Riviera *after* her suicide, Maggie decided to impersonate her dead friend so as to find out what was going on, in which task she was aided and abetted by Mr. Appleby's longtime friend, Dr. Gerrard. Having relayed this information, Maggie exits to inform the police, leaving Jane to slump in shock into the wheelchair so as take it all in. At this point, Bob arrives on the scene and, mistaking Jane for "Penny" from behind, pushes his lover to her death over the cliff edge!

Filming on *Taste of Fear* began in the South of France on 24 October 1960. Following the completion of the location footage, which included scenes at Nice Airport, the Villa de la Garoupe and on the Corniche (previously used by Hitchcock in *To Catch a Thief* [1955]), the production moved to Elstree on 14 November, the stages at Bray already being full with the sets for *The Shadow of the Cat* (1961), which was being shot simultaneously (Bray was also recovering from a fire at the time, which further prevented *Taste of Fear* from taking space there).

To helm the film, Carreras and Sangster turned to the highly respected editor Seth Holt, who had cut such Ealing classics as *The Lavender Hill Mob* (1951) and *Mandy* (1952). Given Holt's additional experience as an associate producer and his recent turn to direction with the underworld thriller *Nowhere to Go* (1958), he seemed like the ideal candidate, especially when put in tandem with the veteran Ealing cinematographer Douglas Slocombe, who had lensed such favorites as *The Man in the White Suit* (1951) and *The Titfield Thunderbolt* (1953). The ideal team, they keep a firm hand on the convoluted plot, pacing the action so that the holes in the narrative don't become *too* apparent. Meanwhile, their decision to shoot the film in black and white, despite its glamorous Riviera backdrop, undoubtedly works in its favor, helping to heighten the tension during the many shadowy nighttime sequences, key among them the genuinely shocking scene in which "Penny" first discovers her father's glassy-eyed body in the summerhouse (this is possibly the most genuine jump-out-of-your-seat scene to be found in *any* Hammer film).

Holt was also blessed with the casting of the American actress Susan Strasberg in the leading role of Penny/Maggie. The daughter of acting guru Lee Strasberg, she cleverly manages to highlight Penny's vulnerability without over-sentimentalizing the role, retaining the character's sense of independence, despite her (albeit faked) disability ("Don't treat me as if I were a mental defective," she admonishes Jane and the doctor at one point, only to later confess to Bob that "Being physically dependent on other people doesn't exactly build up your confidence"). It was also something of a casting *coup* to get the leading British actress Ann Todd to play the seemingly pleasant stepmother. The former wife of director David Lean, for whom she had starred in three films, Todd's impeccable credentials brought kudos to the production, especially given that she had also previously worked with Hitchcock in Hollywood on *The Paradine Case* (1948). Meanwhile, her audience identification as a player of well-bred roles helps to gloss over the fact that she is actually the instigator of the murderous plot ("Did you expect me to be like the wicked stepmother in the fairy stories?" she asks Penny at one point, only to later live up to the image).

Less impressive is Ronald Lewis as Bob the chauffeur, his performance being somewhat bland, while Christopher Lee, obviously cast to make the doctor appear to be the true villain of the piece, doesn't quite convince thanks to his comical Clouseau-like French accent. Nevertheless, the four main players make a cohesive unit, and give the impression that they could easily have played the piece just as effectively as a four-hander on stage.

Elsewhere, Jimmy Sangster's dialogue cleverly gives several clues as to the plot's eventual outcome. "You must be dead," says Jane to Penny after her long journey. Of course, the real Penny actually *is* dead! Meanwhile, Dr. Gerrard reveals that he regards Penny's disability to be "hysterical paralysis," adding that "There are no reasons this person could not get out of her chair and walk," which proves to be equally true. Also note that when Penny gets up in the middle of the night to investigate a banging French window, which leads to the discovery of her father in the summerhouse, the action is cleverly staged so that it looks as if she is about to *climb* out of bed before remembering that she has to physically *pull* herself into her nearby wheelchair (a feat she obviously undertakes for the benefit of the *audience* at this stage, given that no one from the house is around to *see* her get out of bed). Indeed, when Jane enters Penny's bedroom in the morning, she is curious as to how the girl managed to get out of bed and to the chair where she is reading, to which comes the flat reply, "I crawled."

Meanwhile, Seth Holt manages to stage several startling scenes in addition to the discovery of Penny's dead father in the summerhouse, the best of them being the later discovery by Bob of the body in the swimming pool. Beautifully lit and shot by underwater cameramen Egil Woxholt and John Jordan, the sequence has a dreamy quality to it, thanks to the gently swaying weeds in the pool. Indeed, it recalls a very similar sequence in Charles Laughton's *Night of the Hunter* (1955), in which Shelley Winters' body is found in very similar circumstances. However, as superbly staged as the sequence is, it does reveal a major design flaw. As seen from above, the swimming pool looks astonishingly small—certainly no more than ten feet by twelve; more a hip bath than a swimming pool—yet once Bob is underwater, it seems to grow, Tardis-like, in size. So much so that it takes the chauffeur an inordinately long time to explore the lagoon-like depths and find the body, which surely would have been visible from the surface in any case.

Filming on *Taste of Fear* concluded on 7 December 1960, and during the post-production period, the film was scored by Clifton Parker, whose cleverly orchestrated music features a piano motif at key points, by way of reflecting the fact that Bob and Jane use taped piano music to make Penny think that she's going mad (naturally, the piano is discovered to be firmly locked during the following investigation).

At the same time, work began on the ad campaign, which in many ways reflected the promotional techniques used by Hitchcock for *Psycho*. For that film, the unprecedented step had been taken of preventing latecomers from entering the auditorium once the picture had started, thanks to Hitchcock's insistence that patrons see it "from the beginning—or not at all!" He also requested that audiences should not reveal the ending of the picture, on the proviso that "It's the only one we have." Similarly, for *Taste of Fear* (or *Scream of Fear* as it was known in America), patrons were handed special cards with which they pledged "not to reveal any of the plot or the unusual ending of this motion picture." The film's poster proved equally inventive, given that it featured a startling shot of Strasberg screaming her head off. Suitably impressed by this stark design, the MPAA International Film Relations Committee voted the poster the best of the year.

Released in the UK by British Lion Columbia on 4 April 1961, and in America by Columbia on 22 August, the film proved to be a major commercial success. It also generated plenty of positive reviews. Commented *The Times*, "It plays its particular brand of three-card trick with ingenuity and without scruple," to which Penelope Huston added, "All those creaking shutters, flickering candles, wavering shadows and pianos playing in empty rooms still yield a tiny *frisson*." Elsewhere, *Variety* found the film to be a "contrived but expertly executed mystery shocker," while *Cue* thought it to be "a taut, scary, well-acted little murder mystery."

Recalled Christopher Lee of his role as the red herring, "Although this wasn't a typical part for me in a Hammer picture—or a typical Hammer picture—it's one of my favorites. Perhaps for these reasons: I played a 'good guy' for once, but one that the audience doesn't initially trust, because, I'm afraid, *I* was playing him; Jimmy Sangster wrote a very clever script; and the film was beautifully directed by Seth Holt."[3] In fact Lee considers *Taste of Fear* to be "the best film that I was in that Hammer ever made. It had the best director, the best cast and the best story."[4] Said Jimmy Sangster of Christopher Lee's casting: "'Why Chris Lee?' people asked me when they heard. 'He's Dracula and the Mummy, the ultimate villain.' For me he wasn't the ultimate villain, he was the ultimate red herring. He loved the part too. I read somewhere that he considered it the best role he ever played in a Hammer film which even I have to admit is a rather strange choice. But who am I to argue with him?"[5] Meanwhile, of the film itself Sangster observed, "Even now, after 40 years, it holds up well. It is exciting, suspenseful, scary, and it has more twists than most other movies of its type. If that sounds like I'm blowing my own trumpet, I am. And why not? I have little enough to say about most of the movies I wrote and/or produced and/or directed and, for me, this one stands out."[6] **Additional notes:** While Jimmy Sangster had successfully launched himself as a producer and had also escaped being typecast as a writer of gothic horror with this film, he now found himself freshly typecast as a writer of psycho-thrillers, several more of which he would be requested to make during his tenure at Hammer, among them *Maniac* (1963), *Paranoiac* (1963), *Nightmare* (1964), *Crescendo* (1970) and *Fear in the Night* (1972). Christopher Lee had already played a character named Dr. Pierre Gerrard in Hammer's *The Man Who Could Cheat Death* (1959), which had also been scripted by Jimmy Sangster. While in Hollywood later in his career, Sangster penned a further number of psycho-thrillers, among them *A Taste of Evil* (1971, TVM), an unofficial variation on *Taste of Fear* (with a good dash of *Nightmare*), albeit this time involving the rather more troubling plot element of child rape.

Production companies: Hammer/Falcon. Distributor: Columbia (UK, U.S.). Producer: Jimmy Sangster. Executive producer: Michael Carreras. Director: Seth Holt. Screenplay: Jimmy Sangster. Cinematographer: Douglas Slocombe. Music: Clifton Parker. Music director: John Hollingsworth. Supervising editor: James Needs. Editor: Eric Boyd-Perkins. Production design: Bernard Robinson. Art director: Thomas Goswell [uncredited]. Assistant art director: Bill Constable. Makeup: Basil Newall. Hair: Eileen bates. Costumes: Dora Lloyd. Special effects: Les Bowie. Special effects assistants: Ian Scoones [uncredited], Kit West [uncredited]. Sound: Leslie Hammond, Len Shilton, E. Mason. Sound editor: James Groom. Second unit photography: Len Harris [uncredited], Harry Oakes [uncredited]. Underwater photography: Egil Woxholt [uncredited], John Jordan [uncredited]. Assistant director: David Tomblin. Second assistant director: Terry Lens [uncredited]. Production manager: Bill Hill. Camera operator: Desmond Davis. Continuity: Pamela Mann. Casting: Stuart Lyons. Assistant to Michael Carreras: Ian Lewis [uncredited]. Stills: George Higgins [uncredited]. Publicity: Dennison Thornton [uncredited]. Unit publicist: Colin Reid [uncredited]. **Cast:** Susan Strasberg (Penny Appleby/Maggie Frencham), Ann Todd (Jane Appleby), Ronald Lewis (Bob), Christopher Lee (Dr. Pierre Gerrard), Leonard Sachs (Spratt), Fred Johnson (Father), John Serret (Inspector Legrand), Anne Blake (Marie), Richard Klee (Plainclothesman [uncredited]), Fred Rawlings (Plainclothesman [uncredited]), Rodney Burke (Policeman [uncredited]), Gordon Sterne (Policeman [uncredited]), Heinz Bernard (Plainclothesman [uncredited]), Brian Jackson (Plainclothesman [uncredited]), Frederick Schrecker (Plainclothesman [uncredited]), Bernard Brown (Gendarme [uncredited]), Madame Lobegue (Swiss Air Hostess [uncredited]). **DVD availability:** Sony (UK R2 PAL)

### Taste the Blood of Dracula

GB, 1970, 95m, Technicolor, widescreen [1.85:1], RCA, cert X

Given that Christopher Lee had stated that he

**Scream and scream again. Susan Strasberg exercises her vocal chords in this startling American poster for *Taste of Fear* (1961), which was released in the States as *Scream of Fear* (Hammer/Falcon/Columbia).**

would make no more Dracula films following the completion of *Dracula Has Risen from the Grave* (1968), the screenplay for the studio's fourth official Dracula production initially eschewed the character entirely (though it should be noted that Anthony Hinds *had* already completed a script featuring the Count that, though initially discarded, was eventually used for the series' following episode, *Scars of Dracula* [1970]).

Consequently, like *The Brides of Dracula* (1960) and *The Kiss of the Vampire* (1963) before it, Anthony Hinds' new script featured one of the Count's disciples, a penniless and depraved young British aristo named Lord Courtley who, having met three Victorian gentlemen who are keen on experiencing the seamier pleasures of life, coerces them into buying the dead Count's artefacts (his cloak, clasp and ring, plus a phial of his dried blood) so as to perform the ultimate black mass ("Would you be willing to sell your souls to the Devil?" Courtley asks the three men, having accused them of becoming "bored to death" with everything their "narrow imaginations can suggest").

Unfortunately, the ceremony does not go according to plan. Having added his own blood to that of the Count's, Courtley drinks the concoction, only to collapse on the floor of the derelict church in which the Satanic rite is being carried out. Fearing for their own lives, the three gentlemen leave Courtley for dead and return to their respective homes. However, having ingested Dracula's blood, Courtley finds himself transformed into a vampire, and thus vows vengeance on the men and their families.

Although the film had been scripted as a non–Dracula *Dracula*, James Carreras had by no means given up on trying to persuade Christopher Lee—who was also a personal friend—to return to the franchise, if only for the sake of the studio and the jobs his absence might subsequently endanger (Warner Bros. had threatened to cancel their financial involvement in the project if Lee was not a part of the package). Using a mixture of diplomacy and blackmail, Carreras finally persuaded the star to don the fangs, cape and red contact lenses again, but the actor was far from impressed with the hastily amended script, which now, somewhat ingeniously, has Courtley transform into Dracula himself after having been left for dead in the church by the three gentlemen ("They have destroyed my servant; they will *be* destroyed," the Count proclaims).

Lee needn't have been so concerned about his involvement in the enterprise, as the film, for which he was paid £8,000, remains one of the better entries in the declining series, thanks to its incident-packed narrative, which concentrates as much on the romantic entanglements of the offspring of the three gentlemen as it does on their own seedy exploits, all of which are briskly and imaginatively handled by the film's dynamic director Peter Sasdy. Fresh from television, where he had already helmed two episodes of *Journey to the Unknown* (1968, TV) for Hammer, *Taste the Blood of Dracula* marked Sasdy's feature debut, and he brought to it a knowing visual panache, and was certainly unafraid to

experiment with the camera equipment at his disposal (for example, during Courtley's transformation into Dracula, Sasdy pulse-zooms the camera into the Count's face, a gimmick that surely would have found no favor with Hammer's old guard directors).

In addition to Sasdy's brisk and visually inventive direction, the film also benefits from a particularly lush score by James Bernard (which includes organ work during the black mass), some inventive low budget art direction by Scott MacGregor (the fussy Victorian interiors of which recall the work of his predecessor, Bernard Robinson) and a stronger cast than usual. As William Hargood, Samuel Paxton and Jonathan Secker, the three corrupt gentlemen who together visit a brothel secreted behind a poor house on the last Sunday of each month on the pretext of doing "charity work" in the East End, the performances of Geoffrey Keen, Peter Sallis and John Carson effectively emphasize the double standards of each character. "You are a sexually mature young woman and I will not have you displaying yourself in that provocative manner," Hargood chastises his daughter after church, though he doesn't seem to have any qualms over consorting with a whore his daughter's age later on the same Sabbath (he even seems to take a lascivious pleasure in whipping his daughter after she has returned from a party he has forbidden her to attend).

As the corrupt Lord Courtley, Ralph Bates conveys a suitably supercilious air ("He's the very Devil himself," observes the proprietor of the whorehouse where Courtley meets the three men), while Linda Hayden's Alice Hargood—who becomes one of Dracula's acolytes—carefully balances her performance between virginal innocence and an emerging sexual allure. As for Christopher Lee's Dracula, he is very much on the sideline, influencing events rather than taking part in them (observed Christopher Lee: "Good cast, good production, good story—except that Dracula didn't really belong in it!"[7]). Consequently, his dialogue is pared to the bone ("The *first*," "The *second*," "The *third*," he somewhat pointlessly intones after he has been avenged against each of the men). Nevertheless, there are compensations to be found in the excellent supporting cast, among them Gwen Watford as Hargood's careworn wife Martha, the voluptuous Isla Blair as Alice's doomed friend Lucy, and Michael Ripper as the inept copper investigating the series of killings instigated by Dracula ("We can't do much for him out there, except take him out of the flower beds," he says of the late Hargood, who has been bludgeoned to death with a spade).

As for the screenplay itself, it offers a blend of tried and tested situations: Dracula's peripheral involvement in the action stems from *Dracula—Prince of Darkness* (1966), while the illicit meetings between Alice and her beau Paul recall the equally illicit meetings between Maria and Paul in *Dracula Has Risen from the Grave*. There are some new situations, though, among them the gentlemen's visit to the brothel (no doubt included to spice up the action) and the hypocritical stances they take on morality once back in the comfort of their homes. Invention wears a little thin with the eventual de-

mise of Dracula, however. Having climbed into the upper reaches of the church, from where he throws organ pipes at his pursuers, the Count is caught in the light of a cross in one of the stained glass windows, which causes him to fall onto the altar below, where he subsequently disintegrates.

Filming on *Taste the Blood of Dracula* began at Elstree on 27the October 1969 and ran until 5 December, with the chilly location work taking place in Black Park, Tyke's Water Lake and Highgate Cemetery (note the constant cold breath on the actors, who must have been frozen). Advertized with the tagline "Drink a pint of blood a day" in the UK (a send up of the Milk Marketing Board's then-familiar slogan of "Drinka pinta milka day"), the film was trade shown on 6 May 1970 and premiered with the studio's *Crescendo* (1970) at the New Victoria Cinema on 7 May. Both films then went on general release in the UK care of Warner Pathé on 7 June. The film's U.S. release, also on 7 June care of Warner Bros., was meanwhile accompanied by the risible Joan Crawford shocker *Trog* (1970). *Variety* praised *Taste* for its "Smart special effects, excellent Arthur Grant Technicolor lensing and liberal use of blood," before adding that, "Christopher Lee can now play Dracula in his sleep and looks occasionally as if he is doing so." Elsewhere, *Today's Cinema* found the film to be "not as eerie as previous episodes but packed with incident and dripping with rich red blood," while the *New York Post* noted that it was "directed and acted with the usual stylishness of Hammer Films." The *Sunday Express* described the film as "a better-than-average Hammer horror which addicts will enjoy with a giggle and a shiver." More amusingly, the *Daily Mirror* observed that, "Horror addicts are invited to *Taste the Blood of Dracula*. Wine connoisseurs will probably pronounce it 'a robust, eccentric red wine, not witty, but full of body; 1970 vintage but not suited to all tastes.'"

Of the film, Christopher Lee noted, "Hammer was making the Dracula pictures too closely together at this time; remember, six or seven years separated the first two, not six or seven months. No wonder audiences got tired of it all. I certainly did."[8] However, he did concede that, "It had the best cast but after an initial burst the story drooped."[9] Meanwhile, of the company's usual run in with the censors, producer Aida Young remembered, "John Trevelyan was very sympathetic toward Hammer. He liked Hammer because there was no pretension—I mean, if a film was called *Taste the Blood of Dracula* then you couldn't really pretend."[10] **Additional notes:** Les Bowie provided an uncredited matte painting of the mist-shrouded church for the film. The nudity in the brothel sequence was trimmed for the film's U.S. release. The climactic scene from *Dracula Has Risen from the Grave* is used in the prologue, though Christopher Lee's screams are dubbed by another actor for some reason. Keep an eye out for the poor back projection work in the opening carriage scene. Some sources claim that Vincent Price was attached to the picture at one point (presumably in the meaty role of Hargood). Elements from an unsolicited script submitted to Hammer titled *Dracula's Feast of Blood*, penned by Kevin Francis, were incorporated into the film's screenplay by hands other than Anthony Hinds', and for which Francis was subsequently compensated for by Hammer, who had considered but rejected his original efforts. Francis subsequently announced the title as a Tyburn project in 1974, but it failed to materialize. Recalled Francis of Hammer's plagiarism of his work, "They had to pay me a large sum of money before they could release *Taste the Blood of Dracula*."[11] Parts of Lord Courtley's invocation had already been used in Hammer's *The Vengeance of She* (1968), in which they were spoken by the character Men-Hari. The disintegration scene from *Taste* was re-used (albeit in reverse) for the resurrection scene in the following film, *Scars of Dracula* (1970). The end credits have the Snake girl down as having been played by Malaika Martin, though it would appear her name was actually Malaika Mandes.

Production companies: Hammer/Warner Bros./Seven Arts. Distributors: Warner Pathé Distributors (UK [ABC circuit]), Warner Bros. (U.S.). Producer: Aida Young. Director: Peter Sasdy. Screenplay: John Elder (Anthony Hinds). Cinematographer: Arthur Grant. Music: James Bernard. Music director: Philip Martell. Editor: Chris Barnes. Art director: Scott MacGregor. Costumes: Brian Owen-Smith. Special effects: Brian Johncock, Les Bowie [uncredited], Bob Archer [uncredited], Terry Schubert [uncredited], Mike Tilley [uncredited]. Make-up: Gerry Fletcher. Hair: Mary Bredin. Recording supervisor: Tony Lumkin. Sound: Ron Barron. Sound editor: Roy Hyde. Dubbing mixer: Dennis Whitlock. Boom operator: Keith Batten [uncredited]. Camera operator: Neil Binney [uncredited]. Focus puller: Bob Jordan [uncredited]. Production manager: Christopher Sutton. Construction manager: Arthur Banks. Assistant director: Derek Whitehurst. Second assistant director: Nick Granby [uncredited]. Third assistant director: Lindsey C. Vickers [uncredited]. Stunts: Peter Diamond [uncredited], Eddie Powell [uncredited], Peter Munt [uncredited]. Continuity: Geraldine Lawton. Poster: Tom Chantrell [uncredited]. **Cast:** Christopher Lee (Count Dracula), Linda Hayden (Alice Hargood), Ralph Bates (Lord Courtley), Anthony Corlan (Paul Paxton), John Carson (Jonathon Secker), Geoffrey Keen (William Hargood), Peter Sallis (Samuel Paxton), Isla Blair (Lucy Paxton), Roy Kinnear (Weller), Gwen Watford (Martha Hargood), Russell Hunter (Felix), Michael Ripper (Cob), Martin Jarvis (Jeremy Secker), Shirley Jaffe (Betty [the Hargoods' maid]), Keith Marsh (Father), Peter May (Son), Malaika Martin (Snake girl), Reginald Barratt (Vicar), Maddy Smith (Dolly), Lai Ling (Chinese girl), June Palmer (Redheaded prostitute [uncredited]), Amber Blare (Bordello girl [uncredited]), Vicky Gillespie (Bordello girl [uncredited]), Peter Brace (Christopher Lee's stunt double [uncredited]). **DVD availability:** Warner (U.S. R1 NTSC), as part of the *4 Film Favorites: Draculas* box set, which also includes *Dracula* (1958), *Dracula Has Risen from the Grave* (1968) and *Dracula A.D. 1972* (1972); Warner (U.S. R1 NTSC, UK R2 PAL), extras include a trailer only; Warner (U.S. R1 NTSC), as a double bill with *The Curse of Frankenstein* (1957). **Blu-ray availability:** Warner (A/1). **CD availability:** *The Hammer Film Music Collection: Volume One* (GDI Records), which contains the *Main Title*; *Taste the Blood of Dracula* (GDI Records), which contains the entire score; *Dracula: Classic Scores from Hammer Horror* (Silva Screen), which contains six newly recorded cues: *The Blood of Dracula*; *Romance: The Young Lovers/Shadow of the Tomb*; *Ride to the Ruined Church*; *Romance: At Dusk*; *Dracula Triumphant/Pursuit/The Death of Lucy* and *The Victory of Love*

### Tate, Harry

Tate recorded the sound for Hammer's Robin Hood picture *Sword of Sherwood Forest* (1960). His other credits include *The Sound Barrier* (1952), *The Red Beret* (1953), *A Kid for Two Farthings* (1955), *The Green Man* (1956) and *The Small World of Sammy Lee* (1963). **Hammer credits:** *Sword of Sherwood Forest* (1960)

### Taub, Angela

British born Taub (1934–, aka Angela Dunsford) worked as the production secretary on Hammer's *Quatermass 2* (1957). Her other credits in this capacity include episodes of *International Detective* (1959–1961, TV), while her work as a continuity girl takes in episodes of *Colonel Crock* (1955, TV) and *Much Winding Winter Sports* (1955, TV). **Hammer credits:** *Quatermass 2* (1957 [uncredited])

### Tavares, Arthur

Working as both an actor and an editor on both sides of the Atlantic, American born Tavares (1884–1954, aka Arturo Tavares) edited Hammer's musical drama *Song of Freedom* (1936), which proved to be his last editing credit. His other work as a cutter includes *Lilies of the Field* (1924), *Puppets* (1926), the Spanish language version of *The Cat and the Canary* (1930), the Spanish language version of *Dracula* (1931), *Strictly Dishonorable* (1931) and *Charing Cross Road* (1935). His credits as an actor include *Daughter of the Sheriff* (1912), *Hungry Eyes* (1918) and *Fortune's Mask* (1922). **Hammer credits:** *Song of Freedom* (1936)

### Taylor, Don

In films from 1943 with *The Human Comedy* following stage experience in college, this light American leading man (1920–1998) is perhaps best remembered for playing the groom in *Father of the Bride* (1951) and its sequel, *Father's Little Dividend* (1951). In the Army Air Force during World War II, where he continued to act in army productions, his other credits include *Girl Crazy* (1943), *Winged Victory* (1944), in which he played Danny "Pinkie" Scariano, the role he'd played in the original Army Air Force production, *Song of the Thin Man* (1947), *The Flying Leathernecks* (1951) and *The Bold and the Brave* (1957), while in 1954 he travelled to Britain to play a transatlantic Robin Hood in Hammer's *Men of Sherwood Forest* (1954). He also appeared in episodes of such series as *Robert Montgomery Presents* (1950–1957, TV), *Lux Video Theatre* (1950–1959, TV), *Schlitz Playhouse of Stars* (1951–1959, TV) and *Burke's Law* (1963–1966, TV).

In 1956, Taylor began directing with episodes of *Chevron Hall of Stars* (1956, TV), and went on to helm episodes of such series as *Bachelor Father* (1957–1962, TV), *Dr. Kildare* (1961–1966, TV), *Vacation Playhouse* (1963–1967, TV) and *Night Gallery* (1970–1973, TV). He began directing features with *Everything's Ducky* (1961) and went on to helm such high profile projects as *Escape from the Planet of the Apes* (1971), *Tom Sawyer* (1973), *The Island of Dr. Moreau* (1977), *Damien: Omen II* (1978) and *The Final Countdown* (1980). He also helmed such TV movies as *Drop-Out Father* (1982, TVM), *My Wicked, Wicked Ways* (1985, TVM), which he also co-wrote, *Classified Love* (1986, TVM), which he also produced, and *The Diamond Trap* (1988, TVM). Married twice, his first wife was actress Phyllis Avery (1922–2011), to whom he was married between 1944 and 1956. His second wife, whom he met while directing her in *The Crocodile Case*, a 1958 episode of *Alfred Hitchcock Presents* (1955–1962, TV), was actress Hazel Court (1926–2008), whom he married in 1963. She appeared in two Hammer films: *The Curse of Frankenstein* (1956) and *The Man Who Could Cheat Death* (1959). **Additional notes:** Taylor was originally scheduled to helm Hammer's *Visa to Canton* (1960), but pulled out of the project at the last minute, forcing Michael Carreras, who was producing, to also direct. However, Taylor did go on to star in *The Savage Guns* (1962), a western directed by Michael Carreras for Carreras's own company Capricorn Productions. This had originally been slated as a Hammer project to be titled *The Brutal Land*, but Carreras took the property with him when he temporarily left the studio in the early sixties (Taylor replaced Carreras's original choice, Kerwin Mathews, who would go on to star in *The Pirates of Blood River* [1962] for Hammer). **Hammer credits:** *Men of Sherwood Forest* (1954, as Robin Hood)

### Taylor, Elaine

Best remembered for playing the pretty but cauliflower-eared Shirley Blair in Hammer's *The Anniversary* (1968), this British actress (1943–) came in for a barrage of insults during the course of the film's action care of her fiancé's mother played by Bette Davis ("You're a bit of a cretin on the quiet, aren't you?" observes the Hollywood legend at one point). Her other credits include *Casino Royale* (1967), *Half a Sixpence* (1967), having already appeared in the stage production, *Diamonds for Breakfast* (1968), *Lock Up Your Daughters!* (1969) and *The Games* (1970), while her TV appearances include episodes of *The Benny Hill Show* (1955–1968, TV), *Strange Report* (1968–1970, TV) and *The Organization* (1972, TV), as well as such TV movies as *Sharing Richard* (1988, TVM) and *Till Death Us Do Part* (1992, TVM). Her husband is actor Christopher Plummer (1929–, full name Arthur Christopher Orme Plummer), whom she wed in 1970. **Hammer credits:** *The Anniversary* (1968, as Shirley Blair)

### Taylor, Ernest

Following work on such films as *Dreaming* (1944) and *Here Comes the Sun* (1945), this British make-up artist (1913–1987) went to work at Ealing, where he was the make-up man on such classics as *Pink String and Sealing Wax* (1945), *Nicholas Nickleby* (1947), *It Always Rains on Sunday* (1947), *Passport to Pimlico* (1949), *Kind Hearts and Coronets* (1949), *Whisky Galore!* (1949), *The Blue Lamp* (1949), *The Lavender Hill Mob* (1951), *The Man in the White Suit* (1951) and *Mandy* (1952). He later worked on seven episodes of Hammer's *Journey to the Unknown* (1968, TV). Of these, *Poor Butterfly* also appeared in the compendium film *Journey to Midnight* (1968, TVM), *Paper Dolls* appeared in the compendium film *Journey into Darkness* (1968, TVM) and *Matakitas Is Coming* appeared in the compendium film *Journey to the Unknown* (1969, TVM). He also worked on *Moon Zero Two* (1969) for Hammer, among his tasks here being to make up such characters as Yellow man, Green man and Red man. **Hammer credits:** *Eve* (1968, TV [episode of *Journey to the Unknown*]), *Poor Butterfly* (1968, TV [episode of *Journey to the Unknown*]), *Paper Dolls* (1968, TV [episode of *Journey to the Unknown*]), *Miss Belle* (1968, TV [episode of *Journey to the Unknown*]), *Jane Brown's Body* (1968, TV [episode of *Journey to the Unknown*]), *Matakitas Is Coming* (1968, TV [episode of *Journey to the Unknown*]), *Stranger in the Family* (1968, TV [episode of *Journey to the Unknown*]), *Journey into Darkness* (1968, TVM), *Journey to Midnight* (1968, TVM), *Journey to the Unknown* (1969, TVM), *Moon Zero Two* (1969)

### Taylor, Frank (French)

Taylor played Constable Williams in the Hammer shocker *X—The Unknown* (1956). His other credits include *The Black Rider* (1954) and *Geordie* (1955), plus an episode of *ITV Play of the Week* (1955–1968, TV). **Hammer credits:** *X—The Unknown* (1956, as Constable Williams [uncredited])

### Taylor, G.

Taylor worked as a stagehand on Hammer's *Blood from the Mummy's Tomb* (1971). **Hammer credits:** *Blood from the Mummy's Tomb* (1971 [uncredited])

### Taylor, Geoffrey

This British racing driver and engineer (1903–1966) can be seen as a driver in the Hammer second feature *Mask of Dust* (1954). He also doubled for the leading man Richard Conte. Taylor founded the Alta Car and Engineering Company in 1929, and their cars took place in many races, including Grand Prix events and the first ever Formula One race. **Hammer credits:** *Mask of Dust* (1954, as Driver, also Richard Conte's stunt double)

### Taylor, Gilbert

Following a lengthy apprenticeship that began in 1929 at Gainsborough, during which he gained experience as a camera assistant and operator on such films as *Third Time Lucky* (1930), *Rookery Nook* (1930), *Many Waters* (1931), *Number Seventeen* (1932), *Nell Gwyn* (1934), *The Lambeth Walk* (1940), *Brighton Rock* (1947) and *My Brother Jonathan* (1948), this British cinematographer (1914–2013) graduated to become one of the pre-eminent cameramen of his generation. He photographed his first film, *The Guinea Pig*, in 1948, following which he went on to work on such key

films as *Seven Days to Noon* (1950), *Ice Cold in Alex* (1958), *Dr. Strangelove* (1964), *A Hard Day's Night* (1964), *Repulsion* (1965), *Frenzy* (1972), *The Omen* (1976), *Star Wars* (1977), *Dracula* (1979) and *Flash Gordon* (1980), working with such top flight directors as Stanley Kubrick, Richard Lester, Roman Polanski, Alfred Hitchcock, Richard Donner and George Lucas. He also photographed a number of rather more routine productions in the fifties and sixties, among them the Charlie Drake vehicle *Sands of the Desert* (1960), which was partially financed by Hammer, who were also behind the psychological thriller *The Full Treatment* (1961), which features location work in the South of France. Taylor also photographed episodes of *The Avengers* (1961–1969, TV), *The Baron* (1966–1967, TV), *Randall and Hopkirk (Deceased)* (1969–1971, TV) and *The Pathfinders* (1972–1973, TV). He also photographed the effects for *The Dam Busters* (1954), otherwise photographed by Erwin Hillier, directed one episode of *Department S* (1969–1970, TV), and provided additional photography for *2001: A Space Odyssey* (1968) and *Damien: Omen II* (1978). His later credits include *The Bedroom Window* (1987), *Voyage of the Rock Aliens* (1987) and *Don't Get Me Started* (1994), plus various commercials. **Hammer credits:** *Sands of the Desert* (1960), *The Full Treatment* (1961)

### Taylor, Grant

This British actor (1917–1971, real name Ronald Grant Taylor) played the role of Sergeant Ellis in Hammer's *Quatermass and the Pit* (1967). His other credits include *The Siege of Pinchgut* (1959) and *Calamity the Cow* (1967), plus episodes of *The Saint* (1962–1969, TV), *The Champions* (1968–1969, TV) and *UFO* (1970–1971, TV). **Hammer credits:** *Quatermass and the Pit* (1967, as Sergeant Ellis)

### Taylor, Jack

Taylor can be seen as Brownie in Hammer's *The Stranger Came Home* (1954). He also had minor supporting roles in *I Only Arsked!* (1958) and *Paranoiac* (1963). His other credits include *Robin Hood and His Merrie Men* (1952), *The Trollenberg Terror* (1958), *Sentenced for Life* (1960), *Carry On Constable* (1960), *Carry On Regardless* (1961), *Shadow of Fear* (1963) and *Carry On Spying* (1964), plus episodes of *The Adventures of Robin Hood* (1955–1960, TV), *Man from Interpol* (1960–1961, TV) and *The Saint* (1962–1969, TV). **Hammer credits:** *The Stranger Came Home* (1954, as Brownie [uncredited]), *I Only Arsked!* (1958, unnamed role [uncredited]), *Paranoiac* (1963, as Sailor [uncredited])

### Taylor, Larry *see* Taylor, Laurie

### Taylor, Laurie

This prolific British actor (1918–2003, aka Larry Taylor and Laurence Taylor) played minor supporting roles in several of Hammer's late forties/early fifties productions and returned in the sixties for a bit part in *The Curse of the Mummy's Tomb* (1964). He began his film career in 1946 with a small role in *The Captive Heart*. He went on to appear in *Take a Powder* (1953), *Robbery Under Arms*

(1957), *Swiss Family Robinson* (1960), *Zulu* (1964), *Arabesque* (1966), *The Last Valley* (1970), *The Creeping Flesh* (1973), *Skeleton Coast* (1987) and *The Mangler* (1995), plus episodes of *Sword of Freedom* (1957, TV), *The Baron* (1966–1967, TV) and *The Adventurer* (1972–1973, TV). His son is stuntman Rocky Taylor (1945–, real name Laurie Taylor), who worked on several episodes of *Hammer House of Horror* (1980, TV). **Hammer credits:** *Dick Barton Strikes Back* (1949, as Nick), *Wings of Danger* (1952, as O'Gorman), *Lady in the Fog* (1952, unnamed role [uncredited]), *The Gambler and the Lady* (1953, as Shadow [uncredited]), *Five Days* (1954, as Bill [uncredited]), *Third Party Risk* (1955, as Spanish thug [uncredited]), *The Curse of the Mummy's Tomb* (1964, as Swordsman [uncredited])

### Taylor, Maxine

Taylor had a minor supporting role in Hammer's *The Dark Road* (1948). Her other credits include *Around the World in 80 Days* (1956), plus episodes of *Theatre 625* (1964–1968, TV) and *Nicholas Nickleby* (1968, TV). **Hammer credits:** *The Dark Road* (1948, unnamed role)

### Taylor, Robert Brooks

Taylor had a minor role in Hammer's *The Revenge of Frankenstein* (1958). **Hammer credits:** *The Revenge of Frankenstein* (1958, as Groom [uncredited])

### Taylor, Rocky

A stalwart of the Bond franchise, this British stuntman, stunt co-ordinator and bit player (1945–, real name Laurie Taylor) worked on various episodes of *Hammer House of Horror* (1980, TV). His many other credits include *Dr. No* (1962), *From Russia with Love* (1963), *Goldfinger* (1964), *The Dirty Dozen* (1967), *A Bridge Too Far* (1977), *The Wild Geese* (1978), *Never Say Never Again* (1983), *Blue Ice* (1992), *The World Is Not Enough* (1999), *The Mummy Returns* (2001), *Children of Men* (2006), *John Carter* (2012), *World War Z* (2013), *Avengers: Age of Ultron* (2015) and *Angel Has Fallen* (2019), plus episodes of *Brideshead Revisited* (1981, TV), *Pie in the Sky* (1994–1997, TV), *Waking the Dead* (2000–2009, TV), *Honest* (2008, TV) and *Game of Thrones* (2011–2019, TV). Following an accident on *Death Wish 3* (1985), in which he broke his back and was badly burned, he concentrates on working as a stunt arranger and co-ordinator, though he does still occasionally perform. His father was the actor Laurie Taylor (1918–2003, aka Larry Taylor and Laurie Taylor), who appeared in several films for Hammer, among them *Lady in the Fog* (1952) and *The Curse of the Mummy's Tomb* (1964). **Hammer credits:** *Hammer House of Horror* (1980, TV [uncredited])

### Taylor, Roy

Along with Josie McAvin, Taylor worked as one of the assistant art directors on Hammer's *Creatures the World Forgot* (1971). His other credits include *Mister Kingstreet's War* (1973). **Hammer credits:** *Creatures the World Forgot* (1971)

### Taylor, S.

Taylor was one of Shepperton's master painters, and as such worked on the Hammer war film

*Yesterday's Enemy* (1959), which was primarily shot at the studio because of overcrowding at Bray. **Hammer credits:** *Yesterday's Enemy* (1959 [uncredited])

### Taylor, Shaw

Known to TV audiences for hosting the long-running crime detection series *Police Five* (1962–1990, TV), this British presenter (1924–2015, real name Eric Taylor) also hosted such shows as *Tell the Truth* (1955–1990, TV), *Dott* (1958–1960, TV) and *Glamour* (1962–1973, TV). An occasional actor, he appeared in Hammer's *X—The Unknown* (1956) as a police radio operator. His other films include *The Carringford School Mystery* (1958), *Adventures of a Private Eye* (1977) and *The Medusa Touch* (1978). **Hammer credits:** *X—The Unknown* (1956, as Police radio operator [uncredited])

### Taylor, Siobhan

This British actress (1950–) appeared in Hammer's *The Damned* (1963) as Mary. Her other credits include *A Dog of Flanders* (1960), *The Young Detectives* (1963), *A Promise of Bed* (1969) and *Options* (1988), plus the TV series *Swallows and Amazons* (1963, TV), in which she played Susan Walker. **Hammer credits:** *The Damned* (1963, as Mary)

### Taylor, Totti Truman

This British actress (1915–1981) had a supporting role in the Hammer second feature *Delayed Flight* (1964). Her other credits include *The Woman in the Hall* (1947), *Not So Dusty* (1956), *Dr. Crippen* (1962), *Chitty Chitty Bang Bang* (1968) and *Confessions of a Window Cleaner* (1974), plus episodes of *Tales from Dickens* (1958–1959, TV), *Hancock's Half Hour* (1956–1960, TV) and *Doctor at Large* (1971, TV). Also on stage. **Hammer credits:** *Delayed Flight* (1964, as Doctor)

### Tayman, Robert

This British actor (1948–) is best known to Hammer fans for playing Count Mitterhaus in *Vampire Circus* (1972), although he actually made his debut with the company a few years earlier with a bit part in the space western *Moon Zero Two* (1969), in which he appears as a card player. His other credits include *Up Pompeii* (1971), *Up the Chastity Belt* (1971), *House of Whipcord* (1974), *The Internecine Project* (1974) and *The Stud* (1978), plus episodes of *Doctor in the House* (1969–1970, TV), *Spyder's Web* (1972, TV), *Fall of Eagles* (1974, TV) and *The Devil's Crown* (1978, TV). On stage from 1965 (including stints with The Royal Court, Peter Brook and The National Theater), he now teaches acting. Note that Tayman's performance in *Vampire Circus* was completely re-voiced by David de Keyser during post-production. Commented the film's composer, David Whitaker, of Tayman's performance in the film, "I thought the very effeminate vampire at the opening of the picture seemed extraordinarily camp at the time—to me it almost seemed like a send-up."[12] Recalled Tayman of his role, "It certainly wasn't the typical Christopher Lee–type thing…. One had to have this compelling, almost animal-like quality underneath…. And we managed to get that on a number of takes.

We managed to get the strength down."[13] **Hammer credits:** *Moon Zero Two* (1969, as Card player), *Vampire Circus* (1972, as Count Mitterhaus)

### Te Wiata, Inia

New Zealand born Te Wiata (1915–1971) can be seen playing Fahid in the Charlie Drake comedy *Sands of the Desert* (1960), which was partially financed by Hammer. A noted bass baritone opera singer, his other film credits include *The Seekers* (1954), *Pacific Destiny* (1956) and *In Search of the Castaways* (1961), plus episodes of *Saber of London* (1954–1960, TV), *The Saint* (1962–1969, TV) and *The Troubleshooters* (1965–1972, TV). He also guest starred on such shows as *Toast of the Town* (1948–1971, TV) and *The Worker* (1965–1970, TV), the latter again with Charlie Drake. His second wife (of two) was actress Beryl Te Wiata (1925–2017, real name Beryl Margaret Mcmillan), whom he married in 1959. **Hammer credits:** *Sands of the Desert* (1960, as Fahid)

### Technicolor

Formed as a corporation in 1915 by Herbert Kalmus, Daniel Comstock and Barton Prescott, this color process was originally developed as a two-strip format of red and green in 1916 and first used on *The Gulf Between* (1917). Over the years it has developed to take in a three-strip process (available from 1932) a photochemical process (available from 1935) and a revised photochemical process (available from 1997). Hammer began to use Technicolor in the late fifties following experience with Eastmancolor (the two companies linked up in 1951, with Eastmancolor—also known as WarnerColor, DeLuxe and Metrocolor—often processed by Technicolor). The first Hammer film to be shot in Technicolor was the documentary short *Operation Universe*, which was made in 1957, but not released until 1959. Consequently, *Dracula* (1958) stands as the first Hammer feature to be released (in the UK only) in the process, although it was filmed on Eastmancolor stock (the U.S. release was in WarnerColor). Likewise, *The Mummy* (1959) was shot on Eastmancolor stock, but processed by Technicolor. By the sixties, Technicolor had supplanted Eastmancolor as the color process of choice for Hammer—and for most of the film industry.

Note that though *Visa to Canton* (1960) was filmed in Technicolor, it was released in black and white in America. The same fate also befell *The Old Dark House* (1963), while *Fanatic* (1965) was released in Technicolor in the UK and Eastmancolor in the U.S. As for the Hammer films released in America by Twentieth Century–Fox from the mid-sixties

onwards, among them *Dracula—Prince of Darkness* (1966), *Frankenstein Created Woman* (1967) and *The Mummy's Shroud* (1967), these were all shot and released in Technicolor in the UK, but struck in DeLuxe in America, given Fox's close ties with DeLuxe.

Commented the trade paper *Motion Picture Exhibitor* in May 1958 of Hammer's imaginative use of the process in *Dracula*, "The use of Technicolor has transformed what could have been an ordinary horror film into one of vivid terror."

Other films shot or developed in the process include *Rio Rita* (1929), *Mystery of the Wax Museum* (1933), *Snow White and the Seven Dwarfs* (1937), *Gone with the Wind* (1939), *The Spanish Main* (1945), *Cinderella* (1950), *The Titfield Thunderbolt* (1953), *Solomon and Sheba* (1959), *The Deadly Bees* (1966), *Robin Hood* (1973), *Arthur* (1981), *The Cotton Club* (1984), *Batman* (1989), *Executive Decision* (1996), *Seabiscuit* (2003), *Black Swan* (2010) and *Captain America: Civil War* (2016). **Hammer credits:** *Operation Universe* (1957 [released 1959]), *Dracula* (1958 [processing, UK only]), *The Revenge of Frankenstein* (1958), *The Hound of the Baskervilles* (1959), *The Mummy* (1959 [processing only]), *The Man Who Could Cheat Death* (1959), *The Brides of Dracula* (1960), *Sands of the Desert* (1960), *The Two Faces of Dr. Jekyll* (1960), *Visa to Canton* (1960 [UK only]), *The Curse of the Were-*

This eye-catching poster for *The Hound of the Baskervilles* (1959) bigs up the fact that it was shot in Technicolor (Hammer/United Artists).

PETER CUSHING·CHRISTOPHER LEE·YVONNE FURNEAUX
*Directed by TERENCE FISHER*  *A HAMMER FILM PRODUCTION*
*Screenplay by JIMMY SANGSTER*  *DISTRIBUTED BY UNIVERSAL PICTURE*

*Left:* **Color was clearly a selling point in this simple but bold ad for** *The Mummy* **(1959). (Hammer/Rank/Universal International)** *Above:* **British poster for** *The Revenge of Frankenstein* **(1958), billed as being in Supernatural Technicolor (Hammer/Cadogan/ Columbia).**

wolf (1961), *The Phantom of the Opera* (1962, [UK processing only]), *Captain Clegg* (1962 [UK processing only]), *The Scarlet Blade* (1963), *The Old Dark House* (1963 [UK only]), *The Devil-Ship Pirates* (1964), *The Gorgon* (1964), *The Curse of the Mummy's Tomb* (1964), *Fanatic* (1965 [UK only]), *She* (1965), *The Brigand of Kandahar* (1965 [UK only]), *Dracula—Prince of Darkness* (1966 [UK only]), *The Plague of the Zombies* (1966 [UK only]), *Rasputin—The Mad Monk* (1966 [UK only]), *The Reptile* (1966 [UK only]), *The Witches* (1966, [UK only]), *One Million Years B.C.* (1966 [UK only]), *The Viking Queen* (1967 [UK only]), *Frankenstein Created Woman* (1967 [UK only]), *The Mummy's Shroud* (1967 [UK only]), *Quatermass and the Pit* (1967 [UK only]), *A Challenge for Robin Hood* (1967 [UK only]), *The Anniversary* (1968 [UK only]), *The Vengeance of She* (1968 [UK only]), *The Devil Rides Out* (1968 [UK only]), *Slave Girls* (1968 [UK only]), *The Lost Continent* (1968, [UK only]), *Dracula Has Risen from the Grave* (1968), *Frankenstein Must Be Destroyed* (1969), *Moon Zero Two* (1969), *Wolfshead: The Legend of Robin Hood* (1969 [released 1973]), *Crescendo* (1970), *Taste the Blood of Dracula* (1970), *When Dinosaurs Ruled the Earth* (1970), *Scars of Dracula* (1970), *The Horror of Frankenstein* (1970), *Lust for a Vampire* (1971), *Creatures the World Forgot* (1971), *On the Buses* (1971), *Hands of the Ripper* (1971), *Dr. Jekyll and Sister Hyde* (1971), *Blood from the Mummy's Tomb* (1971), *Fear in the Night* (1972), *Straight on Till Morning* (1972),

Mutiny on the Buses (1972), *Demons of the Mind* (1972), *Nearest and Dearest* (1973), *Love Thy Neighbour* (1973), *Man at the Top* (1973), *Holiday on the Buses* (1973), *The Satanic Rites of Dracula* (1974), *Frankenstein and the Monster from Hell* (1974), *Shatter* (1974), *Man About the House* (1974), *To the Devil a Daughter* (1976), *Let Me In* (2010)

### Techniscope

This widescreen process was used to film a couple of Hammer productions in the sixties, beginning with *The Curse of the Mummy's Tomb* (1964). Other films shot in the process include *The Ipcress File* (1965), *For a Few Dollars More* (1965), *Dr. Who and the Daleks* (1965), *Thunderbirds Are Go* (1966), *The Good, the Bad and the Ugly* (1966), *The Naked Runner* (1967), *Once Upon a Time in the West* (1968) and *A Fistful of Dynamite* (1971). **Hammer credits:** *The Curse of the Mummy's Tomb* (1964), *Dracula—Prince of Darkness* (1966)

### Ted Kavanagh Associated (Ltd.) *see* Kavanagh, Ted

### Tee, Elsa

This British actress (1917–2006) played the role of Victoria David in the Hammer featurette *Death in High Heels* (1947). Her other credits include *Heaven Is Round the Corner* (1944), *Twilight Hour* (1945), *Here Comes the Sun* (1946) and *School for Randle* (1949). **Hammer credits:** *Death in High Heels* (1947, as Victoria David)

### Telezynska, Isabella (Izabella)

This Polish actress (1928–2013, aka Iza Teller/ Isa Teller) can be seen as Margaret, the woman

whose demonic baby memorably claws its way from her belly in Hammer's *To the Devil a Daughter* (1976). Her other credits, among them several for director Ken Russell, include *The Debussy Film* (1965, TVM), *Always on Sunday* (1965, TVM), *Billion Dollar Brain* (1967), *Isadora* (1968), *The Music Lovers* (1970), *The Devils* (1971), *Ludwig* (1973), *Bestia* (1979), *Pandemonium* (1982) and *The Mother* (2003), plus episodes of *QB VII* (1974, TV), *Count Dracula* (1977, TV), *Randall and Hopkirk (Deceased)* (2000–2001, TV), *New Tricks* (2003–2015, TV) and *House of Saddam* (2008, TV). **Hammer credits:** *To the Devil a Daughter* (1976, as Margaret)

### Temple, William F.

This British novelist (1914–1989, aka Temple Williams) had his 1949 science fiction drama *Four Sided Triangle* adapted for the screen by Hammer as a second feature in 1953 (the novel originated as a short story from 1939). His other books include *The Dangerous Edge* (1951), *Martin Magnus, Planet Rover* (1954), *Martin Magnus on Mars* (1955), *Martin Magnus on Venus* (1956), *The Automated Goliath* (1961), *Shoot at the Moon* (1966) and *The Fleshpots of Sansato* (1968). He also penned a several short stories. **Hammer credits:** *Four Sided Triangle* (1953)

### Temple-Smith, John

Working as a producer from the early fifties following experience in the RAF and as a test pilot in Canada during the war, British born Temple-Smith (1923–2010) formed the production company Major Films, through which he made such low-budget films as *The Girl on the Pier* (1953), *Profile* (1954), *One Way Out* (1955), which he also wrote and which was shot at Bray, *Find the Lady* (1956),

*Account Rendered* (1957) and *The Big Chance* (1957). A frequent collaborator with the director Peter Graham Scott, the duo made the pirate film *Captain Clegg* (1962) as a co-production between Major and Hammer, Temple-Smith having bought the remake rights to *Dr. Syn* (1937), which was based upon the novels by Russell Thorndike. Temple-Smith later returned to Hammer to make the much-derided historical epic *The Viking Queen* (1966), which he produced and wrote the story for. This time Don Chaffey was in the director's chair. Remembered Temple-Smith of his two helmsmen, "Peter was a great director. He really gave it the artist's eye. He could be very cross at times, but the artists liked to work with him. He could get better performances out of them than they would have done otherwise. I worked with Don Chaffey on *The Viking Queen* and he had a good spatial and visual eye. He had been an art director. But he was never in empathy with his artists. He would just tell them what to do."[14] His other films include *The Island of Dr. Moreau* (1977). **Additional notes:** Temple-Smith also worked on a screenplay for *She* (1965) for Hammer in 1962/3;

however, following re-writes by Berkley Mather and the film's director Robert Day, this was rejected and replaced by a new adaptation by David T. Chantler. Temple-Smith was also briefly connected to *The Witches* (1966) as a producer in 1965, when the project was being touted to Universal. **Hammer credits:** *Captain Clegg* (1962, producer), *The Viking Queen* (1966, producer, story)

### Ten Seconds to Hell

GB, 1959, 94m, bw, widescreen [1.85:1], Klangfilm-Eurocord, cert A

Originally to have been titled *The Phoenix* after the 1955 Lawrence P. Bachmann novel upon which it is based (which had been acquired by Hammer in 1955), this story about six members of a German bomb disposal team who vie for the attentions of a French widow in 1945 Berlin was filmed by Hammer in that city's famous Ufa studios.

The film was a major undertaking by Hammer's usual standards, given that it was filmed entirely abroad, was helmed by a top American director, Robert Aldrich, and starred two major Hollywood names, Jeff Chandler and Jack Palance. Consequently, the film was launched as a co-production with Seven-Arts, an American company headed by producer Ray Stark, whose silent partner was none other than Eliot Hyman, who had already invested in a number of Hammer productions, among them *The Curse of Frankenstein* (1957).

Filming began in Berlin on 24 February 1958, and ran into trouble almost from the start, with Aldrich (used to producing his own films) taking full control of the production, which subsequently ran over schedule and, more importantly, over budget, much to the irritation of Michael Carreras, who found himself an outsider on his own film. Unfortunately, despite Aldrich's demands (which included re-writing the script and hiring his own production personnel), the film isn't any better for his total control over proceedings, being a slow-moving and ponderous affair, notwithstanding the potentially exciting subject matter of instant death amid the rubble ("Everyone makes mistakes—in this business you only make one," the men are warned by their commander, Major Haven). Indeed, from its droning opening narration, which introduces the men one by one, through to the climax of self-sacrifice (only one member of the team survives), the film is something of an endurance test.

Because of its failings, when United Artists released the film in the UK on 15 June 1959 (the U.S. release, also by UA, followed on 17 July), it failed to excite audiences, despite a strong poster campaign, the strap line for which read, "In ten seconds … thousands will be blown to hell!" The critics were similarly unimpressed, with *Variety* dismissing the film as being too "downbeat," despite the angst-ridden performances of its two square-jawed stars.

However, making the film did prove enjoyable for one member of the crew, the legendary production designer Ken Adam, who recalled, "It was an incredible experience. Berlin in 1958 was fantastic, because it was like an island in no-man's land. Everyone in Berlin wanted to have a good time. We were working at the Ufa Studios in Tempelhof, and because the Berlin Wall didn't exist, my laborers came from both the East and West. Half the studio workers commuted from the East. I was very lucky to find an old villa in the Ballenstedter Strasse near the Kurfursten Damm, and of course I gave big parties and we had a ball all the time!"[15] **Additional notes:** Advance publicity for the film (when the film was still titled *The Phoenix*) listed Anthony Nelson Keys as its associate producer. Bachmann's novel was re-printed by Fontana as a tie-in.

Production companies: Hammer/Seven Arts. Distributor: United Artists (UK, U.S.). Producer: Michael Carreras. Director: Robert Aldrich. Screenplay: Lawrence P. Bachmann, Robert Aldrich, Teddi Sherman, based on the novel *The Phoenix* by Lawrence P. Bachmann. Cinematographer: Ernest Laszlo. Music: Kenneth V. Jones. Music director: John Hollingsworth. Supervising editor: James Needs. Editor: Henry Richardson. Assistant editor: Chris Barnes [uncredited]. Post-synch assistants: Chris Greenham [uncredited], Rusty Coppleman [uncredited]. Production designer: Ken Adam. Costumes: Molly Arbuthnot. Camera operators: Len Harris, Herbert Geier. Focus puller: Harry Oakes [uncredited]. Assistant directors: Rene Dupont, Frank Winterstein. Sound: Heinz Garbowski. Sound editor: Roy Hyde. Production managers: Basil Keys, George Mohr. Continuity: Phyllis Crocker. **Cast:** Jeff Chandler (Karl Wirtz), Jack Palance (Eric Koertner), Martine Carol (Margot Hofer), Virginia Baker (Frau Bauer), Richard Wattis (Major Haven), Jimmy Goodwin (Globke), Dave Willock (Peter Tillig), Robert Cornthwaite (Hoeffler), Wes Addy (Sulke), Nancy Lee (Ruth Sulke [uncredited]), Charles Nolte (Doctor [uncredited]), Jim Hutton (Workman [uncredited]). **Blu-ray availability:** Kino Lorber (A/1)

### Teng, Te Hsiang

Teng (aka Chak Teung Dang and Teng Tak Tseung) had a minor role in Hammer's *The Legend of the 7 Golden Vampires* (1974). His other credits include *Shi san tai bao* (1970), *Dragon's Teeth* (1974), *Si qiu* (1976) and *Full Moon Scimitar* (1979), while his work as a stunt co-ordinator/action director includes *Snake Shadow Lama Fist* (1976), *Swift Sword* (1980), in which he also appeared, *Demon of the Lute* (1983) and *The Supreme Swordsman* (1984). **Hammer credits:** *The Legend of the 7 Golden Vampires* (1974, as Rickshaw man [uncredited])

Incendiary artwork for *Ten Seconds to Hell* (1959). Sadly, despite the talent involved, the film was more of a damp squib (Hammer/Seven Arts/United Artists).

*Tennis Court* see *Hammer House of Mystery and Suspense*

**Tennyson, Walter** *see* **D'Eyncourt, Walter**

### Terra Filmkunst GMBH Berlin

This Berlin–based German production company co-financed Hammer's last theatrical horror film for some thirty years, *To the Devil a Daughter* (1976), the opening credits for which bill it as a Hammer/Terra Anglo/German co-production. Founded in the early twenties, other films produced by the company, among them a handful of international co-productions in the sixties and seventies, include *Hanneles Himmelfahrt* (1922), *Das velorene Tal* (1934), *Der Strom* (1942), *Quax in Afrika* (1947), *The Vengeance of Fu Manchu* (1967), *The Blood of Fu Manchu* (1968), *L'iguana della lingua di fuoco* (1971), *Histoire d'O* (1975), *Cross of Iron* (1977) and *Happy Weekend* (1983). The company also worked as a distributor, releasing such titles as *Die verliebte Dachstube* (1937), *Johannisfeuer* (1939) and *Unser kleiner Junge* (1941). NB: please pronounce the company's name with care! **Hammer credits:** *To the Devil a Daughter* (1976)

### Terraine, Molly

Terraine worked as the dialogue director on the Hammer thriller *Blood Orange* (1953). Her other credits in this capacity include *The Tales of Hoffmann* (1951). Her credits as an actress include *Twice Upon a Time* (1953), while her work as a director includes episodes of *Kaleidoscope* (1946–1953, TV), which frequently featured members of the Rank Charm School (officially known as the J. Arthur Rank Company of Youth), for which she taught acting, among her pupils being the young Christopher Lee. **Hammer credits:** *Blood Orange* (1953)

### *The Terror of the Tongs*

GB, 1961, 79m, Eastmancolor, RCA, cert X

Like *The Stranglers of Bombay* (1959), with its exploration of the notorious Thuggee cult, this historical piece set in 1910 Hong Kong exploits as its theme another form of ritual murder, this time the hatchet killings as practiced by the much-feared Red Dragon Tong, "an organization that thrived on vice, terror and corruption," as the opening scrawl informs us. The story of a British Captain who attempts to bring the secret society and its evil leader Chung King to book, the project was originally to have been titled *Terror of the Hatchet Men*, and was the first film to be officially produced by Kenneth Hyman following his uncredited work as an associate producer on *The Hound of the Baskervilles* (1959) and *The Stranglers of Bombay*. However, like *The Stranglers of Bombay* before it, the film would end up less a historical charade and more a horrific come on, thanks to its scenes of mutilation and "bone scraping."

Following the arrival of production designer Bernard Robinson at Hammer in 1956, a policy was devised by which sets were re-cycled from film to film (and even in the *same* film). Now came the next logical step: to produce two films that would require similar settings, enabling the studio to fur-

ther trim back costs. Consequently, the idea was hatched to film *The Terror of the Tongs* back-to-back with another Oriental thriller, *Visa to Canton* (1960). Given that the second film would have a contemporary setting, it was believed the sets could be modified enough to avert suspicion. In any case, the films would not be released on the same bill, so it was assumed that audiences would be none the wiser.

As scripted by Jimmy Sangster, who was contracted to the film on 1 February 1960, *The Terror of the Tongs* went on the floor at Bray on 19 April that year, with former actor Anthony Bushell on-board as director, backed by the expected technical talent of the time. Top-lining the cast as the evil Tong crimelord Chung King was Christopher Lee, who had been busy making films in Europe since his last appearance for Hammer in *The Two Faces of Dr. Jekyll* (1960). Joining him was Geoffrey Toone as the hero, Captain Jackson Sale, a British merchant skipper whose determination to rid the Hong Kong waterfront of the Tongs is motivated by the death of his daughter at their hands. Supporting them were such familiar faces as Yvonne Monlaur as the Tong bond slave who helps the Captain, Charles Lloyd-Pack, Roger Delgado and Ewen Solon, all of whom, like Lee, would be required to play Chinese, assisted by the special eye make-up provided by Roy Ashton and Colin Guard. Christopher Lee would of course go on to play the ultimate Chinese villain, Fu Manchu, in five subsequent films for producer Harry Alan Towers, beginning with *The Face of Fu Manchu* (1965). However, as the actor recalled, his brush with the kind of make-up required to play such a role did not bode well for the future. "The eye make-up was murder. It's the most uncomfortable make-up I've ever had to wear."[16]

Filming on *The Terror of the Tongs* took in excess of six weeks and concluded on 30 May. Inevitably, given its subject matter, the film raised concerns

with the BBFC once cut and scored, primarily over the violence, which was basically its *raison d'etre* ("See drug-crazed assassins carrying out their hate-filled ritual murders!" exclaimed the film's poster, perhaps a little too gleefully). By today's standards, the film is mild beer indeed, yet some of the sadism still works, despite the lackluster direction of Anthony Bushell, who can't seem to stage a convincing fight sequence to save his life. Nevertheless, the film benefits enormously from Bernard Robinson's opulently dressed sets and Arthur Grant's rich Eastmancolor photography, his first color work for the studio, save for some uncredited second unit Technicolor work on *The Brides of Dracula* (1960), which was otherwise photographed by Jack Asher. As for Christopher Lee's relishable villain, which is little more than a glorified cameo, he easily walks away with the picture ("Have you ever had your bones scraped?" he memorably asks the captain at one point before one of his minions carries out the gruesome task).

Following a trade show on 12 September 1961 at the Columbia Theater, the film was premiered at the London Pavilion on 29 September on a double bill William Castle's *Psycho* rip-off *Homicidal* (1961), following which it went on general release in the UK on the ABC circuit care of British Lion Columbia in November. "The horror kings of Britain and America combine to thrill you!" exclaimed the frontage of the Pavilion, which featured a giant portrait of Christopher Lee in full Oriental make-up, while the poster claimed, "You've never had it so ghoul!" in clear reference to PM Harold McMillan's 1957 claim that Britons had "never had it so good."

The film's U.S. release, care of Columbia, for which it was again billed with *Homicidal*, had occurred a few months earlier on 15 March (though for some Stateside dates, *Tongs* played with *The Warrior Empress* [1960] or Hammer's *Sword of Sherwood Forest* [1960], the latter of which must

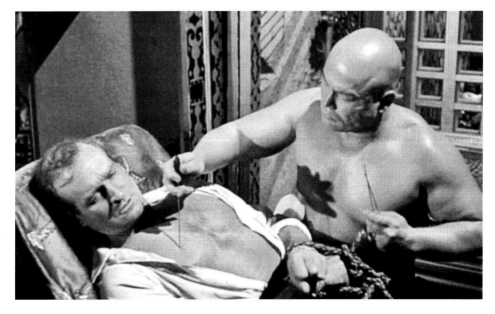

**Getting the point. Milton Reid wields the instruments of torture as Geoffrey Toone prepares for the worst in *The Terror of the Tongs* (1961) (Hammer/Merlin/British Lion Columbia/Columbia).**

have made for a curious double bill). The film's press book offered the usual come-ons: "See ... the dreaded Chinese needle torture," it proclaimed. However, the reviews, especially in the UK, were mostly negative. "No different from a hundred crime thrillers, sneered the *Sunday Telegraph*, while the *Daily Mirror* described it as a "lethargic secret society melodrama." Screenwriter Jimmy Sangster seemed to agree: "The old adage that you can't make a good movie from a bad script is amply demonstrated here. On the other hand, I don't think the assembled company would have made a much better movie even if the script had been good. Apart from the line producer, Ken Hyman, I don't think anybody was too sure what they were doing."[17] Indeed, despite its subject matter, the film is surprisingly short on genuine thrills, and becomes something of a chore to endure well before it reaches its climax. **Additional notes:** Although *The Terror of the Tongs* was made before *Visa to Canton*, it was released after it. Christopher Lee underwent on-camera make-up tests for the film on 13 April, six days before the commencement of principal photography. He'd already sported similar make-up for *The Nightingale*, a 1954 episode of *Tales of Hans Andersen* (1954–1955, TV), and, in addition to his work on the subsequent Fu Manchu films, would do so again for *The Devil's Daffodil* (1961). S.K. Lam was hired as an interpreter on *Tongs*, given the number of Oriental extras and bit players required for the crowd scenes. As part of the premiere ballyhoo, drama students were encouraged to attend the screening in fancy dress, with the winner of the best costume seemingly being offered a walk-on part in Hammer's upcoming production of *The Phantom of the Opera* (1962). The film also marked the first time Christopher Lee received top billing in a full-length feature, despite having played the title characters in *Dracula* (1958) and *The Mummy* (1959), both of which were top-lined by Peter Cushing. The Pavilion hoarding featuring Christopher Lee can be seen in a shot in *The Day of the Triffids* (1962), as Howard Keel and Janina Faye pass through Piccadilly Circus. The film's screenplay was novelized by Jimmy Sangster and published by Digit. William Castle, whose *Homicidal* was double-billed with *The Terror of the Tongs*, would go on to make *The Old Dark House* (1963) with Hammer. Hammer was by no means the first company to re-use and re-dress sets: in the thirties and forties, Universal re-used several sets in their gothic horrors. For example, in addition to their much-used back lot village square set, the spiral stone staircase leading to Frankenstein's cliff-top lab in *Frankenstein* (1931) later appeared as part of the Carfax Abbey crypt set in the opening scene of *Dracula's Daughter* (1936), while a hall and staircase seen in Talbot Castle in *The Wolf Man* (1941) also appeared in Dr. Bohmer's chateau in *The Ghost of Frankenstein* (1942). RKO also carried out the practice: an elaborate staircase seen in *The Magnificent Ambersons* (1942) can also be spotted in *The Seventh Victim* (1941), which was made second but released first, and *The Curse of the Cat People* (1944).

Production companies: Hammer/Merlin. Distributors: British Lion Columbia (UK [ABC cir-

Enter the dragon. Nicely rendered artwork for *The Terror of the Tongs* (1961) (Hammer/Merlin/ British Lion Columbia/Columbia).

cuit]), Columbia (U.S.). Producer: Kenneth Hyman. Executive producer: Michael Carreras. Associate producer: Anthony Nelson Keys. Director: Anthony Bushell. Screenplay: Jimmy Sangster. Cinematographer: Arthur Grant. Music: James Bernard. Music director: John Hollingsworth. Supervising editor: James Needs. Editor: Eric Boyd-Perkins. Assistant editors: Chris Barnes [uncredited], Paul Smith [uncredited]. Production design: Bernard Robinson. Art director: Thomas Goswell. Costumes: Molly Arbuthnot, Rosemary Burrows [uncredited]. Make-up: Roy Ashton, Colin Garde [uncredited]. Hair: Frieda Steiger. Sound: Jock May. Boom: Jim Perry [uncredited]. Sound assistant: Maurice Smith [uncredited]. Sound editor: Alban Streeter. Production manager: Clifford Parkes. Assistant art director: Don Mingaye [uncredited]. Assistant director: John Peverall. Second assistant directors: Hugh Harlow [uncredited], Joe Levy [uncredited]. Third assistant director: Dominic Fulford [uncredited]. Special effects (mattes): Les Bowie [uncredited]. Camera operator: Len Harris. Focus puller: Harry Oakes [uncredited]. Camera grip: Albert Cowlard [uncredited]. Clapper boy: Alan McDonald [uncredited]. Sound camera operators: Michael Sale [uncredited], Al Thorne [uncredited]. Sound maintenance: Charles Bouvet [uncredited]. Construction manager: Arthur Banks [uncredited]. Master carpenter: Charles Davis [uncredited]. Master painter: Lawrence Wrenn [uncredited]. Master electrician: Jack Curtis [uncredited]. Master rigger: Ronald Lenoir [uncredited]. Master plasterer: Stan Banks [uncredited]. Studio manager: A.F. Kelly [uncredited]. Props: Tommy Money [uncredited],

Peter Allchorne [uncredited]. Props buyer: Eric Hillier [uncredited]. Production secretary: Ann Skinner [uncredited]. Casting: Dorothy Holloway [uncredited]. Production accountant: Ken Gordon [uncredited]. Accountant: W.H.V. Able [uncredited]. Cashier: Peter Lancaster [uncredited]. Continuity: Tilly Day, Pauline Wise (trainee). Sign writer: Mr. Doo [uncredited]. Interpreter: S.K. Lam [uncredited]. Stills: Tom Edwards [uncredited]. Publicist: Colin Reid [uncredited]. Processing: Pathé. Poster: John Stockle [uncredited]. **Cast:** Christopher Lee (Chung King), Yvonne Monlaur (Lee), Marne Maitland (Beggar), Geoffrey Toone (Captain Jackson Sale), Brian Worth (Harcourt), Roger Delgado (Wang How), Ewen Solon (Tang How), Marie Burke (Maya), Charles Lloyd-Pack (Doctor), Richard Leech (Inspector Dean), Tom Gill (Beamish [uncredited]), Barbara Brown (Helena Sale), Burt Kwouk (Mr. Ming), Bandana Das Gupta (Anna [uncredited]), Milton Reid (Guardian [uncredited]), Eric Young (Confucius [uncredited]), Johnny Arlan (Executioner [uncredited]), Michael Hawkins (Priest [uncredited]), Harold Goodwin (Sailor [uncredited]), Santso Wong (Sergeant [uncredited]), Arnold Lee (Spokesman [uncredited]), Andy Ho (Lee Chung [uncredited]), June Barry (Tong room girl [uncredited]), Mary Rose Barry (Tong room girl [uncredited]), Audrey Burton (Tong room girl [uncredited]), Marialla Capes (Tong room girl [uncredited]), Ruth Calvert (Tong room girl [uncredited]), Katie Cashfield (Tong room girl [uncredited]), Louise Dickson (Tong room girl [uncredited]), Patty Dalton (Tong room girl [uncredited]), Pauline Dukes (Tong room girl [uncredited]), Valerie Shevaloff

(Tong room girl [uncredited]), Barbara Smith (Tong room girl [uncredited]), Hazel Gardner (Tong room girl [uncredited]), Julie Shearing (Tong room girl [uncredited]), Valerie Holman (Tong room girl [uncredited]), Ann Scott (Girl [uncredited]), Julie Alexander (unnamed role [uncredited]), Ronald Ing (unnamed role [uncredited]), Peter Gray (unnamed role [uncredited]), Jules Ki-Ki (unnamed role [uncredited]), Sui Lin (unnamed role [uncredited]), Walter Randall (unnamed role [uncredited]), Michael Peake (unnamed role [uncredited]), Poing Ping Sam (unnamed role [uncredited]), Steven Scott (unnamed role [uncredited]), Cyril Shaps (unnamed role [uncredited]), Vincent Wong (unnamed role [uncredited]). **DVD availability:** Sony (U.S. R1 NTSC), as part of the *Icons of Adventure* box set, Sony (UK R2 PAL)

### Terror Street see 36 Hours

### Terry, Sir John

Knighted in 1976 for his services to the film industry, Terry (1913–1995) was a Hammer board member between 1991 and 1994. Trained as a lawyer, he was long associated with the National Film Finance Corporation (first as a solicitor in 1949, later as its managing director from 1958–1978). He was also instrumental in founding the National Film School in 1970, and later helped to form the British Screen Advisory Council.

### Tey, Josephine

This British (Scottish) novelist and playwright (1896–1952, real name Elizabeth Mackintosh, aka Gordon Daviot) had the rights to her 1949 thriller *Brat Farrar* bought by Hammer in 1954, although it wouldn't be until 1963 that it appeared on screen as *Paranoiac*, despite being announced for production in 1955 and 1958. Her other books include *A Shilling for Candles* (1936), which was filmed by Alfred Hitchcock as *Young and Innocent* (1937), and *The Franchise Affair* (1948), which was filmed in 1950. She also wrote under the name of Gordon Daviot. Her works under this particular pseudonym include the novel *The Man in the Queue* (1929) and the plays *Youthful Folly* (1934), which was filmed in 1934, and *Richard of Bordeaux* (1932), which was televised in 1955 and remade in 1988 as a TV movie. **Hammer credits:** *Paranoiac* (1963)

### Thatcher, Billy

This British actor (1921–1964) can be seen as Ted Burton in Hammer's *The Adventures of PC 49—The Case of the Guardian Angel* (1949). His other credits include *Perfect Strangers* (1945), *Walking on Air* (1946), *Fortune Lane* (1947) and *No Place for Jennifer* (1950), plus episodes of *BBC Sunday-Night Theatre* (1950–1959, TV), *Dixon of Dock Green* (1955–1976, TV) and *Whack-O!* (1956–1972, TV). **Hammer credits:** *The Adventures of PC 49—The Case of the Guardian Angel* (1949, as Ted Burton)

### Thater, Heinke

Thater can be seen as a Rock girl in Hammer's *Creatures the World Forgot* (1971). **Hammer cred-** its: *Creatures the World Forgot* (1971, as Rock girl [uncredited])

### That's Your Funeral

GB, 1973, 81m, Eastmancolor, Westrex, cert A

Following the success of their 1971 big screen spin-off of *On the Buses* (1969–1973, TV), it was perhaps inevitable that Hammer would look to other sitcom hits to undergo similar treatment in a bid to reap similar financial rewards. Over the following years they would turn to such long-running favorites as *Nearest and Dearest* (1968–1973, TV), *Love Thy Neighbour* (1972–1976, TV) and *Man About the House* (1973–1976, TV). Surprisingly, they also decided to transfer this comedy about the undertaking business to the big screen. Penned by Peter Lewis, the series had been inspired by a one-off episode of *Comedy Playhouse* (1961–1975, TV) titled *Last Tribute* (1970, TV). This was then turned into a seven-part series, which was broadcast by the BBC in 1971.

Having decided to go ahead with the project, Hammer hired Peter Lewis to write the screenplay himself. They also recruited all the key cast members from the show, including Bill Fraser, who would be reprising his role of the boastful Basil Bulstrode, Raymond Huntley as his boss Emmanuel Holroyd, and David Battley as their gormless junior Percy. Meanwhile, comedy specialist John Robins was brought in to direct, while the rest of the production crew was filled with Hammer regulars, from producer Michael Carreras down to construction manager Arthur Banks.

Like the series, the film is set in the North of England and centers round the activities of Holroyd's Funeral Directors, a small family concern run by Emmanuel Holroyd with assistance from his right hand man Basil Bulstrode. As the story opens, Holroyd finally sees off their long-standing competition, Grimthorpe's. "From now on, apart from t' Co-Op, this town's all ours," crows Holroyd to Bulstrode. However, their monopoly doesn't last long, for soon after, a new rival, The Haven of Rest, appears on the scene ("The Haven of Rest treats your loved ones best!"). With their smartly-appointed shop and modern, with-it techniques, The Haven of Rest would seem to have Holyrod's beaten at their own game, but as Bulstrode observes of the flamboyant purple décor when he and Percy go round to take a closer look, "Our customers like to pass over in black and white, not ruddy Technicolor."

However, The Haven of Rest is not all it would seem. Following a mix up with two coffins, Holroyd's team discovers that their rival is also a front for hash smugglers, who are using the caskets as a means of getting the illegal substance into the country from Europe. But it isn't until one consignment has been cremated and they've inadvertently got high on several of the cigarettes that Percy has managed to swipe that the penny finally drops (comments Bulstrode as the smoke from the burning hash billows out of the crematorium chimney, "These furnaces have never been right since they changed over to North Sea gas").

A somewhat variable concoction of gags and situations, the film is little more than an excuse to run through every funeral joke in the book. A good deal of these are dead on arrival, though some bright quips can be found amid the dross. "Honestly, half the time he doesn't know his hearse from his elbow," comments Bulstrode of Percy at one point, while later, during a high-speed hearse chase (perhaps the film's best-staged sequence) he jokes of their pursuers, "They're flogging a dead hearse."

Unimaginatively directed and photographed by John Robins and cinematographer David Holmes respectively, the film looks flat and cheap throughout. It also suffers from a particularly irksome "comedy" score by David Whitaker, which makes much use of jazzed-up funeral music. The opening credits even manage to misspell the title, missing the apostrophe from the word *That's* (though it's present in the poster). Yet despite its faults, the film isn't without its moments. The performances of the three leads are certainly an asset, and without them the film would be a lot less amusing than it is. Thanks to his vast experience, Fraser manages to wring the most out of each comic situation (the look on his face as a hash cigarette he is smoking begins to kick in is priceless). Meanwhile, Huntley is all bluff Northern unctuousness as Holroyd, while Battley's gawp-mouthed Percy makes Stan Laurel's comedy persona seem like Einstein by comparison. The leads aside, the film also features a nice comic turn by Hammer regular Michael Ripper as a flustered railway porter, whose mix-up with the coffins acts as a catalyst for the unfolding events ("You all look a-same, you undertakers. You're like Chinese!" he comments, having given the wrong casket to the wrong company). The supporting cast also features plenty of well known faces, even if they are given too little to do, among them Richard Wattis, Bob Todd, Michael Robbins, Dennis Price, Sue Lloyd, Frank Thornton, Eric Barker and Roy Kinnear.

Sadly, the script is no longer entirely PC. The porter's comment about the Chinese aside, there is also the matter of an unfortunate exchange regarding the skin color of a body between two employees at The Haven of Rest. The characters are Miss Peach and Eugene Soul, played by Sue Lloyd and Dennis Price respectively, and the dialogue, in which they discuss the shade of make-up to be applied to a corpse, goes as follows:

Miss Peach: What about the complexion, Mr. Soul?

Mr. Soul: Well, I was toying with, er, honey tan at this instant, Miss Peach.

Miss Peach: I saw him more as a case for toasted beige.

Mr. Soul: Oh, pooh-pooh, Miss Peach! I'm not against a bit of touching up, but we don't want people to think we're bringing in coa-coas, you know!

This jaw-dropping moment aside, there are also one or two other things to look out for. Note, for example, that the unveiling of a statue towards the end of the film takes place in the grounds of Pinewood Studios, with the magnificent Heatherden Hall in the background. Also note the gell on the windows of the council boardroom, stuck on to help diffuse the in-coming light for the camera. Perhaps the nicest touch, however, is to have several members of the technical crew make cameo appearances as mourners at a graveside during the opening credits, among them producer Michael Carreras, production supervisor Roy Skeggs, screenwriter Peter Lewis, art director Scott Mac-Gregor, sound recordist Les Hammond, production manager Ron Jackson, assistant director Bill Cartlidge, continuity girl Leonora Hail and director John Robins, who presides over the proceedings as the vicar.

On the floor at Pinewood between 7 June and 7 July 1972 (as well as on location in the surrounding environs), *That's Your Funeral* was, like *On the Buses*, proclaimed "A Hammer Special Comedy Presentation" in the opening credits, and was released in the UK care of Rank in July 1973 (though the film carries a 1972 copyright). Commented Clive Jeavons of the film in the *Monthly Film Bulletin*, "Another nail in the British film industry's coffin, this grey comedy is depressingly unfunny even by TV spin-off standards." **Additional notes:** Some sources (notably IMDb), claim that the film was released in the UK as early as December 1972.

Production companies: Hammer/Rank. Distributor: Rank (UK). Producer: Michael Carreras. Production supervisor: Roy Skeggs. Director: John Robins. Screenplay: Peter Lewis, based upon his TV series. Cinematographer: David Holmes. Music: David Whitaker. Music director: Philip Martell. Editor: Archie Ludski. Art director: Scott MacGregor. Assistant art director: Don Picton. Costumes: Rosemary Burrows. Make-up: Eddie Knight. Hair: Jeanette Freeman. Sound: Les Hammond. Sound editor: Jimmy Groom. Dubbing mixer: Ken Barker. Re-recording mixers: Graham V. Hartstone [uncredited], Otto Snel [uncredited]. Production manager: Ron Jackson. Construction manager: Arthur Banks. Assistant director: Bill Cartlidge. Runners: Phil Campbell [uncredited], Brian Reynolds [uncredited]. Camera operator: Rodney "Chick" Anstiss. Continuity: Leonora Hail. Casting: James Liggat. Publicity: Jean Garioch [uncredited]. **Cast:** Bill Fraser (Basil Bulstrode), Raymond Huntley (Emmanuel Holroyd), David Battley (Percy), Dennis Price (Eugene Soul), Richard Wattis (Simmonds), John Ronane (Roland Smallbody), Sue Lloyd (Miss Peach), Roy Kinnear (Mr. Purvis), Dudley Foster (Mr. Grimthorpe), Michael Ripper (Arthur [railway]), Bob Todd (Arthur [funeral director]), Frank Thornton (Town clerk), Geoffrey Sumner (Lord Lieutenant), John Sharp (Mayor), Hugh Paddick (Window dresser), Eric Barker (Pusher), Peter Copley (First funeral director), Michael Robbins (Second funeral director), Ken Parry (Porter), Harry Brunning (Invalid), Carol Catkin (Model), Michael Sharvell-Martin (First Policeman [motorway]), John J. Carney (Second Policeman [motorway]), Clifford Mollison (Witherspoon), George Howe (Parson), Anthony Sagar (Policeman [crematorium]), Tommy Mann (Jenkins), Michael Segal (Council chairman), George Roderick (Butler), Geraldine Burnett (Petrol pump attendant), Stacy Davies (Grimthorpe's driver), Michael Knowles (Man with car [petrol station]), Verne Morgan (Pensioner), Claire Ruane (Partner), James Ware (Reporter), Michael Carreras (Mourner [uncred-

ited]), Roy Skeggs (Mourner [uncredited]), Peter Lewis (Mourner [uncredited]), Scott MacGregor (Mourner [uncredited]), Bill Cartlidge (Mourner [uncredited]), Les Hammond (Mourner [uncredited]), Ron Jackson (Mourner [uncredited]), Leonora Hail (Mourner [uncredited]), John Robins (Vicar [uncredited]). **DVD availability:** Amco (Germany R2 PAL). **CD availability:** *The Hammer Comedy Film Music Collection* (GDI Records), which contains *Opening Scenes*, *Opening Credits*, *Race of the Hearses* and *End Credits*

## Theodorakis, Mikis

Best known for his music for the film *Zorba the Greek* (1964), the theme from which became an international hit, this Greek composer (1925–, real name Mihail Theodorakis) has also provided music for such diverse productions as *Barefoot Battalion* (1954), *Ill Met by Moonlight* (1956), *Honeymoon* (1959), *Phaedra* (1961), *The Day the Fish Came Out* (1967), *Z* (1968), *The Trojan Women* (1971), *Serpico* (1973), *Kostas* (1979), *Cavafis* (1981), *Barluschke* (1997), *Fovou tous Ellines…* (2000), *Mariza* (2008) and *Dance Fight Love Die! With Mikis on the Road* (2017). He also scored the Hammer chiller *The Shadow of the Cat* (1961). His other works include an opera, *Ilektra* (1995), and pieces for the 1992 and 2004 Olympic Games. A political activist, Theodorakis has been imprisoned and deported for his beliefs, only to later become an MP and cultural minister. **Hammer credits:** *The Shadow of the Cat* (1961)

### *There Is No Escape* see *The Dark Road*

### *These Are the Damned* see *The Damned*

### *Third Party Risk*

GB, 1955, 70m [UK], 63m [U.S.], bw, RCA, cert U

Made in early 1954, but not released in the UK by Exclusive until 4 April 1955 (hence the 1954 copyright), this murder mystery has a better cast than it really deserves, among them Hollywood import Lloyd Bridges, who stars as Philip Graham, an American songwriter who finds himself accused of murdering his wartime buddy for some microfilm (containing top secret information about "the hydrogelation process" no less) after having agreed drive his friend's car back to London from Spain. Based on the 1953 novel by Nicolas Bentley, its familiar plot—that of an innocent man being accused of murder—was getting more than a little stale, having been trotted out by Hammer on at least half a dozen occasions by now. Adapted for the screen by its producer Robert Dunbar and its director Daniel Birt, the proceedings barely hold one's attention, despite the presence of such reliable supporting players as Finlay Currie, Ferdy Mayne,

Roger Delgado and Hammer staple George Woodbridge.

A tedious and hesitantly directed affair made worse by a particularly irritating score, the film totally lacks atmosphere, its one neat touch being to have the villain of the piece attempt to escape in a giant carnival mask during a festival, only to be betrayed by his faithful dog. Other attempts at thrills—among them a fight and a fire in a warehouse full of theatrical props and costumes—simply fail to come off, however. Meanwhile, the hero is saddled with some gloriously purple prose at times. As he says to one of the girls he encounters in Spain, "You know, this is the Spanish night that every American dreams about. An enormous moon, starry sky, the scent of lilies and tuba roses, lazy fingers strumming on a guitar and a senorita. Above all a senorita—mysterious as the moonbeams, lovelier than the lilies." Amazingly, Lloyd Bridges manages to keep a straight face while saying this claptrap!

Recalled Jimmy Sangster of the movie, "As usual, we were on a tight budget, something I was well aware of because I made it out and, in spite of the fact that most of the movie was supposed to take place in Spain, we never left the studio. Don't ask me how we did it! A couple of bullfight posters, a

**American artwork for *Third Party Risk* (1955), which was released in the States as *Deadly Game* (Hammer/Lippert/Exclusive/Twentieth Century–Fox).**

mantilla for the leading lady, Maureen Swanson, and rattle some castanets on the score…. Olé! Hammer's version of a foreign location—at least in those days."[18] Indeed, an examination of the film proves that it contains *all* these elements, along with a good dose of library footage to help complete the not entirely convincing illusion.

Sangster also made a discovery about one of his colleagues during the making of the film: "I worked out that Tony Hinds had a speaker in his office wired up to the mike on the set. My office had a window that overlooked his office and occasionally I would see Tony run out of his office, jump into his car and drive off heaven knows where. When that happened I knew that within a couple of minutes I'd be getting a call from the set to let me know that some form of shit had hit the fan and would I/could I take care of it because nobody could find the producer. I think Tony believed that if he wasn't around the problem wouldn't escalate. Let the production manager deal with it, that's what he was being paid for."[19]

The movie was re-titled *Deadly Game* for its earlier American release care of Fox on 8 October 1954, for which seven minutes were mercifully trimmed from the running time. **Additional notes:** The so-called microfilm seen in the movie is actually nothing more than a standard roll of Kodak!

Production companies: Hammer/Lippert. Distributors: Exclusive (UK), Twentieth Century–Fox (U.S.). Executive producer: Michael Carreras. Producer: Robert Dunbar. Director: Daniel Birt. Screenplay: Robert Dunbar, Daniel Birt, based on the novel by Nicolas Bentley. Cinematographer: Walter "Jimmy" Harvey. Music: Michael Krein. Editor: James Needs. Art director: J. Elder Wills. Costumes: Molly Arbuthnot. Production manager: Jimmy Sangster. Sound: Syd Wiles. Assistant director: Jack Causey. Second assistant director: Aida Young [uncredited]. Camera operator: Len Harris. Focus puller: Harry Oakes [uncredited]. Sound camera operator: Don Alton [uncredited]. Make-up: Phil Leakey. Hair: Eileen Bates. Continuity: Renee Glynne. Choreography: Lalagia. **Cast:** Lloyd Bridges (Philip Graham), Finlay Currie (Mr. Darius), Maureen Swanson (Lolita), Roger Delgado (Gonzales), Simone Silva (Mitzi Molnaur), Ferdy Mayne (Maxwell Carey), George Woodbridge (Inspector Goldfinch), Peter Dyneley (Tony Roscoe), Mary Parker (Mrs. Zeissman), Russell Waters (Dr. Zeissman), Seymour Green (Rope-Soles), Toots Pound (Lucy [uncredited]), Patrick Westwood (Porter [uncredited]), Leslie Wright (Sergeant Ramirez [uncredited]), Jane Asher (Young girl [uncredited]), Larry Taylor (Spanish thug [uncredited]). **DVD availability:** VCI Entertainment (U.S., all regions), double-billed with *Face the Music* (1954)

### The Thirteenth Reunion see Hammer House of Horror

### 36 Hours

GB, 1953, 80m, bw, RCA, cert A

Based on an original story and screenplay by Steve Fisher (an American writer better known for his many western scripts), this routine second feature thriller top-lines the American star Dan Duryea as a U.S. airman on a thirty-six-hour leave in London, during which hectic period he discovers that his wife, from whom he has been away for a long period, has gone missing. However, in trying to solve the mystery of her disappearance in the time he has left, he is himself arrested for her murder….

Put before the cameras at Bray in May 1953, the film was helmed by the prolific second feature director Montgomery Tully, who cracked through the proceedings with efficiency if not style, ably supported by Hammer's now firmly established crew of technicians. The results, which are very much of their period, may not be particularly exciting to watch today, but they kept the increasingly busy Bray ticking over nicely until bigger and better things came along.

The film was belatedly released in the UK by Exclusive on 25 October 1954. For its earlier American release on 18 November 1953, it was re-titled *Terror Street* ("Her frame was only the build-up to a frame-up!" teased the posters) and went out with Lippert's *Sins of Jezebel* (1953). **Additional notes:** The film contains some stock music composed by Malcolm Arnold, who had recently worked for Hammer on three films. Steve Fisher had previously worked on the screenplay for Hammer's *Whispering Smith Hits London* (1952).

Production companies: Hammer/Lippert. Distributors: Exclusive (UK), Twentieth Century–Fox (U.S.). Producer: Anthony Hinds. Director: Montgomery Tully. Screenplay/story: Steve Fisher. Cinematographer: Walter "Jimmy" Harvey. Music/conductor: Ivor Slaney (and Malcolm Arnold [stock, uncredited]). Editor: James Needs. Art director: J. Elder Wills. Costumes: Molly Arbuthnot [uncredited]. Furs: Molho [uncredited]. Shoes: Dolcis [uncredited]. Sound: Bill Salter. Production manager: John (Pinky) Green. Assistant director: Jimmy Sangster. Second assistant director: Aida Young [uncredited]. Camera operator: Len Harris. Focus puller: Harry Oakes [uncredited]. Make-up: Phil Leakey. Hair: Nina Broe. Continuity: Renee Glynne. **Cast:** Dan Duryea (Major Bill Rogers), Elsy Albiin (Katie Rogers), Ann Gudrun (Sister Jenny Miller), John Chandos (Orville Hart), Eric Pohlmann (Slossen), Kenneth Griffith (Henry Slossen), Jane Carr (Sister Clair), Michael Golden (Inspector Kevin), Marianne Stone (Pam Palmer), Lee Patterson (Joe [uncredited]), Harold Lang (Harry Cross), Christine Adrian (Mrs. Hart [uncredited]), John Wynn (Detective Sergeant Blake [uncredited]), Russell Napier (Detective [uncredited]), Sheila Berry (Wren [uncredited]), Gabrielle Blunt (Wren [uncredited]), Angela Glynne (Wren [uncredited]), Cleo Rose (Wren [uncredited]), Robert Henderson (Pop [pilot, uncredited]), Kenneth Brown (Policeman [uncredited]), Jacqueline McKenzie (Waitress [uncredited]), Richard Ford (Sergeant [uncredited]), Robert O'Neal (Driver [uncredited]), John Warren (Clerk [uncredited]), Stephen Vercoe (Ned Palmer [uncredited]). **DVD availability:** VCI Entertainment (U.S., all regions), double-billed with *Wings of Danger* (1952)

### Thomas, D.

This supporting actor can be seen as Lord Wembly in the Hammer short *Dick Turpin—Highwayman* (1956). **Hammer credits:** *Dick Turpin—Highwayman* (1956, as Lord Wembly [uncredited])

**Hispanic poster for *Third Party Risk* (1955) (Hammer/Lippert/Exclusive/Twentieth Century–Fox).**

**Thomas, Damien**

Although best known to Hammer fans for playing Count Karnstein in *Twins of Evil* (1971), this Egyptian born actor (1942–) actually began his association with the company three years earlier with a supporting role in *The New People*, an episode of *Journey to the Unknown* (1968, TV) which also appeared in the compendium film *Journey into Darkness* (1968, TVM). His other film credits include *Julius Caesar* (1970), *Henry VIII and His Six Wives* (1972), *Tiffany Jones* (1973), *The Message* (1976), *Sinbad and the Eye of the Tiger* (1977), *Pirates* (1986), *Crisis* (2003), *Never Let Me Go* (2010), *W.E.* (2011) and *The Limehouse Golem* (2016), plus episodes of *The Adventures of Don Quick* (1970, TV), *Jason King* (1971–1972, TV), *Blakes 7* (1978–1981, TV), *Tenko* (1981–1984, TV), *Wish Me Luck* (1987–1990, TV), *Noble House* (1988, TV), *The Brittas Empire* (1991–1997, TV), *Sense and Sensibility* (2008, TV) and *Shalom Kabul* (2016, TV).

Recalled the actor how he came to be cast as Count Karnstein, "I took a screen test, and I thought I was just being given this screen test to act opposite the others who were taking screen tests. But I had no idea I was actually in the running for a principal role. It was quite nice to find out that, in fact, I was up for the role. And even nicer to find out that I got it."[20] Sadly, the film failed to launch Thomas's own career: "After *Twins of Evil*, I was about to face a couple of the worst years of my career. Now when I look back at the film, I don't think I was as bad as I thought I was at the time. Perhaps because John Hough was such a superb, wonderful director who worked at a furious pace."[21] **Hammer credits:** *The New People* (1968, TV [episode of *Journey to the Unknown*], as David Redford), *Journey into Darkness* (1968, TVM, as David Redford), *Twins of Evil* (1971, as Count Karnstein)

**Thomas, Dora**

Thomas worked as the production secretary on Hammer's *The Quatermass Xperiment* (1955). Her other credits include *Up to His Neck* (1954) and *Oh … Rosalinda!!* (1955). She also worked as a continuity girl on *Castle Sinister* (1947) and as a production advisor on *This Is Shell* (1970). **Hammer credits:** *The Quatermass Xperiment* (1955 [uncredited])

**Thomas, Edna** *see* **Tromans, Edna**

**Thomas, Gareth**

Best known for playing Roj Blake in *Blakes 7* (1978–1981, TV), this RADA-trained British (Welsh) actor (1945–2016) also appeared in episodes of such series as *The Avengers* (1961–1969, TV), *Sutherland's Law* (1973–1976, TV), *Star Maidens* (1976, TV), *How Green Was My Valley* (1976, TV), *Children of the Stones* (1977, TV), *By the Sword Divided* (1983–1985, TV), *Knights of God* (1987, TV), *Medics* (1990–1995, TV) and *Torchwood* (2006–2011,TV). He also guested in an episode of *Hammer House of Horror* (1980, TV), in which he played three roles. His film credits include Hammer's *Quatermass and the Pit* (1967), in which he had a small role as a workman, plus *The Ragman's Daughter* (1972), *Smokey Joe's Revenge*

(1974), *Juggernaut* (1974), *Waterland* (1992), *The Witch's Daughter* (1996, TVM), *Merlin* (1998), *Harold Shipman: Doctor Death* (2002, TVM) and *Made in Romania* (2010). **Hammer credits:** *Quatermass and the Pit* (1967, as Workman [uncredited]), *Visitor from the Grave* (1980, TV [episode of *Hammer House of Horror*], as Richard/Policeman/The Swami Guptu Krishna)

**Thomas, Helen**

Credited as an art department assistant on the Hammer comedy *A Weekend with Lulu* (1961), Thomas worked under art director John Howell on the production, which was shot at Shepperton Studios. Her credits as a set dresser/decorator include *Carry On Cabby* (1963), *A Study in Terror* (1965), *Doctor in Clover* (1966), *Carry On Screaming* (1966), *Deadlier Than the Male* (1966), *The Assassination Bureau* (1968), *The Best Pair of Legs in the Business* (1972), *Tales from the Crypt* (1972) and *Craze* (1974), plus episodes of *Danger Man* (1964–1966, TV), *Man in a Suitcase* (1967–1968, TV) and *Strange Report* (1968–1970, TV). She also worked as the assistant art director on *The Boys* (1962). **Hammer credits:** *A Weekend with Lulu* (1961 [uncredited])

**Thomas, Lisa**

Thomas played the role of Sura in Hammer's *One Million Years B.C.* (1966). Her other credits include *Carry On Cowboy* (1965) and *Here We Go Round the Mulberry Bush* (1968), plus episodes of *Gideon's Way* (1964–1967, TV) and *The Baron* (1966–1967, TV). **Hammer credits:** *One Million Years B.C.* (1966, as Sura)

**Thomas, Madoline**

This British (Welsh) actress (1890–1989) can be seen as Mrs. Gladstone in Hammer's *The Black Widow* (1950). Her other film credits include *Painted Boats* (1945), *Blue Scar* (1949), *No Trace* (1950), *Blackout* (1950), *Rogue's Yarn* (1957), *Burke and Hare* (1972) and *Something to Hide* (1972), plus episodes of *Please Sir!* (1968–1972, TV), *Beasts* (1976, TV) and *Juliet Bravo* (1980–1985, TV). **Hammer credits:** *The Black Widow* (1950, as Mrs. Gladstone)

**Thompson, Bob**

According to the BFI database, this British camera operator and cinematographer (1910–2003, real name Harold Arthur Robert Thomson) is "The Man with a Million Names." Frequently credited as H.A.R. Thomson, he has also worked under such names as Harold Thompson, H.R. Thomson, Russell Thomson, Bob Thomson, Bob Thompson, under which guise he operated the camera for Hammer's *The Curse of the Mummy's Tomb* (1964), Robert Thomson, as whom he operated the camera on *Slave Girls* (1968), and Russell Thompson, under which guise he operated the camera for *The Lost Continent* (1968), all of which were directed by Michael Carreras, for whom he'd previously operated on *What a Crazy World* (1963). As H.A.R. Thomson, his credits as a cinematographer include *Big Fella* (1937), *To Dorothy A Son* (1954), *The Naked Prey* (1966) and *No Blade of Grass* (1970), plus episodes of *The Avengers* (1961–1969,

TV). His credits as an operator include *Calling All Stars* (1937), *The Chinese Bungalow* (1940), *Escape* (1948), *Malta Story* (1953), *Doctor at Large* (1957), *The League of Gentlemen* (1960) and *Khartoum* (1966), plus episodes of *Ghost Squad* (1961–1964, TV). He also worked as the second unit operator on *The Quiller Memorandum* (1966), *Where Eagles Dare* (1969), *Kelly's Heroes* (1970) and *11 Harrowhouse* (1974). **Hammer credits:** *The Curse of the Mummy's Tomb* (1964), *Slave Girls* (1968), *The Lost Continent* (1968)

**Thompson, Jill**

Thompson designed the costumes for Hammer's *Dracula Has Risen from the Grave* (1968). Her other credits include *Witchfinder General* (1968). **Hammer credits:** *Dracula Has Risen from the Grave* (1968)

**Thompson, John**

Thompson can be seen as Charles in Hammer's *The Damned* (1963). His other credits include *The Bloody Judge* (1968), on which he also worked as an assistant director, plus episodes of *William* (1962–1963, TV) and *Jezebel ex UK* (1963, TV). **Hammer credits:** *The Damned* (1963, as Charles)

**Thompson, John**

Thompson worked as the executive producer on *The World of Hammer* (1990 [first broadcast 1994], TV). His other credits as an executive producer include *Wicked Willie* (1990, TV). He was also the financial supervisor on *Best of British* (1987–1994, TV) between 1993 and 1994. **Hammer credits:** *The World of Hammer* (1990 [first broadcast 1994], TV)

**Thompson, Mrs.**

Along with Mrs. Croft, Mrs. Thompson ran the Hammer canteen at Bray in the fifties and sixties. Recalled Christopher Lee, "We worked in happy surroundings and had the most wonderful food, which is terribly important on a film."[22] He also noted that, "Our canteen, run by Mrs. Thompson, was the best in the country!"[23] Oliver Reed agreed: "The bread-and-butter pudding, I remember, was superb!"[24]

**Thompson, Peter**

This British actor (1925–) can be seen as the dopey gaoler in Hammer's *Twins of Evil* (1971). His other credits include *The Whisperers* (1967) and *White Cargo* (1973), plus episodes of *Maigret* (1960–1963, TV), *Steptoe and Son* (1962–1974, TV) and *Doomwatch* (1970–1972, TV). **Hammer credits:** *Twins of Evil* (1971, as Gaoler)

**Thompson, Russell** *see* **Bob Thompson**

**Thompson, Sophie**

This British actress (1962–) can be seen as an acolyte in *Guardian of the Abyss* (1980, TV [episode of *Hammer House of Horror*]). Her other TV appearances include episodes of *EastEnders* (1985–, TV), in which she played Stella Crawford between 2006 and 2007, *Thompson* (1988, TV), *Nelson's Column* (1994–1995, TV), *Jonathan Creek* (1997–2004, TV), *Big Top* (2009, TV), *The Borgias* (2011–2013, TV), *Lightfields* (2013, TV) and

*Jericho* (2016, TV), while her occasional film credits include *The Missionary* (1982), *Twenty-One* (1991), *Four Weddings and a Funeral* (1994), *Emma* (1996), *Gosford Park* (2001), *Fat Slags* (2004), *Harry Potter and the Deathly Hallows, Part 1* (2010) and *A Disappearance* (2018). Also much on stage (she won an Olivier Award in 1999 for her performance in *Into the Woods*), her mother is the actress Phyllida Law (1932–) and her father was the actor and writer Eric Thompson (1929–1982); her sister is the actress and writer Emma Thompson (1959–) and her brother-in-law is the actor Greg Wise (1966–). Her husband is the actor Richard Lumsden (1965–), whom she married in 1995. **Hammer credits:** *Guardian of the Abyss* (1980, TV [episode of *Hammer House of Horror*], as First girl)

## Thompson, Wilfred

Thompson worked as the sound editor on Hammer's *Dracula Has Risen from the Grave* (1968). Working primarily in television, his credits here include episodes of *Danger Man* (1964–1966, TV), *The Prisoner* (1967–1968, TV), *Jason King* (1971–1972, TV), *The Adventurer* (1972–1973, TV) and *Return of the Saint* (1978–1979, TV), plus such TV movies as *The Spy Killer* (1969, TVM) and *Foreign Exchange* (1970, TVM). **Hammer credits:** *Dracula Has Risen from the Grave* (1968)

## Thomsett, Sally

This bright and vivacious but disappointingly under-used British actress (1950–) is best remembered for playing Phyllis in *The Railway Children* (1970), which earned her a BAFTA nomination for most promising newcomer to leading film roles. She also played Jo in the long-running sitcom *Man About the House* (1973–1976, TV), a role she repeated for Hammer's 1974 big-screen spin-off. Her other film credits include *Seventy Deadly Pills* (1964), *Danny the Dragon* (1967), *River Rivals* (1967), *Straw Dogs* (1971) and *Baxter!* (1973), while her other TV work includes episodes of *The Very Merry Widow* (1967–1969, TV), *Wicked Women* (1970, TV) and *Wodehouse Playhouse* (1975–1978, TV). She has also appeared in such TV documentaries as *Laughter in the House: The Story of British Sitcom* (1999, TV), *The 100 Greatest Family Films* (2005, TV) and *Crumpet! A Very British Sex Symbol* (2005, TV). **Additional notes:** Thomsett also appeared as Jo in a 1973 edition of the TV comedy special *All Star Comedy Carnival* (1969–1973, TV). **Hammer credits:** *Man About the House* (1974, as Jo)

## Thomson, Alan

Thomson worked as a publicist on a couple of Hammer films in the mid-sixties. Primarily working out of Elstree, his other credits include *Duel in the Jungle* (1954), *The Dam Busters* (1955), *No Trees in the Street* (1958), *Ice Cold in Alex* (1958), *Summer Holiday* (1963) and *The Bargee* (1964). **Hammer credits:** *The Witches* (1966 [uncredited]), *One Million Years B.C.* (1966 [uncredited])

## Thomson, H.A.R. *see* Thompson, Bob

## Thomson, Robert *see* Thompson, Bob

## Thorburn, June

In films from 1952 with *The Pickwick Papers*, this British actress (1931–1967) went on to decorate such films as *True as a Turtle* (1956), *Rooney* (1958), *tom thumb* (1958), *Transatlantic* (1960) and the Hammer swashbuckler *The Scarlet Blade* (1963), in which she made a rather vapid leading lady. Her TV credits include episodes of *Douglas Fairbanks, Jr. Presents* (1953–1957, TV), *Danger Man* (1960–1962, TV) and *Blackmail* (1965–1966, TV). She died in a plane crash. **Hammer credits:** *The Scarlet Blade* (1963, as Clare Judd)

## Thorn, Ronald Scott

This British doctor, author and playwright (1920–1996, real name Ronald Scotthorn Wilkinson) had his 1959 novel *The Full Treatment* turned into a film by Hammer in 1961. Thorne worked on the screenplay with the film's producer-director Val Guest, who had personally acquired the property and brought it to Hammer. Thorn's other novels include *Upstairs and Downstairs*, which was filmed in 1959, *Second Opinion* (1961) and *The Twin Serpents* (1965), while his plays include *Mountain Air* (1948) and *Bed of Roses* (1960). He also co-authored the screenplay for *Doctor in Distress* (1963). **Hammer credits:** *The Full Treatment* (1961)

## Thorndike, Russell

On stage from 1903 following experience as a chorister and training at the Ben Greets Academy, this British actor (1885–1972, real name Arthur Russell Thorndike) went on to become a regular at the Old Vic and the Regent's Park Open Air Theater. In films from 1922, his credits include *Macbeth* (1922), in which he played the title role, *Tense Moments from Great Plays* (1922), *A Shot in the Dark* (1933), *Henry V* (1944), *Caesar and Cleopatra* (1945) and *Richard III* (1955). However, he is best known as the author of seven books featuring the exploits of the pirate Doctor Syn, among them *Doctor Syn: A Smuggler Tale of Romney Marsh* (1915) and *The Shadow of Doctor Syn* (1944), whose adventures have so far been filmed three times, as *Dr. Syn* (1937), Hammer's *Captain Clegg* (1962) and *Dr. Syn, Alias the Scarecrow* (1963). Thorndike also played the role himself on stage. His other books include *The Slype* (1927), *The Forbidden Room* (1933) and *The House of Jeffreys* (1943). His sisters were actresses Dame Sybil Thorndike (1882–1976, full name Agnes Sybil Thorndike), whose biography he penned in 1929, and Eileen Thorndike (1891–1954). His son was actor Daniel Thorndike (1920–2016). **Hammer credits:** *Captain Clegg* (1962 [uncredited])

## Thorne, Al (Alan)

Thorne worked as one of the sound camera operators on the Hammer comedy *The Ugly Duckling* (1959), which led to work on several more productions for the studio in the late fifties/early sixties. His other credits include *A Canterbury Tale* (1944), *The Love Match* (1955) and *The Quiet American* (1958). **Hammer credits:** *The Ugly Duckling* (1959, sound camera operator [uncredited]), *The Mummy* (1959, sound camera operator [uncredited]), *Never Take Sweets from a Stranger* (1960, sound camera operator [uncredited]), *The Terror of the Tongs* (1961, sound camera operator [uncredited]), *Paranoiac* (1963, sound transfer operator [uncredited]), *The Scarlet Blade* (1963, sound camera operator [uncredited]), *The Kiss of the Vampire* (1963, sound camera operator [uncredited]), *Nightmare* (1964, sound camera operator [uncredited]), *The Evil of Frankenstein* (1964, sound camera operator [uncredited]), *The Devil-Ship Pirates* (1964, sound camera operator [uncredited]), *The Gorgon* (1964, sound camera operator [uncredited]), *Frankenstein Created Woman* (1967, sound camera operator [uncredited])

## Thornton, Dennison

One of Hammer's publicists, Irish born Thornton (1909–1977) began his association with the studio with *The Mummy* (1959), on which he worked with Colin Reid. His other credits include *Pygmalion* (1938), *Wuthering Heights* (1970), *Whoever Slew Auntie Roo?* (1971), *Murders in the Rue Morgue* (1971), *Horror Hospital* (1973) and *The Marseille Contract* (1974). Recalled his frequent assistant, Brian Doyle, of Thornton, "Dennison was a lovely man—warm, genial, efficient and very amusing."[25] He began his career as a journalist in Canada before going on to work as a publicist for such studios as Grosvenor Films, Renown, Two Cities and Columbia. **Hammer credits:** *The Mummy* (1959 [uncredited]), *The Stranglers of Bombay* (1959 [uncredited]), *Never Take Sweets from a Stranger* (1960 [uncredited]), *Taste of Fear* (1961 [uncredited]), *A Weekend with Lulu* (1961 [uncredited]), *Paranoiac* (1963 [uncredited]), *The Damned* (1963 [uncredited]), *The Scarlet Blade* (1963 [uncredited]), *The Kiss of the Vampire* (1963 [uncredited]), *The Old Dark House* (1963 [uncredited]), *Nightmare* (1964 [uncredited]), *The Devil-Ship Pirates* (1964 [uncredited]), *The Gorgon* (1964 [uncredited])

## Thornton, Frank

Best known for his role as Captain Stephen Peacock in the long-running sitcom *Are You Being Served?* (1973–1985, TV), a role he repeated for the 1977 film and the TV sequel *Grace and Favour* (1992–1993, TV), this British comedy character actor (1921–2013) sustained a busy career on stage, television and in films. Specializing in snooty, superior types, he began his film career in 1953 with *The Silent Witness*, and went on to appear in such varied titles as *Stock Car* (1955), *Victim* (1961), *The Early Bird* (1965), *Carry On Screaming* (1966), *The Bed Sitting Room* (1969), *The Private Life of Sherlock Holmes* (1970), *Up the Chastity Belt* (1971), *The Three Musketeers* (1973), *Steptoe and Son Ride Again* (1973), *Gosford Park* (2001) and *Back in Business* (2007). He also had a minor role in Hammer's *That's Your Funeral* (1973). His many other TV appearances include episodes of *William Tell* (1958–1959, TV), *HMS Paradise* (1964–1965, TV), *The New Avengers* (1976–1977, TV) and *The Upper Hand* (1990–1996, TV), while in 1997 he joined the cast of another long-running sitcom, *Last of the Summer Wine* (1973–2010, TV), in which he played Herbert "Truly" Truelove, racking up 135 episodes. **Additional notes:** The role of Captain Peacock was subsequently played by John Challis in the 2016 reboot of *Are You Being Served?* (2016, TV). **Hammer credits:** *That's Your Funeral* (1973, as Town clerk)

### Thost, Bruno

This German actor (1936–) can be seen in a minor role in Hammer's *The Lady Vanishes* (1979). His other credits include *Situation* (1973), *Karl May* (1974), *The Tin Drum* (1979), *Swann in Love* (1984), *The Three Musketeers* (1993), *Trefall* (2012) and *My Jurassic Place* (2019), plus episodes of *Holocaust* (1978, TV) and *Julia—Eine ungewohnliche Frau* (1999–2003, TV). **Hammer credits:** *The Lady Vanishes* (1979, as Signal box man)

### *Three Stops to Murder* see *Blood Orange*

### Thrift, Ann

Thrift worked as the production secretary on *Wolfshead: The Legend of Robin Hood* (1969 [released 1973]), which was acquired by Hammer. Her other credits in this capacity include *The Slipper and the Rose* (1976), while her credits as an assistant accountant include *The Witches* (1990) and *The Muppet Christmas Carol* (1992). **Hammer credits:** *Wolfshead: The Legend of Robin Hood* (1969 [released 1973])

### *Thriller* see *Hammer House of Horror*

### *The Thurston Story* see *Dark Road*

### *Ticket to Happiness*

GB, 1959, 30m approx., color, cert U

Long out of circulation, little information is currently available about this short, save that it was produced and directed by Hammer veteran Peter Bryan some time in 1959 and released in the UK by Exclusive in November the same year. According to the BFI database, it would appear to be about a youth club and its patron, a wealthy industrialist, who at first had been opposed to its activities.

Production companies: Hammer/Columbia. Distributor: Exclusive (UK). Producer: Peter Bryan. Director: Peter Bryan. **Cast:** Michael Goodliffe (unnamed role), Elwyn Brook-Jones (unnamed role), Jack Allen (unnamed role)

### Tickle, Frank

This British bit-part player (1893–1955) appeared in Hammer's last pre-war featurette, *The Bank Messenger Mystery* (1936). He also popped up in one of their later post-war second features. His other films include *Two on a Doorstep* (1936), *The Lion Has Wings* (1939), *Atlantic Ferry* (1941), *Henry V* (1944), *The Winslow Boy* (1948), *The Long Dark Hall* (1951) and *Quentin Durward* (1955), plus several episodes of *BBC Sunday-Night Theatre* (1950–1959, TV). **Hammer credits:** *The Bank Messenger Mystery* (1936, unnamed role [uncredited]), *Death of an Angel* (1952, as Sam Oddy)

### Tigon Films

Formed in 1966 by Tony Tenser, this British production company produced a handful of cult horror films in direct competition with Hammer, among them *The Sorcerers* (1967), *Witchfinder General* (1968) and *The Blood on Satan's Claw* (1971),

along with such family fare as *Black Beauty* (1971), which had originally been considered as a project by Hammer in the late sixties, and the sitcom spin-off *For the Love of Ada* (1972). In 1971 the company made a disastrous merger with Hemdale and, intriguingly, rented a suite of offices at Hammer House on Wardour St. (the suite had originally been leased by Grand National Pictures). The company's chairman, Hemdale's Laurie Marsh, who had negotiated the merger, also began to look into merging with Hammer, given the financial difficulties the studio was having at the time (a merger between Hammer and Studio Film Laboratories, aimed at resolving this, had recently soured). An offer of £300,000 was made for the company. This didn't meet with James Carreras's expectations, however, and so the merger was temporarily put on hold. Unfortunately, Michael Carreras had not been privy to these negotiations, and when he discovered what had been taking part behind his back—especially given his position as managing director—this put an additional strain on his by-now fraught relationship with his father. Consequently, Michael Carreras decided to make a bid for the company himself, first in conjunction with Studio Film Laboratories, and finally with Pension Funds Securities, a subsidiary of Imperial Chemical Industries (ICI), securing the deal for £400,000. This proved to be a fatal blow for Tigon, now under the control of the Laurie Marsh Group, and in 1972 Tony Tenser resigned from the LMG board (to form Team Productions), and the Tigon name became merely a distribution utility. LMG distribution would likewise be sold in 1973.

### Tiktin, Jack

Exclusive's branch manager for the city of Cardiff during the fifties, Tiktin remained with the company until 1959, when it wound down.

### *Till Dawn Us Do Part* see *Straight on Till Morning*

### Till, Jenny

This British actress (1940–, full name Jennifer Till) played the role of Lady Marian in Hammer's *A Challenge for Robin Hood* (1967), in which she is disguised as her maidservant Mary for much of the action. Her entire performance was dubbed during post-production. Her other credits include *The Masque of the Red Death* (1964), *Help!* (1965), *Theatre of Death* (1966), *No. 1 of the Secret Service* (1978) and *The First Great Train Robbery* (1978), plus episodes of *Detective* (1964–1969, TV), *Freewheelers* (1968–1973, TV), *The Venturers* (1975, TV) and *Star Maidens* (1976, TV). She was formerly married to the actor and choreographer Leo Kharibian (1927–2001), whom she wed in 1961. **Hammer credits:** *A Challenge for Robin Hood* (1967, as Mary/Lady Marian)

### Tilley, Iris

British born Tilley (1926–2002) worked as the hair stylist on Hammer's *The Curse of the Mummy's Tomb* (1964). Her other credits include *The Long Dark Hall* (1951), *Value for Money* (1955), *The Spanish Gardener* (1956), *What a Whopper!* (1961), *Night of the Eagle* (1962) and *Cairo* (1963). Her

early credits as an assistant stylist include *The Small Back Room* (1949) and *The Third Man* (1949). **Hammer credits:** *The Curse of the Mummy's Tomb* (1964)

### Tilley, Mike

Tilley worked on the effects team for Hammer's *Moon Zero Two* (1969) and *Taste the Blood of Dracula* (1970). His other credits include *Orphans* (1997), *Spice World* (1997), *The Wisdom of Crocodiles* (1998), *Atonement* (2007), *Sherlock Holmes* (2009) and *About Time* (2013). **Hammer credits:** *Moon Zero Two* (1969 [uncredited]), *Taste the Blood of Dracula* (1970 [uncredited])

### Tilling, Bryan (Brian)

British born Tilling (1929–2011) worked as a dubbing editor on all thirteen episodes of *Hammer House of Horror* (1980, TV). His credits as a dialogue editor include *Overlord* (1975), *Alien* (1979), *The Shooting Party* (1985) and *Half Moon Street* (1986), plus episodes of *Forever Green* (1989–1992, TV), while his work as an assistant editor includes *Robbery* (1967), *Man in the Wilderness* (1971), *Confessions from a Holiday Camp* (1977) and *Rosie Dixon—Night Nurse* (1978). He also worked as the sound editor on *Strike It Rich* (1990). **Hammer credits:** *Hammer House of Horror* (1980, TV)

### Tilton, Connie

This actress and stuntwoman (?–2017) can be seen as a Sand mother in Hammer's *When Dinosaurs Ruled the Earth* (1970). Her other credits include *The Seventh Veil* (1945), *Dangerous When Wet* (1953), *Tiger Bay* (1959), *Gorgo* (1960) and *The Haunting* (1963). **Hammer credits:** *When Dinosaurs Ruled the Earth* (1970, as Sand mother)

### Tilvern, Alan

A former barrow boy, this British supporting actor (1918–2003) played the role of Mustafa in the Charlie Drake comedy *Sands of the Desert* (1960), which was partially financed by Hammer. His other credits include *The Small Voice* (1948), *The Master Plan* (1954), *House of Secrets* (1954), *Hot Enough for June* (1963), *Brass Target* (1978), *Firefox* (1982) and *Little Shop of Horrors* (1986), plus a minor role in Hammer's *Rasputin—The Mad Monk* (1966). Also busy on TV, his credits here include episodes of *Douglas Fairbanks, Jr. Presents* (1953–1957, TV), *Crane* (1963–1965, TV), *Poldark* (1975–1977, TV) and *Boon* (1986–1992, TV). **Hammer credits:** *Sands of the Desert* (1960, as Mustafa), *Rasputin—The Mad Monk* (1966, as Patron)

### Tims, Jack

Tims worked as one of Exclusive's many branch managers in the fifties.

### Tingwell, Charles

In British films from 1957 with *The Shiralee* following minor movie roles in his home country, among them *Come Up Smiling* (1939), *Smithy* (1946) and *Always Another Dawn* (1948), this Australian actor (1923–2009, nickname "Bud") is best known for playing Inspector Craddock in four Miss

Marple mysteries: *Murder She Said* (1961), *Murder at the Gallop* (1963), *Murder Most Foul* (1964) and *Murder Ahoy* (1964). His other British films include *Bobbikins* (1959), *Cone of Silence* (1960) and Hammer's *The Secret of Blood Island* (1965), in which he played Major Dryden. However, to genre fans he is best known for playing Alan Kent in *Dracula—Prince of Darkness* (1966), in which he is sacrificed to revive the dead Count. To this day, the sequence remains one of the most memorable in horror film history. Tingwell's other homegrown credits include *Bitter Springs* (1950), *Smiley* (1956), *Breaker Morant* (1980), *Malcolm* (1986), *Evil Angels* (1988), *A Cry in the Dark* (1988), *Amy* (1998), *The Inside Story* (2000) and *Let Me Not* (2007). He also directed episodes of such series as *The Box* (1974–1977, TV), *Prisoner* (1979–1986, TV) and *Newlyweds* (1993–1994, TV). During World War II he served in the RAF and flew in photo reconnaissance missions in North Africa. His daughter is the actress Virginia Tingwell. **Hammer credits:** *The Secret of Blood Island* (1965, as Major Dryden), *Dracula—Prince of Darkness* (1966, as Alan Kent)

Francis Matthews (left) and Charles Tingwell (right) arrive at Castle Dracula in this still from *Dracula—Prince of Darkness* (1966). The smiles will soon be wiped from their faces (Hammer/Associated British Picture Corporation/Seven Arts/Warner Pathé Distributors/Twentieth Century–Fox/Studio Canal).

### Tinker

This was the name of the dog featured in Hammer's *Straight on Till Morning* (1972). **Hammer credits:** *Straight on Till Morning* (1972)

### Tinnell, Robert (Bob)

This American writer, producer and director (1961–) is acknowledged in the credits of *Flesh and Blood—The Hammer Heritage of Horror* (1994, TV). His credits as a director include *Kids of the Round Table* (1995), for which he also provided the story, *Airspeed* (1998), *Believe* (2000), for which he also provided the story, *Requiem for the Damned* (2012 [*The Fall of the House of Usher* seg-

ment]), which he also co-wrote and executive produced, and *Grindsploitation* (2016 [*Grave of the Gods* segment]), his section for which he also wrote, plus episodes of *1863* (2013–2014, TV), his six episodes for which he also scripted. His work as a producer includes *Surf Nazis Must Die* (1987), in which he also appears, and *South of Reno* (1988). His credits as a production manager take in *The Tomb* (1986) and *Prison Ship* (1987), the latter of which he also appeared in. He began his career as a production assistant working on the likes of *Creepshow* (1982) and *Biohazard* (1985). **Hammer credits:** *Flesh and Blood—The Hammer Heritage of Horror* (1994, TV)

### Tintern Productions

This company was formed by Hammer's Brian Lawrence in 1974, through which he collected residuals for the company, including profits from distributors for releases and re-releases, worldwide television sales and super-8 showreels for collectors and film clubs, etc. Lawrence's wife Nessie Kathleen Lawrence also served as a director and as the company secretary.

### Tipaldi, Pearl

Tipaldi (?–1993, real name Pearl Vannin) worked as the hair stylist on Hammer's *Quatermass and the Pit* (1967). Her other credits include *Penny and the Pownall Case* (1948), *Hindle Wakes* (1952), *Bhowani Junction* (1956), *The Angry Hills* (1959), *The Night Fighters* (1960), *Saturday Night and Sunday Morning* (1960), *I Could Go On Singing* (1963), *Accident* (1967) and *Theatre of Blood* (1973), plus a return to Hammer for several other projects in the early seventies. **Hammer credits:** *Quatermass and the Pit* (1967), *The Vampire Lovers* (1970), *Scars of Dracula* (1970), *The Horror of Frankenstein* (1970), *Lust for a Vampire* (1971), *Twins of Evil* (1971), *Straight on Till Morning* (1972)

### Tirard, Anne

This British supporting actress (1917–2003) appeared in the Hammer thriller *The Full Treatment* (1961) as Nicole. Her other credits include *The Frozen Dead* (1966), *Witchfinder General* (1968), *Tess* (1979), *Moonlighting* (1982), *The Chain* (1984), *The Witches* (1990) and *In Your Eye* (1994), plus episodes of *The Avengers* (1961–1969, TV), *Rogue's Gallery* (1968–1969, TV) and *The Young Indiana Jones Chronicles* (1992–1993, TV). Her husband was the actor William Lyon Brown

(1907–1971), whom she married in 1939, and who appeared in *One Million Years B.C.* (1966) and *The Vengeance of She* (1968) for Hammer. **Hammer credits:** *The Full Treatment* (1961, as Nicole)

### To Have and to Hold

GB, 1951, 63m, bw, cert A

The third of four films made by Hammer at Gilston Park, this romantic melodrama has a touch of the *Lady Chatterley's* to it, in that a country gentleman named Brian Harding, learning that he is dying following a riding accident, makes provision for the future happiness of his beloved younger wife June, who has fallen in love with his cousin Max Harding, who has been working as his estate manager (Brian, it seems, tempted Providence by declaring to June that, "I'm almost *too* lucky").

Based on the 1939 play by Lionel Browne, the film was at least a change from Hammer's then current trend of adapting radio crime dramas, although its stiff upper lip attitudes and "country set" personalities have since dated it somewhat. Well enough performed by its three leads—Avis Scott, Patrick Barr and Robert Ayres—the film is more notable for its supporting cast, which includes a good turn by Ellen Pollack as Brian's haughty sister-in-law Roberta de Wynter ("I'll never forgive Brian for engaging a ship's steward as a butler," she complains at one point), and future producer Harry Fine as her bluff husband Robert (Fine would of course go on to produce the "Karnstein trilogy" for Hammer in the seventies). The film also purported to "introduce" future Bond star Eunice Gayson (known for playing Sylvia Trench in the first two movies), despite the fact that she had already appeared in several films. Otherwise, this is a bland programer, handled with a lack of inspiration by director Godfrey Grayson, who also provided the shooting script.

Before the cameras in June 1950, the film was trade shown in March 1951 and finally released in the UK by Exclusive on 2 April the same year.

Production company: Hammer. Distributor: Exclusive (UK). Producer: Anthony Hinds. Director: Godfrey Grayson. Screenplay: Reginald Long, Godfrey Grayson (shooting script), based on the play by Lionel Browne. Cinematographer: Walter "Jimmy" Harvey. Music director: Frank Spencer. Song: *A Midsummer Day* by Frank Spencer (m), Reginald Long (ly). Editor: James Needs. Art director: no credit given. Sound: Edgar Vetter. Second unit director: Derek Greene. Camera operator: Peter Bryan. Loader: Harry Oakes [uncredited]. Assistant director: Jimmy Sangster. Continuity: Renee Glynne. Make-up: Phil Leakey. Hair: Monica Hustler. Production manager: Arthur Barnes. Casting: Prudence Sykes. Production assistant: Michael Carreras [uncredited]. **Cast:** Avis Scott (June Harding), Patrick Barr (Brian Harding), Robert Ayres (Max Harding), Ellen Pollock (Roberta [Bobby] de Wynter), Harry Fine (Robert de Wynter), Richard Warner (Cyril), Eunice Gayson (Peggy Harding), Peter Neil (Dr. Prichard)

### To the Devil a Daughter

GB/Ger, 1976, 93m, Technicolor, widescreen [1.66:1], RCA, cert X

Like the demonic baby that claws its way out of the womb of its unfortunate mother in this diabolical thriller, the birth of *To the Devil a Daughter* likewise proved to be something of a nightmare for Michael Carreras ("…and suddenly the screams of a baby born in Hell!" ran the tagline on the film's American pressbook, though the screams could well have been those of sheer frustration from its uncredited executive producer). Between 1971 and 1973, Hammer had released at total of twenty-one films (seven each year), an impressive number for such a relatively small company, especially given the state of the British film industry. By the time *To the Devil a Daughter* began its lengthy pre-production period, however, the company was struggling to scrape a single project together every two or three years.

Hammer had in the past made two films based upon the works of the popular occult writer Dennis Wheatley: *The Devil Rides Out* (1968) and *The Lost Continent* (1968), the latter taken from *Uncharted Seas*. Neither had been a major commercial success, yet Michael Carreras had remained on friendly terms with the author. After the making of *Man About the House* (1974) in March 1974, Hammer had no films on their production slate, though Carreras had approached Wheatley about getting together for another project. A few years earlier, Christopher Lee and Hammer producer Anthony Nelson Keys had formed a production company named Charlemagne, through which they managed to make one unsuccessful shocker, *Nothing But the Night* (1972). As it transpired, the by now defunct company had also optioned eight of Wheatley's books, among them his 1953 novel *To the Devil a Daughter* and *The Haunting of Toby Jugg* (1959), both of which Carreras subsequently acquired.

Given their original involvement with the property, along with their ties with Hammer, Michael Carreras offered Anthony Nelson Keys the chance to produce the proposed adaptation of *To the Devil a Daughter*, while Christopher Lee was signed as the nominal star. The duo was also offered a percentage of the returns on the resultant film. With this package now in hand, Carreras approached EMI for financing. A deal was subsequently secured, to which was also added a proposed Wheatley television series, *The Devil and All His Works*, a fictional short story compendium based on the author's 1971 factual study of the same name. However, a proposed start date of August 4 1974 proved unattainably optimistic, given that Keys and Lee had only come onboard in June. Indeed, finance from EMI—which only amounted to half the budget—wasn't fully secured until October, leaving it to Carreras to search for the rest of the budget elsewhere.

Initially, writer John Peacock was put onto the script. However, his work proved disappointing, and cost Hammer a potential production deal for the remaining budget with AIP, with whom they'd previously made *The Vampire Lovers* (1970). Consequently, Peacock, who would later work as a story editor on *Hammer House of Mystery and Suspense* (1984, TVM), was replaced by Christopher Wicking who, having penned *Blood from the Mummy's Tomb* (1971) and *Demons of the Mind* (1972) for

Hammer, had recently been working on a couple of film and television projects for the company, neither of which eventually came to fruition (these were *The Sensitive*, a psychic detective series on which he collaborated with Adrian Reid, and the H. Rider Haggard–inspired *Allan Quatermain Esquire: His Quest for the Holy Flower*).

With Peacock now off the picture (though he retains a credit for adaptation), Wicking struggled to get the script into shape, with further re-writes following during filming care of an uncredited Gerald Vaughan-Hughes. As Wicking revealed, "The book was set in 1953, which is a very bad period in terms of recreating it. The whole book is about the effects of the war on the characters, all of which was not just expensive but so remote in the 70s."[26] Meanwhile, Carreras continued to struggle to find finance elsewhere, but was turned down by Universal, Warner Bros. and Avco-Embassy. He also sought to sign a director. Considerations included Ken Russell, Douglas Hickox, Mike Hodges, Jack Gold and Ken Hughes, the latter of whom had written and directed *The House Across the Lake* (1954) for Hammer twenty years earlier. Other directors with a Hammer past were also considered for the film, among them Don Chaffey, Alan Gibson, Silvio Narizzano and Peter Sasdy, while in October 1974, Don Sharp expressed interest in the production, but by the beginning of the New Year he had departed to make *Hennessy* (1975). Eventually, the film landed in the lap of Peter Sykes, who had helmed the Wicking-scripted psycho-thriller *Demons of the Mind* for Hammer.

By the time Sykes joined *To the Devil a Daughter* it was already April 1975. A penalty clause with EMI meant that filming was set to commence two months later on June 30, yet Carreras still had to secure the remainder of the budget. A savior was seemingly found in Constantin Film, a Munich-based production company familiar to Carreras from his European wanderings of the early sixties. Unfortunately, the company soon after withdrew owing to its own financial problems. Time was now quickly running out. Luckily, at practically the last moment, Carreras managed to secure a deal with another German company, Terra Filmkunst GMBH Berlin, which was inked on 16 June 1975, just two weeks before principal photography was due to begin. Further funds were also secured in a loan of $250,000. However, with the loan came interest rates, and with the participation of the various production companies and interested parties came percentage payments (think EMI, ICI's Pension Funds Securities, Terra Filmkunst, Christopher Lee, Anthony Nelson Keys and Dennis Wheatley, who all owned a slice of the film). Consequently, before even a frame had been shot, Hammer's chances of making any money out of *To the Devil a Daughter* were looking increasingly slim.

During the search for a director and the various financial wrangles, Carreras also had to contend with the departure of producer Anthony Nelson Keys, who withdrew in a bid to help cut costs (though he retained his original percentage deal). He was replaced by in-house producer Roy Skeggs, whose biggest venture so far this proved to be. As with everything else, casting was not without its

British poster for *To the Devil a Daughter* (1976), linking its subject matter to two previous diabolical hits, *Rosemary's Baby* (1968) and *The Exorcist* (1973) (Hammer/Terra Filmkunst GMBH Berlin/EMI/Cine Artists/Studio Canal).

problems either, given that there were so many interested parties to please, from investors to distributors to publicists. Suggested names to play occult writer John Verney—who finds himself protecting a young girl from diabolists led by Christopher Lee's ex-communicated priest, Father Michael Rayner—included such surprising choices as Michael Sarrazin, Richard Dreyfuss, Cliff Robertson, Orson Welles, Stacy Keach, Beau Bridges and Peter Fonda. Meanwhile, as the girl, such equally unlikely names as Olivia Newton-John, Jenny Agutter, Lalla Ward, Jane Seymour, Susan Penhaligon, Lynne Frederick and even Twiggy were bandied about.

Eventually, Hollywood stalwart Richard Widmark landed the lead, while newcomer Nastassja Kinski was cast as the girl. But even Widmark's casting had its repercussions. The actor had been a consideration for Verney since October 1974, but his asking price of $130,000 had proved a deterrent (the role had originally been budgeted at a relatively modest $65,000, which is why so many actors had baulked). By now desperate, Carreras bit the bullet and accepted Widmark's price, which led to budget trims elsewhere in the cast. Consequently, David Warner and Jeremy Kemp were out, and replaced by the cheaper Anthony Valentine and Michael Goodliffe respectively. Kinski's fee

was nominal, given her beginner's status, while Denholm Elliott and Honor Blackman, whose fees presumably fell within confines of the budget, filled the remaining key supporting roles.

The cameras eventually began to roll on the £360,000 feature on 1 September 1975. Based at Elstree, the film also made extensive use of locations in and around London, as well as in Germany (several scenes were set on the shores of Lake Herrenschiemsee not far from Munich). The script, which had by now been re-worked a number of times, was still far from seaworthy though, hence the continued re-writes during filming. Yet despite its pre-production problems and its far from smooth shoot, the resultant film for the most part shows few signs of its troubled birth.

It opens with a ceremony that sees Father Michael Rayner excommunicated, following which we cut to "Bavaria—20 years later." A young nun named Catherine Beddows, who has been in the care of Father Michael, is being sent to London to visit her father for her eighteenth birthday, for which the priest has given her a present. In the meantime, the girl's father, Henry Beddows, has contacted an occult writer named John Verney, whom he coerces into meeting Catherine at the airport on his behalf. The girl's father, it would appear, is in trouble with a group of Satanists led by none other than Father Michael, and wants Verney, in return for information about the cult, to look after the girl until things have calmed down. "If Beddows is right, by just taking care of the girl I'll have a hell of a book on my hands if he comes through with that information he promised," Verney tells his agent, Anna Fountain, and her lover David Kennedy, whom he has roped in to looking after Catherine. What Beddows hasn't told Verney is that upon her birth eighteen years earlier, Catherine was promised to Father Michael and his church, The Children of Our Lord, for a demonic ritual. "I think Beddows conned me. It's not *him* they want. It's *Catherine*," observes Verney when the truth begins to dawn on him. As Verney explains to Anna and David, Catherine's birthday actually falls on All Hallows Eve. "This Father Michael is Catherine's godfather, and he's also the leader of their church, which must make her very special to them. Now let's suppose they plan something special for her, tomorrow, her eighteenth birthday, All Hallows Eve. Something that so horrifies her father—and he's *one* of them, for God's sake—he comes to me!"

Beddows has tried to recant

his pact with Father Michael, but to no avail. Indeed, Catherine—who seems unaware of the true nature of the church—is set to become an avatar, the earthly personification of Asteroth via an alliance with a demonic child born of one of Father Michael's acolytes (Catherine's birthday present from Father Michael it transpires is an inverted cross bearing an image of Asteroth). With time now running out, Verney leaves Catherine in the charge of Anna and David so as to get advice from the bishop who excommunicated Father Michael, along with permission to visit the so-called Black Room underneath his church to acquire the required knowledge to void the pact and save Catherine. During Verney's absence, Father Michael contacts Catherine through the power of his mind and wills her to murder Anna, following which she runs from the scene, only to be picked up by George de Grass, the doctor responsible for "delivering" the demonic baby. Having returned home to discover David mourning Anna ("Your girl did well, didn't she?"), Verney and David drive out to Beddows' home, Radley Manor in Guildford, where he breaks in and confronts Catherine's father, who is holed up in the attic amid a pentacle. "If we don't find her, for the rest of her life she'll *be* Asteroth," Verney tells Beddows, who informs them that the pact itself is hidden in a cavity behind a panel in the altar of the nearby Radley Church.

Verney and David thus make their way to the church, where Verney retrieves the long-hidden pact from the altar, only for David to burst into flames and disintegrate to dust when he grabs it, seemingly in place of Beddows, to whom Verney subsequently returns the pact. He then makes for the ritual site, at which Catherine and the demon child, within a circle of blood, have momentarily become one, after which Father Michael kills the re born baby so as to anoint Catherine with its blood. Killing George de Grass with a rock, and then Father Michael with the same weapon, now energized with the blood of a disciple, Verney rescues Catherine amid a mighty wind. But Catherine has spots of blood from the dead demon baby upon her forehead, and it remains unclear as to whether or not Verney has in fact truly "saved" her….

At the core of *To the Devil a Daughter* lies a fairly simple tale of good versus evil, wrapped in a nick-of-time narrative that has our hero racing against the clock to save a young woman from a fate worse than death. This has, however, been tricked out with a variety of diversions and subplots that don't always make complete sense, climaxing in a long-anticipated confrontation scene between Verney and Father Michael that doesn't quite carry the expected impact. Indeed, defeating one of Satan's all-powerful minions simply by throwing a rock at him has always been a cause of consternation for many viewers of the film (pondered an incredulous Christopher Lee, "How do you kill a Satanic character with a rock?"[27]). Nevertheless, despite its faults and the turmoil in which it was made, there is much to appreciate in the film, thanks primarily to the stylish way in which the mumbo jumbo is presented.

An amalgam of elements from *Rosemary's Baby* (1968), *The Exorcist* (1973) and *It's Alive* (1974),

**...and suddenly the screams of a baby born in Hell!**

**WARNING!** THIS MOTION PICTURE CONTAINS THE MOST SHOCKING SCENES THIS SIDE OF HELL!

**TO THE DEVIL...
A DAUGHTER**

American poster for *To the Devil a Daughter* (1976) (Hammer/Terra Filmkunst GMBH Berlin/EMI/Cine Artists/Studio Canal).

the screenplay, which was in the can by 24 October, is little more than a collection of fashionable set-piece elements, including devil worship, demonic childbirth, possession, nightmares, hallucinations and gory deaths, slickly presented by director Peter Sykes via a series of strikingly framed and angled shots. The film may be somewhat involved ("We just couldn't get the script right,"[28] admitted Roy Skeggs), but it certainly looks good throughout. From the opening scene of Father Michael's excommunication, which makes effective use of the colored light cast through a stained glass window and several eye-catching shots of Christ upon the cross, the emphasis is on the visual rather than the verbal. This is just as well, given that the screenplay is fairly devoid of memorable dialogue, save for Verney's observation that, "Ninety-eight per-cent of so-called Satanists are nothing but pathetic freaks who get their kicks out of dancing naked in freezing church yards, and use the Devil as an excuse for getting some sex. But then there's that other two percent. I'm not so sure about them," to which he later adds, "I have a feeling we're dealing with that other two per-cent."

Visual flourishes abound, among them striking aerial shots of London (notably of Big Ben and Tower Bridge), intense close-ups (particularly of Father Michael and the increasingly fraught Henry Beddows), and an eye-catching use of locations, prime among them St. Katharine Docks, where Verney's apartment, with its vaulted brick ceilings, is situated in the converted Ivory House. The film also makes use of the chapel on the Dashwood Estate for the climax (which, as originally scripted, was to have been set in the rather more claustrophobic environs of the crypt of St. Martin's-in-the-Fields in Trafalgar Square). The staging of individual sequences is also highly effective, among them the birth of the demon baby (in which, perhaps mercifully, more is implied that actually shown), Father Michael's attempts to contact Catherine through sheer willpower (the pricking of Catherine's fingers is a nice touch), David's fiery death (performed by stunt man Eddie Powell), and a nightmare sequence in which Catherine, seemingly empathizing with the woman who is at the same time giving birth to the demon baby, dreams that she is being born ("I was clawing my way out"). However, the nudity in the climactic scene, during which Rayner "offers" Catherine to Verney, seems somewhat gratuitous—even questionable—given Kinski's age at the time (she was just fourteen). Otherwise, the film is presented with a professional gloss throughout.

Compared to some Hammer films, the gore is fairly minimal, save for the murder of Anna with a metal comb through her neck, and the climactic sequence in which Catherine seemingly pushes the demonic baby up between her legs and into her womb (sensationalism aside, the point of this indulgent bit of unpleasantness is never made clear, especially given that it does not appear in the original novel). Nevertheless, an air of genuine dread hovers over the proceedings, thanks to the sheer magnetism of Christopher Lee's performance as Father Michael. Never for one moment does one doubt the authenticity of the character's Satanic

**A stab in the dark. Christopher Lee in a German lobby card for *To the Devil a Daughter* (1976) (Hammer/Terra Filmkunst GMBH Berlin/EMI/Cine Artists/Studio Canal).**

powers, nor his influence upon others. Indeed, his threats carry a real charge of menace ("Live in dread, Henry Beddows, and mend your ways," he at one point tells Catherine's poor father, who quite rightly looks concerned). He also effectively conveys Rayner's utter commitment to his cause. During the birth of the demonic baby, he says of its mother, who has rejected an injection of morphine despite the fact that her legs have been tightly bound together, "Margaret knows the only way it must be born. It won't be easy, it won't be pleasant." After the event, he then comfortingly informs her, "Margaret, you shall die now."

We learn little about Verney himself, save that he is a successful writer of occult novels, was divorced five years earlier, and has a daughter of his own. Yet the performance of Richard Widmark (who it appears was frequently less than amiable to work with during shooting) carries equal conviction, thanks to his weather-beaten looks and calmly emphatic manner. The supporting cast is also in good form, particularly Denholm Elliott as Catherine's cowering father, Michael Goodliffe (whose last film this was before his untimely death) as the doctor George de Grass, and Honor Blackman and Anthony Valentine, who make an amusing double act as Anna and David ("Darling, would this go with Wellingtons?" Anna asks David, having tried on Catherine's wimple, to which comes the reply, "Wellington's what?"). Nastassja Kinski meanwhile looks suitably innocent as the young nun, though quite *how* innocent we never really do find out (her lips are in a permanent come-hither pout throughout). Even the minor players leave their mark, among them Brian Wilde as the Black Room attendant ("Our records go back to 1603," he proudly states), Derek Francis

(better known for his blustering comic roles) as the Bishop, and Eva Marie Meineke as Eveline de Grass, who literally donates her lifeblood for the cause.

Technically, the film is also impressive, thanks to David Watkin's expert cinematography, the atmospheric score of Paul Glass, and the tight editing of John Trumper, despite the last-minute excising of certain scenes. Revealed Christopher Lee of the rather tame climax, during which he is hit with a rock by Verney, "When we shot the film, I [originally] recovered, and staggered to my feet. I saw Widmark and Kinski out of the circle; I got up and with the dagger in my hand, ran after them, forgetting the significance of crossing the circle of blood.... The moment I touched it: divine retribution—there was a flash of lightning from on high, which struck me. I was thrown over backwards and I lay on the ground in a crucified position."[29] Michael Carreras had hoped to re-shoot the finale, with Shane Briant appearing as the Devil to do battle with Father Rayner. The sequence was duly scripted by Christopher Wicking, but failed to make it on to film when EMI's Nat Cohen refused additional funds to shoot it.

Thus, *To the Devil a Daughter* appeared before the public in a state less than satisfactory to its makers when released in the UK on 4 March 1976 by EMI following premier engagements in Nottingham and Birmingham. The film opened well enough at the box office and was deemed good enough to be screened at the flagship Odeon Leicester Square in London, but failed to make the distance, with cinemagoers preferring to patronize another demonic thriller, *The Omen* (1976). Still, some of the reviews were quite positive, among them the *Monthly Film Bulletin*, which proclaimed that "Hammer is at last finding successful ways of reworking the Gothic idiom." Others were damning. "Even Christopher Lee, who is used to appearing in spine-chillers beneath his dignity, seems uncomfortable," noted the *Daily Mail*. "About as artistic as picking one's nose in public," commented *Films and Filming*, while the *Evening Standard* warned that it "reduces Dennis Wheatley's Satanic novel to an obsession with gynaecological deliveries, bloodstained wombs, and sacrificial babies."

The film's American release, care of Cine Arts, followed in July the same year. Sadly, *Variety* labelled it a "lackluster occult melodrama," yet found time to describe Christopher Lee as "ever dependable" and the performances of Richard Widmark, Honor Blackman and Anthony Valentine as "serviceable." It also found Nastassja Kinski "moderately appealing as the child-woman novitiate," and felt that "Denholm Elliott turns on the requisite anguish as the fearful father who originally signed the girl over to Lee in order to save his own hide." Unfortunately, the film's biggest critic was Dennis Wheatley himself, who found the film to be thoroughly disgusting and a degradation of his original story. Commented Christopher Lee: "Why the screenplay varied so greatly from Dennis Wheatley's novel was beyond me."[30]

Certainly worthy of being re-evaluated, *To the Devil a Daughter* is by no means the catastrophe some observers have claimed, despite the problems encountered in its making ("It was an absolute nightmare,"[31] admitted Roy Skeggs). A stylish thriller in the idiom of the times, it remains a more-than-worthy addition to Hammer's back catalogue, and is undeniably superior to some of their hole-in-the-wall efforts of the early seventies. Sadly, save for the remake of *The Lady Vanishes* (1979), Hammer's output would henceforth be relegated to the small screen before disappearing completely for some thirty years. **Additional notes:** Christopher Wicking is credited rather casually as Chris Wicking. Director Peter Sykes can be seen in a brief cameo at the airport: he's the one who's bumped into by Constantin de Goguel as he runs out of the terminal in chase of Richard Widmark and Nastassja Kinski. Also at the airport, keep an eye out for the two old biddies who observe Richard Widmark getting out of his car when he first arrives there—one of them points excitedly at him, and seems to be telling her rather more slow-witted friend that, hey, that's Richard Widmark getting out of that car. Hilarious! All the framed photos of the cast seen on desks, etc., in the film (among them stills of Denholm Elliott and Anna Bentinck, as well as the identifying snap of Nastassja Kinski given to Richard Widmark) seem to be their publicity photos. Stuntman Eddie Powell's g-string can be seen during the orgy sequence. Paul Patterson made some minor contributions to the score when composer Paul Glass was running behind schedule; Patterson went on to score four episodes each of *Hammer House of Horror* (1980, TV) and *Hammer House of Mystery and Suspense* (1984, TVM). Michael Goodliffe plays George de Grass in the film, yet the nameplate on the front door of his clinic reads Von Grass. Actor Ed Devereux had his scene in which he is run down by a car cut from the release print. The film ends with a direct quote from Dennis Wheatley: "In light things thrive and bear fruit…. In darkness they decay and die. That is why we must follow the teachings of the Lord of Light." A "making of" book titled *Facts About a Feature Film* by Marjorie Bilbow (with a foreword by Christopher Lee) was issued upon the film's release. The eye-catching St. Katharine's Dock location is also featured in *Czech Mate* (1984, TVM [episode of *Hammer House of Mystery and Suspense*]). The film also features a brief scene at High Canons (doubling as the the the de Grass clinic), already seen in *The Devil Rides Out* (1968) and *The Satanic Rites of Dracula* (1974). The Dashwood estate was home to the infamous Hellfire Club, and the present Lady Dashwood is none other than Marla Landi, who appeared in Hammer's *The Hound of the Baskervilles* (1959). Hammer also owned the rights to another of Dennis Wheatley's John Verney books, *The Satanist*, during this period, which they hoped to film with Christopher Lee and Britt Ekland, though it seems unlikely that Richard Widmark would have returned to the role, given his experiences with Hammer. The opening titles bill the film as a Hammer/Terra Anglo/German Co-production. The film was later re-released on a double bill with *The Devil Rides Out* (1968). Some posters refer to the film as *To the Devil … A Daughter*.

Production companies: Hammer/Terra Filmkunst GMBH Berlin. Distributors: EMI (UK [ABC circuit]), Cine Artists (U.S.). Producer: Roy Skeggs. Executive producer: Michael Carreras [uncredited]. Director: Peter Sykes. Screenplay: Christopher Wicking, John Peacock (adaptation), Gerald Vaughan-Hughes [uncredited], based upon the novel by Dennis Wheatley. Cinematographer: David Watkin. Music: Paul Glass (and Paul Patterson [uncredited]). Music director: Philip Martell. Orchestra "fixer": Harry Martell [uncredited]. Editor: John Trumper. Art director: Don Picton. Set dresser: John Jarvis [uncredited]. Costumes: Laura Nightingale, Eddie Boyce [uncredited]. Special effects: Les Bowie. Make-up: Eric Allwright, George Blackler. Hair: Jeanette Freeman. Recording director: Tony Lumkin. Sound: Dennis Whitlock. Sound editor: Mike Le Mare. Dubbing mixer: Bill Rowe. Assistant director: Barry Langley. Second assistant director: Mike Higgins [uncredited]. Third assistant director: Roy Stevens [uncredited]. Construction manager: Wag Hammerton. Gaffers: Ted Hallows, Steve Birtles [uncredited]. Production manager: Ron Jackson. Production secretary: Jean Clarkson [uncredited]. Camera operator: Ron Robson. Casting: Irene Lamb. Continuity: Sally Jones. Stunts: Vic Armstrong [uncredited]. Stills: Ray Hearne [uncredited]. Publicity: Mike Russell, Davidson Dalling Associates [uncredited]. Production accountant: Ken Gordon. **Cast:** Richard Widmark (John Verney), Christopher Lee (Father Michael Rayner), Denholm Elliott (Henry Beddows), Nastassja Kinski (Catherine Beddows), Honor Blackman (Anna Fountain), Anthony Valentine (David Kennedy), Michael Goodliffe (George de Grass), Eva Marie Meineke (Eveline de Grass), Derek Francis (Bishop), Isabella Telezynska (Margaret), Irene Prador (Matron), Brian Wilde (Black Room attendant), Frances de la Tour (Salvation Army Major), Constantin de Goguel (Kollde), Anna Bentinck (Isabel), Petra Peters (Sister Helle), William Ridoutt (Airport porter), Howard Goorney (Critic), Bill Horsley (Curator), Zoe Hendry (First girl), Lindy Benson (Second girl), Jo Peters (Third girl), Bobby Sparrow (Fourth girl), Ed Devereaux (Reporter [scene deleted, uncredited]), Peter Sykes (Man at airport [uncredited]), Eddie Powell (Christopher Lee and Anthony Valentine's stunt double [uncredited]). **DVD availability:** Anchor Bay (U.S. R1 NTSC), extras include a UK trailer, stills gallery, biographies, a retrospective documentary titled *To the Devil … The Death of Hammer*, featuring Christopher Wicking, Roy Skeggs, Peter Sykes, Gerald Vaughan-Hughes, Christopher Lee, Honor Blackman and Anthony Valentine, plus an interview with stuntman Eddie Powell, which was filmed in 1988 at the Festival of Fantastic Films; Studio Canal/Warner (UK R2 PAL); also available as part of Optimum's *The Ultimate Hammer Collection* (UK R2 PAL). **Blu-ray availability:** Studio Canal (B/2). **CD availability:** *The Hammer Film Music Collection: Volume Two* (GDI Records), which contains *The Seed of Asteroth*

### Tobias, Oliver

This handsome Swiss born actor (1947–, real name Oliver Tobias Freitag) proved to be a fashionable leading man in the late seventies and early eighties thanks primarily to his performance in *The Stud* (1978). In Britain from the age of eight, he trained at the East 15 Acting School and went on to appear in the original 1968 production of the musical *Hair*. His other film credits include *Romance of a Horse Thief* (1971), *'Tis Pity She's a Whore* (1971), *Arabian Adventure* (1979), *A Nightingale Sang in Berkeley Square* (1980), *The Wicked Lady* (1983), *The Brylcreem Boys* (1996), *Grizzly Falls* (1999), *Don't Look Back* (2003), *Eldorado* (2010), *Highway to Hell* (2012) and *Dad's Army* (2016). Also busy on stage and television, his credits for the latter include *Last Video and Testament* (1984, TVM [episode of *Hammer House of Mystery and Suspense*]), in which he plays a businessman out to murder his boss. His other small screen credits include episodes of *Arthur of the Britons* (1972–1973, TV), in which he played the title role, *Jesus of Nazareth* (1977, TV), *Dick Turpin* (1979–1982, TV), *Adventurer* (1987, TV), *Eurocops* (1988–1993, TV), *Vendetta* (1995, TV), *The Knock* (1994–2000, TV) and *Dr. Terrible's House of Horrible* (2001, TV). His father was the actor Robert Freitag (1916–2010, real name Robert Peter Freytag), and his mother the actress Maria Becker (1920–2012). His brother is the actor Benedict Freitag (1952–). **Hammer credits:** *Last Video and Testament* (1984, TVM [episode of *Hammer House of Mystery and Suspense*])

### Todd, Ann

With her immaculate looks and cut-glass accent, this British leading actress (1909–1993) was obviously destined for stardom. On stage from 1928 and in films from 1931 with *These Charming People*, she went on to appear in such popular thirties fare as *The Ghost Train* (1931), *Things to Come* (1936) and *South Riding* (1939) before becoming a major star thanks to her performance in *The Seventh Veil* (1945). In Hollywood briefly to co-star in Hitchcock's *The Paradine Case* (1947), she returned to Britain to appear in *So Evil My Love* (1948), after which she starred in three films for director David Lean (1908–1991), who became her third husband (of three) between 1949 and 1957. These were *The Passionate Friends* (1949), *Madeleine* (1950) and *The Sound Barrier* (1952), the last of which earned her a best actress BAFTA nomination. Todd's subsequent films include *The Green Scarf* (1954), *The Son of Captain Blood* (1963), *The Fiend* (1971), *The Human Factor* (1979) and *Maigret* (1992, TVM), while in the mid-sixties she directed three travelogues: *Thunder in Heaven* (1965), *Thunder of the Gods* (1966) and *Thunder of the Kings* (1967).

In 1961, she starred in the Hammer shocker *Taste of Fear* (1961), in which she turned character expectations on their head by playing a seemingly kind stepmother who ultimately turns out to be of the wicked variety. Remembered writer-producer Jimmy Sangster of Todd, "She was one of the grand ladies of the British screen at the time, but fading fast. A former Mrs. David Lean, she lived in a magnificent house bordering Holland Park in Kensington. It was there one evening when I was having a meeting with Ann about a couple of script points she wanted to go over that she introduced me to her house guest, Ingrid Bergman. I'd like to say that it was the start of something big, but it wasn't."[32] Her second husband was associate producer Nigel Tangye (1909–1988), to whom she was married between 1945 and 1949. **Hammer credits:** *Taste of Fear* (1961, as Jane Appleby)

### Todd, Bob

Much loved for his appearances on television with Benny Hill from the sixties through to the eighties, this balding British comedy character actor (1921–1992) was frequently cast as explosive types, among them the outraged Burgomaster in Hammer's *Scars of Dracula* (1970). In films from 1961 with *Raising the Wind*, his other credits include *Postman's Knock* (1962), *Hot Millions* (1968), *Bachelor of Arts* (1969), *Adolf Hitler—My Part in His Downfall* (1972), *The Four Musketeers* (1974), *The Ups and Downs of a Handyman* (1975), *Confessions of a Pop Performer* (1975), *Superman III* (1983) and *The Return of the Musketeers* (1989). He also appeared in two TV spin-off comedies for Hammer. His other TV appearances include episodes of *It's a Square World* (1960–1964, TV), *Cribbins* (1969–1970, TV), *The Marty Feldman Comedy Machine* (1971–1972, TV) and *The Steam Video Company* (1984, TV). **Hammer credits:** *Scars of Dracula* (1970, as Burgomaster), *Mutiny on the Buses* (1972, as New Inspector), *That's Your Funeral* (1973, as Arthur [funeral director])

### Todd, Brian

Todd can be seen in Hammer's *The Witches* (1966). His other credits include *A Canterbury Tale* (1944), plus an episode of *The Granville Melodramas* (1955, TV). His brother is the actor David Todd (1939–). **Hammer credits:** *The Witches* (1966, as Dancer [uncredited])

### Todd, Dawn

Todd had a minor role in Hammer's *The Anniversary* (1968). Her other credits include *The Great St. Trinian's Train Robbery* (1966) and *Little Dog Lost* (1967). **Hammer credits:** *The Anniversary* (1968, as Child [uncredited])

### Todd, Peter

Todd worked as an assistant editor on several films for Hammer in the late fifties/early sixties. His other credits, among them several shorts and documentaries, include *The Hymac Range* (1966), *An Introduction to Hydraulic Excavators* (1967), *Road South* (1967), *Mechanical Excavating* (1970) and *Team Balance* (1972). **Hammer credits:** *The Revenge of Frankenstein* (1958 [uncredited]), *The Hound of the Baskervilles* (1959 [uncredited]), *The Ugly Duckling* (1959 [uncredited]), *Never Take Sweets from a Stranger* (1960 [uncredited])

### Toguri, David

This Canadian dancer, choreographer and stage director (1933–1997) spent much of his career working in British theater. On stage as a dancer from 1953 with the Volkoff Canadian Ballet, he soon after went to Broadway and then London, where he continued to work on stage as well as on television and in film. He made his film debut as a dancer/actor in Hollywood in *Flower Drum Song* (1961), having appeared in the stage production. His other film appearances include *Three Hats for Lisa* (1965), *You Only Live Twice* (1967), *Welcome to the Club* (1970), *Rentadick* (1972) and *Alicja* (1982).

He began choreographing for films with Hammer's *The Devil Rides Out* (1968), for which he staged the orgiastic woodland Sabbat. Commented *Variety* of the sequence: "[Terence] Fisher's direction makes one of the Satanic orgies a production high spot, aided by some frenzied choreography by David Toguri." His other film credits as a choreographer include *The Perfumed Garden* (1970), *Eskimo Nell* (1974), in which he also appeared, *The Rocky Horror Picture Show* (1975), *Give My Regards to Broad Street* (1984), *Absolute Beginners* (1986), *Scandal* (1988) and *Peter's Friends* (1992). His television credits as an actor include episodes of *The Troubleshooters* (1965–1972, TV), *Armchair Thriller* (1967–1980, TV) and *Rock Follies* (1976, TV), the latter of which he also choreographed. He was also involved with many commercials and pop promos, while for the theater he worked on such diverse shows as *Zorba, Poppy, Little Shop of Horrors* and *Spread a Little Happiness*. **Hammer credits:** *The Devil Rides Out* (1968)

### Toho

This Japanese production company is best known for its man-in-a-rubber-suit monster films, among them many Godzilla epics, including *Godzilla* (1955), *Godzilla versus Hedora* (1971), *Godzilla versus Mechagodzilla* (1974), *Godzilla versus Megalon* (1976) and *Godzilla versus King Ghidorah* (1998). In 1977 Toho was set to make *Nessie* with Hammer, but the project ran aground when Columbia, which was also providing finance, backed out at the eleventh hour.

### Tolan, Michael

The film credits of this American actor (1925–2011, real name Seymour Tuchow) include *John and Mary* (1969), *The Lost Man* (1969), *300 Year Weekend* (1970), *All That Jazz* (1979), *Presumed Innocent* (1990) and *Perfect Stranger* (2007), while his television credits take in the leading role in *Paper Dolls*, an episode of Hammer's *Journey to the Unknown* (1968, TV), which also appears in the compendium film *Journey into Darkness* (1968, TVM). His other TV work includes episodes of *The Web* (1950–1954, TV), *Route 66* (1960–1964, TV), *Here We Go Again* (1973, TV), *Kojak* (1973–1978, TV) and *Murder, She Wrote* (1984–1996, TV). Also busy on stage and radio, his second wife (of two) was actress Rosemary Forsythe (1943–), to whom he was married between 1966 and 1970. **Hammer credits:** *Paper Dolls* (1968, TV [episode of *Journey to the Unknown*], as Craig Miller), *Journey into Darkness* (1968, TVM, as Craig Miller)

### Tomblin, David

British born Tomblin (1930–2005) worked as the assistant director on the Hammer thriller *Taste of Fear* (1961). Regarded as one of the best assistant directors in the business, he worked his way up from third assistant on such films as *The Ghosts of Berkeley Square* (1947) and *Police Dog* (1955), first becoming an AD on *The Anatomist* (1956, TVM) and episodes of *The Count of Monte Cristo* (1956, TV). His other credits as a first assistant include such major films as *The Liquidator* (1965), *Barry Lyndon* (1975), *The Omen* (1976), *A Bridge Too Far* (1977), *Superman* (1978), on which he was the second unit AD, *The Empire Strikes Back* (1980), *Raiders of the Lost Ark* (1981), *Gandhi* (1982), *Never Say Never Again* (1983), *Empire of the Sun* (1987), *Chaplin* (1992), *Braveheart* (1995) and *The Man in the Iron Mask* (1998). He also directed the second unit for *Shaft in Africa* (1973), *Zulu Dawn* (1979), *Superman II* (1980) and *Ever After* (1998). He also worked as a writer, producer, director and assistant director on many television series, most notably *Danger Man* (1964–1966, TV), with whose star, Patrick McGoohan, he went on to work on the cult hit *The Prisoner* (1967–1968, TV), which he produced with McGoohan, and of which he wrote three episodes, two of which he also directed. In 2003 Tomblin earned a special BAFTA award for his outstanding contribution to film. **Hammer credits:** *Taste of Fear* (1961)

### Tomelty, Joseph

Following experience as a playwright, among them *Idolatry at Innishargie* (1942) and *Poor Errand* (1943), this Irish stage actor (1910–1995) went on to appear in thirty films, beginning with the IRA thriller *Odd Man Out* (1947), on which he also worked as an advisor. His other credits include *Treasure Hunt* (1952), *The Sound Barrier* (1952), *Devil Girl from Mars* (1954), *Hobson's Choice* (1954), *Moby Dick* (1956), *Lancelot and Guinevere* (1962) and *The Black Torment* (1964), following which he returned to the stage. He can also be seen as Furnisher Steele in the Hammer thriller *Hell Is a City* (1960). His television credits include episodes of *Douglas Fairbanks, Jr. Presents*

(1953–1957, TV), *Armchair Theatre* (1956–1974, TV), *Police Surgeon* (1960, TV) and *Zero One* (1962–1965, TV). His other plays include *All Soul's Night* (1949), *Down the Heather Glen* (1953) and *Is the Priest at Home?* (1954). His children are writer, director and actress Roma Tomelty (1945–) and actress Frances Tomelty (1945–); his granddaughter is actress Fuschia Sumner (1982–). **Hammer credits:** *Hell Is a City* (1960, as Furnisher Steele)

### Tomlinson, David

Following experience in the Grenadier Guards, this much-liked British comedy character actor (1917–2000) turned to acting in 1936 after appearing in several amateur plays. In films from 1940 with *Garrison Follies*, he went on to appear in over fifty films, securing his name with *Quiet Wedding* (1941) in which he played the best man (he'd previously played the bridegroom on stage, where he was spotted by director Anthony Asquith). Subsequent films include *The Way to the Stars* (1945), *Miranda* (1948), *So Long at the Fair* (1950) and *Carry On Admiral* (1958). Tomlinson also co-starred with Peter Sellers in the Hammer naval comedy *Up the Creek* (1958), the success of which provoked a hasty sequel, *Further Up the Creek* (1958), in which Tomlinson's co-star was this time Frankie Howerd. In the sixties, Tomlinson made a successful move to Hollywood, where he made several films for Walt Disney, among them *Mary Poppins* (1964), in which he played George Banks, *The Love Bug* (1968) and *Bedknobs and Broomsticks* (1971). His remaining films include *Wombling Free* (1977), *Dominique* (1978), *The Water Babies* (1978) and *The Fiendish Plot of Dr. Fu Manchu* (1980), the latter again with Peter Sellers. **Hammer credits:** *Up the Creek* (1958, as Lieutenant Humphrey Fairweather), *Further Up the Creek* (1958, as Lieutenant Humphrey Fairweather)

### Tomlinson, Lionel (Tommy)

Working at the low budget end of the second feature market, this British director (1907–1972, real name Richard Lionel Tomlinson, aka Tommy Tomlinson) helmed Hammer's second post-war featurette, *Death in High Heels* (1947), on which he was credited as Tommy Tomlinson. He also co-directed the quota quickie *Who Killed Van Loon?* (1948) with Gordon Kyle, this time billed as Lionel Tomlinson. Neither could be described as classics. His other credits as a director include *My Hands Are Clay* (1948) and *Take a Powder* (1953), the latter of which he also produced. He began his career as an editor, and his credits in this capacity include *The Limping Man* (1936), *The Terror* (1938), *Hell's Cargo* (1939), *At the Villa Rose* (1940) and *Walking on Air* (1946). **Hammer credits:** *Death in High Heels* (1947, director), *Who Killed Van Loon?* (1948, co-director)

### Tomlinson, Tommy *see* Tomlinson, Lionel

### Toms, Carl

This noted British stage designer (1927–1999) is best known to film fans for his costume work for a number of Hammer productions, among them the diaphanous gowns worn by Ursula Andress in *She* (1965) and the eye-catching but anachronistic doeskin bikini worn by Raquel Welch in *One Million Years B.C.* (1966), since immortalized by Pierre Luigi's portrait of the actress while modeling it. Commented stills photographer Terry O'Neill, who also worked on the film, "It was a great bikini, but a terrible film."[33] Recalled Raquel Welch of her outfit, "Carl Toms, who designed my costume, really outdid himself. He really made the most of this little doeskin number that I was supposed to wear. I, having no dialogue whatsoever, being bored to distraction, used to pull bits and pieces off it during waiting around the set to run from rock A to rock B…. So this costume got smaller and smaller as the production went on. The unit photographer was just having a field day."[34]

Following training at the Royal College of Art and the Old Vic School, Toms went on to design numerous stage productions for the National Theater, The Royal Court and The Old Vic among others, although he only designed one film, *The Winter's Tale* (1967)—which in any case was based upon the Pop Theater stage production seen at the 1966 Edinburgh Festival—plus a version of *Twelfth Night* (1969) for *ITV Sunday Night Theatre* (1969–1974, TV). His other film credits as a costume designer include *The Quiller Memorandum* (1966) and *Rocket to the Moon* (1967). Said Toms of his bikini design for Raquel Welch in *One Million Years B.C.*, "She had such a perfect body that I took a very soft doe skin, stretched it on her and tied it together with thongs. Prehistoric people knew nothing of bust darts and seams!"[35] **Additional notes:** Toms' costumes for *One Million Years B.C.* were re-used for *Slave Girls* (1968), which was shot immediately after, but not released until almost two years later. **Hammer credits:** *She* (1965), *One Million Years B.C.* (1966), *The Vengeance of She* (1968), *Slave Girls* (1968), *The Lost Continent* (1968), *Moon Zero Two* (1969), *When Dinosaurs Ruled the Earth* (1970)

### Toone, Geoffrey

On stage from the age of twenty-one, most notably at The Old Vic, this Irish leading man (1910–2005) entered films in 1938 with *Queer Cargo*. Following wartime service in the Royal Artillery (from which he was invalided out in 1942), he resumed his acting career in 1943, appearing on stage and in films in both Britain and America. His many big screen credits include *Hell Is Sold Out* (1951), *The King and I* (1956), *The Entertainer* (1960), *Dr. Crippen* (1962) and *Dr. Who and the Daleks* (1965), plus episodes of *Crusader* (1955–1956, TV), *Ivanhoe* (1958–1959, TV), *The Odd Man* (1960–1962, TV), *The Persuaders!* (1971–1972, TV), *The New Avengers* (1976–1977, TV), *War and Remembrance* (1988, TV) and *The High Life* (1994–1995, TV). He also played the heroic Captain Jackson Sale in Hammer's Oriental thriller *The Terror of the Tongs* (1961), in which he uncovers a murderous cult. **Hammer credits:** *The Terror of the Tongs* (1961, as Captain Jackson Sale)

### Topps Trading Cards *see* Trading Cards

### Total

This French oil company commissioned several documentaries in the fifties, sixties and seventies extolling the virtues of car travel, among them the Hammer short *Highway Holiday* (1959), which has long been out of circulation. **Hammer credits:** *Highway Holiday* (1959)

### Toto, Ecce Homo

This African actor and bit part player (aka Tony Wane, real name Toto Ware), living in Britain from thirties, can be seen as Mandingo in Hammer's third film, *Song of Freedom* (1936), which starred Paul Robeson. He also appeared in *Sanders of the River* (1935) and *King Solomon's Mines* (1937), both again with Robeson. **Hammer credits:** *Song of Freedom* (1936, as Mandingo)

### Tottenham, Merle

Born in India, this diminutive supporting actress (1901–1958) can be spotted as a maid in Hammer's *Sporting Love* (1936). She also played the role of Alice in the programer *Room to Let* (1950). In Hollywood for a few years in the thirties, her other credits include *Immediate Possession* (1931), *Cavalcade* (1933), in which she reprised her stage role of Annie, *The Invisible Man* (1933), *Night Must Fall* (1937), *Bank Holiday* (1938), *Poison Pen* (1940), *This Happy Breed* (1944), *Sleeping Car to Trieste* (1948) and *The Woman in Question* (1950). **Hammer credits:** *Sporting Love* (1936, as Maid), *Room to Let* (1950, as Alice)

### Tovey, George

This British actor (1914–1982) can be seen in a minor role in Hammer's *Love Thy Neighbour* (1973). His other film credits include *The Secret Partner* (1961), *Never Back Losers* (1961), *Poor Cow* (1967), *Frenzy* (1972), *Baxter!* (1973) and *The Wicked Lady* (1983), while on television he can be seen as the murderous Albert Clements in the pre-credits sequence of *The House That Bled to Death* (1980, TV [episode of *Hammer House of Horror*]). His many other TV credits include episodes of *Quatermass II* (1955, TV), *Steptoe and Son* (1962–1974, TV), *My Old Man* (1974–1975, TV) and *A Fine Romance* (1981–1984, TV). His daughter is the actress Roberta Tovey (1953–). **Hammer credits:** *Love Thy Neighbour* (1973, as Airport porter), *The House That Bled to Death* (1980, TV [episode of *Hammer House of Horror*], as Albert Clements)

### Towb, Harry

This Irish actor (1925–2009) can be seen as Cobb in the Hammer swashbuckler *The Scarlet Blade* (1963). He also had a small role in *Miss Belle* (1968, TV [episode of *Journey to the Unknown*]). In films from 1951 with *The Quiet Woman*, he went on to appear in over forty movies, among them *The Sleeping Tiger* (1954), *The 39 Steps* (1959), *The Blue Max* (1966), *Digby, the Biggest Dog in the World* (1973), *Lassiter* (1983), *Conspiracy of Silence* (2002) and *Gardens with Red Roses* (2009). His many television credits include *Joan and Leslie* (1956–1958, TV), *Gideon's Way* (1965–1966, TV),

*Tottering Towers* (1971–1972, TV), *You and Me* (1974–1992, TV), *Home James!* (1987–1990, TV) and *Comedy Nation* (1998, TV). Also much on stage, he was married to the actress Diana Hoddinot (1945– ). **Hammer credits:** *The Scarlet Blade* (1963, as Cobb [uncredited]), *Miss Belle* (1968, TV [episode of *Journey to the Unknown*], as Bill)

### Townley, Toke

Best known for playing Sam Pearson in the long-running soap *Emmerdale* (1972–, TV, formerly *Emmerdale Farm*) between 1972 and 1984, this British character actor (1912–1984) began his film career in 1949 with *A Man's Affair* following experience as a clerk. Over forty films followed, among them *H.M.S. Defiant* (1962), *The Missing Note* (1961), *The Chalk Garden* (1964) and *Oh! What a Lovely War* (1969). He also appeared in Hammer's *Men of Sherwood Forest* (1954) as Father David, though he is perhaps best remembered by genre fans for his following Hammer film, *The Quatermass Xperiment* (1955), in which he played the unfortunate chemist who comes to a sticky end when hit with Victor Carroon's "cactus arm." Ouch! The experience must have been a traumatic one, for Townley didn't return to Hammer until a quarter of a century later to play a minor role in *Scars of Dracula* (1970). His other TV appearances include episodes of *Tales from Dickens* (1958–1959, TV), *The Avengers* (1961–1969, TV), *Department S* (1969–1970, TV) and *Clouds of Witness* (1972, TV). **Hammer credits:** *Men of Sherwood Forest* (1954, as Father David), *The Quatermass Xperiment* (1955, as Chemist [uncredited]), *Scars of Dracula* (1970, as Waggoner)

### Townsend, Charles

Townsend worked as the production buyer on Hammer's Shepperton-shot comedy *A Weekend with Lulu* (1961). His other credits include *The Small Back Room* (1949) and *Carry On Nurse* (1959). **Hammer credits:** *A Weekend with Lulu* (1961 [uncredited])

### Townsend, Len (Leonard)

Townsend worked as the assistant art director on Hammer's *Dr. Jekyll and Sister Hyde* (1971). His other credits in this capacity include *Lilacs in the Spring* (1954), *King's Rhapsody* (1955) and *Whistle Down the Wind* (1961), plus episodes of *The Avengers* (1961–1969, TV) and *The Baron* (1966–1967, TV). His work as a fully-fledged art director includes *1984* (1956), *Nightmare* (1972) and *Voices* (1973). His other credits include work as a draughtsman on *Madonna of the Seven Moons* (1945) and *Caravan* (1946), and as a set dresser/decorator on *Anna Karenina* (1948), *Trent's Last Case* (1952), *A Night to Remember* (1958) and *Theatre of Death* (1966). **Hammer credits:** *Dr. Jekyll and Sister Hyde* (1971)

### Townsend, Phyllis

Townsend worked as the continuity girl on Hammer's *The Vengeance of She* (1968). Her many other credits include *Man from Tangier* (1957), *Calculated Risk* (1963), *The Face of Fu Manchu* (1965), *I, Monster* (1971), *The Beast Must Die* (1974), *Rising Damp* (1980), *Sahara* (1983), *Indiana Jones*

*and the Temple of Doom* (1984), *Lionheart* (1987) and *Dealers* (1989), plus episodes of *The Zoo Gang* (1974, TV), *Dick Turpin* (1979–1982, TV), *Widows* (1983, TV) and *The Endless Game* (1990, TV). **Hammer credits:** *The Vengeance of She* (1968)

### Tozer, Geoff (Geoffrey)

British born Tozer (1923–1998) worked as the assistant art director on the Hammer thriller *The Full Treatment* (1961). His other credits in this capacity include *The Naked Truth* (1957), *Faces in the Dark* (1960), *The Girl on the Boat* (1962) and episodes of *Strange Report* (1968–1970, TV). His work as a fully-fledged art director/production designer includes *Jigsaw* (1962), *The System* (1964), *Trog* (1970), *Puppet On a Chain* (1971), *Fanny Hill* (1983) and *The Little Drummer Girl* (1984), plus further episodes of *Strange Report*. **Hammer credits:** *The Full Treatment* (1961)

### Tracy

This British vocalist (1951– ), who at the time was under contract to EMI, performed the unfairly dismissed song *Strange Love*, which can be heard in Hammer's *Lust for a Vampire* (1971), which was co-financed and released by EMI. The number's music and lyrics were provided by Harry Robinson and Frank Godwin respectively. The song was presented on the B-side of a Columbia 45, the A-side of which featured *Rock Me in the Cradle (Of Your Lovin' Arms)* by General Johnson, Greg Perry and Ron Dunbar, which was likewise performed by Tracy and arranged by Harry Robinson; the record was produced by Bob Barratt. The film version of *Strange Love* can be found on the GDI CD *The Hammer Vampire Film Music Collection* within the cue titled *The Dream*. Tracy's other singles (A-sides) include *Don't Hold It Against Me* (1966), *Follow Me* (1969 [*The Baying Wolves Theme*]) and *Life's Like That* (1969), all of which were recorded on the Columbia label. **Hammer credits:** *Lust for a Vampire* (1971)

### Trading Cards

Given the gimmicks used to promote Hammer films in the sixties—give-away beards for *Rasputin—The Mad Monk* (1966), fangs and zombie eyes for *The Plague of the Zombies* (1966), etc.–it's surprising that there weren't any trading cards devoted to Hammer until 1976, when the company was practically done and dusted. The first set was produced by Topps, which issued fifty cards under the title Shock Theater, each of which included a piece of Bazooka bubble-gum and a naff joke on the back (referred to as Shocking Laffs). The front of the cards featured a "humorously" captioned color still from one of five Hammer films: *Dracula Has Risen from the Grave* (1968), *Frankenstein Must Be Destroyed* (1969), *Taste the Blood of Dracula* (1970), *Dracula A.D. 1972* (1972) and *The Satanic Rites of Dracula* (1974).

In 1995, a second set of trading cards appeared, this time care of Cornerstone Communications. The featured films were *The Curse of Frankenstein* (1957), *The Brides of Dracula* (1960), *The Curse of the Werewolf* (1961), *Dracula—Prince of Darkness* (1966), *Frankenstein Created Woman* (1967), *Scars of Dracula* (1970) and *Twins of Evil* (1971). A total

of eighty-one cards were produced, along with six "chase" cards featuring artwork by Paul Campbell, four promotional cards and one "Inside Trader" card available to paid up members. A further set of cards followed in 1996, this time featuring stills from *The Quatermass Xperiment* (1955), *Quatermass 2* (1957), *The Hound of the Baskervilles* (1959), *One Million Years B.C.* (1966), *Quatermass and the Pit* (1967), *The Devil Rides Out* (1968), *The Vampire Lovers* (1970), *The Satanic Rites of Dracula* (1974) and *Captain Kronos—Vampire Hunter* (1974). This time, the chase cards included a number of autographs, among them those of Dave Prowse, Ingrid Pitt, Jimmy Sangster and Ian Scoones, along with two Paul Campbell portraits of Oliver Reed in *The Curse of the Werewolf*, depicting his character before and after his transformation. There were also poster reproductions of unmade Hammer films, including *When the Earth Cracked Open* and *Zeppelin v Pterodactyls*.[36]

### The Trading Post

This British special effects house handled the effects for the Hammer science fiction drama *Spaceways* (1953), along with Bowie, Margutti and Co. The company also provided the effects for such films as *Private Potter* (1962), *Help!* (1965), *Half a Sixpence* (1967), *Far from the Madding Crowd* (1967) and *The Magic Christian* (1969). **Hammer credits:** *Spaceways* (1953)

### Travel Film (Distributors), Ltd.

Travel was one of Hammer's many subsidiaries. Based at Hammer House, it directors were James Carreras and Michael Carreras.

### Travers, Bill

In films from 1949 with *Conspirator*, this dependable British leading man (1922–1994, real name William Linden-Travers) is best remembered for the films he made with his second wife, the actress Virginia McKenna (1931– ), whom he married in 1957, and with whom he appeared in such favorites as *The Smallest Show on Earth* (1957), *Born Free* (1966) and *Ring of Bright Water* (1969). His other films include *The Browning Version* (1951), *Bhowani Junction* (1956), *Gorgo* (1960) and *The Belstone Fox* (1973), plus the Hammer programer *Mantrap* (1953), in which he played the supporting role of Victor Tasman. He also co-wrote, co-produced and co-directed *The Lions Are Free* (1967) with James Hill, in which he also appeared; co-wrote, co-produced (with Hill) and starred in *An Elephant Called Slowly* (1969); and directed and co-wrote (again with Hill) *The Lion at World's End* (1971), in which he again appeared (all three with his wife). His sister was the actress Linden Travers (1913–2001, real name Florence Linden-Travers), his son is the actor Bill (Will) Travers, Jr. (1958–, real name William Morrell-Lindon Travers), his nephew was the actor Richard Morant (1945–2011) and his nieces are the actresses Susan Travers (1939–, real name Jennifer Susan Leon) and Penelope Wilton (1946– ). He co-founded the conservation group the Born Free Foundation with McKenna in 1984. **Hammer credits:** *Mantrap* (1953, as Victor Tasman)

## Travis, Daniel

Travis worked on the American casting for all thirteen episodes of *Hammer House of Mystery and Suspense* (1984, TVM), sharing his credit with William J. Kenney. His other credits include *Forty Days of Musa Dagh* (1982), *Good-bye Cruel World* (1983), *Fist Fighter* (1989), *Soultaker* (1990) and *Surface to Air* (1998), plus episodes of *The Fall Guy* (1981–1986, TV). **Hammer credits:** *Hammer House of Mystery and Suspense* (1984, TVM)

## Travis, Richard

This American actor (1913–1989, real name William Justice, aka William [or Dick] Travis) appeared as Kent Foster in scenes shot for the American release of the Hammer prison melodrama *Women Without Men* (1956). His other credits, among them many B-westerns, include *King of the Royal Mounted* (1940), *The Bride Came C.O.D.* (1941), *The Man Who Came to Dinner* (1942), *Mission to Moscow* (1943), *Danger Zone* (1951), *City of Shadows* (1955), *Missile to the Moon* (1958) and *Cyborg 2087* (1966), plus episodes of *The Lone Ranger* (1949–1957, TV), *Code 3* (1957) and *The Legend of Jesse James* (1965–1966, TV). **Hammer credits:** *Women Without Men* (1956, Kent Foster)

## Treacher, Rose

Treacher provided the piano improvisations for Hammer's silent compilation *Made for Laughs* (1952). Her other film credits include *Return Fare to Laughter* (1950), for which she again tickled the ivories. Known for her live silent film accompaniments, she also provided stock music for the De Wolfe music library, for whom she also recorded albums, among them *The Silent Film Era* (1966) and *The Silent Film Era No 2* (1967), for which she penned such evocative cues as *Comedy Chase, The Bar Saloon, Struggle to the Death, Non-Stop Jim* and *The Wild West*. **Hammer credits:** *Made for Laughs* (1942)

## Trechman, Emma

This stage actress contributed to the screenplay of Hammer's third and final Dick Barton adventure, *Dick Barton at Bay* (1950). She also appeared in the early TV plays *Lady Precious Stream* (1938, TV) and *The Ascent of F6* (1938, TV), as well as *Anything But Love* (1951, TV). She also worked as a diction advisor on *Lady Windermere's Fan* (1949). **Hammer credits:** *Dick Barton at Bay* (1950)

## Tregarthen, Jeanette (Jeannette)

This British actress (1920–2010, full name Jeannette Tregarthen Jenkins, usually billed Jeannette Tregarthen) played the role of Monica Harling in the Hammer programer *Meet Simon Cherry* (1949). Her other credits include *Holiday Camp* (1947) and appearances on television in *The Only Way* (1948, TVM), *Corinth House* (1950, TVM), *Mother of Men* (1950, TVM) and *BBC Sunday-Night Theatre* (1950–1959, TV). Also much on stage (especially at the Theater Royal in her home city of Bristol), as well radio. **Hammer credits:** *Meet Simon Cherry* (1949, as Monica Harling)

## Trehy, John

Trehy worked as the production accountant on Hammer's *One Million Years B.C.* (1966). His other credits in this capacity (later as production controller) include *Ryan's Daughter* (1970), *Lady Caroline Lamb* (1972), *Barry Lyndon* (1975), *The Elephant Man* (1980), *Mountains of the Moon* (1990), *CutThroat Island* (1995), *Eyes Wide Shut* (1999) and *Harry Potter and the Prisoner of Azkaban* (2004). He also worked as an associate producer on *Harry Potter and the Goblet of Fire* (2005), and as a co-producer on *Harry Potter and the Order of the Phoenix* (2007) and *Harry Potter and the Deathly Hallows, Part 1* (2010) and *Part 2* (2011). **Hammer credits:** *One Million Years B.C.* (1966 [uncredited])

## Trent, Bill (William)

This sound technician worked as the sound editor on Hammer's *Twins of Evil* (1971). His other credits (either as dubbing editor, sound editor, foley editor or dialogue editor) include *Otley* (1968), *The Blood on Satan's Claw* (1971), *The Alf Garnett Saga* (1972), *Voyage of the Damned* (1976), *Death Ship* (1980), *Biggles* (1986), *Mary Shelley's Frankenstein* (1994), *The Borrowers* (1997) and *Circus* (2000), plus episodes of *The Saint* (1962–1969, TV), *The Champions* (1968–1969, TV) and *The Adventurer* (1972–1973, TV). His son is the editor Michael Trent. **Hammer credits:** *Twins of Evil* (1971)

## Trent, Pauline

This British hair stylist worked on two films for Hammer. Her other credits include *Escape Route* (1952), *Escape by Night* (1953), *The Runaway Bus* (1954), *Father Brown* (1954) and *A Night to Remember* (1958). **Hammer credits:** *The Gambler and the Lady* (1953), *Hell Is a City* (1960)

## Treo Film Exchanges

This American distribution company handled the U.S. release of Hammer's *Song of Freedom* (1936), which wasn't released Stateside until 1938 in a re-edited version. Other films distributed by the company include another British film, *The Lost Chord* (1933), which they released in 1937, and the American-made *Fury Below* (1936). **Hammer credits:** *Song of Freedom* (1936)

## Trevor, Elleston

This prolific British novelist (1920–1995, real name Trevor Dudley Smith, aka T. Dudley-Smith, Adam Hall, Simon Rattray, Lesley Stone, Mansell Black, Warwick Scott and Howard North) had his 1951 book *Dead on Course*, which he co-authored (under the pen-name of Mansell Black) with Packham Webb, adapted for the screen by Hammer as *Wings of Danger* (1952), though the film retained the novel's title for its American release. Also writing as Adam Hall, Simon Rattray and Howard North (among others), his many other works include *Queen in Danger* (1952), which was filmed by Hammer as *Mantrap* (1952), *The Big Pick Up* (1955), which was filmed as *Dunkirk* (1958), *The Pillars of Midnight* (1957), which was filmed as *80,000 Suspects* (1963), *The Flight of the Phoenix* (1964), which was filmed in 1965 and again in

2004, and *The Berlin Memorandum* (1965), which was filmed as *The Quiller Memorandum* (1965), and also formed the basis of the TV series *Quiller* (1975, TV), for which Elleston penned an episode. Hammer also had plans to film his 1950 novel *A Chorus of Echoes*, which failed to make it to the screen. Trevor's son is the matte artist Jean-Pierre Trevor. **Hammer credits:** *Wings of Danger* (1952), *Mantrap* (1953)

## Trevor, John

This supporting actor played a Sapper Captain in the Hammer war film *The Steel Bayonet* (1957). His other credits include episodes of *Fabian of the Yard* (1954–1956, TV), *The Black Brigand* (1956, TV) and *The Count of Monte Cristo* (1956, TV). **Hammer credits:** *The Steel Bayonet* (1957, as Sapper Captain [uncredited])

## Trevor-Davis, J. (John)

Trevor-Davis (sometimes J. Trevor Davies) played an officer in Hammer's *The Two Faces of Dr. Jekyll* (1960). His other credits include *Robbery with Violence* (1958) and *The Court Martial of Major Keller* (1961), plus episodes of *Theatre Royal* (1955–1956, TV) and *Over to William* (1956, TV). He was also originally cast as the uncle in Hammer's *The Curse of Frankenstein* (1957), but for some reason he then lost the role to Raymond Ray. **Hammer credits:** *The Two Faces of Dr. Jekyll* (1960, as Officer [uncredited])

## Trigger, Ian

This British actor (1938–2010) can be seen as a clown in Hammer's *Countess Dracula* (1971). His other credits include *Diamonds for Breakfast* (1968), *Pussycat, Pussycat, I Love You* (1970), *Up Pompeii* (1971), *Up the Chastity Belt* (1971), *Alice's Adventures in Wonderland* (1972) and *The Fantastic Four* (1994), plus episodes of *The Dark Island* (1962, TV), *Tales of Unease* (1970, TV) and *Ace of Wands* (1970–1972, TV). **Hammer credits:** *Countess Dracula* (1971)

## Trinder, Tommy

This British music hall comedian (1909–1989) was at his most popular during the war years. Occasionally in films, his credits include *Almost a Honeymoon* (1938), *The Foreman Went to France* (1942), *Champagne Charlie* (1944) and *You Lucky People* (1954), the latter named after his famous catchphrase. Some sources claim that he can also be spotted briefly as himself in Hammer's *The Damned* (1963). **Hammer credits:** *The Damned* (1963, as Himself [uncredited])

## Tringham, David

This British assistant director (1935–) worked on Hammer's *Slave Girls* (1968), which led to further assignments with the company, among them *The Witches* (1966), which was shot after *Slave Girls* but released before it. His early credits as a third assistant include *The Green Man* (1956) and *A Tale of Two Cities* (1958). He graduated to second assistant on *A Night to Remember* (1958) and to first assistant on *The Third Alibi* (1961). His other AD credits include *Master Spy* (1963), *The Tomb of Ligeia* (1964), *Fathom* (1967), *The Looking Glass*

*War* (1970), *Nobody Ordered Love* (1972), on which he was also an associate producer, *The Great Gatsby* (1974), *Juggernaut* (1974), *Equus* (1977), *Outland* (1981), *The Hunger* (1983), *Henry V* (1989), *The Russia House* (1990), *The Mummy* (1999) and *Bedazzled* (2000). He also wrote and directed the short *The Last Chapter* (1974). **Hammer credits:** *The Witches* (1966), *Slave Girls* (1968), *Captain Kronos—Vampire Hunter* (1974)

## Trio Valencia

This adagio act can be spotted in Hammer's *The Gambler and the Lady* (1953). **Hammer credits:** *The Gambler and the Lady* (1953, as Adagio act [uncredited])

## Tripp, Freddie

Tripp (?–1968) had a supporting role in Hammer's *Face the Music* (1954). His other credits include *Hot Ice* (1950) and episodes of *Stand By to Shoot* (1953, TV) and *The Count of Monte Cristo* (1956, TV). Also in theater, as both an actor and director. **Hammer credits:** *Face the Music* (1954, as Stage manager [uncredited])

## Trolley, Leonard

This British actor (1918–2005) can be seen as Viner in *The Corvini Inheritance* (1984, TVM [episode of *Hammer House of Mystery and Suspense*]). His other TV credits include episodes of *Crane* (1963–1965, TV), *Upstairs, Downstairs* (1971–1975, TV) and *Bergerac* (1981–1991, TV), while his occasional films include *Prelude to Fame* (1950), *A Countess from Hong Kong* (1967), *The Message* (1976), *The Stud* (1978), *Champions* (1984) and *Consuming Passions* (1988). **Hammer credits:** *The Corvini Inheritance* (1984, TVM [episode of *Hammer House of Mystery and Suspense*], as Viner)

## Tromans, Edna

British born Tromans (1929–2010, erroneously billed as Thomas in some sources) worked as the publicist on Hammer's *Demons of the Mind* (1972). Her other credits include *The Rebel* (1961), *Billy Liar* (1963), *2001: A Space Odyssey* (1968), *Sunday Bloody Sunday* (1971) and *Death on the Nile* (1978). She went on to work in America on the likes of *On Golden Pond* (1981), *Making Love* (1982), *Finnegan Begin Again* (1985, TVM), *My Blue Heaven* (1990) and *Doc Hollywood* (1991). **Hammer credits:** *Demons of the Mind* (1972 [uncredited])

## Tromp, Tony

Tromp worked as a unit driver on *Hammer House of Mystery and Suspense* (1984, TVM). His other credits include *Voices* (1995). **Hammer credits:** *Hammer House of Mystery and Suspense* (1984, TVM [uncredited])

## Troughton, Patrick

Best known to sixties television audiences as the second Doctor Who, whom he portrayed between 1966 and 1969 (and later in 1972, 1973, 1983 and 1985), this British character actor (1920–1987) broke into both film and television in the late forties following stage experience with the Old Vic. He made his small screen debut in 1947 and began appearing in films the following year with *Escape* (1948) and *Hamlet* (1948), the latter of which also

featured Hammer stalwarts Peter Cushing and Christopher Lee. Troughton's other early films include *Badger's Green* (1948), *Treasure Island* (1950) and *The Black Knight* (1954). In 1957, he dubbed the voice of the charnel house keeper in Hammer's *The Curse of Frankenstein*, although he had originally been contracted to play the role of Kurt, but the character failed to appear in the final film. Troughton went on to appear before the cameras in a further five films for the company, among them *The Phantom of the Opera* (1962), in which he played the rat catcher, and *Scars of Dracula* (1970), in which he played Dracula's unfortunate manservant Klove, a role previously played by Philip Latham in *Dracula—Prince of Darkness* (1966). Commented director Roy Ward Baker of the actor's performance in the latter, "Patrick Troughton as Dracula's manservant, Klove, was outstanding. His was a genuine performance: no going through the motions for him."[37]

Troughton's other films include *Richard III* (1955), *Jason and the Argonauts* (1963), *The Black Torment* (1964), *Witchfinder General* (1968), *The Omen* (1976), in which he was famously killed with a falling lightning rod, and *Sinbad and the Eye of the Tiger* (1977), while his many TV appearances include episodes of *Robin Hood* (1953, TV), *The Adventures of Robin Hood* (1955–1960, TV), *A Tale of Two Cities* (1965, TV), *Sutherland's Law* (1973–1976, TV) and *Inspector Morse* (1987–2000, TV). His sons are the actors David Troughton (1950–) and Michael Troughton (1955–), and his grandsons are the actors Sam Troughton (1977–) and Harry Melling (1989–). **Hammer credits:** *The Curse of Frankenstein* (1957, as voice of charnel house keeper [uncredited], Kurt [role cut prior to filming]), *The Phantom of the Opera* (1962, as Rat catcher), *The Gorgon* (1964, as Inspector Kanof), *The Viking Queen* (1967, as Tristram), *Scars of Dracula* (1970, as Klove), *Frankenstein and the Monster from Hell* (1974, as Body snatcher)

## Trubshawe, Michael

In films from 1950 with *They Were Not Divided*, this British character player (1905–1985) went on to appear as upper crust types in over forty films. He came to acting following experience in the army with his lifelong friend David Niven, several of whose movies he subsequently appeared in, among them *Around the World in 80 Days* (1956), *The Guns of Navarone* (1961) and *The Pink Panther* (1963). In fact before he appeared on screen himself, a running joke between the two had been that Niven would try to mention Trubshawe's name in every film he appeared in. Trubshawe's other credits include *The Lavender Hill Mob* (1951), *The Rainbow Jacket* (1954), *A Hard Day's Night* (1964) and *The Rise and Rise of Michael Rimmer* (1970). He can also be seen as Sir Roger Clements in the Hammer second feature *The Runaway* (1964). His occasional TV credits include episodes of *No Hiding Place* (1959–1967, TV), *The Avengers* (1961–1969, TV) and *Shirley's World* (1971–1972, TV). **Hammer credits:** *The Runaway* (1964, as Sir Roger Clements)

## Truman-Taylor, Totti *see* Taylor, Totti Truman

## Trumper, John

This prolific British editor (1923–2004) cut Hammer's last theatrical horror film for thirty years, *To the Devil a Daughter* (1976), which had a troubled production. His many other credits, which range from programers to glossy A-features, include *Heart of Gold* (1958), *House of Mystery* (1961), *Strongroom* (1961), *Crooks Anonymous* (1962), *Blind Corner* (1963), *Live It Up* (1963), *Devils of Darkness* (1964), *Coast of Skeletons* (1964), *Victim Five* (1965), *The Face of Fu Manchu* (1965), *The Penthouse* (1967), *Privilege* (1967), *Up the Junction* (1968), *The Long Day's Dying* (1968), *The Italian Job* (1969), *Get Carter* (1971), *The Mutations* (1974), *Alfie Darling* (1975) and *Boyfriends* (1996), plus episodes of *Danger UXB* (1979, TV). He began his career cutting documentary shorts, among them *Instruments of the Orchestra* (1946) and *Waverley Steps: A Visit to Edinburgh* (1948). **Hammer credits:** *To the Devil a Daughter* (1976)

## Trussler, Ellen

Trussler provided the wardrobe for the Hammer second feature *Wings of Danger* (1952). Her other credits include *A Date with a Dream* (1948), *The Interrupted Journey* (1949), *No Trace* (1950) and *The Frightened Man* (1952). **Hammer credits:** *Wings of Danger* (1952)

## Tsau, Johnson

Tsau (sometimes Tsao, aka Sang Chang Tsao Cheng and Johnny Tsao) worked as the art director on Hammer's *The Legend of the 7 Golden Vampires* (1974), which was made back-to-back with *Shatter* (1974), on which he also worked, and on which he is simply credited as Johnson. His many other credits include *Ge qiang yan shi* (1961), *Chuan* (1967), *Chun huo* (1970), *Cleopatra Jones and the Casino of Gold* (1975), *Chinatown Kid* (1977), *Da she* (1980), *Gu* (1981) and *Shui jing ren* (1983). Recalled director Roy Ward Baker of Tsau's work on *The Legend of the 7 Golden Vampires*, "[He was] a charming man who spoke English well and delivered some splendid settings. He was a great man to work with and a bonus in the whole operation."[38] **Hammer credits:** *The Legend of the 7 Golden Vampires* (1974), *Shatter* (1974)

## Tucker, Forrest

In over sixty films from 1940 onwards beginning with *The Westerner*, this American leading man (1919–1986) went on to appear in countless action and western films, among them *Parachute Nurse* (1942), *Sands of Iwo Jima* (1949), *Pony Express* (1953), *Stagecoach to Fury* (1956), *Barquero* (1969) and *The Wild McCullochs* (1975). In 1955, he starred in the Hammer second feature *Break in the Circle*, in which he plays a skipper who is persuaded to help smuggle an East German scientist into Britain. He returned to Hammer two years later to top-line *The Abominable Snowman* (1957), prior to which there had been talk of Tucker starring in a proposed project titled *Captain Morgan, Buccaneer* for the studio, but the proposed production was scrapped following the success of *The Quatermass Xperiment* (1955). Also busy on television, both as a leading performer and guest star, his credits here include episodes of *Crunch and Des* (1955–

1956, TV), in which he starred as Crunch Adams, *Wagon Train* (1957–1965, TV), *F Troop* (1965–1967, TV), in which he starred as Sergeant Morgan O'Rourke, *Alias Smith and Jones* (1971–1973, TV), *Dusty's Trail* (1973–1974, TV), in which he co-starred as Callahan, *The Ghost Busters* (1975, TV), in which he starred as Jake Kong, and *The Love Boat* (1977–1986, TV). Married four times, his wives included the actresses Marilyn Johnson (1922–1960), to whom he was married between 1951 and 1960, and Marilyn Fisk (1939–, aka Marilyn Tucker), to whom he was married between 1961 and 1985. His daughter is the actress Brooke Tucker (1944–, full name Pamela Brooke Tucker). **Hammer credits:** *Break in the Circle* (1955, as Skip Morgan), *The Abominable Snowman* (1957, as Tom Friend)

**Forrest Tucker and Eva Bartok in a scene from *Break in the Circle* (1955) (Hammer/Concanen/Exclusive).**

### Tuckwell, Barry

In Britain from the age of nineteen, this noted Australian musician (1931–) played first horn in several orchestras, among them the Hallé Orchestra, The Scottish National Orchestra and The London Symphony Orchestra. He also played on the soundtrack for a number of Hammer scores, among them James Bernard's music for *She* (1965). His books include *Playing the Horn: A Practical Guide* (1978). He was made an OBE in 1965. **Hammer credits include:** *She* (1965)

### Tully, Brian

Tully (?–2014) can be seen as one of the Sorell clan in Hammer's *Captain Kronos—Vampire Hunter* (1974). His other credits include *For the Love of Ada* (1972) and *The Internecine Project* (1974), plus episodes of *The Saint* (1962–1969, TV), *The Pallisers* (1974, TV) and *Just Good Friends* (1983–1986, TV). **Hammer credits:** *Captain Kronos—Vampire Hunter* (1974, as George Sorell)

### Tully, Montgomery

Following experience as a journalist, this Irish writer and director (1904–1988, real name Geoffrey Montgomery Tully) broke into films in 1929 as an assistant at Publicity Films, where he worked on a number of industrial documentaries, although he didn't gain his first directorial credit until 1937 with *Co-operette*. Further documentaries followed, among them *Behind the Guns* (1940) and *Salute to the Farmers* (1941), after which he joined the war effort. Returning to the cinema in 1945, Tully directed another documentary, *Each for All*, and his first feature, *Murder in Reverse*. In the fifties, he became known for helming all manner of second feature crime thrillers, including many snappy episodes of *Scotland Yard* (1953–1961), among them *Wall of Death* (1956), *The White Cliffs Mystery* (1957) and *Print of Death* (1957). Inevitably, Tully came to the attention of Hammer, who hired him to helm a handful of fifties second features, beginning with *36 Hours* (1953), which he handled with economy though not style. Tully's many other credits include *Mrs. Fitzherbert* (1947), *Dial 999* (1955), *The Hypnotist* (1957), *Clash by Night* (1963), *The Terrornauts* (1967) and *The Hawks* (1968). **Hammer credits:** *36 Hours* (1953), *Five Days* (1954), *The Glass Cage* (1955), *I Only Arsked!* (1958)

### *The Turn of the Screw*

Presented by Hammer Theater of Horror (in association with Sonia Friedman Productions and Act Productions), this adaptation by Rebecca Lenkiewicz of Henry James' 1898 novella was staged at London's Almeida Theater by director Lindsay Posner. Previously the subject of a classic 1961 film *The Innocents* (directed by Jack Clayton, photographed by Freddie Francis and starring Deborah Kerr), as well as a celebrated 1954 opera by Benjamin Britten, the story follows the arrival of a new governess at a remote estate in Bly where she gradually begins to fear that her seemingly angelic charges Miles and Flora are not quite so charming as they appear, and that the corners of the house are haunted by ghostly figures from the recent past….

The play received mixed notices, varying from the impressed to the indifferent. *The Telegraph* described it as a "true, spine-chilling horror with bumps that really *bump* and sleights of hand you didn't expect," adding that "the evocative set and sound effects are pure Hammer." It also averred of the show, "This has the potential to give *The Woman in Black* a run for its money." However, *The Guardian* (which gave it only two stars as opposed to *The Telegraph's* four) lamented that it lacked "the pervasive subtlety of James's story." Meanwhile, *Time Out* noted that it was "indubitably a triumph of atmosphere above all else," though *The Stage* felt that "the show feels slack; there's plenty of texture, but not enough tension." The play ran from 18 January to 16 March 2013.

Production companies: Hammer Theater of Horror/Sonia Friedman Productions/Act Productions. Adaptation: Rebecca Lenkiewicz, from the novella by Henry James. Director: Lindsay Posner.

Design: Peter McKintosh. Music: Gary Yershon. Lighting: Tim Mitchell. Sound: John Leonard. Casting: Julia Horan, Jo Hawes (children). Illusions: Scott Penrose. Assistant director: Alex Brown. **Cast:** Gemma Jones (Mrs. Grose), Anna Madeley (Governess), Caroline Bartleet (Miss Jessel), Laurence Belcher (Miles), Isabella Blake Thomas, Lucy Morton and Emilia Jones (alternating as Flora), Eoion Geoghegan (Peter Quint), Orlando Wells (Sackville)

### Turner, Anna

Long in Britain, this Brazilian actress (1918–2014) had minor roles in Hammer's *Stolen Face* (1952) and *Mantrap* (1953). Her other credits include *The Floating Dutchman* (1952), *The Good Companions* (1957), *Bedazzled* (1967), *Empire of the Sun* (1987) and *Super Grass* (1994), plus episodes of *Dr. Finlay's Casebook* (1962–1971, TV) and *All Creatures Great and Small* (1978–1990, TV). **Hammer credits:** *Stolen Face* (1952, as Maid), *Mantrap* (1953, as Marjorie)

### Turner, Brooks *see* Turner, Robert Brooks

### Turner, Clifford

In films as an assistant at Gaumont-British from 1929, this British editor (1913–1997) went on to cut Hammer's *The Adventures of PC 49—The Case of the Guardian Angel* (1949) and *Celia* (1949). His other credits include *The Small Back Room* (1949) and *Alf's Baby* (1953). **Hammer credits:** *The Adventures of PC 49—The Case of the Guardian Angel* (1949), *Celia* (1949 [uncredited])

### Turner, Frank

Turner worked as the assistant to make-up artist Phil Leakey on Hammer's *The Adventures of PC 49—The Case of the Guardian Angel* (1949). His other credits include *The Depraved* (1957), *Circus of Fear* (1966), *The Plank* (1967) and *Disciple of Death* (1972), plus episodes of *London Playhouse* (1955) and *The Prisoner* (1967–1968, TV). His brothers were the make-up artists Sidney (1913–1978) and George Turner (1903–1962), the latter of whom worked on Hammer's *The Curse of Frankenstein* (1957). **Hammer credits:** *The Adventures of PC 49—The Case of the Guardian Angel* (1949 [uncredited])

### Turner, George

This British make-up artist (1903–1962) was Phil Leakey's assistant on Hammer's *The Curse of Frankenstein* (1957), and his duties included helping to turn Christopher Lee into the Creature. His other credits include *Trunk Crime* (1939), *Pastor Hall* (1940), *Things Happen at Night* (1947), *Just William's Luck* (1948) and *Night Was Our Friend* (1951). His brothers were the make-up artists Sidney (1913–1978) and Frank Turner, the latter of whom worked on Hammer's *The Adventures of PC 49—The Case of the Guardian Angel* (1949). **Hammer credits:** *The Curse of Frankenstein* (1957 [uncredited])

### Turner, Robert Brooks

This British supporting actor (1882–1963, sometimes Brooks Turner or Robert Brooks-

Turner) had minor roles in two Hammer films. His other credits include *Poor Old Bill* (1931), *Quiet Wedding* (1941), *Hatter's Castle* (1942), *Caravan* (1946), *Seven Days to Noon* (1950) and *The Sound Barrier* (1952). **Hammer credits:** *Stolen Face* (1952, as Farmer), *The Revenge of Frankenstein* (1958, as Groom)

### Turner, Stephen

Turner can be seen as the hapless cook Stephan in Hammer's *The Horror of Frankenstein* (1970), in which he is executed for a murder committed by the Monster. His other credits include *Golden Rendezvous* (1977) and *The Final Conflict* (1981), plus episodes of *Little Women* (1970, TV) and *Oppenheimer* (1980, TV). **Hammer credits:** *The Horror of Frankenstein* (1970, as Stephan)

### Turner, Tim

A familiar face in fifties second features, this British supporting actor (1924–1987, real name John Freeman Turner) can be spotted in Hammer's *Mask of Dust* (1954), as well as *Top Secret* (1953), *Night of the Full Moon* (1954), *Police Dog* (1955), *Grip of the Strangler* (1958), *Operation Amsterdam* (1958), *Not a Hope in Hell* (1960) and *Jackpot* (1960). Known for his smooth, mid–Atlantic tones, he provided the voice of Dr. Peter Brady in *The Invisible Man* (1958–1960, TV), and also appeared in an episode as another character (a villain named Nick). His other TV work includes episodes of *Douglas Fairbanks, Jr. Presents* (1953–1957, TV), *White Hunter* (1957–1958, TV) and *International Detective* (1959–1961, TV). He also dubbed Todd Armstrong in *Jason and the Argonauts* (1963) and returned to Hammer to provide the narration for *The Mummy's Shroud* (1967). **Hammer credits:** *Mask of Dust* (1954, as Alvarez), *The Mummy's Shroud* (1967, Narrator [uncredited])

### Turpin, Gerry

Noted for his work for directors Richard Attenborough and Brian Forbes, this British cinematographer (1925–1997) began his career as a focus puller and camera operator, working as the former on Hammer's *Dick Barton Strikes Back* (1949). He went on to shoot a handful of notable sixties productions, including *Peeping Tom* (1960), *Seance on a Wet Afternoon* (1964), which earned him a BAFTA nomination, *The Wrong Box* (1966), *The Whisperers* (1967), which won him a BAFTA, *Morgan: A Suitable Case for Treatment* (1966), *Deadfall* (1968) and *Oh! What a Lovely War* (1969), which won him a second BAFTA. His other credits include *Young Winston* (1972), *The Last of Sheila* (1973) and *The Doctor and the Devils* (1985). His other early credits as a focus puller include *Dead of Night* (1945), *The Happiest Days of Your Life* (1950), *Scrooge* (1951) and *Hobson's Choice* (1954), while his credits as an operator include *Stars in Your Eyes* (1956), *Too Many Crooks* (1959) and *Night of the Eagle* (1962). **Hammer credits:** *Dick Barton Strikes Back* (1949 [uncredited])

### Tushingham, Rita

Something of a sixties icon thanks to her appearances in such era-defining films as *A Taste of Honey* (1961), which won her a BAFTA as most promising newcomer, *The Leather Boys* (1963), *Girl with Green Eyes* (1964), which earned her a best actress BAFTA nomination, *Doctor Zhivago* (1965), *The Knack* (1965), which earned her a second best actress BAFTA nomination, and *Smashing Time* (1967), this gauche British actress (1942–) came to films following stage experience from 1960. Her many other film credits, among them a handful of American and European productions, include *A Place to Go* (1963), *The Trap* (1966), *The Guru* (1969), *An Awfully Big Adventure* (1995), *The Boy from Mercury* (1996), *Out of Depth* (1999), *The Hideout* (2007), *Telstar* (2008), *The Calling* (2009), *Outside Bet* (2012) and *My Name Is Lenny* (2017). She also played Brenda Thompson, the leading role in the Hammer psycho-drama *Straight on Till Morning* (1972), in which she gradually comes to realize that her boyfriend isn't all he appears to be. For a brief period following *Straight on Till Morning*, Tushingham tried to get a production of *Lorna Doone* off the ground, which was to have been co-produced by Hammer and her own production company. Sadly the project failed to come to fruition. Also busy in television, her credits here include episodes of *Armchair Theatre* (1956–1974, TV), *The Human Jungle* (1963–1964, TV), *No Strings* (1974, TV), *Bread* (1986–1991, TV), *Helen West* (2002, TV) and *In the Flesh* (2013–2014, TV). Married twice, Tushingham's husbands were the photographer Terry Bicknell, whom she married in 1962, and the cinematographer Ousama Rawi (1939–), to whom she was married between 1981 and 1996, and who photographed her in *Rachel's Man* (1974) and *The Human Factor* (1975), and directed her in *A Judgment in Stone* (1986). Her daughters are the assistant director Dodonna Bicknell (1964–) and the post-production co-ordinator Aisha Bicknell (1971–, real name Aisha Tushingham). **Hammer credits:** *Straight on Till Morning* (1972, as Brenda Thompson)

### TVi

TVi worked on the post-production of *The World of Hammer* (1990 [first broadcast 1994], TV), along with Fountain Television and Sound Development Studios. They also provided post-production facilities for *The Animals of Farthing Wood* (1993–1995, TV), *The Casting Couch* (1995, TV) and *The Rolling Stones Rock and Roll Circus* (1996, TV), plus tele-cine transfers for *The Match Maker* (1997). **Hammer credits:** *The World of Hammer* (1990 [first broadcast 1994], TV)

### Tweedale, Tony

British born Tweedale (1937–) worked as the publicist on Hammer's *Dracula—Prince of Darkness* (1966). His other credits include *Die, Monster, Die!* (1965) and *The Class of Miss MacMichael* (1978). **Hammer credits:** *Dracula—Prince of Darkness* (1966 [uncredited])

### 20th Century–Fox Film Corporation

Formed in 1935 with the merger of the Fox Film Corporation and Twentieth Century Pictures, this American studio went on to have commercial successes with *The Grapes of Wrath* (1940), *How Green Was My Valley* (1941), *The Song of Bernadette* (1944), *The Robe* (1953), *The Sound of Music* (1965), *Star Wars* (1977) and its various sequels and prequels, *Alien* (1979) and its sequels, *Die Hard* (1988) and its sequels, *X-Men* (2000) and its sequels, *Avatar* (2009) and its sequels, and *Deadpool* (2016) and its sequels. In 1949, the American producer and distributor Robert L. Lippert—who had long been at Twentieth Century–Fox where he operated Screen Guild Pictures, an independent unit making mostly second feature westerns—brokered a *quid pro quo* distribution deal with Hammer's James Carreras, by which Exclusive released Lippert product in the UK, while in return Lippert released Hammer product Stateside via Fox and the sixty cinemas he operated.

This five-year deal was officially announced in August 1950, when Exclusive released Lippert's *The Last of the Wild Horses* (1949). The production deal itself kicked off with *The Last Page* (1952), and went on to include a total of eighteen productions, which were financed by Fox funds that had been frozen in the UK following the Anglo-American agreement of 1948. However, many of these films were either trimmed or re-titled for their Stateside showings. Fox continued to release Hammer films periodically in America following the conclusion of the Lippert deal, among them *Break in the Circle* (1955), which the studio not only held back until 1957, but presented in black and white, despite the fact that it had been shot in Eastmancolor. As was the case with many later productions—among them *Dracula—Prince of Darkness* (1966) and *Rasputin—The Mad Monk* (1966)—their prints were struck in DeLuxe for their U.S. releases, given Fox's close ties with the DeLuxe company, while they were struck in Technicolor for their UK releases.

In addition to their film links with Hammer, Fox also co-financed (along with ABC Television) the seventeen-part anthology series *Journey to the Unknown* (1968, TV), which proved modestly successful with both critics and audiences, but not enough to guarantee a second season, though four compendium movies were derived from the series: *Journey to Midnight* (1968, TVM), *Journey into Darkness* (1968, TVM), *Journey to the Unknown* (1969, TVM) and *Journey to Murder* (1972, TVM). In the seventies, Fox briefly resumed releasing Hammer films in America, this time in their original color formats, while in 1984 they financed a second TV series, *Hammer House of Mystery and Suspense* (1984, TVM), which was broadcast in the U.S. as *Fox Mystery Theater*. **Hammer credits:** *The Last Page* (1952), *Wings of Danger* (1952), *Stolen Face* (1952), *Lady in the Fog* (1952), *The Gambler and the Lady* (1953), *Mantrap* (1953), *The Flanagan Boy* (1953), *Spaceways* (1953), *Blood Orange* (1953), *36 Hours* (1953), *Face the Music* (1954), *Five Days* (1954), *The House Across the Lake* (1954), *The Stranger Came Home* (1954), *Mask of Dust* (1954), *Break in the Circle* (1955 [U.S. release 1957]), *Murder by Proxy* (1955), *Third Party Risk* (1955), *The Glass Cage* (1955), *The Abominable Snowman* (1957), *The Nanny* (1965), *Dracula—Prince of Darkness* (1966), *The Plague of the Zombies* (1966), *Rasputin—The Mad Monk* (1966), *The Reptile* (1966), *The Witches* (1966),

*One Million Years B.C.* (1966), *The Viking Queen* (1967), *Frankenstein Created Woman* (1967), *The Mummy's Shroud* (1967), *Quatermass and the Pit* (1967), *A Challenge for Robin Hood* (1967), *The Anniversary* (1968), *The Vengeance of She* (1968), *The Devil Rides Out* (1968), *Slave Girls* (1968), *The Lost Continent* (1968), *Journey to the Unknown* (1968, TV), *Journey to Midnight* (1968, TVM), *Journey into Darkness* (1968, TVM), *Journey to the Unknown* (1969, TVM), *Countess Dracula* (1971), *Journey to Murder* (1972, TVM), *Vampire Circus* (1972), *Hammer House of Mystery and Suspense* (1984, TVM)

## Twigge, Jenny

This British actress (1950–) can be seen as one of the schoolgirls in Hammer's *Vampire Circus* (1972). Busiest on television, her many credits here include episodes of *Love Story* (1963–1974, TV), *Hadleigh* (1969–1976, TV), *Crown Court* (1972–1984, TV), *Grange Hill* (1978–2008, TV), in which she played Mrs. McGuire between 1982 and 1987, and *Byker Grove* (1989–2006, TV), in which she played Clare Warner between 1989 and 1990. Her other occasional films include *Our Miss Fred* (1972), *The Brute* (1977) and *Holocaust 2000* (1977). **Hammer credits:** *Vampire Circus* (1972, as Schoolgirl [uncredited])

## *Twins of Dracula* see *Twins of Evil*

## *Twins of Evil*

GB, 1971, 87m [UK], 81m [U.S.], Eastmancolor, widescreen [1.78:1], cert X

Hammer's "Karnstein trilogy" came to a lively climax with this generally brisk and energetic saga about a witch-hunting Puritan who is visited by his twin nieces, one of whom turns to the bad and becomes an acolyte of the evil Count Karnstein. The question is, which one?

A follow-up to *The Vampire Lovers* (1970) and *Lust for a Vampire* (1970), the film was again made in conjunction between Hammer and Fantale—who signed a production deal on 5 January 1971—with backing this time provided by Rank. As before, the producers were Harry Fine and Michael Style, while the screenplay, again based on characters from J. Sheridan Le Fanu's *Carmilla*, was by Tudor Gates.

Following his absence from *Lust for a Vampire* owing to the illness and subsequent death of his beloved wife Helen, *Twins of Evil* sees Peter Cushing return to the series, this time as the puritanical Gustav Weil (appropriately pronounced "vile"), whose obsession with destroying evil takes on manic proportions. Not adverse to burning innocent girls at the stake, Weil becomes even more fevered in his pursuits following the arrival of his twin nieces Frieda and Maria Gellhorn, whom he and his wife Katy have agreed to look after following the deaths of their parents. Newly arrived from Venice, they are the epitome of everything fashionable, much to the chagrin of their uncle, who considers them to have prematurely ended their period of mourning, despite their having worn black for two months ("What kind of plumage is *this*?" he chastises them upon first seeing them).

Inevitably, the twins find life with their uncle te-dious in the extreme, especially as they have to be in bed by nine. Consequently, Frieda, the more rebellious of the two, begins to yearn for a more exciting existence, especially after overhearing her uncle tell her aunt about the orgies supposedly taking place up at Castle Karnstein, which the girls can see from their window.

Count Karnstein, with whom Weil has already had a run in, is also keen to explore new pleasures, and to this end has taken to dabbling in Devil worship via a mock sacrifice. However, when this fails to provide the desired thrill, he kills the village girl who has been coerced into the proceedings for real, not realizing that her body lies over the grave of his ancestor, the vampire Mircalla Karnstein, who is subsequently revitalized with the girl's blood. Mircalla thus seduces Count Karnstein, turning him into a vampire too, causing his reflection to disappear from the mirror in front of which they are standing ("We are the undead, and the mirror sees only the living. We walk the earth, but we exist only in hell," she informs him).

Head shot. Peter Cushing holds a model of a freshly beheaded Madeleine Collinson in *Twins of Evil* (1971) (Hammer/Fantale/Rank/Universal).

Meanwhile, the twins have been enrolled at the nearby school for young ladies, where no one seems able to tell the girls apart, save for the music teacher Anton, who, despite Maria's obvious interest in *him*, falls for Frieda, even though she proves to be somewhat outspoken ("I *hate* it here") and seems to be something of a bad girl in waiting ("Perhaps I don't like good men," she replies when Anton suggests that her uncle is essentially good if perhaps misguided). Having met the Count, who happens by the school, her yearning for adventure finally overwhelms her ("Who wants to be good if being good is singing hymns and praying all day long?"), and subsequently spurs a nocturnal visit to the castle, on her way to which she is captured by the Count's loyal manservant Joachim and taken to join the Count for dinner, not realizing that she is about to become one of the courses. "One who is dedicated to the Devil will not die by a vampire's bite, but will become one of the undead—a vampire," the Count informs her before sinking his fangs into her neck.

Still steadfast in his pursuit of evil, Weil next sets his sights on Anton, not realizing that his own niece has now become the very thing he exists to destroy. In fact it isn't long before Weil and his men catch Frieda in the woods, where she has just attacked one of the locals. Claiming that she has also been attacked, Frieda attempts to worm her way out of the situation, but the evidence is damning. "There is blood on your lips," accuses her uncle, before declaiming to the skies that, "The Devil has sent me twins of evil." Indeed, it looks like the innocent Maria is about to be tarred with the same brush, given that she has been kidnapped from her room by Count Karnstein, who replaces her for her sister in the jail cell where she has been incarcerated ("You will be Maria now," the Count informs Frieda. "Unsuspected, good and kind and virginal. Think of the havoc you can cause!").

Thus Frieda attempts to seduce and vampirize Anton, only for him to ward her off with a crucifix. Realizing what has happened, he quickly tracks down Weil and his men, who are about to burn the innocent Maria at the stake ("You've got the wrong girl—you're burning Maria!"). Having been suitably convinced, Weil and his men, accompanied by Anton, hot foot it to the castle; but the Count and Frieda escape down an old tunnel, which leads to the local graveyard, where Frieda is finally beheaded by her uncle. Having escaped back to the castle in the meantime, Karnstein now too meets his fate. "I have waited a long time for this moment," says Weil a little prematurely, only to be killed with the axe with which he plans to dispatch the Count. However, Anton saves the day by staking the Count with a spear, which causes him to disintegrate before the eyes of the remaining Puritans, after which he finally takes Maria into his arms....

Fantale had actually proposed the film to Hammer as *Vampire Virgins*, with Peter Cushing originally set to star as Count Karnstein, out for revenge following the fiery climax of *Lust for a Vampire*. However, the storyline was substantially modified and subsequently went on the floor as the catchier-sounding *Twins of Evil* at Pinewood between 22 March and 30 April, with a budget slightly in excess of £205,000. To appear opposite Cushing as the film's title characters (albeit only one of whom is actually evil), Hammer turned to the charms of real-life twins Madeleine and Mary Collinson, although Kate O'Mara was originally considered to play one of the twins, an idea that was rejected when no one resembling her could be found to play opposite her, though this didn't prevent her from asking, "Why can't I play both parts?"[39] In Britain from 1969, the Maltese twosome had become a modeling sensation after becoming *Playboy*'s first ever twin Playmates in October 1970, by which time they had already started appearing in films, having made their debut in a short, *Halfway Inn* (1969 [geddit?]). Hammer was quick to take note, having cast from the pages of *Playboy* in the past (Susan Denberg, who had starred in *Frankenstein Created Woman* [1967] had appeared in the August 1966 and July 1967 issues of the magazine). But as screenwriter Tudor Gates noted of the twins, "As far as I was concerned this was a picture about

Peter Cushing's character and the twins to me were a coincidental, but necessary part of the formula—the innocence to engage with the evil of the Count."[40]

As Mary Collinson later recalled, "We had no acting experience, and the prospect of working with actors like Peter Cushing was quite frightening. Waiting to see if the parts were ours was awful. Acting was quite different from modeling, but *Twins of Evil* turned into what I still think of as the best experience of our lives."[41]

Also making his Hammer debut was the director John Hough. A TV veteran with several well-regarded episodes of *The Avengers* (1961–1969, TV) under his belt, he had recently made the featurette *Wolfshead: The Legend of Robin Hood* (1969 [released 1973]), which had originally been intended as the pilot for a TV series that failed to materialize, and was subsequently acquired by Hammer as a program filler. He had also just completed a stylish thriller *Eyewitness* (1970). Hough brought the visual zip that had marked his TV work to the production, and was ably assisted by cinematographer Dick Bush. However, as Hough admitted,

it wasn't his plan to alter the Hammer formula and jump on the current bandwagon of more visceral horror, but to actually emulate the house style. "I was a fan of what they were doing. Be less graphic and make it more atmospheric, and intrigue [audiences] in *that* way."[42]

Given the film's restrained finances, Hough and Bush frequently had to find inventive ways of filming the action. Recalled the director, "The budget for the film was relatively low, and all the special effects were achieved by the camera during filming—a far cry from the extensive array of computer-generated imagery now available to the filmmaker. I am still proud of the shots where the vampires and their victims walk in front of mirrors, but only the victim is reflected…. Enthusiasts are still puzzled as to how I did it."[43]

Also contributing to the film's lavish look was art director Roy Stannard. In addition to the stark look of Weil's home and an eye-catching meeting house for the Brotherhood, complete with bleachers-style seating, he also made use of several

*Above:* **Stylish French artwork for *Twins of Evil* (1971). *Right:* An American poster for *Twins of Evil* (1971) (both photographs, Hammer/Fantale/Rank/Universal).**

re-dressed sets from *Countess Dracula* (1971), including the village square and the interior of the Castle Nadasdy, which also includes elements from the castle interior from *Lust for a Vampire*. Also note the dovecote from the courtyard in *Countess Dracula*, which can be seen outside the girls' school, and the use of castle exteriors also seen in *Carry On Henry* (1971). As with the previous episodes in the series, the whole thing was topped off with a splendid score by Harry Robinson, from whom John Hough had requested "a theme suggesting impending doom whenever the Puritans were on screen."[44]

In front of the cameras, the cast was further augmented by the presence of Kathleen Byron, who brings a quiet dignity to the role of Weil's devoted but browbeaten wife Katy; David Warbeck as Anton Hoffer, who cuts a reasonable dash as the nominal hero of the piece; Isobel Black as his ill-fated sister, schoolteacher Ingrid Hoffer; and Dennis Price as Dietrich, the Count's procurer of village girls, a character not dissimilar to his role in *The Horror of Frankenstein* (1970).

The juiciest supporting role, however, went to Damien Thomas as the devilish Count Karnstein ("Damien Thomas was so good-looking that we both fell madly in love with him,"[45] confessed Mary Collinson many years later of her and her sister's feelings for the handsome young actor).

Undoubtedly the best episode in the trilogy, *Twins of Evil* is a generally stylish and fast-moving vampire flick with a little more invention than most of its ilk thanks to its novelty casting ("Torture, terror, sacrifice—times two," ran the tagline). From the opening sequence, which sees Weil and his men riding through the woods in pursuit of their latest victim, through to the gory climax, the film packs in a fair amount of action and incident, including not one but three burnings at the stake, a sacrificial stabbing, a beheading, an eye-gouging, a stomach staking and a machete attack, making this one of the more vicious Hammer films, though it should be noted that the stake burnings pale by comparison to those seen in the similarly themed *Witchfinder General* (1968) and Ken Russell's *The Devils* (1970). The film also contains an abundance of cleavage shots, plenty of bosom bearing, plus a little full-frontal nudity (the village girl on the sacrificial altar is clearly naked under the gauze which is placed over her). There's even a spot of girl-on-girl vampire action (instead of biting Gerta, the Count's plaything, on the neck, Frieda instead sinks her fangs into the girl's left breast). But as John Hough observed, "People thought they saw more sexuality in that [film] than there was."[46]

The film also contains a certain degree of irony, given that the acts of the Puritans prove every bit as depraved as those of Count Karnstein. Observes the Count of Weil, "Some men like a musical evening. Weil and his friends find pleasure through burning innocent girls." Indeed, in what amounts to a mission statement, Weil informs his followers a little too enthusiastically that it is their duty "to seek out the Devil worshippers and to purify their spirits so that they may find mercy at the seat of the Lord—by *burning* them!" Even Frieda notes

the double standards of her uncle early on, commenting to her sister that, "He'd love to find us doing something wrong, just to punish us. It would give him a thrill." In fact Weil's feelings for his nieces may well lean towards the incestuous, given that he isn't above standing outside their bedroom door with a leer on his face. As Frieda also observes, "I know his kind.... I can just imagine. If he came back now and saw the lights on in here, that would give him an excuse to come in..." To which she also adds, "Don't you know men like that? Didn't you ever notice them in the park when we were little girls? With funny staring eyes," which of course takes things in an entirely new direction.

As Weil, Peter Cushing gives one of the standout performances of his career (director John Hough described him as being "superb as Weil"[47]). This was the actor's first film following the death of his beloved wife Helen nine weeks earlier, and he is clearly gaunt with grief, making him all the more mesmerizing to watch, despite Weil being one of the most misguided and least sympathetic characters he ever played. Thankfully, for the sake of the film's balance, the intensity of Cushing's work is well matched by Damien Thomas's performance as the decadent Count Karnstein, whose forebears had been little more than peripheral figures in the previous episodes ("I feel he was one of the best vampires in all Hammer films,"[48] said John Hough of Thomas). Indeed, it is the role of Mircalla—the focus of the first two films—who now becomes one of the peripheral characters, albeit the catalyst for Karnstein's turn to vampirism. In fact Mircalla's diminished role in the proceedings is reflected by the fact that she is here played by Katya

Wyeth, a bit-part actress who had appeared briefly as a pub whore in Hammer's *Hands of the Ripper* (1971). The actress is quite adequate in her moment of glory, but if Hammer had intended on grooming her for bigger things, they failed to materialize.

As the titular twins, the Collinsons certainly look the part, but problems with their accents subsequently saw their performances re-voiced during post-production, but this has little impact on the proceedings (it wasn't for their acting skills that they were hired, after all).

Visually, the film is one of Hammer's more eye-catching entries from the period, thanks to the inventive framing of the action by John Hough and Dick Bush, who between them make the very most of the sets, as well as the location work in the well-trodden environs of Black Park. The ghostly rising of Mircalla from her grave is especially atmospheric (commented Nigel Andrews in the *Monthly Film Bulletin* of this sequence, "The reincarnation of Countess Mircalla, an ectoplasmic shape rising from the sarcophagus and floating in hooded silence towards the terrified Karnstein, is a *tour de force*"). However, we should perhaps draw a discreet veil over her masturbatory fondling of a candle during her subsequent tryst with Karnstein, a miscalculation guaranteed to provoke unwanted chuckles during an otherwise dramatic moment. Pedants for detail will also note a bust of Mircalla during this scene, which gives her death date as 1547, despite the fact that in *The Vampire Lovers* her birth and death dates are given as 1522 and 1545 respectively, while in *Lust for a Vampire* they are 1688 and 1710.

The film's narrative also seems a little choppy at

**Felt-tipped terror. Classic British poster for *Twins of Evil* (1971) (Hammer/Fantale/Rank/Universal).**

times, almost as if certain scenes were excised during post-production. This is particularly apparent during Frieda's nocturnal visits to Castle Karnstein, the timelines for which don't quite fit in with the rest of the action. For example, upon her return, Maria informs Frieda that she pretended to be her during her absence, resulting in her being beaten in her stead by their uncle. However, the absence of this scene—which is significant enough to be discussed by the twins—harms the logic of the central section of the film.

These minor discrepancies aside, the film remains a highly enjoyable romp. Released in the UK by Rank, it was trade shown on 24 September 1971. It premiered at London's New Victoria cinema as the top half of a double with Hammer's own *Hands of the Ripper* (1971) on 3 October, following which it went on general release on 17 October. "Though *Twins of Evil* has its share of the usual Hammer deficiencies—insipid juveniles and some overfamiliar Pinewood locations—it is easily the best of their vampire films for some time," enthused the *Monthly Film Bulletin*, while *Today's Cinema* found it to be "a more plausibly constructed story than most of its kind." Meanwhile, in *Films and Filming*, David McGillivray described the film as "pure Hammer, all throat-fanging and heart-staking and a very different kettle of fish from *Hands of the Ripper*, which is on the same bill." For *Ink*, however, it was "the usual Hammer vampire movie, this time embellished by a pair of indifferent-looking twins." Said John Hough of the finished results, "If cinemagoers don't scream and shudder, I feel I shall have failed."[49]

The film also accompanied *Hands of the Ripper* when released in America by Universal on 13 July 1972 ("In old gothic Europe they had two burning passions: witch hunting and Devil worship," teased the trailer). However, for its Stateside appearance,

the film (at the urging of CIC's Arthur Ables) was given the more exploitable title of *Twins of Dracula*. It was also trimmed by the censor by a whopping five minutes and thirty-six seconds when assessed in February. The trims not withstanding, the film was mostly admired by the critics, with *Variety* praising it for the "good pace" of John Hough's direction. It also reported that "Settings, production values, camerawork and acting are all of a high standard." **Additional notes:** Madeleine Collinson is billed as Madelaine Collinson in the credits (her name is spelled correctly on the poster). The Network DVD release of the movie features a brief, previously unseen schoolroom scene cut from the film before release; this involves the singing of a charming but rather incongruous romantic song composed by Anton Hoffer titled *True Love* and sung by two of the pupils ("Is there really somewhere in this world, Somewhere dreams can be fulfilled, Where the sky is full of golden light, And there is no fear of endless night?" run the opening lines). Perhaps given the memories of *Strange Love* from *Lust for a Vampire*, the scene ended up on the cutting room floor. A fourth film in the Karnstein series, provisionally titled *Vampire Hunters*, was discussed but sadly never materialized. Note the use of an insert shot of a woodland cottage (the interior of which bears little relation to the exterior), which was lifted from *The Horror of Frankenstein* (1970). And keep an eye out of the wobbly gravestone, just after Weil has beheaded Frieda. Also, at one point, Frieda looks out of her bedroom window and observes to Maria, "You can see the light of the castle from here," but there is no light on at the castle. Recalled effects man Bert Luxford of the decapitation scene, which he achieved with help from a huge German sausage and a midget, "John Hough was adamant that I should perform the severing of the head [on behalf of Peter Cushing]. I told him that the only way I'd do it is if he shot half of it in reverse, limiting any potential danger to the actress. I put the machete to her neck and pulled it away…. For the next half of the shot, I substituted my sausage for the neck. We had a little man who was about four foot high, dressed in the girl's costume, with this huge sausage on his head. I then laid into the meat and the machete came away with blood gushing everywhere. If you see the film, it's my hand in Peter Cushing's glove."[50] A seven-inch single of the title

German artwork for *Twins of Evil* (1971) (Hammer/Fantale/Rank/Universal).

theme was released by rock group Essjay to promote the film (with orchestrations care of Mike Batt), while the story was presented as a comic in issue seven of *The House of Hammer*.

Production companies: Hammer/Fantale/Rank. Distributors: Rank (UK), Universal (U.S.). Producers: Harry Fine, Michael Style. Production supervisor: Roy Skeggs. Director: John Hough. Screenplay: Tudor Gates, based upon characters created by J. Sheridan Le Fanu. Cinematographer: Dick Bush. Music: Harry Robinson. Music director: Philip Martell. Editor: Spencer Reeve. Art director: Roy Stannard. Costumes: Rosemary Burrows. Special effects: Bert Luxford [uncredited]. Make-up: George Blackler, John Webber. Hair: Pearl Tipaldi. Sound: Ron Barron. Dubbing mixer: Ken Barker. Sound editor: Bill Trent. Sound camera operator: Stan Samworth [uncredited]. Sound re-recording mixers: Graham V. Hartstone [uncredited], Otto Snel [uncredited]. Assistant director: Patrick Clayton. Second assistant director: David Munro [uncredited]. Third assistant director: Christopher Carreras [uncredited]. Production manager: Tom Sachs. Construction manager: Arthur Banks. Second unit photography/special effects photography: Jack Mills. Camera operator: Dudley Lovell. Continuity: Gladys Goldsmith. Dialogue coach: Ruth Lodge. Casting: Jimmy Liggat

A pensive-looking Peter Cushing in *Twins of Evil* (1971) (Hammer/Fantale/Rank/Universal).

[uncredited]. Stunts: Joe Dunne [uncredited], Peter Munt [uncredited], Vic Armstrong [uncredited]. Poster: Mike Vaughan [uncredited]. Promotional artwork: Tom Chantrell [uncredited]. **Cast:** Peter Cushing (Gustav Weil), Madeleine Collinson (Frieda Gellhorn), Mary Collinson (Maria Gellhorn), Kathleen Byron (Katy Weil), Harvey Hall (Franz), Dennis Price (Dietrich), Isobel Black (Ingrid Hoffer), Damien Thomas (Count Karnstein), Alex Scott (Hermann), David Warbeck (Anton Hoffer), Katya Wyeth (Countess Mircalla), Roy Stewart (Joachim), Inigo Jackson (Woodman), Luan Peters (Gerta), Maggie Wright (Alexa), Sheelah Wilcox (Lady in coach), Judy Matheson (Woodman's daughter), Peter Thompson (Gaoler), Kirsten Lindholm (Girl at stake), Roy Boyd (Man in graveyard [uncredited]), George Claydon (Midget [uncredited]), Cathy Howard (Girl on tomb [uncredited]), Garth Watkins (Chief mock priest [uncredited]), Bill Sawyer (Puritan [uncredited]), Jason James (Puritan [uncredited]), John Fahey (Puritan [uncredited]), Kenneth Gilbert (Puritan [uncredited]), Sebastian Graham-Jones (Puritan [uncredited]), Derek Glynne-Percy (Puritan [uncredited]), Maxine Casson (Schoolgirl [uncredited]), Vivienne Chandler (Schoolgirl [uncredited]), Annette Roberts (Schoolgirl [uncredited]), Janet Lynn (Schoolgirl [uncredited]), Jackie Leapman (Schoolgirl [uncredited]), Doreen Chanter (Schoolgirl [uncredited]), Irene Chanter (Schoolgirl [uncredited]), Sian Houston (Schoolgirl [uncredited]), Peter Stephens (Member of brotherhood [uncredited]), Harry Fielder (Member of brotherhood [uncredited]). **DVD availability:** Carlton (UK R2 PAL); Network (UK R2 PAL), extras include a trailer, a previously deleted scene and program notes; Synapse Films (U.S. R1 NTSC), extras include a feature-length (84m) documentary titled *The Flesh and the Fury: X-Posing Twins of Evil* featuring John Hough and Damien Thomas, a featurette titled *The Props That Hammer Built: The Kinsey Collection*, a trailer, stills and the previously deleted scene. **Blu-ray availability:** Synapse Films (A/1), extras as per the DVD, which is also included; Network (B/2), extras include the trailer, TV spots, the deleted scene, stills and a commemorative booklet. **CD availability:** *The Hammer Film Music Collection: Volume One* (GDI Records), which contains the *Main Title*; *Twins of Evil* (GDI Records), which contains the complete score

### The Two Faces of Dr. Jekyll

GB, 1960, 88m, Technicolor, MegaScope, RCA, cert X

This was Hammer's second take on Robert Louis Stevenson's 1885 novella *The Strange Case of Dr. Jekyll and Mr. Hyde* following their spoof version *The Ugly Duckling* (1959), and like it's predecessor, it failed at the box office, perhaps because—again—the studio tampered with the storyline. This time, instead of turning into a Teddy boy, as had been the case with *The Ugly Duckling*, the staid, middle-aged Dr. Henry Jekyll here turns into the handsome young sadist Edward Hyde, whose indulgences include drink, drugs and pleasures of the flesh. Inevitably, this depraved bill of fare led to

**Under doctor's orders. British artwork for *The Two Faces of Dr. Jekyll* (1960) (Hammer/Columbia/American International).**

much consternation from the BBFC. Commented a concerned John Trevelyan on reading the submitted script, "The three ingredients of sex, violence and horror are here in full measure, and the combination produces a deadly cocktail."[51]

Although one in an increasingly long line of color genre remakes produced by Hammer—also see *The Curse of Frankenstein* (1957), *Dracula* (1958), *The Man Who Could Cheat Death* (1959) and *The Mummy* (1959)—*The Two Faces of Dr. Jekyll* was very much a personal project for producer Michael Carreras, and was originally envisaged (and indeed written) as a prestige vehicle for Laurence Harvey, who had recently secured international stardom with his Oscar-nominated role as Joe Lampton in *Room at the Top* (1958). Unfortunately, Harvey had already been contracted to appear with Elizabeth Taylor in the Hollywood production of *Butterfield 8* (1960) for rather more money than Hammer was able (or willing) to pay, and so the roles of Jekyll and Hyde instead fell to the Canadian actor Paul Massie, though it should be noted that he was originally signed solely to play the role of Hyde, no doubt on the strength of his BAFTA award-winning performance as the army assassin Gene Summers in *Orders to Kill* (1958); however, after a good deal of lobbying, he also bagged the role of the middle-aged Jekyll too, which he plays in Roy Ashton's not-entirely-convincing make-up.

Set in 1874 (eleven years before the novel itself was written), Wolf Mankowitz's script is a surprisingly dull piece of pseudo-intellectualism given the liberties taken with the original material. The basic idea itself is sound enough—that of the attractiveness of evil, and the corruptness of a seemingly decent (i.e., two-faced) society. Commented director Terence Fisher, "Wolf Mankowitz realized that evil wasn't a horrible thing crawling around the street. It's very charming and attractive and seductive. Temptation! That was the only strength of the script, and the only interesting thing, too."[52]

Unfortunately, Mankowitz failed to run with his concept, leaving Fisher somewhat high and dry, though as the director himself later admitted, "You can't always blame the writers…. I don't think I ever tried to love that film very much. It is one of those films out of which I never managed to get the maximum effect."[53] This in turn prompted Mankowitz to concede that "With Larry [Harvey] and a halfway-decent director, Hammer would have had *the* most distinguished film they ever made,"[54] adding that "He [Fisher] didn't understand what the thing was about. He hadn't even read the book. He thought it was just another Hammer horror story."[55]

These recriminations aside, the film additionally suffers from the miscasting of Massie—surprisingly lackluster in both roles—which doesn't help matters, making one wonder why Hammer didn't cast their Monster player in residence Christopher Lee in the parts. That said, Lee *is* onboard as Hyde's corrupt and corrupting friend Paul Allen, and the proceedings undeniably perk up when he's on screen. Recalled the actor, "I'll admit that, initially, I was put off at not playing Jekyll and Hyde. Who wouldn't be? I thought I deserved the opportunity. In retrospect, I'm grateful because I got a very good part. I'm told Paul Allen was written with me in mind. The film was very well made and gave me an unexpected opportunity."[56] Note that Lee did finally play Jekyll and Hyde—albeit re-named Dr. Marlowe and Mr. Blake—in *I, Monster* (1970), yet another commercially unsuccessful variation on the story.

Another actor who would have been equally adept at playing the roles of Jekyll and Hyde was Oliver Reed, who would soon be catapulted to stardom in the lead role in Hammer's *The Curse of the Werewolf* (1961). Here, however, he is confined to a walk-on cameo as a nightclub pimp out to teach Hyde some manners for slighting one of his doxies. Also livening up the cast is the beautiful Dawn Addams as Jekyll's faithless wife Kitty, who ends up being raped by her husband's *alter ego*, while her lover, Paul Allen, is crushed to death by a python belonging to Maria, an exotic dancer with whom Hyde has been having an illicit affair at the Sphinx nightclub. All those with whom Jekyll/Hyde is close are equally two-faced, it would seem, a subtle point that is made much too little of, save for Jekyll's observation that, "In every human personality, two forces struggle for supremacy." Indeed, the lack of any characters one can sympathize with proves to be a major stumbling block for the film. As director Terence Fisher conceded, "You didn't have a single character in that story who was worth tuppence ha'ppny."[57] The film also suffers from a torpid pace (despite its brief eighty-eight minute running time) and sluggish direction that, for the most part, seems to lack enthusiasm. Nevertheless, the production—which was shot on the more accommodating stages of Elstree between 23 November 1959 and 22 January 1960—does have two major pluses: the beautifully lit and composed MegaScope photography of Jack Asher, and the eye-catching production design of Bernard Robinson, with its almost suffocating use of the color red during the nightclub and vice-den sequences, which perfectly reflect the depravity of the period. The film also benefits from a fiery finale, which is excitingly staged and edited. Nevertheless, when compared to the studio's other films of the period, the results seem rather pedestrian and tame thanks to a seemingly over-precautionary approach. This was no doubt a reaction to the screenplay's heady brew of sex and violence, much of which was further trimmed by the censor. Meanwhile, the surplus of subplots detracts from the central story, which in any case fails to grip as it should, resulting in a film of intriguing parts, if not exactly a satisfying whole. Yet like all of Hammer's underdogs—also see *The Curse of the Werewolf* (1961) and *The Lost Continent* (1968)—it does have its champions.

The film was trade shown on 20 August 1960 at the Columbia Theater. Unfortunately, following its premiere at the London Pavilion on 7 October, *The Two Faces of Dr. Jekyll* failed to find favor with either the critics or the public when released on the ABC circuit on 24 October care of Columbia on a double bill with *Heures chaudes* (1959), though some sources state that the film was paired with *La jument verte* (1959). The movie's trailer promised "The century old horror classic filmed as it has never been seen before," which prompted Paul Dehn to sum up the feelings of all when he commented in the *News Chronicle*, "This is not the Jekyll and Hyde I remember." Others were even harsher: "Repellent," blasted *The Times*, while *The Spectator* found it "vulgar and foolish." However,

some publications did look favorably upon the film, among them *Kinematograph Weekly*, which noted that, "The leading players display an exuberance consistent with the lurid tale's Lyceum period," though it proved off the mark when it predicted that, "It'll collect crowds and keep 'em on tenterhooks."

For its American release on 3 May 1961 care of American International, on to which a disappointed Columbia had sold the property, the movie was first re-titled *Jekyll's Inferno* and then, after further consideration, *House of Fright* (this after further cuts and the re-dubbing of some mild profanities—Hades for hell, witch for bitch and darn for damn, etc.). As such it was sent out on a double bill with *Terror in the Haunted House* (1958). Given its content, *Variety* expressed some concern as to its suitability as a "kiddies' matinee film," drawing attention to its "abundant flouting of the moral code—adultery, two rapes and the standard shocker violence." As for the central performance, *The New York Times* found that "Mr. Massie is frankly ridiculous." Yet according to screenwriter Wolf Mankowitz, the movie was most definitely "*not* a horror film."[58] It was, he averred, "a comment on the two-facedness of respectable society."[59] He also claimed that it "contains some comment on the evil of scientific pride divorced from both human and ethical considerations."[60] Despite Hammer's recent successes in the horror genre, *The Two Faces of Dr. Jekyll* had a major impact on both the company, which, for the first time, was seen to be showing signs of major fallibility, and, especially, the career of producer Michael Carreras, for whom the film was seen as a personal indulgence. Indeed, Carreras later commented, "Within the company it set me back a lot,"[61] which seems like an astonishing admission to make given that Hammer was still very much a family enterprise. It has been noted elsewhere that Michael and his father, James Carreras, didn't always see eye to eye. However, this revelation seems to indicate that Henry Jekyll was not the only two-faced person to be found at Hammer during this period; speaking at a board meeting which was not attended by his son, James Carreras commented of the £146,000 film, "A picture of world-wide interest and distribution ought not to cost over £120,000."[62] **Additional notes:** Screenwriter Wolf Mankowitz, composer Monty Norman and lyricist David Heneker had already worked together on the stage musicals *Expresso Bongo* (1958, recorded for TV 1958, filmed 1959) and *Make Me An Offer* (1959, recorded for TV 1966), and it would seem that the triumvirate came to the film as a package. The film was part-financed with a loan from the National Film Finance Corporation. Continuity-wise, one might wonder how Dr. Jekyll grows back his beard after being the clean-shaven Hyde. This could well explain *Variety*'s amusing description of the movie as being "an effective beard remover." The narration for the film's trailer was provided by Valentine Dyall ("If you cannot bear to see a man change before your eyes, then shut them for just a few seconds if you can, and listen for the shuddering sounds to end. They mark the evil transformation of Henry Jekyll to his monstrous other self, the cruel, depraved Edward

Hyde," he intones). Hammer would go on to make yet a further non-straight version of the story with the transgender *Dr. Jekyll and Sister Hyde* (1971).

Production company: Hammer. Distributors: Columbia (UK [ABC circuit]), American International (U.S.). Producer: Michael Carreras. Associate producer: Anthony Nelson Keys. Director: Terence Fisher. Screenplay: Wolf Mankowitz, based upon the novel *The Strange Case of Dr. Jekyll and Mr. Hyde* by Robert Louis Stevenson. Cinematographer: Jack Asher. Music: Monty Norman. Lyrics: David Heneker. Music director: John Hollingsworth. Supervising editor: James Needs. Editor: Eric Boyd-Perkins. Assistant editor: Chris Barnes [uncredited]. Production design: Bernard Robinson. Costumes: Mayo, Molly Arbuthnot. Make-up: Roy Ashton. Hair: Ivy Emmerton. Sound: Jock May. Sound editor: Archie Ludski. Production manager: Clifford Parkes. Studio manager: Arthur Kelly [uncredited]. Chief electrician: Jack Curtis [uncredited]. Master carpenter: Charles Davis [uncredited]. Master painter: Lawrence Wren [uncredited]. Assistant director: John Peverall. Second assistant director: Hugh Harlow [uncredited]. Assistant art director: Don Mingaye [uncredited]. Camera operator: Len Harris. Focus puller: Harry Oakes [uncredited]. Props: Tommy Money [uncredited]. Props buyer: Eric Hillier [uncredited]. Choreographer: Julie Mendez. Casting: Dorothy Holloway [uncredited], Stuart Lyons [uncredited]. Continuity: Tilly Day, Pauline Wise (trainee [uncredited]). Stills: Tom Edwards [uncredited]. Modeller: Margaret Carter (later Robinson [uncredited]). **Cast:** Paul Massie (Dr. Henry Jekyll/Edward Hyde), Dawn Addams (Kitty Jekyll), Christopher Lee (Paul Allen), Francis de Wolff (Inspector), David Kossoff (Ernest Litauer), Norma Marla (Maria), Joy Webster (Jenny), "Tiger" Joe Robinson (Corinthian [uncredited]), William Kendall (Clubman [uncredited]), Frank Atkinson (Groom [uncredited]), John Bonney (Renfrew [uncredited]), Oliver Reed (Pimp [uncredited]), Douglas Robinson (Boxer [uncredited]), Maria Andipa (Gypsy [uncredited]), Percy Cartwright (Coroner [uncredited]), Helen Goss (Nannie [uncredited]), Denis Cleary (Waiter [uncredited]), Janina Faye (Jane [uncredited]), Walter Gotell (Gambler [uncredited]), Felix Felton (Gambler [uncredited]), Anthony Jacobs (Gambler [uncredited]), Roberta Kirkwood (Second brass [uncredited]), Donald Tandy (Plainclothes policeman [uncredited]), Joyce Wren (Nurse [uncredited]), Joan Tyrrell (Major Domo [uncredited]), Arthur Lovegrove (Cabby [uncredited]), Prudence Hyman (Tavern patron [uncredited]), Lucy Griffiths (Tavern patron [uncredited]), Denis Shaw (Tavern patron [uncredited]), Pauline Shepherd (Tavern girl [uncredited]), Zoreen Ismail (Sphinx Girl [uncredited]), Magda Miller (Sphinx Girl [uncredited]), Bandana Das Gupta (Sphinx Girl [uncredited]), Pauline Dukes (Sphinx Girl [uncredited]), Moyna Sharwin (Sphinx Girl [uncredited]), Shirli Scott-James (Sphinx Girl [uncredited]), Hazel Graeme (Sphinx Girl [uncredited]), Carole Haynes (Sphinx Girl [uncredited]), Josephine Jay (Sphinx Girl [uncredited]), Marilyn Ridge (Sphinx Girl [uncredited]), Jean Long (Sphinx Girl [uncredited]), Gundel Sargent (Sphinx Girl [uncredited]), Patricia Sayers (Sphinx Girl [uncredited]), Archie Baker (Singer [uncredited]), Alex Miller (Singer [uncredited]), Ralph Broadbent (Singer [uncredited]), Laurence Richardson (Singer [uncredited]), Anthony Pendrell (Cabinet Minister [uncredited]), Fred Stone (Cabinet Minister [uncredited]), Glenn Beck (Young blood [uncredited]), Rodney Burke (Young blood [uncredited]), Alan Browning (Young blood [uncredited]), Clifford Earl (Young blood [uncredited]), Kenneth Firth (Businessman [uncredited]), Roy Denton (Businessman [uncredited]), George McGrath (Businessman [uncredited]), Mackenzie Ward (Businessman [uncredited]), J. Trevor-Davis (Officer [uncredited]), John Moore (Officer [uncredited]). **DVD availability:** Sony (UK R2 PAL)

### The Two Faces of Evil see Hammer House of Horror

### Tyke's Water Lake

Situated in the Habderdasher's Aske's School estate in Elstree, Hertfordshire, this oft-used location with its familiar-looking redbrick bridge was used in such TV shows as *The Avengers* (1961–1969, TV), *Here Come the Double Deckers!* (1970, TV) and *The Adventures of Sherlock Holmes* (1984–1985, TV), as well as such films as *The Abominable Dr. Phibes* (1971). It can also be seen in a number of Hammer productions, including *Taste the Blood of Dracula* (1970) and *Dracula A.D. 1972* (1972). The school itself can be seen in *The Nanny* (1965). **Hammer credits:** *The Nanny* (1965), *Frankenstein Must Be Destroyed* (1969), *Taste the Blood of Dracula* (1970), *Fear in the Night* (1972), *Dracula A.D. 1972* (1972)

### Tyrrell, Joan

Tyrrell can be seen as the Major Domo in Hammer's *The Two Faces of Dr. Jekyll* (1960). Her other credits include *The Brain Machine* (1955) and *Beyond Therapy* (1987), plus episodes of *Armchair Theatre* (1956–1974, TV). **Hammer credits:** *The Two Faces of Dr. Jekyll* (1960, as Major Domo [uncredited])

# U

### UFA Studios (Universum Film AG/UFA GMBH)

Hammer made their troubled bomb disposal drama *Ten Seconds to Hell* (1959) at the famous German film studio in Berlin, where the cameras began to roll on 24 February 1958. Formed in 1917, and in alliance (via distribution deals) with MGM and Paramount from 1925 (as Parufamet), it produced newsreels, documentaries and feature films on a similar scale to the Hollywood studios, and several noted directors helped to put the facility on the world map during the silent period, notably Fritz Lang, who made such classics as *Dr. Mabuse* (1922), *Die Nibelungen: Siegfried* (1924), *Faust* (1926) and *Metropolis* (1927) there. Other notable

films made at the complex include *Carmen* (1918 [directed by Ernst Lubitsch), *Variety* (1925 [A.E. Dupont]), *The Blue Angel* (1930 [Josef von Sternberg]) and *Triumph of the Will* (1935 [Reni Riefenstahl]). Other famous directors who worked at the studios during its early years include Paul Czinner, F.W. Murnau and William Dieterle. The facility was effectively nationalized in 1937 and was occupied by the Red Army in 1945. It was re-privatized by 1956, and as recently as 2013 underwent a major restructuring. More recent films from UFA, either as a production company or a home territory distributor, include *Riddick* (2013), *Taken 3* (2014), *Naked Among Wolves* (2015), *The Vatican Tapes* (2015) and *The Lake* (2017). **Hammer credits:** *Ten Seconds to Hell* (1959)

### The Ugly Duckling

GB, 1959, 84m, bw, cert U

*The Ugly Duckling* was the first of three films made by Hammer based upon Robert Louis Stevenson's celebrated 1885 novella *The Strange Case of Dr. Jekyll and Mr. Hyde*, yet despite Hammer's propensity for remaking established classics, not one of these films was a straight re-telling of the story (also see *The Two Faces of Dr. Jekyll* [1960] and *Dr. Jekyll and Sister Hyde* [1971]).

This particular version, which was part-financed with a loan from the National Film Finance Corporation, is a comedic take on the legend, specifically produced as a vehicle for Bernard Bresslaw, who had recently scored a hit for Hammer with *I Only Arsed!* (1958). As with that film, the screenplay was provided by gagsters Sid Colin and Jack Davies, based on a story by Colin (or "with ideas stolen from Robert Louis Stevenson" as the credits have it). It sees Bresslaw cast as the bumbling Henry Jekyll who, after having discovered the recipe for his great great grandfather's formula, produces his own batch of the potion, a swig of which transforms him into the tear-away Teddy Hide ("He's a changed man after taking Jekyll's old family remedy," joshed the poster).

Originally to have been titled *Mad Pashernate Love* (after one of Bresslaw's hit singles), the £110,000 film went on the floor at Bray on 4 May 1959, with the plot seeing Hide become involved with a gang of jewel thieves, one of whom is the manager of the local *palais de danse*, where Teddy becomes something of a lothario (these scenes were filmed on location in South London, at the Streatham Locarno). Shooting lasted some six weeks and concluded on 10 June 1959. Unfortunately, the results proved to be a commercial and critical disappointment when released in the UK by Columbia on 10 August 1959, following a trade show at the Columbia Theater on 28 July. Prints of the film were thereafter long out of circulation, leading some to assume that it had been lost. However, when it finally turned up, unheralded, on British TV in 2018, it proved to be far from a lost comedy classic. Indeed, Bresslaw aside, the cast and crew make heavy weather of the proceedings, which become something of a chore to sit through well before the end. **Additional notes:** When Henry Jekyll transforms into Teddy Hide, the soundtrack makes an uncredited use of James Bernard's *Dracula* theme. At one point, Bresslaw makes use of his catchphrase from *The Army Game*: "I only arsed!" Although the family name is clearly Jekyll (as per the sign over their chemist shop), the dance hall features a poster heralding a display of old time dancing by Henry's sister Henrietta Jeckle, while at the climax, after Henry has proved himself a hero, a banner announces it to be "Henry Jeckle Night." Someone clearly wasn't paying attention. Bruce Forsyth, then a TV hit in *Sunday Night at the London Palladium* (1955–1967, TV), was sought

Double trouble. Amusing artwork for the Bernard Bresslaw comedy *The Ugly Duckling* (1959) (Hammer/Columbia).

to appear in the film, but other commitments prevented him from taking part in this, as well as another proposed film, *I'm in Charge* (the title of which was based on one of his Palladium catchphrases). The Jekyll and Hyde story had previously been spoofed in *Abbott and Costello Meet Dr. Jekyll and Mr. Hyde* (1955), which was made by Universal, who were also behind the comedians' encounters with Frankenstein, the Mummy and the Invisible Man. Hammer also seemingly intended to make a serious version of the Jekyll and Hyde story, again with Bresslaw, but the idea was eventually scrapped (said Michael Carreras in an interview for *Kinematograph Weekly* at the time, "The two treatments are so far apart as to be practically unrecognizable. *The Ugly Duckling* will do the straight version some good. It will reacquaint people with the names Jekyll and Hyde"). Jerry Lewis made a similarly themed variation of the story in 1963 titled *The Nutty Professor*, which saw his bumbling college lecturer Professor Julius Kelp turn into the slick-haired crooner Buddy Love; this was later remade as *The Nutty Professor* (1996) starring Eddie Murphy, which in turn spawned a sequel, *Nutty Professor II: The Klumps* (2000).

Production company: Hammer. Distributor: Columbia (UK). Producer: Tommy Lyndon-Haynes. Executive producer: Michael Carreras. Director: Lance Comfort. Screenplay: Sid Colin, Jack Davies, based upon a story by Sid Colin and the novel *The Strange Case of Dr. Jekyll and Mr. Hyde* by Robert Louis Stevenson. Cinematographer: Michael Reed. Music: Douglas Gamley. Music director: John Hollingsworth. Songs: Brian Fahey (theme tune), John Gregory (*Cha-Cha "Chaquito"*). Supervising editor: James Needs. Editor: John Dunsford. Assistant editors: Peter Todd [uncredited], Alan Corder [uncredited]. Production designer: Bernard Robinson. Assistant art director: Don Mingaye. Costumes: Molly Arbuthnot, Rosemary Burrows (assistant [uncredited]), Frank Usher (model dresses). Make-up: Roy Ashton. Hair: Henry Montsash. Choreographer: Lionel Blair. Camera operator: Len Harris. Focus puller: Harry Oakes [uncredited]. Clapper boy/camera loader: Alan MacDonald [uncredited]. Assistant director: John Peverall. Second assistant director: Tom Walls [uncredited]. Third assistant director: Hugh Harlow [uncredited]. Sound: Jock May. Sound assistant: Maurice Smith [uncredited]. Boom operator: Jim Perry [uncredited]. Sound camera operators: Al Thorne [uncredited], Michael Sale [uncredited]. Sound maintenance: Charles Bouvet [uncredited]. Production manager: Don Weeks. Props: Tommy Money, Peter Allchorne [uncredited]. Props buyer: Eric Hillier [uncredited]. Continuity: Marjorie Lavelly. Casting: Dorothy Holloway [uncredited]. Production secretaries: Patricia Green [uncredited], Margot Wardle [uncredited]. Chief accountant: W.H.V. Able [uncredited]. Cashier: Peter Lancaster [uncredited]. Studio manager: Arthur Kelly [uncredited]. Construction manager: Mick Lyons [uncredited]. Master painter: Lawrence Wren [uncredited]. Master plasterer: Arthur Banks [uncredited]. Master carpenter: Charles Davis [uncredited]. Chief electrician: Jack Curtis [uncredited]. Electrical supervisor: George Robinson Cowlard [uncredited]. Publicist: Colin Reid [uncredited]. Stills: Tom Edwards [uncredited]. Drivers: William Epps [uncredited], Sid Humphrey [uncredited], Wilfred Faux [uncredited]. **Cast:** Bernard Bresslaw (Henry Jekyll/Teddy Hide), Jon Pertwee (Victor Jekyll), Reginald Beckwith (Reginald), Maudie Edwards (Henrietta Jekyll), Jean Muir (Snout), David Lodge (Peewee), Michael Ripper (Fish), Harold Goodwin (Benny), Norma Marla (Angel), Keith Smith (Figures), Elwyn Brook-Jones (Dandy), Jess Conrad (Bimbo), Mary Wilson (Lizzie), Gerry Phillips (Tiger), Richard Wattis (Barclay), Michael Ward (Pasco), John Harvey (Detective Sergeant Barnes), Vicki Marshall (Kitten), Alan Coleshill (Willie), Jill Carson (Yum Yum), Nicholas Tanner (Commissionaire), Jean Driant (Blum), Shelagh Dey (Miss Angers), Sheila Hammond (Receptionist), Ian Wilson (Small man), Verne Morgan (Barman), Cyril Chamberlain (Police Sergeant), Reginald Marsh (Reporter), Richard Statman (Reporter), Roger Avon (Reporter), Ian Ainsley (Fraser), Robert Desmond (Dizzy), Alexander Doré (Customer in chemists), Joe Loss and his Orchestra (Themselves), Heather Downham (Margo), Malka Alanat (Fifi), Ann Mayhew (Lucienne), Aldine Honey (Jane), Jacqueline Perrin (Ursula), Helen Pohlman (Amanda), Helga Wahlrow (Rosemary), Jack Armstrong (Dancer), Jamie Barnes (Dancer), Lola Morice (Dancer), Peter Mander (Dancer), Aileen Lewis (Dancer), Richard Duke (Dancer), Stella Kemball (Dancer [billed as Stella Kimball]), Alecia St. Leger (Dancer), Lucy Griffiths (Cellist [uncredited])

## Underdown, Edward

On stage from the age of twenty-four following experience as a jockey, this British actor (1908–1989) made his film debut in 1933 with *The Warren Case*. Subsequent films include *Wings of the Morning* (1937), *They Were Not Divided* (1950), *Beat the Devil* (1954), *The Day the Earth Caught Fire* (1961) and *The Abdication* (1974). He can also be seen in Hammer's *The Camp on Blood Island* (1958) as a British POW. His many TV credits include episodes of *The Saint* (1962–1969, TV), *Doomwatch* (1970–1972, TV) and *The Duchess of Duke Street* (1976–1977, TV). **Hammer credits:** *The Camp on Blood Island* (1958, as Major Dawes)

## *The Unholy Four* see *The Stranger Came Home*

## United Artists

Founded in 1919 by Charles Chaplin, D.W. Griffith, Douglas Fairbanks and Mary Pickford, by way of enabling them to fully control their own output, this independent studio went through several incarnations down the decades, being acquired by various interested parties, among them Howard Hughes. The sixties and seventies were the company's best years, when it produced such worldwide successes as *The Magnificent Seven* (1960), *Tom Jones* (1963), the James Bond series and *Rocky* (1976), although the edifice came crashing down in 1980 with the budgetary over-runs of the over inflated *Heaven's Gate* (1980), which subsequently saw UA acquired by MGM (which became MGM/UA).

It was during the fifties and sixties that United Artists had several dealings with Hammer, beginning with *Cloudburst* (1951), which UA released in America (minus nine minutes), thanks to the contacts of the Hungarian producer Alexander Paal, who also helped to finance the picture. UA also released Hammer's breakthrough film, *The Quatermass Xperiment* (1955) in America, for which it was re-titled *The Creeping Unknown* and shorn of four minutes. Meanwhile, as well as releasing the second Quatermass film (which they again re-titled), United Artists also provided much of the budget, as they did for the war drama *The Steel Bayonet* (1957), which they likewise released. They also released *Ten Seconds to Hell* (1959) and provided finance for and released *The Hound of the Baskervilles* (1959). **Hammer credits:** *Cloudburst* (1951), *The Quatermass Xperiment* (1955), *Quatermass 2* (1957), *The Steel Bayonet* (1957), *Ten Seconds to Hell* (1959), *The Hound of the Baskervilles* (1959)

## United Programmes

This sound system was used to record a handful of Hammer's programers in 1949 and 1950. **Hammer credits:** *Dr. Morelle—The Case of the Missing Heiress* (1949), *The Adventures of PC 49—The Case of the Guardian Angel* (1949), *Meet Simon Cherry* (1949), *The Man in Black* (1950), *Room to Let* (1950), *Someone at the Door* (1950)

## Universal (Universal International/ Universal Pictures)

Founded in 1912 by the German born exhibitor Carl Laemmle, Universal made all manner of films during the silent period, including several highly popular Rudolph Valentino romances. However, with their version of *The Hunchback of Notre Dame* (1923) starring Lon Chaney, the studio became increasingly recognized for their horror films, among them *The Phantom of the Opera* (1925) and, most notably, *Dracula* (1931), which led to a successful run of shockers throughout the thirties and forties. Among these were such classics as *Frankenstein* (1931), *The Mummy* (1932), *The Old Dark House* (1932), *The Invisible Man* (1933), *Bride of Frankenstein* (1935), *Son of Frankenstein* (1939), *The Wolf Man* (1941) and *Abbott and Costello Meet Frankenstein* (1948).

When Hammer announced their own version of *Frankenstein* in 1956, Universal was quick to threaten legal action if the subsequent film, *The Curse of Frankenstein* (1957), in any way infringed their own copyright, especially where the make-up was concerned. However, when the film became an immediate worldwide commercial success, Universal softened its approach and even agreed to distribute and co-finance Hammer's remake of *Dracula* (1958), thus beginning a fruitful association with the company. In fact the commercial success of *Dracula* apparently helped to stave off financial ruin for Universal. Recalled Christopher Lee, "I remember going with Peter Cushing, Jimmy Carreras and Anthony Hinds into the office of Al Daff, president of Universal in New York, and he said, 'Gentlemen, your film has just taken Universal out of bankruptcy.'"[1]

Consequently, Universal now worked with enthusiasm with Hammer, releasing several important genre properties to the studio for the remake treatment, among them *The Invisible Man* (which failed to make it to the screen), *The Phantom of the Opera* and *The Mummy*, the latter of which went before the cameras first in 1959. The film was another major commercial success when released in America by Universal International—so much so that it even managed to out-gross *Dracula* at the box office, confirming that the Hollywood studio's faith in the British company had been warranted.

Interestingly, although the rights were available to them, Hammer chose not to remake Universal's *Werewolf of London* (1935) or *The Wolf Man* (1940), but instead opted to make a version of Guy Endore's novel *The Werewolf of Paris*, the rights to which they sub-contracted from Universal for a hefty fee. In the process, the novel's French setting was transposed to 18th century Spain so as to make use of sets built for an abandoned project titled *The Rape of Sabena* (aka *The Inquisitor*). Unfortunately, the resultant film was not a major commercial success, and remains Hammer's sole big screen foray into the realms of lycanthropy. Equally disappointing in terms of box office was the studio's remake of *The Phantom of the Opera* (1962), which went out on a double bill with *Captain Clegg* (1962). Hammer actively sought an A certificate for the film in the hope of wider box office appeal. Unfortunately, this approach almost completely diluted the film's shocks and gore, much to the chagrin of fans.

However, the studio was on firmer ground with *The Kiss of the Vampire* (1963), which Universal both invested in and distributed in America on a double bill with *Paranoiac* (1963). One of Hammer's better genre pictures, its success did much to restore faith in the company following its string of disappointments. Nevertheless, Universal turned down Hammer's offer to make *The Reptile* (1966) when the production was first announced in 1963 as *The Reptiles* (it would be announced again the following year as *The Curse of the Reptiles* before finally going into production as a Hammer-Seven Arts co-production). However, they did go on to invest in and release (Stateside) Hammer's third Frankenstein picture, *The Evil of Frankenstein* (1964), for which they even allowed the studio to use a variation on Jack P. Pierce's iconographic Monster make-up, as well as fragments of the plots from the old series. The result was something of a mixed bag, but it nevertheless did well at the box office when double-billed with the "mini Hitchcock" *Nightmare* (1964). Universal was also to have been involved in Hammer's remake of *She* (1965), plans for which were announced in 1963, but the project instead ended up being made in association with ABPC. The company was also briefly involved in Hammer's production of *The Witches* (1966) in early 1965, but this came to an end following the U.S. release of *The Secret of Blood Island* (1965), after which Universal abruptly brought an end to their association with Hammer in April that year. Nevertheless, Hammer continued to offer proj-

ects to Universal, among them *The Devil Rides Out* (1968), which was eventually financed by Seven-Arts, and the (unmade) pirate yarn *Mistress of the Seas*. Universal finally became involved with Hammer again in 1971, when it handled the U.S. distribution of *Hands of the Ripper* (1971) and *Twins of Evil* (1971), which were released as a double bill. However, the studio declined to become involved in the financing of *To the Devil a Daughter* (1976) when approached by Michael Carreras. Universal itself remade *The Mummy* in 1999, this time as an Indiana Jones–like adventure, the success of which led to two sequels, *The Mummy Returns* (2001) and *The Mummy: Tomb of the Dragon Emperor* (2008), and a 2017 reboot. **Hammer credits:** *Dracula* (1958), *The Mummy* (1959), *The Brides of Dracula* (1960), *The Curse of the Werewolf* (1961), *The Shadow of the Cat* (1961), *Captain Clegg* (1962), *The Phantom of the Opera* (1962), *Paranoiac* (1963), *The Kiss of the Vampire* (1963), *Nightmare* (1964), *The Evil of Frankenstein* (1964), *The Secret of Blood Island* (1965), *Hands of the Ripper* (1971), *Twins of Evil* (1971)

## Unsworth, Geoffrey

This celebrated British cinematographer (1914–1978) entered the film industry as a camera assistant in 1932, graduating to assistant cameraman on *The Four Feathers* (1939) and operator on *The Life and Death of Colonel Blimp* (1943). He photographed his first film, a documentary short titled *World Garden*, in 1942, and went on to shoot such major productions as *The Blue Lagoon* (1949), *A Night to Remember* (1958) and *North West Frontier* (1959), winning BAFTAs for his work on *Becket* (1964), *2001: A Space Odyssey* (1968), *Cabaret* (1972), which also won him an Oscar, *Alice's Adventures in Wonderland* (1972), *A Bridge Too Far* (1977) and *Tess* (1979), which also won him a second (shared) Oscar. He also earned BAFTA nominations for *Tamahine* (1963), *Murder on the Orient Express* (1974), *Zardoz* (1974) and *Superman* (1978). In the mid-fifties, he also photographed a handful of widescreen musical featurettes for Hammer, which are noted for the fluidity of their camerawork. He was made an OBE in 1976. He was married to the continuity girl Maggie Unsworth (?–2009, aka Margaret Sibley and Margaret Shipway). **Hammer credits:** *The Eric Winstone Bandshow* (1955), *Eric Winstone's Stagecoach* (1956), *The Edmundo Ros Half Hour* (1956)

## Unwin, Geoff

Unwin provided the music for the title song *It's a Great Life on the Buses*, which topped and tailed Hammer's *On the Buses* (1971), which was otherwise scored by Max Harris. Recalled Unwin of his involvement in the film, "I was invited to write the title song for the first *On the Buses* feature film by Philip Martell, head of music at Hammer Films…. At the time I was with EMI Records and beginning to get involved with film music at Elstree Studios. I recorded a demo of the song at Abbey Road Studios with an eighteen-piece line-up featuring ex–Ted Heath big band pianist Frank Horrox on honky tonk. I also used a new vocal group called Quinceharmon who had recently been put under contract

by EMI. The producers of the *On the Buses* movie liked the demo so much that they decided to put it directly on to the soundtrack. So what you hear on the film was only originally intended as a demo!"[2] The song was however subsequently re-recorded for the single release (with no less than Brian Bennett of Shadows fame playing drums). In addition to the public, the record was also released to cinemas to be played before and after each showing of the movie. **Hammer credits:** *On the Buses* (1971)

## Unwin, Stanley

Remembered for his novelty act in which he spoke a form of gobbledygook he named Unwinese, this Pretoria born radio performer and television personality (1911–2002) began his career as a sound engineer at the BBC in 1940 before going on to host his own show, *Unwin Time*. He also appeared in a handful of films, among them *Fun at St. Fanny's* (1955), the Hammer comedy *Further Up the Creek* (1958), *Inn for Trouble* (1960), *Carry On Regardless* (1961), *Hair of the Dog* (1962), *Press for Time* (1966) and *Chitty Chitty Bang Bang* (1968). He also starred in the television series *The Secret Service* (1969, TV), and guested on such shows as *David Nixon's Comedy Bandbox* (1966, TV) and *Tell Tarby* (1973, TV). **Hammer credits:** *Further Up the Creek* (1958, as Porter)

## *Up the Creek*

GB, 1958, 83m, bw, HammerScope, RCA, cert U

Having brought comedy to Hammer with his two Lyons films—*Life with the Lyons* (1954) and *The Lyons in Paris* (1955)—writer-director Val Guest continued the tradition in this reasonably brisk naval farce set aboard the *Barclay*, a rundown shore establishment whose crew try to hide their various black market schemes from their new commander, among them a laundry service and a bakery.

Although David Tomlinson's naïve Lieutenant Fairweather is credited as the star, it is Peter Sellers' wheeler-dealing Bilko-like Bosun who is the real focus of the film. At the time, Sellers was quickly becoming a household name, thanks to his success on radio in *The Goon Show* (1951–1960), and though he had already made a handful of films in supporting roles, among them *The Ladykillers* (1955) and *The Smallest Show on Earth* (1957), his work in *Up the Creek* helped to further establish him as a potential comic lead. Interestingly, James Carreras was not a Sellers fan, and only agreed to his casting if Tomlinson—then considered a bigger box office draw—was given top billing. However, when the film went on to become a major commercial success, it was Sellers that Carreras had to thank.

Recalled Guest of Sellers, "We'd heard of Peter on the radio in *The Goon Show* and seen him on television in *Son of Fred*, but not yet in films, save for a couple of minor appearances. I thought he was a wonderful comic. It was Yo's idea to put him on the screen [Guest's wife Yolande Donlan], so I wrote *Up the Creek* with him in mind."[3]

A co-production with Byron Films (which was run by producer Henry Halsted, who had previously had dealings with Hammer during their resurgence in the late forties), *Up the Creek* was shot at the New Elstree Studios between 11 November and Christmas Eve 1957 (hence the cold breath all round). The film also made use of locations in Weymouth and along the Thames Estuary. The result is a fairly standard British farce with echoes of the Will Hay comedy *Oh, Mr. Porter!* (1937), on which Val Guest had worked as a screenwriter earlier in his career. Packed with familiar comedy faces, among them Wilfrid Hyde-White, Lionel Jeffries and Sam Kydd, the film passes its time adequately enough, providing its fair share of predictable laughs, helped along by the comedy sparring of Tomlinson and Sellers, who though not at their peak, invest the proceedings with a certain energy (commented Sellers of the film's premise, "A good idea insufficiently developed"[4]).

The best exchange occurs early on between an annoyed Commander played by Patrick Cargill and Wilfrid Hyde-White's Admiral Foley. Comments the Commander, "The fact is, sir, I have a very serious complaint," to which comes the shocked retort, "Great Scott, is it catching?" Another memorable touch has the opening credits play over a shot of the statue atop Nelson's column, which subsequently comes to life (as played by Michael Goodliffe) and exclaims of the forthcoming action, "If the story bears any resemblance to the British navy, may I be hoist on a column one-hundred-and-forty-five feet high in the center of London."

Shot in HammerScope, the film—the last Hammer feature to be released by Exclusive—had its premiere at the flagship Warner Bros. Theater in London's Leicester Square on 7 May 1958 (note that Exclusive *did* release one more feature, *Murder at Site 3* [1959], but this was made by another company). *Up the Creek* went on general release on the ABC circuit on 2 June, while its U.S. release care of Dominant followed on 10 November. In fact such was the movie's success ("It was cheap to make and its takings have been fantastic,"[5] noted Sellers), an already-planned sequel, *Further Up the Creek* (1958), was immediately put into production (filming began just twelve days after the London premiere!). However, though David Tomlinson again top-lined, Frankie Howerd was now cast as the second lead, given that Sellers had already moved on to bigger (or should that be smaller?) things with a comic role in the big budget children's fantasy *tom thumb* (1958). A third film in the series was planned by Val Guest, but failed to materialize. **Additional notes:** The film was re-issued by RFI in 1961. Val Guest, cinematographer Arthur Grant and leading man David Tomlinson had already worked together on the similarly-themed navy lark *Carry On Admiral* (1957), though it should be noted that this film was not related to the official *Carry On* series, which was inaugurated a year later by producer Peter Rogers with *Carry On Sergeant* (1958). Guest went on to work with Peter Sellers again on the troubled Bond spoof *Casino Royale* (1967). The surname of Wilfrid Hyde-White is not hyphenated in the credits, while Hugh Latimer is credited as Hugh Lattimer and Peter Wayn as Peter Wayne. Even worse, established character actor Frank Pettingell is credited as Frank Pentingell in both the opening and closing credits. Unbelievable.

Production companies: Hammer/Byron Films/Henry Halsted Productions. Distributors: Exclusive (UK [ABC circuit]), Dominant (U.S.). Producer: Henry Halsted. Director: Val Guest. Screenplay: Val Guest, John Warren, Len Heath. Cinematographer: Arthur Grant. Music: Tony Lowry. Music director: Tony Fones. Editor: Helen Wiggins. Art directors: Elven Webb, Ward Richards. Camera operator: Moray Grant. Production supervisor: Fred A. Swann. Assistant director: John Peverall. Third assistant director: Ted Morley [uncredited]. Sound: George Adams. Make-up: Alec Garfath. Continuity: Gladys Reeve. Technical advisor: Lieutenant Commander J.H. Pidler, R.N. **Cast:** David Tomlinson (Lieutenant Humphrey Fairweather), Peter Sellers (C.P.O. Bosun Docherty), Wilfrid Hyde-White (Admiral Foley), Lionel Jeffries (Steady Barker), Liliane Sottane (Suzanne), Lionel Murton (Perkins), Sam Kydd (Bates), John Warren (Cooky), Reginald Beckwith (Publican), David Lodge (Scouse), Vera Day (Millie), Michael Goodliffe (Nelson), Patrick Cargill (Commander), Frank Pettingell (Station Master), Tom Gill (Flag Lieutenant), Howard Williams (Bunts), Peter Collingwood (Chippie), Barry Lowe (Webster), Edwin Richfield (Bennett), Max Butterfield (Lefty), Malcolm Ranson (Boy), Donald Bissett (Farm laborer), Leonard Fenton (Policeman), Basil Dignam (Captain Coombes), Peter Coke (Price), Jack McNaughton (Petty Officer), Michael Ripper (Decorator), Larry Noble (Chief Petty Officer), Hugh Latimer (Lieutenant Commander), Peter Wayn (Lieutenant), Hazel Sutton (unnamed role [unconfirmed, uncredited]). **DVD availability:** Simply Media (UK R2 PAL); DD Home Entertainment (UK R2 PAL). **CD availability:** *The Hammer Comedy Film Music Collection* (GDI Records), which contains the *Main Title* theme

## Urquhart, Robert

In films from 1952 with *You're Only Young Twice*, this British (Scottish) leading man (1921–1995) is best known to Hammer fans for playing tutor Paul Krempe in *The Curse of Frankenstein* (1957). Urquhart was under contract to ABPC at the time, a fact acknowledged in the opening credits. Despite the actor's best efforts, Krempe is a somewhat dull role, its sole purpose seeming to act as a voice of reason as Frankenstein's experiments become ever more ghoulish. Yet despite this high profile role, Urquhart didn't appear in any further films for Hammer, seemingly because of several negative comments he made in an interview at the time of the film's release regarding horror films. As the actor later recalled, "In this interview I said that there were some things they shouldn't have done [in the film], and I remember getting a letter from Michael Carreras saying, 'This type of publicity could hurt my company enormously.' And I never worked for them again. They were a closed book to me. I was never forgiven."[6] Urquhart nevertheless did go on to appear in over forty other movies, among them *Dunkirk* (1958), *55 Days at Peking* (1963), *The Looking Glass War* (1969) and *The Kitchen Toto* (1987). He was also busy on television, appearing in episodes of such series as *The Flying Doctor* (1959, TV), *Jango* (1961, TV), in

which he played the title role, *The Frighteners* (1972, TV), *The Old Men at the Zoo* (1983, TV) and *The Ruth Rendell Mysteries* (1987–2000, TV).

Interestingly, Urquhart took home the puppy featured in *The Curse of Frankenstein*. Recalled the actor, "Do you remember the little puppy, one of the first experiments? Well, I had that for the rest of its life. We have, I think, had three or four generations from Frankie."[7] Remembered actor Melvyn Hayes of his scenes as the young Victor Frankenstein with Urquhart, "When I came to do the scenes with him, I'd worked on the lines backwards. I was very young, and he was very experienced. He just opened the script and said, 'Shall we have a look at the lines, then?' I thought, I know them backwards…. For me, that was the most important bit, but for him, it was just the next day's shooting."[8]

Urquhart eventually returned to Hammer twenty-three years after *The Curse of Frankenstein* to play a supporting role in *Children of the Full Moon* (1980, TV [episode of *Hammer House of Horror*]), by which time Michael Carreras was no longer involved with the company (the new owners were no doubt unaware of Urquhart's *faux pas*). He was formerly married to the actress Zena Walker (1934–2003), who appeared in *Girl of My Dreams*, an episode of Hammer's *Journey to the Unknown* (1968, TV). **Hammer credits:** *The Curse of Frankenstein* (1957, as Paul Krempe), *Children of the Full Moon* (1980, TV [episode of *Hammer House of Horror*], as Harry)

## Usher, Frank

Usher designed the model costumes for Hammer's *The Ugly Duckling* (1959). **Hammer credits:** *The Ugly Duckling* (1959)

## Ustinov, Tamara

This British actress (1945–) can be seen as Veronica in Hammer's *Blood from the Mummy's Tomb* (1971). Her other credits include *The Blood on Satan's Claw* (1971), *The Last Horror Movie* (2003) and *Into the Light* (2009), while her small screen appearances include episodes of *Paul Temple* (1969–1971, TV), *The Pathfinders* (1972–1973, TV), *The Prime of Miss Jean Brodie* (1978, TV), *Tales of the Unexpected* (1979–1988, TV), *Kavanagh Q.C.* (1995–2001, TV) and *Hex* (2004–2005, TV). Her father was the actor, writer and director Peter Ustinov (1921–2004), her grandfather was the writer and director Reginald Denham (1894–1983) and her grandmother the actress Moyna MacGill (1895–1975). Her half-sister is the actress Pavla Ustinov (1954–) and her aunt is the actress Angela Lansbury (1925–), who appeared in Hammer's remake of *The Lady Vanishes* (1979). She is married to the actor Malcolm Rennie (1947–), whom she wed in 1989. **Hammer credits:** *Blood from the Mummy's Tomb* (1971, as Veronica)

# V

## V.S. (Vernon Sewell) Productions

Formed by the prolific writer-producer-director Vernon Sewell, this small scale British company was created for the production of *Jack of Diamonds*

(1949), which was part financed by Hammer founder Will Hammer. The company's only other credit is for *Ghost Ship* (1952). Also see **Sewell, Vernon**. **Hammer credits:** *Jack of Diamonds* (1949)

**Valencia, Trio** *see* **Trio Valencia**

**Valentine, Anthony**

Best known for such TV series as *Callan* (1969–1972, TV), in which he played Toby Meres, and *Raffles* (1975–1977, TV), in which he played the title character, this dapper British leading actor (1939–2015) began his career as a child, appearing in such films as *No Way Back* (1949), *The Girl on the Pier* (1953) and *The Brain Machine* (1954), and in such TV shows as *The Children of the New Forest* (1955, TV). As a young adult he appeared as one of the unruly Teddy boys in Hammer's *The Damned* (1963), and later returned to play David Kennedy in the company's last theatrical horror film for over thirty years, *To the Devil a Daughter* (1976), on which, for budgetary reasons, he was a last minute replacement for David Warner. He also took top billing in an episode of *Hammer House of Horror* (1980, TV). His other credits include *Escape to Athena* (1979), *The Monster Club* (1980) and *Jefferson in Paris* (1995), plus episodes of *Judge John Deed* (2001–2007, TV), *New Tricks* (2003–2015, TV), *The Last Detective* (2003–2007, TV) and *Chuggington* (2008–2015, TV). He was married to the actress Susan Skipper (1951–, real name Susan Cook), whom he wed in 1982. **Hammer credits:** *The Damned* (1963, as Teddy boy [uncredited]), *To the Devil a Daughter* (1976, as David Kennedy), *Carpathian Eagle* (1980, TV [episode of *Hammer House of Horror*], as Detective Inspector Clifford)

**Valentine, Elizabeth**

Valentine can be seen as one of Dr. Ravna's disciples in Hammer's *The Kiss of the Vampire* (1963). Her other credits include such TV plays as *Not At All* (1962, TV) and *Up the Junction* (1965, TV). **Hammer credits:** *The Kiss of the Vampire* (1963, as Disciple [uncredited])

**Valentine, James**

Valentine can be seen as a sailor in Hammer's *Stolen Face* (1952). His other credits include episodes of *Armchair Theatre* (1956–1974, TV) and *The Sweeney* (1975–1978, TV) and such one-offs as *Spaghetti Two-Step* (1977, TV). **Hammer credits:** *Stolen Face* (1952, as Sailor)

**Valentine, Val**

This prolific British scriptwriter and storywriter (1895–1971, real name Eric Gordon Valentine) is best known for his contributions to several screenplays for the director-producer team of Frank Launder and Sidney Gilliat, among them *Waterloo Road* (1944), *Lady Godiva Rides Again* (1951), *The Belles of St. Trinian's* (1954), *The Constant Husband* (1955), *Blue Murder at St. Trinian's* (1957), *Left Right and Centre* (1959) and *The Pure Hell of St. Trinian's* (1960). His many other credits include *The Rocket Bus* (1929), *Elstree Calling* (1930), *Rich and Strange* (1931), *Shipyard Sally* (1939), *We Dive*

at Dawn (1943), *Old Mother Riley's Jungle Treasure* (1951), *The Ringer* (1952) and *On the Twelfth Day* (1955), as well as the Hammer comedy *A Weekend with Lulu* (1961), for which he provided the story, along with the film's director-producer-screenwriter Ted Lloyd. He also directed one film, *Pyjamas Preferred* (1932), which he also scripted. **Hammer credits:** *A Weekend with Lulu* (1961)

**Valentino, Sal**

This American singer and musician (1942–) penned the number *Alligator Man*, which was performed in Hammer's *Dracula A.D. 1972* (1972) by Stoneground, of which he was also the lead singer. He was formerly a member of the sixties group the Beau Brummels, who appeared in *Village of the Giants* (1965) and *Wild Wild Winter* (1966). He can also be seen in *Medicine Ball Caravan* (1971), again with Stoneground. His more recent albums include *Dreamin' Man* (2006) and *Every Now and Then* (2008). **Hammer credits:** *Dracula A.D. 1972* (1972)

**Valerey, Anne**

This British supporting actress (1926–2013, real name Anne Catherine Firth) played the role of Elaine in the Hammer comedy *What the Butler Saw* (1950). Her other credits include *Cardboard Cavalier* (1949), *The Astonished Heart* (1950), *Folly to Be Wise* (1953) and *One Way Out* (1955), plus episodes of *BBC Sunday-Night Theatre* (1950–1959, TV) and *Saber of London* (1954–1960, TV). She went on to become a writer, and her credits in this capacity include episodes of *Crossroads* (1964–1988, TV), *Angels* (1975–1983, TV), *The Cedar Tree* (1976–1978, TV), *Sally Ann* (1979, TV) and *Tenko* (1981–1984, TV). Her mother was the actress Oriel Paget (1898–1991), and her husband was the writer Nanos Valaoritis (1921–), whom she married in 1946 but subsequently divorced. **Hammer credits:** *What the Butler Saw* (1950, as Elaine)

**Valk, Frederick**

In Britain from 1939, this German born Czech character actor (1895–1956, real name Fritz Valk) made his English-speaking film debut the same year with *Traitor Spy*, prior to which he had appeared in the German film *Der Sohn der Hagar* (1927). Remembered for his role as Dr. Van Straaten in the British horror classic *Dead of Night* (1945), his other films include *Night Train to Munich* (1940), *Dangerous Moonlight* (1941), *Saraband for Dead Lovers* (1948), *The Colditz Story* (1954) and *Zarak* (1956). He also co-starred in the Hammer second feature *The Flanagan Boy* (1953), in which he played boxing promoter Giuseppe Vecchi, whose treacherous wife plans to have him bumped off with the help of a young fighter. His occasional TV credits include episodes of *Wednesday Theatre* (1952–1953, TV) and *Folio* (1955–1959, TV). He was also a highly respected stage actor, best known for his Shakespearian roles. **Hammer credits:** *The Flanagan Boy* (1953, as Giuseppe Vecchi)

**Vampire Circus**

GB, 1972, 87m, Rank-colour, widescreen [1.78:1], Westrex, cert X

This low budget attempt to wring a few more changes out of a well-worn theme remains one of Hammer's most engaging seventies productions, thanks to its stylish direction, its heady mittel-European atmosphere and its accumulation of incident, climaxing in one of the company's goriest finales.

The film was based upon an idea by George Baxt, who it would seem had a fondness for the circus, having already penned the screenplay for *Circus of Horrors* (1960), as well as such classic shockers as *The City of the Dead* (1960) and *Night of the Eagle* (1962), not to mention Hammer's *The Revenge of Frankenstein* (1958), for which he provided additional dialogue, and *The Shadow of the Cat* (1961). Working with the film's producer, Wilbur Stark, Baxt devised a complex revenge drama that was subsequently turned into a full screenplay by Judson Kinberg, himself a writer and producer whose credits included such diverse films as *Reach for Glory* (1962), *Siege of the Saxons* (1963) and *The Magus* (1968).

Given its low budget pedigree, the film (originally known as *Village of the Vampires*) was cast without any major genre stars, and, as a further cost-cutting measure, was required to make use of certain standing sets on the Pinewood back lot, prime among them the village square originally built for *Countess Dracula* (1971), and already seen again in *Twins of Evil* (1971) and, very briefly, *Hands of the Ripper* (1971). The film also marked the feature debut of director Robert Young, a former actor turned documentary maker, who grasped his opportunity with enthusiasm (note that Young was originally offered the Gordon Honeycombe novel *Neither the Sea Nor the Sand* to helm, but Hammer lost the rights and the novel was subsequently acquired and made by other hands).

Set in and around the village of Schtettel, the proceedings open with a lengthy, twelve-minute prologue that sees Anna Mueller, the schoolmaster's wife, abduct a young girl from the forest as a victim for her vampire lover, Count Mitterhaus, in whose thrall she has fallen, and in whose castle she now lives. However, Anna is observed in this act by her cuckolded husband, who follows his wife to the castle, after which he summons a crowd of angry villagers—many of whom have lost their own children to Mitterhaus—to storm the castle and stake the Count. Before he dies, though, Mitterhaus warns that he will be avenged. "None of you will live. The town of Schtettel will die. Your children will die … to give me back my life."

Having been beaten by the villagers, Anna returns to the castle as the locals set explosives to destroy the place. But before the castle goes up in flames, Anna is able to drag Mitterhaus to the crypt, where blood from her lips momentarily revives him. "Circus of Nights. My cousin, Emil…. He will know what you must do," gasps the Count before again expiring, after which Anna makes her escape as the building collapses.

Following the credits, during which fifteen years is shown to pass via the seasons, Schtettel is revealed to be in the grip of a plague ("Twelve dead. Even the priests. If the Lord can't save his own, God knows what's going to happen," says Hauser, one of the villagers). But worse is in store, for soon after The Circus of Nights arrives, having somehow managed to bypass the roadblocks erected to keep the village isolated. "Why have you come?" asks the burgermeister [*sic*] of the gypsy woman seemingly in charge, to which comes the enigmatic reply, "To steal the money from dead men's eyes." The true reason for the circus's visit is even more terrifying, though. Peopled with vampires able to transform into animals, they are out to avenge Count Mitterhaus, among their number being his cousin Emil, who has the ability to turn into a black panther.

As the villagers visit the circus over the following nights, during which they are treated to spectacular displays featuring a comical dwarf, a strongman, brother and sister acrobats and the animals, their numbers begin to dwindle, as the vampires both seduce and murder them. However, after the discovery of the bodies of the Hauser brothers, who were killed by the twin acrobats Helga and Heinrich in the circus's side show the Mirror of Life, the villagers attack the circus, killing the animals. As the action now gathers pace, it is revealed that not only is the gypsy woman the mother of

the twins Helga and Heinrich, but is also Anna! Not a vampire herself, the gypsy woman/Anna determines that the twins should now kill Dora, her own daughter, who has recently returned to the village. But Dora manages to escape into a church. Climbing to its higher reaches, she accidentally dislodges a giant wooden cross, which falls and impales Helga and kills Heinrich too, owing to his closeness to his twin sister.

On the rampage again, the villagers now burn down the circus and shoot the strongman before descending into the castle crypt, where a blood bath ensues, during the confusion of which Emil manages to accidentally bite the gypsy woman, who turns back into Anna as she lies dying. Emil himself is meanwhile killed with the stake taken from the chest of Count Mitterhaus, who subsequently revives, only to be decapitated with a crossbow by Anton Kersh, a heroic local boy who is in love with Dora. The story concludes with the villagers throwing their torches into the crypt as Anton and Dora walk from the carnage, just as a bat screeches from the scene into the night....

*Vampire Circus* has one of the most involved plots to be found in any Hammer film, thanks to the complex relationships between the various characters, which aren't always lucidly conveyed. The fact that the gypsy woman turns out to be Anna, and is therefore the mother of Helga and Heinrich, as *well* as Dora, is perhaps one concept too far, especially given that, in order to keep the revelation a surprise, the roles are played by two different actresses (Domini Blythe and Adrienne Corri respectively). And why the circus takes fifteen years to turn up to mete out revenge is never explained (perhaps they were on a particularly long tour!). This time lapse (between 1810 and 1825) is certainly long enough for Anna/the gypsy woman to bear the twins (who are however played by actors in their early twenties as opposed to their mid-teens), though we never do find out who their father is (could it be Mitterhaus?). Otherwise, the build up of incident, either integral or merely peripheral to the central story, is sufficiently diverting to disguise the fact that this could easily have been another episode in the Karnstein series, with Mitterhaus as Karnstein in all but name.

The film is also more sexually explicit than most Hammer horrors, either in its depiction of love making, such as Anna's sensually staged session with the Count after he has killed Jenny ("One lust feeds the other," he informs her), or in its rather darker hints of paedophilia. Indeed, when it comes to sating his bloodlust, the Count, it seems, has a predilection for pre-pubescent

girls, while many of the later victims are also children, among them the Hauser brothers, who are seduced into the Mirror of Life by Helga and Heinrich (script editor Nadja Regin observed that the screenplay had an "almost pathological obsession with children victims," which she found "strongly reminiscent of the Moors murders"[1]). Thankfully, director Robert Young just about stays on the right side of tact here, treating the perilous situations the various children find themselves in in the manner of an episode from a Grimm's fairytale.

Otherwise, he concentrates his attention on a series of visually diverting set pieces and flourishes, among them the incident-packed pre-credits sequence (a mini movie in itself); an erotic circus dance in which a naked woman—covered in body paint so as to look like a green tiger—is tamed by her master; the acrobatic act of Helga and Heinrich (doubled by circus act Bradforts-Amaros), in which they poetically fly through the air, periodically changing into bats as they do so (note that they are wearing butterfly masks); the various encounters in the Mirror of Life; an episode in which the Schilt family, trying to escape the village, is attacked and ripped to pieces in the woods (despite some fakery involving an all-too-obvious panther puppet); Dora's discovery of their mutilated bodies (prior to which she mistakes a soldier's boot buckles for the eyes of an animal as she hides in the undergrowth); and the bloody Sam Peckinpah–like finale.

Young and his editor Peter Musgrave also make excellent use of several jump cuts during the film. For example, Count Mitterhaus is introduced in front of his portrait via a slick cut, while later the black panther jumps through a curtain and transforms into Emil during the circus show (twice). Best of all, however, is the scene in which Emil enters Mueller's house and seamlessly transforms into the panther as he runs upstairs, where he proceeds to attack the students lodging there (in another clever touch, the students—hitherto unmentioned in the plot, it must be said—are never shown, but merely heard on the soundtrack, at first laughing and singing, then shouting and screaming as the panther attacks them; this may have been a budgetary consideration, but it proves effective, nonetheless).

Astonishingly, all this action (which also includes Dr. Kersh's escape from the village to procure medicine to help combat the plague, which turns out to be "A virulent strain of rabies, carried by bats") is crammed into a tight eighty-seven minute running time. In addition to the brisk staging and editing, the film also boasts a fine score by David Whitaker, who makes effective use of a cimbalom to help accentuate the film's mittel-European setting; he also provides an effective percussion piece featuring drums and guttural male vocals for the Tiger Dance.

In front of the camera, Adrienne Corri (who takes top billing) is suitably voluptuous as the gypsy woman, and she is ably supported by Laurence Payne (who replaced an ill Anton Rodgers) as Mueller, Anthony Corlan as the swarthy Emil (Corlan beat David Essex to the role), Robin Hunter as Hauser, the diminutive Skip Martin as

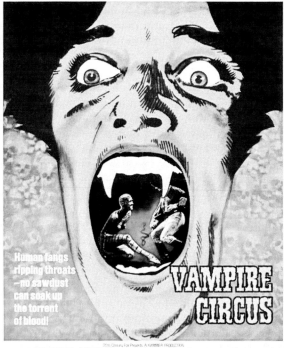

THE GREATEST BLOOD-SHOW ON EARTH!

Human fangs ripping throats —no sawdust can soak up the torrent of blood!

VAMPIRE CIRCUS · ADRIENNE CORRI · LAURENCE PAYNE
THORLEY WALTERS · JOHN MOULDER-BROWN
and ANTHONY CORLAN also starring LYNNE FREDERICK   Produced by WILBUR STARK
Directed by ROBERT YOUNG   Screenplay by JUDSON KINBERG   Color by DeLuxe   PG

"VAMPIRE CIRCUS"

The circus comes to town. Bold artwork for the American release of *Vampire Circus* (1972) (Hammer/Rank/Twentieth Century–Fox).

the mischievous clown Michael (whose far from consistent white make-up he at one point pulls from his face only to reveal more of the same underneath), and the always reliable Thorley Walters as Peter, Schtettel's dithery mayor-cum-burgermeister. The script can't make up its mind whether he's the mayor or the burgermeister (as the credits have it), and has him as both at various points; similarly, Count Mitterhaus is referred to as the Baron at one point by Dr. Kersh.

In addition to its adult cast, the film also features a handful of interesting younger players, among them the innocent-looking Lynne Frederick as Dora, future *Doctor Who* star Lalla Ward as Helga, Robin Sachs as Heinrich, and the floppy-haired John Moulder-Brown—at the time best known for *Deep End* (1970)—as Anton Kersh, the young hero of the piece. As for Robert Tayman's performance as Mitterhaus (which was entirely re-voiced by David de Keyser during post-production), this seems to have divided fans down the years, with many regarding his appearance as being too camp for such a seducer (admittedly, he does look more Jason King than vampire count).

A lively and enjoyable film with more than its usual share of gore for the period ("The greatest blood show on earth" ran the poster tag line), *Vampire Circus* has stood the test of time better than many British horror films of the seventies. "Divertingly entertaining, stylistically fresh and imaginatively produced," enthused *Cinefantastique*, though the *Sunday Telegraph* was of the opinion that "Being facetious is the only defense against abysmal British films."

On the floor at Pinewood and on location in Black Park between 9 August and 21 September 1971, the film was released in the UK by Rank on 30 April 1972 on a double bill with *Explosion* (1970) following a premiere engagement at the New Victoria on 20 April and a trade show on 13 April. Its U.S. release, care of Twentieth Century–Fox (which saw it trimmed by some three minutes), followed on 11 October, for which it was double-billed with *Countess Dracula* (1971). If Hammer intended Mitterhaus to appear in any further films—no doubt hence the cartoon bat escaping into the night at the end—they failed to materialize, given that insufficient audience numbers took up the trailer's invitation "to go through the Mirror of Life … and death." **Additional notes:** The film carries a 1971 copyright. The burning ceiling shot from *Lust for a Vampire* (1970), complete with the falling beam that stakes Carmilla, can be seen during the destruction of Castle Mitterhaus at the top of the film. In addition to the fake panther puppet during the forest attack, the film also contains several other dodgy effects (so pause buttons at the ready, folks!). For example, when Helga puts her hand into a tiger's mouth as a dare, a close-up reveals her hand to be an unconvincing plastic substitute. Meanwhile, the make-up and explosive bladder on the back of the strongman (inevitably played by Dave Prowse) is all too visible just before he gets shot, while during the climax, when Count Mitterhaus grabs the burning end of a torch, he is clearly seen to be wearing a protective glove. Animal advisor Mary Chipperfield doubled

An incident-packed British poster for the incident-packed *Vampire Circus* (1972) (Hammer/Rank/Twentieth Century–Fox).

for Adrienne Corri for some of the scenes featuring the black panther, while producer Wilbur Stark claimed to have directed a handful of shots for the film, among them the circus bat shots and the beheading of Count Mitterhaus. The portrait of Count Mitterhaus was painted by Bernard Robinson's widow, Margaret Robinson. Robert Tayman originally screen tested for the role of a flamboyant circus ringmaster, but the role was subsequently removed from the script and he was instead offered the role of Count Mitterhaus (the ringmaster's duties were instead assumed by Michael the dwarf). In addition to Count Mitterhaus, David de Keyser dubs a number of others in the film, among them Heinz. The film was adapted as a comic in issue seventeen of *The House of Hammer*. Elements from an original story about twin vampires, worked on by Wilbur Stark and John Peacock, were incorporated into the film's screenplay (hence the Helga and Heinrich characters). The film was later re-released on a double bill with *Legend of the Werewolf* (1975).

Production companies: Hammer/Rank. Distributors: Rank (UK [Rank circuit]), Twentieth Century–Fox (U.S.). Producer: Wilbur Stark. Executive producer: Michael Carreras [uncredited]. Production supervisor: Roy Skeggs. Director: Robert Young. Screenplay: Judson Kinberg. Story: George Baxt [uncredited], Wilbur Stark [uncredited]. Cinematographer: Moray Grant. Music: David Whitaker. Music director: Philip Martell. Editor: Peter Musgrave. Art director: Scott MacGregor. Costumes: Brian Owen-Smith, Terry Young (assistant [uncredited]), Marie Feldwick (assistant [uncredited]). Special effects: Les Bowie,

Ray Caple (mattes [uncredited]). Assistant art director: Don Picton. Make-up: Jill Carpenter, Ann Brodie (assistant [uncredited]). Hair: Ann McFadyen, Cathy Kevany [uncredited]. Sound: Claude Hitchcock. Sound editor: Roy Hyde. Dubbing mixer: Ken Barker. Sound re-recording mixer: Graham V. Hartstone [uncredited]. Sound camera operator: Laurie Reed [uncredited]. Boom operator: Keith Batten [uncredited]. Assistant boom operator: Chris Munro [uncredited]. First assistant editor: Roger Wilson [uncredited]. Second assistant editor: Martin Rule [uncredited]. Production manager: Tom Sachs. Construction manager: Arthur Banks. Assistant director: Derek Whitehurst. Second assistant director: Lindsey C. Vickers [uncredited]. Third assistant director: Graham Easton [uncredited]. Stunts: Tim Condren [uncredited], Peter Munt [uncredited], Valentino Musetti [uncredited]. Camera operator: Walter Byatt. Focus puller: Bob Smith [uncredited]. Clapper boy/loader: Peter Carmody [uncredited]. Stills: Ricky Smith [uncredited]. Electrical supervisor: Vic Smith [uncredited]. Grip: Ted Lockhart [uncredited]. Chief draughtsman: Richard Rambaut [uncredited]. Props: Edward Rodrigo [uncredited]. Chargehand props: Danny Skundric [uncredited]. Standby props: W. Bennett [uncredited], Peter Wallis [uncredited]. Scenic artist: Graham Barclay [uncredited]. Carpenter: G.K. Lewin [uncredited]. Stagehand: R.J. Lewin [uncredited]. Painter: R. Fallen [uncredited]. Plasterer: J. Campbell [uncredited]. Plasterer's labourer: T. Kelly [uncredited]. Rigger: H.J. Matthews [uncredited]. Art department runner: Jimmy Carreras [uncredited]. Continuity: June Randall. Casting: James Liggat.

Animal advisor: Mary Chipperfield. Animals: Bradforts-Amaros by courtesy of Billy Smart's Circus. Portrait: Margaret Robinson [uncredited]. Script editor: Nadja Regin [uncredited]. Publicist: Frank Law [uncredited]. Publicity secretary: Julie Smith [uncredited]. Runner: Adrian Delahaye [uncredited]. Driver: Paul Lins [uncredited]. Production secretary: Liz Green [uncredited]. Producer's secretary: Carolyn Brown [uncredited]. Production accountant: Barrie Edwards [uncredited]. Poster: Vic Fair [uncredited]. **Cast:** Adrienne Corri (Gypsy woman/Anna), Laurence Payne (Mueller), Thorley Walters (Peter/Burgermeister [*sic*]), Lynne Frederick (Dora Mueller), John Moulder-Brown (Anton Kersh), Elizabeth Seal (Gerta Hauser), Richard Owens (Dr. Kersh), Anthony Corlan (Emil), Domini Blythe (Anna Mueller), Robin Hunter (Hauser), Lalla Ward (Helga), Robin Sachs (Heinrich), Robert Tayman (Count Mitterhaus), Mary Wimbush (Elvira), Dave Prowse (Strongman), Roderick Shaw (Jon Hauser), Barnaby Shaw (Gustav Hauser), Christina Paul (Rosa), Skip Martin (Michael), Jane Darby (Jenny Schilt), John Bown (Schilt), Sibylla Kay (Mrs. Schilt), Dorothy Frere (Granma [*sic*] Schilt), Sean Hewitt (First soldier), Arnold Locke (Old villager), Jason James (Foreman), Giles Phibbs (Sexton), Milovan and Serena (The Webers), Bradforts-Amaros (doubles for Lalla Ward and Robin Sachs [Helga and Heinrich]), Anna Bentinck (Schoolgirl [uncredited]), Nina Francis (Schoolgirl [uncredited]), Drina Pavlovic (Schoolgirl [uncredited]), Jenny Twigge (Schoolgirl [uncredited]), David de Keyser (Re-voicing of Robert Tayman [uncredited] and Heinz [uncredited]). **DVD availability:** Carlton (UK R2 PAL), extras include a trailer; JVD (Japan R2 NTSC), extras include a trailer, biographies and a stills gallery; CVC (Italy R2 PAL); Spirit Entertainment (UK R2 PAL); Synapse Films (U.S. R1 NTSC), extras include a trailer, stills and a new documentary, *The Bloodiest Show on Earth: Making Vampire Circus*. **Blu-ray availability:** Synapse Films (A/1), extras as per the DVD. **CD availability:** *The Hammer Vampire Film Music Collection* (GDI Records), which contains seven cues from the score, including an alternate version of *The Tiger Dance*; *Dracula: Classic Scores from Hammer Horror* (Silva Screen), which contains a newly recorded version of the *Prologue*

## The Vampire Lovers

GB, 1970, 91m, Movielab, widescreen [1.85:1], cert X

Thanks to the then-recent overhauling of Britain's antiquated classification system, which had barely altered since 1951, a new certificate was introduced to reflect the more liberal attitudes of the late sixties and early seventies. This was the AA certificate, which allowed accompanied fourteen-year-olds in to see certain films that might otherwise have been considered borderline cases. The X certificate, previously for over-sixteens, meanwhile became the province of the over-eighteens, thus allowing for a headier mix of sex and horror. Business being business, Hammer was quick to cash in on the new freedoms on offer, and there was never a better title to exploit this than *The Vampire Lovers*, with its promise sex and horror—and *lesbian* sex at that!

However, the film originated not with Hammer but with Fantale Films, which packaged the project and presented it to the company in October 1969. Fantale was run by producers Harry Fine (a former actor who had appeared in Hammer's *To Have and to Hold* [1951]) and Michael Style, who, in association with their writer Tudor Gates, were looking to break into the horror market. It had originally been Fine's idea to make a film version of J. Sheridan Le Fanu's gothic novella *Carmilla*, which had been serialized in a periodical titled *The Dark Blue* between 1871 and 1872 (some sixteen years before the appearance of Bram Stoker's *Dracula*), and then published in the short story collection *In a Glass Darkly* (1872). However, instead of competing with Hammer, he and his partner chose to go into partnership with the company.

Recalled Fine in the February 28 1970 issue of *Kine Weekly*, "We had an excellent treatment of *Carmilla*, by J. Sheridan Le Fanu, with a screenplay by Tudor Gates. We sat through four Hammer films to get the feel of them. We went into a very careful analysis of the market, too. We are both sick and tired of hearing about the troubled state of the film industry. There is no doubt at all that there is a market for a specialized type of product. And in this case we had a really classic horror story. The story also provides five really meaty women's parts which is very unusual." The gambit proved to be the right one, and the Fantale team subsequently went on to make a further two films with Hammer before striking out on their own in 1971 with the shocker *Fright*.

In looking for help to finance the film, James Carreras eschewed the usual sources and instead turned to Hammer's American "rival" in the horror market, AIP. Formed in 1955 by producers Samuel Z. Arkoff and James H. Nicholson, the company had gone on to make a highly successful string of exploitation pictures, many of them produced and directed by Roger Corman, among them several hits loosely based on the works of Edgar Allan Poe, including *House of Usher* (1960), *The Pit and the Pendulum* (1961) and *The Raven* (1963). AIP had also made *The Tomb of Ligeia* (1964) and *The Masque of the Red Death* (1964) in England, with Hammer's own Arthur Grant the cinematographer on the latter. Given this precedent, Carreras had a poster for *The Vampire Lovers* commissioned and moved in for the kill.

AIP subsequently acquiesced to Carreras' hard sell, and a contract was signed between the two horror giants on 25 November 1969, upon the agreement that the British-based American producer Louis M. Heyward would be on hand to oversee the project as an uncredited executive producer on AIP's behalf (the involvement of Arkoff and Nicholson in the production was negligible; nevertheless, they felt it prudent to have someone of their own on site to keep an eye on their investment, which eventually came in at £165,227, or the then-equivalent of $400,000). Heyward had recently either produced or executive produced a number of genre films for AIP, among them *Curse of the Crimson Altar* (1968), *Witchfinder General* (1968) and *Scream and Scream Again* (1970), and so was well up to par on low budget production methods in the UK. These terms agreed, Carreras then effectively sub-contracted the film out to Fantale, with Harry Fine and Michael Style taking the producer credit between them and Tudor Gates the screenplay credit. Style, Fine and Gates also took a credit for their adaptation of Le Fanu's novella.

To star as the seductive vampiress Carmilla Karnstein, who insinuates her way into a number of households where she wreaks various kinds of havoc, James Carreras turned to the glamorous Polish actress Ingrid Pitt, who had just had a breakthrough role in the international hit *Where Eagles*

**A European ad for *Vampire Circus* (1972), featuring the title in both French and German (Hammer/Rank/Twentieth Century–Fox).**

*Dare* (1969). Recalled the actress of how she came to be cast, "Timing is everything in life. At the after-premiere dinner of *Alfred the Great* I sat next to Hammer's Jimmy Carreras and blew in his ear. He obviously enjoyed it. He told me to come and see him in Wardour Street the following morning."[2] Pitt's tactics—and the mini skirt she wore to the interview—won her the role, despite competition from Shirley Eaton, who was also being considered for the film, but who was dismissed as being too old (despite being born the same year as Pitt–1937–though at the time Pitt was claiming to have been born in 1944). There were also concerns from the Ministry of Labour that a British actress had not been cast.

For the sake of box office, Pitt was supported by a number of well-established hands, prime among them Peter Cushing, who was cast as General Spielsdorf, whose daughter Laura succumbs to Carmilla's charms (Pitt and Cushing were both introduced to the press at a reception held at The Savoy on 13 January 1970, and Pitt was later promoted as "The new horror from Hammer"). The role of Spielsdorf was little more than a glorified cameo for Cushing, but his name added luster to the film, and proved a suitable marketing tool for selling the picture in America. Indeed, it was no coincidence that Cushing was chosen to play a character that, Van Helsing–like, destroys Carmilla at the climax.

Also onboard were such established names as Douglas Wilmer as Baron Hartog, who vows vengeance against the vampiric Karnstein family for killing his sister; George Cole as Morton, whose daughter Emma is also in danger from Carmilla; and Dawn Addams as the mysterious Countess, with whose aid Carmilla is able to worm her way into various unsuspecting households. As well as Miss Pitt, the film also helped to launch such lovelies as Kate O'Mara as the governess Mademoiselle Paradot, who likewise succumbs to Carmilla; Pippa Steele as Spielsdorf's doomed daughter Laura; and Madeline Smith as Emma, whose lifeblood is gradually drained to the point of death by Carmilla. Newcomers among the men included Jon Finch as the dashing Carl Ebhart, who helps to destroy Carmilla and save Emma, and Graham James, as one of several eligible bachelors at a ball thrown by Spielsdorf.

To handle the action, it had been hoped to bring Terence Fisher back into the Hammer fold. Unfortunately, the veteran director was still recovering from an accident that had seen him badly break a leg, and so the equally reliable Roy Ward Baker was instead signed to yield the megaphone. Baker approached the material with caution, noting, "The producers, Harry Fine and Michael Style, were fired with enthusiasm for the script which Tudor Gates had written.... It gradually became apparent that they were even more excited by the possibilities generated by having female vampires and claimed they had uncovered an underlying theme in the original story, which Le Fanu had either discreetly suppressed or perhaps didn't even realize was there. By tradition, when a vampire bites someone, the victim automatically becomes a vampire too. When Carmilla bites a female vic-

*Top:* **The art of seduction. Ingrid Pitt and Madeline Smith in** *The Vampire Lovers* **(1970).** *Bottom: La belle dame sans merci.* **Ingrid Pitt takes advantage of Kate O'Mara in** *The Vampire Lovers* **(1970) (both photographs, Hammer/AIP/Fantale/MGM-EMI/American International).**

tim she not only becomes a vampire—but also a lesbian. This one was full of traps for the unwary."[3]

*The Vampire Lovers* was by no means the first telling of *Carmilla*. Such European productions as *Blood and Roses* (1960) and *Crypt of Horror* (1964) had already touched upon the story (the latter featuring none other than Christopher Lee as Count Ludwig Karnstein), while the British television series *Mystery and Imagination* (1966–1970, TV) had

presented a fifty-minute potted version of *Carmilla* in 1966. However, Hammer's take would emphasize the tale's lesbian element, merely alluded to in the Le Fanu original (commented screenwriter Tudor Gates, "Censorship was in rapid decline ... [and this] allowed me to create the first nude, lesbian vampires, and a picture I little thought at the time would be another cult success."[4] Otherwise, the screenplay adheres to the novella's narrative quite faithfully.

The proceedings commence with a pre-credits sequence in which Hartog vows vengeance against the Karnsteins ("The enemies I sought were no ordinary mortals—they were murderers from beyond the grave"), following which we follow Carmilla's exploits in the Spielsdorf household (where she is known as Marcilla) and the Morton household (where she assumes the name of Mircalla). As Carmilla, whom we first see in a telltale red dress at Spielsdorf's ball, Ingrid Pitt brings an air of genuine mystery to the role, thanks to the natural cadences of her accent. Meanwhile, her considerable physical charms are made use of throughout the film, most memorably in the scenes in which she is seen topless in her bath and, later, makes love with Emma. Mild by today's standards, these brief sequences were considered somewhat daring at the time, and certainly did much to enhance the film's box office appeal ("All the characters are bitten on the breast,"[5] commented Pitt a quarter of a century later, which might explain it!).

Recalled Roy Ward Baker of his players, "I had an excellent cast, with Ingrid Pitt perfect as Carmilla, and Peter Cushing, Madeline Smith, Kate O'Mara and George Cole all giving straightforward, honest performances. But they would, wouldn't they? They all followed my line, which

was to play the thing simply and literally according to the script, without camping it up or deriding the characters. If we had gone over the top, the result would have been risible and might even have been offensive to some."[6] As for the film's look, he noted that, "I decided that the style should be generally realistic but should include magic and suggestions of the supernatural. Elements of fantasy. Moray Grant was the lighting cameraman and he was most enthusiastic…. There were some good atmosphere shots with Carmilla gliding through a graveyard in clouds of dry ice, which look quite unreal. By the way, I am aware that a few snippets of extra nudity were smuggled into the film after I had finished it but no great harm was done."[7]

Despite its commercial success and its continued cult appeal, *The Vampire Lovers* isn't *quite* Hammer at its best. Admittedly, all the right ingredients are there, which *Variety* listed in its review as being "Dank interiors, eerie exteriors and stagecoaches, plenty of blood, a couple of unconvincing decapitations, stakes in the vampire's heart, the sign of the cross, etc." The checklist notwithstanding, the film doesn't quite click as a whole. On the plus side, the cast is well chosen, and Harry Robinson's lush score contributes to the frequently heady atmosphere. Elsewhere, though, director Roy Ward Baker doesn't seem entirely comfortable with the material, while certain sequences don't quite flow as they should. Indeed, the narrative contains a handful of missteps and stumbles, and the editing isn't always confident, while the function of certain characters is never fully explained. What, for example, is the relationship between the Countess and Carmilla? The Countess claims that Carmilla is her daughter to Spielsdorf, which would make the Countess a Karnstein, but Hartog has supposedly destroyed them all, save for Carmilla, hasn't he? If the Countess *isn't* a Karnstein, why is she helping Carmilla? What exactly is in it for her? And how does Spielsdorf know the Countess, given that he is well enough acquainted with her to invite her to his ball? And finally, who exactly is the mysterious man in black who accompanies the Countess and Carmilla on their journeys? Given that he is a vampire, are we supposed to believe that he too is a Karnstein, or merely one of Carmilla's followers?

The film's period look doesn't always convince, either (the story is set in Stiria in 1795). For example, note the modern make-up and hairstyles sported by many of the female cast members (Miss Pitt's false eyelashes are particularly incongruous) and the tennis court with its wire mesh fencing

by the side of General Spielsdorf's home (actually Moor Park Golf Club). Elsewhere, some sets are either over lit (such as the General's ballroom, in which camera shadows can be seen on the backs of dancers), while others appear cramped (such the graveyard, with its poorly painted cyclorama). Some are merely re-dressed from other films, such as the interior of Karnstein castle, which was previously the church set from *Taste the Blood of Dracula* (1970). Sadly, the cumulative effect of all this tends to cheapen and compromise the film.

Still, there are some effective touches, such as the use of green filters during Laura's nightmares, in which she dreams that she is being attacked by a large cat (an idea lifted directly from the Le Fanu text) and the Dorian Gray–like corruption of Carmilla's portrait in Castle Karnstein at the climax. The various stakings and beheadings are also quite efficiently presented, while the love scenes are tastefully—almost coyly—handled. Recalled Ingrid Pitt of these sequences, "The producers weren't too happy about being banned from the set when the nude scenes were being shot. I felt so sorry for them that when I passed them in the corridor wearing only a robe I threw it open and gave them a peek at what they were missing. They certainly lightened their step."[8] Equally, other touches don't quite come off, such as the use of the ghostly shroud in the graveyard, which looks like Bez from The Happy Mondays dancing around in some net curtains.

Budgeted at just over £165,000, *The Vampire Lovers* was on the floor at Elstree between 19 January and 4 March 1970, during which period location work was also undertaken at the aforementioned Moor Park Golf Club, as well as Black Park and Wallhall College in Aldenham, which doubled as the Morton home. Following the submission of the screenplay to the BBFC for vetting, there had been concerns regarding the film's overtly Sapphic content, but these arrived too late to be of concern to the producers, who chose to proceed regardless. Commented the board's Chief Secretary John Trevelyan of the submitted script in a five-page letter sent to Harry Fine, "It contains a lot of material that we would be unhappy about even with an X at eighteen."[9] Yet despite Trevelyan's initial reservations, the film would ultimately be released without any cuts, albeit with the firm stamp of an X certificate.

During filming, Hammer sensed that they were on to a winner, and so announced a sequel before production came to an end. The original title of the sequel was *To Love a Vampire*, but this was later amended to the more exploitable *Lust for a Vampire* (1971). Again, Fantale provided the production services. AIP, however, were notable by their absence, Louis M. Heyward having been less than impressed by the way Hammer managed its business. "I didn't know who was running the company,"[10] he later admitted. Defending Hammer, assistant director Derek Whitehurst commented of the situation, "There were a lot of problems with the American International side. They were always breathing down our neck, and I think that made for a sort of stressed out feeling on the whole production really. There were all sorts of memos passing backwards

**Stylish artwork for the Italian release of *The Vampire Lovers* (1970) (Hammer/AIP/Fantale/MGM-EMI/American International).**

and forwards."[II] Consequently, EMI provided the financing for the follow-up.

Promoted with the tagline "Even the dead can love," *The Vampire Lovers* was both trade shown (at Metro House) and released in the UK on 3 September 1970 by MGM-EMI on a double bill with *Angels from Hell* (1968), making its premiere engagement at London's New Victoria Cinema, during which it was dismissed as being "Not up to the usual standard of Hammer offerings," by the *Monthly Film Bulletin*. It went on general release the following month on 4 October. For its American release care of AIP (whose poster tagline was the rather more visceral "Terror and torture embrace in holy bloodlust"), the film was accompanied by *Cult of the Damned* (1969). On the whole, it met with a better reception Stateside, with the *Philadelphia Daily News* perhaps best describing the film as a "campy, literate, witty and dead-straight vampire movie." Of the performances, *Variety* noted, "Miss Pitt shows a grave and sinister attractiveness, the Misses Steele and Smith are adequate juves…. Cushing, Cole and Wilmer reveal worry, resource and incredulity at appropriate moments. So may audiences." As for the U.S. poster, which featured a seductive but anachronistic shot of Ingrid Pitt posing in a blouse and tights, it ballyhooed: "Torture crypt of the blood nymphs hiding an erotic nightmare of tormented lusts that throb in headless undead bodies." Eh?

Remembered Ingrid Pitt of the film: "To me, *The Vampire Lovers* was a wonderful experience. I loved making the film—I wish I could do it all again! I think there are one or two scenes I'd re-do, but basically I think it's one of the better Hammer films. I think Roy Ward Baker did a wonderful job."[12] **Additional notes:** Ingrid Pitt's seduction of Madeline Smith was voted number seventy-two in Channel Four's *100 Greatest Sexy Moments* (2003, TV). Madeline Smith's performance was entirely re-voiced, as were some of Ingrid Pitt's lines (the latter by Olive Gregg). A clip of *The Vampire Lovers* featuring Ingrid Pitt and Ferdy Mayne can be seen playing on TV in AIP's *The Return of Count Yorga* (1971), albeit with Spanish dialogue! Producer Harry Fine helmed a handful of second unit shots for the film. A paperback tie-in of Le Fanu's *Carmilla* (plus three other stories) was published by Fontana under the title of *The Vampire Lovers* to coincide with the film's release. Elements of the film were later spoofed in *Lesbian Vampire Killers* (2009).

Production companies: Hammer/AIP/Fantale. Distributors: MGM-EMI (UK [ABC circuit]), American International (U.S.). Producers: Harry Fine, Michael Style. Executive producer: Louis M. Heyward [uncredited]. Director: Roy Ward Baker. Screenplay: Tudor Gates. Adaptation: Tudor Gates [uncredited], Harry Fine [uncredited], Michael Style [uncredited], based upon the novella *Carmilla* by J. Sheridan Le Fanu. Cinematographer: Moray Grant. Music: Harry Robinson. Music director: Philip Martell. Editor: James Needs. Art director: Scott MacGregor. Costumes: Brian Cox, Laura Nightingale. Make-up: Tom Smith. Hair: Pearl Tipaldi. Camera operator: Neil Binney. Focus puller: Bob Jordan [uncredited]. Recording direc-

tor: Tony Lumkin. Sound: Claude Hitchcock. Sound editor: Roy Hyde. Dubbing mixer: Dennis Whitlock. Boom operator: Keith Batten [uncredited]. Second unit director: Harry Fine [uncredited]. Production manager: Tom Sachs. Construction manager: Bill Greene. Scene painter: Bob White [uncredited]. Painter: Michael Finlay [uncredited]. Assistant director: Derek Whitehurst. Second assistant director: Nick Granby [uncredited]. Third assistant director: Lindsay Vickers [uncredited]. Runners: Phil Campbell [uncredited], Brian Reynolds [uncredited]. Continuity: Betty Harley. Script editor: Nadja Regin [uncredited]. Stunts: Roy Scammell [uncredited], Roy Street [uncredited], Vic Armstrong [uncredited]. Poster: Mike Vaughan [uncredited]. **Cast:** Ingrid Pitt (Carmilla/Mircalla/Marcilla Karnstein), Peter Cushing (General Spielsdorf), Douglas Wilmer (Baron Hartog), George Cole (Roger Morton), Kate O'Mara (Mademoiselle Paradot), Dawn Addams (The Countess), Madeline Smith (Emma Morton), Ferdy Mayne (Doctor), Pippa Steele (Laura Spielsdorf), Jon Finch (Carl Ebhart), John Forbes-Robertson (Man in Black), Charles Farrell (Kurt), Kirsten Betts (Vampire), Janet Key (Gretchen), Harvey Hall (Renton), Shelagh Wilcocks (Housekeeper), Graham James (First young man at ball), Tom Browne (Second young man at ball), Olga James (Village girl), Joanna Shelley (Woodsman's daughter), Jill Easter (Woodsman's wife [uncredited]), Lindsay Kemp (Pedlar [uncredited]), Sion Probert (Young man in tavern [uncredited]), Vicki Woolf (Landlord's daughter [uncredited]), Dani Retief (Shroud [uncredited]), Mike Horsburgh (Stunt double for Ferdy Mayne [uncredited]), Olive Gregg (partial re-voicing of Ingrid Pitt [uncredited]). **DVD availability:** MGM (U.S. R1 NTSC), extras include a commentary by Ingrid Pitt, Roy Ward Baker and Tudor Gates; MGM/ILC (UK R2 PAL); Midnite Movies (U.S. R1 NTSC), double-billed with *Countess Dracula* (1971); Studio Canal (UK R2 PAL), double-billed with *Lust for a Vampire* (1971). **Blu-ray availability:** Shout Factory (A/1), Final Cut (B/2). **CD availability:** *The Vampire Lovers* (GDI Records), which contains the complete score; *The Hammer Film Music Collection: Volume One* (GDI Records), which contains the *Main Title*

## Van Beers, Stanley

This British supporting actor (1911–1961) can be spotted as the astronaut Ludwig Reichenheim in the "film within the film" sequence from Hammer's *The Quatermass Xperiment* (1955). His other credits include *So Well Remembered* (1947), *Brandy for the Parson* (1952), *The Dam Busters* (1955) and *The Angry Hills* (1959), while his TV work takes in episodes of *Puck of Pook's Hill* (1951, TV), *The Scarlet Pimpernel* (1955–1956, TV) and *Rendezvous* (1957–1961, TV). His wife was the actress Vivienne Burgess (1914–1999), who appeared in *In Possession* (1984, TVM [episode of *Hammer House of Mystery and Suspense*]). **Hammer credits:** *The Quatermass Xperiment* (1955, as Ludwig Reichenheim [uncredited])

## Van Der Merwe, Alwyn

Van Der Merwe can be seen as one of the Rock

people in Hammer's *Creatures the World Forgot* (1971). His other credits include *Bendag vir altyd* (1987), *'N pot vol winter* (1991) and *The Fourth Reich* (1990, TVM), plus episodes of *Ballade vir 'n enkeling* (1987, TV). **Hammer credits:** *Creatures the World Forgot* (1971, as Rock man [uncredited])

## Van Der Zyl, Nikki (Monica)

This German actress and voice-over artist (1935–, real name Monica Van Der Zyl) dubbed the voice of Ursula Andress in a handful of films in the sixties, among them *Dr. No* (1962), Hammer's *She* (1965), *Casino Royale* (1967) and *The Blue Max* (1966). She just missed winning the role of Tatiana played by Daniela Bianchi in *From Russia with Love* (1963), and was Gert Frobe's vocal coach on *Goldfinger* (1964), not that it did him much good as he was eventually dubbed by Michael Collins. She also dubbed Eunice Gayson in both *Dr. No* (1962) and *From Russia with Love* (1963), Shirley Eaton in *Goldfinger*, Claudine Auger in *Thunderball* (1965), Raquel Welch's grunts in *One Million Years B.C.* (1966 [main vocals provided by Nicolette McKenzie]), Mie Hama in *You Only Live Twice* (1967), Susan Denberg in *Frankenstein Created Woman* (1967), Suzy Kendall in *Fraulein Doktor* (1969), Jenny Hanley in *Scars of Dracula* (1970), Jane Seymour in *Live and Let Die* (1973) and Corinne Clery in *Moonraker* (1979). She also worked as a stunt double on *Carry On Cleo* (1963) and *Don't Lose Your Head* (1966), and provided additional vocal dubbing for Hammer's *Slave Girls* (1968). She later became a barrister and painter. In 2011, she unexpectedly turned up on *The Antiques Roadshow* (1979–, TV) with a copy of her *Goldfinger* script and talked briefly about her career, which she later discussed in greater detail in her autobiography *For Your Ears Only* (2013). **Hammer credits:** *She* (1965, voice of Ursula Andress [uncredited]), *One Million Years B.C.* (1966, partial voice of Raquel Welch [uncredited]), *Frankenstein Created Woman* (1967, voice of Susan Denberg [uncredited]), *Slave Girls* (1968, (dubbing of various voices [uncredited]), *Scars of Dracula* (1970, voice of Jenny Hanley [uncredited])

## Van Eyck, Peter

In films in America from 1943 with *Hitler's Children*, prior to which he had worked as a music arranger and manager for songwriter Irving Berlin, and as an assistant for Orson Welles' Mercury Theater, this German born character actor (1911–1969, real name Gotz Von Eick, aka Goetz Van Eyck) was inevitably cast as Nazis during the Hollywood phase of his career. However, following appearances in such films as *Action in the North Atlantic* (1943), *Five Graves to Cairo* (1943) and *The Hitler Gang* (1944), he divided his time between America and Europe, appearing in such films as *Furioso* (1950), *The Desert Fox* (1951), *The Wages of Fear* (1953), *Confidential Report* (1955), *The 1,000 Eyes of Dr. Mabuse* (1960), *The Longest Day* (1962), *The Bridge at Remagen* (1968) and *Code Name Red Roses* (1969). In 1958, he starred in the Hammer thriller *The Snorkel*, in which he played a psychotic husband who contrives to gas his wife to death, only to be undone by the keen observations of his stepdaughter. Recalled screenwriter Jimmy Sangster, "Peter Van Eyck was a pretty big name in those days, with a list of strong supporting roles under his belt. And very good he was too."[13] Van Eyck's first wife (of two) was the actress Ruth Ford (1911–2009), to whom he was married between 1910 and 1945. **Hammer credits:** *The Snorkel* (1958, as Paul Decker)

**Cool in corduroy. Peter Van Eyck in a publicity shot for *The Snorkel* (1958) (Hammer/Clarion/Columbia).**

### Van Eyssen, John

Best known to Hammer fans for playing the doomed Jonathan Harker in the studio's landmark production of *Dracula* (1958), this dapper South African born actor (1922–1995, full name Matthew John D. Van Eyssen) also made appearances in five other Hammer films, beginning with a silent walk on as a poor musician in a café in *The Gambler and the Lady* (1953), soon after which he bagged one of the leads in *Four Sided Triangle* (1953). Following wartime experience in the South African army, Van Eyssen trained at the Central School of Speech and Drama in London, and went on to join the Royal Shakespeare Company. He began appearing in films in 1949 with *The Angel with the Trumpet*. His other credits include *Account Rendered* (1957), *I'm All Right Jack* (1959), *Exodus* (1960) and *The Criminal* (1960).

In 1961 he retired from acting, first to become a literary agent with London Management (later ICM-UK) and went on to manage such heavyweights as Tennessee Williams and Arthur Miller. In 1965 he became a production executive for the British arm of Columbia, and went on to become its worldwide head of production, for which he moved to New York. During his overall time with Columbia he helped to instigate such highly regarded films as *Georgy Girl* (1966), *A Man for All Seasons* (1966) and *Nicholas and Alexandra* (1971). Upon leaving Columbia in 1974, he became an independent producer in America, working on such films as *Daniel* (1983). He returned to London in 1991, where he became involved with the Chelsea Film Festival. His son is the producer, director, creative consultant and advertising mogul David Van Eyssen. **Hammer credits:** *The Gambler and the Lady* (1953, as Musician), *Four Sided Triangle* (1953, as Robin), *Men of Sherwood Forest* (1954, as Will Scarlet), *Quatermass 2* (1957, as The P.R.O.), *Man with a Dog* (1957, as Dr. Langham), *Dracula* (1958, as Jonathan Harker)

### Van Husen, Dan

This German actor (1945–, aka Rudolf Van Husen) can be seen in a supporting role in Hammer's *The Lady Vanishes* (1979). His other hundred-plus credits include *I bastardi* (1968), *Cannon for Cordoba* (1970), *Captain Apache* (1971), *Casanova* (1976), *The Sea Wolves* (1980), *Gotcha!* (1985), *Enemy at the Gates* (2001), *Gellert* (2007), *The Scarlet Worm* (2011), *Tom Sawyer & Huckleberry Finn* (2014) and *Beyond Fury* (2019). **Hammer credits:** *The Lady Vanishes* (1979, as Second killer)

### Van Ost, Valerie

This British actress (1944–, aka Valerie Ost) can be seen as Jane, the SI7 secretary who is kidnapped by Dracula's guards and turned into a vampire in Hammer's *The Satanic Rites of Dracula* (1974). Her other credits include *On the Beat* (1962), *Carry On Cabby* (1963), *Don't Lose Your Head* (1966), *Corruption* (1967), *Mister Ten Per Cent* (1967), *Carry On Doctor* (1968), *Carry On Again Doctor* (1969), *Incense for the Damned* (1970) and *The Insomniac* (1971). Her TV work includes an amusing guest spot in *Dead Man's Treasure*, the classic 1968 episode of *The Avengers* (1961–1969, TV). Other TV appearances include episodes of *Mrs. Thursday* (1966–1967, TV), *Ace of Wands* (1970–1972, TV) and *Bless This House* (1971–1976, TV), plus advertising campaigns for beer and pie fillings in the seventies. She later became a casting director, working on commercials, television series and films, among the latter *Felicity* (1978), *George and Mildred* (1980), *The Apple* (1980), *The Boys in Blue* (1983), *Funny Money* (1983) and *Haunters of the Deep* (1984). **Hammer credits:** *The Satanic Rites of Dracula* (1974, as Jane)

### Vardy, Mike

Vardy helmed Hammer's big screen version of *Man at the Top* (1973), having already helmed seven episodes (out of 23) of the TV series on which it was based (1970–1972, TV). One of his more bizarre jobs on the film was to audition body doubles for a nude scene involving leading lady Nanette Newman. Recalled Vardy, "I spent a rather bizarre lunch-time in Hertfordshire, sitting on a wicker basket in the back of the wardrobe truck, while Laura Nightingale's rather camp assistant wheeled in about eight young ladies for me to see. I had severe indigestion by the end of it."[14] Busiest in television, his work as a director includes episodes of *Mystery and Imagination* (1966–1970, TV), *Van Der Valk* (1972–1977, TV), *London's Burning* (1988–2002, TV), *Capital City* (1989–1990, TV), *Conjugal Rites* (1993–1994, TV) and *Hetty Wainthropp Investigates* (1996–1998, TV). He also produced (with others) *Spring and Autumn* (1972–1976, TV) and *Sadie, It's Cold Outside* (1975, TV). **Hammer credits:** *Man at the Top* (1973)

### Varnals, Wendy

This British actress (1940–) can be seen as Tania in the Hammer second feature *The Runaway* (1964). Her other credits include *Corruption* (1967) and episodes of *No Hiding Place* (1959–1967, TV) and *The Sullavan Brothers* (1964–1965, TV). **Hammer credits:** *The Runaway* (1964, as Tania)

### Varney, Jeanne

Varney can be seen as Mavis in Hammer's *On the Buses* (1971). Her father was Reg Varney (1916–2008), who starred in Hammer's three big screen *On the Buses* spin-offs. **Hammer credits:** *On the Buses* (1971, as Mavis)

### Varney, Reg

Best known for playing bus driver Stan Butler in the long-running sitcom *On the Buses* (1969–1973, TV), of which he appeared in 68 of the 74 episodes, this much-loved British comedy actor (1916–2008) also played the role in Hammer's three big screen spin-offs. He began his career playing the piano in pubs at the age of fourteen, which in turn led to similar work for the stage, cinemas and nightclubs. Following wartime experience with the Royal Electrical and Mechanical Engineers (as a sheet metal worker), his career began to take off on the variety circuit, including work in a double act with Benny Hill. He made his film debut in 1952 in *Miss Robin Hood*, and finally hit the big time as Reg the foreman in highly popular sitcom *The Rag Trade* (1961–1963, TV). A children's series, *The Valiant Varneys* (1964–1965, TV), followed, as did another sitcom *Beggar My Neighbour* (1967–1968, TV). Then, eventually, at the age of fifty-two, came *On the Buses*. By this time Varney was appearing more regularly in films, among them *Joey Boy* (1965), *The Great St. Trinian's Train Robbery* (1966), *Go for a Take* (1971) and *The Best Pair of Legs in the Business* (1972), the latter of which he had also previously filmed for television in 1968. His other TV work includes *Reg Varney* (1973–1974, TV) and *Down the Gate* (1975–1976, TV), several episodes of the latter of which he also wrote, though an attempt to revive *On the Buses* as *Back on the Buses* never happened. However, Varney did tour Australia with a stage version of the series in 1988. After retiring, he devoted much of his time to painting landscapes. His daughter is the actress Jeanne Varney, who appeared in Hammer's *On the Buses*. **Additional notes:** Contrary to some sources, Varney did not appear as Stan Butler in a 1972 edition of the TV comedy special *All Star Comedy Carnival* (1969–1973, TV). He did, however, help to publicize ATMs by making the the first withdrawal from the world's first cash dispensing machine at a Barclays Bank in Enfield in the UK on 27 June 1967. **Hammer credits:** *On the Buses* (1971, as Stan Butler), *Mutiny on the Buses* (1972, as Stan Butler), *Holiday on the Buses* (1973, as Stan Butler)

## Vas, Steven

This Hungarian writer (1894–1967) co-authored the story for Hammer's *Stolen Face* (1952) with Richard Landau and Alexander Paal. His other film credits include *The Crystal Ball* (1943) and *Two Senoritas from Chicago* (1943), for both of which he provided the story. **Hammer credits:** *Stolen Face* (1952)

## Vaughan, Mike

Vaughan designed a number of poster campaigns for Hammer, including the striking artwork for *Twins of Evil* (1971). His other credits include *The Losers* (1968 [1971 UK release]) and *Arabian Adventure* (1979). Note that a collage of images from Vaughan's Hammer work was used as the front cover illustration for Lorrimer's 1973 Hammer book *The House of Horror*. **Hammer credits include:** *The Vampire Lovers* (1970 [uncredited]), *Scars of Dracula* (1970 [uncredited]), *The Horror of Frankenstein* (1970 [uncredited]), *Lust for a Vampire* (1971 [uncredited]), *Hands of the Ripper* (1971 [uncredited]), *Twins of Evil* (1971 [uncredited]), *Blood from the Mummy's Tomb* (1971 [uncredited])

## Vaughan, Peter

Best known to television audiences for playing Harry Grout (Grouty) in the long-running sitcom *Porridge* (1974–1977, TV), this British character actor (1923–2016, real name Peter Ewart Ohm) was frequently cast as menacing or aggressive types. Much on television, in everything from *Interpol Calling* (1959, TV) to *Game of Thrones* (2011–2019, TV), he began appearing in films in 1959 with *The 39 Steps*, following which he went on to perform in over forty further movies, among them *Make Mine Mink* (1960), *The Victors* (1963), *The Naked Runner* (1967), *Straw Dogs* (1971), the big screen version of *Porridge* (1979), *The Missionary* (1983), *The Remains of the Day* (1993), *The Mother* (2003), *Death at a Funeral* (2007), *Is Anybody There?* (2008) and *Albatross* (2011). In 1965 he appeared as the devoted butler Harry in Hammer's *Fanatic*, a performance which *Variety* described as "standout." He also played a thug in *Czech Mate* (1984, TVM [episode of *Hammer House of Mystery and Suspense*]), a role that didn't allow him a single line of dialogue. His other TV work includes episodes of *Our Friends in the North* (1996, TV), which earned him a best actor BAFTA nomination, *The Jury* (2002, TV), and *Lark Rise to Candleford* (2008–2011, TV), as well as such one-offs as *Christmas at the Riviera* (2007, TVM) and *The Antiques Rogue Show* (2009, TVM). He was married to the actress Billie Whitelaw (1932–2014) between 1952 and 1966; she appeared in Hammer's *Hell Is a City* (1960). His second wife was the actress Lillias Walker (1930–), whom he married in 1966. **Hammer credits:** *Fanatic* (1965, as Harry), *Czech Mate* (1984, TVM [episode of *Hammer House of Mystery and Suspense*], as Bull-neck)

## Vaughan, Timothy

Vaughan worked as the assistant art director on *One on an Island* (1968, TV [episode of *Journey to the Unknown*]). His other credits include *There's a Girl in My Soup* (1970), on which he worked as a draughtsman. **Hammer credits:** *One on an Island* (1968, TV [episode of *Journey to the Unknown*])

## Vaughan-Hughes, Gerald

Vaughn-Hughes did uncredited re-writes on Hammer's *To the Devil a Daughter* (1976) while the film was shooting. His other film credits include *Sebastian* (1968) and *The Duellists* (1977), plus episodes of *Armchair Theatre* (1956–1974, TV) and *Murder* (1976, TV). **Hammer credits:** *To the Devil a Daughter* (1976 [uncredited])

## Vaughn, Jimmy

Vaughn worked as a personnel advisor on Hammer's Thuggee thriller *The Stranglers of Bombay* (1959). **Hammer credits:** *The Stranglers of Bombay* (1959 [uncredited])

## Vaz Dias, Selma

This Dutch character actress (1911–1977) played the role of Mrs. Corelli in the Hammer second feature *The Flanagan Boy* (1953). In British films from 1934 with *Jew Suss*, her other credits include *One of Our Aircraft Is Missing* (1942), *Cat Girl* (1957), *Orders to Kill* (1958) and *The Tell-Tale Heart* (1960). Her TV credits include episodes of *Douglas Fairbanks, Jr. Presents* (1953–1957, TV) and *Trial* (1971, TV). **Hammer credits:** *The Flanagan Boy* (1953, as Mrs. Corelli)

## Veendam, Eric

Veendam worked as the assistant director on three films for Hammer, all of which were produced by Henry Halsted. His credits as a production manager include *My Hands Are Clay* (1948), *Night Was Our Friend* (1951) and *Reluctant Heroes* (1951), the latter again for Halsted. **Hammer credits:** *Dick Barton—Special Agent* (1948), *The Dark Road* (1948 [uncredited]), *Dick Barton at Bay* (1950)

## Veevers, Wally

This noted matte artist and effects wiz (1917–1983, full name Walter Joseph Veevers) worked on many major productions during his career. His credits include *Things to Come* (1936), *The Thief of Bagdad* (1940), *Gift Horse* (1952), *Heavens Above!* (1963), *2001: A Space Odyssey* (1968), *The Last Valley* (1970), *Diamonds Are Forever* (1971), *A Bridge Too Far* (1977), *Superman* (1978), which won him a shared BAFTA, *Saturn 3* (1980), *Excalibur* (1981) and *The Keep* (1983), his death during the making of which caused a number of production problems. He also contributed to the special effects for Hammer's *Moon Zero Two* (1969). His father was the cameraman Victor Veevers. **Hammer credits:** *Moon Zero Two* (1969 [uncredited])

## *The Vengeance of She*

GB, 1968, 101m, Technicolor [UK], DeLuxe [U.S.], widescreen [1.66:1], RCA, cert A

Following the enormous international success of *She* (1965), it was inevitable that a sequel would be called for, but its journey to the screen proved to be a convoluted one that, ultimately, was barely worth the effort. As early as December 1964–some five months before the first film's release—Hammer executive James Carreras was trying to set up a sequel, and to this end he pitched the idea of *Ayesha—Daughter of She* to MGM and the independent producer Joseph E. Levine. Neither took the bait. However, following the eventual box office success of *She*, MGM showed renewed interest in the project in early 1966, when it was announced that *She—Goddess of Love* would be made as a co-production, with Anthony Hinds onboard as producer. A screenplay by *Modesty Blaise* co-creator Peter O'Donnell was subsequently written under the title of *The Return of She* (aka *She II*). Haggard's own novel, *Ayesha: The Return of She* (1905), seems not to have been considered as a source for the film.

Unfortunately, although Hammer was able to sign John Richardson to return as the leading man, the studio was unable to persuade Ursula Andress to make a comeback (by this time she was no longer under contract to Hammer's then-partner, Seven Arts, and so refused to appear in the film). Consequently, MGM began to dither about the project, more so when the title was altered again to *She—The Avenger*, by which time Michael Carreras was over-seeing the project behind the scenes, with Aida Young (his former associate producer) now onboard as producer. Recalled Young of her assignment, "As I had been his [Michael's] associate producer on a couple of films, I think I argued I could produce it and they gave it to me."[15]

With Andress now literally out of the picture, a search for a suitable replacement was launched. Among the actresses either considered or audi-

An unsmiling Olinka Berova doesn't look too steady on her feet in this rather awkward publicity shot for *The Vengeance of She* (1968) (Hammer/Seven Arts/ABPC/Warner Pathé Distributors/Twentieth Century–Fox).

tioned for the film were Susan Denberg, Camilla Sparv, Samantha Jones, Britt Ekland, Barbara Bouchet, Julie Kruger-Monsen and Sonia Romanoff. However, it was the Czech actress and former *Playboy* cover girl Olga Shoberova who eventually won the role of Carol, who—in the revised script—finds herself seemingly possessed by the spirit of the long-dead Queen Ayesha. Set in the present day, it follows Carol's adventures as she crosses Europe, inexplicably called to the secret city of Kuma, where Ayesha's lover Killikrates awaits her ("She returned in our time to make two worlds meet in vengeance," exclaimed the trailer, though in the film, Carol turns out not to be the reincarnation of Ayesha at all, thus making it all a lot of fuss over not very much).

Although she had made a handful of films on the Continent, Shoberova was unknown to English-speaking audiences. Consequently, she was given a Hammer makeover and launched as Olinka Berova, under which name she was introduced to the press on 22 June 1967 (commented the 1 July issue of *Kine Weekly* of the arrival of the Czech bombshell, "Olinka Berova, who follows Ursula Andress and Raquel Welch and maintains the Hammer tradition for exciting leading ladies, is the

first actress from this area to star in a major British film"). By this time Cliff Owen had been signed to direct the film, which now carried the title *The Vengeance of She*. This was at the insistence of Hammer's other partner, ABPC, which was at the time considering making a big screen version of the television hit *The Avengers* (1961–1969, TV), and so wanted to avoid any potential confusion.

Better known for his comedies, Owen seemed an unusual choice to helm the film, especially given that Don Sharp had been offered it by Aida Young (he turned it down as he was involved in other projects). Sidney Hayers had also been considered for the job. Nevertheless, it was under Owen's guidance that the long-delayed £352,000 production finally got underway. Filmed between 26 June and 8 September 1967, the crew first made use of locations in Monte Carlo and Almeria (the latter standing in for Israel, which was now considered too dangerous), before returning to England for the interiors, which were shot at Hammer's new base studio, Elstree.

Unfortunately, O'Donnell's script is a somewhat confused affair that really should have been overhauled before going before the cameras. Sadly, this, coupled with the ponderous pace, unspeakable dialogue and unimaginative direction, make heavy weather of what should have been an entertaining blend of romance and fantasy (a more Eurocentric film than most of Hammer's output, it has the look and feel of a Jess Franco production at times). Undeniably, the otherwise wooden Miss Berova certainly looks the part in Carl Toms' diaphanous gowns (which are designed to display her gravity-defying breasts to their best advantage), while the supporting cast includes such well-seasoned players as Edward Judd, André Morell, Noel Willman and Derek Godfrey (whose eyebrows seem to be permanently arched throughout, as well they might be). However, they fail to make bricks without straw, and the movie stands as one of Hammer's more tedious and immediately disposable efforts, save for some attractive location photography by Wolfgang Suschitzky and the spectacular destruction of Kuma at the climax—but it's a long time in coming.

Following a trade show on 21 March 1968, Warner Pathé finally released the much retitled film in the UK on 14 April to complete indifference from both critics and audiences alike. Commented the

*Monthly Film Bulletin*, "The dialogue is literally unspeakable, and the cast mainly to be pitied." The American release, care of Twentieth Century–Fox, for which it was double-billed with Hammer's *The Lost Continent* (1968), followed on 19 June and met a similar fate, thus bringing to an abrupt end any plans the company had of producing a series of films to rival their Dracula and Frankenstein franchises (*Variety* described the film as a "plastic confection" that "lacks thrills and punch," while the *New York Times* labeled it "a scriptwriter's mindless sequel"). In fact the original film made more money when re-released on 10 August 1969 on a double bill with Hammer's *One Million Years B.C.* (1966), bringing in an impressive £190,000.

Remembered producer Aida Young of the film, "We had a lot of problems on that, again on location in the desert. The director, Cliff Owen slipped a disc. It was near the end of the shoot and I didn't want to get a director out so I directed the last few days. I remember that very well, running backwards and forwards with him on a stretcher.... He was lying in bed for quite a few days, while I found work to do without him and then we managed to take him on location on a stretcher."[16] **Additional notes:** Part of the ritual delivered by Men-Hari was later re-used in Hammer's *Taste the Blood of Dracula* (1970), in which it was spoken by Lord Courtley. A brief flashback sequence featuring the earlier incarnation of Ayesha was filmed using Berova, as clips featuring Ursula Andress would all too readily have reminded audiences that she had not returned for the sequel; for this scene, Berova wore Andress' gold costume and headdress from the first film. John Richardson's performance seems to have been re-voiced by David de Keyser. The film carries a 1967 copyright. Some sources state that the film was released in America on 1 May 1968.

Production companies: Hammer/Seven Arts/ABPC. Distributors: Warner Pathé Distributors (UK [ABC circuit]), Twentieth Century–Fox (U.S.). Producer: Aida Young. Director: Cliff Owen. Screenplay: Peter O'Donnell, based on characters created by H. Rider Haggard. Cinematographer: Wolfgang Suschitzky. Music: Mario Nascimbene. Music director: Philip Martell. Conductor: Franco Ferrara [uncredited]. Singer: Bob Fields [uncredited]. Solo saxophone: Tubby Hayes. Supervising editor: James Needs. Editor: Raymond Poulton. Production designer: Lionel Couch. Costumes: Carl Toms, Rosemary Burrows. Special effects: Bowie Films, Ltd. (Les Bowie, Kit West [uncredited], Nicky Allder [uncredited], Bob Cuff [uncredited]). Make-up: Michael Morris. Hair: Mervyn Medalie. Sound: Bill Rowe. Sound editor: Roy Hyde, Jack Knight. Recording director: A.W. Lumkin. Production manager: Dennis Bertera. Assistant director: Terence Clegg. Ritual sequences designed by: Andrew Low. Model maker: Joy Seddon (later Cuff) [uncredited]. Camera operator: Ray Sturgess. Continuity: Phyllis Townshend. Poster: Tom Chantrell [uncredited]. **Cast:** John Richardson (Killikrates), Olinka Berova (Carol), Edward Judd (Philip Smith), Noel Willman (Za-Tor), André Morell (Kassim), Derek Godfrey (Men-Hari), Jill Melford (Sheila Carter),

**Rather cheesy artwork for *The Vengeance of She* (1968), not itself without the whiff of camembert (Hammer/Seven Arts/ABPC/Warner Pathé Distributors/Twentieth Century–Fox).**

Colin Blakely (George Carter), Daniele Noel (Sharna), Gerald Lawson (Seer), George Sewell (Harry), William Lyon Brown (Magus), Zohra Segal (Putri), Derrick Sherwin (Number One), Dervis Ward (Lorry driver), Christine Pockett (Dancer), Charles O'Rourke (Servant), Dana Gillespie (Girl at party [uncredited]), Harry Fielder (Cave dweller [uncredited]), David de Keyser (Re-voicing of John Richardson [uncredited]). **DVD availability:** Anchor Bay (U.S. R1 NTSC), extras include a trailer and TV spots; Anchor Bay/Starz (U.S. R1 NTSC), double-billed with *The Viking Queen* (1967); Studio Canal/Warner (UK R2 PAL). **CD availability:** *She/The Vengeance of She* (GDI Records), which contains the complete score, plus an interview with Mario Nascimbene

### Ventham, Wanda

Although known primarily for her television work, which includes guest appearances and continuing roles in the likes of *The Avengers* (1961–1969, TV), *The Lotus Eaters* (1972–1973, TV), *Hetty Wainthropp Investigates* (1996–1998, TV) and *Lewis* (2006–2015, TV), this glamorous British actress (1935–) has also made a handful of films, among them Hammer's *Captain Kronos— Vampire Hunter* (1974), in which she plays the pivotal role of Lady Durward, having inherited the part from Ingrid Pitt, who turned it down. Trained at the Central School of Speech of Drama, her other film credits include *My Teenage Daughter* (1956), *Carry On Cleo* (1964), *The Knack* (1965), *Death Is a Woman* (1966), *Carry On… Up the Khyber* (1968), *Asylum* (2005) and *Run for Your Wife* (2012). Her second husband is the actor Timothy Carlton (1939–, full name Timothy Carlton Cumberbatch), whom she wed in 1976; their son is the actor Benedict Cumberbatch (1976–), whose parents they played in episodes of *Sherlock* (2010–, TV). **Hammer credits:** *Captain Kronos—Vampire Hunter* (1974, as Lady Durward)

### Vercoe, Stephen

This British actor (1921–1997) can be seen as Ned Palmer in Hammer's *36 Hours* (1953). His other credits include *Appointment in London* (1952), *The Master of Ballantrae* (1953), *The Constant Husband* (1955) and *Les Girls* (1957), plus episodes of *Fabian of the Yard* (1954, TV) and *Captain Gallant of the Foreign Legion* (1955, TV). **Hammer credits:** *36 Hours* (1953, as Ned Palmer [uncredited])

### Verheiden, Mark

This American writer and producer (1956–) is best known for his work on such TV series as *Smallville* (2001–2011, TV), *Battlestar Galactica* (2004–2009, TV), *Heroes* (2006–2010, TV), *Falling Skies* (2011–, TV) and *Hemlock Grove* (2013–, TV). He is also acknowledged in the credits of *Flesh and Blood—The Hammer Heritage of Horror* (1994, TV). **Hammer credits:** *Flesh and Blood—The Hammer Heritage of Horror* (1994, TV)

### Verno, Jerry

Best remembered for playing one of the commercial salesmen in *The 39 Steps* (1935), this British comedian (1895–1975) began his career on the music hall circuit in 1907 as a singer before later turning to comedy. In films from 1931 with *Two Crowded Hours*, his other credits, mostly cameos and bit parts, include *There Goes the Bride* (1932), *Old Mother Riley in Paris* (1938), *The Red Shoes* (1948) and *The Belles of St. Trinian's* (1954). He also had minor roles in Hammer's *Watch It, Sailor!* (1961), in which he played a cab driver, and *The Plague of the Zombies* (1966), in which he played the landlord of the Gardener's Arms. His TV appearances include episodes of *The New Adventures of Charlie Chan* (1957–1958, TV), *Mystery and Imagination* (1966–1970, TV) and *Sanctuary* (1967, TV). On the stage he appeared in everything from musicals to pantomime. **Hammer credits:** *Watch It, Sailor!* (1961, as Cab driver), *The Plague of the Zombies* (1966, as Landlord [uncredited])

### Vernon, Don

Vernon can be seen in Hammer's *The Witches* (1966). His other credits include *The Flesh and the Fiends* (1960), *Half a Sixpence* (1967) and *Macbeth* (1971), plus episodes of *Randall and Hopkirk (Deceased)* (1969–1970, TV) and *Doomwatch* (1970–1972, TV). **Hammer credits:** *The Witches* (1966, as Dancer [uncredited])

### Vernon, Dorothy

This British actress (1894–1952) had a supporting role in Hammer's very first feature production, *The Public Life of Henry the Ninth* (1935), in which she played Mrs. Fickle. Her other credits include *A Cigarette Maker's Romance* (1920), *Flat Number Three* (1934), *Old Mother Riley* (1937) and *My Brother's Keeper* (1948). Her husband was producer John Woolf (1913–1999), whom she married in 1937. **Hammer credits:** *The Public Life of Henry the Ninth* (1935, as Mrs. Fickle)

### Vernon, Richard

A welcome addition to any cast, this British character actor (1925–1997) was frequently called upon to play authority figures and aristocratic types. In films from 1949 with *Stop Press Girl*, his film career took off in the sixties, and went on to include *Village of the Damned* (1960), *The Servant* (1963), *The Tomb of Ligeia* (1964), *Song of Norway* (1970), *The Pink Panther Strikes Again* (1976), *Evil Under the Sun* (1982), *A Month in the Country* (1987) and *Loch Ness* (1996). However, he was best known for his television work, which included appearances in *The Man in Room 17* (1964–1965, TV), *The Duchess of Duke Street* (1976–1977, TV), *Roll Over Beethoven* (1985–1986, TV) and *Class Act* (1994–1995, TV) among many. He also appeared in two Hammer films, first giving an excellent account of himself as the bank clerk Pearson in the thriller *Cash on Demand* (1961), a role he'd previously played in the TV original, *The Gold Inside* (1960, TV). He later played the M-like SI7 head Colonel Matthews in *The Satanic Rites of Dracula* (1974), to which he brought his customary air of dignity. Prior to this, he had also appeared in an episode of *Journey to the Unknown* (1968, TV) for the company. Also on stage and radio, he was married to the actress Benedicta Leigh (1922–

2000) from 1955 to 1990. His daughter is the actress Sarah Vernon (1956–). **Hammer credits:** *Cash on Demand* (1961, as Pearson), *The Madison Equation* (1968, TV [episode of *Journey to the Unknown*], as Sir Gerald Walters), *The Satanic Rites of Dracula* (1974, as Colonel Matthews)

### Vernon, Valerie

This glamorous British actress and model (1926–1975) played the role of Bella in the Hammer second feature *The Glass Cage* (1955). Also on stage, her other credits include *The Delavine Affair* (1955) and an episode of *Saber of London* (1954–1960, TV). **Hammer credits:** *The Glass Cage* (1955, as Bella)

### Verrell, Ronnie

This British musician (1926–2002) played the drums on the soundtrack to Hammer's *Dracula A.D. 1972* (1972). A busy session player, during his career he played with the likes of the Ted Heath Band and the Jack Parnell Orchestra, working for the latter on *Sunday Night at the London Palladium* (1955–1967, TV). He also played for Animal in *The Muppet Show* (1976–1981, TV), and later in life appeared as the drummer with The Skinnerettes in *The Frank Skinner Show* (1995–2005, TV). **Hammer credits:** *Dracula A.D. 1972* (1972)

### Vesnitch, Milovan *see* Milovan and Serena

### Vetri, Victoria

In films and on television in America from the early sixties (at first mostly under the name of Angela Dorian), this glamorous American born actress of Italian and Sicilian descent (1944–, real name Victoria Cecilia Vetry, aka Angela Dorian) had minor roles in the likes of *The Pigeon That Took*

Victoria Vetri displays her charms in this publicity still for *When Dinosaurs Ruled the Earth* (1970). They're presumably dinosaur teeth (Hammer/Warner Pathé Distributors/Warner Bros.).

*Rome* (1962), *Kings of the Sun* (1963), *Chuka* (1967) and *Rosemary's Baby* (1968), before being cast as Sanna, the lead in Hammer's dinosaur epic *When Dinosaurs Ruled the Earth* (1970). Recalled director Val Guest of Vetri, "She'd been a successful model, glamor girl, pin-up and centerfold, all of which hadn't given her much time to take up acting. So how come she was being star-billed in our epic? Well, it seems she had a big admirer in the American distributor's camp who persuaded Jimmy Carreras to cast her in *Dinosaurs* and become the new Raquel Welch. Anyway, she looked great in her leather thong bikini and animal-skin bra. Could Sarah Bernhardt have done that?"[17]

Voted *Playboy* Playmate of the Year in 1968 (prior to which she'd been Miss September 1967), Vetri's other credits include *Night Chase* (1970, TVM), *Incident in San Francisco* (1971, TVM), *Group Marriage* (1973) and *Invasion of the Bee Girls* (1973). Also busy in television, her many credits here include episodes of *Going My Way* (1962–1963, TV), *Destry* (1964, TV), *Batman* (1966–1968, TV), *Land of the Giants* (1968–1970, TV) and *Lucas Tanner* (1974–1975, TV).

**Additional notes:** A sequel to *When Dinosaurs Ruled the Earth* titled *Dinosaur Girl* was proposed, with Vetri attached to star, but nothing became of the announcement. She did however pose for *Playboy* again in 1984, while in 2000 she was voted number fifty-six in the magazine's list of One-Hundred Center-Folds of the Century. In *Rosemary's Baby*, in which she appeared as Angela Dorian, her character is asked if she is Victoria Vetri. Earlier in her career, she apparently turned down the title role in *Lolita* (1962). **Hammer credits:** *When Dinosaurs Ruled the Earth* (1970, as Sanna)

**Poised for action. Victoria Vetri takes up arms in this publicity shot for *When Dinosaurs Ruled the Earth* (1970) (Hammer/Warner Pathé Distributors/Warner Bros.).**

### Vetter, Edgar

With Hammer in their burgeoning days, this British sound recordist and mixer (1913–1988, full name Edward Alfred James Vetter) first worked for the company on *Dr. Morelle—The Case of the Missing Heiress* (1949), on which he was simply billed as Vetter. This led to further employment on *The Adventures of PC 49—The Case of the Guardian Angel* (1949) and several others. He left in 1952 to form a documentary unit, CineVision Productions, with Hammer camera operator Peter Bryan. During the war years, Vetter worked as a correspondent for the BBC, prior to which he had worked for the Winads advertising agency. He also formed a number of sound recording companies during his career, among them Studio 22, Jupiter Recordings and Leomark Recordings. His later sound credits include *The Bolshoi Ballet* (1957), *Dr. Crippen* (1962), *The 300 Spartans* (1962), *The Vulture* (1967), *Stories from a Flying Trunk* (1979) and *Biddy* (1983). **Hammer credits:** *Dr. Morelle—The Case of the Missing Heiress* (1949), *The Adventures of PC 49—The Case of the Guardian Angel* (1949), *Celia* (1949), *Meet Simon Cherry* (1949), *The Man in Black* (1950), *Room to Let* (1950), *Someone at the Door* (1950), *What the Butler Saw* (1950), *The Black Widow* (1950), *The Lady Craved Excitement* (1950), *The Rossiter Case* (1951), *To Have and to Hold* (1951), *A Case for PC 49* (1951), *Cloudburst* (1951), *Death of an Angel* (1952)

### Viccars, Anthony

This British actor (1911–1986, full name Thomas Anthony Viccars, sometimes Antony Viccars) had a minor role in Hammer's *Frankenstein Created Woman* (1967). His other credits include *The Mackintosh Man* (1973) and *On the Game* (1974), plus episodes of *Danger Man* (1960–1962, TV), *The Upchat Line* (1977, TV) and *The Bill* (1984–2010, TV). **Hammer credits:** *Frankenstein Created Woman* (1967, as Second spokesman [uncredited])

### Vickers, Lindsey C.

British born Vickers (1940–) worked as the third assistant director on four Hammer films before graduating to second assistant for two more. Other credits include work as a location manager on *The Sweeney* (1975–1978, TV). **Hammer credits:** *Taste the Blood of Dracula* (1970, third assistant director [uncredited]), *The Vampire Lovers* (1970, third assistant director [uncredited]), *The Horror of Frankenstein* (1970, third assistant director [uncredited]), *Scars of Dracula* (1970, third assistant director [uncredited]), *Blood from the Mummy's Tomb* (1971, second assistant director [uncredited]), *Vampire Circus* (1972, second assistant director [uncredited])

### Vickers, Mike (Michael)

This British composer (1941–), a former guitarist with the sixties group Manfred Mann (which provided songs for the 1968 film *Up the Junction*), scored a number of genre films in the seventies, among them Hammer's *Dracula A.D. 1972* (1972), his music for which combines rock beats and a more traditional orchestral soundtrack to surprisingly good effect, though parts of his score were seemingly re-arranged and re-orchestrated by Hammer composer Don Banks. Vickers' other credits include *The Sandwich Man* (1966), *The Love Box* (1972), *The Sex Thief* (1973), *At the Earth's Core* (1976), *Warlords of Atlantis* (1978) and *The Stud* (1978). Note that Vicker's fellow Manfred Mann band member Paul Jones went on to appear in Hammer's *Demons of the Mind* (1972). Commented music director Philip Martell of his experiences with Vickers on *A.D. 1972*, "Crazy, lazy man.... We got Don Banks to re-do about half of it. The rest of the score I got out of library music."[18] **Hammer credits:** *Dracula A.D. 1972* (1972)

### Vickers, Philip (Phil)

This American born actor (1919–2003) had a walk-on role in Hammer's *Stolen Face* (1952). His other credits include *No Highway* (1951), *Joe Macbeth* (1955) and *The Whole Truth* (1958), plus episodes of *The Quatermass Experiment* (1953, TV) and *The Count of Monte Cristo* (1956, TV). **Hammer credits:** *Stolen Face* (1952, as Solider)

### *The Victim* see *Straight on Till Morning*

### Victor, Charles

This British character actor (1896–1965, real name Charles Victor Harvey) played the role of Inspector Teal in the Hammer second feature *The Saint's Return* (1953). The role had been played by Gordon McLeod in previous episodes. In films from 1935 with *The 39 Steps* following experience as a dancer and stage actor, Victor went on to appear in almost one-hundred films, among them *Major Barbara* (1941), *The Ringer* (1952), *Police Dog* (1955), *The Prince and the Showgirl* (1957) and *The Wrong Box* (1966). He also appeared in episodes of *BBC Sunday-Night Theatre* (1950–1959, TV), *ITV Play of the Week* (1955–1968, TV) and *The Wednesday Play* (1964–1970, TV). **Hammer credits:** *The Saint's Return* (1953, as Inspector Claude Eustace Teal)

### Victor, Stephen

Victor worked as third assistant director on the Hammer swashbuckler *The Scarlet Blade* (1963). He was brought onboard halfway through filming after assistant director Douglas Hermes walked off the production and was replaced by the film's second assistant Hugh Harlow. Victor subsequently returned to the studio for three further assignments. His other credits as a third assistant include *Doomsday at Eleven* (1963) and *Rattle of a Simple Man* (1964), while his work as a second assistant includes *The Eyes of Annie Jones* (1964). **Hammer credits:** *The Scarlet Blade* (1963 [uncredited]), *The Evil of Frankenstein* (1964 [uncredited]), *The Devil-Ship Pirates* (1964 [uncredited]), *The Gorgon* (1964 [uncredited])

## Vidon, Henry (Henri)

This British supporting actor (1908–1978) can be seen as the gardener in the Hammer thriller *The Snorkel* (1958). Working in Britain and on the Continent, his other credits include *Il grido della terra* (1949), *La figlia di Marta Hari* (1954), *The Safecracker* (1958), *Blood of the Vampire* (1958), *Battle of the V-1* (1958) and *Mistress for the Summer* (1960). **Hammer credits:** *The Snorkel* (1958, as Gardener)

## Vigo, David

Vigo produced two second features with Bill Luckwell in conjunction with Hammer and Luckwell (the latter owned by Bill Luckwell). These were *The Runaway* (1964) and *Delayed Flight* (1964), which were shot back-to-back at Bray. Vigo's other credits include *Stéphane Grappelli* (1984). **Hammer credits:** *The Runaway* (1964), *Delayed Flight* (1964)

## Viking

This recording system was used on Hammer's *Dick Barton Strikes Back* (1949). The company was a subsidiary of the Viking Studios, where the film was made. **Hammer credits:** *Dick Barton Strikes Back* (1949)

## *The Viking Queen*

GB, 1967, 91m, Technicolor [UK], DeLuxe [U.S.], widescreen [1.85:1], RCA, cert A

In the 1960s, epic films were all the rage at the box office, and to some extent Hammer had boarded this bandwagon with the likes of *She* (1965) and *One Million Years B.C.* (1966), both of which proved extremely popular. However, their attempt to make a historical epic proper proved to be nothing short of catastrophic.

Set in AD 100 Britain, *The Viking Queen* sees Salina, the warrior queen of the Iceni tribe, fall in love with an invading Roman governor named Justinian, but their affair leads to the revolt of the Druids and, in the case of Salina, suicide (intones Patrick Allen's opening narration, "This was a land where Druid priests held sway over people's minds and prophesied that one day a woman would wear armour and wield a sword against the Romans. A woman who would be called The Viking Queen").

Based upon a story by the film's producer, John Temple-Smith, the screenplay was fleshed out by Clarke Reynolds. Unfortunately, his clunky, modern-sounding dialogue scuppers the film from the get-go. "Bloody country," curses a rain-sodden Roman soldier as he pushes a cart through the muddy English terrain in the opening sequence. Elsewhere it is merely declamatory. "It is written in the clouds … that you will wear armour and carry a sword in your right hand," Salina is told at one point by the Druid priest Maelgan. As for her exchanges with the invading Octavius, they inevitably descend into a trading of threats and insults. "It's only Roman indulgence that allows you to live here," he informs her, to which she retorts, "Your rudeness is only surpassed by your ignorance."

Planned as early as 1964 (with Raquel Welch and Ursula Andress under consideration for the

lead role), the film was shot between 15 June and 18 August 1966, and was based at Ireland's Ardmore Studios, where Hammer had made *Sword of Sherwood Forest* back in 1960. It also made extensive use of the Wicklow Mountains, along with several regiments of the Irish army for some of the bigger combat sequences, which include Salina riding into battle Boadicea-style on a chariot with swords on its wheels. "This land shall run with blood," declares the warrior queen—but not *too* much, the film only being an A certificate ("See the bladed chariots of death challenge Rome's mightiest legions," declared the voiceover in the trailer).

The production was directed by the usually reliable Don Chaffey, who had done such a first rate job with *One Million Years B.C.* Not surprisingly, though, he was somewhat uninspired by the material on offer. That said, Stephen Dade's photography of the verdant countryside is occasionally eyecatching.

Astonishingly, Hammer had high hopes for the film, which it launched on a wave of publicity, promoting Carita, its newly discovered female star, as the latest addition to the stable of Hammer Glamor. However, while the Finnish Carita was physically right for the role of Salina, looking fetching in her various outfits, she was simply too inexperienced as an actress to carry the film, which was also poorly served by its leading man, Hollywood import Don Murray, who was brought in to play Justinian after Christopher Lee wisely turned down the part (Murray was then under contract to Seven Arts, which was co-financing the film as part of an on-going deal with Hammer).

Even the supporting cast, which includes such Hammer familiars as Andrew Keir, an incredibly hammy Donald Houston, Patrick Troughton, Percy Herbert and Niall MacGinnis, fail to make bricks with the soggy straw provided. Despite a budget that finally came in at a substantial £411,000 (£61,000 over the original price-tag), the resultant film looks cheap and rushed, lacking the scale of a true sixties' epic, while the frequent anachronisms further detract from the historical setting (the thing plays like *Carry On Cleo* [1964] without the laughs).

Trade shown at Studio One on 6 March 1967, the film was subsequently released on the ABC circuit by Warner Pathé on 26 March. The film's U.S. release, care of Twentieth Century–Fox, followed on 16 August, for which it was double-billed with

American poster for the double bill of *The Viking Queen* (1967) and *Quatermass and the Pit* (1967), the latter of which was released in the States as *Five Million Years to Earth* (Hammer/Seven Arts/Associated British Picture Corporation/Warner Pathé/Warner Pathé Distributors/Twentieth Century–Fox/Studio Canal).

*Quatermass and the Pit* (1967). Not surprisingly, some of the reviews were withering, among them that by the *Monthly Film Bulletin*, which honed in on the "scrappy and often startlingly anachronistic script." **Additional notes:** The film carries a 1966 copyright.

Production companies: Hammer/Seven Arts/ Associated British Picture Corporation. Distributors: Warner Pathé Distributors (UK [ABC circuit]), Twentieth Century–Fox (U.S.). Producer: John Temple-Smith. Director: Don Chaffey. Screenplay: Clarke Reynolds. Story: John Temple-Smith. Cinematographer: Stephen Dade. Music: Gary Hughes. Music director: Philip Martell. Production design: George Provis. Supervising editor: James Needs. Editor: Peter Boita. Costumes: John Furniss, Hilda Geerdts, Jack Gallagher. Special effects: Allan Bryce. Make-up: Charles Parker. Hair: Bobbie Smith. Sound: H.L. Bird, Bob Jones. Sound editor: Stan Smith. Assistant director: Dennis Bertera. Third assistant director: Mike Higgins [uncredited]. Second unit director: Jack Causey. Second unit cinematographer: John Harris. Gaffer: Bernie Prentice [uncredited]. Production manager:

Rene Dupont. Production liaison: Lieutenant Colonel William O'Kelly. Assistant editor: Dennis Boita [uncredited]. Camera operator: David Harcourt. Master of horse: Frank Hayden. Continuity: Ann Skinner. Stunts: Tim Condron [uncredited], Steve Emerson [uncredited], Sadie Eden [uncredited], Peter Munt [uncredited], Terry Richards [uncredited], Bronco McLoughlin [uncredited], Roy Street [uncredited]. Poster: Tom Chantrell [uncredited]. Stills: George Higgins [uncredited]. **Cast:** Don Murray (Justinian), Carita (Salina), Andrew Keir (Octavian), Donald Houston (Maelgan), Patrick Troughton (Tristram), Nicola Pagett (Talia), Adrienne Corri (Beatrice), Percy Herbert (Catus), Denis Shaw (Osiris), Niall MacGinnis (Tiberion), Wilfred Lawson (King Priam), Sean Caffrey (Fergus), Philip O'Flynn (Merchant), Brendan Matthews (Nigel), Bryan Marshall (Dominic), Gerry Alexander (Fabian), Jack Rodney (Boniface), Patrick Gardiner (Benedict), Paul Murphy (Dalan), Arthur O'Sullivan (Old man), Cecil Sheridan (Shopkeeper), Anna Manahan (Shopkeeper's wife), Nita Lorraine (Nubian slave), Patrick Allen (Narrator [uncredited]). **DVD availability:** Anchor Bay (U.S. R1 NTSC); Anchor Bay/Starz (U.S. R1 NTSC), double-billed with *The Vengeance of She* (1968); Optimum Home Entertainment (UK R2 PAL)

### Viking Studios

Situated on Kensington High St. in London, Viking Studios was used to film the interiors of Hammer's *Dick Barton Strikes Back* (1949). Recalled Jimmy Sangster, who made his Hammer debut on the film as a third assistant director, "The last time I was there, a few years back, it had been turned into a private house and the owner was throwing a grand party in a marquee on the back lawn. He didn't even believe me when I told him his home used to be a movie studio."[19] Note that Viking's own sound recording system was used to record the sound for *Dick Barton Strikes Back*. Other films made at the studios include *The Trial of Madame X* (1948), *A Date with a Dream* (1948), *Fortune Lane* (1948), *Melody Club* (1949) and *A Ray of Sunshine: An Irresponsible Medley of Song and Dance* (1950). **Hammer credits:** *Dick Barton Strikes Back* (1949)

### Villaba, Tadeo

Spanish born Villalba (1935–2009, full name Tadeo Villalba Rodriguez) worked as a production assistant on the Hammer short *Dick Turpin—Highwayman* (1956). He began his career in this capacity in his home country with *Intriga en al escenario* (1953), which he followed with *Richard III* (1955), *The Spanish Gardener* (1956) and *The Pride and the Passion* (1957) among others. He went on to have a lengthy career as a unit/production manager, working in both Britain and on the Continent (especially on Spanish-shot international films), among his many credits being *Around the World in 80 Days* (1956), *Lawrence of Arabia* (1962), *Doctor Zhivago* (1965), *Camelot* (1967), *Patton* (1970) and *Scarab* (1984). He also worked in this capacity on several films for the Madrid-based producer Samuel Bronston, including *King of Kings* (1961),

*El Cid* (1961), *55 Days at Peking* (1963), *The Fall of the Roman Empire* (1964) and *The Magnificent Showman* (1964). He also executive produced a number of films from the early seventies onwards, among them *Gott schutz die Liebenden* (1973), *Pensione paura* (1977), *Pasodoble* (1988), on which he was the associate producer, and *El aliento del diablo* (1993). His father was the set decorator and art director Teddy Villalba (real name Tadeo Villalba Ruiz), his son is the producer Tadeo Villalba hijo (1962–, real name Tadeo Villalba Carmona), and his grandson is the location manager Teddy Villalba. **Hammer credits:** *Dick Turpin—Highwayman* (1956 [uncredited])

### Villiers, Caroline

This British actress (1949–) can be seen as Petra in Hammer's *Captain Kronos—Vampire Hunter* (1974). Her other credits include *All the Fun of the Fair* (1979), and episodes of *Rushton's Illustrated* (1980, TV) and *Frost in May* (1982, TV). **Hammer credits:** *Captain Kronos—Vampire Hunter* (1974, as Petra [uncredited])

### Villiers, James

Known primarily for his sardonic upper-crust roles (once heard, his voice is not forgotten), this fine British character actor (1933–1998, full name James Michael Hyde Villiers) spent a good deal of his career on stage, although he also managed over forty films appearances, beginning with a bit part in *Late Night Final* (1954). Frequently in supporting roles or cameos, his credits include *Nothing But the Best* (1963), *Repulsion* (1965), *Half a Sixpence* (1967), *Otley* (1968), *The Amazing Mr. Blunden* (1972), *For Your Eyes Only* (1981), *Under the Volcano* (1984), *Let Him Have It* (1991) and *The Tichborne Claimant* (1998).

He also appeared in a handful of films for director Joseph Losey, beginning with Hammer's *The Damned* (1963), in which he played the supporting role of Captain Gregory. However, he had much more substantial roles in two further films for Hammer, the first of these being *The Nanny* (1965), in which he is superb as the father of a boy who insists that his nanny is a psychopath. He later appeared in the troubled *Blood from the Mummy's Tomb* (1970), adding luster to the cast as the villainous Corbeck. Both of these films were directed by Seth Holt, who died during the making of the latter. Recalled Villiers of Holt's funeral, "Hammer lent us one of the original hearses from one of their many films, with the plumed horses and the fine carriage with the black drapings and silver trappings, used in every single Dracula film ever made, and we followed along behind this marvellous hearse and buried the old bean."[20] **Additional notes:** Villiers was also considered for the role of George de Grass in Hammer's *To the Devil a Daughter* (1976). **Hammer credits:** *The Damned* (1963, as Captain Gregory), *The Nanny* (1965, as Bill Fane), *Blood from the Mummy's Tomb* (1970, as Corbeck)

### Villiers, Mavis

This Australian born actress (1911–1976, real name Mavis Clare Cooney) had a minor role in Hammer's *Straight on Till Morning* (1972). In films in Hollywood from 1921 with *Little Lord Fauntleroy*, and then in Britain from 1933, her other credits include *King of the Castle* (1936), *Gasbags* (1940), *Pool of London* (1950), *Suddenly, Last Summer* (1959), *Victim* (1961), *The Haunting* (1963), *Promise Her Anything* (1966) and *No Sex Please—We're British* (1973). Her brother was the camera operator Cece Cooney (1906–1993, full name Randolph Cecil Cooney), who worked on five Hammer films, among them *Dracula—Prince of Darkness* (1966) and *Rasputin—The Mad Monk* (1966). **Hammer credits:** *Straight on Till Morning* (1972, as Indian Princess)

### Vincent, Eric

Working out of Shepperton, Vincent maintained the sound equipment on Hammer's *Yesterday's Enemy* (1959), which was shot primarily at the studio because of overcrowding at Bray. His other credits include *They Can't Hang Me* (1955), *The Green Man* (1956) and *The Road to Hong Kong* (1962). **Hammer credits:** *Yesterday's Enemy* (1959 [uncredited])

### Vinson, Malcolm

This British cameraman (1939–) worked as the focus puller on the last of Hammer's Frankenstein and Dracula films. He began his career as a camera assistant on *Womaneater* (1958), graduated to clapper loader on *The Crowning Touch* (1959) and became a focus puller on *Carry On Cowboy* (1965). His other credits as a focus puller include *Tommy* (1975) and *Valentino* (1977). He went on to become a camera operator, sometimes with the second unit, with *The Spaceman and King Arthur* (1979), *Octopussy* (1983), *A View to a Kill* (1985) and *Henry V* (1989). Also working as an operator in TV, his credits here include episodes of *The Professionals* (1977–1983, TV), *Jeeves and Wooster* (1990–1993, TV), *Harry and the Wrinklies* (1999, TV) and *Urban Gothic* (2000, TV). **Hammer credits:** *Frankenstein and the Monster from Hell* (1974 [uncredited]), *The Satanic Rites of Dracula* (1974 [uncredited])

### Visa to Canton

GB, 1960, 75m, Technicolor [UK], bw [U.S.], RCA, cert U

Something of a hark-back to the Exclusive thrillers of the early fifties, *Visa to Canton* was originally intended as a feature-length pilot for a new television action series. Cold War films were just beginning to come into vogue at the time, and the film's story of a Hong Kong–based travel agent cum troubleshooter named Don Benton rescuing a pilot friend who has crash-landed near the border to Red China, only to discover that the crash was instigated so as to pass on vital scientific documents onboard, was at least topical. As penned by veteran scribe Gordon Wellesley, it provided a suitable framework on which to hang the expected scenes intrigue, fisticuffs and romance.

Something of a personal project for producer Michael Carreras, it marked his second time behind the camera as a feature director following his debut with *The Steel Bayonet* (1957). The film went on to the floor at Bray on 9 June 1960, just ten days after the completion of the Eastern shocker *The Terror of the Tongs* (1961), the sets for which it made use of, suitably re-vamped and re-cycled by production designer Bernard Robinson and his team, including a paddle steamer (the *SS Helena* in the Tong film, here the *SS Tong Shan*). Some of the cast also crossed over, including Marne Maitland, Burt Kwouk and Milton Reid. However, it should be noted that the production was originally to have been helmed by the actor-turned-director Don Taylor, who pulled out at the last moment, forcing Carreras to take over the directorial reins, though Taylor did go on to star in *The Savage Guns* (1962), a western directed by Michael Carreras for Carreras's own company Capricorn Productions, so the split can't have been too acrimonious.

As with the Exclusive thrillers, an American name was brought in to head the cast. This time it was the turn of the rather bland Richard Basehart who, as well as appearing in several Hollywood features, had also made several films in Europe, among them *La Strada* (1954), *Il Bidone* (1955) and *Amore e guai* (1958). Supporting him was the veteran British stage actress Athene Seyler as Mao Tai Tai, a Chinese woman obsessed with food and Confucius-like observations ("Flowers of wisdom spring from a well-fed stomach," she informs our

hero at one point). Also onboard was the Austrian character actor Eric Pohlmann as the villain-in-chief Colonel Ivano King, while further down the cast list was future *Pink Panther* star Burt Kwouk as Jimmy, the pilot whose plane crash motivates the plot. Yet despite the talent at hand, the production just doesn't click as a piece of espionage entertainment, perhaps because the ground rules for such had yet to be firmly established by the James Bond franchise, the first film of which was still two years distant. It also doesn't help that the film is perfunctorily staged and has the look of a below average TV episode.

Consequently, Michael Carreras was disappointed when there proved to be no takers for the project as a television pilot (which makes it all the more surprising that it was shot in Technicolor if it was meant for the small screen). Consequently, the film was trimmed of any extreme violence to secure a U certificate and, following a trade show on 20 November 1960, sent out on a double bill with Hammer's Robin Hood romp *Sword of Sherwood Forest* (1960) care of British Lion Columbia on 26 December. For its American release on 22 March 1961, again care of Columbia, the film was re-titled *Passport to China* and presented in black and white. **Additional notes:** The color version of *Visa to Canton* has also been shown on television with the *Passport to China* title clumsily superimposed over the opening title credit. Richard Basehart would also go on to star in Michael Carreras's *The Savage Guns* (1962), which was made during his break from Hammer.

Production companies: Hammer/Swallow. Distributors: British Lion Columbia (UK), Columbia (U.S.). Producer: Michael Carreras. Associate producer: Anthony Nelson Keys. Director: Michael Carreras. Screenplay: Gordon Wellesley. Cinematographer: Arthur Grant. Music/conductor: Edwin Astley. Supervising editor: James Needs. Editor: Alfred Cox. Production design: Bernard Robinson. Art director: Thomas Goswell [uncredited]. Assistant art director: Don Mingaye [uncredited]. Costumes: Molly Arbuthnot. Make-up: Roy Ashton. Hair: Frieda Steiger. Sound: Jock May. Production manager: Clifford Parkes. Assistant director: Arthur Mann. Camera operator: Eric Besche. Continuity: Tilly Day. Modeller: Margaret Carter (later Robinson) [uncredited]. **Cast:** Richard Basehart (Don Benton), Lisa Gastoni

(Lola Sanchez), Athene Seyler (Mao Tai Tai), Eric Pohlmann (Colonel Ivano King), Bernard Cribbins (Pereira), Marne Maitland (Han Po), Burt Kwouk (Jimmy), Alan Gifford (Charles Orme), Hedger Wallace (Inspector Taylor), Milton Reid (Bodyguard [uncredited]), Yvonne Shima (Liang Ti [uncredited]), Gerry Lee Yen (Room boy [uncredited]), Ronald Ing (Sentry [uncredited]), Soraya Rafat (Hostess [uncredited]), Paula Lee Shiu (Croupier [uncredited]), Robert Lee (Officer [uncredited]), Zoreen Ismail (Sweekim [uncredited]), Kevin Scott (unnamed role [uncredited])

### Visitor from the Grave see Hammer House of Horror

**Kathryn Leigh Scott and Simon MacCorkindale share a tense moment in *Visitor from the Grave*, one of the weaker episodes of *Hammer House of Horror* (1980) (Hammer/Cinema Arts International/Chips Productions/ITC Entertainment [an ACC company]/Jack Gill).**

### Vivian, April

Vivian played the role of Polly in the early Hammer short *Polly's Two Fathers* (1936), which was produced and directed by Hammer founder Will Hammer. Her other credits include *Kentucky Minstrels* (1934), *Variety* (1935), *Breakers Ahead* (1935) and *The Academy Decides* (1937). **Hammer credits:** *Polly's Two Fathers* (1936, as Polly)

### Vivian, Bert

This British bit part actress (yes, despite the name!) appeared as one of the Satanists in Hammer's *The Devil Rides Out* (1968). **Hammer credits:** *The Devil Rides Out* (1968, as Satanist [uncredited])

### Vivian, Sydney (Sidney)

This British supporting actor (1901–1984) played Inspector Hood in the Hammer thriller *Dr. Morelle—The Case of the Missing Heiress* (1949) and Inspector Burke in *Dick Barton Strikes Back* (1949), though by the time he appeared in *Whispering Smith Hits London* (1952) for the company he'd been reduced to playing a hotel porter. His other credits include *Mary Had a Little...* (1961),

GO-FOR-BROKE YANK BLASTS BAMBOO CURTAIN!

COLUMBIA PICTURES
**RICHARD BASEHART**
in
**PASSPORT TO CHINA**

ATHENE SEYLER • LISA GASTONI
Written by GORDON WELLESLEY • Produced and Directed by MICHAEL CARRERAS • A HAMMER FILM PRODUCTION

**On target. Arresting American artwork for *Visa to Canton* (1960), which was released in the States as *Passport to China* (Hammer/Swallow/British Lion Columbia).**

*Kill or Cure* (1962), *The Day of the Triffids* (1963), *Hide and Seek* (1964) and *Subterfuge* (1969). His many TV credits include episodes of *The Grove Family* (1954–1957, TV), *Suspense* (1962–1963, TV) and *Doctor in the House* (1969–1970, TV). Note that the opening credits for *Dr. Morelle* list the actor as Sydney Vivian, but by the closing credits he has become Sidney Vivian. **Hammer credits:** *Dr. Morelle—The Case of the Missing Heiress* (1949, as Inspector Hood), *Dick Barton Strikes Back* (1949, as Inspector Burke), *Whispering Smith Hits London* (1952, as Hotel porter)

### Volmer, Daphne

British born Volmer (1928–2006, sometimes Vollmer) worked as the hair stylist on nine episodes of *Hammer House of Horror* (1980, TV), which she followed with eight episodes of *Hammer House of Mystery and Suspense* (1984, TVM). Her film credits include *Escapement* (1958), *Konga* (1961), *2001: A Space Odyssey* (1968), on which she was the assistant stylist, *Barry Lyndon* (1975), *George and Mildred* (1980), *Rising Damp* (1980), *Trail of the Pink Panther* (1982), *Curse of the Pink Panther* (1983), *Lady Jane* (1986) and *Salome's Last Dance* (1988). **Hammer credits:** *The Silent Scream* (1980, TV [episode of *Hammer House of Horror*]), *The Two Faces of Evil* (1980, TV [episode of *Hammer House of Horror*]), *Witching Time* (1980, TV [episode of *Hammer House of Horror*]), *Visitor from the Grave* (1980, TV [episode of *Hammer House of Horror*]), *Rude Awakening* (1980, TV [episode of *Hammer House of Horror*]), *Charlie Boy* (1980, TV [episode of *Hammer House of Horror*]), *Children of the Full Moon* (1980, TV [episode of *Hammer House of Horror*]), *The Thirteenth Reunion* (1980, TV [episode of *Hammer House of Horror*]), *Carpathian Eagle* (1980, TV [episode of *Hammer House of Horror*]), *Czech Mate* (1984, TVM [episode of *Hammer House of Mystery and Suspense*]), *The Sweet Scent of Death* (1984, TVM [episode of *Hammer House of Mystery and Suspense*]), *A Distant Scream* (1984, TVM [episode of *Hammer House of Mystery and Suspense*]), *The Late Nancy Irving* (1984, TVM [episode of *Hammer House of Mystery and Suspense*]), *In Possession* (1984, TVM [episode of *Hammer House of Mystery and Suspense*]), *Black Carrion* (1984, TVM [episode of *Hammer House of Mystery and Suspense*]), *Last Video and Testament* (1984, TVM [episode of *Hammer House of Mystery and Suspense*]), *Mark of the Devil* (1984, TVM [episode of *Hammer House of Mystery and Suspense*]))

### von der Heyde, Barbara

This dancer was a member of the dance troupe The Gojos, which appeared in Hammer's *Moon Zero Two* (1969). Her other appearances with the group include episodes of *Discs a Go-Go* (1961–1967, TV), *Top of the Pops* (1964–2006, TV) and *The Val Doonican Show* (1965–1968, TV). Her other film credits include *Song of Norway* (1970). **Hammer credits:** *Moon Zero Two* (1969)

### Von Kieseritzky, George (Georg)

Von Kieseritzky worked as one of the art directors on Hammer's *The Lady Vanishes* (1979). His other credits, either as art director or production designer, include *John Glueckstadt* (1975), *Ansichten eines Clowns* (1976), *Comeback* (1982), *Super* (1984) and *Auf immer und ewig* (1986). **Hammer credits:** *The Lady Vanishes* (1979)

### Von Schelle, Catherina *see* Schell, Catherine

### Vorhaus, David

Long in Britain, this American electronic music pioneer was noted for his atonal electro-acoustic music, some of which is featured during the black mass sequence in Hammer's *Dracula A.D. 1972* (1972). This was actually taken from the 1969 album *An Electric Storm*, which was the first album by the electronic White Noise Band, which Vorhaus formed the previous year with Delia Derbyshire and Brian Hodgson, who also worked on the piece, titled *The Black Mass: An Electric Storm in Hell*, along with Georgina Duncan and Paul Lytton. Working solo, Vorhaus went on to release a second White Noise album titled *White Noise II—Concerto for Synthesizer* (1974). This was later followed by *White Noise III—Re-Entry* (1980), on which he was joined by Dino Ferari, *White Noise IV—Inferno* (1990), *White Noise V—Sound Mind* (2000) and *White Noise 5.5–White Label* (2006). His other albums include *Velvet Donkey* (1975), *Jammy Smears* (1976), *Electro-Graphics* (1982) and *Digital Tenderness* (2004). His music has also been featured in the children's science fiction series *The Tomorrow People* (1973–1979, TV), along with such films as *The Ballad of Tam Lin* (1970), *The Boy Who Turned Yellow* (1972) and *Phase IV* (1974). He can also be seen in the film *Not Tonight, Darling* (1971). Vorhaus' early work was produced in his own studio, Kaleidophon. In 2005, he was joined in the White Noise Band by Mark Jenkins for a number of tour dates. **Hammer credits:** *Dracula A.D. 1972* (1972 [uncredited])

### Voss, Philip

This British actor (1936–) can be seen as Ernst in Hammer's *Frankenstein and the Monster from Hell* (1974). His other credits include *Hopscotch* (1980), *Octopussy* (1983), *Lady Jane* (1986), *Clockwise* (1986), *Four Weddings and a Funeral* (1994) and *The Brides in the Bath* (2003, TVM), plus episodes of *Suspense* (1962–1963, TV), *Raffles* (1975–1977, TV), *Let Them Eat Cake* (1999, TV), *Dinotopia* (2002–2003, TV), *Law & Order: UK* (2009–2014, TV) and *Vicious* (2013–2016, TV), playing the role of Mason in the latter. **Hammer credits:** *Frankenstein and the Monster from Hell* (1974, as Ernst)

### Vowles, Eric

Vowles worked as standby props on *Hammer House of Mystery and Suspense* (1984, TVM). **Hammer credits:** *Hammer House of Mystery and Suspense* (1984, TVM [uncredited])

---

# W

### WEA Records, Ltd. *see* Warner Brothers

### WPD *see* Warner-Pathé Distributors

### Wade, Johnny (Johnnie)

British born Wade (1933–) can be seen briefly as a taxi driver in *The Corvini Inheritance* (1984, TVM [episode of *Hammer House of Mystery and Suspense*]). His other TV credits include episodes of *Compact* (1962–1965, TV), *Bless This House* (1971–1976, TV) and *Sunburn* (1999–2000, TV), while his occasional films include *The Music Machine* (1979), *George and Mildred* (1980) and *Moscow* (2012). **Hammer credits:** *The Corvini Inheritance* (1984, TVM [episode of *Hammer House of Mystery and Suspense*], as Taxi driver)

### Wagstaff, Elsie

This British character actress (1899–1985) played the role of Aunt Nora in the Hammer comedy thriller *Celia* (1949). Her other credits include *The Show Goes On* (1937), *Old Mother Riley at Home* (1945), *The End of the Affair* (1955), *The Snake Woman* (1960), *Saturday Night and Sunday Morning* (1961), *Whistle Down the Wind* (1961), *Heavens Above!* (1963) and *The Raging Moon* (1970). She can also be seen as an asylum inmate in Hammer's *Frankenstein and the Monster from Hell* (1974), which was shown twenty-five years after her first association with the studio, and marked her final screen appearance. Her TV work includes episodes of *Saber of London* (1954–1960, TV), *Z Cars* (1962–1978, TV) and *Thriller* (1973–1976, TV). **Hammer credits:** *Celia* (1949, as Aunt Nora), *Frankenstein and the Monster from Hell* (1974, as Wild One)

### Wahlrow, Helga

This bit-part player can be seen as Rosemary in the Hammer comedy *The Ugly Duckling* (1959). Her other credits include *The Third Man* (1949) and an episode of *The Andromeda Breakthrough* (1962, TV). **Hammer credits:** *The Ugly Duckling* (1959, as Rosemary)

### Wainwright, Sid

Wainwright worked as a gaffer on Hammer's *Scars of Dracula* (1970) and as an electrical supervisor on *Blood from the Mummy's Tomb* (1971) and *The Satanic Rites of Dracula* (1974). His other credits include *Hoffman* (1970) and episodes of *The Saint* (1962–1969, TV). **Hammer credits:** *Scars of Dracula* (1970, gaffer [uncredited]), *Blood from the Mummy's Tomb* (1971, electrical supervisor [uncredited]), *The Satanic Rites of Dracula* (1974, electrical supervisor [uncredited])

### *Wake Wood*

GB, 2009 90m, color, widescreen [2.39:1], Dolby, cert 18

After being purchased by Cytre Investments in 2007, Hammer finally rose from the grave with the internet serial *Beyond the Rave* (2008). This was soon after followed by the announcement that the company would be returning to feature production with the pagan shocker *The Wake Wood* (later just *Wake Wood*), which—to the initial euphoria of fans—began filming in County Donegal, Ireland on 22 September 2008.

A co-production between Hammer, Fantastic

Films and the LA-based company Spitfire Pictures, with funding provided by the Irish Film Board and additional involvement from the Swedish company Solid Entertainment (hence the curious mix of nationalities in the crew), the film was originally set for an autumn 2009 release in the UK care of Vertigo Films. However, Hammer seemed to distance themselves from the finished film, apparently withdrawing their full backing at one stage (the company's name appears *nowhere* on the film's credits, while the DVD cover simply carries the strapline "Hammer presents," though several of the cast and crew talk up the connection in interviews in the special features).

In fact the movie sat on the shelf for over two years after completion, and for a while appeared even to have been expunged from Hammer's roster of up-coming titles. Instead the company announced that more high profile fare such as *The Resident* (2010) and *Let Me In* (2010) would mark their official return to feature production, which didn't bode well for the low budget *Wake Wood* (*Let Me In* was eventually released first, with *The Resident*—despite its starry cast—likewise held back).

Ultimately, *Wake Wood* went the ignominious route of being released straight to DVD on 28 March 2011 after the briefest of face-saving theatrical showings at just four locations from 25 March, resulting (according to *The Standard*) in an opening weekend box office take of just £1,251. Some sources claimed that the film's delayed appearance was down the vagaries of releasing, which sounded like a rather weak excuse when other low budget films were managing to find a home on the big screen, as well as appreciative audiences. As some concluded, the delay may well have had more to do with the fact that the film wasn't very good—certainly not good enough to re-launch the newly resurrected Hammer on its coat tails, the worry no doubt being that it might well sink the company's ambitions before they had even set sail.

Directed by David Keating (from a script by himself and Brendan McCarthy), the story sees a grieving couple (veterinarian Patrick and his wife, pharmacist Louise), move to the remote community of Wake Wood, so as to better come to terms with the death of their nine-year-old daughter Alice, who has been savaged to death by a crazed dog. Once at Wake Wood, they discover the place to be run by a group of pagans, whose leader, Arthur, reveals that a ritual will allow them three further days with their beloved daughter. However, it remains to be seen what happens after the conclusion of the third day (hence the poster's warning of "Beware those you love the most").

Even at ninety minutes, this is a fairly ponderous and unambitious slice of hokum, notable less for its own style than for its various borrowings, among them elements from *Don't Look Now* (1973), *The Wicker Man* (1973), *Carrie* (1976) and *Pet Sematary* (1989), which several reviewers picked up on. With its straightforward handling and performances (the best of them being Timothy Spall's turn as the tweedy pagan leader Arthur), the film has the look and feel of a television episode writ large. With some judicious trimming it might well have made a good installment of *Hammer*

*House of Horror* (1980, TV), but instead resembles one of the more bloated episodes of *Hammer House of Mystery and Suspense* (1984, TVM). Aidan Gillen and Eva Birthistle are suitably angst-ridden as the grieving parents and little Ella Connolly (whom the film introduces) has a few creepy moments as the resurrected child, even though one never quite believes she is capable of inflicting the death and destruction she does once she goes on the rampage. Otherwise, the cast goes through the proceedings with little fervor. Likewise, save for some pleasant shots of the Irish countryside, Chris Maris's photography is generally unambitious, and Michael Convertino's score (with its echoes of *Tubular Bells* and *Halloween*) adds little in the way of atmosphere, while the dialogue and direction are strictly by the numbers. Sadly, therefore, the sum total is something of a disappointment, particularly given the high hopes that fans no doubt had for the revived company's prospects following its seemingly interminable hibernation.

Given its blink-and-you'll-miss-it appearance in cinemas, critical assessment of the £1.6m film could hardly be described as being full-page. Commented *The Standard* in its brief paragraph of acknowledgment: "David Keating's flesh-ripper owes way too much to superior films (*Don't Look Now*, *The Wicker Man*). It also boasts several dodgy performances, TV-movie camerawork and plot twists that defy belief.... Low expectations are key to enjoying *Wake Wood*. You have been warned." In its equally brief coverage, *Empire* acknowledged Ella Connolly's "well-played" turn as the "creepy resurrected daughter" but otherwise the three-star review was hardly overwhelmingly positive given its use of such half-hearted compliments as "nicely murky" and "familiar but likeable." Like *The Standard*, the magazine also noted the pilfering of other genre works, observing that "this low-key, gritty entry ... follows Stephen King's *Pet Sematary* in offering a gruesome gloss on the theme of being careful what you wish for." It also found that it "fits into a persistent strain of British horror about Pagan communities and unwary incomers." Not exactly a ringing endorsement then. That said, the easily-pleased *News of the World* hailed the film as "an instant folk horror classic," a quote that was naturally seized upon and highlighted on the DVD cover. Fans may beg to differ, and might also ponder why the studio didn't elect to make something a little more affectionately self-referential like the Hammer spoof *Lesbian Vampire Killers* (2009), which, though by no means perfect, at least knew the audience—and genre—it was aiming for. **Additional notes:** Like Hammer's glory days, the film had something of a family atmosphere, given that many of the technical crew had worked together on previous productions, and indeed were actually family members. Production designer John Hand can be spotted in a small role in the film. Director David Keating had originally attempted to set the film up independently before his friend Katrine Boorman (daughter of director John) suggested that he pitch it to Hammer, which he duly did, receiving a positive comeback after just ten days (Boorman receives a thanks in the end credits for her efforts). Commented Keating in *The Standard* of the situa-

tion: "Material-wise, it was a good match." In the film, the township is actually spelled Wakewood (all one word) on a road sign provided by Coastal Signs. The role of the rampaging bull was played by Simple, while the ravening dog was played by Nicko. The film was shot in Donegal, Ireland and at the Ovraby Studios in Sweden. The film's poster artwork bears a striking resemblance to that for *The Ruins* (2008). The screenplay was novelized by K.A. John and published by Hammer Books (via Arrow and Random House). A CD of the film's score announced for release by Perseverance in 2012 failed to appear. Finally, a question: why is the clock on the pharmacy wall always at five-past one?

Production companies: Hammer/Spitfire Pictures/Fantastic Films/Solid Entertainment/RTE/Vertigo Films. Distributor: Exclusive (Worldwide). Producers: Brendan McCarthy, John McDonnell. Executive producers: Simon Oakes, Marc Schipper, Guy East [uncredited]. Co-executive producers: Ben Holden, Patrick Irwin, Allan Niblo, Rupert Preston. Line producer: Natasha Banke. Co-producer: Magnus Paulsson. Director: David Keating. Screenplay: David Keating, Brendan McCarthy. Story: Brendan McCarthy. Cinematographer: Chris Maris. Music: Michael Convertino. Music editor/additional music: P. Daniel Newman. Editor: Tim Murrell, Dermot Diskin. Production designer: John Hand. Art director: Owen Power. Costumes: Louise Stanton, Jo Mapp, Josefin Sandling, William McGovern (trainee). Make-up: Liz Byrne, Deidre Fitzgerald, Kaj Gronberg, Katarina Kovacs, Deidre Fitzgerald, Eloise Anson (assistant). Sound: Felix Andriessens, Naomi Dandridge, Tom Deane, Anders Degerberg, Adele Fletcher, John Nilsson, Martin Schinz, Dominik Schleier, Buster Blaesild, Michael Muller, Lionel Strutt. Sound fx editor: Larz Ginzel. Dialogue editor: Dominik Schleier. ADR editor: Adele Fletcher. Foley editor: Michael Muller. Foley artist: Gunther Rohn. Foley recording: Tonburo Berlin. Re-recording mixer: Martin Schinz. Mixing stage: Elektrofilm. Assistant director: Nick McCarthy. Second assistant director: Marcus Lynch. Third assistant directors: Rosai McCarthy, Anna Harrison. Trainee assistant directors: Jonathon Quinlan, Medb Johnstone. Special effects: Gerry Johnston, Florian Obrecht, Magnus Gillberg, Florian Obrecht, Andreas Schellenberg. Blood and gore: Marcus Gillberg. Titles: Britt Dunse. Props: Chan Kin, Noel Walsh, Kieran Shellard, Zack Zell Jkovymazal, Cheryl Rock, Ian Wallis (trainee). Set designer: Malin Kihlberg. Stunt coordinator: Donal O'Farrell. Camera operator: Ed Lindsley. Clapper/loader: Ewa Gerstrom. Camera trainee: Robbie Kelly. Camera second unit: Stevie Russell, Suzanna Zalodar, J.J. Rolfe. Gaffer: Con Dempsey. Genny operator: C.J. Dempsey. Electricians: Billy Cooley, William Cash. Shake choreographer: Steve Batts. EPK: Steve McCormack. Grip: Set Jonasson. Crane operators: Adam Tsan, Steve O'Brien. Stills: Jesper Lindgren. Colorist: Kevin Shaw. Production manager: Steven Davenport. Production executive: Alan Maher. Business affairs and legal executive: Mark Byrne. Location manager: Brendan O'Sullivan. Assistant location manager: Rossa O'Neill. Location assistants: Donal

McWeeney, Lorcan Berney. Production co-ordinator: Rachel Lysaght. Production assistants: Jurate Kaminskaite, David Nilsson, Jonas Tarestad, Tobias Thuresson, Susann Chandler. Script supervisor: Anna-Maria Ni Chathasaigh. Casting: Maureen Hughes, Anja Schmidt. Casting assistants: Clare McGinley, Thyrza Ging. Production accountant: Rory Mac Dermot. Accounts assistants: Emer Fitzpatrick, Tara Clancy. Financing and tax advisor: John Gleeson. Financial services: Horwath Baston Charlton. Additional financial services: Eilis J. Quinlan and Co. Production lawyers: Jonathan Kelly, Philip Lee and Co. Legal services for Exclusive Film Distribution: Tim Johnson, Emily Spence. Additional legal affairs for Exclusive Film Distribution: John Bridson. Production insurance provided by: John O'Sullivan, Peter Fitzpatrick, Media Insurance Brokers, Ltd. Completion Bond: Neil Calder, Film Finances, Ltd. Model maker: Daniel Bonarelli. Trainee art department: Ciara McKenna. Animal handlers: Mary Owens, Rita Moloney. Veterinary consultant: Roger Wallace. Drivers/transport: Mick Murphy, Tony Mullally, Stephen Moss, Euni Britton. Signs: Coastal Signs. Facilities: Stephen Fearon, Patrick Fisher, Johnny Fortune. Location animal and effects resources: Stephen Loane. Unit nurse: Aoife Bland. Tutors to Ella Connolly: Deidre Martin, Marie Henderson. Craft service: Jurate Kaminskaite. Carpenter: Ulf Bruxe. Made with the support of: Peter Gufstafsson (of the Swedish Film Institution). Body doubles: Jurate Kaminskaite, Anna Maris, Thilde Nilsson, Josefin Sandling, Anders Sjolin, Jonas Tarestad, Agneta Von Platen. Dog trainer: Peter Martensson. Post production facilities Dublin: Windmill Lane. Post production services Berlin: The Post republic GMBH. Post production supervisors: Tim Morris, Michael Reuter. Post production supervisor VFX: Andreas Schellenberg. First assistant editor: John McDonnell. 3D CGI: Richard Merrigan. DI supervisor: Gregor Willie. ADR recording (Dublin): Moynihan & Russell. ADR recording (London): Mayflower Studios. Flame compositing: John Kennedy. Facility co-ordinator: Therese Caldwell. Runners: Lyndzi Doyle, Noelle Gibbons. Camera supplied by: The Production Depot. Sound equipment supplied by: Europe Sound. Facilities vehicles: Irish Film and Television Location Facilities. Post production co-ordinators: Eimear O'Kane, Jean Rice. Post production lab: Arri Munich. Additional music recording: Sean Keating. Theremin: Garvin Browne. Violins: Rodion Raskolinkov, Sophie Delaque. Developed in association with: Bord Scannan Na Hireann/The Irish Film Board. Thanks to: Nic Ransome, Simon Perry, Teresa McGrane, Declan Mills, Janet Moran, Kay Scorah, Amanda Bell, Grace Gageby, Elizabeth Gageby, Garvin Browne, Father Mohan and the staff and Lough Derg, Natasha McGrath, Mary Redberg, Maura Ross, Adopt [sic], Maura Logue, Declan Gillespie, Superintendent Dennedy, An Garda Siochana, Ray Beare, Jean Beare, Pat Britton, Ray Britton, The Cross Bar, Steven Loane, Mrs. Loane, Aideen Doherty, Donegal County Council, Coxilte, Viewback Antiques, Councillor Dara Fencing, Katrine Boorman, Helen at Stock House Ballyshannon, Anne Marie Mc-

Donnell, John McKeon, Greg Hunt, Laura Rourke, Anwar Chentoufi, Dave Hughes, Matt Branton, Fionnuala Gilmartin, Kevin Cooney, Jorgen Andreason, Lara Madden, Stephanie Lodola, Molly Hughes, Michelle and staff at the Garden of Eatin,' Dessie and staff at the Pettigo Inn, Ciara O'Gorman, The people of Pettigo County, Donegal, Agnet and Wilhelm Von Platen, Marcus Galvin, Oressun Film Commission, Anna Maris, Charlotta Nilsson, Karin Brunk Holmovist, Eleni Chandrinou i2i [sic], The National Film School at Iadt Dun Laoghaire, Jean Ricem Paul Freaney, Jocelyn Clarke. **Cast:** Timothy Spall (Arthur), Aidan Gillen (Patrick), Eva Birthistle (Louise), Ella Connolly (Alice), Ruth McCabe (Peggy O'Shea), Brian Gleeson (Martin O'Shea), Dan Gordon (Mick O'Shea), Amelia Crowley (Mary Brogan), John Hand (Arthur's helper), Darragh Hand (Arthur's helper), Tommy McArdle (Tommy), John McArdle (Ben), Aoife Meagher (Deidre), Siobhan O'Brien (Pharmacy customer), Alice McCrea (Lady customer), Johnny Fortune (Mechanic), Steven McDonnell (Boy in field). **DVD availability:** Momentum (UK R2 PAL), extras include interviews and deleted scenes, Dark Sky (U.S. R1 NTSC). **Blu-ray availability:** Dark Sky (A/1), extras include interviews and deleted scenes

### Wake, Tim

Wake worked as a carpenter on Hammer's *Countess Dracula* (1971). His other credits include *Carry On Henry* (1971), *Young Winston* (1972), *The Fifth Element* (1997), *Eyes Wide Shut* (1999), *Quills* (2000) and *Charlie and the Chocolate Factory* (2005). **Hammer credits:** *Countess Dracula* (1971 [uncredited])

### Walden, Sandra (Shandra)

This child actress played a little girl in the Hammer short *A Man on the Beach* (1956). Her other credits include *The Million Pound Note* (1953), *Trouble in the Glen* (1954) and *Next to No Time* (1958), plus episodes of *The Ambermere Treasure* (1955–1956), *Dixon of Dock Green* (1955–1976, TV) and *Those Kids* (1956, TV). **Hammer credits:** *A Man on the Beach* (1956, as Little girl [uncredited])

### Walder, Ernst

This Austrian actor (1927–) appeared as the count's chauffeur in the Hammer comedy *A Weekend with Lulu* (1961). His other credits include *The Safecracker* (1958), *Joey Boy* (1965), *Darling* (1965), *The Quiller Memorandum* (1966), *The Double Man* (1968), *Guns in the Heather* (1968), *Joby* (1975, TVM), *Atom Spies* (1979, TVM) and *Night of the Fox* (1990, TVM), plus episodes of *The Four Just Men* (1959–1960, TV), *Coronation Street* (1960–, TV), *Paul Temple* (1969–1971, TV) and *The Fourth Arm* (1983, TV). **Hammer credits:** *A Weekend with Lulu* (1961, as Count's chauffeur)

### Walder, Lolly

Walder (real name Lorette Walder, aka Lollie Walder) worked as the continuity girl on Hammer's *Creatures the World Forgot* (1971). Her other credits include *The Cape Town Affair* (1967), *The Jackals* (1967), *Staal Burger* (1969), *Die Vervlakste*

*Tweeling* (1969), *Shangani Patrol* (1970) and *Erfgenaam* (1970). She also worked as a production manager on *Lost in the Desert* (1969) and *My Way* (1970). **Hammer credits:** *Creatures the World Forgot* (1971)

### Waldhorn, Gary

This British actor (1943–) can be seen in a supporting role in *Carpathian Eagle* (1980, TV [episode of *Hammer House of Horror*]). A TV regular, he is best known for playing Lionel Bainbridge in the sitcom *Brush Strokes* (1986–1991, TV). His other TV credits include *And the Wall Came Tumbling Down* (1984, TVM [episode of *Hammer House of Horror*]), plus episodes of *Armchair Theatre* (1956–1974, TV), *Seven Faces of Woman* (1974, TV), *Brideshead Revisited* (1981, TV) and *The Vicar of Dibley* (1994–2007, TV), in which he played David Horton. His film credits take in *Zeppelin* (1971), *Hanover Street* (1979) and *The Chain* (1984). Also on stage in the West End and on tour. **Hammer credits:** *Carpathian Eagle* (1980, TV [episode of *Hammer House of Horror*], as Bacharach), *And the Wall Came Tumbling Down* (1984, TVM [episode of *Hammer House of Horror*], as Inspector Crane)

### Walker, Bruce

This British actor (1905–1973, full name Reginald John Bruce Walker) played Dick Barton's loyal sidekick Snowey White in Hammer's second Barton adventure, *Dick Barton Strikes Back* (1949). He also had a minor role in *Dr. Morelle—The Case of the Missing Heiress* (1949). His other credits include *Third Time Lucky* (1948), *Brass Monkey* (1948), *Adam and Evelyne* (1949), *Cardboard Cavalier* (1949) and *A Man's Affair* (1949). **Additional notes:** George Ford played Snowey White in the first and third episodes in the Dick Barton series: *Dick Barton—Special Agent* (1948) and *Dick Barton at Bay* (1950). **Hammer credits:** *Dr. Morelle—The Case of the Missing Heiress* (1949, unnamed role [uncredited]), *Dick Barton Strikes Back* (1949, as Snowey White)

### Walker, Rudolph

This West Indian born actor (1939–) is best known for his roles in the sitcoms *Love Thy Neighbour* (1972–1976, TV), in which he played Bill Reynolds, and *The Thin Blue Line* (1995–1996, TV), in which he played PC Frank Gladstone, as well as the soap opera *EastEnders* (1985–, TV), in which he began appearing in 2001 as Patrick Trueman, going on to clock up over 1,000 episodes. His occasional films include Hammer's *The Witches* (1966), in which he played Mark, *10 Rillington Place* (1970), *Let Him Have It* (1991), *Bhaji on the Beach* (1993) and *The House of Angelo* (1997). He also appeared as Bill Reynolds in Hammer's big screen spin off of *Love Thy Neighbour* (1973), as well as *Man About the House* (1974), in which he made a gag cameo as himself. His other TV work includes episodes of *United* (1965–1967, TV), *Empire Road* (1979, TV) and *Black Silk* (1985, TV). He was awarded an OBE in 2006. **Additional notes:** Walker also appeared as Bill Reynolds in a 1972 edition of the TV comedy special *All Star Comedy Carnival* (1969–1973, TV). **Hammer** credits: *The Witches* (1966, as Mark [uncredited]), *Love Thy Neighbour* (1973, as Bill Reynolds), *Man About the House* (1974, as Himself)

## Walker, Zena

In films sporadically from 1960 with *Danger Tomorrow*, this RADA-trained British actress (1934–2003) spent the majority of her career on stage, having made her debut in 1950 (she went on to win a Tony for her performance in the Broadway version of *A Day in the Death of Joe Egg* in 1968). Her feature credits include *The Hellions* (1961), *Sammy Going South* (1963), *The Likely Lads* (1976) and *The Dresser* (1983). On television from 1956, her credits here include episodes of *Sword of Freedom* (1957, TV), *Albert and Victoria* (1970–1971, TV), *Man at the Top* (1970–1972, TV), *Jemima Shore Investigates* (1983, TV) and *Rosemary & Thyme* (2003–2006, TV), plus an episode of Hammer's *Journey to the Unknown* (1968, TV). Married three times, her first husband was actor Robert Urquhart (1921–1995), who appeared in Hammer's *The Curse of Frankenstein* (1957) and an episode of *Hammer House of Horror* (1980, TV). Her second husband was actor Julian Holloway (1944–), whom she married in 1971, and who re-voiced Horst Janson for Hammer's *Captain Kronos—Vampire Hunter* (1974). **Hammer credits:** *Girl of My Dreams* (1968, TV [episode of *Journey to the Unknown*], as Carrie Clark)

## Wallace House

Situated at 113, Wardour St. London, Wallace House was the home of Exclusive from 1937 (the company purchased the leasehold on 20 July 1937). The building was re-named Hammer House in 1947 in time for the trade show of the recently revived company's first post-war film, *Crime Reporter* (1947). It remains known as Hammer House to this day.

## Wallace, Claude

Wallace co-authored the story *The Kingdom of Zinga* with Dorothy Holloway, which was used as the basis for Hammer's Paul Robeson vehicle, *Song of Freedom* (1936). **Hammer credits:** *Song of Freedom* (1936)

## Wallace, Edna

This noted milliner designed the hats sported by Hy Hazel in Hammer's *Celia* (1949). Another of her creations, Honeybee, was meanwhile featured in the 1958 British Pathé short *Hats and Flowers*. **Hammer credits:** *Celia* (1949)

## Wallace, Hedger

In supporting roles, this British actor (1927–2000), full name Geoffrey Hedger Wallace) can be seen as Inspector Taylor in Hammer's *Visa to Canton* (1960). His other credits include *Double Bunk* (1961), *Dr. Terror's House of Horrors* (1965), *The Oblong Box* (1969) and *The Creeping Flesh* (1972), plus another turn for Hammer in *Nightmare* (1964). His TV work includes episodes of *Man in a Suitcase* (1967–1968, TV) and *Love for Lydia* (1977, TV). **Hammer credits:** *Visa to Canton* (1960, as Inspector Taylor), *Nightmare* (1964, as Sir Dudley)

## Wallis, Jacquie (Jacqueline/Jackie)

This British actress (1942–, real name Jacqueline Wall) is best known to Hammer fans for playing Sabena Ravna in *The Kiss of the Vampire* (1963). Prior to this she trained at London's Corona Stage Academy, during which she appeared in a handful of films, among them *Outcast of the Islands* (1951), *Lady Godiva Rides Again* (1951), *The Stranger Left No Card* (1952) and *The Story of Esther Costello* (1957), following which she moved to Pakistan for a period. She returned two years later and resumed her career with the Hammer classic. Recalled the actress of her performance in *The Kiss of the Vampire*, "I came to the role with a completely open mind. I hadn't read *Dracula*. But I have now! Once you get to know a little about human vampires and their history the whole subject fascinates."[1] Her occasional TV credits include episodes of *No Hiding Place* (1959–1967, TV), *Silent Evidence* (1962, TV), *Hugh and I* (1962–1967, TV) and *The Sentimental Agent* (1963, TV). **Hammer credits:** *The Kiss of the Vampire* (1963, as Sabena Ravna)

## Wallis, Peter

Wallis worked as a standby props man on Hammer's *Vampire Circus* (1972). His other credits as a props man include *Brazil* (1985), *The Princess Bride* (1987), *Memphis Belle* (1990), *GoldenEye* (1995), *Notting Hill* (1999), *The World Is Not Enough* (1999) and *Quills* (2000), plus episodes of *Inspector Morse* (1987–2000, TV). **Hammer credits:** *Vampire Circus* (1972 [uncredited])

## Walls, Tom

British born Walls (1912–1992) was one of Hammer's many second assistant directors, though he briefly graduated to first assistant for *The Snorkel* (1958). His other work as a first assistant includes *Seventy Deadly Pills* (1964) and *The Terrornauts* (1967). He also worked as an associate producer on *Birth of the Beatles* (1979). His father was actor Tom Walls (1883–1949). **Hammer credits:** *The Abominable Snowman* (1957, second assistant director [uncredited]), *The Camp on Blood Island* (1958, second assistant director [uncredited]), *Dracula* (1958, second assistant director [uncredited]), *The Snorkel* (1958, first assistant director), *The Revenge of Frankenstein* (1958, second assistant director [uncredited]), *Further Up the Creek* (1958, second assistant director [uncredited]), *I Only Arsked!* (1958, second assistant director [uncredited]), *The Hound of the Baskervilles* (1959, second assistant director [uncredited]), *The Ugly Duckling* (1959, second assistant director [uncredited]), *Yesterday's Enemy* (1959, second assistant director [uncredited]), *The Mummy* (1959, second assistant director [uncredited]), *The Man Who Could Cheat Death* (1959, second assistant director [uncredited]), *The Stranglers of Bombay* (1959, second assistant director [uncredited]), *Never Take Sweets from a Stranger* (1960, second assistant director [uncredited])

## Walmsley, Anna

Walmsley can be seen as Vera Barscynska in Hammer's *The Revenge of Frankenstein* (1958). Her other credits include episodes of *The Buccaneers*

(1956–1957, TV) and *Saber of London* (1954–1960, TV). **Hammer credits:** *The Revenge of Frankenstein* (1958, as Vera Barscynska)

## Walsh, Dermot

In films from 1946 with *Bedelia*, this Irish leading man (1924–2002, full name James P. Dermot Walsh) went on to become a regular feature in fifties films (surprisingly, he made none for Exclusive). His many credits include *Jassy* (1947), *Ghost Ship* (1952), *The Witness* (1959), *The Tell-Tale Heart* (1960), *Emergency* (1962) and *The Wicked Lady* (1983). However, from the mid-sixties he spent the majority of his time on stage, as well as occasionally on television. His credits here include episodes of *The Pursuers* (1961–1962, TV), *Richard the Lionheart* (1962–1963, TV), in which he played the title role, *Crane* (1963–1965, TV) and *Softly Softly* (1966–1976, TV). He also appeared in *Matakitas Is Coming*, an episode of Hammer's *Journey to the Unknown* (1968, TV), which also appears in the compendium film *Journey to the Unknown* (1969, TVM). Married three times, his first wife was the actress Hazel Court (1926–2008), to whom he was married from 1949 to 1963. She appeared in two films for Hammer: *The Curse of Frankenstein* (1957) and *The Man Who Could Cheat Death* (1959). Their daughter, Sally Walsh (1950–), also appeared in *The Curse of Frankenstein* (mother and daughter played the role of Elizabeth at different ages). His second wife was the actress Diana Scougall (1934–), to whom he was married between 1968 and 1974. His other daughter, by his third marriage, is the actress Elisabeth Dermot Walsh (1974–, real name Elisabeth Clare Louise Walsh). **Hammer credits:** *Matakitas Is Coming* (1968, TV [episode of *Journey to the Unknown*], as Ken Talbot), *Journey to the Unknown* (1969, TVM, as Ken Talbot)

## Walsh, Kay

One of the best loved yet, curiously, most undervalued stars of British cinema, Walsh (1911–2005, real name Kathleen Walsh) began her film career in 1934 with a small role in *How's Chances?* following experience as a dancer on stage. After further minor roles she was put under contract at Ealing, where she went on to co-star in two highly successful George Formby vehicles, *Keep Fit* (1937) and *I See Ice* (1938). However, it was her performance in the classic wartime drama *In Which We Serve* (1942) that secured her name. The film was co-directed (with Noel Coward) by her first husband (of two) David Lean (1908–1991), to whom Walsh was married between 1940 and 1949, and with whom she also went on to work on *This Happy Breed* (1944) and *Oliver Twist* (1948), playing Nancy in the latter. She also contributed to the script of Lean's acclaimed adaptation of *Great Expectations* (1946), which earned her a shared Oscar nomination. Her many other credits as an actress include *Last Holiday* (1950), *Stage Fright* (1950), *Cast a Dark Shadow* (1955), *A Study in Terror* (1965), *Taste of Excitement* (1969), *Scrooge* (1970), *The Ruling Class* (1972) and *Night Crossing* (1982).

She also played the newspaper reporter Stephanie Bax in Hammer's *The Witches* (1966), in which it is revealed (spoiler) that she is the leader of a coven during the climax. The film isn't one of Hammer's best, but Walsh invests the proceedings with energy whenever she's on screen ("Kay Walsh is excellent as the enigmatic journalist," praised *Variety*). The actress also popped up as Mrs. Walker, a landlady with curious nocturnal habits, in *The Last Visitor*, an episode of Hammer's *Journey to the Unknown* (1968, TV), which also appeared in the compendium film *Journey to the Unknown* (1969, TVM). Her other TV credits include episodes of *The Human Jungle* (1963–1964, TV), *Gideon's Way* (1965–1966, TV), *The Baron* (1966–1967, TV) and *Sherlock Holmes and Doctor Watson* (1980, TV), in which she played Mrs. Hudson. **Hammer credits:** *The Witches* (1966, as Stephanie Bax), *The Last Visitor* (1968, TV [episode of *Journey to the Unknown*], as Joan Walker), *Journey to the Unknown* (1969, TVM, as Joan Walker)

### Walsh, Percy

This British character actor (1888–1952) played the role of Professor Mitchell in Hammer's third Dick Barton adventure, *Dick Barton at Bay* (1950). His other films include *Enter the Queen* (1930), *The Man Who Knew Too Much* (1934), *Boys Will Be Boys* (1935), *King of the Damned* (1935), *Let George Do It* (1940), *Secret Mission* (1942), *The Guinea Pig* (1948) and *The Happiest Days of Your Life* (1950). Also on stage. **Hammer credits:** *Dick Barton at Bay* (1950, as Professor Mitchell)

### Walsh, Sally

The daughter of actor Dermot Walsh (1924–2002, full name James P. Dermot Walsh) and actress Hazel Court (1926–2008), British born Walsh (1950–) appeared briefly as the young Elizabeth in Hammer's *The Curse of Frankenstein* (1957); her mother played the role as an adult. Her father can be seen in *Matakitas Is Coming*, an episode of Hammer's *Journey to the Unknown* (1968, TV), which also appeared in the compendium film *Journey to the Unknown* (1969, TVM). Her mother also co-starred in Hammer's *The Man Who Could Cheat Death* (1959). Recalled Hazel Court of her daughter's appearance in *The Curse of Frankenstein*, "They wanted someone who looked like me to play me as a little girl, in one of the flashback scenes, so I suggested Sally. She hated it—*hated* being in it! I think it was all very foreign to her, and she didn't understand it. She still remembers it today, and still doesn't like it!"[2] Which would explain why Walsh made no further film appearances. **Hammer credits:** *The Curse of Frankenstein* (1957, as Young Elizabeth)

### Walter, Jean

Walter worked as the production secretary on Hammer's *The Legend of the 7 Golden Vampires* (1974). Shot in Hong Kong, it was filmed back-to-back with *Shatter* (1974), on which she also worked. Her other credits in this capacity include *The Slipper and the Rose* (1976), *The Boys from Brazil* (1978) and *Heat and Dust* (1983). She went on to become a production manager on such films as *The Chain* (1984), *Lost in London* (1985, TVM) and *The Second Victory* (1986). She was also an executive in charge of production on *The Lady and the Highwayman* (1989, TVM), and a production co-ordinator on *To Be the Best* (1992, TVM). **Hammer credits:** *The Legend of the 7 Golden Vampires* (1974), *Shatter* (1974)

### Walter, Olive

This British actress (1898–1961) had a minor supporting role in Hammer's *Celia* (1949). Her other credits include *The Blue Bird* (1910), *Meet Sexton Blake* (1945), *Take My Life* (1947) and *Stop Press Girl* (1949), plus such early teleplays as *Glorious Morning* (1938, TV) and *The Monkey's Paw* (1939, TV). **Hammer credits:** *Celia* (1949, as Woman in shop [uncredited])

### Walters, Justin

Walters played the young lycanthrope Leon in Hammer's *The Curse of the Werewolf* (1961). The older version was played by the film's star, Oliver Reed. Commented *Variety* of the boy's performance, "There is a restrained portrayal of the budding lycanthrope as a lad by young Justin Walters." His other credits include episodes of *The Idiot* (1966, TV). **Hammer credits:** *The Curse of the Werewolf* (1961, as Leon as a child)

### Walters, M.

This British camera technician worked as the camera grip on the Hammer comedy *A Weekend with Lulu* (1961). **Hammer credits:** *A Weekend with Lulu* (1961 [uncredited])

### Walters, Thorley

Adept at fussy and slightly befuddled roles, this always-welcome British comedy character actor (1913–1991) began his film career in 1935 with *Once in a New Moon*, prior to which he had gained experience on stage, including a period at The Old Vic. His subsequent credits take in over seventy films, among them *The Love Test* (1935), *The Reverse Be My Lot* (1937), *Waltz Time* (1945), *Private's Progress* (1956), *Blue Murder at St. Trinian's* (1957), *Two-Way Stretch* (1960), *The Pure Hell of St. Trinian's* (1960), *Rotten to the Core* (1965), *Oh! What a Lovely War* (1969), *Young Winston* (1972), *The Adventure of Sherlock Holmes' Smarter Brother* (1975) and *The Little Drummer Girl* (1984). However, to Hammer fans, he is best remembered for cherished performances in some of the company's best-regarded horror films, among them *Dracula—Prince of Darkness* (1966), in which he played the fly-eating Ludwig, a variation on the book's Renfield character.

His association with the studio began in 1959 with the wartime comedy *Don't Panic Chaps* in which he played Lieutenant Percy Brown. He then went on to appear in key roles in *Frankenstein Created Woman* (1967), in which he played the Baron's somewhat vague assistant Dr. Hertz, *Frankenstein Must Be Destroyed* (1969), in which he was the easily-irritated Inspector Frisch, and *Vampire Circus* (1972), in which he played the doddery burgermeister [*sic*]. Recalled the actor of Hammer, "I think that the standard Hammer Horrors—looking back on them—were of a high quality, and they've really proved their worth in that people still want to look at them today…. Hammer had built a very high reputation for what they produced."[3]

Walters' TV work includes episodes of *Espionage* (1963–1964, TV), *Misleading Cases* (1967–1974, TV), *The Lotus Eaters* (1972, TV), *Strangers* (1978–1982, TV) and *Minder* (1979–1994, TV). **Hammer credits:** *Don't Panic Chaps* (1959, as Lieutenant Percy Brown), *The Phantom of the Opera* (1962, as Lattimer), *Dracula—Prince of Darkness* (1966, as Ludwig), *Frankenstein Created Woman* (1967, as Dr. Hertz), *Frankenstein Must Be Destroyed* (1969, as Inspector Frisch), *Vampire Circus* (1972, as Peter/Burgermeister [*sic*])

### Walton, Brian

Walton played one of the journalists in Hammer's *Quatermass and the Pit* (1967). His other credits include episodes of *Softly Softly* (1966–1976, TV), *The Fellows* (1967, TV) and *Angels* (1975–1983, TV), plus stage work. **Hammer credits:** *Quatermass and the Pit* (1967, as Journalist [uncredited])

### Walton, Joseph *see* Losey, Joseph

### Walton Studios (aka Nettleford Studios/Hepworth Studios)

This British studio dates back to 1899, when British producer, director and pioneer Cecil Hepworth leased a house in Walton-on-Thames and turned it into a production facility known as Hepworth Studios, from whence he made such brief "actualities" as *The Ladies' Tortoise Race* (1899) and *Procession of Prize Cattle* (1899). Trick films, such as *The Egg-Laying Man* (1900) and *The Eccentric Dancer* (1900) followed, while in 1903 he filmed an adaptation of *Alice in Wonderland*. The hugely successful *Rescued by Rover* appeared in 1905, along with the first of the popular *Tilly* comedies. By this time the studio had expanded, and was soon the home of such literary adaptations as *Oliver Twist* (1912), *David Copperfield* (1913) and *The Vicar of Wakefield* (1913). This literary approach continued well into the twenties with the likes of *Barnaby Rudge* (1915) and *Comin' Thro the Rye* (1916), a remake of which also appeared in 1923. Following Hepworth's bankruptcy in 1923, the studio was sold on to Archibald Nettlefold in 1926, after whom it was renamed. It then played host to a number of low budgeters and quota quickies, among them *Wait and See* (1928), *Two Crowded Hours* (1931), Hammer's *The Mystery of the Mary Celeste* (1935), *Old Mother Riley in Paris* (1938) and *Somewhere in England* (1940). The Ministry of Works commandeered the studio in 1940 for the duration of the war, following which it was acquired by Ernest G. Roy in 1947. In the fifties it played host to such productions as *The Sleeping Tiger* (1954), *Dance Little Lady* (1954) and the Hammer/ACT Films co-production *Don't Panic Chaps* (1959), plus such TV series as *The Adventures of Robin Hood* (1955–1960, TV), by which time it had been acquired by Sapphire Films (the company behind the Robin Hood series), which, in 1955, re-named it yet again as Walton Studios. The facility finally closed its doors in 1961 and was demolished soon afterwards. **Hammer credits:** *The Mystery of the Mary Celeste* (1935), *Don't Panic Chaps* (1959)

## Wang, Chiang

Wang had a supporting role in Hammer's *The Legend of the 7 Golden Vampires* (1974). His other credits include *Xiao sha xing* (1970), *The Lizard* (1972), *The Drug Addicts* (1974), *The Invincible Armour* (1977) and *The Swordsman* (1981). **Hammer credits:** *The Legend of the 7 Golden Vampires* (1974, unnamed role [uncredited])

## Warbeck, David

Following training at RADA, this New Zealand born actor (1941–1997, real name David Mitchell) began appearing in films and on television in minor roles, among his early credits being *Do Me a Favor and Kill Me*, an episode of Hammer's *Journey to the Unknown* (1968, TV), which also appeared in the compendium film *Journey to Murder* (1972, TVM). It looked like he'd gotten his big break when cast as Robin Hood in *Wolfshead: The Legend of Robin Hood* (1969), which was subsequently acquired by Hammer, but the featurette (a failed TV pilot) was not shown in cinemas until 1973. However, by this time Warbeck had started to appear in other films, among them *Trog* (1970) and Hammer's *Twins of Evil* (1971), in which he played the schoolmaster Anton Hoffer, and in which he was directed by John Hough, who had helmed *Wolfshead*. Warbeck went on to work in both Europe and America, becoming something of a cult favorite in the process, among his many credits being *A Fistful of Dynamite* (1971), *Blacksnake* (1973), *Craze* (1973), *The Sex Thief* (1973), *The Beyond* (1981), *The Black Cat* (1981), *Lassiter* (1983), *Miami Horror* (1984), *Breakfast with Dracula: A Vampire in Miami* (1993) and *Razor Blade Smile* (1998). He was also considered for the role of James Bond. His TV work includes episodes of *Spy Trap* (1972–1975, TV), *Thriller* (1973–1976, TV) and *Minder* (1979–1994, TV). Remembered Warbeck of his time on *Twins of Evil*, "Oh, the twins. They were so gorgeous…. They were such sweet kids, they would walk around starkers all the time, completely unselfconscious. It was one of those films where we couldn't wait to get to the set and we used to watch just about everyone else's shots. It was great fun to do, with lots of gags and dear old Peter Cushing."[4] **Hammer credits:** *Do Me a Favor and Kill Me* (1968, TV [episode of *Journey to the Unknown*], as Chris), *Wolfshead: The Legend of Robin Hood* (1969 [released 1973], as Robert of Locksley/Robin Hood), *Twins of Evil* (1971, as Anton Hoffer), *Journey to Murder* (1972, TVM, as Chris)

## Ward, Derek

Ward can be seen as a hunter in Hammer's *Creatures the World Forgot* (1971). He went on to become an editor in South Africa, working on such films as *Tigers Don't Cry* (1976), *Deadly Passion* (1985) and *Alec to the Rescue* (1999). **Hammer credits:** *Creatures the World Forgot* (1971, as Hunter [uncredited])

## Ward, Dervis

This British (Welsh) actor (1923–1996) played the lorry driver who tries it on with Olinka Berova's Carol at the top of Hammer's *The Vengeance of She* (1968). His other credits include *Private Angelo* (1949), *Timeslip* (1956), *Gorgo* (1960), *Deadlier Than the Male* (1966), *To Sir, with Love* (1967), *Dead Cert* (1974) and *The Prince and the Pauper* (1977), plus a return to Hammer for *Mutiny on the Buses* (1972). His TV work includes episodes of *Adventures of a Jungle Boy* (1957, TV), *For Amusement Only* (1968, TV) and *The Protectors* (1972–1973, TV). **Hammer credits:** *The Vengeance of She* (1968, as Lorry driver), *Mutiny on the Buses* (1972, as Angry passenger)

## Ward, Lalla

Best known for playing Romana in *Doctor Who* (1963–1989, TV) between 1979 and 1981 (a role she inherited from Mary Tamm), this British actress (1951–, real name Sarah Ward) has appeared in only a handful of films. She trained at the Central School of Speech and Drama, and soon after leaving made her big screen debut with Hammer's *Vampire Circus* (1972) in which she played the acrobat Helga. Recalled the actress of her role, "Because mine was a small part and dotted about in the film I was called pretty much every day for the five weeks or so shoot at Pinewood Studios, which couldn't have been more fortunate for a first film. The endless hanging about afforded wonderful opportunities to watch and learn and hang out with people who would teach me things."[5] Ward's other credits include *England Made Me* (1972), *Rosebud* (1975) and *The Prince and the Pauper* (1977). She was considered for the role of Catherine Beddows in Hammer's *To the Devil a Daughter* (1976), as well as the role of Karen, but the latter part was cut during the lengthy scripting process. Her other TV work includes episodes of *Dr. Finlay's Casebook* (1962–1971, TV), *The Duchess of Duke Street* (1976–1977, TV) and *Schoolgirl Chums* (1982, TV). Her father was the Viscount Bangor (1905–1993, formerly the Honorable Edward Ward), who was a BBC war correspondent during World Ward II, and her mother was documentary producer and authoress Marjorie Banks (?–1991, later Viscountess Bangor), thus making Ward The Honorable Sarah Ward (her half brother William [1948–] is the current eighth Viscount Bangor). Her grandmother was illustrator Mary Ward (1827–1869), who was the first person to be killed in a motor vehicle accident. Her first husband was her *Doctor Who* co-star Tom Baker (1934–, full name Thomas Stewart Baker), to whom she was married between 1980 and 1982. Her second husband is the writer, presenter and evolutionary biologist Professor Richard Dawkins (1941–, full name Clinton Richard Dawkins), whom she married in 1991, and whose books she occasionally illustrates. Her own books include *Beastly Knits* (1985). She now works primarily as a textile artist. **Hammer credits:** *Vampire Circus* (1972, as Helga)

## Ward, Lawrence

This British actor (1929–2011, real name Michael Ronald Ward, aka Michael Ward) had a supporting role in Hammer's *The Last Page* (1952). His other credits include *Finishing School* (1953) and *Mad About Men* (1954). Working as Michael Ward, he also enjoyed a successful career as a photographer, notably with the *Sunday Times*. Married five times, his second wife was actress Susan Stephen (1931–2000), to whom he was married between 1952 and 1956. She appeared in two films for Hammer: *Stolen Face* (1952) and *The House Across the Lake* (1954). His fifth wife was actress Elizabeth Seal (1933–), whom he married in 1976, and who appeared in Hammer's *Vampire Circus* (1972). **Hammer credits:** *The Last Page* (1952, as Larry)

## Ward, Mackenzie

This British actor (1903–1976) can be spotted in the role of Ashcroft in the Hammer co-feature *The Dark Road* (1948). His other credits include *Syncopation* (1929), *Sons of the Sea* (1939), *Kipps* (1941), *The Happiest Days of Your Life* (1950) and a return to Hammer for a brief appearance as a businessman in *The Two Faces of Dr. Jekyll* (1960), which was his last film appearance. His occasional TV credits include versions of *The Importance of Being Earnest* (1946, TV) and *Rebecca* (1947, TV). **Hammer credits:** *The Dark Road* (1948, as Ashcroft), *The Two Faces of Dr. Jekyll* (1960, as Businessman [uncredited])

## Ward, Michael

Always a welcome face, this fey British character comedian (1909–1997, real name George William Everard Yoe Ward) began his stage career in rep in the early forties following experience as a tutor, and went on to study at the Central School of Speech and Drama. He broke into films in 1947 with *An Ideal Husband*, and went on to make many supporting/cameo appearances in such wide-ranging films as *Trio* (1950), *Private's Progress* (1956), *I'm All Right Jack* (1959), *Smashing Time* (1967) and *Revenge of the Pink Panther* (1978). He also made five *Carry Ons*, including *Carry On Cabby* (1963) and *Carry On Screaming* (1966), while his work for Hammer included appearances in *What the Butler Saw* (1950) and *Frankenstein and the Monster from Hell* (1974). His TV appearances include episodes of *The Adventures of Aggie* (1956–1957, TV), *Sykes* (1972–1979, TV) and *Rising Damp* (1974–1978, TV). **Hammer credits:** *What the Butler Saw* (1950, as Gerald), *Whispering Smith Hits London* (1952, as Receptionist clerk), *The Ugly Duckling* (1959, as Pasco), *Frankenstein and the Monster from Hell* (1974, as Transvest), *Man About the House* (1974, as Gideon)

## Ward, Simon

Following a brief appearance in *If….* (1968), this British leading man (1941–2012) got his big break in Hammer's *Frankenstein Must Be Destroyed* (1969), in which he played Dr. Karl Holst, who finds himself coerced into helping Frankenstein with a brain transplant ("I thought the world had seen the last of you!" Holst exclaims upon discovering the Baron's identity). Following further appearances in *I Start Counting* (1969) and *Quest for Love* (1971), Ward got an even bigger break when he was cast in the leading role of the epic biopic *Young Winston* (1972), which earned him a BAFTA nomination as best newcomer. In demand for the rest of the seventies, his subsequent credits include *The Three Musketeers* (1973), *Dracula* (1973, TVM), *All Creatures Great and Small* (1974), *The Four Musketeers* (1974), *Aces High* (1976) and *The Four*

*Feathers* (1978, TVM), though from the eighties onwards his film appearances were rarer, among them *The Monster Club* (1980), *Supergirl* (1984), *Double X: The Name of the Game* (1992) and *Nightshade* (1995, TVM). However, he remained active on stage and television. In 1974, Hammer had hoped to feature Ward and James Mason in a film titled *The Experiment*, but the production collapsed just two weeks before shooting was scheduled to start. His television appearances include episodes of *The World of Wooster* (1965–1967, TV), *Roads to Freedom* (1970, TV), *A Taste for Death* (1988, TV), *Kurtulus* (1994, TV), in which he again played Churchill, *Judge John Deed* (2001–2007, TV), in which he played Sir Monty Everard, and *The Tudors* (2007–2010, TV), in which he played Bishop Gardiner. His daughter is the actress Sophie Ward (1964–). **Hammer credits:** *Frankenstein Must Be Destroyed* (1969, as Dr. Karl Holst)

**Veronica Carlson and Simon Ward share a tender moment in *Frankenstein Must Be Destroyed* (1969) (Hammer/Warner Bros./Seven Arts/Warner Pathé).**

### Wardle, Margot

Wardle worked as a production secretary on Hammer's *The Ugly Duckling* (1959). **Hammer credits:** *The Ugly Duckling* (1959 [uncredited])

### Ware, James

Ware can be seen as a reporter in Hammer's *That's Your Funeral* (1973), in which he and his interviewees inadvertently get stoned on pot. His other credits include episodes of *The Adventures of Don Quick* (1970, TV), *The Adventurer* (1972–1973, TV), *The Pathfinders* (1972–1973, TV) and *Clayhanger* (1976, TV). **Hammer credits:** *That's Your Funeral* (1973, as Reporter)

### Wark, Victor

Following the departure of Arthur Barnes in 1952, Wark (1913–1993), along with John Green, took over as production managers upon Hammer's permanent return to Down Place, sharing out the various films between themselves for a period.

Wark's other credits in this capacity include *Trottie True* (1949), *Last Holiday* (1950), *The Rainbow Jacket* (1954) and *Stolen Assignment* (1955). He also worked as a location manager on *Uncle Silas* (1947), and as a second assistant director on *Brief Encounter* (1945) and *Great Expectations* (1946). His credits as a director include *Foxhunter: Champion Jumper* (1953), *Smithfield Market* (1961) and *Portrait of a Horsewoman* (1963). **Hammer credits:** *Mantrap* (1953), *Four Sided Triangle* (1953), *Spaceways* (1953)

### Warne, Jo

British born Warne (1938–2017) can be seen in a minor role in *The House That Bled to Death* (1980, TV [episode of *Hammer House of Horror*]). Her many other television credits include episodes of *Follyfoot* (1971–1973, TV), *Spring and Autumn* (1972–1976, TV), in which she played Betty Harris, *Within These Walls* (1974–1978, TV) and *Westbeach* (1993, TV). She also played Peggy Mitchell in *EastEnders* (1985–, TV) in 1991; the role was later taken over by Barbara Windsor, who played the part between 1994 and 2016. Warne's occasional film credits include *Nutcracker* (1982), *Little Dorrit* (1988) and *Consuming Passions* (1988). **Hammer credits:** *The House That Bled to Death* (1980, TV [episode of *Hammer House of Horror*], as First mother)

### Warner, Anthony

Warner can be spotted as a pageboy in Hammer's *Whispering Smith Hits London* (1952). His other credits include an episode of *Emil and the Detectives* (1952, TV). **Hammer credits:** *Whispering Smith Hits London* (1952, as Pageboy)

### Warner, Jack

On stage from the early twenties as a comedian, and in films from 1943 with *The Dummy Talks*, this much-liked British character star (1895–1981, real name Horace John Waters) came to prominence well into middle age in the comedy *Holiday Camp* (1947), in which he played family man Joe Huggett. A major success in Britain, the film spawned three sequels—*Here Come the Huggetts* (1948), *Vote for Huggett* (1949) and *The Huggetts Abroad* (1949)—as well as a long-running radio series. Warner had an even greater success playing the role of copper George Dixon in the crime drama *The Blue Lamp* (1949). Although his character was shot dead at the end of the film, he was nevertheless revived for a television series, *Dixon of Dock Green*, which ran for an incredible twenty-one years between 1955 and 1976, by which time Warner was 82, earning himself the nickname of "world's oldest copper."

Although in over thirty films—among them *The Captive Heart* (1946), *Hue and Cry* (1947), *Train of Events* (1949) and *Forbidden Cargo* (1954)—Warner made only a handful more big screen appearances once his television series was up and running. Prime among these was Hammer's *The Quatermass Xperiment* (1955), in which he played another copper, Inspector Lomax, who helps scientist Bernard Quatermass track down a space monster using nothing more than good old fash-

ioned detective work and a solid helping of homespun humor (comments the God-fearing Lomax of Quatermass's bid to conquer space, "One world at a time's good enough for me!").

Unfortunately, owing to television commitments, Warner didn't return for *Quatermass 2* (1957), and the role of Lomax, now played by John Longden, was noticeably downsized. Warner's remaining films following his sole Hammer outing were *The Ladykillers* (1955), *Home and Away* (1956), *Now and Forever* (1956), *Carve Her Name with Pride* (1957), *Jigsaw* (1962) and *Dominique* (1978). His sisters were the stage and radio comediennes Elsie Waters (1893–1990, full name Florence Elsie Waters) and Doris Waters (1904–1978), who were known for playing two Cockney chars called Gert and Daisy. **Hammer credits:** *The Quatermass Xperiment* (1955, as Inspector Lomax)

### Warner, Patricia

Warner can be seen as one of the schoolgirls in Hammer's *Lust for a Vampire* (1971). **Hammer credits:** *Lust for a Vampire* (1971, as Schoolgirl)

### Warner, Richard

This British actor (1911–1989) played the supporting role of Cyril in Hammer's romantic melodrama *To Have and to Hold* (1951). He also popped up as Edgar in *The Shadow of the Cat* (1961) and as Inspector Barrani (Azi in the first draft script) in *The Mummy's Shroud* (1967). His many other credits include *Golden Arrow* (1949), *The Square Peg* (1959), *Village of the Damned* (1960), *Give a Dog a Bone* (1967), *Mary, Queen of Scots* (1971) and *Dream Demon* (1988), plus episodes of everything from *The Railway Children* (1951, TV), in which he played Perks, to *Miracles Take Longer* (1984, TV). **Hammer credits:** *To Have and to Hold* (1951, as Cyril), *The Shadow of the Cat* (1961, as Edgar), *The Mummy's Shroud* (1967, as Inspector Barrani)

### Warner Brothers (Warner Bros.–Seven Arts/Warner Pathé/Warner Pathé Distributors [WPD]/WEA Records, Ltd.)

Founded in 1923 by the Warner brothers Albert, Harry M., Sam and Jack L., this Hollywood studio became a major player following the success of the first sound features, *Don Juan* (1926), which had a synchronized score, and *The Jazz Singer* (1927), which had songs and fragments of dialogue. Noted for its musicals and gangster thrillers in the thirties, the company has produced many classics down the decades, among them such best picture Oscar winners as *Casablanca* (1942), *My Fair Lady* (1964), *Driving Miss Daisy* (1989) and *Unforgiven* (1992).

In 1956, Warner Bros. began an association with Hammer involving the distribution of certain films in America, the first of these being *X—The Unknown* (1956), which it held back so as to double-bill it with *The Curse of Frankenstein* (1957), in which the studio had invested care of Eliot Hyman; the company also handled the latter film's worldwide distribution, releasing it in WarnerColor in the U.S. (the film was originally shot in Eastmancolor, in which process it was released in the UK). Investment in further Hammer films followed.

Warner also released further Hammer films Stateside, among them *The Abominable Snowman* (1957), while its subsidiary distribution company Warner-Pathé handled the UK release of *Hell Is a City* (1960) and several other productions.

In 1963, Warner Bros. bought 37.5 percent of ABPC, which had strong ties with Hammer. The sixties also saw Warner Bros. merge with Seven Arts, which was run by Eliot Hyman's son Kenneth. Consequently, Seven-Arts became involved in the partial financing of Hammer's *She* (1965) and *One Million Years B.C.* (1966). In 1967, Seven Arts bought out Warner Bros. in a deal worth $125m. This led to a new five-picture production deal between Hammer and Warner Bros./Seven-Arts.

Warner Bros./Seven Arts was in turn taken over by the Kinney Corporation in 1969, selling its share in ABPC to EMI in the process. Now run by Ted Ashley, co-production budgets with Hammer were tightened, and sights aimed at sure-fire box office winners, for which read more Dracula sequels. However, this didn't prevent Warner from turning down the offer to either finance or distribute *The Horror of Frankenstein* (1970) and *Scars of Dracula* (1970), both of which were subsequently made and distributed in the UK by EMI and handled in the U.S. by Continental, though an old, forgotten about contract signed prior to the making of *Dracula Has Risen from the Grave* (1968), giving Warners the right to either sanction or distribute any subsequent Dracula or Frankenstein films, caused Hammer a few headaches during this period.

However, Warners were back for *Dracula A.D. 1972* (1972) and its follow up *The Satanic Rites of Dracula* (1974), both of which they invested in and released under the Columbia-Warner banner, though neither set the box office alight (the latter film was actually sold on to Dynamite Entertainment for release in the U.S.). In 1971 Warner Bros. had been linked to another Dracula project titled *Kali: Devil Bride of Dracula*, an Indian slant on the story that was to have made use of trapped rupees in that country. The project was announced again in 1974 following the release of *The Legend of the 7 Golden Vampires* (1974), the UK distribution of which Warners took over from Avco Embassy (again a by product of the old contract giving Warners the right to either sanction or distribute any subsequent Dracula or Frankenstein films), but the idea was dropped following that film's box office failure, by which time Warner Bros. had in any case extricated its rupees by other means (note that Warners also distributed—via WEA Records, Ltd.—the album version of *The Legend of the 7 Golden Vampires* [1974, LP], which coincided with the release of the film). The studio was also approached by Hammer to help finance *To the Devil a Daughter* (1976), but turned the offer down.

In 1989 Warners again merged, this time with Time Inc., becoming Time-Warner. In 1993, in association with Donner/Shuler Donner, the company announced a deal with Hammer to remake a number of the studio's back catalogue, among them *Stolen Face* (1952), *The Quatermass Xperiment* (1955), *Quatermass and the Pit* (1967) and *The Devil Rides Out* (1968), along with such new titles as *Hideous Whispers* (based upon the novel *The Hiss* by Andrew Laurence). Sadly, despite all the talk of a Hammer revival, nothing came of the deal. **Hammer credits:** *X—The Unknown* (1956), *The Curse of Frankenstein* (1957), *The Abominable Snowman* (1957), *Hell Is a City* (1960), *Sands of the Desert* (1960), *The Scarlet Blade* (1963), *She* (1965), *The Brigand of Kandahar* (1965), *The Nanny* (1965), *Dracula—Prince of Darkness* (1966), *The Plague of the Zombies* (1966), *Rasputin—The Mad Monk* (1966), *The Reptile* (1966), *The Witches* (1966), *One Million Years B.C.* (1966), *The Viking Queen* (1967), *Frankenstein Created Woman* (1967), *The Mummy's Shroud* (1967), *Quatermass and the Pit* (1967), *A Challenge for Robin Hood* (1967), *The Anniversary* (1968), *The Vengeance of She* (1968), *The Devil Rides Out* (1968), *Slave Girls* (1968), *The Lost Continent* (1968), *Dracula Has Risen from the Grave* (1968), *Frankenstein Must Be Destroyed* (1969), *Moon Zero Two* (1969), *Crescendo* (1970), *Taste the Blood of Dracula* (1970), *When Dinosaurs Ruled the Earth* (1970), *Dracula A.D. 1972* (1972), *The Satanic Rites of Dracula* (1974), *The Legend of the 7 Golden Vampires* (1974), *The Legend of the 7 Golden Vampires* (1974, LP)

## Warnercolor

This "in-house" color process was actually a franchised trade name for Eastmancolor, and was used by Warner Bros. for several films in the fifties, among them the U.S. releases of Hammer's *The Curse of Frankenstein* (1957) and *Dracula* (1958). Both had in any case been shot in on Eastmancolor stock. **Hammer credits:** *The Curse of Frankenstein* (1957), *Dracula* (1958)

## Warner-Pathé Distributors (WPD)

Created in 1956 by Warner Brothers as a distribution arm for Associated British Picture Corporation, into which the studio had been investing heavily since 1940, this British distribution company handled many films on behalf of Hammer in the sixties, especially after the company's closer production ties with ABPC following a deal in 1963. In 1969 Warner Bros. sold its share in ABPC to EMI. **Hammer credits:** *Hell Is a City* (1960), *Sands of the Desert* (1960), *The Scarlet Blade* (1963), *She* (1965), *The Brigand of Kandahar* (1965), *The Nanny* (1965), *Dracula—Prince of Darkness* (1966), *The Plague of the Zombies* (1966), *Rasputin—The Mad Monk* (1966), *The Reptile* (1966), *The Witches* (1966), *One Million Years B.C.* (1966), *The Viking Queen* (1967), *Frankenstein Created Woman* (1967), *The Mummy's Shroud* (1967), *Quatermass and the Pit* (1967), *A Challenge for Robin Hood* (1967), *The Anniversary* (1968), *The Vengeance of She* (1968), *The Devil Rides Out* (1968), *Slave Girls* (1968), *The Lost Continent* (1968), *Dracula Has Risen from the Grave* (1968), *Frankenstein Must Be Destroyed* (1969), *Moon Zero Two* (1969), *Crescendo* (1970), *Taste the Blood of Dracula* (1970)

## Warr, Ron

Warr worked as the unit driver for the Hammer thriller *Maniac* (1963). **Hammer credits:** *Maniac* (1963 [uncredited])

## Warren, Adele

Warren can be seen as the tassel-twirling stripper Mimi La Vere in Hammer's *Nearest and Dearest* (1973). **Hammer credits:** *Nearest and Dearest* (1973, as Mimi La Vere [stripper])

## Warren, Anthony

This supporting actor played a German in the Hammer war drama *The Steel Bayonet* (1957). **Hammer credits:** *The Steel Bayonet* (1957, as German [uncredited])

## Warren, Barry

This RADA-trained British actor (1933–1994) is best remembered by Hammer fans for playing Carl Ravna in *The Kiss of the Vampire* (1963). He returned to Hammer for two further films: *The Devil-Ship Pirates* (1964), in which he had a memorable sword fight with Christopher Lee, and *Frankenstein Created Woman* (1967), in which he played one of a trio of toffs who come to regret their loutish behavior. Recalled first assistant director Bert Batt of Warren's sword fight with Lee in *The Devil-Ship Pirates*, "I can still see Christopher struggling manfully through the sword fight. He was quite deft with a sword, but his actor opponent [Warren] ... was not. His accuracy at finding Christopher's knuckles with his blade was first class, however. Mr. Lee left the studio that evening in a not particularly good mood, with his right hand smothered with sticking plasters."[6]

Warren's other credits include *Lawrence of Arabia* (1962) and *Do You Know This Voice?* (1964), while his TV work takes in episodes of *Mary Barton* (1964, TV), *Out of the Unknown* (1965–1971, TV), *The Protectors* (1972–1973, TV), *New Scotland Yard* (1972–1974, TV) and *Lovejoy* (1986–1994, TV). **Hammer credits:** *The Kiss of the Vampire* (1963, as Carl Ravna), *The Devil-Ship Pirates* (1964, as Manuel), *Frankenstein Created Woman* (1967, as Karl)

## Warren, John

Working with Val Guest and Len Heath, this British screenwriter (1916–1977, real name Jack Warner) co-authored the scripts for the Hammer comedies *Up the Creek* (1958) and its sequel, *Further Up the Creek* (1958), which no doubt made use of his wartime experiences in the Royal Navy. His other credits include *Life Is a Circus* (1960), *Two-Way Stretch* (1960), *Operation Snatch* (1962) and *The Wrong Arm of the Law* (1962), all of which were written with Len Heath. Warren also played the role of Cooky in both the *Creek* films, and appeared in minor roles in three further films for Hammer. His other credits as an actor include *The Mark of Cain* (1947), *Up for the Cup* (1950), *Police Dog* (1955), *A Night to Remember* (1958) and *Free Love Confidential* (1968), plus a series of commercials for Surf washing powder in the fifties. **Hammer credits:** *A Case for PC 49* (1951, as Coffee Dan), *Stolen Face* (1952, as Railway guard), *36 Hours* (1953, as Clerk [uncredited]), *Up the Creek* (1958, as Cooky, also co-screenplay), *Further Up the Creek* (1958, as Cooky, also co-screenplay)

## Warren, Kenneth J. (John)

In Britain from 1959, this Australian stage actor

(1929–1973) also made a handful of films, among them *I Was Monty's Double* (1958), *The Criminal* (1960), *Life for Ruth* (1962), *Leo the Last* (1969) and *The Creeping Flesh* (1972). He also had a small role in *Paper Dolls*, an episode of Hammer's *Journey to the Unknown* (1968, TV), which also appeared in the compendium film *Journey into Darkness* (1968, TVM). He also appeared in one theatrical feature for the company. His many TV credits include episodes of *A Tale of Two Cities* (1957, TV), *The World of Tim Frazer* (1960–1961, TV), *Mystery and Imagination* (1966, TV) and *Special Branch* (1969–1974, TV). His son is the actor Damian Warren. **Hammer credits:** *Paper Dolls* (1968, TV [episode of *Journey to the Unknown*], as Joe Blake), *Journey into Darkness* (1968, TVM, as Joe Blake), *Demons of the Mind* (1972, as Klaus)

### Warren, Yvonne *see* Romain, Yvonne

### Warrington, Bill

A shared Oscar winner for his work on *The Guns of Navarone* (1961), the many other credits of this British effects technician (1910–1981) include *Number Seventeen* (1932), on which he worked as a model maker, *In Which We Serve* (1942), *The October Man* (1947), *The Net* (1953), *Ill Met by Moonlight* (1956), *Carve Her Name with Pride* (1958), *A Night to Remember* (1958), *The Heroes of Telemark* (1965), *The Desperados* (1969), *Gold* (1974), *Journey Into Fear* (1975), *Wombling Free* (1977) and *Raiders of the Lost Ark* (1981), plus episodes of the TV series *Danger UXB* (1979, TV). He also headed the effects team for Hammer's second Quatermass film and was involved with several other projects for the studio. **Hammer credits:** *Quatermass 2* (1957), *Yesterday's Enemy* (1959 [uncredited]), *The Mummy* (1959), *The Scarlet Blade* (1963 [uncredited]), *Quatermass and the Pit* (1967 [uncredited])

### Warrington, Kenneth

Warrington played the role of Frank Bevan in Hammer's second post-war production, *Death in High Heels* (1947). His other films include *Strange Cargo* (1936), *The Spy in Black* (1939), *Old Mother Riley at Home* (1945), *Beware of Pity* (1946), *The Silver Darlings* (1947) and *Elizabeth of Ladymead* (1948). **Hammer credits:** *Death in High Heels* (1947, as Frank Bevan)

### Warwick, Christopher

This British child actor (1971–) can be seen in a minor supporting role in *The Sweet Scent of Death* (1984, TVM [episode of *Hammer House of Mystery and Suspense*]). Also on stage, his other credits include an episode of *The Tripods* (1984–1985, TV). As an adult, he went on to direct commercials, music videos and short films, among the latter *Intolerable Redemption* (2004), which he wrote, directed and executive produced. **Hammer credits:** *The Sweet Scent of Death* (1984, TVM [episode of *Hammer House of Mystery and Suspense*], as Boy in park)

### Warwick Dubbing Theater

Formerly situated on Wardour Street in London's Soho, this sound and editing facility was used to record all thirteen episodes of *Hammer House of Mystery and Suspense* (1984, TVM). Other productions to have made use of the facility include *Man in the Wilderness* (1971), *Cities of Spain* (1973), *Mio min Mio* (1987) and *Moonlight Resurrection* (1987). **Hammer credits:** *Hammer House of Mystery and Suspense* (1984, TVM)

### Warwick, Eileen

Warwick worked as the hair stylist on Hammer's *She* (1965), having previously worked with its star, Ursula Andress, on the first James Bond film *Dr. No* (1962). Her other credits include several other Bond films, among them *From Russia with Love* (1963), *Goldfinger* (1964), *Thunderball* (1965), *You Only Live Twice* (1967) and *On Her Majesty's Secret Service* (1969), plus *To Dorothy a Son* (1954), *Corridors of Blood* (1958), *Summer Holiday* (1963), *Woman of Straw* (1964), *The Last Valley* (1970), *Diamonds on Wheels* (1974) and *The Little Prince* (1974). Her occasional TV credits include episodes of *Douglas Fairbanks, Jr. Presents* (1953–1957, TV). **Hammer credits:** *She* (1965)

### Warwick, John

Having appeared in a handful of films in his homeland, among them *In the Wake of the Bounty* (1933), *The Squatter's Daughter* (1933) and *The Silence of Dean Maitland* (1934), this Australian actor (1905–1972, real name John McIntosh Beattle) came to Britain in 1936, where he went on to appear in over fifty films. Among these were *A Yank at Oxford* (1938), *John Halifax* (1938), in which he played the title role, *The Case of the Frightened Lady* (1940), *The Lavender Hill Mob* (1951), *Contraband Spain* (1955) and *Go to Blazes* (1962). He also played Inspector Raynor in the Hammer quickie *Never Look Back* (1952). He later returned to Australia and appeared in such films as *Adam's Woman* (1970) and *That Lady from Peking* (1975), and episodes of *Skippy* (1966–1968, TV), *Contrabandits* (1967–1968, TV) and *Barrier Reef* (1971–1972, TV) His wife was actress Molly Raynor (1905–1976). He also wrote scripts for such series as *Adventures of the Seaspray* (1965–1967, TV) and *Phoenix Five* (1970, TV). **Hammer credits:** *Never Look Back* (1952, as Inspector Raynor)

### Warwick, Norman

This British cinematographer (1920–1994) photographed Hammer's *Dr. Jekyll and Sister Hyde* (1971) and four episodes of *Hammer House of Horror* (1980, TV). His other film credits include several genre pictures for director Freddie Francis, among them *Torture Garden* (1967), *They Came from Beyond Space* (1967), *The Creeping Flesh* (1972), *Tales from the Crypt* (1972), *Tales That Witness Madness* (1973), *Son of Dracula* (1973) and *The Doctor and the Devils* (1985). His other genre titles include *The Abominable Dr. Phibes* (1971), *Dr. Phibes Rises Again* (1972) and *The Godsend* (1980), while his non-genre work takes in *The Last Valley* (1970), *Take Me High* (1974) and *Confessions of a Window Cleaner* (1974). His earlier credits as a camera operator include *The New Lot* (1943), *The Dam Busters* (1954), *Oh ... Rosalinda!!* (1955) and *The Queen's Guards* (1961). He also photographed the second unit for *Ice Cold in Alex* (1958), *Sammy Going South* (1963) and *The Italian Job* (1969). He was married to the actress Hannah

Gordon (1941–), whom he photographed in *Spring and Port Wine* (1970), from 1970. She appeared in *Tennis Court* (1984, TVM [episode of *Hammer House of Mystery and Suspense*]). **Hammer credits:** *Dr. Jekyll and Sister Hyde* (1971), *The House That Bled to Death* (1980, TV [episode of *Hammer House of Horror*]), *The Mark of Satan* (1980, TV [episode of *Hammer House of Horror*]), *Guardian of the Abyss* (1980, TV [episode of *Hammer House of Horror*]), *Growing Pains* (1980, TV [episode of *Hammer House of Horror*])

### Washbourne, Mona

Adept at mousy or twittery roles, this much-liked British character actress (1903–1988) appeared in over fifty films, beginning with an uncredited bit part in *Evergreen* (1934). Her other credits include *Once Upon a Dream* (1948), *The Winslow Boy* (1948), *It's Great to Be Young!* (1956), *Billy Liar* (1963), *Night Must Fall* (1964), *My Fair Lady* (1964), *O Lucky Man!* (1973) and *Stevie* (1978), the latter of which earned her a BAFTA nomination for best supporting actress. She also made humorous contributions to Hammer's *The Gambler and the Lady* (1953), as an etiquette teacher, and *The Brides of Dracula* (1960), as the fussy Frau Lang. Also on television, her work here took in episodes of *ITV Television Playhouse* (1955–1967, TV), *Armchair Theatre* (1956–1974, TV) and *Brideshead Revisited* (1981, TV), in which she played Nanny Hawkins. On stage from 1924, she went on to appear in both the West End and on Broadway. Washbourne's husband was the character actor Basil Dignam (1905–1979), whom she married in 1940, and who appeared in Hammer's *The Quatermass Xperiment* (1955), *Up the Creek* (1958) and *Further Up the Creek* (1958). **Hammer credits:** *The Gambler and the Lady* (1953, as Miss Minter), *The Brides of Dracula* (1960, as Frau Lang)

### Wassell, Graham

Wassell penned the ludicrous teleplay for *Child's Play* (1984, TVM [episode of *Hammer House of Horror*]), the less said about which the better. **Hammer credits:** *Child's Play* (1984, TVM [episode of *Hammer House of Horror*])

### *Watch It, Sailor!*

GB, 1961, 81m, RCA, bw, cert U

The last of several service farces made by Hammer in the late fifties and early sixties—also see *Up the Creek* (1958), *Further Up the Creek* (1958), *I Only Arsked!* (1958) and *Don't Panic Chaps* (1959)—this tame situation comedy about a tar who finds himself accused of fathering a child on the day of his wedding was a sequel to the 1955 stage hit *Sailor Beware*, which had been successfully filmed by Romulus in 1956. Like its predecessor, the follow-up was based on a stage play by Philip King and Falkland L. Carey who, as they did before, also provided the screenplay.

In the previous film, Peggy Mount had top-lined as the the redoubtable Emma Hornett, around whom the Hornett household revolves, while Cyril Smith had co-starred as her much put-upon husband Henry. However, while Smith returned to recreate his role, Mount sadly did not, and was replaced by Marjorie Rhodes. Also replaced from the original film cast were Shirley Eaton (as Shirley Hornett) by Vera Day; Esma Cannon (as Edie Hornett) by Irene Handl; Joy Webster (as Daphne Hornett) by Liz Fraser; Ronald Lewis (as Albert Tufnell) by John Meillon; Thora Hird (as Mrs. Lack) by Miriam Karlin; and Gordon Jackson (as Carnoustie Bligh) by Graham Stark. Also onboard, and taking the starring role (which is actually a glorified cameo), was comedy veteran Dennis Price as Lieutenant-Commander Hardcastle, who finds himself caught up in the action, while comedy veterans Frankie Howerd and Bobby Howes pop up as guest artists, along with Brian Reece, Renee Houston and Arthur Howard.

Set primarily in the Hornett parlor, the action revolves round Albert Tufnell, who finds himself accused of fathering an illegitimate child on the day of his already delayed wedding to Shirley Hornett, much to the inevitable consternation of her dragon-like mother (in fact you could say the incident stirs up a Hornett's nest). A series of arguments and misunderstandings follow, though the happy ending is never very much in doubt.

Unfortunately, though performed with energy by its experienced cast (who are required to do little more than shout at each other and almost willfully misconstrue any given situation), the film—which was shot at Bray in February 1961–lacks the sparkle of its far superior predecessor (the poster promised "A full broadside of broad humored fun!"). Indeed, many of the characters are far from likeable, and it is down to the supporting cast to provide the occasional gems of humor, among them Frankie Howerd in an almost silent turn as a frustrated church organist and Dennis Price, who, as Lieutenant-Commander Hardcastle, has the unenviable task of trying to explain the situation (there turns out to be a question over the paternity of Albert's himself, whose real surname is revealed to be Thimble). In fact, when Hardcastle at one point is offered a sandwich by Irene Handle's demented Edie, he replies, "I've had all I can take today, thank you," and one is inclined to agree. There is also a notable coarsening of language from the predecessor (hell, damn and bastard are freely used), while at one point Albert rather ungallantly calls nosey neighbor Mrs. Lack a "wicked old bitch." All rather surprising for a film rated U.

Routinely handled by director Wolf Rilla and cinematographer Arthur Grant (who fail to make much of Bernard Robinson's drab and claustrophobic sets), the finished film died on its feet at the box office when released in the UK by Columbia on 14 August 1961 following its appearance in London the previous month. **Additional notes:** The film was made via the subsidiary company Cormorant, which was actually a re-branding of Maurice Cowan Productions. Ltd., whose proprietor, Maurice Cowan, produced the film. Anthony Nelson Keys' surname is mistakenly hyphenated in the credits. Note the scene in the parlor just after the party has returned from the aborted wedding ceremony at the church: Edie removes Shirley's veil and takes it away to the kitchen, yet in a close-up a couple of shots later Shirley is wearing it again. What can James Needs have been thinking? One can also see the shadow of the mic boom on the

parlor wall a little later on in the same scene (when Edie emerges from the kitchen with a pot of tea). A third stage play featuring the Hornetts followed: this was *Rock-a-Bye Sailor* (1962). *Watch It, Sailor!* can be seen playing at a cinema in the problem drama *Girl on Approval* (1961).

Production companies: Hammer/Cormorant. Distributor: Columbia (UK). Producer: Maurice Cowan. Executive producer: Michael Carreras. Associate producer: Anthony Nelson Keys. Director: Wolf Rilla. Screenplay: Falkland L. Cary, Philip King, based upon their play. Cinematographer: Arthur Grant. Music: Douglas Gamley. Title song: Horatio Nicholls (music), Tommie Connor (lyrics). Title song sung by: The Dallas Boys. Harmonica solos: Tommy Reilly. Music director: John Hollingsworth. Supervising editor: James Needs. Editor: Alfred Cox. Production designer: Bernard Robinson. Art director: Don Mingaye. Costumes: Rosemary Burrows, Molly Arbuthnot. Make-up: Roy Ashton. Hair: Frieda Steiger. Sound: Jock May, Ken Cameron. Sound editor: Alban Streeter. Production manager: Clifford Parkes. Assistant director: John Peverall. Second assistant director: Dominic Fulford [uncredited]. Camera operator: Len Harris. Focus puller: Harry Oakes [uncredited]. Casting: Stuart Lyons. Continuity: Tilly Day. Stills: Tom Edwards [uncredited]. Poster: John Stockle [uncredited]. **Cast:** Dennis Price (Lieutenant-Commander Hardcastle), Marjorie Rhodes (Emma "Ma" Hornett), Irene Handl (Edie Hornett), Vera Day (Shirley Hornett), Cyril Smith (Henry Hornett), Liz Fraser (Daphne Pink), John Meillon (Albert Tufnell/Thimble), Miriam Karlin (Mrs. Lack), Graham Stark (Carnoustie Bligh), Frankie Howerd (Organist), Renee Houston (Mrs. Mottram), Arthur Howard (Vicar), Bobby Howes (Drunk), Brian Reece (Solicitor), Harry Locke (Ticket collector), William Mervyn (Captain), Marianne Stone (Woman), Diane Aubrey (Bar maid), Jerry Verno (Cab driver)

## Waterman, Dennis

Long before he became famous for such popular TV series as *The Sweeney* (1975–1978, TV), in which he played Detective Inspector George Carter, and *Minder* (1979–1994, TV), in which he played Terry McCann, this British leading man (1948–) found fame as a child actor in the fifties and sixties. In films from 1960 with *Night Train for Inverness*, his other appearances as a youngster include *Snowball* (1960), *Crooks Anonymous* (1962) and *Go Kart Go* (1963), as well as a minor role in Hammer's *The Pirates of Blood River* (1962), in which he played seventeen-year-old Timothy Blackthorne (although only thirteen at the time of filming). Meanwhile, on television, his early credits include such plays as *The Member of the Wedding* (1960, TV) and *All Summer Long* (1960, TV), as well as the series *William* (1962, TV), a version of *Just William*, in which he played the title role. He also co-starred in *Eve*, the pilot episode of Hammer's anthology series *Journey to the Unknown* (1968, TV), in which he played a department store assistant who falls in love with a wax mannequin.

His adult film credits include *Up the Junction* (1968), *A Promise of Bed* (1970), *Fright* (1971),

*The Belstone Fox* (1973), *Sweeney!* (1976), *Sweeney 2* (1978), *Minder on the Orient Express* (1985, TVM), *Vol-au-vent* (1996), *Arthur's Dyke* (2001) and *Back in Business* (2007), while his other TV work takes in *Stay Lucky* (1989–1993, TV), *The Knock* (1994–2000, TV) and another long-runner, *New Tricks* (2003–2015, TV), in which he played Gerry Standing. Waterman also returned to Hammer in adulthood to play the young lead in *Scars of Dracula* (1970).

Married four times, his wives include the actresses Penny Dixon, to whom he was married between 1972 and 1976; Pat Maynard (1942–), to whom he was married between 1977 and 1982, and who appeared in *The House That Bled to Death*, an episode of *Hammer House of Horror* (1980, TV); and Rula Lenska (1947–, real name Roza-Marie Leopoldyna Lubienska), to whom he was married between 1987 and 1998. He is the father (with Maynard) of actress Hannah Waterman (1975–). **Hammer credits:** *The Pirates of Blood River* (1962, as Timothy Blackthorne), *Eve* (1968, TV [episode of *Journey to the Unknown*], as Albert Baker), *Scars of Dracula* (1970, as Simon)

## Waters, Russell

Following appearances in a handful of shorts for director Richard Massingham, among them *Tell Me If It Hurts* (1934), *And So to Work* (1936) and *Daily Round* (1937), this British (Scottish) character actor (1908–1982, full name Andrew Russell Waters) went on to rack up over one-hundred film appearances following wartime experience in the army, among them *The Woman in the Hall* (1947), *Once a Jolly Swagman* (1948), *Seven Days to Noon* (1950), *Reach for the Sky* (1956), *A Night to Remember* (1958), *The Family Way* (1966), *The Wicker Man* (1973), in which he played the harbor master, and *Black Jack* (1979), as well as several more shorts for Massingham, among them comedies and public information films, including *Pool of Contentment* (1946), *Pedal Cyclists* (1947), *The Cure* (1950), *Moving House* (1950) and *Introducing the New Worker* (1951). He also appeared in four films for Hammer, his best known performance for the company being that of Malin, the Eaton family retainer in *The Devil Rides Out* (1968). His TV work includes appearances in such series and one-offs as *Laugh with Me* (1938, TV), *The Swiss Family Robinson* (1939, TV), *Douglas Fairbanks, Jr. Presents* (1953–1957, TV) and *The Borderers* (1968–1970, TV), in which he played Pringle. His son is the actor John Waters (1948–) and his daughter the floor manager Fizz Waters (real name Fiona Waters). **Hammer credits:** *Death of an Angel* (1952, as Walter Grannage), *Third Party Risk* (1955, as Dr. Zeissman), *Yesterday's Enemy* (1959, as Brigadier), *The Devil Rides Out* (1968, as Malin)

## Waterson, Chic

This British cameraman (1924–1997, real name Bernard Frederick Waterson) worked as the camera operator on Hammer's *The Lady Vanishes* (1979). Long at Ealing, where he worked on such classics as *Scott of the Antarctic* (1948), *Whisky Galore!* (1949), *The Cruel Sea* (1953), *The Maggie* (1954) and *The Ladykillers* (1955), his many other credits (among them several for cinematographer Douglas Slocombe, including his Hammer film) take in *Circus of Horrors* (1960), *The Servant* (1963), *The Blue Max* (1966), *The Music Lovers* (1970), *Julia* (1977), *Superman II* (1980), *Raiders of the Lost Ark* (1981), *Indiana Jones and the Temple of Doom* (1984) and *Lady Jane* (1986). His wife was the continuity girl Jean Graham (1922–2003), whom he married in 1952. **Hammer credits:** *The Lady Vanishes* (1979)

### Watford, Gwen

An always-welcome addition to any cast, this noted British stage actress (1927–1994, full name Gwendolyn Watford) also proved popular on television in one-off plays, among them *Night Must Fall* (1957, TV), *The Winslow Boy* (1958 and 1989, TV), *The Barretts of Wimpole Street* (1961, TV) and *Dangerous Corner* (1970, TV). She also appeared in episodes of such series as *White Hunter* (1957–1958, TV), *Shadows of Fear* (1970–1973, TV) and *Sorrell and Son* (1984, TV). Sadly, she made all too few films, among them two for Hammer: *Never Take Sweets from a Stranger* (1960), in which she played an anguished mother whose young daughter has been abused by a town elder, and *Taste the Blood of Dracula* (1970), in which she played the wife of a corrupt Victorian gentleman. Her other film credits include *The Fall of the House of Usher* (1949), *Cleopatra* (1963), *The Very Edge* (1963), *The Ghoul* (1975) and *Cry Freedom* (1987). **Hammer credits:** *Never Take Sweets from a Stranger* (1960, as Sally Carter), *Taste the Blood of Dracula* (1970, as Martha Hargood)

### Watkin, David

This highly respected British cinematographer (1925–2008, full name Francis David Watkin) began his career as a documentary cameraman, notably for British Transport Films, for whom he filmed the likes of *Lancashire Coast* (1957) and *The Coasts of Clyde* (1959) among others, after which he moved into commercials. It was one such commercial, an ad for Shredded Wheat directed by Richard Lester, that led directly to his being hired to photograph Lester's big screen comedy *The Knack* (1965), which is noted for its high contrast look. Watkin went on to photograph several other films for Lester, including *Help!* (1965), *How I Won the War* (1967), *The Bed Sitting Room* (1969), *The Three Musketeers* (1973), *The Four Musketeers* (1974), *Robin and Marian* (1976) and *Cuba* (1979). He also worked for such major directors as Tony Richardson, Ken Russell, Mike Nichols, Franco Zeffirelli, Michael Caton-Jones, Sidney Pollack, Norman Jewison and Hugh Hudson. His many other credits include *The Devils* (1970), *The Boy Friend* (1971), *Mahogany* (1975), *Yentl* (1983), *Out of Africa* (1985), which won him an Oscar and a BAFTA, *Hamlet* (1991), *This Boy's Life* (1993), *Jane Eyre* (1994), *Tea with Mussolini* (1999) and *All Forgotten* (2000). He also photographed Hammer's last theatrical horror film for over thirty years, *To the Devil a Daughter* (1976), which benefits from some excellent framing and angles. He earned additional BAFTA nominations for his work on *The Knack* (1965), *Help!* (1965), *Mademoiselle* (1966),

*The Charge of the Light Brigade* (1968), *Catch-22* (1970), *The Three Musketeers* (1973) and *Chariots of Fire* (1981), as well as the TV series *Jesus of Nazareth* (1977, TV), the latter shared with Armando Nannuzzi. He also photographed the title sequences for *From Russia with Love* (1963) and *Goldfinger* (1964), which were designed by Robert Brownjohn. **Hammer credits:** *To the Devil a Daughter* (1976)

### Watkins, A.W. (Alfred Wilfred)

This prolific British sound technician (1895–1970) worked as the sound supervisor on Hammer's *When Dinosaurs Ruled the Earth* (1970). Long at Denham Studios, where he designed a small theater for recording orchestras, he worked on many films for Alexander Korda. His many credits, over 150 of them, include *A Warm Corner* (1930), *The Private Life of Henry VIII* (1933), *Rembrandt* (1936), *A Yank at Oxford* (1938), *49th Parallel* (1941), *Edward, My Son* (1949), *Bhowani Junction* (1956), *Village of the Damned* (1960), *The Haunting* (1963), *The V.I.P.s* (1963), *Operation Crossbow* (1965), *2001: A Space Odyssey* (1968) and *Goodbye, Mr. Chips* (1969). He was nominated for Oscars for his work on the original *Goodbye, Mr. Chips* (1939), *Knights of the Round Table* (1953), *Libel* (1960) and *Doctor Zhivago* (1965), the latter shared. **Hammer credits:** *When Dinosaurs Ruled the Earth* (1970 [uncredited])

### Watkins, Garth

This British actor (1922–1980) can be seen as the chief mock priest in Hammer's *Twins of Evil* (1971). His other films include *Virgin Witch* (1971) and *Queen Kong* (1976), while his TV work takes in episodes of *The Guardians* (1971, TV), *Trial* (1971, TV) and *Follyfoot* (1971–1973, TV). **Hammer credits:** *Twins of Evil* (1971, as Chief mock priest [uncredited])

### Watkins, Michael

Watkins can be seen as Soames in *Paint Me a Murder* (1984, TVM [episode of *Hammer House of Mystery and Suspense*]). His other TV credits include appearances in *The Naked Civil Servant* (1975, TVM), *All Creatures Great and Small* (1978–1990, TV) and *Minder* (1979–1994, TV), while his occasional films take in *Erotic Inferno* (1975), *Arabian Adventure* (1979), *Venom* (1981), *Bellman and True* (1987) and *Edward II* (1991). **Hammer credits:** *Paint Me a Murder* (1984, TVM [episode of *Hammer House of Mystery and Suspense*], as Soames)

### Watling, Jack

In films as a teenager, beginning with *Sixty Glorious Years* (1938), this British actor (1923–2001) played leading roles in a number of low budget second features, as well as supporting roles in slightly more prestigious productions. In over fifty films, his credits include *Goodbye, Mr. Chips* (1939), *The Way Ahead* (1944), *Once a Sinner* (1950), *A Night to Remember* (1958), *Who Was Maddox?* (1964), *Follow Me* (1972) and *11 Harrowhouse* (1974). He can also be seen in Hammer's *The Nanny* (1965) as Dr. Medman. His TV credits include episodes

of *Stryker of the Yard* (1957, TV), *William Tell* (1958–1959, TV), *The Plane Makers* (1963–1965, TV), *The Power Game* (1965–1969, TV) and *Bergerac* (1981–1991, TV). His wife was the actress Patricia Hicks (1919–2011), whom he married in 1947, and who appeared in Hammer's *The Dark Road* (1948). His children are the actors Dilys Watling (1942–), Deborah Watling (1948–2017) and Giles Watling (1953–). **Hammer credits:** *The Nanny* (1965, as Dr. Medman)

### Watson, Claude

British born Watson (1923–1968) worked as the assistant director on Hammer's *Fanatic* (1965). His other credits include *The Smallest Show on Earth* (1957), on which he was the third assistant director, *The Innocents* (1961), on which he was the second assistant director, and—as first assistant—*The Pumpkin Eater* (1964), *Modesty Blaise* (1966), *Isadora* (1968) and *The Virgin Soldiers* (1969), plus episodes of *The Avengers* (1961–1969, TV). **Hammer credits:** *Fanatic* (1965)

### Watson, Del

Watson can be seen as one of the zombies in Hammer's *The Plague of the Zombies* (1966), strangling Brook Williams' Dr. Peter Tompson during the graveyard dream sequence. Other credits include *The Chimney Sweeps* (1963) and episodes of *Doctor Who* (1963–1989, TV) and *Take a Pair of Private Eyes* (1966, TV). **Hammer credits:** *The Plague of the Zombies* (1966, as Zombie [uncredited])

### Watson, Jack

Best known for his sergeant-major type roles, this tough-looking British character actor (1915–1999, real name Hubert Watson) began his film career in 1945 with the short *Pathé Radio Music Hall* following experience as a musical hall comedian, including a stint as a straight man to his father Nosmo King (1885–1949, real name Vernon Watson). His other films include *The Small Back Room* (1949), *Captain Horatio Hornblower R.N.* (1951), *Peeping Tom* (1960), *The Hill* (1965), *Grand Prix* (1966), *From Beyond the Grave* (1973), *The Wild Geese* (1978), *North Sea Hijack* (1979) and *The Sea Wolves* (1980). He also appeared in a supporting role in *The Gorgon* (1964) for Hammer. His TV work includes episodes of *Detective* (1964–1969, TV), *The Changes* (1975, TV), *Kidnapped* (1978, TV) and *Common as Muck* (1994–1997, TV). Some sources claim that Watson also had a bit part in Hammer's *The Steel Bayonet* (1957). **Hammer credits:** *The Steel Bayonet* (1957, unnamed role [unconfirmed, uncredited]), *The Gorgon* (1964, as Ratoff)

### Watson, John H.

The credits of this British supporting actor (1922–1996) include *Dangerous Cargo* (1954), *The Brain* (1962), *Where the Bullets Fly* (1966) and *Two a Penny* (1968). He can also be seen in supporting roles in a handful of Hammer films, among them *The Scarlet Blade* (1963), in which he played Fitzroy. His TV work includes episodes of *The Adventures of Robin Hood* (1955–1960, TV) and *The Adventures of Ben Gunn* (1958, TV), in which he played Jim Hawkins. **Hammer credits:** *Blood Orange* (1953, as Chauffeur [uncredited]), *The Steel*

Bayonet (1957, as Corporal Bean), *The Scarlet Blade* (1963, as Fitzroy [uncredited]), *The Runaway* (1964, as Hazleton)

## Watson, Ralph

This British actor (1936–) played one of the Taggart family's construction workers in Hammer's *The Anniversary* (1968). His other credits include *McVicar* (1980), *Shooting Fish* (1997) and *A Soldier's Tunic* (2004), plus much TV, including episodes of *The Three Musketeers* (1966, TV), *Edward the Seventh* (1975, TV), *The Fall and Rise of Reginald Perrin* (1976–1979, TV), *Boon* (1986–1992, TV) and *Wycliffe* (1994–1998, TV). **Hammer credits:** *The Anniversary* (1968)

## Wattis, Richard

On stage from 1934 and in films from 1938 with *A Yank at Oxford*, this bespectacled, much-liked British comedy character actor (1912–1975) went on to appear in well over one-hundred films, often as an irritated official. Among his credits are such favorites as *The Happiest Days of Your Life* (1950), *The Belles of St. Trinian's* (1954), *Doctor in the House* (1954), *Around the World in 80 Days* (1956), *Blue Murder at St. Trinian's* (1957), *Carry On Spying* (1964) and *Chitty Chitty Bang Bang* (1968). He was also known for playing Mr. Brown in the long-running sitcom *Sykes* (1972–1979, TV). He crossed paths with Hammer several times during his career, first with a minor part in *Stolen Face* (1952), and later in featured roles in *The Abominable Snowman* (1957) and *That's Your Funeral* (1973). **Hammer credits:** *Stolen Face* (1952, as Wentworth), *Blood Orange* (1953, as Inspector McLeod), *The Abominable Snowman* (1957, as Peter Fox), *Ten Seconds to Hell* (1959, as Major Haven), *The Ugly Duckling* (1959, as Barclay), *That's Your Funeral* (1973, as Simmonds)

## Watts, Frank

Watts (?–1994) photographed nine episodes of *Hammer House of Horror* (1980, TV) and six episodes of *Hammer House of Mystery and Suspense* (1984, TVM), among them *Tennis Court* (1984, TVM), which is notable for its many tilted shots. His other TV credits include episodes of *The Avengers* (1961–1969, TV), *The Champions* (1968–1969, TV), *The Adventurer* (1972–1973, TV), *Space: 1999* (1975–1977, TV) and *Return of the Saint* (1978–1979, TV), while his film credits take in *San Ferry Ann* (1965), *Intimate Games* (1976), *George and Mildred* (1980), *Rising Damp* (1980), *Educating Rita* (1983), *D.A.R.Y.L.* (1985) and *A Hazard of Hearts* (1987, TVM). His credits as an operator include episodes of *The Count of Monte Cristo* (1956, TV) and *Hawkeye and the Last of the Mohicans* (1957, TV). He began as a clapper loader on the likes of *To Dorothy a Son* (1954) and as a focus puller on *Police Dog* (1955). He was the president of the BSC (British Society of Cinematographers) between 1984 and 1986. **Hammer credits:** *The Silent Scream* (1980, TV [episode of *Hammer House of Horror*]), *The Two Faces of Evil* (1980, TV [episode of *Hammer House of Horror*]), *Witching Time* (1980, TV [episode of *Hammer House of Horror*]), *Visitor from the Grave* (1980, TV [episode of *Hammer House of Horror*]), *Rude Awakening* (1980,

TV [episode of *Hammer House of Horror*]), *Charlie Boy* (1980, TV [episode of *Hammer House of Horror*]), *Children of the Full Moon* (1980, TV [episode of *Hammer House of Horror*]), *The Thirteenth Reunion* (1980, TV [episode of *Hammer House of Horror*]), *Carpathian Eagle* (1980, TV [episode of *Hammer House of Horror*]), *Mark of the Devil* (1984, TVM [episode of *Hammer House of Mystery and Suspense*]), *The Corvini Inheritance* (1984, TVM [episode of *Hammer House of Mystery and Suspense*]), *Paint Me a Murder* (1984, TVM [episode of *Hammer House of Mystery and Suspense*]), *Child's Play* (1984, TVM [episode of *Hammer House of Horror*]), *And the Wall Came Tumbling Down* (1984, TVM [episode of *Hammer House of Horror*]), *Tennis Court* (1984, TVM [episode of *Hammer House of Mystery and Suspense*])

## Watts, Freddie

In supporting roles, this British actor (1892–1962) can be seen as a patient in Hammer's second Frankenstein feature, *The Revenge of Frankenstein* (1958). His other credits include *Reunion* (1932), *Thank Evans* (1938), *The Mudlark* (1950), *The Long Haul* (1957), plus episodes of *Murder Bag* (1957–1959, TV) and *Probation Officer* (1959–1962, TV). **Hammer credits:** *The Revenge of Frankenstein* (1958, as Patient [uncredited])

## Watts, Gwendolyn

Best remembered for playing the brassy Rita in *Billy Liar* (1963), this British actress (1937–2000) can also be seen in the part of Gloria in Hammer's *Fanatic* (1965). Her other credits include *Sons and Lovers* (1960), *The System* (1964), *You Must Be Joking!* (1965), *The Wrong Box* (1966), *Carry On Doctor* (1967), *Carry On Again Doctor* (1969) and *Carry On Matron* (1972). Much on television, her credits include episodes of *Walk a Crooked Mile* (1961, TV), *On the Buses* (1969–1973, TV) and *Love Thy Neighbour* (1972–1976, TV). Her husband was actor Gertan Klauber (1932–2008, full name George Gertan Klauber), whom she married in 1959, and who appeared in Hammer's *Don't Panic Chaps* (1959). Her sister is actress Sally Watts (1950–). **Hammer credits:** *Fanatic* (1965, as Gloria)

## Watts, Queenie

This British character actress (1923–1980) came to films and television following experience as a pub landlady and singer. Noted for her "cor blimey" Cockney accent, she is best remembered for the sitcom *Romany Jones* (1972–1975, TV) and its spin-off *Yus, My Dear* (1976, TV), in which she played Lily Briggs to Arthur Mullard's Wally Briggs. The series was created by Ronald Wolfe and Ronald Chesney, the men also behind *On the Buses* (1969–1973, TV). When the Briggses proved popular with TV audiences, Chesney and Wolfe decided to introduce the duo into their third *Buses* film spin-off for Hammer, *Holiday on the Buses* (1973), in which they had many scene-stealing moments. Watts' other film appearances include *Sparrows Can't Sing* (1962), *Alfie* (1966), *Poor Cow* (1967), *Up the Junction* (1968), *Oliver!* (1968), *All Coppers Are…* (1971), *Keep It Up, Jack!* (1974), *Schizo* (1976) and *Come Play with Me* (1977). She was also the subject of a 1964 documentary titled

*Portrait of Queenie.* Her other TV work includes appearances in *Stars and Garters* (1963–1964, TV), *Beryl's Lot* (1973–1977, TV) and *Waterloo Sunset* (1978, TV). She ended her days running the Rose and Crown pub in London's Limehouse. **Hammer credits:** *Holiday on the Buses* (1973, as Lil Briggs)

## Watts, Stephanie

Watts had a minor role in Hammer's *The Brides of Dracula* (1960). Her other credits include *Spare the Rod* (1961) and *Term of Trial* (1962). **Hammer credits:** *The Brides of Dracula* (1960, as Girl [uncredited])

## Waxman, Harry

This British cinematographer (1912–1984) began his career as a camera assistant at British International Pictures in the early thirties. Following further experience at Ealing and Welwyn Studios, he joined the RAF Film Unit during the war, following which he photographed his first feature, *Journey Together* (1945), prior to which he had photographed a handful of shorts, beginning with *Co-operette* (1937). He subsequently went on to photograph such films as *Brighton Rock* (1948), *Father Brown* (1954), *Sapphire* (1959), *Swiss Family Robinson* (1960), *The Family Way* (1966), *Twisted Nerve* (1968), *There's a Girl in My Soup* (1970), *Mr. Forbush and the Penguins* (1971), *The Wicker Man* (1973), *The Pink Panther Strikes Again* (1976) and *The Uncanny* (1977), working for such directors as John and Roy Boulting, Sidney Gilliat and Ken Annakin. He also photographed three films for Hammer, beginning with the lackluster *She* (1965). However, he more than made amends with his excellent work for the Bette Davis vehicle *The Nanny* (1965), which led to his photographing a second film for Davis, *The Anniversary* (1968). Christopher Neame described Waxman as being, "Excellent, though not right in the top line of cameramen. He was recognized throughout the industry as being the most technically learned. His only fault was that he could get himself worked up too easily; nevertheless, when it came to lighting Miss Davis, we were on very safe ground."[7] **Hammer credits:** *She* (1965), *The Nanny* (1965), *The Anniversary* (1968)

## Way, Ann

This diminutive British supporting player (1915–1993) can be seen as a seamstress in Hammer's *Hands of the Ripper* (1971). Her other credits include *The Belles of St. Trinian's* (1954), *The Prime of Miss Jean Brodie* (1968), *Carry On Loving* (1970), *Jabberwocky* (1977), *The Dresser* (1983), *The Dawning* (1988) and *Anchoress* (1993). Her TV credits include episodes of *Bleak House* (1959, TV), *The Goodies* (1970–1981, TV) and *Lovejoy* (1986–1994, TV), though she is perhaps best remembered for playing the role of Mrs. Hall in *Gourmet Night*, the classic 1975 episode of *Fawlty Towers* (1975–1979, TV). **Hammer credits:** *Hands of the Ripper* (1971, as Seamstress [uncredited])

## Way, Eileen

In films sporadically from the early fifties with *Cheer the Brave* (1951), this RADA-trained British actress (1911–1994) can be spotted in the role of

Fernande in the Hammer quickie *Blood Orange* (1953). Her other credits include *Venetian Bird* (1953), *Kidnapped* (1959), *Village of Daughters* (1962), *Drop Dead Darling* (1966) and *Queen of Hearts* (1989). Busiest on television, she also appeared in the early TV plays *The Guy Lord Quex* (1938, TV) and *The Day Is Gone* (1939, TV), as well as episodes of *Barbie* (1955, TV), *The Onedin Line* (1971–1980, TV), *War and Remembrance* (1988, TV) and *Sean's Show* (1992–1993, TV). Also much on stage, including stints in Stratford-upon-Avon and the West End. **Hammer credits:** *Blood Orange* (1953, as Fernande)

## Wayn (Wayne), Peter

This British actor (1927–1995, aka Peter Forbes-Robertson) can be seen as Lieutenant Thornton in Hammer's *The Camp on Blood Island* (1958). He also had a supporting role in *Up the Creek* (1958), for which the credits bill him as Wayne. His other credits include *Womaneater* (1958), *The Naked Edge* (1961) and *Foreign Body* (1986), plus episodse of *My Friend Charles* (1956, TV) and *The Tripods* (1984–1985, TV). **Hammer credits:** *The Camp on Blood Island* (1958, as Lieutenant Thornton), *Up the Creek* (1958, as Lieutenant)

## Weatherley, Peter

This British editor (1930–2015) cut the Bette Davis vehicle *The Anniversary* (1968) for Hammer. He was also brought in to work on the troubled *Blood from the Mummy's Tomb* (1971), on which he replaced Oswald Hafenrichter. His other credits include *Daylight Robbery* (1964), *Mister Moses* (1965), *The Desperate Ones* (1968), *The Limbo Line* (1968), *The Uncanny* (1977), *Alien* (1979) and *Rising Damp* (1980), plus a further return to Hammer for *Fear in the Night* (1972), along with several episodes each of *Hammer House of Horror* (1980, TV) and of *Hammer House of Mystery and Suspense* (1984, TVM). His other small screen work includes the TV movies *The Lady and the Highwayman* (1989, TVM), *A Ghost in Monte Carlo* (1990, TVM) and *Duel of Hearts* (1992, TVM), all three of which were directed by John Hough, as were two of Weatherley's *Hammer House of Mystery and Suspense* episodes (these were *Czech Mate* and *A Distant Scream*). **Hammer credits:** *The Anniversary* (1968), *Blood from the Mummy's Tomb* (1971), *Fear in the Night* (1972), *The Two Faces of Evil* (1980, TV [episode of *Hammer House of Horror*]), *The Mark of Satan* (1980, TV [episode of *Hammer House of Horror*]), *The Thirteenth Reunion* (1980, TV [episode of *Hammer House of Horror*]), *Carpathian Eagle* (1980, TV [episode of *Hammer House of Horror*]), *Growing Pains* (1980, TV [episode of *Hammer House of Horror*]), *Czech Mate* (1984, TVM [episode of *Hammer House of Mystery and Suspense*]), *A Distant Scream* (1984, TVM [episode of *Hammer House of Mystery and Suspense*]), *In Possession* (1984, TVM [episode of *Hammer House of Mystery and Suspense*]), *Last Video and Testament* (1984, TVM [episode of *Hammer House of Mystery and Suspense*]), *The Corvini Inheritance* (1984, TVM [episode of *Hammer House of Mystery and Suspense*]), *Child's Play* (1984, TVM [episode of *Hammer House of Horror*]), *Ten-*

nis Court* (1984, TVM [episode of *Hammer House of Mystery and Suspense*])

## Weaver, Tom

This leading American genre historian (1958–) is acknowledged in the credits of *Flesh and Blood—The Hammer Heritage of Horror* (1994, TV). Best known for writing such books as *Interviews with Science Fiction and Horror Movie Makers* (1988), *It Came from Horrorwood* (1996) and *I Was a Monster Movie Maker* (2001), he has also appeared in or narrated such video documentaries as *Haunted Memories* (2007) and *I Was a Teenage Caveman* (2016), and has written the scripts for several others, among them *Herman Cohen: Cohen My Way* (2003) and *The Movie That Couldn't Die* (2014), the latter of which he also narrated. He has also contributed to a number of DVD commentaries. **Hammer credits:** *Flesh and Blood—The Hammer Heritage of Horror* (1994, TV)

## Weaver, Wyn

This British actor (1871–1951) played the role of Wilfred Wimple in the early Hammer comedy *Sporting Love* (1936). His other credits include *Our Girls and Their Physique* (1920), *Holiday Lovers* (1932), *Gypsy Melody* (1936) and *Knights for a Day* (1937). He also co-authored the play *The Rising Generation* with Laura Leycester, which was filmed in 1928. **Hammer credits:** *Sporting Love* (1936, as Wilfred Wimple)

## Webb, Antony

The British actor (1934–) played the role of a party guest dressed as Lord Nelson in *Poor Butterfly*, an episode of Hammer's *Journey to the Unknown* (1968, TV), which also appeared in the compendium film *Journey to Midnight* (1968, TVM). His other TV credits include episodes of *Dixon of Dock Green* (1955–1976, TV), *Doctor Who* (1963–1989, TV), *Warship* (1973–1977, TV), *Napoleon and Love* (1974, TV), *The Bill* (1984–2010, TV) and *She's Out* (1995, TV). Also on stage. **Hammer credits:** *Poor Butterfly* (1968, TV [episode of *Journey to the Unknown*], as Nelson), *Journey to Midnight* (1968, TVM, as Nelson)

## Webb, Bob (Robert)

Webb worked as a publicist on a couple of Hammer films in the mid-sixties. His other credits include *The Roman Spring of Mrs. Stone* (1961), *Billy Budd* (1962) and *Wonderful Life* (1964). **Hammer credits:** *The Witches* (1966 [uncredited]), *One Million Years B.C.* (1966 [uncredited])

## Webb, Elven

This British art director (1910–1979) designed the sets for the Hammer comedy *Up the Creek* (1958), sharing his credit with Ward Richards. His other credits include *It's a Wonderful World* (1956), *Beat Girl* (1960), *Cleopatra* (1963), which earned him a shared Oscar, *The Taming of the Shrew* (1967), which earned him a shared Oscar nomination, *Play Dirty* (1968), *Monte Carlo or Bust!* (1969) and *The Kremlin Letter* (1970). His earlier credits as a draughtsman and assistant art director include *The Way Ahead* (1944), *Brief Encounter* (1945), *The Red Shoes* (1948), *The Sound Barrier*

(1952) and *The Colditz Story* (1955). **Hammer credits:** *Up the Creek* (1958)

## Webb, Geoffrey

While working in radio in the forties, this British dramatist worked with Edward J. Mason as a scriptwriter on one of the most popular post-war radio series, *Dick Barton—Special Agent*, whose daring exploits ran as a day-time serial on the BBC's Light Program between 1946 and 1951, regularly pulling in an impressive fifteen million listeners. Hammer subsequently made three films about the character, himself actually the creation of a BBC producer named Norman Collins. Webb's other radio credits include many episodes of *The Archers* (1950–), on which he worked between 1951 and 1962 (again mostly with Edward J. Mason, with whom he was a founding writer). **Hammer credits:** *Dick Barton—Special Agent* (1949, original radio serial), *Dick Barton Strikes Back* (1949, original radio serial), *Dick Barton at Bay* (1950, original radio serial)

## Webb, Lincoln

Webb played the role of Charlie in Hammer's *Love Thy Neighbour* (1973). Other credits include *Scream and Scream Again* (1970), *Carry On Up the Jungle* (1970) and *Barry McKenzie Holds His Own* (1974), plus episodes of *Doctor at Large* (1971, TV) and *Doctor at Sea* (1974, TV). **Hammer credits:** *Love Thy Neighbour* (1973, as Charlie)

## Webb, Packham

This writer (1908–1973, full name Thomas Charles Packham Webb) co-authored the 1951 novel *Dead on Course* with Elleston Trevor. This was subsequently filmed by Hammer as *Wings of Danger* (1952). His other books include *Special Assignment* (1947) and *Midnight Intruder* (1950). **Hammer credits:** *Wings of Danger* (1952)

## Webb, Roger

This British composer, songwriter, conductor, arranger and recording artist (1934–2002) penned the catchy title theme for the TV series *Hammer House of Horror* (1980, TV). Amazingly, he received no credit for his efforts. His other TV themes include *Shadows of Fear* (1970–1973, TV) and *George and Mildred* (1976–1979, TV). He also contributed music to such series as *Strange Report* (1968–1970, TV), *Love Thy Neighbour* (1972–1976, TV), *Miss Jones and Son* (1977–1978, TV), *The Gentle Touch* (1980–1984, TV) and *Sylvania Waters* (1992, TV). His film work includes scores for *Bartleby* (1970), *One Brief Summer* (1970), *Burke and Hare* (1972), *Au Pair Girls* (1972), *The Amorous Milkman* (1975), *Bedtime with Rosie* (1975), *What's Up Nurse?* (1977), *The Godsend* (1980), *The Boys in Blue* (1986) and *Here's My Girl* (1987). He also wrote numbers for various artists, including Shirley Bassey, Johnny Mathis, Rex Harrison and Bette Davis. His songs (with lyrics by regular collaborator Dee Shipman) include *Sad Song Lady*, *The Rainbow Bridge* and *Making It By Myself*. **Hammer credits:** *Hammer House of Horror* (1980, TV [uncredited])

## Webber, John

Webber worked as Tom Smith's make-up assistant on Hammer's *The Horror of Frankenstein* (1970) and as a make-up artist on *Twins of Evil* (1971), sharing his credit with George Blackler on the latter. His other credits include *What a Carry On* (1949), *Over the Garden Wall* (1950), *Man in the Moon* (1960), *Three Hats for Lisa* (1965), *The Man Who Haunted Himself* (1970), *The Seven-Per-Cent Solution* (1976), *Gandhi* (1982) and *Indiana Jones and the Temple of Doom* (1984), plus episodes of *The Professionals* (1977–1983, TV) and *A Woman of Substance* (1984, TV). **Hammer credits:** *The Horror of Frankenstein* (1970, make-up assistant [uncredited]), *Twins of Evil* (1971, make-up)

## Webber, Robert

In films from 1951 with *Highway 301* following acting experience in the Marines during the war, this American leading man (1924–1989) went on to appear in *Twelve Angry Men* (1957), *The Nun and the Sergeant* (1962), *The Sandpiper* (1965), *The Dirty Dozen* (1967), *The Choirboys* (1978), *Private Benjamin* (1980), *SOB* (1981) and *Wild Geese II* (1985). He also starred as the amnesiac Christopher Smith in the Hammer thriller *Hysteria* (1965). Unfortunately, Webber didn't get on with the film's leading lady, Lelia Goldoni, and the set was consequently a tense one. Revealed the film's producer and screenwriter Jimmy Sangster, "Webber was a mean-minded guy. Whenever the two of them were on the set at the same time, it cast a pall of gloom. I'm sure we had some light moments, but the overall memory is of an unhappy movie."[8] Director Freddie Francis concurred: "I enjoyed working with Robert Webber as little as I've ever enjoyed working with anybody. He was impossible."[9]

Webber's many TV appearances include episodes of *Starlight Theatre* (1950–1951, TV), *Robert Montgomery Presents* (1950–1957, TV), *The Greatest Show on Earth* (1963–1964, TV), *Banacek* (1972–1974, TV), *Police Woman* (1974–1978, TV) and *Moonlighting* (1985–1989, TV). Married twice, his first wife was the actress Miranda Jones (1934–1973), to whom he was married between 1953 and 1958. He should not be confused with the British actor of the same name, who also worked for Hammer. **Hammer credits:** *Hysteria* (1965, as Christopher Smith)

## Webber, Robert

In supporting roles, this British actor (1903–1980) can be seen as the monk-turned-manservant Brother Martin in *The New People*, an episode of Hammer's *Journey to the Unknown* (1968, TV), which also appeared in the compendium film *Journey into Darkness* (1968, TVM). His many other TV credits include episodes of *Sixpenny Corner* (1955–1956, TV), *Dixon of Dock Green* (1955–1976, TV), *The Six Proud Walkers* (1962, TV), *Alcock and Gander* (1972, TV) and *Love Thy Neighbour* (1972–1976, TV). His occasional films include *Don't Ever Leave Me* (1949), *The Extra Day* (1956) and *Fate Takes a Hand* (1962). He should not be confused with the American actor of the same name, who also worked for Hammer. **Hammer credits:** *The New People* (1968, TV [episode of *Journey to the Unknown*], as Brother Martin [Manservant])

## Webster, Joy

This British actress (1934– ) can be seen as Jenny in Hammer's *The Two Faces of Dr. Jekyll* (1960), as well as Isobel in *The Curse of the Werewolf* (1961). Her other credits include *Sailor Beware* (1956), *Shoot to Kill* (1961), *During One Night* (1961) and *Jungle Street* (1961), plus episodes of *Saber of London* (1954–1960, TV) and *The Avengers* (1961–1969, TV). She was also a hostess on *Film Fanfare* (1956–1957, TV) and *For Love or Money* (1959–1961, TV). **Hammer credits:** *The Two Faces of Dr. Jekyll* (1960, as Jenny), *The Curse of the Werewolf* (1961, as Isobel)

## Webster-Brough, Jean

This British supporting actress (1900–1954) played the minor role of Mrs. Daniels in the Hammer sci-fi quickie *Spaceways* (1953). Her other credits include *Cheer Boys Cheer* (1939) and *Distant Trumpet* (1952), plus such TV plays as *Bardell Against Pickwick* (1946, TV) and *Mr. Bowling Buys a Newspaper* (1950, TV). **Hammer credits:** *Spaceways* (1953, as Mrs. Daniels [uncredited])

## Weedon, Martin

Weedon can be seen in a brief role in *The Corvini Inheritance* (1984, TVM [episode of *Hammer House of Mystery and Suspense*]). His other credits include episodes of *Doctor Who* (1963–1989, TV), *Stalky & Co.* (1982, TV), *The Hello Goodbye Man* (1984, TV) and *The Bill* (1984–2010, TV). **Hammer credits:** *The Corvini Inheritance* (1984, TVM [episode of *Hammer House of Mystery and Suspense*], as Business man)

## *A Weekend with Lulu*

GB, 1961, 89m [U.S. 91m], bw, Westrex, cert A

One of several innocuous comedies made by Hammer in the late fifties/early sixties, this romp about a weekend holiday gone awry might easily have been titled *Carry On Caravanning* given the number of faces onboard familiar from the popular comedy series, among them Bob Monkhouse, Shirley Eaton, Leslie Phillips, Sid James and Kenneth Connor. The story, provided by the film's producer Ted Lloyd and comedy veteran Val Valentine, couldn't be simpler: a group of English holidaymakers end up in France while on a caravanning weekend having accidentally boarded a cross-Channel train and ferry (as Fred Scrutton, the leader of the party notes of their dilemma, "We're stuck in the middle of Europe with no papers for the car, no passports and no foreign cur-

rency, and the whole flamin' lot chattering away in shorthand!")

Although the production was executive produced by Michael Carreras and directed by John Paddy Carstairs—who had previously helmed *Sands of the Desert* (1960), which Hammer had invested in—the film was made primarily by talent from outside the regular Hammer family. Shot at Shepperton Studios between 3 October and 10 December 1960, the film is little more than a collection of linked sketches on a theme, with the hapless Brits encountering confusion with the usual "foreign" types, among them the expected dirty postcard seller, a madam and her "girls" and a randy French aristocrat ("It's that French count that I don't trust," observes Leslie Phillips' Timothy Gray after the aristo has made a pass at his girlfriend Deidre, though the actor's astonishing emphasis on the word *count* leaves one in no doubt as to what he really means—and in an A certificate too!). Even the Tour de France is woven into the narrative, along with plenty of mishaps and pratfalls

An amusing ad for *A Weekend with Lulu* (1961). Potential audiences may have been disappointed to learn that Lulu is not the woman depicted, but the caravan seen at the bottom of the poster. At least she's *en suite* (Hammer/Columbia).

inside the caravan, some of them already familiar from such films as *The Long, Long Trailer* (1954). This being a British film, there is also plenty of trouser dropping and a good dose of lavatory humor (not sure that the caravan has a toilet, Irene Handle's Florence Proudfoot exclaims, "I was gonna have a bob down in the bushes," which doesn't really bear thinking about).

Adequately performed by a cast proficient with such nonsense, the film is of note for Bob Monkhouse's role as the chirpy Cockney Fred Scrutton, which is easily his most endearing film performance, and Alfred Marks' appearance as the randy count, which has a genuine touch of the Charles Boyers to it. It also contains cameos by a number of familiar faces, among them Sydney Tafler, Graham Stark, Tutte Lemkow, Edie Martin and Judith Furse.

The finished film went on general release on 10 April 1961 care of Columbia ("Belly laughs all over La Belle France!" exclaimed the poster). More surprisingly, it even managed a few Stateside bookings, again care of Columbia (St. Louis from 1 November 1961 and New York from 23 May 1962); however, in a reversal of the usual practice, the film's U.S. running time was actually *expanded* by two minutes, and it was apparently accompanied with sub-titles, presumably to help explain such colloquialisms as lolly, scarper, rozzers, have a butchers and twenty-five nicker! Sadly, the film is rarely seen today, not even on television, which is a shame, for while overlong, it provides a fair share of undemanding fun. And just in case you were wondering, Lulu is the name of the caravan. **Additional notes:** The film's composer Trevor H. Stanford is actually pianist Russ Conway, who appears in the film (Stanford being his real name); the film officially "introduced" him to film audiences.

Production company: Hammer. Distributor: Columbia (UK, U.S.). Producer: Ted Lloyd. Executive producer: Michael Carreras. Director: John Paddy Carstairs. Screenplay: Ted Lloyd. Story: Ted Lloyd, Val Valentine. Cinematographer: Ken Hodges. Music: Trevor H. Stanford (theme). Music director: Tony Osborne (orchestrations and additional music). Supervising editor: James Needs. Editor: Tom Simpson. Production designer: John Howell. Art department assistant: Helen Thomas [uncredited]. Costumes: Maude Churchill. Makeup: Dick Bonnor-Morris. Hair: Bill Griffiths. Second unit photography: Jack Mills (credited as exterior photography). Sound: Bill Salter. Boom operator: Tom Buchanan [uncredited]. Dubbing: Allan Morrison. Production manager: Jacques de Lane Lea. Location manager: Colin Brewer. Assistant director: Chris Sutton. Second assistant director: Patrick Hayes [uncredited]. Third assistant director: Michael Klaw [uncredited]. Construction manager: Jack Bolam [uncredited]. Camera operator: Brian West. Camera grip: M. Walters [uncredited]. Clapper boy: Bob Stilwell [uncredited]. Casting: Stuart Lyons [uncredited]. Continuity: "Splinters" Deason. Stills: Robert Penn [uncredited]. Accountant: W.H.V. Able [uncredited]. Production buyer: Charles Townsend [uncredited]. Publicity: Dennison Thornton [uncredited]. Driv-

ers: Peter Willetts [uncredited], L.C. Wenman [uncredited]. **Cast:** Bob Monkhouse (Fred Scrutton), Leslie Phillips (Timothy Gray), Shirley Eaton (Deidre Proudfoot), Irene Handl (Florence Proudfoot), Alfred Marks (Comte de Grenoble), Sid James (Café patron), Eugene Deckers (Inspector Larue), Kenneth Connor (Tourist), Sydney Tafler (Stationmaster), Graham Stark (Chiron), Russ Conway (French pianist), Harold Berens (Card seller), Tutte Lemkow (Leon), Stuart Hillier (Flying Corsican), Andreas Malandrinos (Lodgekeeper), Ernst Walder (Count's chauffeur), Keith Pyott (Count's butler), Judith Furse (Madame Bon-Bon), Denis Shaw (Bar patron), Heidi Erich (Lulubelle), Edie Martin (Lodgekeeper's wife [uncredited]), Harold Kasket (*Bon-viveur* [uncredited]), Alexis Bobrinskoy (Mayor [uncredited]), Gordon Rollings (Humper [uncredited]), Sally Douglas (Lulubelle [uncredited]), Marie Devereux (Lulubelle [uncredited]), Eve Eden (Lulubelle [uncredited]), Janette Rowsell (Lulubelle [uncredited])

## Weeks, Don

British born Weeks (1904–1988, full name Arthur Donald Weeks) began his association with Hammer as an assistant director on *Quatermass 2* (1957) and *The Steel Bayonet* (1957) but quickly graduated to the post of production manager with *The Curse of Frankenstein* (1957) later the same year (however, though *Quatermass 2* and *The Steel Bayonet* were filmed before *The Curse of Frankenstein*, they were released after it). Such was Weeks' skill he was, on occasion, able to run two films at once, as was the case with *The Curse of the Mummy's Tomb* (1964) and *Hysteria* (1965), whose schedules overran each other. His other credits as an assistant director include *Gert and Daisy Clean Up* (1942), *Somewhere in Civvies* (1943), *Demobbed* (1946), *Holiday Camp* (1947), *Cairo Road* (1950), *Island of Terror* (1966) and *A Swarm in May* (1983), while his other work as a production manager includes *Windom's Way* (1957) and *Cul-de-Sac* (1966). He was the brother of Hammer wardrobe supervisor Molly Arbuthnot (1908–2001, maiden name Molly Weeks) **Hammer credits:** *The Curse of Frankenstein* (1957, production manager), *Quatermass 2* (1957, assistant director), *The Steel Bayonet* (1957, assistant director), *The Abominable Snowman* (1957, production manager), *Man with a Dog* (1957, production manager), *Danger List* (1957, production manager), *Dracula* (1958, production manager), *Clean Sweep* (1958, production manager), *The Snorkel* (1958, production manager), *The Revenge of Frankenstein* (1958, production manager), *I Only Arsked!* (1958, production manager), *The Hound of the Baskervilles* (1959, production manager), *The Ugly Duckling* (1959, production manager), *The Mummy* (1959, production manager), *The Man Who Could Cheat Death* (1959, production manager), *Hell Is a City* (1960, production manager), *The Brides of Dracula* (1960, production manager), *Sword of Sherwood Forest* (1960, production manager), *The Shadow of the Cat* (1961, production manager), *Captain Clegg* (1962, production manager), *The Damned* (1963, production manager), *The Kiss of the Vampire* (1963, produc-

tion manager), *Nightmare* (1964, production manager), *The Evil of Frankenstein* (1964, production manager), *The Devil-Ship Pirates* (1964, production manager), *The Gorgon* (1964, production manager), *The Curse of the Mummy's Tomb* (1964, production manager), *Hysteria* (1965, production manager), *The Secret of Blood Island* (1965, production manager), *The Brigand of Kandahar* (1965, production manager), *Dr. Jekyll and Sister Hyde* (1971, production manager)

## Wei, Lo

This prolific Chinese actor, producer and director (1918–1996, aka Lo Wai and Wai Lo) can be seen as Howe in Hammer's *Shatter* (1974), prior to which he'd had a minor role in *The Legend of the 7 Golden Vampires* (1974). His many credits as an actor include *Da liang shan en chou ji* (1949), *Xiao bai cai* (1955), *Zei mei ren* (1961), *Gui liu xing* (1971) and *Gung foo wong dai* (1981), while his work as a director includes *Zhang fu ri ji* (1953), *Jin pu sa* (1966) and *Long teng hu yue* (1983), the latter of which he also produced. His wife was the actress and producer Liang Hua Liu (1933–2014), whom he married in 1953. **Hammer credits:** *The Legend of the 7 Golden Vampires* (1974, as Cohort [uncredited]), *Shatter* (1974, as Howe)

## Weir, Frank

This bandleader and sax player appeared with his orchestra in the Hammer featurette *Parade of the Bands* (1956). He can also be seen in *Dead of Night* (1945), and as himself in episodes of such TV shows as *New to You* (1946–1950, TV), *Off the Record* (1955–1958, TV), *Festival of British Popular Song* (1956–1957, TV) and *Juke Box Jury* (1959–1967, TV). His albums include *Presenting Frank Weir and His Saxophone* and *Frank Weir—Man and His Music*. **Hammer credits:** *Parade of the Bands* (1956, as himself)

## Weir, Molly

Much on television (especially in cookery programs and commercials), this diminutive Scottish actress (1910–2004, real name Mary Weir) first came to attention in the forties in the radio series *ITMA* (1939–1949, full title *It's That Man Again*) in which she played Tattie. *Life with the Lyons* (1950–1954), another successful radio series, followed in the fifties. This time she played the nononsense housekeeper Aggie Macdonald. The program inspired two big-screen spin-offs from Hammer—*Life with the Lyons* (1954) and *The Lyons in Paris* (1955)—as well as a long-running TV sitcom, also titled *Life with the Lyons* (1955–1960, TV), in all of which Weir appeared as Aggie. In films from 1944 with *2,000 Women*, her other credits include *Madeleine* (1950), *Carry On Regardless* (1961), *What a Whopper* (1961), *The Prime of Miss Jean Brodie* (1969), *Scrooge* (1970), *Bless This House* (1972) and *One of Our Dinosaurs Is Missing* (1975). In 1971 she returned to Hammer for a brief appearance as a maid in *Hands of the Ripper*. Her many other TV appearances include episodes of *Comedy Playhouse* (1961–1975, TV), *Oh, Father!* (1973, TV), *Rentaghost* (1976–1985, TV) and *The High Life* (1994–1995, TV). Her brother was the writer and television presenter Tom Weir (1914–2006).

**Hammer credits:** *Life with the Lyons* (1954, as Aggie Macdonald), *The Lyons in Paris* (1955, as Aggie Macdonald), *Adventures with the Lyons* (1957, serial re-issue of *Life with the Lyons*, as Aggie), *Hands of the Ripper* (1971, as Maude [Madame Bullard's maid])

### Welch, Elisabeth

Long in Britain, this much-admired American born singer (1904–2003) made her stage debut in 1922 and, the following year, introduced the *Charleston* to audiences in the Broadway hit *Runnin' Wild*. In Britain on and off from 1933 onwards, she went on to star opposite Paul Robeson in two films: Hammer's *Song of Freedom* (1936) and *Big Fella* (1937). Her other films include *Death at Broadcasting House* (1934), which marked her screen debut, *Soft Lights and Sweet Music* (1936), *Over the Moon* (1937), *Calling All Stars* (1937), *Fiddlers Three* (1944), *Dead of Night* (1945), *Our Man in Havana* (1959), *Girl Stroke Boy* (1971), *Revenge of the Pink Panther* (1978) and *The Tempest* (1979). However, it was on stage, in cabaret, on the concert platform and in the recording studio where she was most at home, popularizing such classics as *Love for Sale* and *Stormy Weather*. Recalled Welch of her time working with Robeson on *Song of Freedom*, "It was a happy time for me, working with Paul and watching him work. I found him a man of great intensity, both in his work and in his beliefs but—thank goodness—not lacking in humor. We'd sometimes sit outdoors with our lunch trays, chatting about life and living. These were times I can never forget…. The lunch break over, he'd laugh and say, 'To be continued tomorrow,' and back we'd go to the life and lights of the film studio."[10] **Hammer credits:** *Song of Freedom* (1936, as Ruth Zinga)

### Welch, Peter

This British actor (1922–1984) played Richardson in Hammer's *The Secret of Blood Island* (1965), prior to which he'd popped up in a supporting role in *Women Without Men* (1956). His other credits include *Dial 999* (1955), *The Two-Headed Spy* (1958) and *The Secret Partner* (1961), while his many TV credits include episodes of *The Adventures of Robin Hood* (1955–1960, TV), *No Hiding Place* (1959–1967, TV) and *Spy Trap* (1972–1975, TV). **Hammer credits:** *Women Without Men* (1956, as Priest [uncredited]), *The Secret of Blood Island* (1965, as Richardson)

### Welch, Raquel

Best known for her spectacular looks and curvaceous physique rather than her acting ability (hence her self-deprecating comment, "If you have physical attractiveness you don't have to act"), this internationally famous actress and sex symbol (1940–, real name Jo Raquel Tejada) broke into films in 1964 with a small role in *A House Is Not a Home* following experience as a model. After further bit parts in *Roustabout* (1964), *Do Not Disturb* (1965) and *A Swinging Summer* (1965), she hit the big time with the science fiction adventure *Fantastic Voyage* (1966), which she closely followed with the role of Loana in Hammer's prehistoric epic *One Million Years B.C.* (1966), which she has criticized ever since (most recently in a 2015

edition of *Piers Morgan's Life Stories* [2009–, TV]), primarily because she had no dialogue as such, save for the frequently uttered "akeeta" and "neetcha" (which were in any case dubbed by Nicolette McKenzie, thus adding insult to injury [Nikki Van Der Zyl also provided additional grunts for the actress]).

Commented *Kinematograph Weekly* of her performance in *One Million Years B.C.*, "Raquel Welch, in a gracefully ragged doeskin bikini, is an anachronistically attractive heroine." When told that she had to do the film by Fox studio head Dick Zanuck, Welch apparently commented, "Oh, well, you know Steve McQueen got away with *The Blob*. Maybe I can get away with *One Million Years B.C.* Nobody will remember this thing. I can shove it under the carpet."[11] However, she went on to concede, "But people remembered it. And I've been living it down ever since."[12] That said, she has since admitted, "That was the crazy, wonderful, silly but still classic film that made me into Raquel Welch. And gave me the opportunity to make over 30 films I made in my career. It started me off. Dick Zanuck was right to put me into it."[13]

Welch's subsequent credits include *Fathom* (1967), *Bedazzled* (1967), *Myra Breckinridge* (1970), *Hannie Caulder* (1970), *Kansas City Bomber* (1972), *The Last of Sheila* (1973), *The Three Musketeers* (1973), *The Four Musketeers* (1974), *The Prince and the Pauper* (1977), *The Legend of Walks Far Woman* (1979, TVM), *Right to Die* (1987, TVM), *Chairman of the Board* (1998), *Legally Blonde* (2001), *Forget About It* (2006), *House of Versace* (2013, TVM) and *How to Be a Latin Lover* (2017). She was also offered the starring role of pirate queen Anne Bonay in Hammer's proposed *Mistress of the Seas*, but Universal turned the project down in 1970.

Her TV appearances include episodes of *Bracken's World* (1969–1970, TV), *Mork and Mindy* (1978–1982, TV), *Central Park West* (1995–1996, TV), *Sin City* (1996–2002, TV), *American Family* (2002–2004, TV) and *8 Simple Rules* (2002–2005, TV), plus countless chat show spots. She has also appeared on Broadway (in *Woman of the Year* and *Victor/Victoria*) and has released a number of successful fitness videos. Married four times, her husbands include the producer Patrick Curtis (1938–), to whom she was married between 1967 and 1972, and with whom she anonymously produced *The Sorcerers* (1967) through their company Curtwel, and the writer, director, producer and cinematographer André Weinfeld (1947–), to whom she was married between 1980 and 1990. She is the mother of the actor Damon Welch (1959–) and the actress Tahnee Welch (1961–, real name Latanne Rene Welch). **Additional notes:** Welch was hired to play the role of Domino in *Thunderball* (1965), but was subsequently released at the request of Richard Zanuck; the role subsequently went to Claudine Auger. **Hammer credits:** *One Million Years B.C.* (1966, as Loana), *Flesh and Blood—The Hammer Heritage of Horror* (1994, TV, interviewee, special thanks)

### Welden, Ben

This prolific American actor (1901–1997, real name Benjamin Weinblatt) began his film career

in Britain in 1930 with *The Man from Chicago*, which he followed with *Big Business* (1930), *77 Park Lane* (1931), *His Lordship* (1932), *Alibi Inn* (1935) and Hammer's second film, *The Mystery of the Mary Celeste* (1935), in which he appeared as Boas Hoffman. Returning to America in 1936, he went on to rack up many more titles, among them *Maytime* (1937), *Kid Galahad* (1937), *Midnight Manhunt* (1945), *Tough Assignment* (1949), *The Lemon Drop Kid* (1951), *Hidden Guns* (1956) and *Night Passage* (1957). He also popped up in episodes of *I Love Lucy* (1951–1957, TV), *The Abbott and Costello Show* (1952–1953, TV), *Adventures of Superman* (1952–1958, TV) and *Batman* (1966–1968, TV). **Hammer credits:** *The Mystery of the Mary Celeste* (1935, as Boas Hoffman)

### Wellesley, Gordon

This veteran Australian screenwriter (1906–1980) began his film career in Malaya in 1929, where he worked on a handful of documentaries for the government. In Hollywood in the early thirties, he co-authored the screenplay for *Shanghai Madness* (1933). However, it was once he was in Britain that Wellesley's career truly took off, seeing him write (either solo or in collaboration) the screenplays for such films as *Sing As We Go* (1934), *Lorna Doone* (1934), *Night Train to Munich* (1940), which earned him an Oscar nomination for best story, *Flying Fortress* (1942), *The Green Scarf* (1954) and the Hammer Cold War thriller *Visa to Canton* (1960). The head of the scenario department for Independent Producers in the forties, he also worked as a producer on *The High Command* (1937), *The Lost People* (1949) and *The Reluctant Widow* (1950), which he also wrote. He also directed *Rhythm Serenade* (1943), *The Silver Fleet* (1943), which he also wrote, and *Trouble with Junia* (1966). Meanwhile, for the small screen he penned episodes of such series as *Douglas Fairbanks, Jr. Presents* (1953–1957, TV), *International Detective* (1959–1961, TV), *Sir Francis Drake* (1961–1962, TV) and *Beware of the Dog* (1964, TV). He also penned a book about the making of *The Silver Fleet* titled *The Silver Fleet: The Story of the Film Put Into Narrative* (1943). **Hammer credits:** *Visa to Canton* (1960)

### Wells, (Bombadier) Billy

Once Britain's longest-reigning champion heavyweight boxer (until Henry Cooper came on the scene), Wells (1887–1967, aka William Wells) held the title between 1911 and 1919. However, it was on screen in the forties that he found true immortality as the second in a series of bodybuilders who introduced Rank films by beating an enormous gong (the first had been Karl Dane, and Wells in turn was succeeded by Phil Nieman and Ken Richmond). Prior to this, Wells was also used by Hammer to introduce their films in the thirties, for which he was required to hammer an anvil. Recalled camera assistant John Mitchell, "The Hammer logo [was] filmed during one lunch hour,"[14] during the making of the company's first film, *The Public Life of Henry the Ninth* (1935). Wells can also be spotted in minor roles in a handful of films, among them *Kent the Fighting Man* (1916), *The Great Game* (1918), *The Ring* (1927), *Broken Blossoms* (1936), *Concerning Mr. Martin* (1937), *We'll Smile Again* (1942), *Old Mother Riley Detective* (1943), *A Canterbury Tale* (1944) and *The Beggar's Opera* (1953). NB: given that many of Hammer's early films are no longer extant, and several were distributed by other companies, it is difficult to determine how many times Wells' introductory logo was in fact used. **Hammer credits include:** *The Public Life of Henry the Ninth* (1935), *Song of Freedom* (1936)

## Wells, Jerold

Cast primarily in character roles, this British actor (1908–1999, real name Denis Gerald Walls) was featured in many films, among them *The Tyburn Case* (1957), *The Naked Truth* (1957), *Playback* (1962), *Anne of the Thousand Days* (1969), *Vault of Horror* (1973), in which he had his best cameo as a vampire waiter in the opening *Midnight Mess* episode, *Time Bandits* (1981) and *Sword of the Valiant* (1983). He also appeared in three Hammer films, plus *Paper Dolls*, an episode of *Journey to the Unknown* (1968, TV), which also appeared in the compendium film *Journey into Darkness* (1968, TVM). His other TV credits include episodes of *Great Expectations* (1959, TV), in which he played Magwitch, *Man in a Suitcase* (1967–1968, TV), *Devenish* (1977–1978, TV) and *Cribb* (1980–1981, TV). **Hammer credits:** *The Pirates of Blood River* (1962, as Commandant), *Maniac* (1962, as Giles), *Paper Dolls* (1968, TV [episode of *Journey to the Unknown*], as Mayhew), *Journey into Darkness* (1968, TVM, as Mayhew), *Frankenstein and the Monster from Hell* (1974, as Landlord)

## Wells, Sheila (Sheilah)

This American actress (1941–) was featured in the additional scenes shot for the expanded U.S. TV version of Hammer's *The Kiss of the Vampire* (1963). Her many other small screen credits include episodes of *Dr. Kildare* (1961–1966, TV), *The Virginian* (1962–1971, TV), *Dan August* (1970–1971, TV) and *Quincy M.E.* (1976–1983, TV). Her occasional film credits include *Love and Kisses* (1965), *The Scarlett O'Hara War* (1980, TVM) and *The Blues Brothers* (1980). She was married to the actor Fred Beir (1927–1980, full name Frederick Edwin Beir) between 1967 and 1969. **Hammer credits:** *The Kiss of the Vampire* (1963, as Theresa Stangher [expanded U.S. TV version only])

## Welsh, Jane

On stage from the age of eighteen, this British actress (1905–2001, real name Louisa Joyce Tudor-Jones) went on to make a handful of films from the early thirties onwards, among them *The Bells* (1931), *Two Crowded Hours* (1931), *The Chinese Puzzle* (1932), *Bell-Bottom George* (1944), *The Second Mate* (1950) and *Another Time, Another Place* (1958). She also appeared as Mrs. Brown, the title character's mother, in *Just William's Luck* (1947) and its sequel *William Comes to Town* (1948), while in 1953 she had a supporting role in Hammer's *Mantrap*. Married twice, her first husband was the actor Henry Mollison (1905–1985, full name Evelyn Henry Mollison), to whom she was wed between 1928 and 1937; he appeared in Hammer's *What the Butler Saw* (1950). **Hammer credits:** *Mantrap* (1953, as Laura)

## Welsh, John

Following several years' stage experience at Dublin's Gate Theater, this refined Irish character player (1914–1985) made the move to London in 1950, where he continued his stage career and broke into films with *The Accused* (1953). Over fifty films followed, among them *The Case of Soho Red* (1953), *Lucky Jim* (1957), *Attack on the Iron Coast* (1967), *The Pied Piper* (1971), *The Thirty-Nine Steps* (1978) and *Krull* (1983). He also popped up in a handful of Hammer productions, including *Paper Dolls*, an episode of *Journey to the Unknown* (1968, TV), which also appeared in the compendium film *Journey into Darkness* (1968, TVM). His many other TV credits include episodes of *Softly Softly* (1966–1976, TV), *Kizzy* (1976, TV), *The Duchess of Duke Street* (1976–1977, TV), in which he played Merriman, *Brideshead Revisited* (1981, TV) and *Blott on the Landscape* (1985, TV). **Hammer credits:** *Women Without Men* (1956, as Prison Chaplain), *The Revenge of Frankenstein* (1958, as Bergman), *Nightmare* (1964, as Doctor), *Rasputin—The Mad Monk* (1966, as Abbott [uncredited]), *Paper Dolls* (1968, TV [episode of *Journey to the Unknown*], as Bart Brereton), *Journey into Darkness* (1968, TVM, as Bart Brereton)

## Wenman, L.C.

Wenman worked as one of the drivers on the Hammer comedy *A Weekend with Lulu* (1961). **Hammer credits:** *A Weekend with Lulu* (1961 [uncredited])

## Wenzel, Edgar

Wenzel (1919–1980) can be spotted in a minor role in Hammer's *The Lady Vanishes* (1979). His other credits include *Nackt, wie Gott sie schuff* (1958), *Waldrausch* (1962), *Charlys Nichten* (1974) and *Fabian* (1980). **Hammer credits:** *The Lady Vanishes* (1979, as Waiter)

## West, Brian

The work of this British cameraman (1928–) includes *Waltz Time* (1945), on which he was a camera assistant, *The Weak and the Wicked* (1945), on which he was the clapper loader, *The Passionate Stranger* (1957), on which he was the focus puller, Hammer's *A Weekend with Lulu* (1961), on which he was the camera operator, and *Oliver!* (1968), on which he photographed the second unit. His work as a fully-fledged cinematographer includes *The Ceremony* (1963), *Billy Two Hats* (1974), *Russian Roulette* (1975), *Yesterday's Hero* (1979), *Finders Keepers* (1984), *84 Charing Cross Road* (1987), *Fire in the Dark* (1991, TVM) and *Ellen Foster* (1997, TV). He also photographed seven episodes of *Hammer House of Mystery and Suspense* (1984, TVM). His other TV work includes episodes of *Holocaust* (1978, TV), *A Man Called Intrepid* (1979, TV), *Remington Steele* (1982–1987, TV) and *Matlock* (1986–1995, TV). **Hammer credits:** *A Weekend with Lulu* (1961, camera operator), *Czech Mate* (1984, TVM [episode of *Hammer House of Mystery and Suspense*], cinematographer), *The Sweet Scent of Death* (1984, TVM [episode of *Hammer House of Mystery and Suspense*], cinematographer), *A Distant Scream* (1984, TVM [episode of *Hammer House of Mystery and Suspense*], cinematographer), *The Late Nancy Irving* (1984, TVM [episode of *Hammer House of Mystery and Suspense*], cinematographer), *In Possession* (1984, TVM [episode of *Hammer House of Mystery and Suspense*], cinematographer), *Black Carrion* (1984, TVM [episode of *Hammer House of Mystery and Suspense*], cinematographer), *Last Video and Testament* (1984, TVM [episode of *Hammer House of Mystery and Suspense*], cinematographer)

## West, Kit

A shared Oscar winner for his work on *Raiders of the Lost Ark* (1981) and a BAFTA winner (also shared) for his work on *Return of the Jedi* (1983), this British special effects technician (1936–2016, real name Christopher John West) began his career in the early sixties, working as an assistant to Les Bowie on a number of Hammer films. His other credits include *First Men in the Moon* (1964), *Billion Dollar Brain* (1967), *Some Girls Do* (1969), *Dracula* (1973, TVM), *The Pink Panther Strikes Again* (1976), *The Wild Geese* (1978), *The Big Red One* (1980), *Dune* (1984), *Universal Soldier* (1992), *Daylight* (1996), *Enemy at the Gates* (2001), *Doom* (2005) and *City of Ember* (2008). He was also Oscar nominated (with others) for his work on *Young Sherlock Holmes* (1985) and *Dragonheart* (1996). **Hammer credits:** *Taste of Fear* (1961 [uncredited]), *The Shadow of the Cat* (1961 [uncredited]), *Captain Clegg* (1962 [uncredited]), *The Pirates of Blood River* (1962 [uncredited]), *Paranoiac* (1963 [uncredited]), *The Damned* (1963 [uncredited]), *The Scarlet Blade* (1963 [uncredited]), *The Kiss of the Vampire* (1963 [uncredited]), *The Old Dark House* (1963 [uncredited]), *Nightmare* (1964 [uncredited]), *The Evil of Frankenstein* (1964 [uncredited]), *The Devil-Ship Pirates* (1964 [uncredited]), *She* (1965 [uncredited]), *One Million Years B.C.* (1966 [uncredited]), *Quatermass and the Pit* (1967 [uncredited]), *The Vengeance of She* (1968 [uncredited]), *Moon Zero Two* (1969)

## West, Lockwood

On stage from 1931 and in films from 1948 with *A Song for Tomorrow*, this British character actor (1905–1989, full name Harry Lockwood West) appeared in almost fifty films, ranging from second features, such as the Hammer comedy thriller *Celia* (1949), in which he played Dr. Cresswell, to such A-features as *Last Holiday* (1950), *Private's Progress* (1956), *Tunes of Glory* (1960), *The Running Man* (1963), *The Dresser* (1983) and *Young Sherlock Holmes* (1985). He also returned to Hammer two more times, appearing in *The Man Who Could Cheat Death* (1959), again as a doctor, and *The Satanic Rites of Dracula* (1974), in which he played the corrupt General Sir Arthur Freeborne. His many TV appearances include episodes of *Pride and Prejudice* (1952, TV), *The Prisoner* (1967–1968, TV) and *Valentine Park* (1985–1988, TV).

His son is actor Timothy West (1934–) and his grandsons actors Samuel West (1966–) and Joseph (Joe) West. **Hammer credits:** *Celia* (1949, as Dr. Cresswell), *The Man Who Could Cheat Death* (1959, as Doctor), *The Satanic Rites of Dracula* (1974, as General Sir Arthur Freeborne)

### West, Norma

This South African born actress (1943–) can be seen as Sarah Tarrant in Hammer's *Man at the Top* (1973). Her other credits include *The Projected Man* (1966) and *Battle Beneath the Earth* (1967), plus episodes of *Londoners* (1965, TV), *Supernatural* (1977, TV), *Lovejoy* (1986–1994, TV) and *A Touch of Frost* (1992–2010, TV). **Hammer credits:** *Man at the Top* (1973)

### West, Wilton

West had a minor role in the Hammer B-picture *River Patrol* (1948). **Hammer credits:** *River Patrol* (1948, unnamed role)

### Westbrook, Tommy

British born Westbrook (1934–) worked as a carpenter on the Hammer thriller *Maniac* (1963). His many other credits include *The Disappearance* (1977), *Shanghai Surprise* (1986), *The Lair of the White Worm* (1988), *The Rainbow* (1989), *The Crying Game* (1992), *Four Weddings and a Funeral* (1994) and *Richard III* (1995), plus episodes of *Inspector Morse* (1987–2000, TV). **Hammer credits:** *Maniac* (1963 [uncredited])

### Westcott, Helen

This American actress (1928–1998, real name Myrthas Helen Hickman) played the role of Christine Halpert in *The Face in the Tombstone Mirror*, the pilot episode of Hammer's aborted television series *Tales of Frankenstein* (1958, TV). In films as a child, she made her debut with *Thunder Over Texas* (1934), and went on to appear in *A Midsummer Night's Dream* (1935), *The New Adventures of Don Juan* (1948), *The Charge at Feather River* (1953), *Studs Lonigan* (1960) and *I Love My Wife* (1971). She also appeared in episodes of *The Lone Wolf* (1954–1955, TV), *Mannix* (1967–1975, TV) and *Switch* (1975–1978, TV). Her father was actor Gordon Westcott (1903–1935, real name Myrthus Hickman). Her first husband (of two) was actor Don Gordon (1926–2017, full name Donald Walter Guadagno), to whom she was married between 1948 and 1953. **Hammer credits:** *Tales of Frankenstein: The Face in the Tombstone Mirror* (1958, TV, as Christine Halpert)

### Westerby, Robert

In films from 1947 with *The White Unicorn*, this British screenwriter (1909–1968) worked on the scripts for *Broken Journey* (1948), *War and Peace* (1956) and *The Three Lives of Thomasina* (1963) among others. He also worked on the screenplay for the Hammer second feature *Break in the Circle* (1955) with the film's director Val Guest. His TV credits include episodes of *Douglas Fairbanks, Jr. Presents* (1953–1957, TV), *Sword of Freedom* (1957, TV) and *The Alfred Hitchcock Hour* (1962–1965, TV). **Hammer credits:** *Break in the Circle* (1955 [uncredited])

### Western Electric

This sound system was used to record Hammer's *The Steel Bayonet* (1957). Used in both the U.S. and the U.K., other films recorded with the system include *Animal Crackers* (1930), *A Star Is Born* (1937), *Royal Wedding* (1951) and *The Story of Gilbert and Sullivan* (1953). **Hammer credits:** *The Steel Bayonet* (1957)

### Westhorpe, Wayne

Westhorpe can be seen as Olive's baby in *Mutiny on the Buses* (1972), in which he spends most of the film making rude noises on his potty. Wonder if his mates down the pub know this? The role was subsequently played by Adam Rhodes in *Holiday on the Buses* (1973). **Hammer credits:** *Mutiny on the Buses* (1972, as Olive's baby)

### Westlake, Donald E.

Best known for his Parker novels, of which several have been filmed to varying degrees of success, this prolific American novelist and screenwriter (1933–2008, aka Richard Stark, Samuel Holt and Tucker Coe among others) had his 1959 story *One on a Desert Island* (also known as *One Man on a Desert Island*) adapted by Oscar Millard as *One on an Island* for the Hammer series *Journey to the Unknown* (1968, TV). Films adapted from his novels include *Point Blank* (1967 [novel, *The Hunter*, 1962–first in the Parker series—writing as Richard Stark]), *The Hot Rock* (1972 [novel 1970]), *The Bank Shot* (1974 [novel 1972]), *Slayground* (1983 [novel 1971, writing as Richard Stark]), *Two Much* (1996 [novel 1975]), *Payback* (1999 [novel, *The Hunter*, 1962, writing as Richard Stark]), *Jimmy the Kid* (1999 [novel 1974]), *What's the Worst That Could Happen?* (2001 [novel 1996]) and *Parker* (2013 [novel, *Flashfire*, 2000, writing as Richard Stark]). His screenplays include *Cops and Robbers* (1973), *The Stepfather* (1987) and *The Grifters* (1990), the latter of which earned him an Oscar nomination. **Hammer credits:** *One on an Island* (1968, TV [episode of *Journey to the Unknown*])

### Westley, Bill

British born Westley (1939–) worked as the third assistant director on Hammer's *Quatermass and the Pit* (1967). He graduated to second assistant director on *Frankenstein Must Be Destroyed* (1969) and *Love Thy Neighbour* (1973). His work as a first assistant includes *Confessions of a Pop Performer* (1975), *Confessions of a Driving Instructor* (1976), *Confessions from a Holiday Camp* (1977), *Stand Up, Virgin Soldiers* (1977), *Who Dares Wins* (1982), *The Killing Fields* (1984), *City of Joy* (1992), *Dark Blood* (1993 [released 2012]), *Rob Roy* (1995), *The Jackal* (1997) and *The Fourth Angel* (2004), plus episodes of *The Sweeney* (1975–1978, TV) and *The Professionals* (1977–1983, TV). **Hammer credits:** *Quatermass and the Pit* (1967, third assistant director [uncredited]), *Frankenstein Must Be Destroyed* (1969, second assistant director [uncredited]), *Love Thy Neighbour* (1973, second assistant director [uncredited])

### Weston, Bill

This British stunt co-ordinator, stunt performer and occasional bit-part actor (1941–2012) arranged the stunt work for Hammer's *Moon Zero Two* (1969), in which he also appeared as a Green man. His other credits as a stunt man or stunt arranger include *The Fighting Prince of Donegal* (1966), *You Only Live Twice* (1967), *On Her Majesty's Secret Service* (1969), *Star Wars* (1977), *Superman* (1978), *Raiders of the Lost Ark* (1981), *Brazil* (1985), *Batman* (1989), *Titanic* (1997), *Sahara* (2005), *The Da Vinci Code* (2006) and *Robin Hood* (2010), while his appearances as a performer include *2001: A Space Odyssey* (1968), *The Living Daylights* (1987) and *Enduring Love* (2004). His TV work includes episodes of *Lovejoy* (1986–1994, TV) and *Tales from the Crypt* (1989–1996, TV). **Hammer credits:** *Moon Zero Two* (1969, as Green Man [uncredited])

### Weston, Leslie

This British actor (1896–1975) had a supporting role in the Hammer second feature *The Last Page* (1952). His other credits include *Glamour Girl* (1938), *My Brother Jonathan* (1948), *Last Holiday* (1950), *Above Us the Waves* (1955) and *The House of the Seven Hawks* (1959), plus episodes of *Dixon of Dock Green* (1955–1976, TV), *Boyd Q.C.* (1956–1964, TV), *The Count of Monte Cristo* (1956, TV) and *Shadow Squad* (1957–1959, TV). **Hammer credits:** *The Last Page* (1952, as Mr. Bruce)

### Weston, Paul

This stuntman and actor (1940–) can be seen as a guard in Hammer's *The Satanic Rites of Dracula* (1974). He also worked as one of the stunt arrangers on Hammer's *The Lady Vanishes* (1979). His other credits include *You Only Live Twice* (1967), *Live and Let Die* (1973), *The Spy Who Loved Me* (1977), *Superman II* (1980), *Aliens* (1986), *Frankenstein Unbound* (1990), *Dragonheart* (1996), *Sleuth* (2007) and *Skyfall* (2012), plus episodes of *The Avengers* (1961–1969, TV), *Supergran* (1985–1987, TV), *New Tricks* (2003–2015, TV) and *Just William* (2010, TV). **Hammer credits:** *The Satanic Rites of Dracula* (1974, as Guard 2), *The Lady Vanishes* (1979, stunt arrangements)

### Westrex

This sound system was used to record a number of Hammer productions, including their ill-fated American TV venture *Tales of Frankenstein* (1958, TV). Used on both sides of the Atlantic, the system was also used to record such films as *A Hill in Korea* (1956), *The Scapegoat* (1959), *One, Two, Three* (1961), *Landru* (1963), *Patton* (1970) and *Jaws* (1975). **Hammer credits:** *Tales of Frankenstein* (1958, TV), *Yesterday's Enemy* (1959), *A Weekend with Lulu* (1961), *Maniac* (1963), *Hysteria* (1965), *Creatures the World Forgot* (1971), *Vampire Circus* (1972), *Nearest and Dearest* (1973), *That's Your Funeral* (1973)

### Westwater, Rosalie

This British actress (1922–1985) can be seen as a caroler in Hammer's *Women Without Men* (1956). Her other credits include *Interlude* (1968), *The Rise and Rise of Michael Rimmer* (1970) and *Naughty!* (1971), plus episodes of *David Copperfield* (1956,

TV), *Mysteries and Miracles* (1965, TV) and *Macbeth* (1970, TV). She was married to the actor Kevin Stoney (1921–2008, full name Thomas Kevin Harvest Stoney) from 1953; he appeared in Hammer's *The Shadow of the Cat* (1961) and *Cash on Demand* (1961), plus an episode of *Hammer House of Horror* (1980, TV). **Hammer credits:** *Women Without Men* (1956, as Caroller [uncredited])

### Westwood, Patrick

This British actor (1924–2017) had a supporting role in the Hammer thriller *Third Party Risk* (1955). His many other credits include *A Gunman Has Escaped* (1948), *House of Secrets* (1956), *My Wife's Family* (1962), *Guns in the Heather* (1969) and *The Last Valley* (1970), while his TV credits take in episodes of *The Quatermass Experiment* (1953, TV), *The Saint* (1962–1969, TV), *Space: 1999* (1975–1977, TV) and *Shelley* (1979–1983, TV). His wife was actress Viola Merrett (1921–), whom he married in 1950. **Hammer credits:** *Third Party Risk* (1955, as Porter [uncredited])

### Wetherall, Virginia *see* Wetherell, Virginia

### Wetherell, Eric

This British bit-part player also worked as Christopher Lee's stand-in on many films for Hammer.

### Wetherell, Virginia

In films from 1963 with *The Partner*, this British actress (1943–, aka Virginia Wetherall) notched up supporting roles in the likes of *Alfie* (1966) and *Curse of the Crimson Altar* (1968) before bagging two female leads for exploitation director Pete Walker in *The Big Switch* (1968) and *Man of Violence* (1970). She returned to supporting roles thereafter, appearing in *A Clockwork Orange* (1971), *Disciple of Death* (1972), *Dracula* (1973, TVM), *Minder on the Orient Express* (1985, TVM) and *Love Is the Devil* (1998). She also notched up two Hammer films in the early seventies: *Dr. Jekyll and Sister Hyde* (1971) and *Demons of the Mind* (1972). She was also considered for the role of Isabel in Hammer's *To the Devil a Daughter* (1976). Her TV work includes episodes of *Doctor Who* (1963–1989, TV), *The Troubleshooters* (1965–1972, TV) and *The Gentle Touch* (1980–1984, TV). Wetherell was married to the actor Ralph Bates (1940–1991) from 1973. He appeared in four films for Hammer: *Taste the Blood of Dracula* (1970), *The Horror of Frankenstein* (1970), *Lust for a Vampire* (1971) and *Dr. Jekyll and Sister Hyde* (1971). Their children are actress Daisy Bates (1974–) and actor and composer Will (William) Bates (1977–). **Hammer credits:** *Dr. Jekyll and Sister Hyde* (1971, as Betsy), *Demons of the Mind* (1972, as Inge)

### *What the Butler Saw*

GB, 1950, 61m, bw, cert U

The fourth of five films shot by Hammer in and around Oakley Court, this tame comedy, based upon a 1950 radio serial by Edward J. Mason (who also co-wrote the screenplay), tells the unlikely story of an earl who, having returned home to his snooty family after a ten-year hunting expedition, finds himself in the awkward position of having to hide a native princess who has followed him back to England because she has fallen for the charms of his straitlaced butler.

A by-the-numbers affair, the film has the look and feel of a threadbare theatrical rep production, with performances to match, save for the ever-reliable Edward Rigby as the earl, who brings a welcome dose of warmth and humor to the proceedings. The rest of the cast, however, often awkwardly fumble their way through the thinly conceived and flatly handled proceedings, some of which are surprisingly vulgar for a U-cert film of the period. Indeed, the insinuating title aside, the film includes a lascivious wolf-whistle in the opening title music, shots of the earl taking a bath, among them a back view taking in a few millimeters of flabby ass crack (and we're talking Edward Rigby's ass crack here!), an exceptionally low cut sarong for the visiting Princess Lapis, a scene in which she takes a impromptu bath in the scullery's Belfast sink, and a scene at a cocktail party at which she arrives stark naked (albeit shot from the neck up) only to be ushered behind a convenient screen by the butler. A remark in the opening scene must also have raised eyebrows at the time: as the under-butler ties up a banner across the main entrance welcoming the earl home, the watching cook, Mrs. Thimble, observes, "You're drooping in the middle, Perks," at which he pointedly looks down at his crotch.

Otherwise, there is very little to laugh at here, save for a running gag about the continued worry of the earl's grandson that discovery of the semiclad Lapis by the authorities could imperil "the dignity" of his position at the Foreign Office. This aside, the plot is padded out with a romantic encounter by the earl's granddaughter, a would-be ballerina who is wooed by a visiting journalist, and a chase climax about the house in which a love potion that Lapis has intended for the butler ends up being inadvertently imbibed by the grandson and the reporter, who subsequently compete with each other for her attentions. No wonder the earl decides to pack up and return abroad at the finish, swapping places with his faithful butler, who by now has finally copped off with Lapis (and not before time). "This is terrible," says the earl's sister, Lady Mary, of all the commotion at one point, and indeed it is.

Made in January 1950 and trade shown in June, the film was released in the UK by Exclusive on 11 September the same year. **Additional notes:** The film "introduces" Mercy Haystead as Lapis, and features a relatively early appearance by comedy stalwart Michael Ward, who would go on to make a further three films for Hammer.

Production company: Hammer. Distributor: Exclusive (UK). Producer: Anthony Hinds. Director: Godfrey Grayson. Screenplay: A.R. Rawlinson, Edward J. Mason, based on the radio serial by Edward J. Mason [uncredited]. Story: Roger Good, Donald Good. Cinematographer: Walter "Jimmy" Harvey. Music director: Frank Spencer. Editor: James Needs. Art director: Denis Wreford. Assistant director: Jimmy Sangster. Second assistant director: Bill Shore [uncredited]. Sound: Edgar Vetter. Boom operator: Percy Britten [uncredited]. Production manager: Arthur Barnes. Camera operator: Peter Bryan. Loader: Harry Oakes [uncredited]. Focus pullers: Michael Reed [uncredited], Jack Howard [uncredited]. Chief electrician: Jack Curtis [uncredited]. Electricians: Richard Jenkins [uncredited], Percy Harms [uncredited], Charles Stanbridge [uncredited]. Construction: Freddie Ricketts [uncredited], Mick Lyons [uncredited]. Continuity: Renee Glynne. Casting: Prudence Sykes. Make-up: Phil Leakey. Hair: Monica Hustler. Props buyer: Jim Day [uncredited]. Props: Tommy Money [uncredited]. Stagehand: Jim Prizeman [uncredited]. Stills: John Jay [uncredited]. Production assistant: Michael Carreras [uncredited]. **Cast:** Edward Rigby (The Earl), Mercy Haystead (Lapis), Michael Ward (Gerald), Peter Burton (Bill Fenton), Henry Mollison (Bembridge), Anne Valery (Elaine), Eleanor Hallam (Lady Mary), Tonie MacMillan (Mrs. Thimble), Mollie Palmer (Maudie), Norman Pitt (Policeman), George Bishop (General), Howard Charlton (Perks), Alfred Harris (Bishop)

### Whatmough, Susan (Sue)

Whatmough worked as the casting director on Hammer's *Moon Zero Two* (1969). Her other credits include *Fanny Hill* (1983), *Bloodbath at the House of Death* (1984), *Ordeal by Innocence* (1984) and *Life Is Sweet* (1991), plus episodes of *The Agatha Christie Hour* (1982, TV), *Spooky* (1983, TV), *Rumpole of the Bailey* (1978–1992, TV) and *Supergran* (1985–1987, TV). **Hammer credits:** *Moon Zero Two* (1969)

### Whatling, Johnny

Whatling worked as a dressing props chargehand on Hammer's *Blood from the Mummy's Tomb* (1971). His other credits include *The Raging Moon* (1970), on which he was the chief propman. **Hammer credits:** *Blood from the Mummy's Tomb* (1971 [uncredited])

### Wheatley, Alan

In films from 1936 with *Conquest of the Air*, this British character actor (1907–1991) is best remembered for playing the Sheriff of Nottingham in the classic television series *The Adventures of Robin Hood* (1955–1960, TV), of which he appeared in eighty-one episodes out of 144. Following experience as a newsreader on BBC radio during the war, he continued his career thereafter with over forty other productions, among them *Caesar and Cleopatra* (1945), *Brighton Rock* (1947), *The Pickwick Papers* (1952), *The Duke Wore Jeans* (1958) and *A Jolly Bad Fellow* (1964). He also made a handful of films for Hammer, beginning with *Whispering Smith Hits London* (1952), though it should be noted that the more marquee-friendly Peter Cushing played the Sheriff of Nottingham in *Sword of Sherwood Forest* (1960), Hammer's big screen version of *The Adventures of Robin Hood*. Wheatley also narrated the documentary short *Elizabethan Express* (1954), and appeared in such TV plays and series as *The Importance of Being Earnest* (1937, TV), *The Chance of a Lifetime* (1939, TV), *BBC Sunday-Night Theatre* (1950–1959, TV), *Sherlock Holmes* (1951,

TV), in which he played Holmes, *Douglas Fairbanks, Jr. Presents* (1953–1957, TV), *The Avengers* (1961–1969, TV) and *Department S* (1969–1970, TV). Also much on stage. **Hammer credits:** *Whispering Smith Hits London* (1952, as Hector Reith), *Spaceways* (1953, as Dr. Smith), *The House Across the Lake* (1954, as Inspector MacLennan), *The Shadow of the Cat* (1961, as Inspector Rowles)

## Wheatley, Dennis

Best known for his occult thrillers, this prolific British author (1897–1977) began writing at the age of thirty-six following a career as a wine merchant. Several of his books have been turned into films, among them *Forbidden Territory* (1934 [novel 1933]) and *The Secret of Stamboul* (1936 [from *The Eunuch of Stamboul*, 1935]). Three of his books were also filmed with varying degrees of success by Hammer following a strong recommendation from Christopher Lee (who starred in two of them). They were *The Devil Rides Out* (1968, [novel 1934]), *The Lost Continent* (1968 [from *Uncharted Seas*, 1938]) and *To the Devil a Daughter* (1976 [novel 1953]). It would seem that Wheatley was quite impressed with the film version of *The Devil Rides Out*, sending a telegram to director Terence Fisher, which read, "Saw film yesterday. Heartiest congratulations, grateful thanks for splendid direction."[15] Recalled Christopher Lee, "He [Wheatley] was indeed very pleased with the picture, and rightly so. It stuck pretty close to the book."[16]

Lee's production company, Charlemagne, which he formed with Hammer producer Anthony Nelson Keys, acquired the rights to eight of Wheatley's books in the early seventies, among them *To the Devil a Daughter* and *The Haunting of Toby Jugg* (1948), both of which were sold on to Hammer when Charlemagne was wound up. However, only *To the Devil a Daughter* made it to the screen following a prolonged pre-production period (*Toby Jugg* was eventually filmed by the BBC as *The Haunted Airman* in 2006). Sadly, Wheatley's reaction this time was less than favorable. Recalled screenwriter John Peacock, "I know he was besides himself with anger over it."[17]

Other books by Wheatley considered for adaptation by Hammer include *The Ka of Gifford Hilary* (1956), which was announced in 1967, and *The Satanist* (1960). A short story television series provisionally entitled *The Devil and All His Works* was also mooted in 1974, but this also came to nothing (the title was derived from Wheatley's 1971 factual book). His many other books include *Such Power Is Dangerous* (1933), *Red Eagle* (1937), *Mediterranean Night* (1942), *The Second Seal* (1950), *The Rape of Venice* (1959), *Dangerous Inheritance* (1965), *The Ravishing of Lady Mary Ware* (1971) and *The Deception Planners* (1980). Wheatley also contributed to the screenplay for *An Englishman's Home* (1940). **Hammer credits:** *The Devil Rides Out* (1968), *The Lost Continent* (1968), *To the Devil a Daughter* (1976)

## Wheatley, E.D.

Wheatley was one of Shepperton's master carpenters, and as such worked on the Hammer war

drama *Yesterday's Enemy* (1959), which was shot primarily at the studio because Bray was already overcrowded with other productions. **Hammer credits:** *Yesterday's Enemy* (1959 [uncredited])

## Wheelan, Roy

Wheelan worked as the camera car driver on *Hammer House of Mystery and Suspense* (1984, TVM). **Hammer credits:** *Hammer House of Mystery and Suspense* (1984, TVM [uncredited])

## Wheeler, Brian

Wheeler worked as a dressing props chargehand on Hammer's *Blood from the Mummy's Tomb* (1971). **Hammer credits:** *Blood from the Mummy's Tomb* (1971 [uncredited])

## Wheeler, Charles

Wheeler operated the boom for Hammer's *The Witches* (1966) and *Frankenstein Created Woman* (1967). His other credits include *Back-Room Boy* (1942), *Shadow of the Eagle* (1950), *Aunt Clara* (1954), *The Pure Hell of St. Trinian's* (1960) and *The Sicilians* (1964), plus episodes of *From a Bird's Eye View* (1971, TV). **Hammer credits:** *The Witches* (1966 [uncredited]), *Frankenstein Created Woman* (1967 [uncredited])

## Wheeler, Paul

This Jamaican born writer (1934–) co-wrote the teleplay for *Eve*, the pilot episode of Hammer's anthology series *Journey to the Unknown* (1968, TV). A former Foreign Office worker, his many other television credits include episodes of *Detective* (1964–1969, TV), *Poldark* (1975–1977, TV),

*Minder* (1979–1994, TV), *The Darling Buds of May* (1991–1993, TV) and *Holby City* (1999–, TV), while his big screen credits include *Caravan to Vaccares* (1974), *Ransom* (1975) and *The Legacy* (1978). **Hammer credits:** *Eve* (1968, TV [episode of *Journey to the Unknown*])

## *When Dinosaurs Ruled the Earth*

GB, 1970, 100m [UK], 96m [U.S.], Technicolor, widescreen [1.85:1], RCA, cert A

Prepared as a sequel-of-sorts to the highly successful *One Million Years B.C.* (1966), this lively if childish prehistoric romp follows the adventures of Sanna, a blonde cave girl set to be sacrificed to the sun by her tribe. Managing to escape her fate, she is subsequently swept out to sea, following which she is taken in by another tribe, befriended by a baby dinosaur, and romanced by a fisherman named Tara.

The novelist J.G. Ballard prepared the initial treatment for the film. The film's producer Aida Young subsequently offered this to Val Guest to flesh out into a workable script, which he did at his holiday home in Malta. Recalled Guest, whose last film for Hammer had been *The Full Treatment* (1961), "Aida came to Malta to see me while I was on holiday. We had a little pad there, and she came to see me about making a dino picture. She said they sort of had a storyline that had been scripted by somebody. Well, once she told me the story I said, 'That's great—let me see a script.' That's when she said, 'See a script? You're the one who's going to write it!'"[18]

Thus signed to the project, Guest set about writ-

**Sacrificial lamb. Victoria Vetri prepares to meet her maker in this scene from *When Dinosaurs Ruled the Earth* (1970) (Hammer/Warner Pathé Distributors/Warner Bros.).**

ing the screenplay, creating a workable prehistoric "language" for his cast to speak in lieu of actual lines. Meanwhile, the cast and technical crew were assembled. To star in the film, Hammer turned to an American bit-part actress and former *Playboy* centerfold named Angela Dorian who, under the rather more exotic-sounding name of Victoria Vetri, had appeared in a handful of films in Hollywood, among them the 1968 hit *Rosemary's Baby.* Suitably nubile and equally at home in Carl Toms' abbreviated costumes as had been Raquel Welch in the previous film, Vetri was ideal casting. Supporting Vetri in her big break were Robin Hawdon as the lovelorn fisherman Tara, and Hammer regular Patrick Allen as tribe leader Kingsor (Allen also did double duty as the film's narrator, speaking its only English dialogue, informing us that it is "A time of beginnings, of darkness, of light, of the sun, the earth, the sea, of man …"). Meanwhile, behind the scenes, the American stop-motion expert Jim Danforth was put in charge of animating the film's various dinosaurs. In this and the production's many other effects chores he was assisted by David Allen, Allan Bryce, Roger Dicken and Brian Johnson.

As had *One Million Years B.C.* before it, *When Dinosaurs Ruled the Earth* made excellent use of the lunar-like terrain to be found in the Canary Islands, where the cameras began turning on 12 October 1968 (Val Guest recalled that the film was shot mostly on the sparsely inhabited island of Fuerteventura, which "looked ideally prehistoric with all its volcanic rock, sand dunes and waterfalls"[19]). Naturally, the effects themselves were added much later, which meant that the cast had to react to "invisible" creatures during the action scenes. Recalled Val Guest, "This wasn't difficult for me, but it was terribly difficult for the actors. When we were on location in the Canary Islands there was a prop man there in a string vest holding a long pole with a cap on the end of it, and *that* was our dinosaur! The actors had to react to that! And more power to them for doing it! It wasn't difficult for me because we had storyboards to work with, so we knew what the finished scene was going to look like."[20]

Once location shooting was completed, the unit moved to Shepperton Studios, where Guest had made *Yesterday's Enemy* for Hammer back in 1959. Here a number of cave sequences were shot, along with close-ups for the action sequences. Live action filming was completed by 8 January 1969, following which Danforth and his team began the long and arduous task of adding in the various effects, the majority of which were shot at Hammer's old haunt, Bray (which the company had vacated on 19 November 1966 for Elstree). In fact so long did post-production take (over sixteen months), the film wasn't ready for release in the UK care of Warner Pathé until 25 October 1970, during which period composer Mario Nascimbene added his sweeping score, complete with his distinctive percussive embellishments. As a consequence of the overrun, some effects sequences had to be dropped, among them a battle between the cavemen and giant ants. The climactic tidal wave sequence was also modified.

The production schedule may have been a lengthy one, but the results paid dividends at the box office, earning in excess of $1.25m in America alone (where its running time was trimmed by four minutes). However, while audiences flocked to the movie—it debuted in San Francisco on 10 February 1971, again care of Warners—the critics were a little more cautious in their welcome. Commented *Variety,* "This is one of those simple sci-fi prehistoric films which do no harm," to which the *Hollywood*

*Top and bottom:* **Robin Hawdon takes a dive to save Victoria Vetri in *When Dinosaurs Ruled the Earth* (1970) (Hammer/Warner Pathé Distributors/Warner Bros.).**

*Reporter* added, "When a movie is this bad it's somehow rather comforting." The *New York Times* was a little kinder, averring that, "If you have a special taste for nonsense, there's a fine sort of idiocy about *When Dinosaurs Ruled the Earth.*" One thing the critics *were* certain about, though, was the quality of the film's special effects, which the *San Diego Union* described as "first class," while *Films and Filming* regarded them as the production's "most engaging aspect." Said Val Guest of the movie, "It's not my favorite picture, but it seems to be very popular. It's always popping up on television."[21]

Getting to know you. Robin Hawdon and Victoria Vetri get a little closer in *When Dinosaurs Ruled the Earth* (1970) (Hammer/Warner Pathé Distributors/Warner Bros.).

The film does nevertheless have several drawbacks, among them its budget, its naïve and meandering plot, its excessive running time and some poorly integrated studio work. Yet there are undeniable pluses in Dick Bush's fine photography, Mario Nascimbene's memorable music, and the effects work of Jim Danforth and his colleagues. In fact Danforth and Roger Dicken went on to earn an Oscar nomination for their sterling efforts, making this Hammer's sole nod from the Academy of Motion Picture Arts and Sciences. Sadly, the film lost out in its category to *Bedknobs and Broomsticks* (1971), which, to add insult to injury, was the only other nominee. **Additional notes:** A promotional short titled *Beauties and Beasts* was shown in cinemas prior to the film's release, and featured footage of Victoria Vetri and an interview with James Carreras in which he ballyhooed Miss Vetri's attributes, commenting, "It's very difficult to be precise about what qualities of a girl capture my interest. A good face and figure of course. But it's more than that—she has to have a special kind of magnetism. I can't describe it, but I know it when I see it, and Victoria Vetri has it I'm sure!" A scene in which Miss Vetri is seen topless during a skinny-dipping sequence was cut from the American and British prints of the film, though the film still features quite a lot of bare flesh for an A certificate. Sequences featuring a triceratops and a dimetrodon were cut during the scripting period. Mattes created for the film by Peter Melrose eventually went unused. The film carries a 1969 copyright. Its sound was recorded at Pinewood. The film's UK poster boasted that the movie was "A Hammer film greater than *One*

*Million Years B.C.*" A proposed sequel titled *Dinosaur Girl* was announced in 1971, but failed to materialize. Instead, Hammer made *Creatures the World Forgot* (1971). A banner featuring the phrase "When dinosaurs ruled the earth" can be seen at the climax of *Jurassic Park* (1993); remnants of it can also be seen in *Jurassic World* (2015).

Production company: Hammer. Distributors: Warner Pathé Distributors (UK [ABC circuit]), Warner Bros. (U.S.). Producer: Aida Young. Executive producer: Michael Carreras [uncredited]. Director: Val Guest. Screenplay: J.G. Ballard, Val Guest. Cinematographer: Dick Bush. Music: Mario Nascimbene. Music director: Philip Martell. Editor: Peter Curran. Art director: John Blezard. Costumes: Carl Toms, Brian Owen-Smith. Special effects: Jim Danforth, David Allen, Allan Bryce, Roger Dicken, Brian Johnson, Martin Gutteridge [uncredited], Garth Inns [uncredited], Brian Humphrey [uncredited], Ray Caple (mattes [uncredited]), Doug Ferris (mattes [uncredited]), Les Bowie (mattes [uncredited], facilities [uncredited]), Peter Melrose (mattes [unused, uncredited]). Make-up: Richard Mills. Hair: Joyce James. Sound supervisor: A. W. Watkins [uncredited]. Sound mixer: Kevin Sutton. Dubbing mixer: Ted

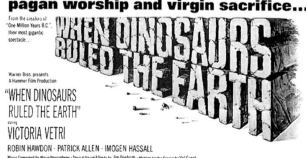

Enter an age of unknown terrors, pagan worship and virgin sacrifice...

*Left:* Shell shocked. Victoria Vetri takes refuge in the shell of a dinosaur egg in *When Dinosaurs Ruled the Earth* (1970). *Right:* A schoolboy's dream. Action-packed artwork for *When Dinosaurs Ruled the Earth* (1970) (Hammer/Warner Pathé Distributors/Warner Bros.).

Karnon [uncredited]. Sound editor: Frank Goulding. Production manager: Christopher Sutton. Construction manager: Albert Blackshaw. Assistant director: John Stoneman. Assistant directors, second unit: Carlos Gil, Miguel Gil. Second unit director: Jim Danforth. Second unit cinematographer: Johnny Cabrera. Camera operator: Ronnie Fox Rogers. Continuity: Josephine Knowles. Second unit continuity/script supervisor: Susanna Merry. Stunts: Steve Emerson [uncredited], Peter Pocock [uncredited]. Narrator: Patrick Allen [uncredited]. Poster: Tom Chantrell [uncredited]. **Cast:** Victoria Vetri (Sanna), Robin Hawdon (Tara), Patrick Allen (Kingsor), Drewe Henley (Khaku), Patrick Holt (Ammon), Sean Caffrey (Kane), Magda Konopka (Ulido), Imogen Hassall (Ayak), Jan Rossini (Rock girl), Carol-Anne Hawkins (Yanni), Billy Cornelius (Hunter), Ray Ford (Hunter), Maria O'Brien (Omah), Connie Tilton (Sand mother), Maggie Lynton (Rock mother), Jimmy Lodge (Fisherman). **DVD availability:** Warner Bros. (UK R2 PAL); Warner Bros. (U.S. R1 NTSC), double-billed with *Moon Zero Two* (1969). **Bluray availability:** Warner Bros. (all regions). **CD availability:** *One Million Years B.C.* (Legend), which contains eight cues from the score; *The Hammer Film Music Collection: Volume One* (GDI Records), which contains the *Main Title*; *The Monster Movie Music Album* (Silva Screen), which con-

tains a newly recorded *Hammer Stone-Age Suite* featuring the *Main Title* and *Storm Over the Sea*

## Wherry, Daniel

This British actor (1908–1955) can be seen as Dr. Taren in Hammer's *Whispering Smith Hits London* (1952). His other credits include *The Voice of Merrill* (1952) and *Black Orchid* (1953), plus the TV play *Kid Flanagan* (1948, TV) and an episode of *Douglas Fairbanks, Jr. Presents* (1953–1957, TV). **Hammer credits:** *Whispering Smith Hits London* (1952, as Dr. Taren)

### *Whispering Smith Hits London*

GB, 1952, 82m, bw, RCA, cert A

Known as *Whispering Smith vs. Scotland Yard* in America, where it was released by RKO minus five minutes, this tedious second feature crime drama features a character already seen in the American-made western *Whispering Smith* (1948), which had starred Alan Ladd as the title character, a government agent who discovers that his friend is involved in a series of train wreck robberies that he is investigating (the novel had previously been filmed in 1916, the year of its publication, as well as 1917 [as *Money Madness*], 1926 and 1927 [as *Whispering Smith Rides*]). Unfortunately, neither Alan Ladd nor his co-star Robert Preston returned for the modern day follow up, leaving it to American import Richard Carlson to step into the shoes vacated by Ladd. This time, Smith investigates the apparent suicide of a young woman while in London, but his findings lead him to suspect that it was in fact murder.

The film was the second of a handful of productions made in association with the American producer Sol Lesser and his son Julian (who co-produced without credit). Made at Down Place in May 1951, the film was trade shown in January 1952 and then released in the UK by Exclusive on 3 February on a double bill with Robert Lippert's *The Lost Continent* (1952).

Though the character of Whispering Smith was created by Frank H. Spearman, the film's screenplay was actually based on an original story titled *Where Is Sylvia?* by the screenwriter John Gilling, who received a screen credit for the story and adaptation on the film's U.S. prints and a credit for the story and screenplay on the UK prints (no mention is made of its origins in *Where Is Sylvia?* in either case). Gilling subsequently had a falling out with Hammer over the matter, and didn't work for the company again until *The Shadow of the Cat* (1961). Gilling also shared his work on the screenplay with Steve Fisher, who received

sole screenplay credit on the film's American prints, while Gilling received sole screenplay credit on the British prints.

Recalled Gilling of the film's reception, "[It] was a roaring co-feature success."[22] Watching it, one may well be inclined to wonder why, despite some intriguing names in the supporting cast, among them Herbert Lom, Danny Green, Stanley Baker, Laurence Naismith, Rona Anderson and Dora Bryan, the latter as a temperamental performer known as La Fosse (interestingly, a performer named Lorraine La Fosse used to appear on stage with Will Hammer in his troupe Will Hammer Entertainers—coincidence, one wonders?). **Additional notes:** Some British posters claim the film to be a U certificate. A sequel titled *Whispering Smith Investigates* was proposed, but never realized, Hammer having acquired a number of Whispering Smith stories. An American television series starring Audie Murphy titled *Whispering Smith* meanwhile appeared in 1961, though Hammer had no involvement with this. In the Alan Ladd film, Smith's first name is Luke, while here it has been changed to Steve. Other Whispering Smith films include *Whispering Smith Speaks* (1935).

Production companies: Hammer/Lesser. Distributors: Exclusive (UK), RKO (U.S.). Producers: Anthony Hinds, Julian Lesser [uncredited]. Director: Francis Searle. Screenplay: John Gilling [credited on UK version, uncredited on U.S. version], Steve Fisher [credited on U.S. version, uncredited on UK version]. Character: Frank H. Spearman. Story: John Gilling [credited on UK version, credited as story and adaptation on U.S. version]. Cinematographer: Walter "Jimmy" Harvey. Music/conductor: Frank Spencer. Music played by: The Royal Philharmonic Orchestra. Editor: James Needs. Assistant director: Jimmy Sangster. Sound: Jack Miller. Camera operator: Peter Bryan. Focus puller: Harry Oakes [uncredited]. Production manager: Arthur Barnes. Continuity: Renee Glynne. Make-up: Phil Leakey. Hair: Anne Box. Casting: Michael Carreras. **Cast:** Richard Carlson (Steve "Whispering" Smith), Greta Gynt (Louise), Herbert Lom (Ford), Danny Green (Cecil), James Raglan (Superintendent Meaker), Reginald Beckwith (Manson), Rona Anderson (Anne), Alan Wheatley (Hector Reith), Dora Bryan (La Fosse), Stanley Baker (First reporter), Lionel Grose (Second reporter), Ian Wilson (Small tough), Laurence Naismith (Parker), Michael Ward (Receptionist clerk), Daniel Wherry (Dr. Taren), Stuart Nichol (Martin), Christine Silver (Mrs. Penston), Vic Wise (Maxie), Ben Williams (Taxi driver), Middleton Woods (Station porter), Sidney Vivian (Hotel porter), Tony Frost (Secretary), June Bardsley (Maid), Michael Hogarth (Police Constable), John Wynn (Police Sergeant), Anthony Warner (Pageboy), John Singer (First photographer), John Kyle (Second photographer), Arthur Mullard (unnamed role [uncredited])

### *Whispering Smith vs. Scotland Yard* see *Whispering Smith Hits London*

## Whitaker, David

Following training at London's Guildhall School

Standing proud. Victoria Vetri is clearly the focus of this German poster for *When Dinosaurs Ruled the Earth* (1970) (Hammer/ Warner Pathé Distributors/Warner Bros.).

of Music and work as music arranger for Decca and CBS Records, this British composer, conductor, arranger and songwriter (1931–2012, aka David Sinclair Whitaker) launched his film career with *Hammerhead* (1968). He went on to score a number of genre films, among them *Scream and Scream Again* (1970), *Vampira* (1974), *Dominique* (1978) and *The Sword and the Sorcerer* (1982), for which he penned a rousing Korngold-esque soundtrack. He also provided the music for three Hammer films, beginning with *Dr. Jekyll and Sister Hyde* (1971), for which he supplied a charming waltz theme and an impressive *faux* piano concerto. He followed this with *Vampire Circus* (1972), another rich, diverse and beautifully orchestrated score that is arguably his best work for the cinema. He also scored the comedy *That's Your Funeral* (1973), which is arguably his worst (the use of jazzed up funeral music might have seemed like a good idea at the time, but it now sounds dated and tinny and does the film no service at all).

Recalled Whitaker of the second assignment, "After seeing *Vampire Circus* I decided it definitely needed a big score. At that time the Hammer formula for an orchestra line-up comprised around 120 musicians, and it was really up to the composer to decide how they would be utilized. With guidance from Hammer's musical director Philip Martell I spread them as I saw fit. I think we used about 60 players per session."[23]

Whitaker's non-genre credits include *Don't Raise the Bridge, Lower the River* (1968), *The Desperados* (1969), *Run Wild, Run Free* (1969), *Subterfuge* (1969), *Harry, He's Here to Help* (2000), *Lemming* (2005) and *Lady Godiva* (2008). He also scored a number of sex romps, among them *Mistress Pamela* (1973), *The Playbirds* (1978), *Confessions from the David Galaxy Affair* (1979), *Queen of the Blues* (1979) and *Mary Millington's True Blue Confessions* (1980), the latter of which was scored in conjunction with the De Wolfe music library. He also scored episodes of a number of television series, among them *Heartbeat* (1992–2009, TV), of which he scored over 200 episodes, *The Royal* (2003–2009, TV) and *The Royal Today* (2008, TV). Prior to his film career, he had a hit with the tune "Toy Piano Bosa Nova" (1963), which led to a contract with Ember Records.

Commented Philip Martell of Whitaker, "He can do very good work if he's left alone…. He had more talent than he shows."[24] Meanwhile, of Martell, Whitaker remembered, "He is an awfully good conductor. On one occasion, doing one of my pictures, he got somewhere about eighteen and twenty minutes of music in a two-and-a-half hour session. And no click track! He didn't even take any notice of my markings. He goes on a stop watch which is about the size of Big Ben."[25] **Additional notes:** For the Orion video release of *Scream and Scream Again*, Whitaker's music was replaced with a new (and vastly inferior) electronic score by Kendall Schmidt; this was a result of issues over the music rights with AIP. Whitaker's music has been restored for the DVD release. **Hammer credits:** *Dr. Jekyll and Sister Hyde* (1971), *Vampire Circus* (1972), *That's Your Funeral* (1973)

## White, Bob (Robert)

This scenic artist worked as a scene painter on Hammer's *The Vampire Lovers* (1970) and *Scars of Dracula* (1970). His other credits include *Richard III* (1955) and *A Shot in the Dark* (1964). **Hammer credits:** *The Vampire Lovers* (1970 [uncredited]), *Scars of Dracula* (1970 [uncredited])

## White, Carol

Best known for her performances in such Ken Loach-directed dramas as *Up the Junction* (1965, TV), *The Coming Out Party* (1965, TV), *Cathy Come Home* (1966, TV) and *Poor Cow* (1967), this British actress (1943–1991, full name Carole Joan White) began her film career as a child, first appearing in *Kind Hearts and Coronets* (1949), *Doctor in the House* (1954), *Circus Friends* (1956) and *Carry On Teacher* (1959) among others. She matured into more adult roles in such films as *Linda* (1960) and *The Man in the Back Seat* (1961). Her other credits, among them later work in America, include *Never Let Go* (1960), *The Fixer* (1968), *Dulcima* (1971), *Made* (1972), *The Squeeze* (1977), *Nutcracker* (1982) and *Talking Walls* (1987), plus episodes of *The Avengers* (1961–1969, TV), *Gideon's Way* (1965–1966, TV) and *Hawaii Five-O* (1968–1980, TV). She also appeared in Hammer's *Slave Girls* (1968) as Gido. Tragically, she suffered a turbulent private life and eventually died from a drug overdose. Her first husband (of three) was musician Mike King. Her sister is actress Jane White. **Hammer credits:** *Slave Girls* (1968, as Gido)

## White, Ethel Lina

This British (Welsh) writer (1876–1944) has had her novel *The Wheel Spins* filmed three times under the title of *The Lady Vanishes*, first by Hitchcock in 1938, later by Hammer in 1979, and then (badly) by the BBC in 2013. The Hitchcock version was originally to have been titled *Lost Lady*. Other filmed works include *Some Must Watch* (1933), which was filmed as *The Spiral Staircase* in 1945, 1975 and 2000 (TVM), and *Her Heart in Her Throat* (1942), filmed as *The Unseen* (1945). Her other novels include *The Wish Bone* (1927), *Put Out the Light* (1931), which was filmed as a 1969 episode of *Detective* (1964–1969, TV), *Step in the Dark* (1938) and *They See in Darkness* (1944). **Hammer credits:** *The Lady Vanishes* (1979)

## White, Ian

White played a television announcer in Hammer's *Quatermass and the Pit* (1967). His other credits include *Up the Chastity Belt* (1971), plus episodes of *Private Investigator* (1958–1959, TV), *On Trial* (1960, TV), *Dr. Finlay's Casebook* (1962–1971, TV), *Virgin of the Secret Service* (1968, TV) and *General Hospital* (1972–1980, TV). Also on stage. **Hammer credits:** *Quatermass and the Pit* (1967, as Television announcer [uncredited])

## White, Jackie

White played one of the vampire disciples in Hammer's *The Kiss of the Vampire* (1963). Her other credits include *The Beauty Jungle* (1964), which made use of her physical attributes, given that she had been crowned Miss United Kingdom in 1962. She went on to become an expert on an-

tique dolls. Her husband was the businessman and record impresario Adrian Jacobs (1929–1997), and their son is the actor, writer, producer and director Jon Jacobs (1966–). **Hammer credits:** *The Kiss of the Vampire* (1963, as Disciple [uncredited])

## White, Joanna (Joanne)

White can be seen in the closing scenes of *The House That Bled to Death* (1980, TV [episode of *Hammer House of Horror*]), in which she plays the older version of Sophie Peters. The character's younger self was played by Emma Ridley. **Hammer credits:** *The House That Bled to Death* (1980, TV [episode of *Hammer House of Horror*], as Sophie Peters [older])

## White, Jon Manchip

This British (Welsh) author and screenwriter (1924–2013) had his 1953 novel *The Last Race* adapted into a film by Hammer in 1954 titled *Mask of Dust*. White's own screenplays include *Mystery Submarine* (1963 [from his play *Decoy*]), *Crack in the World* (1965) and *Naked Evil* (1966 [from his play *The Obi*]). For television, he adapted the Elizabeth Gaskell novel *Cranford* (1951, TV) and contributed scripts to such series as *The Avengers* (1961–1969, TV) and *Witch Hunt* (1967, TV). He also wrote several history books, among them *Ancient Egypt: Its Culture and History* (1952), *Marshall of France: The Life and Times of Maurice, Comte de Saxe* (1962) and *Everyday Life of the North American Indians* (1979). White also penned two screenplays for Hammer: *Day of Grace* (1957), which he co-wrote with Francis Searle, and *The Camp on Blood Island* (1958), which he co-wrote with Val Guest (White himself provided the story and first draft screenplay). He also had two further books optioned by Hammer, but they never made it to the screen. These were *Build Us a Dam* (1955) and *The Mercenaries* (1958), the latter of which had a draft script penned by White in 1962. **Hammer credits:** *Mask of Dust* (1954, novel), *Day of Grace* (1957, story, co-screenplay), *The Camp on Blood Island* (1958, story, co-screenplay)

## White, Leslie (Les)

White appeared in a minor role in Hammer's *Rasputin—The Mad Monk* (1966). His other credits include *The Deadly Affair* (1966) plus episodes of *Public Eye* (1965–1975, TV) and *The Baron* (1966–1967, TV). **Hammer credits:** *Rasputin—The Mad Monk* (1966, as Cheeky man [uncredited])

## White, Maureen

White worked as the production secretary on the Hammer thriller *Paranoiac* (1963), which led to work a handful of further productions. Her other credits include *Zulu* (1964) and *The Rocky Horror Picture Show* (1975). She also worked as a production assistant on *The Masks of Death* (1984, TVM). **Hammer credits:** *Paranoiac* (1963 [uncredited]), *The Kiss of the Vampire* (1963 [uncredited]), *The Old Dark House* (1963 [uncredited]), *Nightmare* (1964 [uncredited]), *The Evil of Frankenstein* (1964 [uncredited]), *The Gorgon* (1964 [uncredited]), *The Witches* (1966 [uncredited])

## White, Meadows

This British actor (1901–1973) can be seen as a night watchman in Hammer's *Frankenstein Must Be Destroyed* (1969). His other credits include *The Last Rose of Summer* (1937), *I See Ice* (1938), *A Run for Your Money* (1948), *Ghost Ship* (1952) and *Fiend Without a Face* (1958), plus much television work, including episodes of *The Buccaneers* (1956–1957, TV), *Bleak House* (1959, TV), *The Saint* (1962–1969, TV), *The Fenn Street Gang* (1971–1973, TV), *Colditz* (1972–1974, TV) and *Six Days of Justice* (1972–1975, TV). **Hammer credits:** *Frankenstein Must Be Destroyed* (1969, as Night watchman [uncredited])

## White, Valerie

This South African born actress (1915–1975) played the Governor in the Hammer prison melodrama *Women Without Men* (1956). On stage in Britain from 1942, her other films include *My Learned Friend* (1943), *The Halfway House* (1944), *Hue and Cry* (1946) and *Travels with My Aunt* (1972). Her TV work includes episodes of *Maigret* (1960–1963, TV), *Upstairs, Downstairs* (1971–1975, TV), *Dial M for Murder* (1974, TV) and *Affairs of the Heart* (1974–1975, TV). Her husband was the actor Albert Lieven (1906–1971, real name Albert Fritz Liévin-Lièvin), who appeared in *The Dark Light* (1951) for Hammer. **Hammer credits:** *Women Without Men* (1956, as Governor)

## Whitear, George

Whitear worked for Hammer as a stills man on *Dracula A.D. 1972* (1972). Most associated with the Bond films, his many other credits include *Diamonds Are Forever* (1971), *Shout at the Devil* (1976), *The Eagle Has Landed* (1976), *Yanks* (1979), *The Empire Strikes Back* (1980), *Outland* (1981), *Octopussy* (1983), *A View to a Kill* (1985), *The Living Daylights* (1987), *Licence to Kill* (1989), *GoldenEye* (1995) and *Tomorrow Never Dies* (1997), plus episodes of *Act of Will* (1989, TV) and *Press Gang* (1989–1993, TV). **Hammer credits:** *Dracula A.D. 1972* (1972 [uncredited])

## Whitehouse, Denis

Whitehouse worked as the assistant editor on Hammer's *Shatter* (1974). His other credits in this respect include *The Spy Who Came in from the Cold* (1965), *Otley* (1968), *The Wicker Man* (1973), *The Four Feathers* (1977, TVM) and *Sunburn* (1979). **Hammer credits:** *Shatter* (1974)

## Whitehurst, Derek

This British assistant director (1928–2005) came to Hammer following work on *The Errol Flynn Theatre* (1955, TV), which was also shot at Bray. A former camera assistant at Gainsborough, where he worked on such films as *Caravan* (1946), he went on to work for a number of other studios, first as a clapper loader on *The Story of Robin Hood and His Merrie Men* (1952), and then as a focus puller on *The Red Beret* (1953). His first film for Hammer was *The Curse of Frankenstein* (1957). He had to wait eleven years for his second job with the company, which was on the TV series *Journey to the Unknown* (1968, TV), of which he worked on four episodes. Of these, *Poor Butterfly* also appeared in the compendium film *Journey to Midnight* (1968, TVM), while *The New People* also appeared in the compendium film *Journey into Darkness* (1968, TVM). Along with Jimmy Sangster and Arthur Banks, he was involved in the making of both *The Curse of Frankenstein* and its remake, *The Horror of Frankenstein* (1970), though of the latter he observed, "I felt it was a bit off-key…. I think the approach was a bit foreign to us all."[26]

Whitehurst's other credits include *The Key Man* (1957), *The Projected Man* (1966), *The Oblong Box* (1969), *Percy* (1971), *Malachi's Cove* (1974) and *The Godsend* (1980), plus episodes of *The Sweeney* (1974–1978, TV), *The Professionals* (1977–1983, TV) and *Terrahawks* (1983–1986, TV). He also worked as location manager on *Fanny Hill* (1983) and *The Doctor and the Devils* (1985), and as the second unit production manager on *Edge of Sanity* (1989).

Recalled Whitehurst of his first experience with Hammer: "There was nothing at Bray then. There was just the house and one tiny stage. We shot *The Curse of Frankenstein* in the winter, which was bitterly cold. There was no central heating!"[27] Meanwhile, of the film's leading man, Peter Cushing, he remembered, "Seeing him do anything vicious on-screen was always such a shock, because there was nothing vicious about him at all. He was very charming and gentle…. And Peter was very athletic. There was lots of swagger and thrust, and those little sets at Bray couldn't really stand up to it when he was belting around."[28] **Hammer credits:** *The Curse of Frankenstein* (1957), *Poor Butterfly* (1968, TV [episode of *Journey to the Unknown*]), *Miss Belle* (1968, TV [episode of *Journey to the Unknown*]), *The New People* (1968, TV [episode of *Journey to the Unknown*]), *Somewhere in a Crowd* (1968, TV [episode of *Journey to the Unknown*]), *Journey into Darkness* (1968, TVM), *Journey to Midnight* (1968, TVM), *Taste the Blood of Dracula* (1970), *The Vampire Lovers* (1970), *The Horror of Frankenstein* (1970), *Scars of Dracula* (1970), *On the Buses* (1971), *Blood from the Mummy's Tomb* (1971), *Vampire Circus* (1972), *The Satanic Rites of Dracula* (1974), *Frankenstein and the Monster from Hell* (1974), *Man About the House* (1974)

## Whitelaw, Billie

Acclaimed for her work in the plays of Samuel Beckett, this British stage actress (1932–2014) began her career on radio at the age of eleven as Henry in *Norman and Henry Bones*. On stage from 1950, she began making films soon after, among them *The Fake* (1953), *Companions in Crime* (1954) and *The Sleeping Tiger* (1954). Her other big screen work includes key performances in Hammer's *Hell Is a City* (1960), which earned her a BAFTA nomination for most promising newcomer to leading film roles, *Charlie Bubbles* (1968), which, along with her work in in *Twisted Nerve* (1968), won her a BAFTA for best supporting actress, *Frenzy* (1972), *Gumshoe* (1972), *Nightwatch* (1973), *The Omen* (1976), for which she received a best supporting actress BAFTA nomination for her role as Mrs. Baylock, *Maurice* (1987), *The Krays* (1990), which earned her another BAFTA nomination for best supporting actress, *Quills*

(2000) and *Hot Fuzz* (2007). She was also considered for the role of Anna Fountain in Hammer's *To the Devil a Daughter* (1976). Her TV work includes appearances in such plays and series as *The Secret Garden* (1952, TV), *Dixon of Dock Green* (1955–1976, TV), *Wicked Women* (1970, TV), *Napoleon and Love* (1972, TV), in which she played Josephine, *The Sextet* (1972, TV), which won her a best actress BAFTA, *Wessex Tales* (1973, TV), which earned her a best actress BAFTA nomination, *The Secret Garden* (1987, TVM), *Firm Friends* (1992–1994, TV) and *A Dinner of Herbs* (2000, TV). Married twice, her first husband was the actor Peter Vaughan (1923–2016, real name Peter Ewart Ohm), to whom she was married between 1952 and 1966; he appeared in Hammer's *Fanatic* (1965) and *Czech Mate* (1984, TVM [episode of *Hammer House of Mystery and Suspense*]). Her second husband was the writer Robert Muller (1925–1998), whom she married in 1967. She was made a CBE in 1991. **Hammer credits:** *Hell Is a City* (1960, as Chloe Hawkins)

## Whiteley, Annette

Briefly busy in her teens and early twenties, this British actress (1946–) can be seen as Meg in the Hammer swashbuckler *The Devil-Ship Pirates* (1964). Her other credits include *Girl on Approval* (1961), in which she played the title role, *The Yellow Teddybears* (1963) and *The Black Torment* (1964), plus episodes of *Z Cars* (1962–1978, TV), *Crossroads* (1964–1988, TV) and *Sanctuary* (1967–1968, TV). Her father was the actor Jack Le White (1912–1999, aka Albert Arthur Whiteley), who appeared in Hammer's *Further Up the Creek* (1958). Her husband is musician Howard Conder, whom she married in 1965. **Hammer credits:** *The Devil-Ship Pirates* (1964, as Meg)

## Whitemore, Hugh

Following experience as an actor, this British playwright and dramatist (1936–2018) went on to have a busy career in television, penning such series and one-offs as *Dan, Dan, the Charity Man* (1966, TV), *Party Games* (1968, TV), *Killing Time* (1970, TV), *Cider with Rosie* (1971, TV), which earned him a BAFTA nomination, *84 Charing Cross Road* (1975, TV), *I Remember Nelson* (1982, TV), *Rebecca* (1979, TV), *Boy in the Bush* (1984, TV), *Breaking the Code* (1996, TV), which earned him a shared BAFTA nomination, *A Dance to the Music of Time* (1997, TV), *The Gathering Storm* (2002, TVM), which won him a shared Emmy, and *Into the Storm* (2009, TVM). His film credits include *All Neat in Black Stockings* (1969), Hammer's big-screen version of *Man at the Top* (1973), *The Bluebird* (1976), *Stevie* (1978), which was based upon his 1977 play, *84 Charing Cross Road* (1987), which earned him a BAFTA nomination, *Jane Eyre* (1996) and *My House in Umbria* (2003). **Hammer credits:** *Man at the Top* (1973)

## Whiting, Edward G.

An occasional backer of low budget British films, Whiting put some money into Hammer's *Dr. Morelle—The Case of the Missing Heiress* (1949), which was billed as a Hammer/Edward G. Whiting production. His other credits as a producer include

*Dangerous Seas* (1931), *Commissionaire* (1933), *Oh, What a Night* (1935), *Schweik's New Adventures* (1945) and *The Adventures of Jane* (1949), the latter of which he also co-wrote and co-directed. **Hammer credits:** *Dr. Morelle—The Case of the Missing Heiress* (1949)

## Whiting, Gordon

This British actor (1918–2002) played the second of two footmen in the Castillo Siniestro scenes of Hammer's *The Curse of the Werewolf* (1961). James Bond veteran Desmond Llewelyn played the other. Whiting's other credits include *Decameron Nights* (1953), *Beau Brummell* (1954), *The Man Who Wouldn't Talk* (1958), *A Night to Remember* (1958) and *The Railway Children* (1970), in which he played the Russian. Busy on television, his many credits here include episodes of *BBC Sunday-Night Theatre* (1951, TV), *The Adventures of Robin Hood* (1955–1960, TV), *Manhunt* (1969–1970, TV), *Boon* (1986–1992, TV) and *Hannay* (1988–1989, TV). **Hammer credits:** *The Curse of the Werewolf* (1961, as Footman [uncredited])

## Whitley, William P. (Bill)

American born Whitley (1908–1976) photographed the additional American-shot scenes for Hammer's *Women Without Men* (1956), which were directed by Herbert Glazer. A prolific cameraman, he began his career as a camera assistant on *The Lady Who Dared* (1931), and went on to work as an operator on *45 Fathers* (1937), *Mr. Moto's Last Warning* (1939) and *Last of the Buccaneers* (1950), as well as the TV series *Adventures of Superman* (1952–1958, TV). He became a cinematographer with *A Yank in Korea* (1951), which he followed with *King of the Congo* (1952), *Cat-Women of the Moon* (1953), *Tarzan's Hidden Jungle* (1955) and *The Three Stooges in Orbit* (1962), plus much series television, including *The Lone Ranger* (1949–1957, TV), of which he photographed 39 episodes, *Men into Space* (1959–1960, TV), of which he photographed 37 episodes, and *Bonanza* (1959–1973, TV), of which he photographed 87 episodes, earning three shared Emmy nominations for the latter. **Hammer credits:** *Women Without Men* (1956)

## Whitlock, Dennis (Denis)

This sound technician began his career as an assistant boom operator on the likes of *The Agitator* (1945) and *The Hasty Heart* (1949), and went on to become a boom operator on *The Magic Box* (1951), *Oh ... Rosalinda!!* (1955) and *The Roman Spring of Mrs. Stone* (1961). He began working as a sound recordist on such TV series as *The Saint* (1962–1969, TV), *Gideon's Way* (1965–1966, TV) and *The Champions* (1968–1969, TV), and graduated to features with Hammer's *The Lost Continent* (1968), on which he was the sound mixer. This in turn led to further work with the company, mostly in the capacity of dubbing mixer. His other credits, either as recordist or mixer, include *Mister Jerico* (1970, TVM), *The Man Who Haunted Himself* (1970), *The Abominable Dr. Phibes* (1971), *Dr. Phibes Rises Again* (1972), *In Celebration* (1974) and *A Voyage Round My Father* (1982, TVM), plus episodes of *Jason King* (1971–1972, TV),

TV), *The Adventurer* (1972–1973, TV), *The New Avengers* (1976–1977, TV) and *Rumpole of the Bailey* (1978–1992, TV). **Hammer credits:** *The Lost Continent* (1968, sound mixer [as Denis Whitlock]), *Taste the Blood of Dracula* (1970, dubbing mixer), *The Vampire Lovers* (1970, dubbing mixer), *Scars of Dracula* (1970, dubbing mixer), *Blood from the Mummy's Tomb* (1971, dubbing mixer), *Fear in the Night* (1972, dubbing mixer), *Straight on Till Morning* (1972, dubbing mixer), *Love Thy Neighbour* (1973, dubbing mixer), *Man at the Top* (1973, dubbing mixer), *The Satanic Rites of Dracula* (1974, dubbing mixer), *Shatter* (1974, dubbing mixer), *Man About the House* (1974, dubbing mixer), *To the Devil a Daughter* (1976, sound)

## Whitman, Stuart

In films from 1951 with *When Worlds Collide*, this craggy-looking American leading man (1928–) proved at home in a number of westerns, among them *Silver Lode* (1954), *Seven Men from Now* (1956), *These Thousand Hills* (1958), *The Comancheros* (1961) and *Rio Conchos* (1965). He successfully guyed his image in the all-star knockabout *Those Magnificent Men in Their Flying Machines* (1965), but was also at home in other roles, earning himself a best actor Oscar nomination for his role as a sex offender in *The Mark* (1961). His other hundred-plus credits include *The Longest Day* (1962), *Shock Treatment* (1964), *The Last Escape* (1968), *Breakout* (1971), *Night of the Lepus* (1972), *The Cat Creature* (1973, TVM), *Blazing Magnum* (1976), *White Buffalo* (1977), *The Monster Club* (1980), *Deadly Embrace* (1989), *Improper Conduct* (1994) and *The President's Man* (2000, TVM). He also appeared in episodes of *The Range Rider* (1951–1953, TV), *Highway Patrol* (1955–1959, TV), *Cimarron Strip* (1967–1968, TV), which he also produced, *Ellery Queen* (1975–1976, TV), *Fantasy Island* (1978–1984, TV), *Knots Landing* (1979–1993, TV) and *Superboy* (1988–1992, TV), in which he played Jonathan Kent.

In 1974 Whitman played the title role in Hammer's Hong Kong-shot action thriller *Shatter* (1974). Sadly, the production was a troubled one, and after three weeks of shooting, producer Michael Carreras fired director Monte Hellman and finished the film himself. Revealed Whitman of this situation, "I would like to have finished the film with Monte Hellman, yes. I would have liked that. Carreras was an okay guy, but he wasn't a director."[29] Ouch! **Hammer credits:** *Shatter* (1974, as Shatter)

## Whitsun-Jones, Paul

This British (Welsh) actor (1923–1974) can be seen as Sergeant Danvers in Hammer's *Dr. Jekyll and Sister Hyde* (1971). In films from the early fifties, his other credits include *The Diamond* (1954), *The Moonraker* (1957), *Room at the Top* (1958), *Tunes of Glory* (1960), *Doctor in Distress* (1963), *The Masque of the Red Death* (1964) and *Keep It Up, Jack!* (1974). He was also known to television audiences as Porthos in *The Three Musketeers* (1954, TV), and went on to appear in many other series, including episodes of *Huntingtower* (1957, TV), *Bonehead* (1957–1962, TV), *Wild,*

*Wild Women* (1969, TV) and *Scotch on the Rocks* (1973, TV). **Hammer credits:** *Dr. Jekyll and Sister Hyde* (1971, as Sergeant Danvers)

## Whittaker, Albert Smith

Whittaker worked as Exclusive's publicity consultant between 1958 and 1959. A former cinema manager, he had also worked as Universal's theater controller and exploitation director before joining Exclusive.

## Whittaker, Ian

This British supporting actor (1928–) appeared for Hammer several times, beginning with the war drama *The Steel Bayonet* (1957), in which he played Private Wilson. His other credits include *Cosh Boy* (1952), *Dr. Crippen* (1962), *My Wife's Family* (1962), *Billy Budd* (1962) and *Operation Snatch* (1962), plus episodes of *Douglas Fairbanks, Jr. Presents* (1953–1957, TV), *The Adventures of Robin Hood* (1955–1960, TV) and *Tell It to the Marines* (1959, TV). **Hammer credits:** *The Steel Bayonet* (1957, as Private Wilson), *Clean Sweep* (1958, as Ian Watson), *The Revenge of Frankenstein* (1958, as Boy [uncredited]), *Further Up the Creek* (1958, as Lofty), *The Secret of Blood Island* (1965, as Mills)

## Whittaker, Michael

This British costume designer (1918–1995) provided the Lincoln greens for Hammer's first color production, *Men of Sherwood Forest* (1954). This was his second Robin Hood movie, having already costumed Disney's *The Story of Robin Hood and His Merrie Men* (1952). His other credits include *The Black Rose* (1950), which earned him an Oscar nomination, *The Naked Heart* (1950) and *Flesh and Blood* (1951), plus episodes of *The Avengers* (1961–1969, TV). He actually began his film career as an actor, and appeared in such films as *Flying Fortress* (1942) and *In Which We Serve* (1942), following which he turned his attention to the fashion industry and film costuming. **Hammer credits:** *Men of Sherwood Forest* (1954)

## Whittington, Margery

Whittington worked as the props buyer on the Hammer thriller *Maniac* (1963). Her other credits include *Two-Way Stretch* (1960) and *The Hellfire Club* (1961). She also worked as an assistant art director on *Midnight Episode* (1950) and *Around the World in 80 Days* (1956). **Hammer credits:** *Maniac* (1963 [uncredited])

## Whittle, Marjorie

British born Whittle (1921–2007) worked as the hairstylist on the Hammer comedy *Further Up the Creek* (1958). Her other credits include *The Gentle Sex* (1943), on which she was the assistant stylist, following which she graduated to stylist with *On Approval* (1944), *Against the Wind* (1948), *Meet Mr. Callaghan* (1954), *The Vicious Circle* (1957), *Strictly Confidential* (1959), *Assignment K* (1968) and *Before Winter Comes* (1969). **Hammer credits:** *Further Up the Creek* (1958)

### *Who Killed Van Loon?*

GB, 1948, 51m, bw, cert A

Based on a radio drama, this little seen crime support about a Dutch girl who finds herself framed for the murder of a diamond merchant was something of a hodgepodge. Financed by Gordon Kyle, who also directed, the film encountered difficulties when funds ran out during production. It was at this point that Hammer stepped in, providing the cash to complete the abandoned project. To this end, Anthony Hinds called back the principals for several days of additional shooting under the stewardship of Lionel Tomlinson, who had recently helmed *Death in High Heels* (1947) for the company, and whose experience as an editor no doubt came in handy when it came time to make sense of the footage.

Trade shown in February 1948, the film was released in the UK by Exclusive on 30 June, following which it quickly disappeared into the quota quickie wilderness ("It's British—It's 'Exclusive,'" cried the posters, but it's doubtful anyone was listening). Of passing interest, the film carries a rare producer credit for James Carreras. **Additional notes:** According to Leslie Halliwell's 1985 autobiography *Seats in All Parts*, a company called Adelphi was later involved with the film's exhibition to cinema bookers (Halliwell worked as a booker for the Rex in Cambridge in the early fifties), yet neither the BFI database nor IMDb lists the company as a distributor/exhibitor either for the film's first run or for any re-issues (perhaps they didn't manage any); likewise, Denis Gifford's *British Film Catalogue, Volume 1* doesn't mention the company in connection with the film either. Other films distributed by Adelphi include *Bait* (1949), *Let's Go Crazy* (1951), *Alf's Baby* (1953), *The Crowded Day* (1954) and *You Lucky People* (1955), but nothing else by Hammer or Exclusive.

Production companies: Hammer/Gordon Kyle. Distributor: Exclusive (UK). Producers: Gordon Kyle, James Carreras. Directors: Gordon Kyle, Lionel Tomlinson. Screenplay: Peter Creswell. Editor: Douglas Myers. **Cast:** Raymond Lovell (Johann Schmidt), Kay Bannerman (Anna Kreuger), Robert Wyndham (Inspector Oxley), John Dodsworth (Ian Ferguson), Milton Rosmer (Simmonds), Patricia Laffan (Peggy Osborn), Beth Ross (unnamed role [uncredited]), Graham Russell (unnamed role [uncredited]), Paul Sheridan (unnamed role [uncredited])

## Wickham, Jeffrey

This British actor (1933–2014, sometimes Jeffry Wickham) can be seen in a supporting role in *Carpathian Eagle* (1980, TV [episode of *Hammer House of Horror*]). His other TV credits include episodes of *An Age of Kings* (1960, TV), *The Baron* (1966–1967, TV), *Edward the Seventh* (1975, TV), *Sapphire and Steel* (1979–1982, TV), *Peak Practice* (1993–2002, TV) and *Black Mirror* (2011, TV), while his big screen credits include *S\*P\*Y\*S* (1974), *Another Country* (1984), *The Remains of the Day* (1993), *Vera Drake* (2004) and *Scoop* (2006). Much involved with the actors' union Equity, he was once its president. His wife was the actress Clair Stewart, and their children are the actors Rupert Wickham (1964–) and Saskia Wickham

(1967–). **Hammer credits:** *Carpathian Eagle* (1980, TV [episode of *Hammer House of Horror*], as Edgar)

## Wicking, Christopher

Following experience as a technician for the BBC and as a journalist for *Cahiers du Cinema*, this British writer (1943–2008) turned his hand to screenwriting, and quickly gained a name for himself in the horror genre. He began his career working for AIP's British arm, earning his first credit for *The Oblong Box* (1969), for which he supplied additional dialogue. He then went on to adapt Peter Saxon's 1966 novel *The Disorientated Man* as *Scream and Scream Again* (1970) for the company, which he followed with a co-screenplay credit for *Cry of the Banshee* (1970). This inevitably brought him to the attention of Hammer, for whom he adapted Bram Stoker's 1903 novel *The Jewel of Seven Stars* as *Blood from the Mummy's Tomb* (1971). This in turn led to work on *Demons of the Mind* (1972), which he based upon a story by himself and the film's producer Frank Godwin. Recalled the film's production manager Christopher Neame of the script, "This one was good. It moved laterally to look at the gothic horror world in a way different from the expected one, with much visual imagery used to tell the story. Yes, it's fair to say some of the dialogue is a bit heavy-handed, but that is probably because of an imbalance between what is heard and what is seen."[30]

Having by this time befriended Michael Carreras ("Michael and I discovered that we had all sorts of things in common,"[31] recalled Wicking), he next approached Hammer about making *The Sensitive*, a film (and possible television spin-off series) about a psychic investigator, on which he had collaborated with Adrian Reid. Following some initial interest, however, the idea fell by the wayside, and Wicking instead found himself working on another subsequently abandoned film-cum-series, *Allan Quatermain Esquire: His Quest for the Holy Flower*. He then scripted Hammer's last horror feature for some three decades, *To the Devil a Daughter* (1976), basing his screenplay on an adaptation of the Dennis Wheatley 1953 novel by John Peacock. The production was a troubled one though, and Wicking continued to re-write during filming. (Gerald Vaughan-Hughes also contributed to the script.) Following the completion of the film, Wicking continued his association with Michael Carreras and Hammer, albeit on a less formal footing, given the company's by-now parlous state. Commented Wicking, "The unspoken relationship we had was that as and when some funding turned up, I would be put in charge of a second-string low-budget department, developing people—trying to make the equivalent of the Corman movies of the sixties. I had all sorts of ideas, including comic books. I talked to Stan Lee about doing a Marvel-Hammer connection. But it all came to nothing … because we had no money to afford to pay anyone to develop it."[32]

Wicking did contribute to an unproduced screenplay for *Vampirella* in early 1976, but like everything else Hammer attempted to launch during this period, the project came to nothing. He

also provided the screenplay for *Nessie*, which he based upon a story by Michael Carreras and Euan Lloyd, and a treatment by John Starr. His work was subsequently re-written by Bryan Forbes, who was set to helm the project, which likewise collapsed following the withdrawal of its major backer, Columbia.

Wicking's other screen credits include *Venom* (1971), *Medusa* (1973), *Lady Chatterley's Lover* (1981), *Absolute Beginners* (1986), *Dream Demon* (1988), *The Way to Dusty Death* (1995, TVM) and *On Dangerous Ground* (1996, TVM). He also worked as a script consultant on *The Dive* (1989) and contributed scripts to such series as *The Professionals* (1978–1983, TV), *Jemima Shore Investigates* (1983, TV) and *Powers* (2004, TV). **Additional notes:** Wicking is listed in the "thanks to" credits of the BBC documentary *Hammer—The Studio That Dripped Blood* (1987, TV). **Hammer credits:** *Blood from the Mummy's Tomb* (1971, screenplay), *Demons of the Mind* (1972, co-story, screenplay), *To the Devil a Daughter* (1976, co-screenplay)

## Widd, Mike (Michael)

Widd worked as the production accountant on all thirteen episodes of *Hammer House of Horror* (1980, TV). His other credits include *George and Mildred* (1980) and *Cry Freedom* (1987), on which he was the location accountant, plus episodes of *Minder* (1979–1994, TV) and *Reilly: Ace of Spies* (1983, TV). He was also the associate producer on *A Day in Summer* (1989, TVM). **Hammer credits:** *Hammer House of Horror* (1980, TV)

## Widescreen

From the mid-fifties onwards, Hammer experimented with a number of widescreen processes. Their first widescreen movie was *Face the Music* (1954), which was available for screening in two formats: the standard Academy ratio of 1.33:1 and a widescreen version at 1.85:1, though this widescreen format was rather cheekily achieved by simply "cropping" the Academy version, rather than by using a widescreen lens. Hammer's first official widescreen film was the musical short *Cyril Stapleton and the Show Band* (1955), which was filmed in CinemaScope, using a lens loaned to Hammer by Twentieth Century–Fox, with which the company had ties. A further five CinemaScope musical featurettes followed, along with a handful of dramatic shorts and travelogues, among them *The Eric Winstone Band Show* (1955), *Just for You* (1956) and *Dick Turpin—Highwayman* (1956). Other widescreen processes used by the company include such catchpenny names as HammerScope, MegaScope and StrangloScope, the latter used as a come-on for *The Stranglers of Bombay* (1959).

## Widmark, Richard

Noted for his villainous roles, this intense American character star (1914–2008) began his film career following experience as a drama teacher. He earned an Academy Award nomination for best supporting actor for his film debut, *Kiss of Death* (1947), in which he played Tommy Udo, a psychopathic killer who memorably shoves an old lady in a wheelchair down a flight of stairs (the scene was deemed so shocking at the time that the censor cut it from British prints). With his distinctive voice and cold stare, he was always watchable, no matter what the quality of the film (critic James Agee once said of him, "It is clear that murder is one of the kindest things he is capable of"). His many other credits include *Road House* (1948), *Halls of Montezuma* (1950), *Judgment at Nuremberg* (1961), *The Secret Ways* (1961), which he also produced and co-directed (without credit), *The Bedford Incident* (1965), which he also produced (without credit), *Madigan* (1967), *Murder on the Orient Express* (1974), *Coma* (1978), *Who Dares Wins* (1982) and *True Colors* (1991). His TV appearances include *Vanished* (1971, TVM), *Benjamin Franklin* (1974, TV), in which he played the title role, *A Gathering of Old Men* (1987, TVM) and *Cold Sassy Tree* (1989, TVM), plus a spin-off of *Madigan* (1972, TV).

Widmark also starred as the occult writer John Verney in Hammer's underrated *To the Devil a Daughter* (1976). The actor was not the first choice for the role (among them such curious choices as Richard Dreyfuss, Peter Fonda, Beau Bridges and Michael Sarrazin), yet he brought to it his accustomed intensity, despite expressing his displeasure during the film's troubled production history. Recalled producer Roy Skeggs of Widmark's not always courteous attitude, "He called us Mickey Mouse productions. I don't blame him in a way. In the second week of shooting he called me at 4 a.m. one morning and told me he was getting the first flight to Los Angeles. I managed to get to him by 6 a.m., sat on the edge of his bed and persuaded him to stay. He did the same the next week, and I went to him again. When it happened again I ignored him."[33]

Widmark's first wife was the actress-turned-screenwriter Jean Hazelwood (1916–1997, full name Ora Jean Hazelwood), to whom he was married between 1942 and her death in 1997. His second wife was the stage producer, lyricist and socialite Susan Blanchard (1928–), to whom he was married from 1999. **Hammer credits:** *To the Devil a Daughter* (1976, as John Verney)

## Wiggins, Bill

This British poster artist designed the posters for several classic Hammer horrors, including *Dracula* (1958) and *The Mummy* (1959), the latter of which, produced during pre-production, caused contention with the film's star, Peter Cushing, who felt that the depiction of the Mummy with a policeman's torch shining through its torso didn't play fair with audiences, and so insisted that a scene be inserted into the film showing him spearing the monster through the chest in a bid to help justify the image. Wiggins' other campaigns include those for *Away All Boats* (1956), *Doctor Blood's Coffin* (1960), *The Lost World* (1960) and *The Day of the Triffids* (1962). **Hammer credits:** *Dracula* (1958 [uncredited]), *The Mummy* (1959 [uncredited]), *The Curse of the Werewolf* (1961 [uncredited]), *Frankenstein and the Monster from Hell* (1974 [uncredited])

## Wiggins, Helen

This British editor cut the Hammer comedy *Up the Creek* (1958). Her other credits include *Murder at the Festival* (1952), *The Devil's Pass* (1957), *Not Wanted on Voyage* 1957), *Nudist Paradise* (1958) and *Don't Talk to Strange Men* (1962). **Hammer credits:** *Up the Creek* (1958)

## Wilcocks, Shelagh (Sheelah)

This British actress (1910–1992, real name Sheelah Eloise Wilcocks, aka Sheelah Wilcox) can be seen as the housekeeper in Hammer's *The Vampire Lovers* (1970), prior to which she played a nurse in *Wolfshead: The Legend of Robin Hood* (1969 [released 1973]), which was subsequently acquired by Hammer. As Sheelah Wilcox, she also had a small role in Hammer's *Twins of Evil* (1971) as a snooty coach passenger. Her other credits include *A Nice Girl Like Me* (1969), *Deviation* (1971) and *Pope Joan* (1972), plus much television, including episodes of *William Tell* (1958–1959, TV), *Ace of Wands* (1970–1972, TV), *Poldark* (1975–1977, TV), *Nanny* (1981–1983, TV) and *London's Burning* (1988–2002, TV). **Hammer credits:** *Wolfshead: The Legend of Robin Hood* (1969 [released 1973], as Nurse), *The Vampire Lovers* (1970, as Housekeeper), *Twins of Evil* (1971, as Lady in coach [as Sheelah Wilcox])

## Wilcox, Elizabeth

Wilcox worked as the continuity girl on Hammer's *A Challenge for Robin Hood* (1967) and later returned for *The Satanic Rites of Dracula* (1974). Her other credits include *Bottoms Up* (1960), *Postman's Knock* (1962) and *Voices* (1973), plus episodes of *The Avengers* (1961–1969, TV), *The Saint* (1962–1969, TV), *The Champions* (1968–1969, TV), *Department S* (1969–1970, TV) and *Randall and Hopkirk (Deceased)* (1969–1970, TV). **Hammer credits:** *A Challenge for Robin Hood* (1967), *The Satanic Rites of Dracula* (1974)

## Wilcox, John

Following training in the camera department of British and Dominion from 1930, this prolific British cinematographer (1905–1979) became an operator on such films as *Peg of Old Drury* (1935). During the war, Wilcox served with the Army Kinematograph Unit, for which he shot *The New Lot* (1943) and *Think It Over* (1945). Following the war, he continued to work as an operator on the likes of *The Winslow Boy* (1948), as well as an occasional second unit cameraman on such productions as *The Macomber Affair* (1947), *The Third Man* (1949) and *State Secret* (1950). His credits as a fully fledged cinematographer meanwhile include *Mr. Denning Drives North* (1951), *Outcast of the Islands* (1952), *Cockleshell Heroes* (1955), *Curve Her Name with Pride* (1958), *The Mouse That Roared* (1959), *Summer Holiday* (1963), *Where's Jack?* (1969), *Steptoe and Son* (1972) and *The Hound of the Baskervilles* (1977). He was also the preferred cameraman of cinematographer-turned-director Freddie Francis, for whom he shot nine features, among them *The Skull* (1965), *The Psychopath* (1966), *The Deadly Bees* (1966), *Craze* (1973) and *The Ghoul* (1975). This association began with the Hammer thriller *Nightmare* (1964), and went on to include two further Francis-directed assignments for the studio. Wilcox later returned for *The Legend of the 7 Golden Vampires* (1974), on which he shared the cinematography credit with Roy Ford, and *Shatter* (1974), on which he shared his credit with Ford and Brian Probyn. Both productions were filmed in Hong Kong. Said Freddie Francis of Wilcox, "I thought John was a fine cameraman. John was not as fast as Arthur Grant. He was a better cameraman, but he wasn't as fast as Arthur."[34]

Wilcox should not be confused with the British production manager of the same name, who was the son of producer-director Herbert Wilcox, and who himself worked on Hammer's *One Million Years B.C.* (1966). To confuse matters further, Wilcox the cinematographer worked as a camera operator for Herbert Wilcox in the thirties. There was also a third John Wilcox, a make-up artist, to muddy the waters further. **Hammer credits:** *Nightmare* (1964, cinematographer), *The Evil of Frankenstein* (1964, cinematographer), *Hysteria* (1965, cinematographer), *The Legend of the 7 Golden Vampires* (1974, co-cinematographer), *Shatter* (1974, co-cinematographer)

## Wilcox, John

This British production manager (1921–2002) was the son of the respected producer and director Herbert Wilcox (1890–1977). His many credits include Hammer's *One Million Years B.C.* (1966), plus *The Yangtse Incident* (1957), *The Queen's Guards* (1961), *Up Jumped a Swagman* (1965), *Up the Front* (1972), *Are You Being Served?* (1977) and *Black Island* (1979). He should not be confused with the cinematographer of the same name, who also worked for Hammer in the sixties, as well as a camera operator for Herbert Wilcox in the thirties. Yet another John Wilcox also worked for Hammer as a make-up artist. His sister was the actress Pamela Bower (1919–1984, real name Pamela Marie Wilcox) and his stepmother was the actress Anna Neagle (1904–1986, real name Florence Marjorie Robertson). **Hammer credits:** *One Million Years B.C.* (1966)

## Wilcox, John

This make-up artist worked uncredited as a supervisor on Hammer's *Dr. Jekyll and Sister Hyde* (1971). His other credits include *The Woman in the Hall* (1947), *Esther Waters* (1948), *Madeleine* (1950), *Blind Man's Bluff* (1952), *Never Let Go* (1960), *Don't Lose Your Head* (1966) and *Deadlier Than the Male* (1967). He should not be confused with the cinematographer or the production manager of the same name, who both also worked for Hammer. **Hammer credits:** *Dr Jekyll and Sister Hyde* (1971 [uncredited])

## Wilcox, Paula

A sitcom favorite since her appearance as Beryl in *The Lovers* (1970–1971, TV), this saucer-eyed British actress (1949–, full name Mary Paula Wilcox) went on to appear in the equally popular *Man About the House* (1973–1976, TV), in which she played Chrissy Plummer. Her other TV work includes episodes of *The Apprentices* (1969, TV), *On the House* (1970, TV), *Miss Jones and Son* (1977–1978, TV), *The Bright Side* (1985, TV), *Blue Heaven* (1994, TV), *The Smoking Room* (2004–2005, TV), *Rock & Chips* (2010–2011, TV), *Mount Pleasant* (2011–2015, TV) and *Upstart Crow*

(2016–, TV). Her film work includes the big-screen spin-offs of *The Lovers!* (1973) and *Man About the House* (1974), the latter produced by Hammer. Also on stage. Her first husband (of two) was actor Derek Seaton (1943–1979), whom she married in 1970. **Additional notes.** Wilcox also appeared as Chrissy Plummer in a 1973 edition of the TV comedy special *All Star Comedy Carnival* (1969–1973, TV). **Hammer credits:** *Man About the House* (1974, as Chrissy Plummer)

### Wilcox, Sheelah *see* Wilcocks, Shelagh

### Wild, Jeanette

Wild can be seen as Suzy in Hammer's *On the Buses* (1971) and as Jill in *Dr. Jekyll and Sister Hyde* (1971). Prior to this she also popped up in a bit role in *Slave Girls* (1968). Her other credits include *Her Private Hell* (1968), *Zeta One* (1969) and *The Fiend* (1971), plus episodes of *Up Pompeii* (1969–1970, TV), *Monty Python's Flying Circus* (1969–1974, TV), *Miss Jones and Son* (1977–1978, TV), *Leave It to Charlie* (1978–1980, TV) and *How's Your Father?* (1979–1980, TV). She was married to the biographer and entertainment journalist Tony Crawley (1938–, full name Anthony Francis Crawley) between 1961 and 1969. **Hammer credits:** *Slave Girls* (1968, unnamed role [uncredited]), *On the Buses* (1971, as Suzy), *Dr. Jekyll and Sister Hyde* (1971, as Jill)

### Wild, Katy

This British (Welsh) actress (1940–) is best remembered for playing the mute girl in Hammer's *The Evil of Frankenstein* (1964), bringing a touch of much-needed pathos to the somewhat ramshackle proceedings. In films following experience in repertory theater, her other credits (among them four more for her Hammer director Freddie Francis) include *On the Run* (1963), *Traitor's Gate* (1964), *Dr. Terror's House of Horrors* (1965), *The Deadly Bees* (1966), *They Came from Beyond Space* (1967) and *Decline and Fall ... of a Birdwatcher* (1968), as well as episodes of such TV series as *Sheep's Clothing* (1960, TV), *Marriage Lines* (1961–1966, TV) and *Z Cars* (1962–1978, TV). In 1968 she

**A publicity shot of Katy Wild during the making of *The Evil of Frankenstein* (1964) (Hammer/ Universal/Rank/Universal International).**

moved to Australia, where she continued her career mostly on television, appearing in episodes of *Good Morning, Mr. Doubleday* (1969, TV), *Spyforce* (1971–1973, TV), *Our Man in the Company* (1973–1974, TV), *Bluey* (1976–1977, TV), *Sons and Daughters* (1982–1987, TV) and *G.P.* (1989–1996, TV), as well as the occasional film, among them *Adam's Woman* (1970) and *The Settlement* (1984). **Hammer credits:** *The Evil of Frankenstein* (1964, as Mute)

### Wilde, Brian

Best known to TV audiences for playing Foggy Dewhurst in the seemingly endless sitcom *Last of the Summer Wine* (1973–2010, TV), of which he appeared in 116 episodes between 1976 and 1997, this much-liked, RADA-trained British character actor (1927–2008) is also remembered for his work in *Porridge* (1974–1977, TV), in which he played the gullible prison warder Mr. Barrowclough. In addition to the big screen version of *Porridge* (1979), his film work includes supporting roles in two Hammer productions, plus *Street Corner* (1953), *Night of the Demon* (1957), *Life for Ruth* (1962), *You Only Live Twice* (1967), *Carry On Doctor* (1968), *Connecting Rooms* (1970), *No Sex Please—We're British* (1973), *Alfie Darling* (1975) and *Adventures of a Taxi Driver* (1976). Prolific on television, his many other credits include episodes of everything from *Douglas Fairbanks, Jr. Presents* (1953–1957, TV) to *The Ghosts of Motley Hall* (1976–1978, TV). His wife was actress Eva Stewart, whom he married in 1960, and his son is editor Andrew Wilde. **Hammer credits:** *Rasputin—The Mad Monk* (1966, as Brute [uncredited]), *To the Devil a Daughter* (1976, as Black Room attendant)

### Wilde, Janice

Wilde (sometimes Wild) designed the costumes for *Child's Play*, an episode of *Hammer House of Horror* (1984, TVM), taking over from series regular Laura Nightingale, who designed all the rest; prior this, Wilde had worked on the series as a wardrobe assistant. Her other credits include *Tangiers* (1985) and *Split Second* (1992), plus episodes of *The Comic Strip Presents* (1982–2012, TV) and *Mike & Angelo* (1989–2000, TV). **Hammer credits:** *Czech Mate* (1984, TVM [episode of *Hammer House of Mystery and Suspense*], wardrobe assistant [uncredited]), *The Sweet Scent of Death* (1984, TVM [episode of *Hammer House of Mystery and Suspense*], wardrobe assistant [uncredited]), *A Distant Scream* (1984, TVM [episode of *Hammer House of Mystery and Suspense*], wardrobe assistant [uncredited]), *The Late Nancy Irving* (1984, TVM [episode of *Hammer House of Mystery and Suspense*], wardrobe assistant [uncredited]), *In Possession* (1984, TVM [episode of *Hammer House of Mystery and Suspense*], wardrobe assistant [uncredited]), *Black Carrion* (1984, TVM [episode of *Hammer House of Mystery and Suspense*], wardrobe assistant [uncredited]), *Last Video and Testament* (1984, TVM [episode of *Hammer House of Mystery and Suspense*], wardrobe assistant [uncredited]), *Mark of the Devil* (1984, TVM [episode of *Hammer House of Mystery and Suspense*], wardrobe assistant [uncredited]), *The Corvini Inheritance* (1984, TVM

[episode of *Hammer House of Mystery and Suspense*], wardrobe assistant [uncredited]), *Paint Me a Murder* (1984, TVM [episode of *Hammer House of Mystery and Suspense*], wardrobe assistant [uncredited]), *And the Wall Came Tumbling Down* (1984, TVM [episode of *Hammer House of Mystery and Suspense*], wardrobe assistant [uncredited]), *Child's Play* (1984, TVM [episode of *Hammer House of Horror*], costumes), *Tennis Court* (1984, TVM [episode of *Hammer House of Mystery and Suspense*], wardrobe assistant [uncredited])

### Wilder, Richelle

Wilder became Hammer's secretary in 1991. In 1993 she moved to California to take charge of Hammer's office at Warner Bros. in Burbank during the company's dealings with Donner/Shuler Donner. She is acknowledged in the credits of *Flesh and Blood—The Hammer Heritage of Horror* (1994, TV). Her own credits as a producer include episodes of the animated TV series *Freefonix* (2007, TV), on which she also worked as a story editor. Her other credits as a script editor include episodes of *Dennis & Gnasher* (2009–2013, TV) and *Rogue* (2013–2017, TV). She was also involved with the script development for *An Ideal Husband* (1999) and *Flushed Away* (2006). **Hammer credits:** *Flesh and Blood—The Hammer Heritage of Horror* (1994, TV)

### Wilding, April

British born Wilding (1941–2003) played the role of Catherine (Anna's mother) in Hammer's *Hands of the Ripper* (1971). Her other credits include *The Frightened City* (1961), *Breath of Life* (1962) and *Secrets of a Windmill Girl* (1966), plus episodes of *Stranger in the City* (1962, TV), *The Saint* (1962–1969, TV) and *Play for Today* (1970–1984, TV). **Hammer credits:** *Hands of the Ripper* (1971, as Catherine)

### Wiles, Sid (Sidney/Syd)

This British sound technician (1899–1973) worked on such productions as *O.H.M.S.* (1937), *The Lady Vanishes* (1938), *Night Train to Munich* (1940), *Kipps* (1941), *Millions Like Us* (1943), *It's Not Cricket* (1949), *The Kidnappers* (1953), *Depth Charge* (1960) and *Panic* (1963), plus episodes of *The Cheaters* (1960–1962, TV). He also notched up a handful of credits for Hammer in the fifties. **Hammer credits:** *Never Look Back* (1952), *Mask of Dust* (1954), *The Stranger Came Home* (1954), *Men of Sherwood Forest* (1954), *Third Party Risk* (1955), *Don't Panic Chaps* (1959)

### Wilkinson, Albert

This diminutive British actor (1938–) can be seen as a circus midget in Hammer's *Countess Dracula* (1971). His other film credits include *Willy Wonka and the Chocolate Factory* (1971), in which he played an Oompa Loompa, *Wombling Free* (1978), in which he sweated it out in one of the Womble suits, and *Labyrinth* (1986), in which he played a goblin. His TV appearances include the controversial 1974 *South Africa* episode of *The Goodies* (1970–1982, TV). **Hammer credits:** *Countess Dracula* (1971, as Circus midget)

## Wilkinson, Arthur

This British songwriter, composer and orchestrator (1919–1968) scored the Hammer comedy *Life with the Lyons* (1954). His other credits as a composer include *The Calendar* (1948), *The Weaker Sex* (1948), *The Limping Man* (1953) and *The Flying Eye* (1955), plus episodes of such series as *Crime on Our Hands* (1954, TV) and *Ukridge* (1968, TV), as well as the TV version of *Life with the Lyons* (1955–1960, TV). He also worked as an arranger on *Things Happen at Night* (1947), and provided additional music for *The Chiltern Hundreds* (1949). His records include two pastiche Beatles discs, *Beatle Cracker Suite* (1965) and *The Beatle Concerto* (1967). **Hammer credits:** *Life with the Lyons* (1954), *Adventures with the Lyons* (1957, serial re-issue of *Life with the Lyons*)

## Wilkinson, Helen

Wilkinson worked as the period design consultant on *Wolfshead: The Legend of Robin Hood* (1969 [released 1973]), making it one of the more authentic looking Robin Hood adventures of the period. The film was subsequently acquired by Hammer. **Hammer credits:** *Wolfshead: The Legend of Robin Hood* (1969 [released 1973])

## Wilkinson, Marc

Scoring films from 1968 with *If….*, the credits of this French born composer and conductor (1929–) also include *The Royal Hunt of the Sun* (1968), *The Blood on Satan's Claw* (1971), *The Triple Echo* (1972), *The Hireling* (1973), *Eagle's Wing* (1978), *The Fiendish Plot of Dr. Fu Manchu* (1980), in which he can also be spotted as a conductor, *Looks and Smiles* (1981), *Enigma* (1982) and *Coming Through* (1985). Also busy in the theater, his TV work includes episodes of *Days of Hope* (1975, TV), *Quatermass* (1979), *Tales of the Unexpected* (1979–1988, TV) and an episode of *Hammer House of Horror* (1980, TV). He received a joint BAFTA nomination for his work on *The Bell* (1982, TV) and *A Voyage Round My Father* (1982, TVM). **Hammer credits:** *Visitor from the Grave* (1980, TV [episode of *Hammer House of Horror*])

## Wilkinson, Nick

This stuntman worked on various episodes of *Hammer House of Horror* (1980, TV), most notably *The Silent Scream*, on which he was Peter Cushing's stunt double. His other credits include *For Your Eyes Only* (1981), *Krull* (1983), *Batman* (1989), *Son of the Pink Panther* (1993), *First Knight* (1995), *Bridget Jones's Diary* (2001), *Doomsday* (2008), *Johnny English Reborn* (2011) and *Mr. Turner* (2014), plus episodes of *Casualty* (1986–, TV), *Waiting for God* (1990–1994, TV), *Silent Witness* (1996–, TV) and *Shameless* (2004–2013, TV). **Hammer credits:** *Hammer House of Horror* (1980, TV [uncredited]), *The Silent Scream* (1980, TV [episode of *Hammer House of Horror*], as Peter Cushing's stunt double)

## Willard, Edmund

This British stage actor (1884–1956) also appeared in a handful of films, among them Hammer's second feature, *The Mystery of the Mary Celeste* (1935), in which he played Toby Bilson, who is shot to death by Bela Lugosi's mad seaman, Anton Lorenzen. His other films include *A Window in Piccadilly* (1928), *Rembrandt* (1936), *Dark Journey* (1937), *Pastor Hall* (1940) and *Up in the World* (1956), plus episodes of *BBC Sunday-Night Theatre* (1950–1959, TV), *Happy and Glorious* (1952, TV) and *The Scarlet Pimpernel* (1955–1956, TV). **Hammer credits:** *The Mystery of the Mary Celeste* (1935, as Toby Bilson)

## Willard, Lola

British born Willard (1912–1997) had a bit part in Hammer's *Straight on Till Morning* (1972), which was directed by her son, Peter Collinson (1936–1980). Her other credits include an episode of *The Diary of Samuel Pepys* (1958, TV). **Hammer credits:** *Straight on Till Morning* (1972, as Customer)

## Willetts, Peter

Willets worked as one of the drivers on the Hammer comedy *A Weekend with Lulu* (1961). **Hammer credits:** *A Weekend with Lulu* (1961 [uncredited])

## Willey, Francis

Willey can be seen as one of Squire Hamilton's young bloods in Hammer's *The Plague of the Zombies* (1966). His TV credits include a couple of episodes of *Doctor Who* (1963–1988, TV). **Hammer credits:** *The Plague of the Zombies* (1966, as Young blood)

## Williams, Arthur

Williams can be seen playing the role of Endobo the witch doctor in Hammer's *Song of Freedom* (1936). Also on stage, his other credits include *A Message from Mars* (1913). **Hammer credits:** *Song of Freedom* (1936, as Endobo [witch doctor, uncredited])

## Williams, Ben (Benjamin)

This British supporting actor (1892–1960) appeared in a handful of Hammer's second features. In films from the early thirties with *The Good Companions* (1933) following experience as a coal miner, his many other credits (in excess of one-hundred) include *Boys Will Be Boys* (1935), *Bank Holiday* (1938), *Contraband* (1940), *Waterloo Road* (1945), *The Black Rose* (1950), *The Teckman Mystery* (1954) and *Hell Drivers* (1957), plus episodes of *The Scarlet Pimpernel* (1955–1956, TV), *The Count of Monte Cristo* (1956, TV) and *Stryker of the Yard* (1957, TV). **Hammer credits:** *The Dark Road* (1948, as Sergeant), *Dick Barton at Bay* (1950, as Captain [uncredited]), *Whispering Smith Hits London* (1952, as Taxi driver), *Stolen Face* (1952, unnamed role [uncredited]), *Face the Music* (1954, as Gatekeeper [uncredited])

## Williams, Billy

This noted British cinematographer (1929–) began his career as an assistant to his father, cinematographer Billie Williams (1895–1966), working on documentaries and newsreels for the likes of the Air Force and the Colonial Film Unit. He went on to work as the second unit cameraman on Hammer's *Someone at the Door* (1950), for which he shot the exteriors in the grounds of Oakley Court "with telling effect," as the trade paper *The Cinema Studio* noted at the time. He became known for his work on a number of commercials, which in turn led to several high profile features, among them *Billion Dollar Brain* (1967), *The Magus* (1968), which earned him a BAFTA nomination, *Women in Love* (1969), which earned him BAFTA and Oscar nominations, *Sunday Bloody Sunday* (1971), which earned him another BAFTA nomination, *Voyage of the Damned* (1976), *On Golden Pond* (1981), which earned him a second Oscar nomination, and *Dreamchild* (1985). His other credits include *Five Guineas a Week* (1956), *San Ferry Ann* (1965), *Zee and Co.* (1971), *Saturn 3* (1980), *The Rainbow* (1988) and *Driftwood* (1997). He also photographed the Iraq sequences for *The Exorcist* (1973). He finally won an Oscar for his work on *Gandhi* (1982), which he shared with Ronnie Taylor. He was the president of the British Society of Cinematographers between 1975 and 1977, and was made an OBE in 2009. **Hammer credits:** *Someone at the Door* (1950 [uncredited])

## Williams, Brook

The son of the celebrated actor-playwright Emlyn Williams (1905–1987), this British actor (1938–2005) is best known to Hammer fans for playing the rather vapid Dr. Peter Tompson in *The Plague of the Zombies* (1966), in which his wife Alice is not only zombified by the local squire, but is then beheaded before his very eyes by his colleague Sir James Forbes when she rises from the grave. In films from the early sixties, Williams' other screen credits (among them several with his close friend Richard Burton) include *The V.I.P.s* (1963), *The Heroes of Telemark* (1965), *Where Eagles Dare* (1969), *Anne of the Thousand Days* (1969), *The Raging Moon* (1970), *Villain* (1971), *Equus* (1977), *The Wild Geese* (1978), *The Medusa Touch* (1978), *North Sea Hijack* (1979), *Pascali's Island* (1988), *The Children* (1990) and *England, My England* (1995), plus episodes of *The Avengers* (1961–1969, TV), *Here's Lucy* (1968–1974, TV) and *Wagner* (1983, TV). He also worked as the dialogue coach on *Wild Geese II* (1985). His brother is the novelist Alan Williams (1935–). **Hammer credits:** *The Plague of the Zombies* (1966, as Dr. Peter Tompson)

## Williams, Cedric

Although Hammer's cinematographer in residence but for a short period, Williams (1913–1999) nevertheless managed to notch up quite a prolific collection of credits during his year-long stay with the company, which began in November 1948 with the filming of *Dr. Morelle—The Case of the Missing Heiress* (1949) and concluded in October 1949 with the making of *Room to Let* (1950). In films from the early thirties as an assistant cameraman, his other credits as a cinematographer include *Comin' Thro' the Rye* (1947), *The Fatal Night* (1948), *Third Time Lucky* (1949), *The Fake* (1953), *It's a Great Day* (1955), *Police Dog* (1955), *The Flaw* (1955), *The Gelignite Gang* (1956), *Blue Horizons* (1957) and *Breath of Life* (1963). He also photographed a few documentaries, among them *The Road to Canterbury* (1956) and *The Story of Regent*

*Street* (1962), as well as episodes of *Douglas Fairbanks, Jr. Presents* (1953–1957, TV).

Recalled Jimmy Sangster of Williams, "While turning out very reasonable-looking movies, [he] took too long to light the scenes in the first place, and then was quite capable of deciding after take two or three that he wanted to change the lights."[35] Recalled Williams of his experiences with Hammer, "James Carreras was a brilliant salesman, and I remember quite distinctly that on the *Dick Barton* film cans that went out to the cinemas there was a special notice in red ink. It read: 'To the chief projectionist. Dear Chief, When it comes to the critical moment at the end of the film, make sure you use full amplification, blast them out of their seats, this is the sort of effect we want.'"[36] **Hammer credits:** *Dr. Morelle—The Case of the Missing Heiress* (1949), *Dick Barton Strikes Back* (1949), *The Adventures of PC 49—The Case of the Guardian Angel* (1949), *Celia* (1949), *Meet Simon Cherry* (1949), *The Man in Black* (1950), *Room to Let* (1950)

## Williams, Charles

Though best remembered for his romantic composition *The Dream of Olwyn*, which featured in the 1947 film *While I Live*, this British composer and conductor (1893–1978, real name Isaac Cozerbreit) also worked on such films as *Kipps* (1941), *Quiet Weekend* (1946) and *The Romantic Age* (1949). A talented pianist and violinist, he made his concert debut at the age of twelve and went on to study music at the Royal Academy of Music. Following military experience during the First World War (in which he served with the Band of the King's Royal Rifles) he continued his studies and joined the J.H. Squire Octet. He formed his own band, The Charles Williams Octet, in 1920, and also started to play in various pit orchestras, including the Royal Opera House. He began conducting in 1923–the same year he also began recording. In 1929 he made an uncredited contribution to the score for Hitchcock's first sound film, *Blackmail*. Over the following years Williams contributed to over forty scores (often uncredited, either as a conductor or the composer of additional music), working primarily for Gaumont-British and Gainsborough. Among his credits are *Dr. Syn* (1937), *The Lady Vanishes* (1938), *Cottage to Let* (1941), *The Way to the Stars* (1945), *Noose* (1948) and *You Can't Escape* (1956). His 1949 piece *Jealous Lover* was also adapted into Adolph Deutsch's score for *The Apartment* (1960). His concert and easy listening pieces include *The Humming Top* (1938), *The Night Has Eyes* (1942), *Model Railway* (1951) and *London Fair* (1955). His other well-known piece is *The Devil's Gallop*, which was used as the signature tune for the popular post-war radio serial *Dick Barton* (1946–1947). Still well known to this day, this theme was also used by Hammer for their three subsequent Barton movies (albeit all without credit). It also features briefly (again without credit) in Hammer's *The Lady Craved Excitement* (1950), when, during a particularly hairy moment, one of the characters ponders, "What would Dick Barton do?" **Hammer credits:** *Dick Barton—Special Agent* (1948 [uncredited]), *Dick Barton Strikes*

*Back* (1949 [uncredited]), *Dick Barton at Bay* (1950 [uncredited]), *The Lady Craved Excitement* (1950 [uncredited])

## Williams, Charlie

This cheeky, much-liked British stand-up comedian (1928–2006) is best known for his appearances on TV's *The Golden Shot* (1967–1975, TV) and *The Comedians* (1971–1974, TV). A former professional footballer, he also took on the occasional dramatic role, including that of club comedian George Harvey in Hammer's *Man at the Top* (1973). **Hammer credits:** *Man at the Top* (1973)

## Williams, Elmo

This noted American editor (1913–2015, full name James Elmo Williams) learned his craft in Britain while apprenticed to fellow American Merrill G. White at British and Dominion Studios, cutting many films for the producer-director Herbert Wilcox, among them *Victoria the Great* (1937) and *Nurse Edith Cavell* (1939). When Wilcox went to America to direct *Irene* (1940) for RKO, Williams followed, and remained at the studio for several years, editing *No, No, Nanette* (1940), again for Wilcox, *Nocturne* (1946) and *Dick Tracy Meets Gruesome* (1947) among others. Following work as a freelance editor, during which period he cut *High Noon* (1952), which earned him a shared Oscar, and *20,000 Leagues Under the Sea* (1954), which earned him an Oscar nomination, Williams went to work for the British arm of Twentieth Century–Fox (he eventually became European Managing Director and, upon his return to America, Vice President in charge of worldwide production). At the time, Fox had a production deal with Hammer via the producer Robert Lippert, for whom Williams directed the prison melodrama *Women Without Men* (1956). Williams' many other credits include *The Tall Texan* (1953), which he directed, *The Vikings* (1958), which he edited, *The Big Gamble* (1960), for which he directed the second unit, *The Longest Day* (1962), on which he was an associate producer, *Caravans* (1978), which he produced, and *Ernest Goes to Camp* (1987), on which he was an executive producer. He was also involved with the TV series *Tales of the Vikings* (1960, TV), which he produced and directed. He became the head of worldwide production for Fox in the seventies, and personally produced the Pearl Harbor epic *Tora! Tora! Tora!* (1970). His wife was the writer and lyricist Lorraine Williams (1919–2004, maiden name Lorraine Bennet Cunningham), whom he married in 1940; she penned the lyrics for *Long Ago Guy* (music by Douglas Gamley), which was featured in *Women Without Men*. Williams wrote about his experiences in *Elmo Williams: A Hollywood Memoir* (2006). **Hammer credits:** *Women Without Men* (1956)

## Williams, F.A.

Williams can be spotted as the butler in the Hammer programer *Room to Let* (1950). **Hammer credits:** *Room to Let* (1950, as Butler)

## Williams, Frank

Best known for playing the bespectacled vicar, the Reverend Timothy Farthing, in *Dad's Army* (1968–1977, TV), this British actor (1931–) was extremely well suited to the role, given that he went on to serve as a member of the General Synod of the Church of England. In films from 1953 as an extra in *The Story of Gilbert and Sullivan*, he subsequently appeared in dozens of movies, among them Hammer's *The Glass Cage* (1955), almost always in minor supporting roles. His other credits include *The Extra Day* (1956), *Inn for Trouble* (1960), *A Stitch in Time* (1963), *Countdown to Danger* (1967), the big screen version of *Dad's Army* (1971), *Jabberwocky* (1977), *Revenge of the Pink Panther* (1978), *The Echoes of Empire* (2012), in which he played Churchill, and the remake of *Dad's Army* (2016), again as the Reverend Timothy Farthing. Even busier on television, his work here includes a brief appearance in *The Indian Spirit Guide* (1968, TV [episode of *Journey to the Unknown*]) as a séance guest. This episode also appeared in the compendium film *Journey to Midnight* (1968, TVM). His other TV work includes episodes of *The Army Game* (1957–1961, TV), in which he played Captain Pocket, *The Rivals of Sherlock Holmes* (1971–1973, TV), *Minder* (1979–1994, TV), *Boon* (1986–1992, TV) and *You Rang, M'Lord?* (1988–1993, TV), in which he played the bishop. He also provided the story for the short *Murder by Appointment* (2009) and penned the one-off *The Golden Years* (2011, TV), appearing in the latter. He also contributed stories to *New Scotland Yard* (1972–1974, TV). **Hammer credits:** *The Glass Cage* (1955, as Spectator [uncredited]), *The Indian Spirit Guide* (1968, TV [episode of *Journey to the Unknown*], as Séance guest), *Journey to Midnight* (1968, TVM, as Séance guest)

## Williams, Howard

This British supporting actor (1932–) can be seen as Michaels in *Quatermass 2* (1957), which led to work on a further four Hammer films, all of which were helmed by Val Guest, who also directed him in *It's a Wonderful World* (1956) and *Carry On Admiral* (1957). His other credits include *Birthright* (1951), *Reach for the Sky* (1956) and *Life Is a Circus* (1960), plus episodes of *Tales from Dickens* (1958, TV) and *Compact* (1962–1965, TV). **Hammer credits:** *Quatermass 2* (1957, as Michaels), *The Camp on Blood Island* (1958, as Prisoner [uncredited]), *Up the Creek* (1958, as Bunts), *Further Up the Creek* (1958, as Bunts), *Yesterday's Enemy* (1959, as Davies [uncredited])

## Williams, J.B.

Active as a writer, director and producer, British born Williams (1903–1965, full name James Bailiff Williams) can be seen in one of his rare acting roles as a judge in Hammer's *The Mystery of the Mary Celeste* (1935). His credits as a director include *White Cargo* (1929), which he also co-produced and scripted, and *The Chinese Bungalow* (1930), which he co-directed, co-scripted and co-produced. His other screenplay credits (usually as co-author or adapter) include *Owd Bob* (1938), *The Stars Look Down* (1939), *We Dive at Dawn* (1943), for which he also provided the story, and *London Belongs to Me* (1948). He also penned episodes of *Douglas Fairbanks, Jr. Presents* (1953–1957, TV), *International Detective* (1959–1961, TV) and *No Hiding Place* (1959–1967, TV). He certainly seems to have had his fingers in some fairly interesting pies. **Hammer credits:** *The Mystery of the Mary Celeste* (1935, as Judge [uncredited])

## Williams, Kate

This British actress (1941–) is best known for playing Joan Booth, the long-suffering wife of bigot Eddie Booth, in the hit sitcom *Love Thy Neighbour* (1972–1976, TV). She also played the role in Hammer's 1973 big screen spin-off. A familiar face on British TV throughout the seventies and eighties, her occasional film credits include *Poor Cow* (1967), *Melody* (1971), a return to Hammer for *Holiday on the Buses* (1973), in which she played Inspector Blake's girlfriend, also named Joan, *Quadrophenia* (1979), *Party Party* (1983), *Little Dorrit* (1988), *The Mystery of Edwin Drood* (1993) and *Hughie Green, Most Sincerely* (2008, TVM). Her other TV appearances include episodes of *Dixon of Dock Green* (1955–1976, TV), *Widows* (1983, TV), *Widows 2* (1985, TV), *EastEnders* (1985–, TV), in which she played Liz Turner between 2006 and 2010, *Time After Time* (1994–1995, TV), *She's Out* (1995, TV), *Family Affairs* (1997–2005, TV) and *Man Down* (2013–2015, TV). **Additional notes:** Williams also appeared as Joan Booth in a 1972 edition of the TV comedy special *All Star Comedy Carnival* (1969–1973, TV). **Hammer credits:** *Love Thy Neighbour* (1973, as Joan Booth), *Holiday on the Buses* (1973, as Joan)

## Williams, Kit

Williams can be seen as Henry in Hammer's *The Damned* (1963). His other credits include *The Girl on a Motorcycle* (1968), plus episodes of *Suspense* (1962–1963, TV), *Son of the Sahara* (1966, TV) and *Mrs. Thursday* (1966–1967, TV). **Hammer credits:** *The Damned* (1963, as Henry)

## Williams, Lorraine

American born Williams (1919–2004, maiden name Lorraine Bennet Cunningham) provided the lyrics for the song *Long Ago Guy* (music by Douglas Gamley), which was featured in the Hammer prison melodrama *Women Without Men* (1956). This was directed by her husband, Elmo Williams (1913–2015, full name James Elmo Williams), whom she married in 1940. She also wrote the screenplay for the documentary *The Cowboy* (1954), which was co-produced, directed, photographed and edited by her husband, and for which she penned the lyrics to such songs as *The Meadowlark, Cowboy Saturday Night* and *Dodge City Trail* (music by Axel Johnson). She likewise penned the lyrics to Ron Goodwin's catchy title theme for *Those Magnificent Men in Their Flying Machines* (1965), which was made under the aegis of her husband (as managing director of Fox's European arm). She later contributed to the screenplay of *Caravans* (1978), which was produced by her husband, and appeared in *Man, Woman and Child* (1983), which was likewise produced by her husband. **Hammer credits:** *Women Without Men* (1956)

## Williams, Reg

Williams worked in the publicity department during Hammer's years at Bray. Among the films he worked on was *The Plague of the Zombies* (1966). **Hammer credits include:** *The Plague of the Zombies* (1966 [uncredited])

## Williams, Roger

This British actor (1900–1975) can be seen as a villager in Hammer's *Captain Kronos—Vampire Hunter* (1974). His other credits include *Meet Mr. Callaghan* (1954) and *Swingin' Along* (1960), plus episodes of *ITV Play of the Week* (1955–1968, TV), *Boyd Q.C.* (1956–1964, TV) and *Armchair Theatre* (1956–1974, TV). **Hammer credits:** *Captain Kronos—Vampire Hunter* (1974, as Villager [uncredited])

## Williams, Simon

This dashing-looking British actor (1946–) first came to attention as Captain James Bellamy in the phenomenally successful *Upstairs, Downstairs* (1971–1975, TV), which led to work on such TV series as the ground-breaking sitcom *Agony* (1979–1981, TV), in which he played Laurence Lucas, *Kinvig* (1981, TV), *Don't Wait Up* (1983–1990, TV), in which he replaced Richard Heffer, and *Agony Again* (1995, TV), as well as guest shots on everything from *Hammer House of Mystery and Suspense* (1984, TVM) to *The Bletchley Circle* (2012–2014, TV). His film credits include *Joanna* (1968), *The Touchables* (1968), *The Blood on Satan's Claw* (1971), *Three for All* (1974), *The Incredible Sarah* (1976), *The Prisoner of Zenda* (1979), *The Gathering Storm* (2002, TVM), *Lady Godiva* (2008), *Run for Your Wife* (2012), *Silent Hours* (2015) and *Viceroy's House* (2017). Also busy on stage, his parents were the actors Hugh Williams (1904–1969) and Margaret Vyner (1914–1993). His brother is the poet Hugo Williams (1942–) and his sister was the actress Polly Williams (1950–2004, aka Polly Havers [following her marriage to actor Nigel Havers]). His first wife was the actress Belinda Carroll (1945–), whose sister Kate O'Mara (1939–2014, real name Kate Carroll) appeared in Hammer's *Captain Clegg* (1962), *The Vampire Lovers* (1970) and *The Horror of Frankenstein* (1970). His second wife, whose mother was the actress Celia Johnson (1908–1982), is the actress Lucy Fleming (1947–, real name Eve Lucinda Fleming), whom he married in 1986, and who appeared in Hammer's *Rasputin—The Mad Monk* (1966). His children (with Carroll) are actors Tam Williams (1971–, full name Tamlyn Williams) and Amy Williams (1976–). **Hammer credits:** *The Late Nancy Irving* (1984, TVM [episode of *Hammer House of Mystery and Suspense*], as Bob Appleyard)

## Williams, Terry

Williams can be spotted in Hammer's *The Witches* (1966). **Hammer credits:** *The Witches* (1966, as Dancer [uncredited])

## Williamson, Alastair (Alister/Alistair)

This busy Australian born bit player (1918–1999) can be seen as Sam in Hammer's Manchester-shot thriller *Hell Is a City* (1960). He began his screen career in Australia with an episode of *The Flying Doctor* (1959, TV) and an appearance in *The Sundowners* (1960). His other British credits include *Saturday Night and Sunday Morning* (1960), *Crooks in Cloisters* (1963), *The Return of Mr. Moto* (1965), *The Deadly Bees* (1966), *The Oblong Box* (1969), *The Last Shot You Hear* (1970) and *The Abominable Dr. Phibes* (1971), plus three further cameos for Hammer. His TV work takes in episodes of *Nick of the River* (1959, TV), *The Third Man* (1959–1965, TV), *Upstairs, Downstairs* (1971–1975, TV) and *That's My Boy* (1981–1986, TV). **Hammer credits:** *Hell Is a City* (1960, as Sam), *The Curse of the Werewolf* (1961, as Policeman [uncredited]), *The Evil of Frankenstein* (1964, as Landlord [uncredited]), *The Gorgon* (1964, as Janus Cass)

## Williamson, Malcolm

Following some work on documentaries in his homeland, among them *Inland with Sturt* (1951) and *The Timber Getters* (1952), this noted Australian composer (1931–2003) was invited by Hammer's resident music director John Hollingsworth to make his feature debut with *The Brides of Dracula* (1960), for which he provided a strident score in the James Bernard manner, accompanied by a judicious use of organ (the *News Chronicle* described Williamson's music as "diabolically bodeful"). Busy with concert pieces and documentaries for much of the sixties, Williamson eventually returned to Hammer at the behest of Hollingsworth's successor, Philip Martell, to score two more films for the studio. These were *Crescendo* (1970), for which he provided a mock piano concerto, and *The Horror of Frankenstein* (1970). Remembered Williamson of the latter, "I did not enjoy it at all…. I used the tuba to personify the creature, but the final effect was ludicrous."[37] Commented Philip Martell of Williamson's film music, "Malcolm has no sense of humor in music. I don't know how many pictures he's sunk because of that. He takes himself so seriously, he loves himself so much that he spoils the music in adoration of himself."[38]

Williamson's other film credits include *Nothing But the Night* (1972) and *The Masks of Death* (1984, TVM), while in 1980 he scored an episode of *Hammer House of Horror*. In 1975, he succeeded Arthur Bliss as Master of the Queen's Musick, while in 1976 he was made a CBE. **Additional notes:** In *Crescendo*, Williamson doubled for actor James Olsen during the playing of the concerto. Williamson's music for Hammer was also featured in the documentary *Peter Cushing—A One-Way Ticket to Hollywood* (1989, TV). **Hammer credits:** *The Brides of Dracula* (1960), *Crescendo* (1970), *The Horror of Frankenstein* (1970), *Visitor from the Grave* (1980, TV [episode of *Hammer House of Horror*])

## Williamson, Paul

This British actor (1929–) can be seen in the Hammer second feature *The Runaway* (1964). He was also featured in the little-seen *Delayed Flight* (1964), with which it was filmed back to back. His other film credits include *Return to Sender* (1963), *Venom* (1981), *The Accidental Tourist* (1988), *In Too Deep* (1990), *Emma* (1996) and

*Namastey London* (2007), plus a return to Hammer for *Man at the Top* (1973). His many TV appearances include episodes of *The Scarlet Pimpernel* (1955–1956, TV), *Redcap* (1964–1966, TV), *Callan* (1967–1972, TV), *Telford's Change* (1979, TV), *Keeping Up Appearances* (1990–1995, TV) and *Broken News* (2005, TV). He is also familiar from such TV ad campaigns as those for Ferrero Rocher (in which he played the butler) and Werther's Originals. **Hammer credits:** *The Runaway* (1964, as Thomas), *Delayed Flight* (1964, as Shentor), *Man at the Top* (1973, as Tarrant)

### Willis, Alan

Willis worked as an assistant editor on Hammer's *Paranoiac* (1963) and as second assistant editor on *Nightmare* (1964). His other credits include *Mister Jerico* (1970, TVM), on which he was the sound editor, *The Disappearance* (1977), on which he was the first assistant editor, the series *Harry's Game* (1982, TV), on which he was the dubbing editor (and which earned him a shared BAFTA nomination), and *May We Borrow Your Husband?* (1986, TVM), on which he was the dubbing editor. He also worked as a music editor on a number of series, including *Man in a Suitcase* (1967–1968, TV), *The Champions* (1968–1969, TV), *The Protectors* (1972–1973, TV), *The Professionals* (1977–1983, TV) and *Seagull Island* (1981, TV). **Hammer credits:** *Paranoiac* (1963 [uncredited]), *Nightmare* (1964, second assistant editor [uncredited])

### Willis, Connie (Constance)

British born Willis (1924–1992) worked as the continuity girl on Hammer's courtroom drama *Never Look Back* (1952). She later returned for the adventure-thriller *Break in the Circle* (1955), which was shot on multiple locations. Her other credits take in *The Spider and the Fly* (1949), *Trio* (1950), *Star of India* (1954), *The Man Who Knew Too Much* (1956), *Vertigo* (1958), *633 Squadron* (1964), *A Shot in the Dark* (1964), *Goldfinger* (1964), *A Man for All Seasons* (1966), *To Catch a Spy* (1971), *The Return of the Pink Panther* (1975), *A Bridge too Far* (1977), *Death on the Nile* (1978), *Lion of the Desert* (1981) and *Death Wish 3* (1985). **Hammer credits:** *Never Look Back* (1952), *Break in the Circle* (1955)

### Willis, Jim

Willis (?–1995) recorded the sound for Hammer's *Captain Kronos—Vampire Hunter* (1974). His other credits include *Custer of the West* (1967), *The Deserter* (1971), *The Little Prince* (1974), *Confessions of a Pop Performer* (1975), *Conan the Barbarian* (1982), *The Trouble with Spies* (1987 [filmed 1984]) and *The Rift* (1990). **Hammer credits:** *Captain Kronos—Vampire Hunter* (1974)

### Willman, Noel

On stage from 1938, this Irish character actor (1918–1988) is best remembered for playing the sect leader Dr. Ravna in Hammer's *The Kiss of the Vampire* (1963), a role he played with a single expression on his face, so as to emphasize the character's noble bearing. However, even Willman must have laughed to himself during the filming of the climax, in which Ravna and his sect are destroyed by a horde of bats. Recalled effects assistant Ian

Scoones, "I had to have my hand between his [Willman's] legs with this stick with a bat on the end, coming through a hole in his costume as if it was attacking his neck. At the rushes the next day, Tony Keys said, 'Christ, we can't use that, it looks like he's being wanked off!'"[39] Commented director Don Sharp of Willman's performance as Ravna, "He was good, wasn't he? Although he was playing a baddie, he was never overtly threatening. He was just this very polite gentleman. The idea of the corruption underneath the class also offered a great mixture."[40] Commented Willman of being cast, "I chose to associate myself for three very good reasons. It paid for a wonderful vacation. Secondly, I like the director, Don Sharp, very much. He was stylish and a surprising pro in the sense that it was his first attempt at making something like this. And most importantly, it was a good script…. I always felt it was rather camp to play a vampire and be in a Hammer horror, and God knows, it didn't hurt Peter Cushing."[41] Meanwhile, of his performance he revealed, "I focused on Ravna's power…. I understand how easy it could be to send all this up, and I chose to play him withdrawn and immobile…. Believe me, the effect worked marvelously and Don Sharp seemed to be very pleased."[42]

Willman spent the majority of his career in the theater as both an actor and director (he won a Tony for his direction of *A Man for All Seasons* on Broadway in 1962), but found time to make over twenty films, among them *The Pickwick Papers* (1952), which marked his screen debut, *Beau Brummell* (1954), *The Man Who Knew Too Much* (1956), *Carve Her Name with Pride* (1958), *Doctor*

*Zhivago* (1965) and *The Odessa File* (1974), in which he played the Nazi Franz Bayer. He also returned to Hammer for two further films: *The Reptile* (1966), in which he played the father of the title creature, and *The Vengeance of She* (1968), in which he played Za-Tor.

Commented *Kinematograph Weekly* of his performance in *The Reptile*, "Noel Willman, whose saturnine features always have a sinister aura, plays Dr. Franklyn with reserve, dignity and considerable effect." In describing his role in *The Vengeance of She*, Willman commented, "I played what can only be termed an Egyptian hairdresser in a Catherine Lacey make-up."[43] His TV work includes episodes of *The Count of Monte Cristo* (1956, TV), *The Third Man* (1959–1965, TV) and *Edward the Seventh* (1975, TV). **Hammer credits:** *The Kiss of the Vampire* (1963, as Dr. Ravna), *The Reptile* (1966, as Dr. Franklyn), *The Vengeance of She* (1968, as Za-Tor)

### Willock, Dave

In films from 1939, this busy American supporting actor (1909–1990) can be seen in the likes of *Good Girls Go to Paris* (1939), *Legion of Lost Flyers* (1939), *Hellzapoppin* (1941), *Chicago Deadline* (1949), *It Came from Outer Space* (1953) and *Send Me No Flowers* (1964). He can also be seen as Peter Tillig in Hammer's *Ten Seconds to Hell* (1959). His TV work includes episodes of *Schlitz Playhouse of Stars* (1951–1959, TV), *Your Jeweler's Showcase* (1952–1953, TV), *The Ford Television Theatre* (1952–1957, TV), *Boots and Saddles* (1957–1958, TV), in which he played Lieutenant Binning, and *Margie* (1961–1962, TV), in which he played Har-

Noel Willman's intentions towards Jennifer Daniel seem to be less than honorable in this moment from *The Kiss of the Vampire* (1963). However, the image is deceptive. In the film he is actually putting her robe *on* (Hammer/Universal/Rank/Universal International).

vey Clayton. **Hammer credits:** *Ten Seconds to Hell* (1959, as Peter Tillig)

## Willoughby, Charles

Working with effects supervisor Bill Warrington, Willoughby provided the effects for the Hammer war drama *Yesterday's Enemy* (1959). **Hammer credits:** *Yesterday's Enemy* (1959 [uncredited])

## Wills, J. Elder

Something of a multi-talent, this British writer, producer, director and designer (1900–1970, full name James Ernest Elder Wills, aka Bunty or Buntie Wills) was also one of Hammer's first board members, being with the company from the very beginning in November 1934. Following experience as a scenic artist for the London stage, primarily at the Theater Royal, Drury Lane, Wills turned his attention to films in 1927 with *Poppies of Flanders*, and went on to have a prolific career, designing over fifty productions, among them *The Informer* (1929), *Sing As We Go* (1934), *No Limit* (1935), *Her Last Affair* (1935), Hammer's *The Mystery of the Mary Celeste* (1935) and *Against the Wind* (1947), the latter of which was also based on his wartime experiences, which involved his being appointed Head of Sabotage and Camouflage (these experiences were also the subject of a 1957 biography, *Sabotage*, by Leslie Bell). As a director, he made his debut with the puppet series *Little People Burlesques* (1930), among them *Tom Mixup* (1930), *Our Dumb Friend* (1930) and *Kuster Beaton* (1930). His live-action debut followed with *M'Blimey* (1931), which he also co-wrote.

He went on to helm two films for Hammer: *Song of Freedom* (1936), which starred Paul Robeson, and *Sporting Love* (1936), on which he also worked as an art director under his nickname, Bunty Wills (sharing his credit with Norman Arnold). Recalled Robeson's *Song of Freedom* co-star Elisabeth Welch of Wills, "He was a known director. He was a charming man, and that's all I know."[44] Wills' other films as a director included *Tiger Bay* (1933), which he also designed and co-wrote, *Everything in Life* (1936), which he also designed, and *Big Fella* (1937), which he again designed, this time as Buntie Wills, and which again starred Paul Robeson and Elisabeth Welch (he also produced the film, albeit without credit).

Following the demise of Hammer in 1937 and his wartime experiences, Wills went to work as a designer for other studios, working on such productions as *Against the Wind* (1948), *Valley of Eagles* (1951) and *Blackmailed* (1951). However, following Hammer's revival in 1946, he returned to the fold, designing many low budget productions for the company, among them the studio's breakthrough film, *The Quatermass Xperiment* (1955), which turned out to be one of his last for the company, thus leaving the door open for Bernard Robinson to take over his mantle for the designing of the forthcoming gothic horrors. Wills' remaining credits include *The Young Jacobites* (1960) and *A Circle of Deception* (1960). **Additional notes:** Some sources claim that Wills worked as an uncredited assistant art director on *Song of Freedom*; this seems feasible given his work

as a designer, as well as the fact that he went on to work with the film's credited art director, Norman Arnold, on Hammer's *Sporting Love*. John Elder, the writing pseudonym of producer Anthony Hinds, is a corruption of Wills' name. The American prints of *The Saint's Return* (1953) misspell his name as J. Elderwills. **Hammer credits:** *The Mystery of the Mary Celeste* (1935, art director), *Song of Freedom* (1936, director), *Sporting Love* (1936, director, co-art director), *The Gambler and the Lady* (1953, art director), *Mantrap* (1953, art director), *Four Sided Triangle* (1953, art director), *The Saint's Return* (1953, art director), *Spaceways* (1953, art director), *Blood Orange* (1953, art director), *36 Hours* (1953, art director), *Face the Music* (1954, art director), *Five Days* (1954, art director), *The House Across the Lake* (1954, art director), *The Stranger Came Home* (1954, art director), *Men of Sherwood Forest* (1954, art director), *Mask of Dust* (1954, art director), *Break in the Circle* (1955, art director), *Murder by Proxy* (1955, art director), *Third Party Risk* (1955, art director), *The Quatermass Xperiment* (1955, art director), *The Glass Cage* (1955, art director)

## Wilmer, Douglas

Best known for playing the title character in *Sherlock Holmes* (1964–1965, TV), this busy, RADA-trained British character actor (1920–2016) also appeared in over fifty films, ranging from the low budget to the epic, among them *Passport to Treason* (1956), *Richard III* (1956), *El Cid* (1961), *Jason and the Argonauts* (1963), *The Fall of the Roman Empire* (1964), *The Brides of Fu Manchu* (1966), in which he played Nayland Smith, *The Vengeance of Fu Manchu* (1967), again as Nayland Smith, *The Golden Voyage of Sinbad* (1973), *The Adventure of Sherlock Holmes' Smarter Brother* (1975), again as Sherlock Holmes, *Revenge of the Pink Panther* (1978) and *Octopussy* (1983). He also appeared in a handful of Hammer productions, beginning with *Men of Sherwood Forest* (1954), which marked his big screen debut, though he is best known to genre fans for playing Baron Hartog in *The Vampire Lovers* (1970). Meanwhile, on television, he co-starred in *Do Me a Favor and Kill Me*, an episode of Hammer's *Journey to the Unknown* (1968, TV), which also appeared in the compendium film *Journey to Murder* (1972, TVM). His other TV work includes episodes of *BBC Sunday-Night Theatre* (1950–1959, TV), *The Adventures of Robin Hood* (1955–1960, TV), *The Rivals of Sherlock Holmes* (1971–1973, TV), this time as Professor Van Dusen, *Space: 1999* (1975–1977, TV), *Blind Justice* (1988, TV) and *Sherlock* (2010–, TV), in which he made a belated appearance as a member of the Diogenes Club. His work in the theater meanwhile took in many Shakespearean roles. He wrote about his career in his memoir *Stage Whispers* (1999).

Recalled Wilmer of his appearance as Baron Hartog, "The part I had in *The Vampire Lovers* didn't interest me. The only thing that interested me was how I was supposed to cut some woman's head off and have it go flying through the air via some special effect. I wanted to see it just for that moment. The rest of it I found, frankly, rather a

bore."[45] Indeed, his opinion of the film seems to have been rather low: "I don't remember anything about it except that there was a Polish actress who was very attractive and very masculine."[46] That'd be Ingrid Pitt, then. **Hammer credits:** *Men of Sherwood Forest* (1954, as Sir Nigel Saltire), *The Right Person* (1956, as Hans Rasmussen/Robbie), *Do Me a Favor and Kill Me* (1968, TV [episode of *Journey to the Unknown*], as Harry Vantese), *The Vampire Lovers* (1970, as Baron Hartog), *Journey to Murder* (1972, TVM, as Harry Vantese)

## Wilson, Hal

Along with director Ben R. Hart, cinematographer Brooks-Carrington and actor John Blythe, this British producer (1899–?) formed Knightsbridge, a small-scale production company which, following the making of a documentary short titled *Old Father Thames* (1946)—a Knightbridge/Wilson-Hart co-production which had been released by Exclusive, and which Wilson had co-directed with Hart—went on to co-finance two films with Hammer. The first of these was *Crime Reporter* (1947), which marked Hammer's return to production following a hiatus during the war. The second film was *River Patrol* (1948). Wilson's other credits as a producer include *It's a Wonderful Day* (1949), a solo venture for Knightsbridge, which he also wrote and directed, while his other films as a director include *The Spirit of Variety* (1937), *Round About Robin Hood* (1948), the final Knightbridge production, and *The Royal Pageant of the Thames* (1954). He also worked as a technical supervisor on *Walking on Air* (1946), and as a production manager on *Ha'penny Breeze* (1950), *Penny Points to Paradise* (1951) and *My Death Is a Mockery* (1952). **Hammer credits:** *Crime Reporter* (1947), *River Patrol* (1948)

## Wilson, Ian

This diminutive British character actor (1901–1987) appeared as Lord Stockridge, who is saved from drowning in the early Hammer short *Polly's Two Fathers* (1936). In films from 1914 with *Always Tell Your Wife*, he went on to notch up well over one-hundred screen appearances in such films as *A Master of Craft* (1922), *Shooting Stars* (1927), *The Merry Men of Sherwood* (1932), *Let George Do It* (1940), *The Magic Box* (1951), *I'm All Right Jack* (1959), *Carry On Cruising* (1962), *Ouch!* (1967) and *The Wicker Man* (1973). He also popped up in a number of Hammer's fifties second features, had a minor role in the studio's Jekyll and Hyde spoof *The Ugly Duckling* (1959), and played the murderous dwarf in *The Phantom of the Opera* (1962). His TV appearances include episodes of *Quatermass II* (1955, TV), *Quatermass and the Pit* (1958–1959, TV) and *Saber of London* (1954–1960, TV). He should not be confused with the cinematographer Ian Wilson, who photographed Hammer's *Captain Kronos—Vampire Hunter* (1974). **Hammer credits:** *Polly's Two Fathers* (1936, as Lord Stockridge), *The Lady Craved Excitement* (1950, as Mugsy), *Whispering Smith Hits London* (1951, as Small tough), *The Last Page* (1951, as Mushroom book customer), *The Flanagan Boy* (1953, as Man in audience [uncredited]),

*The Saint's Return* (1953, unnamed role [uncredited]), *The Glass Cage* (1955, as Eating punter [uncredited]), *The Ugly Duckling* (1959, as Small man), *The Phantom of the Opera* (1962, as Dwarf), *The Runaway* (1964, as Caretaker)

### Wilson, Ian

Working closely with director Brian Clemens, this British cinematographer (1939–) provided Hammer's *Captain Kronos—Vampire Hunter* (1974) with its distinctive look, prompting critic Alan R. Howard writing in the *Hollywood Reporter* to praise the film's "exquisite visuals by photographer Ian Wilson." Wilson had previously worked with Clemens and his producing partner Albert Fennell on the thriller *And Soon the Darkness* (1970), which led directly to his Hammer assignment. An early graduate of the London Film School, Wilson began his film career in 1963 with the documentary short *Gala Day*. His many other credits include such diverse titles as *The Private Right* (1970), *Mafia No!* (1967), *The Committee* (1968), *Tell Me Lies* (1968), *Bartleby* (1970), *Up Pompeii* (1971), *Up the Chastity Belt* (1971), *The House in Nightmare Park* (1973), *Gawain and the Green Knight* (1973), *The Butterfly Ball* (1976), *Privates on Parade* (1982), *Wish You Were Here* (1987), *Checking Out* (1988), *Edward II* (1991), *The Crying Game* (1992), *Backbeat* (1994), *A Christmas Carol* (1999, TVM), which earned him an Emmy nomination, *Below* (2002), *Niagara Motel* (2005) and *Primo* (2007). He also photographed and co-directed (with Ned Sherrin) a short titled *The Cobblers of Umbridge* (1972), which spoofed the long-running radio series *The Archers* (1950–). His TV work includes episodes of *The New Avengers* (1976–1977, TV), again for Clemens and Fennell, *Quatermass* (1979, TV), *Danger UXB* (1979, TV) and *The Flame Trees of Thika* (1981, TV), the latter of which earned him a BAFTA nomination. He should not be confused with the actor Ian Wilson, who also worked for Hammer. **Hammer credits:** *Captain Kronos—Vampire Hunter* (1974)

### Wilson, Mary

This glamorous British actress played a model in the Hammer comedy *Further Up the Creek* (1958). She can also be spotted in *The Ugly Duckling* (1959) as Lizzie. **Hammer credits:** *Further Up the Creek* (1958, as Vicky [model]), *The Ugly Duckling* (1959, as Lizzie)

### Wilson, Neil

This British supporting actor (1916–1975) can be seen as Russell in Hammer's *X—The Unknown* (1956). He later returned to Hammer to play a guard in *The Damned* (1963), the schoolmaster in *The Horror of Frankenstein* (1970) and a policeman in *Dr. Jekyll and Sister Hyde* (1971). His many other credits include *The Lavender Hill Mob* (1951), *Offbeat* (1961), *She Knows Y'Know* (1962), *The Partner* (1963) and *Staircase* (1969), while his TV work takes in episodes of *The Quatermass Experiment* (1953, TV), *Dixon of Dock Green* (1955–1976, TV), in which he played PC Tubb Barrell, *On Trial* (1960, TV), *Dr. Finlay's Casebook* (1962–1971, TV), in which he played Sergeant Gilbey, *Alcock and Gander* (1972, TV) and *Warship* (1973–1977,

TV). **Hammer credits:** *X—The Unknown* (1956, as Russell [uncredited]), *The Damned* (1963, as Guard [uncredited]), *The Horror of Frankenstein* (1970, as Schoolmaster), *Dr. Jekyll and Sister Hyde* (1971, as Older policeman)

### Wilson, Paul

This British cameraman (1925–2014) operated the camera on Hammer's *Fanatic* (1965), which was photographed by Arthur Ibbetson, for whom he frequently operated. In films from 1942 as a second assistant cameraman at Shepherd's Bush Studio, his early career was interrupted by war service in the Navy as a photographer of enemy territory, though he did manage to slip in a few assignments as camera assistant during this period, including *The Man in Grey* (1943), *Time Flies* (1944) and *Love Story* (1944). Following the war he graduated to first assistant cameraman on such films as *Miranda* (1947), *The Sound Barrier* (1952) and *Father Brown* (1954). His work as a camera operator includes *Solomon and Sheba* (1959), *I Could Go On Singing* (1963), *A Hard Day's Night* (1964), *Help!* (1965), *Where Eagles Dare* (1969), *The Looking Glass War* (1970), *The Railway Children* (1970), *Willy Wonka and the Chocolate Factory* (1971), *Frenzy* (1972) and *The Three Musketeers* (1973). He also photographed the comedy *The Ritz* (1976), and worked as the second unit cameraman on *Juggernaut* (1974), *Royal Flash* (1975) and *Robin and Marian* (1976), all of which were helmed by Richard Lester, the director he has most frequently worked with (having also operated on several of his films). He later became a respected effects photographer on such big budget films as *Superman* (1978), *Moonraker* (1979), which earned him a shared Oscar nomination, *Batman* (1989), *Cape Fear* (1991), *GoldenEye* (1995), *Tomorrow Never Dies* (1997), *The World Is Not Enough* (1999), *Harry Potter and the Philosopher's Stone* (2001) and *Die Another Day* (2002), often working for effects director Derek Meddings. **Hammer credits:** *Fanatic* (1965)

### Wilson, Rebecca

This actress and dancer played one of the harem girls in the Hammer comedy *I Only Arsed!* (1958). Her TV credits include episodes of *BBC Sunday-Night Theatre* (1950–1959, TV) and *BBC Sunday-Night Play* (1960–1963, TV). **Hammer credits:** *I Only Arsed!* (1958, as Harem girl [uncredited])

### Wilson, Roger

Wilson worked as the first assistant editor on Hammer's *Vampire Circus* (1972). His other credits as an assistant include *The Love Box* (1972) and *The Amazing Mr. Blunden* (1972). He went on to become an editor/supervising editor, and worked on such films as *The Camerons* (1974) and *God's Outlaw* (1986) and such television series as *Minder* (1979–1994, TV), *Widows* (1983, TV), *Widows 2* (1985, TV), *She's Out* (1995, TV) and *Ultimate Force* (2002–2006, TV). His father was editor Frederick Wilson (1912–1944). **Hammer credits:** *Vampire Circus* (1972 [uncredited])

### Wilson, Ronald

This Canadian supporting actor and bit-part

player (1930–2014, sometimes Ronnie Wilson) had a minor role in Hammer's second Quatermass film. His other credits as an actor include *The Dam Busters* (1955), *I Was Monty's Double* (1958), *The Hand* (1960) and *Element of Doubt* (1961). He went on to become a prolific director in television, helming episodes of such series a *Thirty-Minute Theatre* (1961–1965, TV), *The Brothers* (1972–1976, TV), *To Serve Them All My Days* (1980–1981, TV), *The Bretts* (1987–1989, TV) and *EastEnders* (1985–, TV). **Hammer credits:** *Quatermass 2* (1957, as Man in car)

### Wilson, Ron

Wilson is acknowledged in the credits of *Flesh and Blood—The Hammer Heritage of Horror* (1994, TV). **Hammer credits:** *Flesh and Blood—The Hammer Heritage of Horror* (1994, TV)

### Wilson, Sue

Wilson played the role of Noo in Hammer's *Creatures the World Forgot* (1971). **Hammer credits:** *Creatures the World Forgot* (1971, as Noo)

### Wimbush, Mary

Primarily on stage, radio (from 1945) and television, and only occasionally in films, this British character actress (1924–2005) can be seen as Elvira in Hammer's *Vampire Circus* (1972). Her other credits include *Oh! What a Lovely War* (1969), which earned her a best supporting actress BAFTA nomination, *Butley* (1971) and *Fragment of Fear* (1971), while her television work includes *Jeeves and Wooster* (1990–1993, TV) in which she played Aunt Agatha between 1990 and 1992 (the role was subsequently played by Elizabeth Spriggs). Her other TV work includes episodes of *Jude the Obscure* (1971, TV), *Poldark* (1975–1977, TV) and *Heartbeat* (1992–2009, TV). She was married to the actor Howard Marion-Crawford (1914–1969) between 1946 and 1954; he appeared in Hammer's *Five Days* (1954). **Hammer credits:** *Vampire Circus* (1972, as Elvira)

### Winart

This British distribution company re-issued Hammer's silent comedy compilation *Made for Laughs* (1952) in 1958, for which it trimmed seventeen minutes from the original thirty-four minute running time. **Hammer credits:** *Made for Laughs* (1952)

### Winbolt, John

British born Winbolt (1922–1992) worked as the camera operator on Hammer's *Moon Zero Two* (1969) and *Crescendo* (1970), both of which were photographed by Paul Beeson. He began his career as a clapper loader on *Dead of Night* (1945), was the second unit camera operator on *They Made Me a Fugitive* (1947) and the focus puller on *Noose* (1948). His other work as an operator includes *The Golden Disc* (1958), *The Nudist Story* (1960), *From Russia with Love* (1963), *Goldfinger* (1963), *Thunderball* (1965) and *Mosquito Squadron* (1969), plus episodes of *The Champions* (1968–1969, TV), *Here Come the Double Deckers!* (1970–1971, TV) and *The Protectors* (1972–1973, TV). **Hammer credits:** *Moon Zero Two* (1969), *Crescendo* (1970)

## Winchester Pictures

In the mid-nineties, Winchester Pictures announced plans to make a handful of new features with Hammer. Sadly, nothing came of the proposals.

## Wincott, Geoffrey

This British actor (1901–1973, full name William Geoffrey Wincott) played the role of villain-in-chief Dr. Sigmund Casper in Hammer's *Dick Barton—Special Agent* (1948). Known for his work as an announcer for the BBC, Wincott's other credits are mostly for the small screen, among them guest spots in such shows as *Dixon of Dock Green* (1955–1976, TV), *Jennings at School* (1958, TV), *William* (1962–1963, TV), *The Troubleshooters* (1965–1972, TV), *Elizabeth R* (1971, TV) and *Microbes and Men* (1974, TV). His occasional film credits include *Bronco Bullfrog* (1970) and *Deviation* (1971). **Hammer credits:** *Dick Barton—Special Agent* (1948, as Dr. Sigmund Casper [uncredited])

## Windsor Studios

According to the BFI's database, scenes for the Hammer featurette *River Patrol* (1948) were seemingly shot at this facility, about which little information is extant, save that it was briefly busy in the late forties with a number of shorts, featurettes and documentaries, several of them helmed by Paul Rotha. Other films made or partially made there include *A House on a Hill* (1947), *The Centre* (1947), *The World Is Rich* (1947), *The Balance* (1947), *History of Printing* (1947), *History of Writing* (1947), *First Rhapsody* (1947), *Starlight Stone* (1947), *A Sister to Assist 'Er* (1947) and *A Man's Affair* (1949). **Hammer credits:** *River Patrol* (1948)

## *Wings of Danger*

GB, 1952, 73m, bw, RCA, cert U

Based on the 1951 novel *Dead on Course* by Packham Webb and Elleston Trevor (the latter writing as Mansell Black), this second feature thriller about a pilot who saves his missing buddy—who has faked his own death—from the wiles of some ruthless gold smugglers was the second film made under the auspices of Hammer's production deal with the American producer Robert L. Lippert (it was also director Terence Fisher's second film for Hammer following the Lippert-financed *The Last Page* [1952]). For it, the American star Zachary Scott was imported to play the lead character of Richard Van Ness, and was supported by a better cast than usual, among them Robert Beatty, Diane Cilento (whom the film "introduced") and Kay Kendall.

Made in September 1951 at the Riverside Studios in Hammersmith, London, during a break in Hammer's lease on Down Place, the film, which was released in the UK by Exclusive on 16 May 1952, is very much of its period. Unfortunately, despite some reasonable action highlights, including a chase between a car and a motorbike, and a fight in a ruined tower where the smugglers are hiding out, it is sluggishly directed and ultimately fails to take off thanks to an overabundance of inert dialogue scenes care of screenwriter John Gilling.

Robert Beatty as the missing friend Nick Talbot gets the best line; when discovered by Scott's character, his is response is, "Why can't you let a man die in peace?" Meanwhile, the neatest touch has the smugglers disguising the gold in the shape of some innocuous-looking tools, which recalls a similar idea in *The Lavender Hill Mob* (1951), in which stolen gold is smuggled out of France in the guise of miniature Eiffel Towers. The film also remains of passing note for marking the first of three films to be scored by the celebrated composer Malcolm Arnold, who would go on to work with David Lean, winning an Oscar for *The Bridge on the River Kwai* (1957). **Additional notes:** At Robert Lippert's instigation, producer Jack Leewood was sent over from Hollywood to iron out any overtly British idioms that might cause problems for the film's 1 April American release, which was care of Twentieth Century–Fox, who changed the title back to that of the novel, *Dead on Course*.

Production companies: Hammer/Lippert. Distributors: Exclusive (UK), Twentieth Century–Fox (U.S.). Producer: Anthony Hinds. Director: Terence Fisher. Screenplay: John Gilling, based on the novel *Dead on Course* by Elleston Trevor and Packham Webb. Cinematographer: Walter "Jimmy" Harvey. Music: Malcolm Arnold. Music played by: The London Philharmonic Orchestra. Editor: James Needs. Art director: Andrew Mazzei. Costumes: Ellen Trussler. Sound: Bill Salter. Assistant director: Jimmy Sangster. Casting: Michael Carreras. Camera operator: Peter Bryan. Focus puller: Harry Oakes [uncredited]. Production manager: Arthur Barnes. Continuity: Renee Glynne. Make-up: Phil Leakey. Hair: Bill Griffiths. Chief electrician: Jack Curtis [uncredited]. Stills: Tom Edwards [uncredited], John Jay [uncredited]. Publicist: Bill Luckwell [uncredited]. **Cast:** Zachary Scott (Richard Van Ness), Robert Beatty (Nick Talbot), Kay Kendall (Alexia de la Roche), Diane Cilento (Jeanette), Colin Tapley (Inspector Maxwell), Naomi Chance (Avril Talbot), Arthur Lane (Boyd Spencer), Jack Allen (Truscott), Ian Fleming (Talbot), Harold Lang (Snell), Laurie Taylor (O'Gorman), Nigel Neilson (Duty Officer), Darcy Conyers (Signal operator), Douglas Muir (Doctor), Sheila Raynor (Nurse), Courtney Hope (Mrs. C. Smith), Kathleen Stuart (Receptionist), Anthony Miles (Sam), June Ashley (Blonde), June Mitchell (Blonde), Natasha Sokolova (Blonde), James Steele (First Flying Officer [uncredited]), Russ Allen (Second Flying Officer [uncredited]). **DVD availability:** VCI Entertainment (U.S., all regions), double billed with *36 Hours* (1953)

## Winitsky, Alex

Winitsky worked as one of the executive producers on Hammer's *The Lady Vanishes* (1979). His other credits in this capacity include *End of the Game* (1975), *The Seven-Per-Cent Solution* (1976), *Swing Shift* (1984) and *You Ruined My Life* (1987, TVM), while his work as a producer takes in *Cross of Iron*

(1977), *House Calls* (1978), *Silver Bears* (1978), *Cuba* (1979), *Stanley and Iris* (1990) and *Circle of Friends* (1995), plus the TV series *Cadets* (1988, TV). His production company, Alex Winitsky/Arlene Sellers Productions, which he ran with his producing partner Arlene Sellers, was also behind the TV version of *House Calls* (1979–1982, TV). **Hammer credits:** *The Lady Vanishes* (1979)

## Winslip, Geoff

Winslip worked as a knife thrower (doubling for Marne Maitland) in *The Indian Spirit Guide*, an episode of Hammer's *Journey to the Unknown* (1968, TV), which also appears in the compendium film *Journey to Midnight* (1968, TVM). He also worked as a marksman on a 1968 episode of *Dad's Army* (1968–1977, TV), for which he was credited as Geoff Winship. **Hammer credits:** *The Indian Spirit Guide* (1968, TV [episode of *Journey to the Unknown*], as Knife thrower), *Journey to Midnight* (1968, TVM, as Knife thrower)

## Winstone, Eric

Popular from the late thirties onwards, and especially in the fifties, this British bandleader, piano-accordionist, composer and lyricist (1915–1974) appeared in two musical shorts for Hammer: *The Eric Winstone Bandshow* (1955), for which he also co-wrote (with Brian Fahey) the number *Fanfare Boogie*, which won an Ivor Novello award, and *Eric Winstone's Stagecoach* (1956). He also scored three featurettes for the company: the drama *The Right Person* (1956), the travelogue *Copenhagen* (1956), which he co-scored with John Hotchkiss, and the period adventure romp *Dick Turpin—Highwayman* (1956), for which he also penned a jaunty title song performed by Dennis Hale. His other credits include *Don Chicago* (1945), in which he appeared as a bandleader, and *Tin Pan Alley* (1951), a documentary about songwriters in which he appeared as himself. His radio work included contributions to the popular series *Music While You Work* (1940–1967). Other numbers penned by Winstone include *Happy Hippo*, *Our Mr. Meredith*, *Clarion Call*,

**Musical notes. A portrait of Eric Winstone (Hammer).**

*Stage Coach, Choo Choo Special* and *Trafficscape,* while his albums include *Eric Winstone Plays 007* (1973). **Hammer credits:** *The Eric Winstone Bandshow* (1956, as himself, co-music), *The Right Person* (1956, music), *Copenhagen* (1956, co-music), *Eric Winstone's Stagecoach* (1956, as himself), *Dick Turpin—Highwayman* (1956, music)

### Winter, Heinz

This Austrian actor (1925–1991) can be seen in a supporting role in Hammer's *The Lady Vanishes* (1979). His other credits include *The Fifth Musketeer* (1979), *Fausses notes* (1982, TVM) and *The Living Daylights* (1987). **Hammer credits:** *The Lady Vanishes* (1979, as Hotel manager)

### Winter, Pauline

This British actress (1917–2015) played the role of Laverne in Hammer's *Women Without Men* (1956). Her other credits include *Girl in the News* (1940), *Death Goes to School* (1953) and *The Ipcress File* (1965), plus episodes of *O.S.S.* (1957–1958, TV) and *Mackenzie* (1980, TV). Her husband was the actor Philip Dale (1916–1973), whom she married in 1939. **Hammer credits:** *Women Without Men* (1956, as Laverne [uncredited])

### Winter, Vincent

Best remembered for playing little Davy in *The Kidnappers* (1953)—a film which earned him and co-star Jon Whiteley an honorary Oscar each—this Scottish child actor (1947–1998) can also be seen in *The Dark Avenger* (1955), *Time Lock* (1956), *Gorgo* (1960), *Greyfriars Bobby* (1963) and *The Three Lives of Thomasina* (1963). He also played Ian in the Hammer short *Day of Grace* (1957), fighting to save his pet dog from being drowned by his stern uncle. Winter turned his back on acting in 1964, yet returned to work in the film industry in the early seventies in a variety of capacities, including second assistant director on Hammer's *Fear in the Night* (1972), assistant director on *Royal Flash* (1975), *Superman* (1978) and *The Spaceman and King Arthur* (1979), and production/unit manager/supervisor on *Superman II* (1980), *For Your Eyes Only* (1981), *Superman III* (1983), *Indiana Jones and the Temple of Doom* (1983), *The Color Purple* (1985) and *The Wind in the Willows* (1996). He also worked as the model unit manager on *CutThroat Island* (1996), as a producer on *The Rainbow Thief* (1990) and as an associate producer on *Under Suspicion* (1991). **Hammer credits:** *Day of Grace* (1957, as Ian), *Fear in the Night* (1972, second assistant director [uncredited])

### Winterstein, Frank

Winterstein worked as an assistant director on Hammer's troubled bomb disposal melodrama *Ten Seconds to Hell* (1959). His other credits as an assistant director include *Derby* (1949), *Lissy* (1957), *The Tomb of Love* (1959), *Sherlock Holmes and the Deadly Necklace* (1962), on which he also directed a few additional scenes, *Genghis Khan* (1965) and *The Peking Medallion* (1967), on which he again directed additional scenes. His work as production manager includes *Dollars* (1971), *Who?* (1974) and *The Squeeze* (1977). **Hammer credits:** *Ten Seconds to Hell* (1959)

### Wise, Pauline *see* Harlow, Pauline

### Wise, Vic

This British actor (1900–1976) had a minor supporting role in Hammer's *Whispering Smith Hits London* (1952). His other credits include *It Happened One Sunday* (1944), *There Is Another Sun* (1951), *Charley Moon* (1956), *The 39 Steps* (1959), *The Cuckoo Patrol* (1967) and *School for Sex* (1968), plus episodes of *Douglas Fairbanks, Jr. Presents* (1953–1957, TV), *Out of This World* (1962, TV) and *Tottering Towers* (1971–1972, TV), in which he played Benny the Nose. **Hammer credits:** *Whispering Smith Hits London* (1952, as Maxie)

### *The Witches*

GB, 1966, 91m, Technicolor [UK], DeLuxe [U.S.], widescreen [1.78:1], RCA, cert X

Perhaps because it reflected the tastes of its star, *The Witches* is one of Hammer's more genteel horrors. However, while it doesn't grab one's throat like some of the company's more visceral efforts, it passes the time adequately enough, especially if one doesn't expect too great a pay off from its rather sedate build up.

The project was instigated by the Hollywood actress Joan Fontaine, best known for her work with Hitchcock, which took in the leading roles in both *Rebecca* (1940) and *Suspicion* (1941), the latter of which had won her a best actress Oscar. Yet, as with many of her contemporary female stars of the forties, Fontaine found her film career stalling by the late fifties. So, like Bette Davis, Joan Crawford, Tallulah Bankhead and Fontaine's sister Olivia de Havilland, Fontaine decided to turn to horror in a bid to revitalize her standing. Consequently, in 1962 she bought the rights to the 1960 shocker *The Devil's Own* (aka *The Little Wax Doll*) by Norah Lofts (writing as Peter Curtis), which she offered to Seven Arts, which in turn suggested the film to Hammer two years later (likewise, Hammer tried to interest Universal in the project in 1965, during which period John Temple-Smith was briefly attached to the project as a producer).

Given Fontaine's (albeit dwindling) status, this would be a reasonably prestigious project, and to this end Nigel Kneale was brought in to adapt Lofts' book for the screen. Recalled the writer, "I read the book and thought it was all right, up to a point. The interesting part for me was the very ordinary-seeming country setting, with all its double meanings and sinister things popping through occasionally."[47] Meanwhile, the directorial reigns were handed to the reliable if unadventurous Cyril Frankel, whose previous film for Hammer had been the controversial *Never Take Sweets from a Stranger* (1960). Thanks to his careful handling of this film, the director recalled that there was a tacit understanding that, "When Hammer had a more sensitive and serious film than their usual horror, blood and thunder I would be considered."[48] Yet despite this so-called understanding, Frankell didn't work for the company again until twelve years later when he helmed the far from serious and sensitive

Looking daggers. Kay Walsh wields a sacrificial blade during the climax of *The Witches* (1966). Michele Dotrice (hands across stomach) looks on (Hammer/Seven Arts/Associated British Picture Corporation/Warner Pathé Distributors/Twentieth Century–Fox/Studio Canal).

*Tennis Court* (1984, TVM [episode of *Hammer House of Mystery and Suspense*). The remainder of the production company numbered many Hammer staples, key among them cinematographer Arthur Grant, while the cast contained such reliable names as Kay Walsh, Alec McCowen, Gwen Ffrangcon-Davies, Leonard Rossiter and Michelle Dotrice.

More concerned with intrigue than horror, the story sees teacher Gwen Mayfield arrive in the rose-strewn English village of Heddaby, where she is to assume the post of head mistress at the local school. Recently returned from darkest Africa, where she fell foul of a local witch doctor, it transpires that Mayfield is recovering from a nervous breakdown. However, her troubles are far from over, for it appears that the village is under some kind of dark influence. Someone is also trying to drive her insane with voodoo paraphernalia. The threat is all too real though, for its transpires that the majority of the villagers belong to a coven of witches, the intent of their leader seemingly being to sacrifice one of the schoolmarm's pupils.

Given the subject matter, one can imagine what a genre director of such standing as Terence Fisher or John Gilling would have made of *The Witches*. Unfortunately, Cyril Frankel fails to make the most of the story's various situations, and while the production is professionally mounted with solid performances from Fontaine and, especially, Kay Walsh as Stephanie Bax, a local journalist who turns out to be the leader of the coven, the movie simply fails to ignite ("Doesn't spark off enough horror and tension to make the picture more than routine entertainment," condemned *Variety*). Indeed, the dialogue and situations are exceptionally tame, with Stephanie's explanation of witchcraft being the film's only interesting line ("It's a sex thing, of course. Mostly women go in for it—*older women*"). Astonishingly, the film was awarded an X certificate.

Filmed at Bray and on location in the nearby village of Hambledon between 18 April and 10 June 1966, the production was a particularly smooth one. Sadly, the good working practices of both cast and crew failed to translate to the screen, and, following a trade show at Studio One on 14 November 1966, the film was greeted with indifference when it was released on the ABC circuit in the UK by Warner Pathé on a double bill with *Death Is a Woman* (1966) on 9 December. The film's American release, care of Twentieth Century–Fox, followed on 15 March 1967, for which it was re-titled *The Devil's Own* ("Watch for the witches—they're watching for you!" exclaimed the American trailer).

Of the film's beginning, *Kinematograph Weekly* commented, "The film opens with an exciting African sequence prior to the credits, but is then content to amble along in the quite pleasing atmosphere of village life." Observed the *Motion Picture Exhibitor*, "This import should do okay as part of the program with a fairly interesting plot, all be it on the far-fetched side, adequate performances, and serviceable direction and production. The use of color heightens the more scary scenes, which are not for the very young." As for its ending, Nigel

**Kay Walsh (in headgear) presides over the orgiastic finale of *The Witches* (1966) as Ingrid Brett writhes on the altar. Michele Dotrice looks rather pleased with herself in the background (Hammer/Seven Arts/Associated British Picture Corporation/Warner Pathé Distributors/Twentieth Century–Fox/Studio Canal).**

Kneale noted, "There's nothing as funny as people imagining they're witches. It's naturally comic. I think a cleverer director would have faced that possibility of it all turning to laughs and he would have managed to make it really horrible, creepy and threatening."[49]

Despite his serious and sensitive approach and his apparent dismissal of Hammer's blood and thunder output, Cyril Frankell could well have taken a leaf from Terence Fisher's approach to such scenes, which would reach their apex in *The Devil Rides Out* (1968). Also, at ninety-one minutes, the film is far too long to sustain interest, and could have done with some judicious editing, for while some of the early village scenes intrigue, there is far too much dithering about over not very much. Consequently, the climax is a very long time coming, and when it arrives, it disappoints on almost every level. **Additional notes:** The opening music from the film was later used as a DVD stinger for films in *The Ultimate Hammer Collection*. The novel, again credited to Peter Curtis, was re-printed by Pan as a tie-in. In 2011, it was re-printed yet again by Hammer (care of Random House). The village of Hambledon later played host to the Lew In Fulci horror film *The Black Cat* (1981), which was originally to have starred Peter Cushing, but eventually went before the cameras with Patrick Magee in the role of Professor Robert Miles, though not before Donald Pleasence had also been offered the part; other productions filmed in the village include *A Bunch of Amateurs* (2008) and a 1995 three-part

entry for *The Ruth Rendell Mysteries* (1987–2000, TV) titled *Vanity Dies Hard*.

Production companies: Hammer/Seven Arts/ Associated British Picture Corporation. Distributors: Warner Pathé Distributors (UK [ABC circuit]), Twentieth Century–Fox (U.S.). Producer: Anthony Nelson Keys. Director: Cyril Frankel. Screenplay: Nigel Kneale, based upon the novel *The Devil's Own* by Peter Curtis (Norah Lofts). Cinematographer: Arthur Grant. Music: Richard Rodney Bennett. Music director: Philip Martell. Supervising editor: James Needs. Editor: Chris Barnes. Assistant editor: Tony Lenny [uncredited]. Second assistant editor: Colin Needs [uncredited]. Production design: Bernard Robinson. Art director: Don Mingaye. Draughtsman: Ken Ryan [uncredited]. Costumes: Molly Arbuthnot, Harry Haynes. Make-up: George Partleton. Hair: Frieda Steiger. Sound: Ken Rawkins. Sound editor: Roy Hyde. Boom operator: Charles Wheeler [uncredited]. Production manager: Charles Permane. Assistant director: David Tringham. Second assistant director: Terence Churcher [uncredited]. Third assistant director: Christopher Neame [uncredited]. Camera operators: Cece Cooney, David Harcourt [uncredited]. Focus pullers: Bob Jordan [uncredited], Phil Finch [uncredited]. Clapper loader: Eddie Collins [uncredited]. Choreography: Denys Palmer. Continuity: Anne Deeley. Production secretary: Maureen White [uncredited]. Casting: Irene Lamb. Scenic artist: Feliks Sergejak [uncredited]. Stunts: Peter Diamond [uncredited], Peter

Munt [uncredited], Sadie Eden [uncredited]. Stills: Tom Edwards [uncredited]. Publicity: Alan Thomson [uncredited], Bob Webb [uncredited]. Poster: Tom Chantrell [uncredited]. **Cast:** Joan Fontaine (Gwen Mayfield), Kay Walsh (Stephanie Bax), Alec McCowen (Alan Bax), Gwen Ffrangcon Davies (Granny Rigg), Duncan Lamont (Bob Curd), Leonard Rossiter (Dr. Wallis), Michele Dotrice (Valerie), John Collin (Dowsett), Martin Stephens (Ronnie Dowsett), Ingrid Brett (Linda Rigg), Ann Bell (Sally), Shelagh Fraser (Mrs. Creek), Viola Keats (Mrs. Curd), Bryan Marshall (Tom), Carmel McSharry (Mrs. Dowsett), Kitty Attwood (Mrs. McDowall [uncredited]), Prudence Hyman (Maid [uncredited]), John Barrett (Mr. Glass [uncredited]), Catherine Finn (Nurse [uncredited]), Charles Rea (Sergeant [uncredited]), Rudolph Walker (Mark [uncredited]), Lizbeth Kent (Villager [uncredited]), Artro Morris (Porter [uncredited]), Willie Payne (Adam [uncredited]), Yemi Ajibade (Mark [uncredited]), Ken Robson (Dancer [uncredited]), Roy Desmond (Dancer [uncredited]), Terry Williams (Dancer [uncredited]), Brian Todd (Dancer [uncredited]), Don Vernon (Dancer [uncredited]), Fred Peck (Coven member [uncredited]). **DVD availability:** Anchor Bay (U.S. R1 NTSC), extras include the U.S. trailer, two TV spots and an episode of *The World of Hammer* (1990 [first broadcast 1994], TV) titled *Wicked Women*; Anchor Bay/Stars (U.S. R1 NTSC), double-billed with *Slave Girls* (1966 [as *Prehistoric Women*]); Optimum Home Releasing (UK R2 PAL). **Blu-ray availability:** Studio Canal (B/2), extras include a documentary *Hammer Glamour*. **CD availability:** *The Hammer Film Music Collection: Volume Two* (GDI Records), which contains the *Main Title*

### Witching Time see *Hammer House of Horror*

### Withers, Ken (Kenneth J.)

This Belgian born cameraman (1928–) operated the camera for Hammer's *Countess Dracula* (1971) and all thirteen episodes of *Hammer House of Mystery and Suspense* (1984, TVM), which must have required real stamina. He began his career as a clapper loader on *You're Only Young Twice* (1952), became a camera assistant on *The Beachcomber* (1954) and a focus puller on *The Black Knight* (1954), *Lawrence of Arabia* (1962) and *Doctor Zhivago* (1965). He began operating on *Lord Jim* (1965) and went on to work on such films as *Sinful Davey* (1969), *Julius Caesar* (1970), *Age of Innocence* (1977), *Escape to Victory* (1981), *Spies Like Us* (1985), *Trial by Jury* (1994) and *The Real Blonde* (1997). He also photographed *Erotic Fantasies* (1971) and episodes of *Remington Steele* (1982–1987, TV), and worked as an additional photographer on *White Nights* (1985). **Hammer credits:** *Countess Dracula* (1971), *Hammer House of Mystery and Suspense* (1984, TVM)

### Witkin, Jacob

Witkin can be seen as the woodcutter/werewolf in *Children of the Full Moon* (1980, TV [episode of *Hammer House of Horror*]), in which he makes a memorable shock appearance at a bedroom win-

dow. In films and television in both Britain and America, his big screen credits include *Love and Death* (1975), *Arabian Adventure* (1979), *Matinee* (1993), *Showgirls* (1995), *Arizona Seaside* (2007), *West of the Moon* (2010), *Phantom* (2013) and *Broken Vows* (2015), while his small screen appearances include guest spots in everything from *The Professionals* (1977–1983, TV) to *Terminator: The Sarah Connor Chronicles* (2008–2009, TV). He has also provided vocals for several video games, among them *Conqueror: A.D. 1086* (1995), *Summoner 2* (2002) and *The Mummy: Tomb of the Dragon Emperor* (2008). **Hammer credits:** *Children of the Full Moon* (1980, TV [episode of *Hammer House of Horror*], as Woodcutter)

### Witty, Christopher

This British child actor (1950–) can be seen as William in Hammer's *The Damned* (1963). His other credits include *The Passionate Stranger* (1957), *Rockets in the Dunes* (1960), *Masquerade* (1965), *Baby Love* (1968) and *The Railway Children* (1970), in which he played Jim, a role he'd already played in the 1968 television series. His other TV work includes episodes of *Man from Interpol* (1960–1961, TV), *Ghost Squad* (1961–1963, TV) and *William* (1962–1963, TV), in which he played Ginger. **Hammer credits:** *The Damned* (1963, as William)

### Wladon, Jean

Working in Britain in the sixties, the credits of this French actor (aka Jean Vladon) include Hammer's *One Million Years B.C.* (1966), in which he played Ahot. His other credits include *Battle of Britain* (1969) and an episode of *UFO* (1970–1971, TV). **Hammer credits:** *One Million Years B.C.* (1966, as Ahot)

### Wojtczak, Tessa

This British born actress (1958–) made a brief appearance as an assassin at the top of *Czech Mate* (1984, TVM [episode of *Hammer House of Mystery and Suspense*]). Her other TV work includes *The Insurance Man* (1986, TVM), *The Widowmaker* (1990, TVM) and *A Casualty of War* (1990, TVM), while her occasional film credits include *Sammy and Rosie Get Laid* (1987) and *Gut Instinct* (2005). She also works as a voice over artist. **Hammer credits:** *Czech Mate* (1984, TVM [episode of *Hammer House of Mystery and Suspense*], as Girl on bridge)

### Wolfe, David see Bauer, David

### Wolfe, De see De Wolfe

### Wolfe, Ronald

Along with his partner Ronald Chesney, this British writer (1922–2011, real name Harvey Ronald Wolfe-Luberoff) created and penned a number of successful sitcoms, among them *The Rag Trade* (1961–1963 and 1977–1978, TV), *Meet the Wife* (1964–1966, TV), *Romany Jones* (1973–1975, TV) and *Yus, My Dear* (1976, TV). However, they are best known for creating and writing the hugely popular *On the Buses* (1969–1973, TV), which in turn produced a spin-off series, *Don't Drink the Water* (1974–1975, TV), and an Ameri-

can copy, *Lotsa Luck* (1973, TV). Hammer also made three feature films based upon the series, all of which Chesney and Wolfe wrote and produced. A fourth film, *Still at It on the Buses*, was discussed but failed to materialize, as did a big screen transfer of *The Rag Trade*, to have been titled *The Rag Trade Goes Mod*. **Hammer credits:** *On the Buses* (1971), *Mutiny on the Buses* (1972), *Holiday on the Buses* (1973)

### Wolfe, Tony

Wolfe worked as the sound recordist on *One on an Island* (1968, TV [episode of *Journey to the Unknown*]). His other credits include *The Trap* (1966), on which he was the recordist, and *The Double Man* (1967), on which he was the sound mixer. **Hammer credits:** *One on an Island* (1968, TV [episode of *Journey to the Unknown*])

### Wolfit, Sir Donald

Said to have been the inspiration for "Sir" in the 1980 Ronald Hardwood play *The Dresser*, which was filmed in 1983 and 2015 (TVM), this old school actor-manager (1902–1968, real name Donald Woolfitt) was knighted in 1957 for his services to the theater, among them having toured Shakespeare in the provinces. In films from 1931 with *Down River*, he went on to appear in *Drake of England* (1935), *Svengali* (1954), which earned him a best actor BAFTA nomination, *Room at the Top* (1958), which earned him a second best actor BAFTA nomination, *The Mark* (1961), *Lawrence of Arabia* (1962), *Life at the Top* (1965) and *The Charge of the Light Brigade* (1968). He also appeared in the Hammer short *A Man on the Beach* (1956), in which he played Carter. This film was scripted by Jimmy Sangster, who also scripted the Hammeresque *Blood of the Vampire* (1958) in which Wolfit played Dr. Callistratus, giving a richly hammy performance worthy of comparison to Tod Slaughter. His occasional TV appearances include episodes of *Saber of London* (1954–1960, TV), *Tales from Dickens* (1958–1959, TV), *Ghost Squad* (1961–1963, TV) and *Play of the Month* (1965–1983, TV). Married three times, his wives included actresses Chris Castor (1896–1986), to whom he was married between 1928 and 1934, and Rosalind Iden (1911–1990), to whom he was married from 1948. His daughter (with Castor) was the actress Margaret Wolfit (1929–2008). **Hammer credits:** *A Man on the Beach* (1956, as Carter)

### Wolfshead: The Legend of Robin Hood

GB, 1969, 56m, Technicolor, cert U

So, the question is: is this actually a Hammer film? For years, the argument has been batted backwards and forwards. The official answer is no, but yes, kind of. The film—a variation on the much-told Robin Hood story—was originally conceived and executed by others, and was then bought by Hammer, to whom it is copyrighted in the end credits. However, it was then left it on the shelf for several years before MGM-EMI gave it a brief and belated release in 1973 as a support to the Cliff Richard musical *Take Me High* (1973), since when it has occasionally—but only occasionally—popped up on television, sometimes under the title *The Legend of Young Robin Hood*.

As director John Hough explained, "It was never started as a Hammer production at all. It was invested in by a group of NASSA space rocket engineers! They wanted to make a picture that reflected ye olde England. So we made *Wolfshead*, which was produced by a guy called Bill Anderson, and it was going to be a pilot for a TV show [hence the involvement of London Weekend Television]. The TV shows were never commissioned, and the film was then bought up by Hammer after the event."[50] Clearly considered a Hammer film by the studio, this is confirmed by the inclusion of a clip from the production in the *Costumers* episode of *The World of Hammer* (1990 [first broadcast 1994], TV).

A brisk and entertaining variation on an over-familiar tale, the film presents a harsher, more realistic view of mediaeval life than most Robin Hood adventures, thanks primarily to the fact that it was shot entirely on location in North Wales, with authentic detail provided by the film's period design consultant Helen Wilkinson. The film also utilizes several talents that were soon to become "officially" involved with Hammer, prime among them director John Hough (credited as Johnny Hough), who invests the proceedings with his customary visual panache, making the most of the opportunities provided by the wintry woodland settings and craggy backdrops, which he and cinematographer David Holmes capture from a variety of eye-catching angles. Holmes would go on to photograph two of Hammer's seventies comedy spin-offs, while Hough would go on to helm the fondly regarded *Twins of Evil* (1971), which would also feature David Warbeck, here seen as a suitably dashing Robin Hood. The always-reliable Kathleen Byron, who would also feature in *Twins of Evil*, meanwhile brings a touch of gravitas to the proceedings as Robin's mother, Katherine of Locksley, while the supporting players include Dan Meaden as John Little, Ciaran Madden as Lady Marian and David Butler as Will Stukely. Butler also penned the screenplay, and would go on to become a top writer for television, among his credits being an episode of *The Legend of Robin Hood* (1975, TV).

A little gem, the film's only drawback is its rather abrupt ending, in which Robin's friends swear allegiance to him in his fight against injustice, with their adventures presumably to have continued with the next installment, which of course never materialized. Sadly, the reaction of the NASSA rocket scientists to the finished product is not known. **Additional notes:** According to the opening narration, a "wolfshead" is "an outlaw whose head was worth no more than a wolf's." The film is copyrighted to Hammer Film Productions, Ltd.

Production companies: LWT/Anderson. Distributor: MGM-EMI (UK). Producer: Bill Anderson. Director: John Hough (credited as Johnny Hough). Screenplay: David Butler. Cinematographer: David Holmes. Music: Jack Sprague, Bernie Sharp. Music director: Don Innes. Editor: Bob Dearberg. Period design consultant: Helen Wilkinson. Sound mixer: Sid Squires. Dubbing editor: John Beaton. Costumes: Felix Evans. Make-up: Jim Hydes. Hair: Katie Dawson. Fight arranger: Alf Joint. Camera operator: Urnee Robinson. Gaffer: George Boner. Production manager: Laurie Green-

wood. First assistant director: Ron Purdie. Continuity: Kay Perkins. Production secretary: Ann Thirft. **Cast:** David Warbeck (Robert of Locksley/Robin Hood), Kathleen Byron (Katherine of Locksley), Ciaran Madden (Lady Marian Fitzwalter), Dan Meaden (John Little of Cumberland), Kenneth Gilbert (Friar Tuck), Joe Cook (Much), Derrick Gilbert (Wat), David Butler (Will Stukely), Roy Boyd (Geoffrey of Doncaster), Patrick O'Dwyer (Tom), Christopher Robbie (Roger of Doncaster), Peter Stephens (Abbot of St. Mary's), Pamela Roland (Adele), Kim Braden (Alice), Roy Evans (Gyrth), Inigo Jackson (Legross), Sheelah Wilcocks (Nurse), Will Knightley (Abbot's secretary), Reg Lever (Old Wat), Sheraton Blount (Abbie), Nicholas Jones (Squire)

### *The Woman in Black*

GB, 2012, 95m, color, Panavision, Dolby, cert PG-13 (U.S.), 12A (UK)

Announced in February 2010, this version of the 1983 best-selling Susan Hill novel had the kudos of featuring Harry Potter himself, Daniel Radcliffe, in the leading role of Arthur Kipps, a young solicitor who, sent to the remote Eel Marsh House to deal with a dead client's papers, finds himself inveigled in a complex plot involving the ghost of a scorned woman out for vengeance.

Initial reports claimed that the film would be shot in 3D, but this was later discounted after director James Watkins—previously known for the thriller *Eden Lake* (2008)—claimed he wasn't happy with the format. The $15m film therefore went before the cameras "flat" at Pinewood and on location at the Bluebell Railway and Colne Valley Railway between 26 September and 4 December 2010. Based upon a script by Jane Goldman, the film was designed by Kave Quinn, whose main task was to make the central location, Cotterstock Hall (situated near Peterborough), look a far more daunting place than it did in real life.

Following the box office disappointments of *Wake Wood* (2009), *Let Me In* (2010) and *The Resident* (2010), hopes were no doubt high at Hammer that this would be the one to place the renewed company firmly on the cinematic map with audiences when released in the U.S. on 3 February 2012 ("Do you believe in ghosts?" enticed the poster). In fact, thanks to the pulling power of Radcliffe, the film went on to take an impressive $21m on its opening weekend in America (the usually quiet Super Bowl Weekend), for which it played on 2,855 screens, coming in just behind *Chronicle*, which took the top spot with $22m from 2,907 screens. When it opened in the UK the following week, it did even better and managed to bag the all-important number one spot, which it retained for three weeks, towering over its nearest rival, *The Muppets* (2012). The film eventually went on to rake in over $128m worldwide (it subsequently took an additional $11.3m in DVD and Blu-ray sales).

The reviews were also generally more positive than those that had greeted the studio's previous outings. "A classical British ghost story that lives up to the color in its title," commented the *Northwest Herald*, which went on to describe the old

manor as "the dictionary illustration of a haunted house." In the UK, the verdict in *Total Film* was that the movie was "a heritage horror so classical it almost veers towards camp," though the review did acknowledge "Radcliffe's committed performance and [director] Watkins' willingness to do anything for a scare," an opinion also echoed in *The Metro*, which noted that "there are some satisfying look-behind-you jumps." Meanwhile, *The Standard* awarded the movie a healthy four stars, despite a few general carps about the production: "If you like your ghost movies subtle, then look away now," it warned, adding that "It shouldn't work, but somehow it does." As for its star it added that, "His occasional woodenness fits with the schlock and when he's good he's gripping. Seems like there's life in the old boy yet. Harry Potter, RIP." Other recommendations included "Smart and spooky" from *Time Out*, and "Horror for the Potter generation" from *The Observer*, while the *Daily Mirror* warned, "You'll be jumping out of your seat."

A resolutely old-fashioned scare fest with rather too many unsubtle "jump" moments and a preponderancy towards overly dark photography in which it is often hard to discern what is happening, the film is nevertheless technically assured, with solid performances from Radcliffe and fellow Potter veteran Ciaran Hinds as Mr. Daily, the local man who befriends Kipps. It also benefits from generally well-judged production values, notably the interior and exterior of Eel Marsh House, elements of which recall the gothic baronial halls of Hammer's glory years. As passable as the results are, however, the film never quite escapes the clichés of its genre, and at times embraces them all too readily, so that while one jumps at the jolts (both aural and visual), one can predict their arrival almost to the second, while the muttering locals and their dire warnings could easily have been lifted from any of the studio's back catalogue (albeit here minus the rather better character playing by the likes of Michael Ripper and George Woodbridge). The film is perfectly summed up by a rather telling exchange between Kipps and Mr. Daily. "What's going on?" asks the young solicitor at one point, to which comes the reply, "Complete nonsense!" **Additional notes:** Such was the film's success that as its takings edged past the $75m mark, Hammer announced that a sequel (see below) was already in the pipeline. The original novel had previously been filmed for television in 1989, with a script by Nigel Kneale. In this version, the role of Arthur (here Kidd not Kipps) was played by Adrian Rawlins, who, co-incidentally, went on to play James Potter (father of Harry) in the Harry Potter films. The book was also adapted into a highly successful stage play in 1987 by Stephen Mallatratt; this was first performed at the Stephen Joseph Theater in Scarborough, and subsequently went on tour. It has also played at the Fortune Theatre in London since 1989. There have also been two radio adaptations (presented in 1993, with Robert Glenister as Arthur Kipps, and 2004 with James D'Arcy in the role). Mark Gatiss—who had documented the history of Hammer in an episode of his TV series *A History of Horror with Mark Gatiss* (2010, TV)—was originally approached to pen the screenplay. Several of the technical crew had previously worked with director James Watkins on *Eden Lake*. Some scenes were trimmed for the UK print in order to achieve a 12A release (other countries, including Sweden and South Korea, rated the film as high as a 15).

Production companies: Hammer/Alliance Films/Cross Creek Pictures/Talisman. Distributors: Momentum (UK), CBS (U.S.). Executive producers: Guy East, Roy Lee, Nigel Sinclair, Tyler Thompson, Marc Schipper, Tobin Armbrust, Neil Dunn. Producers: Richard Jackson, Simon Oakes, Brian Oliver. Co-producers: Paul Ritchie, Todd Thompson, Ben Holden. Director: James Watkins. Screenplay: Jane Goldman, based upon the novel and play by Susan Hill. Cinematographer: Tim Maurice-Jones. Music: Marco Beltrami. Editor: Jon Harris. Production designer: Kave Quinn. Set decorator: Niamh Coulter. Costumes: Keith Madden, Emma Hutton, Nikia Nelson, Holly Smart. Makeup: Sidony Etherton, Jeremy Woodhead. Make-up effects: Chris Fitzgerald, Paul Hyett. Production manager: Jennifer Wynne. Production co-ordinator: Adele Steward. Assistant production co-ordinator: Alice Syed. Location manager: Chris Moore. Assistant location manager: Kevin Jenkins. Location scouts: Vinnie Jassal, Davis Seaton. Post-production supervisor: Jeanette Haley. First assistant director: Dominic Fysh. Second assistant director: Emma Stokes. Third assistant director: Tom Browne. Sound: Hugo Adams, Mark Appleby, James Kum, Michael Gassert, Ivor Talbot, Tarn Willers. Special effects: Daniel Nielsen, Haken Blomdahl, Fiorenza Bagnariol, Mitch Crease, Urban Forsberg, Aura Shannon, Rob Pizzey, Malin Persson, Marcus Hindborg, Timothy P. Jones, Elin Lindahl, Linus Lindbalk, Martin Malmqvist, Mervyn New, Kaveh Montazer. Casting: Karen Lindsay-Stewart. Assistant art directors: Andrew Palmer, Jessica Sinclair. Art department assistant: Damian Leon Watts. Standby art director: Huw Arthur. Visual research: Tina Charad. Graphic artist: Andrew Payne. Standby painter: Mary Pat Sheahan. Props: John Fox, Jack Garwood, Toby Wagner, Quentin Davies, Jamie Wilkinson, Simon Wilkinson. Greensmen: Craig Whiteford, Ian Whiteford. Stunt co-ordinator: Andy Bennett. Second unit photography: Alan Stewart. Aerial photography: Jeremy Braben. Camera operator: Julian Morson. Camera assistants: Luke Cairns, Rob Gilmour, Basil Smith, Kat Spencer, Felix Pickles (trainee), Alex Teale (trainee). Video assist operator: Nuria Perez. Best boy: Martin Conway. Loader: Rana Darwish. Grips: Terry Williams, David Armstrong, David Holliday, Cassius McCabe. Focus pullers: Nathan Mann, Tom McFarlings. Riggers: Graham Baker, Darren Flindall, Ian Franklin. Gaffers: Pat Sweeney, Sean Monesson. Electrician: Maiya Rose (trainee). Senior digital film editor: Emily Greenwood. Digital intermediate head of department: Patrick Malone. Colorists: Jamie Payne, Rose-Ellen Saunders. Production assistants: Giles Barron, Holly Gardner, Rosanne (Rosie) Coker, Sam Weeden, Harry Graves (trainee). Music consultant: Joel Sill. Music editor: Tony Lewis. Script supervisor: Caroline Bowker. Story editor: Jon Croker. Accountants: John Miles, Daniel Budd, Nazmeen Dhansey, Edward Taroghion. Production secretaries: Annie Clapton, Joel Clarke, Sheerin Khosrowshahi-Maindoab. Titles: Matt Curtis. Stills: Nick Wall. Stunts: Nellie Burroughes, Paul Lowe, Gary Arthurs, Sam Parham, Marc Mailley. Assistant to Brian Oliver: John Doherty. Assistant to James Watkins: Lee Francis. Medical co-ordinator: Elton Farla. **Cast:** Daniel Radcliffe (Arthur Kipps), Ciaran Hinds (Mr. Daily), Janet McTeer (Mrs. Daily), Sidney Johnston (Nicholas Daily), Shaun Dooley (Fisher), Mary Stockley (Mrs. Fisher), Roger Allam (Mr. Bentley), Alexia Osborne (Victoria Hardy), Teresa Churcher (Mrs. Hardy), Alfie Field (Tom Hardy), Alisa Khazanova (Alice Drablow), Aoife Doherty (Lucy Jerome), Liz White (Jennet Humfrye [The Woman in Black]), Misha Handley (Joseph Kipps), Paul J. Dove (Butcher), John R. Walker (Archer), Lucy May Barker (Nursemaid), Neil Broome (Villager), Lee Steele (Fisherman), David Burke (PC Collins), Emma Shorey (Fisher girl), Molly Harmon (Fisher girl), Ellisa Walker-Reid (Fisher girl), Sophie Stuckey (Stella Kipps), Jessica Raine (Nanny), Indira Ainger (Girl on train), William Tobin (Charlie Hardy), Victor McGuire (Gerald Hardy), Cathy Sara (Mrs. Jerome), Tim McMullan (Mr. Jerome), Sidney Johnston (Nicholas Daily), Ashley Foster (Nathaniel Drablow). **DVD availability:** Momentum (UK R2 PAL), extras include a behind the scenes documentary, cast and crew interviews, an audio commentary with director James Watkins and screenwriter Jane Goldman, photo galleries, storyboards, a red carpet special and (exclusive to HMV) a lenticular (3D) slip cover which features the title character creeping up on an unsuspecting Daniel Radcliffe (She's *behind* you!); CBS (U.S. R1 NTSC). **Blu-ray availability:** Sony (A/1), Momentum (B/2). **CD availability:** Silva America, which contains 22 cues, among them *Tea for Three Plus One*, *In the Graveyard* and *Summoning the Woman in Black*

### The Woman in Black 2: Angel of Death

GB, 2015, 98m, color, widescreen, cert 15

Announced during the successful box office run of *The Woman in Black* (2012), this $15m sequel was Hammer's first opportunity to create a new ongoing franchise in some decades. Set forty years following the events of the first film, it is based on a new story by Susan Hill concerning a young teacher's experiences at Eel Marsh House during World War II, when the place is being used as a shelter for evacuated children, among them a young boy named Edward who has just lost both his parents in the blitz.

Scripting duties this time were handled by Jon Croker, a former Harry Potter production assistant turned story editor known in the industry for his work on such films as *Attack the Block* (2011), *The Deep Blue Sea* (2011), *The Iron Lady* (2011) and *The Last Passenger* (2012), while the directing chores were handed to Tom Harper, best known for his work on *The Scouting Book for Boys* (2009) and episodes of *Misfits* (2009–2013, TV) and *Peaky Blinders* (2013–, TV). The cast was meanwhile headed by Phoebe Fox as the young schoolmarm Eve Parkins, Helen McCrory as her frosty superior, Jeremy Irvine as a handsome RAF pilot who befriends Eve during her journey to Eel Marsh House, and Oaklee Pendergast as the damaged Edward, with Leanne Best taking over the title role from Liz White, here out to continue her vengeance on Eve's young charges ("She never forgives. She never forgets. She never left," ran the tagline).

However, the multi-million dollar question was, would the film appeal at the box office minus the presence of Daniel Radcliffe, who had been so valuable in helping turn the first film into such a success? With a worldwide take of $48.8m (of which $26.5m originated in America) the sequel—which was released on 1 January 2015 in the UK and a day later in the U.S. by Momentum and Relativity Media respectively—certainly wasn't a commercial disappointment, though compared to its predecessor, it wasn't a runaway hit either. The reviews, meanwhile, were generally mixed. *Variety* described the film as "a handsomely made but dramatically inert and not very scary sequel," while of its spectral title character it observed, "boy does she take her sweet time about making a full-fledged appearance." Meanwhile, *The Guardian* opined that it "essentially works the same scares again, mechanically and noisily," though it did aver that it was "a more elegant film than the first." Elsewhere, *The Telegraph* noted that the film's underwater climax—in which the RAF pilot sacrifices himself so as to save Eve and Edward from the clutches of the title character—was "murky and unsatisfying." Indeed, this last observation pretty much sums up the entire film given the consistently monochromatic quality of George Steel's cinematography, which at times is not so much atmospheric as barely decipherable, particularly during many of the night time scare sequences, which, as with most genre films of late, rely too heavily on shock cuts and unexpected loud noises. Given the familiarity of the narrative—which at times becomes a little too morbid in its bid to place children in deadly peril—the actors perform their duties well enough, particularly Phoebe Fox as the vulnerable teacher and Jeremy Irvine as the RAF pilot who it transpires has some demons of his own to conquer. That said, it's an often wearyingly predictable journey to the waterlogged climax. Certainly by no means as bad as one might have expected, but then again, hardly as good as one might have hoped. **Additional notes:** The film's working title was *The Woman in Black: Angel of Death*, a title to which it reverted for its UK DVD release. The story was also novelized under this title by Martyn Waites and published by Hammer in 2013 as an appetite whetter for the film. Actor Adrian Rawlins, who appears here as Dr. Rhodes, played the lead role of Arthur Kidd in the 1989 TV movie version of *The Woman in Black*; the role was subsequently played by Daniel Radcliffe (re-named Arthur Kipps) in Hammer's 2012 remake.

Production companies: Hammer/Alliance Films/Da Vinci Media Ventures/Vertigo Entertainment/Talisman/Exclusive Media Group. Distributors: Momentum (UK), Relativity Media (U.S.). Executive producers: Neil Dunn, Guy East, Roy Lee, Nigel Sinclair, Richard Toussaint, Mark Schipper. Co-executive producers: Ross Jacobson,

Toby Moores, Sheldon Rabinowitz, Mark Roberts, Wendy Rutland. Producers: Tobin Armbrust, Ben Holden, Richard Jackson, Simon Oakes. Associate producers: Susan Hill, Aliza James, Jillian Longnecker, Laura Wilson, Spyro Markesinis. Co-producers: Jane Hooks, Ian Watermeier. Screenplay: Jon Croker. Story: Susan Hill. Director: Tom Harper. Cinematographer: George Steel. Music: Marco Beltrami, Brandon Roberts, Marcus Trumpp. Jennet Humphrye nursery rhyme composed by: Jack Arnold. Editor: Mark Eckersley. Production designer: Jacqueline Abrahams. Supervising art director: Andrew Munro. Art directors: Claudio Campana, Toby Riches. Set decorator: Jille Azis. Standby art director: Richard Usher. Costumes: Annie Symons. Make-up and hair: Cate Hall, Emilie Yong, Andrea Cracknell, Sharon Colley, Cat Corderoy, Samantha Kininmonth, Sophie Slotover, Hannah Edwards, Charlotte Wood, Jo Nielsen, Frankie Francis, Jess Heath, Richard Glass, Selen Hurer, Chris Lyons, Adam James Phillips, Liz Phillips, Stuart Richards, Jemma Scott-Knox-Gore, Laura Schalker, Jacqui Rathore, Gerrold Vincent. First assistant directors: Adam Lock, Phil Booth (second unit). Second assistant director: Jamie D. Allen, James Manning (second unit). Third assistant directors: Alex Currie-Clark, Rory Broadfoot (second unit), David Keadell (unit base). Production manager: Eve Swannell. Location manager: Ben Gladstone, Alex Gladstone (second unit). Assistant location manager/location scout: Peter Gray. Location assistants: Hayley Kasperczky, Toby Lomas. Post production coordinator: Alexander Montgomery. Post-production manager: Jeanette Haley. Post production assistant: Georgina Miles. Unit manager: John David Gunkle, Michael Stapleton (second unit). Production co-ordinator: Deryn Stafford. Assistant production co-ordinator: Catherine Booton. Sound designer: Andy Kennedy. Sound mixer: Ian Voigt, Dylan Voigt (second unit, also sound maintenance). Sound re-recording mixers: Stuart Hilliker, Forbes Noonan. Assistant re-recording mixer: James Ridgway. Supervising sound editor/sound designer: Lee Walpole. Sound effects editors: Joe Beal, Alex Ellerington. Assistant sound editor: Matthew Mewett. Foreign language mixer: Matthew Pavolaitis. ADR recordist: Juraj Mravec. Foley editor: Philip Clements. Foley recordist: Catherine Thomas. Foley artists: Peter Burgis, Andie Derrick, Sue Harding. Sound assistant: Ben Jeffes. Dialogue editor: Jeff Richardson. Sound facility manager: Jess Pegram, Arthur Lavis (support). Re-recorded at: Boom Post, London. Special effects: Lucy Ainsworth-Taylor, Asa Shoul, Alison Arnott, Henry Badgett, Angela Barson, Roni Rodrigues, Patrick Hall, Jan Guilfoyle, Yannick Cibin, Finlay Duncan, Daniel Gardiner, James Corless, Luke Moorcock, Maimunah Yahkup, Nick Rideout, Alan Senior, Johnny Hafnar, Dominic Blake, Nik Smith, Simon Rowling, James Willis, Andy Collings, Paul Carter, Tony Langley, James Cattell, Roni Rodrigues, Peter [Petko] Zhivkov, Stanley Jones, Qian Han, Alexander Kirichenko, Naveen Shukla, Patrick Hall, Francesco [misspelled Francessco in the credits] Russo, Marek Solowiej, Victor Georgiev, Eglantine Boinet, Martin Hohnle, Nic Birm-

ingham, Yannick Cibin, Tony Abejuro, Lee Dexter, Sarah Byers, Robin Hinch, Alison Arnott, Steve Knafou, Caroline Steiner, Tony Abejuro, Philip Charles-Sweeting, Ntana Key, Panos Theodropoulos, Finlay Duncan, Luke Moorcock, Bluebolt, Elements Special Effects. Construction manager: Jamie Powell. Production buyer: Katie Ralph. Casting: Julie Harkin, Harry Parker, Kevin Riddle, Louis Elman. Props: Steve Register, Nick Thomas, Chris Allen, Chris Felstead, Patrick Dunn, Owen Mann, Stuart Rankmore, Arthur Williams, David Sutheran, Guto Humphreys, James Mannell. Carpenters: Lee Boom, Dave Bull, Mark Morrow, John Park, Lee Compton, Gavin Gordon, Dave Perschky, Karthik Poduval. Plasterers: Matt Barrett, Stanley Apperley, Dave Grainger, Brian Gooch, Brad Syrett, Max Connolly. Décor and lettering artist: Clive Ingleton. Painters: Thomas Kingsley, Christopher Gardner, Ian Zawadzki. Décor and lettering artist: Clive Ingleton. Standby painter: Keith Connolly, Nick Bowen (second unit). Standby carpenter: Nick Smith, Robert McMillan (second unit). Standby stage hand: Anthony Edwards (second unit). Art department assistant: Helen Negus. Art department trainees: Tamsin Gandhi, Laura Miller. Junior draughts persons: Max Klaentschi, Damian Leon Watts. Petty cash buyers: Caroline Barton, Viera Zvonarova. Head greensman: Tim Lanning. Storeman: Paul Carter. Work experience: Luke Dass, Katie Boyce, Harriet Claridge, Josh Deighton, Amy Battey, Lerato Moloisane. Standby rigger: Mark Norris. Storyboard artist: Jenny Turner, Robert Castillo. Stunts: Justin Pearson, Gary Arthurs, Andy Bennett, Craig Garner, Annabel Canaven, Belinda McGinley, Christian Knight, Heather Phillips. Wardrobe: Rebecca Tredget, Chloe Reynolds, Aisha Kascioglu, Penny McDonald, Niall O'Shea, Stella Atkinson, Viveene Campbell, Agathe Finney, Vincent Dumas, Heidi McQueen-Prentice, Fliss Jaine, Alison Lyons, Martin Clarke, Gerrold Vincent, Kate Walling, Ceri Price. Camera and electrical (operator, grips, electricians, riggers, gaffers, etc.): Jon Beacham, Richard Copeman, Harry Bowers, Mark Hutton, Hannah McKimm, Stewart Monteith, Jem Morton, Ryan Huffer, Alison Lai, Tom Gough, Michael Hill, Richard Cornelius, Barry Davies, Andy Edridge, John Donne, Stephen Finch, Wick Finch, Will Finch, Graeme McCormick, Patrick O'Flynn, Andy Purdy, Ian Ogden, Nick Wall, Tim Wooster, David Tanner, Lisa Trinder, Scott Hillier, James Shovlar, Thomas Storey, Jack Ridout, Dave Ridout, Garry Ridgwell, Lee Godfrey, Michael Stapleton, Gideon Jenson, Mark Milsome, Phoebe Arnstein, Alexandra Voiku, Grant Taylor, Mark Norris. Editorial: Steven Worsley, Kelly Allum, Jateen Patel, Francois Kamffer, Thom Berryman, Tom Cairns, Michelle Cort, Tim Drewett, Laura Daniel, Stratton Farrar, Justin Lanchbury, Josh Miller, Alexander Montgomery, Steve Owen. Music department: Charles M. Barsamian, John Kurlander, Tara Moross, Tyson Lozensky, Will Akbar, Harry Langston, Tom McFarling, Stuart Sheppard, John Warhurst. Underwater photography: Tim Wooster. Underwater unit: Sean Connor, Richard Copeman, Mark Campany, Pip Keeling, David Tanner, Dave Shaw, Lisa Birch, David Murrell, Jonjo Stickland,

John Ainley, Clint Swann, Gerald Gadd, Shane Roberts. Transportation: Michael Geary, Julian Chapman, Ram Gounder, Martin Giles, Richard Grady, David Lloyd, John Hall, Jason Stedmon, Lee Pellett, Rob McKenna, Rachel Lydiate, Clive King, Guy Drayton, Tony French, Ben Michael, Jennie Mills, Sam Boardman, Tim Shuttleworth, Ray Amber. Production assistant: Marie Allcorn. Unit publicist: Kate Lee, Freud Communications. Clearances: Charles Edwards. Stills: Nick Wall. Electronic press kit producer: Andrew Dillon (for DMS). Chaperones: Benjamin Perkins, Nicola Allpress, Mike Allpress, Linda Matthews, Paula O'Neill, Louise Pearce, Paula Simmons, Rachel Crouch, Nicola Brimblecombe, Ruth Wright. Tutors: Sefton Hewitt, Kevin McHale, Esther Davis, Hayley Catchpole (assistant). Artiste PA: Richard Oxford. Runners: Harry Greaves, Matthew Shipley, Sarah Townsend, Viva Stuart, Jeanette. Sutton, Jack Wren, Aaron Hopkins. Artiste PA: Richard Oxford. Catering: Hot Goblin, Chris Blyth, Shot Stop, Graham Walters. Security: James Brodie, Sean Desmond, Bob Mitchell. Health and safety advisors: Jake Edmonds, Jim Clarke, Kevin McGill. Medical: Nikki Saben (second unit). Finance legal: Ben Grantham. Legal services: Kami Naghdi. Assistant to Simon Oakes: Puffin Hepworth. Assistant to Richard Jackson: Adam Jackson. Assistant to Tom Harper: Jack Peters. Assistant to Ben Holden and Jane Hooks: Louise Pocock. Assistant to Tobin Armbrust: Justine Winkler. Production assistants: Rafferty Thwaites, Tom Ivens. Creative executive: Jeni Jones. Production secretary: Rachel Linehan. Research: Julie Summers. Movement double: Teresa Mahoney. Production accountant: Rob Seager. Assistant accountants: Chrissy Murray, Christine Samways. Post production accountant: Lara Sargent. Post production assistant accountant: Louise Green. Cashier: Laura Cowcher. Payroll: Sargent-Disc Ltd. London. Script supervisor: Marnie Paxton-Harris, San [sic] Davey (second unit). Main and end titles: Matt Curtis, AP. Post production facilities: Molinaire. Score recorded and mixed at: Pianella Studios. Environmental consultant: Melanie Dicks. Additional production personnel/companies: Laura Metcalfe, Len Brown, Gareth Parry, Matt James, Theresa Crooks, Kirsty Dua, Tom Sugden, Jamie Welsh, Mike Andrews, Jonathan Dickinson, Lizzie Newsham, Jordan Seigel, Buck Sanders, Charles M. Barsamian, Chris Piccardo, Cutting Edge, Pinewood Digital, James Corless, Avye Leventis, Julie Summers, The Casting Network, Ann Koska, Sally King, Translux International, Joe Fitzpatrick, Stuart Spencer, Lee Sheffield, Richard Cowden, Norman Parr, David Kelly, Rachel Mears, Terry Lydiate, Tibor Bulak, Media Coaches, Westway Coaches, Paul Creasey, Alex Wright, Shot Stop, Take 2 Films, Fintage Cam, HireWorks, InC [sic] Productions, Nationwide Platforms, Panalux, C& D Rigging, Motorhouse, A-Z Animals, Charles Edwards, Hireworks, Powell Plasterwork and Construction, Fatts, Wavevend, TVS-UK, Kriss Brown, Location Assist, Sean Desmond, Andy White, The Reel Eye Company, Cloud 12, Codex, Sky Media Travel, Cutting Edge Group, Lil and Kate London Ltd, Access Conference Connections, Joy Montgomery,

Team Air Express, BBC Motion Gallery, Media Insurance Brokers Ltd, John O'Sullivan, Lee & Thompson LLP, Reno Antoniades, Angela Scurrah, Rebecca Pick, Babok & Robins LLP, Barry S. Babok, Stroock & Stroock & Lavan LLP, Glen Mastroberte, Field Fisher Waterhouse LLP, Tim Johnson, Barry Smith, Film Finances, Matt Warren, Stephen Joberns, Shipley's LLP, Commercial Bank, Adam J. Korn, Jeff Colvin, Chris Lytton, Alex Walton, Roland Wieshofer, Patrice Theroux, Nelson Kuo-Lee, Giles Willits, Natasha Payne, eOne [*sic*] Film Productions, Catherine McNamara, Llewellyn Radley, Sleepy Dog, Wendy Rutland, Toby Moores, Manu Propria Entertainment, Bill Grantham, Corner Piece Capital LLC. Thanks to: Dasym Investments, Frank Botman, Mark Ramakers, Jonne de Leeuw, Alex Brunner, Kim Troy, Simon Faber, Rob Carlson, Josh Varney, Jack Thomas, Grant Parsons, Stephen Hatton, Aileen McEwan, Ira Schreck, Julie Feldman, Paul Lyon-Maris, Nick Forgacs, Vivien Green, Lucy Fawcett, Laura Engel, Barbara Machin, Neil Calder, Tim Wootton, Damian Mould, Belstaff, Canada Goose, Mac, Dermalogica, Bluebell Railway, The Greenwich Foundation for the Old Royal Naval College, London Underground, Heyford Park Trust, Osea Island, Network Rail, Vintage Carriages Trust, House of Detention. **Cast:** Helen McCrory (Jean Hogg), Phoebe Fox (Eve Parkins), Jeremy Irvine (Harry Burnstow), Adrian Rawlins (Dr. Rhodes), Leanne Best (The Woman in Black), Pip Pearce (James), Jude Wright (Tom), Casper Allpress (Fraser), Alfie Simmons (Alfie), Amelia Crouch (Flora), Ned Dennehy (Hermit Jacob), Oaklee Pendergast (Edward), Leilah de Meza (Ruby), Amelia Pidgeon (Joyce), Hayley Thomas Arnold (Man at station), Eve Pearce (Alice Drablow), Mary Roscoe (Woman in tube), Merryn Pearse (Girl in tube), Keenan Diaper (Ghost child), Olivia Sear (Ghost child), Oscar Cameron (Ghost child), Natasha Wigman (Ghost child), Lucy Dawson (Ghost child), Andreas Bazigos (Ghost Child), Lexie Marie Freeman Cook (Ghost child), Georgina Vane (Ghost child), Katherine Brown (Ghost child), Annabel Hindley (Ghost child), Chloe Mitchell Ghost child), Ben Huish (double for Oaklee Pendergast), Claire Rafferty (Clara [uncredited]), Hayley Joanne Bacon (Woman at station [uncredited]), Claire Ashton (Civilian [uncredited]), Richard Banks (Londoner [uncredited]), Jorge Leon Martinez (Londoner [uncredited]), Shane Salter (Soldier [uncredited]), Leigh Dent (Train passenger [uncredited]), David Norfolk (Fire Chief [uncredited]), Victoria Fayne (Mother [uncredited]), Faith Elizabeth (Mother [uncredited]), Karol Steele (Nurse [uncredited]), Samantha Moran (Nurse [uncredited]), Julie Vollono (Rail traveller [uncredited]), Fabio Vollono (Rail traveller [uncredited]), Harry Jones (Boy at station [uncredited]), Ryan Parker (Soldier [uncredited]), Chris Cowlin (Airman [uncredited]), David Few-Cooper (Soldier [uncredited]), Matthew David McCarthy (Milkman [uncredited]). **DVD availability:** Entertainment One (UK R2 PAL), extras include a deleted scene and several short behind the scenes documentaries, among them *Pulling Back the Veil, Designing Fear, From Page to Screen*

and *Hammer's Legacy*; Twentieth Century–Fox (U.S. R1 NTSC). **Blu-ray availability:** Entertainment One (B/2), Twentieth Century–Fox (A/2), extras for both include the trailer, a deleted scene, and two documentaries: *Pulling Back the Veil* and *Chilling Locations*. **CD availability:** Varese Sarabande, which contains 19 cues, among them *Jennet Humphrye Lost Her Baby, First Night* and *Locked in the Nursery*

### Women Without Men

GB, 1956, 73m, bw, RCA, cert A

This melodrama about an American showgirl, Angie Booth, who breaks out of a British prison so as to meet with her lover, Nick Randall, on New Year's Eve, was the last film to be made under Hammer's long-standing deal with the American producer Robert Lippert. The movie was the only feature made by Hammer in 1955, during which the company concentrated on short subjects while awaiting the box office outcome of *The Quatermass Xperiment* (1955). In fact James Carreras had considered pulling the plug on *Women Without Men*, but given that pre-production was at such an advanced stage, it was eventually considered more cost effective to go ahead with filming as planned.

As with all of Hammer's Lippert productions, the movie top-lined an American star—in this case Beverly Michaels—supported by company regulars both in front of and behind the cameras (though the director, Elmo Williams, was, like his leading lady, an American import). Originally to have been titled *Prison Story*, the movie was filmed at Bray and on nearby locations in early 1955 and released in the UK by Exclusive on 14 June 1956. For its American release by Fox in April of the same year, the film was re-titled *Blonde Bait*, and included additional scenes directed by Herbert Glazer featuring Richard Travis, Bill Cavanagh, Harry Lauter and John Phillips. These scenes were photographed by William P. Whitley, with Bert Sterbach working as the production manager and Glen Glenn as the sound recordist. The plot was also substantially reworked, so much so that Paul Carpenter's role as Nick Randall was completely cut from the print. The role was subsequently re-cast with a completely different actor, Jim Davis, with Randall now (incredibly) a Nazi spy.

Observed production manager Jimmy Sangster of the finished product, "That was a diabolical little picture."[51] A generally routine affair trading in clichéd

characters and situations, it nevertheless benefits from some reasonably earnest performances, chief among them that of leading lady Beverly Michaels as Angie ("Like most women in prison, I'm here because of a man") and supporting player Thora Hird as the comical Granny Rafferty (the actress was only forty-five at the time). Avril Angers as pickpocket Bessie Brown and Hermione Baddeley as a disgruntled landlady who finds herself with three escaped convicts in her rundown boarding house also provide good back up. The technical credits are adequate but no more, though the film does pick up reasonable speed and resource once its leading lady and two fellow inmates go on the run. **Additional notes:** Crew shadow can be seen on the road during the climactic car chase as Granny drives round a country road bend. Lyricist Lorraine Williams was the wife of director Elmo Williams. This was the last Hammer film of long-serving cinematographer Walter "Jimmy" Harvey, save for a brief return in the sixties to photograph *The Runaway* (1964) and *Delayed Flight* (1964), which were made back to back. Some sources erroneously claim that the American starlet Cleo Moore appears in the film; this misconception may

American poster for *Women Without Men* (1956), released in the States as the superficially attractive *Blonde Bait* (**Hammer/Lippert/Hammer/Twentieth Century–Fox**).

arise from the fact that the actress appeared in such similarly titled and themed productions as *Bait* (1954) and *Women's Prison* (1955) around the same the time.

Production companies: Hammer/Lippert. Distributors: Hammer (UK), Twentieth Century–Fox (U.S.). Producer: Anthony Hinds. Director: Elmo Williams (and Herbert Glazer [U.S. scenes only]). Screenplay: Val Guest [uncredited], Richard H. Landau [uncredited]. Story: Richard Landau. Cinematographer: Walter "Jimmy" Harvey (and William P. Whitley [U.S. scenes only]). Music: Leonard Salzedo. Song: *Long Ago Guy* (music Douglas Gamley, lyrics Lorraine Williams). Music director: John Hollingsworth. Editor: James Needs. Art director: John Elphick [uncredited]. Costumes: Molly Arbuthnot. Make-up: Phil Leakey. Hair: Monica Hustler. Sound: Bill Sweeney (and Glen Glenn [U.S. scenes only]). Production manager: Jimmy Sangster (and Bert Sternbach [U.S. scenes only]). Assistant director: Bill Shore. Camera operator: Len Harris. Focus puller: Harry Oakes [uncredited]. Continuity: Renee Glynne [uncredited]. **Cast:** Beverly Michaels (Angie Booth), Joan Rice (Cleo Thompson), Avril Angers (Bessie Brown), Hermione Baddeley (Grace), Thora Hird (Granny Rafferty), Paul Carpenter (Nick Randall), Ralph Michael (Julian Lord), Gordon Jackson (Percy Thompson), Sheila Burrell (Babs Sullivan), Olwen Brookes (Hackett), April Olrich (Margueritte), Valerie White (Governor), Eugene Deckers (Pierre), Maurice Kaufmann (Danny), David Lodge (Prison Officer), Bill Shine (Reveller), Michael Golden (Bargekeeper), Betty Cooper (Chief Matron Evans), John Welsh (Prison Chaplain), Muriel Young (Helen Braddock [uncredited]), Charles Saynor (Man at doorway [uncredited]), Irene Richmond (Guard [uncredited]), Douglas Argent (Reveller [uncredited]), Sidney Brahms (Reveller [uncredited]), Stratford Johns (Reveller [uncredited]), Fanny Carby (Brooker [uncredited]), Pat Edwards (Caroller [uncredited]), Rosalie Westwater (Caroller [uncredited]), Edna Landor (Caroller [uncredited]), Joan Harrison (Caroller [uncredited]), Margaret Flint (Hennessey [uncredited]), Doris Gilmore (Loveland [uncredited]), Thomas Glen (Policeman [uncredited]), George Roderick (Policeman [uncredited]), John Ruddock (Policeman [uncredited]), Mark Kingston (Operator [uncredited]), Valerie Frazer (Inmate [uncredited]), Mona Lilian (Inmate [uncredited]), Anne Loxley (Inmate [uncredited]), Katherine Feliaz (Mrs. Rizzione [uncredited]), Oscar Nation (Mr. Rizzione [uncredited]), Yvonne Manners (Mason [uncredited]), Verne Morgan (Barrowman [uncredited]), Babs Love (Scrubber [uncredited]), Toots Pound (Scrubber [uncredited]), Vi Stevens (Scrubber [uncredited]), Peter Welch (Priest [uncredited]), Pauline Winter (Laverne [uncredited]), Anthony T. Miles (Civilian [uncredited]), John Phillips (Cunard [uncredited]), Jim Davis (Nick Randall [additional U.S. scenes only]), Richard Travis (Kent Foster [additional U.S. scenes only]), Paul Cavanagh (Inspector D.N. Hedges [additional U.S. scenes only]), Harry Lauter (U.S. State Department Security Chief [additional U.S. scenes only])

## Wong, Diana

Long in Britain, this Malaysian born actress (?–2012) played the role of Miss Almond Blossom in Hammer's second post-war featurette, *Death in High Heels* (1947). Also a writer, she contributed to the long-running radio series *Children's Hour* (1922–1964). Her husband was the actor, broadcaster and writer Roy Plomley (1914–1985), whom she married in 1942 and who co-wrote two films for Hammer: *Dr. Morelle—The Case of the Missing Heiress* (1949) and *Celia* (1949). **Hammer credits:** *Death in High Heels* (1947, as Miss Almond Blossom)

## Wong, Santso

This Oriental actor played a sergeant in Hammer's *The Terror of the Tongs* (1961). His other credits include three episode of *Doctor Who* (1963–1989, TV). **Hammer credits:** *The Terror of the Tongs* (1961, as Sergeant [uncredited])

## Wong, Vincent

Born in Jamaica, Wong (1928–2015, real name Vivian Warren Chen) had a minor role in Hammer's *The Terror of the Tongs* (1961). His other credits include *Silver Dream Racer* (1980), *Privates on Parade* (1982), *Little Shop of Horrors* (1986), *Batman* (1989), *Ashes to Ashes* (1999), *Die Another Day* (2002) and *Batman Begins* (2005), plus episodes of *W. Somerset Maugham* (1969–1970, TV), *Space: 1999* (1975–1977, TV) and *Jonathan Creek* (1997–2004, TV). He was also in the original TV version of *Yesterday's Enemy* (1958, TV), which was remade for the big screen by Hammer the following year. **Hammer credits:** *The Terror of the Tongs* (1961, unnamed role [uncredited])

## Wood, Colin

Wood worked as a boom operator on *Hammer House of Mystery and Suspense* (1984, TVM). His other credits include *Exposé* (1976), *Let's Get Laid* (1977), *Nijinsky* (1980), *Lassiter* (1984), *The Last Emperor* (1987), *The Russia House* (1990), *True Blue* (1996), *Tomorrow Never Dies* (1997), *Love Actually* (2003) and *1408* (2007), plus episodes of *The Strauss Dynasty* (1991, TV), *The Young Indiana Jones Chronicles* (1992–1993, TV) and *Holby City* (1999–, TV). **Hammer credits:** *Hammer House of Mystery and Suspense* (1984, TVM [uncredited])

## Wood, Ean

This British (Manx) editor (1937–2010) worked as the first assistant editor on Hammer's *Blood from the Mummy's Tomb* (1971). His other credits as an assistant editor include *Cry of the Banshee* (1970 and *Prey* (1978). His work as an editor includes *Not Tonight, Darling* (1971), the screenplay for which he also co-wrote, while his credits as a sound editor include *The Beast Must Die* (1974) and *Second Best* (1994). He also directed a handful of documentaries and instructional films, among them *How to Get the Best Out of a Plough* (1964), *An Introduction to Mining Electronics* (1977) and *An Introduction to Computer Logic* (1979). **Hammer credits:** *Blood from the Mummy's Tomb* (1971 [uncredited])

## Wood, Fred

This British actor worked as a bit part player and extra on several Hammer films in the sixties and seventies, popping up in crowd scenes and a variety of non-speaking roles. His other credits include *Star Wars* (1977) and *Superman II* (1980), plus episodes of *Gone to Seed* (1992, TV), in which he played Toothy. **Hammer credits include:** *The Curse of the Werewolf* (1961, as Villager [uncredited]), *The Phantom of the Opera* (1962, as Stage hand [uncredited]), *Captain Clegg* (1962, as Villager [uncredited]), *The Kiss of the Vampire* (1963, as Gravedigger [uncredited]), *The Evil of Frankenstein* (1964, as Fairground spectator [uncredited]), *Dracula—Prince of Darkness* (1966, as Mourner [uncredited]), *Lust for a Vampire* (1971, Patron at inn [uncredited]), *Demons of the Mind* (1972, as Villager at staking [uncredited])

## Wood, Gilbert

This British painter (1904–1982, full name Gilbert McConnell-Wood) worked as a scenic artist on Hammer's *The Hound of the Baskervilles* (1959) and *Never Take Sweets from a Stranger* (1960). His other credits include *Much Too Shy* (1942), *Latin Quarter* (1946), *Last Holiday* (1950), *Becket* (1964), *Invasion* (1966), *Alfie* (1966), *Don't Lose Your Head* (1966) and *All the Way Up* (1970). **Hammer credits:** *The Hound of the Baskervilles* (1959 [uncredited]), *Never Take Sweets from a Stranger* (1960 [uncredited])

## Wood, John

This respected British stage actor (1930–2011) can be seen as a doctor in Hammer's *Stolen Face* (1952). Working in both Britain and America, his other credits include *Idol on Parade* (1959), *Invasion Quartet* (1961), *Postman's Knock* (1962), *Just Like a Woman* (1966), *Which Way to the Front?* (1970), *Somebody Killed Her Husband* (1978), *War Games* (1983), in which he played Falken, *Ladyhawke* (1985), *Richard III* (1995) and *The White Countess* (2005), plus episodes of *Kenilworth* (1957, TV), *Matlock Police* (1971–1976, TV) and *Lewis* (2006–2015, TV). He won a best actor Tony Award in 1976 for *Travesties* and a best actor Evening Standard Award in 1991 for *King Lear*. He was made a CBE in 2007. **Hammer credits:** *Stolen Face* (1952, as Dr. Jack Wilson)

## Wood, Mary Laura

This British supporting actress (1924–1990) appeared in a handful of fifties and sixties second features, among them *Valley of Eagles* (1951), *Hour of Decision* (1957), *Escort for Hire* (1960), *Scent of Mystery* (1960) and *Fate Takes a Hand* (1962), plus the Hammer programer *Mantrap* (1953). Her TV work includes episodes of *BBC Sunday-Night Theatre* (1950–1959, TV), *Douglas Fairbanks, Jr. Presents* (1953–1957, TV) and *The Count of Monte Cristo* (1956, TV). Also on stage. **Hammer credits:** *Mantrap* (1953, as Susie Martin)

## Wood, Victoria

Wood can be seen as one of the wolf children in *Children of the Full Moon* (1980, TV [episode of

*Hammer House of Horror*]). Her other credits include an episode of *Mackenzie* (1980, TV). **Hammer credits:** *Children of the Full Moon* (1980, TV [episode of *Hammer House of Horror*], as Sophy)

## Woodbridge, George

A regular feature of Hammer films from the early fifties onwards, this rotund, gravel-voiced British supporting actor (1907–1973) began his film career with *Tower of Terror* (1941), which led to appearances in over one-hundred films and featurettes, among them *The Big Blockade* (1942), *The October Man* (1947), *An Inspector Calls* (1954), *Two-Way Stretch* (1960), *The Iron Maiden* (1962), *Where's Jack?* (1969), *Diamonds on Wheels* (1972) and *Along the Way* (1973). He made his Hammer debut with *Cloudburst* (1951), in which he played one of his most regular roles, that of a policeman, after which he went on to make a total of eleven appearances for the company in the likes of *Dracula* (1958), *The Mummy* (1959) and *The Reptile* (1966), frequently playing friendly yokels and landlords, although he was quite capable of playing darker roles, as per his vicious janitor in *The Revenge of Frankenstein* (1958).

Woodbridge ended his career playing Inigo Pipkin in the children's lunchtime serial *Inigo Pipkin* (1973, TV), which continued after his death as *Pipkins* (1973–1981, TV). His other TV work includes episodes of *Stryker of the Yard* (1957, TV), in which he played Sergeant Hawker, *No Hiding Place* (1959–1967, TV) and *You're Only Young Twice* (1971, TV).

It was Woodbridge who suggested to Anthony Hinds that Hammer might make a film about Rasputin, which eventually appeared as *Rasputin—The Mad Monk* (1966). Despite it being his suggestion, Woodbridge did not appear in the film. Jimmy Sangster described Woodbridge as "A very large, rotund, jovial man and one of those actors directors are so fond of in that he remembered his lines and didn't trip over the furniture."[52] He also appeared on stage from 1928. **Hammer credits:** *Cloudburst* (1951, as Sergeant Ritchie), *The Flanagan Boy* (1953, as Inspector), *Third Party Risk* (1954, as Inspector Goldfinch), *Day of Grace* (1957, as Mr. Kemp), *Dracula* (1958, as Landlord), *The Revenge of Frankenstein* (1958, as Janitor), *The Mummy* (1959, as Constable Blake), *Curse of the Werewolf* (1961, Dominique), *The Scarlet Blade* (1963, as Town Crier [uncredited]), *Dracula—Prince of Darkness* (1966, as Landlord), *The Reptile* (1966, as Old Garnsey)

## Woodhouse, Barbara

This Irish animal trainer (1910–1988, maiden name Barbara Kathleen Vera Blackburn) came to national attention in the UK for her TV series *Training Dogs the Woodhouse Way* (1980, TV), thanks to her eccentric personality and barked commands of "Sit!" and "Walkies!" Prior to her television fame, she provided and trained animals for films, among them a bearded collie named Jeanne of Bothkennar, which played Dan in the Hammer short *Day of Grace* (1957), and a Great Dane, which played the Hound from Hell in *The Hound of the Baskervilles* (1959). She also made a handful of shorts through her own production company, Woodhouse, among them *Sinner to Saint* (1959), which she produced and directed, *Trouble with Junia* (1966), which she wrote and produced, and *Along the Way* (1973), which she wrote and produced (the latter care of another production company named Junia, presumably after the Great Dane featured in *Trouble with Junia*). She also authored several books, among them *Difficult Dogs* (1957), *Almost Human* (1976), *No Bad Dogs* (1982) and *Barbara's World of Horses and Ponies: Their Care and Training the Woodhouse Way* (1984). **Hammer credits:** *Day of Grace* (1957 [uncredited]), *The Hound of the Baskervilles* (1959 [uncredited])

## Woodhouse, Hugh

This British writer (1934–2011) provided an unused synopsis for Hammer's abandoned *Tales of Frankenstein* television series in 1958. His film credits include *Nearly a Nasty Accident* (1961), *Dentist on the Job* (1961) and *Mystery Submarine* (1963), while his other TV work includes episodes of *Colonel Trumper's Private War* (1961, TV) and *Supercar* (1961–1962, TV).

## Woodiwiss, John

British born Woodiwiss (1909–1987) worked as the sound maintenance technician on a handful of films for Hammer in the mid-fifties. His other credits include *Miracle in Soho* (1957), on which he worked on the dubbing crew, and *Too Many Crooks* (1959), on which he was a sound recordist. He also worked on sound for episodes of *Melissa* (1964, TV), *Paul Temple* (1969–1971, TV) and *Doomwatch* (1970–1972, TV). **Hammer credits:** *Face the Music* (1954 [uncredited]), *The House Across the Lake* (1954 [uncredited]), *Break in the Circle* (1955 [uncredited]), *The Quatermass Xperiment* (1955 [uncredited])

## Woodnutt, John

This British supporting actor (1924–2006) can be seen as Lieutenant Wyatt in the Hammer swashbuckler *The Scarlet Blade* (1963). On stage from the age of eighteen, his other credits include *Inn for Trouble* (1960), *Oh! What a Lovely War* (1969) and *Who Dares Wins* (1982), plus much television work, including episodes of *ITV Play of the Week* (1955–1968, TV), *Callan* (1967–1972, TV), *Rogue's Gallery* (1968–1969, TV), *Crown Court* (1972–1984, TV), *Knightmare* (1987–1994, TV), in which he played Merlin, and *Jeeves and Wooster* (1990–1993, TV), in which he played Sir Watkyn Bassett. **Hammer credits:** *The Scarlet Blade* (1963, as Lieutenant Wyatt [uncredited])

## Woodpecker Productions, Ltd.

One of Hammer's many subsidiary companies, Woodpecker was created to finance the thriller *Cash on Demand* (1961). **Hammer credits:** *Cash on Demand* (1961)

## Woods, Karen

Woods worked as "assistant to producer" on all thirteen episodes of *Hammer House of Mystery and Suspense* (1984, TVM). She also worked on *The World of Hammer* (1990 [first broadcast 1994], TV), on which she is credited as being "for Hammer Films" along with Graham Skeggs and Wendy Smith. **Hammer credits:** *Hammer House of Mystery and Suspense* (1981, TVM, assistant to producer), *The World of Hammer* (1990 [first shown 1994], TV, "for Hammer Films")

## Woods, Middleton

This British supporting actor and entertainer (1886–1974) can be seen in minor roles in a handful of Hammer films in the fifties, including *The Curse of Frankenstein* (1957) and its sequel, *The Revenge of Frankenstein* (1958), albeit in different roles. His other credits include *The Man Who Wouldn't Talk* (1958), *Dead Man's Evidence* (1962) and *La spada del Cid* (1965), plus episodes of *The Adventures of Robin Hood* (1955–1960, TV), *Dixon of Dock Green* (1955–1976, TV) and *Gideon's Way* (1965–1966, TV). **Hammer credits:** *Whispering Smith Hits London* (1952, as Station porter), *The Curse of Frankenstein* (1957, as Lecturer), *The Revenge of Frankenstein* (1958, as Patient [uncredited]), *The Man Who Could Cheat Death* (1959, as Little man)

## Woods, Peter

Woods worked as the camera grip on three films for Hammer in the early seventies, and later returned to work on *Hammer House of Mystery and Suspense* (1984, TVM). His other credits include *Alien* (1979), on which he was the key grip for the effects unit. **Hammer credits:** *Scars of Dracula* (1970 [uncredited]), *The Horror of Frankenstein* (1970 [uncredited]), *Blood from the Mummy's Tomb* (1971 [uncredited]), *Hammer House of Mystery and Suspense* (1984, TVM [uncredited])

## Woods, William

Woods (1916–1998) provided the teleplay for *The Beckoning Fair One*, an episode of Hammer's *Journey to the Unknown* (1968, TV). His other credits include *Manuela* (1957), and episodes of *Armchair Theatre* (1956–1974, TV), *No Hiding Place* (1959–1967, TV) and *Suspense* (1962–1963, TV). He also penned the 1942 novel *The Edge of Darkness—A Novel of Occupied Norway*, which was filmed in 1943 as *Edge of Darkness*. **Hammer credits:** *The Beckoning Fair One* (1968, TV [episode of *Journey to the Unknown*])

## Woodthorpe, Peter

Best remembered for playing the corrupt hypnotist Professor Zoltan in Hammer's *The Evil of Frankenstein* (1964), this British character actor (1931–2004) came to films in 1963 with *Father Came Too* following stage and television experience from 1955. Much on stage on both sides of the Atlantic, his other film credits include *The Blue Max* (1966), *The Charge of the Light Brigade* (1968), *The Mirror Crack'd* (1980), *The Madness of King George* (1994) and *Jane Eyre* (1996). He also appeared in Hammer's *Hysteria* (1965) as the fashion photographer Marcus Allan. His TV work includes episodes of *The Adventures of Aggie* (1956–1957, TV), *Wagner* (1983, TV), *Inspector Morse* (1987–2000, TV) and *David Copperfield* (2000, TV). He also provided the voice of Gollum for the animated version of *The Lord of the Rings* (1978), as well as the 1981 BBC radio production, and Pigsy for *Monkey* (1978–1980, TV), the dubbed version of *Saiyuki*. **Hammer credits:** *The Evil of Frankenstein* (1964, as Professor Zoltan), *Hysteria* (1965, as Marcus Allan)

### Woodville, Catherine (Katherine)

On stage from the age of sixteen, and working in both Britain and America, this British actress (1938–2013) played the role of Elsa Connelly in Hammer's *The Brigand of Kandahar* (1965). Her other credits include *Clue of the New Pin* (1961), *The Party's Over* (1963), *The Crooked Road* (1964), *Black Gunn* (1972) and *Where's Willie?* (1978). Her TV work includes episodes of *The Avengers* (1961–1969, TV), *Star Trek* (1966–1969, TV), *Kung Fu* (1972–1975, TV), *Wonder Woman* (1976–1979, TV) and *Eight Is Enough* (1977–1981, TV). She went on to train and breed horses. Married three times, her husbands were actor Patrick Macnee (1922–2015, full name Daniel Patrick Macnee), to whom she was married between 1965 and 1969, and who appeared in Hammer's *Dick Barton at Bay* (1950), the director Jerrold Freeman (1941–) from 1970 to 1975, and actor Edward Albert (1951–2006, real name Edward Laurence Heimberger), from 1979. Her daughter (with Albert) is singer-songwriter and occasional actress Thais Albert (1980–). **Hammer credits:** *The Brigand of Kandahar* (1965, as Elsa Connelly)

### Woofe, Eric

This British actor (1930–2013) played the role of Henry de Courtenay in Hammer's *A Challenge for Robin Hood* (1967). His other credits include *Maddalena* (1971) plus episodes of *United* (1965–1967, TV), *Mr. Rose* (1967–1968, TV), *The Black Tulip* (1970, TV) and *The Strauss Family* (1972, TV). **Hammer credits:** *A Challenge for Robin Hood* (1967, as Henry de Courtenay)

### Woolf, Victor

This British actor (1911–1975) can be seen in a minor role in Hammer's *Frankenstein and the Monster from Hell* (1974). His other credits include *The Harvest Shall Come* (1942) and *The Two-Headed Spy* (1958), plus appearances in such TV plays and series as *Androcles and the Lion* (1946, TV), *Toad of Toad Hall* (1946, TV), *The Adventures of Robin Hood* (1955–1960, TV), in which he played Derwent, *The Prisoner* (1967–1968, TV) and *Ooh La La!* (1968–1973, TV). **Hammer credits:** *Frankenstein and the Monster from Hell* (1974, as Lotch)

### Woolf, Vicki

This British actress (1942–) can be seen as the landlord's daughter in Hammer's *The Vampire Lovers* (1970). She can also be spotted in *Hands of the Ripper* (1971) as a whore. Her other credits include *The Hands of Orlac* (1960), *Jeri Boy* (1966), *Carry On… Up the Khyber* (1968), *Some Will, Some Won't* (1969), *The Great Waltz* (1972) and *Confessions of a Pop Performer* (1975), plus episodes of *Sir Francis Drake* (1961–1962, TV), *Wodehouse Playhouse* (1975–1978, TV), *Minder* (1979–1994, TV) and *Three Up, Two Down* (1985–1989, TV). **Hammer credits:** *The Vampire Lovers* (1970, as Landlord's daughter [uncredited]), *Hands of the Ripper* (1971, as Second cell whore)

### Wooll, Nigel

British born Wooll (1941–) began his career as a third assistant director, working on such films as *Carry On Spying* (1964), *The Intelligence Men* (1965), *Funeral in Berlin* (1966), *Deadfall* (1968) and two films for Hammer. He became a second assistant on *Some Girls Do* (1969) and a first assistant on *The Kremlin Letter* (1970). He later worked as a production manager on *The Prince and the Pauper* (1977), on which he was also the first assistant director, *Force Ten from Navarone* (1978), *Yanks* (1979), *Reds* (1981), *Krull* (1983), *Patriot Games* (1992) and *Miss Potter* (2006), the latter of which he also executive produced. He also worked as an associate producer on *The Dresser* (1983), *Ishtar* (1987) and *Jasmine's Revolution* (2013), as a co-producer on *Shining Through* (1992), as a line producer on *W.E.* (2011), as a producer on *Year of the Comet* (1992) and *The Hatching* (2014), and as an executive producer on *Son of the Pink Panther* (1993) and *Admissible Evidence* (2010). **Hammer credits:** *Fanatic* (1965 [uncredited]), *Slave Girls* (1968 [uncredited])

### Woolner, L.R.

Woolner was one on the board of directors of Bray Studios between 1958 and 1964. He joined Hammer's board of directors in 1959, via their subsidiary company Falcon.

### Woolrich, Cornell

This American mystery writer (1903–1968, full name Cornell George Hopley-Woolrich, aka William Irish and George Hopley) has had a number of his novels and stories adapted for the cinema, among them *Convicted* (1938 [from *Face Work*]), *Street of Chance* (1942 [from *The Black Curtain*]), *The Leopard Man* (1943 [from *Black Alibi*]), *Fall Guy* (1947 [from *Cocaine*]), *Rear Window* (1954 and 1998, TVM), *The Bride Wore Black* (1967), *Mrs. Winterbourne* (1994 [from *I Married a Dead Man*]) and *Original Sin* (2001 [from *Waltz into Darkness*]). His stories have also proved popular on television in such anthology series as *The Ford Television Theatre* (1952–1957, TV), *Alfred Hitchcock Presents* (1955–1962, TV), *Thriller* (1960–1962, TV), *The Alfred Hitchcock Hour* (1962–1965, TV) and Hammer's *Journey to the Unknown* (1968, TV), which featured his story *Jane Brown's Body*. His wife was the actress Violet Virginia Blackton (1910–1965, aka Violet Blackton), to whom he was married between 1930 and 1933. **Hammer credits:** *Jane Brown's Body* (1968, TV [episode of *Journey to the Unknown*])

### Wordsworth, Richard

The great-great grandson of the poet Wordsworth, this British character actor (1915–1993) made his screen debut as the doomed astronaut Victor Carroon in Hammer's breakthrough film *The Quatermass Xperiment* (1955). Wordsworth's played the role entirely in mime, drawing on years of theater experience (he was on stage from the age of twenty-three and was noted for his work in Shakespeare), yet despite the increasingly monstrous contortions Carroon's body undergoes, he manages to retain our sympathy for the character's plight throughout the film. Recalled the movie's director, Val Guest, "Richard Wordsworth's wordless performance as the astronaut has a great deal of sensitivity. I thought he had a very fine face for the film—sort of ethereal. He always said that his first shot in any film was in a space suit, opening the door of a crashed rocket and having fourteen hoses directed at him!"[53]

Although he made several more films, including another three for Hammer, Wordsworth will forever be remembered for his work as Carroon ("That film has been with me ever since," he commented in a *Radio Times* interview in 1972), although his emaciated Dr. Keiller in the POW drama *The Camp on Blood Island* (1958) and his

**Richard Wordsworth and his "cactus" arm are the focus of this well-rendered Italian poster for *The Quatermass Xperiment* (1955) (Hammer/Concanen/Lippert/Exclusive/United Artists).**

slavering beggar from *The Curse of the Werewolf* (1961) are also pretty memorable. Commented director Val Guest of Wordsworth's performance in the POW film, "Again, he looked right, with his thin, gaunt appearance. He looked as if he has been in a Japanese prison camp."[54] Meanwhile, of his experiences on *The Curse of the Werewolf*, Wordsworth recalled, "Just before shooting, I had to come down to London to get fitted for fangs. When I got to the studio nobody seemed to know anything about it. Anyway, I finally found someone who knew and he said, 'Oh, no—no fangs. The censor says no fangs. You can have either the fangs or relations with the girl but not both.' Well, Oliver Reed had to be born, so we had to choose relations with the girl."[55]

Wordsworth's other credits include *The Man Who Knew Too Much* (1956), *Time Without Pity* (1957), *The Moving Toyshop* (1964), *Lock Up Your Daughters!* (1969) and *Song of Norway* (1970), while on television he appeared in episodes of *R3* (1964, TV), *The Regiment* (1972, TV) and *Campion* (1989–1990, TV). Mostly on stage, his many appearances included a one-man show about his great-great grandfather titled *The Bliss of Solitude*. Remembered the actor of his time with Hammer, "I've worked in quite a few Hammer films and always enjoyed it."[56] **Additional notes:** Though Wordsworth made his official film debut in *The Quatermass Xperiment*, he had already appeared as an extra in *Caesar and Cleopatra* (1945) along with future Dick Barton star Don Stannard. According to the film's production co-ordinator Renee Glynne, who went on to become Hammer's most prolific continuity girl, the duo "were listed on the call-sheet as 'Caesar's Geezers.'"[57] **Hammer credits:** *The Quatermass Xperiment* (1955, as Victor Carroon), *The Camp on Blood Island* (1958, as Dr. Keiller), *The Revenge of Frankenstein* (1958, as Up Patient), *The Curse of the Werewolf* (1961, as Beggar)

## Workman, John

One of Hammer production managers, British born Workman (1920–1973) inherited the post from Jimmy Sangster on *Quatermass 2* (1957). His other credits include *The Little Ballerina* (1948), *It's a Great Day* (1955), *The Naked Truth* (1957), *Seventy Deadly Pills* (1964) and *The Body Stealers* (1969), plus episodes of *The Adventures of Aggie* (1956–1957, TV) and *The Third Man* (1959–1965, TV). **Hammer credits:** *Quatermass 2* (1957), *The Steel Bayonet* (1957)

## The World of Hammer

GB, 1990 [first broadcast 1994], 13x25m, color, TV

By 1990, Hammer had seemingly ground to a halt. Despite Roy Skeggs' best efforts to launch a series of projects, finance just wasn't forthcoming, and the company lay dormant production-wise, not having actually made anything since *Hammer House of Mystery and Suspense* (1984, TVM), which had been some six years earlier. Consequently, Skeggs decided to raise Hammer's profile by agreeing to this series of clip shows that would present the studio's rich past in all its glory, and hopefully drum up some new business in the process.

Made in conjunction with Best of British Film and Television (which was a Media Investments PLC company), the series was to use the same format as the long-running *Best of British* (1987–1994, TV), which had clocked up an amazing 57 twenty-five-minute episodes chronicling the highlights of British cinema. This format had been created by Ashley Sidaway, Robert Sidaway, Maurice Sellar and Lou Jones, who between them wrote the scripts and produced the shows, which were narrated by British cinema stalwart John Mills. The Sidaways would re-use the template for *The World of Hammer*, which would offer an overview of the studio's legendary archive via a series of thirteen twenty-five-minute programs, each of which would be themed, concentrating on such topics as Dracula, sci-fi and chillers. To narrate the series, Oliver Reed, who had launched his career at Hammer, returned to do the honors, while Brian Bennett provided the sweeping theme tune, although James Bernard's famous Dracula motif actually opens the credits, being the Hammer equivalent of MGM's roaring lion or the James Bond gun barrel (this brief sting was actually lifted from the soundtrack of *Dracula A.D. 1972* [1972]).

The results are a very mixed bag, given that little or no production history is relayed in the narration. Indeed, the be all and end all of the show is the selection of clips themselves, which, aside from the very occasional exception, are presented in the standard 4:3 format, thus robbing the photography of its widescreen framing and resulting in some cropped close-ups. That said, the majority of the clips are well chosen and in good condition, save for those from *Dracula* (1958), which look grainy and suffer from a number of unfortunate clicks and sputters on the soundtrack. The main title montage (repeated at the end) is nicely put together, however, and features clips from such films as *The Quatermass Xperiment* (1955), *The Mummy* (1959), *The Brides of Dracula* (1960), *The Kiss of the Vampire* (1963), *She* (1965), *One Million Years B.C.* (1966), *Dracula—Prince of Darkness* (1966), *Dracula Has Risen from the Grave* (1968), *The Anniversary* (1968) and *Frankenstein and the Monster from Hell* (1974), among others. The credits' striking-looking typeface is meanwhile nicely done in the style of *The Brides of Dracula*, and opens with the statement, "Roy Skeggs Presents for Hammer Films—A Hammer Film Production."

Sadly, little interest was shown in the series, which also took care to display Hammer's non-genre fare, including their war films and costumers. In fact the show lay on the shelf for an incredible four years before Channel Four decided to air it in the UK in 1994 in a late night slot. **Additional notes:** Sadly, the series does not feature any interviews or behind the scenes material. It was originally planned as a twenty-six-episode series. Program titles that went by the wayside include *Comedy*, *Pursuers and Pursued: Chase and Detection*, *Radio and Television Spin-Offs*, *Henchmen*, *The Supernatural*, *The Occult and Demonology*, *Carmilla and Other Female Vampires*, *Good v Evil: The Church in Hammer Films*, *Hammer in the Far East* and *In the Family: Studies of Family Life*.

The series' episode-to-episode credits are as follows:

Production companies: Best of British Film and Television Productions/Media Investments PLC/Hammer. Producer: Robert Sidaway. Presented by: Roy Skeggs. Executive producer: John Thompson. Written and created by: Ashley Sidaway, Robert Sidaway. Narrator: Oliver Reed. Title theme: Brian Bennett. Series editor: Ashley Sidaway. On line editor: Mike Peatfield. Assistant editors: Amanda Jenks, Alyssa Osment. Sound: Paul Hamilton. Production assistant: Caroline Beecham. Production manager: Evan M. Jones. Production Secretary: Joanne Atkins. For Hammer Films: Graham Skeggs, Karen Woods, Wendy Smith. Post production: Sound Development Studios, Fountain Television, Tvi. Film archivists: John Herron, Steve Rickerby, Mike Dragesic, Steve Leroux. Best of British format created by: Ashley Sidaway, Maurice Sellar, Robert Sidaway, Lou Jones

The episodes are:

### Hammer Stars: Peter Cushing

This program pays tribute to the much-loved Cushing, presenting clips of his work as Van Helsing and Baron Frankenstein, as well as his roles in other films, among them Sherlock Holmes. Here, the clips hail from *The Curse of Frankenstein* (1957), *The Abominable Snowman* (1957), *The Hound of the Baskervilles* (1959), *The Mummy* (1959), *The Brides of Dracula* (1960), *She* (1965), *Twins of Evil* (1971), *Fear in the Night* (1972) and *Frankenstein and the Monster from Hell* (1974). First broadcast 12 August 1994.

### Dracula and the Undead

A fairly self-explanatory episode, this program features clips from *Dracula* (1958), *The Brides of Dracula* (1960), *The Kiss of the Vampire* (1963), *Dracula—Prince of Darkness* (1966), *Scars of Dracula* (1970), *Captain Kronos—Vampire Hunter* (1974) and *The Legend of the 7 Golden Vampires* (1974). Note that *The Kiss of the Vampire* is mentioned as being a 1964 production in the narration, but is credited as being made in 1962 in the end credits. Likewise, *Dracula—Prince of Darkness* is mentioned as being a 1966 production in the narration, but 1965 in the end credits. There are several other such inconsistencies throughout the series. First broadcast 19 August 1994.

### Lands Before Time

Another self-explanatory episode, this time featuring clips from *One Million Years B.C.* (1966), *She* (1965), *The Viking Queen* (1967), *The Vengeance of She* (1968), *Slave Girls* (1968), *The Lost Continent* (1968), *Blood from the Mummy's Tomb* (1971) and *Creatures the World Forgot* (1971). First broadcast 26 August 1994.

### Vamp

A look at the female vampire in Hammer films, featuring clips from *Dracula* (1958), *The Kiss of the Vampire* (1963), *The Brides of Dracula* (1960), *The Vampire Lovers* (1970), *Lust for a Vampire* (1970), *Twins of Evil* (1971) and *Captain Kronos—Vampire Hunter* (1974). Interestingly, the narration does not distinguish the Karsteins in *Captain Kronos—Vampire Hunter* from the Karnsteins in *The Vampire Lovers* and its sequels. First broadcast 1 September 1994.

### Wicked Women

Evil women are the focus of this episode, with examples taken from the studio's non-genre output as well as their horror films. To this end, the performances of Bette Davis, Tallulah Bankhead and Lizabeth Scott are featured, along with the likes of Kay Walsh and Ingrid Pitt. Note that following the opening titles, the program features additional new music over the opening selection of clips; this was presumably composed by Brian Bennett, who provided the theme tune, but there is no mention of this in the credits. Clips featured are from *The Black Widow* (1950), *Stolen Face* (1952), *The Nanny* (1965), *Fanatic* (1965), *The Witches* (1966), *The Anniversary* (1968), *Countess Dracula* (1970) and *Dr. Jekyll and Sister Hyde* (1971). First broadcast 9 September 1994.

### Trials of War

Its horror films aside, Hammer has covered a wide variety of other subjects, and this episode examines its war films, which have featured stories dealing with combat, prisoner of war camps, bomb disposal and post-war espionage. The studio has also dealt with the lighter side of conflict with a number of comedies, which are also featured. Clips hail from *Break in the Circle* (1955), *The Steel Bayonet* (1957), *The Camp on Blood Island* (1958), *Up the Creek* (1958), *Further Up the Creek* (1958), *I Only Arsked!* (1958), *Ten Seconds to Hell* (1959), *Yesterday's Enemy* (1959), *The Secret of Blood Island* (1965) and *The Lady Vanishes* (1979). Note that *Yesterday's Enemy* is mistakenly listed as *Yesterdays Enemies* in the end credit roll. First broadcast 16 September 1994.

### Sci-Fi

Hammer of course had its big breakthrough with science fiction, and this episode tracks the company's connections with the genre, taking in the adventures of Dick Barton and, inevitably, Professor Bernard Quatermass. Clips are taken from *Dick Barton Strikes Back* (1949), *Spaceways* (1953), *The Quatermass Xperiment* (1955), *X—The Unknown* (1956), *Quatermass 2* (1957), *The Damned* (1963), *Frankenstein Created Woman* (1967) and *Quatermass and the Pit* (1967). Note that Oliver Reed at one point refers to *The Quatermast Xperiment!* First broadcast 23 September 1994.

### Mummies, Werewolves and the Living Dead

Again, the title pretty much says it all. This episode contains clips from *The Mummy* (1959), *The Curse of the Werewolf* (1961), *Captain Clegg* (1962), *The Curse of the Mummy's Tomb* (1964), *The Plague of the Zombies* (1966), *The Mummy's Shroud* (1967), *Blood from the Mummy's Tomb* (1971) and *The Legend of the 7 Golden Vampires* (1974). Of course, the marsh phantoms seen in *Captain Clegg* prove to be far from supernatural— a point the program fails to relay. First broadcast 30 September 1994.

### Chiller

Like the program dedicated to Hammer's war films, this one looks at another aspect of the studio's output, the chiller, though *Thriller* might

have been a better title given the mix of films featured (in fact the IMDb features artwork for the episode under the title *Thriller*). This time the back catalogue takes in *Whispering Smith Hits London* (1952), *The Last Page* (1952), *Hell Is a City* (1960), *Taste of Fear* (1961), *Maniac* (1963), *Paranoiac* (1963), *Straight on Till Morning* (1972), *Shatter* (1974) and *Czech Mate* (1984, TVM [episode of *Hammer House of Mystery and Suspense*]). First broadcast 7 October 1994.

### The Curse of Frankenstein

This episode is devoted to the exploits of Baron Frankenstein, yet takes care to include a clip from *Four Sided Triangle* (1953), which ventured into the same territory. Interestingly, there are no clips included from *Frankenstein Must Be Destroyed* (1969), nor, for that matter, *Tales of Frankenstein: The Face in the Tombstone Mirror* (1958, TV), although selections from all the other films in the series are featured, including *The Curse of Frankenstein* (1957), *The Revenge of Frankenstein* (1958), *The Evil of Frankenstein* (1964), *Frankenstein Created Woman* (1967), *The Horror of Frankenstein* (1970) and *Frankenstein and the Monster from Hell* (1974). The narration claims that the only time the role of Frankenstein was played by an actor other than Peter Cushing was when Ralph Bates essayed the part in *The Horror of Frankenstein*, though this isn't strictly accurate, given that Anton Diffring played the character in *Tales of Frankenstein* (one might also argue that Melvyn Hayes played him in *The Curse of Frankenstein*, albeit in his younger form). Note that instead of the usual typeface for the program's title, it instead uses the opening explanatory caption (read by Oliver Reed) and title card from *The Curse of Frankenstein*. First broadcast 14 October 1994.

### Hammer Stars: Christopher Lee

This program examines the work of Hammer's other top star, Christopher Lee, and displays the actor's versatility above and beyond his signature role of Dracula. This time the clips are from *The Curse of Frankenstein* (1957), *Dracula* (1958), *The Hound of the Baskervilles* (1959), *The Mummy* (1959), *The Devil-Ship Pirates* (1964), *She* (1965), *Dracula—Prince of Darkness* (1966), *Rasputin—The Mad Monk* (1966), *The Devil Rides Out* (1968), *Scars of Dracula* (1970) and *To the Devil a Daughter* (1976). First broadcast 21 October 1994.

### Hammer

A potted history of the studio, but lacking any real history—just the expected parade of clips, which this time are taken from *Cloudburst* (1951), *Men of Sherwood Forest* (1954), *Quatermass 2* (1957), *The Curse of Frankenstein* (1957), *The Steel Bayonet* (1957), *The Camp on Blood Island* (1958), *Dracula* (1958), *The Nanny* (1965), *The Plague of the Zombies* (1966), *One Million Years B.C.* (1966), *Quatermass and the Pit* (1967), *That's Your Funeral* (1973) and *Holiday on the Buses* (1973). Note that the narration erroneously claims that *Holiday on the Buses* was made in 1970. No mention is made of the studio's beginnings in the thirties, or of its founding board members. First broadcast 28 October 1994.

### Costumers

Like *Trials of War* and *Chiller*, this program examines Hammer's many costume dramas, among them several of its Robin Hood adventures, including *Wolfshead: The Legend of Robin Hood* (1969), which is a Hammer film by proxy (the company bought the film, which was made by other hands, though it wasn't shown unit 1973). The other clips are taken from *Dick Turpin—Highwayman* (1956), *The Stranglers of Bombay* (1959), *Sword of Sherwood Forest* (1960), *The Pirates of Blood River* (1963), *The Scarlet Blade* (1963), *The Devil-Ship Pirates* (1964), *The Brigand of Kandahar* (1965), which Oliver Reed admits to being his worst film in the narration, and *A Challenge for Robin Hood* (1967). Note that *Wolfshead: The Legend of Robin Hood* is simply credited as *Wolfshead* in the end scroll. First broadcast 4 November 1994. **DVD availability:** DD Home Entertainment (UK R2 PAL); extras include a stills gallery

## Worth (London) Ltd.

The London branch of the House of Worth, this fashion house is credited for providing the "production facilities" for the Hammer thriller *Blood Orange* (1953). The business was established in Paris in 1858 by Charles Frederick Worth (1825–1895), who is said to be the father of *haute couture*, and who did much to revolutionize the fashion industry (he was the first person to use live models and to sew brand labels into his garments). The company went on to have shops in Biarritz and Cannes. It ceased to trade in 1956, but the brand was revived in 1999. **Hammer credits:** *Blood Orange* (1953)

## Worth, Brian

In films from the late thirties, this British actor (1914–1978) appeared in such productions as *Ask a Policeman* (1938), *The Arsenal Stadium Mystery* (1939), *The Lion Has Wings* (1939), *Cardboard Cavalier* (1949), *The Battle of the River Plate* (1956), *Ill Met by Moonlight* (1956), *On Her Majesty's Secret Service* (1969) and *The Boy Who Turned Yellow* (1972). He also played Harcourt in Hammer's *The Terror of the Tongs* (1961). His TV work includes episodes of *Douglas Fairbanks, Jr. Presents* (1953–1957, TV), *The Buccaneers* (1956–1957, TV), *Quatermass and the Pit* (1958–1959, TV) and *The Protectors* (1972–1974, TV). He retired from acting to run a Spanish restaurant in London called La Parra, while during the war, his fluency in Spanish saw him head the Spanish section in the Special Operations Executive between 1941 and 1946. **Hammer credits:** *The Terror of the Tongs* (1961, as Harcourt)

## Worth, Martin

Worth penned the teleplay for *A Distant Scream* (1984, TVM [episode of *Hammer House of Mystery and Suspense*]). This was based on his 1971 teleplay *The Last Witness*, which had originally been written for the anthology series *Out of the Unknown* (1965–1971, TV). His other credits for television include episodes of *Douglas Fairbanks, Jr. Presents* (1953–1957, TV), *William Tell* (1958–1959, TV), *Public Eye* (1965–1975, TV), *Doomwatch* (1970–1972,

TV), *The Onedin Line* (1971–1980, TV), *Heidi* (1974, TV), *Survivors* (1975–1977, TV), *Poldark* (1975–1977, TV) and *C.A.T.S. Eyes* (1985–1987, TV). **Hammer credits:** *A Distant Scream* (1984, TVM [episode of *Hammer House of Mystery and Suspense*])

### Woxholt, Egil

This noted Norwegian second unit cameraman and underwater specialist (1926–1991) helped to photograph the impressive alpine action sequences for the James Bond epic *On Her Majesty's Secret Service* (1969). Starting as a second unit operator on *Miranda* (1948), he also worked as a clapper loader on *The Happiest Days of Your Life* (1950), as the underwater camera operator on *The Silent Enemy* (1958), the underwater photographer on *Mysterious Island* (1961), the second unit camera operator on *Thunderball* (1965), the underwater photographer on *Captain Nemo and the Underwater City* (1969), the additional photographer on *The Call of the Wild* (1972), the second unit camera operator on *Greystoke: The Legend of Tarzan, Lord of the Apes* (1984), and the additional photographer on *A View to a Kill* (1985). He also worked on Hammer's *Taste of Fear* (1961) for which (with John Jordan) he photographed the atmospheric underwater swimming pool sequences. Other credits include *The Heroes of Telemark* (1965) and *Baby: Secret of the Lost Legend* (1985), on both of which he was the second unit director and second unit camera operator. He also photographed the effects for the television series *War and Remembrance* (1988, TV), which earned him a shared Emmy for best special effects. His sister was actress Greta Gynt (1916–2000, real name Margrethe Woxholt, aka Greta Woxholt), who appeared in Hammer's *Whispering Smith Hits London* (1952) and *The Runaway* (1964). **Hammer credits:** *Taste of Fear* (1961 [uncredited])

### Wozniak, Daniel

Wozniak had a minor supporting role that sees him assassinated in the opening moments of *Czech Mate* (1984, TVM [episode of *Hammer House of Mystery and Suspense*]). His other credits include episodes of *Polskie drogie* (1977, TV), *Dom* (1980–2000, TV) and *The Paradise Club* (1989–1990, TV). His occasional films include *They Never Slept* (1990), *The Russia House* (1990) and *The Waiting Time* (1999, TVM). He also wrote, directed, produced, photographed and narrated the documentary *Siestas and Olas: A Surfing Journey Through Mexico* (1997). **Hammer credits:** *Czech Mate* (1984, TVM [episode of *Hammer House of Mystery and Suspense*], as Man on bridge)

### Wragg, Bob

As a member of The Dallas Boys, Wragg performed the title song for the Hammer comedy *Watch It, Sailor!* (1961). His appearances with the group include spots on such shows as *Six-Five Special* (1957–1958, TV), *Oh Boy!* (1958–1959, TV), *International Cabaret* (1966–1978, TV) and *Saturday Variety* (1972, TV). **Hammer credits:** *Watch It, Sailor!* (1961)

### Wrather, Edgar

Wrather worked as the stills cameraman on two

films for Hammer. **Hammer credits:** *Dr. Morelle—The Case of the Missing Heiress* (1949 [uncredited]), *The Adventures of PC 49–The Case of the Guardian Angel* (1949 [uncredited])

### Wreford, Denis

Working for Hammer in the late forties/early fifties, this art director and occasional production designer (1905–1988) designed the sets for such low budget programers *Celia* (1949) and *Room to Let* (1950), which were filmed in the cramped confines of Dial Close and Oakley Court respectively. His other credits include *The Grand Escape* (1946), *Nothing Venture* (1948), *Make Me An Offer* (1954), *The Diamond* (1954), *The Heart Within* (1957) and *Make Mine a Million* (1965), plus episodes of *The Dickie Henderson Half-Hour* (1958–1959, TV), *Gert and Daisy* (1959, TV) and *Guy Operetta* (1959, TV). **Hammer credits:** *Celia* (1949), *Meet Simon Cherry* (1949), *The Man in Black* (1950), *Room to Let* (1950), *Someone at the Door* (1950), *What the Butler Saw* (1950)

### Wren, Joyce

This British supporting actress (1913–2005) played a nurse in Hammer's *The Two Faces of Dr. Jekyll* (1960). A noted puppeteer, she worked in this capacity on such series as *Spyder's Web* (1972, TV), *Cloppa Castle* (1978–1979, TV) and *The Munch Bunch* (1980, TV). Her other acting credits include an episode of *Armchair Theatre* (1956–1974, TV). **Hammer credits:** *The Two Faces of Dr. Jekyll* (1960, as Nurse [uncredited])

### Wren, Richard

Wren had a minor supporting role in *Carpathian Eagle* (1980, TV [episode of *Hammer House of Horror*]). His big screen credits include *The Wicker Man* (1973), *Escort Girls* (1974), *The Eagle Has Landed* (1976), *Bear Island* (1979) and *Yellowbeard* (1983), while his other TV work includes episodes of *Wings* (1977–1978, TV), *The Strange Affair of Adelaide Harris* (1979, TV) and *Kessler* (1981, TV). **Hammer credits:** *Carpathian Eagle* (1980, TV [episode of *Hammer House of Horror*], as Rowley [chauffeur])

### Wrenn, Lawrence

Wrenn was Hammer's master painter from the mid-fifties onwards, and as such he supervised the painting of the sets for such major productions as *Dracula* (1958), *The Hound of the Baskervilles* (1959) and *The Mummy* (1959). Recalled art director Don Mingaye of Wrenn's talents, "If we needed, as we sometimes did, a stained glass window, he would do it. If we had to produce a teak door or a teak bar or marble work, he would do it. If he marbled a fireplace, you would have an awful job just looking at it to say it wasn't marble."[58] **Hammer credits include:** *The Camp on Blood Island* (1958 [uncredited]), *Dracula* (1958 [uncredited]), *The Revenge of Frankenstein* (1958 [uncredited]), *The Hound of the Baskervilles* (1959 [uncredited]), *The Ugly Duckling* (1959 [uncredited]), *The Mummy* (1959 [uncredited]), *The Man Who Could Cheat Death* (1959 [uncredited]), *The Stranglers of Bombay* (1959 [uncredited]), *Never Take Sweets from a Stranger* (1960 [uncredited]), *The Two Faces*

*of Dr. Jekyll* (1960 [uncredited]), *The Curse of the Werewolf* (1961 [uncredited]), *The Terror of the Tongs* (1961 [uncredited]), *The Shadow of the Cat* (1961 [uncredited]), *Cash on Demand* (1961 [uncredited]), *The Phantom of the Opera* (1962 [uncredited]), *Captain Clegg* (1962 [uncredited]), *The Pirates of Blood River* (1962 [uncredited]), *Paranoiac* (1963 [uncredited]), *The Damned* (1963 [uncredited]), *The Scarlet Blade* (1963 [uncredited]), *The Kiss of the Vampire* (1963 [uncredited]), *The Old Dark House* (1963 [uncredited]), *Nightmare* (1964 [uncredited]), *The Evil of Frankenstein* (1964 [uncredited]), *The Devil-Ship Pirates* (1964 [uncredited]), *The Gorgon* (1964 [uncredited])

### Wrenn, Trevor

British born Wrenn (1936–) worked as one of the two focus pullers on the Hammer thriller *Maniac* (1963), the other being Tommy Fletcher. His other credits include *I'm All Right Jack* (1959), on which he was the clapper loader, and *Play Dirty* (1968), on which he was the second camera operator. He went on to become a cinematographer, working on such films as *Scream and Die!* (1973), *Gollocks! There's Plenty of Room in New Zealand* (1973) and *Symptoms* (1974). He also directed *Erotic Inferno* (1975). **Hammer credits:** *Maniac* (1963 [uncredited])

### Wrigg, Ann

British born Wrigg (1915–2004) played the role of Miss Payne in *Stranger in the Family*, an episode of Hammer's *Journey to the Unknown* (1968, TV). Her film credits include *Counterspy* (1953), *The Painted Smile* (1962) and *The Ghost Goes Gear* (1966), while her other TV work includes episodes of *Suspense* (1962–1963, TV), *Hadleigh* (1969–1976, TV) and *Angels* (1975–1983, TV). **Hammer credits:** *Stranger in the Family* (1968, TV [episode of *Journey to the Unknown*], as Miss Payne)

### Wright, George

Wright worked as a driver on Hammer's *Blood from the Mummy's Tomb* (1971). **Hammer credits:** *Blood from the Mummy's Tomb* (1971 [uncredited])

### Wright, Julia

Wright played the pub singer in Hammer's *Dr. Jekyll and Sister Hyde* (1971), in which she performed the Brian Clemens-penned ditty *He'll Be There*, though her vocals were actually provided on the soundtrack by Jackie Lee. Her other credits include *Oh! What a Lovely War* (1969) and *Private Road* (1971). **Hammer credits:** *Dr. Jekyll and Sister Hyde* (1971, as Singer)

### Wright, Leslie

This British (Scottish) actor played supporting roles *Five Days* (1954) and *Third Party Risk* (1955) for Hammer. His other credits include episodes of *Puck of Pook's Hill* (1951, TV), *Z Cars* (1962–1968, TV) and *Suspense* (1962–1963, TV). He soon after moved to Australia, where he went on to appear in episodes of *Adventures of the Seaspray* (1965–1967, TV), *Skyways* (1979–1981, TV), *Prisoner* (1979–1986, TV) and *Sons and Daughters* (1982–1987, TV), as well as such occasional films as *Harlequin* (1980), *Shame* (1988) and *Blackfellas* (1993).

**Hammer credits:** *Five Days* (1954, as Hunter), *Third Party Risk* (1955, as Sergeant Ramirez [uncredited])

### Wright, Maggie

This British supporting actress (1944–) played a tart in Hammer's *Rasputin—The Mad Monk* (1966). Her other credits include *Goldfinger* (1964), *What's New Pussycat?* (1965), *Hammerhead* (1968), *One More Time* (1970), *Side by Side* (1975), *Joseph Andrews* (1977) and *Scrubbers* (1983), plus a return to Hammer for a featured role in *Twins of Evil* (1971). Her TV work includes episodes of *Gideon's Way* (1965–1966, TV), *Jason King* (1971–1972, TV) and *Robin's Nest* (1977–1981, TV). Also on stage, notably in a 1968 production of *Faustus*, in which she was the first actress to appear fully nude in a legitimate British stage production. She later moved to the Far East to run a bar, *Maggie's Tree*, in Phuket. **Hammer credits:** *Rasputin—The Mad Monk* (1966, as Tart [uncredited]), *Twins of Evil* (1971, as Alexa)

### Wright, Tony

Initially on stage in South Africa following experience as a whaler (!), this beefy British actor (1925–1986) got his big break playing the title role in Hammer's boxing melodrama *The Flanagan Boy* (1953). He subsequently went on to appear in such features as *Jumping for Joy* (1956), *Broth of a Boy* (1959), *Journey into Nowhere* (1962), *The Liquidator* (1965), *All Coppers Are…* (1972), *The Creeping Flesh* (1972) and *Can I Come Too?* (1979), albeit it increasingly minor roles. He also popped up in episodes of *Colonel March of Scotland Yard* (1954–1956, TV), *The Saint* (1962–1969, TV), *The Jensen Code* (1973, TV), *Follow Me* (1977, TV) and *Into the Labyrinth* (1981–1982, TV). Between acting jobs he worked as a sales rep for the *South Londoner* Group of Newspapers in the late sixties/early seventies. Wright's father was the actor and screenwriter Hugh E. Wright (1879–1940). He was married to the actress Janet Munro (1934–1972, real name Janet Neilson Horsburgh) between 1956 and 1959; her father, the comedian Alex Munro (1911–1986, real name Alexander Neilson Horsburgh), later had a brief role in Hammer's *Holiday on the Buses* (1973), while her second husband, the actor Ian Hendry (1931–1984), to whom she was married between 1963 and 1971, appeared in Hammer's *Captain Kronos—Vampire Hunter* (1974). **Hammer credits:** *The Flanagan Boy* (1953, as Johnny Flanagan)

### Wu, Li

Wu handled the props for Hammer's *The Legend of the 7 Golden Vampires* (1974). His other credits include *Chou lian huan* (1972) and *Wu du* (1978). **Hammer credits:** *The Legend of the 7 Golden Vampires* (1974)

### Wyer, Reg (Reginald)

During his busy career, this British cinematographer (1901–1970) lensed a wide variety of films, among them *So Long at the Fair* (1950), *Operation Amsterdam* (1959), *Carry On Teacher* (1959), *Dentist in the Chair* (1961), *The Fast Lady* (1963) and *Rocket to the Moon* (1967), plus several atmo-

spheric horror films, including *Night of the Eagle* (1962), *Unearthly Stranger* (1963), *Devils of Darkness* (1965), *Island of Terror* (1966) and *Night of the Big Heat* (1967). In films from 1918 as an operator, he began photographing documentaries during World War II for the Ministry of Information. He made his feature debut with *The Seventh Veil* (1945), by which time he had also co-produced one film, *The Unholy Quest* (1934), and co-written another, *Men of Rochdale* (1944). He also photographed five films for Hammer, beginning with *Never Look Back* (1952). **Hammer credits:** *Never Look Back* (1952), *Mantrap* (1953), *Four Sided Triangle* (1953), *Spaceways* (1953), *The Brigand of Kandahar* (1965)

### Wyeth, Katya

This British actress (1948–, sometimes Kathja Wyeth) can be seen as a pub whore in Hammer's *Hands of the Ripper* (1971), following which she was elevated to the role of Countess Mircalla in *Twins of Evil* (1971), a part previously played by Ingrid Pitt in *The Vampire Lovers* (1970) and Yutte Stensgaard in *Lust for a Vampire* (1970). Wyeth's other credits include *Inspector Clouseau* (1968), *A Clockwork Orange* (1971), *Confessions of a Window Cleaner* (1974), *I'm Not Feeling Myself Tonight* (1976) and *No. 1 of the Secret Service* (1978), plus a return to Hammer for a featured role in *Straight on Till Morning* (1972), in which she plays a shop assistant who is brutally slain with a Stanley knife. Her TV work includes episodes of *The Avengers* (1961–1969, TV), *Dead of Night* (1972, TV) and *Space: 1999* (1975–1977, TV). **Hammer credits:** *Hands of the Ripper* (1971, as First pub whore), *Twins of Evil* (1971, as Countess Mircalla), *Straight on Till Morning* (1972, as Caroline)

### Wykehurst Park

Situated in Bolney, East Sussex, Wykehurst Park was featured in Hammer's *Demons of the Mind* (1972). Built in the 1870s in the style of a mock schloss, the one-hundred-and-five room mansion has been used as a family home, a hotel and a haven for Canadian soldiers preparing to join the D–Day landings during the war. Situated amid one-hundred-and-eighty acres of parkland, other films shot at Wykehurst include *Oh! What a Lovely War* (1969), *The Legend of Hell House* (1973), *The Eagle Has Landed* (1976) and *Holocaust 2000* (1977). **Hammer credits:** *Demons of the Mind* (1972)

### Wymark, Patrick

This intense British character actor (1920–1970, real name Patrick Carl Cheeseman) is best known for his impersonations of Winston Churchill, whom he voiced in the documentaries *The Finest Hours* (1964) and *The Other World of Winston Churchill* (1964), and played (in profile) in *Operation Crossbow* (1965) and *A King's Story* (1965). He also played memorable supporting roles in *Repulsion* (1965), *Witchfinder General* (1968), *Where Eagles Dare* (1969), *Cromwell* (1970) and *The Blood on Satan's Claw* (1971), while his television work includes *The Plane Makers* (1963–1965, TV) and *The Power Game* (1965–1966, TV), in both of

which he played the ruthless John Wilder. One of his least convincing roles was that of the Japanese prison camp commandant Major Jocomo in Hammer's *The Secret of Blood Island* (1965). Also on stage, he was married to the actress and playwright Olwen Wymark (1932–2013, maiden name Olwen Margaret Buck); their children include the actress Jane Wymark (1952–) and the actor Tristram Wymark (1962–). **Hammer credits:** *The Secret of Blood Island* (1965, as Major Jocomo)

### Wyndham, Dennis

This South African born bit-part player (1887–1973) had a minor role in Hammer's first film, *The Public Life of Henry the Ninth* (1935), and can also be can be spotted as an outlaw in *Men of Sherwood Forest* (1954) and as an onlooker in *The Glass Cage* (1955). In films from the silent era, particularly in comedies (he worked several times with Will Hay, George Formby and Arthur Lucan), his other credits include *Lorna Doone* (1920), *Juno and the Paycock* (1930), *Oh, Mr. Porter!* (1937), *Sailors Don't Care* (1940), *Old Mother Riley's Ghosts* (1941), *Bell-Bottom George* (1944), *Oliver Twist* (1948), in which he memorably punches the title character in the street, and *Ramsbottom Rides Again* (1956), plus an episode of *The Quatermass Experiment* (1953, TV). His wife was the actress Poppy Wyndham (1893–1928, maiden name Elsie Mackay). **Hammer credits:** *The Public Life of Henry the Ninth* (1935, unnamed role [uncredited]), *Men of Sherwood Forest* (1954, as Outlaw [uncredited]), *The Glass Cage* (1955, as Onlooker [uncredited])

### Wyndham, Robert

This British supporting actor (1905–1947) played the role of Inspector Oxley in the Hammer quota quickie *Who Killed Van Loon?* (1948). His other credits include *For Those in Peril* (1944), *Champagne Charlie* (1944), *The Captive Heart* (1946) and *Against the Wind* (1948). **Hammer credits:** *Who Killed Van Loon?* (1948, as Inspector Oxley)

### Wyngarde, Peter

This dapper, French born leading man (1927–2018, real name Cyril Louis Goldbert) is best known for playing author-agent Jason King in the series *Department S* (1969–1970, TV) and its spin-off *Jason King* (1971–1972, TV), which were noted for his character's flamboyant fashions and equally flamboyant coif. A frequent guest star in the sixties, his credits here include episodes of *The Avengers* (1961–1969, TV), *The Baron* (1966–1967, TV), *The Prisoner* (1967–1968, TV) and *The Champions* (1968–1969, TV). He later appeared as a 17th century Satanist and his modern day reincarnation in *And the Wall Came Tumbling Down* (1984, TVM [episode of *Hammer House of Horror*]). He began his acting career following experience in advertising and the law, and made his film debut with a brief uncredited role in Hammer's *Dick Barton Strikes Back* (1949). His other film credits take in *The Siege of Sidney Street* (1960), *The Innocents* (1961), in which he played the corrupt gardener Peter Quint, *Night of the Eagle* (1962), *Flash Gordon* (1980), in which he played Klytus, and

*Tank Malling* (1988). Also on stage, including roles in Brecht and Shakespeare, as well as musicals. He also recorded an album, *Peter Wyngarde* (1970, reissued on CD in 1998 as *When Sex Leers Its Inquisitive Head*). His later credits include the narration of the documentary *How to Be Sherlock Holmes: The Many Faces of a Master Detective* (2014, TV). His uncle was the actor Louis Jouvet (1887–1951, full name Jules Eugene Louis Jouvet). **Hammer credits:** *Dick Barton Strikes Back* (1949, as Soldier [uncredited]), *And the Wall Came Tumbling Down* (1984, TVM [episode of *Hammer House of Horror*], as Daniel/General Hawswell)

## Wynn, John

Wynn played Best in Hammer's *The Quatermass Xperiment* (1955). Prior to this he had minor roles in three further films for the company. His other credits include *The Chiltern Hundreds* (1949), *Over the Garden Wall* (1950), *Betrayed* (1954), *Storm Over the Nile* (1955) and *Safari* (1956). **Hammer credits:** *Whispering Smith Hits London* (1952, as Police Sergeant), *The Saint's Return* (1953, unnamed role [uncredited]), *36 Hours* (1953, as Detective Sergeant Blake [uncredited]), *The Quatermass Xperiment* (1955, as Best [uncredited])

## Wynn-Jones, David

British born Wynn-Jones (1944–) worked as first assistant camera on Hammer's *Captain Kronos—Vampire Hunter* (1974) and their remake of *The Lady Vanishes* (1979). His other credits include work as a clapper loader on *The Dirty Dozen* (1967), *2001: A Space Odyssey* (1968) and *Where Eagles Dare* (1969), as a focus puller on *10 Rillington Place* (1971), *Vault of Horror* (1973), *The Man with the Golden Gun* (1974) and *Venom* (1981), as a camera operator on *The Bitch* (1979), *Death Wish 3* (1985) and *Bullseye!* (1990), and as first assistant camera on *Conduct Unbecoming* (1975), *Superman* (1978), *Victor/Victoria* (1982) and *Champions* (1984). **Hammer credits:** *Captain Kronos—Vampire Hunter* (1974), *The Lady Vanishes* (1979)

## Wynne, Don (Donald)

British born Wynne (1918–1993, full name Donald Molison Wynne) worked as the production manager on Hammer's *Dick Barton Strikes Back* (1949). His other credits in this capacity include *The Fatal Night* (1948), *The Clouded Crystal* (1948), *Vengeance Is Mine* (1949), *On Such a Night* (1956), *The Big Chance* (1957) and *Account Rendered* (1957), plus an episode of *Fabian of the Yard* (1954–1956, TV). He also worked as an assistant director on *The Phantom Shot* (1947) and *Third Time Lucky* (1948), and later produced the TV series *Beware of the Dog* (1964, TV). His father was the actor, writer, producer and director Bert Wynne (1889–1971, real name Herbert Wynne). **Hammer credits:** *Dick Barton Strikes Back* (1949)

# X

## X—The Unknown

GB, 1956, 78m, bw, RCA, cert X

Following the making of *The Quatermass Xperiment* (1955), Hammer cancelled its proposed roster of feature productions, save for *Women Without Men* (1956), and concentrated instead on widescreen shorts while awaiting the film's box office outcome. Once this had been assured, the studio turned its back on the B-thriller, which had effectively been its bread and butter for the past decade, and fully embraced the hybrid world of X-rated sci-fi/horror. To this end producer Anthony Hinds asked production manager Jimmy Sangster—who had recently penned his first screenplay for the featurette *A Man on the Beach* (1956)—to come up with an exploitable subject along the lines of their Quatermass film. Not keen to take on the job at first, Sangster was persuaded otherwise following a hasty story conference with Hinds and Michael Carreras. The result, for which Sangster was paid £450, was *X—The Unknown*, and like *The Quatermass Xperiment*, the emphasis was on the all-important X-factor.

This time, instead of a threat from outer space, the title monster hails from *inner* space in the form of radioactive magma which surfaces from a fissure following an explosion on the Scottish moors during army exercises ("It rises from 2000 miles beneath the earth to melt everything in its path!" exclaimed the poster). Recalled Jimmy Sangster of the project's genesis, "For *X—The Unknown*, the pitch was simply, 'A monster from the earth's core creates havoc and mayhem when it bursts through the crust of the earth's surface.' I admit, it doesn't sound like much these days, but back then it was enough to get the project going."[1] Of course, this premise also had its practical side, as Sangster noted: "We wouldn't have to build any space ship sets, which were inclined to be large and expensive."[2]

An American atomic scientist named Dr. Adam Royston is subsequently brought in when it is revealed that the soldiers involved in the exercise are suffering from radiation burns. Following the death of a local lad and the disappearance of radioactive materials from a hospital, Royston concludes that the creature—luridly described in the script as being "a dark, seething, putrid mass, writhing with corruption and hideous rottenness"[3]—needs radium to survive. "Energy can only be fed by more energy—or radiation, if you like," explains the doctor. Consequently, plans are hatched to shut down the nearby cobalt-powered research station before the sludge can absorb its energy and run completely amok. Unfortunately, Royston and his men are unable to prevent the creature from attacking the plant, and so the good doctor reverts to plan B, which involves neutralizing the monster with sonic waves.

With financial input from Sol Lesser (who had previously invested in several Exclusive B-features), the film went before the cameras during an exceptionally chilly January in 1956, with the Scottish exteriors filmed at a water-logged gravel pit at Ger-

rards Cross (nearby Beaconsfield Studios acted as a base for the less-than-comfortable night-time shooting). The interiors were meanwhile filmed on a variety of stages at Bray (note the cold breath on the actors in some scenes, especially in the hospital following the boy's death).

Initially sitting in the director's chair was one Joseph Walton, who was in fact the exiled American director Joseph Losey, whose Hollywood career had been brought to an abrupt halt following his blacklisting by the House Un-American Activities Committee, which had accused him of harboring Communist sympathies. Losey had thus made his way to Britain, where he attempted to resurrect his career, among his first projects being the Sangster-scripted Hammer featurette *A Man on the Beach* (1956), which he directed under his real name. Unfortunately, the clutch of HUAC and the blacklist was far-reaching, and following hints that *X—The Unknown* might not be granted a showing in the all-important American market if Losey were its director (pseudonym or not), not to mention objections from the film's virulently anti-communist star, he was quietly dropped from the project, supposedly the victim of pneumonia—an entirely plausible excuse given the film's chilly location work. Consequently, the veteran Ealing director Leslie Norman was quickly brought in to replace Losey on the picture. Sadly, the brusque Norman was not well liked by the cast or crew, hence the frequent presence on set of executive producer Michael Carreras to help jolly proceedings along. Recalled camera operator Len Harris of the situation, "The director was rather trying for everybody…. The whole unit had a row with him at some time or other."[4]

Despite its brisk running time and intriguing premise, *X—The Unknown* is but a pale imitation of *The Quatermass Xperiment*, let down chiefly by its obviously low budget, some tedious padding, and some less than special effects. However, the assertion by a BBFC reader that the script was "a mixture of scientific hokum and sadism in equal parts without benefit of wit or humor,"[5] seems like a bit of an over-reaction today. These deficiencies aside, Gerald Gibbs' stark black and white cinematography adds to the film's brooding atmosphere, as does James Bernard's unsettling string and percussion score (a stylistic hold over from the Quatermass film), while the radiation burns provided by make-up man Phil Leakey look uncomfortably convincing. A sequence involving the flesh melting from a lab technician's face to reveal the skull underneath is also neatly—and still quite shockingly—put over.

Cast-wise, Hollywood import Dean Jagger makes a suitably determined Dr. Royston in the established Brian Donlevy/Quatermass tradition. In fact Hammer had wanted the film to feature the Quatermass character, but this idea was nixed by Nigel Kneale—though had the proposal been accepted, presumably Brian Donlevy would have been asked to reprise the role. The voice of reason throughout, it is Royston who concludes that, "This thing can take up any shape it needs to." He also asks the all-important question, "How do you kill mud?" Meanwhile, the supporting players feature a variety of familiar faces, several at early stages in their careers, among them Edward Chapman, Leo McKern, William Lucas, Michael Ripper, Anthony Newley, Kenneth Cope and Fraser Hines. So-called "female interest" is mercifully kept to a minimum in the guise of Marianne Brauns' Zena.

Although by no means a major hit like *The Quatermass Xperiment*, *X—The Unknown* nevertheless proved popular enough when, following a trade show in August 1956, it was showcased at the London Pavilion on 21 September and then released on the ABC circuit by Exclusive on a double bill with the French thriller *Les diaboliques* (1954) on 5 November 1956 ("Machine gun bullets! Dynamite! Flame throwers! Nothing can stop it!" screamed the poster). For its U.S. release by Warner Bros. the movie was held back until 25 June 1957, when it was double-billed with Hammer's *The Curse of Frankenstein* (1957); it also did double bill service on the drive-in circuit with *The Cyclops* (1957) from 28 July. *Variety* described the film as "a highly imaginative and fanciful meller, with tense dramatic overtones." It also praised the film for being "made with creditable slickness" and for telling "a story which is completely absorbing, though totally unbelievable."

Recalled Jimmy Sangster, "There's a line in the movie—'Let's not conjure up visions of nameless horrors creeping about in the night'—which is exactly what I set out to do. Conjure up nameless horrors."[6] The critic for the *News Chronicle* agreed: "The plot convinces us less by trick horror effects—bowel-loosening though these often are—than by the fact that it has been admirably acted." **Additional notes:** Producer Anthony Hinds did some uncredited work on the screenplay. The Gerrards Cross gravel pit was later used as a location for Hammer's *The Mummy's Shroud* (1967). *X—The Unknown* was originally to have been released in the U.S. by RKO, thanks to Sol Lesser's connection with the Hollywood studio, but the distribution rights were eventually sold on to Warner Bros. following concerns by RKO that the film's title sounded too much like to their war drama *Toward the Unknown* (1957). Why they simply didn't change the film's title isn't known, given that this was common practice at the time. However, it should be noted that the film's British trailer, which is narrated by Valentine Dyall, carries an RKO distribution credit ("The menace that can kill, but cannot be killed!" it warned audiences), and that RKO did eventually release the film Stateside a month on from its partnering with *The Curse of Frankenstein*, this time, as has been noted, on a double bill *The Cyclops* (1957). Had the movie been passed off as a Quatermass sequel, some sources indicate that the chosen title would have been *Quatermass and the Slime*.[7] The film's opening credits carry the following acknowledgment: "The Producers wish to acknowledge the co-operation received from the War Office during the production of this film." The Hollywood film *The Blob* (1958) shares a very similar concept with *X—The Unknown* but didn't appear until two years later.

Production companies: Hammer/Sol Lesser. Distributors: Exclusive (UK [ABC circuit]), Warner Bros. (U.S.). Producer: Anthony Hinds. Exec-

Twice the terror. *X—The Unknown* (1956) does double duty with *The Cyclops* (1957). Drive-ins never had it so good (Hammer/Sol Lesser/Exclusive/Warner Bros./RKO).

utive producer: Michael Carreras. Associate producer: Mickey Delamar [uncredited]. Director: Leslie Norman (following the departure of Joseph Losey, working as Joseph Walton). Screenplay: Jimmy Sangster (and Anthony Hinds [uncredited]). Cinematographer: Gerald Gibbs. Music: James Bernard. Music director: John Hollingsworth. Editor: James Needs. Art director: Ted Marshall [uncredited]. Costumes: Molly Arbuthnot. Camera operator: Len Harris. Second camera operator: John Reid [uncredited]. Focus puller: Harry Oakes [uncredited]. Clapper loader: Michael Rutter [uncredited]. Assistant editors: Henry Richardson [uncredited], Bill Bouvet [uncredited]. Sound: Cliff Sandell [uncredited]. Sound mixer: Jock May. Sound editor: Alfred Cox. Sound camera operator: Michael Sale [uncredited]. Sound maintenance: Charles Bouvet [uncredited]. Boom operator: Jimmy Perry [uncredited]. Make-up: Phil Leakey. Special effects: Jack Curtis, Bowie-Margutti, Ltd., Roy Field [uncredited], Ray Caple [uncredited], Brian Johncock [uncredited]. Assistant director: Christopher Sutton. Second assistant director: Roy Stevens [uncredited]. Third assistant director: Hugh Harlow [uncredited]. Production manager: Jimmy Sangster. Continuity: June Randall. Production secretary: Margaret Quigley [uncredited]. Stills: Tom Edwards [uncredited]. Draughtsman: Don Mingaye [uncredited]. Construction manager: Freddie Ricketts [uncredited]. Chief electrician: Jack Curtis [uncredited]. Master plasterer: Arthur Banks [uncredited]. Props: Tommy Money [uncredited]. Publicist: Bill Batchelor [uncredited]. **Cast:** Dean Jagger (Dr. Adam Royston), Edward Chapman (Edward Elliott), Leo McKern (Inspector McGill), Jameson Clark (Jack Harding), Anthony Newley (Private "Spider" Webb), Marianne Brauns (Zena), Ian MacNaughton ("Haggis"), William Lucas (Peter Elliott), Peter Hammond (Lieutenant Bannerman), Michael Ripper (Sergeant Grimsdyke), John Harvey (Major Cartwright), Jane Aird (Vi Harding), Kenneth Cope (Private Lancing), Frazer Hines (Ian Osborne), Michael Brooke (Willie Harding), Edwin Richfield (Old soldier), Norman Macowan (Old Tom), Neil Hallet (Unwin), Neil Wilson (Russell [uncredited]), John Stone (Gerry [uncredited]), Stevenson Lang (Reporter [uncredited]), Edward Judd (Soldier [uncredited]), Brian Peck (Soldier [uncredited]), Lawrence James (Guard [uncredited]), Archie Duncan (Police Sergeant Yeardye [uncredited]), John Stirling (Police driver [uncredited]), Shaw Taylor (Police radio operator [uncredited]), Frank Taylor (Constable Williams [uncredited]), Brown Derby (Vicar [uncredited]), Barry Steele (Soldier [uncredited]), Philip Levene (Security man [uncredited]), Anthony Sagar (Gateman [uncredited]), Stella Kemball (Nurse [uncredited]), Robert Bruce (Dr. Kelly [uncredited]), Max Brimmell (Hospital director [uncredited]), Angela Crow (Girl [uncredited]), Raymond Dudley (unnamed role [uncredited]). **DVD availability:** Anchor Bay (U.S. R1 NTSC), extras include a trailer and an episode of *The World of Hammer* (1990 [first broadcast 1994], TV) titled *Sci-Fi*; Anchor Bay (U.S. R1 NTSC), double-billed with *Four Sided Triangle* (1953); DD Home Entertainment (UK R2 PAL), extras include a commentary and filmed interview with Jimmy Sangster; Icon Home Entertainment (UK R2 PAL); Simply Media (UK R2 PAL), double-billed with *The Abominable Snowman* (1957). **Blu-ray availability:** Shock (R/1), as an extra with *The Quatermass Xperiment*. **CD availability:** *The Devil Rides Out: The Film Music of James Bernard* (Silva Screen), which contains a newly recorded *Quatermass Suite*, which features the cues *Radiation* and *Requiem* from *X—The Unknown*

# Y

## Yaltan, Jaron

This Indian actor (1921–2002) can be seen as Harish Taranath, whose suicide at the beginning of Hammer's *Man at the Top* (1973) motivates the plot. His other credits include *The Little Hut* (1957), *North West Frontier* (1959) and *Harem* (1985), plus episodes of *Danger Man* (1964–1966, TV), *The Troubleshooters* (1965–1972, TV), *The Regiment* (1972–1973, TV) and *Sexton Blake and the Demon God* (1978, TV). **Hammer credits:** *Man at the Top* (1973, as Harish Taranath)

## Yanai, Yoshihide

This Japanese actor (1900–1972) can be seen as the villainous Chang in Hammer's *Dick Barton at Bay* (1950). His other credits include *Patricia Gets Her Man* (1937) and *The Mudlark* (1950), plus two episodes of *BBC Sunday-Night Theatre* (1950–1959, TV). **Hammer credits:** *Dick Barton at Bay* (1950, as Chang)

## Yardley, Stephen

Best known to TV audiences for playing PC May in *Z Cars* (1962–1978, TV), William "Spider" Scott in *The XYY Man* (1976–1977, TV) and Ken Masters in *Howards' Way* (1985–1990, TV), this busy British television actor (1942–) also appeared in episodes of *The Mask of Janus* (1965, TV), *The Guardians* (1971, TV), *Secret Army* (1977–1979, TV), in which he played Max Brocard, *Remington Steele* (1982–1987, TV) and *Hex* (2004–2005, TV). He can also be seen in a supporting role in *The Corvini Inheritance* (1984, TVM [episode of *Hammer House of Mystery and Suspense*]). His occasional films include *Funny Money* (1982), *Slayground* (1983) and *The Innocent Sleep* (1996). His second wife is the actress Jan Harvey (1947–). **Hammer credits:** *The Corvini Inheritance* (1984, TVM [episode of *Hammer House of Mystery and Suspense*], as Knowles)

## Yates, Sefton

Yates had a minor role in Hammer's *The Dark Road* (1948). **Hammer credits:** *The Dark Road* (1948, unnamed role)

## Yeardye, Tom (Tommy)

This British stuntman (1930–2004) doubled for Norman Mitchell (playing the highwayman Rooks) in the Hammer short *Dick Turpin—Highwayman* (1956). His other credits include *The Long Haul* (1957), in which he doubled for Victor Mature, and *Climb Up the Wall* (1960). He also doubled for Rock Hudson during his career. Away from films, Yeardye was a not only a successful restaurateur, but went on to co-found the Vidal Sassoon hair care empire. His wife was the model Ann Davis, and their daughter, Tamara Mellon (1967–, maiden name Tamara Yeardye), co-founded Jimmy Choo Shoes, in which he also invested. **Hammer credits:** *Dick Turpin—Highwayman* (1956, stunt double for Norman Mitchell [uncredited])

## Yen, Gerry Lee

This Oriental supporting actor had a minor role in Hammer's *Visa to Canton* (1960). **Hammer credits:** *Visa to Canton* (1960, as Room boy [uncredited])

## Yen-Lien, Pen *see* Lien, Peng Yen

## Yeoman (Yeoman Films, Ltd.)

This production company was originally formed by actor Richard Greene and producer Sidney Cole, through which they made their hit television series *The Adventures of Robin Hood* (1955–1960, TV). The company was also used to co-produce the big-screen spin off with Hammer under the title *Sword of Sherwood Forest* (1960). **Hammer credits:** *Sword of Sherwood Forest* (1960)

## *Yesterday's Enemy*

GB, 1959, 95m, bw, MegaScope [1.33:1], Westrex, cert A

One of several wartime pictures made by Hammer in the late fifties, this jungle-set drama sees a platoon of British soldiers led by the ruthless Captain Langford take over a Malayan village in 1942, resulting in unexpected consequences for both sides ("The most controversial war drama ever filmed!" exclaimed the posters). As with the harrowing *The Camp on Blood Island* (1958), the film is efficiently directed by Hammer veteran Val Guest, working from a screenplay by Peter Newman, which itself was based upon his own television play (first broadcast by the BBC on 14 October 1958), making this one in a long line of small to big screen transfers produced by Hammer during this period.

Owing to the crowded production schedule at Bray (1958/1959 was one of Hammer's busiest), much of *Yesterday's Enemy* was filmed at Shepperton Studios, where principal photography commenced on 12 January 1959 on an impressive jungle set created by production designer Bernard Robinson and his team. As with his gothic sets, Robinson designed the jungle environ in such a way that the foliage could be rotated, so as to give the impression of an ever-changing landscape, which also included a stretch of swampy river. Recalled Val Guest of the film, "My only worry was how to shoot a complex, realistic jungle war film when your budget won't allow even a quick trip to the nearest jungle. The answer is you get a brilliant art director like Hammer's Bernard Robinson, who not only fills an entire stage at Shepperton with Burmese jungle, but builds different sections of it on revolves so that without having to move the unit it can be turned around to look like entirely different locations."[1]

Five weeks later, the production returned to Bray where, beginning on 16 February, filming continued on a swamp set which had been built on the main stage. Principal photography concluded in early March, following which the film went through the editing process. When it came to scoring, director Val Guest was adamant that the film should play without a conventional music track. Instead, working closely with the sound department, he orchestrated the film with jungle sound effects, which helped to make the sweaty tropical environment all the more believable for audiences. Indeed, the film came in for a certain amount of praise for its realistic approach. Referring to it as a "small-scale *River Kwai*," the *Monthly Film Bulletin* admired the production for depicting war as "a dirty, degrading, senseless waste of human life," while *Films and Filming* applauded it for its sincerity and its exploration of "the real meanings and qualities of courage."

A surprisingly claustrophobic film, *Yesterday's Enemy* benefits enormously from Arthur Grant's mobile camera work (the film opens with some impressive tracking and overhead shots in the swamp). The background aural track is also highly convincing, with only the boxy recording of the dialogue giving away the game that the film was shot on a soundstage (shouted dialogue sometimes

**An impassioned poster for *Yesterday's Enemy* (1959) (Hammer/Columbia).**

echoes off the rafters). Likewise, the performances are highly convincing, notably by the leading man Stanley Baker as Captain Langford, who pays the ultimate sacrifice when the village is invaded by a platoon of Japanese soldiers. Solid support is also provided by Guy Rolfe as the platoon's padre and Gordon Jackson as Sergeant Mackenzie. Other familiar faces include Philip Ahn as Yamazaki, the leader of the Japanese platoon, and, way down the cast list, future *Pink Panther* legend Burt Kwouk as a Japanese soldier.

*Yesterday's Enemy* received its premiere in Tokyo on 11 July 1959. It opened in London on 14 September, while a gala screening followed on 17 September at the Empire, Leicester Square in aid of the Burma Star Association, after which the guest of honor, Lord Louis Mountbatten, told Val Guest that he recognized parts of the jungle! Recalled the director, "Not having the courage to tell him it was the large stage at Shepperton, I lied diplomatically."[2] The film finally went on general release on the ABC circuit on 19 October. Its U.S. release, again care of Columbia, followed on 3 March 1960.

As well as the critics, *Yesterday's Enemy* also impressed the British Film Academy, garnering nominations for best British film, best film from any source, best actor (Stanley Baker) and best supporting actor (Gordon Jackson). *Sapphire* (1959) went on to claim the best British picture gong, as well as the awards for best actor (Nigel Patrick) and supporting actor (Michael Craig), while *Ben-Hur* (1959) took the prize for best film from any source. Notwithstanding, simply being taken seriously by such an august body must surely have made all at Hammer very proud indeed. **Additional notes:** The film was part-financed with a loan from the National Film Finance Corporation. Although Hammer's resident music director John Hollingsworth was contracted to work on the film, he concurred with director Val Guest that the film would work best without a music track, but still managed to pocket his fee for advice given. Peter Newman's screenplay was novelized by Maurice Moiseiwitsch and published by Corgi.

Production company: Hammer. Distributor: Columbia (UK [ABC circuit], U.S.). Producer: Michael Carreras. Director: Val Guest. Screenplay/technical advisor: Peter Newman, based upon his television play. Cinematographer: Arthur Grant. Music: None. Music director: John Hollingsworth (advisory capacity only [uncredited]). Supervising editor: James Needs. Editor: Alfred Cox. Production design: Bernard Robinson. Costumes: Molly Arbuthnot. Special effects: Bill Warrington [uncredited], Charles Willoughby [uncredited]. Makeup: Roy Ashton. Hair: Henry Montsash. Sound: Buster Ambler, Red Law, John Cox. Sound editor: Roy Hyde. Sound cameraman: Jimmy Dooley [uncredited]. Boom operator: Peter Dukelow [uncredited]. Sound maintenance: Eric Vincent [uncredited]. Assistant art director: Don Mingaye [uncredited]. Assistant director: John Peverall. Second assistant director: Tom Walls [uncredited]. Third assistant director: Hugh Harlow [uncredited]. Camera operator: Len Harris. Focus puller:

Harry Oakes [uncredited]. Camera loader/clapper boy: Alan McDonald [uncredited]. Grip: Albert Cowlard [uncredited]. Props: Frank Burden [uncredited], T. Frewer [uncredited]. Props buyer: Eric Hillier [uncredited]. Production supervisor: Tommy Lyndon-Haynes. Continuity: Beryl Booth. Stills: Tom Edwards [uncredited]. Publicist: Colin Reid [uncredited]. Casting: Dorothy Holloway [uncredited]. Construction manager: Jack Bolam [uncredited]. Master painter: S. Taylor [uncredited]. Master plasterer: S. Rodwel [uncredited]. Master Carpenter: E.D. Wheatley [uncredited]. Electrical engineer: S.F. Hillyer [uncredited]. Production secretary: Doreen Jones [uncredited]. **Cast:** Stanley Baker (Captain Langford), Guy Rolfe (Padre), Leo McKern (Max), David Oxley (Doctor), Gordon Jackson (Sergeant Mackenzie), Philip Ahn (Yamazaki), Richard Pasco (Lieutenant Hastings), Percy Herbert (Wilson), Bryan Forbes (Dawson), Russell Waters (Brigadier), Wolfe Morris (Informer), David Lodge (Perkins), Barry Lowe (Turner), Burt Kwouk (Japanese Soldier), Edwina Carroll (Suni [uncredited]), Alan Keith (Bendish [uncredited]), Howard Williams (Davies [uncredited]), Barry Steele (Brown [uncredited]), Nicholas Brady (Orderly [uncredited]), Arthur Lovegrove (Patrick [uncredited]), Timothy Bateson (Simpson [uncredited]), Donald Churchill (Elliott [uncredited]), Geoffrey Bayldon (Soldier [uncredited]). **DVD availability:** Sony (UK R2 PAL)

### Ying, Liu Ya

Ying can be seen in a minor role in Hammer's *Shatter* (1974). Her other credits include *Nu ji zhong ying* (1973), *Yu mo* (1974), *Shao nian yu Shao fu* (1974) and *Die xian* (1980). **Hammer credits:** *Shatter* (1974, as Leber's girl)

### Yong, Liu Ka *see* Yung, Liu Chia

### Yorke, Terry

This stuntman and bit part player (1926–2003, aka Terry York) doubled for Philip Friend (playing Dick Turpin) in the Hammer featurette *Dick Turpin—Highwayman* (1956). His other credits, either as a stuntman or stunt arranger, include *The Guns of Navarone* (1961), *Where Eagles Dare* (1969), *Theatre of Blood* (1973), *Superman II* (1980) and *Time Bandits* (1981). He also worked as the assistant director on the second unit for *Circus World* (1964). His credits as an actor include *Late Night Final* (1954), *The Long Duel* (1967), *The Pink Panther Strikes Again* (1976), *The Stud* (1978) and *The Passage* (1979), plus episodes of *The Adventures of Robin Hood* (1955–1960, TV), *Space: 1999* (1975–1977, TV) and *Dempsey and Makepeace* (1985–1986, TV). **Hammer credits:** *Dick Turpin—Highwayman* (1956, stunt double for Philip Friend [uncredited])

### Yospa, Manny

This British cameraman (1918–2002, real name Emanuel Yospa) worked as a focus puller on three of Hammer's fifties co-features. His other credits include *Thursday's Child* (1943), *Aventure malgache* (1944), *The Halfway House* (1944), *Quartet*

(1948), *The Huggetts Abroad* (1949), *The Bulldog Breed* (1960) and *In the Doghouse* (1961). **Hammer credits:** *The Gambler and the Lady* (1953 [uncredited]), *Mantrap* (1953 [uncredited]), *Four Sided Triangle* (1953 [uncredited])

### Young, Aida

This British producer (1920–2007) first came to Hammer in 1952 to work as a second assistant director on *Mantrap* (1953) following experience as an assistant director on documentaries from 1948. Like others who worked for Hammer, she gradually climbed the company ladder. She also gained experience elsewhere, such as on the hit TV series *Danger Man* (1960–1966, TV), which she produced for a while, and with Michael Carreras, whose Capricorn Productions she joined in 1963, working as his associate producer on *What a Crazy World* (1963). She remained Carreras's associate producer upon his return to Hammer on such films as *She* (1965) and *Slave Girls* (1968). Commented Young of her relationship with Carreras, in what at the time was very much a male-dominated industry, "Michael was highly amused by me, having a woman there, but we got on terribly well and we were friends socially as well. So I learnt a lot from him."[3]

Following work as an associate producer for director Ken Annakin on *The Long Duel* (1967), Young finally graduated to full producer status at Hammer with *The Vengeance of She* (1968), which she followed with the box office hit *Dracula Has Risen from the Grave* (1968), the success of which led to her producing a further four films for Hammer, culminating with the glossy period shocker *Hands of the Ripper* (1971). However, according to director Freddie Francis, who worked with Young on *Dracula Has Risen from the Grave*, she was little more than an intermediary: "One really worked for Tony [Hinds]; she happened to be there but she was a sort of go-between and had no real say. We certainly worked together, but under Tony's instructions."[4] Francis also observed perhaps a little ungenerously of Young that, "I don't think Aida was as dedicated as we were."[5] As for Young's own thoughts on Hammer, she commented, "I still think Hammer was a wonderful company and I have always been sorry for its demise."[6] However, as for her career turning to horror, she initially did admit that, "Horror films were not in my remit. And I had never seen a horror film, because I hadn't wanted to. I wasn't interested at all in horror films. I was snotty about them, you know. I still had a hangover from my documentary days when the only things worth seeing were films that had been made by great German, Italian and French directors and our documentary filmmakers."[7] Yet once she got into the stride of things, she admitted to having "had a whale of a time!"[8]

Young's other big screen credits include the TV sit-com spin-offs *Steptoe and Son* (1972), *Steptoe and Son Ride Again* (1973) and *The Likely Lads* (1976), whist for television she produced *Mousey* (1974, TVM) and *The Thief of Baghdad* (1978, TVM), both of which were released theatrically in the UK, and the series *Covington Cross* (1992, TV).

Commented composer Mario Nascimbene of Young, with whom he worked on three films for Hammer, "She was a very nice person, very intelligent."[9] As for Hammer's output during their glory days at Bray, Young noted, "We didn't have enormous budgets. We worked very long hours in very cramped facilities. It was only a big old house. And we did remarkable things. If you look at the old horror films that we made in that old house … you'd think we'd shot at MGM or Pinewood."[10] **Additional notes:** Young helped to direct the last three days of *The Vengeance of She* with Cliff Owen, after he had slipped a disk while on location in the desert. Although *The Vengeance of She* was made after *Slave Girls*, it was released first. Young also did the casting for *Scars of Dracula*. **Hammer credits:** *Mantrap* (1953, second assistant director [uncredited]), *Four Sided Triangle* (1953, second assistant director [uncredited]), *The Flanagan Boy* (1953, second assistant director [uncredited]), *The Saint's Return* (1953, second assistant director [uncredited]), *36 Hours* (1953, second assistant director [uncredited]), *Five Days* (1954, second assistant director [uncredited]), *Life with the Lyons* (1954, second assistant director [uncredited]), *The Stranger Came Home* (1954, second assistant director [uncredited]), *Mask of Dust* (1954, second assistant director [uncredited]), *Break in the Circle* (1955, second assistant director [uncredited]), *Murder by Proxy* (1955, second assistant director [uncredited]), *Third Party Risk* (1955, second assistant director [uncredited]), *The Quatermass Xperiment* (1955, second assistant director [uncredited]), *Adventures with the Lyons* (1957, serial re-issue of *Life with the Lyons*, second assistant director [uncredited]), *She* (1965, associate producer), *One Million Years B.C.* (1966, associate producer), *The Vengeance of She* (1968, producer), *Slave Girls* (1968, associate producer), *Dracula Has Risen from the Grave* (1968, producer), *Taste the Blood of Dracula* (1970, producer), *When Dinosaurs Ruled the Earth* (1970, producer), *Scars of Dracula* (1970, producer, casting), *Hands of the Ripper* (1971, producer)

## Young, Arthur

This British actor and musician (1898–1959), the Novachord a specialty, can be seen as Hyson in Hammer's *Five Days* (1954). His other credits include *Radio Parade of 1935* (1934), *Victoria the Great* (1937), *Spare a Copper* (1940), *San Demetrio London* (1943), *No Smoking* (1955) and *The Gelignite Gang* (1954), while his TV work takes in episodes of *St. Ives* (1955, TV), *The Scarlet Pimpernel* (1955–1956, TV) and *The Count of Monte Cristo* (1956, TV). He also worked on stage. His wife was the actress Beatrice Kane (1898–2004), whom he married in 1924, and who appeared in Hammer's three Dick Barton movies (though her scenes were excised from the third). **Hammer credits:** *Five Days* (1954, as Hyson)

## Young, Eric (Ric)

This RADA-trained British actor can be seen as Confucius in Hammer's Oriental thriller *The Terror of the Tongs* (1961). His other credits include *Satan Never Sleeps* (1962), *The Face of Fu Manchu* (1965),

*Invasion* (1966), *The Brides of Fu Manchu* (1966), *Pretty Polly* (1967), *The Chairman* (1969), *Games Girls Play* (1974), *High Road to China* (1983), *Indiana Jones and the Temple of Doom* (1984), *The Last Emperor* (1987), *Nixon* (1995), in which he played Mao Tse-Tung, *The Transporter* (2002) and *Getting Back to Zero* (2013), plus episodes of *The Avengers* (1961–1969, TV), *Out of the Unknown* (1965–1971, TV), *Return of the Saint* (1978–1979, TV), *Tenko* (1981–1984, TV), *Night Man* (1997–1999, TV) and *Alias* (2001–2006, TV). His credits as a writer include *Oy Vey!* (2007), which he also executive produced and appeared in, and *The Lair* (2011). **Hammer credits:** *The Terror of the Tongs* (1961, as Confucius [uncredited])

## Young, Jeremy

The British actor (1934–) can be seen as a court messenger in Hammer's *Rasputin—The Mad Monk* (1966). His other credits include *The Wild and the Willing* (1962), *Crooks and Coronets* (1969), *Frenzy* (1972) and *Photographing Fairies* (1997), plus episodes of *The Avengers* (1961–1969, TV), *Department S* (1969–1970, TV), *The New Avengers* (1976–1977, TV), *The Tripods* (1984–1985, TV) and *Murder in Mind* (2001–2003, TV). Married twice, his first wife was actress Coral Atkins (1936–2016), whom he married in 1959. His second wife was actress Kate O'Mara (1939–2014), to whom he was married between 1961 and 1976; she appeared in Hammer's *Captain Clegg* (1962), *The Vampire Lovers* (1970) and *The Horror of Frankenstein* (1970). **Hammer credits:** *Rasputin—The Mad Monk* (1966, as Court messenger [uncredited])

## Young, Joan

On stage from the age of fifteen, this British actress (1900–1984, real name Joan Wragge) turned to films in 1937 with *Victoria the Great*, following which she appeared in the likes of *The Fallen Idol* (1948), *Trottie True* (1949), *Time, Gentlemen, Please!* (1952), *The Admirable Crichton* (1957), *Carry On Constable* (1960) and *The Last Shot You Hear* (1968). She can also be seen as Mrs. Caporal in Hammer's *Blood from the Mummy's Tomb* (1971). The daughter of music hall performers, Young also worked in variety, and was popular on radio in the wartime series *Navy Mixture* (1944–1947). Her many TV credits include episodes of *Dixon of Dock Green* (1955–1976, TV), *Sykes* (1972–1979, TV) and *All Creatures Great and Small* (1978–1990, TV). **Hammer credits:** *Blood from the Mummy's Tomb* (1971, as Mrs. Caporal)

## Young, Morris

Hired by Exclusive in 1945 to promote the company's catalogue of shorts and features, Young went on to handle the London circuits for Exclusive. He left the company when it was wound down in the late fifties, moving to United Artists, where he eventually went on to become the company's managing director.

## Young, Muriel

This British actress (1923–2001) appeared in the role of Helen Braddock in the Hammer prison melodrama *Women Without Men* (1956), though at the time she was better known to television au-

diences as a continuity announcer for Associated-Rediffusion (from 1955), playing herself as such in the 1959 film *I'm All Right Jack*. In the late fifties and early sixties, she also began presenting children's programs, among them *Small Time* (1955–1959, TV) and *The Five O'Clock Club* (1963–1966, TV). In 1969 she became head of children's television for Granada, and produced such music programs as *Lift Off* (1969–1974, TV, later *Lift Off with Ayshea*), *Shang-a-Lang* (1975, TV), which starred boy band sensation the Bay City Rollers, and *Arrows* (1976, TV). She also directed (and occasionally produced) *Marc* (1977, TV), which starred Marc Bolan, and produced the long-running cinema magazine *Clapperboard* (1972–1982, TV). Her other film appearances include *The Story of Gilbert and Sullivan* (1953), *Man in Demand* (1955), *The Constant Husband* (1955) and *Can Heironymus Merkin Ever Forget Mercy Humppe and Find True Happiness?* (1966), plus episodes of *Saber of London* (1954–1960, TV) and *The Adventures of Robin Hood* (1955–1960, TV). Prior to all this she had worked as a model and stage actress, beginning at her uncle's rep theater in Henley-on-Thames. She was married to the director Cyril Coke (1914–1993) from 1954; his father, the actor Edward Rigby (1879–1951, real name Edward Coke), appeared in Hammer's *What the Butler Saw* (1950). **Hammer credits:** *Women Without Men* (1956, as Helen Braddock [uncredited])

## Young, Polly

Young worked as the hair stylist on the Hammer quickie *Spaceways* (1953) and the Charlie Drake comedy *Sands of the Desert* (1960). Her many other credits include *Laughter in Paradise* (1951), *Look Back in Anger* (1959), *Dr. Crippen* (1962) and *Crooks in Cloisters* (1963). **Hammer credits:** *Spaceways* (1953), *Sands of the Desert* (1960)

## Young, Raymond

This British supporting actor (1918–2011) played the role of Christopher Boswell in the Hammer second feature *Death of an Angel* (1952). His other credits include *Adam and Evelyne* (1949), *Venetian Bird* (1953), *Goldfinger* (1964), *36 Hours* (1964), *The Love Box* (1972), *The Thirty-Nine Steps* (1978) and *Young Toscanini* (1988), plus episodes of *The New Adventures of Charlie Chan* (1957–1958, TV), *Callan* (1967–1972, TV) and *Jeeves and Wooster* (1990–1993, TV). **Hammer credits:** *Death of an Angel* (1952, as Christopher Boswell)

## Young, Robert

Following experience as an actor (for which he trained at LAMDA), British born Young (1933–, full name Robert William Young) turned his hand to direction, making commercials, documentaries and shorts, among the latter *The Goldfish Bowl* (1970), which brought him to the attention of Michael Carreras, who subsequently offered him the 1969 Gordon Honeycombe novel *Neither the Sea Nor the Sand* to direct. Unfortunately, Hammer subsequently lost the rights to the novel (which was eventually made by Tigon in 1972), and so Young instead made his big screen debut with Hammer's *Vampire Circus* (1972). Despite the film's low budget, he brought a certain visual flair to the proceedings, imbuing them with a heady mittel–European atmosphere. Commented the film's assistant director, Derek Whitehurst, "The film had tremendous pacing and a good story. Robert Young did a very good job."[11] Unfortunately, despite his efforts, Young wasn't invited back to helm another feature for the studio. Commented the director, "At that time, they were going off on a different direction.... What would I have done? Certainly not *On the Buses*, for God's sake, you know?"[12] However, he did eventually return to the Hammer fold at the behest of Roy Skeggs to direct *Charlie Boy*, an episode of *Hammer House of Horror* (1980, TV). He was also set to helm an adaptation of the Andrew Laurance novel *The Hiss* (aka *Hideous Whispers*) for the company, but the project stalled following several attempts to bring it to the screen.

Young's other credits include *Romance with a Double Bass* (1975), which he also co-wrote, *Keep It Up Downstairs* (1976), *The World Is Full of Married Men* (1979), *Splitting Heirs* (1993), *Fierce Creatures* (1997), which was finished by Fred Schepisi when a lengthy re-shoot was required, *Captain Jack* (1998), *Eichmann* (2007), *Wide Blue Yonder* (2010), which he also produced, and *Curse of the Phoenix* (2014), which he again produced. His other credits as a producer include *Son of Nosferatu* (2011). His TV work includes episodes of *Robin of Sherwood* (1984–1986, TV), *Jeeves and Wooster* (1990–1993, TV), *GBH* (1991, TV) and *The Inspector Lynley Mysteries* (2001–2007, TV). **Hammer credits:** *Vampire Circus* (1972), *Charlie Boy* (1980, TV [episode of *Hammer House of Horror*])

### Young, Terry

Young worked as a wardrobe assistant on Hammer's *Vampire Circus* (1972). Other credits include *You Only Live Twice* (1967) and *The Last of Sheila* (1973). **Hammer credits:** *Vampire Circus* (1972 [uncredited])

### Young, Tony (Anthony)

Following experience as an editor at Gainsborough from 1945, this British director (1921–1966) gained further experience as a cameraman before notching up his first directorial credit, *Penny Points to Paradise* (1951). His other films include *My Death Is a Mockery* (1952), *Hands of Destiny* (1954), which he also produced, *Port of Escape* (1956), which he also co-wrote, and *Hidden Homicide* (1958), which he also co-wrote. In 1964 he directed two second features back to back at Bray. These were *The Runaway* (1964) and the *Delayed Flight* (1964), both of which were Hammer/Luckwell co-productions. His TV work includes episodes of *Douglas Fairbanks, Jr. Presents* (1953–1957, TV) and *The Telegoons* (1963–1964, TV). **Ham-**

**mer credits:** *The Runaway* (1964), *Delayed Flight* (1964)

### Young's Dress Hire

Young's provided the wedding dress and morning suits for the wedding scene in Hammer's *Four Sided Triangle* (1953). Now also known as Suits You, they remain in business today and have many shops up and down the UK. **Hammer credits:** *Four Sided Triangle* (1953)

### Yu Ling, Barbara

Ling (1938–1997) can be seen as the high priestess Chin Yang in Hammer's *The Satanic Rites of Dracula* (1974). Her other film credits include *Ping Pong* (1986), *Hardware* (1990) and *Peggy Su!* (1997), plus episodes of *The Avengers* (1961–1969, TV), *The Prisoner* (1967–1968, TV) and *Tenko* (1981–1984, TV). **Hammer credits:** *The Satanic Rites of Dracula* (1974, as Chin Yang)

### Yung, Liu Chia

This Chinese actor (1944–, aka Liu Ka Yong, Lau Kar-Wing and Lau Ka Wing) can be seen as Hsi Kwei, one of the vampire hunting brothers in Hammer's *The Legend of the 7 Golden Vampires* (1974). His many other credits include *Jin ou* (1967), *Master of the Flying Guillotine* (1975), *Game of Death* (1978), *Tang lang* (1978), *Kickboxer* (1989), *Seun sing* (2006) and *Choyleefut: Speed of Light* (2011). He also had a minor role in Hammer's *Shatter* (1974) under the name of Liu Ka Yong. He has also worked as an assistant director, action director and fight choreographer, as well as a director (for which he is sometimes billed as Lau Kar-Wing), among his credits here being such action flicks as *Shi lai yun dao* (1985), *Xiao sheng pa pa* (1986) and *Shou hu fei long* (1991). His brother is the actor, fight choreographer and director Liu Chia-Liang (1936–2013, aka Lau Kar Leung), who co-choreographed the action sequences for *The Legend of the 7 Golden Vampires*. **Hammer credits:** *The Legend of the 7 Golden Vampires* (1974, as Hsi Kwei), *Shatter* (1974, as First bodyguard [billed as Liu Ka Yong])

### Yunus, Tariq

This Indian actor (1946–1994) had a supporting role as a World Food Council representative in *Growing Pains* (1980, TV [episode of *Hammer House of Horror*]). He also popped up in episodes of *The Regiment* (1972–1973, TV), *Father Brown* (1974, TV), *Gangster* (1976–1978, TV) and *Inspector Morse* (1987–2000, TV). His film credits include *Figures in a Landscape* (1970), *East of Elephant Rock* (1976), *Who Dares Wins* (1982), *The Fourth Protocol* (1987), *The Deceivers* (1988) and *Bollywood* (1994). **Hammer credits:** *Growing Pains* (1980, TV [episode of *Hammer House of Horror*], as Charles Austin)

# Z

### "Zaro"

"Zaro" can be seen as Chief Firecloud in the Hammer comedy *Life with the Lyons* (1954). **Hammer credits:** *Life with the Lyons* (1954, as Chief Firecloud)

### Zenios, George

Zenios (real name Giorgos Zenios) can be seen as an Arab reporter in Hammer's *The Mummy's Shroud* (1967). His other film credits include *Woman of Straw* (1964), *Gia poion na vrexi!* (1976), *Avrianos polemistis* (1984), *The Fourth Protocol* (1987) and *The Catch* (2016). His TV work, including later appearances in Cyprus, takes in episodes of *No Hiding Place* (1959–1967, TV), *Studio Four* (1962, TV), *The Regiment* (1972–1973, TV), *Sunburn* (1999–2000, TV), *Deixe mou to filo sou* (2006, TV), *Diet Please* (2009, TV), *3s kai o Kokos* (2010, TV) and *Kokkino nyfiko* (2017, TV). **Hammer credits:** *The Mummy's Shroud* (1967, as Arab reporter [uncredited])

### Zevic, Stanley

Frequently cast as Slavic types (Russian officers and thugs, etc.), Zevic can be spotted in a minor supporting role in Hammer's *Break in the Circle* (1955). His other credits include *The Iron Petticoat* (1956), *Anastasia* (1956) and *Battle of the V-1* (1958), plus episodes of *BBC Sunday-Night Theatre* (1950–1959, TV) and *Assignment Foreign Legion* (1956, TV). **Hammer credits:** *Break in the Circle* (1955, as Second Russian)

### Zillah, Muriel

This British supporting actress (1909–2000) can be seen as Mrs. Coombe in the Hammer featurette *Danger List* (1957). Her other credits include *Happidrome* (1943), plus episodes of *Dixon of Dock Green* (1955–1976, TV), *Harpers West One* (1961–1963, TV) and *No Strings* (1967, TV). **Hammer credits:** *Danger List* (1957, as Mrs. Coombe)

### Zuber, Marc

In Britain from childhood, this Indian actor (1944–2003) can be seen as a guard in Hammer's *The Satanic Rites of Dracula* (1974). His other credits include *A Private Enterprise* (1975), *The Wind and the Lion* (1975), *Sweeney 2* (1978), *The Sea Wolves* (1980), *Foreign Body* (1986), *Shirley Valentine* (1989), *Doorie* (1989), *Robin Hood: Prince of Thieves* (1991) and *Jinnah* (1998), while his many television credits take in episodes of *The Onedin Line* (1971–1980, TV), *Blakes 7* (1978–1981, TV), *The Bill* (1984–2010, TV), *The Darling Buds of May* (1991–1993, TV) and *Grease Monkeys* (2003, TV). **Hammer credits:** *The Satanic Rites of Dracula* (1974, as Guard 1)

# Appendix

Among the many films announced for production by Exclusive and Hammer down the years,
the following failed to make it before the cameras for various reasons.

**All Hallow's Eve:** Proposed adaptation of the 1945 Charles Williams novel about "the attempts of two dead women to remain in contact with the living world."[1]

**Allan Quatermain Esquire: His Quest for the Holy Flower:** Announced in 1974, this proposed feature was to have followed the search for a mythical bloom by the popular H. Rider Haggard character Allan Quatermain (familiar from the 1885 novel *King Solomon's Mines* and its various sequels and film adaptations). Loosely based on Haggard's *Allan and the Holy Flower* (1915), Christopher Wicking was duly set to script the project, which, had it been successful, it was hoped would be spun off into a television series. However, Hammer was unable to find suitable backing for the proposal, which was subsequently shelved.

**The Amazon Queen:** Proposed exotic action adventure.

**The Amorous Prawn:** Proposed adaptation of the 1959 hit West End comedy by Anthony Kimmins, announced in 1961. It was eventually filmed in 1962 by British Lion/Covent Garden, starring Joan Greenwood, Ian Carmichael and Cecil Parker.

**And Then Frankenstein Created Woman:** Announced in 1959 as a follow-up to *The Curse of Frankenstein* (1957) and *The Revenge of Frankenstein* (1958), this episode eventually emerged as *Frankenstein Created Woman* (1967).

**Armchair Detective:** Based upon the radio series by Ernest Dudley, the creator of *Dr. Morelle*, this mystery-thriller was eventually made by Meridian Films in 1952, with Dudley himself co-writing the screenplay and also taking the leading role (as himself).

**The Beetle:** Announced in 2005 as a co-production between Hammer, Random Harvest (Harvest Pictures III) and Stan Winston Productions.

**The Big Wheel:** Originally announced in 1960, this boardroom drama about the wheelings and dealings of a giant corporation was to have been a Columbia co-production based on the 1949 novel by John Brooks, which had been adapted for the screen by Jimmy Sangster. Said Sangster of the project, "Why I ever wrote it I can't imagine and why Hammer were interested is even more perplexing. Anyway, they didn't make it."[2]

**Black Beauty:** Hammer considered a film version of the 1877 Anna Sewell classic in the late sixties, but it fell by the wayside. Tony Tenser eventually produced a version of the story in 1971 for Tigon starring Mark Lester. A previous version had been made in America in 1946, whilst a popular British TV series titled *The Adventures of Black Beauty* appeared in 1972. A second television series, *The New Adventures of Black Beauty* (1990–1991, TV) followed, as did a further big screen remake in 1998.

**Black Chiffon:** Announced in 1956

**The Black Hole of Calcutta:** Announced in 1960, this proposed follow-up to *The Stranglers of Bombay* (1959) was to have been scripted by producer Anthony Hinds; however, the project was abandoned following *Stranglers'* disappointing box office show.

**The Black Opal:** Set to have started shooting at Bray on 12 September 1955 under the direction of Terence Fisher, this second feature thriller was cancelled at the last moment.

**Black Sabbath:** Proposed feature based upon the R.P. Blount novel *Charlie* about "the adopted son of a union between Satan and a member of a black magic coven" who is "governed by his stillborn brother from beyond the grave,"[3] as the press release had it.

**Blood of the Foreign Legion:** Proposed action epic announced in August 1963 and again in 1967. Set in the Sahara Desert, the film was to have been an adventure in the manner of *The Camp on Blood Island* (1958), with Peter Cushing set to star. Anthony Hinds was to produce from a script by Peter Bryan.

**Blood Will Have Blood:** Less a proposal and more of a promotional piece, this apparent follow-up to *Demons of the Mind* (1972) was supposedly put forward in 1977 by one Bennett Byron Sims (either a pseudonym or a fabrication), and was to have been a modern take on the werewolf legend (note that the lycanthropic elements found in the original screenplay for *Demons of the Mind*—itself first known as *Blood Will Have Blood*—had mostly been suppressed). The project was said to be a co-production between Hammer and a company known as Cinema Shares (presumably another fabrication).

**Brainstorm:** Announced in August 1963, this psychological thriller was to have been another entry in Hammer's string of "mini Hitchcocks" penned by Jimmy Sangster. It was later re-titled *The Claw* and announced again in 1968, with Freddie Francis set to direct and Anthony Nelson Keys to produce. It finally emerged, somewhat belatedly, as *Fear in the Night* (1972), with Sangster co-writing, producing and directing. Recalled Sangster of the film's lengthy development: "*The Claw* had been set on a houseboat moored near a big house, which I suggested could be Oakley Court. I must have been feeling nostalgic. Michael Styson [who went on to re-write the script] came up with the idea of transferring the story to a cottage and a nearby boarding school. This was all that was needed. He did a quick re-write and I gave it back to Michael Carreras who decided that at last it was worth making."[4]

**Brat Farrar:** The rights to this 1949 novel by Josephine Tey about a fake heir were bought by Hammer in 1954 and the project was announced for production in 1955, but it never materialized. It was next mooted as part of the studio's 1958–1959 program, at which point it was to have been directed by Joseph Losey from a script by Paul Dehn, with Dirk Bogarde penciled in to star. However, when Columbia suggested that the film might not be commercial, it was put on the back burner again until the success of *Taste of Fear* (1961) prompted new interest in the thriller. Consequently, it finally made it before the cameras as *Paranoiac* (1963). However, by this time, the script was by Jimmy Sangster, the director was Freddie Francis and the star Oliver Reed.

### Break Out

**The Bride of Newgate Gaol (aka Midnight Jones and The Reluctant Virgin):** Based on the 1950 novel by John Dickson Carr, this costly period drama, scripted by Jimmy Sangster, was initiated in 1965 and officially announced in 1967 and again in 1971. However, its budget, estimated at a robust £325,000, proved to be too much of a commitment and the project was subsequently abandoned at the planning stage.

**The Brutal Land (aka The San Siado Killings):** Originally penned by Peter Newman, this Mexican-set western about a gunfighter who holes up at a ranch to recover from his wounds finally saw the light of day as *The Savage Guns* (1962). Announced as a Hammer production in 1959 with Stanley Baker set to star and Michael Carreras to produce, it was eventually directed in Spain under the title *Tierra brutal* by Carreras through his own company Capricorn Productions, which he formed in December 1960 following his temporary departure from Hammer after the plug was pulled on *The Rape of Sabena*. By this time the script had been re-written by Edmund Morris. The movie, which was produced by Carreras's longtime friend Jimmy Sangster, starred Richard Basehart, who had previously appeared in Hammer's *Visa to Canton* (1960). The film's co-stars were Don Taylor, who had played Robin Hood in *Men of Sherwood Forest* (1954), and Alex Nicol, who had starred in *Face the Music* (1954) and *The House Across the Lake* (1954). No other Hammer personnel were involved in the production, which was filmed on location in Spain.

**Build Us a Dam:** Proposed adaptation of the 1955 Jon Manchip White novel of the same name. Announced in 1957, it was to have been filmed on location in Tanganyika, with Val Guest onboard as director.

**Bury Him Darkly:** Announced in 1970 (complete with poster artwork), this adaptation of the 1969 John Blackburn novel was penned by Jimmy Sangster, with Anthony Nelson Keys set to produce. The project was originally intended as a Charlemagne production (the company run by Keys and Christopher Lee), and was announced again in 1973.

**Callan:** Announced in 1974, this big screen version of the popular TV series (1967–1972, TV) was eventually made by EMI and Magnum Productions, with Edward Woodward reprising his title role as the intelligence officer, here under the direction of Don Sharp.

**The Camera:** Before he wrote either *A Man on the Beach* (1956) or *X—The Unknown* (1956), Jimmy Sangster penned this short story, which he submitted to Tony Hinds for possible production. Whilst Hinds found the script to be okay, he didn't want to film it, but *was* sufficiently impressed with Sangster's writing style, which resulted in his being allowed to adapt the Victor Canning story *Chance at the Wheel* as *A Man on the Beach*. The rest, as they say, is history.

**Captain Morgan, Buccaneer:** Proposed action adventure featuring the notorious pirate, set to star Forrest Tucker, who had already starred in *Break in the Circle* (1955) for the company, with *The Abominable Snowman* (1957) yet to come.

**The Captives:** Announced in 1963.

**Chaka Zulu—The Black Napoleon:** Based upon the 1892 H. Rider Haggard novel *Nada the Lily—A Tale of the Zulus*, this epic was announced in 1974 with an accompanying poster by Tom Chantrell, and was set to be shot in South Africa, with Christopher Lee to star as a white hunter who is told of the story of the East African leader and despot.

**Charter to Danger:** Announced in 1957, this Val Guest-scripted adaptation of the 1954 Eliot Reed novel was to follow the adventures of an American soldier of fortune whilst ostensibly on holiday in Spain (note that Eliot Reed was a pseudonym for the novelist Eric Ambler, who wrote the book in collaboration with Charles Rodda).

**Charters and Caldicott:** Proposed spin-off TV series featuring the cricket-mad Englishmen from *The Lady Vanishes* (1979), with Ian Carmichael and Arthur Lowe set to repeat their big screen roles. The BBC eventually made an unrelated series with the same title in 1985, starring Robin Bailey and Michael Aldridge.

**Children of the Wolf:** This 1971 play by John Peacock was bought by Hammer the same year, and was set to be directed by Seth Holt, who, before his untimely death, developed the material with the playwright. Recalled Peacock, "Seth and I worked on the script for quite a long time."[5] The project remained at Hammer, and was later revived by director John Hough in the mid–eighties, but again it failed to make it to the screen. Note that the play's star, Shane Briant, went on to make several films for Hammer, and was originally set to reprise his stage role in the proposed film version.

**Children of the Wolf:** Proposed thriller set to star Lesley-Anne Down, with John Hough onboard as director. Announced in 1994.

**A Chorus of Echoes:** Proposed adaptation of the 1950 Elleston Trevor novel, announced in 1957.

**The Criminal:** Originally intended as a Hammer production, this Jimmy Sangster–scripted gangster thriller was sold on to producer Jack Greenwood at Merton Park when its star, Stanley Baker, insisted that Joseph Losey direct it. The film was released in 1960, and was known as *The Concrete Jungle* in America.

**Dance Band Story:** Proposed musical featurette, to be produced and directed by Michael Carreras, in the style of his other half-hour programmers of the period.

**Dante's Inferno:** Announced in 1971, this was proposed as another Hammer-AIP collaboration following *The Vampire Lovers* (1970), and was to have been based on Dante Alighieri's 1320 poem *The Divine Comedy*, the "Inferno" segment of which had been filmed in 1924 and 1935.

**The Daphne Du Maurier Hour (aka The Breaking Point):** Along with *The House on the Strand*, in 1987, Hammer acquired a number of other Daphne Du Maurier titles, and intended to film them as a thirteen-part series of tele-features.

**The Daring Dexters:** Proposed film version of the BBC's circus-set radio serial that first aired in June 1947.

**The Day the Earth Caught Fire:** Announced in 1993 as part of the Warner Bros. package, this was to have been a remake of Val Guest's 1961 non–Hammer classic (made by British Lion and Pax). Production was to commence in 1995, with Jan De Bont set to direct with Tom Hanks in the lead.

**Dead of Night:** Announced in 1978, this was to have been a remake of the classic Ealing portmanteau of 1945, with the setting now seemingly switched to wartime Soho. The multi-story format had of course already been successfully exploited by Hammer's rival Amicus in the sixties and seventies, but by now had run its course. Indeed, one of their films, *From Beyond the Grave* (1973), had already featured a variation on *The Haunted Mirror* sequence from *Dead of Night*, albeit based on a different story, *The Gate Crasher*, by R. Chetwynd-Hayes.

**Death Rattle:** This epic western about the last days of the American Indian was on the drawing board at Hammer in early 1976 and was announced again in 1978, but like everything else proposed during this period, it came to nothing. A proposed co-production with MOS Films, it was to have been filmed in South Africa on a healthy $1.3m budget. The script was written by Bima Stagg, and Jimmy Sangster was onboard as associate producer. Unfortunately, all those approached to star turned it down, among them such diverse talents as James Coburn, Candice Bergen, Joni Mitchell and Robert Mitchum. Michael Carreras and Tom Sachs were set to produce.

**The Deathshead-Vampire:** This Peter Bryan script (aka *The Vampire-Beast Craves Blood*) was subsequently sold to Tigon, who filmed it as *The Blood Beast Terror* (1967). Directed by Vernon Sewell, the film starred Peter Cushing, Robert Flemyng and Wanda Ventham.

**The Deer Slayer:** Proposed adaptation of the 1841 novel by James Fenimore Cooper, announced in 1956.

**The Devil and All His Works:** This short story anthology series for television was mooted in 1974 during pre-production on the screen version of the Dennis Wheatley novel *To the Devil a Daughter* (1976). The title derives from a 1971 factual study by Wheatley on demonology, though the proposed series would have been fictional, and to this end Don Houghton conceived eight storylines. However, the box office failure of the feature put paid to the TV show. Anthony Nelson Keys was set to produce, with Christopher Lee to have been involved in some of the stories.

**The Devil Rides Out:** Proposed remake of the 1968 Hammer classic, announced as part of the 1993 Warner Bros. deal. Christopher Lee expressed a strong interest in reprising his role of the Duc de Richeleau, whilst Joe Date was mooted as a possible director.

**Dick Barton in Darkest Africa:** Announced in 1949, this proposed fourth film in the Dick Barton series was cancelled following the death of leading man Don Stannard in a car crash. Scripted by John Gilling, there were apparently plans to shoot the film in Kenya, which seems a bit extravagant given Hammer's tight budgets.

**Dinosaur Girl:** Announced in 1971, this was a proposed sequel to *When Dinosaurs Ruled the Earth* (1970), and was again to have starred Victoria Vetri. Unfortunately, we got *Creatures the World Forgot* (1971) instead.

**Disaster in Space:** Announced in 1970, this proposed sequel to *Moon Zero Two* (1969), again scripted by Michael Carreras, failed to materialize following that film's disastrous performance at the box office. A *Moon Zero Two* TV spin-off also crashed and burned as a consequence.

**The Disciple (aka Disciple of Death):** Following his appearance as Count Karnstein in *Lust for a Vampire* (1970), Mike Raven tried to interest Hammer in a script about Satanic worship that he had written under his real name, Churton Fairman. Though it announced the project and even gave the production a start date of September 1971 (with Jimmy Sangster involved as producer and director), the studio eventually passed on the piece, which Raven went on to part-finance himself. Made for Chromage in 1972 under the title *Disciple of Death*, the film was written and produced by Raven (again using his real name) in conjunction with its director Tom Parkinson. Raven also played the leading role. Commented Raven of his script, "I tried to write a genuine Gothic tale without using either of the two standard prototypes—Frankenstein or Dracula. What I tried to do was produce an original tale which contained the elements that should go into a Gothic, yet would come across as completely fresh and unusual."[6]

**The Disciple of Dracula:** This Jimmy Sangster screenplay was one of several potential sequels to *Dracula* (1958). Hammer not being a company that liked to waste anything, elements from the script were subsequently worked into both *The Brides of Dracula* (1960) and *The Kiss of the Vampire* (1963).

**Disciple of Vengeance:** Submitted in 1967, this storyline by Colin Cowie was about a vengeful ventriloquist's dummy, but was turned down no doubt owing to its similarities to *Dead of Night* (1945) and *Devil Doll* (1963).

**Dr. Jekyll and Mr. Hyde:** Announced in 1959, this proposed "straight" version of the story was to act as a companion piece to studio's spoof *The Ugly Duckling* (1959), whose star, Bernard Bresslaw, was again to take on the lead roles(s), for which he underwent make-up tests with Roy Ashton. Instead, Hammer made *The Two Faces of Dr. Jekyll* (1960).

**Dr. Morelle—The Case of the Crooked Steeple:** Proposed sequel to *Dr. Morelle—The Case of the Missing Heiress* (1949).

**Doctors Wear Scarlet:** Terence Fisher tried and failed to interest Hammer in filming Simon Raven's 1960 novel, which was eventually made as *Incense for the Damned* (1970) by director Robert Hartford-Davis (credited as Michael Burrowes), with Peter Cushing and Patrick Mower starring. A troubled production, the finished film was re-cut against the wishes of its director (hence his use of a pseudonym) and wasn't trade shown until 1972, following which it stayed on the shelf until 1976.

**Doreen Gray:** Proposed distaff version of the Oscar Wilde novel, *The Picture of Dorian Gray*, previously filmed in 1945, and here set to star Mia Farrow, with Roy Skeggs and Brian Lawrence in the producers' chairs. Intended as a Hammer-Cinema Arts co-production.

**Dracula:** Announced 1978, from a story by John Elder (Anthony Hinds).

**Dracula:** Yet another version of the story, announced in 1980 during the production of *Hammer House of Horror* (1980, TV), to be produced by Roy Skeggs and Brian Lawrence. Commented Skeggs at the time, "People may have wondered why we have announced another Dracula since there have been so many Dracula pictures made recently. We say that there has never been a Dracula series like those made by Hammer starring Christopher Lee. We have the know-how, the tradition and the experience. Already we are conducting a worldwide search for a suitable actor to portray our new Dracula."[7]

**The Dracula Odyssey:** Hammer announced a number of attempts to re-launch their Dracula cycle in the seventies, among them this Amicus-style compendium of four stories set in various times and places, taken from the perspectives of his female victims. Announced in 1976, one of the tales, *The Lady Was a Vampire*, was penned by Don Houghton. The film was to have been produced by Michael Carreras and Tom Sachs.

**Dracula—The Beginning (aka Dracule):** Announced in 1984, the title tells pretty much everything in this failed attempt to re-launch the *Dracula* story afresh from the start. John Hough was attached to the project as director, and had hoped to lure Christopher Lee back to the role.

**Dracula Walks the Night:** Sadly, despite a press release in 1974, this tantalising project proved to be a hoax, which is a shame, as Terence Fisher was supposedly set to direct a script by Jimmy Sangster and Richard Matheson featuring Vlad the Impaler, Van Helsing, Sherlock Holmes and his sidekick Dr. Watson. It has not been revealed who the hoaxer was, and Hammer denied the project ever existed as far as they were concerned.

**Dracula ... Who?:** This screenplay—a comedic twist on *Dracula*—was penned by none other than Hammer's own Ingrid Pitt, who came up with the idea whilst filming *The Wicker Man* (1973) in Scotland with Christopher Lee. According to the actress, "The Count wants to become a vegetarian and live like a normal person. The Countess—me—ain't interested, though."[8] At one point, Robert Young—the director of *Vampire Circus* (1972)–was attached to the project when it was in development with Hammer. The screenplay knocked around for years, and was announced again as late as in 1996 by Gary Kurtz, who had produced such George Lucas blockbusters as *American Graffiti* (1973), *Star Wars* (1977) and *The Empire Strikes Back* (1980).

**Dracula's Feast of Blood:** This unsolicited screenplay by Kevin Francis was submitted to Hammer in the spring of 1969, but officially rejected by James Carreras and Brian Lawrence on 19 May. Unfortunately, elements from this script subsequently found their way into Hammer's *Taste the Blood of Dracula* (1970), for which the studio duly compensated Francis, who later announced the title as a Tyburn production in 1974, but it failed to appear.

**Easy Virtue:** Proposed television adaptation of the celebrated 1924 Noel Coward stage play, set to star Joan Collins, Denholm Elliott and either Maggie Smith or Angela Lansbury.

**The Ecstasy of Dorian Gray:** Announced in 1970 and again in 1971, this was to have been a variation on the Oscar Wilde novel *The Picture of Dorian Gray*, originally filmed to great effect by MGM in 1945.

**Emergency Call/Trail of Blood:** In 1951, two separate but similarly-themed medical dramas were submitted to Hammer by Vernon Harris and Lewis Gilbert. These were *Trail of Blood* and *Emergency Call*, both of which resolved themselves with the hunt for a rare blood type to save a life. Recalled Gilbert, "The ten-page treatment I came up with I sent to Exclusive Films. Their boss was James Carreras, who was also the head of Exclusive's subsidiary Hammer Films. He had been dropping heavy hints about getting a film out of me. Reaction came almost immediately with a telephone call, most unusual. Exclusive liked the treatment very much, but as they already had something much too similar they could not proceed with my story or the other person's until some kind of arrangement had been arrived at."[9] Gilbert, who had just begun to make a name for himself as a director, and Harris, who had already co-written *The Adventures of PC 49–The Case of the Guardian Angel* (1949) and *A Case for PC 49* (1951) for Hammer, consequently decided to pool their resources and combine the two scripts. The resultant effort was subsequently offered to Butchers (for whom Gilbert had already worked) and made the following year under Gilbert's title of *Emergency Call*. Gilbert and Harris successfully went on to collaborate for over thirty years on such projects as *Albert RN* (1953), *Reach for the Sky* (1956), *The Admirable Crichton* (1957), *Carve Her Name with Pride* (1958), *Moonraker* (1979) and *Educating Rita* (1983), with Harris working as either screen writer or script editor.

**The Experiment:** Announced in 1974, this John Gould script set within an asylum was to be financed with money from a Canadian tax shelter and was to have been a co-production between Hammer and Almerline Productions, with James Mason and Simon Ward set to star. Unfortunately, the project collapsed just two weeks before the proposed start date.

***Eye for An Eye:*** Announced 1974, this thriller was to have involved the implantation of a tiny camera into the eye of a young man so that a cripple can experience life by watching the images transmitted from the camera, but the young man is driven to madness and murder by the pressure the device causes on his brain. Comparisons to *The Sorcerers* (1967) would surely have been inevitable.

***The Fairytale Man:*** Announced in 1973, this Faustian comedy was written by Jimmy Sangster with Vincent Price in mind, with Harold Cohen onboard as producer. Cohen had produced two American TV movies with Sangster based on Sangster's first two novels. These were *private i* (1967), which was made as *The Spy Killer* (1969, TVM), and *Foreign Exchange* (1969, TVM [novel 1968]), both of which were directed by Roy Ward Baker. Unfortunately, budgetary problems scuppered the project, which Sangster subsequently bought back from Hammer and sold on to Disney, who made it as the disappointing *The Devil and Max Devlin* (1981), by which time it had been re-written by Mary Rodgers (Sangster shares a story credit with Rodgers, whilst she receives a sole screenplay credit). Recalled Sangster, "My only consolation in the affair (apart from the money) was the fact that I got to share a screen credit with the daughter of Richard Rodgers ... that's the Richard Rodgers who wrote all the great musicals. Would that his daughter had been as good a screenwriter as her father was a musician."[10]

***Frankenstein Trapped:*** Submitted and subsequently rejected story by Bob Baker.

***Friar Tuck:*** Announced in 1956, this self-explanatory title was discussed as a follow-up to *Men of Sherwood Forest* (1954), with Reginald Beckwith set to re-create the role of the portly monk. Terence Fisher was discussed as a possible director.

***Gateway to Hell:*** Proposed follow-up to *The Devil Rides Out* (1968), based upon Dennis Wheatley's 1970 novel, and again featuring the Duc de Richleau. Like *Strange Conflict* (see own entry), it didn't get past the proposal stage following the failure of *The Devil Rides Out* at the American box office.

***The Godmother:*** Following her work with Hammer on the big screen version of *Nearest and Dearest* (1973), Hammer considered making this spoof of *The Godfather* (1972) with Hylda Baker ("Hylda Baker is *The Godmother*—Need we say more?" queried the promotional artwork, which consisted of a particularly poor sketch of the star with a rose between her teeth). Perhaps wisely, the project was quietly dropped following its announcement in 1972 (though Baker did mention it on an episode of *Russell Harty Plus* [1972–1977, TV]).

***The Goldfish Bowl:*** Announced in 1972, this Jimmy Sangster script was another of his psychological thrillers.

***Hallowe'en House of Horror:*** Proposed collection of TV specials, submitted to America's ABC in 1978, involving clips from old Hammer films and a linking story (to be penned by Jimmy Sangster and Al Taylor) about a TV star seeking shelter in an old house, the books in which prompt the clips. The follow-ups were provisionally titled *Behind the Scenes of the Hallowe'en House of Horror* and *The Other Rooms in the Hallowe'en House of Horror*. One wonders if the success of John Carpenter's *Halloween* (1978) had any influence on the title.

***The Hammer Horror Zone:*** Announced for broadcast in 2000, this proposed forty-five-minute/hour-long animated series was to have been made under license by Abrams Gentile Entertainment (AGE), and was to have presented a re-telling of several classic Hammer horror films. Story editor Ron Kaehler and producer Anthony Gentile wrote two pilot scripts for the show in 1998. These were *Disciples of Dracula*, which was to have melded elements from *The Brides of Dracula* (1960) and *The Kiss of the Vampire* (1963), and *Howl of the Werewolf*, a re-telling of *The Curse of the Werewolf* (1961).

***Hammer Horrors:*** Proposed twenty-six-part hour-long TV series, announced in 1972 and again in 1973 for the 1974 season. No relation to the later *Hammer House of Horror* (1980, TV), it was intended as a collection of remakes, which Michael Carreras hoped to also release on videocassette. Commented the producer, "*Hammer Horrors* was to have been made up of remakes of the classic Hammer films and was to have included stories featuring Dracula, Frankenstein, the Werewolf, the Mummy, Zombies, the Reptile, the Stranglers, the Phantom of the Opera, and other old friends."[11]

***Hammer House of Horror:*** Season two of the 1980 TV series, cancelled following problems with financial backers. Anthony Read was again onboard as story editor, whilst Ingrid Pitt was to have been involved as a writer.

***Hammer House of Horrors:*** Announced in 1977 and 1978, and not be confused with the later anthology series *Hammer House of Horror* (1980, TV), this package of ninety-minute TV movies (rehashed from several previous ideas and proposals) included such titles as *The Insatiable Thirst of Dracula* and *The Golem* (both scripted by Don Houghton), *Werewolf of Moravia* and remakes of several Hammer classics. Fuller theatrical versions of the TV movies with extra scenes of sex and violence were supposedly part of the deal. The series was intended as a German co-production with Constantin Films, with episodes to be divided between Britain and Germany. Seemingly, Michael Carreras's idea was to cast the films with unknowns from a nation-wide talent contest searching for new stars, a bad idea that almost single-handedly scuppered the project. Note that Tyburn was preparing a Golem-style project at the same time, which likewise failed to appear.

***Hammer House of Mystery and Suspense— Season 2:*** Planned follow up to *Hammer House of Mystery and Suspense* (1984, TVM), which was abandoned after a sea change at Fox. Among the proposed storylines, of which thirteen had been planned and worked out according to story editor John Peacock, was *The Housekeeper* by Nigel Kneale (previously announced in connection with *The Haunted House of Hammer*). Commented Peacock of the shelved story, "It would also make a marvelous feature actually."[12]

***The Hammer House of Mystery and Suspense:*** In 1982, just before Hammer went on to make *Hammer House of Mystery and Suspense* (1984, TVM), they produced a brochure to entice backers. This contained a number of mock episode titles and plot synopses, none of which were subsequently scripted or used when it was decided that the emphasis this time round would not be on horror and gore. The proposed titles were *Half a Pound of Tuppeny Cyanide*, *Gallow Bait*, *Death Wrapped for Christmas*, *Saraband for Sara*, *Diary of a Country Killer*, *The Lady Is for Burning*, *Deadly Night Maid*, *Death's Pretty Children*, *Scream and Scream Again*, *Give Me Back My Body*, *The Evil That Men Do*, *By the Light of the Blood Red Moon* and *He Who Shrieks Loudest*.

***The Hammer Mystery Theatre:*** Proposed thirteen-part hour-long TV series, featuring stories compiled by Hammer's script supervisor John Peacock. Writers penciled in for involvement included Nigel Kneale (presumably with the unused *Housekeeper* script again), James Follett, Jill Hyem, Jimmy Sangster, Andrew Laurance, Jesse Lasky, Jr., and Pat Silver.

***The Hammer TV Playhouse of Shock and Suspense:*** Proposed umbrella title for a season of thirty-nine Hammer features, seemingly scuppered by the fact that the copyright of the proposed films actually belonged to the backers and distributors and not to Hammer. Among the package of titles were to have been *The Quatermass Xperiment* (1956), *Dracula* (1958) and *The Curse of the Werewolf* (1961).

***Hammerhead:*** Proposed thriller, announced in 1964.

***Hate (aka Sounds from Hell):*** Proposed horror film with a rock background, set up as a co-production with Gerry Anderson of Supermarionation fame. Michael Carreras tried to revive the project by himself as late as 1988.

***The Haunted House of Hammer:*** Proposed TV series in the vein of *Hammer House of Horror* (1980, TV) and *Hammer House of Mystery and Suspense* (1984, TVM). This one at least sounded viable, but failed to materialize. It was still in the pipeline as late as 1994, with finance to be provided by Majestic Films. The American producer Steve Krantz, best known for the cartoon feature *Fritz the Cat* (1971), was attached to the project at one point. Commented the press release, "Over the past three years, the Hammer script department has collected and collated over 700 ghost stories from writers, past and present, in preparation for a definitive series of the most chilling and terrifying ghost tales to reach the screen."[13] It was hoped that some twenty-six half-hour episodes would be made (later reports had it as forty-four hour-long episodes), of which the first thirteen were officially announced. These were: *Which One?* (by R.Chetwynd-Hayes), *The Sweeper, The Cottage in the Wood, The Coatstand, And Give Us Yesterday, Afterward* (by Edith Wharton), *Markland the Hunter, The Shelter, The Wanderer* (by R. Chetwynd-Hayes), *A Strange Case of Drowning, The Four-Poster* (by Terry Tapp), *The Housekeeper* (by Nigel Kneale) and *The Summons*. Other proposed stories (among them several by R. Chetwynd-Hayes and one by Anthony Hinds writing as John Elder) included *Something Comes in from the Grave* (by R. Chetwynd-Hayes), *The Ghost Who Limped* (by R. Chetwynd-Hayes), *The Doll's Ghost* (by F. Marion Crawford), *The Ghost of Sherlock Holmes* (by Leslie Halliwell—yes, *that* Leslie Halliwell), *Graveyard Lodge* (by Heather Vineham), *Oh, Whistle and I'll Come to You, My Lad* (by M.R. James [a remake of the 1968 *Omnibus* classic, later remade for TV in 2010]), *Alice in Bellington Lane* (by R. Chetwynd-Hayes), *The Sad Ghost* (by R. Chetwynd-Hayes), *The Ghouls* (by R. Chetwynd-Hayes), *Welcombe Manor* (by Roger Mallison), *Keep the Gaslight Burning* (by R. Chetwynd-Hayes), *The Cupboard* (by Jeffrey Farnol), *Norton Camp* (by William Charlton), *The Lamp* (by Agatha Christie), *Cold Fingers* (by R. Chetwynd-Hayes), *The Rock Garden* (by Heather Vineham), *The Prescription* (by Marjorie Bowen), *The Water Ghost of Harrowhy Hall* (by J.K. Bangs), *The Haunted Doll's House* (by M.R. James), *I Can't Come, Mummy—I'm Dead* (by John Elder) and *Tomorrow's Ghost* (by R. Chetwynd-Hayes). Further stories under consideration (among them a second John Elder tale) included *Mariners* (by Terry Tapp), *The Judge's House* (by Bram Stroker), *The Body Snatcher* (by Robert Louis Stevenson [a remake of the 1945 Val Lewton classic]), *Run for the Tunnel* (by R. Chetwynd-Hayes), *The Man Who Stayed Behind* (by R. Chetwynd-Hayes), *Canon Alberic's Scrapbook* (by M.R. James), *Come and Get Me* (by Elizabeth Walter) and *The Dead Still Live, My Darling* (by John Elder).[14]

**The Haunting of Lady Jane:** This episode of *Hammer House of Mystery and Suspense* (1984, TVM), about the haunting of a boat, was abandoned at the behest of Fox, despite being penned by TV veteran by Dennis Spooner. It was replaced with a script titled *Child's Play*. Read the synopsis: "The *Lady Jane* is a cabin cruiser with a mind of its own. It moors, banks, steers … and even brings justice to its passengers." Hmm, perhaps it's just as well it was dropped.

**The Haunting of Toby Jugg:** Proposed adaptation of Dennis Wheatley's 1948 novel, announced in 1967, with Richard Matheson approached (but not contracted) to write the screenplay, and Christopher Lee announced to star. The option subsequently lapsed, but was again acquired by Hammer in 1974 at the same time as *To the Devil a Daughter*. However, only the latter made it to the screen following a convoluted pre-production period, and its resultant box office failure put paid to any other Wheatley adaptations. Terence Fisher, who had been enthusiastic about the book, was earmarked as a possible director (commented Fisher of the story: "I'd love to make it. Because it has everything in it, you see. It has the supernatural, it has this wonderful emotional quality as between boy and girl, you know. That's what's exciting about it").[15] As late as 1978, Val Guest was commissioned to pen a script and possibly direct. The story was eventually filmed by the BBC in 2006 as *The Haunted Airman* and televised on BBC4 on Halloween.

**Headhunter:** Submitted by Bob Baker, this story outline was subsequently rejected.

**Helen of Coral Creek:** Based upon a screenplay by John Gilling, this proposed spoof of *Helen of Troy* was suggested to James Carreras by the writer-director in the mid-sixties, but on this occasion the Colonel didn't take the bait.

**Hell Is a City:** Proposed to Screen Gems and ATV in 1967, this crime series was based upon Hammer's 1960 film of the same name. Long in gestation, the idea was still knocking around as late as 1974, when it was submitted to Granada and Thames for consideration.

**Hellrake:** This novel by Don Houghton was optioned by Hammer and turned into a screenplay by its author, but it failed to make it before the cameras.

**A Heritage of Horror: The Story of Hammer Films:** Announced in 1978, this was to have been a TV clip show highlighting Hammer's glorious past. One wonders if the title was inspired by David Pirie's Hammer-centric study *A Heritage of Horror: The English Gothic Cinema 1946–1972* (1973)?

**Hideous Whispers (aka The Hiss):** Announced in 1989, this was to have been an adaptation of the 1981 Andrew Laurance novel *The Hiss* (originally published in 1969 as *Catacomb*). The screenplay was by John Hockley and Laurance himself (real name Andre Joseph Launay), with Robert Young set to direct. It was also announced in 1993 as part of the Warner Bros. package.

**A Holiday for Simon:** Announced in 1956.

**House of Evil:** Announced in 1971.

**The House on the Strand:** Proposed adaptation of the 1969 Daphne Du Maurier novel, with Val Guest attached as scriptwriter. Announced in 1987 and again in 1990, this time with Jan Hartman onboard as the screenwriter. Other scriptwriters involved in the project include John Peacock and Paul Annett, with the latter set to direct, with finance to be provided by The Weintraub Group. Commented the press release, "Set in contemporary London and in the picturesque cornwall of the present day and the 14th century, it tells of a man's attempt to escape the problems of his gray, confused lifestyle and failing marriage.

Through drug-induced hallucinations, he experiences colorful, exciting encounters of a primitive and sometimes brutal age, until finally his total pre-occupation with visiting his fantasy world destroys him."[16] Pierce Brosnan and Lesley-Anne Down were at one point pencilled in to star.

**I Am Legend:** Also known as *The Night Creatures*, a title that was eventually used for the U.S. release of Hammer's *Captain Clegg* (1962), this proposed screen version of Richard Matheson's 1954 novel was long on the cards at Hammer, Anthony Hinds having acquired the rights for the company in 1957. Matheson even came to Britain to work on the screenplay, whilst Val Guest was set to direct. Sadly, the production never gelled. The script was then sold on to the American producer Robert L. Lippert, with whom Hammer had had dealings, and was eventually made as *The Last Man on Earth* (1963) starring Vincent Price (albeit with a new script by William Leicester, Furio Monetti, Ubaldo Ragona and Richard Matheson [writing under the assumed name of Logan Swanson]). A remake, *The Omega Man*, starring Charlton Heston, later appeared in 1971. Neither was very good. As late as the early seventies, director Terence Fisher was still interested in helming a production of the story, though the Heston version no doubt put paid to this. The story was remade again in 2007 as *I Am Legend*, this time as a vehicle for Will Smith.

**I Hate You … Cat!:** This proposed Spanish co-production (supposedly one of twenty-six) was announced in 1974.

**I'm in Charge:** Proposed in 1959, this film project derived its title from one of the various catchphrases used by comedian Bruce Forsyth on his hit TV show *Sunday Night at the London Palladium* (1955–1967, TV). Hammer had hoped to feature Forsyth in *The Ugly Duckling* (1959), but when commitments prevented him from appearing they proposed a star vehicle that would instead feature him as a "crazy courier on a foreign holiday tour."[17] The project was eventually sold on, but failed to materialize elsewhere.

**In the Sun:** Announced in 1969 and again in 1970, this science fiction story was about a spaceship that is pulled by gravity into the sun, where its astronauts subsequently discover a world of aliens under the surface. Following the disaster of *Moon Zero Two* (1969), it was cancelled.

**The Indian Mutiny:** Proposed period adventure scripted by Anthony Hinds.

**The Insatiable Thirst of Dracula:** Announced in 1973, this was one of several Dracula projects bandied about by the studio during this period (at one stage it was suggested that the film should star the winner of a proposed national talent competition). The project, scripted by Don Houghton, was announced again in 1977 as part of a package of proposed TV movies under the title *Hammer House of Horrors* (not to be confused with the later anthology series *Hammer House of Horror* [1980,

TV]). Houghton's script for *The Golem* was also part of the package.

***Inspector Hornleigh:*** A popular radio character, Hornleigh had already appeared in three films starring Gordon Harker. These were *Inspector Hornleigh* (1938), *Inspector Hornleigh on Holiday* (1939) and *Inspector Hornleigh Goes to It* (1940). The radio series was created by Hans Privin and was part of the *Monday Night at Eight* program.

***The Invisible Man:*** Proposed remake of the 1933 Universal film, announced during the period that Hammer was granted access to the Hollywood studio's library of horror classics for the remake treatment following the success of *Dracula* (1958).

***The Island***

***Jack the Ripper Goes West:*** Announced in 1978 and again in 1979, this was to have been produced by Euan Lloyd from a script by Scot Finch dating back to 1974, when Lloyd had hoped to make it for his own company, with Peter Collinson set to direct and Christopher Lee approached (but not signed) to star. It was to have seen the notorious serial killer carry on his murderous deeds in America (the idea seems to have been inspired by the 1935 classic *The Ghost Goes West*, which sees the ghost of a Scottish castle transported to America when the building is taken there stone by stone by a millionaire). In 1974, a similar premise was explored in the western *A Knife for the Ladies*, whilst in 1985 a TV movie titled *Terror at London Bridge* had the spirit of Jack the Ripper turning up at Lake Havasu, Arizona, where the original London Bridge was transported stone-by-stone.

***Jeb:*** Part of a proposed film slate with Pictures in Paradise, this project was penned by the Kiwi writer Nick Ward, best known for the screenplay *Stickmen* (2001).

***Journey to the Unknown II:*** Proposed second season of the 1969 Hammer/Fox show.

***Just for Kicks:*** This World Cup comedy was announced in 1972 with promotional artwork as abysmal as the dreadful, punning title.

***The Ka of Gifford Hilary:*** Proposed adaptation of Dennis Wheatley's 1956 novel about an English nobleman who, whilst involved with the struggle against Russia, finds himself a witness to his own death. Announced in 1967.

***Kali: Devil Bride of Dracula (aka Kali ... Bride of Dracula, Devil Bride for Dracula, High Priest of Vampires, Dracula—High Priest of Vampires, High Priest for the Vampires*** and ***Dracula in India):*** Just as *The Legend of the 7 Golden Vampires* (1974) had introduced the Count to the Far East, this new story was set to take him to India. The journey never happened, but was announced twice: first in 1971, with an Anthony Hinds/John Elder script, and again in 1974, this time in the form of a revised Don Houghton script. This second incarnation seems to have been intended as a possible follow-on to *The Legend of the 7 Golden Vampires*, with Peter Cushing set to return as Van Helsing. Recalled Michael Carreras, "I worked that out for Warner Bros. They had an enormous amount of blocked rupees in India, and wanted to use them to make a film…. I went to India, and researched the material. Suddenly, while we were in pre-production, the Indian government changed its monetary policy and gave Warner Bros. all their blocked rupees. Consequently, they didn't want to make a picture in India any more. Since the script was specifically tailored for India, it couldn't be adapted to another location."[18]

***King Charles and the Roundheads (aka The Cavalier):*** This historical drama was announced in 1955, with Val Guest onboard as writer-director. After much re-writing, it eventually emerged as *The Scarlet Blade* (1963).

***King Kong:*** Following the success of *One Million Years B.C.* (1966), Hammer approached effects wiz Ray Harryhausen about a remake of the 1933 classic. Unfortunately, this never got past the discussion stage, as RKO, which owned the rights, deemed that only sequels to the story could be made, as per their own *Son of Kong* (1933). Given that such Japanese follow-ups as *King Kong vs. Godzilla* (1962) and *King Kong Escapes* (1967) had by this time also been released, the idea was sadly shelved, although it was still being discussed as late as 1971. A fully-fledged remake of *King Kong* finally appeared in 1976 care of the Italian producer Dino de Laurentiis. A second remake by Peter Jackson followed in 2005.

***The Lady Vanishes:*** Announced in 1973 as part of a two-film deal with Samuel Z. Arkoff and AIP (the other film being *Mistress of the Seas*), this remake of the 1938 Hitchcock classic fell through when Hammer and Rank (who were also part of the deal) refused to Americanize the script, which was penned by Brian Hayles in 1974. It was eventually made by Hammer as a theatrical feature in 1979, with a screenplay by George Axelrod.

***The Lair of the White Worm:*** This 1911 Bram Stoker novel about a female vampire and an ancient snake god was adapted on spec by Don Houghton in 1974 in the hope that it would be optioned by Hammer. It wasn't. The novel was eventually filmed by producer-director Ken Russell in 1988 from his own screenplay adaptation.

***Lorna Doone:*** Hammer announced this version of the 1869 R.D. Blackmore novel in 1972 as a co-production with Rita Tushingham's own company, Tushing-ham having just appeared in *Straight On Till Morning* (1972) for Hammer. The story of a farmer who falls in love with an outlaw's daughter, it had previously been filmed in 1934 with Victoria Hopper and John Loder, and again in 1951 (in Hollywood) with Barbara Hale and Richard Greene. Tushingham's *Straight On Till Morning* leading man, Shane Briant, was set to co-star. Producer Michael Carreras also hoped to sign Oliver Reed for the film, but when the former Hammer star proved unavailable, the project was cancelled.

***Love in Smoky Regions:*** Announced in 1960, this "hot sex comedy"[19] as James Carreras described it, was to have been a Columbia co-production.

***Love Thy Neighbour Again:*** Announced in 1973, this sequel to *Love Thy Neighbour* (1973) failed to appear when the first film tanked at the box office.

***Madam Kitty:*** Proposed four-hour TV miniseries based upon the 1974 Peter Norden novel about a Berlin brothel and its Nazi clientele, previously filmed by Tinto Brass as *Salon Kitty* (1976).

***The Man Who Laughed:*** Announced in 1971, this proposed remake of the 1928 Conrad Veidt vehicle *The Man Who Laughs* was to have been filmed in Germany.

***The Man with Two Shadows:*** Announced in 1960, this adaptation of Robin Maugham's 1958 novel was to have been penned by the author himself. Set in 1946, it followed the exploits of a former British army officer, sent to the Middle East as a secret agent, only to find his mission in peril when he develops a second personality, the result of a head wound received in the war. Val Guest was pencilled in to direct on location in Tangiers.

***The Mercenaries:*** Proposed adaptation of Jon Manchip White's 1958 novel of the same name, for which White penned a draft script in 1962.

**Intriguing artwork for the unmade *Kali: Devil Bride of Dracula* (Hammer).**

*Miss Dangerfield:* Proposed screen version of the six-part 1947 BBC radio series *The Fabulous Miss Dangerfield.* It was announced in 1949.

*Mistress of the Seas:* This pirate yarn about real life pirate queen Anne Bonay was pitched to Universal by Michael Carreras in 1970, but was ultimately turned down, despite the creation of some tantalizing promotional artwork and the fact that Raquel Welch had been offered the lead role. Announced again in 1972, it was also revived in 1973 as a possible co-production between Hammer and Samuel Z. Arkoff during the period when Arkoff was involved in Rank/Hammer's remake of *The Lady Vanishes* (1979), but again fell by the wayside when Arkoff pulled out of the project, despite a script having been prepared by Val Guest (Arkoff seemingly pulled out when Rank and Hammer refused to Americanize the script for *The Lady Vanishes*). This script resurfaced in 1982 as *Pirate Anne,* which was to have starred Bo Derek and been produced by her husband John Derek, but nothing became of the enterprise, though Guest again worked on the screenplay. Other hands eventually filmed the story as *Cut-Throat Island* (1995), but the costly production was not a commercial success.

*Monster of the Night:* Announced in 1971, 1972 and again in 1973.

*Moulin Rouge:* Proposed thirteen-part TV series, announced in 1989, about the celebrated Paris nightclub and those who frequented it, such as Oscar Wilde, and those who appeared there on stage, including Jane Avril, the last of the original Can-Can dancers. The episode titles were as follows: *Rags to Riches, The Boneless Wonder, Too Fat for the Dance, Slander, The Good Jockey, Oscar, I'd Rather Have a Bow-Wow, Golden Helmets, The Footit and Chocolat Show, Cabin 54, On Tour, Vice in Their Eyes* and *Crazy Jane.* Majestic films was involved in the project as a distributor.

*Mrs. Dale's Diary:* Proposed big screen version of the popular radio drama serial, which first began broadcasting in 1948. It was announced in 1949.

*Murder in Safety*

*Murders at the Folies Bergere:* This project was put into development with Fantale Films following their success with *The Vampire Lovers* (1970), *Lust for a Vampire* (1970) and *Twins of Evil* (1971). It was subsequently re-titled *Terror in the Moulin Rouge, Murders in the Moulin Rouge* and, finally, *The Soho Murders,* but it soon after disappeared from the schedules. Britain's top female impersonator Danny La Rue was set to star at one point. Instead he made the wartime comedy *Our Miss Fred* (1972), which proved to be his only feature film.

*The Mutation:* Announced in 1964, this screenplay by Anthony Hinds (writing as John Elder) involved a research scientist at an atomic plant who becomes suffused with radioactive power.

*My Wife Next Door:* Announced in 1973, this was to have been a big screen transfer of the 1972 BBC sitcom starring John Alderton and Hannah Gordon, which had been created by Richard Waring and Brian Clemens.

*Nearer and Dearer:* Following their big screen version of the sitcom *Nearest and Dearest* (1973), Hammer considered making a follow-up. However, the idea was dropped when the film failed to perform as expected at the box office.

*Neither the Sea Nor the Sand:* Hammer eventually lost the rights to this 1969 novel by newsreader Gordon Honeycombe about love surviving death, but not before trying to set up the project with director Robert Young, who instead went on to direct *Vampire Circus* (1972) for the company. The novel was subsequently acquired by Tigon (in conjunction with Portland Films and LMG) and was directed by Fred Burnley from a script by Honeycombe and Rosemary Davies.

Up in flames. Poster artwork for the unmade *Mistress of the Seas,* which sank without trace (Hammer).

*Nessie* (aka *Nessie—Monster from the Past*): Planned as a major, blockbuster-style production, this proposed $7m fantasy was to see the legendary Loch Ness Monster grow to Godzilla-like proportions after ingesting a highly toxic chemical named Mutane 4, following which it goes on the rampage, wrecking a hovercraft and an oil rig before finally being destroyed in the South China Seas. Based upon a story devised by Michael Carreras and Euan Lloyd, this idea was subsequently turned into a treatment by John Starr and a screenplay by Christopher Wicking. This in turn was re-written by Bryan Forbes, who was set to direct. Set up as a co-production between Hammer, Columbia, David Frost's Paradine Productions and Toho (which presumably would be providing the rubber suit), the film—which was announced in 1976—was to begin shooting on 1 May 1977. David Frost declared that the resultant film "would make *Jaws* look like a toothpaste commercial."[20] Unfortunately, a change of management at Columbia saw the Hollywood studio withdraw from the project, which limped on in search of a new backer until March 1978, when Toho also withdrew, causing its collapse. Undeterred, Michael Carreras attempted to launch *Nessie* again in May 1979 for a summer 1980 release, by which time the budget had ballooned to $10m (perhaps it too had had a dose of Mutane 4?). Pinewood was penciled in

for the proposed shoot, with Michael Anderson onboard as director and Richard Harris and Katherine Ross approached to star. Roger Moore and Gregory Peck—who at the time were starring in *The Sea Wolves* (1980) for Euan Lloyd—were also considered casting. Yet despite Carreras's concerted efforts, the project again collapsed.

*Never Let Go:* Announced in 1958, this African-set treasure hunt adventure was to have been written and directed by Val Guest.

*The Nightmare Giver:* Submitted and rejected in 1960, this screenplay by David Chester, with its echoes of Freddy Krueger to come, involved a creature that invades the dreams of his victims before visiting them in reality.

*One Million Years B.C.:* Hammer approached Twentieth Century–Fox about the possibility of turning their dinosaur hit into a TV series. Instead, the two companies linked up to make *Journey to the Unknown* (1968, TV).

*Our Mare River:* Proposed £250,000 star-studded West African-set action adventure based upon the 1959 stage hit by Beverley Cross concerning a mutiny onboard a tramp steamer. Announced in 1960, it was to have been helmed by Hammer regular Val Guest and financed by Columbia. James Carreras described the project as "an extraordinary, tension-crammed drama."[21]

Michael Carreras was set to produce the project, which was to be filmed in HammerScope, on location in Sierra Leone, with Robert Shaw repeating his stage role of Captain John Sewell (other members of the original stage cast included such up-coming names as Michael Caine, Norman Mitchell, Bryan Pringle, Dudley Foster and Dudley Sutton, whilst the play was directed by Sam Wannamaker).

**Panic at Madame Tussaud's:** Announced in 1949, this proposed thriller was seemingly set to star Francis Clare and Harry Fine, the latter of whom would go on to produce Hammer's "Karnstein trilogy," as well as appear in *To Have and to Hold* (1951).

**Payment in Fear:** Described as "a special Hammer action adventure" in the promotional artwork prepared by Keenan Forbes, this African-set thriller failed to make it beyond the initial development stage. It was announced in 1972.

**Perfect Sight:** Announced in 2005 as a co-production between Hammer, Random Harvest (Harvest Pictures III) and Stan Winston productions.

**The Picture of Dorian Gray:** This proposed adaptation of the 1891 Oscar Wilde novel—previously filmed in 1945 and first published in *Lippincott's Monthly Magazine* in 1890–was abandoned following the failure of *The Two Faces of Dr. Jekyll* (1960). Two later projects, *The Ecstasy of Dorian Gray* and *Doreen Gray*, also failed to materialize.

**The Pit of Doom (aka The Pit):** Announced in 1966.

**The Plague of Dracula:** Proposed Dracula story set at the time of the Great Plague of London in 1665.

**Poison Pen**

**Prime Evil:** Project brought to Hammer by director John Hough.

**The Progress of Julius:** Proposed four-hour mini series scripted by Allan Prior based upon the 1933 novel by Daphne Du Maurier about a man named Julius Levy, who rises from poverty to give "the world fast food at cheaper prices."[22]

**Quatermass and the Pit:** Proposed remake of the 1967 Hammer classic, announced as part of the Warner Bros. package of remakes. Commented Nigel Kneale of the proposal (which gave him another opportunity to moan), "I'd much prefer they didn't do it. If it turned out to be a bastardized version then I would fight tooth and nail to have my name taken off it."[23]

**The Quatermass Experiment/The Quatermass Xperiment:** Proposed $30m remake of the 1955 Hammer classic, announced in 1993 as part of a package of proposed remakes by Warner Bros. and Donner/Shuler Donner following the signing of a six-figure deal with Hammer. Sean Connery and Anthony Hopkins were mooted as possible stars to fill the professor's raincoat. Said Roy

Skeggs of the proposed remake, "And it will still be titled 'Xperiment.'"[24] Commented Nigel Kneale of the film's script, penned by Dan O'Bannon, "It's very clever and much closer to my original BBC script than the Hammer thing.... Logically, it all works, and he uses my original ending. But I think the whole thing has died on them— it's too intellectual, so I don't think it will see the light of day."[25] It didn't.

**Quatermass 4:** Announced in 1969, this proposed fourth installment in the Quatermass franchise was eventually made for television by Euston Films, with John Mills in the role of the Professor. Simply titled *Quatermass* (1979, TV), the four-part series was also released theatrically in some territories in a trimmed down version known as *The Quatermass Conclusion*. Co-starring Simon MacCorkindale and Barbara Kellerman, the production was directed by Piers Haggard from a script by Nigel Kneale.

**Raffles—Gentleman Crook:** Proposed one-hour television series, to be executive produced by Don Houghton, announced in 1973 for the 1974 season. A television film titled *Raffles—The Amateur Cracksman* eventually appeared in 1975, and was followed by a thirteen-part series in 1977, but they were made by Yorkshire Television, with Anthony Valentine in the role of the gentleman crook.

**The Rag Trade Goes Mod:** Proposed big screen version of the popular TV sitcom, which aired between 1961 and 1963, with Peter Jones, Reg Varney and Miriam Karlin. Announced in 1971, the idea no doubt came into being following the unexpected success of Hammer's big screen version of *On the Buses* (1971), also starring Reg Varney. Instead, Hammer made two further *Buses* films, whilst *The Rag Trade* was eventually revived on TV in 1977, this time without Reg Varney, but with the addition of his *On the Buses* co-star Anna Karen, who reprised her role as the gormless Olive for the series, which again co-starred Peter Jones and Miriam Karlin.

**The Rape of Sabena (aka The Inquisitor):** Announced in 1959 and again in 1960, this historical drama set during the Spanish Inquisition was to have been produced by Michael Carreras and directed in black and white by John Gilling from a script by Peter Newman, with Kieron Moore onboard as the nominal star. However, when Columbia, which was investing in the project, objected to the film on the grounds that it was too far removed from Hammer's trademark horror fare, the plug was pulled. The Catholic Church had also raised concerns about the film's subject matter (recalled Anthony Hinds, "We got a tip that the Catholic Church would ban the picture"[26]). Un-

Enticing artwork for the unmade *Payment in Fear*, one of many Hammer projects which fell by the wayside (Hammer).

fortunately, by this time, the film had been given a start date of 5 September 1960. Consequently, the sets had already been designed by Bernard Robinson, several of which had been erected on the back lot. However, these were subsequently made use of in the Spanish-set horror film *The Curse of the Werewolf* (1961), which was originally scheduled to have been shot back-to-back with *Sabena*. Elements of the unused screenplay later turned up in *The Lost Continent* (1968).

**Reason:** Proposed screenplay by Andy Cull, who ran a South London video store. Could he have been the next Tarantino? We'll never know, as the project stalled at the start line.

**Restless:** Announced in 1973, this suspense thriller was to have been based on a screenplay by Gerry O'Hara, who had helmed an episode of Hammer's *Journey to the Unknown* (1968, TV).

**The Return of the Werewolf:** Proposed werewolf story, announced in 1972.

**The Revenge of Dracula (1958, aka Dracula the Damned and Dracula II):** Announced in 1958 following the worldwide success of *Dracula* (1958), this proposed sequel was long-delayed following Christopher Lee's initial refusal to repeat the role. Instead, Hammer made *The Brides of Dracula* (1960). The *Dracula* follow-up eventually emerged—after much development—as *Dracula—Prince of Darkness* (1966).

***The Revenge of King Tutankhamen:*** Proposed television dramatization of the discoveries of Howard Carter and Lord Carnavon in the Valley of the Kings in 1922, based upon a 1977 book *Behind the Mask of Tutankhamen* by Barry Wynne. The TV movie was instead made by HTV in 1980 under the title of *The Curse of King Tut's Tomb*.

***The Revenge of the Children (aka The Children):*** Announced in 1974, this story involved two brain-damaged twins out to avenge themselves on their parents.

***Robin Hood and the King's Ransom:*** This swashbuckler was planned for production in July and August of 1964, but failed to materialize, despite Hammer's past success with this genre. They did eventually go on to make *A Challenge for Robin Hood* (1967).

***The Robinson Family:*** Proposed screen version of the BBC radio serial.

***The Rocky Horror Show:*** First staged in 1973, Richard O'Brien's phenomenally successful musical was turned into the cult film *The Rocky Horror Picture Show* (1975) by producer Michael White, but not before Hammer had tried to get it off the ground. Having been impressed by the show, Michael Carreras had wanted to make it as a Hammer film, but failed to secure American financing for the project. Had Hammer made the film, it could well have been the shot in the arm that they so desperately needed in the mid-seventies (as it is, the finished film features scenes shot at Hammer's old haunt, Oakley Court).

***Rosemary's Baby:*** Terence Fisher tried to interest Hammer in a production of the 1967 best-selling Ira Levin thriller, but it was not to be. The book was eventually filmed to commercial and critical acclaim by Roman Polanski in 1968.

***Ruffians:*** Announced in 1960 as a Columbia co-production and intended to go on the floor at Bray in 1962 after the completion of *The Phantom of the Opera* (1962), this biker drama was to have been adapted by Alun Owen from his 1960 TV play.

***Safari:*** Proposed in 1961, this Africa-set television series was originally pitched to Screen Gems, with whom Hammer had made the unsuccessful *Tales of Frankenstein* (1958, TV). Michael Carreras even went on a trip to scout locations, but nothing came of the project

***The Satanist:*** Announced in 1975 as a possible follow-up to *To the Devil a Daughter* (1976), this Dennis Wheatley project was taken from his 1960 novel (aka *The Black Magician*). Adapted for the screen by Brian Hayles, it was again to have featured the occult writer John Verney, and was set to star Christopher Lee and Britt Ekland (given his hatred of making *To the Devil a Daughter*, it seems unlikely that Richard Widmark would have returned as Verney for the follow up). EMI and Tyburn also attempted to get the project off the ground, but it failed to materialize (while it was at Tyburn, the film was to have been helmed by

Freddie Francis from a script by Anthony Hinds, with Peter Cushing, Shirley Bassey [!] and Orson Welles penciled in to star). Note that Don Houghton had previously turned down an offer to adapt the book for the screen

***The Savage Jackboot:*** Scripted by Don Houghton, who was also set to produce, this story of violent resistance set in France in 1945 was submitted to Paramount for consideration in 1972, and was accompanied by a mock up poster by Tom Chantrell featuring Peter Cushing in full Nazi regalia ("From the pages of Europe's bloodiest chapter…" ran the accompanying tagline). Shane Briant was also connected to the project. The Hollywood studio instead proposed a budget of £1.5m on the understanding that either Yul Brynner or Jack Palance could instead be secured. They couldn't, and so the film failed to materialize.

***The Scavengers:*** Tom Sachs attempted to launch this project on behalf of Hammer in early 1976.

***The Scent of New-Mown Hay:*** Proposed adaptation of the 1958 John Blackburn novel about a nameless pestilence that is wiping out the female population. Announced in 1972.

***The Scott Report on Sex, Wife-Swapping and the Permissive Society:*** This comedy vehicle for TV star Terry Scott was announced in 1972 following the success of Hammer's sitcom spin-off *On the Buses* (1971), and was based upon his TV series *Scott On…* (1964–1974, TV).

***Second-Hand Death:*** This episode of *Hammer House of Mystery and Suspense* (1984, TVM), scripted by John Peacock, was abandoned at the behest of Fox.

***See No Evil:*** Proposed thriller about a blind girl being terrorized by a killer in an old house, based upon a Jimmy Sangster script, which he was also set to produce. A very similarly-plotted but unrelated film titled *Blind Terror* eventually appeared in 1971; scripted by Brian Clemens and directed by Richard Fleischer, it starred Mia Farrow. Interestingly, the film's American title was *See No Evil*.

***The Sellout:*** This independently written screenplay by Judson Kinberg and Murray Smith was brought to Hammer in 1975 by Tom Sachs, who had worked on a number of films as a production manager for the company before launching himself as an associate producer elsewhere. Hammer wasn't able to get the script off the ground, and so Sachs took it to producer Josef Shaftel, who had better luck with it. The film was subsequently made as a Warner-Oceanglade-Amerifilm co-production and released in 1975. Richard Widmark and Oliver Reed starred and Peter Collinson directed, with Sachs onboard as associate producer

***The Sensitive:*** In 1974, Christopher Wicking approached Hammer with this idea for a film and possible TV spin-off series about a psychic investigator, on which he had collaborated with Adrian Reid. However, after some initial interest, Wicking was instead sidelined into working on two other

projects: *Allan Quatermain Esquire: His Quest for the Holy Flower* and *To the Devil a Daughter* (1976).

***Shatter:*** During the making of the Hong Kong based thriller *Shatter* (1974), Michael Carreras nurtured plans to produce a spin-off TV series starring Stuart Whitman and Peter Cushing. However, after the finished film lay on the shelf for several years before receiving a desultory release (and reviews), the plan was quietly abandoned.

***Shoot:*** Announced in 1972, this thriller was to have been filmed in Australia in association with George Brown Films.

***Silver Spoon***

***The Sins of Rasputin:*** Provisionally scheduled to go before the cameras in 1961, this project eventually resurfaced as *Rasputin—The Mad Monk* (1966) in a fictionalized (ie: less litigious) version of the actual historical events.

***A Small Man's Guide:*** Announced in 1979, this proposed TV comedy series was to have been based on the 1976 book *Ronnie Corbett's Small Man's Guide … or How to Aspire to Greater Heights* by the diminutive television comedian, who was also set to star.

***Stand and Deliver:*** Proposed dramatization of the life of highwayman Jonathan King, announced in 1956, the same year that Hammer made *Dick Turpin—Highwayman*. Terence Fisher was discussed as a possible director.

***Still at It on the Buses (aka On the Buses 4):*** Discussed as a further continuation of Hammer's successful *On the Buses* franchise, this fourth installment failed to materialize. It was announced in 1973 following the opening of *Holiday on the Buses*, and was to have been set in Sicily.

***Stolen Face:*** Proposed remake of Hammer's 1952 production about obsession and plastic surgery, announced in 1993 as part of the Warner Bros. package that failed to materialize.

***Stones of Evil:*** This project was promoted with a mock-up poster by Tom Chantrell, but failed to make it before the cameras. Based upon the 1974 novel by Bryan Cooper, it was to have followed the adventures of a stonemason in ancient Britain who finds himself involved in the building of a giant henge.

***Strange Conflict:*** Proposed follow-up to *The Devil Rides Out* (1968), based upon Dennis Wheatley's 1941 novel, again set to star Christopher Lee as the Duc de Richleau.

***The Strange Story of Linda Lee:*** An adaptation of the 1972 Dennis Wheatley novel, this was penned in 1974 by Don Houghton in the hope that Hammer would option the screenplay. They didn't.

***Supernatural:*** In August 2003, a co-production deal was announced between Hammer and Chris Brown's Australian company Pictures in Paradise to produce a slate of low budget horror films intended for theatrical release and, more particularly, DVD. Six movies were planned over a five-year period, of which this and *Jeb* were announced. Commented Brown of the deal, "Working with Hammer is the realization of an ambition I've had since my earliest days in the business. Hammer is one of the truly great influences in gothic cinema and without doubt the world's leading horror brand."[27] Script development for the company was handled by writer-director-producer Chris Fitchett, who penned *Supernatural*.

**The Sword of Robin Hood:** Announced in 1972, 1973 and again in 1979, this was yet another variation on the Robin Hood story, this time intended for television (as half-hour adventures), though why Hammer decided to pursue this project when they had left *Wolfshead: The Legend of Robin Hood* (1969) to gather dust until 1973 remains a mystery. Two episodes were actually penned by Don Houghton. These were *The Devil on Horseback*, which blended elements from Houghton's boyhood short story *Death versus the Vampire* and Hammer's own *Captain Clegg* (1962), with Robin warding off the Sheriff of Nottingham by disguising his men as skeletal horse-riders, and *Escape from the Darkness*, in which Robin disguises himself as a beggar so as to rescue Maid Marian, who has been falsely imprisoned for treason.

**Tale of a City:** Proposed drama set to star Joyce Cummings and Michael Hawley. It was announced in 1949.

**Tales of Frankenstein: Frankenstein Meets Dr. Varno:** As scripted by Jerome Bixby, this was to have been the second episode of Hammer's aborted television series *Tales of Frankenstein* (1958, TV). Further synopses for the series already submitted by Jimmy Sangster, A.R. Rawlinson and Peter Bryan were subsequently abandoned, although elements from Bryan's story, which involved hypnosis, were later used in *The Evil of Frankenstein* (1964), which was written by producer Anthony Hinds under his pen name John Elder.

**Tall Tales of Great Britain:** Proposed TV series, announced in 1972.

**Taxi:** Proposed screen version of the BBC radio series.

**That's Hammer:** No doubt taking its inspiration from the *Carry On* compilation *That's Carry On* (1978), this clip show was first announced in 1978. With a narration penned by Don Houghton, the project was to have been a co-production between Rank and the BBC, but was felled by problems acquiring the rights to the various clips, given that Hammer's back catalogue was actually owned by a variety of other film companies rather than Hammer itself. It was announced again in 1983, this time as a fifty-two-episode half-hour series, with Peter Cushing proposed as the host/narrator. This clip show format was eventually used for the TV series *The World of Hammer* (1990 [first broadcast 1994], TV), by which time the copyright issues had been resolved.

**To Kill a Stranger:** This thriller penned by "Karnstein" scribe Tudor Gates was announced in 1974.

**Too Many Ghosts:** Announced in 1963, this was to have been a second co-production between Hammer and William Castle following their collaboration on *The Old Dark House* (1963), but it soon fell by the wayside given the problems with the first project.

**Tower of London:** Proposed series of two-hour tele-films set around the London landmark. This was announced in 1973 for the 1974 season, with Don Houghton set to produce. In the trade ads, the proposal was described as "A series of two-hour 'star name' excursions into the dark mystique that has shrouded this incredible symbol of power for centuries." A better title might have been *Grabbing at Straws*.

**The Unquenchable Thirst of Dracula:** Set in India in the 1930s, this unfilmed screenplay by Anthony Hinds eventually turned up as a radio play broadcast on BBC Radio 4 on 28 October 2017. Adapted by Mark Gatiss and Laurence Bowen, it was directed by Gatiss, and featured Michael Sheen, Anna Madeley and Lewis Macleod (as Dracula). "An Indian summer for the Prince of Darkness!" ran the accompanying publicity blurb.

**Untitled Benny Hill project:** Announced in 1972.

**Untitled comedy project for TV's The Two Ronnies:** Announced in 1972.

**Untitled Father Shandor project:** Priest and vampire hunter Father Sandor (minus the 'h') had featured in *Dracula—Prince of Darkness* (1966) and was later revived for a series of comic strip adventures in the *House of Hammer* magazine in the mid-seventies. Having seen a copy of one of the strips, Michael Carreras tried to interest American backers in a feature film. Recalled the magazine's editor Dez Skinn, "Michael Carreras actually took copies of our first Shandor story to the States as a potential film. I told him the story and he took the penciled drawings which hadn't even been inked, let alone lettered, to potential backers in America. Unfortunately, he couldn't remember the original story, so he made up a totally different one. When he got back he said can you change the story because that's not the one he'd told the Americans."[28]

**Untitled Jimmy Hanley project:** After he had appeared in *Room to Let* (1950) for Hammer, it was reported in the trade paper *The Cinema Studio* that Hanley had been approached by James Carreras and Tony Hinds to direct at least one of their second features, but nothing came of the announcement.

**Untitled Lyons project:** Proposed third comedy featuring the Lyons family following on from *Life with the Lyons* (1954) and *The Lyons in Paris* (1955).

**Untitled Mini Series:** Announced in 1984, this untitled project was to have been about the Nazis' experiments with drugs during World War II.

**Untitled Mummy project:** In early 1970, Anthony Hinds was requested to pen a new Mummy screenplay for Hammer. This untitled project was to have been directed and co-written by Jimmy Sangster, but it was called off by James Carreras on 22 April following disinterest from potential distributors, and so never saw the light of day. However, this didn't prevent the studio from going on to make *Blood from the Mummy's Tomb* (1971), an adaptation of Bram Stoker's 1903 novel *Jewel of the Seven Stars*.

**Untitled period project:** Following the release of *The Public Life of Henry the Ninth* (1935), Hammer announced an untitled historical project to take place during the period of Louis XV, but the film failed to materialize. Instead, the company turned its attention to the Bela Lugosi vehicle *The Mystery of the Mary Celeste* (1935).

**Untitled Peter Bryan featurette:** Given that Exclusive had distributed a handful of 3D films in the fifties, among them *Cat Women of the Moon* (1953) and *Robot Monster* (1953), it was announced in 1954 that Peter Bryan would helm a 3D featurette for Hammer, but the film never materialized.

**Untitled prehistoric project:** After the making of *Creatures the World Forgot* (1971), itself a sequel of sorts to *One Million Years B.C.* (1966) and *When Dinosaurs Ruled the Earth* (1970), Hammer planned a fourth prehistoric epic, but the project was eventually cancelled by Michael Carreras.

**Untitled twin vampire project:** This story about twin vampires, developed by producer Wilbur Stark and writer John Peacock, was subsequently added to *Vampire Circus* (1972) as a subplot featuring the characters of Helga and Heinrich. The story bore no relation to *Twins of Evil* (1971), which was a different kettle of fish entirely.

**Up the Creek sequel:** Following the success of the Peter Sellers comedy *Up the Creek* (1958), Hammer quickly put a follow up into production titled *Further Up the Creek* (1958), which this time starred Frankie Howerd. Unfortunately, it didn't perform as well at the box office, and so plans for a third installment were abandoned. Recalled writer-director Val Guest, who had been involved in the first two films, "I was planning vague ideas for a third film but Frankie's agent, 'Scruffy' Dale, got far too big for his boots. He demanded millions for another film and what with one thing and another the project was washed up. But Frankie would have definitely been in any further films I made 'up the creek.' He was a successful film comedian and a wonderful man."[29]

**Upstairs, Downstairs:** A big screen adaptation of this much-loved period television drama (1970–1975, TV) was considered by Hammer in 1972.

**Vampire Hunters:** Announced in 1972, this was discussed as a further entry in the Karnstein series, with the script to be provided by Tudor Gates. Sadly, this fourth episode in the on-going saga failed to materialize.

**Vampire Virgins:** Announced in 1972 and again in 1973, this proposed follow-up to *Lust for a Vampire* (1971) was to have starred Peter Cushing as a vengeful Count Karnstein. However, it was substantially re-worked and ultimately became *Twins of Evil* (1971).

**Vampirella:** In August 1975 Michael Carreras placed an ad in *Famous Monsters of Filmland* asking its readers "What will Hammer do next?" The response was overwhelming: to make a film of James Warren's popular comic strip *Vampirella*, which followed the exploits of a female space vampire. However, despite promoting the idea at the New York "Monstercon" in November of the same year, and touting round a story treatment prepared by Jimmy Sangster, the project eventually hit the rocks when Columbia turned it down. AIP, which had likewise been approached as a backer, also lost interest following negotiations with James Warren over merchandising rights and a failed attempt to secure an A-list Hollywood star for the supporting role of Pendragon, although Michael Carreras had John Gielgud penciled in to play one of the supporting characters. By this time Sangster's treatment had been scripted and re-written by the likes of Christopher Wicking, Lew Davidson, John Starr and Michael Carreras (writing as Henry Younger), with Peter Cushing and Playboy Playmate Barbara Leigh set to star (Caroline Munro was also a consideration for the title role, whilst Richard Roundtree was thought of to play a black descendant of Van Helsing, presumably a by-product of the then-current blaxploitation phase). At various times of devel-

opment, Gordon Hessler and then John Hough were onboard as director ("I always wanted to make *Vampirella* .... I was a fan of the comics,"[30] Hough admitted). Said Michael Carreras of the project somewhat optimistically, "It was really going to be geared for the college kids and young marrieds and have all the tongue-in-cheek you could get away with. They were the people who would've been in tune with what we were trying to do anyway; it would've been marvellous and been playing everywhere forever."[31] Sadly, it was not to be. Admitted Carreras many years later, "The fact that it didn't get made is still my greatest disappointment."[32] A *Vampirella* film finally appeared in 1996; produced by Roger Corman, it was directed by Jim Wynorski, and quickly sank without trace.

**Fever dream. Artwork for the unmade *Victim of His Imagination* (Hammer).**

**Bat out of hell. An ad announcing the making of *Vampirella*. Sadly, it didn't come to pass (Hammer).**

**Vault of Blood:** Announced in 1971, and again in 1972 and 1973, this shocker never made it before the cameras. Amicus of course made the similar-sounding *Vault of Horror* (1973).

**Vengeance of Wurdalak:** Proposed Spanish co-production, seemingly set to star Peter Cushing and Spanish horror star Paul Naschy. Based on a story by Leon Tolstoy, this had previously been filmed as a segment in the Italian portmanteau horror *Black Sabbath* (1963). It was announced in 1973.

**Victim of His Imagination:** Following the making of *Blood from the Mummy's Tomb* (1971), which was based upon Bram Stoker's *The Jewel of Seven Stars*, the film's producer, Howard Brandy, proposed another Stoker-orientated project. This was a fact and fantasy story about the author's life leading up to the writing of *Dracula*. The project was announced in 1972 and poster art was drawn up for the film. A script was also commissioned from Don Houghton, whilst Shane Briant was cast as Stoker and Christopher Lee as actor-manager Henry Irving. De-

spite this flurry of activity, the film was dropped from the schedules in 1973.

**Vlad Tepes (aka *The Impaler* and *Lord Dracula*):** Following the making of *Countess Dracula* (1971), its producer Alexander Paal hoped to set up a project about the real Dracula, Vlad Tepes, at Hammer, with Mike Raven in the title role. However, James Carreras turned the idea down for fear of alienating Christopher Lee, whose services the company needed more than ever in the early seventies. Recalled Mike Raven, "Paal was trying to get the Carreras stamp to make it a Hammer film."[33] In 1974, by which time Lee had played Dracula for the last time, the film was offered to director Ken Russell, who found the project somewhat lacking. In a written response to the offer, he replied, "Thanks for thinking of me ... please don't misunderstand me. I would like to make a horror film with you—a *real* one."[34] Producer Tom Sachs tried to re-launch the project again in early 1976, but despite his concerted efforts it failed to materialize. By now intended as a serious historical piece rather than an out-and-out horror film, Yul Brynner was penciled in to star. This version of the story was based on a 1974 BBC radio play called *Lord Dracula* by Brian Hayles starring Kenneth Haigh (as Vlad Tepes), Nigel Stock and Don Henderson. Other stars linked to the project at one time or another included Richard Harris, Alec Guinness and Richard Burton, whilst Val Guest was also involved at one stage as the writer and potential director. The project was later announced in the eighties once Hammer had been taken over by Roy Skeggs and Brian Lawrence, and again in the nineties. Michael Carreras also hoped to present an elaborate production of the story on stage, complete (according to writer John Peacock) with galloping horses on a treadmill. Recalled Carreras of his various attempts to launch the film, "I was never able to find one company that would say, 'OK, we will take on the entire cost.' It was always, 'If you can find a co-producer,' or 'If you can find under-writing for the below-the-line costs.' At that point, it should have been given to somebody whose total time could have been concentrated on that one project. Unfortunately, I never had that time."[35]

**The Vultures:** Proposed action adventure, "To be produced on location in Australia," as the press release had it. It was later re-announced in 1972 as *A Gathering of Vultures*.

**Waiting Revenge:** Peter Cushing enjoyed working on Hammer's pirate adventure *Captain Clegg* (1962) so much that in 1972 he penned a twenty-two-page treatment for a follow-up that sadly never saw the light of day.

**The Weir of Hermiston:** Proposed adaptation of Robert Louis Stevenson's unfinished 1896 novel.

**Werewolf Wedding:** Another rejected Bob Baker storyline.

**When the Earth Cracked Open (aka *The Day the Earth Cracked Open*):** One of several large-scale fantasy action adventures proposed by Hammer in the seventies, this costly-sounding production was to have been based on a screenplay by Don Houghton. First announced in 1969, and then again in 1971, it failed to make it much beyond some intriguing promotional artwork by Tom Chantrell featuring one of the film's potential stars, Caroline Munro (the project bears a title already connected with a previously mooted Ray Harryhausen project).

**When the Earth Cracked Open:** Following work on *One Million Years B.C.* (1966), effects legend Ray Harryhausen and Hammer tried to get a remake of *King Kong* off the ground. Sadly their efforts came to nothing. In 1972 they tried to launch another caveman-and-dinosaurs epic, and Harryhausen sketched out some storyboards for the proposed film. Commented Harryhausen, "Neither project came to fruition and I am not too sad about *Kong*, but the second idea did have some possibilities…. I did rough out some basic ideas as storyboards of giant ants, dinosaurs and a tentacled beast but that's as far as it went."[36] The title was later re-used for an unmade science fiction epic by Hammer.

**Whispering Smith Investigates:** Proposed sequel to *Whispering Smith Hits London* (1952).

**The White Witch of Rose Hall:** Proposed adaptation of the 1970 Harold Underhill novel *Jamaica White* about an Englishwoman named Annie Palmer and her involvement with voodoo, set to be filmed in Jamaica ("Three times married. Three times a murderess," exclaimed the press release).

**The Whites Grew Pale:** This original screenplay by Hugo Lous about racial intolerance in the Dutch East Indies was purchased by Hammer in 1959. Peter Newman, who had scripted Hammer's *Yesterday's Enemy* (1959) from his own tele-play, was hired to turn the piece into a play, a novel and a film. The property was sold on to Michael Carreras's Capricorn Productions in 1960, but only the play ever surfaced.

**They Used Dark Forces:** Proposed adaptation of the 1964 Dennis Wheatley novel involving one of several adventures featuring Gregory Sallust. Here he parachutes into Nazi Germany, his objective being to penetrate the rocket installation at Peenemunde. He also becomes involved with a Mocata-like Satanist named Ibrahim Malacou. MGM's *Operation Crossbow* (1965) subsequently presented a similar wartime mission.

**Zeppelin v Pterodactyls:** Despite some tantalizing artwork prepared to promote it, this fantasy-adventure unfortunately failed to take flight. It was announced in 1969, and was provisionally titled *Raiders of the Stone Ring*, and was based on a story treatment by effects technicians David Allen, Jim Danforth and Dennis Muren (Allen and Danforth were working on Hammer's *When Dinosaurs Ruled the Earth* [1970] at the time). Commented Allen of the studio's involvement, "Hammer simply had their own banal ideas. They said something like, 'We feel that this film would be just as exciting if we had an enemy tribe wearing strange headgear.'"[37] For which see the Mud Men in *Creatures the World Forgot* (1971). After Hammer abandoned the project, Allen continued to work on it under the new title of *The Primevals*, which was subsequently acquired by Empire Films. Note that a pterodactyl attacks a bi-plane in AIP's *The People That Time Forgot* (1977).

*Requiescat in pace ultima*
Inscription on the Van Helsing family gravestone, *Dracula A.D. 1972* (1972)

# Notes

## Introduction

1. This was actually the Beeb's third—and best—season of horror double bills, which ran from 1975 to 1983. This particular season went out under the umbrella title *Dracula, Frankenstein and Friends*. The showing of *Dracula—Prince of Darkness* I'd seen the previous year turned out to be the last film in the second series, which went out under the title *Masters of Terror*. • 2. John Kenneth Muir, *Horror Films of the 1970s* (McFarland, 2002), p. 67. • 3. John McCarty, *The Modern Horror Film* (Citadel Press, 1990). • 4. *Shivers*, #31, July 1996, p. 38.

## A

1. Unpublished interview with the author. • 2. *Ibid*. • 3. Marcus Hearn and Alan Barnes, *The Hammer Story* (Titan, 1997), p. 27. • 4. Unpublished interview with the author. • 5. Christopher Frayling, *Ken Adam: The Art of Production Design* (Faber, 2005), p. 98. • 6. *Ibid.*, p. 99. • 7. *Little Shoppe of Horrors*, #18, September 2006, p. 31. • 8. *Little Shoppe of Horrors*, #17, November 2005, p. 47. • 9. *Ibid.* • 10. *Ibid.*, p48. • 11. *Ibid.*, p49. • 12. Denis Meikle, *A History of Horrors* (Scarecrow, 2001), p. 277. • 13. Christopher Neame, *Rungs on a Ladder: Hammer Films Seen Through a Gauze* (Scarecrow, 2003), p. 90. • 14. Bruce Sachs and Russell Wall, *Greasepaint and Gore* (Tomahawk, 1991), p. 133. • 15. Wayne Kinsey, *Hammer Films: The Bray Studios Years* (Reynolds & Hearn, 2002), p. 301. • 16. *Little Shoppe of Horrors*, #13, November 1996, p. 78. • 17. Kinsey, *Hammer Films: The Bray Studios Years*, p. 304. • 18. Wayne Kinsey, *Hammer Films: The Elstree Studios Years* (Tomahawk, 2007), p. 36. • 19. Jimmy Sangster, *Inside Hammer* (Reynolds & Hearn, 2001), p. 121. • 20. Roy Ward Baker, *The Director's Cut* (Reynolds & Hearn, 2000), p. 125. • 21. *Ibid.*, p. 126. • 22. *Ibid.*, p. 126. • 23. Sangster, *Inside Hammer*, p. 117. • 24. *Ibid.*, p96. 25. *Shivers*, #33, September 1996, p. 38. • 26. Marcus Hearn, *The Mummy* (GDI Records, 1999), CD liner notes. • 27. Hearn and Barnes, *The Hammer Story*, p. 85. • 28. *Ibid.*, p. 87. • 29. *Hammer Horror*, #4, June 1995, p. 11. • 30. Sachs and Wall, *Greasepaint and Gore*, p. 39. • 31. *Ibid.*, p. 74. • 32. *Ibid.*, p49. • 33. Meikle, *A History of Horrors*, p. 91. • 34. Sachs and Wall, *Greasepaint and Gore*, p. 40. • 35. *Little Shoppe of Horrors*, #14, December 1999, p. 65. • 36. Sachs and Wall, *Greasepaint and Gore*, p. 39. • 37. Kinsey, *Hammer Films: The Bray Studios Years*, p. 188. • 38. Sachs and Wall, *Greasepaint and Gore*, p. 85. • 39. *Ibid.*, p111. • 40. *House of Hammer* #2, p. 39. • 41. Sachs and Wall, *Greasepaint and Gore*, p. 126. • 42. *Ibid.* • 43. *Fangoria*, #35, p. 35. • 44. Sachs and Wall, *Greasepaint and Gore*, p. 131. • 45. *Little Shoppe of Horrors*, #14, December 1999, p. 65. • 46. Sachs and Wall, *Greasepaint and Gore*, p. 149. • 47. *Ibid.*, p. 153. • 48. *Ibid.*, p. 155. • 49. *Ibid.*, p. 7. • 50. *Ibid.* • 51. *Ibid.*, p. 81.

## B

1. Wayne Kinsey, *Hammer Films: The Bray Studios Years* (Reynolds & Hearn, 2002), p. 296. • 2. *Britain's Most Watched TV* (Objective Productions, 2005). •

3. Wayne Kinsey, *Hammer Films: The Elstree Studios Years* (Tomahawk, 2007), p. 67. • 4. Roy Ward Baker, *The Director's Cut* (Reynolds & Hearn, 2000), p. 124. • 5. *Ibid.*, p. 128. • 6. Ingrid Pitt, *Life's a Scream* (Heinemann, 1999), p. 208. • 7. Baker, *The Director's Cut*, p. 130. • 8. *Ibid.*, p. 131. • 9. *Little Shoppe of Horrors*, #16, August 2004, p. 44. • 10. Baker, *The Director's Cut*, p. 131. • 11. *Ibid.*, p. 139. • 12. David Miller, *The Complete Peter Cushing* (Reynolds & Hearn, 2005), p. 146. • 13. *Hammer Horror*, #3, May 1995, p. 36. • 14. John Walker [ed], *Halliwell's Who's Who* (Harper-Collins, 2003), p. 31. • 15. Joel Lobenthal, *Tallulah! The Life and Times of a Leading Lady* (Aurum, 2005), p. 521. • 16. Kinsey, *Hammer Films: The Bray Studios Years*, p. 187. • 17. *Hammer Horror*, #7, September 1995, p. 38. • 18. *Little Shoppe of Horrors*, #10/11, July 1990, p. 96. • 19. Kinsey, *Hammer Films: The Elstree Studios Years*, p. 33. • 20. *Little Shoppe of Horrors*, #4, April 1978, p. 65. • 21. Bruce Sachs and Russell Wall, *Greasepaint and Gore* (Tomahawk, 1991), p. 160. • 22. Jimmy Sangster, *Inside Hammer* (Reynolds & Hearn, 2001), p. 19. • 23. Baker, *The Director's Cut*, p. 135. • 24. *Fear in the Night*, DVD commentary. • 25. *Ibid.*, p. 76. • 26. *Little Shoppe of Horrors*, #8, May 1984, p. 76. • 27. Kinsey, *Hammer Films: The Bray Studios Years*, p. 270. • 28. Kinsey, *Hammer Films: The Elstree Studios Years*, p. 177–178. • 29. Andy Murray, *Into the Unknown: The Fantastic Life of Nigel Kneale* (Headpress, 2006), p. 43. • 30. *Little Shoppe of Horrors*, #12, April 1994, p. 98. • 31. *Hammer House of Mystery and Suspense—Volume 1*, DVD liner notes. • 32. *Little Shoppe of Horrors*, #12, April 1994, p. 83. • 33. *Shivers*, #34, October 1996, p. 38. • 34. *Music from the Movies* #9, Summer 1995, p. 37. • 35. *Little Shoppe of Horrors*, #10/11, July 1990, p. 96. • 36. *Shivers*, #38, September 1996, p. 38. • 37. *Ibid.*, p. 39. • 38. *Film Review Special*, #53, August 2004, p. 67. • 39. *Shivers*, #33, September 1996, p. 39. • 40. *Ibid.* • 41. *Ibid.* • 42. *Shivers*, #34, October 1996, p. 38. • 43. *Ibid.* • 44. *Film Review*, #580, p. 84, April 1999. • 45. *Little Shoppe of Horrors*, #10/11, July 1990, p. 103. • 46. *Soundtrack!* Vol 11, #43, September 1992, p. 23. • 47. *Ibid.* • 48. *Shivers*, #34, October 1996, p. 38. • 49. *Soundtrack!* Vol 11, #43, September 1992, p. 23. • 50. *Shivers*, #34, October 1996, p. 38. • 51. *She*, CD liner notes, GFD, 2001. • 52. *Shivers*, #34, October 1996, p. 38. • 53. *Ibid.* 54. *Ibid.*, p. 38–39. • 55. *Ibid.*, p. 39. • 56. *Ibid.* 57. *Ibid.*, p38. • 58. *Ibid.*, p. 39. • 59. *Shivers*, #33, September 1996, p. 39. • 60. *Little Shoppe of Horrors*, #10/11, July 1990, p. 96. • 61. *Ibid.*, p. 90. • 62. *Little Shoppe of Horrors*, #12, April 1994, p. 111. • 63. Marcus Hearn and Alan Barnes, *The Hammer Story* (Titan, 1997), p. 140. • 64. *The Knowledge*, 28 October 2006, p. 17. • 65. *Fangoria*, #63, May 1987, p. 61. • 66. *The Knowledge*, 28 October 2006, p. 16. • 67. Hearn and Barnes, *The Hammer Story*, p. 148. • 68. *The Knowledge*, 28 October 2006, p. 16. • 69. *Little Shoppe of Horrors*, #16, August 2004, p. 62. • 70. *Ibid.* • 71. *Ibid.*, p. 63. • 72. Kinsey, *Hammer Films: The Elstree Studios Years*, p. 103. • 73. *Ibid.*, p. 190. • 74. *Little Shoppe of Horrors*, #10/11, July 1990, p. 61. • 75. Brian McFarlane, *An Autobiography of British Cinema* (Methuen/BFI, 1997), p. 259. • 76. *Little Shoppe of Horrors*, #13, November 1996, p. 67. • 77. *Little*

*Shoppe of Horrors*, #19, September 2007, p. 66. • 78. Christopher Lee, *Tall, Dark and Gruesome* (Victor Gollancz, 1997), p. 210. • 79. *Little Shoppe of Horrors*, #13, November 1996, p. 97. • 80. *Little Shoppe of Horrors*, #12, April 1994, p. 63. • 81. *Blood from the Mummy's Tomb*, CD liner notes, 2002, GDI Records. • 82. *Ibid.* • 83. *Ibid.* • 84. Hearn and Barnes, *The Hammer Story*, p. 145. • 85. *Blood from the Mummy's Tomb*, CD liner notes, 2002, GDI Records. • 86. Louis Paul, *Tales from the Cult Film Trenches* (McFarland, 2008), p. 168. • 87. Christopher Neame, *Rungs on a Ladder: Hammer Films Seen Through a Soft Gauze* (Scarecrow, 2003), p. 98. • 88. Neame, *Rungs on a Ladder: Hammer Films Seen Through a Gauze*, p. 101. • 89. *Little Shoppe of Horrors*, #12, April 1994, p. 85. • 90. Jan Read, *Young Man in Movieland* (Scarecrow, 2004), p. 116. • 91. Neame, *Rungs on a Ladder: Hammer Films Seen Through a Gauze*, p. 104. • 92. *Film Review Special*, #53, August 2004, p. 68. • 93. *Little Shoppe of Horrors*, #10/11, July 1990, p. 61. • 94. Hearn and Barnes, *The Hammer Story*, p. 44. • 95. *Little Shoppe of Horrors*, #4, June 1978, p. 77. • 96. Kinsey, *Hammer Films: The Bray Studios Years*, p. 171. • 97. *Little Shoppe of Horrors*, #18, 2006, p. 46. • 98. Derek Pykett, *Michael Ripper Unmasked* (Midnight Marquee Press, 1999), p. 121. • 99. Neame, *Rungs on a Ladder: Hammer Films Seen Through a Gauze*, p. 13. • 100. *Hammer Horror*, #4, June 1995, p. 13. • 101. *Little Shoppe of Horrors*, #10/11, July 1990, p. 96. • 102. McFarlane, *An Autobiography of British Cinema*, p. 524. • 103. *Little Shoppe of Horrors*, #4, June 1978, p. 35. • 104. *Ibid.*, p. 26. • 105. Sangster, *Inside Hammer*, p. 19. • 106. *Straight on Till Morning*, DVD commentary. • 107. HammerWeb—Shane Briant interview. • 108. *Little Shoppe of Horrors*, #14, December 1999, p. 85. • 109. *Ibid.*, p. 82. • 110. Miller, *The Complete Peter Cushing*, p. 87. • 111. Sachs and Wall, *Greasepaint and Gore*, p. 75. • 112. *Little Shoppe of Horrors*, #19, September 2007, p. 42. • 113. Sachs and Wall, *Greasepaint and Gore*, p. 75. • 114. Jimmy Sangster, *Inside Hammer* (Reynolds & Hearn, 2001), p. 60. • 115. *Ibid.*, p. 60. • 116. *Ibid.*, p. 18. • 117. *The World of Hammer*, narration. • 118. Brian McFarlane, *An Autobiography of British Cinema* (Methuen/BFI, 1997), p. 103. • 119. Neame, *Rungs on a Ladder: Hammer Films Seen Through a Gauze*, p. 110. • 120. Sachs and Wall, *Greasepaint and Gore*, p. 44. • 121. *Ibid.*, p. 145. • 122. Lee, *Tall, Dark and Gruesome*, p. 231. • 123. *Kinematograph Weekly*, 5 May 1960.

## C

1. *Hammer Horror*, #4, June 1995, p. 28. • 2. Unpublished interview with the author. • 3. Unpublished interview with author. • 4. Val Guest, *So You Want to Be in Pictures* (Reynolds & Hearn, 2001), p. 133. • 5. *Little Shoppe of Horrors*, #17, November 2005, p. 41. • 6. *Little Shoppe of Horrors*, #4, April 1978, p. 40. • 7. *Little Shoppe of Horrors*, #17, November 2005, p. 24. • 8. *Captain Kronos* DVD, liner notes, DD Video. • 9. Marcus Hearn and Alan Barnes, *The Hammer Story* (Titan, 1997), p. 159. • 10. *Ibid.* • 11. *ABC Film Review*, August 1972, p. 17. • 12. *Captain Kronos* DVD, liner notes, DD Video, 2003. • 13. *Ibid.*

• 14. *Ibid.* • 15. *Ibid.* • 16. *Ibid.* • 17. *Fangoria,* #63, May 1987, p. 62. • 18. *Ibid.* • 19. *Captain Kronos* DVD, liner notes, DD Video, 2003. • 20. *Little Shoppe of Horrors,* #17, November 2005, p. 39. • 21. Jimmy Sangster, *Inside Hammer* (Reynolds & Hearn, 2001), p. 14. • 22. Tom Johnson and Mark A. Miller, *The Christopher Lee Filmography* (McFarland, 2004), p. XVIII. • 23. *Little Shoppe of Horrors,* #8, May 1984, p. 90. • 24. *The Frankenstein Film Music Collection,* CD liner notes, GDI Records, 2000. • 25. *Little Shoppe of Horrors,* #10/11, July 1990, p. 103. • 26. *Ibid.* • 27. *Ibid.* • 28. *Little Shoppe of Horrors,* #8, May 1984, p. 14. • 29. Jon Burrows, *Legitimate Cinema: Theatre Stars in British Films, 1908–1918* (University of Exeter Press, 2003), p. 7. • 30. Allen Eyles and Robert Adkinson, Nicholas Fry, *House of Horror* (Lorrimer, 1973), p. 8. • 31. Denis Meikle, *A History of Horrors* (Scarecrow, 2001), p. 206. • 32. *Shivers,* #36, December 1996, p. 34. • 33. Brian McFarlane, *An Autobiography of British Cinema* (Methuen/BFI, 1997), p. 524. • 34. Tudor Gates, *Scenario: The Craft of Screenwriting* (Wallflower, 2002), p. 71–72. • 35. Meikle, *A History of Horrors,* p. 269. • 36. Sangster, *Inside Hammer,* p. 139. • 37. *Flesh and Blood: The Hammer Heritage of Horror,* Heidelburg/Hammer/Bosutow Media Group, 1994. • 38. Unpublished interview with the author. • 39. Eyles, Adkinson and Fry, *House of Horror,* p. 9. • 40. Sangster, *Inside Hammer,* p. 41. • 41. *Flesh and Blood: The Hammer Heritage of Horror,* Heidelburg/Hammer/Bosutow Media Group, 1994. • 42. Eyles, Adkinson and Fry, *House of Horror,* p. 17–18. • 43. Hearn and Barnes, *The Hammer Story,* p. 7. • 44. *Ibid.,* p. 10. • 45. *Little Shoppe of Horrors,* #12, April 1994, p. 49. • 46. Sangster, *Inside Hammer,* p. 41. • 47. Hearn and Barnes, *The Hammer Story,* p. 9. • 48. Wayne Kinsey, *Hammer Films: The Bray Studios Years* (Reynolds & Hearn, 2002), p. 19. • 49. Eyles, Adkinson and Fry, *House of Horror,* p. 9. • 50. Meikle, *A History of Horrors,* p. 295. • 51. *Fangoria,* #61, February 1987, p. 59. • 52. Meikle, *A History of Horrors,* p. 295. • 53. Eyles, Adkinson and Fry, *House of Horror,* p. 10. • 54. Sangster, *Inside Hammer,* p. 85. • 55. Eyles, Adkinson and Fry, *House of Horror,* p. 9. • 56. *Ibid.,* p. 11. • 57. Meikle, *A History of Horrors,* p. 269. • 58. Hearn and Barnes, *The Hammer Story,* p. 135. • 59. Eyles, Adkinson and Fry, *House of Horror,* p. 11. • 60. Meikle, *A History of Horrors,* p. 269. • 61. Hearn and Barnes, *The Hammer Story,* p. 165. • 62. *Fangoria,* #63, May 1987, p. 63. • 63. Meikle, *A History of Horrors,* p. 295–296. • 64. Christopher Neame, *Rungs on a Ladder: Hammer Films Seen Through a Soft Gauze* (Scarecrow, 2003), p. 10. • 65. *Hammer House of Mystery and Suspense,* DVD documentary, DD Entertainment, 2005. • 66. Hearn and Barnes, *The Hammer Story,* p. 171. • 67. *Fangoria,* #63, May 1987, p. 68. • 68. *Little Shoppe of Horrors,* #10/11, July 1990, p. 150. • 69. *Ibid.,* p. 153. • 70. *The Hammer Quatermass Film Music Collection,* CD liner notes, GDI Records, 1999. • 71. *Blood from the Mummy's Tomb,* CD liner notes, GDI Records, 2002. • 72. *Little Shoppe of Horrors,* #10/11, July 1990, p. 97. • 73. Festival of Fantastic Films, Manchester, September 1994. • 74. *Little Shoppe of Horrors,* #18, 2006, p. 28. • 75. *Ibid.* • 76. *Hammer House of Mystery and Suspense,* DVD documentary, DD Entertainment, 2005. • 77. *Hammer Horror,* #3, May 1995, p. 34. • 78. *Little Shoppe of Horrors,* #12, April 1994, p. 83–84. • 79. *Hammer Horror,* #7, September 1995, p. 36. • 80. *Hammer House of Mystery and Suspense,* DVD documentary, DD Entertainment, 2005. • 81. Meikle, *A History of Horrors,* p. 4. • 82. *Little Shoppe of Horrors,* #4, April 1978, p. 36. • 83. Sangster, *Inside Hammer,* p. 16. • 84. *Hammer Horror,* #7, September 1995, p. 38. • 85. Kinsey, *Hammer Films: The Bray Studios Years,* p. 287. • 86. Hearn and Barnes, *The Hammer Story,* p. 148. • 87. *Captain Kronos* DVD, liner notes, DD Video, 2003. • 88. Howard Maxford, *Hammer, House of Horrors: Behind the Screams* (Batsford, 1996), p. 18. • 89. *Hammer Horror,* #3, May 1995, p. 40. • 90. *Ibid.,* p. 7. • 91. *Hammer Horror,* # 3, May 1995, p. 41. • 92. *Little Shoppe of Horrors,* #18, 2006, p 77. • 93. Neame, *Rungs on a Ladder: Hammer Films Seen Through a Gauze,* p. 114. • 94. Sangster, *Inside Hammer,* p. 142. • 95. *Little Shoppe of Horrors,* #14, December 1999, p. 50. • 96. *Little Shoppe of Horrors,* #8, May 1984, p. 79. • 97. *Twins of Evil,* CD liner notes, GDI Records, 2000. • 98. *Little Shoppe of Horrors,* #14, December 1999, p. 53. • 99. Wayne Kinsey, *Hammer Films: The Elstree Studios Years* (Tomahawk, 2007), p. 316. • 100. Bruce Sachs and Russell Wall, *Greasepaint and Gore* (Tomahawk, 1991), p. 95. • 101. Kinsey, *Hammer Films: The Bray Studios Years,* p. 223. • 102. Sachs and Wall, *Greasepaint and Gore,* p. 49. • 103. *Ibid.,* p. 108–109. • 104. Kinsey, *Hammer Films: The Bray Studios Years,* p. 274. • 105. *Dark Terrors,* #18, May 2002, p. 28. • 106. *Shivers,* #32, August 1996, p. 45. • 107. Ingrid Pitt, *Life's a Scream* (Heinemann, 1999), p. 214. • 108. Albert J. Luxford and Gareth Owen, *Albert J. Luxford, the Gimmick Man* (McFarland, 2002), p. 135. • 109. Hearn and Barnes, *The Hammer Story,* p. 143. • 110. Pitt, *Life's a Scream,* p. 214. • 111. Hazel Court, *Hazel Court: Horror Queen* (Tomahawk, 2008), p. 83. • 112. Tom Weaver, *Return of the B Science Fiction and Horror Heroes* (McFarland, 2000), p. 43. • 113. *Hammer Horror,* #1, March 1995, p. 13. • 114. Court, *Hazel Court: Horror Queen,* p. 76. • 115. Weaver, *Return of the B Science Fiction and Horror Heroes,* p. 42–43. • 116. *The Times,* April 9 2008. • 117. *Ibid.* • 118. *Little Shoppe of Horrors,* #19 September 2007, p. 80–81. • 119. *Shivers,* #100, November 2002, p. 60. • 120. *Little Shoppe of Horrors,* #18, September 2006, p. 87. • 121. Ed Sikov, *Dark Victory: The Life of Bette Davis* (Aurum, 2007), p. 359. • 122. *Little Shoppe of Horrors,* #15, November 2001, p. 34. • 123. *Little Shoppe of Horrors,* #13, November 1996, p. 23. • 124. John Murray, *The Remarkable Michael Reeves* (Cinematics, 2002), p. 108. • 125. *Ibid.* • 126. Sangster, *Inside Hammer,* p. 125. • 127. Murray, *The Remarkable Michael Reeves,* p. 109. • 128. *Little Shoppe of Horrors,* #10/11, July 1990, p. 103. • 129. *Hammer International Journal* #4. • 130. *Hammer House of Mystery and Suspense,* DVD documentary, DD Entertainment, 2005. • 131. *Film Review,* March 1998, p. 57. • 132. Sangster, *Inside Hammer,* p. 28. • 133. Meikle, *A History of Horrors,* p. 39. • 134. *Little Shoppe of Horrors,* #3, February 1974, p. 59. • 135. *Film Review,* March 1998, p. 58. • 136. Johnson and Miller, *The Christopher Lee Filmography,* p. 65. • 137. Kinsey, *Hammer Films: The Bray Studios Years,* p. 61. • 138. Doug Bradley, *Behind the Mask of the Horror Actor* (Titan, 2004), p. 149. • 139. Hearn and Barnes, *The Hammer Story,* p. 24. • 140. Kinsey, *Hammer Films: The Bray Studios Years,* p. 73. • 141. Christopher Lee, *Tall, Dark and Gruesome* (Victor Gollancz, 1997), p. 182. • 142. David Miller, *The Complete Peter Cushing* (Reynolds & Hear, 2005), p. 62. • 143. Court, *Hazel Court: Horror Queen,* p. 79. • 144. Sangster, *Inside Hammer,* p. 32–33. • 145. *Film Review,* March 1998, p. 57. • 146. *Hammer Horror,* #1, March 1995, p. 35. • 147. *Shivers,* #38, September 1996, p. 39. • 148. Lee, *Tall, Dark and Gruesome,* p. 183. • 149. Alan Frank, *Horror Films* (Hamlyn, 1977), p. 67. • 150. HFCGB, *The Films of Peter Cushing* (HFCGB, 1975), p. 24. • 151. Bradley, *Behind the Mask of the Horror Actor,* p. 150. • 152. Court, *Hazel Court: Horror Queen,* p. 79. • 153. *Ibid.,* p. 81. • 154. *Film Review,* March 1998, p. 61. • 155. Sarah Streeter, *Transatlantic Crossings: British Feature Films in the USA* (Continuum, 2002), p. 157. • 156. Johnson and Miller, *The Christopher Lee Filmography,* p. 64. • 157. *Hammer—The Studio That Dripped Blood,* documentary, BBC, 1987. • 158. Sachs and Wall, *Greasepaint and Gore,* p. 62. • 159. *Fangoria,* #7, p. 53. • 160. Sachs and Wall, *Greasepaint and Gore,* p. 92. • 161. Kinsey, *Hammer Films: The Bray Studios Years,* p. 207. • 162. Meikle, *A History of Horrors,* p. 136. • 163. *Fandom's Film Gallery* #3, 1978. • 164. *Ibid.* • 165. Eyles, Adkinson and Fry, *House of Horror,* p. 19. • 166. *Ibid.* • 167. Miller, *The Complete Peter Cushing,* p. 61. • 168. Lee, *Tall, Dark and Gruesome,* p. 182. • 169. *Famous Monsters of Filmland,* August 1978. • 170. *Shivers,* #61, January 1999, p. 61. • 171. Johnson and Miller, *The Christopher Lee Filmography,* p. 82. • 172. *Evening Bulletin.* • 173. *The Frankenstein Film Music Collection,* CD liner notes, GDI Records, 2000. • 174. Pitt, *Life's a Scream,* p. 210. • 175. *Flesh and Blood: The Hammer Heritage of Horror,* Heidelburg/Hammer/Bosutow Media Group, 1994. • 176. Miller, *The Complete Peter Cushing,* p. 141. • 177. *Shivers,* #38, February 1997. • 178. Eyles, Adkinson and Fry, *House of Horror,* p. 20. • 179. *Ibid.* • 180. *Ibid,* p. 19. • 181. *Ibid,* p. 20. • 182. *Ibid.* • 183. *BBC News,* mid–80s. • 184. Sachs and Wall, *Greasepaint and Gore,* p. 75–76. • 185. *Fangoria,* #63, May 1987, p. 59. • 186. *British Film Forever,* BBC, 2007. • 187. Court, *Hazel Court: Horror Queen,* p. 78. • 188. Johnson and Miller, *The Christopher Lee Filmography,* p. 64.

## D

1. Wayne Kinsey, *Hammer Films: The Bray Studios Years* (Reynolds & Hearn, 2002), p. 218. • 2. *Dark Terrors,* #18, May 2002, p. 12. • 3. Val Guest, *So You Want to Be in Pictures* (Reynolds & Hearn, 2001), p. 161. • 4. *Little Shoppe of Horrors,* #10/11, June 1990, p 60. • 5. Brian McFarlane, *An Autobiography of British Cinema* (Methuen/BFI, 1997), p. 258. • 6. Kinsey, *Hammer Films: The Bray Studios Years,* p. 310. • 7. Marcus Hearn and Alan Barnes, *The Hammer Story* (Titan, 1997), p. 93. • 8. Ed Sikov, *Dark Victory: The Life of Bette Davis* (Aurum, 2007), p. 359. • 9. *Ibid,* p. 360. • 10. *Evening Standard Metro Life,* 21–27 January 2005, p. 16. • 11. Christopher Neame, *Rungs on a Ladder: Hammer Films Seen Through a Soft Gauze* (Scarecrow, 2003), p. 47. • 12. Kinsey, *Hammer Films: The Bray Studios Years,* p. 187. • 13. *Little Shoppe of Horrors,* #13, November 1996, p. 52. • 14. Tom Johnson and Mark A. Miller, *The Christopher Lee Filmography* (McFarland, 2004), p. 142. • 15. *Dark Terrors,* #18, May 2002, p. 29–30. • 16. *Ibid.,* p. 29. • 17. Hearn and Barnes, *The Hammer Story,* p. 17. • 18. *Film Review, Special* #53, 2004, p. 67. • 19. *Dark Terrors,* #18, May 2002, p. 18. • 20. Denis Meikle, *A History of Horrors* (Scarecrow, 2001), p. 239–240. • 21. Hearn and Barnes, *The Hammer Story,* p. 55. • 22. Meikle, *A History of Horrors,* p. 257. • 23. *Hammer Horror,* #5, July 1995, p. 10. • 24. Neame, *Rungs on a Ladder: Hammer Films Seen Through a Gauze,* p. 24. • 25. Kinsey, *Hammer Films: The Bray Studios Years,* p. 257. • 26. *The Devil Rides Out* CD, GDI Records, 2000, recorded interview with Christopher Lee. • 27. *Ibid.* • 28. Christopher Lee, *Tall, Dark and Gruesome* (Victor Gollancz, 1997), p. 235. • 29. *The Devil Rides Out* CD, GDI Records, 2000, liner notes. • 30. *Ibid.* • 31. *Dark Terrors,* #13, 1996, p. 34. • 32. *Shivers,* #85, December 2000, p. 36. • 33. *Dark Terrors,* #13, 1996, p. 35. • 34. Lee, *Tall, Dark and Gruesome,* p. 215. • 35. Kinsey, *Hammer Films: The Bray Studios Years,* p. 274. • 36. Hearn and Barnes, *The Hammer Story,* p. 79. • 37. Kinsey, *Hammer Films: The Bray Studios Years,* p. 276. • 38. *Dark Terrors,* #13, 1996, p. 35. • 39. *Shivers,* #85, December 2000, p. 36. • 40. Johnson and Miller, *The Christopher Lee Filmography,* p. 131. • 41. *Ibid.,* p. 132. • 42. Jimmy Sangster, *Inside Hammer* (Reynolds and Hearn, 2001), p. 99–100. • 43. Meikle, *A History of Horrors,* p. 7. • 44. Kinsey, *Hammer Films: The Bray Studios Years,* p. 15. • 45. *Hammer Horror,* #3, May 1995, p. 35. • 46. *Hammer Horror,* #7, September 1995, p. 37. • 47. Kinsey, *Hammer Films: The Bray Studios Years,* p. 268. • 48. *Dark Terrors,* #18, May 2002, p. 19. • 49. *Little Shoppe of Horrors,* #13, November 1996, p. 122. • 50. *Ibid.* • 51. Sangster, *Inside Hammer,* p. 54. • 52. *Hammer Horror,* #1, March 1995, p. 13–14. • 53. Sangster, *Inside Hammer,* p. 105. • 54. Roy Ward Baker, *The*

*Director's Cut* (Reynolds & Hearn, 2000), p. 135. • 55. *Ibid.*, p. 136. • 56. *Ibid.* • 57. Hearn and Barnes, *The Hammer Story*, p. 149. • 58. *Ibid.* • 59. Wayne Kinsey, *Hammer Films: The Elstree Studios Years* (Tomahawk, 2007), p. 266. • 60. Kinsey, *Hammer Films: The Bray Studios Years*, p. 287. • 61. *Shivers*, #31, July 1996, p. 36. • 62. *Film Review Special, #53*, August 2004, p. 67. • 63. *Ibid.* • 64. I.Q. Hunter [ed], *British Science Fiction Cinema* (Routledge 1999), p. 51. • 65. *Film Review Special, #53*, August 2004, p. 67. • 66. *Ibid.* • 67. Guest, *So You Want to Be in Pictures*, p. 132. • 68. Andy Murray, *Into the Unknown: The Fantastic Life of Nigel Kneale* (Headpress, 2006), p. 56. • 69. *Little Shoppe of Horrors*, #10/11, June 1990, p. 8. • 70. *Cinefantastique*, February 1994. • 71. Sangster, *Inside Hammer*, p. 15–16. • 72. Hearn and Barnes, *The Hammer Story*, p. 10. • 73. *Little Shoppe of Horrors*, #10/11, June 1990, p. 6. • 74. *Ibid.* • 75. Kinsey, *Hammer Films: The Bray Studios Years*, p. 85. • 76. *Film Review, #580*, April 1999, p. 80. • 77. *Ibid.* • 78. *Ibid.* • 79. *Ibid.* • 80. Kinsey, *Hammer Films: The Bray Studios Years*, p. 94. • 81. Lee, *Tall, Dark and Gruesome*, p. 185. • 82. Lee, *Tall, Dark and Gruesome*, p. 185. • 83. *Photon #27*, 1975, p. 30. • 84. *Starlog #6*, 1992, p. 47. • 85. James Marriott, *Virgin Film: Horror Films* (Virgin, 2004), p. 48. • 86. *Ibid.* • 87. Bruce Sachs and Russell Wall, *Greasepaint and Gore* (Tomahawk, 1991), p. 73–74. • 88. *Ibid.*, p. 74. • 89. Lee, *Tall, Dark and Gruesome*, p. 186. • 90. Kinsey, *Hammer Films: The Bray Studios Years*, p. 101. • 91. *Film Review, #580*, April 1999, p. 84. • 92. *Ibid.* • 93. *Ibid.* • 94. Kinsey, *Hammer Films: The Bray Studios Years*, p. 111. • 95. Sarah Street, *Transatlantic Crossings: British Feature Films in the USA* (Continuum, 2002), p. 161. • 96. *Film Review, #580*, April 1999, pp. 83–84. • 97. *Ibid.*, p. 85. • 98. *Ibid.* • 99. Streeter, *Transatlantic Crossings: British Feature Films in the USA*, p. 161. • 100. Hearn and Barnes, *The Hammer Story*, p. 7. • 101. *Shivers*, #34, October 1996, p. 39. • 102. *Little Shoppe of Horrors*, #12, 1994, p. 98. • 103. Johnson and Miller, *The Christopher Lee Filmography*, p. 237. • 104. *Ibid.* • 105. Allen Eyles and Robert Adkinson, Nicholas Fry, *The House of Horror* (Lorrimer, 1973), p. 15. • 106. *Hammer Horror, #6*, August 1995, p. 27. • 107. *Little Shoppe of Horrors*, #13, November 1996, p. 55. • 108. Johnson and Miller, *The Christopher Lee Filmography*, p. 186. • 109. *Ibid.* • 110. *Ibid.*, p. 185. • 111. *Hammer Horror, #6*, August 1995, p. 11. • 112. Johnson and Miller, *The Christopher Lee Filmography*, p. 187. • 113. *Hammer Horror, #6*, August 1995, p. 28. • 114. Johnson and Miller, *The Christopher Lee Filmography*, p. XVII [sic]. • 115. *Hammer Horror, #6*, August 1995, p. 11. • 116. *Ibid.* • 117. *Ibid.* • 118. Johnson and Miller, *The Christopher Lee Filmography*, p. 187. • 119. Johnson and Miller, *The Christopher Lee Filmography*, p. 132. • 120. Jimmy Sangster, *Inside Hammer* (Reynolds & Hearn, 2001), pp. 113–114. • 121. Gareth Owen. *Albert J. Luxford, the Gimmick Man* (McFarland, 2002), p. 132. • 122. *Ibid.*, p. 115. • 123. *Ibid.* • 124. *Ibid.*, p. 114. • 125. Neame, *Rungs on a Ladder: Hammer Films Seen Through a Gauze*, p. 7. • 126. Johnson and Miller, *The Christopher Lee Filmography*, p. 151. • 127. *Hammer Horror*, #3, May 1995, p. 15–16. • 128. *Starburst*, Winter Special 1989, p. 62. • 129. Sangster, *Inside Hammer*, 2001, p. 114. • 130. Sachs and Wall, *Greasepaint and Gore*, p. 80.

**F**

1. Wayne Kinsey, *Hammer Films: The Bray Studios Years* (Reynolds & Hearn, 2002), p. 56. • 2. *Hammer Horror*, #7, September 1995, p. 33. • 3. *Ibid.* • 4. *Little Shoppe of Horrors*, #15, November 2001, p. 35. • 5. *Ibid.*, p. 37. • 6. Ingrid Pitt, *Life's a Scream* (Heinemann, 1999), p. 213–214. • 7. Wayne Kinsey, *Hammer Films—The Elstree Studios Years* (Tomahawk,

2007), p. 39. • 8. Denis Meikle, *A History of Horrors* (Scarecrow, 2001), p. 227. • 9. *Little Shoppe of Horrors*, #10/11, July 1990, p. 7. • 10. *Little Shoppe of Horrors*, #14, December 1999, p. 30. • 11. Kinsey, *Hammer Films: The Bray Studios Years*, p. 38. • 12. Bruce Sachs and Russell Wall, *Greasepaint and Gore* (Tomahawk, 1991), p. 119. • 13. *Hammer Horror, #6*, August 1995, p. 9. • 14. Sachs and Wall, *Greasepaint and Gore*, p. 119. • 15. *Ibid.*, p. 115. • 16. *Ibid.*, p. 120. • 17. *Hammer Horror, #6*, August 1995, p. 14. • 18. *Hammer Horror, #6*, August 1995, p. 15. • 19. *Hammer Horror, #6*, August 1995, p. 16. • 20. Marcus Hearn and Alan Barnes, *The Hammer Story* (Titan, 1997), p. 12. • 21. McFarlane, *An Autobiography of British Cinema*, p. 524.

**F**

1. Jimmy Sangster, *Inside Hammer* (Reynolds & Hearn, 2001), p. 16. • 2. Joel Lobenthal, *Tallulah! The Life and Times of a Leading Lady* (Aurum, 2005), p. 515. • 3. *Ibid.* • 4. *The New York Times*. • 5. Lobenthal, *Tallulah! The Life and Times of a Leading Lady*, p. 519. • 6. Wayne Kinsey, *Hammer Films: The Bray Studios Years* (Reynolds & Hearn, 2002), p. 160. • 7. *Little Shoppe of Horrors*, #14, December 1999, p. 58. • 8. *Little Shoppe of Horrors*, #19, September 2007, p. 81. • 9. *Fear in the Night*, DVD commentary, Anchor Bay. • 10. *Ibid.* • 11. David Miller, *The Complete Peter Cushing* (Reynolds & Hearn, 2005), p. 135. • 12. *Little Shoppe of Horrors*, #15, November 2001, p. 75. • 13. *Little Shoppe of Horrors*, #16, August 2004, p. 36. • 14. *Little Shoppe of Horrors*, #19, September 2007, p. 7. • 15. Allen Eyles and Robert Adkinson, Nicholas Fry, *The House of Horror* (Lorrimer, 1973), p. 13. • 16. *Ibid.* • 17. *Ibid.*, p. 13–14. • 18. Sangster, *Inside Hammer*, p. 15. • 19. Marcus Hearn and Alan Barnes, *The Hammer Story* (Titan, 1997), p. 23. • 20. Eyles, Adkinson and Fry, *House of Horror*, p. 14. • 21. Hearn and Barnes, *The Hammer Story*, p. 23. • 22. Eyles, Adkinson and Fry, *House of Horror*, p. 14. • 23. *Hammer Horror, #6*, August 1995, p. 46. • 24. *Cinefantastique*, Vol 4, #3, p. 26, 1973. • 25. *The Hammer Film Music Collection*, CD liner notes, GDI Records, 2000. • 26. Eyles, Adkinson and Fry, *House of Horror*, p. 15. • 27. Wayne Kinsey, *Hammer Films: The Elstree Studios Years* (Tomahawk, 2007), p. 345. • 28. Hearn and Barnes, *The Hammer Story*, p. 161. • 29. *Hammer Horror, #1*, March 1995, p. 13. • 30. *The Devil Rides Out*, CD interview, GDI Records, 2000. • 31. Tom Johnson and Mark A. Miller, *The Christopher Lee Filmography* (McFarland, 2004), p. 66. • 32. Kinsey, *Hammer Films: The Bray Studios Years*, p. 282. • 33. *Little Shoppe of Horrors*, #10/11, 1990, p. 96. • 34. Christopher Neame, *Rungs on a Ladder: Hammer Films Seen Through a Gauze* (Scarecrow, 2003), p. 6. • 35. Johnson and Miller, *The Christopher Lee Filmography*, p. 66. • 36. *Fangoria*, #63, May 1987, p. 60. • 37. *Shivers*, #42, June 1997, p. 20. • 38. *Films and Filming*, July 1964, p. 8. • 39. Eyles, Adkinson and Fry, *House of Horror*, p. 15. • 40. *Little Shoppe of Horrors*, #19, September 2007, p. 5. • 41. *Ibid.*, p. 37. • 42. Alan Frank, *Horror Films* (Hamlyn, 1977), p. 12. • 43. Sangster, *Inside Hammer*, p. 16–17. • 44. Neame, *Rungs on a Ladder: Hammer Films Seen Through a Gauze*, p. 22. • 45. Meikle, *A History of Horrors*, p. 240. • 46. *Little Shoppe of Horrors*, #16, August 2004, 56. • 47. *Shatter*, DVD commentary. • 48. *Hammer Horror, #1, March 1995*, p. 36–37. • 49. *Four Sided Triangle*, DVD liner notes, DD Entertainment, p. 9. • 50. *Hammer Horror, #6*, August 1995, p. 8. • 51. Wheeler Winston Dixon, *The Films of Freddie Francis* (Scarecrow Press, 1991), p. 76. • 52. *Little Shoppe of Horrors*, #4, April 1978, p. 47. • 53. Kinsey, *Hammer Films: The Bray Studios Years*, p. 289. • 54. Brian McFarlane, *An Autobiography of British Cinema* (Methuen/BFI, 1997), p. 210. • 55. Harvey

Fenton [ed], *Flesh & Blood Compendium* (FAB Press, 2003), p. 158. • 56. *Ibid.* • 57. McFarlane, *An Autobiography of British Cinema*, p. 211. • 58. Hearn and Barnes, *The Hammer Story*, p. 131. • 59. *Fangoria*, #63, May 1987, p. 60. • 60. Hearn and Barnes, *The Hammer Story*, p. 161. • 61. *Ibid.* • 62. Miller, *The Complete Peter Cushing*, p. 141. • 63. Hearn and Barnes, *The Hammer Story*, p. 161. • 64. *Hammer Horror*, #5, p. 10. • 65. John Kenneth Muir, *Horror Films of the 1970s* (McFarland, 2002), p. 56. • 66. Miller, *The Complete Peter Cushing*, p. 6. • 67. *Ibid*, p. 142. • 68. *Little Shoppe of Horrors*, #3, February 1974, p. 52. • 69. Sangster, *Inside Hammer*, p. 15. • 70. *Little Shoppe of Horrors*, #15, November 2001, p. 119. • 71. Val Guest, *So You Want to Be in Pictures* (Reynolds & Hearn, 2001), p. 138. • 72. Robert Ross, *The Complete Frankie Howerd* (Reynolds & Hearn, 2001), p. 111.

**G**

1. *Soundtrack! Vol 11, No 43*, September 1992, p. 23. • 2. Wayne Kinsey, *Hammer Films: The Bray Studios Years* (Reynolds & Hearn, 2002), p. 273. • 3. Tudor Gates, *Scenario: The Craft of Screenwriting* (Wallflower, 2002), p. 71. • 4. *Little Shoppe of Horrors*, #8, May 1984, p. 43. • 5. Gates, *Scenario: The Craft of Screenwriting*, p. 72. • 6. *Little Shoppe of Horrors*, #16, August 2004, p. 39. • 7. Quentin Falk and Dominic Prince, *Last of a Kind: The Sinking of Lew Grade* (Quartet Books, 1987), p. 110. • 8. *Little Shoppe of Horrors*, #14, December 1999, p. 7. • 9. *Little Shoppe of Horrors*, #12, April 1994, p. 60. • 10. *Little Shoppe of Horrors*, #14, December 1999, p. 118. • 11. Kinsey, *Hammer Films: The Bray Studios Years*, p. 267. • 12. Denis Meikle, *A History of Horrors* (Scarecrow, 2001), p. 194. • 13. *Little Shoppe of Horrors*, #4, April 1978, p. 57. • 14. *Ibid.* • 15. *Shivers*, #31, July 1996, p. 36. • 16. *Little Shoppe of Horrors*, #12, April 1994, p. 106. • 17. *Ibid.*, p. 107. • 18. *Hammer Horror, #7*, September 1995, p. 37. • 19. *Ibid.*, p. 39. • 20. Jimmy Sangster, *Inside Hammer* (Reynolds & Hearn, 2001), p. 18. • 21. Christopher Neame, *Rungs on a Ladder: Hammer Films Seen Through a Soft Gauze* (Scarecrow, 2003), p. 105. • 22. Kinsey, *Hammer Films: The Bray Studios Years*, p. 289. • 23. *Ibid.*, p. 335. • 24. Marcus Hearn and Alan Barnes, *The Hammer Story* (Titan, 1997), p. 13. • 25. Kinsey, *Hammer Films: The Bray Studios Years*, p. 189. • 26. *Ibid.*, p. 78. • 27. *Ibid.*, p. 283. • 28. *Ibid.* • 29. Bruce Sachs and Russell Wall, *Greasepaint and Gore* (Tomahawk, 1991), p. 127. • 30. Sachs and Wall, *Greasepaint and Gore*, p. 127. • 31. *Little Shoppe of Horrors*, #9, April 1986, p. 90. • 32. David Miller, *The Complete Peter Cushing* (Reynolds & Hearn, 2005), p. 101. • 33. Tom Johnson and Mark A. Miller, *The Christopher Lee Filmography* (McFarland, 2004), p. 135. • 34. *Little Shoppe of Horrors*, #4, April 1978, p. 57. • 35. *Ibid.* • 36. *Ibid.*, p. 107. • 37. Wayne Kinsey, *Hammer Films: The Elstree Studios Years* (Tomahawk, 2007), p. 260. • 38. Neame, *Rungs on a Ladder: Hammer Films Seen Through a Gauze*, p. 23. • 39. Kinsey, *Hammer Films: The Elstree Studios Years*, p. 22. • 40. *Ibid.*, p. 103–104. • 41. Neame, *Rungs on a Ladder: Hammer Films Seen Through a Gauze*, p. 27. • 42. *Little Shoppe of Horrors*, #4, April 1978, p. 57. • 43. *Ibid.* • 44. Christopher Lee, *Tall, Dark and Gruesome* (Victor Gollancz, 1997), p. 235. • 45. *Hammer Horror, #6*, August 1995, p. 50. • 46. Sangster, *Inside Hammer*, p. 41. • 47. Albert J. Luxford and Gareth Owen, *Albert J. Luxford, the Gimmick Man*, (McFarland, 2002), p. 134. • 48. *Little Shoppe of Horrors*, #17, November 2005, p. 49. • 49. *Ibid.* • 50. *Little Shoppe of Horrors*, #8, May 1984, p. 41. • 51. Unpublished interview with the author. • 52. Unpublished interview with the author. • 53. Val Guest, *So You Want to Be in Pictures* (Reynolds & Hearn, 2001), p. 131. • 54. Unpublished interview with the author. • 55.

Unpublished interview with the author. • 56. Brian McFarlane, *An Autobiography of British Cinema* (Methuen/BFI, 1997), p. 259. • 57. Unpublished interview with the author. • 58. *Hammer House of Mystery and Suspense*, DVD documentary (DD Entertainment, 2005. • 59. Guest, *So You Want to Be in Pictures*, Val Guest, p. 179. • 60. *Hammer House of Mystery and Suspense*, DVD documentary (DD Entertainment, 2005. • 61. Unpublished interview with the author. • 62. *Little Shoppe of Horrors*, #10/11, July 1990, p. 99.

# H

1. Christopher Neame, *Rungs on a Ladder: Hammer Films Seen Through a Soft Gauze* (Scarecrow, 2003), p. 103. • 2. *Little Shoppe of Horrors*, #16, August 2004, p. 38. • 3. *Hammer—The Studio That Dripped Blood*, BBC, 1987. • 4. *Ibid.* • 5. *Little Shoppe of Horrors*, #10/11, July 1990, p 58. • 6. *Little Shoppe of Horrors*, #13, November 1996, p. 15. • 7. Marcus Hearn and Alan Barnes, *The Hammer Story* (Titan, 1997), p. 171. • 8. *Hammer House of Mystery and Suspense*, DVD liner notes, DD Entertainment, 2005/*The Evening Standard*. • 9. Hearn and Barnes, *The Hammer Story*, p. 173. • 10. *Hammer House of Mystery and Suspense*, DVD liner notes, DD Entertainment, 2005. • 11. *Hammer House of Mystery and Suspense*, DVD liner notes, DD Entertainment, 2005/*The Evening Standard*. • 12. Hearn and Barnes, *The Hammer Story*, p. 171. • 13. *Little Shop of Horrors* #8, May 1984, p. 17. • 14. Hearn and Barnes, *The Hammer Story*, p. 25. • 15. *Hammer House of Mystery and Suspense*, DVD liner notes, DD Entertainment, 2005. • 16. *Little Shoppe of Horrors*, #8, May 1984, p. 14. • 17. *Hammer House of Mystery and Suspense*, DVD documentary, DD Entertainment, 2005. • 18. Hearn and Barnes, *The Hammer Story*, p. 174. • 19. *Little Shoppe of Horrors*, #8, May 1984, p. 14. • 20. *Hammer House of Mystery and Suspense*, DVD documentary, DD Entertainment, 2005. • 21. *Ibid.* • 22. *Ibid.* • 23. *Ibid.* • 24. *Ibid.* • 25. *Ibid.* • 26. *Ibid.* • 27. *Little Shoppe of Horrors*, #8, May 1984, p. 13. • 28. *Hammer House of Mystery and Suspense*, DVD documentary, DD Entertainment, 2005. • 29. *Ibid.* • 30. *Little Shoppe of Horrors*, #8, May 1984, p. 13. • 31. *Hammer House of Mystery and Suspense*, DVD documentary, DD Entertainment, 2005. • 32. *Ibid.* • 33. *Little Shop of Horrors* #8, May 1984, p. 15. • 34. *Hammer House of Mystery and Suspense*, DVD documentary, DD Entertainment, 2005. • 35. *Ibid.* • 36. *Little Shoppe of Horrors*, #8, May 1984, p. 13. • 37. *Ibid.* • 38. *Hammer House of Mystery and Suspense*, DVD documentary, DD Entertainment, 2005. • 39. *Ibid.* • 40. *Ibid.* • 41. *Dark Terrors*, #18, May 2002, p. 9. • 42. Brian McFarlane, *An Autobiography of British Cinema* (Methuen/BFI, 1997), p. 524. • 43. *Dark Terrors*, #18, May 2002, p. 9. • 44. *Ibid.* • 45. *Ibid.* • 46. *Ibid.*, p. 12. • 47. Denis Meikle, *A History of Horrors* (Scarecrow, 2001), p. 138. • 48. *Little Shoppe of Horrors*, #14, December 1999, p. 71. • 49. *Dark Terrors*, #18, May 2002, p. 12. • 50. *Ibid.* • 51. Patricia Warren, *Elstree: The British Hollywood* (Columbus, 1988), p. 137. • 52. Derek Pykett, *Michael Ripper Unmasked* (Midnight Marquee Press, 1999), p. 121. • 53. Hearn and Barnes, *The Hammer Story*, p. 89. • 54. *Hammer Horror*, #6, August 1995, p. 18. • 55. *Little Shoppe of Horrors*, #13, November 1996, p. 57. • 56. Meikle, *A History of Horrors*, p. 215. • 57. *Ibid*, p. 220. • 58. *Dark Terrors*, #18, May 2002, p. 14. • 59. *Ibid.* • 60. *Ibid.* • 61. Meikle, *A History of Horrors*, p. 234. • 62. *Film Review*, #580, April 1999, p. 83. • 63. Meikle, *A History of Horrors*, p. 280. • 64. *Hammer House of Mystery and Suspense*, DVD documentary, DD Entertainment, 2005. • 65. *Little Shoppe of Horrors*, #10/11, July 1990, p. 101. • 66. *Fangoria*, #63, May 1987, p. 56. • 67. *Flesh and Blood: The Hammer Heritage of Horror*, Heidelburg/Hammer/Bosutow Media Group,
1994. • 68. *Hammer—The Studio That Dripped Blood*, BBC, 1987. • 69. *Hammer House of Mystery and Suspense*, DVD documentary, DD Entertainment, 2005. • 70. *Ibid.* • 71. *Dark Terrors*, #18, May 2002, p. 5. • 72. BBC News website, 10 May, 2007. • 73. *Ibid.* • 74. *The Devil Rides Out*, CD interview, GDI Records, 2000. • 75. Allen Eyles and Robert Adkinson, Nicholas Fry, *The House of Horror* (Lorrimer, 1973), p. 17. • 76. *Starburst*, Winter Special 1989, p. 60. • 77. Meikle, *A History of Horrors*, p. 295. • 78. *Ibid.*, p. 295. • 79. *Little Shoppe of Horrors*, #4, April 1978, p. 31. • 80. *Flesh and Blood: The Hammer Heritage of Horror*, Heidelburg/Hammer/Bosutow Media Group, 1994. • 81. Hearn and Barnes, *The Hammer Story*, p. 7. • 82. *Little Shoppe of Horrors*, #13, November 996, p. 52. • 83. Hearn and Barnes, *The Hammer Story*, p. 85. • 84. Roy Ward Baker, *The Director's Cut* (Reynolds & Hearn, 2000), p. 140. • 85. Hearn and Barnes, *The Hammer Story*, p. 146. • 86. *Films Illustrated*, 1971. • 87. Baker, *The Director's Cut*, p. 131. • 88. *Little Shoppe of Horrors*, #10/11, July 1990, p. 157. • 89. *Little Shoppe of Horrors*, #12, April 1994, p. 112. • 90. *Ibid.* • 91. *Ibid.*, p. 113. • 92. Wayne Kinsey, *Hammer Films: The Bray Studios Years* (Reynolds & Hearn, 2002), p. 274. • 93. Meikle, *A History of Horrors*, p. 296. • 94. Kinsey, *Hammer Films: The Bray Studios Years*, p. 23. • 95. *Little Shoppe of Horrors*, #4, April 1978, p. 76. • 96. *Little Shoppe of Horrors*, #14, December 1999, p. 67. • 97. *Jason and the Argonauts* DVD, *The Ray Harryhausen Chronicles*, documentary, Columbia/Lorac Productions Inc., Julian Seddon Films, 1997. • 98. Kinsey, *Hammer Films: The Bray Studios Years*, p. 351. • 99. Ray Harryhausen and Tony Dalton, *The Art of Ray Harryhausen* (Aurum, 2005), p. 76. • 100. Jimmy Sangster, *Inside Hammer* (Reynolds & Hearn, 2001), p. 16. • 101. *Little Shoppe of Horrors*, #10/11, July 1990, p. 159. • 102. *The Blood on Satan's Claw: An Angel for Satan*, DVD documentary, Anchor Bay, 2003. • 103. *Film Review*, March 1998, p. 46. • 104. *Ibid.* • 105. Kinsey, *Hammer Films: The Bray Studios Years*, p. 339. • 106. Sangster, *Inside Hammer*, p. 15. • 107. *Hammer Horror*, #3, May 1995, p. 35. • 108. Sangster, *Inside Hammer*, p. 15. • 109. *Hammer Horror*, #5, July 1995, p. 14. • 110. McFarlane, *An Autobiography of British Cinema*, p. 259. • 111. *Shatter*, DVD commentary. • 112. *Captain Kronos—Vampire Hunter*, DVD liner notes, DD Video, 2003. • 113. *Little Shoppe of Horrors*, #12, April 1994, p. 60. • 114. Neame, *Rungs on a Ladder: Hammer Films Seen Through a Gauze*, p. 25. • 115. *Ibid.*, p. 28. • 116. Kinsey, *Hammer Films: The Bray Studios Years*, p. 187. • 117. Neame, *Rungs on a Ladder: Hammer Films Seen Through a Gauze*, p. 106. • 118. Eyles, Adkinson and Fry, *House of Horror*, p. 9. • 119. McFarlane, *An Autobiography of British Cinema*, p. 525–526. • 120. Unpublished interview with the author. • 121. Val Guest, *So You Want to Be in Pictures* (Reynolds & Hearn, 2001), p. 131. • 122. Neame, *Rungs on a Ladder: Hammer Films Seen Through a Gauze*, p. 11. • 123. *Little Shoppe of Horrors*, #5, August 1980, p. 19. • 124. *Little Shoppe of Horrors*, #12, April 1994, p. 48. • 125. Meikle, *A History of Horrors*, p. 177. • 126. Neame, *Rungs on a Ladder: Hammer Films Seen Through a Gauze*, p. 11. • 127. *Dark Terrors*, #18, May 2002, p. 14. • 128. *Little Shoppe of Horrors*, #10/11, July 1990, p 56. • 129. Meikle, *A History of Horrors*, p. 227. • 130. *Captain Kronos—Vampire Hunter*, DVD liner notes, DD Video, 2003. • 131. Hearn and Barnes, *The Hammer Story*, p. 89. • 132. Neame, *Rungs on a Ladder: Hammer Films Seen Through a Gauze*, p. 11. • 133. Hearn and Barnes, *The Hammer Story*, p. 10. • 134. *Little Shoppe of Horrors*, #4, April 1978, p. 57. • 135. Sangster, *Inside Hammer*, p. 12. • 136. *Hammer Horror*, #6, August 1995, p. 9. • 137. Alan Frank, *Horror Films* (Hamlyn, 1977), p. 15. • 138. *Hammer Horror*, #1, March 1995, p. 50. • 139. *Film Review Special*, #53, August 2004, p. 67. • 140. *Little Shoppe of Horrors*, #18, September 2006, p. 71. • 141. *Ibid.*, p. 73. •
142. *Flesh and Blood: The Hammer Heritage of Horror*, Heidelburg/Hammer/Bosutow Media Group, 1994. • 143. *Little Shoppe of Horrors*, #12, April 1994, p. 59. • 144. David Huckvale, *Hammer Film Scores and the Musical Avant-Garde* (McFarland, 2008), p. 8. • 145. Hearn and Barnes, *The Hammer Story*, p. 59. • 146. Lee, *Tall, Dark and Gruesome*, p. 207. • 147. *Ibid.*, p. 207. • 148. John Walker [ed], *Halliwell's Who's Who* (Harper-Collins, 2006), p. 233. • 149. *Blood from the Mummy's Tomb*, CD liner notes, GDI Records, 2002. • 150. *The Knowledge*, 28 October 2006, p. 17. • 151. Sangster, *Inside Hammer*, p. 117. • 152. *Hammer Horror*, #6, August 1995, p. 16. • 153. *Hammer Horror*, #6, August 1995, p. 17. • 154. Hearn and Barnes, *The Hammer Story*, p. 138. • 155. *Shivers*, #36, December 1996, p. 34. • 156. Sangster, *Inside Hammer*, p. 129–131. • 157. *Little Shoppe of Horrors*, #16, August 2004, p. 92. • 158. *Hammer House of Mystery and Suspense*, DVD documentary, DD Entertainment, 2005. • 159. *Ibid.* • 160. *Ibid.* • 161. *Ibid.* • 162. *Ibid.* • 163. *Little Shoppe of Horrors*, #16, August 2004, p. 92. • 164. *Ibid.*, p. 93. • 165. Hearn and Barnes, *The Hammer Story*, p. 38. • 166. Kinsey, *Hammer Films: The Bray Studios Years*, p. 134. • 167. Lee, *Tall, Dark and Gruesome*, p. 198. • 168. *Shivers*, #34, October 1996, p. 38. • 169. Sangster, *Inside Hammer*, p. 16. • 170. *Dark Terrors*, #13, 1996, p. 38. • 171. Robert Ross, *The Complete Frankie Howerd* (Reynolds & Hearn, 2001), p. 111. • 172. Guest, *So You Want to Be in Pictures*, Val Guest, p. 126. • 173. *Little Shoppe of Horrors*, #10/11, July 1990, p. 96. • 174. *Shivers*, #85, December 2000, p. 86. • 175. Alan Hume with Gareth Owen, *A Life Through the Lens* (McFarland, 2004), p. 66. • 176. *Little Shoppe of Horrors*, #4, April 1978, p. 47. • 177. *Little Shoppe of Horrors*, #12, April 1994, p. 99. • 178. Sangster, *Inside Hammer*, p. 62. • 179. *Little Shoppe of Horrors*, #14, December 1999, p. 96. • 180. *Dark Terrors*, #18, p. 10. • 181. *Little Shoppe of Horrors*, #17, November 2005, p. 62. • 182. *Ibid.* • 183. Sangster, *Inside Hammer*, p. 92. • 184. *Ibid.*, p. 93. • 185. *Ibid.*

# I

1. Wayne Kinsey, *Hammer Films: The Elstree Studios Years* (Tomahawk, 2007), p. 212. • 2. *Ibid.*

# J

1. *Captain Kronos—Vampire Hunter*, DVD liner notes, p. 11. • 2. Marcus Hearn and Alan Barnes, *The Hammer Story* (Titan, 1997), p. 159. • 3. *Little Shoppe of Horrors*, #18, September 2006, p. 63. • 4. *Little Shoppe of Horrors*, #13, November 1996, p. 101. • 5. Jimmy Sangster, *Inside Hammer* (Reynolds & Hearn, 2001), p. 134–135. • 6. *Film Review Special*, #53, 2004, p. 67. • 7. *Little Shoppe of Horrors*, #10/11, July 1990, p. 97. • 8. *Little Shoppe of Horrors*, #18, September 2006, p. 67. • 9. Edith De Rham, *Joseph Losey* (Andre Deutsch, 1991), p. 122. • 10. *House of Hammer* #14, p. 23. • 11. Tom Weaver, *I Was a Monster Movie Maker* (McFarland, 2001), p. 177. • 12. *Dark Terrors*, #18, May 2002, p. 14. • 13. Denis Meikle, *A History of Horrors* (Scarecrow, 2001), p. 222.

# K

1. *Little Shoppe of Horrors*, #12, April 1994, p. 108. • 2. *Shivers*, #42, June 1997, p. 20. • 3. Marcus Hearn and Alan Barnes, *The Hammer Story* (Titan, 1997), p. 117. • 4. *Shivers*, #31, July 1996, p. 35. • 5. *Shivers*, #31, July 1996, p. 37. • 6. *Little Shoppe of Horrors*, #12, April 1994, p. 109. • 7. *Ibid.* • 8. Roy Ward Baker, *The Director's Cut* (Reynolds & Hearn, 2000), p. 131. • 9. Christopher Neame, *Rungs on a Ladder: Hammer Films Seen Through a Soft Gauze* (Scarecrow, 2003), p. 6. • 10. *Shivers*, #42, June 1997, p. 20. • 11. *Hammer Horror*, #4, June 1995, p. 11. •

12. *Little Shoppe of Horrors*, #4, April 1978, p. 57. • 13. *Ibid.* • 14. Bruce Sachs and Russell Wall, *Greasepaint and Gore* (Tomahawk, 1991), p. 119. • 15. *Shivers*, #85, December 2000, p. 86. • 16. *Ibid.* • 17. *Ibid.* • 18. *The Hammer Vampire Film Music Collection*—liner notes, GDI Records, 2000. • 19. Sachs and Wall, *Greasepaint and Gore*, p. 79. • 20. *The Hammer Vampire Film Music Collection*—liner notes, GDI Records, 2000. • 21. Sim Branaghan, *British Film Posters* (BFI, 2006), p. 105. • 22. *Starburst* #265, September 2000, p. 56. • 23. I.Q. Hunter [ed], *British Science Fiction Cinema* (Routledge, 1999), p. 50. • 24. *Ibid.*, p. 51. • 25. *Ibid.* • 26. *Shivers*, #31, July 1996, p. 33. • 27. Andy Murray, *Into the Unknown: The Fantastic Life of Nigel Kneale* (Headpress, 2006), p. 55. • 28. *Ibid.*, p. 92–93.

## L

1. *Hammer Horror*, #3, May 1995, p. 36. • 2. Maurice Sellar, *Best of British—A Celebration of Rank Film Classics* (Sphere, 1987), p. 61. • 3. *Film Review Special*, #53, August 2004, p. 67. • 4. *Little Shoppe of Horrors*, #19, September 2007, p. 80. • 5. *Little Shoppe of Horrors*, #12, April 1994, p. 49. • 6. *Ibid.*, p. 50. • 7. Wayne Kinsey, *Hammer Films: The Elstree Studios Years* (Tomahawk, 2007), p. 135. • 8. Jimmy Sangster, *Inside Hammer* (Reynolds & Hearn, 2001), p. 14. • 9. Marcus Hearn and Alan Barnes, *The Hammer Story* (Titan, 1997), p. 12. • 10. Christopher Neame, *Rungs on a Ladder—Hammer Films Seen Through a Soft Gauze* (Scarecrow, 2003), p. 10. • 11. Denis Meikle, *A History of Horrors* (Scarecrow, 2001), p. 206. • 12. *Little Shoppe of Horrors*, #13, November 1996, p. 51. • 13. Wayne Kinsey, *Hammer Films: The Bray Studios Years* (Reynolds & Hearn, 2002), p. 28. • 14. *Little Shoppe of Horrors*, #6, July 1981, p. 36. • 15. Christopher Lee, *Tall, Dark and Gruesome* (Victor Gollancz, 1997), p. 182. • 16. *Hammer Horror*, #7, September 1995, p. 38. • 17. *Shivers*, #50, February 1998, p. 18. • 18. Allen Eyles and Robert Adkinson, Nicholas Fry, *The House of Horror* (Lorrimer, 1973), p. 16. • 19. *Ibid.* • 20. *Film Review*, March 1998, p. 59. • 21. *Ibid.* • 22. *Ibid.* • 23. Tom Johnson and Mark A. Miller, *The Christopher Lee Filmography* (McFarland, 2004), p. 64. • 24. Doug Bradley, *Behind the Mask of the Horror Actor* (Titan, 2004), p. 150. • 25. *Ibid.* • 26. Johnson and Miller, *The Christopher Lee Filmography*, p. XV [*sic*]. • 27. *Ibid.*, p. 64. • 28. Lee, *Tall, Dark and Gruesome*, p. 183. • 29. *Ibid.*, p. 182. • 30. *Film Review*, #580, April 1999, p. 82. • 31. *Hammer—The Studio That Dripped Blood*, BBC TV, 1987. • 32. *The AFI'S 100 Top Film Stars*, Channel 4, 2003. • 33. *Film Review*, #580, April 1999, p. 83. • 34. Eyles, Adkinson and Fry, *House of Horror*, p. 17. • 35. *Ibid.* • 36. Johnson and Miller, *The Christopher Lee Filmography*, p. 76. • 37. Lee, *Tall, Dark and Gruesome*, p. 184. • 38. *Ibid.*, p. 188. • 39. *Film Review*, #580, April 1999, p. 83. • 40. *Ibid.*, p. 82. • 41. Lee, *Tall, Dark and Gruesome*, p. 184. • 42. John Brosnan interview, 1976. • 43. *The Mummy*, CD liner notes, GDI Records, 1999. • 44. *Ibid.* • 45. Bradley, *Behind the Mask of the Horror Actor*, p. 154. • 46. Meikle, *A History of Horrors*, p. 115. • 47. Kinsey, *Hammer Films: The Bray Studios Years* p. 275. • 48. *Shivers*, #85, December 2000, p. 36. • 49. Meikle, *A History of Horrors*, p. 159. • 50. Kinsey, *Hammer Films: The Bray Studios Years*, p. 283. • 51. *She*, CD liner notes, GDI Records, 2001. • 52. Lee, *Tall, Dark and Gruesome*, p. 231. • 53. Eyles, Adkinson and Fry, *House of Horror*, p. 15. • 54. Johnson and Miller, *The Christopher Lee Filmography*, p. 178. • 55. *Fangoria*, #63, May 1987, p. 59. • 56. Lee, *Tall, Dark and Gruesome*, p. 306. • 57. *Ibid.*, p. 306. • 58. *Ibid.* • 59. Hearn and Barnes, *The Hammer Story*, p. 163. • 60. *Shivers*, #52, April 1998, p. 20. • 61. *Fangoria*, #63, May 1987, p. 60. • 62. *Flesh and Blood: The Hammer Heritage of Horror*, Heidelburg/Hammer/Bosutow Media Group, 1994. • 63. *Ibid.* • 64. Eyles, Adkinson and Fry, *House of Horror*, p. 15. • 65. *Ibid.* • 66. Johnson and Miller, *The Christopher Lee Filmography*, p. XVI [*sic*]. • 67. *Ibid.*, p. 64. • 68. *Fangoria*, #63, May 1987, p. 59. • 69. *Ibid.* • 70. Johnson and Miller, *The Christopher Lee Filmography*, p. 64. • 71. *Ibid.*, p. 415. • 72. Louis Paul, *Tales from the Cult Film Trenches* (McFarland, 2008), p. 147. • 73. Roy Ward Baker, *The Director's Cut* (Reynolds & Hearn, 2000), p. 139. • 74. *Ibid.* • 75. *Ibid.* • 76. *Ibid.*, p. 140. • 77. *Ibid.* • 78. *Ibid.*, p. 139. • 79. *Ibid.*, p. 140. • 80. *Hammer Horror*, #7, September 1995, p. 39. • 81. Baker, *The Director's Cut*, p. 140. • 82. David Miller, *The Complete Peter Cushing* (Reynolds & Hearn, 2005), p. 146. • 83. *Shivers*, #38, February 1997, p. 7. • 84. *The Hammer Vampire Film Music Collection*, liner notes, GDI Records, 2000. • 85. *The Lost Continent*, CD liner notes, GDI Records, 2000. • 86. *Little Shoppe of Horrors*, #16, August 2004, p. 77. • 87. Kinsey, *Hammer Films: The Bray Studios Years*, p. 30. • 88. *Little Shoppe of Horrors*, #13, November 1996, p. 10. • 89. Kinsey, *Hammer Films: The Bray Studios Years*, p. 187. • 90. *The Knowledge*, 28 October 2006, p. 17. • 91. Kinsey, *Hammer Films: The Bray Studios Years*, p. 255. • 92. *The Knowledge*, 28 October 2006, p. 17. • 93. Louis Paul, *Tales from the Cult Film Trenches*, p. 170. • 94. *Fear in the Night*, DVD commentary, Anchor Bay. • 95. *Little Shoppe of Horrors*, #13, November 1996, p. 120. • 96. Hearn and Barnes, *The Hammer Story*, p. 10. • 97. Bruce Sachs and Russell Wall, *Greasepaint and Gore* (Tomahawk, 1991), p. 105. • 98. Hearn and Barnes, *The Hammer Story*, p. 73. • 99. Kinsey, *Hammer Films: The Bray Studios Years*, p. 222. • 100. *Little Shoppe of Horrors*, #12, April 1994, p. 58. • 101. Tom Weaver, *I Was a Monster Movie Maker* (McFarland, 2001), p. 135. • 102. *Little Shoppe of Horrors*, #10/11, July 1990, p. 163. • 103. Alan Frank, *Monsters and Vampires* (Octopus, 1976), p. 12. • 104. Jonathan Rigby, *English Gothic* (Reynolds and Hearn, 2002), p. 21, via Gary Don Rhodes, *Lugosi* (McFarland, 1997). • 105. *Shatter*, DVD commentary, Anchor Bay. • 106. *Little Shoppe of Horrors*, #8, May 1984, p. 40. • 107. *The Hammer Vampire Film Music Collection*, liner notes, GDI Records, 2001. • 108. Hearn and Barnes, *The Hammer Story*, p. 142. • 109. *Ibid.* • 110. Kinsey, *Hammer Films: The Bray Studios Years*, p. 217. • 111. *The Hammer Vampire Film Music Collection*, liner notes, GDI Records, 2001. • 112. *Little Shoppe of Horrors*, #8, May 1984, p. 40. • 113. Sangster, *Inside Hammer*, p. 137. • 114. *The Hammer Vampire Film Music Collection*, liner notes, GDI Records, 2001. • 115. Weaver, *I Was a Monster Movie Maker*, p. 137. • 116. *The Hammer Vampire Film Music Collection*, liner notes, GDI Records, 2001. • 117. Sangster, *Inside Hammer*, p. 137. • 118. *Little Shoppe of Horrors*, #10/11, July 1990, p. 96. • 119. *The Hammer Vampire Film Music Collection*, liner notes, GDI Records, 2001. • 120. Howard Maxford, *Hammer, House of Horrors: Behind the Screams* (Batsford, 1996), p. 110. • 121. *The Hammer Vampire Film Music Collection*, liner notes, GDI Records, 2001. • 122. *Ibid.* • 123. Wheeler Winston Dixon, *The Films of Freddie Francis* (Scarecrow Press, 1991), p. 76. • 124. *Little Shoppe of Horrors*, #10/11, July 1990, p. 97. • 125. Albert J. Luxford and Gareth Owen, *Albert J. Luxford, the Gimmick Man* (McFarland, 2002), p. 132. • 126. Val Guest, *So You Want to Be in Pictures* (Reynolds & Hearn, 2001), p. 126.

## M

1. Wayne Kinsey, *Hammer Films: The Bray Studios Years* (Tomahawk, 2007), p. 120. • 2. *Little Shoppe of Horrors*, #8, May 1984, p. 55. • 3. Kinsey, *Hammer Films: The Bray Studios Years*, p. 347. • 4. *Little Shoppe of Horrors*, #4, April 1978, p. 35. • 5. Jimmy Sangster, *Inside Hammer* (Reynolds & Hearn, 2001), p. 21. • 6. *Dark Terrors*, #18, May 2002, p. 29. • 7. Sangster, *Inside Hammer*, p. 21. • 8. Sachs and Wall, *Greasepaint and Gore*, p. 49. • 9. Tom Johnson and Mark A. Miller, *The Christopher Lee Filmography* (McFarland, 2004), p. 84. • 10. *Ibid.*, p. 84. • 11. Sangster, *Inside Hammer*, p. 54. • 12. Tom Weaver, *Return of the B Science Fiction and Horror Heroes* (McFarland, 2000), p. 45. • 13. *Ibid.* • 14. Tom Johnson and Deborah Del Vecchio, *Hammer Films: An Exhaustive Filmography* (McFarland, 1996), p. 225. • 15. Sangster, *Inside Hammer*, p. 82. • 16. *Ibid.*, p. 85. • 17. Marcus Hearn and Alan Barnes, *The Hammer Story* (Titan, 1997), p. 48. • 18. *Hammer Horror*, #3, May 1995, p. 40–41. • 19. Sangster, *Inside Hammer*, p. 55. • 20. Kinsey, *Hammer Films: The Bray Studios Years*, p. 68. • 21. *Little Shoppe of Horrors*, #4, April 1978, p. 69. • 22. *Shivers*, #34, October 1996, p. 38. • 23. *The Vampire Lovers*, CD liner notes, GDI Records, 2000. • 24. *The Hammer Vampire Film Music Collection*, CD liner notes, GDI Records, 2000. • 25. Dennis Meikle, *A History of Horrors* (Scarecrow, 1996), p. 296. • 26. *Soundtrack!* Vol 11, No 43, September 1992, p. 23. • 27. *Little Shoppe of Horrors*, #10/11, July 1990, p. 94. • 28. *Ibid.* • 29. *The Curse of the Mummy's Tomb*, CD liner notes, GDI Records, 2000. • 30. *Ibid.* • 31. *Little Shoppe of Horrors*, #10/11, July 1990, p. 98. • 32. Sangster, *Inside Hammer*, p. 18–19. • 33. *Ibid.*, p. 18. • 34. *Little Shoppe of Horrors*, #13, November 1996, p. 119. • 35. *Starburst*, Winter Special 1989, p. 60. • 36. Sachs and Wall, *Greasepaint and Gore*, p. 81. • 37. *Starburst*, Winter Special 1989, p. 60. • 38. *Hammer Horror*, #2, April 1995, p. 19. • 39. *Starburst*, Winter Special 1989, p. 62. • 40. *Little Shoppe of Horrors*, #12, April 1994, p. 118. • 41. *Ibid.*, p. 9. • 42. *Little Shoppe of Horrors*, #16, August 2004, p. 57. • 43. *Little Shoppe of Horrors*, #10/11, July 1990, p. 99. • 44. *Ibid.*, p. 140. • 45. *Hammer Horror*, #6, August 1995, p. 28. • 46. Val Guest, *So You Want to Be in Pictures* (Reynolds & Hearn, 2001), p. 128. • 47. Sangster, *Inside Hammer*, p. 19. • 48. Kinsey, *Hammer Films: The Bray Studios Years* (Tomahawk, 2007), p. 15. • 49. Sangster, *Inside Hammer*, p. 41. • 50. *Little Shoppe of Horrors*, #4, April 1978, p. 67. • 51. *Ibid.* • 52. Kinsey, *Hammer Films: The Bray Studios Years*, p. 187. • 53. *Ibid.*, p. 177. • 54. Sangster, *Inside Hammer*, p. 62. • 55. Roy Ward Baker, *The Director's Cut* (Reynolds & Hearn, 2000), p. 128. • 56. *Ibid.* • 57. *Dark Terrors*, #18, May 2002, p. 14. • 58. Baker, *The Director's Cut*, p. 129. • 59. Kinsey, *Hammer Films: The Bray Studios Years*, p. 116. • 60. *Hammer Horror*, #7, September 1995, p. 39. • 61. *Hammer Horror*, #5, July 1995, p. 8. • 62. *Little Shoppe of Horrors*, #30, May 2013, p. 89. • 63. Peter Cushing, *Peter Cushing: Past Forgetting* (Weidenfeld and Nicolson, 1988), p. 77. • 64. *The Mummy*, CD liner notes, GDI Records, 1999. • 65. Johnson and Miller, *The Christopher Lee Filmography*, p. 87. • 66. *The Guardian*, 1999. • 67. Sachs and Wall, *Greasepaint and Gore*, p. 60. • 68. Johnson and Miller, *The Christopher Lee Filmography*, p. 88. • 69. *The Mummy* CD, opening introduction by Christopher Lee, GDI Records, 1999. • 70. Johnson and Miller, *The Christopher Lee Filmography*, p. 88. • 71. Christopher Neame, *Rungs on a Ladder: Hammer Films Seen Through a Soft Gauze* (Scarecrow, 2003), p. 29. • 72. *Little Shoppe of Horrors*, #4, April 1978, p. 58. • 73. Hearn and Barnes, *The Hammer Story*, p. 141. • 74. *Little Shoppe of Horrors*, #12, April 1994, p. 99. • 75. Hearn and Barnes, *The Hammer Story*, p. 141. • 76. *Little Shoppe of Horrors*, #17, November 2005, p. 39. • 77. *ABC Film Review*, June 1972. • 78. Neame, *Rungs on a Ladder: Hammer Films Seen Through a Gauze*, p. 118. • 79. Gary D. Rhodes, *Lugosi* (McFarland, 2006), p. 295. • 80. *Ibid.* • 81. *Little Shoppe of Horrors*, #23, October 2009, p. 80. • 82. Gregory William Mank, *Bela Lugosi and Boris Karloff: The Expanded Story of a Haunting Collaboration* (McFarland, 2009),

p. 266), care of *Vampire Over London: Bela Lugosi in Britain*.

## N

1. Jimmy Sangster, *Do You Want It Good or Tuesday?* (Midnight Marquee Press, 1997), p. 84. • 2. Howard Maxford, *Hammer, House of Horror: Behind the Screams* (Batsford, 1996), p. 79. • 3. Joe Lobenthal, *Tallulah! The Life and Times of a Leading Lady* (Aurum, 2005), p. 521. • 4. *She/The Vengeance of She*, GDI Records, 2001 (recorded interview with Mario Nascimbene). • 5. *Little Shoppe of Horrors*, #10/11, July 1990, p. 96. • 6. *Ibid.*, p. 98. • 7. Sue Harper and Vincent Porter, *British Cinema of the 1950s: The Decline of Deference* (Oxford University Press, 2003), p. 11 [quoting the National Film Finance Corporation's Second Annual Report to 31 March 1951, paragraph 13]. • 8. Allen Eyles and Robert Adkinson, Nicholas Fry, *The House of Horror* (Lorrimer, 1973), p. 9. • 9. *Ibid.* • 10. Denis Meikle, *A History of Horrors* (Scarecrow, 2001), p. 4. • 11. Christopher Neame, *Rungs on a Ladder: Hammer Films Seen Through a Soft Gauze* (Scarecrow, 2003), p. X [*sic*]. • 12. Neame, *Rungs on a Ladder: Hammer Films Seen Through a Gauze*, p. 86. • 13. *Flesh and Blood: The Hammer Heritage of Horror*, Heidelburg/Hammer/Bosutow Media Group, 1994. • 14. *Little Shoppe of Horrors*, #17, November 2005, p. 37. • 15. Wayne Kinsey, *Hammer Films: The Elstree Studios Years* (Tomahawk, 2007), p. 33. • 16. *Ibid.* • 17. *Hammer Horror*, #3, May 1995, p. 36–37. • 18. Wayne Kinsey, *Hammer Films: The Bray Studios Years* (Reynolds & Hearn, 2002), p. 159. • 19. *Dark Terrors*, #18, May 2002, p. 12. • 20. *Little Shoppe of Horrors*, #4, April 1978, p. 35. • 21. *Dark Terrors*, #17, p. 35–36. • 22. Jimmy Sangster, *Inside Hammer* (Reynolds & Hearn, 2001), p. 90. • 23. *Ibid.* • 24. Wayne Kinsey, *Hammer Films: The Bray Studios Years* (Reynolds & Hearn, 2002), p. 44–45. • 25. Sangster, *Inside Hammer*, p. 25. • 26. Brian McFarlane, *An Autobiography of British Cinema* (Methuen/BFI, 1997), p. 441.

## O

1. Marcus Hearn and Alan Barnes, *The Hammer Story* (Titan, 1997), p. 10. • 2. Jimmy Sangster, *Inside Hammer* (Reynolds & Hearn, 2001), p. 12. • 3. *Dark Terrors*, #18, May 2002, p. 12. • 4. Ingrid Pitt, *Life's a Scream* (Heinemann, 1999), p. 209–210. • 5. *Little Shoppe of Horrors*, #8, May 1984, p. 73. • 6. *Ibid.*, p. 73–75. • 7. Christopher Neame, *Rungs on a Ladder: Hammer Films Seen Through a Soft Gauze* (Scarecrow, 2003), p. 103. • 8. *Little Shoppe of Horrors*, #4, April 1978, p. 35. • 9. Wayne Kinsey, *Hammer Films: The Elstree Studios Years* (Tomahawk, 2007), p. 270. • 10. *Little Shoppe of Horrors*, #12, April 1994, p. 83. • 11. *Ibid.* • 12. Ray Harryhausen and Tony Dalton, *Ray Harryhausen: An Animated Life* (Aurum, 2003), p. 198. • 13. *The Times Magazine*, 10 December 2005, p. 4. • 14. *Dark Terrors*, #18, p. 30. • 15. *Ibid.*

## P

1. Ingrid Pitt, *Life's a Scream* (Heinemann, 1999), p. 213. • 2. *Hammer Horror*, #3, May 1995, p. 41. • 3. *Little Shoppe of Horrors*, #13, November 1996, p. 42. • 4. Jimmy Sangster, *Inside Hammer* (Reynolds & Hearn, 2001), p. 87. • 5. *Ibid.*, p. 88. • 6. *Ibid.*, p. 58. • 7. Pitt, *Life's a Scream*, p. 212. • 8. *Hammer Horror*, #7, September 1995, p. 38. • 9. *Hammer House of Mystery and Suspense*, DVD documentary, DD Entertainment, 2005. • 10. *The Knowledge*, 28 October 2006, p. 16. • 11. *Ibid.* • 12. *Ibid.* • 13. Bruce Sachs and Russell Wall, *Greasepaint and Gore* (Tomahawk, 1991), p. 143. • 14. *Little Shoppe of Horrors*, #5 (aka *The Hammer Journal* #1), August 1980. • 15.

*Ibid.* • 16. *Little Shoppe of Horrors*, #12, April 1994, p. 59. • 17. *Little Shoppe of Horrors*, #9, April 1986. • 18. *Little Shoppe of Horrors*, #10/11, July 1990, p. 103. • 19. *Little Shoppe of Horrors*, #14, December 1999, p. 120. • 20. *Fangoria*, #74, p. 54. • 21. Denis Meikle, *A History of Horrors* (Scarecrow, 2001), p. 159. • 22. Tom Johnson and Mark A. Miller, *The Christopher Lee Filmography* (McFarland, 2004), p. 100. • 23. *Dark Terrors*, #17, p. 23. • 24. Tom Johnson and Deborah Del Vecchio, *Hammer Films: An Exhaustive Filmography* (McFarland, 1996), p. 220. • 25. *Little Shoppe of Horrors*, #14, December 1999, p. 64. • 26. *Dark Terrors*, #17, p. 25. • 27. Johnson and Miller, *The Christopher Lee Filmography*, p. 112. • 28. Wayne Kinsey, *Hammer Films: The Bray Studios Years* (Reynolds & Hearn, 2002), p. 227. • 29. *Shivers*, #42, June 1997, p. 19. • 30. Marcus Hearn and Alan Barnes, *The Hammer Story* (Titan, 1997), p. 78–79. • 31. John Trevelyan, *What the Censor Saw*, (Michael Joseph, 1973). • 32. Kinsey, *Hammer Films: The Bray Studios Years*, p. 228. • 33. Johnson and Miller, *The Christopher Lee Filmography*, p. 114. • 34. Sangster, *Inside Hammer*, p. 96. • 35. Pitt, *Life's a Scream*, p. 206. • 36. *Ibid.* • 37. *The Vampire Lovers*, CD liner notes, GDI Records, 2000. • 38. Pitt, *Life's a Scream*, p. 209. • 39. *Ibid.*, p. 212. • 40. *Ibid.*, p. 212. • 41. *Shivers*, #32, August 1996, p. 45. • 42. *Ibid.* • 43. *Shivers*, #38, February 1997, p. 5. • 44. Albert J. Luxford and Gareth Owen, *Albert J. Luxford, the Gimmick Man* (McFarland, 2002), p. 133. • 45. Sachs and Wall, *Greasepaint and Gore*, p. 142. • 46. *Ibid.*, p. 145. • 47. Christopher Lee, *Tall, Dark and Gruesome* (Victor Gollancz, 1997), p. 231. • 48. *Hammer Horror*, #3, May 1995, p. 16. • 49. Sachs and Wall, *Greasepaint and Gore*, p. 160. • 50. *Ibid.*, p. 62. • 51. *The Stage*, 2000, obituary. • 52. Sachs and Wall, *Greasepaint and Gore*, p. 61. • 53. www.janinafaye.com. • 54. *Hammer Horror*, #7, September 1995, p. 39. • 55. Hearn and Barnes, *The Hammer Story*, p. 94. • 56. *Little Shoppe of Horrors*, #8, May 1984, p. 79. • 57. *Little Shoppe of Horrors*, #4, April 1978, p. 104. • 58. Wayne Kinsey, *Hammer Films: The Elstree Studios Years* (Tomahawk, 2007), p. 351–352. • 59. John Mitchell, *Flickering Shadows: A Lifetime in Film* (Harold Martin & Redman, 1997), p. 24. • 60. *Ibid.* • 61. *Little Shoppe of Horrors*, #4, April 1978, p. 90/*Shivers*, #64, April 1999, p. 56–59.

## Q

1. Andy Murray, *Into the Unknown: The Fantastic Life of Nigel Kneale* (Headpress, 2006), p. 92. • 2. Wayne Kinsey, *Hammer Films: The Elstree Studios Years* (Tomahawk, 2007), Wayne Kinsey, p. 18–19, via *Little Shoppe of Horrors*, #4, April 1978, p. 44. • 3. *The Hammer Quatermass Film Music Collection*, CD liner notes, GDI Records, 1999. • 4. *The Hammer Quatermass Film Music Collection*, CD liner notes, GDI Records, 1999. • 5. *Ibid.* • 6. Roy Ward Baker, *The Director's Cut* (Reynolds & Hearn, 2000), p. 124. • 7. Christopher Neame, *Rungs on a Ladder: Hammer Films Seen Through a Gauze* (Scarecrow, 2003), p. 37. • 8. I.Q. Hunter [ed], *British Science Fiction Cinema* (Routledge, 1999), p. 54. • 9. Baker, *The Director's Cut*, p. 125. • 10. *Shivers*, #31, July 1996, p. 35. • 11. Murray, *Into the Unknown: The Fantastic Life of Nigel Kneale*, p. 96. • 12. Unpublished interview with the author. • 13. I.Q. Hunter [ed], *British Science Fiction Cinema* (Routledge, 1999), p. 53. • 14. *Ibid.* • 15. *Film Review Special*, #53, August 2004, p. 65. • 16. *Ibid.* • 17. Marcus Hearn and Alan Barnes, *The Hammer Story* (Titan, 1997), p. 21. • 18. Catherine Johnson, *Telefantasy* (BFI, 2005), p. 17–18. • 19. I.Q. Hunter [ed], *British Science Fiction Cinema* (Routledge, 1999), p. 50. • 20. *Film Review Special*, #53, August 2004, p. 65. • 21. *Ibid.* • 22. *Ibid.*, p. 65–66. • 23. *Ibid.*, p. 66. • 24. Val Guest, *So You Want to Be in Pictures* (Reynolds & Hearn, 2001), p. 131. • 25. *Film Review Special*,

#53, August 2004, p. 67. • 26. Guest, *So You Want to Be in Pictures*, p. 126. • 27. *Ibid.*, p. 131. • 28. *Film Review Special*, #53, August 2004, p. 67. • 29. *Ibid.*, p. 68. • 30. Jimmy Sangster, *Inside Hammer* (Reynolds & Hearn, 2001), p. 22. • 31. *Evening Standard*, 2 April 2014. • 32. *Ibid.* • 33. David Miller, *The Complete Peter Cushing* (Reynolds & Hearn, 2005), p. 72.

## R

1. Ed Sikov, *Dark Victory: The Life of Bette Davis* (Aurum, 2007), p. 360–361. • 2. Marcus Hearn and Alan Barnes, *The Hammer Story* (Titan, 1997), p. 119. • 3. Wayne Kinsey, *Hammer Films: The Elstree Studios Years* (Tomahawk, 2007), p. 290. • 4. *Ibid.*, p. 336. • 5. *Hammer Horror*, #4, June 1995, p. 11. • 6. Christopher Neame, *Rungs on a Ladder: Hammer Films Seen Through a Soft Gauze* (Scarecrow, 2003), p. 15. • 7. *Shivers*, #85, December 2000, p. 37. • 8. Tom Johnson and Mark A. Miller, *The Christopher Lee Filmography* (McFarland, 2004), p. 155. • 9. *Ibid.*, p. 155. • 10. Denis Meikle, *A History of Horrors* (Scarecrow, 2001), p. 232. • 11. Tom Weaver, *I Was a Monster Movie Maker* (McFarland, 2001), 137. • 12. Hearn and Barnes, *The Hammer Story*, p. 142. • 13. *Hammer Horror*, #4, June 1995, p. 16. • 14. *Hammer Horror*, #2, April 1995, p. 35. • 15. *Ibid.*, p. 37. • 16. Bruce Sachs and Russell Wall, *Greasepaint and Gore* (Tomahawk, 1991), p. 89. • 17. Meikle, *A History of Horrors*, p. 136. • 18. Sachs and Wall, *Greasepaint and Gore*, p. 89. • 19. *Ibid.*, p. 94. • 20. *Little Shoppe of Horrors*, #15, November 2001, p. 57. • 21. Meikle, *A History of Horrors*, p. 306. • 22. *Films and Films Illustrated*, 1971. • 23. *Little Shoppe of Horrors*, #4, April 1978, p. 58. • 24. Sachs and Wall, *Greasepaint and Gore*, p. 150. • 25. *Ibid.*, p. 151. • 26. Jimmy Sangster, *Screenwriting: Techniques for Success* (Reynolds & Hearn, 2003), p. 22. • 27. David Miller, *The Complete Peter Cushing* (Reynolds & Hearn, 2005), p. 71–72. • 28. *Ibid.*, p. 72. • 29. Jimmy Sangster, *Inside Hammer* (Reynolds & Hearn, 2001), p. 52. • 30. *Shivers*, #33, September 1995, p. 39. • 31. *Little Shoppe of Horrors*, #12, April 1994, p. 83. • 32. *Little Shoppe of Horrors*, #13, November 1996, p. 12. • 33. *Little Shoppe of Horrors*, #12, April 1994, p. 74. • 34. Hearn and Barnes, *The Hammer Story*, p. 52. • 35. Sangster, *Inside Hammer*, p. 58. • 36. *Shivers*, #50, February 1998, p. 22. • 37. Stephen Bourne, *Elisabeth Welch: Soft Lights and Sweet Music* (Scarecrow, 2005), Stephen Bourne, p. 46, taken from *Film Weekly*, 23 May 1936. • 38. *Little Shoppe of Horrors*, #4, April 1978, p. 43. • 39. Wayne Kinsey, *Hammer Films: The Bray Studios Years* (Reynolds & Hearn, 2002), p. 175. • 40. *Little Shoppe of Horrors*, #9, April 1986, p. 95. • 41. *Ibid.* • 42. Sangster, *Inside Hammer*, p. 76. • 43. Neame, *Rungs on a Ladder: Hammer Films Seen Through a Gauze*, p. 14. • 44. *Little Shoppe of Horrors*, #4, April 1978, p. 31. • 45. *Little Shoppe of Horrors*, #15, November 2001, p. 65. • 46. *Hammer: The Studio That Dripped Blood*, 1987, TV documentary. • 47. Meikle, *A History of Horrors*, p. 307. • 48. *Little Shoppe of Horrors*, #10/11, July 1990, p. 100. • 49. *The Vampire Lovers*, CD liner notes, GDI Records, 2000. • 50. *Ibid.* • 51. *The Hammer Vampire Film Music Collection*, CD liner notes, GDI Records, 2001. • 52. *Little Shoppe of Horrors*, #10/11, July 1990, p. 102. • 53. *Ibid.*, p. 94. • 54. *Twins of Evil*, CD liner notes, GDI Records, 2000. • 55. David Huckvale, *Hammer Film Scores and the Musical Avant-Garde* (McFarland, 2008), p. 93. • 56. *Little Shoppe of Horrors*, #10/11, July 1990, p. 102. • 57. *Ibid.* • 58. *Ibid.* • 59. *Ibid.*, p. 96. • 60. *Timeshift: How to Be Sherlock Holmes—The Many Faces of a Master Detective* (2013, TV [first broadcast 2014]). • 61. *The Frankenstein Film Music Collection*, CD liner notes, GDI Records, 2000. • 62. *Little Shoppe of Horrors*, #15, November 2001, p. 42. • 63. Jimmy Sangster, *Do You Want It*

*Good or Tuesday?* (Midnight Marquee Press, 1997), p. 90. • 64. Christopher Neame, *Rungs on a Ladder: Hammer Films Seen Through a Soft Gauze* (Scarecrow, 2003), p. 46. • 65. Sikov, *Dark Victory: The Life of Bette Davis*, p. 369.

## S

1. Denis Meikle, *A History of Horrors* (Scarecrow, 2001), p. 287. • 2. Jimmy Sangster, *Inside Hammer* (Reynolds & Hearn, 2001), p. 16. • 3. *Little Shoppe of Horrors*, #13, November 1996, p. 100. • 4. Sangster, *Inside Hammer*, p. 16. • 5. Christopher Neame, *Rungs on a Ladder: Hammer Films Seen Through a Soft Gauze* (Scarecrow, 2003), p. 52. • 6. Sangster, *Inside Hammer*, p. 13. • 7. *Ibid.*, p. 15. • 8. Jimmy Sangster, *Screenwriting: Techniques for Success* (Reynolds & Hearn, 2003), p. 10. • 9. *Ibid.*, p. 22. • 10. *Film Review*, March 1998, p. 58. • 11. *Ibid.*, p. 57. • 12. Sangster, *Screenwriting: Techniques for Success*, p. 19. • 13. *Ibid*, p. 20. • 14. Sangster, *Inside Hammer*, p. 41. • 15. *Ibid.*, p. 41–42. • 16. *Ibid.*, p. 96. • 17. *Ibid.*, p. 104. • 18. *Ibid.*, p. 106. • 19. *Shivers*, #36, December 1996, p. 36. • 20. Sangster, *Inside Hammer*, p. 127. • 21. *Blood from the Mummy's Tomb*, liner notes, GDI Records, 2002. • 22. *Ibid.* • 23. *Ibid.* • 24. Marcus Hearn and Alan Barnes, *The Hammer Story* (Titan, 1997), p. 142. • 25. *Inside Hammer*, p. 155. • 26. Sangster, *Screenwriting: Techniques for Success*, p. 21. • 27. *Shivers*, #38, September 1996, p. 44–46. • 28. *Little Shoppe of Horrors, #19*, September 2007, p. 5. • 29. *Inside Hammer*, p. 155. • 30. Ingrid Pitt, *Life's a Scream* (Heinemann, 1999), p. 213. • 31. Pitt, *Life's a Scream*, p. 213. • 32. *Little Shoppe of Horrors*, #13, November 1996, p. 92. • 33. *Fangoria*, #41, p. 19. • 34. Christopher Lee, *Tall, Dark and Gruesome* (Victor Gollancz, 1997), p. 234. • 35. John Kenneth Muir, *Horror Films of the 1970s* (McFarland, 2002), p. 290. • 36. Tom Johnson and Mark A. Miller, *The Christopher Lee Filmography* (McFarland, 2004), p. 261. • 37. *Little Shoppe of Horrors*, #12, April 1994, p. 99. • 38. *Scars of Dracula*, CD liner notes, GDI Records, 2000. • 39. *Ibid.* • 40. Wayne Kinsey, *Hammer Films: The Elstree Studios Years* (Tomahawk, 2007), p. 198. • 41. *Ibid.*, p. 196. • 42. *Scars of Dracula*, CD liner notes, GDI Records. • 43. Roy Ward Baker, *The Director's Cut* (Reynolds & Hearn, 2000), p. 132. • 44. Hearn and Barnes, *The Hammer Story*, p. 139. • 45. Baker, *The Director's Cut*, p. 131. • 46. *Shivers*, #38, February 1997, p. 4. • 47. Johnson and Miller, *The Christopher Lee Filmography*, p. 223. • 48. *The Lost Continent*, CD liner notes, GDI Records, 2000. • 49. *Ibid.* • 50. *Ibid.* • 51. Hearn and Barnes, *The Hammer Story*, p. 44. • 52. *Ibid.*, p. 173. • 53. Festival of Fantastic Films, Manchester, 1994. • 54. *Little Shoppe of Horrors*, #14, December 1999, p. 56. • 55. *Ibid.* • 56. Sangster, *Inside Hammer*, p. 14. • 57. Brian McFarlane, *An Autobiography of British Cinema* (Methuen/BFI, 1997), p. 521. • 58. *Little Shoppe of Horrors*, #17, 2005, p 36. • 59. *Hammer Horror*, #7, September 1995, p. 37. • 60. McFarlane, *An Autobiography of British Cinema*, p. 524. • 61. *Hammer Horror*, #3, May 1995, p. 35. • 62. McFarlane, *An Autobiography of British Cinema*, p. 524. • 63. Hearn and Barnes, *The Hammer Story*, p. 7. • 64. McFarlane, *An Autobiography of British Cinema*, p. 258. • 65. *Little Shoppe of Horrors*, #4, April 1978, p. 78. • 66. *Fangoria*, #63, May 1987, p. 61. • 67. McFarlane, *An Autobiography of British Cinema*, p. 530. • 68. *Ibid.*, p. 529. • 69. Meikle, *A History of Horrors*, p. 191. • 70. Wayne Kinsey, *Hammer Films: The Bray Studios Years* (Reynolds & Hearn, 2002), p. 205. • 71. *Ibid.*, p. 300. • 72. *Shivers*, #85 December 2000, p. 85–86. • 73. Hearn and Barnes, *The Hammer Story*, p. 76. • 74. *Shivers*, #85, December 2000, p. 38. • 75. Kinsey, *Hammer Films: The Bray Studios Years*, p. 270. • 76. *Little Shoppe of Horrors*, #10/11, July 1990, p. 52.

• 77. *Shivers*, #42, June 1997, p. 20. • 78. Hearn and Barnes, *The Hammer Story*, p. 173. • 79. *Shivers*, #85, December 2000, p. 38. • 80. *Shatter*, DVD commentary, Anchor Bay. • 81. *Ibid.* • 82. *Ibid.* • 83. Hearn and Barnes, *The Hammer Story*, p. 165. • 84. *Shatter*, DVD commentary, Anchor Bay. • 85. *Little Shoppe of Horrors*, #13, November 1996, p. 53. • 86. *Ibid.* • 87. *Shatter*, DVD commentary, Anchor Bay. • 88. Sachs and Wall, *Greasepaint and Gore*, p. 137. • 89. Johnson and Miller, *The Christopher Lee Filmography*, p. 143. • 90. *Ibid.*, p. 143. • 91. *Little Shoppe of Horrors*, #12, April 1994, p. 102. • 92. *Ibid.*, p. 98. • 93. *Shivers*, #31, July 1996, p. 36. • 94. Kinsey, *Hammer Films: The Elstree Studios Years*, p. 33. • 95. Hearn and Barnes, *The Hammer Story*, p. 150. • 96. *Ibid.*, p. 169. • 97. *Hammer House of Mystery and Suspense*, DVD documentary, DD Entertainment, 2005. • 98. *Ibid.* • 99. *Ibid.* • 100. *Ibid.* • 101. Neame, *Rungs on a Ladder: Hammer Films Seen Through a Gauze*, p. 18. • 102. David Pirie, *The New Heritage of Horror* (IB Tauris, 2008), p. 61. • 103. *Ibid.* • 104. *Fangoria*, #63, p. 61. • 105. *Hammer Horror*, #2, April 1995, p. 37. • 106. *Little Shoppe of Horrors*, #13, November 1996, p. 105. • 107. *Cinema Retro*, Vol 1, #3, 2005, p. 14. • 108. David Miller, *The Complete Peter Cushing* (Reynolds & Hear, 2005), p. 141. • 109. *Little Shoppe of Horrors*, #8, May 1984, p. 68. • 110. Kinsey, *Hammer Films: The Elstree Studios Years*, p. 351. • 111. Louis Paul, *Tales from the Cult Film Trenches* (McFarland, 2008), p. 218–219. • 112. Neame, *Rungs on a Ladder: Hammer Films Seen Through a Gauze*, p. 119. • 113. Kinsey, *Hammer Films: The Elstree Studios Years*, p. 185. • 114. McFarlane, *An Autobiography of British Cinema*, p. 236. • 115. Sangster, *Inside Hammer*, p. 41. • 116. Stephen Bourne, *Elisabeth Welch: Soft Lights and Sweet Music* (Scarecrow, 2005), p. 47. • 117. Kinsey, *Hammer Films: The Bray Studios Years*, p. 24. • 118. Sangster, *Inside Hammer*, p. 15. • 119. *Little Shoppe of Horrors*, #14, December 1999, p. 69. • 120. *The Devil Rides Out*, CD interview, GDI Records, 2000. • 121. Sangster, *Inside Hammer*, p. 12. • 122. Meikle, *A History of Horrors*, p. 51. • 123. *Little Shoppe of Horrors*, #8, May 1984, p. 71. • 124. *The Hammer Vampire Film Music Collection*, CD liner notes, GDI Records, 2001. • 125. *Ibid.* • 126. *Little Shoppe of Horrors*, #14, December 1999, p. 47. • 127. *Ibid.* • 128. *Straight on Till Morning*, DVD commentary, Anchor Bay. • 129. Sangster, *Inside Hammer*, p. 17–18. • 130. Hearn and Barnes, *The Hammer Story*, p. 47. • 131. *Dark Terrors*, #18, May 2002, p. 43. • 132. Hearn and Barnes, *The Hammer Story*, p. 47. • 133. Sangster, *Inside Hammer*, p. 75. • 134. *Little Shoppe of Horrors, #4*, April 1978, p. 107. • 135. Sangster, *Inside Hammer*, p. 135. • 136. *Ibid.* • 137. Hearn and Barnes, *The Hammer Story*, p. 22. • 138. *Starburst*, Winter Special 1989, p. 11–12. • 139. *Hammer Horror*, #7, September 1995, p. 39. • 140. *Little Shoppe of Horrors*, #13, November 1996, p. 93. • 141. *Little Shoppe of Horrors*, #12, April 1994, p. 69.

## T

1. David Pirie, *The New Heritage of Horror* (I.B. Tauris, 2008), p. 87. • 2. *Little Shoppe of Horrors*, #4, April 1978, p. 35. • 3. Tom Johnson and Mark A. Miller, *The Christopher Lee Filmography* (McFarland, 2004), p. 107. • 4. Marcus Hearn and Alan Barnes, *The Hammer Story* (Titan, 1997), p. 61. • 5. Jimmy Sangster, *Inside Hammer* (Reynolds & Hearn, 2001) p. 70. • 6. *Ibid.*, p. 73. • 7. Johnson and Miller, *The Christopher Lee Filmography*, p. 219. • 8. *Ibid.*, p. 219. • 9. Christopher Lee, *Tall, Dark and Gruesome* (Victor Gollancz, 1997), p. 305. • 10. Hearn and Barnes, *The Hammer Story*, p. 87. • 11. *Ibid.*, p. 131. • 12. *Little Shoppe of Horrors*, #10/11, July 1990, p. 105. • 13. *Little Shoppe of Horrors*, #30, May 2013, p. 81. • 14. *Little Shoppe of Horrors*, #17, November 2005, p.

39. • 15. Christopher Frayling, *Ken Adam: The Art of Production Design* (Faber, 2005), p. 99. • 16. Wayne Kinsey, *Hammer Films: The Bray Studios Years* (Reynolds & Hearn, 2002), p. 188. • 17. Sangster, *Inside Hammer*. • 18. *Ibid.*, p. 18. • 19. *Ibid.*, p. 18. • 20. *Little Shoppe of Horrors*, #8, May 1984, p. 78. • 21. *Ibid.* • 22. *Film Review*, March 1998, p. 59. • 23. Hearn and Barnes, *The Hammer Story*, p. 7. • 24. Denis Meikle, *A History of Horrors* (Scarecrow, 2001), p. 136. • 25. *Little Shoppe of Horrors*, #10/11, July 1990, p. 6. • 26. *Little Shoppe of Horrors*, #12, April 1994, p. 72. • 27. Johnson and Miller, *The Christopher Lee Filmography*, p. 279. • 28. Hearn and Barnes, *The Hammer Story*, p. 165. • 29. Meikle, *A History of Horrors*, p. 282. • 30. Johnson and Miller, *The Christopher Lee Filmography*, p. 279. • 31. Hearn and Barnes, *The Hammer Story*, p. 165. • 32. Sangster, *Inside Hammer*, p. 76. • 33. *The Times Magazine*, 10 December 2005, p. 4. • 34. *Little Shoppe of Horrors*, #12, April 1994, p. 83. • 35. *Today's Cinema*, 1 October 19 • 71. • 36. *Shivers*, #36, December 1996, p. 38. • 37. Roy Ward Baker, *The Director's Cut* (Reynolds & Hearn, 2000), p. 131. • 38. *Ibid.*, p. 139. • 39. *Little Shoppe of Horrors*, #8, May 1984, p. 72. • 40. Wayne Kinsey, *Hammer Films: The Elstree Studios Years* (Tomahawk, 2007), p. 271. • 41. *Twins of Evil*, CD liner notes, GDI Records, 2000. • 42. *Hammer House of Mystery and Suspense*, DVD documentary, DD Entertainment, 2005. • 43. *Twins of Evil*, CD liner notes, GDI Records, 2000. • 44. *Ibid.* • 45. *Ibid.* • 46. *Hammer House of Mystery and Suspense*, DVD documentary, DD Entertainment, 2005. • 47. *Twins of Evil*, CD liner notes, GDI Records, 2000. • 48. *Ibid.* • 49. Maurice Sellar, *Best of British: A Celebration of Rank Film Classics* (Sphere, 1987), p. 136. • 50. Albert J. Luxford and Gareth Owen, *Albert J. Luxford, the Gimmick Man* (McFarland, 2002), p. 127–128. • 51. Kinsey, *Hammer Films: The Bray Studios Years*, p. 168. • 52. *Cinefantastique*, Vol 4:3, p. 24. • 53. *Little Shoppe of Horrors*, #9, 1986, p. 89. • 54. Meikle, *A History of Horrors*, p. 115. • 55. *Ibid.*, p. 119. • 56. Johnson and Miller, *The Christopher Lee Filmography*, p. 100. • 57. *Cinefantastique*, Vol 4:3, p. 24. • 58. Hearn and Barnes, *The Hammer Story*, p. 48. • 59. *Ibid.* • 60. *Ibid.* • 61. Meikle, *A History of Horrors*, p. 121. • 62. Hearn and Barnes, *The Hammer Story*, p. 49.

## U

1. Wayne Kinsey, *Hammer Films: The Bray Studios Years* (Reynolds & Hearn, 2002), p. 127. • 2. www.elstreecalling.co.uk/geoffunwinfeature.htm. • 3. Unpublished interview with the author. • 4. Roger Lewis, *The Life and Death of Peter Sellers* (Arrow, 1995), p. 474. • 5. Roger Lewis, *The Life and Death of Peter Sellers* (Arrow, 1995), p. 477. • 6. *Hammer Horror*, #1, March 1995, p. 43. • 7. *Ibid.* • 8. *Hammer Horror*, #1, March 1995, p. 35.

## V

1. Marcus Hearn and Alan Barnes, *The Hammer Story* (Titan, 1997), p. 154. • 2. *The Vampire Lovers*, CD liner notes, GDI Records, 2000. • 3. Roy Ward Baker, *The Director's Cut* (Reynolds & Hearn, 2000), p. 129. • 4. Tudor Gates, *Scenario: The Craft of Screenwriting* (Wallflower, 2002), p. 71. • 5. *The Perfect Vamp Movie*, Visual Voodoo/Channel Four, 2005. • 6. Baker, *The Director's Cut*, p. 130. • 7. *Ibid.* p130, 131. • 8. *The Vampire Lovers*, CD liner notes, GDI Records 2000. • 9. *Ibid.* • 10. Denis Meikle, *A History of Horrors* (Scarecrow, 2001), p. 236. • 11. *The Vampire Lovers*, CD liner notes, GDI Records 2000. • 12. *Shivers*, #31, July 1996, p. 47. • 13. Jimmy Sangster, *Inside Hammer* (Reynolds & Hearn, 2001), p. 41. • 14. *Dark Terrors*, #17, p. 35–36. • 15.

Wayne Kinsey, *Hammer Films: The Elstree Studios Years* (Tomahawk, 2007), p. 43. • 16. *Ibid.*, p. 45. • 17. Val Guest, *So You Want to Be in Pictures* (Reynolds & Hearn, 2001), p. 160–161. • 18. *Little Shoppe of Horrors*, #10/11, July 1990, p. 97. • 19. Sangster, *Inside Hammer*, p. 12. • 20. Hearn and Barnes, *The Hammer Story*, p. 143.

## W

1. *Little Shoppe of Horrors*, #10/11, July 1990, p. 64. • 2. Tom Weaver, *Return of the B Science Fiction and Horror Heroes* (McFarland, 2000), p. 43. • 3. *Little Shoppe of Horrors*, #10/11, July 1990, p. 155–156. • 4. *Little Shoppe of Horrors*, #16, August 2004, p. 89. • 5. *Little Shoppe of Horrors*, #30, May 2013, p. 75. • 6. Wayne Kinsey, *Hammer Films: The Bray Studios Years* (Reynolds & Hearn, 2002), p. 275. • 7. Christopher Neame, *Rungs on a Ladder: Hammer Films Seen Through a Gauze* (Scarecrow, 2003), p. 46. • 8. Kinsey, *Hammer Films: The Bray Studios Years*, p. 289. • 9. *Ibid.* • 10. Stephen Bourne, *Elisabeth Welch: Soft Lights and Sweet Music* (Scarecrow, 2005), p. 47. • 11. *Little Shoppe of Horrors*, #12, April 1994, p. 82. • 12. *Ibid.* • 13. *Ibid.*, p. 83. • 14. John Mitchell, *Flickering Shadows—A Lifetime in Film* (Harold Martin & Redman, 1997), p. 24. • 15. *The Devil Rides Out*, CD liner notes, GDI Records, 2000. • 16. *Ibid.* • 17. *Hammer House of Mystery and Suspense*, DVD documentary, DD Entertainment, 2005. • 18. Unpublished interview by the author. • 19. Val Guest, *So You Want to Be in Pictures* (Reynolds & Hearn, 2001), p. 159. • 20. Unpublished interview by the author. • 21. *Ibid.* • 22. *Little Shoppe of Horrors*, #4, April 1978, p. 57. • 23. *The Hammer Vampire Film Music Collection*, CD liner notes, GDI Records, 2000. • 24. *Little Shoppe of Horrors*, #10/11, July 1990, p. 97. • 25. *Ibid.*, p. 105. • 26. *Little Shoppe of Horrors*, #8, May 1984, p. 53. • 27. David Miller, *The Complete Peter Cushing* (Reynolds & Hear, 2005), p. 62. • 28. *Ibid*, p. 61. • 29. *Shatter*, DVD commentary, Anchor Bay. • 30. Neame, *Rungs on a Ladder: Hammer Films Seen Through a Gauze*, p. 105. • 31. Meikle, *A History of Horrors*, p. 277. • 32. *Ibid.*, p. 279. • 33. Marcus Hearn and Alan Barnes, *The Hammer Story* (Titan, 1997), p. 165. • 34. Wheeler Winston Dixon, *The Films of Freddie Francis* (Scarecrow, 1991), p. 83. • 35. Jimmy Sangster, *Inside Hammer* (Reynolds & Hearn, 2001), p. 16. • 36. *Hammer Horror*, #1, March 1995, p. 48. • 37. *Little Shoppe of Horrors*, #10/11, July 1990, p. 103. • 38. *Ibid.*, p. 95. • 39. Kinsey, *Hammer Films: The Bray Studios Years*, p. 260. • 40. *Shivers* #85, December 2000, p. 86. • 41. *Little Shoppe of Horrors*, #12, April 1994, p. 111. • 42. *Ibid.* • 43. *Ibid.* • 44. Bourne, *Elisabeth Welch: Soft Lights and Sweet Music*, p. 45. • 45. *Little Shoppe of Horrors*, #16, August 2004, p. 58. • 46. *Ibid.* 47. Hearn and Barnes, *The Hammer Story*, p. 108. • 48. *Ibid.* • 49. *Ibid.* • 50. *Hammer House of Mystery and Suspense*, DVD documentary, DD Entertainment, 2005. • 51. *Dark Terrors*, #18, May 2002, p. 28. • 52. Sangster, *Inside Hammer*, p. 41. 53. *Film Review Special, #53*, August 2004, p. 67. • 54. *Hammer Horror*, #7, September 1995, p. 15. • 55. *Ibid.* • 56. *Ibid.* • 57. *Ibid.*, p. 37. • 58. Kinsey, *Hammer Films: The Bray Studios Years*, p. 187.

## X

1. Jimmy Sangster, *Screenwriting: Techniques for Success* (Reynolds & Hearn, 2003), p. 18. • 2. Marcus Hearn and Alan Barnes, *The Hammer Story* (Titan, 1997), p. 18. • 3. Wayne Kinsey, *Hammer Films: The Bray Studios Years* (Reynolds & Hearn, 2002), p. 43. • 4. *Ibid.*, p. 44. • 5. *Ibid.*, p. 41. • 6. Sangster, *Inside Hammer*, p. 23. • 7. Andy Murray, *Into the Unknown: The Fantastic Life of Nigel Kneale* (Headpress, 2006), p. 53.

## Y

1. Val Guest, *So You Want to Be in Pictures* (Reynolds & Hearn, 2001), p. 135. • 2. *Ibid.* • 3. Wayne Kinsey, *Hammer Films:The Bray Studios Years* (Reynolds & Hearn, 2002), p. 299. • 4. *Hammer Horror*, #6, August 1995, p. 11. • 5. *Flesh and Blood: The Hammer Heritage of Horror*, TV documentary, Heidelburg/Hammer/Bosutow Media Group, 1994. • 6. *Little Shoppe of Horrors*, #12, April 1994, p. 11. • 7. *Little Shoppe of Horrors*, #13, November 1996, p. 63. • 8. *Ibid.* • 9. *She/The Vengeance of She* (CD interview, GDI Records), 2001. • 10. *Hammer: The Studio That Dripped Blood*, TV documentary, BBC, 1987. • 11. *Little Shoppe of Horrors*, #8, May 1984, p. 53. • 12. *Little Shoppe of Horrors*, #30, May 2013, p. 66.

## Appendix

1. *Little Shoppe of Horrors*, #10/11, July 1990, p. 21. • 2. Jimmy Sangster, *Inside Hammer* (Reynolds & Hearn, 2001), p. 147. • 3. *Little Shoppe of Horrors*, #10/11, July 1990, p. 21. • 4. Sangster, *Inside Hammer*, p. 139. • 5. *Hammer House of Mystery and Suspense*, DVD documentary, DD Entertainment, 2005. • 6. *Hammer Horror*, #4, June 1995, p. 18. • 7. *Little Shoppe of Horrors*, #10/11, July 1990, p. 111. • 8. *Shivers*, #32, August 1996, p. 47. • 9. Lewis Gilbert, *All My Flashbacks* (Reynolds & Hearn, 2010), p. 120. • 10. Sangster, *Inside Hammer* (Reynolds & Hearn, 2001,), p. 147. • 11. *Little Shoppe of Horrors*, #10/11, 1990, p. 113. • 12. *Hammer House of Mystery and Suspense*, DVD documentary, DD Entertainment, 2005. • 13. *Little Shoppe of Horrors*, #10/11, July 1990, p. 19. • 14. *Ibid.*, p. 19–20. • 15. *Little Shoppe of Horrors*, #19, September 2007, p. 67. • 16. *Little Shoppe of Horrors*, #10/11, July 1990, p. 20. • 17. Hearn and Barnes, *The Hammer Story*, p. 46. • 18. *Fangoria*, #63, May 1987, p. 63. • 19. *Dark Terrors*, #13, 1996, p. 22. • 20. *Hammer Horror*, #6, August 1995, p. 6. • 21. *Dark Terrors*, #13, 1996, p. 22. • 22. *Little Shoppe of Horrors*, #10/11, July 1990, p. 22. • 23. *Hammer Horror*, #7, September 1995, p. 20. • 24. *Cinefantastique*, February 1994. • 25. *Hammer Horror*, #7, September 1995, p. 20. • 26. Marcus Hearn and Alan Barnes, *The Hammer Story* (Titan, 1997), p. 56. • 27. *Little Shoppe of Horrors*, #16, August 2004, p. 18. • 28. *Dark Terrors*, #13, 1996, p. 40. • 29. Robert Ross, *The Complete Frankie Howerd* (Reynolds & Hearn, 2001), p. 111. • 30. *Hammer House of Mystery and Suspense*, DVD documentary, DD Entertainment, 2005. • 31. Hearn and Barnes, *The Hammer Story*, p. 169. • 32. *Ibid.* 33. *Hammer Horror*, #4, June 1995, p. 18. • 34. Hearn and Barnes, *The Hammer Story*, p. 135. • 35. *Ibid.* 36. Ray Harryhausen and Tony Dalton, *The Art of Ray Harryhausen* (Aurum, 2005), p. 75–76. • 37. *Little Shoppe of Horrors*, #10/11, July 1990, p. 129.

# Bibliography

Annakin, Ken. *So You Wanna Be a Director?* Sheffield: Tomahawk Press, 2001.

Armstrong, Vic, and Robert Sellers. *The True Adventures of the World's Greatest Stuntman.* London: Titan, 2011.

Atkins, Rick. *Let's Scare 'Em.* Jefferson, N.C.: McFarland, 1997.

Baker, Barbara. *Let the Credits Roll.* Jefferson, N.C.: McFarland, 2003.

Barnes, Alan. *Sherlock Homes on Screen: The Complete Film and TV History.* London: Reynolds & Hearn, 2002.

Barr, Charles. *Ealing Studios,* revised edition. London: Studio Vista, 1993.

Bentley, Chris. *The Complete Gerry Anderson: The Authorized Episode Guide.* Richmond: Reynolds & Hearn, 2003.

Bergan, Ronald. *The United Artists Story.* London: Octopus, 1986.

Billman, Larry. *Film Choreographers and Dance Directors.* Jefferson, N.C.: McFarland, 1997.

Black, Andy, and Steve Earles. *The Dead Walk.* Hereford: Noir, 2008.

Boot, Andy. *Fragments of Fear.* London: Creation Books, 1996.

Bourne, Stephen. *Elisabeth Welch: Soft Lights and Sweet Music.* Lanham, Md.:Scarecrow Press, 2005.

Bradley, Doug. *Behind the Mask of the Horror Actor.* London: Titan, 2004.

Branaghan, Sim. *British Film Posters: An Illustrated History.* London: BFI, 2006.

Bright, Morris. *Pinewood Studios: 70 Years of Fabulous Film-Making.* London: Carroll & Brown, 2007.

Bryce, Allan, editor. *Amicus: The Studio That Dripped Blood.* Liskeard: Stray Cat, 2000.

Butters, Wes. *Whatshisname: The Life and Death of Charles Hawtrey.* Sheffield: Tomahawk Press, 2010.

Campbell, Phil, and Brian Reynolds. *Running Scared.* London: Peveril Publishing, 2014.

Cettle, Robert. *Serial Killer Cinema.* Jefferson, N.C.: McFarland, 2003.

Chester, Lewis. *All My Shows Are Great: The Life of Lew Grade.* London: Aurum, 2012.

Chibnall, Steve. *Quota Quickies: The Birth of the British 'B' Film.* London: BFI, 2007.

_____, and Julian Petley, editors. *British Horror Cinema.* London: Routledge, 2002.

Christie, Ian, and Andrew Moor. *The Cinema of Michael Powell: International Perspectives on an English Film-Maker.* London: BFI, 2005.

Cohen, John. *Lost Treasures of the Odeons. 1329 Forgotten Films !!:* John Cohen, 2007.

Coldstream, John. *Dirk Bogarde: The Authorised Biography.* London: Weidenfeld & Nicolson, 2004.

Cook, Pam, editor. *Gainsborough Pictures.* Washington, D.C.: Cassell, 1997.

Cotter, Robert Michael "Bobb." *The Women of Hammer Horror–A Biographical Dictionary and Filmography.* Jefferson, N.C.: McFarland, 2013.

Court, Hazel. *Hazel Court: Horror Queen.* [Place of publication not identified]: Tomahawk Press, 2008.

Davies, Glen. *Last Bus to Bray: The Unfilmed Hammer.* [Place of publication not identified]:Hemlock, 2010.

Décharné, Max. *King's Road.* London: Weidenfeld & Nicolson, 2005.

Deeley, Michael. *Blade Runners, Deer Hunters and Blowing the Bloody Doors Off: My Life in Cult Movies.* London: Faber and Faber, 2008.

Dendle, Peter. *The Zombie Movie Encyclopedia.* Jefferson, N.C.: McFarland, 2001.

Dixon, Wheeler Winston. *The Films of Freddie Francis.* Lanham, Md.: Scarecrow Press, 1991.

Duncan, Paul, editor. *The James Bond Archives.* Köln; London: Taschen, 2012.

Dyson, Jeremy. *Bright Darkness: The Lost Art of the Supernatural Horror Film.* London: Cassell, 1997.

Eames, John Douglas. *The Paramount Story.* London: Octopus, 1985.

_____, and Ronald Bergan. *The MGM Story,* revised edition. London: Hamlyn, 1993.

Elley, Derek. *Variety Movie Guide 1999.* London: Boxtree, 1999.

Evans, Jeff. *The Penguin TV Companion.* London: Penguin, 2001.

Everman, Welch. *Cult Horror Films.* New York: Citadel, 1993.

Everson, William K. *Classics of the Horror Film.* Secaucus, N.J.: Citadel, 1974.

Eyles, Allen, and Robert Adkinson, Nicholas Fry, editors. *The House of Horror.* London: Lorrimer, 1973.

Falk, Quentin. *The Golden Gong.* London: Columbus, 1987.

_____, and Dominic Prince. *Last of a Kind: The Sinking of Lew Grade.* London: Quartet Books, 1987.

Fane-Saunders, Kilmeny, editor. *Radio Times Guide to Films 2007.* London: BBC Worldwide, 2006.

Fenton, Harvey, and David Flint. *Ten Years of Terror: British Horror Films of the 1970s.* Guildford: FAB, 2001.

Fenton, Harvey, editor. *Flesh & Blood Companion.* Guildford: FAB, 2003.

Fentone, Steve. *AntiCristo.* Guildford: FAB, 2000.

Feramisco, Thomas M. *The Mummy Unwrapped.* Jefferson, N.C.: McFarland, 2008.

Filmer, Alison J., and Andre Golay. *Harrap's Book of Film Directors and Their Films.* London: Harrap, 1989.

Fischer, Dennis. *Science Fiction Film Directors, 1895–1998.* Jefferson, N.C.: McFarland, 2000.

Forbes, Bryan. *A Divided Life.* London: Heinemann, 1992.

Frank, Alan. *The Horror Film Handbook.* London: Batsford, 1982.

_____. *Horror Films.* London: Hamlyn, 1977.

_____. *The Movie Treasury: Horror Movies.* London: Octopus, 1974.

_____. *The Movie Treasury: Monsters and Vampires.* London: Octopus, 1976.

_____. *The Science Fiction and Fantasy Film Handbook.* London: Batsford, 1982.

Fraser, John. *Close Up: An Actor Telling Tales.* London: Oberon, 2004.

Frayling, Christopher. *Ken Adam: The Art of Production Design.* London: Faber and Faber, 2005.

Gates, Tudor. *Scenario: The Craft of Screenwriting.* London: Wallflower, 2002.

Gifford, Denis. *The British Film Catalogue, Volume 1:*

*Fiction Film, 1895–1994,* third edition. London: Fitzroy Dearborn, 2001.

_____. *Movie Monsters.* London: Studio Vista/Dutton, 1974.

_____. *A Pictorial History of Horror Movies.* London: Hamlyn, 1973.

Gilbert, Lewis. *All My Flashbacks.* London: Reynolds & Hearn, 2010.

Glut, Donald F. *The Frankenstein Archive.* Jefferson, N.C.: McFarland, 2002.

Guest, Val. *So You Want to Be in Pictures.* London: Reynolds & Hearn, 2001.

Hailsham, Joe. *It's Scary Already.* Pasqual Enterprises/Grass International, 2008.

Hall, Sheldon. *Zulu: With Some Guts Behind It.* Sheffield: Tomahawk Press, 2005.

Hallenbeck, Bruce G. *Hammer Fantasy and Sci-Fi,* British Cult Cinema series. Bristol, England: Hemlock Books, 2011.

_____. *The Hammer Vampire,* British Cult Cinema series. Bristol, England: Hemlock Books, 2010.

Halliwell, Leslie. *The Dead That Walk.* London: Grafton Books, 1986.

_____. *Double Take and Fade Away.* London: Grafton Books, 1987.

_____. *Halliwell's Harvest.* London: Grafton, 1986.

_____. *Seats in All Parts,* paperback edition. London: Grafton Books, 1986.

_____, and John Walker. *Halliwell's Film Guide 2007.* London: HarperCollins Entertainment, 2006.

_____. *Halliwell's Who's Who in the Movies.* London: HarperCollins Entertainment, 2006.

Halliwell, Leslie, and Philip Purser. *Halliwell's Television Companion.* London: Grafton Books, 1986.

Hamilton, John. *Beasts in the Cellar.* London: FAB P., 2005.

Hannsberry, Karen Burroughs. *Bad Boys: The Actors of Film Noir, Vols 1 & 2.* Jefferson, N.C.: McFarland, 2008.

Hardy, Phil, editor. *The Aurum Encyclopedia: Science Fiction.* London: Aurum, 1995.

_____. *The Aurum Film Encyclopedia: Horror.* London: Aurum, 1996.

Harper, Sue, and Vincent Porter. *British Cinema of the 1950s: The Decline of Deference.* Oxford: Oxford University Press, 2003.

Harryhausen, Ray, and Tony Dalton. *The Art of Ray Harryhausen.* London: Aurum, 2005.

_____. *A Century of Model Animation.* London: Aurum, 2008.

_____. *Ray Harryhausen: An Animated Life.* London: Aurum, 2003.

Hayes, R.M. *Trick Cinematography.* Jefferson, N.C.: McFarland, 1984.

Hayward, Anthony, and Deborah Hayward. *TV Unforgettables.* Enfield: Guinness, 1993.

Hearn, Marcus. *The Art of Hammer.* London: Titan, 2010.

_____. *Hammer Glamour.* London: Titan, 2009.

_____. *The Hammer Vault.* London: Titan, 2011.

_____, and Alan Barnes. *The Hammer Story.* London: Titan, 1997.

Hirschhorn, Clive. *The Columbia Story.* London: Hamlyn, 1999.

913

_____. *The Universal Story,* revised edition. London: Hamlyn, 2000.

_____. *The Warner Bros. Story.* London: Octopus, 1980.

Holston, Kim R., and Tom Winchester. *Science Fiction, Fantasy and Horror Film Sequels Series and Remakes.* Jefferson, N.C.: McFarland, 1997.

Huckvale, David. *Hammer Film Scores and the Musical Avant-Garde.* Jefferson, N.C.: McFarland, 2008.

_____. *Hammer Films' Psychological Thrillers, 1950–1972.* Jefferson, N.C.: McFarland, 2014.

_____. *James Bernard, Composer to Count Dracula.* Jefferson, N.C.: McFarland, 2006.

Hume, Alan, and Gareth Owen. *A Life Through the Lens.* Jefferson, N.C.: McFarland, 2004.

Hunter, I.Q. *British Science Fiction Cinema.* New York: Routledge, 1999.

Hunter, Jack. *Eyes of Blood.* London: Glitter Books, 2012.

_____. *Intercepting Fist: The Films of Bruce Lee and the Golden Age of Kung-Fu Cinema.* London: Glitter, 2005.

Hutchings, Peter. *British Film Makers: Terence Fisher.* Manchester: Manchester University Press, 2001.

James, Simon R.H. *London Film Location Guide.* London: Batsford, 2007.

Jewell, Richard B., and Vernon Harbin. *The RKO Story.* London: Octopus, 1982.

Johnson, Catherine. *Telefantasy.* London: BFI, 2005.

Johnson, Tom, and Deborah Del Vecchio. *Hammer Films: An Exhaustive Filmography.* Jefferson, N.C.: McFarland, 1996.

Johnson, Tom, and Mark A. Miller. *The Christopher Lee Filmography.* Jefferson, N.C.: McFarland, 2004.

Jones, Stephen. *The Essential Monster Movie Guide.* London: Titan, 1999.

Joslin, Lyndon W. *Count Dracula Goes to the Movies.* Jefferson, N.C.: McFarland, 1999.

Katz, Ephraim. *The Film Encyclopedia,* second edition. New York: HarperCollins, 1994.

Keaney, Michael F. *British Film Noir Guide.* Jefferson, N.C.: McFarland, 2008.

Kerekes, David, editor. *Creeping Flesh: The Horror Fantasy Handbook.* Manchester: Headpress, 2003.

Kinsey, Wayne. *Hammer Films: A Life in Pictures.* Sheffield: Tomahawk Press, 2008.

_____. *Hammer Films: The Bray Studios Years.* London: Reynolds & Hearn, 2002.

_____. *Hammer Films: The Elstree Studios Years.* Sheffield: Tomahawk Press, 2007.

_____. *Hammer Films: The Unsung Heroes.* Sheffield: Tomahawk Press, 2010.

_____, and Gordon Thomson. *Hammer Films On Location.* Peveril, 2012.

Klepper, Robert K. *Silent Films, 1897–1996.* Jefferson, N.C.: McFarland, 1999.

Lane, Andy, and Paul Simpson. *The Bond Files.* London: Virgin, 2002.

Langley, Roger. *Patrick McGoohan: Danger Man or Prisoner?* Sheffield: Tomahawk Press, 2007.

Lee, Christopher. *Tall, Dark and Gruesome.* London: Gollancz, 1997.

Lennig, Arthur. *The Immortal Count: The Life and Films of Bela Lugosi.* Lexington : University Press of Kentucky, 2003.

Lentz, Harris M., III. *Feature Films, 1960–1969.* Jefferson, N.C.: McFarland, 2001.

Leonard, Geoff, Pete Walker, and Gareth Bramley. *John Barry: The Man with the Midas Touch.* Bristol: Redcliffe, 2009.

Lewis, Roger. *The Life and Death of Peter Sellers.* London: Arrow, 1995.

Lisanti, Tom. *Glamour Girls of Sixties Hollywood.* Jefferson, N.C.: McFarland, 2008.

Lobenthal, Joel. *Tallulah! The Life and Times of a Leading Lady.* London: Aurum, 2005.

Long, Stanley. *X-Rated–Adventures of an Exploitation Filmmaker.* London: Reynolds & Hearn, 2008.

Luxford, Albert J., with Gareth Owen. *Albert J. Luxford, the Gimmick Man.* Jefferson, N.C.: McFarland, 2002.

Maasz, Ronnie. *A Cast of Shadows: A Cameraman's Journey.* Lanham, Md.: Scarecrow Press, 2004.

MacNab, Geoffrey. *J. Arthur Rank and the British Film Industry.* London: Routledge, 1994.

Mank, Gregory William. *Bela Lugosi and Boris Karloff: The Expanded Story of a Haunting Collaboration.* Jefferson, N.C.: McFarland, 2009.

Marriott, James. *Horror Films.* London: Virgin Books, 2004.

_____, and Kim Newman. *Horror.* London: Andre Deutsch, 2006.

Mavis, Paul. *The Espionage Filmography.* Jefferson, N.C.: McFarland, 2001.

Maxford, Howard. *The A–Z of Horror Films.* London: B.T. Batsford, 1996.

_____. *The A–Z of Science Fiction & Fantasy Films.* London: B.T. Batsford, 1997.

_____. *Hammer, House of Horror–Behind the Screams.* London: B.T. Batsford, 1996.

Mayer, Geoff. *Roy Ward Baker* [British Film Makers series]. Manchester and New York: Manchester University Press, 2004.

McCann, Graham. *Bounder! The Biography of Terry-Thomas.* London: Aurum, 2008.

McCarty, John. *The Fearmakers.* London: Virgin, 1995.

_____. *Hammer Films.* Harpenden: Pocket Essentials, 2002.

_____. *The Modern Horror Film.* New York: Citadel Press, 1990.

McFarlane, Brian. *An Autobiography of British Cinema.* London: Methuen, 1997.

_____. *The Encyclopedia of British Film,* second edition. London: Methuen, 2005.

McGee, Mark Thomas. *Beyond Ballyhoo.* Jefferson, N.C.: McFarland, 1989.

_____. *Roger Corman—The Best of the Cheap Acts.* Jefferson, N.C.: McFarland, 1988.

McKay, Sinclair. *A Thing of Unspeakable Horror: The History of Hammer Films.* London: Aurum, 2007.

Meikle, Denis. *A History of Horrors.* Lanham, Md.: Scarecrow Press, 1996.

_____. *Jack the Ripper: The Murders and the Movies.* London: Reynolds & Hearn, 2002.

Miller, David. *The Complete Peter Cushing.* London: Reynolds & Hearn, 2005.

Mitchell, John. *Flickering Shadows–A Lifetime in Film.* Malvern : Harold Martin, 1997.

Muir, John Kenneth. *Horror Films of the 1970s.* Jefferson, N.C.: McFarland, 2002.

Murphy, Robert. *Sixties British Cinema.* London: BFI, 1992.

Murray, Andy. *Into the Unknown: The Fantastic Life of Nigel Kneale.* Manchester: Headpress, 2006.

Murray, John B. *The Remarkable Michael Reeves: His Short and Tragic Life.* London: Cinematics, 2002.

Myers, Harry, John Willis and Gareth Owen. *Pictures and Premieres.* London: Hale, 2007.

Naha, Ed. *The Films of Roger Corman: Brilliance on a Budget.* New York: Arco, 1982.

Neame, Christopher. *Principal Characters: Film Players Out of Frame.* Lanham, Md.: Scarecrow Press, 2005.

_____. *Rungs on a Ladder: Hammer Films Seen Through a Soft Gauze.* Lanham, Md.: Scarecrow Press, 2003.

Nollen, Scott Allen. *Robin Hood: A Cinematic History of the English Outlaw and His Scottish Counterparts.* Jefferson, N.C.: McFarland, 2008.

Nourmand, Tony. *James Bond Movie Posters.* London: Boxtree, 2001.

O'Brien, Daniel. *SF:UK.* London: Reynolds & Hearn, 2000.

_____. *Spooky Encounters: A Gwailo's Guide to Hong Kong Horror.* Manchester: Headpress, 2003.

Odell, Colin, and Michelle Le Blanc. *Vampire Films.* Harpenden: Pocket Essentials, 2008.

O'Neill, James. *Terror on Tape.* New York: Billboard Books, 1994.

Owen, Gareth, and Brian Burford. *The Pinewood Story.* London: Reynolds & Hearn, 2000.

Pattison, Barrie. *The Seal of Dracula.* London: Lorrimer, 1975.

Paul, Louis. *Tales from the Cult Film Trenches.* Jefferson, N.C.: McFarland, 2008.

Peary, Danny. *Cult Movie Stars.* New York: Simon & Schuster, 1991.

Perkins, Roy, and Martin Stollery. *British Film Editors.* London: BFI, 2004.

Perry, George. *Movies from the Mansion: A History of Pinewood Studios,* third edition. London: Pavilion, 1986.

Petrie, Duncan. *The British Cinematographer.* London: BFI, 1996.

Pirie, David. *A New Heritage of Horror.* London: I.B. Tauris, 2008.

_____. *The Vampire Cinema.* London: Hamlyn, 1977.

Pitt, Ingrid. *Life's a Scream.* London: Heinemann, 1999.

Pitts, Michael R. *Horror Film Stars.* Jefferson, N.C.: McFarland, 2002.

_____. *Western Movies,* revised edition. Jefferson, N.C.: McFarland, 1997.

Puchalski, Steven. *Slimetime–A Guide to Sleazy, Mindless Movies,* revised and updated edition. Manchester: Headpress/Critical Vision, 2002.

Pykett, Derek. *British Horror Film Locations.* Jefferson, N.C.: McFarland, 2008.

_____. *Michael Ripper Unmasked.* Baltimore, Md.: Midnight Marquee Press, 1999.

Pym, John, editor. *Time Out Film Guide 2007, 15th Edition.* London: Time Out Guides, 2006.

Quinlan, David. *Quinlan's Character Stars,* third edition. London: Reynolds & Hearn, 2005.

_____. *Quinlan's Film Directors,* second edition. London: B.T. Batsford, 1999.

_____. *Quinlan's Film Stars,* fifth edition. London: B.T. Batsford, 2000.

_____. *Quinlan's Illustrated Directory of Film Comedy Stars.* London: B.T. Batsford, 1992.

Rance, P.T.J. *Martial Arts.* Virgin Books, 2005.

Read, Jan. *Young Man in Movieland.* Lanham, Md.: Scarecrow Press, 2004.

Rham, Edith De. *Joseph Losey.* Andre Deutsch, 1991.

Rhodes, Gary Don. *Lugosi.* Jefferson, N.C.: McFarland, 2006.

Rigby, Jonathan. *Christopher Lee: The Authorised Screen History,* second edition. London: Reynolds & Hearn, 2003.

_____. *English Gothic: A Century of Horror Cinema,* third edition. London: Reynolds & Hearn, 2004.

_____. *Studies in Terror.* Cambridge: Signum Books, 2011.

_____. *Euro Gothic—Classics of Continental Horror Cinema,* Signum Books, 2016.

Ross, Jonathan. *The Incredibly Strange Film Book.* London: Simon and Schuster, 1993.

Ross, Robert. *The Complete Frankie Howerd.* London: Reynolds & Hearn, 2001.

_____. *The Complete Sid James.* London: Reynolds & Hearn, 2000.

Russell, Jamie. *Book of the Dead.* Guildford: FAB Press, 2005.

Sachs, Bruce, and Russell Wall. *Greasepaint and Gore: The Hammer Monsters of Roy Ashton.* Sheffield : Tomahawk Press, 1991.

Sangster, Jimmy. *Do You Want It Good or Tuesday?* Baltimore, Md.: Midnight Marquee Press, 1997.

_____. *Inside Hammer.* London: Reynolds & Hearn, 2001.

_____. *Screenwriting: Techniques for Success.* London: Reynolds & Hearn, 2003.

Schlossheimer, Michael. *Gunmen and Gangsters.* Jefferson, N.C.: McFarland, 2002.

Schreck, Nikolas. *The Satanic Screen.* [Place of publication not identified]: Creation Books, 2001.

Scivally, John Cork and Bruce. *James Bond: The Legacy.* London: Boxtree, 2002.

Sellar, Maurice, with Lou Jones, Robert Sidaway and

Ashley Sidaway. *Best of British: A Celebration of Rank Film Classics.* London: Sphere, 1987.

Sellers, Robert. *The Battle for Bond.* Sheffield: Tomahawk Press, 2007.

_____. *Very Naughty Boys: The Amazing True Story of HandMade Films.* London: Metro, 2004.

_____. *Cult TV: The Golden Age of ITC.* London: Plexus, 2006.

Senn, Bryan. *A Year of Fear.* Jefferson, N.C.: McFarland, 2007.

Shaw, Tony. *British Cinema and the Cold War.* London: I.B. Tauris, 2006.

Sheridan, Simon. *Keeping the British End Up.* London: Reynolds & Hearn, 2001..

Shubrook, Martin. *Special Effects Superman: The Art and Effects of Derek Meddings.* Shubrook Bros., 2008.

Sigoloff, Marc. *The Films of the Seventies,* 2000 reprint. Jefferson, N.C.: McFarland, 1984.

Sikov, Ed. *Dark Victory: The Life of Bette Davis.* London: Aurum, 2007.

Silver, Alain, and James Ursini. *The Vampire Film,* third edition. New York: Limelight Editions, 1997.

Skal, David J. *Hollywood Gothic–The Tangled Web of Dracula from Novel to Stage to Screen.* London: Deutsch, 1992.

_____. *The Monster Show: A Cultural History of Horror.* London: Plexus, 1993.

Smith, Gary Allen. *Epic Films,* second edition. Jefferson, N.C.: McFarland, 2004.

Speed, F. Maurice. *Film Review.* London: Macdonalds, 1946.

_____. *Film Review.* London: Macdonalds, 1947.

_____. *Film Review.* London: Macdonalds, 1948.

Stanley, John. *Creature Features.* New York: Berkley Boulevard, 2000.

Stine, Scott Aaron. *The Gorehound's Guide to Splatter Films of the 1960s and 1970s.* Jefferson, N.C.: McFarland, 2001.

Street, Sarah. *Transatlantic Crossings: British Feature Films in America.* New York: Continuum, 2002.

Stritto, Frank J. Dello, and Andi Brooks. *Vampire Over London: Bela Lugosi in Britain.* Houston: Cult Movie Press, 2000.

Sweet, Matthew. *Shepperton Babylon: The Lost Worlds of British Cinema.* London: Faber and Faber, 2005.

Sylvester, David, Philip French, Christopher Frayling, and Ken Adam. *Moonraker, Strangelove and Other Celluloid Dreams: The Visionary Art of Ken Adam.* London: Serpentine Gallery, 1999.

Taylor, Rod. *The Guinness Book of Sitcoms.* Enfield: Guinness, 1994.

Thomas, Nicholas, editor. *International Dictionary of Films and Filmmakers–1: Films,* second edition. Chicago: St. James Press, 1990.

_____. *International Dictionary of Films and Filmmakers—3: Actors and Actresses,* second edition. Chicago: St. James Press, 1992.

Thomas, Tony, and Aubrey Solomon. *The Films of Twentieth Century Fox,* second edition. Secaucus, N.J.: Citadel, 1985.

Thompson, Nathaniel. *DVD Delirium, Volume 1.* Guildford: FAB, 2002.

_____. *DVD Delirium, Volume 1 Redux.* Guildford: FAB, 2006.

_____. *DVD Delirium, Volume 2.* Guildford: FAB, 2003.

_____. *DVD Delirium, Volume 3.* Guildford: FAB, 2006.

Thrower, Stephen, editor. *Eyeball Compendium.* Guildford: FAB, 2003.

Tookey, Christopher. *The Critics' Film Guide.* London: Buxtree, 1994.

Trevelyan, John. *What the Censor Saw.* London: Joseph, 1973.

Upton, Julian. *Fallen Stars.* Manchester: Headpress, 2004.

Vacche, Angela Dalle, and Brian Price, editors. *Color: The Film Reader.* London: Routledge, 2006.

Vazzna, Eugene Michael. *The Silent Film Necrology: Second Edition.* Jefferson, N.C.: McFarland, 2001.

Walker, Mark, editor. *Film Music,* third edition. Harrow, Middlesex: Gramophone/Arcam, 1998.

Warren, Bill. *The Evil Dead Companion.* London: Titan, 2000.

_____. *Keep Watching the Skies! American Science Fiction Movies of the Fifties.* Jefferson, N.C.: McFarland, 1997.

Warren, Patricia. *British Film Studios,* second edition. London: Batsford, 2001.

_____. *Elstree: The British Hollywood.* London: Columbus, 1988.

Weaver, Tom. *I Was a Monster Movie Maker.* Jefferson, N.C.: McFarland, 2001.

_____. *Return of the B Science Fiction and Horror Heroes.* Jefferson, N.C.: McFarland, 2000.

_____. *A Sci-Fi Swarm and Horror Horde.* Jefferson, N.C.: McFarland, 2010.

Winner, Michael. *Unbelievable: My Life in Restaurants and Other Places.* London: J.R. Books, 2010.

Wisdom, Norman, and William Hall. *Don't Laugh at Me.* London: Century, 1992.

Wright, Bruce Lanier. *Nightwalkers.* Dallas: Taylor, 1995.

# Newspapers, Magazines, Programs, Press/Publicity Material

*Cinema Retro* (Vol 1, #1, January 2005)
*Cinema Retro* (Vol 1, #2, May 2005)
*Cinema Retro* (Vol 1, #3, 2005)
*Cinema Retro* (Vol 2, #6, 2006)

*The Dark Side* (#40, June/July 1994)
*Dark Terrors* (#13, 1996)
*Dark Terrors* (#18, May 2002)
*Daughter of the Night: Carmilla on Screen* (Tim Greaves, Kevin Collins; One Shot, 1994)
*Fangoria* (#12, April 1981)
*Fangoria* (#63, May, 1987)
*Fantasynopsis #2* (1989)
*Film Review* (#F90, March 1998)
*Film Review* (#580, April 1999)
*Film Review Special* (#53, August 2004)
*Flesh & Blood* (#2, Autumn 1993)
*Flesh & Blood* (#3, 1994)
*Flesh & Blood* (#4, 1995)
*Hammer at the Barbican* (1996 [program])
*Hammer Horror: Collectors' Special* (1994)
*Hammer Horror* (#1–7, March 1995–September 1995)
*Ingrid Pitt: Queen of Horror* (Tim Greaves; One Shot, 1996)
*Kinematograph Weekly* (1947, 1962–1971)
*Little Shoppe of Horrors* (#1–35, 1972–2015)
*Music from the Movies* (#8, Spring 1995)
*Music from the Movies* (#9, Summer 1995)
*Satellite Times* (September 1996)
*Shivers* (#31, July 1996)
*Shivers* (#32, August 1996)
*Shivers* (#33, September 1996)
*Shivers* (#34, October 1996)
*Shivers* (#36, December 1996)
*Shivers* (#38, February 1997)
*Shivers* (#39, March 1997)
*Shivers* (#42, June 1997)
*Shivers* (#50, February 1998)
*Shivers* (#52, April 1998)
*Shivers* (#61, January 1999)
*Shivers* (#64, April 1999)
*Shivers* (#85, December 2000)
*Shivers* (#100, November 2002)
*Soundtrack!* (Vol 11, #43, September 1992)
*The Stage* (2000)
*Starburst* (Winter Special 1989)
*Starburst* (#265, September 2000)
*The Times* (17/09/05)

# Internet Resources

www.bafta.org
www.bfi.org.uk
www.christopherleeweb.com
www.epguides.com
www.imdb.com
www.tvtome.com

# Index

Numbers in **bold italics** indicate pages with illustrations

# Index

# Index

Wing Commander 150
Winged Victory 786
The Wingless Bird 674
Wings 152, 472, 549, 573, 643, 688, 884
Wings of Danger 12, 13, 21, 23, 32, 35, 42, 70, 86, 114, 122, 127, 141, 171, 249, 260, 262, 274, 276, 310, 313, 330, 369, 382, 395, 397, 405, 412, 429, 450, 463, 469, 478, 485, 502, 506, 514, 548, 558, 562, 573, 591, 592, 599, 600, 610, 672, 693, 709, 713, 727, 732, 755, 763, 767, 774, 782, 787, 795, 807, 808, 810, 848, 871
Wings of Mystery 305, 426, 689
Wings of the Apache 327
Wings of the Morning 818
Wings Over Africa 43, 309
Wings Over Everest 140
Wink to Me Only 379
Winnie the Pooh and the Honey Tree 91
Winning Widows 134, 485
The Winslow Boy 30, 141, 150, 172, 184, 214, 313, 391, 403, 430, 499, 596, 671, 798, 844, 846, 863
Winston Churchill: The Wilderness Years 84, 264, 375
Winter Glory 134
Winter in the Garden 192
Winter of 1917 95
A Winter's Tale 69
The Winter's Tale 414, 424, 805
Wipeout 564
Wire in the Blood 557
Wire Service 32, 74, 122, 537, 612
Wiretappers 263
The Wisdom of Crocodiles 798
The Wish Bone 858
Wish Me Luck 65, 121, 305, 796
Wish You Were Here 392, 492, 530, 589, 870
Wish You Weren't Here 396
Wishbaby 270
The Witch Boy 710
Witch Hunt 858
Witchcraft 128, 378, 388, 427, 447, 474, 502, 540, 592, 676, 733
Witchcraft and Necromancy 99
Witchery 459
The Witches 10, 19, 25, 26, 35, 36, 37, 45, 46, 72, 75, 123, 127, 135, 142, 145, 192, 194, 198, 205, 218, 247, 249, 265, 269, 271, **278**, 285, 296, 324, 340, 369, 375, 385, 420, 421, 434, 447, 449, 451, **452**, 453, 459, 467, 468, 470, 493, 506, 539, 540, 549, 552, 561, 569, 580, 591, 614, 620, 622, 626, 628, 650, 656, 671, 673, 692, 696, 698, 702, 706, 730, 731, 750, 764, 780, 789, 790, 797, 798, 799, 804, 807, 808, 810, 819, 831, 838, 840, 843, 848, 855, 860, 867, **872**, **873**, 883
Witches' Brew 726
Witchfinder General 18, 32, 69, 109, 112, 154, 184, 187, 208, 219, 340, 365, 392, 432, 436, 453, 513, 521, 564, 676, 706, 729, 730, 782, 796, 798, 799, 808, 813, 824, 885
Witching Time 14, 30, 35, 50, 54, 69, 266, 271, 305, 339, 340, 460, 478, 549, 605, 625, 665, 673, 727, 754, 836, 847
The Witch's Daughter 796
The Witch's Head 335
With Love from London 129
With Uncle Bill at the Zoo: Beaks and Claws 485

Within These Walls 58, 63, 64, 85, 122, 179, 191, 297, 392, 420, 460, 476, 500, 564, 687, 707, 708, 777, 778, 842
Withnail & I 67, 70, 601, 752
The Witness 64, 611, 838
Witness for the Prosecution 10, 91, 307, 311, 423, 599
Wittgenstein 664
Wives and Daughters 104, 143
The Wizard 495
The Wizard of Baghdad 745
The Wizard of Oz 180, 557
Wizards vs. Aliens 557
Wo ai shen xian zhe 502
Wodehouse Playhouse 34, 387, 595, 797, 881
Wokenwell 243
Wolf Dog 39, 595, 764
Wolf Hall 243
The Wolf Man (1941) 169, 170, 321, 562, 747, 781, 792, 818, 819
Wolf Man's Maker 747
The Wolf of Wall Street 515
The Wolfman (2010) 37, 155, 170, 271
Wolfshead: The Legend of Robin Hood 14, 42, 63, 64, 67, 68, 90, 91, 141, 187, 190, 254, 308, 328, 369, 403, 408, 420, 423, 425, 433, 434, 460, 497, 506, 525, 552, 555, 557, 602, 628, 651, 693, 698, 700, 734, 760, 764, 779, 789, 798, 812, 841, 863, 864, 874, 883
Wolfshead: The Legend of Young Robin Hood 525
The Wolverine 216
Wolves 537
The Wolves of Kromer 676
The Wolves of Willoughby Chase 41, 44
A Woman Alone 447
A Woman at War 694
A Woman Called Golda 307, 392
The Woman Disputed 132
The Woman for Joe 418
The Woman from China 241
The Woman from Hell 426
Woman Hater 55
The Woman He Loved 375
Woman in a Dressing Gown 315, 317, 454, 563
The Woman in Black: Angel of Death 876
The Woman in Black 2: Angel of Death 7, 52, 92, 261, 263, 368, 369, 377, 398, 459, 634, 635, 664, 809, 876
Woman in Gold 7, 329
The Woman in Question 671, 805
The Woman in the Hall 283, 736, 744, 788, 845, 863
Woman in the Rain 597
The Woman in White 393, 536
The Woman Juror 269
A Woman of Mystery 418
A Woman of No Importance 132, 139
Woman of Rome 165, 263
Woman of Straw 83, 181, 844, 891
A Woman of Substance 188, 614, 727, 734, 753, 761, 849
Woman of the Year 851
A Woman Possessed 131, 718
Woman to Woman 55, 554
The Woman with No Name 25, 34
Womaneater 198, 389, 392, 718, 834, 848
Womanhood 9
A Woman's Devotion 390
Woman's Hour 137
A Woman's Law 33
Woman's Own 683

A Woman's Place Is in the Home 562
A Woman's Temptation 399, 454
The Wombles 155
Wombling Free 56, 150, 193, 300, 386, 417, 430, 805, 844, 864
The Women 151, 277, 314
Women and Diamonds 204
Women and Sport 87
Women Aren't Angels 25, 527
Women in Love 22, 24, 320, 375, 388, 473, 501, 675, 743, 864
Women of Twilight 74, 85, 427, 546, 570
Women Without Men 15, 16, 19, 28, 57, 69, 72, 82, 89, 102, 103, 105, 120, 139, 142, 186, 187, 191, 248, 251, 263, 268, 277, 297, 302, 311, 312, 313, 315, 332, 333, 369, 379, 382, 397, 398, 402, 419, 425, 431, 447, 454, 468, 469, 473, 474, 478, 499, 500, 502, 505, 511, 513, 535, 557, 558, 569, 587, 591, 600, 604, 622, 632, 645, 663, 672, 687, 689, 690, 698, 705, 710, 713, 718, 725, 743, 744, 764, 765, 769, 778, 807, 851, 852, 853, 854, 860, 861, 866, 867, 872, **878**, 886, 890
Women's Prison 879
The Women's Room 321
The Wonder 744
Wonder Woman 580, 881
Wonderful Day 83
A Wonderful Heritage: The Hadley Story 428
Wonderful Life 30, 45, 377, 384, 508, 515, 584, 612, 704, 749, 848
Wonderful Lips 88
The Wonderful Story 470
The Wonderful World of the Brothers Grimm 179
Wonderwall 143, 242, 524, 556, 678, 767
Woobinda, Animal Doctor 554
The Woodchoppers' Ball 253
The Wooden Horse 89, 187, 320, 327, 620, 627, 699, 727, 744, 766
The Woodlanders 89
Woof! 204, 430, 628, 747
The Wooing of Anne Hathaway 430, 548
The Word 210, 267
A Word with Alf 562
Words for Battle 92
Work and Wages 459
Work Is a Four-Letter Word 197, 311, 314, 497, 702, 760
The Worker 16, 84, 239, 317, 549, 747, 788
A World Apart 157
The World at Their Feet 460
World Gardern 819
World in Action 323, 432
The World in His Arms 253
The World Is Full of Married Men 46, 58, 417, 447, 690, 707, 891
The World Is Not Enough 20, 56, 210, 251, 324, 371, 376, 386, 458, 503, 562, 580, 646, 647, 687, 787, 838, 870
The World Is Rich 870
The World of Hammer 7, 26, 44, 45, 49, 50, 51, 102, 162, 166, 175, 202, 215, 225, 230, 239, 280, 282, 337, 352, 367, 369, 391, 430, 433, 434, 484, 495, 510, 553, 578, 579, 611, 626, 642, 656, 658, 670, 675, 682, 689, 717, 730, 736, 744, 747, 748, 750, 754, 757, 796, 810, 875, 880, 882, 887

The World of His Own 158, 455
The World of Paul Slickey 391
World of Plenty 777
World of Sport 454
The World of Survival 501
The World of Suzie Wong 485, 743, 762
The World of the Beachcomber 468, 610
The World of Tim Frazer 267, 388, 407, 844
The World of Wooster 104, 648, 842
The World Owes Me a Living 89, 449, 451, 731
The World Ten Times Over 777
World Theatre 242
World War Z 787
The World We Knew 699
World's End 622, 643
The World's Smallest Country 263
Worlds Within Worlds 455
Worm's Eye View 91, 277, 280, 336, 391, 513
The Worst Week of My Life 244, 539
Worth Living For 38
Worzel Gummidge 394, 434, 629, 677, 777
Worzel Gummidge Down Under 394, 629
Worzel Gummidge Turns Detective 26
Wrath of the Titans 773
Wreck Raisers 697
The Wrecker 689
The Wright Pianoforte Tutor 596
Write Me a Murder 461
Written in the Stars 149
The Wrong Arm of the Law 34, 39, 155, 387, 402, 403, 430, 450, 520, 573, 612, 744, 843
The Wrong Box 44, 46, 69, 128, 149, 241, 244, 301, 505, 520, 765, 782, 810, 832, 847
The Wrong Man 558
The Wrong Move 455
The Wrong Side of the Sky 520
The Wrong Trousers 709
Wrongfully Accused 140
Wu da han 126
Wu du 885
Wu guan 125
Wu ha dan 627
Wu Lang ba gua gun 125
Wu ye lan hua 299
Wuthering Heights 44, 58, 86, 88, 92, 138, 176, 180, 280, 392, 419, 519, 582, 610, 667, 761, 797
Wycliffe 9, 155, 315, 671, 847
The Wyvern Mystery 476

X-15 216
The X Files 431
X-Men 82, 126, 216, 810
X-Men: Dark Phoenix 216
X-Men: Days of Future Past 216
X-Men: First Class 56, 216
X-Men Origins: Wolverine 613
X-Men 2 150
X—The Man with X-Ray Eyes 210
X—The Unknown 5, 7, 10, 19, 33, 39, 42, 48, 50, 66, 67, 70, 72, 81, 82, 85, 94, 96, 108, 111, 114, 123, 129, 136, 143, 149, 156, 158, 165, 171, 178, 192, 197, 241, 243, 244, 249, 263, 269, 270, 282, 306, 313, 336, 362, 369, 370, 376, 379, 381, 395, 397, 402, **426**, 427, 431, 445, 450, 459, 470, 477, 495, 497, 503, 508, 509, 513, 514, 525, 531, 537, 539, 547, 551, 561, 564, 579, 591, 595, 599, 600, 626, 628, 650, 656, 657, 664,